MOON HANDBOOKS

# PATAGONIA

WAYNE BERNHARDSON

PATAGONIA
ARGENTINA
URUGUAY
CHILE
PACIFIC OCEAN
OCEAN
Tacuarembó
Villa María
Rosario
Río Cuarto
San Luis
MENDOZA
Viña del Mar
VALPARAISO
SANTIAGO
RANCAGUA
Cordillera de los Andes
Trinidad
Junín
BUENOS AIRES
LA PLATA
Montevideo
Río de la Plata
Río Desaguadero
Salado
TALCA
Malargüe
Pehuajó
SANTA ROSA
Santa Isabel
Olavarría
Azul
CONCEPCIÓN
Río
Chos Malal
Neuquén
Mar del Plata
Bahía Blanca
TEMUCO
Zapala
NEUQUÉN
Río Colorado
Choele Choel
Junín de los Andes
Valdivia
San Martín de los Andes
Río Limay
Río Negro
Osorno
Lago Nahuel Huapi
VIEDMA
Carmen de Patagones
Golfo San Matías
Sierra Grande
San Carlos de Bariloche
PUERTO MONTT
El Bolsón
Ancud
Castro
Puerto Madryn
Península Valdes
Golfo Nuevo
Trelew
RAWSON
Río Chubut
Esquel
Chaitén

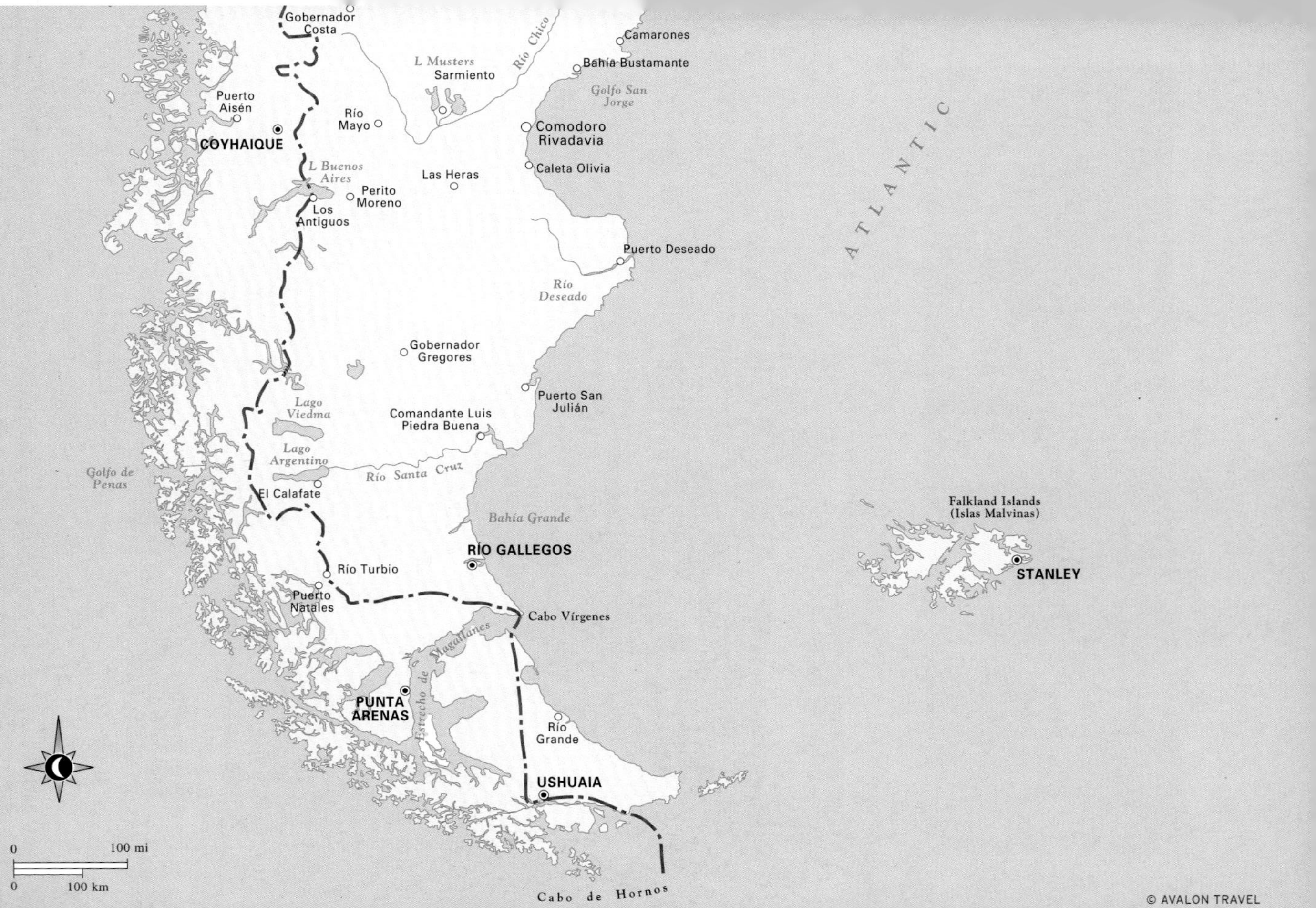

© AVALON TRAVEL

# Contents

# Discover Patagonia

Where the South American continent tapers to its tip, Patagonia is a land of legend that's inspired the imagination ever since the first fantastic tales – the Magellan expedition's account of South Atlantic giants and hidden cities of gold – reached the Old World. Patagonia is also the land that drew Bruce Chatwin, in the 1970s, to research a family anecdote about a giant ground sloth. Unlike the Patagonian giants, these megafauna existed (though not within human memory), and Chatwin's resulting literary travelogue – not totally free of the fictions that have typified so much writing about Patagonia – revived the region's mystique. Today, though air travel has often made the exotic familiar, Patagonia remains a destination whose staggering landscapes evoke exploration and mystery. Increasing numbers of visitors are imagining their own Patagonia on the shores, steppes, rivers, lakes, forests, and mountains of southernmost Argentina, Chile, and the Falkland Islands.

Northernmost Patagonia's forested lakes districts remind visitors of North America's Pacific Northwest or the European Alps. Only New Zealand, Norway, and the Alaskan panhandle can equal Chile's Pacific fjords and Tierra del Fuego's wildlands. The Falklands boast the best assemblage of Antarctic wildlife this side of the frozen continent. Among its attractions, Patagonia counts four UNESCO World Biosphere Reserves and four World Heritage Sites. In Argentina, these include the wildlife-

packed Atlantic coastline of Península Valdés, the aboriginal rock art of Cueva de las Manos, and Glaciar Perito Moreno, a grinding river of ice that's a feast for the eyes and the ears. Chile boasts the araucaria forests of its lake district, the chapels and churches of the Chiloé archipelago, the ice fields of Laguna San Rafael, and the igneous pinnacles of Torres del Paine.

Patagonia is also rich with culture. Chile's lake district is still home to the resilient Mapuche, who defended their territory against the Spaniards and their successors for over three centuries. In southernmost Patagonia and Tierra del Fuego, sheep farmers created a distinctive cultural landscape, with dispersed settlements that have become vacation attractions in themselves.

Following Magellan's expedition, Patagonia became an enduring symbol of the unknown, a place where anything was possible. Today, some five centuries later, Patagonia still excites the imagination and lures adventurous travelers to discover it for themselves.

# Planning Your Trip

## ▸ WHERE TO GO

Patagonia is notoriously hard to define, but for purposes of this guide, it's a pragmatic matter that corresponds closely to political geography.

### Buenos Aires

While it's no longer cheap, South America's highest-profile capital is reason enough to visit the country—many visitors spend weeks or even months enjoying its first-rate hotels, innovative cuisine, all-night entertainment, nonstop shopping, and matchless cultural resources. Despite its international sophistication, it's also a city of intimate neighborhoods where no one is truly anonymous.

### Santiago de Chile

Patagonia's other gateway capital remains one of the continent's most underrated cities—even though it ranked No. 1 on *The New York Times*'s list of places to go in 2011. While it lacks the international profile of its

### IF YOU HAVE . . .

- **ONE WEEK:** Visit Buenos Aires, El Calafate and the Glaciar Perito Moreno, and Torres del Paine.
- **TWO WEEKS:** Add El Chaltén, Tierra del Fuego (possibly including the Cruceros Australis voyage from Punta Arenas to Ushuaia), and Santiago. Alternatively: Add Laguna San Rafael (including parts of the Carretera Austral and Termas de Puyuhuapi, or the ferry from Puerto Natales to Puerto Montt).
- **THREE WEEKS:** Add Península Valdés and Bariloche, or Parque Pumalín and Pucón.
- **FOUR WEEKS:** Add the Falkland Islands or Chiloé and vicinity.
- **SIX WEEKS:** Add a road trip along RN 3 and RN 40 (Argentina) or the entire Carretera Austral (Chile).

Catedral Metropolitana, Plaza de Armas, in Santiago de Chile

Argentine neighbor, Santiago's setting at the base of the Andes is more impressive, and its hotels, food, and entertainment scenes are catching up rapidly—not least because Chile is the continent's most politically stable and prosperous country.

## Northern Argentine Patagonia

Argentine Patagonia consists of Neuquén, Río Negro, Chubut, and Santa Cruz provinces. In this guide, northern Argentine Patagonia comprises Neuquén and Río Negro plus northwesterly parts of Chubut.

While most of Argentine Patagonia is arid steppe, the densely forested sector near the Chilean border boasts numerous national parks. San Carlos de Bariloche is the country's playground for hiking, skiing, rafting, kayaking, and fly-fishing.

## The Chilean Lakes District

The Sur Chico (Lesser South), popularly called the Chilean lakes district, is a wonderland of rivers, lakes, forests, and volcanoes that comprises the Araucanía (Region IX) and Los Lagos (Region X); the latter includes the Chiloé archipelago. It is common to cross the Andes into Argentine Patagonia here; it's also the official starting point for the Carretera Austral, the southern highway that links parts of southern Chile to the mainland.

## Aisén and Continental Chiloé

Chile's Aisén (Region XI) is mostly wild islands-and-highlands country. In this guide, it also includes the southernmost part of Los Lagos (Region X), often known as "continental Chiloé."

Running most of the region's length, the Carretera Austral is one of Patagonia's greatest road trips, but off-highway sights like Laguna San Rafael and other national parks and reserves are also highlights. Parque Pumalín is one of South America's most audacious private conservation initiatives.

## Southern Argentine Patagonia

In this guide, southern Argentine Patagonia consists of Chubut province (excluding the lakes

# DEFINING PATAGONIA

Most literary accounts of Patagonia, from Darwin's *Voyage of the Beagle* to Bruce Chatwin's classic *In Patagonia,* deal primarily with sprawling Argentine Patagonia, not the lesser-known narrow strip of Pacific Chile in the same latitudes.

Part of the difficulty in defining Patagonia derives from the fact that, in Argentina, there's broad agreement that it's the enormous territory south of the Río Colorado, comprising the provinces of Neuquén, Río Negro, Chubut, and Santa Cruz, and the Argentine sector of Tierra del Fuego. Yet, Neuquén province's northernmost point is only slightly southeast of the Chilean city of Talca, part of a Mediterranean vineyard zone that is clearly not Patagonia. There are no formal boundaries in Chilean Patagonia, though nearly everybody would agree that Region XI (Aisén) and Region XII (Magallanes) are at least part of it. Other northerly areas would like to partake of the Patagonian mystique.

One academic collection places Patagonia between 39° and 55° south latitude, its northern boundary slightly south of the Chilean city of Temuco and almost precisely at the Argentine provincial capital of Neuquén. This would expand Chilean Patagonia's traditional boundaries and substantially reduce Argentine Patagonia by excluding much of Neuquén province.

Ecologically speaking, the same collection posits four vegetation zones: Patagonian steppe, *coigüe*-dominated southern beech forest, Magellanic moorland, and ice fields and glaciers. This approach would disregard Neuquén's northerly steppe and some forested Andean areas.

No portrayal of Patagonia can overlook its native peoples. Many were mobile hunter-gatherers, like the land-based Tehuelche and the coastal Kawéskar, Selk'nam, and Yámana, or the trans-Andean Mapuche (Araucanians), who disregarded political borders. It was the combative Mapuche, in fact, whose presence marked the frontier on both sides of the border – deterring colonial Spain and making Argentine and Chilean colonization precarious almost until the 20th century.

In reality, Patagonia does not lend itself to any easy, precise definition. Like the people, plants, and animals that migrate with the season, the years, the decades, the centuries, and even millennia, it shifts with time and perspective. Pinning it down is less important than appreciating and enjoying what it's offered in the past, still offers today, and will offer tomorrow.

guanacos in Parque Nacional Torres del Paine

district) and Santa Cruz province. Its coastline is a scenic cornucopia of whales, seals, penguins, and other wildlife, while Santa Cruz province is famous for the Glaciar Perito Moreno, a crackling outlier of the Campo de Hielo Sur, the southern Patagonian ice sheet.

Two legendary highways, the coastal RN 3 and the interior RN 40 (Patagonia's "loneliest road") connect the region with northerly provinces.

## Magallanes

South of Aisén, much of Chilean Patagonia consists of jagged mountains and islands set among inland seas; copious rain and snow feed rivers and the glaciers of the Campo de Hielo Sur. Pristine woodlands still cover the mountainsides in much of the region, whose biggest draw is the igneous spires of Parque Nacional Torres del Paine. The only significant city is Punta Arenas, though growing Puerto Natales is a gateway to Torres del Paine; Puerto Williams is the last major settlement north of Antarctica. Local cruise ships now visit Cape Horn, South America's southernmost point.

a petrified forest just inland from Bahía Bustamante in southern Argentine Patagonia

## Argentine Tierra del Fuego

Across the Strait of Magellan from the continent, Chile and Argentina share the broad steppes and mountainous sub-Antarctic grandeur of the Isla Grande de Tierra del Fuego, where Ushuaia is the world's southernmost city and Parque Nacional Tierra del Fuego was Argentina's first coastal national park.

*Stella Australis* passengers hiking to Glaciar Águila in Magallanes

### The Falkland Islands (Islas Malvinas)

In the open South Atlantic, more than 500 kilometers east of the mainland, the Falkland Islands acquired international notoriety in 1982, when an Argentine dictatorship invaded to enforce a long-standing territorial claim to the British-held islands. The British regained them 10 weeks later; since then, the Falklands have prospered under a commercial-fishing-license regime. They've also become a magnet for cruise ships and a handful of independent adventurers who come to see abundant sub-Antarctic wildlife and enjoy local hospitality.

king penguins in the Falkland Islands

## ▸ WHEN TO GO

The fact that the southern spring, summer, and fall months correspond to the Northern Hemisphere's coldest seasons adds to Patagonia's appeal. Still, seasonal wildlife migrations and Andean ski resorts make it a destination even during the austral winter.

snow-covered rocks and flowering shrubs at Chile's Torres del Paine

The Andean lakes district is a traditional summer destination, with locales like Bariloche and Pucón as busy as the ocean beaches; it's also a magnet for fly-fishing enthusiasts October-April. Bariloche is the focus of Argentina's ski industry June–August.

Farther south, El Calafate, gateway to Glaciar Perito Moreno, offers many services October-April, and even for July holidays. Península Valdés is a special case that depends on South Atlantic wildlife—July's midwinter arrival of right whales brings the first tourists, who keep coming with the influx of elephant seals, orcas, and penguins until the end of March.

Tierra del Fuego is primarily a summer destination, though it also has a ski season. The city of Ushuaia is the gateway to Antarctica, where the spring breakup of pack ice determines the season.

Falklands tourism depends on the wildlife

calendar. Migratory Magellanic and rockhopper penguins and elephant seals begin arriving in October and stay until March, or even a little later. That said, there's some wildlife at all seasons, even though access becomes more difficult in winter.

## BEFORE YOU GO

When planning any trip to Patagonia, don't overlook the fact that this is an enormous territory—far larger than most of the world's countries—and logistics can be complicated. Unless your trip is an open-ended overland excursion, this means choosing from numerous options, both as to destinations and means of transportation. Capital cities like Buenos Aires and Santiago are compact and easy to travel around, but visiting other high-profile destinations like Argentina's Perito Moreno Glacier and Chile's Torres del Paine require either two- to three-hour flights or 15- to 30-hour bus trips. Driving is an option, but for most visitors this will mean a rental car from a provincial airport or city.

### Passports and Visas

U.S. and Canadian citizens traveling to Argentina and Chile need passports but not advance visas. Passports are also necessary for checking into hotels, cashing travelers checks, or even credit card transactions. Both countries routinely grant foreign visitors 90-day entry permits in the form of a tourist card. Both also collect a substantial "reciprocity" fee from certain nationalities, including Americans, Canadians, and Australians, at their major international airports in Buenos Aires and Santiago.

Visitors to the Falkland Islands, including Britons, must have passports, return or onward tickets, and sufficient funds to cover their stay; they may need to arrange accommodations in

winter in the Falkland Islands

advance. A Visa or MasterCard is proof of sufficient funds. Visitors must also have adequate medical coverage, including emergency evacuation insurance.

## Vaccinations and Health Insurance

Theoretically, Argentina and Chile demand no proof of vaccinations, but if you are coming from a tropical country where yellow fever is endemic, authorities could ask for a vaccination certificate. Traveling to Patagonia or elsewhere without adequate medical insurance is risky. Before leaving home, purchase a policy that includes evacuation in case of serious emergency.

## Transportation

Getting There: Most visitors arrive in Patagonia by air, via the international airport of Buenos Aires, Aeropuerto Internacional Ministro Pistarini (BUE), or Santiago, Aeropuerto Internacional Arturo Merino Benítez (SCL). Some arrive overland and others by ship. Chile's LAN has the only commercial flights to the Falkland Islands.

trans-Andean bus ride

Overland travel from the north can be challenging, but once you reach Argentina or Chile, it's easy enough. Argentina and Chile share numerous border crossings; in both countries' lakes districts, trans-Andean bus service is fairly common, but many southerly crossings lack public transportation.

For those choosing an aquatic route, the main international crossings are the popular bus-boat-bus shuttle between Argentina's San Carlos de Bariloche and Chile's Puerto Montt, and the cruise between Punta Arenas and Ushuaia.

Getting Around: Argentina has an extensive network of domestic airports and a handful of airlines centered on Buenos Aires, serving many destinations from Buenos Aires south to Ushuaia, Tierra del Fuego. Chile's domestic airports are located in Temuco, Pucón, Osorno, Puerto Montt, Chaitén, Balmaceda (Coyhaique), and Punta Arenas.

In both countries, buses along the principal highways are frequent, spacious, and comfortable—sometimes even luxurious. Fares are reasonable by international standards.

If you're visiting for several months, buying a vehicle is worth consideration. To rent a car, you must present a valid driver's license, have a valid credit card, and be at least 25 years old.

## What to Take

Luggage: For budget travelers planning months in Patagonia, a spacious but lightweight backpack and a small daypack for local excursions is the best choice. Even for non-backpackers, light luggage and a small daypack are advisable. Small but sturdy lightweight locks are advisable for all sorts of luggage.

Clothing: The climate in Buenos Aires is mild in spring and autumn, hot and humid in summer, and cool but not cold in winter.

a mild day at the Feria de San Pedro Telmo in Buenos Aires

For summer, light cottons are the rule, but bring a sweater and a light jacket as well. For winter, a warm jacket and rain gear are advisable. Santiago has a dry-summer, wet-winter climate; summer days can be hot, but nights invariably cool off. The Andean lakes district gets the brunt of Pacific storms, and good rain gear and warm footwear are essential for hikers. Warm clothing is imperative in high altitudes and latitudes; in southernmost Patagonia and Tierra del Fuego, state-of-the-art wet-weather gear is more than advisable.

Camping Gear: In addition to wet-, cold-, and wind-resistant clothing, warm sleeping bags and a sturdy tent are imperative. In much of the region, drinking water is potable straight from the stream, but some sort of purification system is a good idea, just in case. In some national parks, primarily in Argentina, wood fires are prohibited. An adaptable multi-fuel camp stove is the best choice.

Rental gear is available in the gateways to some of the prime hiking areas, such as Bariloche, Puerto Natales, and El Chaltén.

Odds and Ends: Since public toilets sometimes lack toilet paper, travelers should always carry some. A compact pair of binoculars is a good idea for birders and others who enjoy wildlife and the landscape.

trekking across Glaciar Perito Moreno with the helpful addition of crampons

# Explore Patagonia

## ▶ THE BEST OF PATAGONIA

This 10-day itinerary focuses on highlights for first-timers, including Argentina's Perito Moreno Glacier, Chile's Torres del Paine, and one of South America's largest penguin colonies. A possible extension goes to the "uttermost part of the earth" at Ushuaia, the world's southernmost city, in Argentine Tierra del Fuego.

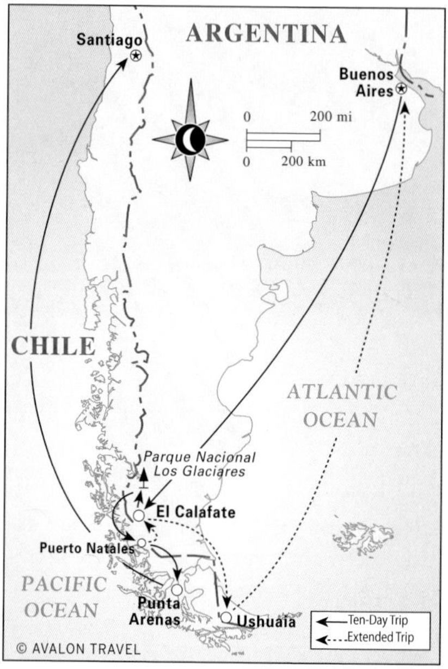


### Day 1

Plan a morning arrival at Aeropuerto Internacional Ministro Pistarini (Ezeiza) and transfer to a Buenos Aires hotel, leaving the afternoon free for sightseeing and the evening for a tango floor show.

### Days 2-3

After breakfast, fly to El Calafate and take an afternoon excursion to a nearby *estancia* (ranch) for an *asado* (barbecue). The following morning, go on a full-day excursion to the groaning, deep blue Glaciar Perito Moreno in Parque Nacional Los Glaciares.

a boat tour of Glaciar Perito Moreno

## Days 4-5

Take a scenic morning bus trip or drive to El Chaltén, the trekking mecca in the Sector Fitz Roy of Parque Nacional Los Glaciares. With an early arrival and good weather, it'll be a swift hike to view the glaciated needle of Cerro Torre. Spend the next morning on a full-day hike to Laguna de los Tres, with stupendous views of Cerro Fitz Roy, followed by an evening return to El Calafate.

## Days 6-8

Bus to the bustling Chilean town of Puerto Natales, gateway to Parque Nacional Torres del Paine. Stay overnight in Natales; the next day, plan on a scenic day hike in the vicinity or in the park, with afternoon options for short hikes or a horseback ride. The next morning, hike the short but strenuous trail to the tarns beneath the Torres themselves; on the following day, you'll still have several hiking options. In the evening, return to Puerto Natales.

## Day 9

Travel across the Magellanic steppe to Punta Arenas, with a short detour to the Magellanic penguin colony at Pingüinera Seno Otway, or, if the timing is right, ride the afternoon ferry to the larger colony on Isla Magdalena, in the Strait of Magellan. There are also quicker Zodiac trips to Isla Magdalena.

## Day 10

In Chile's underrated capital of Santiago, a morning flight leaves the afternoon free for sightseeing and a seafood lunch at the Mercado Central, followed by a nighttime departure from Aeropuerto Internacional Arturo Merino Benítez. With a later departure from Punta Arenas, there would be time to visit that city's exceptional Museo Regional and transfer directly to the international flight.

Parque Nacional Torres del Paine

## USHUAIA AND TIERRA DEL FUEGO EXTENSION

## Day 9

Return to El Calafate by bus, possibly working in an afternoon excursion to bird-watching or rock-art sites, and have dinner at one of the city's outstanding restaurants.

## Days 10-11

Tierra del Fuego is a magical world, and its capital of Ushuaia, reached by a one-hour flight from El Calafate, is the starting point for wildlife-viewing excursions on the legendary Beagle Channel. The next morning, plan a full-day excursion to Parque Nacional Tierra del Fuego, which has multiple short hiking trails, but save some time for Ushuaia's Museo Marítimo de Ushuaia, which is actually a prison museum.

## Days 12-13

Back in Buenos Aires, after overflying Argentina's endless Atlantic coastline, the afternoon and evening are free for sightseeing and a tango floor show; the following day is open for exploring the city before an evening departure flight.

# EXPLORE THE NATURAL WORLD: PAST AND PRESENT

In its more than 1.1 million square kilometers, divided between Chile and Argentina, Patagonia can offer an astonishing diversity of natural environments. Nearly the entire coastline abounds in wildlife, including elephant seals, penguins, and sea lions, but the great distances require time and money to see them—public transportation is fine along the main highway but poor off it. The same is true of the Patagonian steppes, home to the llama-like guanaco and the ostrich-like rhea, and the southern Andean forests beyond the main tourist clusters. In terms of its natural assets, Tierra del Fuego is a southern extension of Patagonia.

Northern Argentine Patagonia boasts major paleontological sites in and around the city of Neuquén, and in and around the city of Trelew, near Puerto Madryn, as well as the wildlife mecca of Península Valdés. Along much of the Andes, but particularly on the Chilean side, volcanism is an active presence.

## Day 1

After an early-morning arrival at Aeropuerto Internacional Arturo Merino Benítez in Santiago, transfer to your hotel and start sightseeing, including seafood lunch at the picturesque Mercado Central and a visit to the information offices of Conaf, the country's main national parks and conservation agency. Alternatively, in lieu of a hotel, ride a comfortable sleeper bus to Temuco, gateway to the upper Biobío's araucaria forests.

## Day 2

From Temuco, reached by sleeper bus or flight from Santiago, rent a car to explore the streams, gallery forests, and araucaria woodlands of Parque Nacional Tolhuaca and the upper Biobío, with accommodations at Malalcahuello. Bring binoculars for bird-watching.

## Day 3

Plan a full-day hiking excursion to araucaria forests above Malalcahuello, on the slopes of Volcán Lonquimay, with a post-hike soak at the nearby hot-springs resort.

## Days 4-5

Take a leisurely drive of the upper Biobío through Lonquimay and forested, thinly populated Pehuenche country, entering Parque Nacional Conguillío via the southern Melipeuco approach. After a visit to the visitors center for orientation, camp or find or *cabaña* accommodations nearby.

## WILDLIFE ENCOUNTERS

Nearly the entire Patagonian coastline abounds in wildlife, such as elephant seals, penguins, sea lions, and numerous bird species. The numerous national parks and reserves in both Chile and Argentina afford the Patagonian traveler a unique and unparalleled wildlife experience. These are the top destinations for prime wildlife viewing.

**Península Valdés**
(Southern Argentine Patagonia, page 336)
On Argentina's Atlantic coast, the World Heritage Site of Península Valdés is famous for southern right whales, which breed and birth there during the winter months. Yet at different seasons, there are also orcas, elephant seals, Magellanic penguins, and sea lions, while grazing guanacos and sprinting rheas roam the interior grasslands.

**Área Natural Protegida Punta Tombo**
(Southern Argentine Patagonia, page 350)
The South American continent's largest single Magellanic penguin colony (a quarter million pairs come ashore each spring to nest!) is a top destination for penguin watchers. In addition, giant petrels, kelp and dolphin gulls, king and rock cormorants, oystercatchers, and steamer ducks all breed within the reserve.

**Parque Interjurisdiccional Marino Costero Patagonia Austral**
(Southern Argentine Patagonia, page 352)
In Chubut province, this recently declared park consists of a wildlife-rich coastal strip, including islands, that extends from Camarones to Cabo dos Bahías, with an easy access point and accommodations at Bahía Bustamante.

**Parque Marino Francisco Coloane**
(Magallanes, Chile, page 428)
One of Chile's first maritime reserves, this park was created to investigate the southern humpback whale's feeding grounds. Orcas, Magellanic penguins, sea lions, cormorants, and many other southern seabirds populate the 67,000-hectare park.

**Falkland Islands** (page 490)
For wildlife lovers, the Falkland Islands are a sub-Antarctic Galapagos, rich with elephant seals, fur seals, sea lions, and massive nesting colonies of penguins (including five or more species), black-browed albatrosses, cormorants, and many unusual smaller birds. Prime destinations include **Volunteer Point** and wildlife lodges at **Carcass Island, Pebble Island, Sea Lion Island,** and **Saunders Island.** Whales can be found offshore near Saunders February-May.

A king cormorant scavenges for nesting material on Saunders Island in the Falklands.

On the following day, try any of several hikes among Conguillío's lava fields and signature monkey-puzzle forests, where the birdlife resembles that at Malalcahuello.

*alerce* (false larch) in Parque Natural Pumalín

## Days 6-7

Depart in the morning for Lago Villarrica, with accommodations in Villarrica or Pucón. Plan an excursion to the Termas Geométricas hot springs or an afternoon rafting on the Río Trancura.

The next morning—weather and seismic conditions permitting—tackle a strenuous full-day climb to the crater of Volcán Villarrica, one of the continent's most active volcanoes. Alternatively, spend a full day hiking to the Andean lakes of nearby Parque Nacional Huerquehue where, with luck, Andean condors glide overhead.

## Day 8

Return to Temuco and bus to Puerto Varas, spending a leisurely afternoon on the shores of Lago Llanquihue, in the shadow of Volcán Osorno's perfect snow-capped cone. Alternatively, take a shuttle to the ski area, where, even in summer, the lifts carry hikers close to the snow line for panoramic views.

## Days 9-10

Take an air taxi or ferry to Chaitén, gateway to the temperate rainforests of Parque Natural Pumalín. Find accommodations in Chaitén or, depending on availability, camp or stay in cabañas near park headquarters in Caleta Gonzalo.

The following morning, you have your choice of several full-day hiking excursions within Parque Natural Pumalín. *Alerce* (false larch) forests are the attraction here, but it's possible to see foxes, pudus, and pumas, not to mention sea lions offshore.

## Day 11

Return by air taxi or ferry/bus combination to Puerto Varas for overnight.

## Days 12-13

Pray for fine weather on the classic, full-day bus-boat combo to Bariloche, Argentina, via Lago Todos los Santos. Stay in or near Bariloche.

The road to Chaitén passes dramatic volcanic peaks.

The next morning, tour Bariloche and its Museo de la Patagonia Francisco P. Moreno, emphasizing natural history and conservation in Argentina's national park system.

In the afternoon, plan an excursion on Parque Nacional Nahuel Huapi's Circuito Chico, a loop that includes a stiff trail hike to Cerro López for panoramic views of the Andes and Lago Nahuel Huapi. Alternatively, boat to the lake's Isla Victoria, formerly home to the park system's ranger school.

## Day 14

From Bariloche, a smooth paved highway rounds Nahuel Huapi's eastern shore and then turns northwest to Villa La Angostura, where a long but not taxing day hike leads to the myrtle forest of Parque Nacional Los Arrayanes and back; those with less stamina can take a comfortable boat either or both ways.

## Day 15

Drive north along the Siete Lagos route to San Martín de los Andes, stopping for a lunchtime *asado* (barbecue) and a visit to Parque Nacional Lanín, with spectacular views of its namesake volcano. Find accommodations in San Martín or Junín de los Andes.

Lago Nahuel Huapi, near Bariloche

## Day 16

From the Andes cross the steppe to Parque Nacional Laguna Blanca, a shallow lake created by a lava-flow dam that's home to black-necked swans and many other birds, including rheas and flamingos. Continue across the steppe to Plaza Huincul's Museo Municipal Carmen Funes, an upgraded paleontological museum, and then go north on graveled RP 17 to Centro Paleontológico Lago Los Barreales, northwest of Neuquén city; if summer water levels are too high for a complete tour of the dinosaur excavation site here, there are several good wineries in the vicinity. Stay in the provincial capital of Neuquén.

## Day 17

Continue on to Villa El Chocón, a hydroelectric-company town that contains the Museo Paleontológico Municipal Ernesto Bachmann, another of Neuquén province's several paleontological museums and dinosaur excavations. Continue south on RN 237 to Bariloche for a comfortable overnight sleeper bus to Puerto Madryn.

## Days 18-20

Start the day at Puerto Madryn with a visit to the Ecocentro Puerto Madryn, an environmental museum. In the afternoon, take time for in-town beach activities such as diving or windsurfing.

The following morning, depart early by tour bus or rental car for Península Valdés, where, depending on the season, there'll be elephant seals, penguins, orcas, or right whales. Many other species—rheas, guanacos, and sea lions, for instance—are present all year.

The morning after, plan a full-day rental-car excursion to the gigantic Magellanic penguin colony at Punta Tombo, south of Trelew. On the way back, visit Trelew's state-of-the-art Museo Paleontológico Egidio Feruglio, and take Welsh tea at Gaiman.

## Days 21-22

Catch a morning flight to Buenos Aires, with the afternoon and evening free for sightseeing and perhaps a tango floor show. Leave the following day free for exploring Buenos Aires before your evening departure flight.

*Giganotosaurus*, one of the world's largest carnivorous dinosaurs, at Villa El Chocón's Museo Bachmann

# SOUTHERN PATAGONIA ROAD TRIP

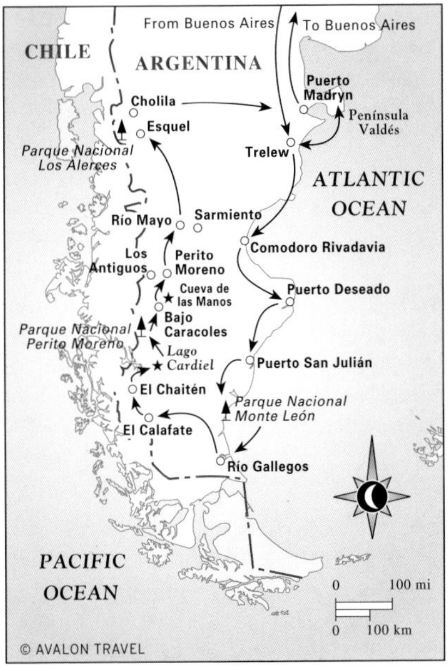


Because of Patagonia's vast expanses, overland travel tends to be for those with plenty of time. Most routes are well-served by reasonably priced public transportation, but those who can afford a vehicle can usually do them more efficiently and stop to see appealing second-tier sights. Four-wheel-drive may not be necessary, but a high-clearance vehicle is worth the extra bucks.

Parallel to RN 3, the mother of all Argentine roads is RN 40, from the Bolivian border in Jujuy province to the Chilean border in Patagonia's Santa Cruz province. It's in Patagonia, though, that RN 40 has acquired an international reputation as *the* adventurous route between the northern lakes and southern glaciers. Only in the last few years has there been any semi-regular public transportation between Perito Moreno and El Calafate, and between Perito Moreno and Bariloche. While the route south from Perito Moreno to Calafate is in the process of being fully paved, for the moment any trip south of Río Mayo will still seem like an expedition, and travelers should be prepared for several days' rugged travel—and weeks, if they want to explore off the main route.

As late as the 1980s, coastal RN 3 was

road-tripping on RP 23, heading west with a sunset view of Cerro Fitz Roy

nearly as rugged as RN 40 is now; today, it's entirely paved though discontinuous, and parts of the connector roads through the Chilean sector of Tierra del Fuego remain unsurfaced. Still, RN 3 glows with the charisma of the world's southernmost highway, the Patagonian road that leads from Buenos Aires to Tierra del Fuego's tip. To grasp the vastness that so impressed the first Europeans, and to view prodigious concentrations of wildlife, "Ruta Tres" is still a matchless itinerary.

## Day 1

Arrive at Aeropuerto Internacional Ministro Pistarini (Ezeiza) and transfer to a Buenos Aires hotel, leaving the afternoon free for sightseeing.

## Day 2

Take a morning flight to Trelew and transfer north on RN 3 to the coastal city of Puerto Madryn, with an afternoon visit to the Ecocentro Puerto Madryn, an environmental museum. This leaves time for the beach, more active pursuits such as diving or windsurfing, or even an excursion to Área Natural Protegida Punta Loma, which has a big sea lion colony and many seabirds.

## Day 3

Plan a full-day rental-car excursion to Península Valdés, where, depending on the season, there'll be elephant seals, penguins, orcas, or right whales. Many other species—such as rheas, guanacos, and sea lions—are present all year. Consider a night at one of the peninsula's accommodations, such as Estancia Rincón Chico.

## Day 4

Depart in the morning, heading south on RN 3 to Trelew, to visit Museo Paleontológico Egidio Feruglio, a state-of-the-art paleontology museum, followed by a badlands hike through the *in situ* paleontological park Geoparque Paleontológico Bryn Gwyn, near Gaiman. Enjoy a late afternoon Welsh tea and overnight at Gaiman.

## Day 5

On an eastbound lateral from RN 3, Área Natural Protegida Punta Tombo's massive

southern right whale, Península Valdés

## GLACIER GAZING

Measuring some 16,800 square kilometers, the Campo de Hielo Sur (southern continental ice field) feeds some of the most southerly glaciers this side of Antarctica. On ferries and cruise ships, visitors can watch the ice meet the sea there and on the Isla Grande de Tierra del Fuego; on the landward side, they can drive to some of the largest ones, with catamaran alternatives on some larger lakes, and the most active can climb on top of the ice and into glacial caverns.

Glaciar Perito Moreno

**Laguna San Rafael** (Aisén, Chile, page 287)
Ferries, catamarans, and even small cruise ships sail to remote Laguna San Rafael, where the Campo de Hielo Norte meets the sea but might not do so much longer—a natural laboratory for global warming studies, it's receding rapidly.

**Glaciar O'Higgins** (Aisén, Chile, page 321)
From Villa O'Higgins, the terminus of the Carretera Austral, the vessel that carries cyclists to the alternative Cruce de Lagos, the rugged overland border crossing to El Chaltén, continues to this scenic outlier of the Campo de Hielo Sur.

**Parque Nacional Los Glaciares**
(Southern Argentine Patagonia, page 383)
Parque Nacional Los Glaciares, a UNESCO World Heritage Site, is home to the famous **Glaciar Perito Moreno,** 250 square kilometers in area and 30 kilometers in length. Easily reached overland, it intermittently explodes from the weight of the water behind it when the advancing ice dams a nearby lake.

In the same park, the even larger Upsala and Viedma glaciers are accessible by catamaran, and on both the Moreno and the Viedma it's possible to go ice-climbing with experienced guides. At the same time, don't overlook El Calafate's new glacier museum, the **Glaciarium.**

**The Fjords of Fuegia**
(Magallanes, Chile, page 433)
Luxury cruises, on relatively small vessels, visit Chilean Tierra del Fuego's Avenida de los Glaciares on weekly circuits between Punta Arenas and the Argentine city of Ushuaia. Most visitors take the trip in one direction or the other; if the weather cooperates, the luckiest get to go ashore at Cape Horn.

**The Channels of the Kawéskar**
(Magallanes, Chile, page 448)
On multi-day cruises from Puerto Natales to Puerto Edén and back, passengers can catch a glimpse of South America's longest glacier, **Glaciar Pío XI,** a staggering 62 kilometers in length and 6 kilometers wide. Many others, such as **Glaciar Amalia,** also get views up close and personal. On a catamaran day-trip from Natales, it's possible to see the **Fiordo de la Montaña,** part of the Kawéskar itinerary that's home to five major glaciers.

Magellanic penguin colony is the continent's largest. From Punta Tombo, a drive along the desolately scenic coastline past Cabo Raso to isolated Camarones for lunch, and on to Bahía Bustamante for accommodations and excursions to offshore islands or a nearby petrified forest.

## Days 6-7

Southbound on RN 3, make a brief stop at Comodoro Rivadavia's first-rate petroleum museum, Museo Nacional del Petróleo, before continuing to picturesque Puerto Deseado and its unique estuary, the Reserva Natural Provincial Ría Deseado, an outstanding eastbound detour off the highway.

The next morning, go on a full-day excursion on the Ría Deseado, home to penguins, cormorants, many other seabirds, and especially dolphins. Or, time and conditions permitting, sail to offshore Isla Pingüinos, site of the world's northernmost rockhopper colony, along with Magellanics and many sea lions.

## Day 8

Drive south on RN 3 to Puerto San Julián, where Magellan's crew wintered in 1520 and Sir Francis Drake later put down a mutiny. Its harbor and offshore islands are also home to large populations of dolphins and Magellanic penguins.

## Day 9

Continue on to the stunning headlands of Parque Nacional Monte León, a short detour off the main road. Check the tide tables at the park visitors center on the highway at the former *estancia*'s *casco,* in order to be able to walk the beach, enter the sea caves, and approach the cormorant-covered Isla Monte León. You'll find exceptional accommodations at Hostería Monte León, in the nearby town of Comandante Luis Piedra Buena, or when camping at the park itself.

elephant seal pup on the coast of Argentine Patagonia, near Puerto Deseado

## Day 10

Departing in the morning or afternoon, head south on RN 3 to Río Gallegos, capital of Santa Cruz province. Find accommodations in town or at the remote Estancia Monte Dinero, near the large Magellanic penguin colony at Reserva Provincial Cabo Vírgenes, the easternmost point of the Strait of Magellan.

## Days 11-12

After a visit to Gallegos's Museo Regional Provincial Padre Jesús Molina, make a post-lunch departure for El Calafate, gateway to Parque Nacional Los Glaciares; en route, northwest-bound RP 5 becomes briefly contiguous with northbound RN 40. Time permitting, visit a working *estancia* (ranch) for an *asado* (barbecue). Otherwise, dine at one of El Calafate's fine restaurants.

The following morning, take a full-day overland excursion to the Glaciar Perito Moreno in Parque Nacional Los Glaciares.

## Days 13-16

East of El Calafate, retake northbound RN 40 and then westbound RP 23 to El Chaltén, in Sector Fitz Roy of Parque Nacional Los Glaciares. With an early arrival and good weather, you can make a swift hike to view Cerro Torre's namesake glaciated needle. Find accommodations in or near town.

The following morning, plan on a demanding full-day hike to Laguna de los Tres, for views of Cerro Fitz Roy. On the next day, take a full-day boat excursion to Glaciar Viedma, including a short hike on the glacier itself. With a midafternoon return on a long summer day, there's time to drive north on RP 23 to Lago del Desierto, near the Chilean border.

Schedule an extra day here in case of bad weather, and if every day's fine, do another hike to Loma del Pliegue Tumbado for its panoramas of the Fitz Roy range.

## Day 17

In the morning, return to northbound RN 40, passing Tres Lagos en route to Lago Cardiel, over what is traditionally the ruggedest part of La Cuarenta (RN 40). Check into accommodations at Estancia La Angostura, Estancia La Siberia, or in Gobernador Gregores.

## Days 18-19

Depart in the morning for Parque Nacional Perito Moreno, an 80-kilometer westbound detour on RP 37, staying at Estancia Menelik or Estancia La Oriental, or camping.

The next morning, hike to the summit of Cerro León, which has panoramic views across the eastern steppe, west toward the Andes on the Chilean border, with numerous condors and guanacos en route.

## Day 20

In the morning return to RN 40 toward Bajo Caracoles and Cueva de las Manos, the world-famous rock-art site. The only real accommodations option along the route is Estancia Cueva de las Manos, north of Bajo Caracoles, which offers the option of a short but scenic hike to the site, rather than a drive northeast from Bajo Caracoles on RP 41. Otherwise, continue to the town of Perito Moreno; alternatively, make a westbound detour on RP 41 from Bajo Caracoles to Paso Roballos and then north on RP 11 to Los Antiguos, a lush "banana belt" town on the south shore of Lago Buenos Aires.

Cerro Fitz Roy

La Trochita, Patagonia's famous narrow-gauge railway

## Day 21

Head to Río Mayo and Sarmiento, gateway to a spectacular petrified-forest badlands. Find accommodations in or near Sarmiento, which requires a detour on eastbound RP 20.

## Days 22-23

Today it's a long day's drive to Esquel, a short detour off RN 40 and the terminus of the famous narrow-gauge railway La Trochita (the so-called "Old Patagonian Express"). The next morning, make an excursion on La Trochita to the Mapuche hamlet of Nahuel Pan. In the afternoon visit the historic Welsh mill town of Trevelin, its Museo Histórico Regional Molino Viejo, and surrounding historic sites; in late afternoon, have a traditional Welsh tea in lieu of dinner.

## Days 24-25

Head toward the Andes and Parque Nacional Los Alerces on RN 259 and RP 71; the park offers camping, cabañas, and hotels. Take a day hike on any of several accessible trails.

The following morning, plan a full-day lake excursion to the *alerce* forests of Parque Nacional Los Alerces.

## Day 26

Northbound on RP 71, Butch Cassidy's restored Patagonian cabin at Cholila is the main attraction, along with RN 40's Museo Leleque, a Benetton-sponsored historical museum at Leleque. Loop back south to Esquel for accommodations.

## Day 27

On the long RN 25 drive across the Patagonian steppe to Trelew or Puerto Madryn, the main reward is the canyon scenery of the middle Chubut valley, at Paso de los Indios and Valle de los Mártires; carry empanadas from Esquel, as the few restaurants are dire.

## Day 28

This is a rest and relaxation day at Puerto Madryn.

## Days 29-30

Catch a morning flight to Buenos Aires, leaving the afternoon and evening free for sightseeing and perhaps a tango floor show. You'll have most of the following day free for exploring Buenos Aires before your evening departure flight.

# BUENOS AIRES

South America's highest-profile capital, Buenos Aires, has evolved dramatically since its shaky colonial origins. Massive post-independence immigration and prosperity turned a cozy "Gran Aldea" (Great Village) into a "Paris of the South" with broad avenues, colossal monuments, and mansard-capped mansions.

In the 20th century, Buenos Aires experienced spectacular spurts of growth and even more spectacular economic and political disasters. Yet somehow, like its melancholy signature music and dance, the tango, it's retained its identity and mystique.

Despite Argentina's problems, the Río de la Plata's megalopolis still has much to offer urban explorers in a city that truly never sleeps. It's one of the most underrated destinations on an underrated continent—even during the 2002 economic and political crisis, *Travel + Leisure* called it Latin America's top tourist city.

Foreign visitors often conflate the city with Argentina—though provincial Argentines adamantly assert, "Buenos Aires is *not* Argentina." Despite a cosmopolitan outlook, many Porteños ("residents of the port") identify more strongly with their own Gran Aldea barrios or neighborhoods. Like New Yorkers, they often seem brash and assertive, their accent setting them apart from the provincial residents.

Buenos Aires has a humid coastal climate resembling that of Washington D.C. for most of the year, with particularly hot and muggy summers. Unlike Washington, though, Buenos Aires has mild winters, and it has snowed only once in the last century. The daily maximum temperature averages 30.4°C in January; it's

© WAYNE BERNHARDSON

## HIGHLIGHTS

**Plaza de Mayo:** Buenos Aires's historic center is ground zero for public life in Argentina (page 35).

**Café Tortoni:** For nearly a century and a half, the Avenida de Mayo's traditional gathering place has been an island of stability in a tumultuous ocean of political, social, and economic upheaval (page 35).

**Teatro Colón:** Having celebrated Argentina's bicentennial with a major restoration, the continent's most important performing arts venue retains its style and dignity (page 41).

**Plaza Dorrego:** Antiques vendors and spirited performers clog San Telmo's principal plaza and surrounding streets every Sunday (page 42).

**Cementerio de la Recoleta:** For both the living and the dead, the barrio of Recoleta is the capital's prestige address (page 49).

**Museo de Arte Latinoamericano de Buenos Aires (MALBA):** For decades, even during dictatorships, Argentina has had a thriving modern art scene, but Palermo's striking Latin American art museum has given it a focal point (page 51).

**Museo Eva Perón:** Promoted by Evita's partisans, Argentina's first museum dedicated to a woman is as notable for what it omits as for what it includes (page 51).

**Museo Argentino de Ciencias Naturales:** In the decidedly untouristed barrio of Caballito, this improving museum sheds light on Argentina's impressive dinosaur discoveries of recent decades (page 53).

LOOK FOR TO FIND RECOMMENDED SIGHTS, ACTIVITIES, DINING, AND LODGING.

slow to cool off until the early morning hours. In July, the coolest month, the daily maximum averages 13.9°C.

## PLANNING YOUR TIME

Buenos Aires deserves as much time as possible, but Patagonia-bound visitors with limited time will have to pick and choose. Anyone planning an extended stay should consult the author's *Moon Buenos Aires.*

Presuming no more than two days in town, visitors should focus on central highlights like the Plaza de Mayo and vicinity, the Teatro Colón, the southern barrios of San Telmo and La Boca, the famous Recoleta cemetery, plus the art museums of Palermo.

## HISTORY

Buenos Aires dates from the 1536 landing of Pedro de Mendoza, but his party failed to survive supply shortages and Querandí attacks. Juan de Garay refounded the city in 1580, but for nearly two centuries it was a backwater, subordinate to Spain's viceregal capital of Lima.

Mendoza's lasting legacy was the escaped livestock that transformed the surrounding *pampas* (grasslands) into a fenceless ranch. Feral cattle and horses, nearly free for the taking, spawned Argentina's gaucho culture.

Buenos Aires had few markets, though, because low-value hides were too bulky to ship to Spain via Lima and Panama. This led to vigorous contraband with British and Portuguese vessels in the Paraná delta and obliged Spain to make Buenos Aires capital of the Virreinato del Río de la Plata (Viceroyalty of the River Plate).

Late colonial Porteños resisted British invasions in 1806 and 1807, but those invasions hastened the Revolution of May 1810, the beginning of the end of Spanish rule. In 1816, the Provincias Unidas del Río de la Plata (United Provinces of the River Plate) formally declared independence.

Following decades of disorder, isolationist caudillo Juan Manuel de Rosas took command of Buenos Aires province, ruling it from 1829 until 1852. When Rosas took power, the provincial capital's population was nearly 60,000; shortly after his departure, it reached 99,000.

Rosas's overthrow and exile brought explosive growth—the city's population more than doubled, to 230,000, by 1875. In 1880, it became the federal capital and, by the early 20th century, Latin America's first city with more than a million inhabitants.

## From Gran Aldea to Cosmopolitan Capital

Federalized Buenos Aires's first mayor, Torcuato de Alvear, soon imposed his vision on the newly designated capital. Instead of the intimate Gran Aldea (Great Village), Buenos Aires would become a cosmopolitan showpiece. Where single-story houses had lined narrow colonial streets, broad boulevards like the Avenida de Mayo soon linked majestic public buildings.

Newly landscaped spaces like the Plaza de Mayo, Plaza del Congreso, and Plaza San Martín reflected an ambitious country's aspirations. Some, though, castigated Alvear for favoring upper-class barrios like Recoleta and Palermo over immigrant neighborhoods like San Telmo and La Boca.

As European immigrants streamed into Buenos Aires, such inequitable treatment exacerbated social tensions. In 1913, it became the first South American city to open a subway system, even as large families on subsistence wages squeezed into *conventillos* (tenements) in poorer neighborhoods. The tension between rich and poor often exploded into open conflict.

In the 1930s, the military dictatorship that overthrew President Hipólito Yrigoyen further obliterated narrow colonial streets to create broad thoroughfares like Corrientes and Santa Fe, as well as the cross-town Avenida 9 de Julio. Despite lip service to working-class interests, the populist Perón regimes of the 1940s and 1950s splurged on pharaonic projects, heavy and heavily subsidized industry,

© EDUARDO RIVERO/123RF

the Congreso Nacional in Buenos Aires

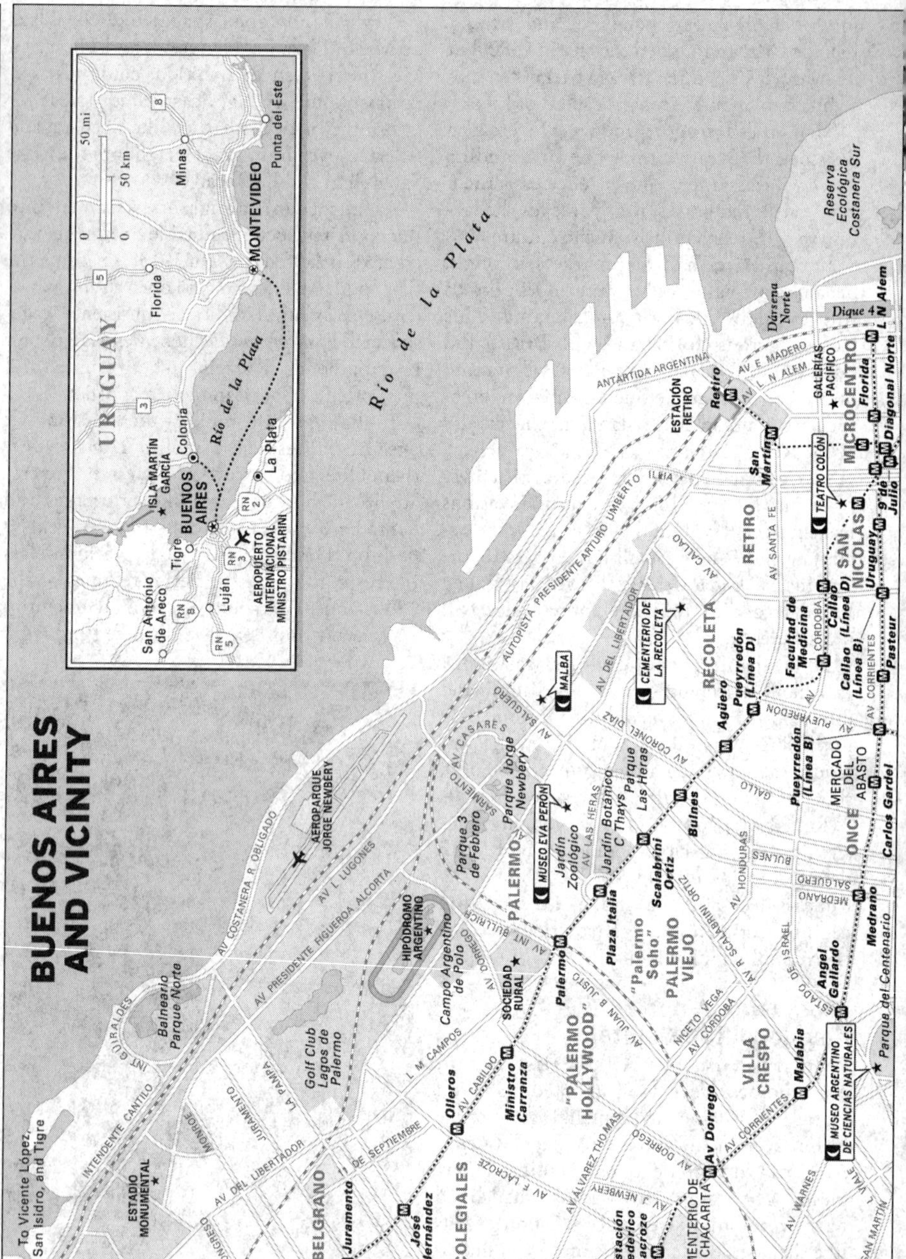
BUENOS AIRES AND VICINITY
Río de la Plata
URUGUAY
MONTEVIDEO
Punta del Este
Minas
Florida
Colonia
ISLA MARTÍN GARCÍA
BUENOS AIRES
Tigre
San Antonio de Areco
Luján
La Plata
AEROPUERTO INTERNACIONAL MINISTRO PISTARINI
0 50 mi
0 50 km
To Vicente López, San Isidro, and Tigre
ESTADIO MONUMENTAL
Balneario Parque Norte
AEROPARQUE JORGE NEWBERY
HIPÓDROMO ARGENTINO
Golf Club Lagos de Palermo
Campo Argentino de Polo
SOCIEDAD RURAL
Parque 3 de Febrero
Parque Jorge Newbery
PALERMO
MUSEO EVA PERÓN
Jardín Zoológico
Jardín Botánico C Thays
Parque Las Heras
MALBA
CEMENTERIO DE LA RECOLETA
RECOLETA
RETIRO
ESTACIÓN RETIRO
Dársena Norte
Dique 4
Reserva Ecológica Costanera Sur
GALERÍAS PACÍFICO
MICROCENTRO
TEATRO COLÓN
SAN NICOLÁS
ONCE
MERCADO DEL ABASTO
"PALERMO HOLLYWOOD"
"Palermo Soho"
PALERMO VIEJO
VILLA CRESPO
MUSEO ARGENTINO DE CIENCIAS NATURALES
Parque del Centenario
CEMENTERIO DE LA CHACARITA
BELGRANO
COLEGIALES
Juramento
José Hernández
Olleros
Ministro Carranza
Palermo
Plaza Italia
Scalabrini Ortiz
Bulnes
Agüero
Pueyrredón (Línea D)
Facultad de Medicina
Callao (Línea D)
Callao (Línea B)
Pueyrredón (Línea B)
Carlos Gardel
Medrano
Angel Gallardo
Malabia
Av Dorrego
Estación Federico Lacroze
Pasteur
Uruguay
9 de Julio
Diagonal Norte
Florida
L N Alem
San Martín
Retiro
AV COSTANERA R. OBLIGADO
AV PRESIDENTE FIGUEROA ALCORTA
AV L LUGONES
AV DEL LIBERTADOR
AUTOPISTA PRESIDENTE ARTURO UMBERTO ILLIA
ANTÁRTIDA ARGENTINA
AV E MADERO
AV L N ALEM
AV SANTA FE
AV CALLAO
CÓRDOBA
AV CORRIENTES
AV PUEYRREDÓN
AV CORONEL DÍAZ
AV LAS HERAS
AV SARMIENTO
AV CASARES
AV SALGUERO
AV INT BULLRICH
AV DORREGO
AV JUAN B JUSTO
AV R SCALABRINI ORTIZ
NICETO VEGA
AV CÓRDOBA
AV HONDURAS
GALLO
BULNES
SALGUERO
MEDRANO
ESTADO DE ISRAEL
AV CABILDO
L M CAMPOS
LA PAMPA
JURAMENTO
MONROE
INTENDENTE CANTILO
INT GUIRALDES
11 DE SEPTIEMBRE
AV CONGRESO
AV F LACROZE
AV ALVAREZ THOMAS
AV J NEWBERY
AV WARNES
VIALE
AV SAN MARTÍN

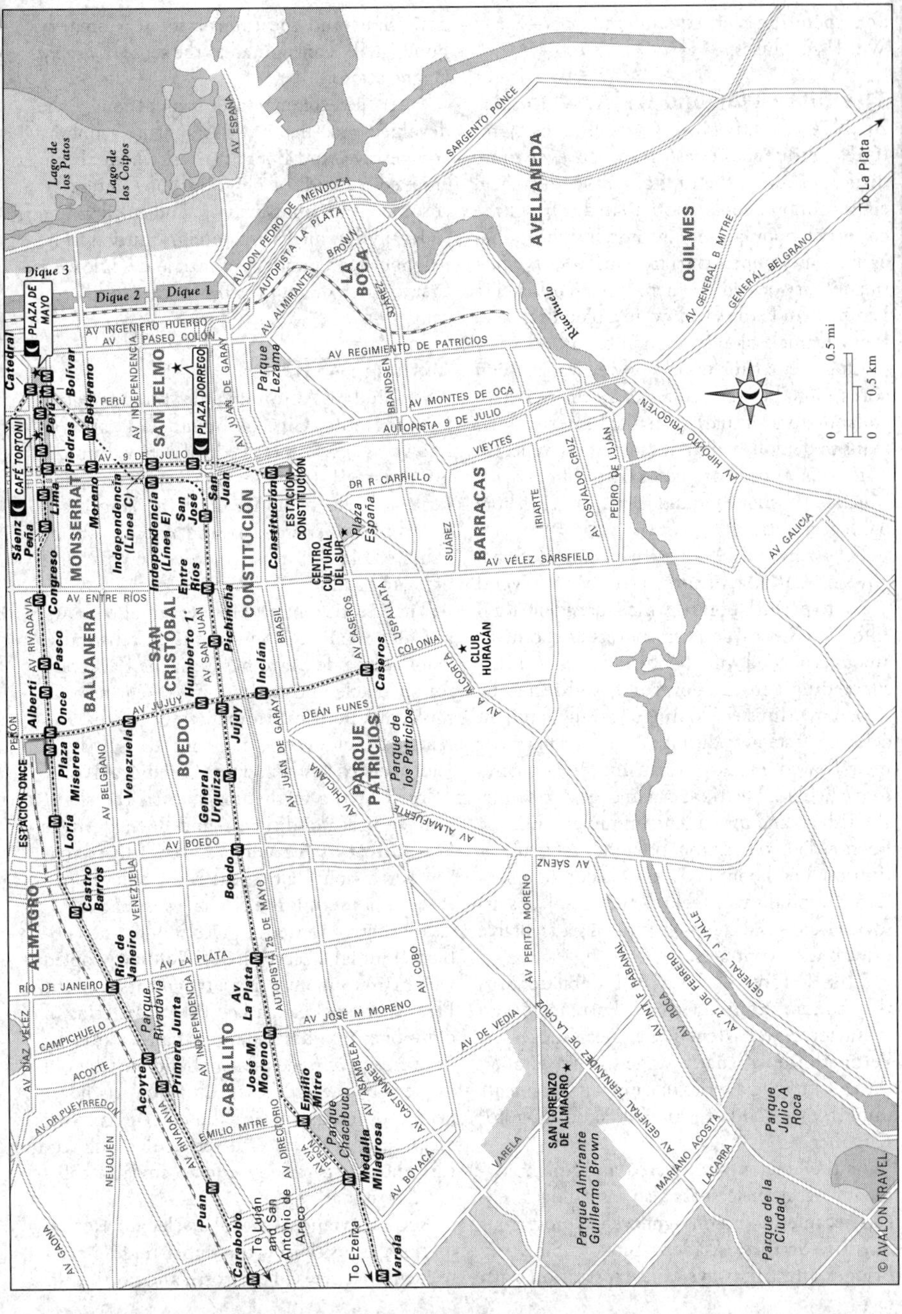
AVELLANEDA
QUILMES
LA BOCA
SAN TELMO
MONSERRAT
BALVANERA
SAN CRISTOBAL
CONSTITUCIÓN
BOEDO
ALMAGRO
CABALLITO
PARQUE PATRICIOS
BARRACAS
PLAZA DE MAYO
PLAZA DORREGO
CAFÉ TORTONI
Catedral
Bolívar
Belgrano
Perú
Piedras
Lima
Sáenz Peña
Congreso
Moreno
Independencia (Línea C)
Independencia (Línea E)
San José
San Juan
Constitución
ESTACIÓN CONSTITUCIÓN
CENTRO CULTURAL DEL SUR
Plaza España
Entre Ríos
Pichincha
Humberto 1˚
Jujuy
Inclán
Caseros
CLUB HURACÁN
Pasco
Alberti
Once
Plaza Miserere
ESTACIÓN ONCE
Venezuela
General Urquiza
Boedo
Loria
Castro Barros
Río de Janeiro
Av La Plata
José M. Moreno
Emilio Mitre
Medalla Milagrosa
Varela
Acoyte
Primera Junta
Puán
Carabobo
Parque Rivadavia
Parque Chacabuco
Parque Lezama
Parque de los Patricios
SAN LORENZO DE ALMAGRO
Parque Almirante Guillermo Brown
Parque de la Ciudad
Parque Julio A Roca
Lago de los Patos
Lago de los Coipos
Dique 1
Dique 2
Dique 3
Riachuelo
AV INGENIERO HUERGO
AV PASEO COLÓN
AV INDEPENDENCIA
AV 9 DE JULIO
AV JUAN DE GARAY
AV ENTRE RÍOS
AV RIVADAVIA
AV SAN JUAN
AV JUJUY
AV BELGRANO
AV BOEDO
VENEZUELA
AV LA PLATA
RÍO DE JANEIRO
CAMPICHUELO
ACOYTE
AV DÍAZ VÉLEZ
AV DR PUEYRREDÓN
NEUQUÉN
AV GAONA
EMILIO MITRE
AV RIVADAVIA
AV DIRECTORIO
AUTOPISTA 25 DE MAYO
AV JOSÉ M MORENO
AV COBO
AV ASAMBLEA
AV CASTAÑARES
AV EVA PERÓN
AV BOYACÁ
AV DE VEDIA
AV PERITO MORENO
VARELA
AV FERNÁNDEZ DE LA CRUZ
AV GENERAL FERNÁNDEZ
MARIANO ACOSTA
LACARRA
AV INT F RABANAL
AV ROCA
AV 27 DE FEBRERO
GENERAL J J VALLE
AV SÁENZ
AV ALMAFUERTE
AV CHICLANA
DEÁN FUNES
AV CASEROS
BRASIL
USPALLATA
COLONIA
AV A ALCORTA
AV VÉLEZ SARSFIELD
SUÁREZ
IRIARTE
AV OSVALDO CRUZ
PEDRO DE LUJÁN
DR R CARRILLO
VIEYTES
AUTOPISTA 9 DE JULIO
AV MONTES DE OCA
AV REGIMIENTO DE PATRICIOS
BRANDSEN
AV ALMIRANTE BROWN
AUTOPISTA LA PLATA
AV DON PEDRO DE MENDOZA
AV ESPAÑA
SARGENTO PONCE
AV HIPÓLITO YRIGOYEN
AV GALICIA
AV GENERAL B MITRE
AV GENERAL BELGRANO
PERÚ
PERÓN
To La Plata
To Luján and San Antonio de Areco
To Ezeiza
0 0.5 mi
0 0.5 km
© AVALON TRAVEL

and spending that squandered post–World War II surpluses.

### The Dirty War and Its Aftermath

By 1970, as sprawling Gran Buenos Aires (Greater Buenos Aires) absorbed ever more distant suburbs, the capital and vicinity held eight million people, more than a third of the country's population. Chronic instability became almost open warfare until 1976, when the military ousted the inept President Isabelita Perón (Juan Perón's widow) in a bloodless coup that became a bloody reign of terror.

One pretext for taking power was civilian corruption, but the military and their civilian collaborators similarly attracted international loans to demolish vibrant but neglected neighborhoods and create colossal public works. Much of the money found its way into offshore bank accounts.

Following the 1983 return to constitutional government, Argentina underwent several years' hyperinflation in which President Raúl Alfonsín's Radical government wasted enormous amounts of good will. President Carlos Menem's succeeding Peronist government, directed by Economy Minister Domingo Cavallo, brought a decade of stability during which foreign investment flowed into Argentina, and Buenos Aires in particular. The financial and service sectors flourished, and urban renewal projects like the Puerto Madero riverfront brought a sense of optimism. The boom had a dark side, though, a "crony capitalism" in which the president's associates enriched themselves through favorable privatization contracts.

Even before the late-2001 debt default, the economy contracted and Porteños began to suffer. After Menem's hapless successor, Fernando de la Rúa, resigned in December, the country had a series of caretaker presidents until the May 2003 election of Peronist Néstor Kirchner.

As the economy stagnated and unemployment rose, homelessness also rose and scavengers became a common sight even in prosperous barrios. Strikes, strident pickets blocking bridges and highways, and frustration with politicians and the International Monetary Fund (IMF) contributed to the sense of *bronca* (aggravation).

After the economy hit bottom, though, the devalued peso made the Argentine economy competitive, and Buenos Aires, which always enjoyed a blend of neighborhood integrity, cosmopolitan sophistication, and cultural life, suddenly boomed with foreign tourists. The neighboring republics of Brazil and Chile were first to catch on, but the rest of the world soon caught up.

## ORIENTATION

The Ciudad Autónoma de Buenos Aires (Autonomous City of Buenos Aires), also known as the Capital Federal, lies within the boundaries formed by the Río de la Plata, its Riachuelo tributary, and the ring roads of Avenida General Paz and Avenida 27 de Febrero. Most visitors see only a key handful of its 47 barrios.

The historic center is **Monserrat** (also known as Catedral al Sur, "South of the Cathedral"), whose Plaza de Mayo has been the flashpoint for spectacle and debacle in Argentina's tumultuous politics. Immediately north, **San Nicolás** includes the compact, densely built **Microcentro** (also known as Catedral al Norte, "North of the Cathedral"), with the shopping and theater districts, and Buenos Aires's Wall Street in "La City." Eastward, stretching north–south along the river, redeveloped **Puerto Madero** is the city's newest barrio.

Southern Monserrat gives way to the cobbled colonial streets of **San Telmo,** peopled with artists and musicians, tango bars, and the Plaza Dorrego flea market, plus a scattering of old-money families and more than a scattering of *conventillos* (tenements) abandoned by old money. To the southeast, **La Boca** has never been prosperous, but it has a colorful history, an extravagantly colorful vernacular architecture and artists' colony, and an enviable community solidarity.

Across Avenida Córdoba, elegant **Retiro** marks a transition to the upper-middle-class residential barrios to the north and northwest.

Immediately northwest, **Recoleta** retains that elegance in one of the world's most exclusive graveyards, where many affluent Argentines have elected to spend eternity. Barrio Norte, a mostly residential area overlapping Retiro and Recoleta, is more a real estate contrivance than a barrio per se.

Beyond Recoleta, broad avenues lead to the open spaces of **Palermo,** a middle- to upper-middle-class barrio with the city's finest dining and wildest nightlife. Woodsy **Belgrano** is a mostly residential barrio with an assortment of museums and other cultural resources.

# Sights

Buenos Aires's sights are mostly easily grouped by the barrios described above, though a few outlying barrios have scattered points of interest.

## MONSERRAT/CATEDRAL AL SUR AND VICINITY

The barrio's axis is the **Avenida de Mayo,** which links the **Casa Rosada** presidential palace (1873–1898) with the **Congreso Nacional** (National Congress, 1908). The perpendicular **Avenida 9 de Julio** splits Monserrat in half.

### Plaza de Mayo

The Plaza de Mayo derives its name from the date of the Revolution of 1810, but it owes its fame to the massive demonstrations that have taken place here in support and protest of the Peróns, the Falklands/Malvinas war, and other political causes.

At the plaza's northwest corner, the imposing **Catedral Metropolitana** (1827) holds the remains of national icon José de San Martín. At the southwest corner, only part of the colonial **Cabildo de Buenos Aires** (1725–1765) survived construction of the Avenida de Mayo. If the economy were as solid as the northeast corner's neoclassical **Banco de la Nación** (1939), Argentina would be a global powerhouse.

© WAYNE BERNHARDSON

The Cabildo is one of the few colonial buildings in downtown Buenos Aires.

### Café Tortoni

First among the Avenida de Mayo's surviving landmarks, the legendary Café Tortoni (Av. de Mayo 825, tel. 011/4342-4328, www.cafetortoni.com.ar) dates from 1858. One of Buenos Aires's most fiercely if quietly traditional places, the Tortoni has made no concessions to the 21st century and only a few to the 20th: Upholstered chairs and marble tables stand among sturdy columns beneath a ceiling punctuated by stained-glass vitreaux; the wallpaper looks original between the dark-stained wooden trim; and the walls are decorated with pictures, portraits, and *filete,* the traditional calligraphy of Porteño sign-painters.

Among the patrons acknowledged on the walls are tango singer Carlos Gardel, La Boca painter Benito Quinquela Martín, dramatists

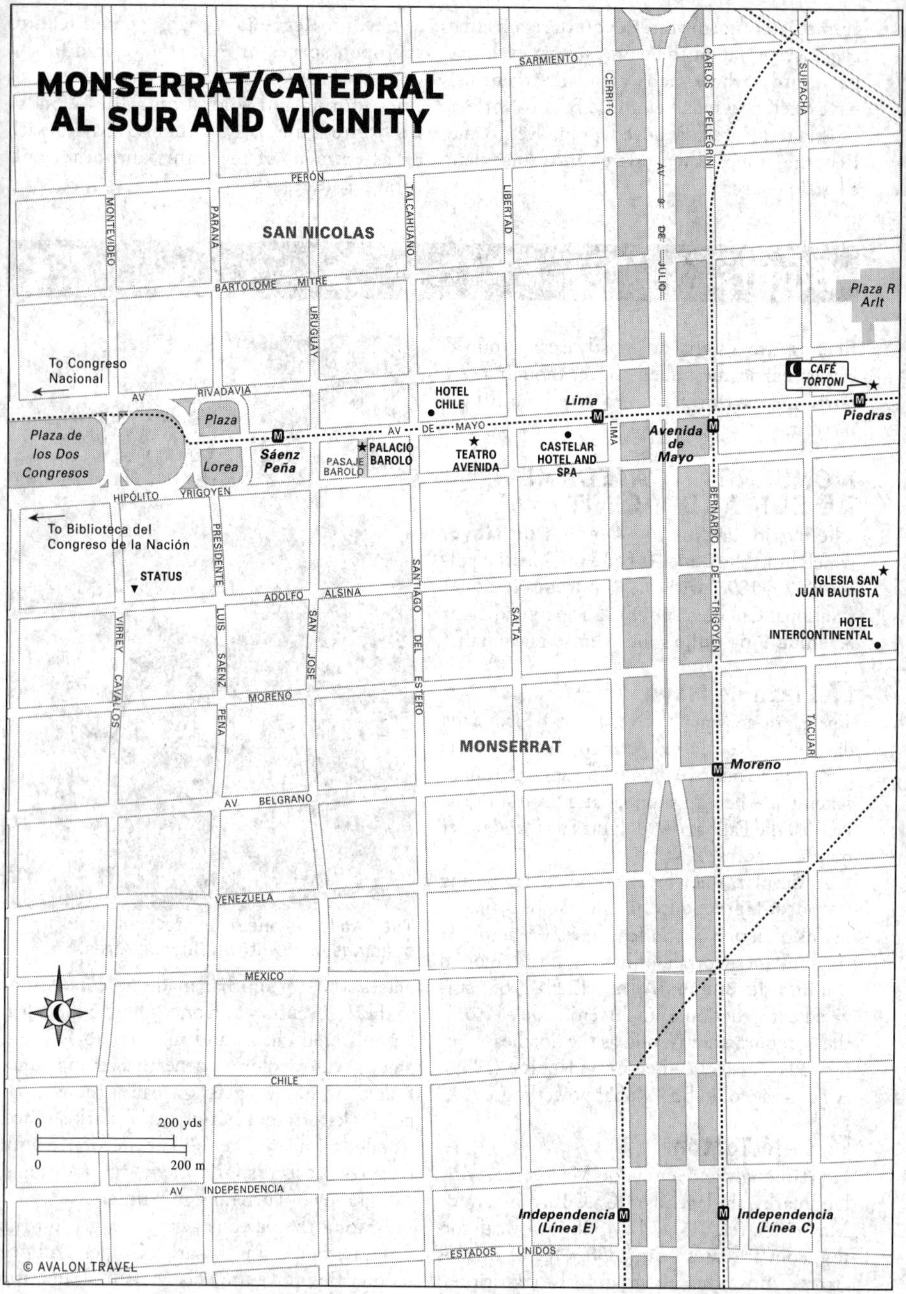
MONSERRAT/CATEDRAL AL SUR AND VICINITY
SAN NICOLAS
MONSERRAT
SARMIENTO
PERÓN
BARTOLOME MITRE
AV RIVADAVIA
AV DE MAYO
HIPÓLITO YRIGOYEN
ADOLFO ALSINA
MORENO
AV BELGRANO
VENEZUELA
MEXICO
CHILE
AV INDEPENDENCIA
ESTADOS UNIDOS
MONTEVIDEO
PARANÁ
URUGUAY
TALCAHUANO
LIBERTAD
CERRITO
CARLOS PELLEGRINI
AV 9 DE JULIO
LIMA
BERNARDO DE IRIGOYEN
SUIPACHA
TACUARI
PRESIDENTE LUIS SAENZ PEÑA
SAN JOSE
SANTIAGO DEL ESTERO
SALTA
VIRREY CAVALLOS
To Congreso Nacional
To Biblioteca del Congreso de la Nación
Plaza de los Dos Congresos
Plaza Lorea
Sáenz Peña
PASAJE BAROLO
PALACIO BAROLO
HOTEL CHILE
TEATRO AVENIDA
CASTELAR HOTEL AND SPA
Lima
Avenida de Mayo
CAFÉ TORTONI
Piedras
Plaza R Arlt
STATUS
IGLESIA SAN JUAN BAUTISTA
HOTEL INTERCONTINENTAL
Moreno
Independencia (Línea E)
Independencia (Línea C)
0 200 yds
0 200 m
© AVALON TRAVEL

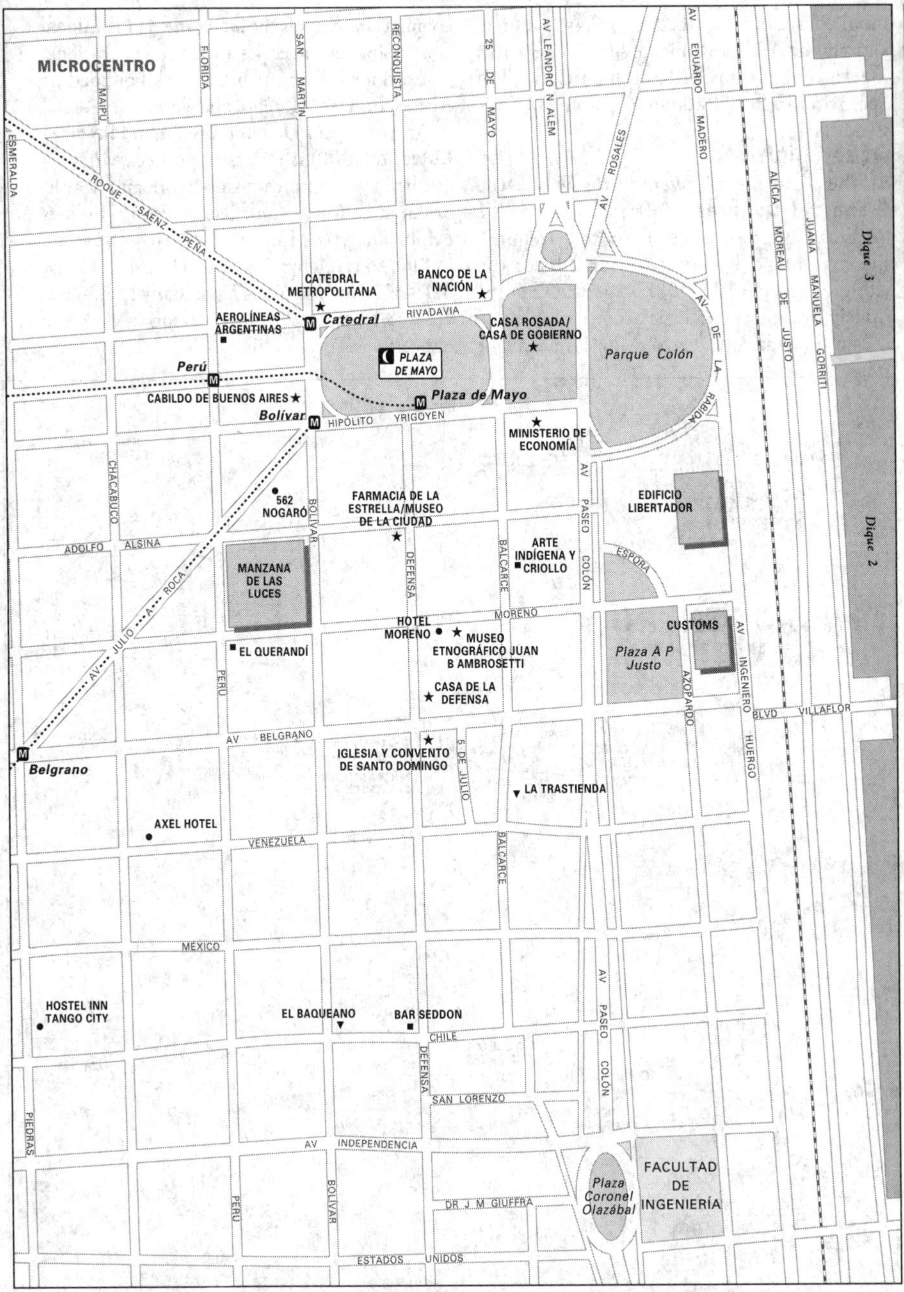
MICROCENTRO
CATEDRAL METROPOLITANA
BANCO DE LA NACIÓN
AEROLÍNEAS ARGENTINAS
Catedral
CASA ROSADA/ CASA DE GOBIERNO
PLAZA DE MAYO
Parque Colón
Perú
Plaza de Mayo
CABILDO DE BUENOS AIRES
Bolívar
MINISTERIO DE ECONOMÍA
562 NOGARÓ
FARMACIA DE LA ESTRELLA/MUSEO DE LA CIUDAD
EDIFICIO LIBERTADOR
ARTE INDÍGENA Y CRIOLLO
MANZANA DE LAS LUCES
HOTEL MORENO
MUSEO ETNOGRÁFICO JUAN B AMBROSETTI
CUSTOMS
Plaza A P Justo
EL QUERANDÍ
CASA DE LA DEFENSA
IGLESIA Y CONVENTO DE SANTO DOMINGO
Belgrano
LA TRASTIENDA
AXEL HOTEL
HOSTEL INN TANGO CITY
EL BAQUEANO
BAR SEDDON
Plaza Coronel Olazábal
FACULTAD DE INGENIERÍA
Dique 3
Dique 2
ESMERALDA
MAIPÚ
FLORIDA
SAN MARTÍN
RECONQUISTA
25 DE MAYO
AV LEANDRO N ALEM
AV ROSALES
AV EDUARDO MADERO
ALICIA MOREAU DE JUSTO
JUANA MANUELA GORRITI
ROQUE SAENZ PEÑA
RIVADAVIA
AV DE LA RABIDA
HIPÓLITO YRIGOYEN
CHACABUCO
BOLÍVAR
AV PASEO COLÓN
ADOLFO ALSINA
DEFENSA
BALCARCE
ESPORA
MORENO
AV JULIO A ROCA
PERÚ
AZOPARDO
AV INGENIERO HUERGO
BLVD VILLAFLOR
AV BELGRANO
5 DE JULIO
VENEZUELA
MÉXICO
CHILE
SAN LORENZO
AV INDEPENDENCIA
PIEDRAS
DR J M GIUFFRA
ESTADOS UNIDOS

Luigi Pirandello and Federico García Lorca, and pianist Arthur Rubinstein; more recently, the Tortoni has hosted King Juan Carlos I of Spain and Hillary Rodham Clinton.

## Other Sights

At the west end of Avenida de Mayo, the **Plaza del Congreso** (officially, Plaza de los Dos Congresos, 1904), another frequent site for political demonstrations, faces the Congreso Nacional (1908), Argentina's notoriously dysfunctional legislature.

South of Plaza de Mayo, Monserrat's major colonial landmark is the **Manzana de las Luces,** comprising several ecclesiastical and educational institutions filling an entire block bounded by Alsina, Bolívar, Moreno, and Perú.

At Alsina and Defensa, the **Farmacia de la Estrella** (1900) is a classic apothecary distinguished by magnificent woodwork and health-oriented ceiling murals. Its exterior windows exhibit materials from the upstairs **Museo de la Ciudad** (Defensa 219, tel. 011/4343-2123 or 011/4331-9855, 11 A.M.–7 P.M. daily Mar.–Jan., US$0.80, free Wed.), specializing in elements of everyday Porteño life.

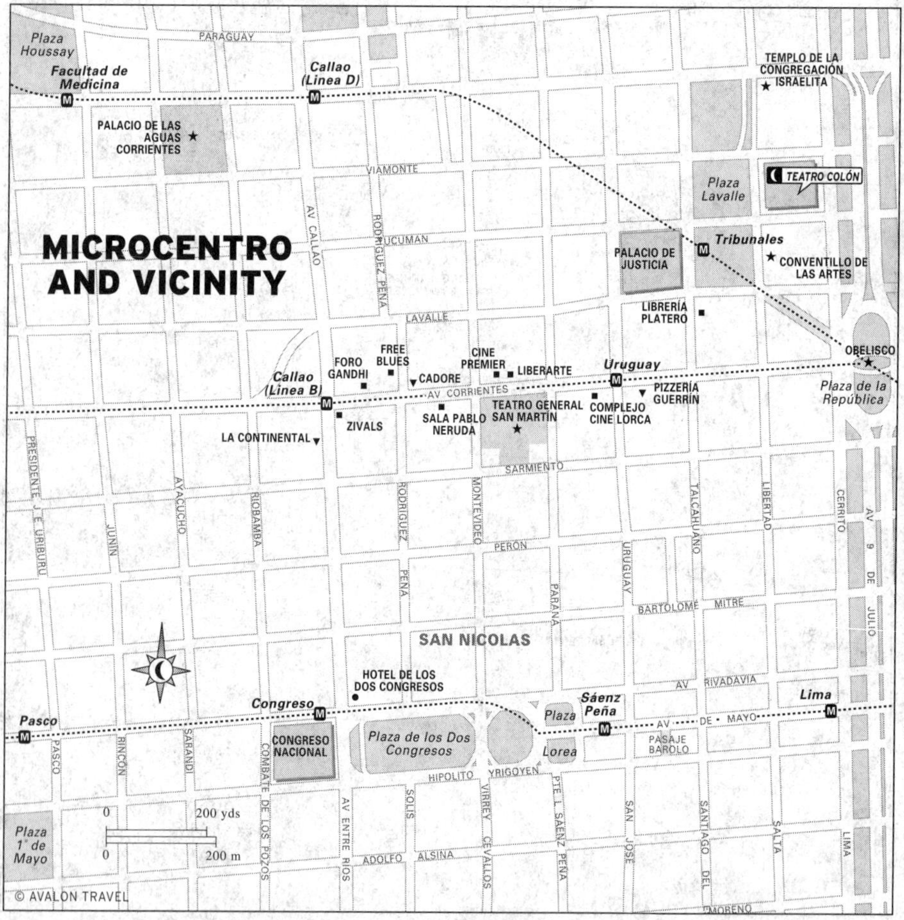

A block south, the **Museo Etnográfico Juan B. Ambrosetti** (Moreno 350, tel. 011/4345-8196, www.museoetnografico.filo.uba.ar, 1–7 P.M. Tues.–Sun. and 3–7 P.M. Sat.–Sun. Feb.–Dec., US$0.75, free for retirees) has superb archaeological, ethnographic, and ethnohistorical displays on the Tierra del Fuego archipelago. There are guided tours weekends at 4 P.M.

From the roof of the **Casa de la Defensa** (Defensa 372), Porteños poured boiling oil on British invaders in 1806–1807. Half a block south, at Avenida Belgrano, the 18th-century **Iglesia y Convento de Santo Domingo** shares grounds with the Instituto Nacional Belgraniano, a patriotic institute that contains the tomb of Argentine flag designer General Manuel Belgrano.

## MICROCENTRO AND VICINITY

Formally known as San Nicolás, the area bounded by Avenida Córdoba, Avenida Madero, Avenida Rivadavia, and Avenida Callao encompasses the city's traditional financial, commercial, and entertainment centers. The area between Avenida 9 de Julio and the riverfront, immediately north of the Plaza

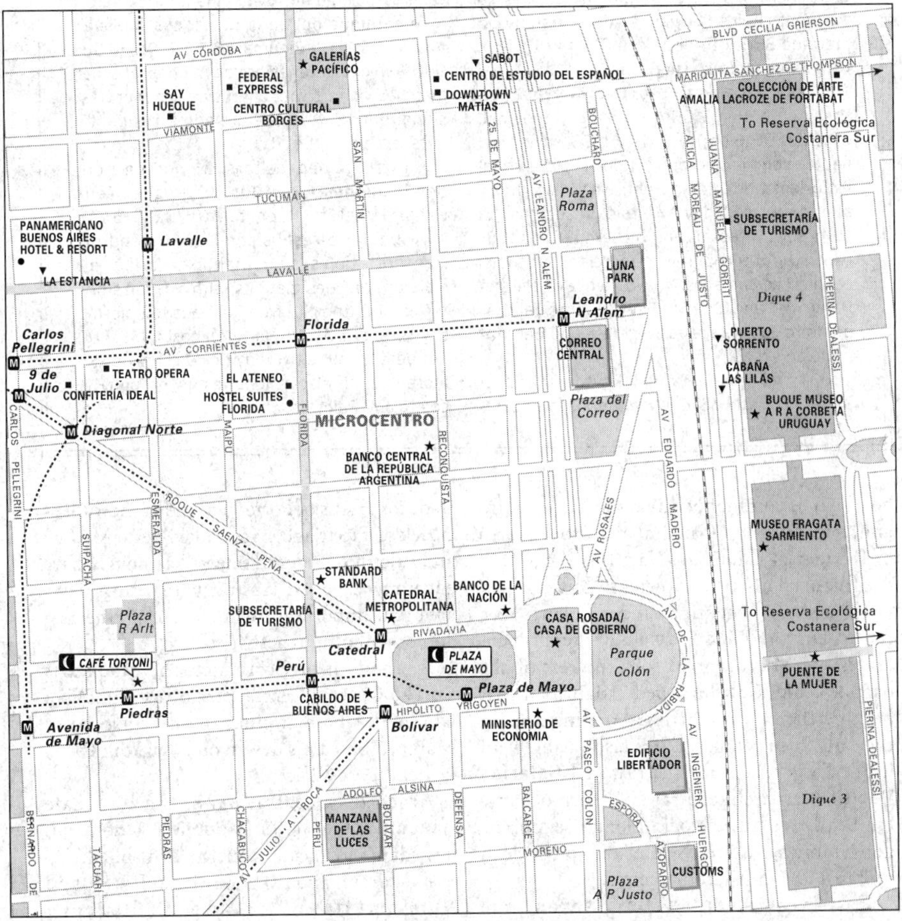

## ORGANIZED TOURS

Some of the city's best guided tours are available through the municipal tourist office on Saturday and Sunday, often but not always with English-speaking guides. The complete schedule appears on the city government's website (www.bue.gov.ar). In case of rain, the tours are canceled, and they usually do not take place in the summer months of January and February.

For conventional tours of the capital and vicinity, including the Microcentro, Recoleta and Palermo, and San Telmo and La Boca, a frequent choice is **Buenos Aires Visión** (Esmeralda 356, 8th floor, tel. 011/4394-2986, www.buenosaires-vision.com.ar).

Highly recommended **Eternautas** (Av. Presidente Julio A. Roca 584, 7th floor, tel. 011/5031-9916 or 011/15-4173-1078, www.eternautas.com) is an organization of professional historians who offer inexpensive walking tours and longer half-day excursions, such as "El Otro Sur," a fascinating three-hour bus tour (US$30 pp) through working-class southern barrios like Barracas, Nueva Pompeya, Parque Patricios, and Boedo. They also go farther afield to such places as La Plata and San Antonio de Areco.

By its very name, **Tangol** (Florida 971, Local 31, tel. 011/4312-7276, www.tangol.com) combines those two Porteño passions, tango and soccer *(igo-o-ol!)*, in its offerings. It also does excursions farther afield in Buenos Aires province and elsewhere. For a commercial website it's surprisingly informative as well.

**Travel Line Argentina** (Viamonte 640, 9th floor, tel. 011/4393-9000, www.travelline.com.ar) conducts specialty excursions such as its "Evita Tour" (four hours, US$55), which takes in the CGT labor headquarters, Luna Park Stadium, the Perón and Duarte residences, and other locales associated with Evita's meteoric career.

One unique option is **Cicerones de Buenos Aires** (J. J. Biedma 883, tel. 011/5258-0909, www.cicerones.org.ar), a nonprofit that matches visitors with enthusiastic nonprofessional guides who can provide a resident's perspective on the city.

For self-guided visitors, a good new option is **Buenos Aires Bus** (Av. Roque Sáenz Peña 846, 10th floor, tel. 011/5239-5160, www.buenosairesbus.com), an on-and-off transportation system that links various attractions and destinations, with a dozen stops throughout the city from La Boca to Palermo (9 A.M.–8 P.M.). A 24-hour ticket costs US$17.50 per person, but a two-day ticket is only US$5 more; there is also a nightlife bus through Recoleta and Palermo.

de Mayo, is commonly called the Microcentro and, occasionally, "Catedral al Norte." North of Rivadavia, Calle San Martín is the axis of the financial district, known as "La City."

Named for Argentina's independence day, the 16-lane **Avenida 9 de Julio** literally separates the Microcentro from the rest of the barrio. **Calle Florida,** a pedestrian mall that became the city's smartest shopping area in the early 20th century, is less fashionable than it once was except for the restored **Galerías Pacífico,** an architectural landmark occupying nearly an entire block. Don't overlook its dome murals, inspired by the famous Mexican muralist Davíd Alfaro Siqueiros.

East–west **Avenida Corrientes,** the traditional axis of Porteño nightlife, now takes a back seat to trendier areas like Puerto Madero and Palermo. Widened sidewalks, though, have encouraged pedestrian traffic to return in an area still important for its theaters, cinemas, and other cultural activities.

At the foot of Corrientes, the beaux arts **Correo Central** (central post office, 1928) is a landmark whose original architect, Norberto Maillart, based his design on New York City's General Post Office.

Argentina's central bank, the Italianate **Banco Central de la República Argentina,** has identical facades on the 200 blocks of San Martín and Reconquista. Its **Museo Numismático Dr. José E. Uriburu**

(Reconquista 266, tel. 011/4393-0021, 10 A.M.–3 P.M. weekdays, free) helps explain the country's volatile economic history.

At Avenida 9 de Julio and Corrientes, the 67.5-meter **Obelisco** (Obelisk, 1936) is a city symbol erected for the 400th anniversary of Pedro de Mendoza's landing. From the Obelisco, the Diagonal Roque Sáenz Peña ends at **Plaza Lavalle,** where the **Palacio de Justicia** ("Tribunales" or Law Courts, 1904) has lent its colloquial name to the neighborhood.

Across the plaza is the stately, newly renovated **Teatro Colón** (1908) opera house. To its north, fronting on Libertad and protected by bulky concrete planter boxes, the **Templo de la Congregación Israelita** (1932) is the capital's largest synagogue. Do not photograph this or any other Jewish community site without express permission.

© WAYNE BERNHARDSON

**Marking the 400th anniversary of the founding of Buenos Aires, the Obelisco is the local counterpart of the Washington Monument.**

## Teatro Colón

Possibly the continent's most important performing arts venue, the ornate Colón reopened in 2010 after a bicentennial makeover. Moved from an earlier Plaza de Mayo site, the current theater dates from 1908; Francesco Tamburini's Italian Renaissance structure replaced the city's first railway station.

Occupying a lot of more than 8,000 square meters, with floor space of nearly 38,000 square meters on seven levels, the Colón opened with a performance of Verdi's *Aida*. Seating 2,478 patrons, with standing room for another 700, it's one of the country's most ornate buildings, its **Gran Hall** outfitted with Verona and Carrara marble, the **Salón de los Bustos** studded with busts of famous figures from European classical music, and the **Salón Dorado** (Golden Salon) modeled on palaces like Paris's Versailles and Vienna's Schönbrunn.

The main theater itself follows lines of French and Italian classics, with world-class acoustics; a rotating disc aids rapid scene changes. The orchestra accommodates up to 120 musicians. Seating ranges from comfortably upholstered rows to luxury boxes, including a presidential box with its own Casa Rosada phone line and a separate exit. Presidential command performances take place on the winter patriotic holidays of May 25 and July 9.

Argentine lyric theater dates from the early 19th century, with early European artists arriving in the 1820s. Since its opening, the current theater's who's who of performers has included Igor Stravinsky, María Callas, Mikhail Baryshnikov, George Balanchine, and Yo-Yo Ma, not to mention world-renowned orchestras and dance companies. At times, though, it's let its hair down to accommodate performers like folksinger Mercedes Sosa, the rhythm-and-blues unit Memphis La Blusera, and rock guitarist-songwriter Luis Alberto Spinetta.

The Teatro Colón (box office at Libertad 621, tel. 011/4378-7344, www.teatrocolon.org.ar) presents some 200 events per annum between May and November. Both events and guided tours were suspended until the theater reopened, but for the latest information contact the Teatro Colón (Viamonte 1168, tel. 011/4378-7132, visitas@teatrocolon.org.ar,

US$15 pp nonresident adults, US$5 Argentine residents, children up to age 6 free); tours last 50 minutes and go behind the scenes as well.

## PUERTO MADERO

Born amidst 19th-century corruption, modern Puerto Madero has reclaimed a riverfront that languished off-limits during the 1976–1983 military dictatorship. Comparable, in some ways, to Baltimore's Inner Harbor and London's Docklands, its focus is four rectangular *diques* (basins) bordered by brick warehouses recycled into stylish lofts, offices, restaurants, bars, and cinemas.

Sequentially numbered from south to north, the four rectangular basins include a 450-berth yacht harbor at Dique No. 3; docked on the west side, the **Museo Fragata *Sarmiento*** (tel. 011/4334-9386, 10 A.M.–7 P.M. daily, US$0.60, children under 5 free) is an early-20th-century naval training vessel.

Spanish architect Santiago Calatrava's **Puente de la Mujer** is a modernistic pedestrian suspension bridge whose rotating center section allows vessels to pass between Dique No. 3 and Dique No. 2. At the northernmost Dique No. 4, the **Buque Museo A.R.A. *Corbeta Uruguay*** (tel. 011/4314-1090, 10 A.M.–7 P.M. daily, US$0.60) rescued Norwegian explorers Carl Skottsberg and Otto Nordenskjöld from Antarctica in 1903. Dating from 1874, it's the oldest Argentine vessel still afloat.

Toward the barrio's north end, the **Hotel de Inmigrantes** was Argentina's Ellis Island for European immigrants; it's now the **Museo Nacional de la Inmigración** (Av. Antártida Argentina 1355, tel. 011/4317-0285, museodelainmigracion@migraciones.gov.ar, 10 A.M.–5 P.M. weekdays, 11 A.M.–6 P.M. weekends, free).

## SAN TELMO

San Telmo, with its narrow colonial streets, antiques shops, and street fairs, appeals to Argentines and foreigners alike. Six blocks south of Plaza de Mayo, it's a fine walkers' neighborhood—especially Sundays, when authorities close most of Calle Defensa to motor vehicles.

After elite families fled an 1870s yellow fever epidemic to northern barrios like Palermo and Belgrano, San Telmo became an area where impoverished immigrant families could find a foothold in *conventillos,* abandoned mansions where large families filled small spaces—often a single room. Today it's a mixed neighborhood where *conventillos* still exist, but young professionals have also recycled crumbling apartment buildings and even industrial sites into lofts. It's also closely linked to tango, or at least the high-priced spectacle with professional dancers.

While colonial Spanish law dictated rectangular city blocks of equal size, San Telmo breaks the rules. North–south **Calle Balcarce,** for instance, doglegs between Chile and Estados Unidos, crossing the cobblestone alleyways of **Pasaje San Lorenzo** and **Pasaje Giuffra.** The **Casa Mínima** (Pasaje San Lorenzo 380) takes the vernacular *casa chorizo* (sausage house) style to an extreme: This two-story colonial adobe is barely wider than an average adult male's armspread.

To the east, on Paseo Colón's **Plaza Coronel Olazábal,** Rogelio Yrurtia's massive sculpture ***Canto al Trabajo*** (Ode to Labor), a tribute to hardworking pioneers, is a welcome antidote to pompous equestrian statues elsewhere.

San Telmo's heart, though, is **Plaza Dorrego** (Defensa and Humberto Primo), site of the hectic weekend flea market. At Defensa and Avenida Brasil, a statue of Pedro de Mendoza guards the entrance to **Parque Lezama,** where Mendoza ostensibly founded the city in 1536.

### Plaza Dorrego

Six days a week, Plaza Dorrego is a shady square where Porteños sip *cortados* and nibble lunches from nearby cafés. Sundays, though, it swarms with visitors who stroll among antiques stalls at the **Feria de San Pedro Telmo,** the most famous of the capital's street fairs. Items range from soda siphons to brightly painted *filete* plaques with *piropos* (aphorisms), oversized antique radios, and many other items. The plaza and side streets also fill with *tangueros* (tango dancers), puppet theaters, hurdy-gurdy

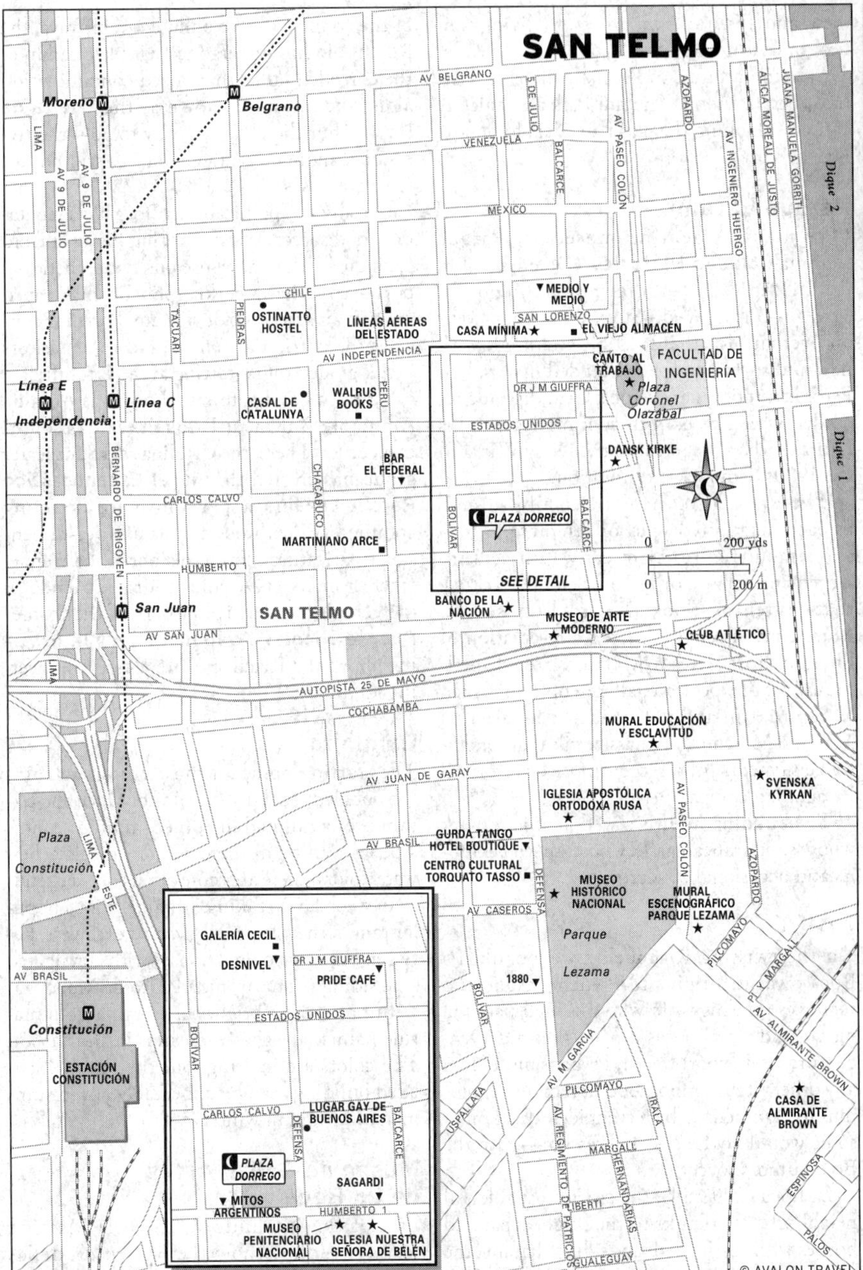


© AVALON TRAVEL

men, and a glut of *estatuas vivas* ("living statues" or costumed mimes).

Starting around 9–10 A.M., the *feria* lasts into late afternoon. The sidewalk and balcony cafés overlooking the plaza are ideal for enjoying the show.

### Parque Lezama

Like many Argentine museums, Parque Lezama's **Museo Histórico** (Defensa 1600, tel. 011/4307-1182, informes@mhn.gov.ar, 11 A.M.–6 P.M. Wed.–Sun., free) underwent an overhaul for the 2010 bicentennial, with new and surprisingly evenhanded material on Peronism (note Juan Perón's Grundig tape recorder, which he used to communicate to his faithful), the state terror of the Dirty War, and the 1980s democratic restoration.

There are also thematic exhibits, such as early daguerreotypes of famous but also anonymous figures from early-19th-century Argentina, that border on a social history that's often overlooked in such museums. More conventionally, there's a re-creation of liberator José de San Martín's French bedroom-in-exile, portrait galleries of figures such as San Martín and independence intellectual Mariano Moreno, and massive oils that romanticize General Julio Argentino Roca's brutal Patagonian campaigns.

The building itself is a well-kept landmark whose subterranean gallery hosts special exhibits and occasional concerts.

## LA BOCA

On the twisting Riachuelo's west bank, La Boca owes its origins to French Basque and Genovese immigrants who manned packing plants and warehouses during the mid-19th-century beef export boom. Perhaps more than any other city neighborhood, it remains a community, symbolized by fervent identification—some would say fanatical obsession—with the Boca Juniors soccer team.

La Boca is, literally, the city's most colorful neighborhood, thanks to the brightly painted houses with corrugated zinc siding that line the curving **Caminito,** once a rail terminus. One of the country's most polluted waterways, the **Riachuelo** has undergone a visible cleanup of the corroded hulks that oozed contamination along the meander known as the **Vuelta de Rocha,** but there's a long way to go—the riverside is more presentable, but it's still not for sensitive noses.

Socially and politically, La Boca has a reputation for disorder and anarchy, but the late Benito Quinquela Martín, whose oils sympathetically portrayed its hard-working inhabitants, helped make it an artists' colony. Many Porteños consider the barrio dangerous, and some visitors prefer guided tours starting at the Caminito.

La Boca's real gateway, though, is Avenida Almirante Brown, at Parque Lezama's southeast corner. There, the Catalinas del Sur theater group has erected the **Mural Escenográfico Parque Lezama,** a sprawling mural depicting community life through colorful three-dimensional caricatures. From the foot of the avenue, where it intersects Avenida Pedro de Mendoza, the remaining massive girders of the former **Puente Nicolás Avellaneda** (1940), towering above the Riachuelo, are a civil engineering landmark.

### Caminito

The starting point for most visitors remains the cobbled, curving Caminito. Once the terminus of a railroad line, the Caminito is now a pedestrian mall where painters display their watercolors (there are more artists on weekends than weekdays). Taking its name from a popular tango, the passageway veers northwest, between brightly colored houses with corrugated zinc siding, from Avenida Pedro de Mendoza.

Initially, these bright colors came from marine paints salvaged from ships in the harbor. The colors are inviting, but the poorly insulated buildings can be unbearably hot in summer and frigid in winter.

### Museo de Bellas Artes de La Boca

East of the Caminito, Quinquela Martín's former studio is now the Museo de Bellas Artes de la Boca (Pedro de Mendoza 1835, tel.

© WAYNE BERNHARDSON

La Boca's vibrant Caminito is one of the city's most-visited sights.

011/4301-1080, 11 A.M.–5:30 P.M. Tues.–Sun., US$0.80).

### Estadio Alberto J. Armando

For residents, the key landmark is the Estadio Alberto J. Armando, the soccer stadium better known as **La Bombonera,** at Brandsen and Del Valle Iberlucea; murals of barrio life cover the walls along the Brandsen side. It's now home to the **Museo de la Pasión Boquense** (Brandsen 805, tel. 011/4362-1100, www.museoboquense.com, 10 A.M.–6 P.M. daily), a thunderous homage to the passion for soccer and its role in the community. Admission costs US$5 per person, or US$8 per person with a guided stadium tour.

## RETIRO

Popularly describing the area surrounding **Plaza San Martín,** Retiro takes in much of the terrain north of Avenida Córdoba and overlaps the Barrio Norte sector. Once literally a retreat, it originated as an isolated colonial monastery on the *barranca* (terrace) above the river, but by 1862, General San Martín's equestrian statue marked its definitive urbanization. On the centenary of the Liberator's birth in 1878, the original property was declared Plaza San Martín.

From the late 19th century, surrounding streets became Buenos Aires's most elite residential area. The most extravagant residence, dating from 1909, was the **Palacio Paz** (Av. Santa Fe 750), a 12,000-square-meter Francophile mansion built for newspaper magnate José C. Paz. On the north side, dating from 1905, the art nouveau **Palacio San Martín** was originally a three-house complex built for the Anchorena family. At the plaza's southeastern edge, dating from 1935, the 33-story **Edificio Kavanagh** (Florida 1035) was Buenos Aires's first skyscraper.

At the northeast corner, the marble **Monumento a los Caidos de Malvinas** commemorates those who died in the 1982 Falkland Islands war with Britain. Across Avenida del Libertador, the former Plaza Britania is now the **Plaza Fuerza Aérea**

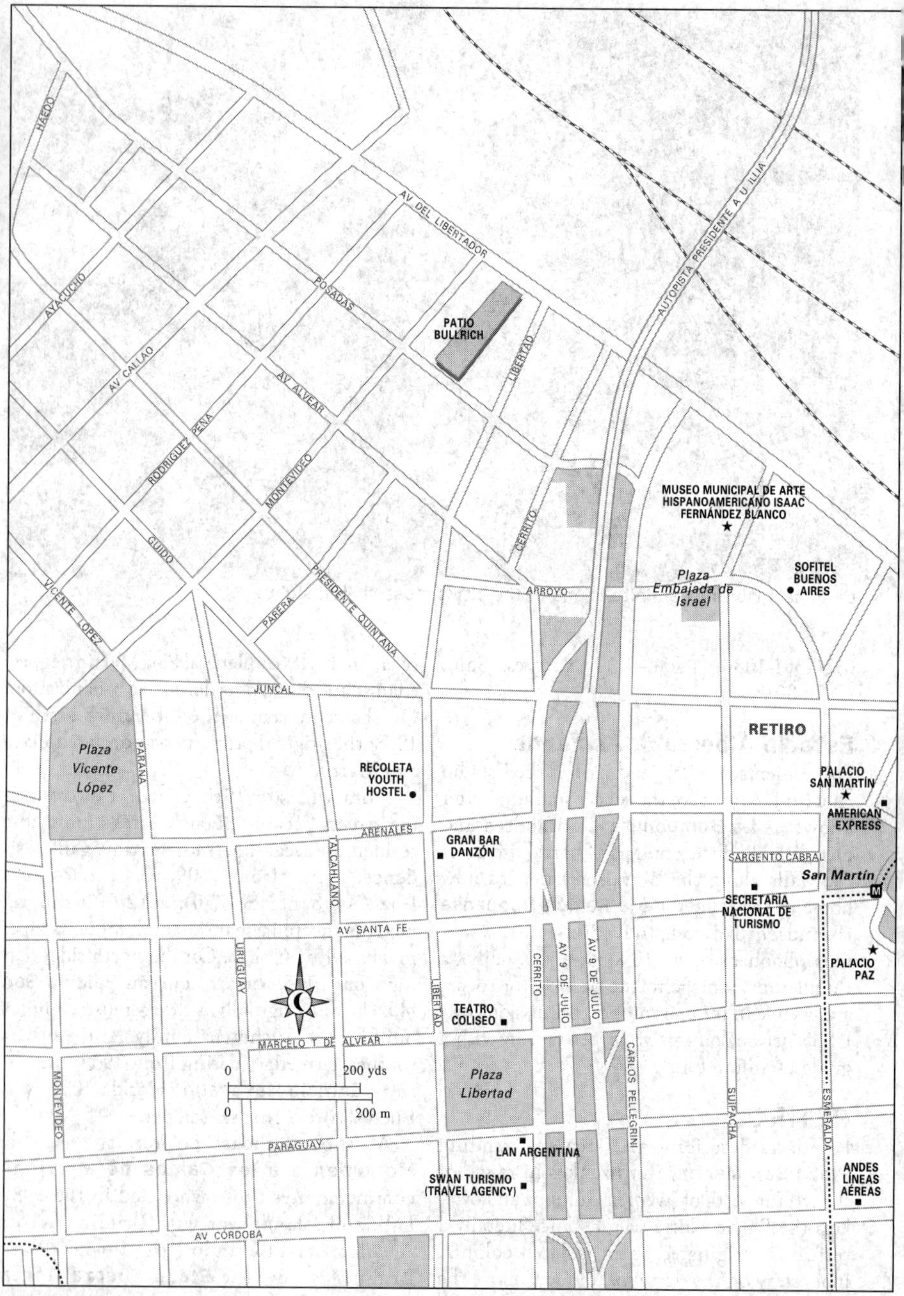
HAEDO
AV DEL LIBERTADOR
AUTOPISTA PRESIDENTE A U ILLIA
AYACUCHO
POSADAS
PATIO BULLRICH
LIBERTAD
AV CALLAO
AV ALVEAR
RODRIGUEZ PEÑA
MONTEVIDEO
MUSEO MUNICIPAL DE ARTE HISPANOAMERICANO ISAAC FERNÁNDEZ BLANCO
CERRITO
GUIDO
SOFITEL BUENOS AIRES
ARROYO
Plaza Embajada de Israel
VICENTE LOPEZ
PARERA
PRESIDENTE QUINTANA
JUNCAL
RETIRO
Plaza Vicente López
PARANÁ
RECOLETA YOUTH HOSTEL
PALACIO SAN MARTÍN
AMERICAN EXPRESS
ARENALES
GRAN BAR DANZÓN
SARGENTO CABRAL
San Martín
TALCAHUANO
SECRETARÍA NACIONAL DE TURISMO
AV SANTA FE
URUGUAY
CERRITO
AV 9 DE JULIO
AV 9 DE JULIO
PALACIO PAZ
LIBERTAD
TEATRO COLISEO
MARCELO T DE ALVEAR
CARLOS PELLEGRINI
0
200 yds
Plaza Libertad
0
200 m
MONTEVIDEO
SUIPACHA
ESMERALDA
PARAGUAY
LAN ARGENTINA
SWAN TURISMO (TRAVEL AGENCY)
ANDES LÍNEAS AÉREAS
AV CÓRDOBA

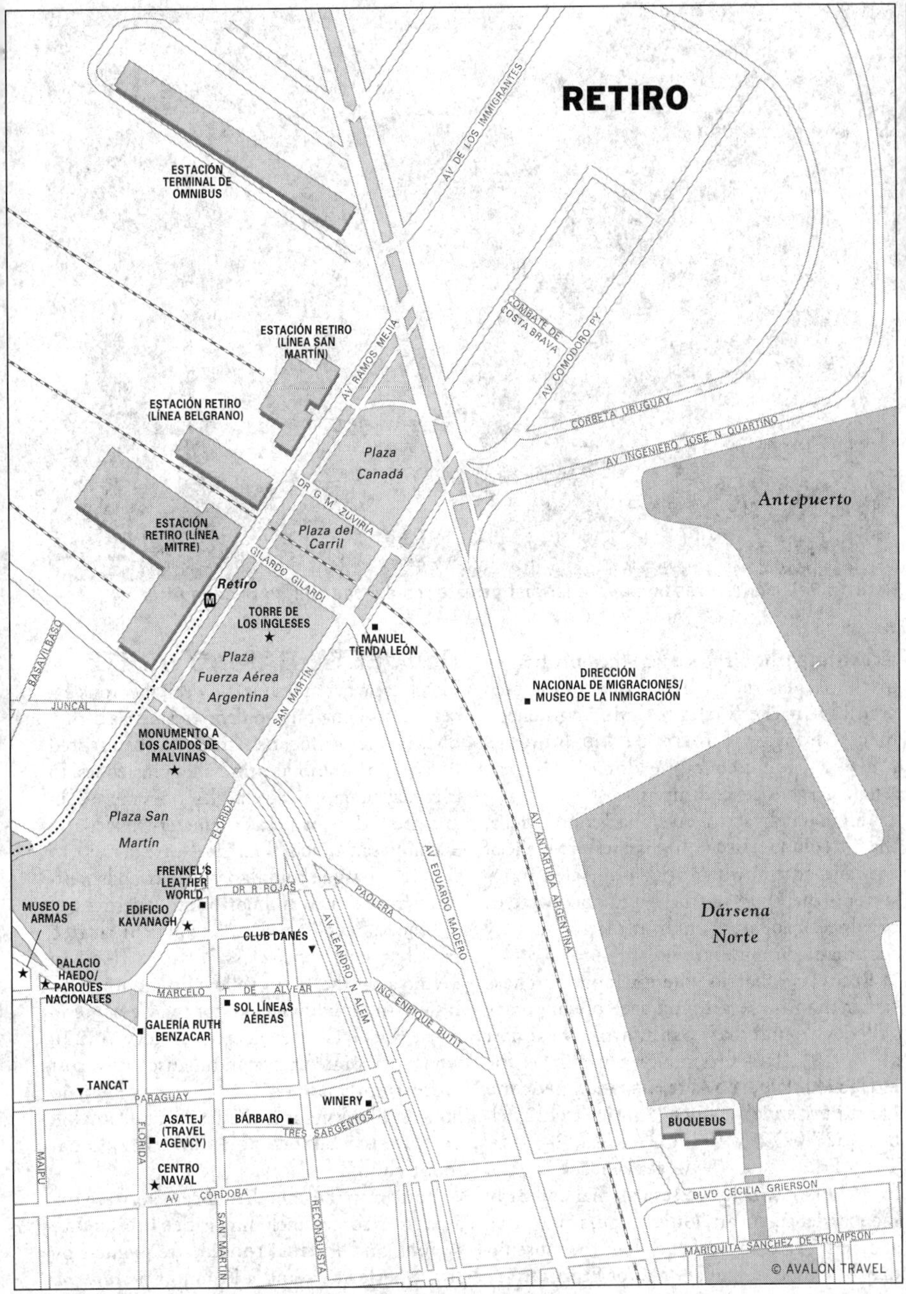
RETIRO
ESTACIÓN TERMINAL DE OMNIBUS
AV DE LOS INMIGRANTES
ESTACIÓN RETIRO (LÍNEA SAN MARTÍN)
AV RAMOS MEJÍA
COMBATE DE COSTA BRAVA
AV COMODORO PY
ESTACIÓN RETIRO (LÍNEA BELGRANO)
CORBETA URUGUAY
AV INGENIERO JOSÉ N QUARTINO
Plaza Canadá
DR G M ZUVIRÍA
Plaza del Carril
Antepuerto
ESTACIÓN RETIRO (LÍNEA MITRE)
GILARDO GILARDI
Retiro
TORRE DE LOS INGLESES
MANUEL TIENDA LEÓN
Plaza Fuerza Aérea Argentina
SAN MARTÍN
BASAVILBASO
JUNCAL
DIRECCIÓN NACIONAL DE MIGRACIONES/ MUSEO DE LA INMIGRACIÓN
MONUMENTO A LOS CAIDOS DE MALVINAS
Plaza San Martín
FLORIDA
AV ANTÁRTIDA ARGENTINA
AV EDUARDO MADERO
FRENKEL'S LEATHER WORLD
DR R ROJAS
PAOLERA
MUSEO DE ARMAS
EDIFICIO KAVANAGH
CLUB DANÉS
AV LEANDRO N ALEM
Dársena Norte
PALACIO HAEDO/ PARQUES NACIONALES
MARCELO T DE ALVEAR
ING ENRIQUE BUTTY
SOL LÍNEAS AÉREAS
GALERÍA RUTH BENZACAR
TANCAT
PARAGUAY
WINERY
BÁRBARO
TRES SARGENTOS
BUQUEBUS
ASATEJ (TRAVEL AGENCY)
MAIPÚ
FLORIDA
CENTRO NAVAL
AV CÓRDOBA
BLVD CECILIA GRIERSON
SAN MARTÍN
RECONQUISTA
MARIQUITA SÁNCHEZ DE THOMPSON
© AVALON TRAVEL

© WAYNE BERNHARDSON

Retiro's Palacio Paz was one of the largest private residences built in Buenos Aires.

**Argentina** (the air force was the only branch of the Argentine military that performed credibly in the war). Its enduring centerpiece, though, is **Torre de los Ingleses** (1916), a Big Ben clone donated by the Anglo-Argentine community.

Immediately across Avenida Ramos Mejía, the **Estación Retiro** (1915) is a restored relic of the railroad era, when British-operated trains served Argentina's northern and northwestern provinces. Today, though, it receives mostly suburban commuter trains.

Retiro is a barrio where people purchase rather than make art, and the contemporary galleries around Plaza San Martín are almost all worth a look. Its major museum is the **Museo Municipal de Arte Hispanoamericano Isaac Fernández Blanco** (Suipacha 1422, tel. 011/4327-0272 or 011/4327-0228, 2–7 P.M. Tues.–Fri., 11 A.M.–7 P.M. weekends, US$0.25, free Thurs.), which stresses colonial and early independence-era art. Guided tours take place at 3 and 5 P.M. on weekends, but the museum may be closed in January and/or February.

## RECOLETA/BARRIO NORTE

Recoleta, where the line between vigorous excess and serene but opulent eternity is a thin one, is one of Buenos Aires's most touristed barrios, and one of its prime shopping zones. In everyday usage, "Recoleta" describes the area in and around its namesake cemetery, but it also encompasses much of Barrio Norte, a residential area of vague boundaries that extends westward from Retiro and north into Palermo.

Once a bucolic outlier, Recoleta urbanized rapidly when upper-class Porteños fled San Telmo after the 1870s yellow fever outbreaks. It's internationally known for the Cementerio de la Recoleta (Recoleta Cemetery, 1822), whose elaborate crypts and mausoleums cost more than many—if not most—Porteño houses. Flanking it is the Jesuit-built **Iglesia de Nuestra Señora de Pilar** (1732), a baroque church.

Bordering the church and cemetery are sizable green spaces, including **Plaza Intendente Alvear** and **Plaza Francia,** frequented by street performers and a legion of *paseaperros* (professional dog walkers). On the southeastern corner, along Robert M. Ortiz, are some of Buenos Aires's most traditional cafés, most notably **La Biela.**

Alongside the church, the **Centro Cultural Ciudad de Buenos Aires** (Junín 1930, tel. 011/4803-1040, www.centroculturalrecoleta.org, 2–9 P.M. Tues.–Fri. and 10 A.M.–9 P.M. weekends and holidays, free except for some areas) is one of the capital's most important cultural centers.

Facing Plaza Francia, the Museo Nacional de Bellas Artes (1933) is the national fine-arts museum. Several other plazas stretch along Avenida del Libertador, northwest of the museum toward Palermo.

## Cementerio de la Recoleta

For quick and dead alike, Recoleta is Buenos Aires's most prestigious address; its roster of postmortem residents represents wealth and power as surely as the inhabitants of surrounding Francophile mansions and luxury apartments hoard their assets in overseas bank accounts. Socially, the cemetery is more exclusive than the neighborhood—cash can buy an impressive residence, but not a surname like Alvear, Anchorena, Mitre, Pueyrredón, or Sarmiento.

Its top attraction, though, is the crypt of Eva Perón, who overcame humble origins with a relentless ambition that brought her to the pinnacle of power with her husband, General and President Juan Perón, before her death in 1952. Even Juan Perón, who lived until 1974, failed to qualify for Recoleta.

There were other ways into Recoleta, though. One unlikely occupant is boxer Luis Angel Firpo (1894–1960), the "wild bull of the Pampas," who nearly beat Jack Dempsey for the world heavyweight championship in 1923. Firpo, though, had pull—his sponsor was landowner Félix Bunge, whose family owns some of the cemetery's most ornate constructions.

The Cementerio de la Recoleta (Junín 1790, tel. 011/4803-1594, 7 A.M.–6 P.M. daily, free) is the site for many guided on-demand tours

© WAYNE BERNHARDSON

**Outside Cementerio de la Recoleta, Plaza Francia's Sunday market attracts all kinds of street performers.**

through travel agencies; the municipal tourist office sponsors occasional free weekend tours.

### Museo Nacional de Bellas Artes

Argentina's traditional fine-arts museum mixes works of well-known European artists such as Picasso and Van Gogh with Argentine counterparts, including Antonio Berni, Cándido López, Benito Quinquela Martín, Prilidiano Pueyrredón, and Lino Spilimbergo. In total, it houses about 11,000 oils, watercolors, sketches, engravings, tapestries, and sculptures. Among the most interesting works are López's detailed oils, which re-create the history of the Paraguayan war (1864–1870) despite his having lost his right arm to a grenade.

The Museo Nacional de Bellas Artes (Av. del Libertador 1473, tel. 011/4803-0802, www.mnba.org.ar, 12:30–8:30 P.M. Tues.–Fri., weekend hours start at 9:30 A.M., free) offers guided tours at 4 and 6 P.M. Tuesday–Friday, and at 5 and 6 P.M. on weekends.

## PALERMO

Buenos Aires's largest barrio, Palermo boasts wide-open spaces thanks to 19th-century dictator Juan Manuel de Rosas, whose estate stretched almost from Recoleta all the way to Belgrano. After his exile, the property passed into the public domain and, ironically enough, the sprawling **Parque 3 de Febrero** takes its name from the date of his defeat in 1852.

Once part of the capital's unsavory *arrabales* (margins), its street corners populated by stylish but capricious *malevos* (bullies) immortalized in Jorge Luis Borges's stories, Palermo hasn't entirely superseded that reputation—in some areas, poorly lighted streets still make visitors uneasy. Yet it also has exclusive neighborhoods such as **Barrio Parque,** also known as **Palermo Chico,** with embassies, single-family mansions, some of Buenos Aires's highest property values, and several key museums.

Across Avenida del Libertador, the **Botánico** is an upper-middle-class enclave taking its name from the **Jardín Botánico Carlos Thays** (Av. Santa Fe 3951, tel. 011/4831-4527, 8 A.M.–6 P.M. daily, free), a lovely botanical garden infested with feral cats. Once a neighborhood of imposing *palacetes,* the Botánico is still affluent but less exclusive than when, in 1948, Eva Perón enraged the neighbors by making one of those mansions into a home for single mothers that's now a museum in her memory.

Opposite nearby Plaza Italia, the rejuvenated **Jardín Zoológico** (Av. Las Heras s/n, tel. 011/4806-7412, www.zoobuenosaires.com.ar, 10 A.M.–6 P.M. Tues.–Sun.) is an ideal outing for visitors with children (free up to age 12). General admission costs US$3 per adult.

The real action is slightly northwest at **Palermo Viejo,** where **Plaza Serrano** (also known as **Plaza Cortázar**) has become a major axis of Porteño nightlife. Palermo Viejo further subdivides into **Palermo Soho** and the more northerly **Palermo Hollywood,** where many TV and radio producers have located facilities. Shaded by sycamores, many streets still contain low-rise *casas chorizos* (sausage houses) on deep, narrow lots. At the northern end of the barrio, **Las Cañitas** is a gastronomic and nightlife area challenging Palermo Viejo among partygoers.

### Museo de Motivos Argentinos José Hernández

It's tempting to call this the "museum of irony": Argentina's most gaucho-oriented institution stands in one of the country's most urbane, affluent, and cosmopolitan neighborhoods. Named for the author of the *gauchesco* epic *Martín Fierro,* it specializes in rural Argentiniana.

Even more ironically, oligarch Félix Bunge built the derivative French-Italianate residence with marble staircases and other lavish features, and exhibits depict gentry like the Martínez de Hoz family—one of whom was the 1976–1983 dictatorship's economy minister—as symbols of a romantic open-range lifestyle.

That said, the museum's worthwhile collections range from magnificent silverwork and vicuña textiles by contemporary Argentine artisans to pre-Columbian pottery, indigenous crafts, and even a typical *pulpería* (rural store).

The Museo de Arte Popular José Hernández (Av. del Libertador 2373, tel. 011/4803-2384, www.museohernandez.org.ar, 1–7 P.M. Wed.–Fri., 10 A.M.–8 P.M. weekends and holidays) charges US$0.30 admission except Sunday, when it's free. It's normally closed in February.

### Museo Nacional de Arte Decorativo

Matías Errázuriz Ortúzar and his widow, Josefina de Alvear de Errázuriz, lived less than 20 years in the ornate beaux arts building (1918), which now houses the national decorative art museum. Its inventory consists of 4,000 items from the family's collections, ranging from Roman sculptures to contemporary silverwork, but mostly Asian and European pieces from the 17th to 19th centuries. Many items are anonymous; the best known are by Europeans like Manet and Rodin.

The Museo Nacional de Arte Decorativo (Av. del Libertador 1902, tel. 011/4802-6606, www.mnad.org.ar, 2–7 P.M. Tues.–Sun., US$1.25, free Tues.) offers guided English-language tours Tuesday–Saturday at 2:30 P.M. It's closed the last week of December and first week of January.

### Museo de Arte Latinoamericano de Buenos Aires (MALBA)

Dedicated to Latin American art, Buenos Aires's most deluxe museum is a striking steel-and-glass structure that devotes one entire floor to Argentine businessman and founder Eduardo F. Constantini's private collections, featuring prominent artists like the Mexicans Frida Kahlo and Diego Rivera, but there are also works by Antonio Berni, Chilean Robert Matta, Uruguayan Pedro Figari, and others. The second floor offers special exhibitions.

The Museo de Arte Latinoamericano de Buenos Aires (Av. Figueroa Alcorta 3415, tel. 011/4808-6500, www.malba.org.ar, noon–9 P.M. Wed., noon–8 P.M. Thurs.–Mon. and holidays, US$4, US$1.25 Wed.) also has a cinema and hosts many events.

### Museo Eva Perón

Eva Perón, the charismatic spouse of populist president Juan Domingo Perón, made a point of antagonizing her political opponents, or, in her words, "the oligarchy." At her most combative, to the anger and dismay of neighbors, she chose the upscale Botánico for the **Hogar de Tránsito No. 2,** a shelter for single mothers from the provinces. Even more galling, her Fundación de Ayuda Social María Eva Duarte de Perón took over an imposing three-story mansion to house the transients on their way to the capital.

Since Evita's 1952 death, middle-class multistory apartment blocks have mostly replaced the elegant single-family houses and distinctive apartments that then housed the Porteño elite (many have moved to exclusive northern suburbs). Fifty years later, on the July 26 anniversary of her death—supporting novelist Tomás Eloy Martínez's contention that Argentines are "cadaver cultists"—Evita's great-niece María Carolina Rodríguez officially opened the museum "to spread the life, work, and ideology of María Eva Duarte de Perón."

What it lacks is critical perspective. Rather than a balanced account of her life, the museum's is a professionally presented chronological homage that sidesteps the demagoguery and personality cults that typified both Evita and her charismatic husband.

The Museo Eva Perón (Lafinur 2988, tel. 011/4807-9433, www.museoevita.org, 11 A.M.–7 P.M. Tues.–Sun., US$3) has a museum store with a selection of Evita souvenirs and a fine café-restaurant as well. Guided English-language tours, bookable in advance, cost US$5.

## BELGRANO

North of Palermo, linked to downtown by Subte, bus, and train, Belgrano remains a barrio apart. In fact, it was once a separate city and then, briefly in the 1880s, the country's capital; the Congress met at what is now the **Museo Histórico Sarmiento** (Cuba 2079, tel. 011/4781-2989, www.museosarmiento.gov.ar, 1–5:30 P.M. Sun.–Fri., US$0.60, free Thurs.),

## EVITA ON TOUR

Eva Perón became famous for her visit to Europe in 1947, when, as representative of an Argentina that emerged from World War II as an economic powerhouse, she helped legitimize a shaky Franco regime in Spain and, despite missteps, impressed other war-ravaged European countries with Argentina's potential. But even her death, five years later, didn't stop her from touring.

Millions of Argentines said adios to Evita in a funeral cortege that took hours to travel up Avenida de Mayo from the Casa Rosada to the Congreso Nacional, where her corpse lay in state. She then found a temporary resting place at the headquarters of the Confederación General del Trabajo (CGT, the Peronist trade union), where the shadowy Spanish physician Pedro Ara gave the corpse a mummification worthy of Lenin in hopes of a monument to honor her legacy.

Evita remained at the CGT until 1955, when anti-Peronist General Pedro Aramburu took power and ordered her removal. Eventually, after a series of whistle stops that included the office of a mummy-smitten military man, Aramburu shipped her to an anonymous grave near Milan, Italy – even as a cadaver, Evita symbolized Peronism's durability.

Despite banning the party, Aramburu had reason to worry. For many years, while Perón lived in luxury near Madrid, Argentines dared not even speak his name. In 1970, though, as Argentine politics came undone, left-wing Montoneros guerrillas kidnapped Aramburu and demanded to know Evita's whereabouts.

When Aramburu refused to answer, they executed him and issued a statement that they would hold the body hostage until Evita was returned to "the people." A common slogan of the time was "Si Evita viviera, sería Montonera" (If Evita were alive, she would be a Montonera); the cynical Perón encouraged leftist militants to help return him to power, even as he privately despised them.

The police found Aramburu's body before any postmortem prisoner swap could take place, but a notary to whom Aramburu had confided came forward with information on Evita's whereabouts. In September 1971, Perón was stunned when a truck bearing Evita's casket and corpse arrived at his Madrid residence; remarried to dancer María Estela (Isabelita) Martínez, he neither expected nor wanted any such thing. His bizarre spiritualist adviser, José López Rega, though, used the opportunity to try to transfer Evita's essence into Isabelita's body, as the mummy remained in the attic.

In 1973, Perón finally returned – leaving Evita in Madrid – and was soon elected president with Isabelita as his vice president. Meanwhile, the Montoneros once again kidnapped Aramburu – from his Recoleta crypt – until Evita's return.

Angry but ill and senile, Perón died the next year, but his widow – now president – flew Evita's corpse on a charter from Madrid to Buenos Aires. Evita remained at the presidential residence at Olivos, just north of the capital, until March 1976, when General Jorge Rafael Videla's junta overthrew Isabelita.

At Recoleta, Evita finally achieved the respectability that she envied and resented in others during her rise to power. Though she was an illegitimate child who went by her mother's surname, Ibarguren, she landed in the family crypt of her father, Juan Duarte, a provincial landowner – only a short walk from Aramburu's tomb.

Even now, Evita's wanderings may not be over. In mid-2002, there were rumors of yet another move – to San Telmo's Franciscan convent at Defensa and Alsina (ironically enough, it was set afire by Peronist mobs in 1955, but it's also the burial place of her confessor, Pedro Errecart). Another possibility is the new mausoleum at Juan Perón's *quinta* (country house) in the southern suburb of San Vicente, which holds his remains after a chaotic move from Chacarita in late 2006 (when a brawl between rival unions erupted into gunfire).

Isabelita, for her part, was even willing to see Evita lie alongside her late husband. The main objection, it seems, is that Isabelita, former caretaker president Eduardo Duhalde, and other Peronist politicians like the idea better than the Duarte heirs do.

honoring President Domingo F. Sarmiento. Sarmiento never lived here, but the exhibits contain many personal possessions and a model of his provincial San Juan birthplace; it also chronicles the near–civil war of the 1880s that resulted in Buenos Aires's federalization. Guided tours take place Sunday at 4 P.M.

Only a block off Cabildo, **Plaza General Manuel Belgrano** hosts a crafts market (www.feriaplazabelgrano.com) open on weekends and holidays; immediately east, at Vuelta de Obligado 2042, the landmark **Iglesia de la Inmaculada Concepción** (1865), known as **La Redonda** for its circular floor plan, figures in Ernesto Sabato's psychological novel *On Heroes and Tombs.*

The **Museo Casa de Yrurtia** (O'Higgins 2390, tel. 011/4781-0385, www.casadeyrurtia.gov.ar, 3–7 P.M. Tues.–Fri. and Sun., US$0.30) was home to sculptor Rogelio Yrurtia (1879–1950), creator of San Telmo's *Canto al Trabajo* and other works that challenged the pomposity of Argentine public art. Guided tours, at no additional expense, take place at 3 P.M. Tuesday–Friday and at 4 P.M. Sunday.

## OUTER BARRIOS

Beyond its most touristed barrios, Buenos Aires has a variety of worthwhile sights ranging from the mundane to the morbid. Some are less accessible by Subte, but have regular *colectivo* (city bus) service.

### Museo Argentino de Ciencias Naturales

The westerly barrio of Caballito gets few tourists, but its largest open space, **Parque Centenario,** is a good area to see an unadorned but improving neighborhood popular with urban homesteaders. Its impressive natural history museum veers between the stuff-in-glass-cases approach and more sophisticated exhibits offering ecological, historical, and cultural context. Dating from 1937, its quarters are only a third the size of the original grandiose project but include decorative details such as bas-relief spiderwebs around the main entrance and sculpted owls flanking the upper windows.

The main floor contains geological and paleontological exhibits, including the massive Patagonian specimens *Giganotosaurus carolini* (the world's largest carnivorous dinosaur) and *Argentinosaurus huinculensis* (an herbivore whose neck alone measures about 12 meters). The second floor stresses South American mammals (including marine mammals), comparative anatomy, amphibians and reptiles, birds, arthropods, and botany.

The Museo Argentino de Ciencias Naturales Bernardino Rivadavia (Angel Gallardo 490, tel./fax 011/4982-0306, www.macn.secyt.gov.ar, 2–7 P.M. daily, US$0.80 for visitors age 7 and older) is about equidistant from the Malabia and Angel Gallardo stations on Subte Línea B.

### Cementerio de la Chacarita and Vicinity

For most cadavers, Buenos Aires's second cemetery is more affordable than Recoleta, but eternity at the Cementerio de la Chacarita can still mean notoriety. Many high-profile Argentines, in fields ranging from entertainment to religion and politics, reside here, and the lines between these categories can be blurry.

The most universally beloved is tango singer Carlos Gardel, victim of a 1935 plane crash. Hundreds of admirers from around the globe have left dedicatory plaques, many thanking him for miracles, and every June 26 *Gardelianos* jam the cemetery's streets—platted like a small city—to pay homage.

In terms of devotion, only faith-healer-to-the-aristocracy Madre María Salomé can approach Gardel; on the second of every month—she died October 2, 1928—white carnations cover her crypt. Other famous figures include aviator Jorge Newbery; tango musicians Aníbal "Pichuco" Troilo and Osvaldo Pugliese; poet Alfonsina Storni; painter Benito Quinquela Martín; and theater and film comedian Luis Sandrini.

Certainly the most notorious, though, was Juan Domingo Perón, who moved to a new mausoleum at his San Vicente country house a few years ago. In June 1987, stealthy vandals entered his Chacarita crypt, amputating and stealing the caudillo's hands; anti-Peronists speculated, despite lack of evidence, that the thieves sought Perón's fingerprints for access to supposed Swiss bank accounts.

The Cementerio de la Chacarita (Guzmán 680, tel. 011/4553-9338, www.cementeriochacarita.com.ar, 7 A.M.–6 P.M. daily) covers 95 blocks with a total of 12,000 burial vaults, 100,000 gravesites, and 350,000 niches. It's a short walk from Estación Federico Lacroze (Subte Línea B). The website is unofficial but informative.

Besides Chacarita, there are two contiguous but formally separate cemeteries: the **Cementerio Alemán** (German Cemetery, Av. Elcano 4530, tel. 011/4553-3206, 7 A.M.–6 P.M. daily) and the **Cementerio Británico** (British Cemetery, Av. Elcano 4568, tel. 011/4554-0092, 7 A.M.–6 P.M. daily).

The Británico is more diverse, with tombs belonging to Armenian, Greek, Irish, Jewish, and other immigrant nationalities. Lucas Bridges, the son of pioneer Anglican missionaries in Tierra del Fuego and author of the classic Fuegian memoir *The Uttermost Part of the Earth,* lies here after dying at sea en route from Ushuaia to Buenos Aires.

# Entertainment and Shopping

## ENTERTAINMENT AND EVENTS

Buenos Aires is a 24-hour city with as much to offer as New York or London. Argentines in general and Porteños in particular are night people—discos and dance clubs, for instance, may not even *open* until 1 A.M. or so, and they stay open until dawn. Not everything takes place at those hours, though, and since a deadly fire in late 2004 there are more municipal restrictions on live music venues and hours.

Every Buenos Aires daily has thorough event listings, especially in end-of-the-week supplements. For tickets to events at many major venues, contact **Ticketek** (tel. 011/5237-7200, www.ticketek.com.ar), which adds a US$1 service charge per ticket. It has brick-and-mortar outlets in the Microcentro (Viamonte 560, Locales 6 and 8), in Barrio Norte at Lee-Chi (Rodríguez Peña 1034), in San Telmo at La Trastienda (Balcarce 460), and in Recoleta at the Centro Cultural Recoleta (Junín 1930).

For discount tickets to tango shows, cinemas, and live theater, try these ticket agencies *(carteleras):* **Cartelera Espectáculos** (Lavalle 742, Local 2, tel. 011/4322-1559), **Cartelera Baires** (Av. Corrientes 1382, Local 24, tel. 011/4372-5058, www.cartelerabaires.com), and **Cartelera Vea Más** (Av. Corrientes 1660, Local 2, tel. 011/6320-5319).

### Cafés

No single place embodies tradition better than Monserrat's **Café Tortoni** (Av. de Mayo 825, tel. 011/4342-4328, www.cafetortoni.com.ar). Most come for coffee and croissants, but there's live tango and the bar serves good mixed drinks, accompanied by a *tabla* of cold cuts and cheeses that easily feeds two people.

Despite a partial rehab, the **Confitería Ideal** (Suipacha 384, tel. 011/5265-8069, www.confiteriaideal.com) remains one of the city's most traditional settings. With its worn upholstery and cracked floors, the Ideal served as a set for Madonna's *Evita* debacle, and it hosts downstairs tango shows (for spectators) and upstairs *milongas* (for aspiring dancers) Wednesday and Thursday around 3 P.M.

Recoleta's **La Biela** (Av. Quintana 596/600, tel. 011/4804-0449, www.labiela.com) is a classic breakfast spot. In good weather try the patio, beneath the palm and *palo borracho* trees and the giant *gomero* or *ombú,* which needs wooden beams to prop up its sprawling branches. It's slightly more expensive to eat outside, where the service can be inconsistent.

## Bars and Clubs

The distinction between cafés and bars is more a continuum than a dichotomy. Some bars call themselves pubs, pronounced as in English, and many of those call themselves Irish.

Relocated to Monserrat, **Bar Seddon** (Defensa 695, tel. 011/4342-3700) has made a successful transition to the capital's oldest neighborhood. Behind its street-side restaurant, **La Trastienda** (Balcarce 460, tel. 011/4342-7650, www.latrastienda.com) has recycled a Monserrat warehouse into an attractive theater that hosts both live music and drama.

**Downtown Matías** (Reconquista 701, tel. 011/4311-0327, www.matiaspub.com.ar) is the Microcentro branch of Buenos Aires's oldest Irish-style pub. San Telmo's **Mitos Argentinos** (Humberto Primo 489, tel. 011/4362-7810, www.mitosargentinos.com.ar) has retooled as a *rock nacional* pub with live music Friday and Saturday.

Retiro's **Bárbaro** (Tres Sargentos 415, tel. 011/4311-6856, www.barbarobar.com.ar) takes its punning name from a *lunfardo* (street slang) term roughly translatable as "cool." Bordering Barrio Norte, **Milión** (Paraná 1048, tel. 011/4815-9925, www.milion.com.ar) is a tapas bar set in a magnificent 1913 mansion, with garden, patio, and interior seating. **Gran Bar Danzón** (Libertad 1161, tel. 011/4811-1108, www.granbardanzon.com.ar) is a sophisticated wine bar, with a sushi special at happy hour (7–9 P.M.), and doubles as a restaurant with separate dining area.

Recoleta's **Buller Brewing Company** (Presidente Ramón Ortiz 1827, tel. 011/4808-9061) is a brewpub offering seven different styles of beer served with tapas, seafood, and pizza. Palermo Hollywood's cavernous **Niceto Club** (Niceto Vega 5510, tel. 011/4779-6396, www.nicetoclub.com) has become one of the area's top live music venues; it's open Thursday, Friday, and Saturday nights.

Restored to its old Palermo location, beneath the Parque Tres de Febrero railroad tracks, **The Roxy** (Av. Casares and Av. Sarmiento, no phone, www.theroxybsas.com.ar) draws performers of the stature of Charly García. It also operates Palermo Hollywood's **Roxy Live Bar** (Niceto Vega 5542), down the block from Niceto Club.

## Jazz

**Clásica y Moderna** (Av. Callao 892, tel. 011/4812-8707, 8 A.M.–2 A.M. Sun.–Thurs., 8 A.M.–4 A.M. Fri.–Sat.) is a hybrid bookstore-café–live jazz venue that has occupied the same Barrio Norte location since 1938. Performers here have included Susana Rinaldi, Mercedes Sosa, and Liza Minnelli. Regulars get better service than strangers.

## Tango and *Milonga*

Many but not all tango venues are in the southerly barrios of Monserrat and San Telmo. Professional shows range from straightforward, low-priced programs to extravagant productions at high (often excessive) cost. *Milongas* are participatory bargains for those who want to learn.

Monserrat's legendary **Café Tortoni** (Av. de Mayo 825, tel. 011/4342-4328, www.cafetortoni.com.ar) offers song-and-dance shows at its Sala Alfonsina Storni, separated from the main part of the café, for around US$10–18 per person plus drinks and food.

Dating from 1920, the elegant **El Querandí** (Perú 302, tel. 011/5199-1770, www.querandi.com.ar) is another classic; for US$80 per person, the nightly dinner (starting at 8:30 P.M.) and show (starting at 10:30 P.M.) occupies the upper end of the scale.

One of San Telmo's classic venues, occupying a late-18th-century building, **El Viejo Almacén** (Balcarce and Av. Independencia, tel. 011/4307-6689, www.viejo-almacen.com.ar) charges US$78 per person including dinner at its restaurant, directly across the street.

Literally in the shadow of the Mercado del Abasto, part of a project to sustain the legacy of the "Morocho del Abasto" in his old neighborhood, the **Esquina Carlos Gardel** (Carlos Gardel 3200, tel./fax 011/4867-6363, www.esquinacarlosgardel.com.ar) has nightly shows from US$65 (show only) to US$92 pp (with dinner); there are also more expensive VIP seats.

© WAYNE BERNHARDSON

Tango singer Soledad Villamil performs at Centro Cultural Torquato Tasso.

For those who want to learn instead of watch, the best options are neighborhood *milongas.* Organized events charge US$2–3 with a live orchestra, less with recorded music. For classes, a good clearinghouse is Monserrat's **Academia Nacional del Tango** (Av. de Mayo 833, tel. 011/4345-6968, www.anacdeltango.org.ar), alongside the Café Tortoni. For the truly committed, it even offers a three-year tango degree.

San Telmo's **Centro Cultural Torquato Tasso** (Defensa 1575, tel. 011/4307-6506, www.torquatotasso.com.ar) offers outstanding live tango music shows (but no dancing) on Friday and Saturday usually at 10 P.M., a free Sunday-night *milonga* at 10 P.M., and tango lessons every day.

Balvanera's **Italia Unita** (Perón 2535, tel. 011/4953-8700, www.saboratango.com.ar) hosts tango floor shows, but after 10:30 P.M. Saturday night it hosts a *milonga* that often features live music. Constitución's **Niño Bien** (Humberto Primo 1462, tel. 015/4147-8687) has an elegant Thursday-night *milonga* from 10:30 P.M. that gets crowded early, as it has one of the best dance floors. Palermo's **Salón Canning** (Scalabrini Ortiz 1331, tel. 011/4832-6753) hosts the **Parakultural** (www.parakultural.com.ar), a more avant-garde *milonga* that incorporates electronica, on Monday, Tuesday, and Thursday from 11 P.M.

## Classical Music and Opera

The classical music and opera season lasts March–November but peaks in winter, June–August. For nearly a century the premier venue has been the **Teatro Colón** (Libertad 621, tel./fax 011/4378-7344, www.teatrocolon.org.ar).

Other options include the Microcentro's **Teatro Ópera** (Av. Corrientes 860, tel. 011/4326-1335), which seats 2,500; Monserrat's **Teatro Avenida** (Av. de Mayo 1212, tel. 011/4381-0662, www.balirica.org.ar); and Retiro's **Teatro Coliseo** (Marcelo T. de Alvear 1125, tel. 011/4816-5943).

## Cultural Centers

Adjacent to the Galerías Pacífico, the **Centro Cultural Borges** (Viamonte and San Martín, tel. 011/5555-5359, www.ccborges.org.ar, 10 A.M.–9 P.M. Mon.–Sat., noon–9 P.M. Sun., US$2.50 pp) features permanent exhibits on Argentina's most famous literary figure as well as rotating fine-arts programs and performing-arts events.

Recoleta's **Centro Cultural Ciudad de Buenos Aires** (Junín 1930, tel. 011/4803-1040, www.centroculturalrecoleta.org, 2–9 P.M. Tues.–Fri., 10 A.M.–9 P.M. weekends and holidays) is one of the city's outstanding cultural venues, with many free or inexpensive events. There are guided visits (tel. 011/4803-4057) Wednesday at 6 P.M. and Saturday at 3 and 5 P.M.

### Gay Venues

Buenos Aires has a vigorous gay scene, centered mostly around Recoleta, Barrio Norte, and Palermo Viejo, with a handful of venues elsewhere. Lots of gay men hang out on Avenida Santa Fe between Callao and Pueyrredón, a good area to meet people and learn the latest. The monthly publication *La Otra Guía* (www.laotraguiaweb.com.ar) lists gay-oriented and gay-friendly businesses.

### Events

Buenos Aires observes all the usual holidays and many special events as well. The summer months of January and February are generally quiet; things pick up after school starts in early March.

Dates for the renascent pre-Lenten **Carnaval** (Carnival), in February or March, vary from year to year; unlike Brazil's massive festivities, Carnaval here means neighborhood *murgas* (street musicians and dancers); celebrations take place on weekends rather than during the entire week.

Mid-April's **Feria del Libro** (www.el-libro.com.ar) is Latin America's largest book fair, a fixture on the literary scene for nearly three decades. Late April's **Festival Internacional de Cine Independiente** (International Independent Film Festival, www.bafici.gov.ar) has grown impressively over the past decade.

For more than a century, late July's **Exposición Internacional de Ganadería, Agricultura y Industria Internacional** (www.ruralarg.org.ar), the Sociedad Rural's annual livestock show at the Predio Ferial, has been one of the capital's biggest events.

The **Festival Buenos Aires Tango** (www.festivaldetango.gov.ar) starts around mid-August, immediately before the Mundial de Tango (World Tango Championships), which run to the end of the month. It's a decentralized series of performances at smaller, often intimate venues, offering opportunities to see and hear not just established artists but also developing performers.

## SHOPPING

The main shopping areas are the Microcentro, along the Florida pedestrian mall toward Retiro; Retiro, around Plaza San Martín and along Avenida Santa Fe; Recoleta, near the cemetery; and the tree-lined streets of Palermo Viejo, with stylish shops among the newest restaurants and bars. Street markets take place in San Telmo, Recoleta, and Belgrano.

### Shopping Centers

Over the past decade-plus, developers have recycled many older buildings into upmarket malls for one-stop shopping. The most notable is the Microcentro's magnificent **Galerías Pacífico** (Florida and Córdoba, tel. 011/5555-5100, www.galeriaspacifico.com.ar).

Once a livestock auction house, Retiro's **Patio Bullrich** (Av. del Libertador 750, tel. 011/4814-7400, www.shoppingbullrich.com.ar) has become a palatial commercial space with nearly 70 shops, plus restaurants and cinemas, on four levels.

### Antiques

Sunday's **Feria de San Pedro Telmo,** one of the city's biggest tourist attractions, fills Plaza Dorrego with antiques and bric-a-brac. There are also many dealers in galleries with small street-side frontage, including **Galería Cecil** (Defensa 845, tel. 011/4307-0259) and **Galería de la Defensa** (Defensa 1179, no phone).

## *FERIAS* OF BUENOS AIRES

For sightseers and spontaneous shoppers alike, Buenos Aires's diverse *ferias* (street fairs) are one of the city's greatest pleasures. The most prominent is Sunday's **Feria de San Pedro Telmo**, which fills Plaza Dorrego and surrounding streets – authorities close Calle Defensa to vehicle traffic – with booths full of antiques, *filete* paintings, and other crafts. There are professional tango musicians and dancers, and dozens more street performers range from embarrassingly mundane to truly innovative. Lasting roughly 10 A.M.–5 P.M., it also offers sidewalk cafés and upscale antiques shops.

So successful is the Feria de San Pedro Telmo that it's aided the now-thriving **Feria Parque Lezama**, a Sunday crafts fair that's gradually spread north from its namesake park up Calle Defensa and under the freeway; only the broad Avenida San Juan has managed to stop it. Parque Lezama also gets Sunday street performers, though not as many as Plaza Dorrego.

In La Boca, the **Feria Artesanal Plazoleta Vuelta de Rocha** (Av. Pedro de Mendoza and Puerto de Palos) takes place weekends and holidays 10 A.M.–6 P.M.; along the length of the nearby Caminito, painters, illustrators, and sculptors sell their works in the **Feria del Caminito,** open 10 A.M.–6 P.M. daily.

After San Telmo, the most frequented is probably Recoleta's crafts-oriented **Feria Plaza Intendente Alvear.** Immediately northeast of the Centro Cultural Recoleta, also strong on street performers, it's stretched south along Junín; hours are 9 A.M.–7 P.M. weekends and holidays.

On weekends and holidays, crafts stalls cover most of Belgrano's main square at the easygoing **Feria Artesanal Plaza General Manuel Belgrano** (Juramento and Cuba). Hours are 9 A.M.–7 P.M. or even later (when it's better).

## Art Galleries

Buenos Aires has a thriving modern-art scene, with the most innovative galleries in Retiro and Recoleta. Retiro's **Galería Ruth Benzacar** (underground at Florida 1000, tel. 011/4313-8480, www.ruthbenzacar.com) showcases some of the capital's and the country's most avant-garde artists.

**Galería Rubbers** (Av. Alvear 1595, Recoleta, tel. 011/4816-1864, www.rubbers.com.ar) is an excellent contemporary gallery.

## Books and Music

Buenos Aires's signature bookstore is the Microcentro's **El Ateneo** (Florida 340, tel. 011/4325-6801, www.tematika.com.ar), with a huge selection on Argentine history, literature, and coffee-table souvenir books, plus domestic travel titles (it's also a publishing house).

The most elegant outlet, though, is Barrio Norte's affiliated **El Ateneo Grand Splendid** (Av. Santa Fe 1880, tel. 011/4813-6052), a recycled cinema that made *The Guardian*'s list of the world's 10 best bookstores. **Zivals** (Av. Callao 395, Congreso, tel. 011/4371-7500, www.zivals.com) is an excellent independent store. In addition to books, El Ateneo, El Ateneo Grand Splendid, and Zivals all carry quality CDs.

The specialist **Librería Platero** (Talcahuano 485, Tribunales, tel. 011/4382-2215, www.libreriaplatero.com.ar) has an enormous stock of new and out-of-print books (the latter in the basement stacks).

**Librerías Turísticas** (Paraguay 2457, tel. 011/4963-2866 or 4962-5547, www.libreriaturistica.com.ar) has a wide choice of maps and guidebooks, including its own guides to the capital's cafés.

San Telmo's **Walrus Books** (Estados Unidos 617, tel. 011/4300-7135, www.walrus-books.com.ar, 10 A.M.–8 P.M. Tues.–Sun.) carries an ample selection of English-language books well beyond the usual Stephen King potboilers.

### Crafts

Monserrat's **Arte Indígena y Criollo** (Balcarce 234, tel. 011/4343-1455, www.arteyesperanza.com.ar) stocks a representative sample of indigenous crafts from around the country. Palermo's **Arte Étnico Argentino** (El Salvador 4656, tel. 011/4832-0516, www.arteetnicoargentino.com) specializes in textiles, specifically clothing from the Andean northwest and woolen rugs from the Mapuche of Patagonia, along with rustically styled furniture.

### Leather Goods and Footwear

Retiro has several leather specialists, starting with **Frenkel's Leather World** (Florida 1055, tel. 011/4311-2300, www.frenkelsleather.com.ar), which sells crafts as well. Italian immigrant Luciano Bagnasco created one of the capital's most enduring shoemakers in **Guido Mocasines** (Rodríguez Peña 1290, Barrio Norte, tel. 011/4813-4095, www.guidomocasines.com.ar).

### Wine

Retiro's **Winery** (Av. Leandro N. Alem 880, tel. 011/4311-6607, www.winery.com.ar) sells Argentine wines by the glass and also carries a stock of imported wines. It has several other branches around town.

Near the U.S. Embassy, Palermo's **Terroir** (Buschiazzo 3040, tel. 011/4778-3408, www.terroir.com.ar) is an elite wine shop, with access to limited vintages in addition to the usual fine wines, but it's not utterly unaffordable.

# Accommodations and Food

## ACCOMMODATIONS

Buenos Aires has abundant accommodations in all categories. Since 2002's economic implosion, some opportunistic hoteliers have established higher rates for foreigners; if they insist on this, there's little you can do except go elsewhere or, if your language skills are good enough, try to argue the point. Advertised rates at top-end hotels often exclude the 21 percent IVA, but prices listed here do include taxes.

Note that many accommodations, especially hostels that have both dorms and private rooms, have rates that overlap the categories below.

### Under US$25

Over the past several years, youth hostels have sprung up like tango halls in Gardel's time, and most of them are good to excellent at modest prices. Some but not all are Hostelling International affiliates.

It actually lies within Retiro, but HI affiliate **Recoleta Youth Hostel** (Libertad 1216, tel. 011/4812-4419, www.trhostel.com.ar, US$10–13 pp dorm, US$42–55 d with private bath) still boasts an excellent location—arguably the most prestigious address of any hostel in the city. Rates are higher on weekends.

Rates at Monserrat's **Hostel Inn Tango City** (Piedras 680, tel. 011/4300-5776, www.hostel-inn.com, US$11 pp dorm, US$40 d), an HI affiliate, include breakfast, kitchen facilities, free Internet, and even dinner Monday–Thursday. It's even dog-friendly, but owners must take responsibility for their canine companions.

In a primo location, the Microcentro's **Hostel Suites Florida** (Florida 328, tel. 011/4325-0969, www.hostelsuites.com, US$11 pp dorms, US$40 s, 49 d) is a converted hotel with institutional architecture, but they've spiced it up with decorative touches and theme floors for Carlos Gardel, Che Guevara, and other figures from Argentine history. While it's lively and occasionally rowdy, the sleeping quarters are far from the common areas; an activities board that shows what's going on around town.

It's not quite the design hostel it aspires to be, but San Telmo's **Ostinatto Hostel** (Chile 680, tel. 011/4362-9639, www.ostinatto.com.ar, US$11 pp dorm, US$50–53 s or d with private bath) has done some daring innovations while keeping prices modest, even low, in an ideal location. It features a bar-restaurant, a rooftop terrace that hosts barbecues, and even a mini-cinema, and offers at least one free-of-charge activity per day.

## US$25-50

Near the Facultad de Medicina, **Hotel del Prado** (Paraguay 2385, tel. 011/4961-1192, www.hoteldelprado-ba.com.ar, US$38 s or d) is a plain but tastefully remodeled older building with a quiet interior, good beds, and friendly owner-operators. Rooms have private bath, cable TV, telephone, and ceiling fans but no air-conditioning; there are discounts for extended stays.

Congreso's **Hotel Chile** (Av. de Mayo 1297, tel./fax 011/4383-7877, www.hotelchile.com.ar, US$37 s, US$45 d) is an art nouveau monument offering modernized rooms with private baths, cable TV, and telephones. Corner balcony rooms on the upper floors enjoy panoramic views of the Congreso and, by craning your neck eastward, the Plaza de Mayo and Casa Rosada; the decibel level rises from the street, though.

## US$50-100

On a block-long street where original cobbles still show through slabs of pavement, Palermo Soho's **Che Lulu Guest House** (Emilio Zolá 5185, tel. 011/4772-0289, www.luluguesthouse.com, US$55–70 d with breakfast) is an artist-inspired B&B where seven small but colorful rooms with rustically styled furniture go for bargain prices; the cheaper rooms have shared bath. Their main shortcoming is limited closet space, which can mean living out of a suitcase or backpack.

At **Hotel de los dos Congresos** (Rivadavia 1777, tel. 011/4372-0466, www.hoteldoscongresos.com, US$79 s, US$84 d), the stately exterior is a misleading approach to a refurbished interior, where spacious and comfortable rooms with cable TV, air-conditioning, telephone, and other standard amenities come with a buffet breakfast. Slightly more expensive loft rooms have spiral staircases and whirlpool tubs.

In Palermo's "Villa Freud" neighborhood, the French-run **Hotel Costa Rica** (Costa Rica 4137, tel. 011/4864-7390, www.hotelcostarica.com.ar, US$70 d with shared bath, US$95–140 d with private bath) falls at the affordable end of the boutique hotel scale. Restored to their original configurations, with high ceilings in what was once a crowded family hotel, its 25 rooms are well-furnished but plain and frills-free (no TV, for instance). While less convenient than some barrio hotels, it's still easy walking distance to the restaurants and bars of Palermo Soho.

Falling somewhere between a B&B and a boutique hotel, the **Soco Buenos Aires Hotel** (Lavalle 3119, tel. 011/4864-2032, www.socohotels.com, US$96–108 s or d) unites two classic residences immediately behind the Abasto Shopping mall, with an expansive and luminous lobby. In an area with an improving gastronomic scene and nightlife, specifically tango-oriented, it has only eight rooms, and preserves the high ceilings and natural woodwork of the original structures.

Opposite Parque Lezama, its name derived from a *lunfardo* (slang) term meaning "shelter," the **Gurda Tango Hotel Boutique** (Defensa 1521, tel. 011/4307-0646, www.gurdahotel.com, US$97–157 s or d) is a cozy "sausage house" dating from 1922 recycled into a boutique-style hotel, with contemporary amenities such as air-conditioning and radiant heating. Its seven rooms display individualized decor, including a mix of classic and modern furniture. The larger, more expensive rooms have Jacuzzis.

## US$100-150

For years, Buenos Aires has had a handful of gay-oriented or gay-friendly bed-and-breakfasts, but Monserrat's "hetero-friendly" **Axel Hotel** (Venezuela 647, tel. 011/4136-9400, www.axelhotels.com, US$133–339 plus IVA) is the first full-service hotel built and run with the homosexual market in mind. Architecturally, its creative use of transparent glass in the reception area, staircases, and even the rooftop health club pool—its shimmering waters visible from the ground level—metaphorically suggest that those who stay here have nothing to hide. The decor of its 48 midsized guest rooms and common areas is modern and boutique-ish.

One of the capital's most historic lodgings, dating from 1929, Monserrat's **Castelar Hotel & Spa** (Av. de Mayo 1152, tel. 011/4383-5000, www.castelarhotel.com.ar, from US$143 s or d) has hosted the likes of Spanish dramatist Federico García Lorca, Chilean Nobel Prize–winning poet Pablo Neruda, and Nobel Prize scientist Linus Pauling. Embellished with Carrara marble, it offers comfortable, well-equipped rooms with breakfast and access to its own spa.

Barrio Norte's bright **Design Suites** (Marcelo T. de Alvear 1683, tel./fax 011/4814-8700, www.designsuites.com, US$145–210 s or d) has a heated pool, gym, restaurant room service, and daily newspaper delivery (of the guest's choice). Each of its 40 suites has cable TV, telephone, Internet and fax connections, kitchenette, minibar, air-conditioning, strongbox, and hot tub.

Devaluation briefly made Monserrat's four-star **562 Nogaró** (Diagonal Presidente Julio A. Roca 562, tel. 011/4331-0091, www.562nogaro.com, from US$149 s or d) a bargain, but prices have returned to international levels. Dating from 1930 but renovated a few years ago, this French-style, 150-room hotel offers in-room safes and Internet connections.

## US$150-200

Near the Obelisco, the **Panamericano Buenos Aires Hotel and Resort** (Carlos Pellegrini 525, tel. 011/4348-5000, www.panamericano.us, US$149–179 s or d, with more expensive suites) consists of an older (slightly cheaper) south tower and a newer north tower. Both are comfortable, but the north-tower rooms are technologically superior. All of its 400 rooms have access to amenities including gym and rooftop pool; its restaurant, **Tomo I,** is widely considered one of the capital's best.

Built from scratch, rather than recycled, Palermo Soho's deceptively named **Five Cool Rooms Buenos Aires** (Honduras 4742, tel. 011/4774-8783, www.fivebuenosaires.com, US$131–290 s or d) is a design hotel with a total of 17 rooms in three categories: small, medium, and large (the "five" derives from the number of brothers and sisters who own the place). The management deserves truth-in-labeling credit for the 11 "smalls," but in truth they're a bit bigger than the name implies; king-size beds, though, occupy most of the floor space. The capacious common areas, including a reading room, two large patios, and an even larger rooftop terrace with a whirlpool tub, compensate for any small interior spaces. The entire hotel enjoys a quiet seclusion uncommon among the abundant restaurants, bars, and shops.

In a painstakingly remodeled *casa chorizo* (sausage house), **Malabia House** (Malabia 1555, tel./fax 011/4832-3345 www.malabiahouse.com.ar, US$153–205 s or d) is a bed-and-breakfast with magnificent natural light, glistening wood floors, handsome furnishings, and small but attractive patios. Standard ground-floor rooms have external private baths; the more expensive upstairs rooms have air-conditioning and interior baths.

As their father's Republican party took a thumpin' in the 2006 U.S. midterm elections, the Bush twins partied in Palermo, and every taxi driver in town learned about **Hotel Home Buenos Aires** (Honduras 5860, tel. 011/4779-1008, www.homebuenosaires.com, US$183–254 s or d). Even U2 stayed here (and welcomed other hotel guests to *their* party) when they played Buenos Aires, but you needn't be a big name to enjoy its imaginative design, spacious rooms and suites, and ample common spaces, including a large garden with pool that's uncommon in this part of town.

In a recycled six-story printshop, Monserrat's **Hotel Moreno** (Moreno 376, tel. 011/6091-2001, www.morenobuenosaires.com, from US$199 d) calls itself a "no-frills deluxe" hotel with 39 large rooms and lofts with limited decor and amenities—little or no artwork, for

© WAYNE BERNHARDSON

Monserrat's Hotel Moreno has rooftop views.

instance, and relatively small flat-screen TVs. It retains classic features, such as grillwork elevators and staircase vitreaux; a rooftop bar and terrace offer fine views. In low season (April through July except Easter) some rooms can go for as little US$97.

### Over US$200

Monserrat's high-rise **Hotel Intercontinental** (Moreno 809, tel. 011/4340-7100, www.intercontinental.com, US$215–350 s or d) consistently makes best-hotels lists in magazines like *Travel & Leisure.* More than half the 305 rooms are nonsmoking. Corporate and other discount rates are possible.

Each of the 11 rooms at Palermo Soho's **Legado Mítico Buenos Aires** (Gurruchaga 1848, tel. 011/4833-1300, www.legadomitico.com, US$240–300 plus 21 percent taxes) takes its theme from a historic figure in Argentina's past (this is perhaps the first time that such bitter enemies as Eva Perón and writer Victoria Ocampo have appeared under the same roof). Its decor is a blend of classic and contemporary, with French-style furnishings often side by side with modern designs; ironically, one of the largest and most luxurious rooms is "The Idealist," dedicated to Ernesto "Che" Guevara, but Guevara's family background placed him among the Argentine elite.

Of all the city's hotels, Retiro's **Sofitel Buenos Aires** (Arroyo 841, tel. 011/4131-0000, www.sofitel.com, from US$270 plus taxes) comes closest to matching the Alvear Palace's classic Parisian elegance. Its lobby an architectural masterpiece, this modernization of the neoclassical Torre Mihanovich (1929) manages to blend the Francophile tradition with current design trends and modern functions. The slightly more expensive "luxury" rooms have larger bathrooms and slightly better views on one of the city's quietest blocks, known for its upscale art galleries.

Since 1928, the ☾ **Alvear Palace Hotel** (Av. Alvear 1891, tel. 011/4805-2100, www.alvearpalace.com, from US$360 s or d) has symbolized elegance and luxury—not to mention wealth and privilege. This is one place that, despite devaluation, maintains both its standards and its prices for accommodations with Egyptian-cotton sheets and Hermés toiletries. Francophobes, though, may find the *ancien régime* decor cloying.

There's no faux modesty in the name of French architect Philippe Starck's latest project, which turned a landmark Puerto Madero granary into the five-star-plus **Faena Hotel & Universe** (Marta Salotti 445, tel. 011/4010-9000, www.faenahotelanduniverse.com, from US$485 s or d). From outside, it's not evident that this redbrick structure is even a hotel, but its interior is a revelation of continental style. The rooms and their furnishings look so Parisian as to be incongruous with the building, but there's no denying their quality and sophistication. In its "universe," the Faena also sells "experiences," such as polo with pros and workshops with famous photographer Aldo Sessa.

## FOOD

While prices are rising, dining out remains affordable by global standards, at quality ranging from good to world-class.

### Monserrat

Almost but not quite in San Telmo (the opposite side of the street is) **El Baqueano** (Chile 494, tel. 011/4342-0802, www.restoelbaqueano.com, 7 P.M.–midnight Tues.–Sat.) is a one-of-a-kind restaurant specializing in Patagonian products and, in addition, wild game dishes from throughout the country. To sample the kitchen's diversity, the best choices are the nightly five- and seven-course tasting menus (US$28–33 pp, with a two-person minimum), which samples items such as ñandú (rhea) carpaccio and *yacaré* (caiman) empanadas, in addition to more conventional dishes such as Patagonian lamb and duck pâté. It's a quiet place, with soothing decor and assiduous service.

### Microcentro and Vicinity

**Pizzería Guerrín** (Av. Corrientes 1372, tel. 011/4371-8141, from 8 A.M. daily) is a one-of-a-kind that sells by the slice at the stand-up counter—the oniony *fugazza* (and *fugazzetta*) are exquisitely simple and simply exquisite. **La Continental** (Callao 361, tel. 011/4374-1444, www.lacontinental.com, 7 A.M.–1 A.M. Sun.–Thurs., to 2 A.M. Fri.–Sat.), which has more than a dozen branches around town, is a good backup.

Several tourist-oriented *parrillas* make a fetish of staking their steaks over hot coals in circular barbecue pits, tended by bogus gauchos in full regalia, behind picture windows. While they play for the cliché and serve too many people for individual attention, the quality is good and prices are reasonable at **La Estancia** (Lavalle 941, tel. 011/4326-0330, www.asadorlaestancia.com.ar, lunch and dinner daily).

Possibly downtown's best restaurant, the banker's favorite **Sabot** (25 de Mayo 756, tel. 011/4313-6587, weekday lunch only) serves Italian-Argentine dishes of the highest quality in a very masculine environment—women are few but not unwelcome—with good-humored professional service. Moderately expensive by current standards, most entrées, like *matambre de cerdo* (pork flank steak) and *chivito* (roast goat), plus some fish dishes, cost in the US$10–15 range. A pleasant surprise is the *mate de coca*, a tea made from fresh coca leaves (for digestive purposes only).

### Puerto Madero

Even though Puerto Madero's food is mostly unimpressive, the barrio draws foreigners from nearby luxury hotels because its restaurants don't flinch at dinnertimes as early as 7 P.M.

Opposite Dique No. 4, the best *parrilla* is **Cabaña Las Lilas** (Alicia Moreau de Justo 516, tel. 011/4313-1336, www.laslilas.com, noon–4 P.M. and from 8 P.M. daily). Often packed for lunch despite soaring prices, it offers complimentary champagne and snacks while you wait, but its admittedly fine *bife de chorizo* (similar to a porterhouse) has skyrocketed to US$30.

**Puerto Sorrento** (Alicia Moreau de Justo 410, tel. 011/4319-8731, www.sorrentorestaurant.com.ar, noon–1:30 A.M. daily) is the best seafood choice, and it has an excellent three-course *almuerzo ejecutivo* (midday special, literally "businessman's lunch") for US$18 including soft drink, beer, or wine.

## San Telmo and Vicinity

Despite San Telmo's tourist allure, most restaurants here are better lunchtime bargains than dinnertime indulgences, but the scene's improving.

**Medio y Medio** (Chile 316, tel. 011/4300-1396, 9 A.M.–2 or 3 A.M. Mon.–Sat.) bursts with lunchgoers seeking the Uruguayan caloric overload *chivito,* a steak sandwich piled high with lettuce, cheese, tomato, and bacon; a fried egg crowns the *chivito al plato,* which includes a slab of beef plus potato salad, green salad, and fries.

Dating from 1864, **Bar El Federal** (Carlos Calvo 399, tel. 011/4300-4313, from 8 A.M. daily) looks its age—in a positive way, with its worn tiled floors and intricate carved wooden bar. The house specialty is turkey ravioli (US$5), with a choice of sauces; there's refreshingly cold hard cider on tap.

Despite the large multiple dining rooms at **DesNivel** (Defensa 855, tel. 011/4300-9081, lunch Tues.–Sun., dinner daily), Sunday visitors to Plaza Dorrego form long queues outside for *parrillada* and pasta at bargain prices. Opposite Parque Lezama, **1880** (Defensa 1665, tel. 011/4307-2746, lunch and dinner Tues.–Sat.) is a traditional *parrilla* with plenty of barrio atmosphere, including *filete* ornaments by Martiniano Arce.

Recently reopened in its classic dining room—dark mahogany woodwork and Spanish tiles—the **Casal de Catalunya** (Chacabuco 863, tel. 011/4361-0191, cuinacatalana@hotmail.com, lunch Tues.–Sun., dinner daily) specializes in Catalonian seafood, tapas, and the occasional standard Argentine item. Many dishes are made with garlic, about which Argentines are unenthusiastic.

Really two restaurants in one, **Sagardi** (Humberto Primo 319, tel. 011/4361-2538, www.sagardi.com.ar, noon–4 P.M. and from 8 P.M. daily) serves elaborate elaborate Basque and Spanish seafood in its semi-private dining

© WAYNE BERNHARDSON

Spanish-style tapas are a popular option at San Telmo's Sagardi.

room, but the street side is a tapas bar with varied *pintxos* (bar snacks) ideal for a light but diverse and relatively inexpensive lunch. Pay by the toothpick for prosciutto, salmon, artichoke with chopped tomato, sardines, and the like.

## La Boca

La Boca's offerings are limited, but the food's good enough for lunch—most people visit during the daytime, anyway—and even an occasional dinnertime foray.

**Banchero** (Suárez 396, tel. 011/4301-1406, noon–4 P.M. and from 8 P.M. daily) is the original site of the pizzeria that claims to have invented the onion-and-mozzarella *fugazzetta.* Whether or not that's true, theirs is one of the best.

In an area where taxis are obligatory at night and maybe advisable even in the daytime (though some cabbies have trouble finding it), **El Obrero** (Agustín Cafferena 64, tel. 011/4362-9912, noon–4 P.M. and from 8 P.M. Mon.–Sat.) is where celebrities go slumming for steaks. Its walls plastered with images of soccer icon Diego Maradona and little else, it draws an international clientele on the order of Bono and Robert Duvall. There's no printed menu—check the chalkboards, where most items run US$5–6.

At the other extreme, celebrity chef Francis Mallman's **Patagonia Sur** (Rocha 801, tel. 011/4303-5917, www.restaurante-patagoniasur.com, lunch Thurs.–Sun., dinner Thurs.–Sat.), one of his several gourmet restaurants in Argentina and Uruguay, seems out of place here, and it's expensive (around US$80 pp for a three-course dinner without wine), but Mallman's Argentine beef, seafood, and other regional dishes are always worth consideration.

## Retiro

Danish *smørrebrød* might seem an improbable alternative here, but the **Club Danés** (Av. Leandro N. Alem 1074, 12th floor, tel. 011/4312-5442, weekday lunch only) is cheap *and* appetizing, with lunch specials in the US$8 range—plus exceptional views of Puerto Madero.

**Tancat** (Paraguay 645, tel. 011/4312-5442, noon–12:30 A.M. Mon.–Sat.) is a first-rate *tasca,* an informal Spanish bar/restaurant with good-natured service and lunches US$8–15; don't miss the prosciutto-like *jamón serrano* appetizer. There are few tables, but lunchgoers jam into the long wooden bar, backed by shelves of wine covered with business cards, posters, and photos.

## Recoleta/Barrio Norte

**José Luis** (Av. Quintana 456, tel. 011/4807-0606, lunch and dinner Mon.–Sat.) is an Asturian seafood restaurant that stresses fresher and lighter dishes than most of its counterparts. Entrées are mostly in the US$10 range and up.

Internationally recognized **Oviedo** (Beruti 2602, tel. 011/4822-5415, www.oviedoresto.com.ar, lunch and dinner Mon.–Sat.) is a formal restaurant that specializes in seafood, such as a shrimp risotto (US$17), but also serves Patagonian lamb and standards like beef, with most entrées in the US$15–25 range.

## Palermo

Palermo is, without question, the center of innovation in Argentine dining, mostly in Palermo Soho but also in Palermo Hollywood, the Botánico, and Las Cañitas.

Among the Botánico's best, **Bella Italia Café Bar** (Repúblic Arabe Siria 3330, tel. 011/4807-5120, www.bellaitalia-gourmet.com.ar, 7 A.M.–1 A.M. daily) serves items such as squash gnocchi (US$7) with a subtle cream sauce, as well as fine cannelloni and salads.

**Guido** (Bulevar Cerviño 3943, tel. 011/4802-1262, www.guidorestaurant.com.ar, from 7 P.M. Tues.–Sat., 1–5 P.M. Sat.–Sun.) is a trattoria that has expanded an already outstanding menu notable for a nightly risotto (US$10) and a separate three-course dinner (also US$10), plus inexpensive pizzas. The decor is cinematic, the service is attentive, and there's an extensive list of wines by the glass.

**Mark's Deli & Coffee House** (El Salvador 4701, tel. 011/4832-6244, 8:30 A.M.–9:30 P.M. Mon.–Sat., 10 A.M.–7 P.M. Sun.) is a U.S.-style deli, bright and cheerful with indoor and patio seating and outstanding sandwiches (about US$5); there's a small selection of wines by the glass and large and tasty glasses of lemonade.

In the Botánico, cozy **Nemo** (Cabello 3672, tel. 011/4802-5308, danieljosecid@hotmail.com, lunch and dinner daily) serves light entrées, including seafood-based pastas (around US$8–12) and a diverse fish menu (US$10–15) that includes at least one freshwater catch. It has limited sidewalk seating. *Buenos Aires Herald* food writer Dereck Foster calls it the capital's "consistently best seafood restaurant."

Just when it seems that Peruvian food here can't get any better, along comes **Bardot** (Honduras 5237, tel. 011/4831-1112, www.restobardot.com, from noon Tues.–Fri., from 1 P.M. Sat.–Sun.), with dishes such as *mero a lo macho* (grouper with a shrimp sauce, US$13), Buenos Aires's best pisco sours (two-for-one on Wed.), and near flawless service. For those who want to sample Peru's gastronomic diversity, there's a Sunday buffet (1–4 P.M., US$18) that includes a bit of everything, including the pisco sour.

Unique in the city, Palermo Hollywood's **Jangada** (Bonpland 1670, tel. 011/4777-4193, www.restaurantejangada.com, lunch and dinner daily) specializes in two-person platters (US$20–25) of Paraná river fish such as *boga, pacú,* and *surubí.* Reservations are advisable.

The *parrilla* of the moment is **La Cabrera** (Cabrera 5099, tel. 011/4831-7002, www.parrillalacabrera.com.ar, lunch and dinner daily), where the *bife de chorizo* (US$10) is big enough for two hungry diners and comes with a sampler of side dishes. For an excellent and cheaper alternative, try the distinctly unfashionable **El Trapiche** (Paraguay 5099, tel. 011/4772-7343, lunch and dinner daily), where a single portion of beef can suffice for two or even three diners.

**Sa Giara** (Gurruchaga 1806, tel. 011/4832-5062, www.sagiara.com.ar, Tues.–Sun. lunch, Thurs.–Sat. dinner) brings something new to Italian-Argentine cuisine with Sardinian *curligionis,* resembling Chinese or Japanese pot stickers but stuffed with sweet potato (US$11) or three meats (beef, lamb, and pork, US$13). The villa-style venue also offers inexpensive sandwiches of prosciutto, artisanal cheeses, and the like.

At the casual **Social Paraíso** (Honduras 5182, tel. 011/4831-4556, www.socialparaiso.com.ar, lunch Tues.–Sun., dinner Tues.–Sat.), the US$7 lunch specials feature items like *bondiola* (pork loin) with a tabbouleh salad. Entrées such as stuffed chicken breast with mozzarella and bacon, or Patagonian lamb with grilled vegetables, fall into the US$8–11 range. It also has innovative desserts and wines by the glass.

One of Buenos Aires's most creative restaurants, Palermo Hollywood's **Olsen** (Gorriti 5870, tel. 011/4776-7677, olsen@fibertel.com.ar, from noon Tues.–Sat., from 10 A.M. Sun.) serves what might be called Scandinavian criollo cuisine, with dishes like ravioli with goat cheese and pork roast with raspberry sauce, for upwards of US$10. The bar serves the standard aperitifs but also a literally dizzying variety of vodka-based cocktails. Open for lunch and dinner Tuesday–Sunday, and at 10 A.M. Sunday for brunch, Olsen has also devoted part of its deep lot to a sculpture garden that replicates a Scandinavian boreal forest of birches, cypresses, and pines.

Though not so fashionable, Palermo Hollywood's **Lobby** (Nicaragua 5944, tel.

© WAYNE BERNHARDSON

Palermo's Olsen serves Patagonian specialties with a Scandinavian touch.

011/4770-9335, 9 A.M.–midnight daily) is a hybrid restaurant, wine bar, and wine retailer with inexpensive but outstanding breakfast and lunch menus, including sandwiches, vegetarian dishes, and seafood salads. The by-the-glass wine options are excellent, but they also sell bottles off the wall for a token corkage fee, and there is sidewalk seating.

### Belgrano

On a quiet Belgrano block, the stylishly cozy **Pura Tierra** (3 de Febrero 1167, tel. 011/4899-2007, www.puratierra.com.ar, 8 P.M.–12:30 A.M. Mon.–Sat.) is one of the city's top restaurants for a creative menu that incorporates fresh, natural, local ingredients into tantalizing starters such as ceviche and a wild boar salad (US$9), entrées such as corvina with portobello mushrooms (US$15) and *bondiola* (pork shoulder, US$16), and remarkable desserts. On top of that, its sommelier provides some of the savviest wine recommendations, at reasonable prices, to accompany them. One of the best options for a romantic dinner or a small group of friends, Pura Tierra offers a 10 percent discount for cash payments.

# Information and Services

## INFORMATION

The **Ministerio de Turismo** (Av. Santa Fe 883, Retiro, tel. 011/4312-2232 or 0800/5550016, www.turismo.gov.ar) is open 9 A.M.–5 P.M. weekdays; there's a branch at Aeropuerto Internacional Ezeiza (tel. 011/4480-0292) and another at Aeroparque Jorge Newbery (tel. 011/4771-0104). Both airport branches are open 8 A.M.–8 P.M. daily.

The municipal **Subsecretaría de Turismo** (www.bue.gov.ar) maintains several information kiosks: in the Microcentro (Florida 100, 8:30 A.M.–6:30 P.M. daily); in Retiro (Florida and Marcelo T. de Alvear, 9 A.M.–5 P.M. Mon.–Sat.); in Recoleta (Quintana 596, 10 A.M.–5 P.M. daily); at Puerto Madero's Dique 4 (Av. Alicia Moreau de Justo 200, tel. 011/4315-4265, 9:30 A.M.–7:30 P.M. daily); and at the Retiro bus terminal (tel. 011/4313-0187, daily 7:30 A.M.–1 P.M. weekdays only). All distribute maps and brochures, and usually have English-speaking staff.

## SERVICES

Buenos Aires has a capital city's selection of services, many of which keep long hours.

### Money

The ubiquitous ATMs are most convenient for changing money. In the La City financial district, *casas de cambio* along San Martín between Corrientes and the Plaza de Mayo usually offer the best exchange rates for U.S. cash, euros, and travelers checks. For travelers checks, they normally charge a commission or pay a lower rate than for cash, but **American Express** (Arenales 707, Retiro, tel. 011/4310-3000) cashes its own checks for no commission.

### Postal Services

The **Correo Central** (Sarmiento 151, 8 A.M.–8 P.M. weekdays, 10 A.M.–1 P.M. Sat.) is a landmark building worth a visit in its own right; there are many other branch offices. International parcels exceeding one kilogram must go from the **Correo Internacional** (Antártida Argentina near Retiro train station, tel. 011/4316-7777, 11 A.M.–5 P.M. weekdays).

**Federal Express** (Maipú 753, tel. 011/4393-6054) offers private courier service.

### Communications

*Locutorios* for faxes and long-distance calls are so plentiful that it's unnecessary to mention any in particular. Many have Internet connections, but there are also countless storefronts devoted exclusively to Internet service, and wireless Internet is almost ubiquitous.

### Travel Agencies

North of Plaza San Martín, Retiro's **American**

**Express** (Arenales 707, tel. 011/4310-3000, www.americanexpress.com.ar) offers the usual services of a travel agency.

**Swan Turismo** (Cerrito 822, 9th floor, Retiro, tel. 011/4129-7926, www.swanturismo.com.ar) is a full-service agency with a reputation for navigating some of the Argentine travel system's eccentricities.

In the Galería Buenos Aires, the nonprofit **Asatej** (Florida 835, 3rd floor, Retiro, tel. 011/4311-6953, www.asatej.com) is good at searching out the best airfares for anyone, not just students; it is also a Hostelling International affiliate. Another good choice is **Say Hueque** (Viamonte 749, 6th floor, tel. 011/5199-2517, www.sayhueque.com), especially for independent travelers.

### Libraries

The **Biblioteca Nacional** (National Library, Agüero 2502, Recoleta, tel. 011/4808-6000, www.bn.gov.ar) is open 9 A.M.–9 P.M. weekdays, noon–7 P.M. weekends. It holds frequent special exhibitions, lectures and literary events, and free concerts.

### Immigration

For visa extensions, the **Dirección Nacional de Migraciones** (Av. Antártida Argentina 1355, tel. 011/4317-0237) is open 8 A.M.–1 P.M. weekdays.

### Medical Services

Public hospitals include Recoleta's **Hospital Rivadavia** (Av. Las Heras 2670, tel. 011/4809-2000) and Palermo's **Hospital Municipal Juan Fernández** (Cerviño 3356, tel. 011/4808-2600).

The **Hospital Británico** (Perdriel 74, Barracas, tel. 011/4304-1082, www.hospitalbritanico.org.ar) is a highly regarded private hospital. Argentine presidents have had arthroscopies and soccer star Diego Maradona did detox at Belgrano's **Clínica Fleni** (Montañeses 2325, tel. 011/5777-3200, www.fleni.org.ar), but it does not handle every specialty.

# Getting There and Around

## GETTING THERE

Buenos Aires is the main port of entry for overseas visitors, and the hub for domestic travel.

### Air

Most international flights arrive and depart from the suburban airport at Ezeiza (Aeropuerto Internacional Ministro Pistarini), though a handful from neighboring countries use close-in Aeroparque Jorge Newbery. Both airports are operated by the private concessionaire **Aeropuertos Argentinos 2000** (tel. 011/5480-6111, www.aa2000.com.ar).

**Aerolíneas Argentinas** (Perú 2, Monserrat, tel. 011/4320-2000) flies to destinations ranging from Puerto Iguazú on the Brazilian border to Ushuaia in Tierra del Fuego.

Serving a growing number of domestic destinations, **LAN Argentina** (Cerrito 866, tel. 0810/9999526) is the local affiliate of Chile's successful and reliable international airline.

Aeroparque-based **Andes Líneas Aéreas** (Av. Córdoba 775, tel. 0810/7772-6337, www.andesonline.com) is a new private airline flying to Puerto Madryn and northerly Argentine cities. **Sol Líneas Aéreas** (Marcelo T. de Alvear 510, tel. 0810/4444765, www.sol.com.ar) flies south to Comodoro Rivadavia, Río Gallegos, Río Grande, and Ushuaia, also from Aeroparque.

**Líneas Aéreas del Estado** (LADE, Perú 714, San Telmo, tel. 011/4361-7071, www.lade.com.ar) is the Argentine air force's commercial aviation branch. Miraculously surviving budget crises and privatizations, it flies to southern Buenos Aires province and Patagonia on a wing and a subsidy.

### Bus

Buenos Aires's main bus station is Retiro's **Estación Terminal de Ómnibus** (Av. Ramos Mejía 1860, tel. 011/4310-0700, www.tebasa.com.ar). The sprawling three-story building hosts nearly 140 separate bus companies that cover the entire country and international destinations as well. It's walking distance from the northern terminus of Subte Línea C, at the Retiro train station.

Passengers leave from the first-floor *andenes* (platforms). Companies occupy more than 200 *ventanillas* (ticket windows) on the second floor, roughly organized by geographical region; for readers of this guide, the most important is Zona Sur (South Zone, windows 1–21, 23, 25, 27–30, 32–34, and 101).

On the departure level, the Centro de Informes y Reclamos (tel. 011/4310-0700) provides general information and also oversees taxis; direct any complaint about drivers to them. There is a separate tourist office, open 7:30 A.M.–1 P.M. only.

Reservations are a good idea during summer (Jan.–Feb.) and winter (late July) holidays, and also on long weekends like Semana Santa (Holy Week).

## GETTING AROUND

### Airports

Buenos Aires has two airports, both operated by the private concessionaire **Aeropuertos Argentinos 2000** (tel. 011/5480-6111, www.aa2000.com.ar). The main international facility is **Aeropuerto Internacional Ministro Pistarini,** 35 kilometers southwest of downtown, popularly called Ezeiza after its namesake suburb. The other is Palermo's **Aeroparque Jorge Newbery** (Av. Costanera Rafael Obligado s/n), which is primarily domestic but handles some international flights from neighboring countries.

International passengers leaving from Ezeiza pay a US$30.50 departure tax, payable in local currency or U.S. dollars; US$18 of this is normally collected on departure. On flights shorter than 300 kilometers to neighboring countries, such as Uruguay, the tax is only US$6; on domestic flights from Aeroparque, it's about US$3. These latter fees are normally included in the ticket price.

There are various options for getting to and from the airports, ranging from *colectivos* (city buses) to shuttles, metered taxis, and *remises* (meterless taxis).

***Colectivos*** are the cheapest option, but they are more practical for close-in Aeroparque than distant Ezeiza, as they take circuitous routes on surface streets. To Aeroparque (about US$0.30), the options are No. 33 from Plaza de Mayo, the Microcentro, and Retiro; No. 37-C (Ciudad Universitaria) from Plaza del Congreso, Avenida Callao, Avenida Las Heras, and Plaza Italia; No. 45 northbound from Plaza Constitución, Plaza San Martín, or Retiro; and No. 160-C or 160-D from Avenida Las Heras or Plaza Italia. Return buses leave from the Avenida Costanera Rafael Obligado, a short walk outside the terminal.

To Ezeiza (about US$0.75), the backpackers' pick is the No. 86-A (Aeropuerto), from La Boca to Plaza de Mayo, Plaza del Congreso, and onward, but the roundabout route can take two hours. *Servicio diferencial* buses cost more (US$2.60) but have comfortable reclining seats. At Ezeiza, both leave from just outside the Aerolíneas Argentinas terminal, a short distance from the main international terminal.

**Manuel Tienda León** (Av. Madero and San Martín, Retiro, tel. 011/4315-5115 or 0810/8885366, www.tiendaleon.com.ar) runs frequent buses to and from Ezeiza (US$12) and to Aeroparque (US$4); buses from Ezeiza make connections to Aeroparque for domestic flights and also include door-to-door taxi service from Tienda León's Retiro terminal.

Offering door-to-door services, **taxis** and ***remises*** are no more expensive than shuttles for three or more people. Manuel Tienda León and many other companies, such as **Transfer Express** (tel. 0800/4444872) and **Naon Remises** (tel. 011/4545-6500), have *remises* to Aeroparque (US$6) and Ezeiza (US$25–35). Both usually tack on tolls to Ezeiza (about US$1).

## *Colectivos* (Buses)

Most visitors need to know relatively few of Buenos Aires's bus routes. Detailed city atlases have abbreviated pocket versions available at kiosks and bookstores, but Porteño riders are also generous with information. Fares (around US$0.30) depend on distance; on hearing your destination, the driver enters the fare in the automatic ticket machine, which takes only coins and gives small change. Rechargeable electronic tickets are in the works.

## Subway

Popularly known as the Subte, South America's first underground railway has modernized, but some antique cars (with varnished but worn woodwork) and elaborately tiled but chipped station murals help recall the early 20th century's prosperity and optimism.

Concessionaire **Metrovías** (www.metrovias.com.ar) has improved rolling stock, extended existing lines, remodeled older stations and built new ones, and replaced *fichas* (tokens) with electronic tickets.

## RIDING THE SUBTE

Operated by the private concessionaire Metrovías, the state-owned Subterráneos de Buenos Aires comprises five alphabetically designated lines *(líneas)*, four of which (A, B, D, and E) begin in Monserrat or the Microcentro and serve outlying northern and western barrios with numerous stations in between. Línea C is a north-south connector line between major railway stations at Retiro and Constitución.

An additional north-south connector line, Línea H, now links Once and outlying southern barrios, beneath Avenida Pueyrredón and Avenida Jujuy, to Avenida Caseros. Línea E is undergoing a 2.1-kilometer extension from Bolívar station (Plaza de Mayo) to Retiro, due to be completed in 2012.

Subte hours are 5 A.M. to about 11 P.M. Monday-Saturday, but the system opens later (around 8 A.M.) and closes earlier (about 10:30 P.M.) Sundays and holidays, when services are less frequent. Fares are about US$0.30; to save time, purchase magnetic tickets in quantities of 2, 5, 10, or 30 rides, or a rechargeable Monedero ticket. Two or more people may legally use the same ticket by passing it back and forth across the turnstile; you do not need a ticket to exit the system.

Before going through the turnstiles, be sure of which direction you're headed; at some stations, trains in both directions use the same platform, but at others the platforms are on opposite sides. Some stations have one-way traffic only; in those cases, the next station down the line usually serves one-way traffic in the other direction.

For complaints or problems, contact Metrovías's Centro de Atención al Pasajero (tel. 0800/5551616 toll-free).

### SUBTE ROUTES

**Línea A** begins at Plaza de Mayo in Monserrat and runs beneath Avenida Rivadavia to Carabobo, in the barrio of Flores.

**Línea B** begins at Avenida Leandro Alem in the Microcentro and runs beneath Avenida Corrientes to Federico Lacroze in the barrio of Chacarita, where it connects with the suburban Ferrocarril Urquiza. A recent northwesterly extension continues to Tronador and Avenida los Incas and is due to reach Villa Urquiza.

**Línea C** connects Retiro (which has northern suburban commuter surface rail lines) with Constitución, the transfer point for southern suburban commuter surface lines; Línea C also has transfer stations for all other Subte lines.

**Línea D** begins at Catedral on Plaza de Mayo and runs beneath Avenida Santa Fe and Avenida Cabildo through Palermo and Belgrano to Congreso de Tucumán in the barrio of Núñez.

**Línea E** begins at Bolívar on the Avenida de Mayo (though a northern extension to Retiro is under construction) and goes to Plaza de los Virreyes in the barrio of Flores. At Plaza de los Virreyes, there's a light-rail extension known as the Premetro.

**Línea H** now runs crosstown from Avenida Corrientes, at Línea B's Estación Pueyrredón, south to Caseros, with additional transfer stations at Once (Línea A) and Humberto Primo (Línea E).

# SANTIAGO DE CHILE

For most visitors, sprawling Santiago de Chile, its Mediterranean hillsides, and the snow-covered Andean crest are their first impressions of the country. Santiago may lack Buenos Aires's international profile, but its finest attractions can match or, in some cases, surpass those of Argentina's capital.

Since the 1990 return to constitutional government and subsequent economic expansion, the city has improved greatly. Both individuals and businesses, for instance, have restored or rehabbed houses and buildings in once run-down Barrio Brasil, and entrepreneurs have replaced unsalvageable structures with tasteful contemporary apartments. Barrio Bellavista has enjoyed a gastronomic and nightlife boom, and international commerce flourishes in Providencia and Las Condes. Despite the publicity, the powerful 8.8 earthquake of February 2010 barely slowed the city down.

The mega-city of Santiago is really many cities, consisting of 32 different *comunas* (boroughs) with separate governments. Most sights are in the central city's colonial nucleus and adjacent boroughs like Recoleta, Independencia, and Quinta Normal, and eastern suburbs like Providencia, Las Condes, and Ñuñoa.

Five million people, more than a third of all Chileans, live in Gran Santiago (Greater Santiago). The locus of political and economic power, the capital has grown at the expense of the regions, but unevenly so—some *comunas* have become prosperous, while others remain desperately poor.

Class-based residential segregation is striking, though less extreme than in cities like

© WAYNE BERNHARDSON

## HIGHLIGHTS

**Plaza de Armas:** Numerous historical buildings and museums surround Santiago's 16th-century plaza, platted by Pedro de Valdivia (page 77).

**Museo Chileno de Arte Precolombino:** In an elegant colonial building, this museum houses an irreplaceable assortment of indigenous artifacts from throughout the Americas (page 83).

**Mercado Central:** North of the Plaza de Armas, this onetime colonial rubbish tip became a produce market and, more recently, a tourist draw for its simpático seafood eateries (page 83).

**Palacio de la Moneda:** Santiago's colonial presidential palace survived the 1973 headlines, and the public is once again welcome to stroll its passages. On the side facing the Alameda, a spectacular subterranean cultural center is an additional attraction (page 84).

**Cerro Santa Lucía:** In the late 19th century, visionary mayor Benjamín Vicuña Mackenna started the transformation of a barren quarry, where Pedro de Valdivia founded Santiago, into a true garden spot (page 85).

**La Chascona (Museo Neruda):** On a cul-de-sac in bohemian Barrio Bellavista, Nobel poet Pablo Neruda's whimsical Santiago residence is a literary pilgrimage site that delights everyone (page 91).

**Viña Cousiño Macul:** Though surrounded by the sprawling capital, the surviving vineyards and subterranean bodegas of this classic Chilean winery are conveniently close for tours and tasting (page 92).

**Viña Concha y Toro:** In the southeastern suburb of Pirque, Concha y Toro is a bit more distant than Cousiño Macul, but it's still a prime visitor destination and one of Chile's best-known vineyards and wineries (page 92).

LOOK FOR TO FIND RECOMMENDED SIGHTS, ACTIVITIES, DINING, AND LODGING.

Lima and Mexico City. There are environmental costs, as well—more than a million automobiles sometimes clog narrow colonial streets. Though sooty diesel buses are mostly a thing of the past, smokestack industry adds its share, aggravating one of the world's worst smog problems—especially in the almost windless autumn months of March and April.

Santiago's Mediterranean climate has a pronounced dry season (November–April) and wet winters (though droughts are not unusual). The daily maximum temperature averages 28°C in January, but it almost always cools off at night, thanks to the elevation. In July, the coolest month, the daily maximum averages 10°C.

## PLANNING YOUR TIME

Presuming only two days, visitors should get to know the central Plaza de Armas and vicinity, including the Mercado Central and the Museo Precolombino, the Palacio de la Moneda, Cerro Santa Lucía, poet Pablo Neruda's "La Chascona" house, and a winery or two. Anyone planning a longer stay should consult the author's *Moon Chile.*

## HISTORY

Conquistador Pedro de Valdivia founded "Santiago del Nuevo Extremo" on February 12, 1541, in a place where "The land is such that there is none better in the world for living in and settling down…because it is very flat, very healthy, and very pleasant. . . ." Valdivia established early good relations with Araucanians, but during his absence in Peru, the Spaniards began to abuse the indigenes; their rebellion nearly destroyed the settlement, which became a precarious armed camp.

The site Valdivia chose proved an enduring one, but not without problems. One was the Mapocho, which often flooded with the spring runoff. Another was the Araucanian raiders, who made its defense costly—between 1600 and 1606, the governing viceroyalty of Lima had to quadruple Chile's military budget to

© WAYNE BERNHARDSON

Throughout its history, Santiago has been vulnerable to earthquakes such as the one that damaged these buildings near the Parque Quinta Normal in 2010.

maintain its presence. By the end of the 16th century, according to historian Eduardo Solar Correa, Santiago's "appearance was sad and miserable." Landed proprietors dominated urban society, though their economic and power base was the countryside.

With the 18th century, though, came material improvements like construction of a cathedral, creation of the Casa de la Moneda (colonial mint) to spur economic activity, *tajamares* (dikes) to contain the floods, and improved roads. Cultural life improved with establishment of what later became the Universidad de Chile.

By Chile's independence in 1810, Santiago was a modest, nondescript city. Charles Darwin, in the 1830s, remarked that "it is not so fine or so large as Buenos Ayres, but it is built after the same model." Earthquakes encouraged utilitarian rather than elaborate construction.

Post-independence Santiago, though, was poised for a boom. The 1850s California Gold Rush created a market for Chilean wheat, wine, and other produce, and the beneficiaries were a landed elite who built splendid city mansions, furnished them extravagantly, and supported exclusive institutions like the Club Hípico (Racing Club). By the 1870s, progressive mayor Benjamín Vicuña Mackenna was transforming areas like Cerro Santa Lucía into public parks, and Venezuelan-born scholar/educator Andrés Bello helped enrich the cultural life of a city whose population exceeded 100,000 by midcentury.

Conflict with Peru and Bolivia in the War of the Pacific (1879–1884) changed the city and country dramatically, in ways that were not immediately apparent. Chilean interests grew wealthy with control of the nitrate-rich Atacama Desert, financing a new round of conspicuous consumption by mining magnates and bringing revenue to the government treasury, but neglect lost much of sprawling, vaguely defined Patagonia to Argentina.

Industrialization initially absorbed excess labor when the nitrate mines failed in the early 20th century, but rural labor conflicts

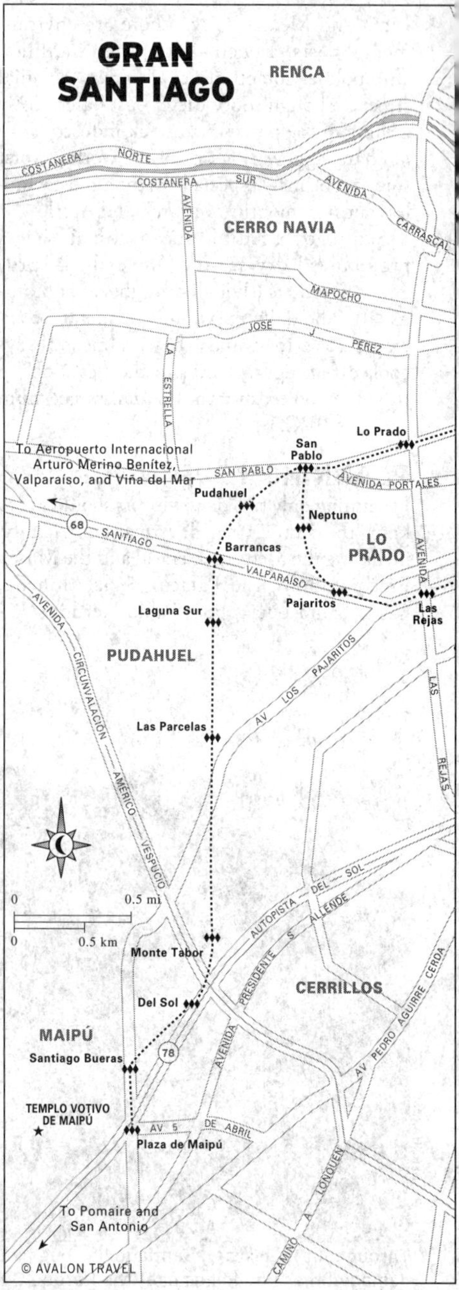

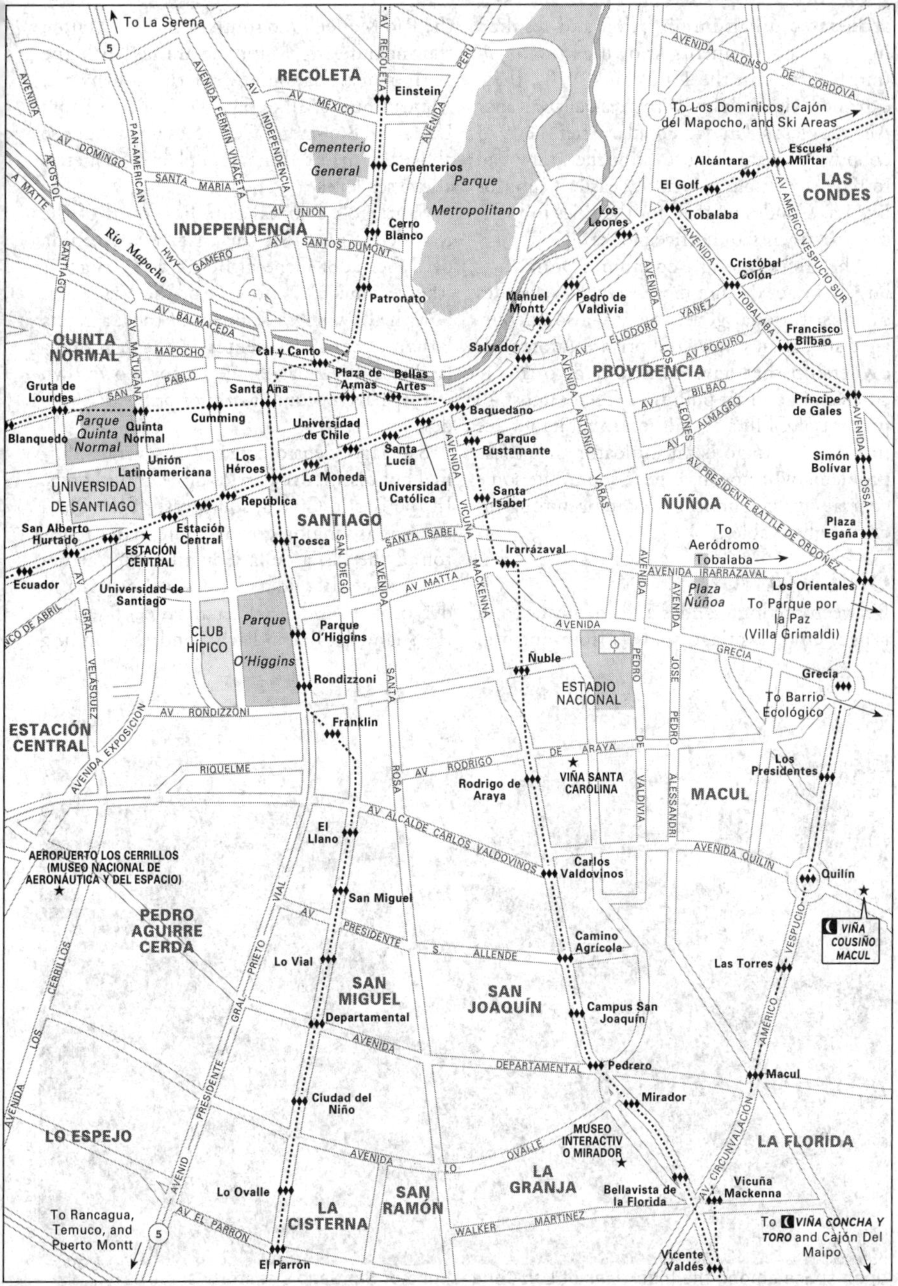

To La Serena
RECOLETA
Einstein
AV. MEXICO
Cementerio General
Cementerios
Parque Metropolitano
AVENIDA ALONSO DE CORDOVA
To Los Dominicos, Cajón del Mapocho, and Ski Areas
Escuela Militar
Alcántara
LAS CONDES
El Golf
Tobalaba
Los Leones
INDEPENDENCIA
Cerro Blanco
Río Mapocho
AV. SANTOS DUMONT
Patronato
Manuel Montt
Pedro de Valdivia
Cristóbal Colón
Francisco Bilbao
QUINTA NORMAL
Cal y Canto
Salvador
PROVIDENCIA
Plaza de Armas
Bellas Artes
Gruta de Lourdes
Santa Ana
Baquedano
Príncipe de Gales
Blanquedo
Parque Quinta Normal
Quinta Normal
Cumming
Universidad de Chile
Parque Bustamante
Santa Lucía
Simón Bolívar
Unión Latinoamericana
Los Héroes
La Moneda
UNIVERSIDAD DE SANTIAGO
Universidad Católica
Santa Isabel
ÑUÑOA
República
SANTIAGO
San Alberto Hurtado
Estación Central
ESTACIÓN CENTRAL
Toesca
Irarrázaval
To Aeródromo Tobalaba
Plaza Egaña
Ecuador
Universidad de Santiago
AVENIDA IRARRAZAVAL
Plaza Ñuñoa
Los Orientales
To Parque por la Paz (Villa Grimaldi)
CLUB HÍPICO
Parque O'Higgins
Parque O'Higgins
Rondizzoni
Ñuble
ESTADIO NACIONAL
Grecia
To Barrio Ecológico
ESTACIÓN CENTRAL
Franklin
AV. RONDIZZONI
Rodrigo de Araya
VIÑA SANTA CAROLINA
Los Presidentes
MACUL
El Llano
AV. ALCALDE CARLOS VALDOVINOS
AEROPUERTO LOS CERRILLOS (MUSEO NACIONAL DE AERONÁUTICA Y DEL ESPACIO)
Carlos Valdovinos
Quilín
San Miguel
PEDRO AGUIRRE CERDA
Camino Agrícola
VIÑA COUSIÑO MACUL
Lo Vial
Las Torres
SAN MIGUEL
SAN JOAQUÍN
Departamental
Campus San Joaquín
Pedrero
Macul
Ciudad del Niño
Mirador
LO ESPEJO
MUSEO INTERACTIV O MIRADOR
LA FLORIDA
LA GRANJA
Lo Ovalle
Bellavista de la Florida
Vicuña Mackenna
To Rancagua, Temuco, and Puerto Montt
LA CISTERNA
SAN RAMÓN
To VIÑA CONCHA Y TORO and Cajón Del Maipo
El Parrón
Vicente Valdés

accelerated urban immigration and resulted in squatter settlements known as *callampas* (mushrooms). In the 1960s and 1970s, these exploded with activism with President Salvador Allende's leftist Unidad Popular; after the 1973 coup by General Augusto Pinochet, they had to bide their time as wealthy eastern suburbs like Las Condes reached for the skies in high-rise apartments and office blocks.

The dictatorship's economic policies—largely intact despite more than two decades of constitutional government—also encouraged suburban sprawl and private automobile ownership that have contributed to traffic congestion and air pollution. That almost 40 percent of Chile's 17 million inhabitants live in Gran Santiago is an indicator that these problems will not disappear soon, but some central city neighborhoods are becoming increasingly livable.



## ORIENTATION

Between the high Andes and the lower coast range, Gran Santiago sprawls from north of the Río Mapocho to south of the Río Maipo; the meandering Mapocho unites with the Maipo near Talagante, to the southwest. Andean outliers like 635-meter Cerro Santa Lucía and 869-meter Cerro San Cristóbal rise above the city's sedimentary plain, 550 meters above sea level.

Santiago's colonial core lies south of the Mapocho, north of the east–west Avenida del Libertador General Bernardo O'Higgins (the "Alameda"), and east of the Vía Norte Sur, the downtown segment of the Carretera Panamericana. Its center is the rectangular Plaza de Armas. Some narrow downtown streets have become *paseos* or *peatonales* (pedestrian malls).

Santiago Centro consists of several informal but distinctive barrios or neighborhoods. In the Barrio Cívico, southwest of the Plaza de Armas, major government offices surround the Plaza de la Constitución; farther west, once-dilapidated Barrio Brasil is undergoing a residential renaissance. South of the Alameda, Barrio París Londres's winding

© WAYNE BERNHARDSON

open space among the high-rises of Las Condes, one of Santiago's easterly suburbs

streets break the grid pattern, as do those of Barrio Lastarria, east of Cerro Santa Lucía.

Beyond Santiago Centro, several other *comunas* have sights and services, most notably the easterly suburbs of Providencia and Las Condes. Some of these boast their own distinctive neighborhoods: North of the Mapocho, the restaurant and nightlife mecca of Barrio Bellavista lies half in Recoleta, half in Providencia. Providencia's traditional point of identification is Plaza Baquedano, universally known as Plaza Italia, where the eastbound Alameda becomes Avenida Providencia.

Las Condes and Vitacura are affluent eastward extensions of Providencia. Independencia, Quinta Normal, and Estación Central have fewer sights, except for major museums and parks, and a few key services such as long-distance bus terminals.



# Sights

Central Santiago has the highest density of sights in or around the Plaza de Armas, Plaza de la Constitución, Cerro Santa Lucía, and Barrio Bellavista, with a handful elsewhere. The municipal tourist authority, with separate offices near the Plaza de Armas and on Cerro Santa Lucía, offers free walking tours that include admission to some of the best museums; check for the most current itineraries.

## PLAZA DE ARMAS AND VICINITY

On its west side, the plaza's oldest surviving landmark is the **Catedral Metropolitana,** begun in 1748 but, because of earthquakes and fires, not completed until 1830. Italian architect Joaquín Toesca designed its neoclassical facade, modified with late-19th-century Tuscan touches.

On the north side, the next oldest structure is the **Municipalidad de Santiago** (1785). Immediately west, the **Palacio de la Real Audiencia** (1804) houses the Museo Histórico Nacional; at the corner of Paseo Puente, the French-style **Correo Central** (Post Office, 1882) replaced the original government house. Half a block east of the plaza, dating from 1769, the **Casa Colorada** (Merced 860) houses the municipal tourist office and city museum.

One block from the southwest corner of the plaza, the **Palacio de la Real Aduana** (Royal Customs House, Bandera 361) now accommodates the exceptional Museo Chileno de Arte Precolombino (Chilean Museum of Pre-Columbian Art).

One block north of the plaza, built of massive blocks, the **Templo de Santo Domingo** (begun in 1747, finished in 1808) stands at 21 de Mayo and Monjitas; two blocks north is the **Mercado Central,** the landmark central market that's a major tourist draw for its seafood restaurants.

From 1913 until 1987, trains to Valparaíso, northern Chile, and Mendoza (Argentina) used Eiffel-influenced architect Emilio Jecquier's monumental **Estación Mapocho;** closed in 1987 and reopened as a cultural center, it hosts events like Santiago's annual book fair. In the nearby Cal y Canto Metro station, parts of the foundations of the colonial **Puente Cal y Canto** bridge over the Mapocho have been exposed to view.

### Museo Histórico Nacional (Palacio de la Real Audiencia)

After 1609, the Real Audiencia housed Chile's colonial supreme court, but earthquakes destroyed its quarters in both 1647 and 1730. Architect Juan José de Goycolea y Zañartu designed the current neoclassical building (1808), but its clock tower dates from Mayor Benjamín Vicuña Mackenna's late-19th-century term.

Three years later, during the independence struggle, the first Congreso Nacional met here, but royalists restored the Real Audiencia from 1814 to 1817. That same year, the Cabildo of

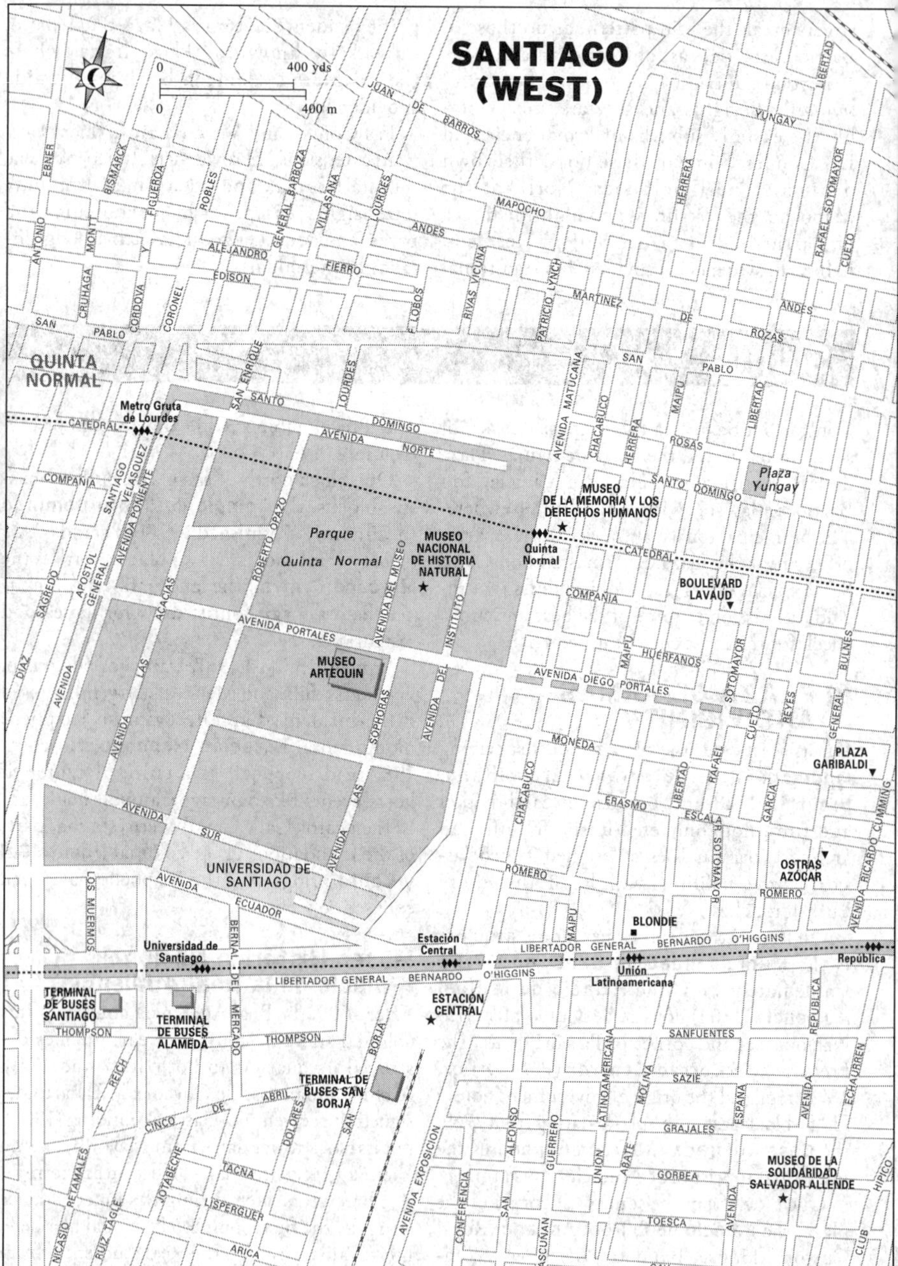
SANTIAGO
(WEST)
0
400 yds
0
400 m
QUINTA NORMAL
Metro Gruta de Lourdes
Parque Quinta Normal
MUSEO NACIONAL DE HISTORIA NATURAL
MUSEO DE LA MEMORIA Y LOS DERECHOS HUMANOS
Quinta Normal
Plaza Yungay
BOULEVARD LAVAUD
MUSEO ARTEQUIN
PLAZA GARIBALDI
OSTRAS AZÓCAR
UNIVERSIDAD DE SANTIAGO
BLONDIE
Universidad de Santiago
Estación Central
Unión Latinoamericana
República
TERMINAL DE BUSES SANTIAGO
TERMINAL DE BUSES ALAMEDA
ESTACIÓN CENTRAL
TERMINAL DE BUSES SAN BORJA
MUSEO DE LA SOLIDARIDAD SALVADOR ALLENDE
JUAN DE BARROS
YUNGAY
LIBERTAD
MAPOCHO
ANDES
ALEJANDRO
FIERRO
EDISON
MARTINEZ DE ROZAS
SAN PABLO
SANTO DOMINGO
AVENIDA NORTE
CATEDRAL
COMPAÑIA
ROSAS
HUERFANOS
AVENIDA DIEGO PORTALES
AVENIDA PORTALES
MONEDA
ERASMO ESCALA
ROMERO
AVENIDA SUR
AVENIDA ECUADOR
LIBERTADOR GENERAL BERNARDO O'HIGGINS
THOMPSON
SANFUENTES
SAZIE
GRAJALES
GORBEA
TOESCA
GAY
TACNA
LISPERGUER
ARICA
CINCO DE ABRIL
EBNER
BISMARCK
FIGUEROA
ROBLES
GENERAL BARBOZA
VILLASANA
LOURDES
ANTONIO MONTT
CRUHAGA
CORDOVA
CORONEL
F. LOBOS
RIVAS VICUÑA
PATRICIO LYNCH
HERRERA
RAFAEL SOTOMAYOR
CUETO
SAN ENRIQUE
AVENIDA MATUCANA
CHACABUCO
MAIPU
SANTIAGO
VELASQUEZ
AVENIDA PONIENTE
ROBERTO OPAZO
AVENIDA DEL MUSEO
INSTITUTO
SAGREDO
APOSTOL
GENERAL DIAZ
AVENIDA LAS ACACIAS
SOPHORAS
AVENIDA LAS
BULNES
REYES
GENERAL GARCIA
AVENIDA RICARDO CUMMING
LOS MUERMOS
BERNAL DEL MERCADO
SAN BORJA
DOLORES
F. REICH
RETAMALES
NICASIO
RUIZ TAGLE
JOTABECHE
AVENIDA EXPOSICION
CONFERENCIA
SAN ALFONSO
BASCUNAN
GUERRERO
UNION LATINOAMERICANA
ABATE MOLINA
ESPAÑA
AVENIDA REPÚBLICA
ECHAURREN
CLUB HIPICO

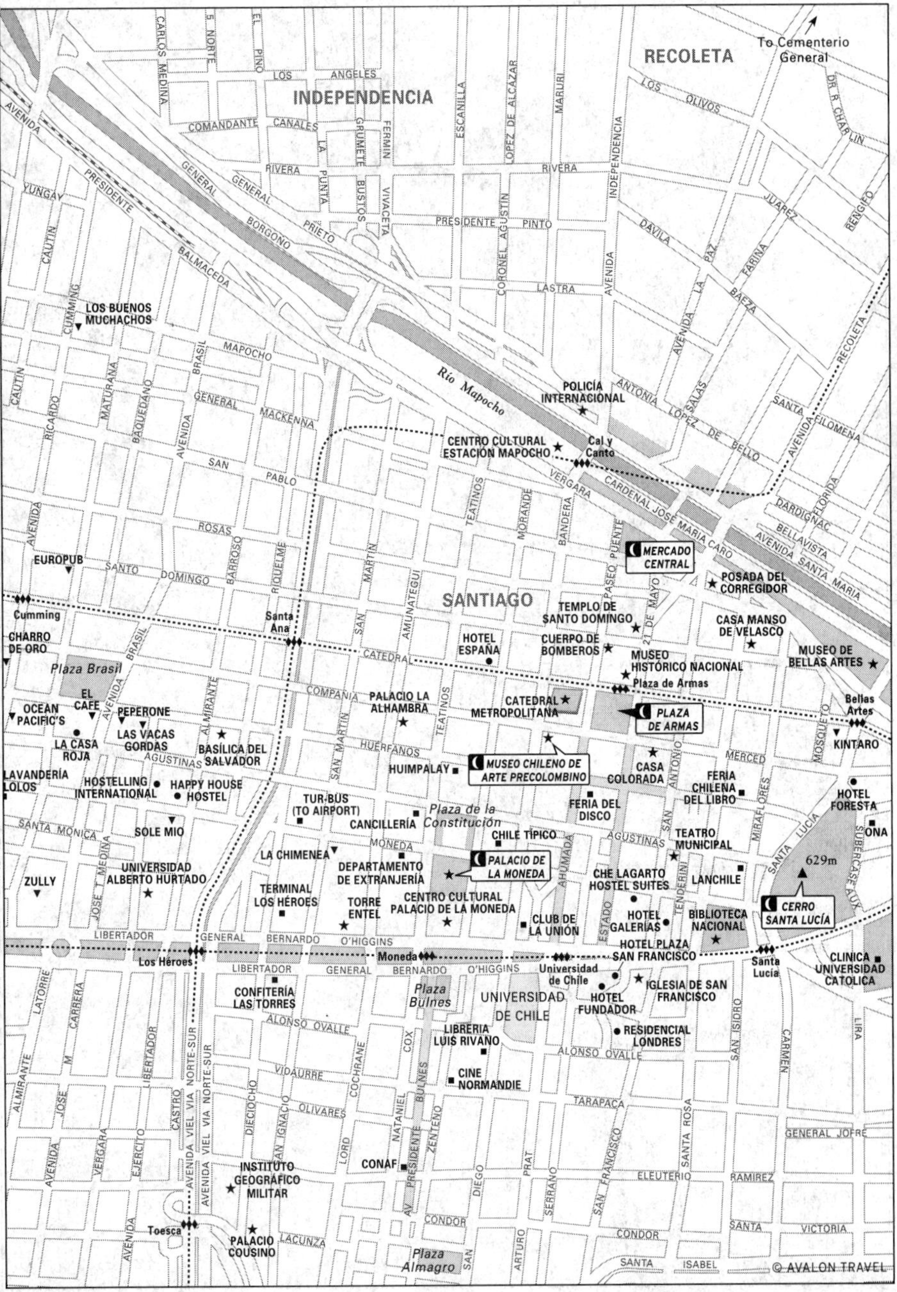

To Cementerio General
RECOLETA
INDEPENDENCIA
SANTIAGO
Río Mapocho
LOS BUENOS MUCHACHOS
POLICÍA INTERNACIONAL
CENTRO CULTURAL ESTACIÓN MAPOCHO
Cal y Canto
MERCADO CENTRAL
POSADA DEL CORREGIDOR
EUROPUB
TEMPLO DE SANTO DOMINGO
CASA MANSO DE VELASCO
Cumming
Santa Ana
HOTEL ESPAÑA
CUERPO DE BOMBEROS
MUSEO HISTÓRICO NACIONAL
MUSEO DE BELLAS ARTES
CHARRO DE ORO
Plaza Brasil
Plaza de Armas
EL CAFE
CATEDRAL METROPOLITANA
PALACIO LA ALHAMBRA
PLAZA DE ARMAS
Bellas Artes
OCEAN PACIFIC'S
PEPERONE
LAS VACAS GORDAS
BASÍLICA DEL SALVADOR
LA CASA ROJA
KINTARO
MUSEO CHILENO DE ARTE PRECOLOMBINO
HUIMPALAY
CASA COLORADA
LAVANDERÍA LOLOS
HOSTELLING INTERNATIONAL
HAPPY HOUSE HOSTEL
FERIA CHILENA DEL LIBRO
HOTEL FORESTA
TUR-BUS (TO AIRPORT)
Plaza de la Constitución
CANCILLERÍA
FERIA DEL DISCO
SOLE MIO
CHILE TÍPICO
TEATRO MUNICIPAL
ONA
LA CHIMENEA
DEPARTAMENTO DE EXTRANJERÍA
PALACIO DE LA MONEDA
CHE LAGARTO HOSTEL SUITES
LANCHILE
629m
UNIVERSIDAD ALBERTO HURTADO
ZULLY
TERMINAL LOS HÉROES
TORRE ENTEL
CENTRO CULTURAL PALACIO DE LA MONEDA
CLUB DE LA UNIÓN
HOTEL GALERÍAS
BIBLIOTECA NACIONAL
CERRO SANTA LUCÍA
HOTEL PLAZA SAN FRANCISCO
Los Héroes
Moneda
Universidad de Chile
Santa Lucía
CLINICA UNIVERSIDAD CATOLICA
CONFITERÍA LAS TORRES
Plaza Bulnes
UNIVERSIDAD DE CHILE
HOTEL FUNDADOR
IGLESIA DE SAN FRANCISCO
LIBRERÍA LUIS RIVANO
RESIDENCIAL LONDRES
CINE NORMANDIE
CONAF
INSTITUTO GEOGRÁFICO MILITAR
Toesca
PALACIO COUSINO
Plaza Almagro
© AVALON TRAVEL

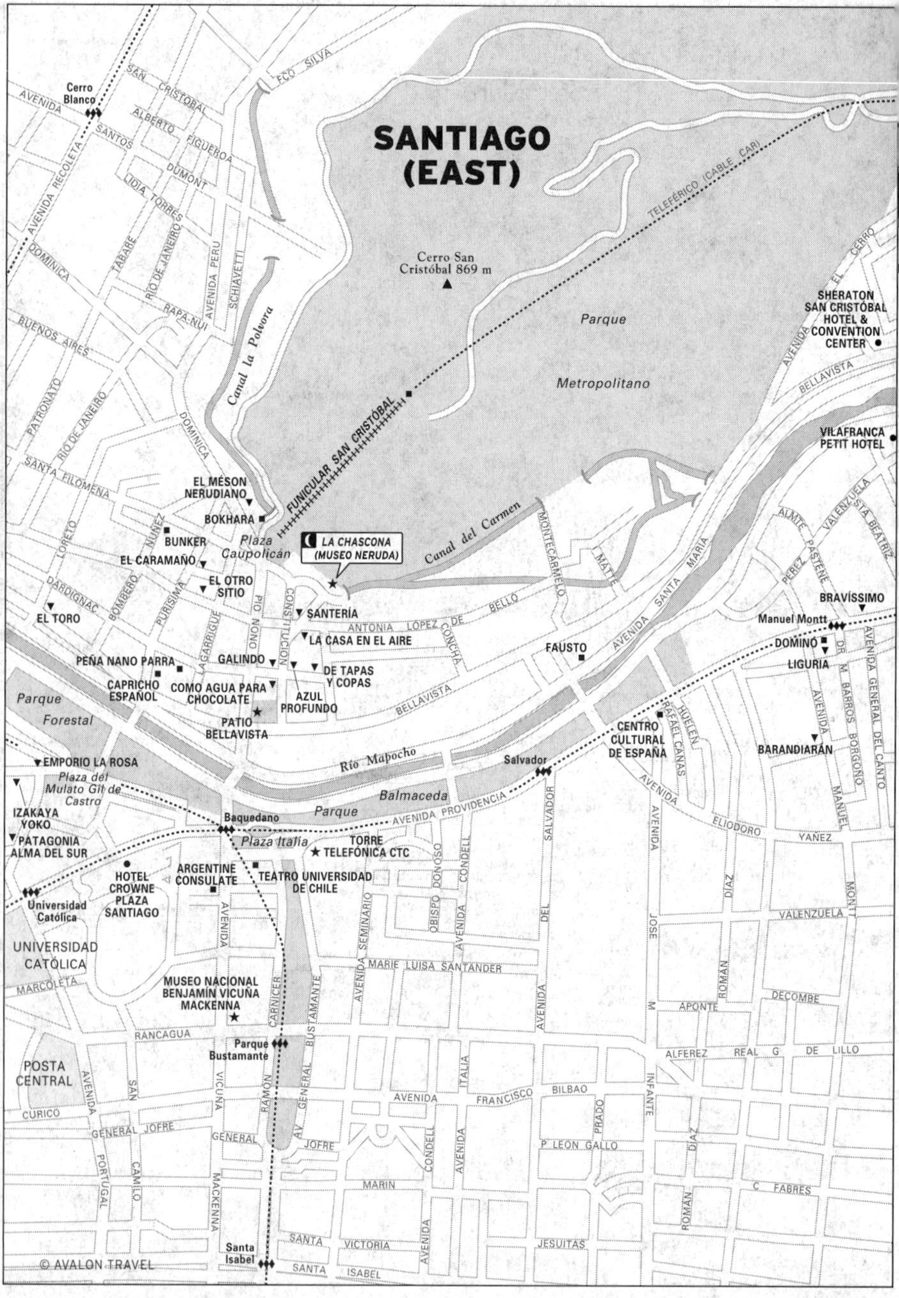
SANTIAGO (EAST)
Cerro San Cristóbal 869 m
Parque Metropolitano
TELEFÉRICO (CABLE CAR)
FUNICULAR SAN CRISTÓBAL
LA CHASCONA (MUSEO NERUDA)
Plaza Caupolicán
Canal la Polvora
Canal del Carmen
Cerro Blanco
SHERATON SAN CRISTÓBAL HOTEL & CONVENTION CENTER
VILAFRANCA PETIT HOTEL
EL MÉSON NERUDIANO
BOKHARA
BUNKER
EL CARAMAÑO
EL OTRO SITIO
EL TORO
SANTERÍA
LA CASA EN EL AIRE
GALINDO
DE TAPAS Y COPAS
PEÑA NANO PARRA
CAPRICHO ESPAÑOL
COMO AGUA PARA CHOCOLATE
AZUL PROFUNDO
PATIO BELLAVISTA
FAUSTO
BRAVÍSSIMO
Manuel Montt
DOMINÓ
LIGURIA
BARANDIARÁN
CENTRO CULTURAL DE ESPAÑA
Salvador
Parque Forestal
EMPORIO LA ROSA
Plaza del Mulato Gil de Castro
IZAKAYA YOKO
PATAGONIA ALMA DEL SUR
Río Mapocho
Parque Balmaceda
Baquedano
Plaza Italia
TORRE TELEFÓNICA CTC
HOTEL CROWNE PLAZA SANTIAGO
ARGENTINE CONSULATE
TEATRO UNIVERSIDAD DE CHILE
Universidad Católica
UNIVERSIDAD CATÓLICA
MUSEO NACIONAL BENJAMÍN VICUÑA MACKENNA
Parque Bustamante
POSTA CENTRAL
Santa Isabel
AVENIDA RECOLETA
DOMINICA
BUENOS AIRES
PATRONATO
RÍO DE JANEIRO
SANTA FILOMENA
LORETO
BOMBERO NUÑEZ
PURÍSIMA
LAGARRIGUE
DARDIGNAC
PÍO NONO
CONSTITUCIÓN
ANTONIA LÓPEZ DE BELLO
CONCHA
BELLAVISTA
MONTECARMELO
MATTE
AVENIDA SANTA MARÍA
AVENIDA EL CERRO
ALMTE PASTENE
PEREZ VALENZUELA
STA BEATRIZ
DR M BARROS BORGOÑO
AVENIDA GENERAL DEL CANTO
AVENIDA MANUEL MONTT
AVENIDA PROVIDENCIA
RAFAEL CAÑAS
HUELEN
AVENIDA ELIODORO YÁÑEZ
AVENIDA SALVADOR
AVENIDA JOSÉ M INFANTE
DÍAZ
VALENZUELA
ROMÁN DÍAZ
DECOMBE
APONTE
ALFEREZ REAL
G DE LILLO
AVENIDA FRANCISCO BILBAO
PRADO
P LEON GALLO
C FABRES
MARIE LUISA SANTANDER
OBISPO DONOSO
AVENIDA CONDELL
AVENIDA SEMINARIO
AVENIDA VICUÑA MACKENNA
CARNICER
AV GENERAL BUSTAMANTE
RAMÓN CARNICER
RANCAGUA
MARCOLETA
CURICO
GENERAL JOFRE
PORTUGAL
SAN CAMILO
AVENIDA ITALIA
MARIN
SANTA VICTORIA
JESUITAS
SANTA ISABEL
SAN CRISTÓBAL
ALBERTO
SANTOS DUMONT
FIGUEROA
LIDIA TORRES
TABARE
RAPA-NUI
AVENIDA PERU
SCHIAVETTI
ECO SILVA
© AVALON TRAVEL

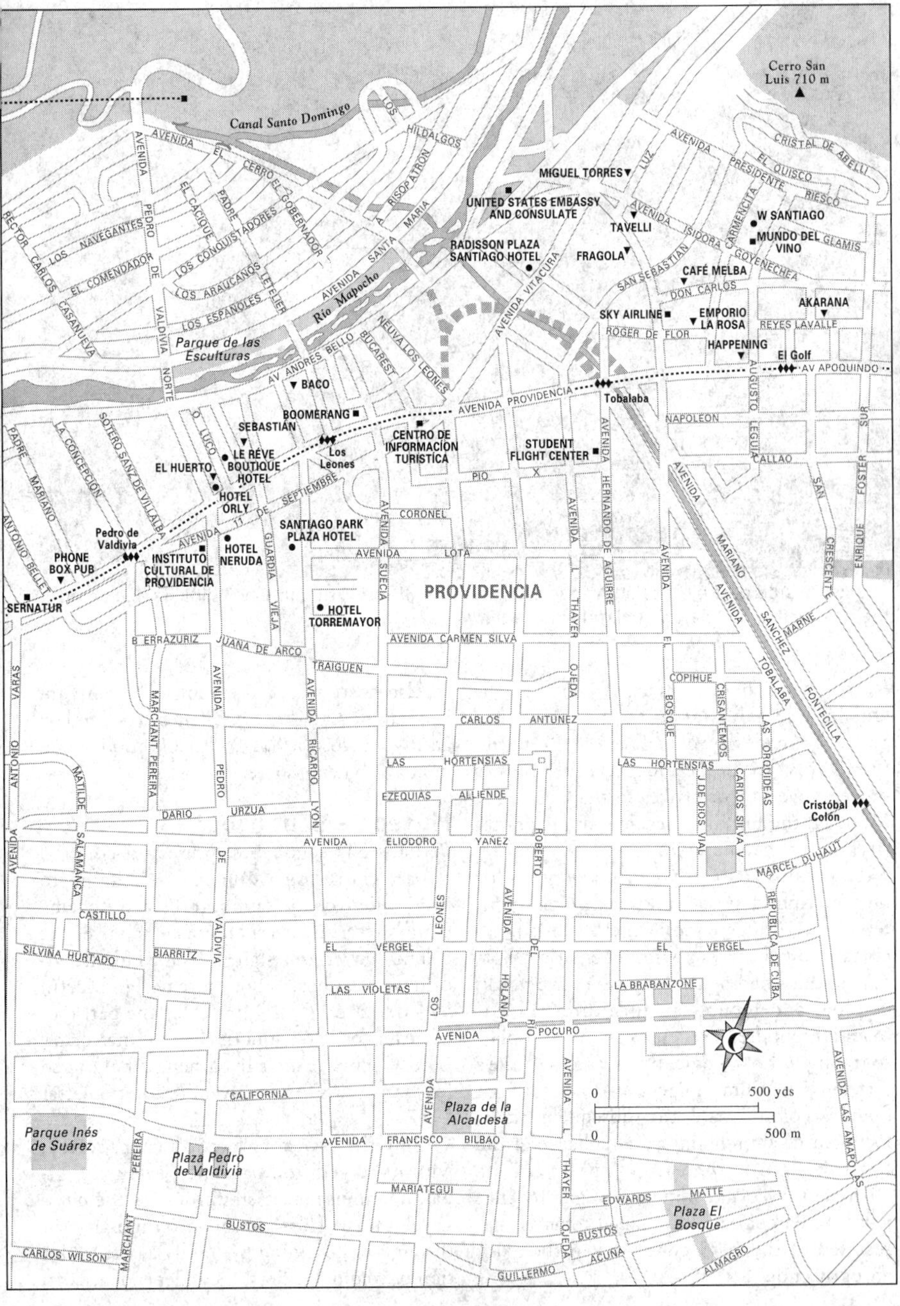
Cerro San Luis 710 m
Canal Santo Domingo
Río Mapocho
Parque de las Esculturas
MIGUEL TORRES
UNITED STATES EMBASSY AND CONSULATE
RADISSON PLAZA SANTIAGO HOTEL
TAVELLI
FRAGOLA
W SANTIAGO
MUNDO DEL VINO
CAFÉ MELBA
AKARANA
SKY AIRLINE
EMPORIO LA ROSA
HAPPENING
El Golf
AV APOQUINDO
Tobalaba
BACO
BOOMERANG
SEBASTIÁN
LE RÊVE BOUTIQUE HOTEL
EL HUERTO
HOTEL ORLY
Los Leones
CENTRO DE INFORMACIÓN TURÍSTICA
STUDENT FLIGHT CENTER
SANTIAGO PARK PLAZA HOTEL
Pedro de Valdivia
PHONE BOX PUB
INSTITUTO CULTURAL DE PROVIDENCIA
HOTEL NERUDA
SERNATUR
HOTEL TORREMAYOR
PROVIDENCIA
Cristóbal Colón
AVENIDA PROVIDENCIA
AVENIDA 11 DE SEPTIEMBRE
AVENIDA VITACURA
AVENIDA ANDRES BELLO
AVENIDA SANTA MARIA
AVENIDA LOTA
AVENIDA CARMEN SILVA
AVENIDA ELIODORO YAÑEZ
AVENIDA PRESIDENTE RIESCO
AVENIDA ISIDORA GOYENECHEA
AVENIDA TOBALABA
AVENIDA FRANCISCO BILBAO
AVENIDA RICARDO LYON
AVENIDA LOS LEONES
AVENIDA HOLANDA
AVENIDA PEDRO DE VALDIVIA
AVENIDA SUECIA
AVENIDA HERNANDO DE AGUIRRE
AVENIDA EL BOSQUE
AVENIDA MARIANO SANCHEZ FONTECILLA
AVENIDA LAS AMAPOLAS
AVENIDA RIO POCURO
AVENIDA THAYER OJEDA
AVENIDA ANTONIO VARAS
LAS HORTENSIAS
CARLOS ANTUÑEZ
EL VERGEL
LAS VIOLETAS
CALIFORNIA
MARIATEGUI
BUSTOS
CARLOS WILSON
GUILLERMO ACUÑA
EDWARDS MATTE
ALMAGRO
NAPOLEON
CALLAO
ROGER DE FLOR
REYES LAVALLE
DON CARLOS
SAN SEBASTIAN
EL QUISCO
CRISTAL DE ABELLI
GLAMIS
CARMENCITA
AUGUSTO LEGUIA SUR
ENRIQUE FOSTER SUR
SAN CRESCENTE
MARNE
COPIHUE
CRISANTEMOS
LAS ORQUIDEAS
J DE DIOS VIAL
CARLOS SILVA V
MARCEL DUHAUT
REPUBLICA DE CUBA
LA BRABANZONE
ROBERTO DEL RIO
ALLIENDE
EZEQUIAS
URZUA
DARIO
MATILDE SALAMANCA
CASTILLO
SILVINA HURTADO
BIARRITZ
MARCHANT PEREIRA
B ERRAZURIZ
JUANA DE ARCO
TRAIGUEN
GUARDIA VIEJA
CORONEL
PIO X
NUEVA LOS LEONES
BUCAREST
O LUCO
SOTERO SANZ DE VILLALBA
LA CONCEPCION
PADRE MARIANO
ANTONIO BELLET
RECTOR CARLOS CASANUEVA
LOS NAVEGANTES
EL COMENDADOR
LOS CONQUISTADORES
LOS ARAUCANOS
LOS ESPAÑOLES
EL CACIQUE
PADRE LETELIER
EL CERRO
EL GOBERNADOR
RISOPATRON
HILDALGOS
LUZ
Plaza de la Alcaldesa
Parque Inés de Suárez
Plaza Pedro de Valdivia
Plaza El Bosque
0 500 yds
0 500 m

© WAYNE BERNHARDSON

**The north side of the Plaza de Armas includes a wealth of 19th-century buildings, including the post office and national history museum.**

Santiago met here to make Argentine general José de San Martín head of state, but San Martín declined in favor of Bernardo O'Higgins. After President Manuel Bulnes moved government offices to the Casa de la Moneda, the building became municipal offices and then a museum.

Following a professional makeover, this once moribund museum (Plaza de Armas 951, tel. 02/4117000, www.dibam.cl/historico_nacional) now deserves a visit. Thematically, its collections encompass Mapuche silverwork, colonial and republican furniture and art, material folklore, textiles, weapons, and photography. Chronologically, it traces Chile's development from indigenous times through Spanish colonial rule, the subsequent establishment of church and state, collapse of the Spanish empire, the early republic and its 19th-century expansion, the oligarchy that ruled parliament, and the failed reforms that resulted in the 1973 coup—when the story abruptly ends.

Also hosting special exhibits, the museum is open 10 A.M.–5:30 P.M. Tuesday–Sunday; admission costs US$1.25 except Sunday and holidays, when it's free.

## Museo de Santiago

Perhaps Santiago's best-preserved colonial house, the **Casa Colorada** was home to Mateo de Toro y Zambrano, who became Chile's interim governor, at age 83, after the colonial governor resigned. Named for its reddish paint, it hosted both José de San Martín and Bernardo O'Higgins after the battle of Chacabuco (1817), and the famous mercenary Lord Cochrane later lived here. Abandoned for many years, it underwent restoration after 1977.

Only the two-story facade facing Merced, with its forged iron balconies, is truly original. The museum itself chronicles the city's development from the pre-Columbian past through its founding by Valdivia, the evolution of colonial society, the independence era, and its transformation under 19th-century mayor Benjamín Vicuña Mackenna. The history is particularly vivid in the models of historical buildings and dioramas of events such as the 1863 fire that destroyed the Iglesia de la Compañía.

The Museo de Santiago (Merced 860, tel. 02/324546, 10 A.M.–6 P.M. Tues.–Fri., 10 A.M.–5 P.M. Sat., 11 A.M.–2 P.M. Sun. and holidays, US$1 pp) reopened in mid-2011 after a major remodel.

### Museo Chileno de Arte Precolombino

The late architect Sergio Larraín García-Moreno donated a lifetime's acquisitions to stock this exceptional museum in the former colonial Real Casa de Aduana (Royal Customs House, 1805). Following independence, the neoclassical building became the Biblioteca Nacional (National Library) and then the Tribunales de Justicia (Law Courts) until a 1968 fire destroyed most of its interior and archives. Flanked by twin patios, a broad staircase leads to the upstairs exhibits.

The permanent collections from Mesoamerica and the central and southern Andes are impressive; there are smaller displays on the Caribbean, the Amazon, and Andean textiles. Particularly notable are the carved wooden *chemamull,* larger-than-life-size Mapuche funerary statues. The museum also possesses Aguateca's Stele 6, from a Late Classic Maya site in Guatemala's Petén lowlands that's suffered severe depredations from looters.

The Museo Chileno de Arte Precolombino (Bandera 361, tel. 02/6887348, www.precolombino.cl) is open 10 A.M.–6 P.M. Tuesday–Sunday; it closes on Friday, Saturday, and Sunday of Semana Santa (Holy Week) and on May 1, September 18 and 19, Christmas, and New Year's. Admission costs US$6 but is free for US$2 for students and free for children to age 13.

### Mercado Central

In 1817, Bernardo O'Higgins himself shifted the disorderly market on the Plaza de Armas to an area once known as "the Dominican rubbish dump" on the Mapocho's south bank, a few blocks north. When fire destroyed the informal installations on the new Plaza de Abasto in 1864, municipal authorities hired Manuel Aldunate to create more permanent facilities, but the current structure (1872) is mainly the work of Fermín Vivaceta.

Street-side storefronts have concealed the original facade except on the Ismael Valdés Vergara side, where it faces the river and opens onto a new plaza; there are entrances, however, on San Pablo, Paseo Puente, and 21 de Mayo. From the interior, the wrought-iron superstructure, embellished with the Chilean flag's recurring lone star, provides an airy setting for merchants to display their fresh fruit, vegetables, and seafood—according to journalist Robb Walsh, "a display of fishes and shellfish so vast and unfamiliar that I felt I was observing the marine life of another planet."

Lunching and people-watching at tables set among the produce is a popular pastime for foreigners and tourists alike. The smallish restaurants on the periphery are cheaper and nearly as good as the two or three that monopolize the prime central sites.

## BARRIO CÍVICO AND VICINITY

Straddling the Alameda, several blocks southwest of the Plaza de Armas, the Barrio Cívico is the country's political and administrative center. Facing the **Plaza de la Constitución,** the recently repainted, late-colonial **Palacio de la Moneda** is the locus of presidential authority. At 10 A.M. on even-numbered days, there's a presidential changing-of-the-guard ceremony here.

In a development that rankles Pinochet diehards, a dignified statue of former President Salvador Allende overlooks the plaza's southeast corner, with a plaque inscribed with words from his last radio address: "I have faith in Chile and her destiny," September 11, 1973.

Across the street, at Moneda and Morandé, the **Intendencia de Santiago** (1914–1916) features an attractive corner entrance and a spectacular interior cupola. French architect Emilio Jecquier designed the flatiron-style **Bolsa de Comercio** (Stock Exchange, La Bolsa 84), begun in 1914 but delayed when World War I disrupted the arrival of materials from New York. Immediately south, reached by a cobbled passageway but fronting on the Alameda, the members-only **Club de la Unión** (1925) gave stockbrokers a place to schmooze on their lunch hours.

## Palacio de la Moneda

Never intended as the seat of government, the neoclassical Moneda became the presidential palace in 1846, when Manuel Bulnes moved his residence and offices to the former colonial mint. It made global headlines in 1973, when the air force strafed and bombed it in General Pinochet's coup against President Salvador Allende, who shot himself to death before he could be taken prisoner.

Around 1730, during an economic depression, local government requested the Spanish crown to establish a local mint. But Madrid, itself short of resources, designated businessman Francisco García Huidobro as treasurer of a mint at Huérfanos and Morandé—perhaps one of the earliest privatizations on record. When that mint proved inadequate, architect Joaquín Toesca began work on a new facility in 1784 but died six years before its completion in 1805.

Pinochet's regime restored the building to Toesca's original design by 1981, but it's no longer the presidential residence. Ricardo Lagos, the first Socialist elected president since Allende, opened the main passageway for one-way public traffic from the Plaza de la Constitución entrance to the Plaza de la Libertad exit, 10 A.M.–6 P.M. weekdays only.

For a more thorough guided tour, contact the Dirección Administrativa del Palacio de la Moneda (Morandé 130, tel. 02/6714103, visitas@presidencia.cl) at its office beneath Plaza de la Constitución. Normally, arranging a visit takes a couple of days with a written or emailed request.

The Moneda's most impressive addition, new

© WAYNE BERNHARDSON

Beneath the Plaza de la Ciudadanía, the Centro Cultural Palacio La Moneda presents a diversity of arts, cultural, and entertainment events.

in 2006, is the subterranean **Centro Cultural Palacio La Moneda;** between the palace and the Alameda, beneath the lawns and reflecting pools of the Plaza de la Ciudadanía, broad pedestrian ramps descend to a luminous subterranean facility with a gigantic atrium flanked by special exhibit galleries and other facilities.

## CERRO SANTA LUCÍA AND VICINITY

East of Paseo Ahumada and north of the Alameda, the promontory called Welén by the Mapuche was where Pedro de Valdivia held out against the indigenous forces that threatened to expel the Spaniards from the Mapocho valley. Nearly three centuries later, in 1822, the Scotswoman María Graham marveled at the view of:

> *...the city, its gardens, churches, and its magnificent bridge all lit up by the rays of the setting sun...what pen or pencil can impart a thousandth part of the sublime beauty of sunset on the Andes?*

It took visionary mayor Benjamín Vicuña Mackenna to realize Santa Lucía's potential, as his efforts—along with convict labor and donations from wealthy citizens—transformed a barren quarry into an urban Eden with more than 60 hectares of gardens, fountains, and statuary—including his own tomb.

From the summit, approached by meandering footpaths and reached by a steep climb to a tiny parapet, there are stupendous views of the Andes—at least on a clear day—and panoramas of the city and Cerro San Cristóbal. A lower but broader terrace offers less panoramic but almost equally impressive views toward Providencia and the Andes.

Royalists built **Fuerte Hidalgo** (1816) toward the park's north end to defend against Chilean revolutionaries. On its lower northeastern slope, the **Jardín Japonés** (Japanese Garden) is a more recent addition; along the Alameda, look for the tile mural of Nobel Prize poetess Gabriela Mistral.

Fenced except around its lowest periphery and steepest slope, Cerro Santa Lucía has two main entrances: from the Alameda just east of Plaza Vicuña Mackenna, where twin staircases nearly encircle the fountains of **Plaza Neptuno,** and by a cobbled road from the east end of Agustinas. There's also a modern glass elevator, at the east end of Huérfanos, that's often out of service. In an exaggerated effort to improve security, authorities require all visitors to sign in (as if muggers would do so), but the park's not really dangerous.

Hours are 9 A.M.–8 P.M. daily, but the best introduction is a guided tour (English and Spanish) starting from its municipal tourist-office branch at 10 A.M. Monday and 11 A.M. Saturday and Sunday. Tours include Vicuña Mackenna's tomb and the still-functioning gun emplacement (several years ago, authorities halted the customary but startling midday cannon shot because of neighbors' complaints; broader public pressure restored the tradition at a lower decibel level).

Between Cerro Santa Lucía and Paseo Ahumada, the most imposing landmark is the classicist **Biblioteca Nacional** (National Library, 1914–1927) facing the Alameda between MacIver and Miraflores. Two blocks north, the neoclassical **Teatro Municipal** (Municipal Theater, 1857) has seen performances by Sarah Bernhardt, Igor Stravinsky, Plácido Domingo, Anna Pavlova, and the Chilean classical pianist Claudio Arrau.

## BARRIO PARÍS LONDRES AND VICINITY

South of the Alameda, the major landmark is the **Iglesia y Convento de San Francisco** (Alameda 834), Chile's oldest colonial building (1618) and a survivor of repeated fires and earthquakes; its former convent is also home to the **Museo de Arte Colonial,** an ecclesiastical art collection.

Until the early 1920s, the Franciscans controlled much of this area, but a financial crisis forced them to sell 30,000 square meters to developer Walter Lihn. Lihn demolished several buildings and patios, and their gardens, but architects Roberto Araya and Ernesto Holzmann designed an intimately livable neighborhood of meandering cobbled streets in their place.

Betraying the neighborhood's legacy, the house at **Londres 40** was a torture center during Pinochet's dictatorship. Two blocks west of Iglesia San Francisco, the **Casa Central de la Universidad de Chile** (1863–1872), the state university's main campus, stretches along the Alameda.

### Iglesia y Convento de San Francisco



Pedro de Valdivia himself established the Ermita del Socorro to house an image of the Virgen del Socorro—to which he credited Santiago's survival from Mapuche attacks—that he had brought to Chile. In 1554, in exchange for 12 city lots, the Franciscans built a church to house the image, but an earthquake destroyed the original structure in 1583. After finishing the present church in 1618, they built a pair of cloisters and gradually added patios, gardens, a refectory, and other structures. Earthquakes toppled the original towers in 1643 and 1751, but Fermín Vivaceta's 19th-century clock tower has withstood every tremor since. The interior is notable for its Mudejar details and carved cypress doors.

Over four and a half centuries, the Franciscans have kept faith with Valdivia by continuing to host the Virgen del Socorro. In addition, its **Museo de Arte Colonial** (Londres 4, tel. 02/6398737, www.museosanfrancisco.cl, US$2 pp) is open 10 A.M.–1 P.M. and 3–6 P.M. Tuesday–Saturday, 10 A.M.–2 P.M. Sunday, but it's closed January 1, May 1, Good Friday, September 11, 18, and 19, and Christmas.

## BARRIO LASTARRIA AND VICINITY

East of Cerro Santa Lucía, between Parque Forestal and the Alameda, Barrio Lastarria is a neighborhood of narrow streets and cul-de-sacs that's home to several intimate restaurants and bars.

The barrio's main axis is its namesake street, José Victorino Lastarria, whose **Plaza del Mulato Gil de Castro** is an adaptive reuse uniting several early-20th-century buildings into a commercial/cultural cluster with two notable museums: the **Museo Arqueológico de Santiago** and the eye-catching **Museo de Artes Visuales.** Between Rosal and Merced, Lastarria has become an attractive pedestrian mall.

To the north, the Mapocho's banks and floodplain were home to slums and rubbish dumps until the early 20th century, when mayor Enrique Cousiño redeveloped it as the **Parque Forestal,** stretching from Estación Mapocho on the west to the Pío Nono bridge on the east. Shaded with mature trees and dotted with statues and fountains, it's a verdant refuge from summer's midday heat.

Toward the west, directly north of Cerro Santa Lucía, stands the **Museo Nacional de Bellas Artes,** the city's traditional fine-arts museum. South across the Alameda, toward downtown, is the central campus of the **Universidad Católica** (Catholic University, 1913).

### Museo de Artes Visuales

With a permanent collection of 1,400 pieces by 400 contemporary Chilean artists, among them Roberto Matta and Alfredo Jaar, Santiago's visual-arts museum, in the Plaza del Mulato Gil complex, opened in early 2001. About 140 of these pieces, ranging from engravings to paintings, photographs, and sculptures, are on display at any one time.

Architect Cristián Undurraga's design incorporates 1,400 square meters of display space. Flawless lighting accentuates individual pieces in half a dozen spacious galleries, which feature high ceilings and polished wooden floors. The English translations are better than at some Chilean museums, but a reliance on cognates makes some of them a bit vague.

Privately owned and financed, the Museo de Artes Visuales (MAVI, Lastarria 307, tel. 02/6649397, www.mavi.cl) is open 10:30 A.M.–6:30 P.M. Wednesday–Monday; it's also closed January 1, May 1, September 17, and December 25. Admission costs US$2 for adults, US$1 for children 8–12, but is free Sunday.

The MAVI now subsumes the **Museo Arqueológico de Santiago** (Lastarria 321, tel. 02/6383502). With excellent but stagnant exhibits on Chile's indigenous peoples from pre-Columbian times to the present, Santiago's archaeological museum ("ethnohistorical" might be more accurate) is worthwhile for an introductory visit, but repeat visits are unlikely to reveal new material.

### Museo de Bellas Artes

Built for Chile's independence centennial and fashioned after Paris's Petit Palais, Santiago's neoclassical fine-arts museum is the pride of Parque Forestal. Collections range from colonial and religious art to nearly contemporary figurative and abstract works by artists like the recently deceased Roberto Matta. It also has a sample of French, Italian, and Dutch painting, and prestigious special exhibits. While Bellas Artes is a traditional museum, its ambitious website is making the works of 2,000 Chilean artists accessible to the world in a "museum without walls."

Despite some exterior earthquake damage, the Museo de Bellas Artes (José Miguel de La Barra s/n, tel. 02/4991660, www.mnba.cl, US$1.20, US$0.60 for students and seniors) remains open 10 A.M.–6:50 P.M. Tuesday–Friday.

## BARRIO BRASIL AND VICINITY

West of the Vía Norte Sur, Barrio Brasil was a prestigious early-20th-century residential area that fell upon hard times but has recently rebounded without losing its character. The best way to approach the barrio is the Huérfanos pedestrian suspension bridge that crosses the Vía Norte Sur to an area where recently constituted private universities have rehabbed buildings, salvaged libraries, built collections, and introduced a youthful vigor. It's also good for moderately priced accommodations and food.

The barrio's focus is its lovingly landscaped namesake, **Plaza Brasil.** Dating from 1892, its most impressive landmark has been the neo-Gothic **Basílica del Salvador** (Huérfanos 1781), but severe damage from the 1985 and 2010 earthquakes may require its demolition.

Dating from 1926, the most idiosyncratic building is the German Gothic **Universidad Albert Hurtado** (Cienfuegos 41), whose grinning gargoyles and smiling skulls, jutting out from its facade, always attract attention.

On Santiago Centro's western edge, beyond Barrio Brasil proper, wooded **Parque Quinta Normal** offers relief from a densely built area and is home to several museums. The other main attraction is the **Museo de la Solidaridad Salvador Allende** (Av. República 475, tel. 02/6899479, www.museodelasolidaridad.cl, 10 A.M.–6 P.M. Tues.–Sat., US$1.20 adults, US$0.60 children), a modern-art collection and cultural center.

### Parque Quinta Normal

At the western edge of Santiago Centro, Parque Quinta Normal is a traditional open space whose 40 hectares were the city's first de facto botanical garden. It also provides playgrounds, soccer fields, tennis courts, skating rinks, and pools, and a cluster of museums.

© WAYNE BERNHARDSON

The Puente Huérfanos, a pedestrian suspension bridge, connects downtown Santiago with Barrio Brasil.

SANTIAGO DE CHILE

## TORTURE TOURS

It's harder to tell in happier times but, from 1973 to 1990, Chile experienced one of the most vicious and durable military dictatorships ever on a continent that was notorious for them. Yet there are numerous reminders of those sad years, even if most of them are relatively inconspicuous (such as the headquarters of Constramet metal workers union, Avenida Santa Rosa 101, which simply displays a plaque with the names of some 60 members who disappeared under General Augusto Pinochet's regime). A couple of them, though, are more outspokenly eloquent.

### PARQUE POR LA PAZ

Perhaps the most subtly eloquent memorial to the dictatorship's victims, Peñalolén's Parque por la Paz (Park for Peace) occupies the grounds of the former Villa Grimaldi, the principal torture center for the Directorio de Inteligencia Nacional (DINA), General Manuel Contreras's ruthless intelligence service. Before it closed, more than 200 political prisoners died at the isolated mansion, and many more were interrogated and tortured.

In the regime's final days, the military bulldozed nearly every building to destroy evidence, but the nonprofit Fundación Parque por la Paz has transformed the property into a pilgrimage site that commemorates the victims without any overt political posturing. It has permanently locked the original street-side gates, by which prisoners entered the grounds, with a declaration that they are "never to be opened again."

Parque por la Paz (Av. Arrieta 8401, tel. 02/2925229, www.villagrimaldicorp.cl, free) is open 10 A.M.-2 P.M. and 3-6 P.M. daily (guided tours at 10:30 A.M., noon, and 3 P.M. Tues.-Fri.). From Metro Plaza Egaña (Línea 4), Transantiago buses 513 and D09 pass nearby.

**La Bicicleta Verde** (Av. Santa María 227, Oficina 12, tel. 02/5709338, www.labicicletaverde.com) is the only operator offering alternative "Human Rights Legacy" tours that take in Parque por la Paz, the Cementerio General, and the Fundación Pinochet.

### MUSEO DE LA MEMORIA Y DE LOS DERECHOS HUMANOS

More central, and more comprehensive than Villa Grimaldi, the glistening new Museo de la Memoria is a three-story monument whose glass exterior and reflecting pool establish transparency as an architectural and cultural value. Its interior exhibits vividly document the abuses of the Pinochet years and the slow return to democracy.

On the ground level, the museum starts innocuously enough in displaying the written accounts of human rights violations, such as the "Rettig Report," that began to appear in the aftermath of the regime. The powerful visual material begins with huge wall photos of the violent coup against President Salvador Allende, along with live footage of the events on multiple screens (though the English subtitles are sometimes misleading) and a sample of the front pages of Santiago dailies (whose coverage was truly disgraceful).

Having suffered some damage in the 2010 earthquake, the partially reopened **Museo Nacional de Historia Natural** (Natural History Museum) is a research facility that also has public exhibits on archaeology, ethnography, physical anthropology, mineralogy, paleontology, botany, and zoology. Dating from 1830, when the government contracted French naturalist Claude Gay to inventory Chile's natural resources, the Museo de Historia Natural (tel. 02/6804624, www.mnhn.cl) is open 10 A.M.–5:30 P.M. Tuesday–Saturday and 11 A.M.–5:30 P.M. Sunday. Admission costs US$1.20 for adults, US$0.60 for kids, but is free Sundays and holidays except January 1, Easter Sunday, May 1, September 18–19, November 1, and December 25, when it's closed.

Parque Quinta Normal's main entrance is on Matucana at the west end of Compañía, with other gateways on Avenida Portales, Santo Domingo, and Apostól Santiago; it now has its

© WAYNE BERNHARDSON

Museo de la Memoria

In addition, the material here includes a site-by-site catalog of detainment camps and torture centers with video links, while the second floor covers demands for accountability of the missing, with a computer database of individual cases. A separate exhibit deals with popular culture, stressing the contributions of folk music *peñas* and the works of *arpilleras* (quilters) as indicators of resistance. The third floor is open for special exhibitions, such as late 2010's account of Spanish refugees in Chile after Francisco Franco's forces defeated the Republicans in that country's civil war.

The Museo de la Memoria (Matucana 501, tel. 02/3651165, www.museodelamemoria.cl) is open 10 A.M.–6 P.M. Tuesday–Sunday. Admission is free, but donations are welcome. It has its own access to the Metro Quinta Normal station (Línea 5).



own Metro station. Grounds are open 8 A.M.–8:30 P.M. Tuesday–Sunday.

## Palacio Cousiño

South of the Alameda, 19th-century Calle Dieciocho was an aristocratic area of Parisian-style mansions long before the oligarchy moved to the eastern suburbs. One of its keystone families was the Cousiños, Portuguese immigrants who made fortunes in wine and mining.

Funds for the Palacio Cousiño (1878) came from the estate of Luis Cousiño, an art collector who inherited his father's mining fortune (Luis Cousiño died young, but his widow Isidora Goyenechea continued construction). The three-story house has marble staircases, a music hall, winter garden, and even a one-person elevator, the country's first.

The Palacio remained in family hands until 1941, when the city purchased it for a museum and as a guesthouse for high-profile visitors like Charles DeGaulle, Marshal Tito, and Golda

Meir. A 1968 fire, which destroyed the third-floor interior, prevented England's Queen Elizabeth II from spending the night on her state visit.

The Palacio Cousiño (Dieciocho 438, tel. 02/6985063, www.palaciocousino.co.cl) is open 9:30 A.M.–1:30 P.M. daily and 2:30–5 P.M. weekdays only. Admission, including guided tours in Spanish or English, costs US$6 for adults, US$2 for children.



## PROVIDENCIA AND VICINITY

At the east end of the Alameda, lively **Plaza Italia** (formally known as Plaza Baquedano) marks the boundary of the *comuna* of Providencia, the westernmost of the affluent eastern suburbs that also include Las Condes, Vitacura, and Ñuñoa. While this mostly staid, middle-class to upper-middle-class area has shopping malls that seem straight out of the San Fernando Valley, it also has Bohemian enclaves like Barrio Bellavista (Santiago's main restaurant and nightlife area) and bar-hopper zones like Avenida Suecia. Except in compact Bellavista, points of interest are more spread out than in Santiago Centro, but public transportation is good.

From Plaza Italia, the northbound Puente Pío Nono (Pío Nono bridge) crosses the Mapocho to **Barrio Bellavista.** The area's most conspicuous landmark is the 31-story **Torre Telefónica CTC** (Av. Providencia 111), the company headquarters in the form of a (now nearly antique) 140-meter cell phone!

South of Plaza Italia, Avenida Vicuña Mackenna separates the *comunas* of Santiago Centro, on the one hand, and Providencia and Ñuñoa, on the other. On the Providencia side, the **Museo Nacional Benjamín Vicuña Mackenna** (Av. Vicuña Mackenna 94, tel. 02/2229642) honors the mayor, historian, journalist, and diplomat responsible for the capital's 1870s modernization. Hours are 9:30 A.M.–1 P.M. and 2–5:50 P.M. Monday–Saturday; admission costs US$1.20 for adults, half that for students and seniors.

On the Mapocho's north bank between the Padre Letelier and Pedro de Valdivia bridges, the open-air **Parque de las Esculturas** (Av. Santa María 2201, tel. 02/2232700, www.proviarte.cl, 10 A.M.–7 P.M. daily) showcases abstract works by contemporary Chilean sculptors. It also has an enclosed gallery with rotating exhibitions.

## BARRIO BELLAVISTA AND VICINITY

At the foot of massive Cerro San Cristóbal, compact Bellavista is a walker's delight. In daytime, Santiaguinos cross the Pío Nono bridge to stroll its leafy streets, parks, and plazas and enjoy modest lunch specials at innovative restaurants. At night, they crowd the same places for elaborate dinners before a night at nearby bars, discos, salsa clubs, theaters, and other diversions. Daytime visitors, by the way, may not even realize that this is a nightlife center—most dance clubs, for instance, do not *open* until 1 A.M. or so, and few have prominent signs.

While most visitors see Bellavista as a single neighborhood, the recently rehabbed **Avenida Pío Nono** is a dividing line between the two *comunas* that compose the barrio—rough-edged Recoleta to the west and modish Providencia to the east. There's more style than substance to this, as security-obsessed Providencia makes more conspicuous efforts to prevent auto burglaries and other petty crime in what is, for the most part, a safe area.

On weekends, Pío Nono itself is a frenetic blend of crafts market, cheap sidewalk restaurants, and beer joints. While not so bad as that might sound, it's less appealing than the barrio's perpendicular and parallel side streets.

For a notion of Bellavista's best, relax on a bench at **Plazuela Camilo Mori,** a small triangular plaza at Antonia López de Bello and Constitución. Walking north, turn into the cul-de-sac at Márquez de la Plata, where poet Pablo Neruda lived at the house he called **La Chascona,** now a museum. A short walk northwest, **Plaza Caupolicán** is the main entry point to the 722-hectare **Parque Metropolitano,** a hillside and hilltop public park. A funicular railway carries visitors past the city zoo to the summit, whose terrace offers exceptional views on clear days; from there, a *teleférico* (cable gondola) connects the park to eastern Providencia.

On the Recoleta side, at the north end of Avenida La Paz, famous figures from Chile's past are among the two million who repose in the **Cementerio General** (General Cemetery, 1897).

### La Chascona (Museo Neruda)

Inconspicuous from the street side of its cul-de-sac, Pablo Neruda's hillside house is by no means extravagant—in fact, it may be the most conventional of his three houses (the others, also open for visits, are in Valparaíso and the beach community of Isla Negra). Opposite the house, a small amphitheater tucked into the slope is an ideal complement to the residence, restored since its military sacking in 1973 (Neruda, a committed Salvador Allende supporter, died only about a month after the coup).

The Fundación Neruda (Márquez de La Plata 0192, tel. 02/7378712, www.fundacionneruda.org) offers hour-long guided tours by reservation, 10 A.M.–6 P.M. Tuesday–Sunday. Guided tours in Spanish cost US$5 per adult, US$2 for students or seniors; in English or French, it's US$7 per person. The museum also operates a café, bookstore, and souvenir shop.

### Cementerio General

Among the cemetery's Gothic, Greek, Moorish, and Egyptian-style sepulchers, all but two of Chile's presidents are interred (Bernardo O'Higgins's remains rest in the Alameda's Altar de la Patria, and Gabriel González Videla lies in his native La Serena). Other notable figures include diplomat Orlando Letelier (killed by a car bomb in Washington, D.C., under orders from a Pinochet subordinate); Venezuelan-born educator Andrés Bello; and cultural icon, folksinger, and songwriter Violeta Parra. Nobel Prize poets Gabriela Mistral and Pablo Neruda originally rested here as well, but Mistral's body was moved to her Elqui valley birthplace and Neruda's to his Isla Negra beach residence.

Salvador Allende moved in the other direction—after 17 years in Viña del Mar, he regained his freedom to travel after the Pinochet dictatorship's demise and has a monumental memorial here. Another indicator of change is sculptor Francisco Gazitúa's *Rostros* (Faces), memorializing the regime's victims.

The Cementerio General (Av. La Paz s/n, tel. 02/7379469 www.cementeriogeneral.cl) is open 8:45 A.M.–5 P.M. weekdays but closes at 2 P.M. on weekends and holidays.

## OUTLYING SIGHTS

Several points of interest are scattered elsewhere around town.

### Los Dominicos

One of few survivors from colonial Las Condes, the **Iglesia y Convento San Vicente Ferrer de los Dominicos** sits on lands that Pedro de Valdivia seized from Mapuche cacique Apoquindo for Valdivia's mistress, Inés de Suárez. Eventually willed to the Dominican order, the property deteriorated during a century-plus of litigation, but the Dominicans managed to add its twin Byzantine domes in 1847.

Alongside the church, where Avenida Apoquindo dead-ends at Padre Hurtado, **Los Graneros del Alba** (Av. Apoquindo 9085) is Santiago's biggest crafts market, also popular for its country cuisine and impromptu entertainment. Popularly known as "Los Dominicos," it's open 10 A.M.–7:30 P.M. daily all year. Since the extension of the Metro's Línea 1 here in December 2009, it's much easier to reach.

### Estadio Nacional

South of Providencia and east of Santiago Centro, middle-class Ñuñoa has few landmarks but enjoys a vigorous cultural life on and around **Plaza Ñuñoa,** thanks partly to nearby campuses of the Universidad Católica and the Universidad de Chile.

With the Andean front range in the distance, Ñuñoa's one unforgettable landmark is the Estadio Nacional (National Stadium, Av.

Grecia 2001). First famous for the 1962 World Cup, it became infamous as an impromptu prison camp after the 1973 coup, when some 7,000 Allende sympathizers (and suspected sympathizers) were incarcerated. Many were tortured and more than a few were executed (including folksinger Victor Jara and U.S. citizens Charles Horman and Frank Teruggi). Today, the stadium is once again the site of the country's most important soccer matches, and it's within reasonable walking distance of Línea 5's Ñuble station.



### Viña Cousiño Macul

In the southeastern *comuna* of Peñalolén, Cousiño Macul is one of Chile's oldest wineries, in the same family since Matías Cousiño purchased the vineyards in 1856. Its cellars and Museo del Vino (Wine Museum) are open for Spanish- and English-language tours weekdays at 11 A.M., noon, and 3 and 6 P.M. and Saturday at 11 A.M. and noon. Tours cost US$14; the accompanying tasting, held in an attractive bar cum sales room, includes one varietal and one reserve vintage, in a souvenir glass. The house produces cabernet, merlot, chardonnay, sauvignon blanc, and riesling.

Viña Cousiño Macul (Av. Quilín 7100, tel. 02/3514135, www.cousinomacul.cl, ventas@cousinomacul.cl) is a 20-minute walk from Quilín station, on the Metro's Línea 4.

### Viña Concha y Toro

In suburban Pirque, Viña Concha y Toro (Victoria Subercaseaux 210, tel. 02/4765269, www.conchaytoro.com) offers guided English-language tours of its vineyards, grounds, cellars, and museum, with tasting (US$14 pp), between 10 A.M. and 5 P.M. daily except holidays. Reservations are advisable, but it's sometimes possible to join an existing group that might include—who knows?—Mick Jagger, Bono, Helmut Kohl, Nicaraguan poet Ernesto Cardenal, and others who have toured the facilities. A separate wine bar is open 10 A.M.–6:30 P.M. daily.

# Entertainment and Shopping

## ENTERTAINMENT AND EVENTS

Just as it's the center of Santiago's restaurant scene, Barrio Bellavista is the city's nightlife focus—in a neighborhood where most clubs don't *open* until after midnight and hardly anybody goes before 2 A.M., it's hard to believe that, during Pinochet's dictatorship, Santiaguinos endured an 11 P.M. curfew.

There are also nightspots in and around Santiago Centro, around Providencia's Avenida Suecia, and near Plaza Ñuñoa, in the largely middle-class borough of the same name. Many bars and dance clubs, especially gay venues, have no obvious public signs except during opening hours.

### Bars

Bellavista's **La Casa en el Aire** (Antonia López de Bello 0125, tel. 02/7356680, www.lacasaenelaire.cl) is a direct descendant of 1960s and 1970s *peñas,* with folkloric music, storytelling, films, and the like in an alternative milieu. Down the block, **Altazor** (Antonia López de Bello 0189, tel. 02/7779651, www.baraltazor.cl) is a blues-and-folk venue, while **Peña Nano Parra** (Ernesto Pinto Lagarrigue 80, tel. 02/7356093) is more traditional. The consistently best rock-music locale is Plaza Ñuñoa's **La Batuta** (Jorge Washington 52, tel. 02/2747096, www.batuta.cl).

North of Avenida Providencia, Avenida Suecia and cross streets are home to a swarm of theme-oriented bars that tend toward kitsch, but the drinks are good, often imaginative, and a bargain during happy hours that can last until midnight. Australian-run **Boomerang** (General Holley 2285, tel. 02/3345081) has been the most durable.

## Discos and Dance Clubs

**Blondie** (Alameda 2879, tel. 02/6817793, www.blondie.cl; Metro Unión Latinoamericana) is a four-floor dance club, featuring occasional live acts, that accommodates up to 2,000 people at a time—two-thirds of those on the main floor. Admission starts around US$5–6.

## Nightclubs

Several venerable venues hold stage and floor shows, often featuring clichéd cultural staples such as the *cueca,* along with typical cuisine such as *pastel de choclo.* The most interesting is **Confitería Las Torres** (Alameda 1570, tel. 02/6986220, www.confiteriatorres.cl), a magnificent 19th-century building that hosts live tango on weekends. If you can't visit Buenos Aires's Café Tortoni, this is a worthy alternative.

South of the Alameda, the garish **Los Adobes de Argomedo** (Argomedo 411, tel. 02/2222104, www.losadobesdeargomedo.cl) is popular for foreign tour groups' farewell dinners (around US$26), but it gets plenty of Chileans as well. The floor show is participatory—get ready to *cueca.*

In the same location since 1939, Barrio Brasil's cavernous **Los Buenos Muchachos** (Av. Ricardo Cumming 1031, tel. 02/6980112, www.losbuenosmuchachos.cl) seats up to a thousand people for lunch or dinner and floor shows (around US$27) with its own orchestra. The above-average food is not *that* far above average; prices are farther above average. The service is excellent, and there's an effectively isolated tobacco-free dining room.

## Gay and Lesbian Venues

Bellavista's Recoleta side is home to most of Santiago's gay clubs. The most discreet is **Capricho Español** (Purísima 65, tel. 02/7777674), whose patrons often meet for a quiet drink and/or dinner before a night out.

Open every night, **Bokhara** (Pío Nono 430, tel. 02/7321050, www.bokhara.cl, US$3–4 cover) is home to a lively scene that looks bigger than it is—plenty of hangers-on crowd the entrance without actually entering. A bit less central, **Fausto** (Av. Santa María 0832, tel. 02/7771041, www.fausto.cl, US$4 cover) draws a mixed-age crowd on separate levels linked by broad staircases that encourage interaction.

Holding up to a thousand partygoers on Thursday, Friday, and Saturday nights, the gigantic **Bunker** (Bombero Núñez 159, tel. 02/7773760, www.bunker.cl) appeals to those who can afford the US$10-plus cover charge; for lesbians, it operates **Femme by Bunker** (Bombero Núñez 169, tel. 02/7382301), immediately next door. Several other gay clubs and bars dot the same street.

## Cultural Centers

New in 2006, the **Centro Cultural Palacio La Moneda** (Plaza de la Ciudadanía 26, tel. 02/3556500, www.ccplm.cl) is in a class of its own. In addition to its gigantic atrium and special exhibit galleries, facilities include the **Cineteca Nacional** (national film archive, with regular repertory programs) and a sprawling crafts shop displaying museum-quality pieces from artisans around the country (not all of these are for sale). General admission costs US$2 for adults, half that for children, but is free until noon weekdays.

The **Instituto Chileno-Norteamericano de Cultura** (Moneda 1467, tel. 02/6777070, www.norteamericano.cl) sponsors art exhibits and other events, and has an English-language library. The most elaborate and active foreign cultural center, though, is Providencia's **Centro Cultural de España** (Av. Providencia 927, tel. 02/7959700, www.ccespana.cl), which sponsors events nearly every night.

## Cinema

Several multiscreen cinemas, both in Santiago Centro and outlying *comunas,* show current films, often in English with Spanish subtitles. Children's films and animated features normally appear in Spanish. For locations and phone numbers, see any Santiago newspaper.

## Performing Arts

Santiago has many live theater and music venues, with offerings ranging from serious classical and contemporary drama to vulgar burlesque, and from traditional folk to rock and classical; the best source of information is the entertainment section of the daily *El Mercurio.*

The landmark **Teatro Municipal** (Agustinas 794, tel. 02/4638888, www.municipal.cl) is Santiago's most prestigious performing-arts venue, hosting classical music, opera, and occasional popular musicals. Only opening performances are truly formal, and Santiaguinos sometimes appear in surprisingly casual clothes; during operas, a translation of the libretto is projected above the stage so that it's easier to follow the plot (if you read Spanish).

Musicians rave about the acoustics at the **Teatro Universidad de Chile** (Av. Providencia 043, tel. 02/9782480, www.teatro.uchile.cl), best known for ballet and classical music, though it hosts the occasional rock event.

### Festivals

September's patriotic holidays are an excuse for parties and parades, but the month can be contentious—September 11, the date of Pinochet's coup, usually sees disturbances around Providencia's Avenida 11 de Septiembre. September 18, **Día de la Independencia** (Independence Day), means cheerful barbecues in the parks, but September 19's **Día del Ejército** (Armed Forces Day) is more divisive.

At the Estación Mapocho, November's 10-day **Feria de Libro** (Book Festival, www.filsa.cl) draws both Chilean writers and internationally recognized authors.

## SHOPPING

Santiago may not be one of the great shopping meccas, but quality handicrafts and antiques from around the country are widely available. Many visitors, of course, take home Chilean wines.

### Books

The **Feria Chilena del Libro** (Huérfanos 623, tel. 02/6396758, www.feriachilenadellibro.cl) is a chain with several branches elsewhere. For academic and antiquarian tastes, try downtown's **Librería Luis Rivano** (San Diego 111, Local 7, tel. 02/6723164) or Providencia's **Librería Chile Ilustrado** (Av. Providencia 1652, tel. 02/2358145). At the same address, **Books** sells used English-language paperbacks at fairly high prices.

Barrio Lastarria's antiques fair

© WAYNE BERNHARDSON

Vitacura's **Librería Eduardo Albers** (Av. Vitacura 5648, tel. 02/2185371, www.texto.cl) has a selection of guidebooks and other general-interest books in English and German.

### Music

For CDs or tapes of present and past Chilean music, try the **Feria del Disco** (Ahumada 286, tel. 02/5928921, www.feriadeldisco.cl).

### Handicrafts

Downtown's best souvenir shops are **Chile Típico** (Moneda 1025, Local 149, tel. 02/6965504) and **Huimpalay** (Huérfanos 1162, tel. 02/6721395), with premium prices. Cerro Santa Lucía's **Centro de Exposición de Arte Indígena** (Alameda 499, tel. 02/6323668), in the semisubterranean Grutas del Cerro Welén, has Mapuche, Aymara, and Rapanui crafts; it's open 10 A.M.–6 P.M. Monday–Saturday, closing an hour later in summer.

Bellavista is best for lapis lazuli jewelry, at locales like **Lapiz Lazuli House** (Bellavista 04, tel. 02/7321419, www.lapislazulihouse.cl).

In the Bellas Artes neighborhood, **Ona** (Victoria Subercaseaux 295, tel. 02/6321859, www.onachile.com) carries a wide selection of quality Andean handicrafts from throughout Chile and even parts of Bolivia and Peru, commissioned from notable artisans. The best include delicately carved and painted wooden birds, *krin* (woven horsehair items including dolls and butterflies), Mapuche silver, textiles, and pre-Columbian reproductions.

### Antiques

For the best antiques selection, visit Bellavista shops such as **Arte del Mundo** (Dardignac 67, tel. 02/7352507). Barrio Lastarria is home to an active weekend antiques fair.

### Wine

If visiting wineries isn't on your agenda but buying wine is, Providencia's **Baco** (Santa Magdalena 116, tel. 02/2314444, www.bacobistro.cl) is the retail outlet of its nearby restaurant. In the same building as the W Hotel, Las Condes's **El Mundo del Vino** (Isidora Goyenechea 3000, tel. 02/5801173, www.elmundodelvino.cl) is a wine supermarket.



# Accommodations and Food

## ACCOMMODATIONS

Nearly all the budget to midrange accommodations are in and around Santiago Centro, with luxury hotels in Providencia and Las Condes. Most midrange and top-end hotels discount IVA for foreign visitors. Many upper-range hotels belong to international chains.

Unless otherwise indicated, hotels listed here are in Santiago Centro; some of them are more closely defined by barrio. Many hotels in other *comunas* are oriented towards business travelers but still welcome ordinary travelers or tourists.

### US$10-25

Relocated after the 2010 earthquake damaged its previous digs, **Che Lagarto Hostel Suites** (San Antonio 60, tel. 02/6383568, www.chelagarto.com, US$9–15 pp in dorms, US$55 d with private bath) occupies spiffy new quarters, in a central location, with a casual atmosphere.

### US$25-50

Also relocated, after the 2010 earthquake collapsed an entire three-story in its previous location, Barrio Brasil's **Happy House Hostel** (Moneda 1829, tel. 02/6884849, www.happyhousehostel.com, US$14–18 pp in dorms, US$60 s, US$70 d) has truly turned a century-old mansion into a "boutique design hostel" that isn't quite finished, but what it has is spectacular: huge private rooms with state-of-the-art overhead showers, high ceilings, a modern kitchen for dorm backpackers, and a swimming pool with a bar and two large wooden decks.

Two of the ground-level bedrooms, though, get noise from the busy street.

In the winding cobbled streets south of the Alameda, such good value that reservations are imperative, **Residencial Londres** (Londres 54, tel. 02/6339192, www.londres.cl, US$18 pp with shared bath, US$20 pp with private bath) has real charm but may not be able to keep pace with some of the newer backpacker favorites. Breakfast costs US$3 extra.

A dull burgundy facade masks the interior of Barrio Brasil's **La Casa Roja** (Agustinas 2113, tel. 02/6964241, www.lacasaroja.cl, US$14 pp, US$42–50 d), a sprawling 19th-century mansion that bids to become a backpackers' boutique hostel—though with 85 or so beds, it's perhaps a bit too large for that. Australian owner Simon Shalders has restored period details while modernizing the baths and creating a contemporary kitchen—not to mention a garden pool with a swim-up bar plus a batting cage (for cricket, but adaptable for baseball). Even the eight-bed dorms don't feel cramped, and with large common areas scattered through the building, the place never seems crowded. There are also private rooms with or without private baths.

Used mostly by groups and a steady influx of independent foreigners, **Hostelling International** (Cienfuegos 151, tel. 02/6718532, www.hisantiago.cl, US$18–20 pp in dorms) has spacious common areas (including a bar), dorm-style accommodations (four beds per room), a few doubles (without and with private bath, US$54–60), free wireless Internet, and cheap laundry service. Its cafeteria has lunches and dinners.

## US$50-100

At the north end of Cerro Santa Lucía, the underrated **Hotel Foresta** (Subercaseaux 353, tel. 02/6396261, www.forestahotel.cl, US$44 s, US$56 d with a so-so breakfast) offers excellent value for money. In the past, it's suffered from traffic noise, but recent street improvements have helped.

Nicely modernized, **Hotel España** (Morandé 510, tel. 02/7704500, www.hotelespania.com,

© WAYNE BERNHARDSON

Barrio Brasil's La Casa Roja is the only Santiago hostel with a swim-up bar.

US$60 s, US$75 d) has spacious cheerful rooms with contemporary baths, exceptional natural light on the fourth floor in particular, plus cable TV, Internet connections, and electronic strong boxes. It's also kept its rates stable despite the appreciating Chilean peso.

Few traditional townhouses survive among Providencia's high-rises, but a Catalan couple has converted two of them into the tobacco-free **Vilafranca Petit Hotel** (Pérez Valenzuela 1650, tel. 02/2351413, www.vilafranca.cl, US$82 s, US$98 d with breakfast), whose only drawback is the rush-hour drone from nearby Avenida Andrés Bello. Engagingly furnished, the eight rooms vary from cozy attic doubles to spacious suites, all with private baths, plus amenities such as cable TV and wireless Internet; the common areas include a comfortable living room, with plenty of reading material, and a shady patio.

## US$100-150

Decorated with museum piece artifacts from the Chilean countryside, downtown's **Hotel Galerías** (San Antonio 65, tel. 02/4707400, www.hotelgalerias.cl, US$132 s, US$143 d) is a theme hotel that, despite its romantic ruralism, has contemporary conveniences, including wireless Internet and a terraced pool. With 162 rooms, its deceptively inconspicuous street-side entrance leads to spacious facilities that are an enclave of calm in a busy neighborhood.

A converted apartment building, **Hotel Neruda** (Av. Pedro de Valdivia 164, tel. 02/6790700, www.hotelneruda.cl, US$140–190 s, US$160–230 d) is a business-oriented facility, with contemporary conveniences including free wireless Internet, plus a gym, sauna, and rooftop pool in an adjacent building.

At Providencia's **Hotel Santiago Park Plaza** (Ricardo Lyon 207, tel. 02/3724000, www.parkplaza.cl, US$149–241 s or d), the antique-studded foyer belies the modernity of its wired rooms and recreational facilities, including a glassed-in rooftop plunge pool. The 104 rooms in this European-style hotel vary considerably in size, however.

## US$150-200

Las Condes's **Radisson Plaza Santiago Hotel** (Av. Vitacura 2610, tel. 02/2036000, www.radisson.cl, US$165–230 s or d) caters primarily to business travelers; each room comes with its own cell phone, for instance, and it occupies part of Santiago's World Trade Center. There are also, of course, amenities such as a rooftop pool, a gymnasium, and whirlpool tubs, and views of the Andes to the east.

## Over US$200

Business-oriented **Hotel Plaza San Francisco** (Alameda 816, tel. 02/6393832, www.plazasanfrancisco.cl, US$200–230 s or d) often gets celebrity clientele such as Mia Farrow, Plácido Domingo, and even the Dalai Lama. Some of its 148 rooms have Asian design touches. In the summer off-season, there may be discounts for "standard" rooms.

Overlooking the Mapocho from the base of Cerro San Cristóbal, with garden space that other luxury hotels lack, Providencia's **Sheraton San Cristóbal Hotel & Convention Center** (Av. Santa María 1742, tel. 02/2335000, www.sheraton.com/santiago, US$199–389 s or d with buffet breakfast) is where Bob Dylan holes up when he plays Santiago. The rooms are stylishly decorated and feature beautiful views, but for those who want to explore the city, this hotel is a little isolated and definitely not pedestrian-friendly.

New in 2010, at the base of Cerro San Cristóbal, **The Aubrey** (Constitución 299, tel. 02/9402800, www.theaubrey.com, US$240–550 s or d) has seamlessly transformed a derelict 1930s residence into a 15-room boutique hotel (four rooms, newly constructed, occupy a separate wing). While the street can get busy and the zoo is next door, the double-paned windows keep this handsomely restored and recycled building quiet; it also includes a branch of the outstanding Valparaíso restaurant Pasta e Vino (which is open to the public at large for dinner).

Also new in 2010, Providencia's **Le Rêve Boutique Hotel** (Orrego Luco 023, tel. 02/7576000, www.larevehotelcl, US$241 s or

d) appeals to Francophiles in its architecture and furnishings (except for the lobby, which is surprisingly modernist). According to the front desk personnel, at least, Parisians have said they feel at home here.

The first of its kind in South America, Las Condes's **W Santiago** (Isidora Goyenechea 3000, tel. 02/7770000, www.whotels.com, US$269–539 s or d) is a 196-room unit that occupies the upper 17 floors of a 21-story convention center complex crowned by its panoramic swimming pool and rooftop bar. Including several restaurants, two bars, and a clothing boutique, it aims to provide casual luxury—if you want to bring along your howler monkey, they won't say no.

Virtually self-contained, downtown's business-oriented **Hotel Crowne Plaza Santiago** (Alameda 136, tel. 02/6381042, www.crowneplaza.cl, US$284 s or d) features recreational facilities, including a gymnasium, swimming pool, dozens of shops, and even its own post office. All the 293 rooms in this 22-story hotel have luxury furniture, marble baths, and free Internet access.

Alongside the Parque Arauco shopping center, Las Condes's skyscraping copper-plated **Marriott Santiago Hotel** (Av. Kennedy 5741, tel. 02/4262000, www.marriott.cl, from US$329 s or d) is one of Santiago's tallest buildings. It projects a contemporary gentility, especially in its luminous atrium, but nonconformist celebrity guests are often among its clientele—check to see if Ozzy Osbourne's in the adjacent room.

In Las Condes, the 310-room high-rise **Grand Hyatt Santiago** (Av. Kennedy 4601, tel. 02/9501234, www.hyatt.cl, from US$389 s or d) has made *Condé Nast Traveler*'s top 10 list of Latin American hotels several times; its lofty atrium, topped by a glass dome, lets natural light stream inside. Rates for midsize to capacious rooms, some with stupendous Andean panoramas, also include access to a gymnasium, a swimming pool, and tennis courts.

© WAYNE BERNHARDSON

From its rooftop bar, the W Santiago has spectacular Andean and city views.

SANTIAGO DE CHILE

## FOOD

On a global level, Santiago's diverse and innovative gastronomy is an underappreciated secret. The distribution of restaurants mirrors that of hotels, with cheaper eateries downtown and most upscale restaurants in Providencia and Las Condes—though Barrio Bellavista, across the Río Mapocho, offers the most original dining and congenial ambience.

### Santiago Centro

Santiago cafés have finally broken through the "coffee with legs" barrier to become places such as **Emporio La Rosa** (Merced 291, tel. 02/6389257, www.emporiolarosa.cl, 8 A.M.–9:45 P.M. weekdays, 9 A.M.–9:45 P.M. weekends), which serves excellent breakfasts and lunches (less than US$10), with outstanding juices and Argentine-style *medialunas* (croissants) and empanadas.

For whimsical decor, traditional Chilean food, and equally reasonable prices (less than US$10 for a full meal), there's **La Chimenea** (Príncipe de Gales 90, tel. 02/6970131, www.lachimenea.cl, 10 A.M.–2 A.M. Mon.–Thurs., 10 A.M.–4 A.M. Fri., noon–4 A.M. Sat.); in the same location since 1952, it keeps long hours and often has live music and even films.

In Barrio Lastarria, near Cerro Santa Lucía, **Patagonia** (José Victorino Lastarria 96, tel. 02/6643830, 8 A.M.–1 A.M. weekdays, 9 A.M.–1 A.M. weekends) has shifted from a café with a creative sandwich menu to a full-fledged restaurant and wine bar that enjoys one of the neighborhood's widest sidewalks for outdoor dining, With most entrées around US$9–11 for pastas and US$17 for lamb with polenta, it's probably still best for sandwiches (around US$9), but the *parrillada patagónica* of grilled beef, lamb, venison, wild boar, and vegetables (US$42 for two) is unique here.

**Kintaro** (Monjitas 460, tel. 02/6382448, www.kintaro.cl, lunch and dinner Mon.–Sat.) is one of Santiago's cheapest sushi options, with large fresh fish and shrimp plates—more than most diners can consume in a sitting—in the US$12 range. Sashimi and rice-based plates like *donburi* are also on the menu. Not quite so good or diverse, but notably cheaper, is **Izakaya Yoko** (Monjitas 296-A, tel. 02/6321954, lunch and dinner Mon.–Sat.).

### Barrio Brasil

Barrio Brasil's dining options are getting steadily better but, unfortunately, many of them are free-fire zones for tobacco junkies, with no smoke-free areas.

For breakfast, espresso drinks, exceptional sandwiches (large enough for two), and rich desserts, it's hard to top **El Café** (Huérfanos 2064, tel. 02/6880352, 8:30 A.M.–midnight weekdays, 10:30 A.M.–midnight weekends), a cheerful corner place that also provides the morning newspapers. The misleadingly named **Peperone** (Huérfanos 1934, tel. 02/6879180, lunch only Mon.–Sat) is not a pizzeria but rather a tobacco-free *empanadería* with fillings that are far more diverse than most of its Chilean counterparts—baked rather than deep fried, the empanadas can include items such as crab and scallops for around US$3. Fresh fruit juices are also a house specialty.

Long after its opening, **Las Vacas Gordas** (Cienfuegos 280, tel. 02/6971066, closed Sun. evening) still manages to combine high standards with high volume and low prices (US$8–13 for most entrées), but it's almost always crowded and noisy. The fare is primarily *parrillada,* but pasta and fish are also on the menu. For US$2, it may not have the city's best pisco sour, but it's arguably the best value.

Prepared to a soundtrack of *narcocorridos* (Mexican border ballads about drug traffickers), the bargain-priced Mexican tacos (about US$2 each), *antojitos* (short orders such as enchiladas), and more elaborate dinner plates at **Charro de Oro** (Av. Ricardo Cumming 342-A, tel. 02/6972695, lunch and dinner Mon.–Sat.) are too spicy for some Chilean palates, but those who have eaten Mexican food elsewhere will probably not be bothered. Its main drawback is the erratic hours, though it's ostensibly open for lunch and dinner Monday–Saturday.

The best Mexican option, **Plaza Garibaldi** (Moneda 2319, tel. 02/6971418, www.plazagaribaldi.cl, lunch and dinner Mon.–Sat.)

continues to draw diners who at one time wouldn't be caught dead in this area. Brightly decorated, it's operated by the improbably named Jane Holmes, a Chilean who lived many years in exile in Mexico City. The diverse regional Mexican menu merits a visit even for those who live in areas where such food is common. Entrées are mostly in the US$8–12 range; the Mexican beers and strong margaritas are more than authentic.

**Sole Mio** (Moneda 1816, tel. 02/6726342, 1 P.M.–12:30 A.M. Mon.–Sat., 1–5 P.M. Sun.) is a stylish but moderately priced Italian choice, in a spectacularly recycled building; the mezzanine is stunning (though its acoustics are a little *too* good). Unlike many Chilean restaurants, it offers ample distance between tables, and the ground floor is tobacco-free. Also unusual for a Chile restaurant, the ground-floor kitchen is open to public view.

**Ostras Azócar** (Bulnes 37, tel. 02/6816109 or 02/6822293, www.ostrasazocar.cl, 12:30–11:30 P.M. Mon.–Sat., 12:30–4:30 P.M. Sun.) has retained its traditional approach to serve a more affluent clientele; before being seated, everyone enters the oyster bar for freshly shucked samples accompanied by a shot-plus of Chardonnay. A wide selection of sauces accompanies very fresh fish dishes, and the Peruvian-style pisco sours are outstanding.

The barrio's star is **Zully** (Concha y Toro 34, tel. 02/6961378, www.zully.cl, lunch and dinner Mon.–Sat.), an audacious restoration/modernization of a once-crumbling mansion in Barrio Concha y Toro, an intriguing maze of streets just off the Alameda. Expat Michigander Joe Westrate has created an intimate destination-in-itself bar/restaurant with multiple dining rooms, plus a spectacular basement wine bar with an adjacent sunken patio and an equally impressive rooftop terrace; the furniture and place settings, though, are ultra-modern. That's not to mention a creative, visually spectacular menu that changes frequently but includes entrées such as "ostrich" (rhea, US$20). It's expensive, with entrées in the US$15–25 range, but the three-course weekday lunch costs just US$21 (with non-alcoholic drink) or US$27 (with a glass of wine and coffee). There's a big wine list (including a good by-the-glass selection), mostly from Chilean bodegas.

In a similar vein, **Boulevard Lavaud** (Compañía 2789, tel. 02/6825243, www.boulevardlavaud.cl, 9 A.M.–1 A.M. Mon.–Thurs., 9 A.M.–3 A.M. Fri.–Sat., 11 A.M.–5 P.M. Sun.) has recycled an 1868 building into a combination bar/restaurant that also serves, in daytime hours, its historic function as a barbershop (for men and women). Even that doesn't say everything, as it's also integrated an antiques shop into the restaurant—much of the decor along its red-brick walls is for sale. With all that, the food might seem an afterthought, but dishes such as *coq au vin* (US$13) and *duck a l'orange* (US$18) are relatively expensive specialties, and it also serves breakfast, plus a midday menu for US$10; drinks are fairly expensive.

## Barrio Bellavista

North of the Mapocho via the Pío Nono bridge, Bellavista is Santiago's gourmet ghetto, with dozens of fine restaurants virtually side-by-side—but not on Pío Nono itself, where most of the options are little better than greasy spoons. The bulk of the choices are east of Pío Nono, on the Providencia side of the barrio, but there are still fine options on the Recoleta side, to the west.

Surviving in the midst of rampant gentrification by serving outstanding sandwiches and simple but well-prepared Chilean dishes such as *pastel de choclo* (US$9) to a Bohemian clientele, **Galindo** (Dardignac 098, tel. 02/7770116, www.galindo.cl, 12:30 P.M.–2 A.M. Sun.–Thurs., 12:30 P.M.–4 A.M. Fri.–Sat.) is one of the Providencia side's oldest eateries. With its bright new facade, **El Caramaño** (Purísima 257, tel. 02/7377043, 1–4 P.M. and 7 P.M.–12:30 A.M. Mon.–Thurs., to 1:30 A.M. Fri.–Sat.) is less casual than it once was—in the past, it lacked even a street sign and you used to need to bang on the door to get in, lending it a slumming sort of "members only" atmosphere. In the back rooms, diners can still scribble on the walls, and the Chilean specialties, starting around US$10, are reliable.

© WAYNE BERNHARDSON

**The traditional restaurant Galindo bucks the trends of Bellavista, Santiago's gourmet ghetto.**



One of Santiago's best in any category, the Peruvian **El Otro Sitio** (Antonia López de Bello 53, tel. 02/7773059, www.elotrositio.cl, 1 P.M.–midnight Sun.–Thurs., 1 P.M.–1 A.M. Fri.–Sat.) is slightly expensive (US$12–20 and up for entrées) but worth the splurge. The upstairs tables, with views over the atrium, are the most pleasant (on weekends, it's entirely tobacco-free, but on weeknights smokers have the upstairs).

Dining at **Azul Profundo** (Constitución 111, tel. 02/7380288, 12:45–4:30 P.M. and 7:30 P.M.–12:30 A.M. Sun.–Thurs., to 1:30 A.M. Fri.–Sat.) must be the closest possible experience to eating at Pablo Neruda's; its whimsical decor, including its signature deep-blue exterior, a doorway bowsprit, and maritime memorabilia within, could have come straight from the poet's beloved Isla Negra residence. Seafood, of course, is the specialty, and they've put as much effort into its kitchen as its character; though prices for pastas and fish dishes have risen into the US$15–18 range, it's still worth consideration.

Occupying a classic Bellavista mansion, with a small shaded terrace offering views of densely wooded Cerro San Cristóbal, **El Mesón Nerudiano** (Dominica 35, tel. 02/7371542, www.elmesonnerudiano.cl, closed Sun. evening) prepares exceptional fish (especially corvina) and seafood dishes, as well as pastas with seafood sauces, in the US$10–13 range. Downstairs, it has live music, ranging from folk to jazz, several nights per week.

**De Tapas y Copas** (Dardignac 0192, tel. 02/7776477, www.detapasycopas.cl, from 12:45 P.M. Mon.–Sat.) has a broader Spanish menu ranging from the obvious small and inexpensive dishes to beef, fish, and seafood entrées in the US$10–15; the food is above average in concept, less so in execution. Despite a diverse wine list, its name is misleading in that it offers only a handful of those wines by the glass.

Looking like a set from the movie based on its Mexican namesake novel, **Como Agua Para Chocolate** (Like Water for Chocolate, Constitución 88, tel. 02/7778740, www.comoaguaparachocolate.cl, 12:30–4 P.M. and

7:30 P.M.–2 A.M. daily) is one of Bellavista's smartest restaurants. The menu, though, has shifted away from Mexican-Caribbean entrées more toward creative Chilean cuisine with entrées in the US$15–20 range—though the fajitas suggest it hasn't entirely abandoned its origins.

**Santería** (Chucre Manzur 1, tel. 02/7329316, www.santeria.cl, 12:30–3:30 P.M. and 8 P.M.–midnight Tues.–Sat.) sports a Latin American fusion food with Peruvian, Mexican, and Caribbean touches—the ceviches and coconut-tinged shrimp are ideal for fish and seafood lovers. The open-air patio, with wicker furniture, is comfortable and stylish, but the nonsmoking area is relatively small (though effectively segregated). Most entrées are US$12–15, complemented by a variety of sours—including the spicy Mapuche *merkén*.

It's stretching things to call it Bellavista—it's really in Recoleta's Patronato garment district—but Argentine-run **El Toro** (Loreto 33, tel. 02/7375937, 12:30 P.M.–midnight Mon.–Sat., 2–9 P.M. Sun.) has earned a loyal following for its crepes, moderately priced lunches (about US$10), and nonconformist sidewalk atmosphere.

On the Providencia side, the latest development in neighborhood gastronomy is the expanding **Patio Bellavista** (Constitución 70, tel. 02/7774582, www.patiobellavista.cl, noon–2 A.M. Sun.–Wed., noon–4 A.M. Thurs.–Sat.), a refashioned interior patio between Avenida Pío Nono and Constitución that's home to new branches of several successful restaurants as well as some new establishments. The Peruvian institution **Barandiarán** (Constitución 38, Local 52, tel. 02/7370725, 1–11:45 P.M. Sun.–Thurs., 1 P.M.–12:45 A.M. Fri.–Sat.) and the well-established **La Casa en el Aire** (Constitución 40, Local D, noon–midnight Mon.–Sat.) have locales here, while **PizzaSí** (www.pizzasi.cl) is a serviceable pizzeria that doubles as **Backstage,** a bar and Saturday night blues club.

## Providencia

**Liguria** (Av. Providencia 1373, tel. 02/2357914, www.liguria.cl, 8 A.M.–6 A.M. Mon.–Sat.) is a traditional hangout with plain but reliable Chilean meals at moderate prices (less than US$10), but it has only a small nonsmoking area. Nearby **Dominó** (Av. Providencia 1355, www.domino.cl, 8 A.M.–10 P.M. weekdays, 10:30 A.M.–4:30 P.M. Sat.) has excellent sandwiches, fresh juices, and quick service, with several other branches around town.

**Eladio** (Av. 11 de Septiembre 2250, 5th floor, tel. 02/2314224, www.eladio.cl, 12:30–4 P.M. and 8 P.M.–midnight Sun.–Thurs., to 1 A.M. Fri.–Sat.) specializes in beef, but its varied menu will satisfy almost anyone, with inexpensive entrées (US$8–12) and good, cheap pisco sours (about US$2).

**El Huerto** (Orrego Luco 054, tel. 02/2332690, www.elhuerto.cl, 8:30 A.M.–midnight Mon.–Wed., 8:30 A.M.–1 A.M. Thurs.–Fri., 12:30 A.M.–1 A.M. Sat., 12:30–4:30 P.M. Sun.) is a landmark vegetarian restaurant, with dishes so appetizing that even unreconstructed carnivores hardly seem to notice the lack of meat. Having closed its adjacent café in favor of an expansion, it has far more sidewalk seating than in the past; most entrées, such as vegetable curry, fall into the US$10–12 range.

In an old but spacious Providencia house, painted in exuberant primary colors, **Barandiarán** (Manuel Montt 315, tel. 02/2366854, www.barandiaran.cl, lunch Tues.–Sun., dinner Tues.–Sat.) prepares tangy appetizers and ceviches, spicy Peruvian entrées (US$12–15), and a diverse dessert menu.

It's no longer a secret—go early for dinner or call ahead for reservations at **Puerto Perú** (Av. Condell 1298, tel. 02/3639886, www.puertoperu.cl, 1–3:45 and 8–11:45 P.M. Mon.–Sat., 1–3:45 P.M. only Sun.), a once-modest Peruvian place that put the neighborhood south of Avenida Providencia, near the Ñuñoa border, on the gastronomic map. Prices have risen (into the US$12–15 range for entrées), but so has the quality.

Set back from a shady but busy street, **Baco** (Nueva de Lyon 113, tel. 02/2314444, www.bacobistro.cl, 12:30 P.M.–1 A.M. daily) is a wine bar with a mostly Francophile menu such as beef bourguignon (US$14) and crepes

**Baco is one of Santiago's first restaurants with a wide selection of wines by the glass.**

(around US$8), but also the occasional oddity such as gnocchi (US$11). The main dining room, with its semicircular bar and natural woods, is tobacco-free, and there's a big wine-by-the-glass selection displayed on the chalkboard, with vintages from quality niche wineries alongside the traditional giants (each glass bears a circular label around the base so you don't forget what you're drinking).

Providencia has some of the city's best ice creameries, including **Bravíssimo** (Av. Providencia 1406, tel. 02/4217601) and **Sebastián** (Andrés de Fuenzalida 26, tel. 02/2319968).

## Las Condes and Vitacura

For lunches (in the US$6–10 range) and Sunday brunch, the hands-down choice is Kiwi-run **Café Melba** (Don Carlos 2898, tel. 02/2324546, 7:30 A.M.–9 P.M. weekdays, 8 A.M.–5 P.M. weekends). There's sidewalk seating, and the omelets, fresh juices, and similar breakfast fare are unmatchable in their category. The popular **Emporio La Rosa** (Roger de Flor 2894, tel. 02/3611592, www.emporiolarosa.cl, 8 A.M.–9 P.M. weekdays, 9 A.M.–9 P.M. weekends) operates a branch nearby. It serves excellent breakfasts and lunches (less than US$10), with outstanding juices and Argentine-style *medialunas* (croissants) and empanadas.

Under the same ownership, in the shadow of the Ritz-Carlton Hotel, **Akarana** (Reyes Lavalle 3310, tel. 02/2319667, www.akarana-restaurant.cl, noon–midnight daily) is an elegant, full-service restaurant and tapas bar. Occupying one of the area's few surviving World War II vintage houses, with both interior and stylish open-air seating, it serves entrées ranging from pumpkin ravioli (US$18) to New Zealand lamb loin (US$21) and seared Easter Island yellowfin tuna (US$20). There are also individual gourmet pizzas (around US$10) and a midday business lunch (US$18) with choice of entrées and dessert, along with a soft drink or glass of wine.

Except for a few boned cuts, nearby **Happening** (Av. Apoquindo 3090, tel. 02/2332301, www.happening.cl, 12:30 P.M.–12:30 A.M. daily) imports its beef directly from Argentina (sanitary regulations prohibit shipping boned meats across the border). The results are well above average, as are the prices (starting around US$15, but most are higher). There are a couple of fish dishes, the odd pasta, fine desserts, and a gigantic wine list. The building itself is an older house, its interior walls demolished to form a spacious, luminous dining room, with a small nonsmoking section.

On restaurant row, **Miguel Torres** (Isidora Goyenechea 2874, tel. 02/2429360, www.mtvinosytapas.cl, 12:30 A.M.–midnight daily) is the Santiago base of Curicó's landmark winery, offering a fine daily lunch menu (US$16) that includes a starter, main dish, and dessert, with wine by the glass extra—a good selection, but only from its namesake winery. The menu is Mediterranean, as befits a producer whose traditional base is Spain.

Las Condes now has two fine ice creameries within sight of each other: **Fragola** (Av. El Bosque Norte 0166, tel. 02/3332029) and **Tavelli** (Isidora Goyenechea 2891).

# Information and Services

## INFORMATION

Santiago is home to Chile's central tourism agency but also to municipal authorities and some private information sources.

### Tourist Offices

The national tourism service **Sernatur** (Av. Providencia 1550, tel. 02/7318300, www.sernatur.cl) has English-speaking personnel who distribute maps and information on city attractions and services, and brochures on the rest of the country; hours are 8:30 A.M.–6 P.M. weekdays, 9 A.M.–2 P.M. Saturday. Its international airport office (tel. 02/6019320) is open 8:15 A.M.–9:30 P.M. daily.

Half a block east of the Plaza de Armas in the colonial Casa Colorada, the municipal **Oficina de Turismo** (Merced 860, tel. 02/6327785, turims@entelchile.net) also has a satellite office on Cerro Santa Lucía (tel. 02/6644206). Both are open 10 A.M.–6 P.M. Monday–Thursday, 10 A.M.–5 P.M. Friday.

The borough of Providencia has its own **Centro de Información Turística** (Av. Providencia 2359, tel. 02/3742743, www.citi.providencia.cl, 9 A.M.–8 P.M. weekdays, 10 A.M.–7 P.M. weekends).

### National Parks

South of the Alameda, the **Corporación Nacional Forestal** (Conaf, Av. Bulnes 291, tel. 02/3900282 or 02/3900125, www.conaf.cl, 9 A.M.–1 P.M. and 2–4:30 P.M. weekdays only) provides information on national parks and other protected areas; it also has inexpensive maps, as well as books and pamphlets.

### Libraries

The **Biblioteca Nacional** (Alameda 651, tel. 02/3605200), the national library, also has frequent special exhibitions on history, archaeology, and art.

### Newspapers

The notoriously conservative—many would say reactionary—daily *El Mercurio* still publishes paeans to Pinochet, but now does it through guest columnists rather than its own editorial staff. It partially compensates for that with broad international, business, cultural, and entertainment coverage.

The online *Santiago Times* (www.santiagotimes.cl) provides an excellent digest of the Spanish-language press, but full access requires a paid subscription.

## SERVICES

Like accommodations and restaurants, most services are in Santiago Centro, Providencia, and Las Condes, with a few addresses elsewhere.

### Money

ATMs are so abundant that exchange houses have become virtual dinosaurs except for changing travelers checks or leftover cash; the many branches of BancoEstado do not collect a surcharge for foreign ATM cards. Most exchange houses are downtown on Agustinas, between Bandera and Ahumada, but there are others in Providencia and at the airport (where rates are notably lower).

For replacing lost or stolen travelers checks, contact American Express (Isidora Goyenechea 3621, 10th floor, Las Condes, tel. 02/3506700).

### Postal Services

The **Correo Central** (Plaza de Armas 983) is open 8 A.M.–10 P.M. Monday–Friday, 8 A.M.–6 P.M. Saturday. In addition to poste restante (general delivery), it has a philatelic office here and branch offices around town.

For courier service, try **Federal Express** (Av. Providencia 1951, tel. 02/2315250).

### Communications

Long-distance *centros de llamados,* at Metro stations and on the streets, are so ubiquitous that none needs individual mention anymore.

Many of these provide Internet access as well, but there are also Internet specialists charging US$1 per hour or even less.

### Immigration

For visa extensions, visit the **Departamento de Extranjería** (Moneda 1342, Santiago Centro, tel. 02/6725320, 8:30 A.M.–3:30 P.M. daily). Replacing a lost tourist card requires a trip to the **Policía Internacional** (General Borgoño 1052, Independencia, tel. 02/7371292, 8:30 A.M.–12:30 P.M. and 3–7 P.M. weekdays), across the Mapocho from the old railroad station.

### Laundry

Laundries include Santiago Centro's **Lavandería Autoservicio** (Monjitas 507, tel. 02/6321772), Barrio Brasil's **Lavandería Lolos** (Moneda 2296, tel. 02/6995376), and Providencia's **Laverap** (Av. Providencia 1645).

### Travel Agencies

The **Student Flight Center** (Hernando de Aguirre 201, Oficina 401, Providencia, tel. 02/3350395, fax 02/3350394, www.sertur.cl) provides discounts for both students and the general public.

### Photography

For the most complex digital service, visit **Photo Service** (Av. Suecia 84, 8th floor, Providencia, tel. 02/3354460, www.photoservice.cl).

### Medical Services

The **Posta Central** (Av. Portugal 125, Santiago Centro, tel. 02/6341650) is a public clinic; the private **Clínica Universidad Católica** (Lira 40, tel. 02/3846000, www.clinicauc.cl) is nearby. The private **Clínica Alemana** (Av. Vitacura 5951, Vitacura, tel. 02/2129700, www.alemana.cl) is highly regarded.



## Getting There and Around

### GETTING THERE

Santiago has international air links to most South American capitals and some provincial cities, to Europe, North America, and the Caribbean, and across the Pacific. Domestic destinations include Puerto Montt, the gateway to Chilean Patagonia, and the Patagonian cities of Coyhaique and Punta Arenas.

International overland passengers arrive by road from Perú and Argentina, and domestic passengers arrive from many destinations throughout the country.

#### Air

Domestically, **LAN** (Huérfanos 926, tel. 02/5263000) flies northbound to Arica and intermediates, and southbound to Punta Arenas and intermediates. Its main competitor, **Sky Airline** (Av. El Bosque 0117, Las Condes, tel. 02/3525600) has fewer destinations and flights but is growing steadily.

#### Bus

Santiago's four bus terminals are all on or near the Alameda; some companies have offices at more than one.

**Tur-Bus** and **Pullman Bus** are based at the **Terminal de Buses Alameda** (Alameda 3750, tel. 02/2707500, Metro: Universidad de Santiago) and travel to a wide variety of destinations. Most southbound carriers use nearby **Terminal Santiago** (also known as Terminal de Buses Sur, Alameda 3848, tel. 02/3761755, www.terminaldebusessantiago.cl). Some Terminal Santiago buses pick up additional passengers at **Terrapuerto Los Héroes** (Tucapel Jiménez 21, tel. 02/4200099, www.terminaldebuseslosheroes.cl).

Fares can fluctuate both seasonally and among companies, so comparison shopping is advisable. Correlation between distance and price is imperfect—longer trips can be cheaper when competition is greater.

Sample domestic destinations, fares, and

journey times include Temuco (US$16–34, eight hours), Villarrica (US$18–38, 10 hours), Puerto Montt (US$25–45, 13 hours), and Castro (US$32–54, 17 hours).

**Nar-Bus** (tel. 02/7781235, www.narbus.cl) goes to Argentina's Patagonian cities of Junín de los Andes, San Martín de los Andes, and Neuquén, with a change of buses in Temuco. **Cruz del Sur** (tel. 02/7790607) goes to Bariloche, but this requires changing buses in Osorno.

## GETTING AROUND

Santiago has plenty of public transport at reasonable cost, with a particularly outstanding Metro.

### Airport

Serving all international and virtually all domestic flights, the state-of-the-art **Aeropuerto Internacional Arturo Merino Benítez** (tel. 02/6019001, 02/6019709, www.aeropuerto-santiago.cl) is 26 kilometers west of Santiago Centro, in the *comuna* of Pudahuel.

For airport transport to Pudahuel, the cheapest option (US$1.75 pp) is **Centropuerto** (tel. 02/6019883), which has some 40 buses daily from Plazoleta Los Héroes, just off the eastbound lanes of the Alameda outside Los Héroes Metro station. The slightly more expensive **Tur-Bus** (Moneda 1523, tel. 02/8227918) has similar services.

For shuttle services, it's best to ring a day in advance. **Transvip** (tel. 02/6773000) provides door-to-door service for the entire city, starting around US$11 to Santiago Centro; Providencia, Las Condes, and other eastern *comunas* are slightly more expensive. This is the best option for travelers with heavy luggage, or those who arrive late at night.

Hotels can help arrange taxi or radio-taxi service, which can be cost-effective if shared by several people.

### Metro

Carrying upwards of 200 million passengers per year, Santiago's quiet, clean, and efficient Metro (www.metrosantiago.cl) would be the

© WAYNE BERNHARDSON

Despite cosmetic damage in the 2010 quake, Santiago's airport was soon up and running.

© WAYNE BERNHARDSON

Santiago's Metro carries more than 200 million passengers per year.



pride of many European cities. Five interconnected lines cover most points of interest; others, and extensions of existing lines, are under construction. For most visitors, Línea 1, running beneath the Alameda and Avenida Providencia to Los Dominicos, is the most useful line (for what it's worth, there is no Línea 3, but there is a Línea 4-A).

Hours are 6:30 A.M.–10:30 P.M. daily except Sundays and holidays, when it's open 8 A.M.–10:30 P.M. Fares depend on the hour of the day. A *punta* (peak hour) ticket, good 7:15–9 A.M. and 6–7:30 P.M. weekdays, costs US$1.25; during the day and on weekends, the *valle* (mid-hour) fare is about US$1.10, while the early morning and late night *bajo* fare is US$1. The turnstile swallows the ticket, which is not needed to exit the system.

A *tarjeta bip* (multitrip ticket) is more convenient, but the electronic ticket itself requires a US$3 investment that's almost pointless for short-term users. More than one person, though, may use a *bip* ticket by passing it back across the turnstile (this is not illegal).

## Micros (Buses)

Traditionally, city buses have been numerous and cheap, and they have run all day and all night to virtually every part of town—often faster than they should. They have also spewed black diesel clouds into Santiago's already smoggy skies, but the Transantiago (www.transantiago.cl) plan is replacing those dilapidated yellow-and-whites with smart new, cleaner-burning articulated buses. Unfortunately, the transition has been difficult because of insufficient new buses and other glitches.

Along the Alameda are dedicated bus lanes and fixed stops, intended to speed up traffic, and the hope is that the new system will reduce traffic congestion. After the Metro closes, it's the main means of getting around town.

Destinations are marked on window signs and at fixed stops. Buses have automatic fare machines that accept coins but also work with the *tarjeta bip;* hold onto your tickets, as inspectors often ask for them.

## CAR RENTAL AGENCIES IN SANTIAGO

Santiago's numerous car rental agencies, both international franchises and local companies (the latter generally cheaper), are scattered throughout the city. Most airport rentals are franchises. Note that demand is high for economy cars, so reserve well in advance for the best rates.

- **Alameda** (Av. Libertador Bernardo O'Higgins 4332, Estación Central, tel. 02/7790609 or 02/7798545, www.alamedarentacar.cl)
- **Alamo** (Av. Francisco Bilbao 2846, Providencia, tel. 02/6555200, www.alamo.com)
- **Atal** (Av. Costanera Andrés Bello 1051, Providencia, tel. 02/2359222)
- **Automóvil Club de Chile** (Acchi, Av. Vitacura 9511, Vitacura, tel. 02/4311106, www.automovilclub.cl)
- **Avis** (Av. Las Condes 9739, Las Condes, tel. 600/3682000, www.avis.cl)
- **Dollar** (Lo Echevers 200, Quilicura, tel. 02/4904000, www.dollarchile.cl)
- **Econorent** (Av. Manquehue Sur 600, Las Condes, tel. 02/2029002, www.econorent.cl)
- **Euro** (Av. Eduardo Frei Montalva 1762, Renca, tel. 02/4789000, www.eurorentacar.cl)
- **First** (Rancagua 0514, Providencia, tel. 02/2256328, www.firstrentacar.cl)
- **Hertz** (Av. Costanera Andrés Bello 1469, Providencia, tel. 02/3608600, www.hertz.cl)



### *Taxi Colectivos*

Carrying four or sometimes five passengers on fixed routes, *taxi colectivos* cover much of the same ground as Transantiago buses but are slightly more expensive (though often quicker).

### Taxis

Black with yellow roofs, regular taxis charge about US$0.55 to start the meter and US$0.20 more for every subsequent 200 meters. There is also a system of radio taxis with fixed fares within certain zones; among the choices are **Radio Taxi Arauco** (tel. 02/2461114) and **Radio Taxi Alameda** (tel. 02/7764730).

### Car Rental

All the major international agencies and several locals offer rental cars, both at the airport and in town.

# NORTHERN ARGENTINE PATAGONIA

On a bridge over the Río Colorado in southern Buenos Aires province, midway between Bahía Blanca and the Río Negro, a roadside sign reading "Patagonia Starts Here" marks the boundary of southernmost South America's vast, legendary region. No other part of the continent—not even Amazonia—so stimulates the imagination. Ever since Magellan's chronicler Antonio Pigafetta concocted encounters with a giant "so tall that the tallest among us reached only to his waist," the remote southern latitudes have projected a mystique that's been a mixture of anticipation and apprehension.

Geographically, Patagonia is more diverse, with its long Atlantic coastline, boundless steppes, and Andean lakes, forests, and peaks, than simple statistics would suggest. Many of the country's finest wildlife sites and national parks draw visitors from around the globe, but several towns and cities are also worth a visit. Though they vary in quality, increasing numbers of *estancias* (ranches) have become enticing getaways.

In Argentina, Patagonia comprises the area south of the Río Colorado, primarily the provinces of Neuquén, Río Negro, Chubut, and Santa Cruz. While the four provinces' approximately 2 million residents are nearly 5 percent of the country's 40.1 million, they cover more than 27 percent of Argentine territory, an area roughly equivalent to Texas.

Between them, Neuquén and Río Negro provinces, the overland gateways to Patagonia, contain most of the Argentine lakes district, the traditionally popular vacation area on the eastern Andean slope. Along the Chilean

© KEITH WHEATLEY/DREAMSTIME.COM

# HIGHLIGHTS

**Volcán Lanín:** In the northernmost sector of Argentina's fabled lakes district, this snowcapped centerpiece of Parque Nacional Lanín is perhaps the region's most recognizable summit (page 135).

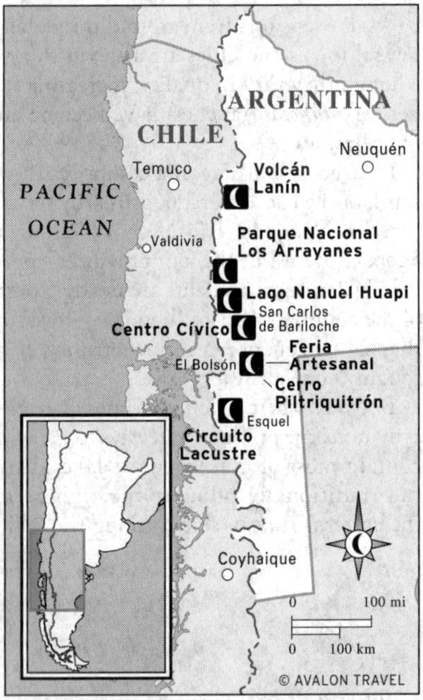


LOOK FOR TO FIND RECOMMENDED SIGHTS, ACTIVITIES, DINING, AND LODGING.

**Parque Nacional Los Arrayanes:** *Arrayán* forests are the highlight of this park on the shore of Lago Nahuel Huapi. The town of Villa La Angostura provides easy access (page 139).

**Centro Cívico:** The buildings surrounding the central square of San Carlos de Bariloche represent the best of Argentine Patagonia's architecture, setting a standard for the entire lakes district with their steep roofs and arched *recovas* (page 143).

**Lago Nahuel Huapi:** From the alluring shoreline of this glacial finger lake, the terrain of Parque Nacional Nahuel Huapi, one of Argentina's most-visited national parks, rises to the forests, pinnacles, and ice fields of the Andes (page 155).

**Feria Artesanal:** This three-times-a-week market surrounding El Bolsón's Plaza Pagano is the perfect place to find local crafts and sample regional food and drink (page 159).

**Cerro Piltriquitrón:** This 2,284-meter granite summit rises east of El Bolsón, where a clear day reveals snow-covered peaks along the Chilean border. There's a parking area at 1,200 meters with a forest of chainsaw stump sculptures nearby (page 165).

**Circuito Lacustre:** The most popular excursion in Parque Nacional Los Alerces is this lake circuit, by boat and by foot, starting at Puerto Limonao, on Lago Futalaufquen's south end, and ending at Puerto Sagrario (page 175).

border, its alpine peaks and glaciers, indigo finger lakes, and dense forests have long been a prime destination; if Patagonia were a country, its logical capital might be the Río Negro resort of San Carlos de Bariloche.

Together, though, the two provinces extend from the Andes to the Atlantic, and the coastal zone features the colonial city of Carmen de Patagones and the Río Negro provincial capital of Viedma, plus a scattering of wildlife reserves and beach resorts. An energy storehouse for its petroleum reserves and hydroelectric resources, the intervening steppe is the site of some of the world's most momentous dinosaur discoveries.

In addition to Río Negro and Neuquén, northern Argentine Patagonia, for the purposes of this guide, includes parts of Chubut Province, most notably the city of Esquel and vicinity, including Parque Nacional Los Alerces, which are most frequently visited from southern Río Negro; southern Argentine Patagonia includes coastal sections of Chubut and all of Santa Cruz Province.

## PLANNING YOUR TIME

Patagonia's highlights could consume a lifetime, so even repeat visitors usually have to make decisions on what to see and do. Because distances are so great, it's often necessary to fly, especially if visiting widely separated areas like the northerly lakes of Neuquén and Río Negro, and southern Patagonia's coastal wildlife areas and massive Andean glaciers.

Unlike the coast, where sights and settlements are often far apart, the Andean lakes district of Neuquén, Río Negro, and northwestern Chubut is a more compact area with dense infrastructure and easy accessibility. A week here can be rewarding for special-interest visitors like fly-fishing aficionados, but general-interest travelers would easily enjoy two weeks or more, and dedicated sports-oriented travelers like climbers could spend a month or an entire summer.

San Carlos de Bariloche makes an ideal hub for excursions in and around the lakes, but towns like San Martín de los Andes, Villa La Angostura, El Bolsón, and Esquel are also good choices—not to mention rural lodges and *estancias.*

In Patagonia's southerly latitudes, January and February are the main vacation months, but they are also the most expensive. The shoulder months of November–December and March–April have less crowding and lower prices, with almost equally good (sometimes better) weather. By April, days are getting shorter, but the region becomes a winter destination, thanks to skiing in Bariloche, San Martín de los Andes, and a few lesser areas.

Note that, throughout Patagonia, overland transportation schedules change from season to season and year to year, and may be disrupted by weather.

### THE PUYEHUE PROBLEM

At the time of writing, the ash-and-pumice eruption of Chile's Puyehue-Córdon Caulle volcano that began in June 2011 continued, closing the international highway that connects Argentina and Chile over the Cardenal Samoré pass. While there were no deaths or even serious injuries in the thinly populated area surrounding the volcano, it resulted in evacuations and economic distress – particularly on the Argentine side, where it nearly smothered the picturesque lakeside town of Villa La Angostura in ash and closed the airport at San Carlos de Bariloche for more than a month.

That derailed the 2011 ski season and, while emergency cleanup efforts were underway, the eruption figured to have repercussions over the coming year or two. Visitors intending to cross the border may have to detour north through Pucón or take the bus-boat-bus shuttle between Puerto Varas and Bariloche; those planning to stay on the Argentine side may find changes in services, particularly accommodations and restaurants.

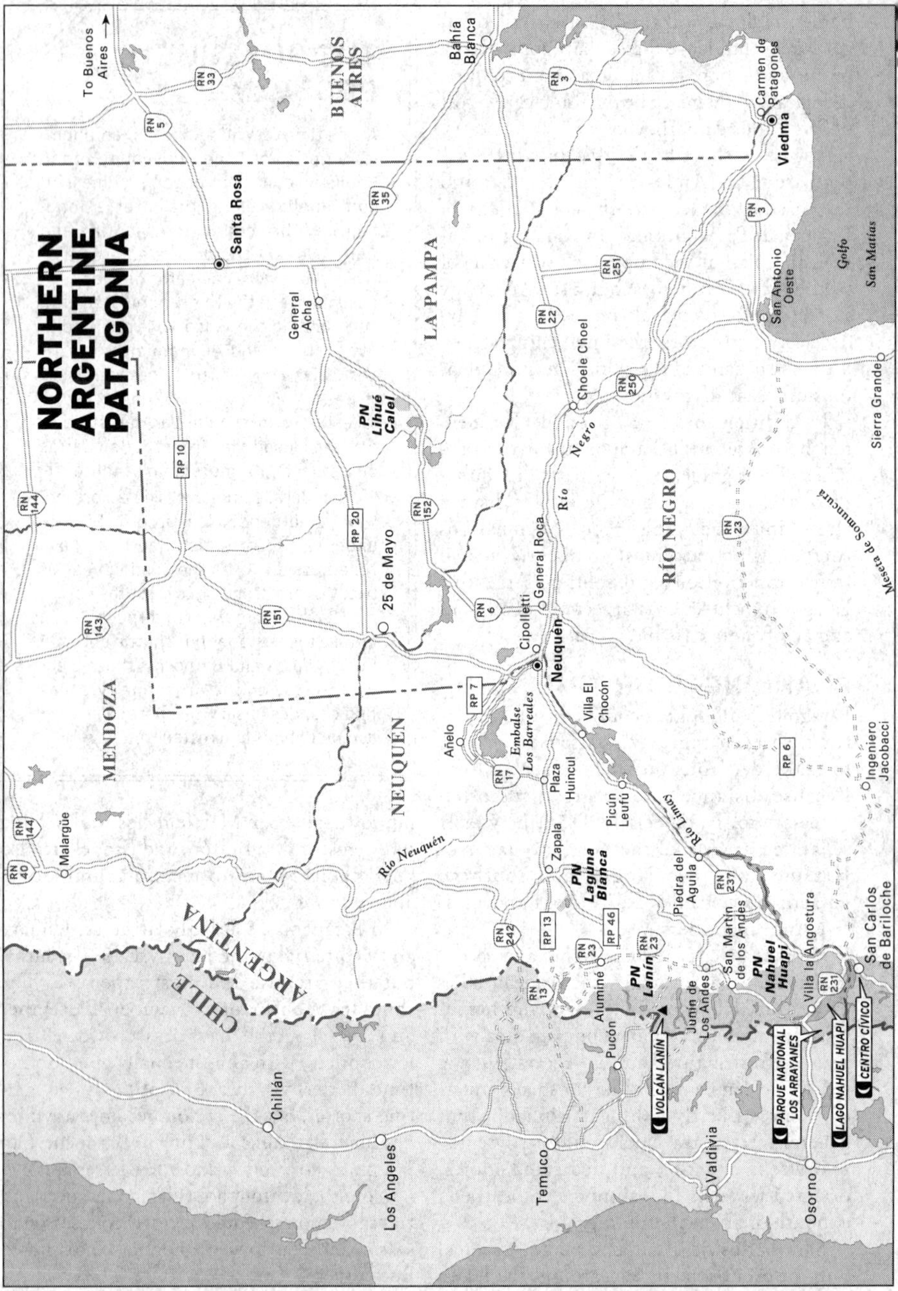
NORTHERN ARGENTINE PATAGONIA
To Buenos Aires
Bahía Blanca
BUENOS AIRES
Santa Rosa
LA PAMPA
General Acha
PN Lihué Calel
Carmen de Patagones
Viedma
San Antonio Oeste
Golfo San Matías
Sierra Grande
Choele Choel
Río Negro
RÍO NEGRO
Meseta de Somuncura
General Roca
Cipolletti
Neuquén
25 de Mayo
MENDOZA
NEUQUÉN
Villa El Chocón
Embalse Los Barreales
Añelo
Plaza Huincul
Picún Leufú
Río Limay
Río Neuquén
Zapala
PN Laguna Blanca
Piedra del Aguila
Malargüe
Ingeniero Jacobacci
San Martín de los Andes
Junín de Los Andes
PN Lanín
PN Nahuel Huapi
Villa la Angostura
San Carlos de Bariloche
Aluminé
Pucón
CHILE
ARGENTINA
Chillán
Los Angeles
Temuco
Valdivia
Osorno
VOLCÁN LANÍN
PARQUE NACIONAL LOS ARRAYANES
LAGO NAHUEL HUAPI
CENTRO CÍVICO
RN 5
RN 33
RN 3
RN 35
RN 251
RN 22
RN 250
RN 144
RP 10
RP 20
RN 152
RN 143
RN 151
RN 6
RP 7
RN 17
RN 23
RP 6
RN 40
RN 242
RP 13
RP 46
RN 13
RN 237
RN 231

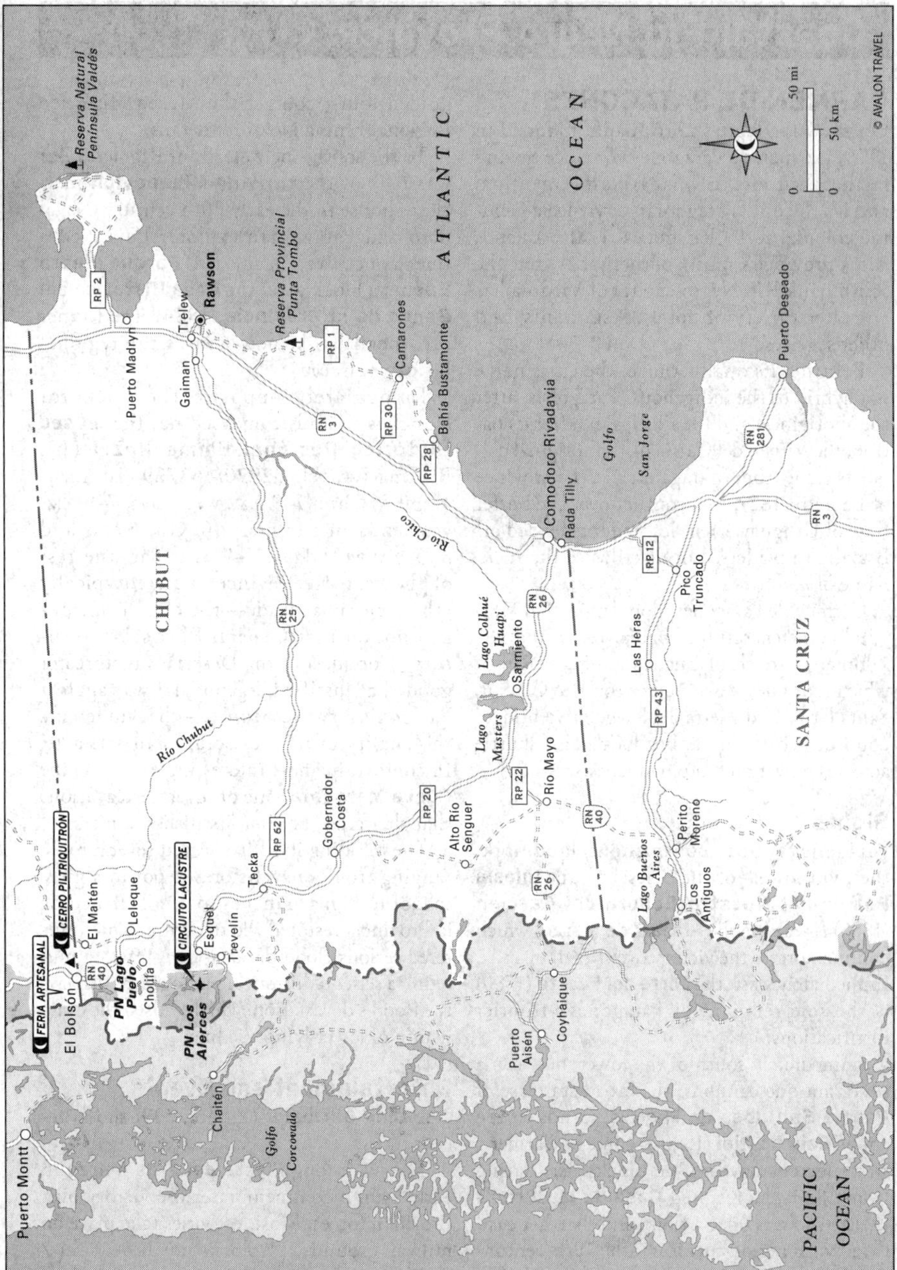
Reserva Natural Península Valdés
Reserva Provincial Punta Tombo
ATLANTIC
OCEAN
Puerto Madryn
Trelew
Rawson
Gaiman
Camarones
Bahía Bustamonte
Comodoro Rivadavia
Rada Tilly
Golfo San Jorge
Puerto Deseado
CHUBUT
SANTA CRUZ
Río Chico
Río Chubut
Lago Colhué Huapi
Lago Musters
Sarmiento
Río Mayo
Alto Río Senguer
Gobernador Costa
Tecka
Esquel
Trevelín
Leleque
El Maitén
El Bolsón
Cholila
PN Lago Puelo
PN Los Alerces
FERIA ARTESANAL
CERRO PILTRIQUITRÓN
CIRCUITO LACUSTRE
Chaitén
Puerto Montt
Golfo Corcovado
Puerto Aisén
Coyhaique
Lago Buenos Aires
Los Antiguos
Perito Moreno
Las Heras
Pico Truncado
PACIFIC OCEAN
RP 2
RP 1
RP 30
RP 28
RN 3
RN 25
RN 26
RN 281
RP 12
RP 43
RP 22
RP 20
RP 62
RN 40
0 50 mi
0 50 km
© AVALON TRAVEL

# Coastal Río Negro Province

## CARMEN DE PATAGONES

On the Río Negro's north bank, founded in 1779, Carmen de Patagones was once Spain's farthest outpost in what is now Argentina, and it's the only Patagonian city with a genuine colonial feel. "Patagones" is also Buenos Aires province's most southerly city, but the south bank Río Negro capital of Viedma has a greater variety of hotels, restaurants, and other services.

Befitting its dual heritage, the city's name is a hybrid of the indigenous (Patagones, after the aborigines) and the European (after its patron, the Virgen del Carmen). The original colonists came from Maragatería, in the province of León; in 1827, in a conflict over the buffer state of Uruguay, their descendants fended off Brazilian invaders. Locals still use the nickname of *maragatos.*

Carmen de Patagones (population 18,095) is 279 kilometers south of Bahía Blanca and 961 kilometers south of Buenos Aires via RN 3, which continues west and then south to Chubut, Santa Cruz, and Tierra del Fuego. Two bridges connect it to Viedma, but locals also shuttle across the river on motor launches.



### Sights

Patagones's most conspicuous landmark, the twin towers of the Salesian-built **Iglesia Parroquial Nuestra Señora del Carmen** (1885) rise above the **Plaza 7 de Marzo,** which commemorates the victory over Brazil in 1827. Immediately west, the **Torre del Fuerte** (1780) is the sole remnant of Patagones's frontier fortifications.

Immediately south of the tower, between a set of antique cannons, the broad staircase of **Pasaje San José de Mayo** descends to the adobe **Rancho Rial** (1820s), home of Carmen's first elected mayor. One block east, dating from 1823, the restored **Casa de la Cultura** (Mitre 27) was once a flour mill. Farther east, fitted with period furniture, the 19th-century **Rancho La Carlota** (Bynon and Mitre) offers guided tours; contact the Museo Histórico Regional Emma Nozzi for details.

To the south, the waterfront Rigoletto Bar was part of the thriving **Mihanovich** merchant house in the early 20th century. Naval hero and Patagonian explorer Luis Piedra Buena once lived in adjacent **Parque Piedra Buena;** a block west, the **Casa Histórica del Banco de la Provincia** (1884), the former provincial bank, now houses the regional history museum.

Immediately opposite the dock for launches to and from Viedma, the **Museo Histórico Regional Emma Nozzi** (J.J. Biedma 64, tel. 02920/462729, 10 A.M.–12:30 P.M. and 7–9 P.M. weekdays, 7–9 P.M. weekends in summer; 10 A.M.–noon and 3–5 P.M.weekdays, 5–7 P.M. Sat. the rest of the year, free) evinces a stereotypically ethnocentric attitude—the clear if unspoken notion that General Roca's 19th-century "Conquest of the Desert" was a greater good that justified a genocidal war against Patagonia's native peoples—that undercuts the quality of its pre-Columbian artifacts. In context, its most interesting exhibit is the **Cueva Maragata,** one of several excavations that sheltered the first Spanish colonists.

The building itself has served several roles, ranging from a naval-stores depot to a girls' school to bank branches to retail. Banco de la Provincia restored the structure, which suffered serious flood damage in 1899, as a museum; a series of historical photographs displays the flood's devastation, which caused the evacuation of lower-lying Viedma.

### Entertainment and Events

The **Cine Garibaldi** (España 209) shows recent films.

The week-long **Fiesta del 7 de Marzo** in early March commemorates the victory over Brazilian forces. Most festivities take place on railway grounds, 11 blocks north of Plaza 7 de Marzo.

## Accommodations and Food

Patagones has decent shoestring accommodations, with private baths, at **Residencial Reggiani** (Bynon 422, tel. 02920/461065, www.internetviedma.com.ar/reggiani, US$25 s, US$45 d), which has a restaurant. The late-19th-century **Hotel Percaz** (Comodoro Rivadavia and H. Yrigoyen, tel. 02920/464104, www.hotelpercaz.com.ar, US$36 s, US$51 d) preserves only a few details of more splendorous times at the dining room, while rooms are disappointingly unattractive.

**Confitería Sabbatella** (Comodoro Rivadavia 218) is fine for breakfast, coffee, or sandwiches. **Neptuno** (Comodoro Rivadavia 310, tel. 02920/461493) is a popular *parrilla* (its *bife de lomo*—tenderloin—costs US$10) that also sells pizza from US$7. More sophistication is found at the **Restaurant del Hotel Percaz** (Comodoro Rivadavia and H. Yrigoyen, tel. 02920/464104), where salmon ravioli in a prawn sauce (US$10) and lamb with a dark beer sauce (US$11) are on the menu together with cheaper short orders of a good standard.

## Information and Services

Well-stocked with maps and brochures, including suggested walking tours, the helpful **Dirección Municipal de Turismo** (Mitre 84, tel. 02920/464819, www.patagones.gov.ar) is open 7 A.M.–1 P.M. and 3–9 P.M. weekdays, 10 A.M.–1 P.M. and 6–9 P.M. weekends in summer; 7 A.M.–7 P.M. weekdays the rest of the year. A new tourist office by the pier is expected to be completed by 2012.

**Banco de la Nación** (Paraguay 2) has an ATM on Plaza 7 de Marzo. **Correo Argentino** (Paraguay 38) is immediately east; the postal code is 8504. Phone and Internet access are available at **Locutorio** (Comodoro Rivadavia and España); Internet access is also available at **Ciber** (Comodoro Rivadavia 327).

## Getting There and Around

Services to and from Patagones's **Terminal de Ómnibus** (Barbieri and Méjico), four blocks north and three blocks east of Plaza 7 de Marzo, are less frequent than Viedma's; several long-distance buses stop at both, however. Nearby Viedma has an airport.

On-demand ***lanchas*** (passenger launches) frequently cross the river to Viedma (6:30 A.M.–10:45 P.M. weekdays, 7 A.M.–9:45 P.M. Sat., 9 A.M.–9.45 P.M. Sun. and holidays, US$0.50).

# VIEDMA

While it lacks Patagones's colonial character, Viedma long ago surpassed its neighbor in services and significance—it's even Río Negro's capital despite its distance from other cities in this Atlantic-to-the-Andes province. Locals swim and kayak along the willow-shaded riverfront, with its restaurants and sailing school.

Founded simultaneously with Patagones, in 1779, Viedma became Patagonia's de facto capital exactly a century later and then, following the "Conquest of the Desert," capital of Río Negro territory. In 1955, it became capital of the new Río Negro province. In the 1980s, President Raúl Alfonsín tried to move the federal capital here from Buenos Aires—a foolishly visionary boondoggle that, fortunately, never came to be.

Viedma (population 52,754) is 280 kilometers south of Bahía Blanca and 440 kilometers north of Puerto Madryn via coastal RN 3. It's 982 kilometers east of Bariloche, Río Negro's largest city, via the Río Negro Valley and Neuquén.

## Sights

On the southwest side of **Plaza Alsina,** the entire block bounded by Yrigoyen, Colón, Rivadavia, and Álvaro Barros is a national historical monument dating from the 1880s, when the Salesian order installed itself here. Among its works were the **Vicariato Apostólico de la Patagonia Septentrional** (Vicarage of Northern Patagonia, 1884–1897), with its neo-Renaissance brick facade and tower.

For many years, the structure served as the **Colegio San Francisco de Sales** (a boys' school) and an orphanage. Since 1976, it's been the **Centro Histórico Cultural Salesiano,** comprising two separate museums: the **Museo**

**Salesiano Cardenal Cagliero** (Rivadavia 34, cell 02920/15-618498, 9 A.M.–1 P.M. and 7–9 P.M. Tues.–Thurs.), presenting the Salesian viewpoint on Patagonian evangelization, and the **Museo Tecnológico del Agua y el Suelo** (Colón 498, 1st floor, tel. 02920/426096, www.museo-dpa.blogspot.com, 10 A.M.–1 P.M. and 6–8 P.M. weekdays in summer; 8:30 A.M.–6 P.M. Mon., Tues., and Fri, 10 A.M.–noon and 2–6 P.M. Wed. and Thurs. the rest of the year, free), focusing on irrigation.

Part of the same complex but facing Plaza Alsina, the **Catedral de la Merced** (1912) replaced an earlier church that came down after the 1899 flood; alongside it, the neoclassical **Obispado de Viedma** (Bishopric of Viedma, 1945) replaced the **Hospital San José.**

Key public buildings cluster around Plaza San Martín, including the **Casa de Gobierno** (Government House), the **Municipalidad** and the dignified **Residencia del Gobernador** (Governor's Residence).

From Thursday through Sunday at 6 P.M. in summer, the catamaran *Curru Leuvu II* (tel. 02920/15-408599) offers 1.5-hour river excursions (US$9 adults, US$2.50 children to age 12) from the **Muelle de Lanchas,** at the foot of 25 de Mayo.



## Events

Viedma's biggest event is January's **Regata del Río Negro** (www.regatadelrionegro.com.ar), a more-than-300-kilometer kayak race from Neuquén and one of the ten races included in the Classic Canoe Marathon World Series.

## Shopping

While a provincial **Mercado Artesanal** (Belgrano 305 and also on Av. Villarino and Belgrano) sells varied handicrafts made by Mapuche artisans, informal craftspeople usually populate Plaza Alsina. For wines and other local produce, try **Vinópolis** (Rivadavia 890, tel. 02920/426225).

## Accommodations

On a quiet residential area nine blocks east of downtown **Residencial Río Mar** (Rivadavia and Santa Rosa, tel. 02920/424188, www.internetviedma.com.ar/residencialriomar, US$28 s, US$45 d) is good enough as a shoestring option and has wireless Internet.

Close to Plaza San Martín **Residencial Roca** (Roca 347, tel. 02920/431241, US$33 s, US$52 d, breakfast extra US$3) is another decent choice with parking and bathrooms with bathtubs.

Overlooking Plaza Alsina, no-frills **Hotel Peumayén** (Buenos Aires 334, tel. 02920/425222, www.hotelpeumayen.com.ar, US$45 s, US$67 d) shows some wear, but yet is a good option in the midrange category with a helpful staff, wireless Internet, air-conditioning, parking, and TV.

Friendly **Hotel Nijar** (Mitre 490, tel. 02920/422833, www.hotelnijar.com, US$53 s, US$78 d) is a modern hotel with good service, comfortable rooms, parking, restaurant, and other amenities, including wireless Internet.

Overlooking the river, there's **Hotel Austral** (Av. Villarino 292, tel. 02920/422615, www.hotelesaustral.com, US$59–78 s, US$75–100 d), which has similar amenities but a better location than the Nijar and includes one floor for smokers. It's worth considering paying the higher rates for larger rooms with river views, otherwise standard rooms at the back are on the smallish side.

## Food

**Camila's Café** (Buenos Aires and Saavedra) is good for coffee and desserts and has wireless Internet.

For its varied menu of a good standard and generous portions, the most popular choice in town is the family-friendly **Sahara Pizza & Pasta** (Saavedra 336, tel. 02920/421092, lunch and dinner daily), where pizzas (from US$9) are offered also in halves at half the price. Pasta, beef, lamb, chicken, fish, and seafood dishes (entrées in the US$8–18 range) complete the list together with creative salads. A popular pizzeria is **Los Tíos** (Belgrano 387, tel. 02920/422790, lunch and dinner daily), with pizzas from US$7.

The waterside **Sal y Fuego** (Av. Villarino

55, tel. 02920/431259, lunch and dinner daily) specializes in fish and seafood with a few pricey dishes (US$12–20). Under same ownership and at the same building, **Café del Sauce** offers cheaper short orders and a terrace ideal for lunch beneath the riverside willow trees.

**Fiore Helados** (Buenos Aires and Aguiar, tel. 02920/426100) serves fine ice cream. Its riverside branch, **Mondo Fiore** (Av. Villarino and Belgrano, tel. 02920/420700), also serves fast food.

## Information

The riverfront **Oficina de Informes Turísticos** (Av. Francisco de Viedma 51, tel. 02920/427171, www.viedma.gov.ar) is open 9 A.M.–9 P.M. daily in summer, 8 A.M.–7 P.M. weekdays and 11 A.M.–7 P.M. weekends the rest of the year.

The **Ministerio de Turismo** (Av. Caseros 1425, tel. 02920/422150) provides information and printed matter for the entire province.

For motorists, **ACA** (tel. 02920/422441) is at Héroes de Malvinas (ex RN 3) Km 962.

## Services

**Banco Patagonia** (Buenos Aires 184) has one of many ATMs. **Tritón Turismo** (Namuncurá 78, tel. 02920/431131, tritonturismo@hotmail.com) changes money, rents cars, and arranges excursions. **Mona Tour** (Laprida 145, tel. 02920/422933, www.monatour.com.ar) organizes city and coastal tours, as well as excursions with *La Trochita* train from Ingeniero Jacobacci if available.

**Correo Argentino** is at Rivadavia 151; the postal code is 8500. Phone services are at Buenos Aires and Colón, while **@rroba** (Colón 202) provides Internet access.

**Lavandería Automática Siglo XXI** (Mitre 343, tel. 02920/15-664086) does the laundry.

**Hospital Artémides Zatti** (Rivadavia 391, tel. 02920/422333) is the public hospital.

## Getting There

**Aerolíneas Argentinas** (Colón 246, tel. 02920/422018) flies two weekly nonstops to Aeroparque Jorge Newbery. **LADE** (Saavedra 576, tel. 02920/424420) flies south to Puerto Madryn, Trelew, and Comodoro Rivadavia, and north to Mar del Plata.

The **Tren Patagónico** (Cagliero s/n, tel. 02920/422130, www.trenpatagonico-sa.com.ar) connects Estación Viedma, on the southeast edge of town, with Bariloche by rail on Friday at 6 P.M. The 19-hour trip costs US$14 in hard-backed *económica,* US$29 in reclining Pullman, or US$57 in *camarote* sleepers; children 5–12 pay half.

Viedma's **Terminal de Ómnibus** (Guido 1660, tel. 02920/426850) is 13 blocks south of downtown. Tickets for **Vía Bariloche** group are also sold downtown (San Martín 57, tel. 02920/421300). Sample destinations, fares, and times include Las Grutas (US$5, 2.5 hours), Puerto Madryn (US$26–37, seven hours), Trelew (US$29–43, eight hours), Neuquén (US$25, eight hours), Comodoro Rivadavia (US$53–76, 13 hours), Buenos Aires (US$67–104, 12–14 hours), Bariloche (US$40–50, 12–15 hours), and Río Gallegos (US$97–131, 24 hours).

## Getting Around

Taxis or *remises* to **Aeropuerto Gobernador Castello** (tel. 02920/425311), five kilometers south of town on RP 51, cost about US$5.

On-demand *lanchas* (passenger launches) frequently cross the river to Carmen de Patagones (6:30 A.M.–10:45 P.M. weekdays, 7 A.M.–9:45 P.M. Sat., 9 A.M.–9.45 P.M. Sun. and holidays, US$0.50) from the Muelle de Lanchas at the foot of 25 de Mayo.

**Tritón Turismo** (Namuncurá 78, tel. 02920/431131) has rental cars. **Avis** is at Hotel Nijar (Mitre 490, tel. 02920/429800, viedma@avis.com.ar).

# GOLFO SAN MATÍAS AND VICINITY

From Viedma, RN 3 turns west and slightly inland toward the port of San Antonio Oeste, paralleling the Golfo San Matías shoreline, but day-trippers and visitors with their own vehicles should consider a detour along coastal RP 1.

Here, about 30 kilometers southeast of Viedma at the mouth of the Río Negro, **Balneario El Cóndor** draws beachgoers from the provincial capital; from Zatti between Álvaro Barros and Mitre, **Empresa Ceferino** (Schieroni 383, tel. 02920/424542) has five buses daily (US$1.50), adding services in summer.

The scenic coastline is a prime **birdwatching** area. Along 12 kilometers starting immediately west of El Cóndor, headlands host about 35,000 active nests of burrowing parrots in the world's largest known colony of Psittaciformes; the area is best visited in the breeding season from November to early January.

RP 1 and La Comarca buses continue another 30 kilometers to **La Lobería,** where the **Reserva Faunística Provincial Punta Bermeja** protects some 3,000 southern sea lions.

West of La Lobería, the pavement ends but RP 1's scenery improves to include massive dunes at **Bahía Creek** and another sea lion colony at **Reserva Provincial Caleta de los Loros,** where more nesting parrots burrow into the headlands. At Punta Mejillón, the highway swerves inland, where it's possible to return to RN 3 via unpaved RP 52, or else continue west toward Puerto San Antonio Este, before which a paved road also turns north to RN 3.



Some 187 kilometers west of Viedma but east of RN 3, summer and weekend visitors swarm the beaches of **Las Grutas** (permanent population 2,708), named for the wave-cut grottoes that have penetrated the sedimentary headlands. Because of a wide tidal range, the beachfront can recede to just tens of meters, suitable for only the most gregarious beachgoers. There are nearly a hundred hotels, *hospedajes,* and campgrounds; for suggestions, visit the **Secretaría Municipal de Turismo** (Av. Río Negro 715, tel. 02934/497470). Las Grutas has frequent bus links to San Antonio Oeste, 16 kilometers northeast.

About 125 kilometers south of San Antonio Oeste and 140 kilometers north of Puerto Madryn, RN 3 passes through **Sierra Grande** (population 6,768), an iron-mining town that's the northernmost point to purchase gasoline at Patagonian prices—cheaper than in Las Grutas or San Antonio Oeste. Southbound drivers should nurse their fuel to get here, while the northbound should top off the tank.

## NEUQUÉN AND VICINITY

Capital of its namesake province, Neuquén is a gateway to the northern Patagonian lakes, but also an ideal base for visiting a triangle of nearby dinosaur sites and cluster of new wineries. At the confluence of two major rivers, it's a clean modern city that benefits from abundant energy resources, its productive financial sector, and the upper Río Negro valley's agricultural plenty. It also has an active cultural life, best exemplified by its fine arts museum.

Where the Río Neuquén and the Río Limay meet, Neuquén (population 233,000) is 537 kilometers east of Bahía Blanca via RN 22, 559 kilometers southwest of Santa Rosa via several paved highways, and 429 kilometers northeast of San Carlos de Bariloche via RN 22, RN 237 and RN 40. RN 22 through the upper Río Negro Valley and west toward Zapala is a narrow highway with heavy truck traffic and dangerously impatient drivers.

### Sights

Nearly all the sights are in the **Parque Central,** the recycled railyard bounded by Avenida San Martín/Avenida Independencia and the streets of Manuel Láinez, Tierra del Fuego, and Sarmiento/Mitre.

The **Sala de Arte Emilio Saraco** (Av. Olascoaga s/n, tel. 0299/4491200, ext. 4390, 8 A.M.–9 P.M. weekdays, 6–10 P.M. weekends and holidays in summer; 8 A.M.–8 P.M. weekdays, 4–8 P.M. weekends and holidays the rest of the year, free) occupies the railroad station's former cargo terminal, with exhibits of contemporary art.

Two blocks east, in a former railway workers' residence, the **Museo de la Ciudad Paraje Confluencia** (Av. Independencia and Pasaje Héroes de Malvinas, tel. 0299/15-5553082, 8 A.M.–8 P.M. weekdays, 6–10 P.M. weekends and holidays in summer; 8 A.M.–8 P.M. weekdays,

4–8 P.M. weekends and holidays the rest of the year, free) traces Neuquén's urban evolution.

**MUSEO NACIONAL DE BELLAS ARTES**

In luminous contemporary quarters in the Parque Central, this is the first provincial branch of the national fine arts museum, with permanent collections of European and Argentine art, complemented by rotating exhibits (Mitre and Santa Cruz, tel. 0299/4491200, ext. 4311, www.mnba-neuquen.com.ar, 10 A.M.–9 P.M. Tues.–Fri., 10 A.M.–2 P.M. and 6–10 P.M. Sat., 6–10 P.M. Sun. and holidays in summer; 10 A.M.–8 P.M. Tues.–Sat., 4–8 P.M. Sun. and holidays in winter, free). Mobile walls-on-wheels separate its 2,000-square-meter interior into manageable spaces as needed, but the shabby gravel parking lot still needs new landscaping commensurate with the building's aspirations.

## Entertainment and Events

**La Casona** (Alvear 59) is a bar with occasional live music, as well as **O'Connell's** (Roca 234). For current films, there's the **Cine Teatro Español** (Av. Argentina 235, tel. 0299/4482486).

January's **Regata del Río Negro** (www.regatadelrionegro.com.ar) is a kayak marathon of over 300 kilometers that starts here and ends a week later in Viedma, included in the Classic Canoe Marathon World Series.

## Shopping

The province of Neuquén sponsors **Artesanías Neuquinas** (Almirante Brown 280, tel. 0299/4423806, www.artesaniasneuquinas.com), with a diverse crafts selection at reasonable prices. **Cardón** (Ministro González 54, tel. 0299/4477331) sells leather goods, *mates,* and silverwork. **Artesanías Mapuches** (Roca 151, tel. 0299/4436750) focuses on indigenous silverwork.

## Accommodations

Nearly all accommodations lie in the scruffy but not unsafe retail area between RN 22 and the Parque Central.

© WAYNE BERNHARDSON

Neuquén's Museo Nacional de Bellas Artes

## NEUQUÉN'S DINOSAUR TRIANGLE

Where there's oil, there are dinosaurs, and Neuquén's sedimentary steppe is one of Argentina's late-Cretaceous hot spots. By rental car, a triangle of sites northwest, west, and southwest of the provincial capital makes an ideal (if long) full-day excursion, though one of these, Lago Barreales, is more difficult to reach and is best in fall and winter. The other two, Plaza Huincul and Villa El Chocón, are easily accessible by public transportation.

**a fossil dinosaur egg in the museum at Lago Los Barreales**

### CENTRO PALEONTOLÓGICO LAGO LOS BARREALES

The best place to see an on-site excavation is this reservoir northwest of Neuquén, where paleontologists demonstrate the separation and rescue of fossil deposits as well as the cleaning and extraction of the fossils themselves. Beasts in the sediments here include the sauropod *Futalognkosaurus* (a long-tailed quadruped with a long neck and small head), teropods (bipedal carnivores with huge claws, such as *Megaraptor*), and ornithopods (small bipedal herbivores), along with bivalves, crocodiles, turtles, and pterosaurs.

Only when the water level falls in autumn, usually in early April, can the expert team, under Jorge Calvo, resume its work, so this is the ideal time to go. There is now an interpretative trail with some fossils in situ, and an improvised museum in a Nissen hut.

On Barreales's north shore, the Centro Paleontológico Lago Los Barreales (Av. Megaraptor 1450, RP 51 Km 65, tel. 0299/15-6329558, www.proyectodino.com.ar) is open 9 A.M.–7 P.M. daily. Guided tours cost US$7 per person for Argentines, US$20 per person for foreigners, and US$4 for children under 12. Foreign university students can hire on to participate in the digs (for a price).

Actually reaching the site can be complicated, but the simplest route is to take RP 7 from Cipolletti almost to Añelo, about 100 kilometers northwest of Neuquén, and then turn south on a gravel road to the north shore of Barreales. It's now well-signed but still requires close attention, and there are plenty of heavy trucks kicking up dust.

### MUSEO MUNICIPAL CARMEN FUNES (PLAZA HUINCUL)

At the oil town of Plaza Huincul, about midway between Neuquén and Zapala, the municipal

Rooms at friendly, centrally located **Hostería Belgrano** (Rivadavia 283, tel. 0299/4480612, www.hosteriabelgrano.com, US$28 s, US$40 d) are small—some claustrophobic—but also immaculate.

**Hotel Ideal** (Av. Olascoaga 243, tel. 0299/4422431, www.interpatagonia.com/hotelideal, US$45 s, US$58 d with breakfast) has clean, comfortable rooms with modern amenities but lacks parking.

**Hotel Huemul** (Tierra del Fuego 335, tel. 0299/4422344, www.huemulhotel.com.ar, US$39 s, US$65 d) is another decent enough choice for one night; quiet, with firm beds and wireless Internet.

A lot better than the cheaper options is the local classic **Hotel Iberia** (Av. Olascoaga 294, tel. 0299/4422372, www.interpatagonia.com/hoteliberia, US$50 s, US$70 d), for its tidy, ample rooms with standard conveniences, including wireless Internet. It's worth paying extra for the more comfortable suite for two people.

Though showing some wear, **Hotel El Prado**

museum's prize exhibit is a replica skeleton of *Argentinosaurus huinculensis,* the world's largest dinosaur at 35 meters long and 18 meters high. So large is the herbivore *A. huinculensis* that an adult male human barely reaches its knee, and one of its dorsal vertebrae measures 1.6 meters.

Former oil worker Guillermo Heredia found the fossil only three kilometers away, along the highway, in 1987. In addition to the imposing skeleton, there are models of the carnivorous *Mapusaurus* and several smaller dinosaurs, a clutch of dinosaur eggs some 80 million years old, and remains of crocodiles found in Picún Leufú, about 75 kilometers to the south.

In expanded quarters along the highway, the Museo Municipal Carmen Funes (Av. Córdoba 55, tel. 0299/4965486, museocarmenfunes@copelnet.com.ar, US$1) is open 9 A.M.-7 P.M. Monday-Friday, 9:30 A.M.-8:30 P.M. weekends and holidays.

Plaza Huincul, 110 kilometers west of Neuquén via RN 22, has an **Oficina de Informes** (RN 22 s/n, tel. 0299/4967637) directly on the highway. Buses from Neuquén are frequent and comfortable.

### MUSEO PALEONTOLÓGICO MUNICIPAL ERNESTO BACHMANN (VILLA EL CHOCÓN)

Plaza Huincul boasts the world's largest herbivore, but Villa El Chocón claims its carnivorous counterpart in *Giganotosaurus carolinii.* Above the Embalse Exequiel Ramos Mexía, an enormous hydroelectric reservoir southwest of Neuquén, the municipal museum also features models of *Carnotaurus* and the smaller *Pianitzkysaurus.* There are also dinosaur tracks in the vicinity.

*G. carolinii* takes its name from amateur paleontologist Rubén Carolini, who discovered the fossil; Rodolfo Coria, Leonardo Salgado, and Jorge Calvo first identified it. Measuring 14 meters in length and 4.65 meters high at the hip, it weighed up to eight tons.

Unfortunately, because the massive hydroelectric dam drowned the Río Limay's sedimentary canyon here, many probable paleontological sites have disappeared beneath the water. The Museo Paleontológico Municipal Ernesto Bachmann (8 A.M.-7 P.M. daily, US$2.50) also offers exhibits on the area's archaeology and a whitewashed history of the dam and former *estancia* owner Manuel Bustigorry.

Villa El Chocón, 80 kilometers southwest of Neuquén via RN 22 and RN 237, originated as a company town during the dam's construction. The **Dirección Municipal de Turismo** (tel. 0299/4901223), at the northern approach to town off RN 22, is open 8 A.M.-7 P.M. daily.

On the shoreline, **La Posada del Dinosaurio** (tel. 0299/4901200, www.posadadinosaurio.com.ar, US$88 d) offers excellent accommodations, with a good, reasonably priced restaurant and outstanding service. Camping also exists nearby.



(Perito Moreno 484, tel. 0299/4486000, www.hotel-elprado.com.ar, US$58–69 s, US$83–98 d) remains one of the city's better values, with large, well-furnished rooms with wireless Internet. In addition, there's an abundant buffet breakfast and superb service.

The best value downtown, **Hotel Suizo** (Carlos H. Rodríguez 167, tel. 0299/4422602, www.hotelsuizo.com.ar, US$78–90 s, US$95–108 d) has very comfortable rooms, attentive service, wireless Internet, parking, and a buffet breakfast.

Downtown's four-star **Hotel del Comahue** (Av. Argentina 377, tel. 0299/4432040, www.hoteldelcomahue.com, US$147–162 s, US$173–190 d) is the overpriced pick of the litter.

## Food

Neuquén is strong on pizza and pasta, at places like the traditional **La Nonna Francesca** (9 de Julio 56, tel. 0299/4300930, lunch and dinner daily) and **La Tartaruga** (Roca 193, tel. 0299/4436880, lunch and dinner daily), where most entrées are in the US$10–15 range.

**Franz y Peppone** (9 de Julio and Belgrano, tel. 0299/4482299, lunch and dinner daily) blends the Teutonic and the Mediterranean, including *salchichas con chucrut* (sausage and sauerkraut, US$8) and pizzas from US$7, in the varied menu.

**La Birra** (Santa Fe 53, tel. 0299/4434344) is a popular, casual restaurant with an Italian-Argentine menu that includes items such as pizza, pasta, and the like in the US$12 range, in a congenial atmosphere with outstanding service. Oddly, for its name it has a limited beer selection.

**Piré** (Diagonal Alvear 29, tel. 0299/4430575) has fine ice creams downtown.

## Information

Directly on RN 22, the **Subsecretaría de Turismo** (Félix San Martín 182, tel. 0299/4424089, www.neuquentur.gov.ar) is open 7 A.M.–9 P.M. daily. In content, accuracy, and usefulness, their maps and brochures are among the country's best.

For motorists, **ACA** is at Rivadavia and the diagonal 25 de Mayo (tel. 0299/4424860).

## Services

**Banco de la Provincia de Neuquén** (Av. Argentina 13) has one of many ATMs. **Cambio Olano** (J.B. Justo 107, tel. 0299/4426192) and **Cambio Pullman** (Alcorta 144, tel. 0299/4422438) are exchange houses.

**Correo Argentino** is at Rivadavia and Santa Fe; the postal code is 8300. **Ciber One** (Av. Olascoaga 331) has both telephone and Internet access.

Neighboring Chile has a **consulate** (tel. 0299/4422727) at La Rioja 241. **Migraciones** (tel. 0299/4422061) is at Santiago del Estero 466.

**Lava Ya** (Av. Independencia 326, tel. 0299/4434318) does the washing.

The **Hospital Regional** (Buenos Aires 450, tel. 0299/4490800) can handle emergencies or routine care.

## Getting There

**Aerolíneas Argentinas** (Santa Fe 52, tel. 0299/4422409) averages three or four flights daily to Aeroparque Jorge Newbery. Travel agencies can handle ticketing for **American Jet** (tel. 0810/3459876, www.americanjet.com.ar), which has services to San Martín de los Andes (five times weekly). **LAN** (Hipólito Yrigoyen 347, tel. 0810/9999526) has daily flights to Aeroparque Jorge Newbery. **Sol** (tel. 0810/4444765) has northbound services to Córdoba and Rosario via Mendoza, and southbound to Ushuaia via Comodoro Rivadavia and Río Gallegos.

About five kilometers west of downtown, Neuquén's shiny **Terminal de Ómnibus** (Planas and Solalique, tel. 0299/4452300) is a hub for provincial, national, and some international bus services (to the Chilean city of Temuco, reservations advisable).

Sample provincial and long-distance destinations, fares, and times include Zapala (US$13, three hours), Bariloche (US$25–40, 5.5 hours), San Martín de los Andes (US$30–43, seven hours), Villa La Angostura (US$35–38, seven hours), Puerto Madryn (US$49–60, 9–11 hours), El Bolsón (US$31–43, 7–8 hours), Mendoza (US$50–79, 11–13 hours), Esquel (US$34–48, 9.5–10.5 hours), Buenos Aires (US$80–113, 14–17 hours), Comodoro Rivadavia (US$60–99, 14–20 hours), and Río Gallegos (US$141–170, 27–29 hours).

Bus companies for Temuco via Zapala and the Pino Hachado pass (US$35–39, 9.5–11 hours) include **Igi Llaima/Narbus** (tel. 0299/4452295), **Andesmar** (tel. 0299/4452493), **El Valle** (tel. 0299/4452265), **Albus** (tel. 0299/4452522), and **Plaza** (tel. 0800/3331970). **El Rápido Internacional** and **CATA** (tel. 0299/4461656) go to Santiago de Chile via Mendoza (US$78, 22 hours).

## Getting Around

**Aeropuerto Internacional J. D. Perón** (tel. 0299/4440244) is seven kilometers west of town via RN 22 (despite its name, there are no international services at present). A taxi or *remise* costs US$10, while the local Indalo bus No. 50B is a cheaper option. For the bus terminal, it's better to take a taxi (US$5).

Car rental agencies include **Avis** (tel.

0299/4441297), **Hertz** (tel. 0299/4440146), and **Localiza** (tel. 0299/4440440), all three at the airport.

## ZAPALA

Argentine backpackers once used forlorn Zapala, the erstwhile end of the line for the Ferrocarril Roca's northern spur, as a takeoff point to the lakes district's least-visited parts. Since the railroad shut down, the town and the bleak surrounding steppe is mainly a convenient stopover en route to San Martín de los Andes, though it has good access to bird-rich Parque Nacional Laguna Blanca.

Zapala (population 32,500) is 184 kilometers west of Neuquén via RN 22 and 244 kilometers northeast of San Martín de los Andes via RN 40 and RN 234. From Zapala RN 40 continues northwest toward Las Lajas, from where RN 242 reaches the Chilean border at Pino Hachado. The main drag is Avenida San Martín, which leads south from a roundabout on RN 22.

### Museo Olsacher

Zapala's modernized mineralogical museum fills a recycled warehouse with minerals from around the world and paleontological exhibits from Neuquén. Its prize exhibit is the remains of the herbivorous dinosaur *Zapalasaurus bonapartei,* but there are also displays on marine reptiles, paleobotany, systematic mineralogy, Argentine economic minerals, and invertebrate and vertebrate paleontology, and a specialized library.

Alongside the bus terminal, the Museo Olsacher (Etcheluz and Ejército Argentino, free) is open 9 A.M.–2 P.M. weekdays only.

### Shopping

Zapala's **Escuela de Cerámica** (Luis Monti 240) has a long tradition in artisanal pottery.

### Accommodations and Food

While accommodations and dining are limited, quality is good. The cheapest are **Hotel Coliqueo** (Etcheluz 159, tel. 02942/421307, US$27 s, US$45 d) and the immaculate **Pehuén Hotel** (Etcheluz and Elena de la Vega, tel. 02942/423135, US$27 s, US$45 d). **Hotel Hue Melén** (Almirante Brown 929, tel. 02942/422407, hotelhuemelen@hotmail.com, US$58 s, US$88 d) also has a restaurant.

For breakfast, coffee, and snacks, there's **El Chancho Rengo** (Av. San Martín and Etcheluz, tel. 02942/422797). Directly on RN 22 near the roundabout, **El Fogón** (Houssay and Bolivia, tel. 02942/15-664781) is a good *parrilla,* where entrées are around US$12. **Helados Don Héctor** (Etcheluz 527) is only so-so compared with ice creameries elsewhere, but it's not a desperation choice.

### Information

Providing information on the province's northernmost lakes district, the **Centro de Informes Turísticos Portal del Pehuén** (RN 22 Km 1398, tel. 02942/424296, turismozapala@yahoo.com.ar) occupies new quarters near the ACA gas station, on the eastern approach to town. Hours are 7 A.M.–9 P.M. daily.

The **Administración de Parques Nacionales (APN)** (Ejército Argentino 217, tel. 02942/431982, www.pnlagunablanca.com.ar, lagunablanca@apn.gov.ar) provides information on Parque Nacional Laguna Blanca.

### Services

**Banco de la Provincia del Neuquén** (Cháneton and Italia) has an ATM.

**Correo Argentino** is at Avenida San Martín 324; the postal code is 8340. **Telefónica** (Etcheluz 527) has long-distance telephones and improved Internet.

For medical needs, try the **Hospital Regional** (Luis Monti 155, tel. 02924/431428).

### Getting There and Around

Downtown's **Terminal de Ómnibus** (Etcheluz and Uriburu, tel. 02924/431090) has provincial and long-distance services; some Chile-bound carriers will pick up passengers here.

Sample destinations, fares, and times include Neuquén (US$13, three hours), San Martín de los Andes (US$18, four hours), and Buenos Aires (US$92–122, 16–20 hours).

Most often, for Buenos Aires, it's easier to transfer in Neuquén.

## PARQUE NACIONAL LAGUNA BLANCA

In the stark volcanic steppe southwest of Zapala, alkaline Laguna Blanca is a shallow, plankton-rich interior drainage lake with breeding populations of the striking black-necked swan. Designated a major international wetland under the Ramsar convention, it's also an ideal **bird-watching** site to spot coots, ducks, grebes, gulls, upland geese, and the occasional flamingo. Even the flightless *choique* (rhea) scurries along the barren shoreline for a drink.

From a junction 10 kilometers south of Zapala via RN 40, paved RP 46 leads 20 kilometers southwest to the park, comprising 11,250 hectares of undulating terrain 1,276 meters above sea level; the lake itself covers 1,700 hectares to a depth of 10 meters.

### Sights

From the roadside visitors center, a short nature trail leads across the steppe to the shoreline for glimpses of the swans, which are always here. Though birdlife is most abundant November–March, the unfortunate introduction of nonnative fish species, such as *perca,* decades ago has affected the birds' diet and, hence, diminished its population; a fishing season in the colder months has been set up to try to reverse the situation.

### Practicalities

On the north side of RP 46, about two kilometers east of the visitors center, a free APN campground offers little shelter from the westerlies that gust across the steppe, but Laguna Blanca really makes a better day trip than an overnight. There's no food or water available—bring everything necessary.

Directly on RP 46, the steadily improving **Centro de Visitantes** has helpful rangers, informative exhibits, and clean toilets. It's open 9 A.M.–6 P.M. daily mid-December–March; the rest of the year it's open weekends and holidays only.

Public transportation is limited, and the only two companies that pass Parque Nacional Laguna Blanca en route to Aluminé do so in the afternoon, after which there are no services back on the same day. Hiring a *remise* for a quick visit and return costs about US$25.



# The Lakes District

## ALUMINÉ AND VICINITY

West of Laguna Blanca, paved RP 46 passes 2,839-meter Cerro Chachil, with more distant views of Volcán Lanín, on the border with Chile, and of fuming Volcán Villarrica, across the line. From the Cuesta de Rahue, where the first araucaria (monkey puzzle) trees make their appearance, the zigzag road descends into the valley of the Río Aluminé, a prime trout and white-water river whose singularly appropriate name derives from a Mapuche compound meaning "glittering jewel."

Aluminé proper is nothing special, but for visitors with their own vehicles, it offers the best services in an area with almost unlimited recreational opportunities in northernmost Parque Nacional Lanín. The southbound route through the Aluminé valley, to Junín de los Andes and San Martín de los Andes, is more scenic than RN 40.

Aluminé (population about 4,100; 900 meters above sea level) is 138 kilometers southwest of Zapala via RN 40, RP 46 (which is gradually being paved), and a paved stretch of RP 23; it is also 102 kilometers north of Junín de los Andes via RP 23, a good but mostly gravel road.

### White-Water Rafting

November and December's heavy runoff makes the Class II–IV Río Aluminé a superb white-water opportunity, but low water the rest of the year makes much of the the rock-strewn riverbed hazardous. Class III–IV trips (from US$45 pp) are over by December, but Class II–III (from US$18 pp) rafting continues through the summer. Contact **Aluminé Rafting** (Villegas 610, tel. 02942/496322, www.interpatagonia.com/aluminerafting, aluminerafting@yahoo.com.ar) or **Neuquén Rafting** (RP 23 Km 1, tel. 02942/15-572572, www.neuquenrafting.com.ar).

### Events

Mid-March's **Fiesta del Pehuén** pays homage to the distinctive monkey puzzle tree that provided sustenance to the region's aboriginal inhabitants. Mapuche communities still harvest the fallen nuts.

### Accommodations and Food

Across from Plaza San Martín, looking better without than within, **Hostería Aluminé** (Cristián Joubert 312, tel. 02942/496174, www.hosteriaalumine.com.ar, US$45 s, US$55 d) has spacious if spartan rooms, but breakfast is US$5 extra.

Aluminé's best, **Hotel de la Aldea** (RP 23 Km 82, tel. 02942/496340, www.hoteldelaaldea.com.ar, US$50 s, US$83 d) is a multistory European-style chalet with comfortable rooms, some with river views, though the beds are little soft. It has wireless Internet and some of the common areas are worn. Rates include an abundant but mediocre breakfast; dinner is notably better.

At Rahue, 16 kilometers south of Aluminé, **Hostería Quillén** (RP 46, tel. 02942/496129, www.interpatagonia.com/quillen, US$64 s, US$80 d) is a comfortable lodge catering primarily to hunters and fishers. Rates include an abundant, diverse breakfast; lunch and dinner are also available. It's open January–mid-April only.

The area's top accommodation, though, is the all-inclusive **Hostería Rural Piedra Pintada** (tel. 02942/496396, www.piedrapintada.com.ar, US$330 pp), 36 kilometers northwest of town on the south shore of Lago Pulmarí. Alongside the aboriginal rock-art site that gives the resort its name, it's a 2,000-hectare property with a dozen luxury doubles and an appealing restaurant serving produce from its own organic garden. It also provides fine access to the northernmost sector of Parque Nacional Lanín and the scenic loop road to Villa Pehuenia.

### Information and Services

For information, consult the diligent **Secretaría de Turismo** (Cristián Joubert and Julio Ayoso, tel. 02942/496001, www.alumine.gov.ar), directly on the central Plaza San Martín. In summer, it also operates a Centro de Informes in the hamlet of Rahue, at the junction of RP 46 and RP 23.

**Banco de la Provincia del Neuquén** (Villegas 392) has an ATM.

**Correo Argentino** is at Villegas 560; the postal code is 8345. There's a *locutorio* (call center) at Juan Benigar 334.

**Nex Sur** (on Av. RIM 26 No. 848) has Internet access.

### Getting There

Aluminé's **Terminal de Ómnibus** (4 de Caballería 139, tel. 02942/496048) occupies a triangular block immediately south of Plaza San Martín. **Albus** leaves a few times daily to Zapala (US$10, three hours) and Neuquén (US$20–30, 5.5–6 hours). In summer it goes daily also to Junín de los Andes (US$8, 2.5 hours) and to San Martín de los Andes (US$10, three hours), with fewer weekly services the rest of the year.

## JUNÍN DE LOS ANDES

Where the steppe meets the sierra, the Río Chimehuín gushes from the base of 3,776-meter Volcán Lanín to become one of Argentina's top trout streams near Junín de los Andes. Styling itself Neuquén's "trout capital," Junín also provides the best access to the central sector of Parque Nacional Lanín, which takes its name from the symmetrical cone along the Chilean border.

In addition to its natural attractions, Junín promotes itself as a pilgrimage site for links to the recently beatified Chilean Laura Vicuña, a young girl who (legend says) willed her own death to protest her widowed mother's affair with an Argentine landowner, and for the ostensible blend of Catholic and Mapuche traditions here. Founded in 1883, during General Roca's so-called "Conquista del Desierto," it's Neuquén's oldest city.

Near the confluence of the Chimehuín and its Curruhué tributary, Junín (population about 12,500) is 387 kilometers southwest of Neuquén via RN 22, RN 40, and RN 234, and 41 kilometers northeast of San Martín de los Andes via RN 234. It's 218 kilometers north of San Carlos de Bariloche via RN 234 and RN 40.

The main thoroughfare is north–south RN 234; the compact city center, a regular grid around Plaza San Martín, lies east between the highway and the river.

## Sights

The **Museo Mapuche** (Padre Milanesio and Ginés Ponte, 9 A.M.–noon and 2:30–7 P.M. weekdays, free) focuses on indigenous artifacts and historical exhibits, but it also displays fossils.

Recent developments reflect Junín's promotion of religious tourism. The modernized **Santuario Nuestra Señora de las Nieves y Beata Laura Vicuña** (Ginés Ponte and Don Bosco) has become an airy, luminous structure incorporating Mapuche elements; it also holds an urn with one of Laura Vicuña's vertebrae. It's open for guided tours 9 A.M.–7 P.M. daily.

In the western foothills, the **Vía Christi** is a stations-of-the-cross footpath climbing 2.5 kilometers to the summit of **Cerro de la Cruz.**

## Entertainment and Events

January's **Encuentro de Artesanos Mapuches** and mid-July's **Semana de Artesanía Aborigen** let the Mapuche showcase their crafts.

Late January's **Feria y Exposición Ganadera** is the landowners' extravaganza of blue-ribbon cattle, horses, and sheep, plus rabbits and poultry. Gauchos show off their skills as well, but they take center stage at mid-February's **Festival del Puestero.**

The pre-Lenten **Carnaval del Pehuén** fills the streets with parades, costumed celebrants, water balloons, and confetti.

## Shopping

Junín's **Paseo Artesanal** (Padre Milanesio 590) and **Paseo del Centenario** (Don Bosco and Coronel Suárez) house a cluster of artisans working in ceramics, leather, wood, and wool.

## Sports and Recreation

Both Argentines and foreigners flock here for **fishing** on the Chimehuín, the Aluminé, their tributaries, and Parque Nacional Lanín's glacial lakes. Catch-and-release is the norm for riverine fishing; for licenses and suggested guides, visit the tourist office on Plaza San Martín. For nonresidents of the country, licenses cost US$25 per day, US$75 per week, or US$105 for the season (Nov.–Apr.), with an additional charge for a trolling permit; passport required.

The **APN** office (Padre Milanesio 570, tel. 02972/492748) provides information on hiking and climbing Volcán Lanín and other excursions within the park.

## Estancia Huechahue

On the Río Aluminé, about 30 kilometers east of Junín via RN 234, the 6,600-hectare Anglo-Argentine Estancia Huechahue is a forested cattle ranch that doubles as a recreational getaway for serious gaucho-style riders, or those who want to become serious riders. October–April, Jane Williams's well-trained horses carry a maximum of 12 guests at a time over the mountainous terrain into Parque Nacional Lanín, or undertake a circuit of various nearby *estancias*.

For accompanying non-riders, or for a change of pace, there's hiking, birding, fishing, swimming, and even tennis. Huechahue also features volcanic caves, Tehuelche rock-art sites, and wildlife including Andean condor nesting sites (not to mention deer and feral boar).

Most visitors arrange packages from overseas; drop-ins are not possible, but with at least a few days' notice it may be possible to arrange a stay (three-day minimum). The basic rate of US$389 per person, in twin-bedded rooms, includes full board (traditional Patagonian fare rather than the European-style cuisine of some *estancias*), drinks (beer, wine, and spirits), hot tub and sauna, and activities (fishing guides and massages are extra). It also includes transportation between Huechahue and San Martín de los Andes' Aeropuerto Chapelco; transportation to or from Bariloche is possible for an additional charge. For details, contact Jane Williams at Estancia Huechahue (www.huechahue.com).

## Accommodations

The riverside **Camping Albergue Mallín Laura Vicuña** (Ginés Ponte 867, tel. 02972/491149, mallinlaura@gmail.com, US$6 pp) has a well-organized site, offering shoestring accommodations also in dorms and in small apartments for 4–8 people.

The roadside **Residencial Marisa** (Blvd. Juan Manuel de Rosas 360, tel. 02972/491175, residencialmarisa@jdeandes.com.ar, US$23 s, US$45 d) has rooms of a basic comfort with private bathrooms and wireless Internet.

Aging but agreeable, the riverside **Hostería Chimehuín** (Coronel Suárez and 25 de Mayo, tel. 02972/491132, hosteriachimehuin@fronteradigital.net.ar, US$50 s, US$65 d) has 23 comfortable rooms with private bathrooms, as well as apartments. Breakfast includes homemade scones and other specialties.

On Junín's northern outskirts, **Hotel Alejandro Primero** (RN 234 and Av. Neuquén, tel. 02972/491182, hotelalejandro1@fronteradigital.net.ar, US$62 s, US$72 d) has good rooms and wireless Internet at the lobby.

Junín's only four-star accommodations, the self-consciously rustic **The Río Dorado Lodge & Fly Shop** (Pedro Illera 448, tel. 02972/491548, www.riodorado.com.ar, US$70 s, US$91 d with buffet breakfast, US$112 s, US$176 d with half board, including wine and beer) has become the default option for foreign tour groups, especially but not exclusively for fly-fishing.

## Food

For pizza and pasta, plus sandwiches and empanadas, the traditional favorite is **Cocinarte** (Ginés Ponte 331, tel. 02972/491504, lunch and dinner daily). It has a credible challenger, though, in **Pizzería Offa** (Padre Milanesio 520, tel. 02972/492577, lunch and dinner daily).

In an attractive building styled after Bariloche's landmark civic center, the awkwardly named **Centro de Turismo** (Padre Milanesio 586, tel. 02972/492555, lunch and dinner daily) has a mostly standard Argentine menu; the standout item is the butter-grilled trout (US$12).

Primarily a *parrilla*, **Ruca Hueney** (Padre Milanesio and Coronel Suárez, tel. 02972/491113, lunch and dinner daily) has a more diverse menu including trout and venison (try the *pollo al ajillo*, garlic chicken, US$10), offers good service even with large numbers of diners, and is now tobacco-free.

Across the plaza, **Tío Tom** (Lamadrid and San Martín, tel. 02972/492510) has Junín's best ice cream.

## Information

Facing Plaza San Martín, the **Subsecretaría de Turismo** (Padre Milanesio 596, tel. 02972/491160, www.junindelosandes.gov.ar, 8 A.M.–9 P.M. daily) answers questions, gives brochures, and sells fishing permits.

Immediately north, the **APN** office (Padre Milanesio 570, tel. 02972/492748, erratic opening times) provides information for Parque Nacional Lanín.

## Services

**Banco de la Provincia del Neuquén** (Av. San Martín and Lamadrid) has an ATM.

**Correo Argentino** is at Coronel Suárez and Don Bosco; the postal code is 8371. For long-distance, use the ***locutorio*** at Padre Milanesio 530, half a block north of the tourist office. **Arroba Computación** (Lamadrid 342) has Internet access.

**Laverap Pehuén** (Ginés Ponte 330) does the washing.

For medical emergencies, contact the **Hospital de Área** (Av. Antártida Argentina and Pasaje 2 de Abril, tel. 02972/492143).

## Getting There and Around

**Aeropuerto Aviador Carlos Campos-Chapelco** (RN 234 Km 24, tel. 02972/428388) lies midway between Junín and San Martín de los Andes. Air and bus schedules change frequently, especially in ski season. **Aerolíneas Argentinas** (Belgrano 949, tel. 02972/410588) flies regularly to Aeroparque Jorge Newbery. **American Jet** (tel. 0810/3459876, www.americanjet.com.ar) has five weekly services to Neuquén.

Services at Junín's **Terminal de Ómnibus** (Olavarría and Félix San Martín, tel. 02972/492038) resemble those at San Martín de los Andes, including trans-Andean buses to Chile.

**Castelli** (tel. 02972/491557) goes hourly to San Martín de los Andes (US$2, 50 min.), less often on Sunday.



# SAN MARTÍN DE LOS ANDES

Barely a century since its founding as a frontier fortress, San Martín de los Andes has become one of the lakes district's most fashionable resorts. Nestled in the hills near Lago Lácar, it owes its appeal to its surrounding scenery, the trout that thrash in Parque Nacional Lanín's lakes and streams, and the ski boom that began at nearby Chapelco in the 1940s.

San Martín itself is picturesque enough, thanks to the legacy of architect Alejandro Bustillo, whose rustically styled Centro Cívico builds on his designs at Bariloche. Unlike Bariloche, San Martín has shunned the high-rise horrors that have degraded Bustillo's legacy there; its biggest blight is the increasingly aggressive marketing of timeshares. The height limit has its own downside in promoting San Martín's perceived exclusivity—in a sense, it's Argentina's Jackson Hole, where fashion often trumps nature.

At Lago Lácar's east end, 642 meters above sea level, San Martín (population 28,000) is 189 kilometers north of Bariloche via RN 40, RN 231, and RN 234; it's 109 kilometers north of Villa La Angostura via RN 234. Via Junín and La Rinconada it's 259 kilometers and a faster alternative from Bariloche.

## Sights

The masterpiece of lavishly landscaped **Plaza San Martín** is Bustillo's former **Intendencia del Parque Nacional Lanín,** which matches the style of its Bariloche counterpart and has influenced architects and designers throughout the region. The exterior consists of roughly hewn blocks, rustically carved beams, attic windows that jut out from the main structure, and wooden roof shingles. Now combining a museum on the park's origins and natural history with its traditional information center, the **Museo del Parque Nacional Lanín** (Emilio Frey 749, tel. 02972/420664, free) is open 8 A.M.–8 P.M. daily in summer, 8 A.M.–8 P.M. weekdays only the rest of the year.

Across the plaza, the **Museo Primeros Pobladores** (Rosas 758, 02972/428676, ext. 2, museoprimerospobladores@yahoo.com.ar, 4–8 P.M. Tues.–Sat. in summer, 2–6 P.M. Tues.–Sat. the rest of the year, free) is a modest effort at acknowledging all the area's cultural influences, from pre-Columbian hunter-gatherers to settled Mapuche farmers and their struggles with the Spanish and Argentine invaders, and the European colonists who helped create the contemporary city. Exhibits include items such as arrowheads, spear points, and ceramics, and there's also an account of Parque Nacional Lanín's creation.

For four nights in 1952, Ernesto Guevara Lynch and his buddy Alberto Granados crashed on hay bales in the national park's barn in San Martín. That, apparently, was reason enough to turn the barn into the interactive **La Pastera Museo del Che** (Sarmiento and Rudecindo Roca, tel. 02972/411994, www.lapasteramuseoche.org.ar, 10 A.M.–1 P.M. and 5–8 P.M. Wed.–Mon., US$2.50 for foreigners), complete with video of Che's career and a shop to market Che souvenirs, including his books and those of his admirers. In reality, it's more a shrine than a museum; if there's a museum to

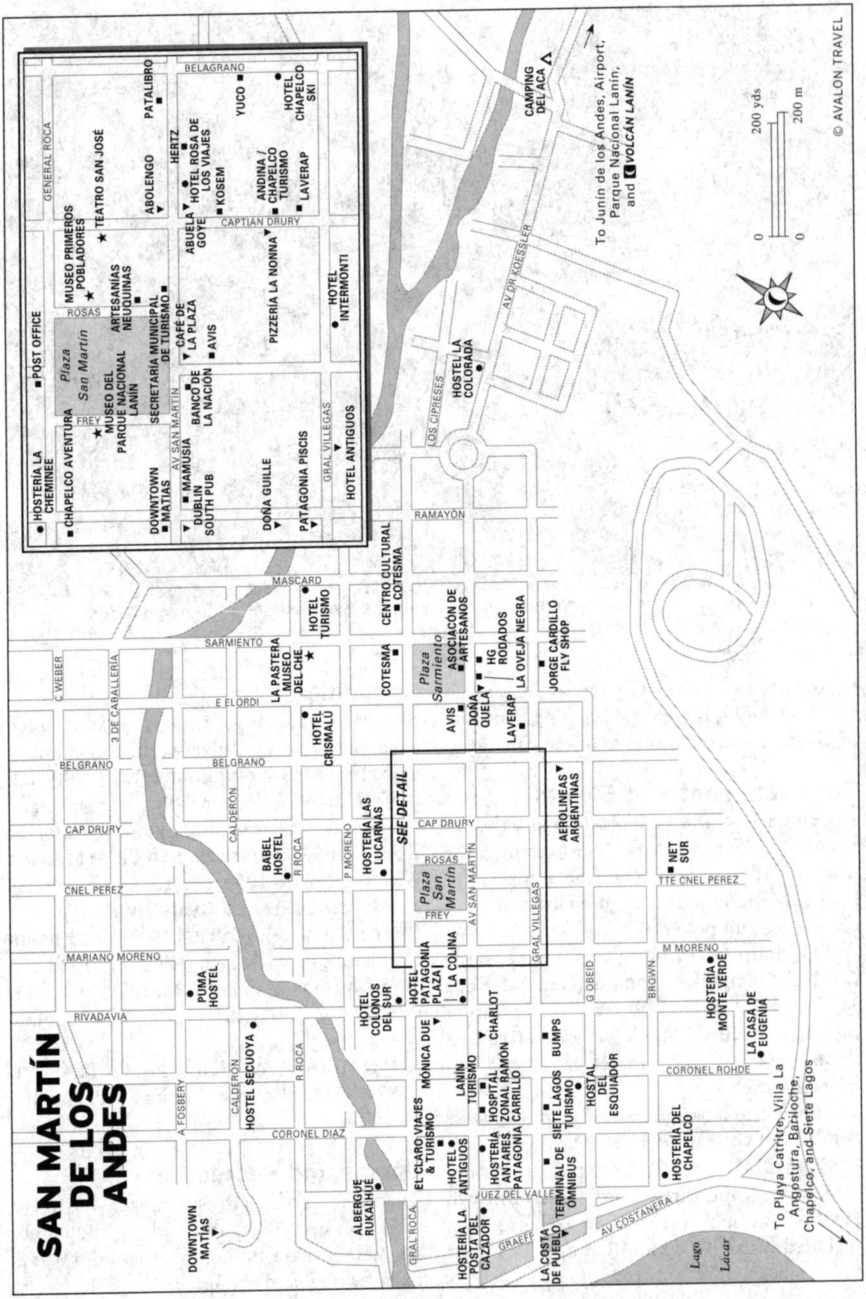


N. ARGENTINE PATAGONIA

© WAYNE BERNHARDSON

the former headquarters of Parque Nacional Lanín, now a museum, in San Martín de los Andes



be founded everywhere Guevara and Granados spent the night, there would be a near infinity of Guevara shrines throughout the Americas.

## Entertainment and Events

At February 4's **Día de la Fundación,** the anniversary of San Martín's 1898 founding, the military still marches down the avenues, followed by firefighters and an equestrian array of gauchos and polo players.

The main performing-arts outlet is the **Centro Cultural Cotesma** (General Roca 1154, tel. 02972/428399), which offers recent movies at its **Cine Amankay.** The **Teatro San José** (Capitán Drury 743, tel. 02972/428676) hosts live theater.

This is also a bar-goer's town, at places like **Dublin South Pub** (Av. San Martín 599, tel. 02972/410141), offering beer, pub grub, sidewalk seating, and wireless Internet; **Downtown Matías** (Av. San Martín 598); and also at its secluded hillside location (Coronel Díaz and Calderón, tel. 02972/421699).

## Shopping

San Martín's souvenir outlets start with Mapuche weavings, silverwork, and carvings at **Artesanías Neuquinas** (Rosas 790, tel. 02972/428396), a provincially sponsored crafts cooperative. There's also a good selection at Plaza Sarmiento's **Asociación de Artesanos** (Av. San Martín 1050, tel. 02972/429097).

For textiles, try **La Oveja Negra** (Av. San Martín 1025, tel. 02972/428039) or **Kosem** (Capitán Drury 836, tel. 02972/427562).

**Mamusia** (Av. San Martín 601, tel. 02972/427560) is a traditional chocolate shop.

**Patalibro** (Av. San Martín 884, tel. 02972/411485) carries books on Patagonia, including some in English.

## Sports and Recreation

Thanks to Lanín's proximity, San Martín is a mecca for everything from hiking and climbing to mountain biking, white-water rafting, trout fishing, and skiing.

## THE SLOPES OF CHAPELCO

Overlooking San Martín de los Andes, at a maximum elevation of 1,980 meters, Cerro Chapelco draws enthusiastic winter crowds to 28 different runs, the longest combination of which is about 5.3 kilometers. The diversity of conditions means it's suitable for both experienced skiers and novices. Several winter sports events take place annually, including the snowboard world cup, snow polo tournaments, and many ski championships.

**Chapelco Aventura** (Mariano Moreno 701, tel. 02972/427845, www.cerrochapelco.com) is the resort office in San Martín. Rental equipment is available onsite but also in town at **Bumps** (Villegas 465, tel. 02972/428491) and **La Colina** (San Martín 532, tel. 02972/427414).

Lift-ticket prices depend on timing; the season runs mid-June–mid-October but is subdivided into low, mid-, and peak season. For current rates, check Chapelco's website.

**HG Rodados** (Av. San Martín 1061, tel. 02972/427345) rents mountain bikes, which are ideal for secondary roads around Lago Lácar and the park.

Argentine rivers generally have lower flows and fewer rapids than their Chilean counterparts, but the Class II–IV Río Aluminé flows through spectacular scenery a couple hours north of San Martín. It's best with the spring runoff in November and December; contact **Siete Lagos Turismo** (Villegas 313, tel. 02972/427877, sietelagostmo@smandes.com.ar) or **Lanín Turismo** (Av. San Martín 437, local 3, tel. 02972/425808, www.laninturismo.com.ar).

Closer to San Martín, the Class II Río Hua Hum provides a gentler experience. Contact **El Claro Viajes & Turismo** (Coronel Díaz 751, tel. 02972/428876, www.elclaroturismo.com.ar), **Net Sur** (Teniente Coronel Pérez 1124, tel. 02972/427929, www.netsurpatagonia.com.ar), or **Yuco** (Belgrano 845, Local 12, tel. 02972/423150).

For hiking and climbing, contact **Rumbo Patagonia** (tel. 02944/15634070, www.rumbopatagonia.com.ar).

For fishing gear and advice, visit the **Jorge Cardillo Fly Shop** (Villegas 1061, tel. 02972/428372).

### Accommodations

Accommodations are abundant, but the best values go fast. Reservations are advisable—and single occupants usually have to pay double rates—in summer, at Semana Santa, and throughout ski season. The municipal tourist office, though, will make every effort to help find the best accommodations in your price range. The credit-card surcharge is usually high.

#### US$10-25

On the Junín highway, the wooded **Camping del ACA** (Av. Koessler 2176, tel. 02972/429430, US$25 per site for two people in summer) is spacious and shady, but the best sites go early. There are other campgrounds north and south of town, in Parque Nacional Lanín.

#### US$25-50

Named for the giant redwood in its garden, the HI affiliate **Hostel Secuoya** (Rivadavia 411, tel. 02972/424485, www.hostelsecuoya.com.ar, US$19 pp, US$43 d) has only two downstairs bathrooms and most of the beds upstairs, in rooms with thin walls. Still, it's friendly and well located, with wireless Internet and breakfast included.

In a red house with sparkling common areas, the 21-bed **Hostel La Colorada** (Av. Koessler 1614, tel. 02972/411041, www.lacoloradahostel.com.ar, US$19 pp) is an independent hostel that has mostly dorms but also one triple with shared bath. Rates include breakfast, use of PCs, and wireless Internet. Its main drawback is its location along the busy access road.

**Albergue Rukalhue** (Juez del Valle 682, tel. 02972/427431, www.rukalhue.com.ar, US$20 pp in dorms, US$61 d) offers respectable hostel accommodations, private rooms, and small apartments, including wireless Internet as well as breakfast in high season. The hostel rate also includes dinner in high season. Breakfast is not served off season.

**Babel Hostel** (Rudecindo Roca 720, tel. 02972/412120, www.babelhostel.com.ar, US$19–21 pp) is a cozy garden hostel with large common areas, dorms, and a double room. It has wireless Internet and breakfasts are included. Peak-season reservations are imperative at HI-affiliated **Puma Hostel** (Fosbery 535, tel. 02972/422443, www.pumahostel.com.ar), an attractive 50-bed facility north of the arroyo.

At one of the town's edges, well-located **Hotel Turismo** (Mascardi 517, tel. 02972/427592, www.hotelturismopatagonia.com, US$38 s, US$50–60 d) belongs to another era for the exterior and dining room's style. One of the best values in town, it has wireless Internet, self-service breakfast, and comfortable rooms—brighter on the street and newer upstairs. Thin walls are its main drawback.



### US$50-100

The handsome classic **Hotel Crismalú** (Rudecindo Roca 975, tel. 02972/427283, www.interpatagonia.com/crismalu, US$50 s, US$65 d) is showing its age but is still reasonable for what it offers. It has wireless Internet.

At the east end of town, on the road toward Junín, **Hostería Parque Los Andes** (RN 234 Km 2, tel. 02972/428211, www.interpatagonia.com/parquelosandes, US$65 s or d) retains its classic style, with bright and improved rooms. After Chilean poet Pablo Neruda fled over the Andes on horseback to avoid political persecution in 1949, he may have shared drinks with Juan Perón in the gallery bar.

**Hotel Rosa de los Viajes** (Av. San Martín 817, tel. 02972/427484, www.interpatagonia.com/rosahotel, US$69 s or d) is rather small and homey, but both foot and auto traffic are heavy in this part of town.

Central **Hotel Chapelco Ski** (Belgrano 869, tel. 02972/427480, www.chapelcoskihotel.com.ar, US$58 s, US$73 d) is a little worn and has limited parking but is otherwise OK.

Near the lake, **Hostería del Chapelco** (Brown 297, tel. 02972/427610, www.delchapelco.com.ar, US$65 s, US$80 d) has the best location of any hotel in its range with its dining room with lake views. It has wireless Internet in common areas and rooms are on the smallish side.

With responsive management, **Hostería Las Lucarnas** (Teniente Coronel Pérez 632, tel. 02972/427085, www.hosterialaslucarnas.com.ar, US$73 s, US$80 d) is a homey choice, with only 10 smallish rooms, a breakfast buffet, and amenities that include cable TV, wireless Internet, strongboxes, and parking. It's a much better value off season.

**Hotel Colonos del Sur** (Rivadavia 686, tel. 02972/427224, www.colonosdelsur.com.ar, US$85 s or d) has smallish rooms, wireless Internet, a hot tub, and a swimming pool.

Sedate **Hotel Intermonti** (Villegas 717, tel./fax 02972/427454, www.hotelintermonti.com.ar, US$73 s, US$88 d) has 24 well-furnished midsize rooms, plus attractive common areas and wireless Internet.

Some upstairs rooms have lake views at **Hostería La Posta del Cazador** (Av. San Martín 175, tel. 02972/427501, www.postadelcazador.com.ar, US$88–103 s or d), a family-run Middle European–style place on a quiet block near the lake, with larger superior rooms, wireless Internet, and parking.

Try also **Hostal del Esquiador** (Coronel Rohde 975, tel. 02972/427674, www.hostaldelesquiador.com.ar, US$93 s, US$98 d), a block from the bus terminal, which has clean pleasant rooms with appealing designer touches.

### US$100-200

**Hotel Antiguos** (Coronel Díaz 753, tel. 02972/411876, www.hotelantiguos.com.ar, US$102 s or d) is a luminous 12-room hotel with natural wood details and some luxuries, including Jacuzzis in every bath. While the rooms are on the small side, they are stylish.

On a quiet location **Hostería Monte Verde**

(Rivadavia 1165, tel. 02972/410129, www.hosteriamonteverde.com.ar, from US$113 s or d) is a functional and very comfortable place, with a swimming pool and sauna, and where more expensive rooms have their own Jacuzzi and fireplace.

Attractively located at the end of a leafy street, **La Casa de Eugenia** (Coronel Díaz 1186, tel. 02972/427206, www.lacasadeeugenia.com.ar, US$150–180 s or d) stands out as a 1927 wooden residence in impeccable condition. Best choice in town, this family-run *hostería* has nine rooms—five suites of which face a manicured garden with a small heated pool—that perfectly combine an old ambience with modern functionality. Breakfast's sweet delicacies are also served at the tea room which is open to nonguests as well.

Four-star **Hotel Patagonia Plaza** (Av. San Martín and Rivadavia, tel./fax 02972/422280, www.hotelpatagoniaplaza.com.ar, from US$138 s, US$173 d) has become one of the city's premier accommodations, with 90 rooms ranging from relatively simple doubles to sprawling suites.

**Hostería La Cheminée** (General Roca and Mariano Moreno, tel. 02972/427617, www.hosterialacheminee.com.ar, US$198 s or d) has upgraded into one of the town's most stylish hotels, featuring an indoor pool, sauna, wine bar, art gallery, and many other distinctive amenities.

### OVER US$200

San Martín's latest luxury option, **Hostería Antares Patagonia** (Av. San Martín 251, tel. 02972/427670, www.antarespatagonia.com.ar, US$240–298 s or d) is a recycled and expanded family mansion, on a large lot, with 10 spacious suites (superior ones have their own Jacuzzi and fireplace), a heated pool, sauna, business center, and other spacious common areas.

## Food

Try **Café de la Plaza** (Av. San Martín and Teniente Coronel Pérez, tel. 02972/428488) for coffee, croissants, sandwiches, desserts and good short orders. Cozy, comfortable **Abolengo** (Av. San Martín 806, tel. 02972/427732) is ideal for rich hot chocolate on a cool night. More excellent chocolate and cakes are at **Abuela Goye** (Av. San Martín 807, tel. 02972/429409), also with outstanding ice cream. Attractive **La Casa de Eugenia** (Coronel Díaz 1186, tel. 02972/427206) is a fine teahouse.

**Pizzería La Nonna** (Capitán Drury 857, tel. 02972/422223) serves about 30 varieties of pizzas (from US$10), including wild boar, trout, and venison, plus calzones and empanadas. It gets noisy, though—either take earplugs, go early or late, or consider takeout.

For lunch or dinner with lake views, there are few tables with the setting to match **La Costa del Pueblo** (Av. Costanera, by the pier, tel. 02972/429289), where the menu includes the Argentine standards (from US$8) and regional specialties (US$15–20).

Reservations are advisable for **Mónica Due** (Rivadavia 759, tel. 02972/423643), which has only seven tables and authentic Italian pastas, from Bologna, served with genuine warmth. Mediocre pesto may be the main shortcoming of Italian-Argentine cuisine, but here it's the real thing. Prices are reasonable, around US$12–14 per entrée.

Dinner lines form early outside popular *parrilla* **Patagonia Piscis** (Villegas 598, tel. 02972/423247), which also serves fish and game (most entrées are in the US$8–15 range). The service can be erratic, though.

A former hotel built in 1910 houses **Doña Quela** (Av. San Martín 1017, tel. 02972/420670), with a varied menu including pasta (from US$8) and trout (from US$15).

For ice cream, try **Charlot** (Av. San Martín 467, tel. 02972/428561), with dozens of imaginative flavors.

## Information

At Plaza San Martín's east end, the **Secretaría Municipal de Turismo** (Av. San Martín and Rosas, tel. 02972/427347, www.sanmartindelosandes.gov.ar) provides advice, maps, and brochures, plus an up-to-the-minute database of accommodations and rates; in peak season, though, high demand can test its resources. Hours are 8 A.M.–9 P.M. daily.

The APN's **Centro de Visitantes del Parque Nacional Lanín** (Emilio Frey 749, tel. 02972/420664, lanin@apn.gov.ar, 8 A.M.–8 P.M. daily in summer, 8 A.M.–8 P.M. weekdays only the rest of the year) provides park information, with a selection of maps and brochures.

## Services

**Banco de la Nación** (Av. San Martín 687) and several others have ATMs. **Andina Internacional** (Capitán Drury 876) is the only exchange house.

**Correo Argentino** (General Roca and Teniente Coronel Pérez) is the post office. **Cotesma** (General Roca and Sarmiento) has telephone and Internet.

**Chapelco Turismo** (Capitín Drury 876, Local 1, tel. 02972/427550) offers conventional excursions to Parque Nacional Lanín, Villa La Angostura, and other destinations.

For laundry, **Laverap** (tel. 02972/428820) has two locations: Capitán Drury 880 and Villegas 972.

**Hospital Zonal Ramón Carrillo** (Av. San Martín and Coronel Rohde, tel. 02972/427211) is central.

## Getting There

Air and bus schedules change frequently, especially in ski season. **Aerolíneas Argentinas** (Belgrano 949, tel. 02972/410588) flies regularly to Aeroparque Jorge Newbery. **American Jet** (tel. 0810/3459876, www.americanjet.com.ar) has five weekly services to Neuquén.

San Martín's **Terminal de Ómnibus** (Villegas 231, tel. 02972/427044) has regional, long-distance, and Chilean connections.

**Castelli** (tel. 02972/491557) goes hourly to Junín de los Andes (US$2, 50 min.), less often on Sunday.

**Ko Ko** (tel. 02972/427422) goes to Villa La Angostura (US$10, 2.5 hours) in summer via the scenic Siete Lagos route, continuing to Bariloche, but most services to Bariloche (US$15, four hours) use the longer but smoother Rinconada route. **Albus** (tel. 02972/428100) and **Vúa Bariloche** (tel. 02972/422800) also go to Villa La Angostura, 3–4 times daily by the Siete Lagos route, with one service to Bariloche.

In summer, Ko Ko goes to the Chilean border at Paso Hua Hum and also to nearby lakes. **Igi-Llaima** (tel. 02972/428100) and **Empresa San Martín** (tel. 02972/427294) alternate service to Pucón (US$25, five hours) and Temuco, Chile (US$25, seven hours), Monday–Saturday; San Martín continues to Valdivia.

Other typical destinations include Neuquén (US$30–43, seven hours) and Buenos Aires (US$110–145, 19–22 hours).

## Getting Around

**Aeropuerto Aviador Carlos Campos-Chapelco** (RN 234 Km 24, tel. 02972/428388) lies midway between San Martín and Junín de los Andes. A taxi costs around US$18.

At the foot of Obeid, **Naviera Lácar y Nonthué** (Av. Costanera s/n, tel. 02972/427380) sails 3–8 times daily to Quila Quina (US$20 round-trip; national park admission fee not included), on Lago Lácar's south shore, and daily in summer to Hua Hum (US$60 round-trip; park admission fee not included).

For rental cars, try **Avis** (Teniente Coronel Pérez and Av. San Martín, tel. 02972/411141) or **Hertz** (Av. San Martín 831, 1st floor, tel. 02972/420280).

# PARQUE NACIONAL LANÍN

In westernmost Neuquén, stretching from Lago Ñorquinco in the north to a diagonal that runs between Lago Nonthué on the Chilean border and Confluencia on RN 40, Parque Nacional Lanín comprises 412,000 hectares of arid steppe, mid-altitude forests ringing glacial lakes and streams, alpine highlands, and volcanic summits. From Aluminé in the north to San Martín de los Andes in the south, several longitudinal highways intersect graveled westbound access roads.

When the eastward-flowing Pleistocene glaciers receded, they left a series of deep finger lakes draining into the Río Limay's upper and lower tributaries. Unlike Parque Nacional Nahuel Huapi, to the south, these lakes and the Valdivian forests surrounding them have suffered less commercial development, but they are recovering from timber exploitation and livestock grazing that persist in some areas.

Most park visitors use either Junín or San Martín as their base.

### Flora and Fauna

Up to 3,000 millimeters of precipitation per annum supports dense humid Valdivian woodlands. Lanín's signature species is the coniferous *pehuén* or monkey puzzle tree *(Araucaria araucana),* for centuries a subsistence resource for the Mapuches and Pehuenches (a sub-group whose own name stresses their dependence on the tree's edible nuts). Along with the broadleaf deciduous southern beech, *raulí,* the *pehuén* forms part of a transitional forest overlapping southern beech species that dominate the more southerly Patagonian forests, such as the *coihue, lenga,* and *ñire.* In places, the solid bamboo *colihue* forms almost impenetrable thickets.

At higher elevations, above 1,600 meters, cold and wind reduce the vegetative cover to shrubs and grasses. At lower elevations, the drier climate supports shrubs and steppe grasses.

Except for its trout, Lanín is less celebrated for its wildlife than for its landscapes. Fortunate visitors may see the secretive spaniel-size deer known as the pudu or the larger Andean huemul. The major predator is the puma, present on the steppes and in the forest, while the torrent duck frequents the faster streams and the Andean condor glides on the heights. The lakes and rivers attract many other birds.

### Sector Aluminé

Immediately west of Aluminé, RP 18 follows the south bank of the Río Rucachoroi for 23 kilometers to Lago Rucachoroi, site of a Mapuche reserve. From Rahue, 16 kilometers south of Aluminé, RP 46 leads west to **Lago Quillén,** a beautiful area of dense forests that's also home to Mapuche families.

Nineteen kilometers north of Aluminé via RP 23, scenic RP 11 climbs westward through araucaria forests along the Río Pulmarí and **Lago Ñorquinco,** the park's northernmost access point. On what would be an excellent mountain-bike route, the road loops north-northeast toward the Chilean border at Icalma and the small Argentine resort of Villa Pehuenia.

### Volcán Lanín

Looming above the landscape, straddling the Chilean border at 3,776 meters above sea level, lopsided Lanín is the literal and metaphorical center of its namesake park. Covered by permanent snow, rising 1,500 meters above any other nearby peak, its irregular cone is a beacon for hundreds of kilometers to the east and, where the rugged terrain permits, to the north and south.

### Sector Lago Tromen

From a junction 16 kilometers north of Junín, northwesterly RP 60 leads to the Chilean border at Paso Mamuil Malal, where Lago Tromen marks the most convenient approach to the summit of **Volcán Lanín.** Because of the

© WAYNE BERNHARDSON

Volcán Lanín rises above the Patagonian steppe.

## ONE TRAIL FOR THE LAKES

In early 2011, Argentina opened the first 22 sections of the **Huella Andina,** a public footpath now covering about 30 percent of its total 560 kilometers across the lakes district's woodlands. Most of the area is protected not only under Argentina's national park administration but since 2007 as part of UNESCO's Andina Norpatagónica World Biosphere Reserve.

The first of its kind in Argentina, the north-south trail will, when finished, connect Neuquén's Lago Aluminé with northwestern Chubut's tiny Lago Baggilt. Like the Sendero de Chile, it uses existing but rehabbed paths for pedestrians, allowing bikers and horseback riders in some sections as well, and demanding a few lake crossings. A distinctive blue and white circle painted alongside the itinerary identifies this route.

As the trail steadily improves, more information will be available at the local APN and tourist offices.



northeasterly exposure, hiking and climbing routes open earlier here than on the southern side, which lies partly in Chile.

Unless you hire a registered national park guide, before climbing Lanín a permission must be obtained from the APN at its onsite Centro de Informes, which will ask to inspect your gear; it should contain crampons, an ice axe, plastic tools, VHF radio, helmet, a portable stove, first-aid kit, and appropriate clothing and peripherals (gloves, hats, insulated jackets, sunglasses, and sunscreen). As the maximum number of hikers authorized to climb at the same time is 60 and reservations are not possible, you might have to wait there.

From the APN's Centro de Informes it's one hour to start the ascent along **Espina de Pescado,** and another hour for the steeper **Camino de Mulas,** which leads after three hours to the **Refugio Militar Nuevo** (elevation 2,315 meters). Less than an hour above is the **Refugio Club Andino Junín de los Andes (CAJA)** (elevation 2,600 meters); beyond here, snow gear is essential for the following 6–7 long hours up to the summit.

### Sector Lago Huechulafquen

About four kilometers north of Junín, RP 61 leads northwest along the Río Chimehuín and Lago Huechulafquen's north shore for 52 kilometers to Puerto Canoa and **Lago Paimún** (at road's end). En route, a few trailheads lead north; the most interesting is the **Cara Sur** (Southern Face) approach to Volcán Lanín along the wooded Arroyo Rucu Leufú.

From the Piedra Mala campground at Lago Paimún, a 30-minute hike goes to **Cascada El Saltillo,** a 20-meter waterfall. In summer when Río Paimún and Arroyo Frutillar are usually fordable, it's possible to walk around Lago Paimún. Otherwise, for US$3 summer hikers can do the boat crossing at La Unión narrows, which separates Huechulafquen and Paimún, to basic **Camping Ecufén,** on Paimún's south shore, one of several Mapuche family-run campsites in the park.

From La Unión, the trail continues through *coihue* and *pehuén* forest for about three hours to **Aila** campground and another eight hours to **Termas de Epulafquen,** where a new resort has made exclusive use of the hot springs there. From Epulafquen, RP 62 returns to Junín de los Andes.

For non-hikers, the **Catamarán José Julián** (Av. San Martín 643, San Martín de los Andes, tel. 02972/429264, www.catamaranjosejulian.com.ar) offers a 90-minute lake excursion from Puerto Canoa over Huechulafquen and Epulafquen (US$24 pp) 3–5 times daily in summer, less frequently the rest of the year.

### Lago Lolog and Lago Lácar

About 15 kilometers north of San Martín, Lago Lolog has several campgrounds and regular summer transportation; it's particularly popular with windsurfers.

San Martín's own Lago Lácar is wilder

© WAYNE BERNHARDSON

Windsurfers flock to Lago Lolog.

toward the Chilean border, where there is camping, hiking, and white-water rafting at the outlet of the Río Hua Hum.

At the foot of Obeid, **Naviera Lácar y Nonthué** (Av. Costanera s/n, tel. 02972/427380) sails 3–8 times daily to Quila Quina (US$20 round-trip; national park admission fee not included), on Lago Lácar's south shore, and daily in summer to Hua Hum (US$60 round-trip; park admission fee not included).

## Accommodations and Food

Except in nearby towns, accommodations and food options are few. Organized campgrounds with hot showers and other services charge slightly more than so-called *agreste* (wild) sites, which cost around US$6 per person.

**Sector Lago Tromen:** Reservations are essential for the four singles and six twin rooms at **Hostería San Huberto** (RP 60 Km 12.5, tel. 02972/421875, www.sanhubertolodge.com.ar, US$300–375 s, US$440–560 d, with full board), which appeals chiefly to fly-fishing fanatics.

**Sector Lago Huechulafquen:** Several Mapuche community-run organized campgrounds offer good services (US$7–8 pp) along the shores of Lago Huechulafquen and Lago Paimún, including **Camping Bahía Cañicul** (RP 61 Km 48), which has a small store, but supplies are cheaper and more diverse in Junín. **Camping Raquithué** (RP 61 Km 54) and **Camping Piedra Mala** (RP 61 Km 60) are other options.

A few kilometers before Lago Paimún, **Hostería Huechulafquen** (RP 61 Km 51, tel. 02972/427598, www.hosteriahuechulafquen.com, US$113 pp with half board) is pleasant enough. **Hostería Paimún** (RP 61 Km 57, tel. 02972/491758, hosteriapaimun@jdeandes.com.ar, US$108 pp with half board, US$120 pp full board) is primarily a fishing lodge.

**Lago Lolog:** Basic **Camping Puerto Arturo** charges US$8 per person.

**Hua Hum:** Westbound from San Martín, gravel RP 48 follows Lago Lácar's and Nonthué's north shores to the Chilean border at Hua Hum. En route, open mid-December through Semana Santa, **Café Quechuquina** (RP 48 Km 30) is a rustic teahouse with exceptional cakes and cookies; hours are noon–7:30 P.M. daily for lunch and tea. Though lacking accommodations, it enjoys lake access and makes an ideal day trip.

## Other Practicalities

In addition to the APN visitor center at San Martín, there are ranger stations at all major lakes and some other points. While the rangers are helpful, they do not, in general, have maps or other printed matter. The US$13 per person (for foreigners) admission fee must be paid at the various park entrances.

San Martín de los Andes and Junín de los Andes are the main gateways, but public transportation is limited. On international buses to Chile, via the northerly Tromen (or Mamuil Malal) pass, through passengers have priority.

# VILLA LA ANGOSTURA AND VICINITY

On Lago Nahuel Huapi's north shore, Villa La Angostura lies within Bariloche's economic orbit. Its proximity to less developed parts of the lake, to Parque Nacional Los Arrayanes, and to the Cerro Bayo winter-sports center, though, has helped established its own identity—with an air of exclusivity—for both Argentines and foreigners. It has excellent accommodations and restaurants, with prices on the high side because it gets hordes of Chilean visitors thanks to the paved international highway.

Villa La Angostura (population 11,100) is 80 kilometers northwest of Bariloche via RN 40 and RN 231 (the highway to Osorno, Chile) and 109 kilometers south of San Martín de los Andes via RN 234, the scenic Siete Lagos (Seven Lakes) route that's now being paved. It's 870 meters above sea level, but the mountains rise sharply from the lakeshore.

Many services line both sides of RN 231 (Av. Arrayanes and its westward extension, Av. Siete Lagos) as it passes directly through El Cruce. Three kilometers south, residential La Villa (also referred to as El Puerto) also has a cluster

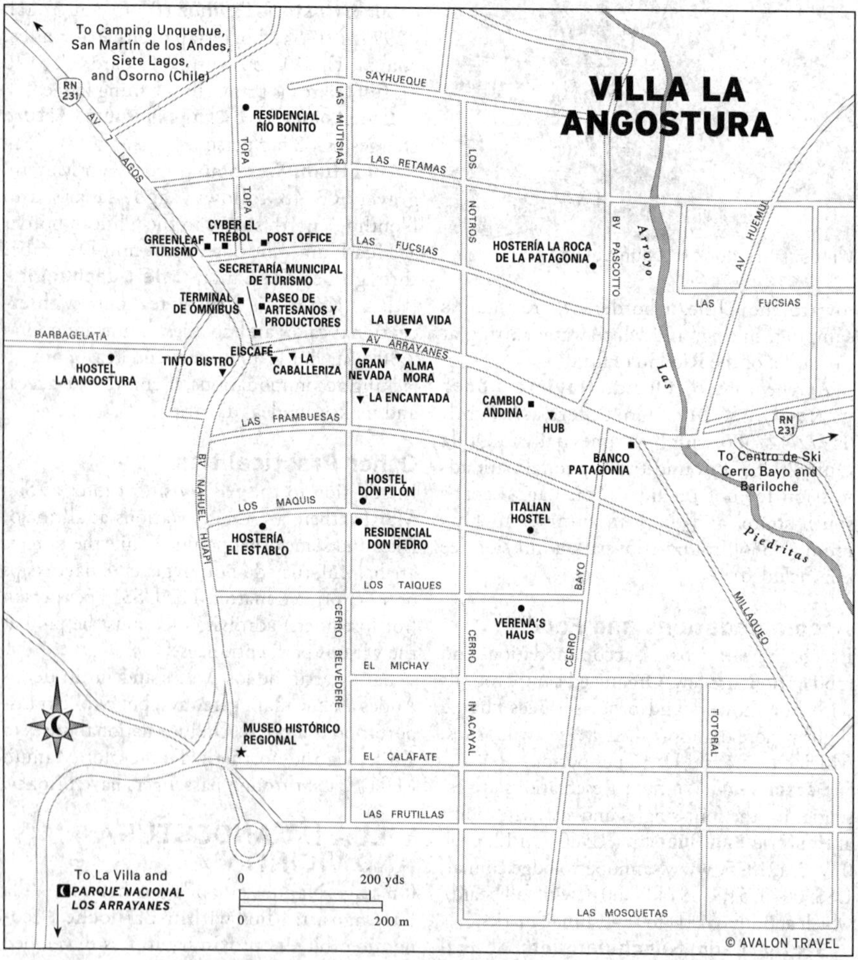

of hotels and restaurants; Parque Nacional Los Arrayanes occupies all of Península Quetrihué, the southward-jutting peninsula linked to La Villa by the isthmus that gives Villa La Angostura its name (The Narrows).

## Sights

Foot, bicycle, and kayak are the best ways to see Villa La Angostura and nearby sights. For hiking in the mountains, where the trails are too steep and narrow for bicycles, consider hiring a taxi or *remise* to the trailhead.

At La Villa, the **Museo Histórico Regional** (Blvd. Nahuel Huapi 1900, 10 A.M.–5 P.M. Tues.–Sat., free) deals primarily with pioneer timber-cutting, the agriculture that followed it, the families who established themselves here, and the binational Mapuche legacy.

From June to September, nine kilometers east of El Cruce, the **Centro de Ski Cerro Bayo** (Las Fucsias 121, Oficina 3, in town, tel. 02944/494189, www.cerrobayoweb.com) operates 12 kilometers of runs ranging from 1,050 to 1,782 meters above sea level, with eight chairlifts and four tow bars. Cerro Bayo also has restaurants and rental equipment on-site; for lift ticket prices, consult the website.

From Avenida Siete Lagos, 800 meters west of El Cruce, the Cacique Antriao road leads to a wide parking area, from which a two-kilometer trail reaches **Mirador Belvedere,** for views along Lago Correntoso to the north, the implausibly short Río Correntoso that connects it to Lago Nahuel Huapi, and the hoary western peaks that mark the Chilean border.

About midway up the forest trail, an eastbound one leads to **Cascada Inacayal,** a 50-meter waterfall. For experienced trekkers only, another trail to 1,992-meter **Cerro Belvedere** climbs through *coihue* forest before dipping into a saddle and then ascending steeply over Cerro Falso Belvedere before continuing to the summit.

## ☾ Parque Nacional Los Arrayanes

Local folklore says Walt Disney's cartoon feature *Bambi* modeled its forest after the *arrayán* woodland at the tip of Península Quetrihué, a former *estancia* that became a national park in 1971. With their bright white flowers, the eye-catching red-barked forests of *Luma apiculata* do bear a resemblance, but a Disney archivist has pointed out that *Bambi* was in production before Walt's 1941 trip to Argentina, and that he never visited the area.

So close to La Villa that it feels more like a sprawling city park—it's larger than the town itself—Los Arrayanes occupies Quetrihué's entire 1,753 hectares, which stretch south into Lago Nahuel Huapi. Its namesake forest covers only about 20 hectares, but the rest of the peninsula bristles with trees like the *maitén* and the southern beeches *coihue* and *ñire,* as well as colorful shrubs like the *notro* and *chilco,* and dense bamboo thickets of *colihue.*

The park's floral standout is the *arrayán,* whose individual specimens reach up to 25 meters and 650 years of age, but it's also ideal for hiking and mountain biking—the undulating 12-kilometer trail to or from the peninsula's tip is a perfect half-day excursion (on a bicycle or doing one way by boat and the other on foot) or a full day by hiking in both directions. Argentine rangers often exaggerate the time needed on certain trails, but the three hours they suggest is about right for this walk in the woods, which passes a pair of lakes. Only at the park portal, near La Villa, are there any steep segments.

Before starting any hike in the park and within the previous 48 hours to the date of the hike, a free form provided at ANP's offices (also available online on the park's webpage) or at the Club Andino must be filled in to keep a record at the national park's *Registro de Trekking* and to show upon park rangers' request. Access for hikers is permitted only up to 1 P.M. and up to 2 P.M. for bikers. Bikes can be rented at La Villa.

At the portal, rangers collect a US$13 admission charge (US$5 for Argentine residents); even those whose only goal is the 20-minute stroll to the panoramic **Mirador Arrayán** must pay the fee. Near the dock at the peninsula's southern tip, a *confitería* with a cozy fireplace serves sandwiches, coffee, and hot chocolate.

From the Bahía Mansa dock near park headquarters, non-hikers can reach the *arrayán* forest in about 45 minutes on the *Catamarán Futaleufú,* run by El Cruce's **Greenleaf Turismo** (Av. Siete Lagos 118, 1st floor, tel. 02944/494405, www.bosquelosarrayanes.com.ar), 1–3 services daily; the cost is US$25 one-way, US$50 round-trip, plus a small boarding tax and the park admission fee.

From the Bahía Brava dock across the isthmus, the newer *Catamarán Patagonia Argentina* (tel. 02944/494463, www.catamaranpatagonia.com.ar) runs a slightly cheaper service (US$24 one-way, US$40 round-trip, plus a small boarding tax and the park's admission fee), 1–3 times daily.

## Shopping and Events

Local artisans, brewers, and other food producers sell their stuff at El Cruce's **Paseo de Artesanos y Productores** (just behind the bus terminal), and also at **Paseo del Puerto** (at Bahía Mansa), daily in summer.

For four days, early February's provincial **Fiesta de los Jardines** (Garden Festival) occupies center stage.

## Sports and Recreation

Hikers must register at APN's office or online (www.nahuelhuapi.gov.ar) within 48 hours prior to starting any hike in the parks.

English-speaking Anthony Hawes operates **Alma Sur Eco Trips** (tel. 02944/15-564724, www.almasur.com), with activities ranging from hiking and riding to mountain biking, fly-fishing, and white-water rafting and kayaking.

## Accommodations

In the recent past, Villa La Angostura was almost exclusively upscale, but recent developments include some fine budget options.

Some 500 meters west of the tourist office, **Camping Unquehue** (Av. Siete Lagos 727, tel. 02944/494103, www.campingunquehue.com.ar, US$10 pp plus US$4 per tent) offers wooded sites, with hot showers in the communal baths. They also run small modern apartments (US$75 for two people).

The well-organized and lively HI-affiliate **Hostel La Angostura** (Barbagelata 157, tel. 02944/494834, www.hostellaangostura.com.ar, US$18 pp, US$55 d) is an imposing alpine-style building on spacious grounds, with wireless Internet and all rooms with private baths; breakfast is included. The quiet, cyclists-oriented **Italian Hostel** (Los Maquis 215, tel. 02944/494376, www.italianhostel.com.ar, US$19 pp, US$55 d, closed May–Sept.) has functional rooms and shared baths, wireless Internet, and a lovely garden and orchard.

On attractive wooded grounds, **Bajo Cero Hostel** (Av. Siete Lagos 1200, tel. 02944/495454, www.bajocerohostel.com, US$20 pp, US$80 d) is well-run and has the usual amenities. Rooms have their own bathrooms.

El Cruce's **Don Pilón** (Belvedere and Los Maquis, tel. 02944/494269, www.hosteldonpilon.com, US$20 pp, US$60 d) is a very well-cared place run by Agustina and Luis, heirs of a local pioneer. Delicious home-made breakfasts, a fireplace, wireless Internet, and parking attract families and couples alike. Discounts for longer stays apply; all rooms have private baths. Two blocks north of the bus terminal, homey and very good value **Residencial Río Bonito** (Topa Topa 260, tel. 02944/494110, www.riobonitopatagonia.com.ar, US$58 d) enjoys a quiet garden setting and has been attractively refurbished thanks to new young owners. It has wireless Internet and parking.

About one kilometer west of El Cruce, **Hostería Las Cumbres** (Av. Siete Lagos s/n, tel. 02944/494945, www.hosterialascumbres.com, US$70 s, US$83 d) is an eight-room, owner-operated hotel that's a fine value.

With friendly management and traditional Euro-Andean style, on a large lot in a quiet area, **Hostería La Roca de la Patagonia** (Blvd. Pascotto 155, tel. 02944/494497, www.larocadelapatagonia.com.ar, US$83 s or d) offers 10 large comfortable rooms and a lounge with a great view on its upper floor, while the dining room is on street level.

Dating from 1938, originally built for the APN, La Villa's lakeside classic **Hotel**

N. ARGENTINE PATAGONIA

**Angostura** (Nahuel Huapi 1911, tel. 02944/494224, www.hotelangostura.com, US$85–98 d) has 20 rooms, some with lake views, and three separate bungalows sleeping up to six people. While its aged floors are creaky and the hot water seeps slowly through the pipes for the morning's first shower, this once-romantic hotel still has style, personality, good beds, no TVs in the rooms, wireless Internet, a restaurant, and friendly service.

El Cruce's **Hostería Verena's Haus** (Los Taiques 268, tel. 02944/494467, www.verenas-haus.com.ar, US$88 s or d) is a bed-and-breakfast—a little overpriced in high season, with comfortable beds, and small but functional baths. It also has off-street parking in a large garden, and wireless Internet through most of the building.

In Puerto Manzano, about six kilometers southeast of El Cruce, the eight-room **Hostería Naranjo en Flor** (Chucao 62, tel. 02944/475320, www.naranjoenflor.com.ar, US$113–150 d) occupies a forested lot with views of Lago Nahuel Huapi and the Andes. Premium rooms have their own fireplace and Jacuzzi. It also has a pool and a restaurant that pulls in nonguests as well.

Set among large lush gardens, **Hostería El Establo** (Los Maquis 56, tel. 02944/494142, www.hosteriaelestablo.com.ar, US$78 s, US$103 d) is an Andean lodge that offers 14 comfortable rooms with individualized decor, plus engaging common areas, with an excellent buffet breakfast. It's one of the town's best values.

Across the Río Correntoso, three kilometers northwest of El Cruce, the historic **Correntoso Lake & River Hotel** (cell 02944/15-619728, tel. 011/4803-0030 in Buenos Aires, www.correntoso.com, US$405–635 s or d) started as a fishing lodge in 1917 and became a major attraction before burning down. Once nearly abandoned, it's undergone a rehab that's restored its former glory plus—there's a spa, a lakeside fishing bar, a wine bar, and an outstanding restaurant as well.

A short distance west of town, the **Sol Arrayán Hotel & Spa** (RN 231 Km 64.5, tel. 02944/488000, www.solarrayan.com, US$260–428 s or d) benefits from a sloping lot that insulates it from highway noise. It benefits even more from assiduous service and 42 luminous lake-view rooms with balconies, plus common areas that include a restaurant, wine bar, and a spa that includes an indoor/outdoor pool.

The area's standout is the Relais & Chateaux affiliate **Las Balsas Gourmet Hotel & Spa** (tel. 02944/494308, www.lasbalsas.com, US$480 d and up), a 12-room, three-suite classic south of El Cruce. All rooms have lake views; rates include unlimited spa access and breakfast, and there's a highly regarded hybrid restaurant with French and traditional Argentine dishes.

## Food

In addition to hotel restaurants, Villa La Angostura offers a diversity of dining options at moderate to upmarket prices.

**Alma Mora** (Av. Arrayanes 156, tel. 02944/488145, lunch and dinner daily) is a fine and modern café and bistro with wireless Internet, a few tables, and comfortable couches. **La Buena Vida** (Av. Arrayanes 167, Local 4, tel. 02944/495200, lunch and dinner daily) is a small, homey place that serves fine pastas with nearly 20 different sauces, such as *sorrentinos Buena Vida* (US$7) with a four-cheese and Patagonian mushroom sauce.

Highly regarded as a budget choice, **Gran Nevada** (Av. Arrayanes 106, tel. 02944/494512, lunch and dinner daily) offers generous portions of the Argentine standards at very low prices (US$5–8). Also popular for its generous portions and more elaborate quality food is **Hub** (Av. Arrayanes 256, tel. 02944/495700, www.hubpatagonia.com, lunch and dinner daily), where most entrées are in the US$13–17 range. Go early before its bar gets too lively.

Not necessarily the area's best, but conceivably its best value, moderately priced **La Encantada** (Cerro Belvedere 69, tel. 02944/495515, lunch and dinner Tues.–Sun.) has a mud oven for roasting trout and lamb (US$15–18), and serves exceptional *ahumados* (smoked appetizers), exquisite trout empanadas, and fine pizzas and pastas, with attentive service (including savvy wine recommendations).

Set on wooded grounds, Puerto Manzano's **Waldhaus** (Av. Arrayanes 6431, tel. 02944/475323, www.saboresdelneuquen.com.ar) serves Continental-style dishes like fondue, goulash, and raclette, with a Patagonian touch. With entrées well upwards of US$20, chef Leo Morsella's restaurant is open for lunch and for dinner (when reservations are obligatory), with a fine wine list.

Under the same ownership as Waldhaus, **La Caballeriza** (Av. Arrayanes 44, tel. 02944/494248, www.lacaballeriza-argentina.com, lunch and dinner daily) is a *parrilla* that has several branches in Buenos Aires, but this is the first in Patagonia. *Cordero a las brasas* (grilled lamb) is served for two people for US$30. It has kept the pastas and desserts of Morsella's previous restaurant, La Macarena (try *negra tentación*, a highly rich chocolate blend).

Reservations are critical at the star of the cuisine scene, the **Tinto Bistro** (Blvd. Nahuel Huapi 34, tel. 02944/494924, www.tintobistro.com). Run by brother-to-royalty Martín Zorreguieta (sister Máxima married Holland's Prince William in 2002), it offers Asian/Mediterranean/Americas fusion food with Patagonian ingredients, on a seasonal variation and with entrées in the US$16–21 range. Open for dinner only, it offers the area's finest wine list (including very expensive vintages). On Thursdays after 1 A.M. in high season it opens as a bar.

The best ice creams are at **Eiscafé** (Av. Arrayanes 40, tel. 02944/495671), which carries a selection of premium ice cream flavors from El Bolsón's Jauja, plus cakes and coffee.

### Information and Services

The **Secretaría Municipal de Turismo** (Av. Arrayanes 9, El Cruce, tel. 02944/494124, www.villalaangostura.gov.ar) is open 8:30 A.M.–9 P.M. daily, closing an hour earlier in winter.

The APN's **Seccional Villa La Angostura** (Blvd. Nahuel Huapi 2193, tel. 02944/494152) is in La Villa, where hikers must register (if they haven't done so already online: www.nahuelhuapi.gov.ar).

Virtually all services are in El Cruce, where **Banco Patagonia** (Millaqueo 10) has an ATM. **Cambio Andina** (Av. Arrayanes 256) is an exchange house. **Correo Argentino** is at Las Fucsias 121; the postal code is 8407. **Cyber El Trébol** (Las Fucsias and Topa Topa) has long-distance phones and Internet connections.

### Getting There

El Cruce's convenient **Terminal de Ómnibus** (Av. Siete Lagos and Av. Arrayanes) has frequent connections to Bariloche, several buses daily to San Martín de los Andes via the scenic Siete Lagos route, and long-distance services to Neuquén. Chile-bound buses from Bariloche stop here, but reservations are advisable because they often run full.

Sample destinations include Bariloche (US$6, 1.5 hours), San Martín de los Andes (US$10, 2.5 hours), and Neuquén (US$34–42, 6–7 hours).

## SAN CARLOS DE BARILOCHE AND VICINITY

If Patagonia ever became independent, its logical capital might be San Carlos de Bariloche, the highest profile destination in an area explorer Francisco P. Moreno once called "this beautiful piece of Argentine Switzerland." It's not just that Bariloche, with its incomparable Nahuel Huapi setting, is the lakes district's largest city, transportation hub, and gateway to Argentina's first national park; in the 1930s, the carved granite blocks and rough-hewn polished timbers of its landmark Centro Cívico set a promising precedent for harmonizing urban expansion with wilder surroundings.

Dating from 1902, Bariloche was slow to grow—when former U.S. president Theodore Roosevelt visited in 1913, he observed:

> *Bariloche is a real frontier village.... It was like one of our frontier towns in the old-time West as regards the diversity in ethnic type and nationality among the citizens.*

*The little houses stood well away from one another on the broad, rough, faintly marked streets.*

When Roosevelt crossed the Andes from Chile, Bariloche was more than 400 kilometers from the nearest railroad, but it boomed after completion of the Ferrocarril Roca's southern branch in 1934. Its rustically sophisticated style has spread throughout the region—even to phone booths—but unrelenting growth, promoted by unscrupulous politicians and developers, has detracted from its Euro-Andean charm. For much of the day, for instance, the Bariloche Center, a multi-story monstrosity authorized by the brief and irregular repeal of height-limit legislation, literally overshadows the Centro Cívico.

As the population has grown from near 50,000 in 1980 to almost 110,000 in 2010, its congested *microcentro* has become a clutter of chocolate shops, hotels, and timeshares, and is notorious for high-school graduation bashes that leave hotel rooms in ruins. Student tourism is declining, in relative terms at least, but Bariloche still lags behind aspirations that were once higher than Cerro Catedral's ski areas. Like other Patagonian destinations, it booms in the summer months of December, January, and February.

Bariloche holds a unique place in Argentine cinema as the location for Emilio Vieyra's *Sangre de Vírgenes* (Blood of the Virgins), a Hammer-style vampire flick that was ahead of its time when shot in 1967 (it's available on DVD). Perhaps Vieyra envisaged the unsavory things to come, but Bariloche's bloodsuckers are only part of the story—the city and its surroundings still have much to offer, at reasonable cost. Many of the best accommodations, restaurants, and other services lie along or near Avenida Bustillo between Bariloche proper and Llao Llao, about 25 kilometers west.

## Orientation

On Lago Nahuel Huapi's southeastern shore, 764 meters above sea level, Bariloche (population 108,205) is 1,596 kilometers from Buenos Aires and 429 kilometers southwest of Neuquén via RN 237 and RN 40, but 835 kilometers west of Viedma, Río Negro province's coastal capital, via RN 3, RP 23, and RN 40. It is 123 kilometers north of El Bolsón via RN 40.

As RN 40 enters Bariloche from the east, it becomes Avenida 12 de Octubre, Avenida Juan Manuel de Rosas, and then Avenida Bustillo, continuing west to Llao Llao. En route, it skirts the landmark Centro Cívico; one block south, the parallel Bartolomé Mitre is the main commercial street in the densely built downtown. North–south streets—some of them staircases—climb steeply from the lakeshore.

## ☾ Centro Cívico

Even with the kitsch merchants who pervade the plaza with Siberian huskies and St. Bernards for photographic poses, and the graffiti defacing General Roca's equestrian statue, the array of buildings that border it would be the pride of many cities around the globe. The view to Lago Nahuel Huapi is a bonus, even when the boxy Bariloche Center blocks the sun.

The Centro Cívico was a team effort, envisioned by architect Ernesto de Estrada in 1936 and executed under APN director Exequiel Bustillo until its inauguration in 1940. When the Municipalidad's **Torre Reloj** (Clock Tower) sounds at noon, figures from Patagonian history appear to mark the hour. Other buildings of interest, with steep-pitched roofs and arched arcades that offer shelter from inclement weather, include the former **Correo** (post office, but now the tourism office) and the **Museo de la Patagonia Francisco P. Moreno.**

Exequiel Bustillo's brother, architect Alejandro Bustillo, designed the **Intendencia del Parque Nacional Nahuel Huapi** (Nahuel Huapi National Park Headquarters, San Martín 24), one block north, to harmonize with the Centro Cívico. As a collective national monument, they represent Argentine Patagonia's best.

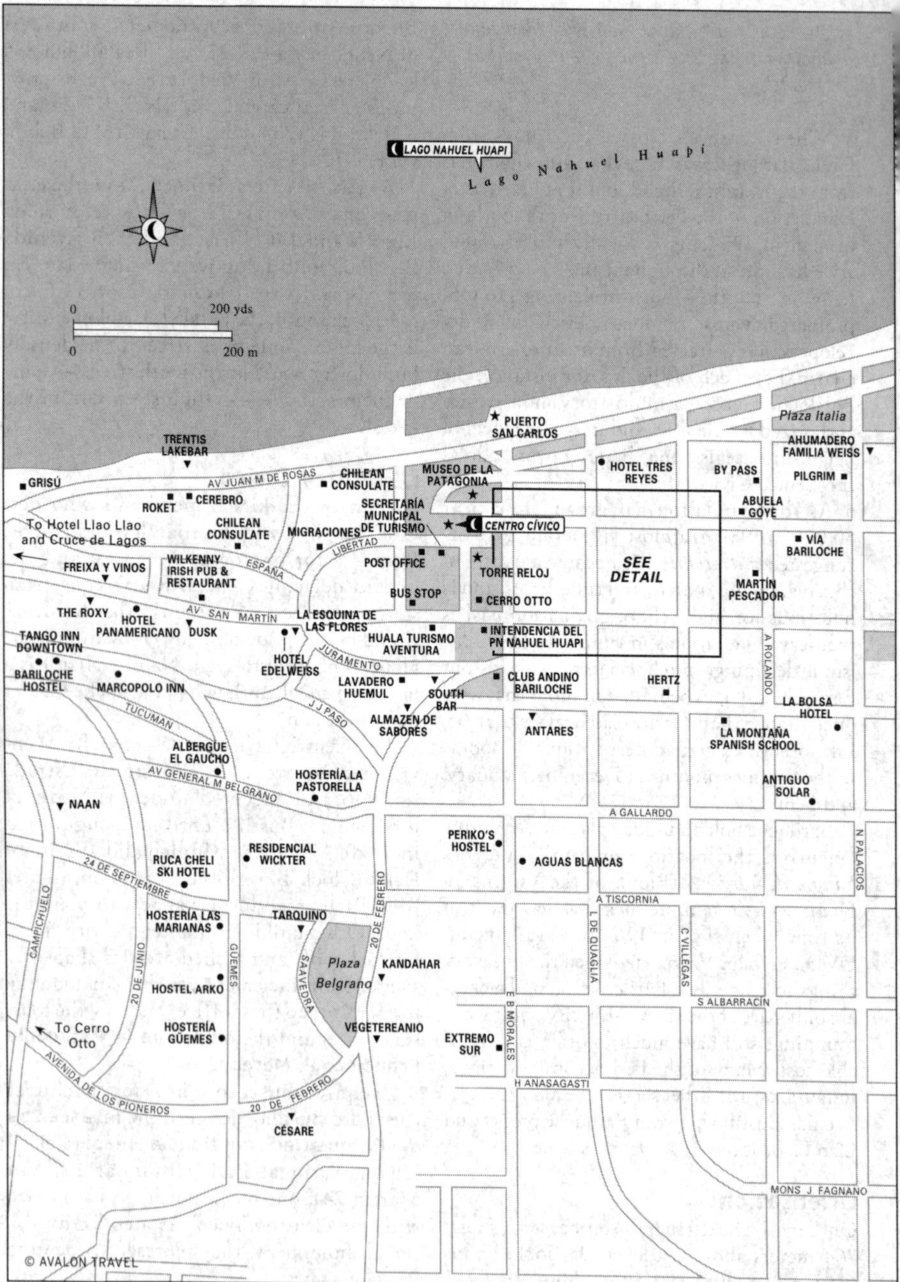
LAGO NAHUEL HUAPI
Lago Nahuel Huapi
0 200 yds
0 200 m
PUERTO SAN CARLOS
Plaza Italia
AHUMADERO FAMILIA WEISS
TRENTIS LAKEBAR
MUSEO DE LA PATAGONIA
HOTEL TRES REYES
BY PASS
PILGRIM
GRISÚ
AV JUAN M DE ROSAS
CHILEAN CONSULATE
ROKET
CEREBRO
SECRETARÍA MUNICIPAL DE TURISMO
CENTRO CÍVICO
ABUELA GOYE
To Hotel Llao Llao and Cruce de Lagos
CHILEAN CONSULATE
MIGRACIONES
LIBERTAD
VÍA BARILOCHE
FREIXA Y VINOS
WILKENNY IRISH PUB & RESTAURANT
ESPAÑA
POST OFFICE
TORRE RELOJ
SEE DETAIL
MARTÍN PESCADOR
BUS STOP
CERRO OTTO
THE ROXY
HOTEL PANAMERICANO
AV SAN MARTÍN
LA ESQUINA DE LAS FLORES
DUSK
TANGO INN DOWNTOWN
HUALA TURISMO AVENTURA
INTENDENCIA DEL PN NAHUEL HUAPI
A ROLANDO
HOTEL EDELWEISS
JURAMENTO
BARILOCHE HOSTEL
MARCOPOLO INN
LAVADERO HUEMUL
SOUTH BAR
CLUB ANDINO BARILOCHE
HERTZ
TUCUMAN
J J PASO
ALMAZEN DE SABORES
ANTARES
LA BOLSA HOTEL
LA MONTAÑA SPANISH SCHOOL
ALBERGUE EL GAUCHO
AV GENERAL M BELGRANO
HOSTERÍA LA PASTORELLA
ANTIGUO SOLAR
NAAN
A GALLARDO
N PALACIOS
PERIKO'S HOSTEL
RESIDENCIAL WICKTER
RUCA CHELI SKI HOTEL
AGUAS BLANCAS
24 DE SEPTIEMBRE
A TISCORNIA
CAMPICHUELO
HOSTERÍA LAS MARIANAS
TARQUINO
20 DE FEBRERO
L DE QUAGLIA
C VILLEGAS
20 DE JUNIO
GUEMES
Plaza Belgrano
KANDAHAR
SAAVEDRA
HOSTEL ARKO
S ALBARRACÍN
E B MORALES
To Cerro Otto
HOSTERÍA GÜEMES
VEGETEREANIO
EXTREMO SUR
H ANASAGASTI
AVENIDA DE LOS PIONEROS
20 DE FEBRERO
CÉSARE
MONS J FAGNANO
© AVALON TRAVEL

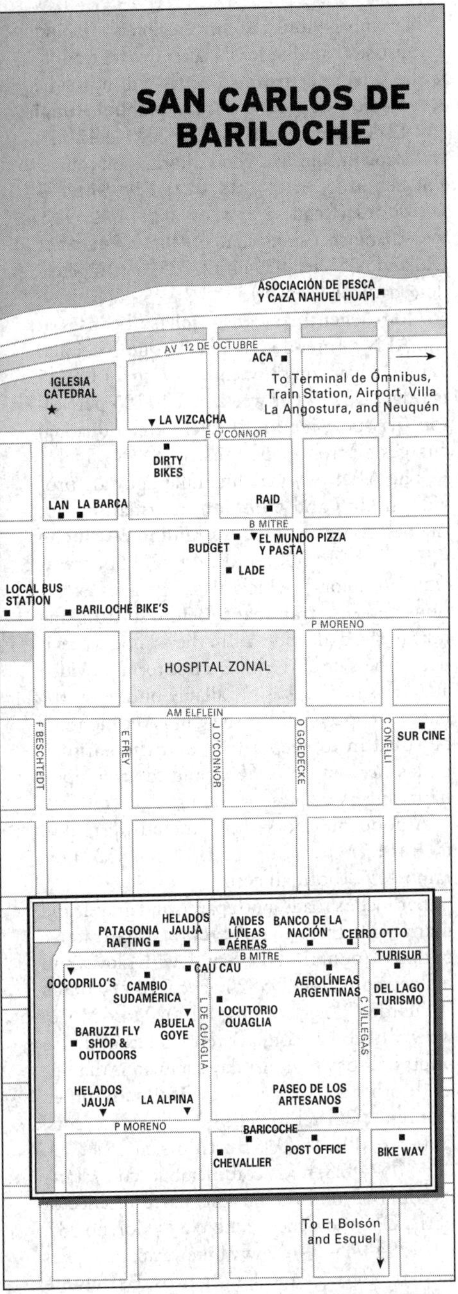


## Museo de la Patagonia Francisco P. Moreno

At the Centro Cívico's northeast corner, Bariloche's Patagonian museum (Centro Cívico s/n, tel. 02944/422309, 10 A.M.–12:30 P.M. and 2–7 P.M. Tues.–Fri., 10 A.M.–5 P.M. Sat., from US$1.25) attempts admirably to place the region (and more) in ecological, cultural, and historical context. Its multiple halls touch on natural history through taxidermy (better than most of its kind); insects (inexplicably including subtropical Iguazú); Patagonia's population from antiquity to the present; the aboriginal Mapuche, Tehuelche, and Fuegian peoples; caudillo Juan Manuel de Rosas; the "Conquista del Desierto" that displaced the indigenous people; and Bariloche's own urban development. There is even material on Stanford geologist Bailey Willis, a visionary consultant who did the region's first systematic surveys in the early 20th century.

## Entertainment

**Sur Cine** (at Shopping Patagonia, Elflein and Onelli, tel. 02944/427189, www.shoppingpatagonia.com.ar) shows recent movies.

A cluster of downtown bars also offer palatable pub grub. Choices include the **Wilkenny Irish Pub & Restaurant** (Av. San Martín 435, tel. 02944/424444, www.wilkennybariloche.com.ar) and the comparable **Pilgrim** (Palacios 167). Popular **Antares** (Elflein 47, tel. 02944/431454, www.cervezaantares.com) is a brewpub with a decent food menu of German specialties and sandwiches to complement the suds. **South Bar** (Juramento 30, tel. 02944/522001) is also popular with the pub-crawlers.

A secluded brewpub is **La Cruz** (Nilpi 789, uphill from Av. Bustillo Km 6.1, tel. 02944/525065, www.cerveceríalacruz.com.ar, closed on Mon.); it opens at 6 P.M. and serves snacks and a few meals with its excellent ales.

For live music, there are two good choices: **The Roxy** (Av. San Martín 580), a bar/restaurant that's a branch of its Buenos Aires namesake, and the nearby **Dusk** (Av. San Martín 490, tel. 02944/400450).

Bariloche nightspots open late—around 1 A.M.—and close around daybreak. The most central is the youthful **By Pass** (Rolando 155, tel. 02944/435681, www.bypass.com.ar). Several others lie a few blocks west of the Centro Cívico: **Cerebro** (Av. Juan Manuel de Rosas 406, tel. 02944/424948, www.cerebro.com.ar), **Roket** (Av. Juan Manuel de Rosas 424, tel. 02944/431940, www.roket.com), and **Grisú** (Av. Juan Manuel de Rosas 574, tel. 02944/422269, www.grisu.com).

## Events

More than just a pretty landscape, Nahuel Huapi has an active cultural life. Llao Llao's **Camping Musical Bariloche** (www.campingmusicalbche.org.ar) sponsors chamber music and brass concerts throughout the year.

March's **Exposición de Otoño** is an end-of-summer flower show. August's **Fiesta Nacional de la Nieve** (National Snow Festival) marks the peak of the ski season.

For one week every October, Llao Llao Hotel & Resort hosts the **Semana Musical Llao Llao** (www.semanamusical.com), an exclusive musical event.

Mid-December brings the **Navidad Coral** (Christmas Chorus) at the cathedral.



## Shopping

Local artisans live off souvenir hunters who frequent the **Paseo de los Artesanos** (Villegas and Perito Moreno, 10 A.M.–9 P.M. daily).

**Freixa y Vinos** (Av. San Martín 597, tel. 02944/436300) carries a wide selection of reds and whites. Chocoholics flock to **Abuela Goye** (Quaglia 219; Mitre 258, tel. 02944/433861, www.abuelagoye.com) and similar locales.

**La Barca** (Mitre 534, Local 3, tel. 02944/436744) has a good selection of books and maps.

## Sports and Recreation

Because of Parque Nacional Nahuel Huapi, Bariloche is the base for outdoor activities ranging from fishing, hiking, and climbing to mountain biking, horseback riding, white-water rafting and kayaking, and skiing.

November–April, the entire region is a **fishing** enthusiast's paradise for its lakes (where trolling is the rule) and streams (for fly-fishing). The **Asociación de Pesca y Caza Nahuel Huapi** (Av. 12 de Octubre and Onelli, tel. 02944/421515, www.apcnh.com) is a good information source. For rental gear, try **Baruzzi Fly Shop & Outdoors** (Urquiza 250, tel. 02944/424922, www.barilochefishing.com) or **Martín Pescador** (Rolando 257, tel. 02944/422275, martinpescador@bariloche.com.ar).

Non-Argentines can purchase licenses at the APN's Intendencia del Parque Nacional Nahuel Huapi on the Centro Cívico for US$25 per day, US$75 per week, or US$105 per season (passport required); there are additional charges for trolling permits.

The APN (www.nahuelhuapi.gov.ar) provides **hiking** and **climbing** information, but the best source is the **Club Andino Bariloche** (20 de Febrero 30, tel. 02944/527966, www.clubandino.org), which also organizes excursions and sells trail maps. Before starting any hike in the park and within the 48 hours previous to the date of the hike, a free form provided at ANP's offices (also available online on the park's webpage) and at the Club Andino must be filled in to keep a record at the national park's *Registro de Trekking* and to show upon park rangers' request.

A good outdoors shop, including rental, is **Raid** (Mitre 860, tel. 02944/522178, ramos1157@hotmail.com).

Bariloche's roads, both paved and gravel, and many wide trails make **cycling** an attractive option. Mountain-bike rental, with gloves and helmet, costs from US$20 per day. **Dirty Bikes** (Eduardo O'Connor 681, tel. 02944/425616, www.dirtybikes.com.ar) rents bikes and also offers half-day to multi-day excursions that include other activities as well. **Bariloche Bikes** (Moreno 520, tel. 02944/424657) also rents. **Bike Cordillera** (Av. Bustillo Km 18.6, tel. 02944/524828, www.cordillerabike.com) starts its tours beyond the busiest, narrowest sector of the Circuito Chico. **Bike Way** (Moreno 237, tel. 02944/456571, www.bikeway.com.ar) has similar offerings and longer trips. **Patagonia**

## THE SLOPES OF BARILOCHE

After decades of decline and eclipse by resorts like Las Leñas (Mendoza), Bariloche is reestablishing itself as a ski destination with new investment and technological improvements at **Catedral Alta Patagonia** (Base Cerro Catedral, tel. 02944/409000, www.catedralalta-patagonia.com), only a short hop west of town. It's still more popular with Argentines and Brazilians than intercontinental travelers, but new snow-making and grooming gear has complemented the blend of 50 beginner-to-advanced runs, and lift capacities have also improved. From a base of 1,030 meters, the skiable slopes rise another 1,100 meters.

As elsewhere, ticket prices depend on timing; the season runs mid-June-mid-October but is subdivided into low, mid-, and peak season. For prices, check the area's website.

Basic rental equipment is cheap, but quality gear is more expensive. In addition to on-site facilities, try downtown's **Raid** (Mitre 860, tel. 02944/522178, ramos1157@hotmail.com) for ski rentals.

There are also cross-country opportunities at close-in Cerro Otto.

**Moto Rent** (tel. 02944/15537554, www.patagoniamotorent.com) rents scooters and motorcycles.

Local **horseback-riding** trips can last from two hours (about US$53) to a full day (US$73 with lunch), with multi-day excursions also possible. The main operators are **Cabalgatas Carol Jones** (Modesta Victoria 5600, tel. 02944/426508, www.caroljones.com.ar) and **Cabalgatas Tom Wesley** (tel. 02944/448193, www.cabalgatastomwesley.com).

For **rafting** and **kayaking,** mostly from September to April, the Río Manso between Lago Steffen and Río Villegas is a Class II–III float midway between Bariloche and El Bolsón to the south, ideal for beginners and families (from US$73). Downstream and near the international border the Río Manso becomes more challenging with some taxing Class IV rapids (from US$78). On some multi-day trips that may include a border crossing, trekking, horseback riding, or cycling is added.

River operators include **Aguas Blancas** (Morales 564, tel. 02944/432799, www.aguas-blancas.com.ar); **Extremo Sur** (Morales 765, tel. 02944/427301, www.extremosur.com); and **Patagonia Rafting** (Mitre 86, 3rd floor, apartment A, tel. 02944/15-531247, www.patagoniarafting.com).

Half-day to four-day-plus kayak touring trips across nearby lakes and on Río Limay are run by **Pura Vida Patagonia** (tel. 02944/15-414053, www.puravidapatagonia.com).

## Accommodations

Bariloche has plentiful accommodations options in all categories, from camping to hostels, B&Bs, hotels, and luxury lodges. Hostels, in particular, have proliferated. The finest hotels are west of the city proper, on and along the Llao Llao road. Though it's usual to find the highest rates in ski season it's not necessarily the rule.

The municipal tourist office keeps a thorough accommodations database, and when summer demand is high, they're an excellent resource. Since many low-priced to midrange hotels cater to high school graduation trips, it's better to avoid them toward the end of December.

### US$10-25

The lakefront **Camping Petunia** (Av. Bustillo Km 13.5, tel. 02944/461969, www.campingpetunia.com, US$10 pp for adults, US$5 pp for kids) is one of numerous campgrounds west of town.

### US$25-50

Most places in this range are hostels that, in addition to dorms, also have private rooms that are mostly better value than an average hotel. They also include breakfast and offer amenities such as wireless Internet, and one even includes dinner in its rates.

On wooded grounds in a quiet barrio west of town, **Alaska Hostel** (Lilinquén 326, tel. 02944/461564, www.alaska-hostel.com, US$12–14 pp, US$28–48 d) is walking distance from Avenida Bustillo Km 7.5. Several buses, including No. 10, 20, and 21, will drop passengers here.

Under the same management, **Periko's Hostel** (Morales 555, tel. 02944/522326, www.perikos.com, US$15 pp, US$40–50 d) has mostly dorm rooms but also some stylish doubles (the cheaper ones have shared bath) on the upper floors. The secluded garden is uncommon in this part of town.

**La Bolsa Hostel** (Palacios 405, tel. 02944/423529, www.labolsadeldeporte.com.ar, US$15 pp, US$50 d) is a well-established hostel.

Only 500 meters west of the bus terminal, the HI affiliate **Tango Inn Soho** (Av. 12 de Octubre 1915, tel. 02944/430707, www.tangoinn.com, US$15 pp for dorms, US$63–73 s or d) has all dorms and private rooms with their own baths, a restaurant, cafeteria, and bar. On a hostel-lined street, also an HI affiliate, the **Tango Inn Downtown** (Salta 514, tel. 02944/400004, www.tangoinn.com, US$17–18 pp, US$80–90 d) offers central accommodations instead with great lake views, all rooms with bathtubs, and free use for doubles occupants of the hot tub.

A quiet, good option is the **Albergue El Gaucho** (Belgrano 209, tel. 02944/522464, www.hostelelgaucho.com, US$18 pp, US$60 d), which in an attractive former family residence has mostly dorms but also a handful of doubles, all with private baths. The staff can manage English, German, and Italian.

Barrio Belgrano's **Hostel Arko** (Güemes 685, tel. 02944/423109, www.eco-family.com, US$18 pp, US$49 d) is a family-run place with a long history in the area and the neighborhood, with good dorms and comfortable private doubles with baths. Thanks to flexible and friendly management and staff, facilities may be used after checkout.

Another hostel on Calle Salta with lake views, friendly **Bariloche Hostel** (Salta 528, tel. 02944/425460, www.barilochehostel.com.ar, US$18 pp, US$63 d) is a converted residence where both dorms and doubles have private baths. The lake panoramas are even better from the deck on the slope behind the house, where there's a magnificently productive pear tree and other fruit trees.

The HI affiliate **Marcopolo Inn** (Salta 422, tel. 02944/400105, www.marcopoloinn.com.ar, US$20 pp, US$85 d) is a converted hotel whose rooms, all with private baths and most with bathtubs, are more spacious than most hostels. Rates include not just breakfast but also dinner.

Well-located places include Barrio Belgrano's **Hostería Güemes** (Güemes 715, tel. 02944/424785, US$50 d), one of the oldest and most hospitable B&Bs.

### US$50-100

Run by a young couple in a 1950s former family residence, **Antiguo Solar** (Ángel Gallardo 360, tel. 02944/400337, www.antiguosolar.com, US$45 s, US$55 d) is a lovely B&B; its warm attentive service and comfort make for an excellent value choice.

Some of the 12 rooms at **Hostería La Pastorella** (Belgrano 127, tel. 02944/424656, www.lapastorella.com.ar, US$49 s, US$70 d) are a little too cozy for comfort, but it does offer a diverse breakfast and amenities including a sauna.

On the Llao Llao road, cozy **Hostería Pájaro Azul** (Av. Bustillo Km 10.8, tel. 02944/461025, www.hosteriapajaroazul.com.ar, US$80 s/d) has eight pine-paneled rooms with mountain views through relatively small windows, along with wireless Internet.

Built in an Austrian style, Barrio Belgrano's **Hostería Las Marianas** (24 de Septiembre 218, tel. 02944/439876, www.hosterialasmarianas.com.ar, US$94 s or d with discounts for cash payment) is a friendly, family-run inn with only 16 rooms—each named for a nearby Andean peak.

Barrio Belgrano's upgraded **Ruca Cheli Village Ski Hotel** (24 de Setiembre 275, tel./fax 02944/424528, www.rucacheli.com.

ar, US$96–112 s or d with buffet breakfast) has reasonably large rooms and obliging management.

### US$100-200

The lakefront **Hotel Tres Reyes** (Av. 12 de Octubre 135, tel. 02944/426121, www.hoteltresreyes.com, US$94–105 s, 100–114 d), a stylishly rehabbed classic dating from 1951, is a reliable downtown hotel whose higher rates correspond to lake views. Some rooms are smallish, but even these almost double their rates in ski season.

It's past its prime, but **La Posada del Ángel** (Av. Bustillo Km 12.6, tel. 02944/461263, www.posadadelangel.com.ar, US$90 s, US$110 d) does enjoy friendly family service, a pool, and five pine-sheltered hectares. The rooms are ample and comfortable, but small windows limit the light and alpine views.

Highly regarded **Posada Los Juncos** (Av. Bustillo Km 20, tel. 02944/448485, www.visitlosjuncos.com, US$150 d) is an exclusive five-room B&B with a restaurant on Bahía Campanario.

**Hotel Edelweiss** (Av. San Martín 202, tel. 02944/445500, www.edelweiss.com.ar, US$157–174 s or d) has 100 spacious standard to superior rooms, plus more elaborate suites. A minimum stay of four nights is required in ski season.

Downtown's most prestigious option is **Hotel Panamericano** (Av. San Martín 536/570, tel. 02944/409200, www.panamericanobariloche.com, US$157–182 s or d), a sprawling complex on both sides of the avenue, linked by glassed-in, elevated bridges. It also holds a casino and a spa, and one of its restaurants, Tinto Bistro, maintains the excellence of its partner in Villa La Angostura. However, it's not up to the standards—not to mention the style or location—of places like the Llao Llao. Rates vary according to view (none or lake).

Part of a golf development at Arelauquen, near Lago Gutiérrez, the 23-room **Pestana Bariloche Ski & Golf Resort** (RP 82 Km 4.5, tel. 02944/476110, www.pestana.com, US$185–335 d) is a recent member of the local luxury lodge sweepstakes. Rates vary according to whether the rooms have mountain or golf course views and more than double in ski season.

### OVER US$200

Llao Llao's **Hotel Tunquelén** (Av. Bustillo Km 24.5, tel. 02944/448600, www.tunquelen.com, US$280–445 s or d) might be the area's top choice were it not for the nearby Llao Llao Hotel & Resort.

Built into the slopes of Península San Pedro, the **Aldebarán Hotel & Spa** (Av. Bustillo Km 20.4, Península San Pedro, tel. 02944/448678, www.aldebaranpatagonia.com, US$341–479 s or d) is a strikingly modern view hotel with panoramas to Cerro Campanario, Cerro López, and beyond. The 10 rustically stylish rooms are enormous, from 35 to 55 square meters plus huge baths, with balconies overlooking the lake. It also boasts a good restaurant and enjoys contemporary spa facilities.

Part of a small exclusive chain, **Design Suites Bariloche** (Av. Bustillo Km 2.5, tel. 02944/457000, www.designsuites.com, US$351–641 s or d) differs from all its kin in setting and architecture. In this case, the common areas consist of a luminous clubhouse with cathedral ceilings and views over Nahuel Huapi, as well as an indoor-outdoor pool, a gym, and sauna facilities. The accommodations proper occupy three separate buildings with greater setbacks from the busy avenue; all rooms enjoy lake views (and whirlpool tubs, some of them with views as well).

Not just a hotel but a landmark in its own right, **Llao Llao Hotel & Resort** (Av. Bustillo Km 25, tel. 0810/2225526, www.llaollao.com, US$466–2,694 s or d) is an Alejandro Bustillo classic dating from 1940, its interior completely renovated in the 1990s and a new wing added in 2007. Rates depend on the room's size (22–160 square meters), views, and amenities, as well as the season.

## Food

For breakfast, coffee, sandwiches, and sweets, try *confiterías* like **La Alpina** (Perito Moreno 98, tel. 02944/425693).

Bariloche abounds in pizzerias, starting with the unpretentious and excellent **Cocodrilo's** (Mitre 5, tel. 02944/426640, lunch and dinner daily), where pizzas start from US$12, though **El Mundo Pizza y Pasta** (Mitre 759, tel. 02944/423461, lunch and dinner daily) has greater variety of pizzas and prices start at US$10. In addition to pizza and similarly priced, **Césare** (20 de Febrero 788, tel. 02944/432060, lunch and dinner daily) prepares around 20 kinds of empanadas.

An attractive residence hidden by two big *pehuenes* houses **Vegetariano** (20 de Febrero 730, tel. 02944/421820, lunch and dinner Mon.–Sat.), where the three (US$6) or five courses (US$8) offered as the meal of the day may include fish.

Across the street from Club Andino, tiny and unpretentious **Almazen de Sabores** (20 de Febrero 40, tel. 02944/422096, lunch Mon.–Fri., dinner Mon.–Sat.) has rapidly gained a reputation as one of the best places to eat in town, allowing the customer's choice of four (US$15 pp) to five (US$17 pp) different courses out of a list of 12 inventive though simple dishes that varies every two months. The lunch menu is more limited than dinner.

On the Llao Llao road, the **Berlina Brew House & Restaurante** (Av. Bustillo Km 11.750, tel. 02944/523336, www.cervezaberlina.com) offers beer samplers and excellent sandwiches, plus pizzas, pastas, and a few standard Argentine dishes such as *bife de chorizo* (sirloin, US$13). It opens at noon and has an outdoor beer garden, with a 6–8 P.M. happy hour.

For *picadas,* pizzas, and draft beer, don't miss **Cervecería Blest** (Av. Bustillo Km 11.6, tel. 02944/461026, www.cervezablest.com.ar, lunch and dinner daily); it closes at midnight.

For smoked *ciervo* (venison), *jabalí* (wild boar), and *trucha* (trout), visit tourist-oriented **Ahumadero Familia Weiss** (Palacios and V.A. O'Connor, tel. 02944/435789, www.restauranteweiss.com, lunch and dinner daily), where entrées are in the US$10–15 range, and specialties include *ciervo a la cazadora* (a venison stew with a side of spätzle for US$11).

**La Vizcacha** (Eduardo O'Connor 630, tel. 02944/422109, lunch and dinner Wed.–Mon.) is a venerable downtown *parrilla.* The full-sized *bife de chorizo* (sirloin, US$18) at **El Boliche de Alberto** (Villegas 347, tel. 02944/434564; Villegas and Elflein, tel. 02944/401040; Av. Bustillo Km 8.8, tel. 02944/462285, www.elbolichedealberto.com, lunch and dinner daily) will challenge all but the most ravenous adolescents; even the half portion (US$15) may be too large for a single diner and some couples.

Primarily a *parrilla* but also serving excellent trout (US$18), **Tarquino** (24 de Septiembre and Saavedra, tel. 02944/434774, www.restaurantetarquino.com.ar, lunch and dinner daily) is a Hansel-and-Gretel construction with high ceilings, erected around living trees. Most entrées, including venison ravioli and *ñoquis* (gnocchi), cost around US$10–15.

Despite the name, **Kandahar** (20 de Febrero 698, tel. 02944/424702, www.kandahar.com.ar, dinner only) does not serve Afghan food, but rather Patagonian game dishes such as a venison casserole garnished with applesauce and red cabbage (US$18), in intimate surroundings with a Sinatra soundtrack. The service is excellent, the kitchen involved, but the dessert menu is weak.

Camouflaged in residential Barrio Belgrano, **Naan** (Campichuelo 568, tel. 02944/421785, dinner only) produces a truly cosmopolitan menu of local dishes with creative touches, complemented by French, Italian, Mexican, and even Vietnamese entrées, in moderately sized but flavorful portions. Entrées start around US$15, the service is highly individual, and two huge picture windows offer panoramas of Bariloche, Nahuel Huapi, and the cordillera behind the lake.

Despite its intimidating size, cavernous **El Patacón** (Av. Bustillo Km 7, tel. 02944/442898, www.elpatacon.com, lunch and dinner daily) has personalized service and meticulously prepared food served in generous portions. Former U.S. president Bill Clinton dined on dishes such as the provoletta appetizer and venison ravioli. Entrées start at US$14.

Bariloche has exceptional ice creameries,

starting with **Abuela Goye** (Quaglia 219; Mitre 258, tel. 02944/433861, www.abuelagoye.com). The real standout, though, is **Helados Jauja** (Mitre and Quaglia; Moreno 48, tel. 02944/437888), whose dizzying diversity includes unconventional wild fruit flavors, half a dozen or more chocolates, and the remarkable *mate cocido.*

## Information

The **Secretaría Municipal de Turismo** (Centro Cívico s/n, tel. 02944/429850, www.bariloche-patagonia.info) is open 8 A.M.–9 P.M. daily, but in peak season it's overrun with visitors seeking accommodations and other information. There are satellite offices at the bus terminal (Av. 12 de Octubre s/n) and at the airport.

The APN's **Intendencia del Parque Nacional Nahuel Huapi** (San Martín 24, tel. 02944/423111, www.nahuelhuapi.gov.ar) is one block south of the tourist office, where hikers must register within 48 hours prior to the start of any hike in the park. Another block south, the **Club Andino Bariloche** (20 de Febrero 30, tel. 02944/527966, www.clubandino.org, 9 A.M.–9 P.M. Mon.–Sat. in summer, afternoons only the rest of the year) provides hiking information.

For motorists, **ACA** is at Avenida 12 de Octubre 785, tel. 02944/423000.

## Services

**Cambio Sudamérica** (Mitre 63) changes foreign cash and travelers checks. **Banco de la Nación** (Mitre 180) is one of many downtown banks with ATMs.

**Correo Argentino** is at Moreno 175; the postal code is 8400.

**Locutorio Quaglia** (Quaglia 220) has phone/fax and Internet.

**Siturismo** (Villegas 222, tel. 02944/436215, www.siturismo.com) is a full-service agency that will arrange a variety of excursions around the area.

**La Montaña Spanish School** (Elflein 251, tel. 02944/524212, www.lamontana.com) charges US$160 per week for 20 hours of instruction.

Chile has a **consulate** (tel. 02944/422842) at España 275 (tel. 02944/423050). For visa matters, visit the **Dirección Nacional de Migraciones** (Libertad 191, tel. 02944/423043).

**Lavadero Huemul** (Juramento 37, tel. 02944/522067) is one of many laundries.

The **Hospital Zonal** (tel. 02944/426100) is at Perito Moreno 601.

## Getting There

Bariloche is northern Argentine Patagonia's transportation hub, with regional and international bus connections.

**LAN** (Mitre 534, Local 1, tel. 02944/427755) flies daily to Buenos Aires. **Andes** (Mitre 106, tel. 02944/425494) flies to Buenos Aires. **Aerolíneas Argentinas** (Mitre 185, tel. 0810/2228-6527) flies to Buenos Aires and El Calafate. Twice a week, there is a flight to Mendoza, Salta, and Iguazú.

Bariloche is something of a hub for **LADE** (John O'Connor 214, tel. 02944/423562), with cheap flights to Buenos Aires and to other Patagonian destinations, but most of these are only weekly, and schedules often change.

On the eastern outskirts of town, across the Río Ñireco, Bariloche's **Terminal de Ómnibus** (Av. 12 de Octubre s/n, tel. 02944/432860) is immediately east of the train station. There are services to Chile, long-distance buses throughout the country, and provincial and regional routes. Some bus companies keep downtown offices where tickets can also be purchased, including **Chevallier** (Moreno 107, tel. 02944/423090) and the **Vía Bariloche** group (Mitre 321, tel. 02944/429012).

Four companies cross the Andes to the Chilean cities of Osorno (US$20–30, 4–6 hours), Valdivia (US$28–30, 7–8 hours), Puerto Varas (US$20–28, 5.5–6.5 hours), and Puerto Montt (US$20–30, 6–7.5 hours): **Andesmar** (tel. 02944/430211), **Bus Norte/Cruz del Sur** (tel. 02944/422818), **Tas Choapa** (tel. 02944/422288), and **Vía Bariloche** (tel. 02944/432444).

Sample domestic destinations include Villa La Angostura (US$6, 1.5 hours), El

Bolsón (US$6–11, 2–2.5 hours), San Martín de los Andes (US$15, four hours), Esquel (US$16–20, 4.5 hours), Neuquén (US$25–40, 5.5 hours), Viedma (US$40–50, 12–15 hours), Trelew (US$43–60, 12–13 hours), Puerto Madryn (US$46–63, 13–14 hours), Comodoro Rivadavia (US$50–63, 13–15 hours), Buenos Aires (US$116–153, 20–25 hours), Río Gallegos (US$93–103, 24 hours), El Calafate (US$113–125, 28 hours, via RN 3, or US$123, 34 hours, via RN 40), and El Chaltén (US$114, 30 hours, via RN 40).

Immediately west of the bus terminal, **Tren Patagónico** (Av. 12 de Octubre s/n, tel. 02944/423172, www.trenpatagonico-sa.com.ar) connects Bariloche with Viedma via **train** on Sunday at 5 P.M. The 19-hour trip costs US$14 in hard-backed *económica,* US$29 in reclining Pullman, or US$57 in *camarote* sleepers; children 5–12 pay half.

**Cruce Andino** (www.cruceandino.com) operates the bus-boat shuttle over the Andes to Puerto Montt, Chile (US$230 pp without lunch; national park admission fee and boarding tax are not included) via Puerto Pañuelo, Puerto Blest, Puerto Frías, Peulla (Chile), Petrohué, and Puerto Varas. With an overnight at Peulla, the trip costs US$370–410 per person, depending on the hotel. For bookings, contact **Turisur** (Mitre 219, tel. 02944/426109, www.turisur.com.ar). It's possible to do this trip in segments or as a round-trip, say from Puerto Pañuelo to Puerto Blest and back.



### Getting Around

**Aeropuerto Teniente Candelaria** (tel. 02944/405016) is 15 kilometers east of Bariloche via RN 40 and RP 80. Micro Ómnibus 3 de Mayo's No. 72 bus goes directly there (US$1.5), while cabs and *remises* cost about US$15.

From Moreno between Palacios and Beschtedt, where **Micro Ómnibus 3 de Mayo** (tel. 02944/425648) has its office at Moreno 480, Línea Catedral goes to Cerro Catedral (US$1.50) hourly 7:15 A.M.–8:15 P.M., via Avenida de los Pioneros or via Avenida Bustillo, alternately.

For most of the day, 3 de Mayo's No. 20 bus goes every 20 minutes to Llao Llao and Puerto Pañuelo (US$1.50), while No. 10 bus goes to Colonia Suiza seven times daily (four of which reach Bahía López), on the Circuito Chico route through Parque Nacional Nahuel Huapi.

Micro Ómnibus 3 de Mayo's No. 50 bus goes to Lago Gutiérrez (US$1.50) every 30 minutes. Their Línea Manso goes twice a month to Río Villegas and El Manso (US$5), on Parque Nacional Nahuel Huapi's southwestern edge.

Bariloche has several car rental agencies, including **Baricoche** (Moreno 115, 1st floor, tel. 02944/427638), **Budget** (Mitre 717, tel. 02944/422482), and **Hertz** (Elflein 190, tel. 02944/423457).

## PARQUE NACIONAL NAHUEL HUAPI

In 1903, Patagonian explorer Francisco Pascasio Moreno donated three square leagues of "the most beautiful scenery my eyes had ever seen," at Lago Nahuel Huapi's west end, near the Chilean border, to "be conserved as a natural public park." Citing the United States' example in creating large public reserves, Moreno's burst of idealism returned part of a personal land grant to the Argentine state. First known as Parque Nacional del Sur, the property became today's Parque Nacional Nahuel Huapi.

Since then, countless Argentine and foreign visitors have benefited from Moreno's civic generosity in a reserve that now encompasses a far larger area of glacial lakes and limpid rivers, forested moraines and mountains, and snow-topped Andean peaks that mark the border. So many have done so, in fact, that it's debatable whether authorities have complied with Moreno's wish that "the current features of their perimeter not be altered, and that there be no additional constructions other than those that facilitate the comforts of the cultured visitor."

Prior to the "Conquest of the Desert," Araucanian peoples freely crossed the Andes via the Paso de los Vuriloches south of 3,554-meter Cerro Tronador. The pass lent its name to Bariloche, which, a century since its 1903

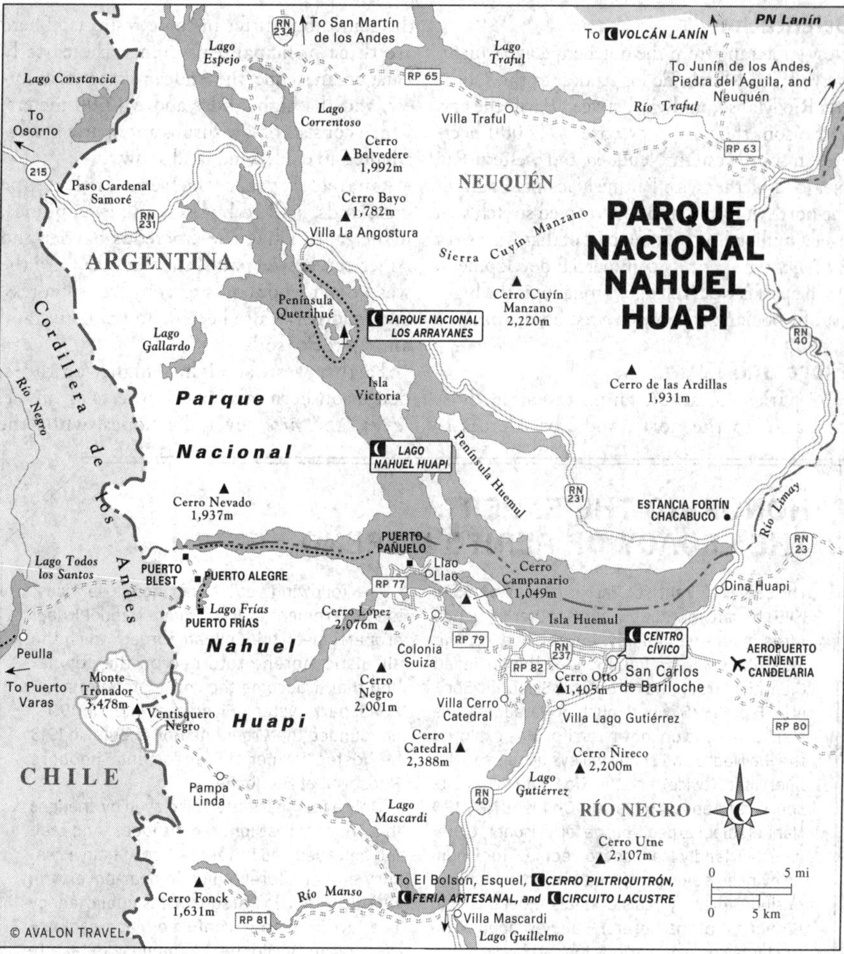


founding, has morphed from lakeside hamlet to a sprawling city whose wastes imperil the air, water, and surrounding woodlands.

For all that, Nahuel Huapi remains a beauty spot that connects two countries via a series of scenic roads and waterways. In 1979, Argentine and Chilean military dictatorships fortified the borders and mined the approaches because of a territorial dispute elsewhere, but a papal intervention cleared the air and perhaps reflected Moreno's aspirations:

*This land of beauty in the Andes is home to a colossal peak shared by two nations: Monte Tronador unites both of them.... Together, they could rest and share ideas there; they could find solutions to problems unsolved by diplomacy. Visitors from around the world would mingle and share with one another at this international crossroads.*

## Orientation

Now stretching from the northerly Lago Queñi, west of San Martín de los Andes, to the southerly Río Manso, midway between Bariloche and El Bolsón, the park now covers 717,000 hectares in southwestern Neuquén and western Río Negro. Together with Parque Nacional Lanín to the north, it forms an uninterrupted stretch well over a million hectares, but part of that is a *reserva nacional* that permits commercial development. At the park's western edge, Tronador is the highest of a phalanx of snow-covered border peaks.

## Flora and Fauna

The park's flora and fauna resemble those of Lanín to the north and Los Alerces to the south, but differ in some respects. There are three principal ecosystems: the easterly Patagonian steppe, the Andean-Patagonian forest, and the high Andes above 1,600 meters, which consists of low shrubs and sparse grasses adapted to cold, wind, and snow.

Guanacos graze the semi-arid steppe grasslands, stalked by foxes and even pumas, while raptors like the cinereous harrier and American kestrel patrol the skies. Toward the west, open woodlands of coniferous cypress, *ñire* (southern false beech), and *maitén* stand among rocky soils.

Farther west, at slightly higher altitudes, dense southern false beech forests of *coihue, lenga,* and *ñire* cover the slopes, while the

### HONORING THE EXPERT: THE LEGACY OF PERITO MORENO

The career of Francisco Pascasio Moreno (1852-1919) began improbably at his father's Buenos Aires insurance agency, but, by age 20, the inquisitive Moreno had founded the Sociedad Científica Argentina (Argentine Scientific Society). From 1875, when much of Patagonia was still hostile and unknown territory, he explored the Río Negro and Limay valleys up to Lago Nahuel Huapi (twice), and the Río Santa Cruz to its source at Lago San Martín. On his 1879-1880 Nahuel Huapi expedition, he fell prisoner to previously friendly Manzanero people – for whom he evinced a sympathy that was unfashionable during General Roca's Conquista del Desierto (Conquest of the Desert) – and escaped down the Limay on a precarious log raft.

In 1884, dedicated to the public good, Moreno donated his natural history collections to the Museo Antropológico y Etnológico de Buenos Aires, which became the Museo de Historia Natural de La Plata, which U.S. surveyor Bailey Willis compared with the Smithsonian Institution. In 1897, recognizing Moreno's knowledge of the region, the government named the *perito* (expert) its delegate to a commission settling border differences with Chile; five years later, he oversaw the placement of permanent boundary markers.

The following year, honoring his services, the government granted him a Nahuel Huapi property near the Chilean border, which the altruistic Moreno returned on the stipulation that it become the cornerstone of a national park system. Five years later, in 1908, he founded the Argentine Boy Scouts; in 1913 he hosted former U.S. president Theodore Roosevelt at Bariloche.

Only a few years later, dismayed by changes in a country that ignored his ideas, and feeling betrayed and bitter like San Martín a century earlier, Moreno died in near poverty in Buenos Aires. In Patagonia, his public legacy is a few frequently confused place-names – a street in Bariloche, his namesake lake to the west, the dusty provincial town of Perito Moreno, Parque Nacional Perito Moreno, and the famous Glaciar Perito Moreno.

Yet according to Bailey Willis (whose own name graces a peak near Bariloche), Moreno was the first to grasp Patagonia's potential as a "national asset" that needed impartial research to be properly unlocked: "Among men of Moreno's nationality, personal ambition is more often than not the ruling motive. But he was selfless where knowledge of the truth was his objective."

shoreline and stream banks burst with a flowering understory of *notro* and climbing vines like *mutisia,* with clusters of the cinnamon-barked *arrayán.*

Near Puerto Blest, rainfall up to 4,000 millimeters per annum supports a humid Valdivian forest of Guaiteca cypress, podocarpus, and tree ferns. Nahuel Huapi, though, lacks Lanín's monkey puzzle forests, and the more southerly *alerce* tree is less abundant than in Chubut province.

Sightings of the huemul (Andean deer) and the miniature deer pudu are rare here. Other mammals include the carnivorous *huillín* (otter) and the *tuco-tuco,* an endemic gopher-like rodent.

Normally ocean-going, the king cormorant has a colony along Lago Nahuel Huapi, where the kelp gull often trails the boats that sail the lake. Nahuel Huapi, its tributary streams, and other lakes teem with trout and other fish.

## Lago Nahuel Huapi

Nahuel Huapi's focal point is its namesake lake, whose finger-like channels converge near the Llao Llao peninsula to form the main part of its 560-square-kilometer surface. With a maximum depth of 454 meters, it drains eastward into the Río Limay, a Río Negro tributary.

In the middle of Nahuel Huapi's northern arm, **Isla Victoria** once housed the APN's park ranger school (since relocated to Tucumán, and then to Córdoba), which trained rangers from throughout the Americas. From Puerto Pañuelo, Turisur's *Modesta Victoria* (Mitre 219, tel. 02944/426109, www.turisur.com.ar) sails once a day to the island (US$47 plus US$13 national park admission fee), while the *Cau Cau* (Quaglia 211; Mitre 139, tel. 02944/431372, www.islavictoriayarrayanes.com, US$55 plus national park admission fee) goes twice; both continue to Parque Nacional Los Arrayanes (which is more accessible from Villa La Angostura, on the north shore).

## Circuito Chico

Bariloche's single most popular excursion leads west out Avenida Bustillo to Península Llao Llao and returns via the hamlet of Colonia

© STEVE KINGSMAN/123RF

Lago Nahuel Huapi

Suiza, at the foot of Cerro López. En route, it passes or touches several points of interest; public buses will pick up and drop off passengers almost anywhere, and it's also popular with cyclists.

For exceptional panoramas of Nahuel Huapi and surroundings, take the **Aerosilla Campanario** (Av. Bustillo Km 17.5, tel. 02944/448151, US$10 pp) to the 1,050-meter summit of **Cerro Campanario.** The chairlift operates 9 A.M.–5:30 P.M. daily, and there is a *confitería* at the summit.

The bus-boat Cruce Andino trip to Chile starts at **Puerto Pañuelo,** but excursions to Isla Victoria and Parque Nacional Los Arrayanes (across the lake) also leave from here. The outstanding cultural landmark is the **Llao Llao Hotel & Resort** (Av. Bustillo Km 25, tel. 0810/2225526, www.llaollao.com), a Bustillo creation opened to nonguests for Wednesday's guided tours (free of charge, previous booking required).

Almost immediately west of Puerto Pañuelo, a level footpath from the parking area leads southwest to an *arrayán* forest in **Parque Municipal Llao Llao;** the trail rejoins with the paved road near **Lago Escondido.** The road itself passes a trailhead for **Cerro Llao Llao,** a short but stiff climb that offers fine panoramas of Nahuel Huapi and the Andean crest. On the descent, the trail joins a gravel road that rejoins the paved road from Puerto Pañuelo, which leads south before looping northeast toward Bariloche; a gravel alternative heads east to **Colonia Suiza,** known for its Sunday crafts fair (also Wednesday in summer), when a spectacular assortment of sweets and desserts and *curanto* (a mixture of beef, lamb, pork, chicken, sausage, potatoes, sweet potatoes, and other vegetables, baked on heated earth-covered stones; booking is necessary and can be made at Abuela Goye shops or by calling tel. 02944/448605) are also on offer.

On any day, try the regional menu at **Fundo Colonia Suiza** (tel. 02944/448619, www.fundocoloniasuiza.com.ar), which is open from noon to 7 P.M. daily (in summer it closes at 8 P.M.). The individual *tabla* of

© WAYNE BERNHARDSON

Architect Alejandro Bustillo's Llao Llao Hotel is Nahuel Huapi's classic hotel.

smoked venison, pork, trout, salami, and cheese (US$11) is an unusual practice (most restaurants have a two-person minimum) and one that's very welcome.

From Colonia Suiza, a zigzag dirt road suitable for four-wheel-drive vehicles and mountain bikes climbs toward the **Refugio López** (tel. 02944/15-580321, www.cerrolopezbariloche.com.ar), 1,620 meters above sea level; farther west and near the junction of the paved and gravel roads, a steep footpath climbs 2.5 hours to the *refugio,* open mid-December–late March.

From Refugio López (a good place to take a break and a beer), the route climbs to **Pico Turista,** a strenuous scramble over rugged volcanic terrain. With an early start, experienced hikers will possibly reach the 2,076-meter summit of **Cerro López.**

Many Bariloche agencies offer the Circuito Chico as a half-day tour (about US$15 pp), but it's also possible (and cheaper) on public transportation.

## Cerro Otto

From Bariloche's Barrio Belgrano, Avenida de los Pioneros intersects a gravel road that climbs gently and then steeply west to Cerro Otto's 1,405-meter summit. While it's a feasible eight-kilometer hike or mountain-bike ride, it's easier via the gondolas of **Teleférico Cerro Otto** (Av. de los Pioneros Km 5, tel. 02944/441035, www.telefericobariloche.com.ar, US$18 pp, US$13 for seniors, and US$10 for children 6–12, 10 A.M.–6 P.M. daily); free transfer from downtown's ticket office at Avenida San Martín and Independencia is included.

On the summit road, at 1,240 meters, the Club Andino's **Refugio Berghof** (tel. 02944/15-271527) serves meals and drinks. Its **Museo de Montaña Otto Meiling,** which honors an early mountaineer who built his residence here, is due to reopen in 2012.

## Cerro Catedral

Cerro Catedral's 2,388-meter summit overlooks **Villa Catedral,** the ski village that serves **Catedral Alta Patagonia,** the area's major winter-sports resort. From Villa Catedral, the chair lifts, **Telesilla Princesa I, II, and III** (US$19 pp, 10 A.M.–5 P.M. daily), carry visitors to **Confitería Punta Princesa.** Hikers can continue along the ridgetop to the Club Andino's 40-bed **Refugio Emilio Frey**

© WAYNE BERNHARDSON

Cerro López

(tel. 02944/15-352222, www.refugiofrey.com, US$15 pp), 1,700 meters above sea level and open all year; the spire-like summits nearby are a magnet for rock climbers.

## Monte Tronador

Its inner fire died long ago, but the ice-clad volcanic summit of Tronador still merits its name (the "Thunderer") when frozen blocks plunge off its face into the valley below. The peak that surveyor Bailey Willis called "majestic in savage ruggedness" has impressed everyone from Jesuit explorer Miguel de Olivares to Perito Moreno, Theodore Roosevelt, and the hordes that view it every summer. Its ascent, though, is for skilled snow-and-ice climbers only.

Source of the Río Manso, Tronador's icy eastern face gives birth to the **Ventisquero Negro** (Black Glacier), a jumble of ice, sand, and rocky detritus, and countless waterfalls. At Pampa Linda, at the end of the Lago Mascardi road, whistle-blowing rangers prevent hikers from approaching the **Garganta del Diablo,** the area's largest accessible waterfall, too closely.

From Pampa Linda, hikers on a two-day trek (requiring access to Chile) can visit Club Andino's basic **Refugio Viejo Tronador,** a kiln-shaped structure that sleeps a maximum of 10 climbers in bivouac conditions, via a trail on the road's south side. On the north side, another trail leads to the 60-bed **Refugio Otto Meiling** (tel. 02944/15-213921), 2,000 meters above sea level. Between early January and March, well-equipped backpackers can continue north to Laguna Frías via the 1,335-meter Paso de las Nubes and return to Bariloche on the previously booked bus-boat shuttle via Puerto Blest and Puerto Pañuelo.

Reaching the Tronador area requires a roundabout drive via southbound RN 40 to Lago Mascardi's south end, where westbound RP 81 follows the lake's southern shore; at kilometer 9, a northbound lateral crosses Río Manso and becomes a single-lane dirt road to Pampa Linda and Tronador's base. Because it's narrow, morning traffic is one-way inbound (10:30 A.M.–2 P.M.), afternoon traffic outbound (4–6 P.M.), and at other times open to cautious two-way traffic (7:30 P.M.–9 A.M.). From December to Easter holidays, **Active Patagonia** (tel. 02944/529875, www.active-patagonia.com.ar) provides transportation from Club Andino's Bariloche headquarters to Pampa Linda at 8 A.M. daily, returning at 5 P.M. (US$25 round trip, two hours).

## Accommodations and Food

Campgrounds are numerous, especially in areas accessible by road. Club Andino *refugios* charge around US$15 per person for overnight stays, US$10 for breakfast, US$15 for lunch or dinner, and US$7 for kitchen use. Though *refugios* don't take reservations for bunks, which are limited, it is always advisable to check first if a numerous group is already accommodated; day hikers can buy simple meals and cold drinks.

Hotels and other accommodations are scattered around various park sectors. At Lago Mascardi's northwest end, on the Pampa Linda road, **Hotel Tronador** (tel. 02944/490550, www.hoteltronador.com, US$128–150 s or d with full board) is a lakes-district classic in the Bustillo tradition. It's open from early November to mid-April.

Near road's end, **Hostería Pampa Linda** (tel. 02944/490517, www.hosteriapampalinda.com.ar, US$125 s, US$165 d with half board, US$185 s, US$276 d with full board) is a rustically contemporary inn that also organizes hikes and horseback rides (at additional cost).

## Information

Before starting any hike in the park and within 48 hours prior to the date of the hike, a free form provided at ANP's offices (also available online on the park's webpage) and at Club Andino must be filled in to keep a record at the national park's *Registro de Trekking* and to show upon park rangers' request.

For detailed park information and hiking registration, contact the **APN** (San Martín 24, tel. 02944/423111, www.nahuelhuapi.gov.ar) or **Club Andino Bariloche** (20 de Febrero 30, tel. 02944/527966, www.

clubandino.org). The *refugios* are good sources of information within the park.

Club Andino's improved trail map, *Refugios, Sendas y Picadas,* at a scale of 1:100,000 with more detailed versions covering smaller areas at a scale of 1:50,000, is a worthwhile acquisition, but Aoneker (www.aoneker.com) publishes more sophisticated versions of some areas. The fifth edition of Tim Burford's *Chile and Argentina: The Bradt Trekking Guide* (Chalfont St. Peter, United Kingdom: Bradt Travel Guides, 2001) covers several trails in detail, but its maps are suitable for orientation only.

## EL BOLSÓN

El Bolsón, Argentine Patagonia's counterculture capital, may be the place to replace your faded tie-dyes, but it's also a beauty spot in a fertile valley between stunning longitudinal mountain ranges that provide fine hiking. So far, despite completion of the paved highway from Bariloche, this self-styled "ecological municipality" and outspoken non-nuclear zone has managed to stymie five-star hotels and ski areas in favor of simpler—earthier, even—services and activities.

El Bolsón's alternative lifestyle, which began in the 1960s, grew as an island of tolerance and tranquility even during the Dirty War dictatorship. More affordable than Bariloche, it embraces visitors, turns its agricultural bounty—apples, cherries, pears, raspberries, strawberries—into delectable edibles, and makes local hops into a distinctive brew. Motorists appreciate that it's the northernmost place to buy gasoline at Patagonian discount prices.

Río Negro's southernmost city, El Bolsón (population 25,000, elevation 300 meters) is 123 kilometers south of Bariloche via RN 40 and 167 kilometers north of Esquel via RN 259 and RN 40. West of the south-flowing Río Quemquemtreu, the Cordón Nevado's snowy ridge marks the Chilean border, while Cerro Piltriquitrón's knife-edge crest rises steeply to the east. Surrounding an artificial lake, the elliptical Plaza Pagano is the town's civic center and the site of its popular street fair.

© WAYNE BERNHARDSON

El Bolsón's Feria Artesanal



### Feria Artesanal

Nearly encircling Plaza Pagano, buskers, bakers, candle-makers, flower arrangers, and other crafts workers have transformed El Bolsón's street fair from a once-a-week gathering to a Tuesday, Thursday, and Saturday event (and in summer, there's a smaller version on Sunday). Forgo a restaurant lunch and snack to the max on the Belgian waffles, empanadas, sandwiches, sausages, and sweets, and wash them all down with freshly brewed draft beer. It starts around 10 A.M. and winds down around 4 P.M. or so.

### Other Shopping

The Mapuche-oriented **Centro Artesanal Cumei Antu** (Av. San Martín 1920) sells indigenous textiles. **Cabaña Micó** (Islas Malvinas 2753, tel. 02944/492691, www.mico.com.ar) sells fresh fruit from its own vines in season, and homemade preserves the rest of the year.

### Entertainment and Events

Founded in 1926, the city celebrates its **Aniversario** on January 28. Local brewers

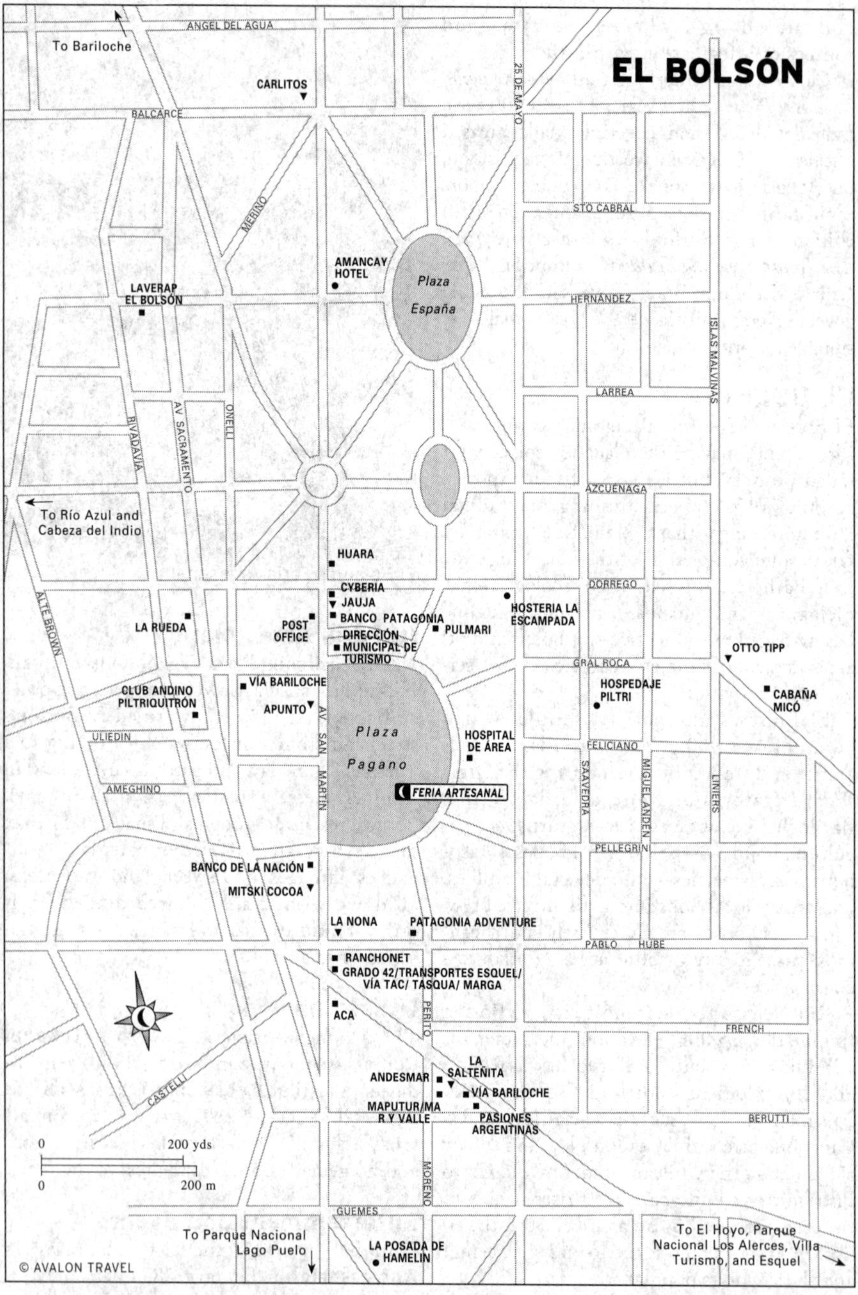


© AVALON TRAVEL

take center stage in mid-February's four-day **Festival Nacional del Lúpulo** (National Hops Festival). In high season, a few evenings a week at Cabaña El Pitío in Villa Turismo, **Languedoc** (Tres Cipreses s/n, www.languedoc.com.ar) performs theatrical medieval and renaissance music concerts.

## Sports and Recreation

Several travel agencies arrange excursions such as boating on Lago Puelo, hiking and climbing, horseback riding, mountain biking, rafting on the Río Azul and the more distant Río Manso, and parasailing. Where logistics are complex, as in reaching some trailheads, these can be a good option.

Operators include **Grado 42** (Av. Belgrano 406, tel. 02944/493124, www.grado42.com), **Pulmari** (Perito Moreno 2871, tel. 02944/492161, pulmariturismo@hotmail.com), and **Huara** (Dorrego 410, tel. 02944/455000, www.huaraviajesyturismo.com.ar).

## Accommodations

El Bolsón has quality accommodations for every budget except the luxury category (though character often compensates for lack of luxury). Some of the best values are not in town, but scattered around the outskirts.

At the north end, directly on the Bariloche highway, **Camping El Bolsón** (RN 40 s/n, tel. 02944/492595, www.cervezaselbolson.com, US$7 pp) operates its own brewery and beer garden.

About three kilometers north of town, **El Pueblito Hostel** (Barrio Luján s/n, tel. 02944/493560, www.elpueblitohostel.com.ar, US$15–17 pp in dorms, US$35–45 d) is a comfortable, sociable place on a large property, with 40 beds but also separate cabañas, some with shared bath and others with private bath, and wireless Internet. From downtown El Bolsón, there are hourly buses between 7:45 A.M. and 8:45 P.M., except at 7:45 P.M.; the first transfer is deducted from the bill.

**Hospedaje Piltri** (Saavedra 2729, tel. 02944/455305, lucas_breide17@hotmail.com, US$18 pp, breakfast extra) is a quiet family-run place whose spacious but sparsely furnished rooms have firm beds. Its main drawback is the insufficient number of shared baths (which are, however, immaculate) when it's crowded.

On secluded grounds in Barrio Turismo just off the road to Cerro Piltriquitrón, HI affiliate **Hostal Altos del Sur** (Tres Cipreses 1237, tel. 02944/498730, www.altosdelsur.bolsonweb.com, US$19 pp, US$60 d, with breakfast) has four- and six-bed dorms, plus a couple doubles, and a detached house for four, all with private baths. Off season the first transfer is free because it's a little isolated and hard to find, but its pristine facilities and amenities (which include two hectares of woodlands, an organic orchard, a library, satellite TV, homebrewed beer, and wireless Internet) make it El Bolsón's best hostel.

West of the highway on El Bolsón's northern outskirts, **Hostería del Campo** (RN 40 s/n, tel. 02944/492297, www.cabaniasdelcampo.com.ar, from US$63 s or d) has quiet motel-style rooms with wireless Internet and covered parking, set among spacious gardens, but breakfast is extra (US$4).

The **Amancay Hotel** (Av. San Martín 3207, tel. 02944/492222, www.hotelamancaybolson.com.ar, US$40 s, US$75 d) is an aging but still-serviceable hotel showing wear but not tear.

The four-room **La Posada de Hamelin** (Granollers 2179, tel. 02944/492030, www.posadadehamelin.com.ar, US$50 s, US$75 d) is one of El Bolsón's best B&Bs.

Under new ownership in 2011, six kilometers north of town, by a signed dirt road that diverges from the Bariloche highway, the riverside **La Casona de Odile** (Barrio Luján s/n, tel. 02944/492753, www.lacasonadeodile.com.ar) has added hostel accommodations (check new rates on the webpage) in its always attractive grounds, remaining open from late spring to early fall.

New in 2008, in a quiet east-side location, **Hostería La Escampada** (Azcuénaga and 25 de Mayo, tel. 02944/483905, www.laescampada.com.ar, US$50 s, US$80 d) is a cozy B&B with wireless Internet, friendly management, and regional style. For a slightly higher rate, superior doubles have their own Jacuzzis.

Close to heaven and at the edge of the wooded slopes of Villa Turismo, **Buena Vida Social Club** (tel. 02944/491729, www.buenavidapatagonia.com, US$75 s, US$90 d, open Dec.–May) is a delightful five-room B&B run by a couple of artists who personally designed the place in an aesthetic fusion of styles. Simple comfort and no TV add to a perfect relaxing stay.

## Food

Given the fresh fruit and vegetables, El Bolsón's food exceeds expectations, though it lacks sophistication. Be sure to give up one lunch in favor of snacking at Plaza Pagano's **Feria Artesanal.** Note that most places in El Bolsón stay open all day, serving breakfast, lunch, and dinner, and many of them have wireless Internet.

**La Salteñita** (Av. Belgrano 515, tel. 02944/493749) serves spicy northern empanadas for takeaway. **Mitski Cocoa** (Av. San Martín 2526, tel. 02944/491878) is an ideal breakfast spot for succulent croissants and hot chocolate. Non-spicy and still tasty empanadas are served at the popular bakery **La Nona** (Av. San Martín 2525, tel. 02944/492413), which has also a few tables outside.



**Otto Tipp** (Islas Malvinas and Roca, tel. 02944/493700) is stylishly Teutonic, with free beer samples in addition to pastas, pizzas, and a *picada* for two that includes smoked venison and wild boar (US$22).

**Carlitos** (Av. San Martín 3410, tel. 02944/455654) is a *parrilla,* where lamb costs US$10 and its *bife de chorizo* (sirloin) is US$11. **Pasiones Argentinas** (Av. Belgrano and Beruti, tel. 02944/483616) serves more elaborate versions of standards such as *bife de chorizo* (US$9), pastas, and grilled lamb (US$12).

**Apunto** (Av. San Martín 2760, tel. 02944/483780) has a varied menu of some elaborate meals such as the potent *bife de chorizo* filled with smoked venison and mozzarella (US$14).

**Jauja** (Av. San Martín 2867, tel. 02944/492448) is probably the best downtown. Vivid flower arrangements set the stage for succulent pastas such as gnocchi with a pine tree mushroom sauce (US$10), vegetarian dishes such as quinoa and millet burger with a side of vegetable aioli (US$9), trout with a white wine sauce (US$13), outstanding homemade bread, and local brews.

Ignore Jauja's in-house desserts, and step just outside to **Helados Jauja** (www.heladosjauja.com), one of the country's top ice creameries, with an almost paralyzing choice of nearly 60 inventive flavors. The author's longstanding favorite is *mate cocido con tres de azúcar* (boiled and slightly sweetened *mate*), though even some Argentines blanch at consuming their favorite bitter infusion in frozen form. *Chocolate profundo,* a bittersweet chocolate mousse, is also interesting.

Set among lavender, a 10-minute drive south on the road to Esquel, **Pirque** (RN 40 Km 1903, tel. 02944/471867) offers a sophisticated menu, including native *perca* fish and cypress mushrooms. Entrées are in the US$13–18 range.

## Information

At Plaza Pagano's north end, the **Secretaría de Turismo** (Av. San Martín and Roca, tel./fax 02944/492604, www.elbolson.gov.ar) provides decent maps of accommodations and other services; it even employs an accommodations specialist who makes suggestions and books hotels. Summer hours are 8 A.M.–10 P.M. daily (8 A.M.–8 P.M. Mon.–Fri., 9 A.M.–8 P.M. weekends the rest of the year).

For hiking and climbing suggestions, visit the **Club Andino Piltriquitrón** (Sarmiento between Roca and Ulieldin, tel. 02944/492600, www.capiltriquitron.com.ar).

For motorists, **ACA** is at Avenida Belgrano and Avenida San Martín (tel. 02944/492260).

## Services

**Banco de la Nación** (Av. San Martín 2598) and **Banco Patagonia** (Av. San Martín and Roca) have ATMs.

**Correo Argentino** is at Avenida San Martín

2806; the postal code is 8430. **Ranchonet** (Av. San Martín and Pablo Hube) has the best Internet connections. Phones and Internet access are also available at **Cyberia** (Av. San Martín and Dorrego).

**Laverap El Bolsón** (José Hernández 223, tel. 02944/493243) does the washing.

The **Hospital de Área** (Perito Moreno s/n, tel. 02944/492240) is behind Plaza Pagano.

### Getting There

El Bolsón lacks a central **bus** terminal, but most companies are within a few blocks of each other, and several travel agencies are not only selling points but bus stops too.

**Andesmar** group (Belgrano and Perito Moreno, tel. 02944/492178) goes to Bariloche, Buenos Aires (with a change in Bariloche), and south to Esquel. **Vía Bariloche** group (Av. Belgrano 556, tel. 02944/493910; Roca and Onelli, tel. 02944/455554) goes to Esquel, Bariloche, Comodoro Rivadavia, Puerto Madryn, Buenos Aires, and northbound destinations as far as San Salvador de Jujuy. **Mar y Valle** (Perito Moreno 2331, tel. 02944/491440) goes to Esquel and Puerto Madryn.

**Grado 42** (Belgrano 406, tel. 02944/493124, www.grado42.com) represents Taqsa/Marga, which goes to El Calafate and El Chaltén, and Transportes Esquel, which goes to Esquel via Parque Nacional Los Alerces, running transfer services to its northernmost stop at Lago Puelo. Grado 42 also operates its own regular service to El Maitén.

The usual destinations are Bariloche (US$6–11, 2–2.5 hours) and Esquel (US$7–17, 2–3 hours), Trelew (US$33–48, 11 hours), and Puerto Madryn (US$38–53, 12 hours). Fares to other northbound destinations are slightly more expensive than those from Bariloche; fares to southbound destinations are slightly cheaper.

### Getting Around

For a small town, El Bolsón has fine public transportation for excursions like Cerro Piltriquitrón and Lago Puelo. There are also abundant radio taxis and *remises.*

For rental bikes and cars, try **Maputur** (Perito Moreno 2331, tel. 02944/491440, maputur@elbolson.com).

## VICINITY OF EL BOLSÓN

One of El Bolsón's virtues is its convenience to trailheads for hiking and secondary roads for mountain biking. Most are just far enough away, though, to require an early start for those without their own vehicle; consider hiring a *remise* (radio taxi) to the trailheads. Hikers should look for *Guía Educativa: Ingreso a los Refugios,* an inexpensive local hiking guide for sale in El Bolsón's tourist office and the Club Andino. Though in Spanish, it summarizes trail descriptions in English, and its basic orientation maps are adequate for initial planning.

Both east and west of town, there are backcountry *refugios* where hikers can either camp or hire a bunk or floor space, and cook or purchase meals. These are fairly basic, but inexpensive and comfortable enough, and the *refugieros* who run them have built a series of connector trails to supplement the access points and create a hikers' circuit.

Two blocks north of Plaza Pagano, westbound Azcuénaga crosses the Quemquemtreu and continues six kilometers to a footpath overlooking its southerly confluence with the Río Azul and, in the distance, Lago Puelo; the short but precipitous northbound trail leads to the natural metamorphic silhouette colloquially known as the **Cabeza del Indio** (Indian's Head). There's now a small admission charge.

About six kilometers north of town via the Bariloche road, a northwesterly gravel road leads to a signed southwesterly turnoff to the municipal **Reserva Forestal Loma del Medio-Río Azul** (US$1 admission charge). Its main attraction is an 800-meter loop trail to the **Cascada Escondida,** where the river follows a fault before tumbling down the tilted face in a classic bridal veil. It's best during spring runoff, when the volume of water turns the single falls into two or three larger ones.

About 10 kilometers north of town by the same main road, but via a northeasterly lateral, the **Cascada Mallín Ahogado** (US$1 admission charge) is a 20-meter waterfall on the Quemquemtreu tributary of the Arroyo del Medio. Diverted for agriculture, it's also best in early spring. The caretaker has carved scale models of traditional oxcarts, wheelbarrows, and the like.

A parallel main road continues 15 kilometers northwest to Club Andino's 70-bunk **Refugio Perito Moreno** (tel. 02944/483433, US$8–10 pp); a small ski area, at a base elevation of 1,000 meters, has a chairlift and a T-bar lift to 1,450 meters. From the *refugio,* the 2,206-meter summit of **Cerro Perito Moreno** is about a three-hour hike. The *refugio* is busiest in summer; meals are also available here.

## Cajón del Azul

Immediately west of Mallín Ahogado, 15 kilometers northwest of El Bolsón, a signed gravel road drops steeply into the canyon of the Río Azul, which flows eastward out of the Andes before turning sharply south at the confluence with the Río Blanco. Beyond the Arco Iris campground, where the road ends, two precarious *pasarelas* (pedestrian bridges) cross the rivers before the trail becomes an up-and-down hike that leads to a sheer-sided gorge. Here, beneath a sturdy log bridge, the spring runoff explodes like a cannon shot.

Just across the bridge, about 3.5 hours from the confluence, **Refugio Cajón del Azul** is open all year. Run by an English-speaking semi-hermit named Atilio who offers a free coffee, tea, or *mate* to every arrival, the *refugio* also offers camping (US$5 pp) and mattresses for overnighters (US$13 pp) in a communal dormitory. Though dark, the rustically comfortable *refugio* even has a water-driven turbine for electricity. Most supplies arrive on horseback, though in summer and fall Atilio's irrigated *chacra* provides fresh apples, cherries, peaches, plums, raspberries, and the like. The westbound trail continues another hour or more to **Refugio El Retamal** (refugioelretamal@hotmail.com, US$13 pp for bunks, US$5 pp for camping).

An alternative northwesterly trail from

© WAYNE BERNHARDSON

Cerro Piltriquitrón rises behind El Bolsón's Plaza Pagano.

the Arco Iris trailhead dead-ends at **Refugio Dedo Gordo** (US$13 pp for bunks, US$5 pp for camping), providing access for experienced hikers to the summit of its namesake 2,065-meter summit. Before the final climb to Refugio Cajón del Azul, a new but poorly signed trail climbs steeply southward and then drops into the drainage of the Arroyo Teno and to **Refugio Hielo Azul** (www.refugiohieloazul.com.ar, US$13 pp for bunks, US$4 pp for camping) This route allows overnight hikers to loop back to El Bolsón.

### Cerro Piltriquitrón

East of El Bolsón, the piedmont rises steadily and then sharply to 2,284-meter Piltriquitrón's granite summit, where a clear day reveals the snow-covered phalanx of peaks along the Chilean border, from Tronador and beyond in the north to Lago Puelo and beyond the Cordón Esperanza in the south. When the clouds clear, Volcán Osorno's Fuji-perfect cone, in Chile, appears almost immediately west of Tronador.

From El Bolsón, a winding dirt road climbs 13 kilometers to a parking area at the 1,200-meter level, where a steep footpath leads to the **Bosque Tallado** (US$4 pp). Here, chainsaw carvers have transformed trunks from a scorched *lenga* forest into 50 memorable sculptures.

Beyond the Bosque Tallado, the trail climbs to the Club Andino's **Refugio Piltriquitrón** at 1,400 meters. Bunks cost US$9 per person, but you need your own sleeping bag; meals are also available. This was once a ski area, and the path climbs even more steeply along the rusty T-bar cable before leveling off and rounding Piltriquitrón; marked by paint blazes, it then climbs steeply over loose talus to the summit. From the *refugio,* it takes about 2–3 hours; carry water and high-energy snacks.

In summer, **Grado 42** (Av. Belgrano 406, tel. 02944/493124, www.grado42.com) goes to the parking area at 9 A.M. daily, returning two hours later. The fare is US$14 round-trip, while a *remise* costs US$20.



# Interior Chubut Province

## PARQUE NACIONAL LAGO PUELO

Fed by four rivers and numerous arroyos, nearly surrounded by forested peaks, Lago Puelo is the turquoise showpiece of its namesake national park. In addition to its scenery, it's popular for camping, swimming, boating, and hiking, and it offers a little-used option for crossing into Chile (unlike most Argentine lakes, Lago Puelo drains toward the Pacific).

Just 15 kilometers south of El Bolsón, Lago Puelo lies across the Chubut provincial line. It encompasses 27,674 hectares of mostly mountainous forested land, except for the Río Azul's lakeshore deltas in the north and the Río Turbio, across the lake to the south. The lake lies only 200 meters above sea level, but the summits rise above 1,500 meters.

### Flora and Fauna

Lago Puelo's flora and fauna closely resemble those of Nahuel Huapi to the north and Los Alerces to the south. Its relatively low elevations and exposure to Pacific storms, though, create a mild lakeshore microclimate that permits the growth of tree species like the *ulmo,* with its showy white flowers, and the *lingue.* The huemul (Andean deer) and pudu (miniature deer) are present but rarely seen.

### Sports and Recreation

Several trailheads start near the Oficina de Informes. The most popular is the **Sendero al Mirador del Lago** to the east, which climbs 130 meters to an overlook.

To the west, the **Senda Los Hitos** fords the Río Azul and leads five kilometers to Arroyo Las Lágrimas, where Chile-bound hikers can complete Argentine border formalities. Thirteen kilometers farther west, well into Chilean territory, Carabineros finish the paperwork; from there, continue to the Chilean town of Puelo, with onward connections to Puerto Montt.

For most visitors, though, sailing the lake is the main attraction. The ***Juana de Arco*** (tel. 02944/498946 in El Bolsón, www.interpatagonia.com/juanadearco) and other smaller boats carry passengers on half-hour excursions (US$13 pp) and also on longer rides, including to Los Hitos with a short trek there (US$38 pp).

### Practicalities

Immediately east of the visitors center is **Camping del Lago** (tel. 02944/499017, US$10 pp), where limited supplies are available.

In addition, there's a site at Arroyo Las Lágrimas (US$7 pp), about five kilometers west on the footpath to the border, and other free sites at Río Turbio, at the lake's south end.

Near the park entrance, where rangers collect US$2.50 per person for Argentine residents, US$5 per person for foreigners, the helpful **Oficina de Informes** (lagopuelo@apn.gov.ar, 9 A.M.–8 P.M. daily in summer, more limited hours the rest of the year) provides practical information on attractions and activities.

From El Bolsón, in summer Transporte La Golondrina **buses** shuttle down Avenida San Martín to the pier and back 14 times daily between 9 A.M. and 10:30 P.M. There are two early morning services that only reach the entrance to the park, which is also the terminal point for all off-season services.



## EL MAITÉN

In 1979, Paul Theroux's overrated opus *The Old Patagonian Express* made the dying narrow-gauge railway that ran south from Ingeniero Jacobacci to Esquel a global household word. Its antique steam locomotives no longer traverse the entire 402-kilometer route, but the dusty township of El Maitén, with its rusting rails, weathered workshops, and twirling turntables, is the best place to savor this picturesque economic folly. Like Esquel, it retains enough rolling stock that committed trainspotters can board this living anachronism and fill their photo albums in the process.

El Maitén (population 6,300) is 70 kilometers southeast of El Bolsón via RN 40 and RP 70. It's 130 kilometers north of Esquel via RN 40 and RN 1s40.

### La Trochita

Gringos may cite the Gospel of Theroux, but Argentines know the train as La Trochita (a diminutive for "gauge") or El Trencito (Little Train). The yards are still open, though only a couple of locomotives (an American Baldwin and a 1922 German Henschel) are in running order; the mostly Belgian cars date from 1922 to about 1960.

February's **Fiesta Nacional del Tren a Vapor** (National Steam Train Festival) fills the handful of hotels and campgrounds. Celebrating the railroad, it also features live music on a new custom-built stage, horseback races, bronco-busting, and regional delicacies.

Two-and-a-half-hour excursions to Desvío Thomae (the first station south of El Maitén) and back (US$38 pp for foreigners) are usually run from January to Easter holidays once or twice weekly, adding more frequencies in January and during the festival. Excursions include a visit to a small but interesting museum at the old station and to the nearby workshops. For reservations, contact **Grado 42** (Av. Belgrano 406, tel. 02944/493124, in El Bolsón; Av. San Martín 1135, tel. 02945/495585, in El Maitén, www.grado42.com).

For current schedules, contact El Maitén's **Dirección de Turismo** (Av. San Martín 992, tel. 02945/495016, www.turismoelmaiten.com.ar), near the railroad tracks, or **Estación El Maitén** (Pellegrini 841, tel. 02945/495190, ferroelmaiten@gmail.com).

### Practicalities

The **Camping Municipal** (US$2 pp) is on the nearby Río Chubut. **Hostería Refugio Andino** (Av. San Martín 1179, tel. 02945/495007, refugioandino12@hotmail.com, US$15 pp) has accommodations, a restaurant, and long-distance phones.

**Grado 42** (tel. 02945/495585) goes daily to El Bolsón (US$8). **Jacobsen** (tel. 02945/495007) goes to Esquel (US$5, two hours) Tuesday, Thursday, and Saturday at 4 P.M.

## ESQUEL

Across the Chubut border, the gateway to Parque Nacional Los Alerces and the end of the line for the "Old Patagonian Express," Esquel is a deceptively tranquil town of wide avenues divided by densely planted medians. It's also a city recently divided by a plebiscite that rejected a nearby gold mine that would have used toxic cyanide to leach the valuable mineral. What's more, it's a place where Mapuche militancy is palpable, in graffiti that says "neither Argentine nor Chilean, but Mapuche."

Esquel (population 32,000) is 167 kilometers south of El Bolsón via RN 40 and RN 259, all of them smoothly paved. Alternatively, many visitors take RP 71, south of the town of Epuyén, directly to Parque Nacional Los Alerces. Esquel is also 608 kilometers west of Trelew via several paved highways across the Patagonian steppe, and 581 kilometers northwest of Comodoro Rivadavia via equally good roads.

The city itself is a compact grid on the north bank of the Arroyo Esquel. Southbound RN 259 leads to a junction to Parque Nacional Los Alerces, the Welsh-settled town of Trevelin, and the Chilean border at La Balsa.

### La Trochita

From its new railway station, next to the old one converted into a museum, La Trochita still makes entertaining excursions to the Mapuche hamlet of Nahuel Pan. Its wooden passenger wagons, with salamander stoves and hard-backed benches, are classics of their era, and the entire line is a national historical monument.

As the train departs, residents leave their houses and cars to wave as it chugs past their backyards and crosses the highway. Each passenger coach has a guide, but the rolling stock



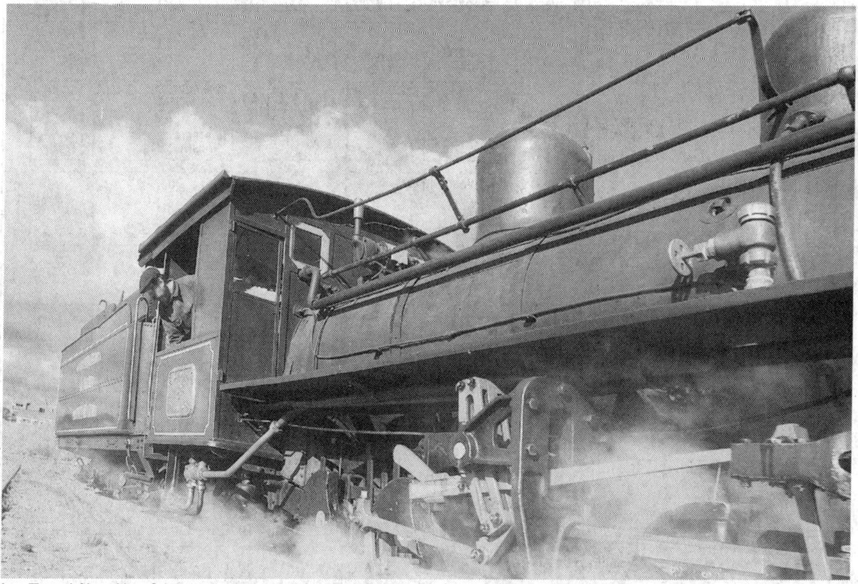

© EDUARDO RIVERA/123RF

La Trochita, the famous narrow-gauge steam train, arrives at Esquel.

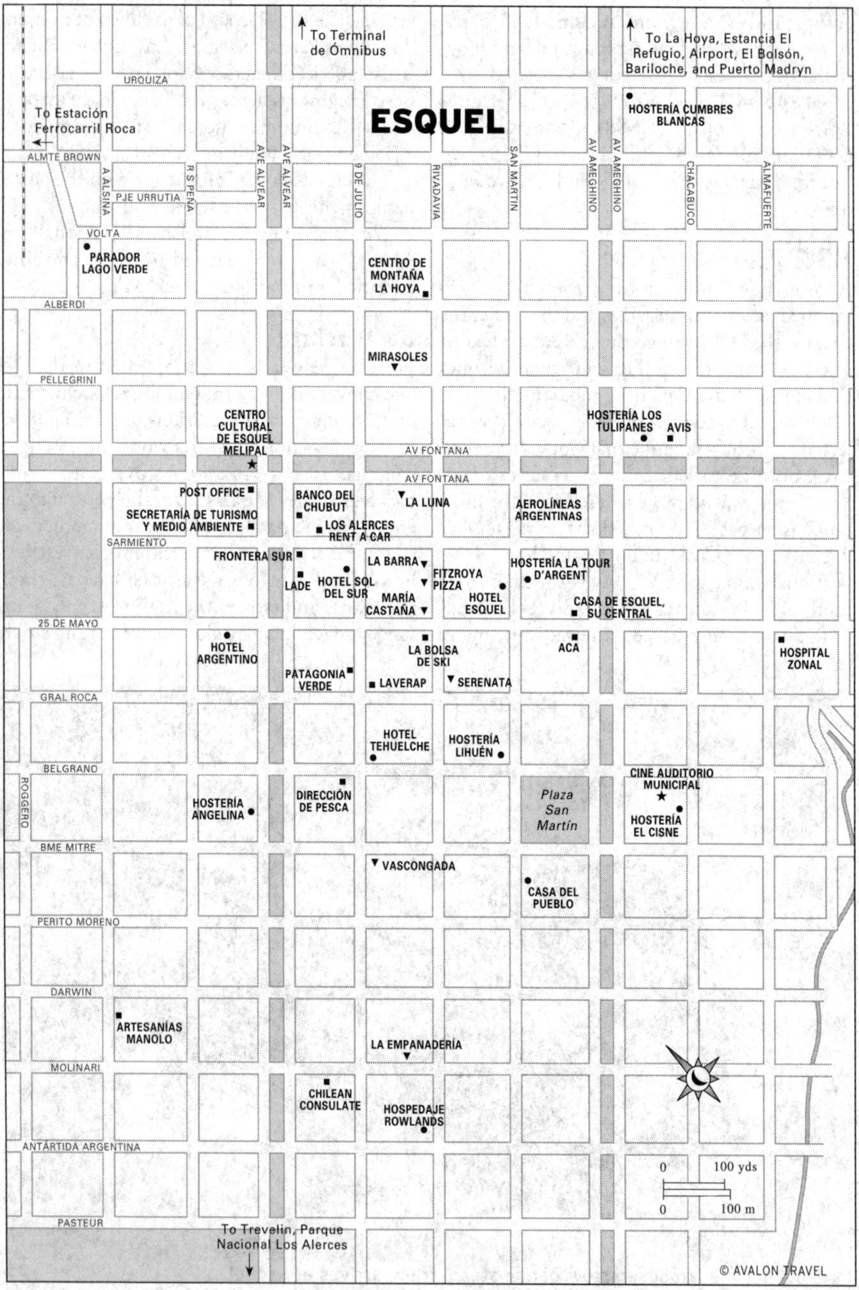
ESQUEL
To Terminal de Ómnibus
To La Hoya, Estancia El Refugio, Airport, El Bolsón, Bariloche, and Puerto Madryn
To Estación Ferrocarril Roca
URQUIZA
ALMTE BROWN
PJE URRUTIA
VOLTA
ALBERDI
PELLEGRINI
AV FONTANA
SARMIENTO
25 DE MAYO
GRAL ROCA
BELGRANO
BME MITRE
PERITO MORENO
DARWIN
MOLINARI
ANTÁRTIDA ARGENTINA
PASTEUR
A. ALSINA
R S PEÑA
AVE ALVEAR
9 DE JULIO
RIVADAVIA
SAN MARTIN
AV AMEGHINO
CHACABUCO
ALMAFUERTE
ROGGERO
HOSTERÍA CUMBRES BLANCAS
PARADOR LAGO VERDE
CENTRO DE MONTAÑA LA HOYA
MIRASOLES
CENTRO CULTURAL DE ESQUEL MELIPAL
HOSTERÍA LOS TULIPANES
AVIS
POST OFFICE
SECRETARÍA DE TURISMO Y MEDIO AMBIENTE
BANCO DEL CHUBUT
LOS ALERCES RENT A CAR
LA LUNA
AEROLÍNEAS ARGENTINAS
FRONTERA SUR
LADE
HOTEL SOL DEL SUR
LA BARRA
FITZROYA PIZZA
MARÍA CASTAÑA
HOTEL ESQUEL
HOSTERÍA LA TOUR D'ARGENT
CASA DE ESQUEL, SU CENTRAL
HOTEL ARGENTINO
LA BOLSA DE SKI
ACA
HOSPITAL ZONAL
PATAGONIA VERDE
LAVERAP
SERENATA
HOTEL TEHUELCHE
HOSTERÍA LIHUÉN
CINE AUDITORIO MUNICIPAL
HOSTERÍA ANGELINA
DIRECCIÓN DE PESCA
Plaza San Martín
HOSTERÍA EL CISNE
VASCONGADA
CASA DEL PUEBLO
ARTESANÍAS MANOLO
LA EMPANADERÍA
CHILEAN CONSULATE
HOSPEDAJE ROWLANDS
0 100 yds
0 100 m
To Trevelin, Parque Nacional Los Alerces
© AVALON TRAVEL

is so noisy that understanding the narration is difficult.

Taking about an hour to reach Nahuel Pan, La Trochita remains another hour before returning to Esquel. In the meantime, there are good oven-baked empanadas, drinks, Mapuche crafts, short horseback rides, and spare time to visit there the **Museo de Culturas Originarias Patagónicas** (open for train arrivals).

Excursions are usually run from October to Easter holidays, plus winter holidays, operating daily services (Mon.–Sat.) in summer and reducing the frequencies the rest of the season to keep only the Saturday service. Foreigners pay US$38 per person, cash only; it's advisable to buy tickets in advance. For details, contact **Estación Esquel** (Roggero and Urquiza, tel. 02945/451403).

## Events and Entertainment

Late February's **Semana de Esquel** marks the city's 1906 founding.

**Hotel Argentino** (25 de Mayo 862) has a great bar with a classic kitchen-sink collection of memorabilia and junk, as well as friendly staff.

In the utterly transformed old bus terminal, the **Centro Cultural de Esquel Melipal** (Av. Fontana and Av. Alvear) encompasses a variety of art and performing arts spaces. The **Auditorium Ciudad de Esquel** (Belgrano 330, tel. 02945/451929) shows first-run movies.

## Shopping

**Artesanías La Estación** (Sarmiento 630) sells crafts, textiles, and other regional produce.

For wood carvings, try **Artesanías Manolo** (Alsina 483). **Casa de Esquel** (25 de Mayo 415, tel. 02945/452544) is a bookstore focused on Patagonia and a crafts outlet. Though well adapted to contemporary times, **Los Vascos** (9 de Julio and 25 de Mayo) still keeps the attractive atmosphere and diversity of goods of an old general store.

## Sports and Recreation

Hiking, climbing, fishing, horseback riding, and rafting and kayaking are all on the docket. Argentina's Río Corcovado is a Class II–III starter river, but the Class V Futaleufú, across the Chilean border, has world-class white water.

**Patagonia Verde** (9 de Julio 926, tel. 02945/454396, www.patagonia-verde.com.ar) arranges activities like hiking, climbing, and riding. **Frontera Sur** (Sarmiento 784, tel. 02945/450505, www.fronterasur.net) organizes water sports like rafting (US$75 for a full day) and kayaking on the Corcovado, as well as hiking, riding, and mountain biking. **Epa Viajes y Turismo** (Av. Fontana 482, tel. 02945/457015, www.grupoepa.com) also does rafting and other activities.

For fishing licenses, contact the **Secretaría de Pesca** (Belgrano 722, tel. 02945/451063), or they can be purchased also at some shops and gas stations; the season runs November–April. **Andrés Müller** (Sarmiento 120, tel. 02945/454572, framumi@ar.inter.net) is a reliable independent fishing guide, while **Rincón Andino** (Miguens 40, tel. 02945/452185, www.rinconandino.com.ar) is a specialist operator.



## Accommodations

Esquel has increased its accommodations, but things can get tight in summer and in ski season. Standards in general are good.

The HI affiliate **Casa del Pueblo** (San Martín 661, tel. 02945/450581, www.esquelcasadelpueblo.com.ar, US$12 pp, US$30 d) is a well-run hostel with a bar and a tidy garden.

**Hospedaje Rowlands** (Rivadavia 330, tel. 02945/452578, gales01@hotmail.com, US$15 pp) has expanded from a simple family house, offering some good private rooms with baths; breakfast costs US$4 more. **Residencial El Cisne** (Chacabuco 778, tel. 02945/452256, hosteria.el.cisne@gmail.com, US$20 s, US$30 d) is comparable.

Backpackers can also try **Parador Lago Verde** (Volta 1081, tel. 02945/452251, www.patagonia-verde.com.ar, US$28 d, breakfast US$5 extra), which offers good value private rooms with baths. The 10-room no-frills **Hostería Los Ñires** (San Martín 820, tel. 02945/452589, www.hotelnires.com, US$38 s, US$50 d) is decent and the place has wireless Internet.

**Hostería los Tulipanes** (Av. Fontana 365, tel. 02945/452748, rubenportscher@yahoo.com.ar, US$40 s, US$55 d) is a family-run hostelry that has added wireless Internet but needs a general renovation. However, the homey atmosphere, warmth in the details (like bedside chocolates), and a diverse breakfast still make for a good choice.

A commonplace facade conceals the spacious, well-furnished rooms at **Hostería Angelina** (Av. Alvear 758, tel./fax 02945/452763, info@hosteriaangelina.com.ar, US$50–60 s, US$60–73 d), whose gregarious owner goes out of his way to make guests feel welcome. Rates include wireless Internet, cable TV, parking, and central heating, while bathrooms in larger superior rooms have bathtubs; the buffet breakfast has 35 different products, including croissants, rice pudding, cakes, ham, cheese, bread, cereal, fruit and fruit salad, coffee, and tea.

New in 2009, **Hotel Sur Sur** (Av. Fontana and Chacabuco, tel. 02945/453858, www.hotelsursur.com, US$50 s, US$63 d) has excellent value accommodations, with functional, light, and simply decorated rooms, including an ample breakfast and wireless Internet.

In the Villa Ayelén neighborhood, opposite the racetrack just south of the town center, **Hostería Canela** (Los Notros and Los Radales, tel. 02945/453890, www.canelaesquel.com, US$115 s or d) is a former teahouse turned bed-and-breakfast with six spacious rooms on immaculate grounds. Hosts Jorge Miglioli and Verónica Ayling speak fluent English, provide an ample breakfast, and offer dining and excursion suggestions.

New in 2010, with every modern comfort but no real luxuries, the **Las Bayas Hotel** (Av. Alvear 985, tel. 02945/455800, www.lasbayashotel.com, US$165–265 s or d) has 10 spacious suites, including a split-level apartment for four, with a long list of amenities, attentive room service, and a restaurant also open to nonguests.

Somewhat overpriced, the 20 midsize-plus rooms at **Hostería Cumbres Blancas** (Av. Ameghino 1683, tel. 02945/455100, www.cumbresblancas.com.ar, US$150 s, US$216 d) look as good as the day they opened in 1997. It also has wireless Internet, a sauna, a restaurant, and grounds that include a mini-golf course and a duck pond. If business is slow, try asking for the lower Argentine rates.

## Food

**María Castaña** (25 de Mayo 605, tel. 02945/451752, 8 A.M.–midnight daily) serves breakfast, coffee, and good sandwiches. **Empanadería** (Molinari 633, noon–10 P.M. daily) bakes a variety of takeaway empanadas.

An ideal stopover when everywhere else is closed, **Serenata** (Rivadavia 939, tel. 02945/455999, noon–11 P.M. daily) is a good choice for coffee, cakes, and sandwiches, and has Esquel's finest ice cream.

**La Luna** (Av. Fontana 656, tel. 02945/453800, lunch and dinner daily) has a list of Argentine standards, including massive *milanesa La Luna,* with bacon, fried eggs, and potatoes (US$11), and offers patio seating. **La Barra** (Sarmiento 638, tel. 02945/454321, lunch and dinner daily) is an unpretentious but excellent *parrilla* that has unexpected treats, such as giant ravioli stuffed with lamb (US$9). When it gets busy, though, the service can suffer.

**Fitzroya Pizza** (Rivadavia 1048, tel. 02945/450512, lunch and dinner daily) is a first-rate pizzeria, with an enormous variety of toppings (from US$8); solo diners can order half portions. Irish-style pubs are a staple in Argentina, but **Killarney's Irish Resto Bar** (Av. Alvear and Sarmiento, tel. 02945/457041, from 8:30 P.M. Mon.–Sat., from 6 P.M. Sun.) is the first of its kind here, good for sandwiches, its draft Heiskel beer, and the great Killarney's salad (US$7).

The bistro-style **Mirasoles** (Pellegrini 643, tel. 02945/456390, dinner only Tues.–Sat.) is good for Italian-Argentine entrées (around US$10–15) like *ñoquis* (gnocchi), appetizers like *mozzarella caprese,* and vegetarian dishes.

**Don Chiquino** (Av. Ameghino 1641, tel. 02945/450035, lunch and dinner daily) has outstanding pastas, such as lasagna (US$15), at a picturesque place run by a magician.

## Information

The **Secretaría de Turismo** (Av. Alvear 1120, tel. 02945/451927, www.esquel.gov.ar, 7 A.M.–11 P.M. daily in summer, 8 A.M.–9 P.M. daily the rest of the year) maintains a thorough database on accommodations and other services here and in Parque Nacional Los Alerces. In summer only, a satellite office at the bus terminal is open daily.

For tourist information on the whole province of Chubut, there is a **Centro de Informes de la Subsecretaría de Turismo** (Sarmiento 635, tel. 02945/451480, infoturismoprovincia@gmail.com, 10 A.M.–8 P.M. daily, extended hours in summer).

For motorists, **ACA** (tel. 02965/452382) is at 25 de Mayo and Avenida Ameghino.

## Services

**Banco del Chubut** (Av. Alvear 1131) has one of several downtown ATMs. For money exchange, try **Artesanías La Estación** (Sarmiento 630).

**Correo Argentino** is at Avenida Alvear 1192; the postal code is 9200. **Su Central** (25 de Mayo 415) has both phone and Internet access, as does **Cyber Club** (Av. Alvear and 25 de Mayo).

Chile's **consulate** (Molinari 754, tel. 02945/451189) is open 8:30 A.M.–1:30 P.M. weekdays.

For laundry (about US$4 per load), try **Laverap** (9 de Julio and Roca, tel. 02945/455959).

For medical services, contact the **Hospital Zonal** (25 de Mayo 150, tel. 02945/450009).

## Getting There

Esquel has limited air services, better bus connections, and rail fantasies.

**Aerolíneas Argentinas** (Av. Fontana 406, tel. 02945/453614) flies thrice weekly to Buenos Aires. **LADE** (Av. Alvear 1085, tel. 02945/452124) usually flies weekly to Bariloche and Buenos Aires, but schedules change frequently.

The **Terminal de Ómnibus** (Av. Alvear 1871, tel. 02945/451584) is a contemporary facility eight blocks northeast of downtown. It has good local and regional services, but long-distance links are better in Bariloche; a small boarding tax is charged.

**Transporte Jacobsen** (tel. 02945/454676) connects Esquel with El Maitén at 1:30 P.M. Tuesday, Thursday, and Saturday.

Jacobsen also serves nearby Trevelin (frequently), La Balsa (2–3 times weekly), Corcovado (four times weekly), and other minor destinations in west and northwestern Chubut. Twice daily in summer (at 7:30 A.M. and 1:30 P.M., it goes to Lago Puelo via Parque Nacional Los Alerces.

**Transportes Esquel** (tel. 02945/453529) goes in summer to Parque Nacional Los Alerces and Lago Puelo at 8 A.M. (connecting with lake excursions) daily. Fares are US$4 to La Villa, US$5 to Bahía Rosales, US$6.50 to Lago Verde and to Lago Rivadavia, US$7.50 to Cholila, and US$13 to Lago Puelo (six hours), where there are easy connections to El Bolsón. An open ticket (US$15) valid throughout the season either north- or southbound allows passengers to stop anywhere en route and continue on any succeeding bus on same direction. Bikes not allowed. Winter services are limited to three weekly.

Typical destinations include Trevelin (US$1, 30 minutes), La Balsa (US$5, 1.5 hours), El Maitén (US$5, two hours), El Bolsón (US$7–17, 2–3 hours), Bariloche (US$16–20, 4.5 hours), Trelew (US$28–40, 8–8.5 hours), Puerto Madryn (US$43, nine hours), Comodoro Rivadavia (US$32–37, eight hours), and Buenos Aires (US$124–173, 24 hours).

## Getting Around

**Aeropuerto Esquel** is 20 kilometers east of town on RN 40; transfer services arranged by travel agencies, taxis, and *remises* are the only options.

**Los Alerces Rent a Car** (Sarmiento 763, tel. 02945/456008, www.losalercesrentacar.com.ar) and **Avis** (Av. Fontana 331, tel. 02945/455062) have rental cars.

## VICINITY OF ESQUEL

In addition to Parque Nacional Los Alerces, Esquel has many other points of interest within an hour or two.

### La Hoya

Only 12 kilometers north of Esquel, La Hoya is a modest ski area that, thanks to its location on the Andes's drier eastern side, gets a fine powder that compensates for its relatively small size. It's substantially cheaper than Bariloche, and the infrastructure is improving, but limited capacity can mean long lift lines.

Ranging from 1,350 to 2,075 meters above sea level, La Hoya has 25 runs totaling about 22 kilometers on 60 hectares. Its modern lifts include the 1,100-meter Telesilla del Bosque, which also carries hikers to high-country trailheads in summer (US$7), and the 1,018-meter Telesilla del Cañadón. In season, it also has a ski school, and the **Fiesta Nacional del Esquí** (National Ski Festival) is celebrated.

Equipment can be rented on-site or in Esquel at several shops, including **Bolsa de Ski** (Rivadavia and 25 de Mayo, tel. 02945/452379, www.bolsadeski.com.ar). For other details, contact **Centro de Actividades de Montaña La Hoya** (Av. Ameghino and Av. Fontana, tel. 02945/453018, www.skilahoya.com).



### Museo Leleque

Midway between Esquel and El Bolsón, on what was one of Argentina's largest *estancias*, the Museo Leleque (RN 40 Km 1440, tel. 02945/452600, ext. 24, www.elmaiten.com.ar/museo.htm, US$1.50) covers Patagonia from prehistory to the present. Funded by fashion icon Carlo Benetton, who purchased the Argentine Southern Land Company and several other Patagonian properties, it houses the collections of Ukrainian immigrant Pablo S. Korschenewski, who left Buenos Aires half a century ago to explore the Patagonian countryside on foot and by horseback.

In the process, Korschenewski amassed over 14,000 artifacts, including arrowheads, bone drills, ceremonial axes, grinding stones, and pottery shards. Striking a chord with Benetton, he persuaded the Italian to turn Leleque's historic buildings, once a general store, hotel, and school, into a contemporary museum that now gets 8,500 visitors, mostly Argentines, per annum. Not just archaeological, the exhibits stress contact and post-contact history of the region's first peoples, regional and oral histories, photographs, and documents. One prize is a receipt signed by Butch Cassidy, who lived in nearby Cholila from 1901 to 1905, under the alias Santiago Ryan.

Administered by the Fundación Ameghino, the Museo Leleque is 90 kilometers north of Esquel. It's open 11 A.M.–5 P.M. Thursday–Tuesday (except holidays), but is closed May–June. The museum has a souvenir shop and a *boliche* for snacks and coffee.

### Cholila

Though it's barely a wide spot in the road, Cholila has become an offbeat pilgrimage site ever since U.S. author Anne Meadows pinpointed the house of *yanqui* outlaws Robert Leroy Parker and Harry Longabaugh in her historical travelogue *Digging Up Butch and Sundance* (3rd edition; Lincoln, Nebraska: University of Nebraska Press, 2003). Bruce Chatwin also told of the Cholila cabin—perhaps taking literary license—in his classic *In Patagonia* (New York: Summit Books, 1977).

Butch and Sundance presumably tried to go straight here, but fled to Chile in 1905 when accused of a robbery in Río Gallegos and the Pinkertons got on their scent. After the 1999 death of the house's elderly occupant, Aladín Sepúlveda, souvenir hunters targeted the unoccupied and crumbling cabin, but the municipality has restored the buildings—in fact, they look livable enough that you almost expect to see cardboard cutouts of Paul Newman and Robert Redford, but there are no exhibits within. In theory, a caretaker collects a small admission charge.

Near Parque Nacional Los Alerces's northeastern entrance, a few kilometers north of Cholila at kilometer 21 of RP 71 near the signed junction to the Casa de Piedra teahouse, the cabin is visible on the west side of the highway; in fact, buses between Puelo and Esquel via Los Alerces pass within sight of it.

Beyond the entrance, a westbound lateral leads to the **Casa de Piedra** (tel. 02945/498056, US$63 d), a hybrid B&B/teahouse that's open from December through Semana Santa. It makes an ideal detour even for day-trippers.

## TREVELIN AND VICINITY

Few settlements in Chubut's Andean interior retain the Welsh imprint, but tranquil Trevelin, with historic houses and teahouses to rival Gaiman, is the exception. Only half an hour from Esquel, it owes its name to a Welsh compound meaning "mill town," after its first flour mill, now a history museum.

Trevelin (population 6,900), 24 kilometers south of Esquel via RN 259, is also unique for its disorienting octagonal Plaza Coronel Fontana, from which the highway continues south as Avenida San Martín; it's the main commercial street and thoroughfare to Corcovado and the Chilean border post of Futaleufú. Other streets fan out from the plaza.

Chile-bound motorists should fill the tank here, as Futaleufú has no gas station and Chilean prices are substantially higher than those in Argentine Patagonia.

### Sights

In 1922, Welsh immigrants founded the Molino Harinero de la Compañía Andes, the flour mill that's now the **Museo Histórico Regional Molino Viejo** (Molino Viejo 488, tel. 02945/480189, 10 A.M.–8 P.M. daily Jan.–Feb, 11 A.M.–6 P.M. the rest of the year, US$1.50 for adults, US$0.80 children under age 12). Commercially closed in 1953, it was then used for wool storage; a fire gutted the interior in 1972, but its solid brick walls survived to house the city's historical museum. Contents include period clothing, furniture, carriages, and agricultural machinery, as well as photographs, maps, and documents. It also devotes space to the Mapuche and Tehuelche and notes an early-20th-century banditry crackdown, by the army, that was tough on honest settlers.

Two blocks northeast of the plaza, the offbeat **Museo Cartref Taid** (Malacara s/n, tel. 02945/480108, 10 A.M.–noon in summer and July, and 3:30–8 P.M. all year, US$1.50, US$2.50 including a guided tour and visit to a pioneer's rebuilt cottage) holds the **Tumba de Malacara,** the final resting place of a horse that helped its rider, Trevelin founder John D. Evans, flee an Araucanian raid during the Argentine army's 1880s war against the indigenes.

At the south end of town, built of brick, the **Capilla Bethel** (Ap Iwan and Laprida) is a Welsh chapel dating from 1910; it has also served as a school.

About 17 kilometers south of Trevelin via RN 259 and a short southbound lateral, **Reserva Provincial Nant-y-Fall** is a provincial park with a 400-meter footpath to a string of waterfalls, the highest of which is 64 meters. Nant-y-Fall's source is **Lago Rosario,** a sub-alpine lake on a Mapuche reservation, 26 kilometers southeast of Trevelin via RN 259, RP 17, and a short eastbound lateral.

Six kilometers west of the access to Nant-y-Fall, the provincial **Estación de Salmonicultura** (salmon hatchery) offers guided tours 8 A.M.–8 P.M. daily in summer, and shorter hours daily the rest of the year. There are several campgrounds and cabañas along RN 259, which leads to the Chilean border.

In the Valle 16 de Octubre, about five kilometers east of Trevelin via gravel road, the historic **Escuela No. 18** stands near the site of a 1902 plebiscite that determined that Trevelin would stay on the Argentine side of the border (the original adobe building no longer exists). The onetime school now holds the **Museo del Plebiscito de 1902,** an outlier of Trevelin's regional museum, which commemorates the 1902 events.

In summer, Plaza Coronel Fontana hosts a weekend **crafts market** that also takes place on holidays. The rest of the year, it takes place alternate Sundays.

### Accommodations

Except for cabañas, which are primarily for family groups, accommodations are few. On high ground a few blocks east of the plaza, the HI affiliate **Casaverde Hostel** (Los Alerces s/n, tel. 02945/480091, www.casaverdehostel.com.ar, US$13 pp in dorms, US$48 d, breakfast extra US$4) is a prize: comfortable rooms and extensive grounds with views of the Andes. It's small, though, so reservations—or good timing—are essential. It also rents bicycles.

Other options include comfortable **Hospedaje Familiar Pezzi** (Sarmiento 353, tel. 02945/480146, hpezzi@intramed.net, US$50 d, summer only) with an ample breakfast, a neat backyard, and discounts for longer stays, and **Hostería Estefanía** (Perito Moreno and Sarmiento, tel. 02945/480148, hosteriaestefania@gmail.com, US$63 d), which has wireless Internet and petulant ownership.

New in 2008, **Hostería Casa de Piedra** (Brown 244, tel. 02945/480357, www.casadepiedratrevelin.com, US$88 s, US$98 d) is a 10-room, two-story bed-and-breakfast of stone and polished natural wood that offers king-size beds, continental or buffet breakfast, and amenities including wireless Internet.



## Food

Welsh teahouses are fewer here than in Gaiman, but the quality is still outstanding. The traditional favorite, in modern quarters, is **Nain Maggie** (Perito Moreno 179, tel. 02945/480232, www.casadetenainmaggie.com), but there's nothing wrong with **La Mutisia** (Av. San Martín 170, tel. 02945/480165). Late-afternoon teas, very filling, cost about US$15 per person.

Trevelin's Irish pub is **San Patricio** (across the street from the tourist office). **Oregon** (Av. San Martín and John Murray Thomas, tel. 02945/480408, lunch and dinner daily, closed on Tues.) is a popular *parrilla,* where the all-you-can-eat option costs US$18, drinks extra.

**Serenata** (on Plaza Fontana) has fine ice cream.

## Information and Services

January–February, the erratic **Dirección de Turismo** (Plaza Coronel Fontana s/n, tel. 02945/480120, www.trevelin.gob.ar) is open 8 A.M.–9 P.M. daily; the rest of the year, hours are 8 A.M.–7 P.M. daily.

**Banco del Chubut** (Av. San Martín and Brown) has an ATM. **Correo Argentino** (Av. San Martín and Brown) is across from the bank; the postal code is 9203.

**Gales al Sur** (Av. Patagonia 186, tel. 02945/480427, www.galesalsur.com.ar) organizes excursions and activities in and around town.

**Hospital Trevelin** (Av. San Martín and Primera Junta, tel. 02945/480132) is nine blocks south of Plaza Coronel Fontana.

## Getting There and Around

In daylight hours, **Transporte Jacobsen** shuttles between Esquel and Trevelin frequently; some buses continue to the Chilean border crossing at La Balsa (Monday and Friday at 8:30 A.M. and 6:30 P.M., US$4). Long-distance travelers have to return to Esquel.

# PARQUE NACIONAL LOS ALERCES

Parque Nacional Los Alerces owes its existence and name to *Fitzroya cupressoides,* the coniferous monarch of the humid Valdivian forests, also known as *lahuán,* false larch or Patagonian cypress. Easily western Chubut's most popular attraction, the park draws campers and fishing aficionados to its forests and finger lakes. Despite a magnificent setting, with snowy Andean summits to the west, hikers find it frustrating because a scant trail network often forces them to walk the shoulders of dusty roads with heavy auto traffic.

## Geography and Climate

About 45 kilometers west of Esquel via RN 259 and RP 71, Los Alerces is a 263,000-hectare unit on the eastern Andean slope. Its highest point is 2,253-meter Cerro Torrecillas, but Pacific storms that penetrate the lower cordillera here make it wetter than most of Argentine Patagonia.

Past glaciations have left navigable finger lakes that provide access to some of the park's finest sights. Summers are mild, with temperatures reaching 24°C with cool nights, but winters average barely 2°C, with ample snowfall.

Most destinations within the park are described with reference to La Villa, the village-like cluster of services at Lago Futalaufquen's south end.

## Flora and Fauna

Besides the *alerce,* the park's other conifers include the Chilean incense cedar and the Guaiteca cypress, both with limited geographical distribution. Most of the rest of the forest consists of the broadleaf southern beeches *coihue, lenga,* and *ñire.* The *arrayán* nears the southern limit of its range here.

For hikers, one of the worst plagues is the *colihue,* a solid bamboo that forms impassable thickets. The aggressive exotic *rosa mosqueta,* a European introduction, is displacing native plants.

In this dense forest, Los Alerces's fauna are less conspicuous, but the Andean deer or huemul is present, along with its distant miniature relative the pudu. Birds include the *chucao* (a common songbird), the austral parakeet, and the Patagonian woodpecker.

## Sights and Recreation

On the Río Desaguadero, west of RP 71 at the south end of Lago Futalaufquen, the **Sendero de las Pinturas Rupestres** is an easy 500-meter nature trail that passes a natural overhang with fading pre-Columbian rock art, some of it clearly geometrical; it then climbs through forest to an overlook with expansive panoramas to the north.

Register with rangers to hike the steep route to the 1,916-meter summit of **Cerro El Dedal,** reached by a trailhead from La Villa; figure about 6–7 hours round-trip to complete the hike. From the road to Puerto Limonao (3.5 km north of La Villa), **Cinco Saltos** is a shorter and easier hike to a series of waterfalls.

From Puerto Limonao, four kilometers north of La Villa, the 25-kilometer **Sendero Lago Krüger** follows Lago Futalaufquen's south shore to the smaller Lago Krüger, which has a campground and a lodge; register with rangers before beginning the hike (a portable stove is obligatory), which has only one campsite, at Playa Blanca, between the trailhead and the lodge for an overnight stay (for inbound hikers only). Daily boat service to Lago Krüger costs about US$30 per person round-trip.

## Circuito Lacustre

Los Alerces's traditional excursion is the "lake circuit" from Puerto Limonao, at Lago Futalaufquen's south end, to the Río Arrayanes outlet of Lago Verde; at **Puerto Mermoud,** a catwalk crosses to Lago Menéndez's **Puerto Chucao,** where another boat continues to **Puerto Sagrario.**

From Puerto Sagrario, passing blue-green **Lago Cisne,** a looping nature trail goes to the **El Alerzal** grove and the landmark **El Abuelo,** the oldest and most impressive *alerce* specimen. While there are guides on the hike to and from El Abuelo, it's possible to separate from the group; it's not possible, though, to hike elsewhere in an area that's mostly limited-access *zona intangible.*

It's possible to start the excursion at either Puerto Limonao (US$49 pp) or Puerto Chucao (US$40 pp), though low water often eliminates the Limonao-Chucao segment. Scheduled departures vary, and in summer an extra afternoon service from Limonao is added to the usual morning excursion. Any Esquel travel agency can make reservations, but it's possible (though not recommended) to purchase tickets here on a space-available basis.

More exclusive boat trips of up to 10 passengers are run by **Glaxiar** (tel. 02945/15-558088, www.glaxiar.com.ar), offering its own lake circuit excursion and a trek to the Torrecillas glacier.

## Accommodations and Food

Los Alerces has numerous campgrounds and other accommodations, mostly near Lago Futalaufquen. In addition to organized campgrounds, formerly free *agreste* (wild) sites now charge for limited services but are much cleaner than in the past.

Accessible by road, organized campgrounds

all have picnic tables, fire pits, toilets with hot showers, and access to groceries and restaurants; some have electrical outlets. Among them are **Camping Los Maitenes** (tel. 02945/471006, US$8 pp), 800 meters from the Intendencia at Futalaufquen's south end; **Camping Bahía Rosales** (tel. 02945/471044, US$8 pp), 15 kilometers from La Villa on the eastern lakeshore; and **Camping Lago Rivadavia** (tel. 02945/452009, US$8 pp), 46 kilometers north of La Villa at its namesake lake's south end.

At Lago Verde, 35 kilometers from La Villa, is the exclusive fishing lodge **Lago Verde Wilderness Resort** (tel. 011/48134340, www.hosteriaselaura.com, from US$500 s or d per bungalow for half board), with comfortable bungalows and a gourmet restaurant.

Reached only by a 25-kilometer footpath or launch from Puerto Limonao, **Hostería & Camping Lago Krüger** (tel. 02945/457015 in Esquel, www.epaexpediciones.com.ar) is the only backcountry campsite and hotel. Having undergone a major renovation, it charges about US$12 per person for camping, US$100 per person with full board in the *hostería*.

For groups of any size, the cheapest non-camping options are places like **Cabañas Tejas Negras** (RP 71, tel. 02945/471046, tejasnegras@infovia.com.ar, US$125 for up to four people), about 12 kilometers north of La Villa.

About five kilometers north of La Villa, **Hostería Quimé-Quipán** (RP 71 s/n, tel. 02945/471021, US$88 s, US$95 d) has simple but comfortable rooms, some with lake views; the restaurant is adequate.

Four kilometers north of La Villa, the park's prestige accommodation is the Bustillo-built **Hostería Futalaufquen** (tel. 02945/471008, www.brazosur.com.ar, US$178–270 s or d with half board, depending on view, in high season). With only nine rooms, it enjoys a privileged end-of-the-road location on Lago Futalaufquen's western shore; distinctive features include beamed Tudor-style ceilings, a walk-in granite fireplace, copper chandeliers, and a polished wooden bar. The restaurant is open to nonguests (reservations only for dinner).

### Other Practicalities

Colloquially known as La Villa, Villa Futalaufquen is the park headquarters. The APN's **Museo y Centro de Informes** (tel. 02945/471015, ext. 23, infoalerces@apn.gov.ar, 8 A.M.–9 P.M. daily mid-Dec.–Mar., 9 A.M.–8 P.M. daily the rest of the year) is both a museum, with history and natural history exhibits, and a helpful ranger information center.

At both the northern Lago Rivadavia (Portada Norte) and eastern La Portada (Portada Centro) entrances, rangers collect a US$13 per person admission charge for foreigners. After 9 P.M., when the tollbooths close, there's no one to collect the charge, but they check on the way out.

In addition to the APN headquarters, La Villa also has a grocery, public telephones, and a first-aid station.

**Transportes Esquel** and **Transporte Jacobsen** buses between Esquel and Lago Puelo pick up and drop off passengers along RP 71 within the park; off season Transportes Esquel buses go only thrice a week to Lago Puelo, and on Monday only to La Villa.

## GOBERNADOR COSTA

Some 180 kilometers south of Esquel, Gobernador Costa is a cowtown with the best services on the long haul between Esquel and Río Mayo on RN 40. Its early-February **Fiesta Provincial del Caballo** is the town's major event. **Río Pico's** nearby streams and lakes, and **Lago General Vintter,** on the Chilean border via partly paved westbound RP 19, are popular with fishers.

### Accommodations and Food

North of the highway, the **Camping Municipal** (2 de Abril and Los Suecos) has hot water and electricity. Owned by a Boer descendant, **Hotel Sudáfrica** (San Martín and Pasteur, tel. 02945/491075, US$25 pp) has all basic rooms with baths, central heating, and parking. **Hostería y Restaurant Mi Refugio** (Av. Roca s/n, tel. 02945/491097, US$45 d) has firm, comfortable beds but is ragged around the edges. Its restaurant serves pretty good versions of Argentine standards.

Across from the tourist office, **El Petiso** (Av. Roca s/n, no phone, lunch and dinner daily) is best for beef.

### Other Practicalities

The helpful **Oficina de Informes Turísticos** (Av. Roca s/n, tel. 02945/491004) is open 9 A.M.–8 P.M. daily.

**Banco del Chubut** (Sarmiento and San Martín) has an ATM.

The bus terminal has services northbound to Esquel, eastbound to Trelew, and southbound to Sarmiento and Comodoro Rivadavia.

## RÍO MAYO

Because public transportation is almost nonexistent on RN 40 between Gobernador Costa and Perito Moreno, only self-propelled southbound travelers normally see the crossroads town of Río Mayo; in fact, few vehicles of any kind use the dull but spine-jarring gravel section that intersects RP 43, the paved route between Comodoro Rivadavia and the Chilean border, 124 kilometers to the south. Despite having little to see, it's a stopover for cyclists, bikers, and motorists, as well as southbound safaris from Bariloche.

Living primarily off the wool trade, though petroleum is making a comeback, Río Mayo (population 2,940) is 233 kilometers south of Gobernador Costa and 274 kilometers west of Comodoro Rivadavia via paved RN 26 and RN 40. There is westbound public transportation on RN 26 to Coyhaique, Chile.

### Events

Featuring sheep-shearing contests and horseback races, early January's **Festival Nacional de la Esquila** is the principal festival.

### Accommodations and Food

**Camping El Labrador** (Belgrano and Sarmiento) charges US$5 per person. Modernized **Hotel Aka-ta** (San Martín 640, tel. 02903/420054, hotelakata@yahoo.com.ar, US$35 s, US$60 d) has rooms with private baths, and an improved but cramped restaurant with erratic wireless Internet.

Reservations are advisable for **Hotel El Viejo Covadonga** (San Martín 573, tel. 02903/420020, covadonga_hotel@yahoo.com.ar, US$13 pp, US$30 s, US$40 d), which has private rooms with baths and breakfast included, as well as cheaper accommodations without. This spruced-up hotel has gracious management and is also the best place to eat.

### Information and Services

At the eastern approach to town is the **Dirección de Cultura y Turismo** (Av. Ejército Argentino s/n, tel. 02903/420400, culturayturismorm@gmail.com, 8 A.M.–noon and 2–6 P.M. weekdays only.

**Banco del Chubut** (Yrigoyen and Antártida Argentina) has an ATM. The **Cooperativa Eléctrica** (9 de Julio 409) has long-distance telephones and Internet access, and also arranges burials (seriously!).

**Hospital Río Mayo** (Sarmiento and Belgrano, tel. 02903/420022) provides medical services.

### Getting There

Schedules are subject to change from Río Mayo's **Terminal de Ómnibus** (Fontana and Irigoyen). **ETAP** (tel. 02903/420164) has daily eastbound services to Comodoro Rivadavia (US$10, four hours), and **Transaustral** has westbound buses to Coyhaique, Chile (US$20, six hours), leaving Wednesday and Saturday at noon (reservations a few days in advance are essential).

# THE CHILEAN LAKES DISTRICT

South of the Río Biobío, popularly known as the "lakes district" for the scenic finger lakes left by receding Pleistocene glaciers, the Sur Chico (Lesser South) has long enticed Chileans and Argentines with its matchless scenery of ice-capped volcanic cones soaring above dense native forests. Only in the past decade-plus have significant numbers of them, plus adventurous foreigners, begun to venture beyond conventional lakeside resorts into the Andean backcountry for hiking, horseback riding, and white-water rafting. National parks and reserves cover large swaths of the cordillera.

Politically, the Sur Chico comprises the Araucanía (Region IX), the newly designated Los Ríos (Region XIV, not covered in this guide), and Los Lagos (Region X), which includes the Chiloé archipelago and, on the mainland across the Golfo de Ancud and the Golfo de Corcovado, what is colloquially known as continental Chiloé. Economically diverse cities such as Temuco, Osorno, and Puerto Montt, which rely on forestry, agricultural services, and manufacturing in addition to tourism, are the gateways, but smaller lakeside towns such as Villarrica, Pucón, and Puerto Varas make better bases for excursions. There are several trans-Andean routes to Argentina, which has its own lakes region centered on the city of Bariloche; Puerto Montt, the de facto terminus of the continental Panamericana, is the hub for air, land, and sea access to Chilean Patagonia and also a gateway to the Argentine side.

Southeast of Temuco, Lago Villarrica is a beehive of activity for access to national parks

© STEVE KINGSMAN/123RF

## HIGHLIGHTS

**Parque Nacional Conguillío:** The monkey puzzle tree's fame was such that, nearly a century ago, the aging pioneer conservationist John Muir went far out of his way to visit the site that now protects much of southern South America's endemic araucaria forests (page 195).

**Parque Nacional Villarrica:** Every summer, hundreds of hikers slog up the snow-covered slopes of Chile's most active volcano, in its namesake national park immediately south of Pucón, for the views and the thrills (page 212).

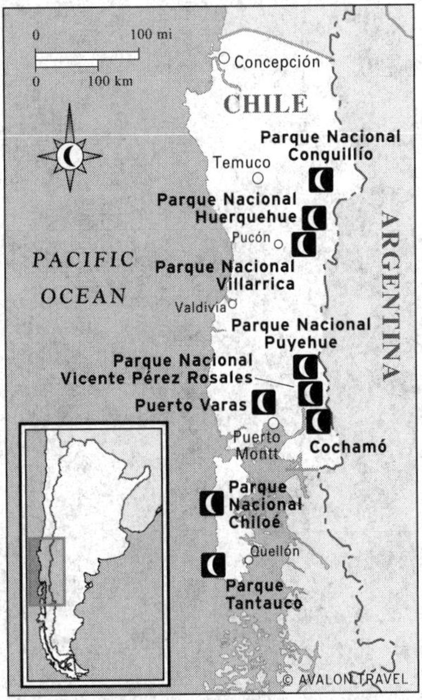


LOOK FOR TO FIND RECOMMENDED SIGHTS, ACTIVITIES, DINING, AND LODGING.

**Parque Nacional Huerquehue:** Just northwest of Pucón, Huerquehue is the place for shaded woodland hikes alongside rushing streams in ruggedly scenic terrain (page 213).

**Parque Nacional Puyehue:** Its remaining forests resemble the rainforest woodlands north and south of it, but the most impressive sight is the barren high country wrought by the lava flows and ash from the 1960 eruption of its namesake volcano (page 218).

**Puerto Varas:** On Lago Llanquihue's western shore, studded with shingled houses that recall the Middle European origins of its earliest settlers, Puerto Varas has the Chilean lakes district's finest services and restaurants, making it the ideal gateway to the bus-boat crossing to the Argentine lakes district city of Bariloche (page 227).

**Parque Nacional Vicente Pérez Rosales:** On the eastern shore of Lago Llanquihue, Volcán Osorno is a beacon of Fuji-like perfection. Ski facilities have recently been upgraded, but the rest of the park is also a summer favorite for climbers and hikers (page 236).

**Cochamó:** Southwest of Puerto Varas, the Cochamó backcountry boasts Yosemite-like granite monoliths surrounded by lush mid-latitude rainforests. Hiking the muddy trails can be a slog, so some visitors prefer horseback excursions (page 239).

**Parque Nacional Chiloé:** On Chiloé's wild west coast, hikers can still traipse through dense dwarf native woodlands (page 265).

**Parque Tantauco:** On southwestern Chiloé's roadless wilderness, Chilean president Sebastián Piñera has created a forest reserve that bids to become one of the country's top ecotourism destinations (page 270).

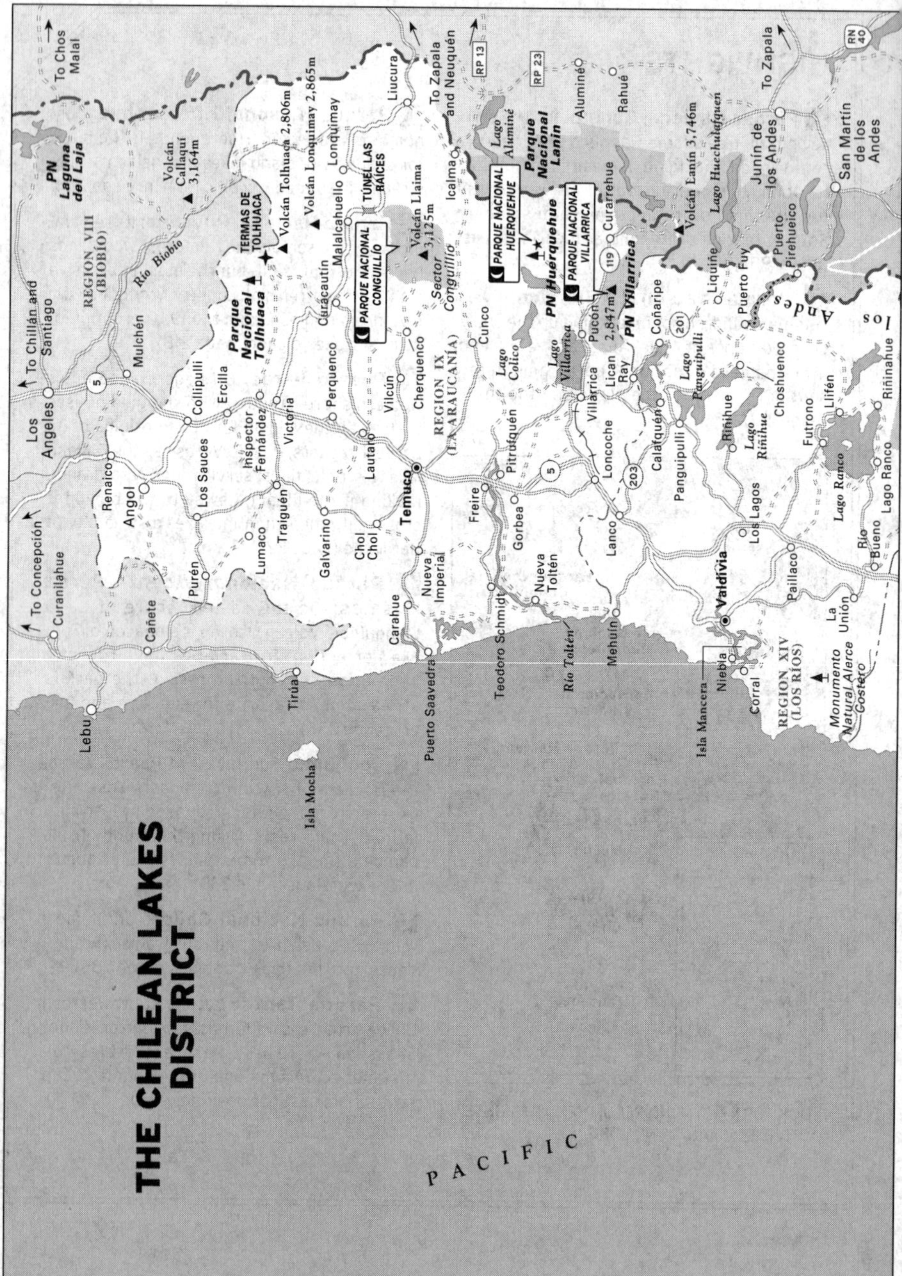
THE CHILEAN LAKES DISTRICT
PACIFIC
Isla Mocha
Lebu
Tirúa
Curanilahue
To Concepción
Cañete
Purén
Angol
Renaico
Los Angeles
To Chillán and Santiago
Mulchén
REGION VIII (BIOBÍO)
Río Biobío
PN Laguna del Laja
To Chos Malal
Volcán Callaquí 3,164m
Collipulli
Ercilla
Los Sauces
Lumaco
Traiguén
Inspector Fernández
Victoria
Parque Nacional Tolhuaca
TERMAS DE TOLHUACA
Volcán Tolhuaca 2,806m
Volcán Lonquimay 2,865m
Lonquimay
Liucura
Malalcahuello
TÚNEL LAS RAÍCES
Curacautín
Perquenco
Galvarino
Lautaro
PARQUE NACIONAL CONGUILLÍO
Volcán Llaima 3,125m
Sector Conguillío
Vilcún
Cherquenco
Chol Chol
Temuco
REGION IX (LA ARAUCANÍA)
Carahue
Nueva Imperial
Puerto Saavedra
Teodoro Schmidt
Freire
Pitrufquén
Cunco
Icalma
To Zapala and Neuquén
RP 13
RP 23
Lago Aluminé
Aluminé
Rahué
Parque Nacional Lanín
PARQUE NACIONAL HUERQUEHUE
PN Huerquehue
Lago Colico
Gorbea
Nueva Toltén
Río Toltén
Mehuín
Lanco
Loncoche
Villarrica
Lago Villarrica
Pucón
Volcán 2,847m
PN Villarrica
PARQUE NACIONAL VILLARRICA
Curarrehue
119
Lican Ray
Coñaripe
Calafquén
Lago Panguipulli
Panguipulli
201
203
5
Liquiñe
Volcán Lanín 3,746m
Lago Huechulafquen
Junín de los Andes
To Zapala
RN 40
San Martín de los Andes
Puerto Pirehueico
Puerto Fuy
Los Andes
Choshuenco
Riñihue
Lago Riñihue
Los Lagos
Valdivia
Niebla
Isla Mancera
Corral
REGION XIV (LOS RÍOS)
Monumento Natural Alerce Costero
Paillaco
La Unión
Río Bueno
Lago Ranco
Futrono
Llifén
Riñinahue

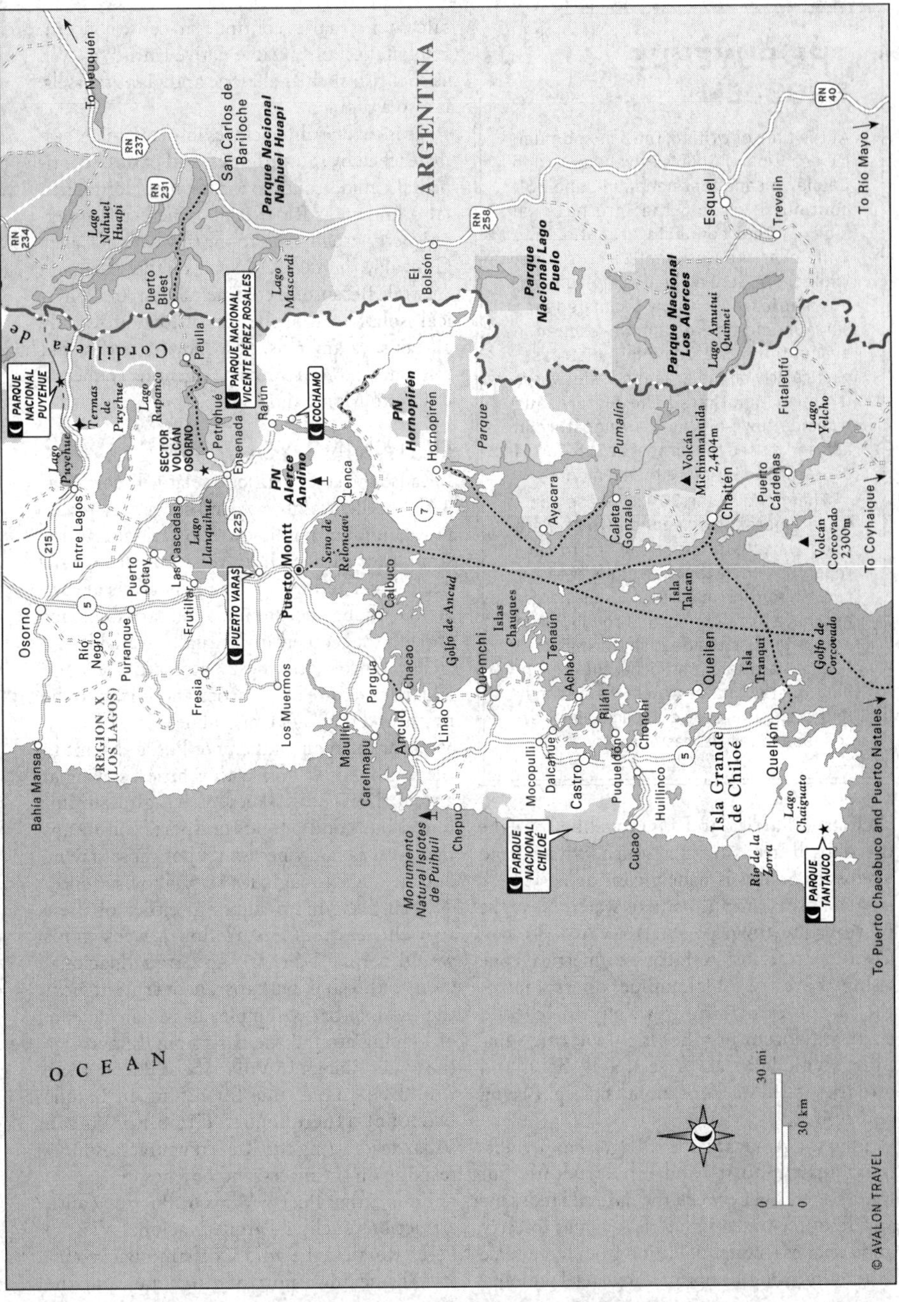
To Neuquén
RN 237
RN 234
RN 231
San Carlos de Bariloche
Parque Nacional Nahuel Huapi
Lago Nahuel Huapi
ARGENTINA
Puerto Blest
Lago Mascardi
El Bolsón
RN 258
Parque Nacional Lago Puelo
Esquel
Trevelin
RN 40
To Río Mayo
Parque Nacional Los Alerces
Lago Amutui Quimei
Futaleufú
Lago Yelcho
Puerto Cárdenas
Volcán Corcovado 2300m
To Coyhaique
Cordillera de
PARQUE NACIONAL PUYEHUE
Termas de Puyehue
Lago Puyehue
Lago Rupanco
Peulla
PARQUE NACIONAL VICENTE PÉREZ ROSALES
SECTOR VOLCÁN OSORNO
Petrohué
Ensenada
Ralún
COCHAMÓ
PN Hornopirén
Hornopirén
Parque
Pumalín
Volcán Michinmahuida 2,404m
Chaitén
Caleta Gonzalo
Ayacara
PN Alerce Andino
Lenca
Entre Lagos
215
Lago Llanquihue
225
Las Cascadas
Puerto Octay
Osorno
5
Río Negro
Purranque
Frutillar
PUERTO VARAS
Puerto Montt
Seno de Reloncaví
7
Calbuco
Isla Talcán
Golfo de Ancud
Islas Chauques
Tenaún
Quemchi
Achao
Quellón
Isla Tranqui
Golfo de Corcovado
Fresia
Los Muermos
REGION X (LOS LAGOS)
Bahía Mansa
Maullín
Pargua
Chacao
Carelmapu
Ancud
Linao
Rilán
Chonchi
Mocopulli
Dalcahue
Castro
Puqueldón
Huillinco
Isla Grande de Chiloé
Quellón
Lago Chaiguata
Monumento Natural Islotes de Puihuil
Chepu
PARQUE NACIONAL CHILOÉ
Cucao
Río de la Zorra
PARQUE TANTAUCO
To Puerto Chacabuco and Puerto Natales
OCEAN
0
30 mi
0
30 km
© AVALON TRAVEL

## THE PUYEHUE PROBLEM

At the time of writing, the ash-and-pumice eruption of Chile's Puyehue-Córdon Caulle volcano that began in June 2011 continued, closing the international highway that connects Argentina and Chile over the Cardenal Samoré pass. While there were no deaths or even serious injuries in the thinly populated area surrounding the volcano, it resulted in evacuations and economic distress – particularly on the Argentine side, where it nearly smothered the picturesque lakeside town of Villa La Angostura in ash and closed the airport at San Carlos de Bariloche for more than a month.

That derailed the 2011 ski season and, while emergency cleanup efforts were underway, the eruption figured to have repercussions over the coming year or two. Visitors intending to cross the border may have to detour north through Pucón or take the bus-boat-bus shuttle between Puerto Varas and Bariloche; those planning to stay on the Argentine side may find changes in services, particularly accommodations and restaurants.

such as Villarrica and Huerquehue, but the district's heart is farther south, where Lago Todos los Santos is widely considered Chile's single most beautiful body of water. Near the picturesque town of Puerto Varas, Volcán Osorno, an almost perfectly symmetrical cone rising above Lago Llanquihue, offers some of the most breathtaking views anywhere. Still, there are dozens of other high volcanic summits, scenic lakes and rivers, and shores and estuaries to fill weeks or months of sightseeing and activities.

Like the Araucanía, Los Lagos has a vigorous tourist industry and infrastructure, but there's a tension between the natural landscape and resource-based industries such as forestry and fisheries—water pollution from large-scale salmon farming in both freshwater lakes and saltwater estuaries continues to cause concern. Exploitation of valuable native finfish, as well as shellfish such as abalone and giant mussels, is also a problem.

This chapter also includes insular Chiloé, easily reached by shuttle ferries, and parts of continental Chiloé, south to the town of Hornopirén (also known as Río Negro), where a summer-only ferry usually sails to the tiny cove of Caleta Gonzalo, the de facto start of the Carretera Austral. Because of continental Chiloé's physical isolation from the rest of Region X, only air taxis, catamarans, slow-moving ferries, and roundabout buses through Argentina connect it to Puerto Montt and Castro.

## PLANNING YOUR TIME

Because the lakes district is relatively compact, with excellent highways and secondary roads, plus abundant public transportation, travel is straightforward. Still, in the summer tourism peak, hotel and rental-car reservations are advisable, though accommodations are abundant enough that something's usually available.

For visitors, the best bases are the Lago Villarrica resorts of Villarrica and Pucón to the north, and the Lago Llanquihue town of Puerto Varas or the mainland city of Puerto Montt to the south. For visitors with vehicles, staying at any of these locales keeps driving to a minimum, but good public transportation means that a car is rarely necessary. For those staying outside town, though, it's helpful to have one.

Seeing the main sights in either of these two clusters requires around a week. This would permit a day trip to Parque Nacional Conguillío and perhaps an overnight near the thermal-baths complex at Malalcahuello, or looping around the park from Temuco via the upper Biobío. In Villarrica or Pucón, there would be ample time for hiking in Parque Nacional Huerquehue, climbing Volcán Villarrica, rafting the Río Trancura, or simply relaxing on the black-sand beaches.

From either Puerto Varas or Puerto Montt, attractions such as Parque Nacional Vicente Pérez Rosales, the wild Cochamó backcountry, the seafood port of Angelmó, and the

Chiloé archipelago are almost equally accessible. Many visitors prefer Puerto Varas, which is quieter and more picturesque and has better services in a more compact area.

## HISTORY

Human presence in the region dates from at least 13,000 years ago, when hunter-gatherers roamed the area around Monte Verde, 35 kilometers west of Puerto Montt. One of the continent's oldest archaeological sites, Monte Verde offered ideal conditions for preservation: Despite the humid climate, more than a meter of volcanic ash and peat covered the remains of mastodons, shellfish, seeds, fruits, and roots consumed by the dozen or so families who lived there. From the remaining refuse, researchers have determined that these bands hunted and foraged within a radius of about 100 kilometers.

Unlike the central Andean highlands of Peru and Bolivia, the pre-Columbian Sur Chico never developed cities or monuments—its people developed agricultural skills, but they were shifting cultivators in dispersed settlements, lacking centralized political authority. In practice, this benefited their resistance to the Inka empire and, later, Spanish invaders; the Mapuche used guerrilla tactics to harass their opponents. More egalitarian than hierarchical, their leadership was interchangeable rather than irreplaceable.

Thus, by the early 1600s, Mapuche resistance had reduced most Spanish settlements south of the Biobío to ashes and ruin. Except for the river port of Valdivia, reestablished in the mid-17th century, the area remained precarious for settlers until a series of treaties between the Chilean government and indigenous forces in the 1880s. Several northerly cities and towns—Victoria, Curacautín, Lonquimay, Temuco, Cunco, Villarrica, and Pucón—were originally a string of fortresses along the Mapuche frontier.

Chile counts more than a million Mapuche among its 16 million citizens. Many have left for the cities, but large numbers still remain in the countryside, where, in the more liberal political climate following the Pinochet dictatorship, they have become more assertive of their rights to ancestral lands.

Part of the controversy dates from the officially encouraged immigration that took place after the mid-19th century, when Santiago recruited German émigrés to settle on and around Lago Llanquihue. In the ensuing years, Llanquihue and other lakes to the north became the region's highways, linking towns like Puerto Varas and Puerto Octay via sail and steamer until the railroad's advent in the early 20th century.

German immigrants have left a palpable imprint on the economy (through commerce and manufacturing), landscape (through dairy farming and other agricultural pursuits), architecture (some of the country's finest European-style houses), and food (Germanic goodies known collectively as kuchen are almost universal). Many other nationalities, mostly Spaniards and Italians, also flowed into the region.



# Araucanía Region

## TEMUCO

Fast-growing Temuco is the gateway to the lakes, numerous national parks, and many other attractions, though its own tourist appeal is limited—while it's a Mapuche market town, the architecture is utilitarian, and economically it relies on agricultural and forest products. Unfortunately, it suffers air-pollution problems, especially in winter, as widespread use of low-quality wood-burning stoves has contributed to frequent respiratory infections.

### History

Temuco dates from February 24, 1881, when President Aníbal Pinto sent Interior Minister Manuel Recabarren, General Gregorio Urrutia,

# TEMUCO

To Museo Nacional Ferroviario
To Rodoviario Araucario, Chillán and Santiago
To Aeropuerto Maquehue, Valdivia, and Puerto Montt
AVENIDA A PINTO
FERIA LIBRE ANÍBAL PINTO
ESTACIÓN FERROCARRILES DEL ESTADO
BUSES IGI LLAIMA/NAR-BUS
TERMINAL DE BUSES RURALES
HOSTAL CASA BLANCA
MATTA
ZENTENO
BUSES INTERCOMUNAL SUR
HOTEL CHAPELCO
GENERAL CRUZ
GENERAL MACKENNA
BUSES JAC
ALDUNATE
MERCADO MUNICIPAL
MULTITOUR
HOTEL NICOLÁS
BANCOESTADO
CASA DE CAMBIO GLOBAL
SKY AIRLINE
LANCHILE
HOTEL AITUÉ
LAVANDERÍA NI-ZU
HOSTAL ALDUNATE
HOTEL FRONTERA
CONAF
BULNES
INSISCOM
TERMINAL BIO BIO
POST OFFICE
HOTEL RP
CIBER CENTER
SERNATUR
Plaza de Armas Aníbal Pinto
HERTZ
AVIS
PRAT
Plaza Manuel Recabarren
Plaza Teodoro Schmidt
EUROPCAR
HOTEL DON EDUARDO
EL CORRALERO
HOTEL TERRAVERDE
V MACKENNA
VICUÑA
MACKENNA
IGLESIA ANGLICANA
LAGOS
LYNCH
Cerro Ñielol
Monumento Natural
Cementerio
LAS HERAS
O'HIGGINS
CARRERA
HOSPITAL REGIONAL
Plaza Teniente Dagoberto Godoy
AULA MAGNA UNIVERSIDAD CATÓLICA
BLANCO
FREIERE
NORTE
PRIETO
PRIETO SUR
Plaza
LAS QUILAS
EL BOSQUE
MUSEO REGIONAL DE LA ARAUCANÍA
CABO RIQUELME
ARRAYAN
THIERS
PHILLIPPI
STA LAURA
LA SUERTE
CARRILLO
DINAMARCA
AUTOMÓVIL CLUB DE CHILE
SANTA MARGARITA
Estero Coilaco
Estero Temuco
TRIZANO
POSADA SELVA NEGRA
SAN FEDERICO
FRANCIA
ESPAÑA
HOCHSTETTER
PIZZERÍA MADONNA
JALISCO
HOTEL DREAMS ARAUCANÍA
CLUB ALEMÁN
URUGUAY
SENADOR ESTEBANEZ
AVENIDA ALEMANIA
AVENIDA HOLANDESA
AVENIDA SAN MARTÍN
AVENIDA CAUPOLICÁN
PEDRO DE VALDIVIA
MANUEL RODRÍGUEZ
BALMACEDA
BARROS ARANA
DIEGO PORTALES
Río Cautín
200 yds
200 m
© AVALON TRAVEL

engineer Teodoro Schmidt, and the Chilean army to found Fuerte de Temuco (originally Fuerte Recabarren). Later that year, the Chileans averted an attack by reaching a treaty agreement, and within 15 years the railroad had arrived. Before the turn of the century, colonists had flooded into the region, their farmers displacing the aboriginal Mapuche, and the population exceeded 7,000. The early push from the railroad sustained that growth well into the 20th century, providing easy access to metropolitan markets and technology.

## Orientation

On the north margin of the braided Río Cautín, Temuco (population about 378,000) is 677 kilometers south of Santiago and 339 kilometers north of Puerto Montt via the Panamericana, which bypasses the city center; the former Panamericana, known as Avenida Caupolicán, divides the city into a compact original grid to the east and an irregular residential area to the west.

## Sights

Temuco's focal point is the recently re-landscaped **Plaza de Armas Aníbal Pinto,** whose showpiece is the massive **Homenaje a la Región de la Araucanía,** a sculpture representing a Mapuche *machi* (female healer), a so-called *soldado de la pacificación* (soldier of the pacification), a *colono* (early colonist), the conquistador and epic poet Alonso de Ercilla, and the Mapuche *toqui* (leader) Kallfulifán. The bandshell gallery hosts rotating cultural exhibits.

Most other landmarks are scattered, such as the gingerbread-style **Iglesia Anglicana Santa Trinidad** (Vicuña Mackenna and Lautaro), the century-old Anglican church, as well as several museums and markets.

Chile's national flower, the *copihue (Lapageria rosea),* flaunts its autumn blooms in the deciduous lowland forest of **Monumento Natural Cerro Ñielol,** a hilly 90-hectare reserve on the north side of Temuco. Several short trails thread among the mixed woodlands, but it's also a historical site—under the shade of **La Patagua del Armisticio,** in 1881, Mapuche leaders finally acceded to the founding of the city. For most of its tens of thousands of yearly visitors, though, it's a place for weekend picnics and similar recreation.

Reached by strolling north on Prat from the Plaza de Armas for about one kilometer, Cerro Ñielol (8:30 A.M.–11 P.M. daily) charges US$2 admission per pedestrian, US$1 for each child.

## Museo Regional de la Araucanía

Housed in the former Carlos Thiers residence (1924), a German immigrant-style national monument, Temuco's regional museum has been undergoing a seemingly endless rehab and reorganization and only recently reopened in full. The early results are encouraging, with exhibits on little-known topics such as the early-20th-century immigration of South African Boers and a Darwin bicentennial exhibit. In the past, though, the museum has seen frequent clashes of philosophy in a region where the indigenous presence is so strong.

The museum (Av. Alemania 084, tel. 045/739952, www.museoregionalaraucania.cl, 9:30 A.M.–5:30 P.M. Tues.–Fri., 11 A.M.–5 P.M. Sat., and 11 A.M.–2 P.M. Sun. and holidays, US$1.25 pp) is about 10 blocks west of the Plaza de Armas.

## Museo Nacional Ferroviario Pablo Neruda

Soon after the railroad's arrival from Angol in 1893, Temuco became a rail hub, where long-distance trains changed locomotives; its original *casa de máquinas* (roundhouse) opened in 1920, housed locomotives used on several branch lines, and also held repair facilities. By the 1930s, though, these installations were inadequate; the current roundhouse was completed between 1937 and 1941. Temuco was the last Chilean base for steam locomotives; the Empresa de los Ferrocarriles del Estado (EFE) maintained it as a repair and reserve center for them until 1983—there were no permanent diesel facilities here until the 1980s—but it closed soon after.

In the aftermath, EFE officials wanted to tear down the roundhouse and sell off its 14 antique steam engines and other rolling stock for scrap, but the persistent Asociación Chilena de Conservación del Patrimonio Ferroviario (ACCPF, Chilean Association for Conservation of Railroad Patrimony) managed to get all of them declared national monuments. Finally, in February 2004, President Ricardo Lagos dedicated the new museum to Pablo Neruda during the poet's centennial year (Neruda's father was a railroad laborer, and Neruda himself wrote many poems about rail travel).

In a 19-hectare facility that includes the roundhouse and extensive lawns with additional stock elevated on rails, the highlights include a luxury presidential railcar that was in service until 2003, an antique sleeper also in service until 2003, and President Carlos Ibáñez del Campo's 1928 Packard limousine—custom-designed so that it could use the rails as well as Chile's then-rudimentary roads.

The museum (Av. Barros Arana 0565, tel. 045/937940, www.museoferroviariotemuco.cl, 9 A.M.–6 P.M. Tues.–Sun., 10 A.M.–6 P.M. weekends, US$2 for adults, US$0.60 for kids), about one kilometer north of the station, also features an art gallery. Northbound buses and *taxi colectivos* on Barros Arana go within two short blocks of the site, saving an unappealing walk through a grubby neighborhood. An occasional summer steam train does a five-hour excursion to and from Victoria (US$12 pp).

## Mercado Municipal

Replacing an earlier market the city had outgrown, the municipal bazaar (1928) is a high-ceilinged landmark that draws tourists with its accomplished crafts and typical restaurants, which vary from the plain and simple to, if not quite sublime, at least good enough. Locals take advantage of abundant fresh produce and utilitarian commodities such as manufactured household goods and clothing.

Two blocks north of the Plaza de Armas, the Mercado Municipal (Manuel Rodríguez 960, tel. 045/203345, www.mercadotemuco.cl, 8 A.M.–8 P.M. Mon.–Sat. and 8:30 A.M.–4 P.M. Sun. in summer, 8 A.M.–7 P.M. Mon.–Sat. and 8:30 A.M.–4 P.M. Sun. and holidays the rest of the year) fills most of the eastern two-thirds of the block bounded by Diego Portales, Bulnes, Manuel Rodríguez, and Aldunate.

## Feria Libre Aníbal Pinto

Comprising more than 700 different stalls, this lively, mainly Mapuche, sometimes disagreeably fragrant produce market fills several blocks south along Avenida Aníbal Pinto and Avenida Barros Arana from the Terminal de Buses Rurales south to the EFE railroad station. In July 2001, members of the indigenous Asociación de Productores de Verduras Ñuke Mapu protested their possible eviction from the market, resisting what they claimed were the mayor's plans to remodel the entire area to their detriment, but the project nevertheless went forward. The Aníbal Pinto sector is now a roofed pedestrian area that looks pretty handsome and is tidier (and more hygienic) than in past years—though it's hardly immaculate.

In addition to fruits and vegetables, there are cheap eateries and assorted Mapuche crafts. Hours are roughly 8 A.M.–5 P.M. daily.

## Entertainment and Events

Temuco isn't exactly a 24-hour city, but there's usually something going on at local cultural facilities or its two universities. The biggest single celebration is February's **Aniversario de la Ciudad,** commemorating the city's founding—at the time, it was really a fortress—on February 24, 1881. During the festivities, a high-quality crafts fair nearly fills the Plaza de Armas.

The **Aula Magna Universidad Católica** (Manuel Montt 56, tel. 045/205421) has an annual event schedule including live theater, music, and films.

## Shopping

There's a good crafts selection at the **Mercado Municipal** (Diego Portales and Aldunate), but also lots of kitsch.

## Accommodations

Temuco's budget accommodations are only so-so, but travelers spending just a little more can get better value. Upper-range choices are generally good.

### US$25-50

**Hostal Aldunate** (Aldunate 864, tel. 045/642438, hostalaldunate864@hotmail.com, US$16–21 s, US$25–30 d, breakfast included) occupies a quiet but still central neighborhood; rates vary according to shared or private bath.

**Hotel Chapelco** (General Cruz 401, tel. 045/749393, www.hotelchapelco.cl, US$30 s, US$50 d) is a respectable option, with private bath, breakfast, and parking, near the train tracks at the east end of downtown.

### US$50-100

Near the Mercado Municipal, **Hotel Nicolás** (General Mackenna 420, tel. 045/210020, www.hotelnicolas.cl, US$46 s, US$54 d with private bath and TV) is undistinguished but more central.

On the residential west side, **Posada Selva Negra** (Tirzano 110, tel. 045/236913, www.hospedajeselvanegra.cl, US$40 s, US$56 d) is a German-run B&B with quiet garden rooms—some singles are small but contain a writing desk, and there's wireless Internet—plus unexpected touches like a soft bathrobe (unusual in this price range). The breakfast nook has a world-class collection of Teutonic kitsch.

**Hotel Aitué** (Antonio Varas 1048, tel. 045/212512, www.hotelaitue.cl, US$78 s, US$90 d but ask for IVA discount) is a business-oriented facility with responsive service.

**Hotel Frontera** (Bulnes 733, tel. 045/200400, www.hotelfrontera.cl, US$79 s, US$91 d, US$104 s or d with IVA discount) is a complex of two facing buildings that include one business-oriented hotel and convention center. The one across the street has greater amenities—swimming pool, gym, and the like—but its only advantage is easier access, as guests at either building are entitled to use all facilities.

### OVER US$100

Downtown's **RP Hotel** (Portales 779, tel. 045/977777, www.hotelrp.cl, US$105 s or d) is a modern 23-room boutique that includes one suite.

At the foot of Cerro Ñielol, **Hotel Panamericano Temuco** (Prat 0220, tel. 045/239999, www.panamericanahoteles.cl, US$100–130 s or d) is a five-star choice by local standards, but not demonstrably superior to the RP.

New in 2010, the five-story **Hotel Dreams Araucanía** (Av. Alemania 0945, tel. 045/379000, www.mundodreams.com, US$112 s or d) is a glass palace that's an integral part of the city's casino. In this mostly residential area, it has better access to the restaurant-and-nightlife strip than do its downtown counterparts.

At **Hotel Don Eduardo** (Andrés Bello 755, tel. 045/214133, www.hoteldoneduardo.cl, US$112–142 s or d), the small dark lobby is a misleading approach to a modern downtown business hotel with smallish but spotless standard rooms, wireless Internet, a decent buffet breakfast, and secure parking. Double-paned windows keep the street noise to a minimum.

## Food

Known best as a crafts market and a sight in itself, the **Mercado Municipal** (Portales and Aldunate) is equally good for straightforward seafood—try **La Caleta** (Puesto 27, tel. 045/213002). Figure about US$10–13 for a good, filling meal; the market, though, is primarily a lunch venue, and most eateries close by 7 P.M.

The only downtown restaurant of any note, **El Corralero** (Vicuña Mackenna 811, tel. 045/401355, lunch and dinner daily) specializes in beef but also offers a sample of fish and seafood dishes, mostly in the US$10–12 range; it provides excellent and congenial service as well. In residential Temuco, though, only a couple blocks west of Hochstetter and just south of Avenida Alemania, the popular **Restaurant Oregon** (Recreo 530, tel. 045/385776, lunch daily, dinner Mon.–Sat.) is a step-plus above most of its *parrilla* competitors, with fish and pastas to supplement the beef. Most entrées fall into the US$10–13 range, the service is attentive and good-natured, and they're flexible about wine-by-the-glass selections.

The popular **Pizzería Madonna** (Av. Alemania 0660, tel. 045/329393, lunch and dinner daily) has fine pastas and a greater diversity of pizzas, ranging from individual to family-size, than most Chilean pizzerias.

**Jalisco** (Hochstetter 435, tel. 045/243254, lunch and dinner daily) is a pub with a Tex-Mex menu. **Club Alemán** (Senador Estébanez 772, tel. 045/240034, lunch and dinner daily), the German club, is a traditional option.

## Information

On the north side of the Plaza de Armas, **Sernatur** (Claro Solar 899, tel. 045/211969, infoaraucania@sernatur.cl) is in the process of repairing quake-damaged offices; meanwhile, it still distributes free city maps and regional leaflets from temporary quarters in the Museo Regional (Av. Alemania 084, tel. 045/739952, 9:30 A.M.–5:30 P.M. Tues.–Fri., 11 A.M.–5 P.M. Sat., and 11 A.M.–2 P.M. Sun. and holidays), about 10 blocks west of the Plaza de Armas.

For motorists, the **Automóvil Club de Chile** (San Martín 0278, tel. 045/910522) is west of the former Panamericana.

**Conaf** (Av. Bilbao 931, 2nd floor, tel. 045/298114) provides national parks information.

## Services

Though it's primarily an administrative and commercial center, Temuco has a full complement of traveler's services as well. **BancoEstado** (Claro Solar 931) collects no foreign service charges at its ATMs; the nearby **Casa de Cambio Global** (Bulnes 655, Local 1) is an exchange house.

**Correos de Chile** (Diego Portales 801) is the post office. **Ciber Center** (Montt 820, 2nd floor) has the best Internet connections, with comfortable workstations.

For laundry, try **Lavanderías Ni-Zu** (Aldunate 842, tel. 045/236893).

The expanding **Hospital Regional** (Manuel Montt 115, tel. 045/212525) is west of the former Panamericana.

## Getting There

Temuco is Araucanía's major transportation hub, with air connections north and south, and abundant bus connections north and south along the Panamericana, and east into and over the Andes.

**LAN** (Bulnes 687, tel. 045/211339) flies several times daily to Santiago and once or twice daily to Puerto Montt. **Sky Airline** (Bulnes 677, tel. 045/747300) flies four times weekly to Santiago and to Puerto Montt.

The chaos of long-distance carriers that once congested downtown streets has been relieved by construction of the **Rodoviario Araucario** (Vicente Pérez Rosales 01609, tel. 045/225005), at the eastern foot of Cerro Ñielol. This has not completely concentrated services—the **Terminal de Buses Rurales** (Av. Aníbal Pinto 032, tel. 045/210494) hosts regional carriers, and several long-distance companies have ticket offices and even terminals around the axis formed with the perpendicular Avenida Balmaceda.

Among the regional carriers at Buses Rurales are **Flota Erbuc** (tel. 045/272204), which goes several times daily to Curacautín via Lautaro or Victoria, continuing to Malalcahuello and Lonquimay; **Nar-Bus** (tel. 045/407740) and **Intercomunal Sur** (Av. Balmaceda 1371, tel. 045/214864), which travel to Cherquenco (for the Llaima sector of Parque Nacional Conguillío), Icalma, Cunco, and Melipeuco; and **Buses Jac,** servicing Villarrica and Pucón, though departures are more frequent from its other office. From its own terminal, **Buses Biobío** (Lautaro 853, tel. 045/210599) links Temuco to Angol.

From the Rodoviario, many carriers connect Temuco with Panamericana destinations from Santiago to Puerto Montt and Chiloé. Some have downtown ticket offices, including **Tur-Bus** (Claro Solar 598, tel. 045/230979) and **Igi Llaima,** which shares facilities with **Nar-Bus** (Miraflores 1535, tel. 045/407777). **Buses Jac** (Av. Balmaceda 1005, tel. 045/210313) shuttles frequently to Villarrica and Pucón, with fewer trips to Lican Ray and to Coñaripe (changing buses in Villarrica in off-season), and a daily service to Curarrehue.

Sample domestic destinations, with

approximate fares and times, include Villarrica (US$2–4, one hour), Pucón (US$4–5, 1.5 hours), Curacautín (US$4, 1.5 hours), Osorno (US$8–11, four hours), Puerto Montt (US$10–14, 5.5 hours), and Santiago (US$25–70, nine hours).

Most Argentina-bound buses use the Paso Mamuil Malal crossing southeast of Pucón (to Junín de los Andes and San Martín de los Andes), but some take the Paso Pino Hachado route, directly east of Temuco via Curacautín and the upper Biobío town of Lonquimay (to Zapala and Neuquén). In addition, there are connections to Bariloche via the Panamericana to Osorno and Ruta 215 east over Paso Cardenal Samoré.

Since the distances are long, the terrain mountainous, and the roads partly gravel, some trans-Andean buses leave early—sometimes as early as 3 A.M. Carriers serving Junín de los Andes and San Martín de los Andes (US$25, six hours) include **Buses San Martín** (tel. 045/258626) and **Buses Ruta Sur** (Miraflores 1151, tel. 045/210079). **Igi Llaima** and **Nar-Bus** (both at Miraflores 1535, tel. 045/407777) alternate daily 5 A.M. services to Zapala and Neuquén (US$32, 10 hours) and also go to San Martín. **Vía Bariloche** (tel. 045/257904) also goes to Neuquén.

### Getting Around

Just six kilometers south of town and west of the Panamericana, Temuco's **Aeropuerto Maquehue** (tel. 045/554801) was due to move to Freire, 30 kilometers south, but a conflict with the Mapuche has indefinitely postponed this move. **Transfer Araucanía** (tel. 045/339900) arranges airport transfers (around US$12 pp), as do taxis from the northeast corner of the Plaza de Armas.

From downtown to the Rodoviario, catch northbound Micro 7 Troncal or Micro 9 from Portales and Bulnes, or *taxi colectivo* 11-P from the corner of Prat and Claro Solar.

For excursions into the backcountry in and around Temuco, especially the circuit through Parque Nacional Conguillío or the upper Biobío, scarce public transportation makes car rental the most convenient option. Rental agencies include the **Automóvil Club de Chile** (Acchi, San Martín 0278, tel. 045/248903), **Avis** (San Martín 755, tel. 045/237575, airport tel. 045/337715), **Europcar** (Vicuña Mackenna 399, tel. 045/232715), and **Hertz** (Andrés Bello 792, tel. 045/318585, airport tel. 045/337019).

## VICINITY OF TEMUCO

There are worthwhile excursions in all directions, but most visitors focus on the Andes to the east. Temuco's **Multitour** (Bulnes 307, Oficina 203, tel. 045/237913, www.chile-travel.com/multitour) has English-speaking guides and a good track record for excursions in and around Temuco—primarily toward the Andean national parks and reserves, but also to westerly Mapuche villages.

### Parque Nacional Tolhuaca

Native woodlands of araucarias and other species adorn the foothill slopes of Parque Nacional Tolhuaca, where the Río Malleco drains south/southwest into marshy Laguna Malleco before plunging toward the coast. Improved access roads have increased visitation, especially in summer and on weekends, but most people stay in the immediate vicinity of Laguna Malleco—the rest of the park remains ideal for camping, hiking, and fishing.

In the Andean precordillera, ranging from 1,000 meters above sea level at Laguna Malleco to 1,821 meters on the summits and ridgelines to the north, Tolhuaca is a compact 6,374-hectare unit on the north bank of Malleco, which flows northwest toward the town of Collipulli. It has a cool humid climate, with an average annual temperature of 9°C and 2,500–3,000 millimeters of rainfall, but with mild, relatively dry summers. The park's namesake peak, 2,806-meter Volcán Tolhuaca, lies beyond its boundaries to the southeast.

At higher elevations, Tolhuaca has nearly pure araucaria stands in well-drained soils, but the dense gallery forests along the Río Malleco consist of *coigüe, olivillo,* and other evergreen species, along with deciduous *raulí* and roble. *Quila* forms almost impenetrable

© WAYNE BERNHARDSON

**Araucaria (monkey puzzle) trees line the road between Liucura and Icalma, southeast of Parque Nacional Conguillío.**

bamboo thickets in some areas. *Junquillos* (reeds) grow in the lakeside sediments, while rhubarb-like *nalcas,* ferns, firecracker fuchsias, mosses, and other water-loving plants grow on the riverbanks.

Except for waterfowl and coypu in Laguna Malleco, Tolhuaca's fauna are inconspicuous, but pumas, pudus (miniature deer), foxes, and skunks all exist here.

As ash and other sediments from the surrounding ridges and peaks sluice into the river and downstream, water-loving reeds are colonizing the shoreline of 76-hectare **Laguna Malleco,** a glacial remnant where Conaf keeps a loaner rowboat for anglers and birders. It's an easy walk from the campground, and swimming is possible in several nearby pools.

From Laguna Malleco's north shore, the 1,800-meter **Sendero El Salto** winds through thick native forest to **Salto Malleco,** a 50-meter cascade that plummets over basalt into the lower drainage. Also from Laguna Malleco, the **Sendero Prados de Mesacura** switchbacks up the north shore to intersect the **Sendero Lagunillas,** which follows the contour east through nearly waterless araucaria woodlands (the porous volcanic soil absorbs almost all precipitation). From a spot about five kilometers east of Laguna Malleco, toward Termas de Tolhuaca, the eight-kilometer **Sendero Laguna Verde** skirts 1,606-meter Cerro Laguna Verde's southwestern slope to arrive at its namesake lake.

At Laguna Malleco, Conaf's shady **Camping Inalaufquén** (tel. 02/1960480, US$24 per site in January and February, US$16 the rest of the year) has 25 sites with barbecue pits, picnic tables, running water, and clean bathrooms with flush toilets and cold showers. Single travelers can seek a discount if it's not crowded. For visitors with their own vehicles and more money, Curacautín's Hotel Termas de Tolhuaca is an option.

Tolhuaca lacks a formal visitors center, but rangers at Laguna Malleco offer daily chats at the outdoor amphitheater. Park admission costs US$6 for adults, US$3 for children.

From Curacautín, 87 kilometers northeast of Temuco via Lautaro or 119 kilometers via Victoria, an improved gravel road reaches the hot-springs resort of Termas de Tolhuaca, 33 kilometers to the north. From Termas de Tolhuaca, a once-hazardous four-wheel-drive road to Laguna Malleco is now passable for ordinary vehicles, at least in summer. *Taxi colectivos* from Curacautín go as far as Termas de Tolhuaca, but it's another nine kilometers to Malleco.

## The Upper Cautín and Biobío

From Victoria, 58 kilometers north of Temuco on the Panamericana, a smooth and scenic two-lane highway goes to Curacautín, Lonquimay, and the upper Biobío, a little-visited and underappreciated area north of Parque Nacional Conguillío. Blessed with its own native forests, rushing rivers, and volcanic grandeur, the upper Biobío is, along with Conguillío, part of a UNESCO World Biosphere Reserve declared to protect its remaining araucaria stands.

In addition to the main road, this area is

also accessible via a shorter paved alternative that heads northeast from Lautaro (30 kilometers north of Temuco). From the upper Biobío, it's also possible to loop back around on good gravel roads to Melipeuco (Conguillío's southern gateway) or back to Temuco.

### CURACAUTÍN

Dating from 1882, when the military established Fuerte Ultra Cautín in Pehuenche territory, Curacautín (population about 13,000) is now the northern access point to Parque Nacional Conguillío and gateway to the upper Río Cautín and upper Biobío. It is 87 kilometers northeast of Temuco via Lautaro or 119 kilometers via the Panamericana and Victoria.

Facing the highway, **Hospedaje Aliwen** (Manuel Rodríguez 540, tel. 045/881437, US$18 pp with shared bath, US$40 s or d with private bath) includes breakfast in its rates. There are few places to eat, the best of which is probably Hotel Central's **La Cabaña** (Yungay 157, tel. 045/881256, breakfast, lunch, and dinner daily), opposite the plaza. **Café Vizzio's** (Serrano 248, tel. 045/881653, lunch and dinner daily) has sandwiches, desserts, and coffee.

On the north side of the Plaza de Armas, the **Oficina de Informaciones Turísticas** (Manuel Rodríguez s/n, tel. 045/464858) is open 8 A.M.–9 P.M. weekdays, 9 A.M.–5 P.M. Saturday, and 9 A.M.–2 P.M. Sunday.

**BancoEstado** (O'Higgins 562) has an ATM. **Correos de Chile** (Yungay 285) is the post office. **Telefónica** (O'Higgins 640-B) has both long-distance service and Internet access, but there are several new Internet outlets.

Three blocks west of the Plaza de Armas, Curacautín's **Terminal Rodoviario** (Ruta 89 and Arica) is directly on the Lonquimay highway. At a separate office, **Tur-Bus** (Serrano 101, tel. 045/882542) has direct Santiago service.

**Flota Erbuc** has five buses daily to and from Temuco (US$3.50) via Victoria and four via Lautaro; there are five to Lonquimay. Getting to Parque Nacional Conguillío is possible only with a taxi.

**Igi Llaima** and **Nar-Bus** pass through town daily en route to Zapala and Neuquén, Argentina (US$23), as does **Buses Plaza;** make reservations in Temuco to guarantee a seat.

### TERMAS DE TOLHUACA

Reached by an improved gravel road that heads north out of Curacautín for 35 kilometers, the once-humble hot-springs resort of Termas de Tolhuaca has morphed into a spa alternative for those who want to visit Parque Nacional Tolhuaca but don't want to camp in the park, which is nine kilometers farther on by road. The resort was founded in 1898, but today's facility is a dramatic improvement over the rustic Russian-built original.

Accommodations at the 100-bed **Hotel Termas de Tolhuaca** (Calama 240, Curacautín, tel. 045/411111, www.tolhuaca.viaje.cl, US$110 pp with full board, US$78 per child under age 10) include unlimited access to pools and baths; it has its own restaurant. Camping costs US$21 per person, including pool access, and there are limited supplies on-site.

### MANZANAR AND VICINITY

Barely a wide spot in the road, 18 kilometers east of Curacautín and 680 meters above sea level, Manzanar is home to **Hotel Termas de Manzanar** (tel./fax 045/881200, www.termasdemanzanar.cl), an aging but still respectable riverside spa hotel 400 meters south of the highway. It offers accommodations options ranging from simple rooms with private baths (US$70 s, US$120 d including breakfast) to suites with private baths and whirlpool tubs (US$190 s or d including breakfast). Full-board packages are also available, and nonguests can use the pools for US$16 per person.

About five kilometers west of Manzanar, the rushing Río Cautín and dense forest shield the immaculate **Hostal Andenrose** (Km 68.5, cell 09/9869-1700, www.andenrose.com, US$46–56 s, US$62–72 d) from any noise or visual pollution on the nearby highway. B&B accommodations, in luminous pinewood rooms with firm beds, include a diverse buffet breakfast. Its gregarious Bavarian owner, English-speaking Hans Schöndorfer, also offers excellent lunches and dinners in the restaurant,

## THE CHILEAN PATH TO CONSERVATION

One of Latin America's most far-sighted conservation projects is the former Lagos administration's **Sendero de Chile,** a foot-, bicycle, and horse path linking the Norte Grande's altiplano, near the Peruvian border, with southern Patagonia's sub-Antarctic tundra. Intended for both environmental and recreational purposes, its initial segments opened in 2001; the ambitious goal was to finish the project by 2010, the bicentennial of Chilean independence. The bicentennial has passed, but progress continues.

Comparable to the United States' Pacific Crest Trail in the terrain it covers, but more like the older Appalachian Trail in that authorities hope to encourage community maintenance, the trail will pass through a representative sample of precordillera and upper Andean ecosystems. There is even the unprecedented possibility of cooperation with Argentina, where the route passes through the vicinity of the Campo de Hielo Sur, the southern Patagonian ice sheet that once engendered a bitter border dispute between the two countries.

Conama, the state environmental agency entrusted with the project, prohibits motorized transport on the two-meter-wide dirt and gravel trail. Mostly following the Andean foothills, the route provides detours to important natural, cultural, or even commercial features, such as archaeological sites, wineries, and crafts markets.

Conama hopes the trail will attract both urban day-trippers and Chilean and foreign outdoor enthusiasts to hike some or all of its length. Along the route there will be rustic cabins and campsites, built in locally appropriate styles, as well as mileage markers and informational panels on flora and fauna. Because one project goal is to encourage local development, there will be special emphasis on local place-names and cultural monuments.

Since early 2001, when Ricardo Lagos himself inaugurated the first kilometer at Parque Nacional Conguillío, thousands of kilometers have opened to the public. This progress may not be so great as it implies, though – parts of it link preexisting trails in national parks, reserves, and monuments. Some segments will pass through private land, and private companies and individuals will become involved.

Conama and its tourism counterpart, Sernatur, are now promoting this as the world's longest hiking trail, in excess of 8,500 kilometers by its presumed completion – whenever that is. To follow its progress, visit the Sendero de Chile website (www.senderodechile.cl), which details access, services, and routes.

and provides transfers from the Curacautín bus terminal. There's also a verdant riverside campground (US$8 pp) for backpackers, with separate toilets and showers.



### MALALCAHUELLO

Ten kilometers east of Manzanar, the hamlet of Malalcahuello occupies a high valley in the shadow of 2,865-meter Volcán Lonquimay (known also as Volcán Mocho). At 980 meters, Malalcahuello is cooler than areas to the west, and nights can get chilly even in summer. Its newest asset is the hot-springs resort Centro Termal Malalcahuello.

Thanks to accessibility to its namesake national reserve—trailheads start near the highway itself—Malalcahuello makes an ideal destination for hikers and riders.

Combined with the contiguous Reserva Las Nalcas to the north, the **Reserva Nacional Malalcahuello** comprises 25,000 hectares of wild high country that also serves as a key forestry research center. Higher than nearby Parque Nacional Tolhuaca, it contains an overlapping forest flora of araucaria with deciduous Andean forest of evergreen *coigüe* and *lenga,* and araucaria with *coigüe* mixed with *ñire.* The fauna resembles Tolhuaca's, though the Andean condor and the *carpintero negro* (black woodpecker) are more common here.

Its summit crater filled by a glacier that spills onto the adjoining flanks, symmetrical

**Volcán Lonquimay** is the reserve's focal point. Slightly northeast of town, it dates from the late Pleistocene but erupted as recently as 1933, almost simultaneously with nearby Volcán Llaima, and lava spilled down its northeastern flanks in 1990. Trails to nearby Cerro Cautín (2.5 hours) and Lonquimay's summit start here, and the Sendero de Chile rounds Lonquimay before descending into town and then continuing toward the Sierra Nevada and Conguillío; trekking maps, for sale at La Suizandina, make hiking here easier.

On the site of an older ski area that was nearly in ruins, Malalcahuello also has a sparkling new resort, the **Corralco Centro de Montaña** (Av. Apoquindo 6275, Las Condes, Santiago, tel./fax 02/2029325, www.corralco.com, US$138–178 with breakfast). After a slow start, the new area has improved its operations but still has some distance to go; lift tickets cost about US$50 per day during the entire mid-June–October season.

**La Suizandina** (Camino Internacional Km 83, tel. 045/1973725 or cell 09/9884-9541, www.suizandina.com, US$26 pp for hostel accommodations, US$58–76 s, US$82–108 d, but ask for IVA discounts) is a combination hostel, cabaña, and guesthouse west of town on the north side of the highway. Multilingual founder Tom Buschor is no longer here, but his managers and staff still provide a Swiss-style breakfast and also serve Swiss specialties such as fondue and rösti for reasonably priced lunches or dinners, accompanied by fresh desserts and Chilean wines. While they no longer promote Suizandina as a campground, it's still possible to camp here economically (US$12 pp, breakfast optional for US$10). Guests get a 15 percent discount at nearby hot-springs resorts.

The **Malalcahuello Thermal Resort & Spa** (Ruta 181 Km 86; Rosario Norte 24, Oficina 1001, Santiago, www.malalcahuello.cl, US$240–360 s or d for hotel accommodations) is a hot-springs mega-project that fits surprisingly well into its natural setting, about two kilometers south of the highway via paved spur. With state-of-the-art indoor pools, spa treatments, and physical therapists, it also has

© WAYNE BERNHARDSON

The Malalcahuello Thermal Resort & Spa is an elaborate hot-springs hotel.

a handful of cabañas and bungalows (starting around US$275 for up to five people, including access to baths but not breakfast), and a so-so restaurant. Outside peak seasons (summer and ski season), rates drop by about 25 percent.

Admission to the pools costs US$24 per adult, US$12 per child. Additional services include massages, mud baths, Jacuzzis, saunas, and the like.

Conaf's Malalcahuello ranger station is a good source for advice; speakers of English, German, French, and Italian can try La Suizandina. There is free "Bibliored" Internet access at the library at the old train station, but also long waits and no wireless Internet.

**Biobío** and **Flota Erbuc** buses between Temuco and Lonquimay go directly past the gates of La Suizandina and the ranger station.

### LONQUIMAY

From Malalcahuello, the highway heads southeast to enter the 1930s' **Túnel Las Raíces,** where a Púa–Lonquimay tourist train ran as recently as the 1990s. Now open to vehicle traffic (toll US$1), the one-lane, 4.5-kilometer tunnel has been upgraded with new pavement and a reinforced roof, but a second parallel tunnel (to permit two-way rather than alternating traffic as at present) remains in the planning stages. This would simplify access to the Pino Hachado border crossing.

Beyond the tunnel (where bicyclists must hitch a lift with a passing pickup) the highway turns northeast to the village of Lonquimay, in the placid upper Biobío drainage—the traditional starting point for descending what was Chile's wildest white-water river until a series of downstream dams submerged the rapids.

Instead of a standard grid, Lonquimay (population about 3,500) has a peculiar ovoid town plan, though still centered on the handsomely refurbished Plaza de Armas. For information, it also has an obliging **Unidad Turística** (O'Higgins and Colón, tel. 045/464842, www.mlonquimay.cl) with a selection of wool sweaters and other local crafts, and restaurants and hotels that traditionally close by March. From Malalcahuello, a steep eastbound dirt road over Cuesta las Raíces is a shorter alternate route to Lonquimay, which is 900 meters above sea level, but it's open in summer and autumn only.

**Lonco Patagonia** (Ruta 89 Km 106.5, tel. 045/891959, cell 09/9283-0846, www.loncopatagonia.galeon.com) offers horseback excursions in the vicinity.

**Hostería Follil Pewenche** (Ignacio Carrera Pinto 110, tel. 045/891110, www.pewenche.cl) has both shared-bath (US$18 s, US$32 d) and private-bath (US$36 s or d) accommodations. **Hostería Donde Juancho** (O'Higgins 1130, tel. 045/891140, www.dondejuancho.cl, US$20 pp, US$50 s or d) also offers accommodations and has a 50-seat restaurant with beef and traditional Chilean dishes. Accommodations prices are negotiable.

At least five **Biobío** and **Flota Erbuc** buses daily connect Lonquimay with Temuco.

### ALTO BIOBÍO

South of Lonquimay, a gravel road tracks south over the Cuesta La Fusta past Lago Galletué, the Biobío's official source and part of Conaf's **Reserva Nacional Galletué;** it continues southeast past the border post of Icalma (for the Argentine town of Aluminé), but there is no public transport across this route. There are numerous simple campgrounds along this main road, which then turns west toward Melipeuco and Parque Nacional Conguillío. From Lonquimay, newly paved Ruta 181 crosses Conaf's **Reserva Nacional Alto Biobío** via the 1,884-meter Paso Pino Hachado, the route used by buses to the Argentine cities of Zapala and Neuquén.

## Melipeuco

In the Río Allipén valley, sited on an ancient mudflow 92 kilometers east of Temuco via Cunco and 45 kilometers west of Icalma, the Mapuche town of Melipeuco is Parque Nacional Conguillío's southern access point and an alternative route into the upper Biobío loop around Lonquimay. In the 1970s, this was a conflictive area in the agrarian reform movement, and the issue remains alive today.

Melipeuco (population about 2,500) operates a summer-only tourist office on Pedro Aguirre Cerda, across from the YPF gas station. There's a crafts market here as well, and free public wireless Internet (at least in the vicinity of the municipality).

The cheapest accommodations are at friendly **Hospedaje Icalma** (Pedro Aguirre Cerda 729, cell 09/9280-8210, US$14 pp with private bath and breakfast), though the rooms are unheated (but have lots of blankets). New in 2010, in a remodeled house of some architectural distinction, **Orígen Melipeuco** (Pedro Aguirre Cerda 384, tel. 09/9662-2250, www.origenmelipeuco.cl, US$36 pp with breakfast) is arguably overpriced for a place with shared baths, but the restaurant is off to an excellent start with specialties from the region, such as smoked pork loin with a pesto purée (US$10). It even serves a respectable sample of wines by the glass, and a credible crème brûlée.

**Nar-Bus** runs around seven buses daily to and from Temuco's Terminal de Buses Rurales (US$3, 1.5 hours). There is no scheduled public transport to Conguillío, but taxis or pickup trucks will take passengers to the visitors center for about US$15–20 one-way.

## PARQUE NACIONAL CONGUILLÍO

Directly east of Temuco, 3,125-meter Volcán Llaima's smoldering crater is Conguillío's most eye-catching feature; since colonial times, Chile's second most active volcano has recorded dozens of violent eruptions. On New Year's Day 2008, in fact, a sudden eruption and lava flow closed the northern access road from Curacautín and forced evacuation of 150 tourists.

Within its 60,833 hectares, though, this UNESCO biosphere reserve also abounds with dozens of other lava flows, secondary cones, alpine lakes, river canyons, and the araucaria forest that it was created to protect—the name Conguillío derives from the Mapudungun *kongüjim*, "to enter the *pewen* forest."

The *pewen*'s fame was such that, in late 1911, the aging pioneer U.S. conservationist John Muir traveled here simply to see, sketch,

© WAYNE BERNHARDSON

In a snowstorm, the lava beds of Parque Nacional Conguillío appear to be steaming.

and photograph the tree in its native habitat—"A glorious and novel sight, beyond all I had hoped for." As he so often did in California's Sierra Nevada, Muir slept in the open air, beneath the trees he came to visit.

For foreigners and Chileans alike, Conguillío is one of Temuco's most popular excursions. It justifies a day trip but merits at least an overnight.

## Geography and Climate

From Temuco, Conguillío's western limit is only about 80 kilometers away via Cherquenco, but by either Curacautín or Melipeuco it's about 120 kilometers. Altitudes range from around 900 meters in the Río Truful Truful valley to 3,125 meters on Llaima's summit. In its northeastern corner, the ruggedly glaciated Sierra Nevada averages above 2,500 meters.

Since most of Conguillío's 2,500 millimeters of precipitation falls as snow between May and September, the mild summers, averaging around 15°C, make its lakes and streams popular recreational destinations. Even in summer, though, occasional heavy rains—if not lava flows—can make the Curacautín road impassable even with four-wheel drive.

## Flora and Fauna

Conguillío originally was two separate parks, the other named Los Paraguas after the umbrella shape of the mature araucaria that, above 1,400 meters, mixes with the southern beeches *coigüe, ñire,* and *lenga. Coigüe* is also common at lower elevations, around 900 meters, but mixed with roble; above 1,200 meters, *raulí* succeeds roble.

Traditionally, Pewenche people collected the coniferous araucaria's nuts, much as indigenous groups gathered piñon nuts in western North America. The name Pewenche means "people of the *pewen,*" the local species of an endemic Southern Hemisphere genus that once enjoyed a greater distribution throughout the Americas.

Because much of Conguillío's terrain consists of barren volcanic slopes, lava fields, and open woodlands, prime wildlife habitat is scarce and so is wildlife. Birds are most common and resemble those at Tolhuaca or Malalcahuello, but the small reptile *lagartija* flourishes in drier environments.

## Sights and Recreation

Towering just west of the park's geographic center, glacier-covered **Volcán Llaima** is a Holocene structure of accumulated lava flows within an eight-kilometer-wide caldera that exploded about 7,200 years ago. It has two active craters, one on the summit and another on its southeastern shoulder. Its early 2008 eruption closed the park for a time, but in good weather the northern access road is passable for almost any motor vehicle.

In **Sector Conguillío,** east of Llaima, the sprawling lava flows of **El Escorial** dammed the Río Truful Truful to form **Laguna Arco Iris** and **Laguna Verde;** to the north, beneath the Sierra Nevada, **Laguna Conguillío** has a similar origin.

Near Conaf's Centro de Información Ambiental at the southwest corner of Laguna Conguillío, the **Sendero Araucarias** is a short woodland nature trail suitable for any hiker. For a longer and more challenging excursion try walking from **Playa Linda,** at the east end of Laguna Conguillío, to the base of the **Sierra Nevada,** which rewards the hiker with overwhelming views through nearly pure araucaria woodland. This extension across the mountains to Termas Río Blanco is a hazardous one on which hikers have died.

At **Laguna Captrén,** at the park's northern entrance, the **Sendero de Chile** was the initial section of the nonmotorized trail intended to unite the country from the Peruvian border to Tierra del Fuego. At Laguna Arco Iris, to the south, an early settler built the wooden **Casa del Colono** as a homestead cabin. From Laguna Verde, also known as Laguna Quililo, a short wooded footpath reaches the beach at **La Ensenada.**

Conaf's **Sendero Cañadon Truful-Truful,** a 900-meter nature trail, follows the river's course where erosion has uncovered the rainbow chronology of Llaima's eruptions and ash falls. Along the 800-meter **Sendero Los Vertientes,** subterranean springs emerge from the volcanic terrain.

From **Sector Los Paraguas,** on the park's west side, well-equipped climbers can scale Llaima; camping is possible in summer, and there's also a *refugio.* There is an alternative route from Captrén, which has better public transport, on the north side. Before climbing, get permission from Conaf in Temuco.

Skiing takes place at Los Paraguas's upgraded **Centro de Ski Las Araucarias** (tel. 045/562313, www.skiaraucarias.cl); it has Temuco offices at Bulnes 351, Oficina 47 (tel. 045/239999). Lift tickets cost US$35–50 per day.

## Accommodations

Along Laguna Conguillío's south shore, Conaf has five campgrounds under private concession: The campground administration is at **Los Ñirres** (44 sites), while there are smaller clusters at **Los Carpinteros** (12 sites), **La Caseta** (12 sites), **El Estero** (10 sites), and **El Hoyón** (10 sites). Rates are US$36 per site for up to six people in summer and during Semana Santa, US$25 the rest of the year. Conaf also sets aside a handful of El Estero sites for bicyclists and backpackers (US$10 pp).

Ten kilometers northwest of Laguna Conguillío, there are several more sites at **Laguna Captrén,** recently reopened after repair of damage from the 2008 eruption. For more information or reservations in Temuco, contact Conaf (tel. 045/298114).

The former cabañas built around massive araucaria trees have been dismantled, but newer and better ones are now available just one kilometer west of park headquarters for US$100 for up to three guests, US$150 for up to seven; off-season rates are about 20 percent lower. For details and reservations, contact Cristián Pérez (Victoria tel. 045/841710, cell 09/9050-2654, cristianevans@hotmail.com).

At Laguna Verde, 18 kilometers northeast of Melipeuco, the private **La Baita Conguillío** (Casilla 492, Villarrica, tel. 045/416410, cell 09/9733-2442, www.labaitaconguillio.cl, US$86 s, US$100 d) has cabañas sleeping 4–8 people and an "eco-lodge" that's more like a traditional Andean hotel.

The modern **Centro de Ski las Araucarias** (tel. 045/562313, www.skiaraucarias.cl) has a variety of accommodations. Its **Refugio Paraguas** has dorm beds (US$20 pp with your own sleeping bag) and one six-bed apartment (US$120), while the **Refugio Pehuén** also has dorms (US$20 pp) and doubles with shared bath (US$48). Facilities at the **Edificio Llaima** (US$140) can sleep up to four.

## Information

At Laguna Conguillío, Conaf's **Centro de Información Ambiental** (tel. 02/1960850, parque.conguillio@conaf.cl) has good natural-history exhibits and a cozy fireplace; it's open 9 A.M.–1 P.M. and 2–6 P.M. daily except in January and February, when it does not close at midday and stays open until 7:30 P.M. It organizes children's programs and hiking excursions and provides evening naturalist talks.

Conaf also has ranger stations at the Laguna Captrén and Truful Truful park entrances, where park admission costs US$8 per person. At the Paraguas ski area, it costs US$2.

## Getting There

Because public transportation is inconvenient to almost every sector of the park, it's worth considering a car rental, but it's not absolutely essential. Even with a car, the steep, narrow, and sometimes muddy road between Laguna Captrén and the park administration can be difficult—in either direction.

Reaching Curacautín and Melipeuco, the northern and southern gateways to the main park loop, is easy enough by public bus. From Curacautín, there's now a twice-daily bus service, at 6:30 A.M. and 5 P.M., to the northern park entrance at Laguna Captrén; from Melipeuco, it's possible to hire a taxi or pickup truck to Conguillío.

Sector Los Paraguas is most difficult to reach by public transportation. At Temuco's Terminal de Buses Rurales, **Nar-Bus** (Pinto 032, tel. 045/407740) goes to the village of Cherquenco (US$2.50) at 11:30 A.M. and 12:30, 4:30, and 5:30 P.M., but from there it's 17 kilometers farther to the Los Paraguas ski lodge.

An alternative route goes from Captrén to Los Paraguas, but with no public transport.

## VILLARRICA

Volcán Villarrica's fiery eruptions may have deterred some settlers, but Mapuche resistance to the Spaniards and Chileans was more effective. In 1552, 50 colonists under Gerónimo de Alderete established Santa María Magdalena de Villarrica, but the Mapuche forced its abandonment several times despite speculation about precious metals nearby (the overly optimistic founding name Villarrica means "Rich Town"). After expelling the Spaniards in 1602, the Mapuche enjoyed nearly three centuries of uninterrupted possession until, in 1883, Chilean colonel Gregorio Urrutia reached an agreement with Mapuche chief Epuléf to regularize the Chilean presence.

Villarrica's 1897 declaration of city status brought an influx of immigrants, many of them German, who transformed the area into a dairy zone and, eventually, a durable resort area with an international reputation.

### Orientation

Some 87 kilometers southeast of Temuco via the Panamericana and Ruta 199, an international highway to Argentina, Villarrica (population about 30,000) lies at Lago Villarrica's southwestern edge, at its Río Toltén outlet. While the town has a regular grid pattern, the focus of activity is not the Plaza de Armas but rather the lakeshore, along with the commercial thoroughfare Avenida Pedro de Valdivia and its perpendicular Camilo Henríquez.

### Sights and Recreation

Stone tools, early Mapuche ceramics, and contemporary indigenous jewelry, silver, and leatherwork constitute the collections of the **Museo Histórico y Arqueológico de Villarrica**

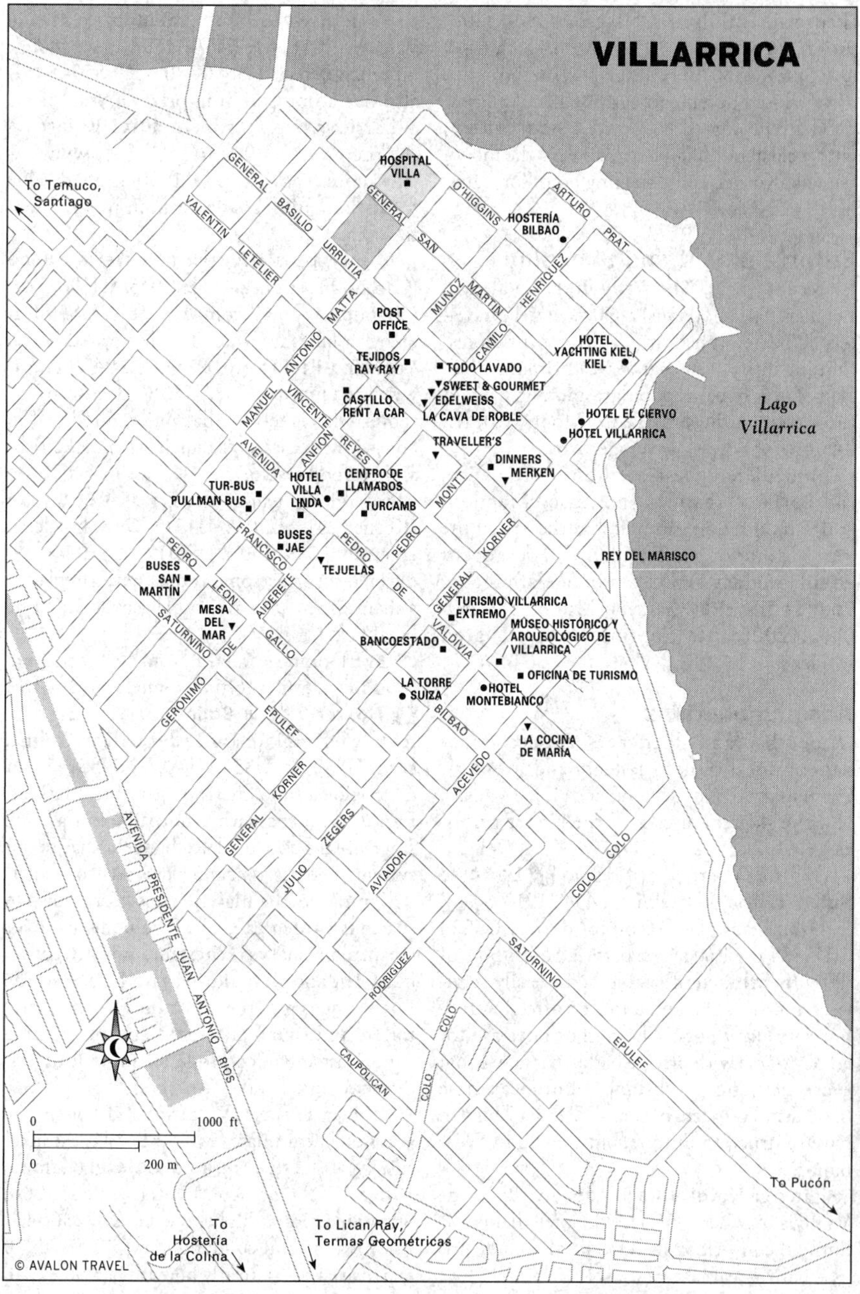


CHILEAN LAKES DISTRICT

(Pedro de Valdivia 1050, tel. 045/415706, 9 A.M.–1 P.M. and 6–10 P.M. Mon.–Sat., 6–10 P.M. Sun., US$0.20). As of late 2010, however, it was closed because of earthquake damage.

The rejuvenated lakefront **Embarcadero,** with a cluster of small jetties toward the foot of General Körner, is the starting point for water-based excursions.

## Entertainment and Shopping

In recent years, **The Travellers** (Valentín Letelier 753, tel. 045/412830, www.thetravellers.cl) has morphed from a diverse fusion restaurant into a bar that serves primarily pub grub, but it remains popular; smoking prevails throughout. **Dinners** (Pedro Montt 390, tel. 045/416745) draws a younger crowd.

Immediately west of the tourist office, the **Feria Artesanal** showcases Mapuche crafts and food in summer, but the rest of the year it's moribund. The daily market opens around midday and closes in late afternoon. **Tejidos Ray-Ray** (Anfión Muñoz 386, tel. 045/412006) is a clothing store strong on woolens.

## Accommodations

As in other lakes district resorts, accommodations prices peak in January and February, but Semana Santa, September's Fiestas Patrias, and the ski season can all see higher prices, as well.

Cyclists in particular flock to **La Torre Suiza** (Bilbao 969, tel./fax 045/411213, www.torresuiza.com, US$16 pp for dorms, US$24 s, US$34 d with shared bath, US$48–60 s or d), with firm, comfortable beds, easily regulated hot showers, and a tobacco-free interior, but squeaky floors. The higher rates are for larger rooms with private baths in a new wing; everyone shares a substantial European-style breakfast. Founders Béat and Claudia Zbinden have returned to Europe, but it's still in Swiss hands.

Rates at **Hotel Villa Linda** (Av. Pedro de Valdivia 678, tel. 045/411392, hotelvillalinda@hotmail.com, US$24 s, US$44 d) include private bath, breakfast, and cable TV.

Modern **Hotel Montebianco** (Pedro de Valdivia 1011, tel. 045/411798, www.hotelmontebianco.cl, US$50–80 s, US$56–84 d) also has an outstanding pizzeria, but it's on Villarrica's busiest street. **Hotel Villarrica** (Körner 255, tel./fax 045/411641, www.cajalosandes.cl, US$77 s or d) offers good value for its tranquil lakeside location in a residential area.

Comfy, rustically styled **Hostería Bilbao** (Camilo Henríquez 43, tel. 045/411186, hosteriabilbao@gmail.com, US$50 s, US$90 d) enjoys a lakeshore site. The renovated **Hotel Yachting Kiel** (Körner 153, tel. 045/411631, www.restaurantkiel.cl, US$80 d) also offers rooms with lake-view balconies, satellite TV, and wireless Internet, plus its namesake fish-and-seafood restaurant.

Set among lush gardens, **Hotel El Ciervo** (Körner 241, tel. 045/411215, www.hotelelciervo.cl, US$89–100 s, US$112–135 d) is a traditional favorite; some rooms have fireplaces, and rates include an ample European-style breakfast.

Overlooking the lake from secluded high ground, the Oregonian owners at TV-free **Hostería de la Colina** (Las Colinas 115, tel./fax 045/411503, www.hosteriadelacolina.com, US$75 s, US$90 d, up to US$135 s or d) provide a full American-style breakfast, attractive gardens with a hot tub, and a large English-language book exchange on the honor system. The best volcano views are from a garden mirador; the highest rates correspond to spacious garden cabañas. The homemade ice cream alone makes the restaurant worth a visit, but Glen and Bev Aldrich also belong to the Los Bosques group (protecting Chile's native forests and rivers) and the Mapuche-oriented Agro Gastronómico program (promoting traditional ingredients and dishes).

Midway between Villarrica and Pucón, the area's only legitimate five-star hotel is the lakeside **Villarrica Park Lake Hotel** (Camino Villarrica Pucón Km 13, tel. 045/450000, www.villarricaparklakehotel.cl, US$286–431 s or d), a tasteful contemporary place with 70 expansive rooms (nearly all with balconies), all of which face the lake. Its relatively small private beach is rockier than it is sandy, but it compensates partly with indoor and outdoor pools, as well as a spa, two bars, and a restaurant. Serious high rollers choose the presidential suite (US$931 per night, usually reserved well ahead of time).

## Food

At the Mercado Fritz crafts market, inexpensive **La Cocina de María** (Aviador Acevedo 600) is a good lunch option for typical Chilean dishes such as chicken with rice, fried chicken, and empanadas.

The unpretentious **Tejuelas** (Gerónimo de Alderete 632, tel. 045/410619, lunch and dinner daily) delivers great value for the price, especially with some of the country's finest homemade bread for sandwiches. The pizza is less appealing, its crust a little heavy despite a diversity of appetizing toppings.

**Sweet Gourmet** (Camilo Henríquez 331, tel. 045/414087) does sandwiches and light meals, but its strength is Chile's best kuchen—the raspberry kuchen topped with flakes of white chocolate is beyond exquisite. **Edelweiss** (Camilo Henríquez 387, tel. 045/413647, breakfast, lunch, and dinner daily) is good for large but inexpensive sandwiches (around US$5), pizzas in the US$7–10 range, and ice cream.

In a lakeside setting, **El Rey del Marisco** (Valentín Letelier 1030, tel. 045/412093, lunch and dinner daily) remains popular for fish and shellfish dishes in the US$9–12 range, but it's been up and down lately. More often than not, the ambitious **Mesa del Mar** (Gerónimo de Alderete 835, tel. 045/419515, www.mesadelmar.cl, lunch and dinner daily) is very good, but on a bad night it's forgettable at best.

New in late 2010, **Merken** (Valentín Letelier 836, tel. 09/7125-1438, lunch and dinner daily) attempts to produce a hybrid Mapuche cuisine with lakes district standards spiced up with its namesake hot peppers *(merkén)*—the only truly spicy seasoning found in Chile. Other specialties include nalca, the rhubarb-like plant that grows widely in the mid-latitude forests here. Midday specials are a bargain at US$4–6 for a three-course meal, but even the à la carte dishes come in under US$10, and the service is a pleasant surprise.

The carnivore's choice, Villarrica's most sophisticated option is **La Cava de Roble** (Valentín Letelier 658, tel. 045/416446, www.lacavaderoble.cl, lunch and dinner daily), which specializes in beef and tasty game dishes such as venison (with a sweet and sour blueberry sauce, US$15) and wild boar. A limited pasta menu is creative—think ravioli stuffed with smoked salmon and abalone (US$10). Unlike most Chilean restaurants outside Santiago, it offers a choice of quality wines by the glass, and there's a spacious terrace for sunny afternoons or fine evenings.

Under new management, **Restaurant Kiel** (General Körner 153, tel. 045/411631, www.restaurantkiel.cl, lunch and dinner daily) has upgraded its quarters and the menu, with seafood specialties in the US$15 range. Here, though, only house wines are available by the glass.

## Information

Well-stocked with maps, brochures, and a roster of accommodations but no prices, Villarrica's municipal **Oficina de Turismo** (Pedro de Valdivia 1070, tel. 045/206619, turis@villarrica.org) keeps long hours in January and February: 8 A.M.–11 P.M. daily; the rest of the year, hours are 9 A.M.–1 P.M. and 2:30–6 P.M. daily except weekends, when it closes half an hour earlier.

## Services

**Turcamb** (Camilo Henríquez 576, Local 6) is the only exchange house. The ATM at BancoEstado (Pedro de Valdivia 957) collects no service charges.

**Correos de Chile** (Anfión Muñoz 315) is the post office. The **Centro de Llamados** (Camilo Henríquez 587) provides both long-distance telephone and Internet service.

For laundry service, try **Todo Lavado** (General Urrutia 699, Local 7, tel. 045/414452).

It used to be necessary to organize excursions such as climbing Volcán Villarrica in Pucón, but **Turismo Villarrica Extremo** (Pedro de Valdivia 910, tel. 045/410900, www.villarricaextremo.com) works with Pucón agencies.

For medical assistance, there's the **Hospital Villarrica** (San Martín 460, tel. 045/411169).

### Getting There and Around

Villarrica has a central **Terminal de Buses** (Av. Pedro de Valdivia 621), but some carriers have individual offices nearby. At the main terminal, **Buses Regionales Villarrica** (tel. 045/411871) has frequent buses to Pucón (US$1.50, 45 minutes), where there are connections to other regional destinations such as Curarrehue and Puesco.

**Buses Jac** (Bilbao 610, tel. 045/467777) shuttles at least every 15–30 minutes between Temuco (US$2–4, one hour) and Pucón (US$1.50, 30 minutes).

Northbound services to Santiago and intermediates on the Panamericana are frequent, but some southbound services require backtracking to Temuco; alternatively, transfer at Freire from any Temuco-bound bus.

Many companies go to Santiago, including **Pullman Bus** (Bilbao 598, tel. 045/414217), Buses Jac, and **Tur-Bus** (Anfión Muñoz 657, tel. 045/411534), which also have direct services to Osorno, Puerto Varas, and Puerto Montt.

Santiago fares start around US$25, with *salón cama* sleepers around US$40. Other sample destinations, fares, and times include Osorno (US$13, 3.5 hours) and Puerto Montt (US$16, five hours).

Local carriers also serve the Argentine cities of Junín de los Andes, with connections to San Martín de los Andes; these buses leave from Temuco and board additional passengers in Villarrica and Pucón. **Buses San Martín** (Pedro León Gallo 583, tel. 045/411584) and **Igi Llaima** (tel. 045/412733), at the main terminal, alternate daily services. For services to Bariloche, it's necessary to return to Temuco or make connections in Osorno.

**Castillo Rent A Car** (Anfión Muñoz 415, tel. 045/411618, www.castillorentacar.cl) is the only car-rental option.

## PUCÓN

At the foot of smoldering Volcán Villarrica, Pucón has gained a name as *the* destination for hikers, climbers, mountain bikers, windsurfers, and white-water rafters and kayakers. Still popular with conventional Chilean holiday-makers, it enjoys a longer season than most lakes district resorts because hordes of youthful international travelers frequent the area from November to April. It has no sights of its own because almost everything worth seeing or doing is outside town, but at day's end everyone swarms to local hotels, restaurants, and bars to party.

That doesn't mean Pucón lacks a serious side. Over the past several years, the landmark cooperative Hostería ¡Ecole!, along with the affiliated Fundación Lahuen, has actively promoted regional forest conservation.

### Orientation

Where the Río Pucón enters the lake, 25 kilometers east of the town of Villarrica via Ruta 119, Pucón (population about 15,000) occupies a compact grid bounded by the lakeshore to the north and west, Avenida Colo Colo to the east, and Volcán Villarrica's lower slopes to the south. Its commercial axis is Avenida Bernardo O'Higgins, which continues as Ruta 119 toward Curarrehue and the Argentine border at Paso Mamuil Malal.

### Entertainment and Events

There's little in terms of formal entertainment venues, but somehow Pucón has plenty to do.

The shell of the colossal Casino de Pucón burned nearly to the ground in late 2007, costing the city its main performing-arts venue and a cinema, but the new **Enjoy Pucón** (Ansorena 121, tel. 045/550000, www.enjoy.cl) casino imports performers of the stature of Spain's Joan Manuel Serrat.

There's a lot of turnover in bars, but several have managed to last more than a few seasons, most notably **Krater** (O'Higgins 447, tel.

Volcán Villarrica looms above the beach at Pucón.

045/441339) and **Mamas & Tapas** (O'Higgins 587, tel. 045/449002). Both places serve food as well, but that's not their forte.

Early February's **Ironman Internacional de Pucón** (Pucón International Triathlon) grows in popularity every year. February 27's **Aniversario de Pucón** celebrates the city's founding.

## Shopping

The **Mercado Artesanal Municipal** (Ansorena 445, daily) and **Artesanos de Pucón** (Alderete 370, daily) both have ample crafts selections. There are also abundant street vendors.

## Accommodations

Pucón has abundant budget accommodations, but the best values are just a bit more expensive.

### US$25-50

In a quiet site only about 100 meters north of the Tur-Bus terminal, Swiss-run **Casa Satya** (Blanco Encalada 190, tel. 045/444093, cpassavant@gmail.com, US$16 pp, US$64 d with breakfast) has doubles and triples with either shared or private bath, plus wireless Internet and access to a full modern kitchen; the higher rates correspond to doubles with private baths. Owner Cristina Passavant also offers massage options ranging from reiki to Thai.

**Residencial Lincoyán** (Lincoyán 323, tel. 045/441144, www.lincoyan.cl, US$20 pp with shared bath) is a plain but friendly family-style place with good beds but no other amenities. Breakfast costs US$5 more.

Just beyond the town's central grid, **Pucón Hostel** (Av. O'Higgins 771, tel. 045/441381, www.puconhostelchile.com, US$20 pp, US$50 s or d) is a sparkling new purpose-built facility that has mostly private rooms with just a few dorm bunks. While it may lack the vigorous vibes of places like ¡Ecole!, it compensates with a friendly family approach that, however, does not interfere with its guests.

Occupying two adjacent houses on the same property, the misleadingly named **Tree House Hostel** (General Urrutia 660, tel. 045/444679,

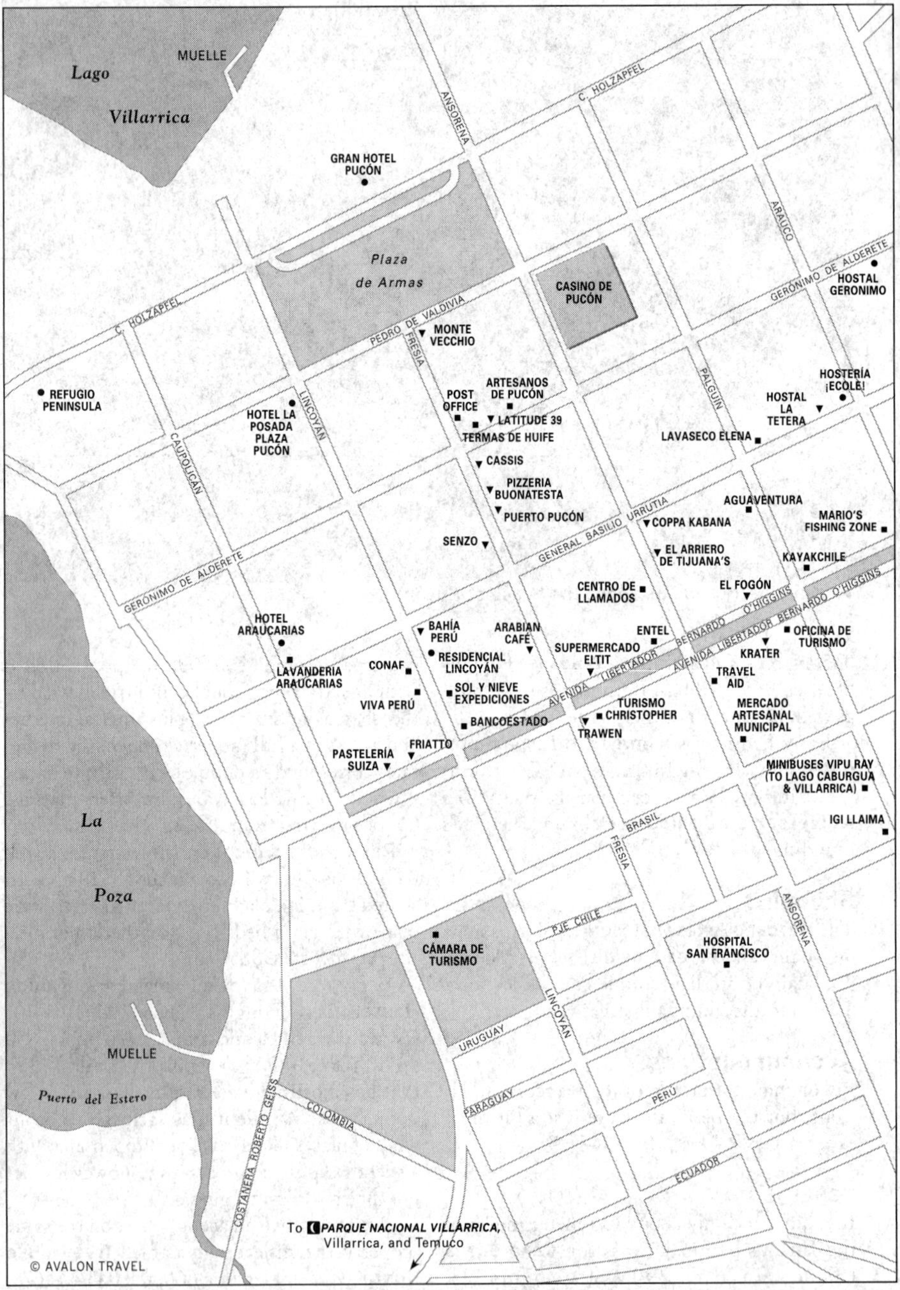


CHILEAN LAKES DISTRICT

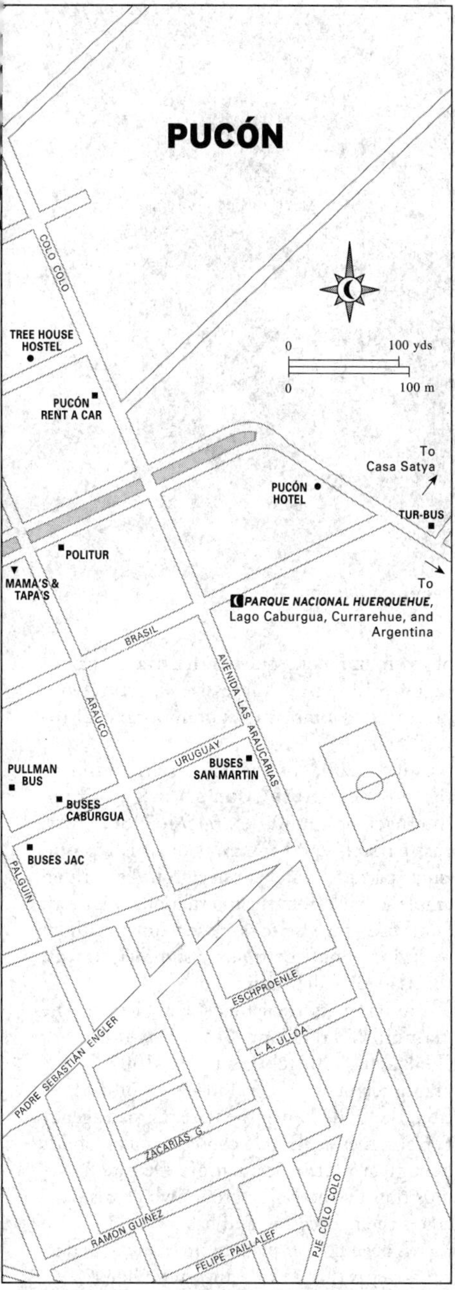


www.treehousechile.cl, US$18–25 pp, US$58 s or d) is an Anglo-Chilean venture with both dorms and private rooms. The beds and other furnishings are both sturdy and stylish, but its actual tree house is just a place to grab a view of Volcán Villarrica.

More than just a comfy bed, **Hostería ¡Ecole!** (General Urrutia 592, tel. 045/441675, www.ecole.cl, US$14–20 pp in dorms, US$34 s, US$40 d with shared bath, US$60–76 s or d with private bath) has become a destination in itself. Owned and operated by a cooperative of Chilean and international environmental advocates, it provides informally stylish B&B-style accommodations (breakfast extra). It also has a moderately priced vegetarian restaurant, a bar, and a book exchange; operates its own excursions; and provides information and advice. It's so popular, though, that reservations are essential in summer and advisable the rest of the year. The cheapest choice is backpackers' bunks, for which you need your own sleeping bag.

### US$50-100

It's a little ragged in some aspects—the rooms have irregular shapes, for instance, and the bathroom linoleum undulates across the floor—but the family-run HI affiliate **Refugio Península** (Holzapfel 11, tel. 045/443398, www.refugiopeninsula.cl, US$30 pp in dorms, US$50 s, US$70 d) compensates with coziness and a quiet lakeshore location. HI members get a small discount.

Alongside ¡Ecole!, the more subdued **Hostal La Tetera** (General Urrutia 580, tel./fax 045/441462, www.tetera.cl, US$55 s, US$62 d with shared bath, US$71 s, US$78 d with private bath) offers equally stylish, comfortable rooms with good beds and individual reading lights, though the walls are a little thin. Still, it attracts a quiet clientele and has some of Pucón's best breakfasts; there's also a good book exchange. Ask for one of the front rooms, whose balconies offer views of Volcán Villarrica; if possible, avoid room 4 (Meli), shaded by ¡Ecole!'s dense fir tree.

**Hostal Gerónimo** (Gerónimo de Alderete

**Hostería ¡Ecole!'s restaurant has an exclusively vegetarian menu.**

665, tel. 045/443762, www.geronimo.cl, US$72 s, US$76 d, up to US$96 s or d) offers immaculate small-to-midsized rooms, some with terrace views of the volcano. The personnel are gracious and helpful, and there's also a pasta-oriented restaurant.

Set on ample grounds, with a large pool, **Hotel La Posada Plaza Pucón** (Pedro de Valdivia 191, tel. 045/441088, www.hotelplazapucon.cl, US$66–101 s, US$82–111 d) has midsized rooms in an older upgraded building. The management is very accommodating.



### US$100-200

With its spa and other upgrades, **Hotel & Spa Araucarias** (Caupolicán 243, tel. 045/441286, www.araucarias.cl, US$80 s, US$120 d) is a fine value with IVA discounts. It also has a small but impressive museum of Mapuche artifacts.

The main shortcoming at **Hotel Malalhue** (Camino Internacional 1615, tel. 045/443130, www.malalhue.cl, US$96–109 s, US$119–130 d) is that it fronts on the eastbound road out of town and, consequently, has traffic day or night. Still, it's an impressive structure with luminous rooms and contemporary Euro-Andean style.

New in 2008, on Pucón's eastern outskirts, the 50-room **Hotel Oasis Park** (Camino Internacional 3000, tel. 045/467960, www.oasispark.cl, US$143–237 s or d) is a promising spa hotel on expansive grounds with an ample setback from the international highway. For those who wish to be close to town without worrying about the frenetic summer crowds, this is a good alternative.

Enjoying its own black-sand beach, the mammoth lakefront **Gran Hotel Pucón** (Holzapfel 190, tel./fax 045/441001, www.granhotelpucon.cl, US$150–244 s or d) dates from the 1930s, when the state railroad agency Ferrocarriles del Estado chose Pucón as Chile's next great tourist destination. Despite its acquisition by the Enjoy group, which also operates the new casino and has money to burn, there's been no conspicuous investment, and its character is that of an aging grand hotel.

### OVER US$200

Two kilometers west of town on the Villarrica road, poised among wooded hillside gardens with immaculate flower beds, pools, and cascades, the Bauhaus-style **Hotel Antumalal** (tel. 045/441011 www.antumalal.com, from US$239 s or d) prides itself on personal service; when you arrive, staff members place a fresh fruit basket in every room and even wash your car. Each of its 22 rooms boasts lake views and a fireplace; the common areas have panoramic views through giant plate-glass windows, as well as a strong wireless Internet signal. In addition to a heated pool and a private beach, it's also added a spa with a hot tub, sauna, and massage services. Half-board rates are also available; the restaurant has been gaining clientele from nonguests as well.

## Food

Pucón's food ranges from simple regional cuisine and fast food—no greasy chain outlets, thankfully—to sophisticated international fare. A good example of the former is **Coppa Kabana** (Urrutia 407, tel. 045/444371, lunch and dinner daily), which serves sandwiches and plain lunches at reasonable prices. **Pastelería Suiza** (O'Higgins 116, tel. 045/441241, breakfast, lunch, and dinner daily) is the classic breakfast spot for tasty pastries.

**Latitud 39** (Gerónimo de Alderete 324, cell 09/7430-0016, www.latitude39chile.com, breakfast, lunch, and dinner Mon.–Sat.) is a U.S.-run café with a diverse menu that includes sandwiches, Mexican food, and Thai dishes, and serves breakfast all day. Prices are moderate, and the spicy tortilla soup (US$6) is great for a cool winter's day. Latitud 39 introduced a novelty—shaved ice—for hot summer days.

Even if there's no room at the inn, don't miss the renovated menu at **Presente** (Urrutia 592, tel. 045/441675, lunch and dinner daily), the vegetarian restaurant at Hostería ¡Ecole!, which focuses on seasonal, locally produced organic products, including Mapuche-derived dishes and spices. For about US$6–10 per entrée, this remains some of the country's best-value food.

The menu at **Trawen** (O'Higgins 311, tel. 045/442024, lunch and dinner daily) does a lot with standards such as ravioli (stuffed with prosciutto, for instance), creative vegetarian dishes, and the freshest local ingredients. There's also a respectable selection of wines by the glass. Across the street, with a steady crowd even in the off-season, **Il Fiore** (O'Higgins 291, tel. 045/442743) offers a wide variety of quality pizza and pastas but is relatively expensive at around US$11 per entrée—the price of the sauce adds another US$3–4.

**Puerto Pucón** (Fresia 246, tel. 045/441592, lunch and dinner daily) is the standard seafood option, but prices have risen dramatically, with most entrées in the US$15 range. **El Fogón** (O'Higgins 480, tel. 045/444904, US$9–15 for entrées) is a traditional *parrilla,* but the town has sprouted a gaggle of new *parrillas* over the past couple of years.

Uruguayans eat even more beef than Argentines, so it's not surprising that the Uruguayan-owned *parrilla* **La Maga** (Gerónimo de Alderete 276, tel. 045/444277, www.lamagapucon.cl, lunch and dinner daily) serves up massive slabs of meat, such as a thick pepper steak (US$21) that's easily large enough for two. The ambience is appealing for families, couples, and even individual diners, everything's cooked precisely to order, and it has made concessions to local custom by producing side dishes such as *merkén*-spiced potatoes, but the elevated prices make it best for a special occasion—or for those who couldn't care less what it costs.

Alongside La Maga, the same owners operate a more moderately priced snack bar in **La Celeste** (Gerónimo de Alderete 266, tel. 045/444046), which specializes in the Uruguayan caloric overload known as the *chivito.* This is not kid goat, as the word would normally suggest, but rather a steak sandwich slathered with fried eggs, bacon, tomatoes, cheese, and mayonnaise, plus a side of fries.

The Argentine-style **Pizzería Buonatesta** (Fresia 243, tel. 045/441434, lunch and dinner daily, US$7–10 for pizzettas) is outstanding. **Senzo** (Fresia 284, tel. 045/449005, lunch and dinner Wed.–Mon.) is also highly regarded for pastas and risottos. The trilogy of pastas (US$15) is a sampler of their agnolotti, ravioli, and tortellini, with diverse sauces, but the kitchen is perhaps a little too quick to deliver the goods.

Pucón's main Mexican option is the modest **El Arriero de Tijuana's** (Ansorena 303, tel. 045/444144, lunch and dinner daily). The **Arabian Café** (Fresia 354, tel. 045/443469, lunch and dinner daily) serves Middle Eastern specialties.

**Bahía Perú** (General Urrutia 211, tel. 045/443820, www.bahiaperu.cl, lunch and dinner daily) falls short of the top echelon of Chile's Peruvian restaurants, but the prices (US$7–14 for most entrées) are fair, the pisco sours suitably tart, and the service exceptional.

**Viva Perú** (Lincoyán 372, tel. 045/444025, lunch and dinner daily) serves arguably lighter versions of Peruvian dishes such as *ají de gallina* (chicken in a walnut sauce, US$11), plus ceviche and Peruvian-style pisco sours. Most entrées fall into the US$8–13 range.

**Cassis** (Fresia 223, tel. 045/449088, breakfast, lunch, and dinner daily) serves sandwiches, coffee, juices, and particularly exquisite desserts, including homemade ice cream and crepes, as well as artisanal chocolates. **Friatto** (O'Higgins 136-B) also serves decent ice cream.

## Information

In summer, Pucón's **Oficina Municipal de Turismo** (O'Higgins 483, tel. 045/293002, www.visitpucon.com) is open 8:30 A.M.–10 P.M. daily; the rest of the year, hours are 8:30 A.M.–7 P.M.

The private **Cámara de Turismo** (Brasil 115, tel. 045/441671, www.puconturismo.cl) is open 9 A.M.–midnight daily in January and February, 10 A.M.–1:30 P.M. and 4–7 P.M. daily the rest of the year.

For national parks, **Conaf** (Lincoyán 336, 1st floor, tel. 045/443781) now has centrally convenient offices.



## Services

**Turismo Christopher** (O'Higgins 335) and **Supermercado Eltit** (O'Higgins 336) change U.S. and Argentine cash. The supermarket now has an ATM, as does **BCI** (Fresia 174).

**Correos de Chile** (Fresia 183) handles the mail. For long-distance telephone and Internet services, there's a **Centro de Llamados** (Ansorena 380), but many restaurants and cafés have wireless Internet.

Speaking Spanish, English, and German, Swiss-run **Travel Aid** (Ansorena 425, Local 4, tel. 045/444040, www.travelaid.cl) is a well-informed travel agency, tour broker, and apartment rental agency that also sells books and maps of the area, region, and country. It's also the local agent for Navimag and Cruce de Lagos.

**Lavaseco Elena** (General Urrutia 520-B, tel. 045/441019) charges about US$6 per load, washed, dried, and folded. **Lavandería Araucarias** (General Urrutia 108, Local 4) is equally efficient.

For medical services, contact **Hospital San Francisco** (Uruguay 325, tel. 045/441177).

## Getting There

In the past there have been occasional summer flights into Pucón. Construction of a new airport 30 kilometers south of Temuco would have shortened the distance to Pucón, but it has been postponed. Even then, the Pucón airfield is not really suitable for commercial flights.

Long-distance bus service is an extension of that from Villarrica. The three main carriers have their own terminals: **Tur-Bus** (O'Higgins 910, tel. 045/443328), **Buses Jac** (Uruguay 505, tel. 045/990880), and **Pullman Bus** (Palguín 555, tel. 045/443331). **Intersur** shares the Tur-Bus terminal, while other companies have separate terminals around the east end of town.

Buses Jac, Tur-Bus, Intersur, and **Igi Llaima** (Palguín 598, tel. 045/441676) go frequently to Santiago, while Tur-Bus also goes to Puerto Montt. Igi Llaima and **Buses San Martín** (Colo Colo 612, tel. 045/443595) both cross the cordillera to Junín de los Andes and San Martín de los Andes, Argentina.

**Minibuses Vipu Ray** (Palguín 550, tel.

## GOING TO THE DOGS

In wintertime, skiing and snowboarding are no longer the only outdoor activities in and around Pucón. While it may not be Alaska or the Yukon, Konrad and Katje Jakob have 30 working huskies that, on the western slopes of Volcán Villarrica, they use for guided tours on individual sleds for experienced – or aspiring amateur – mushers. In summer, though, the same animals are available to pull carts on the area's backroads. Full-moon rides are another option.

About midway between Villarrica and Lican Ray, **Aurora Austral Husky Adventure** (tel. 09/8901-2574, www.novena-region.com) offers day trips for visitors to Pucón and Villarrica, but also sells packages that include accommodations at its own cabañas on their own secluded property.

PHOTO COURTESY OF KONRAD JAKOB

**In winter, the Jakobs offer sled trips on the western slopes of Volcán Villarrica.**

045/413449) and Buses Jac both go frequently to Villarrica (US$1.50, 45 minutes); Vipu Ray has nine buses daily to Caburgua (US$1), while Jac has three or four daily to Curarrehue (US$2.50). In summer, **Buses Caburgua** (Uruguay 540) has four daily to Parque Nacional Huerquehue (US$3); the rest of the year, there are at least two per day.

### Getting Around

Several adventure travel companies on Avenida O'Higgins also rent mountain bikes.

For rental cars, try **Pucón Rent A Car** (Colo Colo 340, tel./fax 045/443052, www.puconrentacar.cl).

## VICINITY OF PUCÓN

The locus of adventure travel in the Andean lakes district, Pucón offers activities ranging from climbing Volcán Villarrica to rafting the Río Trancura, hiking at Huerquehue, horseback riding, fly-fishing, skiing, and visits to nearby thermal baths. Competition—often cutthroat competition—can keep prices low and temperatures high among local operators. Occasionally, though, they cooperate in putting groups together, especially outside the summer peak.

Commercial operators include French-run **Aguaventura** (Palguín 336, tel. 045/444246, www.aguaventura.com), **Kayakchile**

(O'Higgins 524, tel. 045/441584, www.kayakchile.net), **Politur** (O'Higgins 635, tel./fax 045/441373, www.politur.com), and **Sol y Nieve Expediciones** (Lincoyán 361, tel./fax 045/444761, www.solynievepucon.cl).

Best known as a place to stay, noncommercial **Hostería ¡Ecole!** (General Urrutia 592, tel. 045/441675, www.ecole.cl) organizes groups to visit the Fundación Lahuén's nearby Santuario Cañi forest reserve and other excursions; the staff also offers suggestions for independent excursions.

**Mario's Fishing Zone** (O'Higgins 590, tel. 09/9760-7280, www.flyfishingpucon.com) is a fly-fishing operator.

## Cuevas Volcánicas

On Volcán Villarrica's southern slopes, but outside the national park, the misleadingly named "volcanic caves" are really lava tubes that descend 340 meters into the mountainside (unless you're a bat, the darkness at the bottom is absolute). Unfortunately, what was once a professional introduction to volcanism, with bilingual guides and informative displays, has declined and is hard to recommend with any enthusiasm.

Reached by a fork off the road to Parque Nacional Villarrica, the Cuevas Volcánicas (tel. 045/442002, www.cuevasvolcanicas.cl) are 14.5 kilometers south of the main Villarrica–Pucón highway. Some guides can manage English if necessary; admission and the one-hour tour cost US$30 per person for adults, US$20 per person for children, including transport to and from Pucón.

## Río Trancura

Barely half an hour east of Pucón, the Trancura is not one of Chile's premier white-water rivers—there are long calm floats between rapids—but the Class IV waterfalls make parts of the upper river a wild ride indeed. Heavy competition has kept prices down to about US$40–50 per person for the Alto Trancura, US$24–30 for the calmer Bajo Trancura. Both are half-day excursions, either morning or afternoon, but the Alto Trancura means a little longer on the water.

## Hot Springs

The entire volcanic cordon of the Sur Chico is dotted with *termas* (hot springs), but there's a particularly dense concentration around Pucón. Several have been turned into retreats or resorts that vary from basic day-use facilities to upmarket but not-quite-lavish hotels.

On the Río Liucura northeast of Pucón, **Hotel y Termas Huife** is the most upscale option, a modern chalet-style resort with spa facilities in 40°C waters and massage therapy. For US$23 in summer, US$18 the rest of the year, day-trippers can use the outdoor pools. The resort provides its own transportation from Pucón for US$34 round-trip, including outdoor pool access, but infrequent buses also pass near the entrance. Restaurant and cafeteria meals are available.

**Termas Huife** (Gerónimo de Alderete 324, Pucón, tel./fax 045/445970, www.termashuife.cl, US$156–192 s, US$228–288 d) is 30 kilometers northeast of Pucón via Paillaco, on the road to Parque Nacional Huerquehue. The higher rates are in effect mid-December–mid-March only.

Just two kilometers beyond Huife, the minimalist **Termas Los Pozones** (tel. 045/1972350) is a backpacker's alternative; admission to a series of riverside pools ranging 30–40°C costs US$8 per person in the daytime, and US$10 per person at night (when some Pucón travel agencies run tours). Bring food and other supplies, as there's little on-site. There are usually one or two buses daily.

On the highway to Argentina, the **Parque Termal Menetúe** (Camino Internacional Km 30, tel. 045/441817, www.menetue.com) has the best indoor installations in the area. Rates for using the pools are US$22 per person in summer, US$12 the rest of the year; kids pay half. There are also mud baths and massages. Cabaña accommodations cost US$182 double in summer, US$141 double the rest of the year; full-board packages cost around US$126 per person in summer, US$104 per person the rest of the year. Menetúe runs its own daily transfers from Pucón, which includes access to the mud baths, for US$30 in summer, US$25 the rest of the

## PUCÓN MAPUCHE

East of Pucón, along the Río Palguín, two related family enterprises welcome visitors interested in learning about the region's Mapuche heritage through accommodations, meals, and activities. They are also popular with cyclists en route to or from Argentina, as they are either on or near the highway to San Martín de los Andes.

### KILA LEUFÚ

At Palguín Bajo, east of Pucón, Kila Leufú is a working Mapuche farm that offers horseback riding, the chance to participate (or not) in farm activities, a *ruca* (a typical Mapuche shelter) for socializing, and comfortable accommodations, all at affordable prices.

Kila Leufú (tel. 09/9876-4576, www.kilaleufu.cl) is 23 kilometers east of Pucón on the Curarrehue road, just beyond the Cabedañe Bridge and the Termas de Palguín turnoff. Camping costs US$10 per person with breakfast. Accommodations with shared baths cost US$20 per person with breakfast, while rooms with private baths cost US$25 per person. Lunches and dinners, focusing on Mapuche standards, cost US$12.

From Pucón, Curarrehue-bound Buses Jac services pass by Kila Leufú's front door, every half hour until about 8:30 P.M. For further information, contact Irma Epulef (tel. 09/9876-4576, Spanish and Mapudungun only).

### RUKA RAYEN

At Ruka Rayen, only a short distance north, Irma Epulef's daughter, Margot Martínez, and her husband, Peter Krenner, provide accommodations and lead horseback trips nearby and multi-day rides to Termas de Panqui and Parque Nacional Villarrica. Half-day rides cost US$32 per person, full-day rides US$44 per person.

In addition, Ruka Rayen offers accommodations (US$17-20 pp) and camping (US$9 pp), as well as barbecues in its own nearby *ruca*. Margot and Peter (an Austrian) can handle English, German, and French in addition to Spanish. They also rent mountain bikes, lead treks, and have good access to nearby hot springs.

Ruka Rayen (tel. 09/8449-1153, 09/9711-8064, www.rukarayen.com, margotex@yahoo.com) is about 1,300 meters north of the highway via a gravel road at a signed junction just east of Kila Leufú.

year, plus the cost of access to the pools; the transfer is free for those housed at Menetúe.

Southeast of Villarrica, beyond the town of Coñaripe, Ruta 201 leads to a turnoff to the **Termas Geométricas** (Km 16, tel. 09/9442-5420, www.termasgeometricas.cl), a Zen-like hot-springs retreat that's drawn raves for its 17 thermal pools, linked by wooden walkways in a lush sylvan setting. There's also a café, but no accommodations; hours are 10 A.M.–10 P.M. daily in summer, 11 A.M.–8 P.M. daily the rest of the year. Admission costs US$24–32 for adults, US$12–16 for children under age 15, depending on the hour of arrival. Alcohol is forbidden.

## Rancho de Caballos

At Palguín Alto, near Termas de Palguín, the German-run Rancho de Caballos offers a series of three-hour to 10-day riding tours of the backcountry in and around Parque Nacional Villarrica for about US$110 per person per day. In addition to tours, Rancho de Caballos (Casilla 142, Pucón, tel./fax 045/441575, www.ranchodecaballos.com) provides simple cabaña accommodations (US$14 pp), with meals available in addition.

## Corral del Agua

At Curarrehue, about 40 kilometers east of Pucón, a narrow gravel road leads northeast toward Reigolil, and at about the 14-kilometer point an even narrower road dead-ends 11 kilometers later at Corral del Agua, a small private nature reserve and lodge that organizes hiking and horseback excursions into the much larger backcountry of Reserva Nacional Villarrica, along the Argentine border.

One of Corral del Agua's most impressive

sights is the **Salto Malal-co,** a waterfall that spills vertically over a columnar basalt wall that resembles California's Devil's Postpile. There's abundant birdlife, including nesting condors and many lacustrine and riverine species.

For information on programs and accommodations, contact Corral del Agua (cell 09/8398-9774, www.corraldelagua.cl).

### Santuario Cañi

In a high roadless area about 21 kilometers east of Pucón, the Fundación Lahuen administers 400 hectares of mixed araucaria forest in the Santuario Cañi, Chile's initial private nature reserve. A project is underway to create a "Sendero Pehuén" to connect the reserve with Parque Nacional Huerquehue, as part of the ambitious Sendero de Chile project; it will have campgrounds, *refugios,* trail markers, and hygienic facilities.

For the moment, access is limited to guided hikes (around US$30 pp with a minimum of two) under the auspices of the Fundación Lahuen through Hostería ¡Ecole! (Urrutia 592, Pucón, tel. 045/441675, www.ecole.cl) and other local operators. For information in the United States, contact Ancient Forests International (Box 1850, Redway, CA 95560, tel./fax 707/923-4475, www.ancientforests.org).

## PARQUE NACIONAL VILLARRICA

Dominating the skyline south of Pucón, 2,847-meter Volcán Villarrica's glowing crater is a constant reminder that what Spanish conquistador poet Alonso de Ercilla called its "great neighbor volcano" could, at any moment, bury the town beneath a cloud of ash or a lahar of lava and melting snow—or set it aflame in a cataclysm of volcanic bombs. Closely monitored and occasionally closed to climbers, its summit remains one of Pucón's most popular excursions.

More than just the volcano, the park comprises 63,000 hectares of mostly wooded Andean cordillera stretching from Pucón to the 3,746-meter summit of Volcán Lanín, most of which lies within Argentina's Parque Nacional Lanín (would-be climbers must cross the border to the Argentine side).

### Geography and Climate

Immediately south of Pucón, the park ranges from 600 meters above sea level on the lower slopes to 3,746 meters at Volcán Lanín. Barren lava flows and volcanic ash cover much of its surface, but unaffected areas are lushly forested. The other major summit is 2,360-meter Volcán Quetrupillán, halfway to the Argentine border; from Quetrupillán to the east, several alpine lakes are accessible by foot.

Summertime temperatures range from a minimum of about 9°C to a maximum of around 23° C, while wintertime lows average 4°C. Most precipitation falls between March and August, when Pacific storms can drop up to two meters of snow, but rain can fall at any time. The park receives about 2,500–3,500 millimeters rainfall per year.

### Flora and Fauna

At lower elevations, up to about 1,500 meters, mixed araucaria and *Nothofagus* woodlands cover the slopes—the araucaria reaches its most southerly point at Volcán Quetrupillán. The *mañío* (podocarpus), an ornamental in the Northern Hemisphere, also makes an appearance. Native bunch grasses have colonized some volcanic areas.

Among the mammals are pumas, pudus, foxes, and skunks, as well as the aquatic coypus. Waterfowl such as coots and ducks inhabit the lakes and other watercourses, while large raptors such as the black-shouldered kite and peregrine falcon are occasionally sighted in the skies.

### Volcán Villarrica

Chile's most active volcano, Villarrica is a cauldron of bubbling lava and venting steam that's erupted dozens of times, including a 1971 event that expelled 30 million cubic meters of lava in a flow that spread over 14 kilometers.

A strenuous but nontechnical climb, Villarrica requires crampons, an ice ax, rain- and wind gear, high-energy snacks, and a guide—except for those who manage to wrangle one of Conaf's few individual private permits. For those who contract a tour with one of Pucón's adventure travel agencies, it involves a crash course in mountaineering; in good weather, the summit's about six hours from the ski area, but bad weather sometimes forces groups to turn back. When the sulfurous crater is especially active, Conaf closes the route.

While the ascent can be a slog through wet snow, the descent involves body-sledding down the volcano's flanks with only an ice ax for braking. With revaluation of the peso, rates for the trip (US$80–90 pp) have risen notably.

When winter snows cover the lower slopes, the **Centro de Ski Volcán Villarrica** operates four lifts with nine runs ranging 500–1,500 meters in length, but there have been many complaints. Lift tickets cost around US$45 per day in peak season, US$33 per day in the shoulder season; there are also three-day, one-week, and season passes. For more information, contact **Pucón Ski** (Holzapfel 190, tel. 045/441901, www.skipucon.cl) in the Gran Hotel Pucón.

### Sector Quetrupillán

About midway between Volcán Villarrica and **Volcán Quetrupillán,** a rough summer-only road crosses the park from Termas de Palguín to the hot-springs town of Coñaripe. Best suited to four-wheel-drive or at least high-clearance vehicles, though some daring (or foolhardy) Chileans attempt it with ordinary passenger cars, it passes through a scenic araucaria forest that includes the park's only campground.

From Volcán Villarrica's southern slopes, hiking trails cross the park to Termas de Palguín and continue to Puesco, where Buses Jac has a daily bus back to Pucón. For more detail on this hike, which has some hard-to-follow segments, see Tim Burford's *Chile and Argentina: The Bradt Trekking Guide* (Chalfont St. Peter, United Kingdom: Bradt Travel Guides, 2001) or Carolyn McCarthy's *Trekking in the Patagonian Andes* (Melbourne: Lonely Planet, 2009). Conaf now levies a US$14 fee for hikers on this trail.

### Accommodations and Food

In Sector Quetrupillán on the park's southern boundary, on the steep, narrow road between Termas de Palguín and Coñaripe, Conaf's **Camping Chinay** (US$24 in January and February, US$16 the rest of the year) lies in the midst of an araucaria forest, but it sometimes suffers water shortages.

At the ski area, the **Refugio Villarrica** serves cafeteria meals, but skiers stay in Pucón.

### Information

On the road to the ski area, eight kilometers from Pucón, Conaf's Guardería Rucapillán is the best source for information; rangers collect a US$6 per person admission charge (US$3 for children) here. There are ranger stations at Sector Quetrupillán and Sector Puesco.

### Getting There and Around

Transportation is limited except for organized tours. To Sector Rucapillán, only a few kilometers south of Pucón, taxis are the only non-tour option.

## PARQUE NACIONAL HUERQUEHUE

In the scenic Andean precordillera, dotted with alpine lakes, rushing rivers, and waterfalls set among dense native forest, 12,500-hectare Huerquehue has become one of the area's most popular parks. Its proximity to Pucón and a small but accessible network of hiking trails make it ideal for day trips, but overnights are also possible.

### Geography and Climate

Huerquehue is 35 kilometers northeast of Pucón via the hamlet of Paillaco. Elevations range from about 720 meters above sea level near Lago Tinquilco to the 2,000-meter summit of Cerro Araucano, but glaciers and rivers have eroded deep canyons. It receives just over 2,000 millimeters of rainfall per year, mostly between May and September, some falling as snow at higher elevations. While temperatures are generally mild, rain can fall at any time.

### Flora and Fauna

On the park's lower slopes, the dominant forest species is the *coigüe,* while *lenga* gives way gradually to araucaria at higher elevations. Birds, ranging from woodpeckers to thrushes, flit within the forest, while Andean condors sometimes soar among the ridgetops and summits.

### Sendero Ñirrico

Huerquehue is a hiker's park, beginning with this signed nature trail, starting at the parking lot just beyond the park gate, that parallels the shore of Lago Tinquilco. Thanks to this trail, it's no longer necessary to walk along the gravel road that leads to the Lago Verde trailhead, where the park's most popular walk starts (the gravel road is closed to vehicles other than those belonging to Conaf or park inholders).

### Sendero Lago Verde

From the north end of Lago Tinquilco, reached by the Sendero Ñirrico, the well-watered Sendero Lago Verde (Lago Verde Trail) zigzags from 700 meters altitude at the trailhead to 1,300 meters at its namesake lake. Gaps in the *coigüe* woodlands yield glimpses of Volcán Villarrica to the south, while the surrounding ridges sport araucaria forests.

From Tinquilco, it's about two or more hours of steady hiking to **Lago Chico,** where the terrain levels off; at a trail junction beyond Lago Chico, the left fork goes to **Lago Verde,** while the right fork goes to **Lago El Toro** and continues to Conaf's simple **Camping Renahue,** the park's only authorized backcountry campground. From here an eastbound trail continues to **Termas de Río Blanco,** thermal springs linked by gravel road to Cunco, Lago Colico, and Lago Caburgua's north end.

### Sendero Quinchol and Sendero San Sebastián

From the parking lot beyond the park gate, the gravel road north soon intercepts the Sendero Quinchol, which climbs even more steeply than the Sendero Lago Verde through shady southern beech forests to an araucaria-studded Pampa Quinchol, with a short loop through even denser araucaria forests. At roughly the three-kilometer mark, the first stunted monkey-puzzle appears, but it's another kilometer or so to the junction with Sendero San Sebastián, which leads north toward the Pampa Quinchol, with expansive views of nearly all the area's volcanoes. On a clear day, Villarrica, Lanín, and Choshuenco, plus Lago Caburgua, are all within view.

The five-kilometer trail to the Pampa Quinchol takes about two hours; the descent is not much shorter because of its steepness, and there is little or no water. On the return, for variety, take the Sendero Quinchol loop back to the trail junction before returning to the park headquarters.

### Accommodations and Food

On Lago Tinquilco's eastern shore, near the park gate, Conaf's 22-site **Camping Tinquilco** (US$21 per site) can accommodate up to five persons on each of its wooded sites.

Just beyond the park entrance, near the Lago Verde trailhead, the rustically chic Canadian-Chilean ☾ **Refugio Tinquilco** (cell 09/9539-2728, Santiago tel. 02/7777673, www.tinquilco.cl) charges US$20 for hostel-type bunks (with a US$4 surcharge for sheets, if necessary); it also has rooms with king-sized beds (US$52 d with shared bath, US$64 d with private bath). Set on densely wooded grounds, it has its own beach and offers fixed-price breakfasts, lunches, and dinners to guests or nonguests; more elaborate multicourse dinners include aperitifs and wine.

### Information

At the Lago Tinquilco entrance, Conaf's **Centro de Educación e Interpretación Ambiental** is open 10 A.M.–8 P.M. daily in summer. Rangers at the park gate collect a US$8 admission fee (US$4 for children). Refugio Tinquilco is also a good source of information for hiking alternatives beyond the main Lago Verde route.

### Getting There and Around

Thanks to increasing demand, **Buses Caburgua** now offers summer service from Pucón to Huerquehue (US$5) four times daily starting at 8:30 A.M.; the rest of the year, though, it's just twice daily. Most Pucón travel agencies also offer Huerquehue excursions.

# Los Lagos

## OSORNO

More a crossroads than a destination, Osorno relies on dairying, forestry, and manufacturing for its livelihood, but it's the gateway to destinations such as Lago Puyehue, Parque Nacional Puyehue, and Argentina's own Andean lakes region. The city dates from 1558, but the Mapuche uprising of 1599 destroyed it and six other cities within five years, even resulting in the death of Spanish governor Oñez de Loyola.

Spanish authorities needed nearly two centuries to re-found the city in 1793 with the construction of Fuerte Reina Luisa, a riverside fortification that helped keep out the Mapuche. It failed to flourish until the mid-19th century, as overland communications were too arduous—even hazardous—to permit rapid growth of internal markets. This began to change with the mid-19th-century arrival of German immigrants; it accelerated after the so-called "pacification" south of the Biobío in the 1880s, followed by the railroad's arrival in 1895 and its extension to Puerto Montt by 1911. Through most of the 20th century, it achieved steady growth.

### Orientation

Osorno (population about 160,000) is 913 kilometers south of Santiago and 109 kilometers north of Puerto Montt via the Panamericana. Also an east–west crossroads, it's 126 kilometers from the Argentine border at Paso Cardenal Samoré via paved Ruta 215.

Central Osorno, about two kilometers west of the Panamericana, has a slightly irregular grid bordered by the Río Damas to the north, Calles Angulo and Eduvijes to the east, Manuel Rodríguez to the south, and the Río Rahue to the west.

### Sights

Despite its colonial origins, Osorno has few venerable sights—the so-called **Distrito Histórico** west of the Plaza de Armas includes early-20th-century landmarks such as the restored Francophile **Estación de Ferrocarril** (1912); it now houses the **Museo Interactivo de Osorno** (Portales 901, tel. 064/221916, 10:30 A.M.–12:45 P.M. and 3:30–7:30 P.M. Tues.–Sun., shorter winter hours, free), a hands-on science museum.

© WAYNE BERNHARDSON

The Casa Enrique Schüller is part of Osorno's small historic district.

Other area sights include the restored **Sociedad Molinera de Osorno,** a flour mill now occupied by a pasta factory, and many weathered private residences. The ramparts and towers of **Fuerte Reina Luisa** (1793) modestly stand out—these are all that remains of the colonial fortress at the foot of Eleuterio Ramírez.

The de facto historical district, though, is on Juan Mackenna between Avenida Matta and Freire, where half a dozen pioneer houses are national monuments: the **Casa Mohr Pérez** (Mackenna 939), **Casa Enrique Schüller** (Mackenna 1011), **Casa Sürber** (Mackenna 1027), **Casa Germán Stückrath** (Mackenna

1047), **Casa Federico Stückrath** (Mackenna 1069), and **Casa Conrado Stückrath** (Mackenna 1095).

The **Museo Histórico Municipal** (Av. Matta 809, tel. 064/238615, free) exhibits diverse materials ranging from Paleo-Indian archaeology and Mapuche culture to Osorno's colonial founding, its destruction by the Mapuche and subsequent re-founding, the 19th-century city and immigration, and naval hero Eleuterio Ramírez. A natural-history room and a child-oriented interactive basement display round out the features. Occupying the former Schilling Buschmann residence (1929), a handsome neocolonial building with a neglected exterior, the municipal historical museum is open 9 A.M.–5 P.M. Monday–Friday and 2–6 P.M. Saturday. Summer hours are 9:30 A.M.–6 P.M. weekdays except Friday, when it closes an hour earlier, and 2–7 P.M. weekends, with shorter winter hours.

## Shopping

**Detalles Hecho a Mano** (Mackenna 1100, tel. 064/238462) sells regional crafts, but the biggest selection is at **Alta Artesanía** (Mackenna 1069, tel. 064/232446), including wood carvings, woolens, ceramics, copper, and jewelry. At the **Pueblito Artesanal** (Mackenna between Freire and Prat), artisans sell directly to the public along a block of the city's most heavily traveled street.

## Entertainment

**Cine Lido** (Ramírez 650, tel. 064/233890) is a two-screen movie theater. The municipal **Centro Cultural** (Av. Matta 556, tel. 064/238898, 8:30 A.M.–1:45 P.M. and 4–5:15 P.M. daily) hosts theater and music events, along with rotating art exhibits.

## Accommodations

Except in the upper categories, Osorno's accommodations are so-so at best.

East of the bus terminal, **Hospedaje Sánchez** (Los Carrera 1595, tel./fax 064/232560, ximenitasanchez@hotmail.com, US$14 pp) is a modest but passable shoestring choice.

Two blocks east of the Plaza de Armas, standard rates at shingled **Residencial Schulz** (Freire 530, tel. 064/237211, US$16 pp with shared bath, US$40 s or d with private bath) include breakfast; the cheaper rooms are on the uppermost floor.

Four blocks south of the terminal, **Hotel Villa Eduviges** (Eduviges 856, tel./fax 064/235023, www.hoteleduviges.cl, US$44 s, US$53 d with breakfast) occupies a rambling older building that's undergone a haphazard modernization; the shower stalls, in particular, are tiny, but it enjoys a less congested and quieter neighborhood than some other places. It does provide wireless Internet.

Under the same ownership, **Hostal Bilbao** (Bilbao 1019, tel./fax 064/262200, www.hotelbilbao.cl, US$40 s, US$56 d) and **Hotel Bilbao** (Juan Mackenna 1205, tel./fax 064/264444, www.hotelbilbao.cl, US$50 s, US$68 d) are among the best in their range; both have wireless Internet in all rooms.

Rates at **Hostal Rucaitué** (Freire 546, tel. 064/239922, hrucaitue@surnet.cl, US$78 s, US$90 d) include breakfast, TV, and private bath. **Hotel San Pedro** (Bulnes 630, tel./fax 064/242477, hotelpumalal@gmail.com, US$50 s, US$60 d) is a contemporary business-oriented hotel.

**Hotel Lagos del Sur** (O'Higgins 564, tel. 064/245222, www.hotelagosdelsur.cl, US$94 s, US$116 d) is a nearly new hotel with handsomely decorated rooms. The classic **Hotel Waeger** (Cochrane 816, tel. 064/233721, www.hotelwaeger.cl, US$106 s, US$144 d) is a deco-style lodging where German speakers get special attention.

The contemporary **Hotel García Hurtado de Mendoza** (Mackenna 1040, tel. 064/237111, www.hotelgarciahurtado.cl, US$120 s, US$140 d) is holding its own in a city with mostly unexceptional accommodations.

## Food

For real budget meals, nothing's better than the seafood at the numerous *comedores* in the **Mercado Municipal** (Prat and Errázuriz, roughly 8 A.M.–6 P.M. daily)—avoid the *fried* fish, though.

Upstairs from its namesake bakery, **Pastelería Rhenania** (Ramírez 977, tel. 064/235457, www.rhenania.cl, 9 A.M.–9 P.M. Mon.–Fri., 10 A.M.–8 P.M. Sat.) serves sandwiches and pastries. **Dino's** (Ramírez 898, tel. 064/233880, breakfast, lunch, and dinner) also specializes in sandwiches and light meals, as does its franchise rival **Bavaria** (O'Higgins 743, tel. 064/231302, www.bavaria.cl, 10 A.M.–midnight daily). **Bocatto** (Ramírez 938, tel. 064/238000, breakfast, lunch, and dinner) has similar offerings but also pizza and Osorno's best ice cream.

The **Club Alemán,** also known as the **Deutscher Verein** (O'Higgins 563, tel. 064/232784, www.clubalemanosorno.cl, lunch daily, dinner Mon.–Sat.), reflects the German community's significance more in name than in menu, which is standard Chilean. The **Club de Artesanos** (Juan Mackenna 634, tel. 064/230307, noon–11:30 P.M. Mon.–Sat., noon–3:30 P.M. Sun.) is a labor-union restaurant with a good Chilean menu.

**Del Piero** (Manuel Rodríguez 1081, tel. 064/256767, 12:30–3 P.M. and 8 P.M.–midnight Mon.–Sat., 12:30–3 P.M. Sun.) offers pizza and pasta. In the historic Casa Conrado Stückrath, **La Parrilla de Pepe** (Mackenna 1095, tel. 064/239653, lunch daily, dinner Mon.–Sat.) lacks ambience but serves meats cooked to order, has diligent service, and is tobacco-free.

## Information

On the west side of the Plaza de Armas, **Sernatur** (O'Higgins 667, tel. 064/234104, infosorno@sernatur.cl, 8:30 A.M.–1 P.M. and 2:30–5:30 P.M. weekdays) occupies a ground floor office at the Edificio Gobernación Provincial.

At the plaza's southwest corner, the municipal **Departamento de Turismo** (tel. 064/212740, www.osornochile.cl) is an information kiosk open 8:30 A.M.–8 P.M. weekdays and 11 A.M.–6 P.M. Saturday mid-December–mid-March. It keeps a shorter, weekdays-only schedule the rest of the year, closing 1–3 P.M.

The **Automóvil Club de Chile** (Acchi, Manuel Bulnes 463, tel. 064/540080) can help motorists. For national parks information, contact **Conaf** (Martínez de Rozas 430, tel. 064/221301).

## Services

**Turismo Frontera** (Ramírez 959, Local 12) changes cash and travelers checks, while **BancoEstado** (Eleuterio Ramírez 741) has one of many ATMs.

On the west side of the Plaza de Armas, **Correos de Chile** (O'Higgins 645) is the postal service. There is free municipal wireless Internet in and around the Plaza de Armas, and in some other parts of town.

**Lavandería Limpec** (Arturo Prat 678, tel. 064/238966) offers prompt laundry service.

For medical assistance, contact the **Hospital Base** (Av. Bühler 1765, tel. 064/230977); Avenida Bühler is the southward extension of Arturo Prat.

## Getting There

Osorno has limited air connections, but it's a hub for bus services along the Panamericana, throughout the region, and across the Andes to Argentina. **LAN** (Ramírez 802, tel. 064/314900) flies at least daily to Santiago, usually via Temuco or Concepción. **Sky Airline** (Mackenna 1100, tel. 064/318858) flies less often.

The **Terminal de Buses** (Av. Errázuriz 1400, tel. 064/234149) is the long-distance facility. Some but not all regional buses use the Mercado Municipal's **Terminal de Buses Rurales** (Errázuriz 1300, tel. 064/201237).

From the Terminal de Buses Rurales, two companies go to Puyehue and Aguas Calientes: **Buses Expreso Lago Puyehue** (tel. 064/243919) and **Buses Barría** (tel. 064/230628). From 7 A.M. to 9 P.M., there are departures about every half hour on a route that's also served by *taxi colectivos* across the street.

At the main terminal, **Buses Angulo** (tel. 064/234371) goes to the eastern Lago Llanquihue destination of Las Cascadas (US$3) up to seven times daily. **Buses Via Octay** (tel. 064/237043) and **Octay Bus** (tel. 064/213065) go frequently to the northern Lago Llanquihue town of Puerto Octay (US$2).

Many carriers connect Osorno with Panamericana destinations between Santiago in the north and Puerto Montt to the south. Sample destinations, fares, and times include Puerto Montt (US$5, 1.5 hours), Temuco (US$9, three hours), and Santiago (US$34–80, 12 hours).

Services to Punta Arenas (US$85, 28 hours) and to Coyhaique (US$63, 19 hours) start in Puerto Montt and pick up passengers here. Note that buses to Chilean Patagonian destinations use Paso Cardenal Samoré, east of Osorno, but carry through-passengers only—Chilean domestic bus lines may not drop passengers within Argentina.

Most buses across the Andes to Bariloche (US$26, five hours) and other Argentine destinations also begin in Puerto Montt and use Paso Cardenal Samoré.

### Getting Around

**Aeropuerto Carlos Hott Siebert** (tel. 064/232559), also known as Cañal Bajo, is seven kilometers east of Osorno via Avenida Buschmann. It's off the city bus routes, but cabs cost only about US$5.

**Full Travel** (Freire 759, tel. 064/235579, www.fulltravel.cl) provides rental cars.

## VICINITY OF OSORNO

As a land transport hub, Osorno offers excellent access to some of the lakes district's most popular summer resort areas. Among them are Lago Puyehue, Termas de Puyehue and other lesser-known hot-springs resorts in its vicinity, Parque Nacional Puyehue, and the northern and western shores of Lago Llanquihue, including the picturesque towns of Puerto Octay and Frutillar.

### Auto Museum Moncopulli

Opened in 1995, this private automotive museum contains more than 80 historic vehicles, many restored and others awaiting restoration, along with supplementary advertising and marketing materials and other artifacts of the early to mid-20th century. German collector Bernardo Eggers, its creator, specializes in the now-obscure Studebaker, from its 1850s beginnings as a horsecart manufacturer in South Bend, Indiana, to its first electric automobile (1902) and the plant's closure (1966). With its futuristic design, the late 1940s and early 1950s Studebaker was one of the most distinctive automobiles ever manufactured, but it never really caught on with the public.

Professionally arranged, the museum has one shortcoming: a failure to provide any narrative beyond its creator's enthusiasm (there is more info on the Spanish-only website). That said, for anyone traveling the highway to Parque Nacional Puyehue and the Argentine border, it's well worth at least a brief stop. Classic car fans may want to go out of their way to see it.

East of Osorno, the Auto Museum Moncopulli (Ruta 215 Km 25, tel. 064/210744, www.moncopulli.cl, US$5 adults, US$2 students, US$1 children) is generally open 10 A.M.–6 P.M. daily; in summer, it closes two hours later.

## PARQUE NACIONAL PUYEHUE

Barely an hour from Osorno, accessible Puyehue still has plenty of untamed wilderness among its 106,772 hectares of Valdivian rainforest—at least where lava flows and ash from its volcanic vents and summits have not left it as barren as the Atacama. Statistically, it's one of Chile's most visited parks, but statistics can deceive—the highly developed hot-springs resort at Aguas Calientes and its Antillanca ski area draw its mostly Chilean crowds. Except for trails near its hotels and campgrounds, the backcountry gets only small numbers of hikers, and the park is under threat from a proposed hydroelectric project.

### Geography and Climate

Ranging from the lower Río Golgol valley, about 250 meters above sea level, to the 2,240-meter summit of **Volcán Puyehue,** the park is about 80 kilometers east of Osorno and extends to the Argentine border. **Volcán Casablanca**

(1,980 meters) is another major landmark, and the park has abundant creeks, rivers, and lakes that are ideal for fishing.

The annual rainfall, about 5,000 millimeters (with snow at higher elevations), supports verdant Valdivian forest. Temperatures are relatively mild at lower elevations, averaging about 14°C in summer and 5°C in winter, with highs near 25°C and lows around freezing.

## Flora and Fauna

Puyehue's lush lower Valdivian forest is a mixed woodland of species such as *ulmo,* which can reach 40 meters or more in height, along with *olivillo, tineo, mañío,* and *coigüe.*

Beneath the dense canopy grow smaller trees such as the myrtle relative *arrayán,* while the solid bamboo *quila* forms impassable thickets; the endemic *chilco,* along with intensely green ferns and mosses, provides spots of color. The striking *nalca* sports umbrella-sized leaves at the end of edible stalks up to two meters in height.

At some higher elevations, though, lava flows and ash from Volcán Puyehue's 1960 eruption have left the landscape so barren that grasses and shrubs have only recently begun to colonize the area, despite substantial rainfall.

Pudus may inhabit the dense forest, but it's difficult to see them or other woodland and riverine species such as foxes, otters, and coypus. Some 100 or so bird species flit from tree to tree, along with waterfowl such as the *pato cortacorriente* (torrent duck), which fishes in the river rapids, and the condors that soar on the thermals overhead.

## Sights and Recreation

Puyehue consists of three distinct sectors: Aguas Calientes at its southwestern border, Antillanca at its southeastern border, and Anticura, mostly north of Ruta 215.

### AGUAS CALIENTES

From the Termas de Puyehue junction, a paved road leads four kilometers south to **Termas Aguas Calientes** (tel. 064/331710, www.termasaguascalientes.cl), whose highlight is its namesake thermal baths, open to hotel guests, campers, and day-trippers alike. Under the same management as Termas de Puyehue, its rates are more affordable.

Several short nature trails and one longer hike start here. The six-kilometer **Sendero El Pionero** switchbacks through dense Valdivian forest to a ridgetop with panoramic northern vistas of Lago Puyehue, the wooded Río Golgol Valley, and Volcán Puyehue's barren cone, before continuing to Lago Espejo and then returning along the Antillanca road. Along its namesake river, the **Sendero Rápidos del Chanleufú** traverses 1,200 meters of gallery forest. The 11-kilometer **Sendero Lago Bertín** climbs steadily to its namesake lake, where backcountry camping is possible.

### ANTILLANCA

Beyond Aguas Calientes, the road becomes a gravel surface leading another 18 kilometers to the base of Volcán Casablanca, where Antillanca is a popular hotel and ski resort from early June to late October; in summer it's open for hikers, mountain bikers, anglers, and general recreationists even though there's no campground nearby.

Where the public road ends, the Club Andino Osorno maintains a toll road (US$5.50 per vehicle) to the 1,262-meter **Cráter Raihuén,** an extinct volcanic crater, and **Cerro Mirador,** the starting point for several high-country trails. Pay at the hotel office, which opens the gate and provides a helpful topographic map.

Ranging from 1,050 meters at its base to 1,514 meters above sea level on Cerro Haique, the ski area itself has beginner, intermediate, and expert slopes. For more details, contact the Centro Turístico Deportivo Antillanca at the **Club Andino Osorno** (Casilla 765, O'Higgins 1073, Osorno, tel. 064/235114, www.skiantillanca.com).

### ANTICURA

From Termas de Puyehue, Ruta 215 leads northeast up the Golgol Valley for 17 kilometers to Anticura, before continuing to Chilean customs and immigration at Pajaritos and on to the Argentine border. At Anticura, there is camping and access to several short trails and some longer ones.

The 950-meter **Sendero Educativo Salto del Indio** is a signed nature trail leading to a waterfall on the Golgol; its name comes from a local legend that a fugitive Mapuche hid to avoid forced labor in a colonial mine. An overnight excursion up the Río Anticura Valley leads to **Pampa Frutilla,** now part of the Sendero de Chile. Areas east of Pajaritos, the Chilean border post, require Conaf permission to hike or otherwise explore because it's a legal no-man's-land and, unfortunately, this means limited access to large parts of the park.

From El Caulle, two kilometers west of Anticura, a 16-kilometer trail climbs the abrupt flanks of **Volcán Puyehue,** where there's a simple *refugio* and camping is also possible; alternatively, continue through a barren volcanic landscape of fumaroles and lava flows to rustic thermal pools where it's also possible to camp. At the trailhead, though, ex-senator Marcos Cariola's **Turismo El Caulle** (Ruta 215 Km 90, cell 09/9920-3244, www.elcaulle.com) demands a US$14 toll for the right to pass through his property; this includes use of the *refugio,* but Cariola's cattle have eroded parts of the trail. It's possible to hike through to Riñinahue, at Lago Ranco's south end (where there's a US$4 toll), rather than return to El Caulle.

Volcán Puyehue itself is a flat-topped Holocene caldera, measuring 2.4 kilometers in diameter; it sits within a larger caldera measuring five kilometers across. The most recent eruptions have come not from the summit caldera, but from vents on its western, southern, and eastern flanks, and a small cone on the southern flank.



## Accommodations and Food

Some visitors stay at Termas de Puyehue, but park accommodations also include campgrounds and cabañas.

### AGUAS CALIENTES

**Termas Aguas Calientes** (tel. 064/331710, www.termasaguascalientes.cl) operates the 36-site **Camping Chanleufú** (US$29 for up to four persons, open all year). Fees at Chanleufú include firewood and electricity, but access to the pools is additional.

Accommodations at **Cabañas Aguas Calientes** (tel. 064/331710, US$193 for up to four persons) include access to the baths. It also has a cafeteria with a sandwich menu, the more elaborate restaurant **El Arrayán,** and an outdoor *parrilla* in summer only.

### ANTILLANCA

At the ski area, the 73-room **Hotel Antillanca** (Ruta 215 Km 98, tel. 064/235114, www.skiantillanca.cl) has a contemporary sector and an older but more-than-acceptable *refugio.* In the peak season, July–mid-August, hotel "ski week" rates reach US$1,055 double weekly with accommodations, full board, and lift tickets. In the shoulder ski season, prices drop by about 25 percent, and in summer rooms are available for US$53 single, US$75 double in the hotel, US$35 single, US$50 double in the *refugio.*

In Osorno, contact the Centro Turístico Deportivo Antillanca through the Club Andino Osorno (Casilla 765, O'Higgins 1073, tel. 064/242010).

### ANTICURA

Etnoturismo Anticura (cell 09/9177-4672, etnoturismoanticura@gmail.com) runs the eight-site **Camping Catrué** (US$13 d, US$3 each additional person), whose basic facilities include running water, picnic tables, fire pits, and pit toilets; there's also a hostel (US$10 pp with shared bath and kitchen facilities) and cabañas (around US$53 d).

Just west of Anticura, **El Caulle** (Ruta 215 Km 90, cell 09/9641-2000, www.elcaulle.com) operates a *parrilla* just off the highway and has added accommodations (US$14 pp, US$18 pp with breakfast).

## Information

At Aguas Calientes, Conaf's **Centro de Información Ambiental** (tel. 064/1974572, www.parquepuyehue.cl, 9 A.M.–1 P.M. and

## TERMAS DE PUYEHUE

Alone on a winter's night, walking the endless corridors and circuitous staircases at Hotel Termas de Puyehue, you might expect a deranged Jack Nicholson to turn the corner swinging an ax. Unlike *The Shining*'s isolated alpine hotel, though, the Sur Chico's elite hot-springs resort borders a major international highway, stays open all year, and is never isolated by weather, so you're not likely to be snowed in with a madman.

While a recent remodel and expansion has left only a small wing of the original building, Termas de Puyehue retains the stately elegance of a grand country hotel while adding contemporary conveniences to ensure its premier position among Chilean hot-springs resorts. From modest beginnings in 1908, on sprawling wooded grounds near the border of Parque Nacional Puyehue, it now houses up to 300 guests in 138 spacious rooms, some with balconies.

Its thermal spa boasts a huge covered pool and an Olympic-size outdoor pool, and offers whirlpool tubs, massages, mud baths, and algal treatments. For food, there are three restaurants, including the Italian **Olivia Nova,** and a bar. Other amenities include a small museum, a library, game rooms, and even an events hall that hosts classical music concerts. Since 1939, electricity has come from the resort's own small hydroelectric plant.

As of late 2007, however, Termas de Puyehue has reinvented itself as an all-inclusive resort where guests pay one rate for open access to nearly all services (including full board with both alcoholic and nonalcoholic drinks), as well as activities such as horseback riding, mountain biking, and tennis – in addition to its signature thermal pools. Only premium wines and spa treatments are additional.

Now known as Termas de Puyehue Wellness & Spa Resort (Ruta 215, tel. 064/331400, www.puyehue.cl, US$482-896 s, US$538-997 d), it sits at the junction where the main highway continues toward Anticura and the Argentine border; a paved lateral heads to Aguas Calientes, a more modest hot springs, and the Antillanca sector of Parque Nacional Puyehue.

Around major holidays, there may be a minimum stay of three or four days. Outside the peak summer season (Jan.-mid-Mar.), rates drop; 20-25 percent. In summer, day passes for nonguests cost US$80 Monday-Friday, US$90 weekends and holidays; the rest of the year, prices drop by about the same rate.

2–6 P.M. daily, until 7 P.M. in summer) offers daily slide talks in late afternoon during the summer; permanent exhibits focus on natural history (flora and fauna) and topics such as vulcanism. Conaf also maintains an information center at Antillanca, generally open in ski season only.

### Getting There and Around

Paved all the way to the border, Ruta 215 passes directly through the park. From Osorno's Mercado Municipal (Errázuriz 1300), **Buses Expreso Lago Puyehue** (tel. 064/243919) and **Buses Barría** (tel. 064/230628) serve Termas de Puyehue and Aguas Calientes with buses and *taxi colectivos,* with additional service to Anticura and the Chilean border post at Pajaritos.

In winter, the **Club Andino Osorno** (O'Higgins 1073, tel. 064/235114) shuttles between Osorno and the Antillanca ski area.

## PUERTO OCTAY AND VICINITY

From prosaic 19th-century beginnings as a port at Lago Llanquihue's north end, idyllic Puerto Octay has become one of the region's most picturesque locales, with magnificent views across the lake to Volcán Osorno. Local pleasure boats, though, have supplanted the steaming freighters that once connected Octay with Puerto Varas, and it's become a low-key destination for summer holiday-makers who arrive by paved road from Osorno, 50 kilometers northwest. The German immigrant presence is palpable in its architecture, food, the checkerboard landscape of dairy farms and woodlands, and in its apparent middle-class contentment.

Puerto Octay (population about 3,500) also includes Península Centinela, a wooded spit protruding into the lake that's home to hotels and campgrounds. From town, it's possible to travel Llanquihue's western shore to the resort village of Frutillar, or its eastern shore to Ensenada and Parque Nacional Vicente Pérez Rosales, via a road whose northern half is now paved.

## Sights

Puerto Octay dates from 1852, but its architectural legacy of European-style neoclassical and chalet houses dates from the early 20th century. While no structure within Puerto Octay is a recognized national monument, at least a dozen private residences and other buildings contribute to the town's captivating ambience.

One of those buildings is the **Casa de la Cultura Emilio Winkler** (Independencia 591, tel. 064/643327, www.museopuertooctay.cl, 10:15 A.M.–1 P.M. and 3–5 P.M. daily), housing part of the **Museo El Colono,** a well-organized collection of maps, photographs, and other materials on early German colonization. The building is too small, though, to contain an assortment of antique farm equipment that spills out of a barn and onto the grounds of a separate facility (at the point where the gravel road to Península Centinela splits off the paved road to Frutillar). Personnel from the Universidad Austral have helped the facilities and reorganized the exhibits. Admission (US$2) is valid for both sites.

## Puerto Octay Hostal Zapato Amarillo

About two kilometers north of town on the Osorno road, the Swiss-Chilean Zapato Amarillo has become a destination in its own right as much as a place to stay. It provides transfers to La Picada for a five-hour hike to Petrohué (US$47 pp for a minimum of four people, with stops at Saltos del Petrohué and Ensenada on the ride back), and hiking and boating excursions to Lago Rupanco (US$50–58 pp).

Comfortably stylish hostel-type accommodations on ample grounds, with kitchen facilities, cost US$17 per person with breakfast and shared bath October–April, slightly less the rest of the year. It has recently added several doubles with shared or private bath (US$52–63), some of them in free-standing, sod-roofed houses that are truly distinctive. There are fine views of Volcán Osorno across the lawns.

In addition, Zapato Amarillo (tel./fax 064/210787, www.zapatoamarillo.cl) offers initial transfers from Puerto Octay, information, wireless Internet, laundry, rental bikes, and even a small sailboat. Proprietors Armin and Nadia Dübendorfer can handle Spanish, German, English, and French.

## Accommodations

Downtown has camping and basic *hospedajes,* but Avenida Andrés Schmoelz leads south out of Puerto Octay proper for about two kilometers to dead-end on Península Centinela, which has more upscale lodgings but also affordable alternatives. The Puerto Octay Hostal Zapato Amarillo is another reasonable option, a short distance north of town.

Five hundred meters south of the Plaza de Armas, **Camping El Molino** (Costanera Pichi Juan 124, tel. 064/391375, US$24) has lakefront campsites for up to five persons.

The most interesting option is the **Hotel Haase** (Pedro Montt 344, tel. 064/391302, www.hotelhaase.cl, US$17 pp with shared bath, US$41 s or d with private bath), an architectural monument whose common areas are approaching their onetime grandeur; the rooms, mostly with shared bath, lag a little behind, and the floors are squeaky. The management is friendly, and the restaurant has become more consistent.

At road's end, the peninsula's showpiece is the renovated and expanded **Hotel y Cabañas Centinela** (tel./fax 064/391326, www.hotelcentinela.cl, US$142–222 s or d

© WAYNE BERNHARDSON

On the outskirts of Puerto Octay, the Swiss-Chilean Zapato Amarillo offers stylish accommodations with sod roofs.

with breakfast), a chalet-type structure that, in its 1930s heyday, hosted guests such as the Prince of Wales. The 12 rooms retain their original natural wood, but the furniture and baths have been upgraded.

The hotel proper has greater personality than its nearby A-frame cabañas, whose rates start around US$131 double. Off-season rates March–mid-December are about 15–20 percent lower; nonguests may use the restaurant here.

## Food

Puerto Octay has little out of the ordinary—it's mostly Chilean standbys such as **Baviera** (Germán Wulf 582, tel. 064/391460, lunch and dinner daily). At **Puerto Muñoz Gamero** (Muñoz Gamero 107, tel. 064/391435, lunch and dinner daily), the traditional German colonial house outshines the salmon and hake on the limited menu.

About one kilometer north of town on the Osorno highway, **El Fogón de Anita** (tel. 064/391276, www.fogondeanita.cl, lunch daily, dinner Mon.–Sat.) is a fine *parrilla*—try the *asado de tira* (short ribs, US$11). It also prepares exceptional pisco sours and has attentive service in attractive surroundings.

Another option is the **Rancho Espantapájaros** (Camino a Frutillar Km 6, tel. 065/330049, www.espantapajaros.cl, lunch and dinner daily), whose specialty is barbecued boar as the centerpiece of a US$25 buffet that includes wine or beer. There's also a sandwich menu for those who don't care to gorge themselves. That said, there have been some recent negative reports.

The restaurant at **Hotel Centinela,** on the peninsula, is open to the public, with three-course fixed-price dinners (around US$25–30 pp).

## Information and Services

The **Oficina Municipal de Turismo** (Manuel Montt 378) is open 9 A.M.–2:30 P.M. weekdays; on occasion, there's a smaller office (Esperanza 555) alongside the Municipalidad on the Plaza de Armas (9 A.M.–9 P.M. daily Dec.–Feb.).

A more reliable choice is the private **Oficina La Rueda** (Germán Wulf s/n), alongside the church, operated by the aging but exceptionally helpful Octavio (also known by his nickname Punti), who knows Octay as well as or better than anyone else.

Opposite Hotel Haase, **BancoEstado** (Pedro Montt 345) has an ATM.

### Getting There and Around

Buses and minibuses leave from the **Terminal de Buses** (La Esperanza and Balmaceda), half a block south of the Plaza de Armas. **Via Octay** (tel. 064/230118) and **Octay Bus** go to Osorno's main bus terminal (US$2.50) several times daily, while **Thaebus** goes half a dozen times daily to Puerto Montt (US$3) via Frutillar and Puerto Varas. Four times daily, **Arriagada** goes south to Las Cascadas (US$2.50), roughly halfway to Ensenada.

## FRUTILLAR

The region's most self-consciously immaculate example of German colonization, the western Llanquihue village of Frutillar can seem a caricature of Teutonic orderliness—the lakefront is so tidy that, when a thoughtless smoker flips a cigarette butt, some burgher might well materialize to catch it before it hits the ground.

Still, with its almost perfectly preserved European-style houses, Frutillar exudes both style and charm; for a town its size, it also has cultural resources in a fine museum, a state-of-the-art theater, and one of Chile's most important music festivals. Mirrored in Llanquihue's waters, Volcán Osorno soars symmetrically to the east.

### Orientation

Frutillar (population about 15,500) is 63 kilometers south of Osorno and 50 kilometers north of Puerto Montt via the Panamericana. It comprises two separate sectors: Frutillar Alto's busy commercial zone adjoins the Panamericana, while Avenida Carlos Richter leads to tranquil Frutillar Bajo, pinched between the sandy lakeshore and a steeply rising hill, about two kilometers east. Avenida Philippi runs north–south along the lakeshore, linked to the parallel Vicente Pérez Rosales by a series of block-long streets; most services and other points of interest face the lake from the west side of Philippi.

### Sights

Middle European–style architecture is Frutillar Bajo's trademark, in structures such as the 1911 **Iglesia Luterana** (Lutheran Church, Philippi 1000), but German-style houses and other handsome buildings face the entire lakefront.

The highlight is the Universidad Austral's **Museo Colonial Alemán de Frutillar,** an indoor-outdoor facility set among immaculate gardens at the base of the hill. Antique farm machinery in mint condition adorns the grounds; buildings such as the **Molino** (a water-powered mill), the **Casa del Herrero** (a working smithery), the **Campanario** (a storage structure with a conical roof supported by a central pillar), and the **Casa del Colono** (a residence filled with period furniture and household implements) are precise historical reconstructions.

Built partly with German aid, the museum (Vicente Pérez Rosales s/n, tel. 065/421142, www.museosaustral.cl, 9 A.M.–7:30 P.M. daily, US$4 adults, US$2 children) is at the west end of Arturo Prat, one short block from the lakeshore. The museum shop sells souvenirs such as horseshoes forged in the Casa del Herrero and wood carvings of museum buildings.

### Events

Frutillar's major annual event is the **Semanas Musicales de Frutillar** (www.semanasmusicales.cl), a 10-day extravaganza that has showcased classical, jazz, and ethnic music since 1968. From January 27 to February 5, events take place both during the daytime and at night, when performances are both more formal and more expensive. Some recitals take place at the magnificent **Teatro del Lago** (Av. Philippi 1000, tel. 065/422900, www.teatrodellago.cl), a state-of-the-art theater built mostly over the lake; seating about 1,000 spectators within, its exterior gleams with strips of veneer from native woods. The series also

© WAYNE BERNHARDSON

**Frutillar's Teatro del Lago has made a major contribution to the region's arts and entertainment offerings.**

includes concerts in regional cities such as Osorno and Puerto Montt.

The second-largest event is November's **Semana Frutillarina,** celebrating its founding as a lakeport in 1856.

## Accommodations

Frutillar's accommodations scene is strong at the mid- to upscale range, but budget alternatives are limited; during the music festival, prices can spike even higher than regular summer rates. All listings provided here are in Frutillar Bajo, but Frutillar Alto has a handful of cheaper *residenciales.*

Only a block from the beach, **Hospedaje Tía Clarita** (Vicente Pérez Rosales 743, tel. 065/421806, claritaalmonacid@msn.com, US$19–22 pp with breakfast) is a friendly, family-run place that lacks the elaborate German colonial style of Frutillar's more expensive options, but it compensates in other ways. Rates vary according to shared or private bath; rooms with private baths have cable TV.

Also notable for its teahouse, **Hospedaje Trayén** (Philippi 963, tel. 065/421346, tttrayen33@hotmail.com, US$30 pp with breakfast) has rooms with private baths and cable TV; some have balconies with lake views.

**Hotel Residenz am See** (Philippi 539, tel. 065/421539, www.hotelamsee.cl, US$80–100 d) offers rooms with wireless Internet, private baths, a European-style breakfast, and parking. The more expensive rooms have lake views.

At the southern edge of town, the 14 rooms at **Hotel Elun** (Camino Punta Larga Km 2, tel. 065/420055, www.hotelelun.cl, US$85 s, US$105 d) feature natural wood interiors, with lake and volcano views, surrounded by lush gardens. Set back from the street, it's quiet and attractive, with friendly ownership and staff, but the wireless Internet only reaches the rooms nearest the lobby. The restaurant is normally open in summer only but will serve meals on request the rest of the year.

With just eight tasteful rooms, in a house dating from 1911, **Hotel Kaffee Bauernhaus**

(Philippi 663, tel. 065/420003, www.hotelbauernhaus.cl, US$130 s or d) is more a B&B than a hotel, but it's a very fine one. Despite the flat rates, rooms differ in views and amenities.

On a hillock with colorful flower gardens, **Hotel Frau Holle am See** (Antonio Varas 54, tel. 065/421345, www.frauholle-frutillar.com, US$94 s, US$105 d) embodies traditional Frutillar—a lovingly maintained family-run hotel with no frills but utterly reliable.

**Hotel Ayacara** (Philippi 1215, tel./fax 065/421550, www.hotelayacara.cl, US$136–171 s or d) occupies a gabled century-old lakefront mansion; each of its eight rooms—the more expensive enjoy lake views—is distinctive. Rates include a full German-style breakfast, with homemade kuchen.

On the northern outskirts of town, less than a kilometer from where the pavement ends, the **Salzburg Hotel & Spa** (Camino Playa Maqui s/n, tel. 065/421579, www.salzburg.cl, US$140–160 s or d) is a venerable TV-free hotel, most of whose rooms are in a modern new wing overlooking lush gardens with views to Lago Llanquihue and Volcán Osorno. In addition to having a restaurant, it is likely the only accommodation in Chile with its own artisanal brewery on the grounds (open for tours and tasting).

## Food

In summer, look along the lakeshore for stands with fresh raspberries, raspberry jam, and raspberry kuchen, all local specialties. Compared with its accommodations, Frutillar's restaurant are only average, but it has several breakfast and *onces* (afternoon tea) places, starting with the **Salón de Té Trayén** (Philippi 963, tel. 065/421346, breakfast and lunch daily).

For fixed-price meals around US$10, try the firehouse restaurant **Tierra del Fuego** (Philippi 1065, tel. 065/421588, lunch and dinner daily). **Guten Apetit** (Balmaceda 98, tel. 065/421145, lunch and dinner daily) is a *parrilla* with lunchtime specials and assiduous service.

The traditional **Club Alemán** (San Martín 22, tel. 065/421249, lunch and dinner daily) is more formal and more expensive, with dishes such as *pastel de jaiva* (crab soufflé) in the US$12 range among otherwise more Germanic specialties, slightly sugary pisco sours, and generous servings of limited wine-by-the-glass selections.

On the southern outskirts of town, **Lavanda** (Camino Quebrada Honda Km 1.5, cell 09/9269-1684, www.lavandacasadete.cl, 1–8 P.M. Tues.–Sun.) is a new teahouse that's drawn widespread praise, with nearly 50 different teas and creative sandwiches that include wild boar and rhea fillings, but their chocolate cake falls a bit short of its aspirations—stick with the kuchen for sweets. The sandwiches (on bagels) are moderately priced, the teas and sweets fairly expensive at about US$5 each.

## Information

Tourist information has been a black hole for years, but the private **Corporación Turística Frutillar** (Philippi and O'Higgins, tel. 065/420070, www.frutillarchile.cl) has a new office that's open 9 A.M.–7 P.M. daily as a joint operation with Turismo Hornig, a travel agency.

## Services

Frutillar has no exchange houses, but **BancoEstado** (Philippi 403) has an ATM.

**Correos de Chile** (Pérez Rosales and San Martín) delivers the mail and also has Internet service. For long-distance phone calls, there's a **Centro de Llamados** (Av. Philippi and Manuel Rodríguez) in Frutillar Bajo.

Frutillar Alto's **Lavandería Laveli** (San Pedro 436, tel. 065/421555) washes clothes.

For medical services, contact the **Hospital de Frutillar** (Las Piedras s/n, tel. 065/421386).

## Getting There and Around

Buses arrive at and leave from Frutillar Alto; *taxi colectivos* shuttle back and forth to Frutillar Bajo. The major long-distance carriers are **Tur-Bus** (Diego Portales 150, tel. 065/421390) and **Cruz del Sur** (Alessandri 32, tel. 065/421552); both run north (Santiago and intermediates) and south (to Puerto Montt) along the Panamericana. From a small new terminal alongside the Bigger supermarket, **Thaebus** (Alessandri and Manuel Montt) runs half a dozen buses daily to Puerto Octay (US$1.50) and to Puerto Montt (US$1.50).

## PUERTO VARAS

North of Puerto Montt, picturesque Puerto Varas appeals to conventional tourists who loll on Lago Llanquihue's beaches, admire its century-old mansions, sup in some of Chile's best restaurants, and follow the bus-boat crossing to the Argentine resort of Bariloche. Increasing numbers of more adventurous visitors also appreciate the nearby Río Petrohué's white-water rafting, Volcán Osorno's snow-clad slopes, Cochamó's wild backcountry, and other outdoor attractions. To the southeast, beyond Cochamó, a bridge over the Río Puelo also provides an alternative route to Hornopirén and the Carretera Austral.

Varas's architectural heritage, stemming from its German colonization as a 19th-century lake port, lends it its character. A recent building boom has resulted in nondescript housing developments on the outskirts, but it's also brought more stylish infill downtown; many visitors prefer Varas to nearby Puerto Montt, and not just as a base for excursions.

### Orientation

On Llanquihue's southwestern shore, Puerto Varas (population about 30,000) is 996 kilometers south of Santiago, 20 kilometers north of Puerto Montt, and a short distance east of Ruta 5, the Panamericana. The boundaries of its compact central grid are the lakeshore to the east, Diego Portales to the north, San Bernardo to the west, and Del Salvador to the south. On all sides except the shoreline, hills rise steeply toward quiet residential neighborhoods that include many places to stay.

From the corner of Del Salvador, the Costanera becomes paved Ruta 225 to the village of Ensenada, the lakeport of Petrohué in Parque Nacional Vicente Pérez Rosales, and toward the Cochamó backcountry.

### Sights

Other than the lake and its inspiring views toward Volcán Osorno, Varas's main attraction is its Germanic colonial architecture. The most imposing single structure is the **Iglesia del Sagrado Corazón** (1915), a national monument whose steeple soars above the town from the corner of San Francisco and María Brunn. When lit at night, it's best seen from the corner of Imperial and Santa Rosa.

Numerous private residences are national monuments, mostly in residential neighborhoods northwest and west of downtown; the city has recently emphasized its architectural heritage by erecting explanatory signs with brief histories alongside many of them. Examples include the **Casa Kuschel** (1910) at Klenner 299, the **Casona Alemana** (1914) at Nuestra Señora del Carmen 788, the deteriorating **Casa Maldonado** (1915) at Quintanilla 852, **Casa Jupner** (1910) at Miraflores 96, **Casa Opitz** (1913) at Terraplén 861, **Casa Gotschlich** (1932) at Dr. Otto Bader 701-05, and **Casa Yunge** (1932) at San Ignacio 711. A couple of impressive nonmonuments serve as accommodations: the **Casa Schwerter** (1941–1942) at Nuestra Señora del Carmen 873, and the **Casa Hitschfeld** (1930) at Arturo Prat 107.

For some years after the Santiago–Puerto Montt railroad closed, the former **Estación del Ferrocarril** (Klenner s/n) sat empty, but it's been revamped into the Centro Cultural Estación, a gallery and events center. After a brief revival, rail service has been suspended, but there is work underway on the tracks and sleepers.

### Entertainment and Events

Puerto Varas has less nightlife than might be expected in a town with so much tourist traffic. It has filled an unsightly vacant lot with the equally unsightly and pharaonically oversized **Casino de Puerto Varas** (Del Salvador 21, tel. 065/346600), crammed with roulette wheels and slot machines, as well as the new Hotel de los Volcanes.

Far better, though, is **Garage** (Walker Martínez 220, cell 09/8755-7640), a low-key bar (alongside the Copec gas station) that was once an auto repair shop. While it often has fine live music, including jazz, the air quality is toxic. **Urbano** (San Pedro 418) is also popular for drinks.

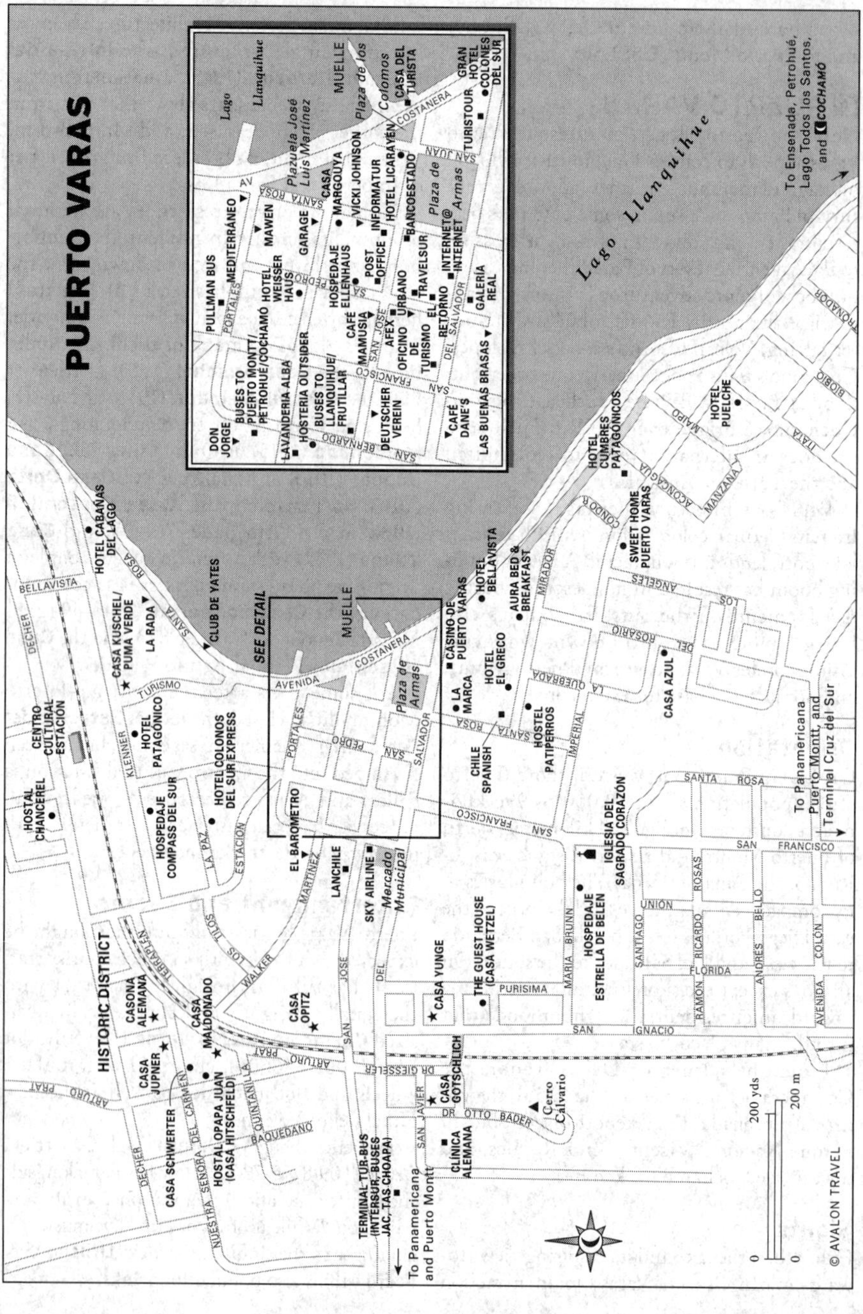
PUERTO VARAS
Lago Llanquihue
SEE DETAIL
MUELLE
HISTORIC DISTRICT
HOSTAL CHANCEREL
CENTRO CULTURAL ESTACIÓN
HOTEL PATAGÓNICO
HOSPEDAJE COMPASS DEL SUR
HOTEL COLONOS DEL SUR EXPRESS
CASA KUSCHEL/ PUMA VERDE
HOTEL CABAÑAS DEL LAGO
LA RADA
CLUB DE YATES
CASONA ALEMANA
CASA MALDONADO
CASA JUPNER
CASA SCHWERTER
HOSTAL OPAPA JUAN (CASA HITSCHFELD)
CASA OPITZ
EL BAROMETRO
LANCHILE
SKY AIRLINE
Mercado Municipal
CASA YUNGE
THE GUEST HOUSE (CASA WETZEL)
CASA GOTSCHLICH
CLÍNICA ALEMANA
TERMINAL TUR-BUS (INTERSUR, BUSES JAC, TAS-CHOAPA)
Cerro Calvario
HOSPEDAJE ESTRELLA DE BELEN
IGLESIA DEL SAGRADO CORAZÓN
CHILE SPANISH
HOSTEL PATIPERROS
HOTEL EL GRECO
LA MARCA
CASINO DE PUERTO VARAS
HOTEL BELLAVISTA
AURA BED & BREAKFAST
SWEET HOME PUERTO VARAS
HOTEL CUMBRES PATAGÓNICOS
HOTEL PUELCHE
CASA AZUL
Plaza de Armas
To Panamericana and Puerto Montt
To Panamericana, Puerto Montt, and Terminal Cruz del Sur
To Ensenada, Petrohué, Lago Todos los Santos, and COCHAMÓ
0 200 yds
0 200 m
BELLAVISTA
DECHER
SANTA ROSA
TURISMO
KLENNER
LA PAZ
ESTACIÓN
TERRAPLÉN
LOS TILOS
WALKER
MARTÍNEZ
SAN JOSÉ
DEL SALVADOR
ARTURO PRAT
DR GIESSELER
QUINTANILLA
BAQUEDANO
NUESTRA SEÑORA DEL CARMEN
SAN JAVIER
DR OTTO BADER
PURISIMA
MARÍA BRUNN
SAN IGNACIO
SANTIAGO
UNIÓN
ROSAS
RICARDO
RAMÓN
FLORIDA
ANDRÉS BELLO
COLÓN
AVENIDA
SAN FRANCISCO
IMPERIAL
LA QUEBRADA
DEL ROSARIO
LOS ANGELES
MIRADOR
CONDOR
ACONCAGUA
MANZANA
MAIPO
ITATA
BIOBÍO
TRONADOR
AVENIDA COSTANERA
PORTALES
SAN PEDRO
Lago Llanquihue
Plazuela José Luis Martínez
Plaza de los Colonos
CASA DEL TURISTA
GRAN HOTEL COLONES DEL SUR
TURISTOUR
BANCOESTADO
Plaza de Armas
HOTEL LICARAYÉN
INFORMATUR
VICKI JOHNSON
CASA MARGOUYA
GARAGE
MAWEN
MEDITERRÁNEO
PULLMAN BUS
HOTEL WEISSER HAUS
HOSPEDAJE ELLENHAUS
POST OFFICE
INTERNET@ INTERNET
GALERÍA REAL
TRAVELSUR
EL RETORNO
URBANO
AFEX
CAFÉ MAMUSIA
OFICINO DE TURISMO
LAS BUENAS BRASAS
CAFÉ DANE'S
DEUTSCHER VEREIN
BUSES TO LLANQUIHUE/ FRUTILLAR
HOSTERIA OUTSIDER
LAVANDERIA ALBA
BUSES TO PUERTO MONTT/ PETROHUÉ/COCHAMÓ
DON JORGE
SAN BERNARDO
SAN JUAN
COSTANERA
© AVALON TRAVEL

More a wine bar than a restaurant, though it does serve food and stronger alcohol, the Costanera's **Bravo Cabrera** (Vicente Pérez Rosales 1071, tel. 065/233441) has a diverse selection of wines by the glass, not all of them from the biggest producers.

Commemorating the city's 1854 founding, the **Aniversario de Puerto Varas** lasts two weeks in late January and early February. Soon thereafter, painters from around the country display their work at the **Concurso de Pintura El Color del Sur.**

## Shopping

At the headquarters for Parque Pumalín, **Puma Verde** (Klenner 299, tel. 065/250079) is the crafts outlet for residents of its surrounding communities. Items for sale range from locally produced honey to souvenirs and quality woolens; in addition, there's a good selection of books on Chilean conservation topics, mostly in Spanish.

For chocoholics, **Vicki Johnson** (Santa Rosa 318, tel. 065/232240) fashions exquisite takeaway truffles in addition to a substantial crafts selection.

## Accommodations

Puerto Varas has abundant accommodations, some of them very distinctive, in all categories. Some of the cheapest are seasonal, but there are always good options.

### US$10-25

New in early 2009, the summer-only **Sweet Home Puerto Varas** (Imperial 092, tel. 065/234570, sweethomeptovaras@gmail.com, US$10 pp, up to US$50 d) is a quirky hostel with fluent English-speaking Chilean management that also offers yoga classes twice weekly. Campers can pitch their tents in the spacious back yard (US$8 pp), and climbers can work out, even in wet weather, on its basement wall and ceiling.

### US$25-50

**Casa Margouya** (Santa Rosa 318, tel. 065/511648, www.margouya.com, US$18

© WAYNE BERNHARDSON

carved salad spoons at the Puma Verde crafts shop in Puerto Varas

CHILEAN LAKES DISTRICT

pp, US$30 s, US$40 d) can lodge up to 17 guests in a variety of singles, doubles, and dorms, which share just two bathrooms. Rates include a buffet breakfast, free tea and coffee, and free Internet access, with Spanish, English, and French spoken. This is one of Varas's livelier accommodations—not for the early-to-bed crowd.

Downtown's labyrinthine **Hospedaje Ellenhaus** (San Pedro 325, tel. 065/233577, www.ellenhaus.cl, US$14 pp with shared bath, US$38 d with private bath) is a step above most other budget places.

In a quiet hilltop neighborhood about a 10-minute walk from the Plaza de Armas, German-run ☾ **Casa Azul** (Manzanal 66, tel. 065/232904, www.casaazul.net, US$16 pp in dorms, US$36 d with shared bath, US$50 d with private bath) has become a favorite for its rustically stylish and comfortable rooms, which enjoy central heating. Rates include kitchen access, but the huge breakfast of muesli and homemade bread costs US$5 extra. The garden includes a bonsai-bounded koi pond and an ungainly but friendly Brazilian fila dog named Butch.

### US$50-100

Easy walking distance from downtown, but in a quiet barrio opposite the old railway station, ☾ **Hospedaje Compass del Sur** (Klenner 467, tel. 065/232044, www.compassdelsur.cl, US$20 pp in dorms, US$44 s, US$54 d) occupies a German colonial–style house with large rooms and kitchen privileges; rates include a standard breakfast, but extras such as muesli, eggs, and real coffee (not Nescafé) cost more. Moderately priced laundry service is also available.

Still nearly pristine after more than a decade, ☾ **Hostería Outsider** (San Bernardo 318, tel./fax 065/232910, www.turout.com, US$45–48 s, US$56–60 d) has consistently provided some of Varas's best value for the price, and has done it with style.

Since its arrival in late 2007, alongside the Iglesia Sagrado Corazón, **Hospedaje Estrella de Belén** (Verbo Divino 422, tel. 065/716551, www.hospedaje-estrelladebelen.cl, US$36–44 s, US$62–66 d) has drawn enthusiastic praise. Services include cable TV and wireless Internet; rates vary according to shared or private bath.

The brown-shingled Casa Hitschfeld, a national monument, is home to **Hostal Opapa Juan** (Arturo Prat 107, tel. 065/232234, www.opapajuan.cl, US$50 s, US$70 d with private bath and breakfast). It may look remote on the map, but **Hostal Chancerel** (Decher 400, tel./fax 065/234221, www.turismochancerel.com, US$50 s, US$72 d) is still less than a 15-minute walk from the Plaza de Armas. Rates include spacious rooms with private baths, breakfast, cable TV, wireless Internet, and central heating. Other meals and German-style *onces* (afternoon tea) are available.

Owned by the casino immediately below it, **Aura Bed & Breakfast** (Mirador 104, tel. 065/492030, www.aurapuertovaras.cl, US$56 s, US$80 d) has almost nothing in common with its glitzy sister—rather, it occupies a staid but agreeably updated German-style house with pleasant personnel and no obvious shortcomings. The casino blocks most of its views, though, except for those from the breakfast nook.

If its rooms had views, the 25-room **Puerto Chico Hotel** (Av. Colonos 60, tel. 065/231000, www.puertochicohotel.cl, US$80 d) would command higher prices than it does, as the decor and amenities match or exceed those of many better-known accommodations. At the same time, it's easy walking distance from the lakeshore and the eastern Costanera.

Its exterior restored to its pioneer style, ☾ **The Guest House** (O'Higgins 608, tel. 065/231521, www.vicki-johnson.com/guesthouse, US$75 s, US$80 d) occupies the German-colonial Casa Wetzel, a national monument. With smartly furnished rooms and ample, well-lighted common spaces, it provides Varas's most intimate accommodations.

### US$100-200

Downtown's **Hotel Weisser Haus** (San Pedro 252, tel. 065/346479, www.weisserhaus.cl, US$110 s or d) is a 10-room bed-and-breakfast that consists of a handsome and architecturally suitable addition to a traditional German colonial–style residence. A couple rooms are small but still well designed, and slightly cheaper.

One of Varas's most distinctive accommodations, featuring natural wood walls enhanced with work by regional artists, the boutique-style **Hotel El Greco** (Mirador 134, tel. 065/233880, www.hotelelgreco.cl, US$112 s, US$120 d) might be the world's greenest hotel in terms of building materials. When the nearby German school moved to new quarters, El Greco's owners salvaged everything from the building and converted what was once a single-story hotel into a four-story building with legitimately traditional style. The current floors, for instance, were once part of the school's gymnasium, and the room doors once opened into classrooms.

In quiet surroundings, some rooms at **Hotel Colonos del Sur Mirador** (Estación 505, tel./fax 065/235555, www.colonosdelsur.cl, US$105–133 s, US$120–145 d, with breakfast) have truly grand views, and, compared with some other places, the hotel has kept its prices stable. However, it now serves as more of an overflow accommodation when there's no room at its rebuilt lakeside sister hotel.

Directly on the Costanera, **Hotel Licarayén** (San José 114, tel. 065/232305, www.hotelicarayen.cl, US$90–100 s, US$120–130 d) has added amenities such as a sauna and gym while keeping prices stable; the more expensive rooms are larger and enjoy lake views.

On the lakeshore just south of the casino, the rapidly modernizing **Hotel Bellavista** (Vicente Pérez Rosales 60, tel. 065/232011, www.hotelbellavista.cl, US$140–240 s or d) has outstanding lake views and improved amenities. Popular with foreign tour groups, it's notably cheaper off-season.

On the lakefront, the 98-room **Gran Hotel Colonos del Sur** (Del Salvador 024, tel. 065/235555, www.colonosdelsur.cl, US$170–320 s, US$190–340 d) is the expanded reconstruction of its namesake, which was leveled by fire a while back. Standard rooms are noticeably smaller than premiums and suites, but those on the lakeside seventh floor are preferable to those facing the casino across the street. In addition to a restaurant, it has a small pool and spa, and a great view lounge on the top floor.

### OVER US$200

**Hotel Puelche** (Itata 695, tel. 065/233600, www.hotelpuelche.com, US$175 s, US$205 d) is a handsome 21-room boutique hotel, in a rustically sophisticated style of stone and wood, on a hill just above the lakeshore. Under the same ownership as Petrohué Lodge, in Parque Nacional Vicente Pérez Rosales, it includes a gym and spa, and is within easy walking distance to Varas's best restaurants. In clear weather, some of the balconied rooms enjoy volcano views.

Stretching impressively above the lakeshore, the hillside **Hotel Cabañas del Lago** (Klenner 195, tel. 065/232291, www.cabanasdellago.cl, US$170 s, US$210 d up to US$370 s or d with breakfast) has equally impressive views and a heated pool. The more expensive corner suites, though, offer views of Osorno as well as the lake and Calbuco.

New in 2009, **Hotel Cumbres Patagónicas** (Imperial 0561, tel. 065/222000, www.cumbrespatagonicas.cl, US$225–325 s or d) is a spa hotel whose luminous common areas stress locally quarried volcanic stone and native woods. On a hillock behind the Costanera, it has some of the finest unobstructed views in town; the 92 rooms include 25 luxury rooms, with their own balconies, and four suites.

Across from the train station, the Spanish Meliá chain rehabbed the rundown casino that sat empty for several years, but then divested itself of the glistening **Hotel Patagónico** (Klenner 349, tel. 065/201000, www.hotelpatagonico.cl, US$200–420 s or d), with 91 contemporary rooms with elaborate common areas and gardens. Some of the rooms, though, suffer minor limitations associated with the remodeling of an existing building, but this still takes its place among Varas's top hotels.

Under the same ownership as the adjacent casino, the **Hotel de los Volcanes** (Del Salvador 021, tel. 065/492000, www.enjoy.cl,

US$215–258 s or d) deserves consideration even by nongamblers—its 50 tastefully decorated rooms, which include several more expensive suites, enjoy spectacular lake and volcano views. Amenities include a pool, a spa, and an elaborate buffet breakfast.

## Food

Puerto Varas has some of Chile's best food, and even run-of-the-mill restaurants can be pretty good. **Café Dane's** (Del Salvador 441, tel. 065/232371, breakfast, lunch, and dinner daily) wins no style points, but its breakfasts, *onces* (afternoon tea), and Chilean specialties, such as *pastel de choclo,* are more than a step above similar fare elsewhere.

**Mawen** (Portales s/n, tel. 065/234020, 8 A.M.–8 P.M. daily) serves fine salads and sandwiches, as well as desserts including kuchen, but is probably most notable for a variety of espresso drinks. **Fuente del Lago** (San Juan 431, Local 3, tel. 065/272787, breakfast, lunch, and dinner) offers good, large sandwiches starting around US$5, plus Kunstmann beer on tap. In the same complex, with only seven tables and 30 spots maximum, **Pastagonia** (San Juan 431, Local B, tel. 065/232399, www.pastagonia.cl, 1–3:15 P.M. and 7:30–11 P.M. Wed.–Sat., 1–3:15 P.M. Sun.) makes a not-yet-convincing attempt to blend Italian cooking with regional specialties—think lasagna with wild boar meat (US$12). Still, the concept is interesting enough it shouldn't be written off.

**El Barómetro** (Walker Martínez 584, tel. 065/346100, lunch and dinner daily) has graduated from a popular meeting place with good sandwiches, desserts, and coffee to a full-fledged restaurant with a more elaborate menu, but loses points for its smoky ambience.

**Café Mamusia** (San José 316, tel. 065/233343, lunch and dinner daily) serves fine Chilean specialties, especially *pastel de choclo,* in the US$8–11 range, with a cheaper fixed-price *menu de casa* at midday; the pisco sours are strong and the kuchen sweet with fresh fruit, but service is erratic. The very traditional **Deutscher Verein** (German Club, San José 415, tel. 065/232246, lunch and dinner daily) offers fixed-price midday meals.

In the Mercado Municipal, **Donde El Gordito** (San Bernardo 560, Local 7, tel. 065/233425, 11:30 A.M.–11 P.M. daily) is a modest seafood venue that's good value for the price. **Don Jorge** (San Bernardo 240, tel. 09/6559759, lunch and dinner daily) is a no-frills locale specializing in beef and Chilean dishes.

The lakeside **Mediterráneo** (Santa Rosa 068, tel. 065/237268, lunch and dinner daily) does fine meats and good fish, mostly in the US$10–15 range, but with wine and dessert it's easy to spend upwards of US$30. For fine summer afternoons and evenings, it has outdoor seating.

**Kaori** (San Ignacio 695, tel. 065/237222, www.kaorirestaurant.cl, noon–11 P.M. Mon.–Fri., 1–11:30 P.M. Sat.) prepares decent sushi (around US$9–10 pp), plus fresh juices, in immaculate modern surroundings.

One of the best values is **Las Buenas Brasas** (San Pedro 543, tel. 065/230953, www.lbb.cl, lunch and dinner daily). From its name (The Good Coals), it sounds like a *parrilla,* but the restaurant is proudest of its fish dishes, especially conger eel (around US$12) and seafood sauces (which cost extra). The service can be a little distracted, but it's so well intentioned that this is a minor flaw.

In the same building as Hostería Outsider, **Trattoria Di Carusso** (San Bernardo 318, tel. 065/233478, lunch and dinner daily) makes tremendous pizza (the crust is especially notable) and seafood. The best pizza choice, with the most diverse toppings, is moderately priced **El Retorno** (San Pedro 465, tel. 065/346441, lunch and dinner daily). If you can put up with zero decor and shaky service, **El Reloj** (San Francisco 310, tel. 065/312475, 9:30 A.M.–12:30 A.M. daily) has excellent pastas and sauces at moderate prices. **Da Alessandro** (Av. Costanera 1290, tel. 065/310583, lunch and dinner daily) gets good reviews from knowledgeable locals for its pizzas, pastas, and seafood.

While it's drawn deserved praise for its grilled meats in the US$11 range and up, the otherwise attractive downtown branch of

**La Marca** (Santa Rosa 539, tel. 065/232021, www.restaurantlamarca.cl, lunch and dinner daily) has not set aside an area for nonsmokers. However, its larger lakeshore branch (Av. Vicente Pérez Rosales 1589, tel. 065/234168, lunch and dinner daily) does have a tobacco-free ground floor, even if the smokers upstairs get better views.

**Ibis** (Vicente Pérez Rosales 1117, tel. 065/232017, www.ibisrest.cl, dinner daily) is one of southern Chile's finest dining experiences, with prices to match. Appetizers cost US$7–20, and most entrées are in the US$12-and-up range; with drinks and side orders, it's easy to spend upwards of US$35 per person. Still, it's one of the best splurges beyond Santiago for dishes such as seafood crepes (US$15) with a sauce made of shrimp, scallops, and abalone; committed carnivores can request dishes from the adjacent **Parrilla Ibis** (Vicente Pérez Rosales 1137). Only Ibis proper has a nonsmoking area.

For fish and seafood, **La Olla** (Ruta 225 Km 0.9, tel. 065/233540, lunch and dinner daily) falls into the upmarket end of the "hearty Chilean cooking" category, with all traditional dishes plus a few, such as corvina with a razor clam sauce (US$12), that transcend the stereotype. In new quarters at the eastern outskirts of town, it still gets crowded, especially on weekends, and parking can be a problem.

The most impressive recent addition to the dining scene, **La Rada** (Santa Rosa 040, tel. 065/718316, www.larada.cl, noon–4 P.M. and 7–11 P.M. daily) specializes in fish, such as vidriola (seasonally available from the Juan Fernández archipelago, US$12), but also exceptional side dishes, including superior salads. What the portions lack in size, they more than compensate for with flavor, and the service is remarkably good.

## Information

The municipal **Oficina de Turismo** (Del Salvador 320, tel. 065/361219, www.puertovaras-chile.cl) is open 9:30 A.M.–9 P.M. daily in summer; the rest of the year, it closes at 7 P.M. At the foot of the pier on the Avenida Costanera, the private **Casa del Turista** (Piedraplén s/n, tel. 065/237956, www.puertovaras.org, 9 A.M.–10 P.M. daily Dec.–Feb., 9 A.M.–1:30 P.M. and 3–7 P.M. daily Mar.–Nov.) usually has an English speaker available.

**Informatur** (San José and Santa Rosa, tel. 065/338542, www.informatur.com), sponsored by an alliance of various service operators, keeps a selective accommodations database.

## Services

**Afex** (San Pedro 414, tel. 065/232377) is the local exchange house; **TravelSur** (San Pedro 451, tel./fax 065/236000) is a general travel agency that also changes money. The ATM at **BancoEstado** (Santa Rosa 414) does not add a service charge on transactions.

**Correos de Chile** (San José 242) is the post office. There are numerous downtown phone and cyber outlets, such as **Internet@Internet** (Del Salvador 264, Local 102).

**Chilean Spanish** (Mirador 160-A, tel. 09/8361-2500, www.chile-spanish.cl) offers Spanish-language classes.

**Lavandería Alba** (Walker Martínez 511, tel. 065/232908) washes clothes.

Atop Cerro Calvario in southwestern Puerto Varas, the **Clínica Alemana** (Dr. Otto Bader 810, tel. 065/232336) provides medical assistance.

## Getting There

Puerto Varas is close to the area's principal airport (Puerto Montt), has good regional and long-distance bus connections, and is also on the popular bus-boat route to Argentina.

**LAN** (Av. Gramado 560, tel. 065/234799) flies out of Puerto Montt, as does **Sky Airline** (San Bernardo 430, tel. 065/231039).

Rather than a central terminal, both regional and long-distance **bus** companies share central offices near the Plaza de Armas as well as slightly less central terminals. Some long-distance carriers from Puerto Montt pick up passengers here; some area carriers have no fixed offices but pick up and drop off passengers en route through the city.

Santiago carrier **Pullman Bus** (Portales 318,

tel. 065/234612) has its own central terminal, while **Cruz del Sur** (Walker Martinez 239-B, tel. 065/231925; terminal at San Francisco 1317, tel. 065/236969) shares offices with **Buses Norte Internacional,** which goes daily to San Carlos de Bariloche, Argentina (US$27, six hours). **Buses Jac** and **Cóndor Bus** (both at Walker Martínez 227, tel. 065/237255) also go to Santiago.

Other northbound carriers to Santiago (US$34–80, 12–13 hours) and intermediates include **Intersur** and **Tur-Bus** (both at San Pedro 210, tel. 065/233787, terminal at Del Salvador 1093, tel. 065/233787) and **Tas Choapa** (Walker Martínez 230, tel. 065/233831). Santiago fares can even be a little higher, depending on the service level; the most expensive are nighttime buses with fully reclining seats.

Puerto Montt–based **Thaebus** shuttles frequently to Puerto Varas (US$1.50), stopping at the corner of San Bernardo and Walker Martínez, as does **Expreso Puerto Varas** (tel. 065/232253); it is commonly known as "Mitsubishi" for its minibus fleet. From 8:30 A.M. to 6 P.M. daily, Expreso Petrohué goes half-hourly to Ensenada (US$3) and Petrohué, on Lago Todos los Santos (US$5). **Buses J.M.** (cell 09/9647-1716) and Thaebus also go to Ensenada and Petrohué, but less often.

From Puerto Montt, **Vía Lago Sur** (cell 09/9224-8109) goes to Cochamó (US$6) and Puelo (US$8), at 8 A.M., noon, and 5 P.M. daily. **Buses Río Puelo** (tel. 065/342004) also goes to Cochamó at 4 and 4:30 P.M. daily, with the latter continuing to Puelo; Varas departures are about half an hour later.

Puerto Varas is one of the intermediate points on the Cruce Andino bus-boat shuttle (US$230 pp) from Puerto Montt to Bariloche (Argentina) via Lago Todos los Santos, so it's possible to purchase tickets and board the bus to Petrohué here. Most of the year, buses leave Puerto Montt at 7:45 A.M. daily for Petrohué; April–mid-September, though, they run Wednesday–Sunday only, leaving Puerto Montt at 9 A.M. For details, contact **Turistour** (Del Salvador 72, tel. 065/437127, www.turistour.cl, www.cruceandino.cl).

### Getting Around

There are no regularly scheduled airport departures, but **Pacific** (tel. 065/237790) will drop off or pick up Varas passengers for US$28 for up to four persons. Otherwise it's necessary to make the connection indirectly via ETM bus from Puerto Montt.

## VICINITY OF PUERTO VARAS

Puerto Varas is the gateway for sights such as Volcán Osorno and Lago Todos los Santos, in Parque Nacional Vicente Pérez Rosales, and the Cochamó backcountry. It's also the staging point for adventure activities such as white-water rafting, hiking, climbing, mountain biking, horseback riding, and fishing. Paved Ruta 225 follows the lakeshore east to Ensenada; at a fork two kilometers farther east, the main road goes northwest to Petrohué, while another paved route heads southeast to Ralún, Cochamó, and Puelo.

Conventional travel agencies include **Turistour** (Del Salvador 72, tel. 065/437127, www.turistour.cl) and **TravelSur** (San Pedro 451, tel./fax 065/236000, www.travelsur.cl). For activities-oriented operators, try **Alsur Expediciones** (Aconcagua 8, tel. 065/232300, www.alsurexpeditions.com), **First Patagonia** (Imperial 699, tel. 065/230907, www.firstpatagonia.cl), and **Miralejos** (San Pedro 311, tel. 065/234892, www.miralejos.cl). Several operators and services in and around Cochamó, including Miralejos, have formed an alliance as **Secret Patagonia** (www.secretpatagonia.cl).

Most adventure-travel agencies rent mountain bikes and other outdoor-sports equipment. Just north of the pier, **Canoas Tour** (Av. Costanera s/n, tel. 065/346928 or 09/9294-0543) rents kayaks for lake use, but **KoKayak** (Ruta 225 Km 40, cell 09/9310-5272, www.kokayak.com) organizes more ambitious kayak trips on the Río Petrohué.

### Ensenada and Vicinity

At Lago Llanquihue's east end, 45 kilometers from Puerto Varas, the shoreline village of Ensenada lies midway between Volcán Osorno's symmetrical cone, to the northeast,

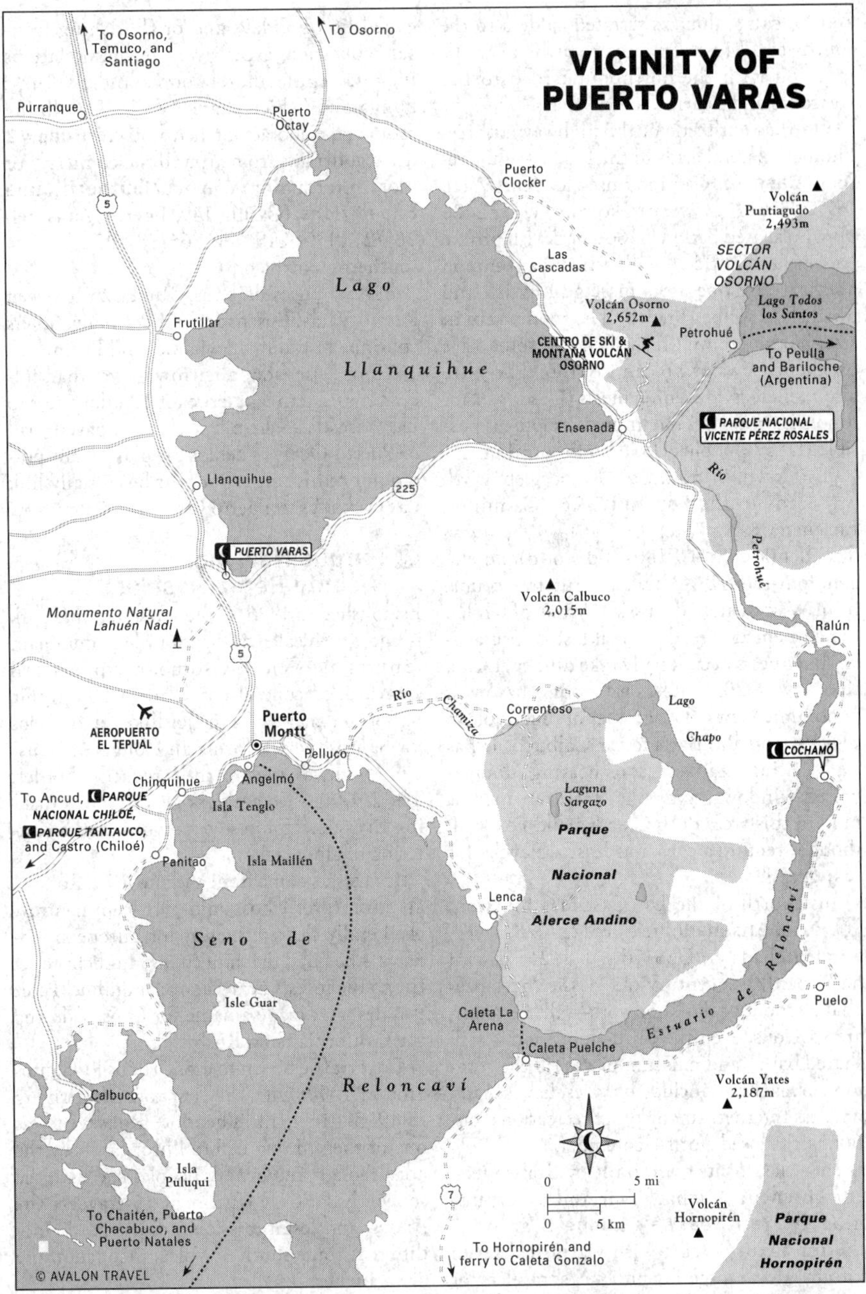
VICINITY OF PUERTO VARAS
To Osorno, Temuco, and Santiago
To Osorno
Purranque
Puerto Octay
Puerto Clocker
Volcán Puntiagudo 2,493m
SECTOR VOLCÁN OSORNO
Las Cascadas
Lago Llanquihue
Volcán Osorno 2,652m
Lago Todos los Santos
Frutillar
CENTRO DE SKI & MONTAÑA VOLCÁN OSORNO
Petrohué
To Peulla and Bariloche (Argentina)
Ensenada
PARQUE NACIONAL VICENTE PÉREZ ROSALES
Río Petrohué
Llanquihue
225
PUERTO VARAS
Volcán Calbuco 2,015m
Monumento Natural Lahuén Ñadi
Ralún
5
Río Chamiza
Correntoso
Lago Chapo
AEROPUERTO EL TEPUAL
Puerto Montt
Pelluco
COCHAMÓ
Angelmó
Chinquihue
To Ancud, PARQUE NACIONAL CHILOÉ, PARQUE TANTAUCO, and Castro (Chiloé)
Isla Tenglo
Laguna Sargazo
Parque Nacional Alerce Andino
Panitao
Isla Maillén
Lenca
Seno de Reloncaví
Estuario de Reloncaví
Isle Guar
Puelo
Caleta La Arena
Caleta Puelche
Volcán Yates 2,187m
Calbuco
Isla Puluqui
0 5 mi
0 5 km
7
Volcán Hornopirén
Parque Nacional Hornopirén
To Chaitén, Puerto Chacabuco, and Puerto Natales
To Hornopirén and ferry to Caleta Gonzalo
© AVALON TRAVEL

and Volcán Calbuco's serrated caldera to the southwest. Most services are at or near the junction with the northbound road to Las Cascadas and Puerto Octay.

On the south side of the highway, a three-kilometer lateral leads to the French-run, five-room **Casa Ko** (Camino Ensenada Km 37, tel. 09/7703-6477, www.casako.com, US$22–26 pp with shared bath, US$60 s or d with private bath) is a solid B&B, with attractive common areas, whose operators manage English and Spanish as well as French. The rooms vary in size, but all are well-furnished and some have excellent views of Volcán Osorno. There are also French-style evening meals (US$19) in addition to breakfast, and limited camping is possible (US$7 pp, plus US$6 pp for breakfast).

Just downhill from Casa Ko, a steep driveway leads to the **Fox Hill B&B** (Camino a Ensenada Km 37, tel. 09/8461-3005, www.foxhillchile.com, US$80–100 s or d), an elegant four-room B&B built and run by a couple from Wisconsin and Russia (by way of Chile); the homemade bread at breakfast is spectacular, but guests occasionally take dinner at Casa Ko. New in 2011, most of its rooms have vast panoramic views of Lago Llanquihue, Volcán Osorno and Puntiagudo, or Calbuco. It has high ceilings, radiant floor heating, double-paned windows, and other features uncommon in this area. Both Casa Ko and Fox Hill, though, require a car, or at least a bicycle, for easy access.

Just north of the Las Cascadas junction, **Hotel Ensenada** (tel. 065/212028, www.hotelensenada.cl, US$156 s, US$214 d with half board) is a century-old classic that oozes character out of the woodwork—all the rooms are spacious, even the third-floor rooms with shared baths, and museum pieces fill the common areas. Rates include bicycles, kayaks, and wireless Internet, among other recreational options. It's closed April–September.

In a class of its own, built by Seattle tech entrepreneur Michael Darland, the punning **Yan Kee Way Lodge** is an over-the-top luxury resort with whimsical (even kitschy) decor targeting big-bucks travelers for expedition holidays and/or fly-fishing (considerably more expensive). Accommodations include regular hotel rooms and two-unit bungalows (which share a wall). The dining room and elaborate kitchen at its **Latitude 42** draw gourmets from around the country. For more information, contact **Southern Chile Expeditions** (Casilla 149, Puerto Varas, tel. 065/212030, U.S. tel. 866/881-9215, www.southernchilexp.com).

Several buses daily use Ruta 225 between Puerto Varas, Ensenada, and Petrohué; others continue to Ralún, Cochamó, and Puelo.

From Ensenada, a narrow gravel road follows the eastern lakeshore for 22 kilometers to Las Cascadas, where it becomes a paved road to Puerto Octay. There is no public transportation on this route, but four buses daily link Las Cascadas to Puerto Octay.

## Parque Nacional Vicente Pérez Rosales

Established in 1926, Chile's first national park is a geographical extravaganza whose dominant features are Volcán Osorno, a symmetrical snowcapped cone often called the "Fujiyama of South America," and fjordlike Lago Todos los Santos, which forms an elongated lacustrine highway toward the Argentine border. The 251,000-hectare park also contains rushing rivers, steep forested canyons, and a scattering of alpine lakes.

It takes its name from Vicente Pérez Rosales, an adventurer whose mid-19th-century travels literally cleared the way for European pioneers—he hired the indigenous Huilliche to set fire to the forests near Lago Llanquihue. Pérez Rosales later made a name for himself during the California Gold Rush.

Boat traffic began to cross Todos los Santos around 1890, with the first tourists arriving in 1903—in 1913, Theodore Roosevelt was one of them. Long before Europeans saw the area, though, indigenous peoples had used the southerly Paso de Vuriloche to traverse the Andes, and Jesuit missionaries used a slightly different route south of Volcán Tronador, the area's highest peak.

## GEOGRAPHY AND CLIMATE

Some 50 kilometers northeast of Puerto Varas via Ruta 225, Parque Nacional Vicente Pérez Rosales ranges from 50 meters above sea level near Ensenada to about 3,460 meters on the summit of Cerro Tronador, a dormant glaciated volcano on the Argentine border. Volcán Osorno's 2,652-meter summit is its most conspicuous feature; other high peaks include 2,493-meter Volcán Puntiagudo on the park's northern border and 1,710-meter Cerro La Picada, northeast of Volcán Osorno.

Several rivers drain into Lago Todos los Santos, most notably the Río Negro; at 191 meters above sea level, the lake is the source of the Río Petrohué, diverted southward into the Golfo de Reloncaví by lava flows that reached Lago Llanquihue's shores just north of Ensenada.

The park receives about 2,500 millimeters of rainfall per year at lower elevations but up to 4,000 millimeters, much of it as snow, near the border. The lake moderates the ambient temperature, which averages about 16°C in summer and 6.5°C in winter, though it gets colder at higher altitude. Summertime highs reach about 25°C.

## FLORA AND FAUNA

Ecologically, up to 1,000 meters above sea level, the dense Valdivian rainforest consists of the southern beech *coigüe* mixed with glossy-leaved *ulmos* and the dense bamboo *quila,* as well as ferns and climbing vines. At higher elevations *coigüe* mixes with the related *lenga;* the rare coniferous *alerce* grows in a few steep areas.

Within the park are 33 mammal species, among them pumas, pudus, foxes, and skunks, and 117 bird species, including torrent ducks, kingfishers, coots, woodpeckers, and hummingbirds. Rainbow and brown trout have been introduced into its lakes and streams, though there are also native trout.

## SIGHTS AND RECREATION

While it hasn't erupted since the mid-19th century, Volcán Osorno's youthful Holocene crater has active fumaroles and is potentially dangerous. From the deck of the *Beagle,* Darwin observed its eruption of January 19–20, 1835:

> *At midnight the sentry observed something like a large star, which gradually increased in size until about three o'clock, when it presented a very magnificent spectacle. By the aid of a glass, dark objects, in constant succession, were seen, in the midst of a great glare of red light, to be thrown up and to fall down. The light was sufficient to cast on the water a long bright reflection.*

Adventure travel operators in Puerto Octay and Puerto Varas offer one-day guided climbs of Osorno, from about US$400 for one person, US$250 per person if there are two. Starting around 4 A.M., it's a challenging ascent, requiring either technical skills on snow and ice or guides with those technical skills, especially to cross crevasses. Conaf, which regulates climbing here, requires one guide for every two climbers on commercial trips; for independent climbers, it requires proof of experience and presentation of gear before permits are issued.

Recent improvements have made Osorno's ski area a viable recreational option in both summer and winter, though it's not likely to draw big crowds away from more elaborate ski areas such as Portillo and Valle Nevado. As it has no accommodations of its own (though a local ski club operates a simple nearby *refugio*), most skiers stay in either Puerto Varas or other lakeside communities.

Facilities include a pair of decent lifts that carry skiers nearly 500 meters above the base elevation of 1,200 meters. At the base, reached by a paved road just north of Ensenada, there's a small cafeteria and a larger restaurant, seating up to 150 patrons for lunch. Lift tickets are moderately priced, and rental gear is available; outside ski season, visitors can still take the lifts (US$20 pp, US$11 pp for kids) for access to the views and high country walks.

For more information on the ski area in both winter and summer, contact **Centro de Ski & Montaña Volcán Osorno** (San Francisco 333,

2nd floor, Puerto Varas, tel. 065/233445, www.volcanosorno.com). **CTS Turismo** (Santa Rosa 560, Local 15, Puerto Varas, tel. 065/237330) provides round-trip transportation (US$35 pp), remaining there for about three or four hours.

At the west end of Todos los Santos, the source of its namesake river, **Sector Petrohué** is most popular as the port for the passenger ferry to Peulla, which leaves mid-morning and returns in early afternoon. Cruce Andino, which operates the ferry, also runs a daily excursion (Jan.–Feb. only) to **Isla Margarita,** an island that rears its head above the middle of the lake, for a minimum of 12 passengers.

Since most of Sector Petrohué lacks an integrated trail network, visiting remote areas requires either hiring a private launch or contracting an activities-oriented tour, but there are a few accessible options. From **Playa Larga,** the black-sand beach north of Petrohué Lodge, the five-kilometer **Sendero Rincón del Osorno** follows the lake's western shore. Six kilometers southwest of Petrohué, on the south side of the highway, Conaf charges US$2.50 admission for the **Sendero Saltos del Petrohué,** a short riverbank trail that follows a series of basalt bedrock rapids and falls too rough for rafting or kayaking. Below the falls, Puerto Varas operators start their Class III–IV descents of the **Río Petrohué** (US$50–60 pp), which is suitable for novice rafters but interesting enough for those with more experience. Sites suitable for rock climbing are nearby.

Where the Río Negro and the Río Peulla empty into Todos los Santos, 20 nautical miles east of Petrohué, the hamlet of **Peulla** traditionally earns its livelihood from tourist traffic that patronizes Hotel Peulla and its restaurant, whether overnight, on day excursions from Petrohué, or en route to Bariloche; there is also a new luxury hotel to supplement the Peulla. Chilean customs and immigration is only a short distance east of here.

Day-trippers and through travelers have time enough to walk to **Cascada de Los Novios,** a waterfall just a few minutes from Hotel Peulla. Only overnighters will have time for the eight-kilometer climb of the **Sendero Laguna Margarita.**



### ACCOMMODATIONS AND FOOD

Park accommodations and food are limited; hotel reservations are advisable.

Just below Volcán Osorno's permanent snow line, 1,200 meters above sea level, the 40-bunk **Refugio Teski Ski Club** (tel. 09/9700-0370, www.teskiclub.cl, US$20 pp using your own sleeping bag, US$30 pp with sheets, US$70 d in a private room) also serves meals. From a turnoff three kilometers north of the Ensenada junction, the *refugio* is a 13-kilometer climb on a smoothly paved road.

On the Río Petrohué's south bank, reached by rowboat shuttle from the visitors center, the no-frills **Hospedaje Küschel** charges US$20 per person for beds, half that for camping. North of the visitors center, Conaf's 24-site **Camping Playa Petrohué** charges US$16 for up to five persons, including firewood.

Rebuilt after a 2002 fire, the Middle European–style **Petrohué Lodge** (tel./fax 065/212025, www.petrohue.com, US$160 s, US$220 d with breakfast) is at least the equal of what had always been a fine hotel. Other rate options include half board (US$175 s, US$250 d) and full board (US$240 s, US$420 d). The fourth floor has the best views but there are no elevators; there is wireless Internet, and its restaurant and bar are open to the public. Otherwise, limited supplies at high prices are available at Petrohué's only shop, and Cruce Andino has a small snack bar at the dock.

At the east end of the lake, the ownership of the venerable Hotel Peulla has built the new, separately managed **Hotel Natura** (tel. 065/560485, www.hotelnatura.cl, US$184 s or d with buffet breakfast) in the manner of an Andean design hotel, with spacious four-star rooms and magnificent natural light throughout; it remains open all year. Lunch or dinner costs an extra US$30 per person.

In 1913, when **Hotel Peulla** (tel. 065/212053, www.hotelpeulla.cl, US$108 s or d with buffet breakfast) opened at the east end of the lake, Theodore Roosevelt was among the first-year

© WAYNE BERNHARDSON

At the west end of Lago Todos los Santos, Petrohué Lodge is walking distance from the dock for the bus-boat crossing to Bariloche.

contingent of visitors. Now serving as an overflow from the Natura, it sometimes closes in winter, but many rooms have been renovated, though it retains a Euro-Andean style and squeaky floors. If space is available, the hotel offers a backpackers' special with half board; many Cruce Andino passengers take the buffet lunch at its restaurant, **Tejuela,** en route to Bariloche. Both hotels have agonizingly but unavoidably slow Internet connections.

For the truly financially challenged, tent camping is possible near the Conaf cabin on the road that leads from the boat dock to the hotels.

### OTHER PRACTICALITIES

At Petrohué, Conaf's **Centro de Visitantes** contains exhibits on the park's geography, geology, fauna, flora, and history.

Several bus companies connect Petrohué with Puerto Varas and Puerto Montt. Mid-September–mid-April, Monday–Saturday, Puerto Montt's Turistour operates 7:45 A.M. buses to Ensenada and Petrohué via Puerto Varas, connecting with its own bus-boat crossing to Bariloche (Argentina). The rest of the year, the Bariloche crossing takes two days, with an obligatory overnight at Hotel Peulla; buses run Monday–Friday only, leaving Puerto Montt at 8:30 A.M.

At Petrohué, a dockside kiosk sells tickets for the three-hour voyage to Peulla, where it connects with the bus to the Argentine border at Puerto Frías and a relay of bus-boat links to Bariloche. Hikers and cyclists can also take this route; round-trip tickets to Peulla cost US$45 for adults, slightly less for children; lunch at Hotel Peulla costs an additional US$20 per person. From Puerto Varas, the fare is US$55; for more details, contact **Turistour** (Del Salvador 72, tel. 065/437127, www.turistour.cl).

## Cochamó and Vicinity

Two kilometers east of Ensenada, where international Ruta 225 continues to Petrohué, another paved road follows the Río Petrohué southeast for 30 kilometers, where it forks as

CHILEAN LAKES DISTRICT

the river enters the Estuario de Reloncaví. While the right fork heads south to Canutillar, the graveled left fork crosses the bridge over the Petrohué and continues to **Ralún,** where another gravel road forks north to **Cayutué,** on the south arm of Lago Todos los Santos.

The main road, though, continues another 15 kilometers to Cochamó, where the 2,111-meter Volcán Yates provides a backdrop for the shingled **Iglesia Parroquial María Inmaculada** and its soaring steeple. The area's big attraction, though, is the yet untamed grandeur of the upper Río Cochamó, where ribbon-like waterfalls tumble over exfoliated granite domes that rise above the luxuriant rainforest.

Still, only small numbers of hikers, dedicated technical climbers, and horseback riders challenge the muddy trail, part of which follows a 19th-century log road that crossed the Andes to Argentina, to the scenic valley of **La Junta** and beyond. Though landowner opposition has stopped a road up the valley to La Junta, the Spanish utility company Endesa has acquired water rights that could lead to road-building and construction of hydroelectric turbines.

From the Río Cochamó's outlet, the gravel road continues south over a new bridge across the Río Puelo and then joins Ruta 7, the Carretera Austral, to **Caleta Puelche.** Here it's possible to double back north toward Puerto Montt via the ferry shuttle to Caleta La Arena, or continue south to Hornopirén, the summer ferry port for southbound travelers.

Cochamó is the base for **Campo Aventura,** an eco-lodge and horse-trekking company that offers one- to ten-day horseback trips to its backcountry camp at La Junta, 17 kilometers east and 300 meters above sea level. Under U.S. ownership, it has expanded its hiking programs, with a full-time guide for those who prefer to travel on foot. They've also trained new horses to replace those that were getting long in the tooth.

The present trail follows the river's north bank as far as La Junta, where it's necessary to ford the river to Campo Aventura's south-bank camp, which has comfortable lodging, camping (US$6 pp with shower access), and its own network of hiking trails. If the river is high, the crossing can be dangerous for hikers and, on rare occasions, even riders, but Campo Aventura has installed its own cable car to simplify the process. Its classic four-day, three-night horseback-riding package costs US$450 per person; for more details, especially on the longer excursions, contact Campo Aventura's Puerto Varas office (San Bernardo 318, tel./fax 065/232910, www.campoaventura.cl). In addition, the company offers boat trips to nearby thermal baths and a sea lion colony, sea kayaking, and fishing and trekking.

Both horseback-tour clients and nonriders stay overnight (US$62 pp with full board) at the three tasteful cabañas at their **Riverside Lodge,** five kilometers south of Cochamó proper and 500 meters east of the Puelo road, on the south side of the bridge over the Río Cochamó; it's also possible to camp here for US$16 per person with breakfast. Seafood and vegetarian lunches and dinners are also available at its restaurant, **La Mesa de los Sabores.**

Open mid-September–mid-May, Campo Aventura has equally stylish if simpler dormitory accommodations at La Junta's **Campo Aventura Mountainside Lodge,** with wood-fired hot showers and a campground as well. Meals, wine, and fresh bread are available, but it's best to make advance arrangements for meals at the riverside lodge. Camping is possible at both sites but, for quality control, on a limited basis only.

### GETTING THERE AND AROUND

From Puerto Montt, **Vía Lagos Sur** (cell 09/9224-8109) and **Buses Río Puelo** (tel. 065/342004) go to Cochamó (US$5) four or five times daily via Puerto Varas. Confirm schedules at Campo Aventura's Varas office, which is near the bus stop and can also arrange transfers by private vehicle or even kayak (even for nonkayakers).

## Lago Tagua Tagua and Vicinity

East of the town of Puelo, surrounded by high forested mountains, Lago Tagua Tagua is the starting point for an adventurous crossing of the Argentine border that begins with a vehicle and passenger ferry at the hamlet of El Canelo. From Puerto Maldonado, at the east end of the lake, daily bus service continues another 32 kilometers to Llanada Grande, but from there it's another 70 kilometers on foot or horseback to the Argentine border at Lago Puelo, about half an hour south of the popular town of El Bolsón.

At the lake's east end, under new ownership, the reopened **Hotel Mítico** (San Pascual 397, Las Condes, Santiago tel. 02/822 8762, Tagua Tagua tel. 02/1961001, www.miticohoteles.com, US$400–550 s or d) has reinvented itself as a diverse activities-oriented lodging instead of the fly-fishing destination it once was (though fly-fishing is still part of the mix). Open all year, the 2,400-square-meter structure has expansive ground-floor common areas in natural wood and midsized rooms with ample private baths; those on the second floor have large balconies with lake views (partially blocked by dense forest).

**Vía Lagos Sur** (cell 09/9224-8109) goes daily at 8 A.M. from Puerto Montt via Puerto Varas to El Canelo (US$10, four hours), connecting at 1 P.M. with the ferry *Caupolicán* to Puerto Maldonado (US$2 for passengers, US$13 for vehicles), where another bus continues to Llanada Grande.

## PUERTO MONTT AND VICINITY

No Chilean city enjoys a more impressive setting than Puerto Montt, where a cordon of forested mountains and snowcapped volcanoes stretches south along Chile's island-studded "Inside Passage." While the midsize port can't match the prosperity and cultural diversity of cities in comparable surroundings, such as Seattle and Vancouver, B.C., improvements are underway. Part of the waterfront, with its dramatic views, has become a park; anchor businesses are helping make downtown a retail mecca; handsome high-rise apartments are filling once-vacant lots; pedestrian malls are sprouting chic sidewalk cafés; and pubs and bars are proliferating.

Puerto Montt owes part of this growth to shipbuilding, extractive industries such as forestry, and the fish-farming sector. As a city whose potential, to this point, exceeds its achievements, the capital of Region X (Los Lagos) remains primarily a gateway to the Andean lakes district, the Chiloé archipelago, Chilean Patagonia, and parts of Argentina. As a transport hub where mainland Chile ends and archipelagic Chile begins, it enjoys air, land, or sea connections in all directions but west. Cruise ships call at its port of Angelmó, though there's barely room for them to maneuver in and out of the congested harbor; the largest vessels have to anchor offshore and shuttle passengers to the pier.

### History

Puerto Montt dates from 1853, when German colonists landed at the north end of the Seno de Reloncaví in what was then called Melipulli, a Huilliche word whose definition—Four Hills—aptly described the site. It grew slowly until 1912, when the railroad cut travel time to Santiago to 26 hours and it became the jumping-off point for southbound colonists headed for continental Chiloé, Aisén, and Magallanes.

In 1960, a massive earthquake destroyed the port and most of what Jan Morris called "structures in the Alpine manner, all high-pitched roofs and quaint balconies." Rebuilt in a mostly utilitarian style, Puerto Montt is only now beginning to sport newer buildings of distinction; the earlier style survives in nearby Puerto Varas.

### Orientation

Puerto Montt (population about 190,000) is 1,016 kilometers south of Santiago via the Panamericana, which bypasses the city center en route to the Chiloé archipelago. Like Valparaíso, it occupies a narrow shelf at the foot of a series of hills, but neither so high nor so steep as those at Valparaíso. Westbound Avenida Diego Portales becomes Avenida Angelmó, the main approach to the ferry, fishing, and forest-products port of Angelmó, which draws tourists to its crafts fair and

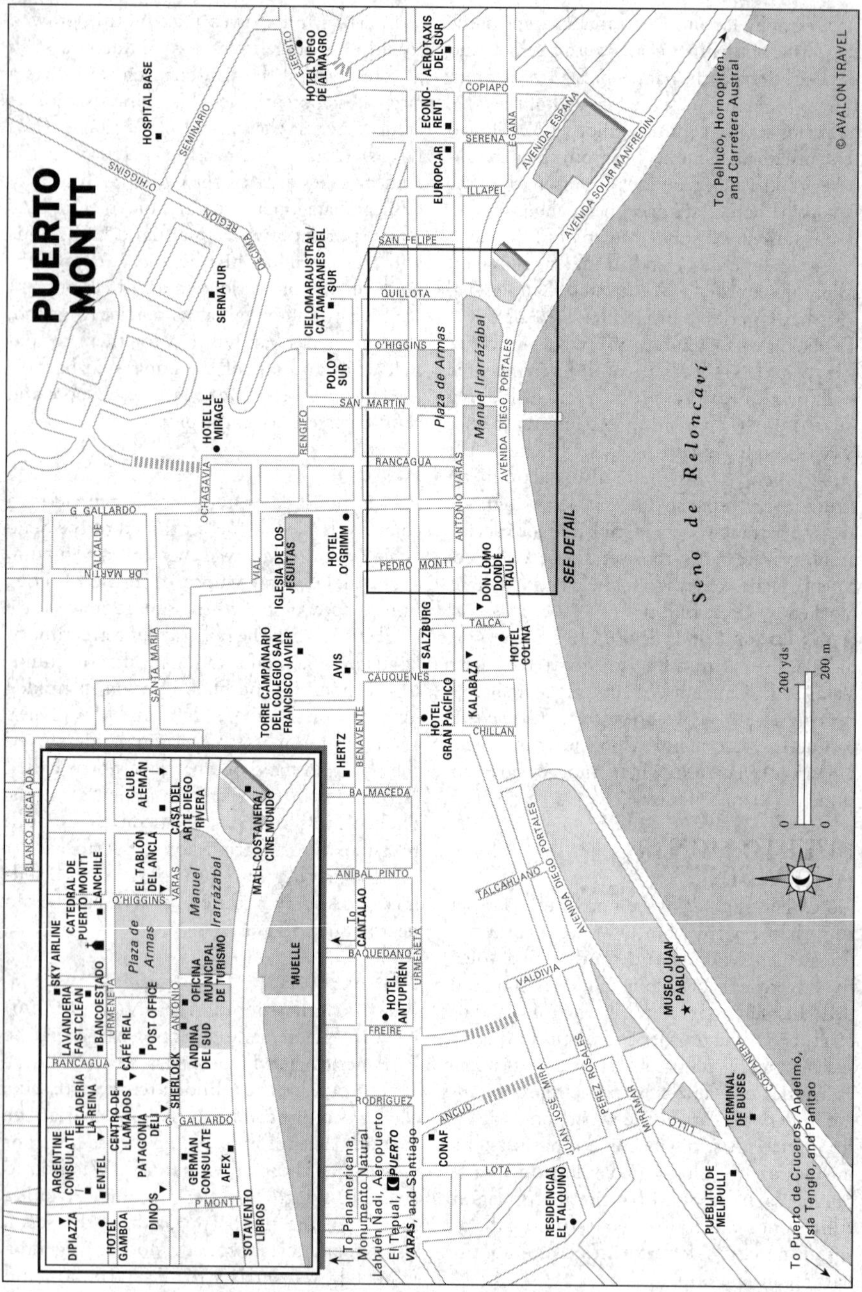


CHILEAN LAKES DISTRICT

seafood restaurants; eastbound, it becomes Avenida Soler Manfredini, the starting point for the discontinuous Carretera Austral, a series of both paved and gravel highways linked, where necessary, by ferries. This highway ends at Villa O'Higgins, 1,240 kilometers to the south in Region XI (Aisén), but most travelers cover at least part of the route via air or ferry from Puerto Montt or Chiloé.

## Sights

Puerto Montt's strength is its magnificent setting, but it also has a handful of architectural monuments and other sights. On the south side of **Plaza Manuel Irarrázaval,** built of *alerce,* the copper-domed, Parthenon-styled **Catedral de Puerto Montt** (1856) is the city's oldest building. Surrounded by woods, the hillside **Torre Campanario del Colegio San Francisco Javier** (1894) rises behind the **Iglesia de los Jesuitas** (1872), at the corner of Guillermo Gallardo and Rengifo.

Though its exterior needs a serious makeover, the waterfront **Museo Juan Pablo II** (Av. Diego Portales 991, tel. 065/223029, museojp@yahoo.com, 9 A.M.–5:45 P.M. weekdays, 10 A.M.–6 P.M. weekends, US$1 adults, US$0.40 children) holds worthwhile collections on natural history, archaeology (including dioramas of the Monte Verde early human site 35 kilometers west of town), anthropology, early Spanish and 19th-century German colonization, and the city's history from its origins as the hamlet of Melipulli to the 1960 earthquake and up to the present. For locals, history's high point is the 1987 visit from Pope John Paul II, also documented here, which resulted in the museum's renaming.

Puerto Montt and **Angelmó,** two kilometers west, have gradually merged along the waterfront, but the port retains its own identity and attracts more visitors than other parts of town, thanks to its sprawling crafts market and gaggle of *marisquerías* (simple fish and seafood eateries) always jammed with lunch and dinner patrons. *Taxi colectivos* out Avenida Diego Portales go directly to the port area, which is also the departure point for southbound ferries.

© WAYNE BERNHARDSON

A copper dome sits atop Catedral de Puerto Montt, built of *alerce* timber.

### Monumento Natural Lahuén Ñadi

Little native forest remains near Puerto Montt, but substantial stands of *alerce, ulmo, mañío, coigüe,* and other species survive in this 200-hectare woodland between the city and Aeropuerto El Tepual, despite the steady encroachment of trophy houses surrounded by high fences and guarded by Rottweilers.

Located on the private Fundo El Rincón, the Conaf-administered park features a small visitors center, a cafeteria, a short nature trail, and one slightly longer hiking trail. Midway between the Panamericana and the airport, a bumpy gravel road leads to the park, about three kilometers north; water can cover parts of the road when rains are heavy, but the surface is firm gravel and vehicles without four-wheel drive pass easily.

Any airport-bound bus will drop you at the junction, which is about a 30-minute walk from the park. Admission costs about US$2, but visits now require authorization from Conaf's Puerto Montt office (Urmeneta 977, 5th floor, tel. 065/486115).

## CHILE'S INSIDE PASSAGE

Even in the darkest days of the 1970s, as Chile chafed under dictatorship and foreign travelers were few, the occasional adventurer still went south in search of a sailing passage through the labyrinth of its southern canals. Then, only a handful managed to secure a berth on the aging rustbucket *Río Baker*. Today, fortunately, it's easier than ever to find a berth on "the poor man's cruise," a three-day voyage through western Aisén and Magallanes.

The Navimag vessel *Evangelistas*, which shuttles the 900 nautical miles between Puerto Montt and Puerto Natales every week, is not a cruise ship. Rather, it's a cargo ferry that also carries passengers in reasonable comfort through some of South America's finest scenery – at least when the weather clears in one of the earth's stormiest regions.

Schedule permitting, from November to March the *Evangelistas* pauses at **Puerto Edén,** a fishing hamlet where the last remaining Kawéskar (Alacaluf) reside, long enough for an optional landing and walk through town (the US$6 pp fee goes entirely to the community). Beyond Puerto Edén, the enthralling scenery includes emerald forests, countless waterfalls, and glaciers that don't quite reach the sea but still glisten when the sun burns through the clouds. Southbound, the ship detours for a view of **Glaciar Pío XI,** with its five-kilometer face, before resuming the journey. Approaching Puerto Natales, passengers grab their backpacks and prepare to head for *hospedajes* and hotels to make their plans for Torres del Paine and Patagonia.

### PRACTICALITIES

Because the *Evangelistas* is larger and faster than the *Puerto Edén,* which used to run this route, the frustration that many passengers felt when weather or mechanical problems caused delays has diminished. The boat sails Friday afternoon all year, returning from Puerto Natales early Tuesday (boarding Monday night), but longer summer days usually mean good visibility even with changeable weather.

A Japanese ferry remodeled in Chile, the *Evangelistas* can carry 337 passengers versus the *Puerto Edén*'s maximum of 175 or so. The former needs only about 60 hours between Puerto Montt and Puerto Natales, even with a stop at Puerto Edén and a detour to Glaciar Pío XI, while the slower *Puerto Edén* often took longer. When demand falls in the off-season, though, the smaller *Puerto Edén* sometimes substitutes for the *Evangelistas*.

The *Evangelistas* has a pub, self-service cafeteria and dining room, and spacious upper decks and terraces. Its eight AAA cabins have two bunks each with individual reading lights (with a separate outlet suitable for charging cell phones or computers), private baths, writing desk, chair, locking closet, regulated heat, and an exterior window. Sixteen AA cabins have two upper and two lower bunks and the same amenities except for desk and chair. Fourteen A cabins have identical amenities but lack exterior windows. The 132 C *literas* (berths) have locking closets and shared baths. If you're susceptible to seasickness, medication is available from the bar; take it well before crossing the Golfo de Penas.



## Entertainment

Built with Mexican aid after the 1960 quake and named for the famous muralist, the **Centro de Arte Diego Rivera** (Quillota 116, tel. 065/261817, www.teatrodiegorivera.cl, 10 A.M.–7 P.M. Mon.–Sat., 3–7 P.M. Sun. and holidays, free) is Montt's main venue for theater, dance, and the occasional film. It also includes several display halls: the **Sala Mexicana,** with rotating exhibits; the **Sala Hardy Wistuba,** named for a mid-20th-century Chilean painter; and the **Pinacoteca Municipal,** the municipal art museum.

Puerto Montt has a smattering of pubs and bars, including the **Salzburg** (Cauquenes 128, tel. 065/293000), which specializes in Frutillar's namesake microbrew, and the **Sherlock** (Antonio Varas 452, tel. 065/288888).

In the former train station, miraculously transformed into the Mall Costanera, the **Cinemundo** (Illapel 10, Local 303, tel. 065/348877, www.cinemundo.cl) shows current movies.

© WAYNE BERNHARDSON

Navimag's ferry *Evangelistas* at anchor at Angelmó (Puerto Montt)

The food is cafeteria food, but it has improved in quality and increased in quantity. Both bridge and cabin staff are friendly, even the food servers, and bar prices (notable for the "Happy Sour" promotion) are moderate. Some people bring their own wine, as the selection is limited. Smoking is allowed outdoors only.

Navimag carries about twice as many foreigners as Chileans on the Puerto Montt–Puerto Natales route, which can still be delayed by bad weather. At the outset, there is an orientation and safety talk. Videos, including exceptional Chilean films, and other entertainment, including a closing-night party, take place on board.

In the course of the voyage, many people make acquaintances and enduring friendships, and even some marriages have resulted. There's easy access to the bridge, the crew are personable and informative, and it's possible to follow the route on their charts. Some passengers, though, bring their own GPS devices and charts, the most comprehensive of which is British Admiralty Chart 561, *Cabo Pilar to Golfo Coronados* (scale 1:750,000).

Reservations are still advisable in the summer peak season; contact **Navimag** (Av. Angelmó 1735, Puerto Montt, tel. 065/432 360, www.navimagferries.com). Fares depend on the season and the quality of the accommodations but range US$300–2,470 per person with full board. Bicycles cost an additional US$50, motorcycles US$127, passenger cars US$417, and light trucks US$492; other vehicles pay a linear meter rate.

## Shopping

Directly opposite the bus terminal, the **Pueblito de Melipulli** (Diego Portales s/n, tel. 065/263524) is a permanent artisans' market, but crafts stalls also line both sides and cover the sidewalks of Avenida Angelmó west of Independencia. Typical items include woolens, copperware, and standard souvenirs.

**Sotavento Libros** (Diego Portales 580, tel. 065/256650) specializes in local and regional history and literature.

## Accommodations

Puerto Montt has abundant accommodations, but many lower-end options are unremarkable if not quite dire; even most at the top lack distinction. Many visitors prefer to stay in Puerto Varas, 20 minutes north, and visit Puerto Montt for the afternoon.

### US$10–25

Uphill from the bus terminal, **Residencial El Talquino** (Pérez Rosales 114, tel. 065/253331, eltalquino@hotmail.com, US$12 pp without breakfast) also offers breakfast (US$5) and kitchen privileges for a small additional charge.

### US$25-50

Northwest of the terminal, **Casa Perla** (Trigal 312, tel. 065/262104, www.casaperla.com, US$18–24 pp with breakfast) offers rooms with shared or private bath, kitchen privileges, and laundry facilities; while it's not Puerto Montt's most appealing neighborhood, the sociable owners speak English, and the cozy common areas include a small library.

**Hotel Gamboa** (Pedro Montt 157, tel. 065/252741, US$20–25 pp) is a vintage hotel with character but distracted management. The sizable rooms retain most of their original style, though some of the modern furniture is tacky; rates vary according to shared or private baths.

Nearer the port, **Hospedaje Rocco** (Pudeto 233, tel./fax 065/272897, www.hospedaje-rocco.cl, US$24 pp in dorms, US$40 s, US$50 d with breakfast) also gets high marks for hospitality, but the rates are high for a place that has shared baths only.

### US$50-100

Near the waterfront, under new ownership, the renovated **Hotel Colina** (Talca 81, tel./fax 065/253501, www.hotelcolina.cl, US$60 s, US$70 d) has undergone a facelift that's compromised its original deco style; the busy nearby avenue makes it not the quietest location. Rates include a buffet breakfast, and the hotel has added a tango bar.

Business-oriented **Hotel Antupirén** (Freire 186, tel. 065/367800, reservas@hotelantupiren.cl, US$60 s, US$70 d) has attentive, efficient service and a good buffet breakfast. Some smaller, slightly cheaper rooms offer less value for the price.

### OVER US$100

Up the hill from downtown, with expansive views of the sound and surrounding volcanoes, **Hotel Diego de Almagro** (Ejército 516, tel. 065/320200, www.dahoteles.com, US$105 s, US$125 d) is the local branch of an excellent chain, but its location is not pedestrian-friendly.

The business-oriented **Hotel Gran Pacífico** (Urmeneta 719, tel. 065/482100, www.hotelgranpacifico.cl, US$111 s, US$129 d) has spacious, comfortable, and immaculate rooms with outstanding views, especially facing southeast, from the higher floors (eighth and ninth are best). Amenities include a gym and a sauna, and what may be the city's best view restaurant on the tenth floor.

## Food

For sandwiches, *onces* (afternoon tea), coffee, and desserts, such as German-style kuchen, try **Café Real** (Rancagua 137, tel. 065/253750, lunch and dinner daily), **Kalabaza** (Antonio Varas 629, tel. 065/266010, lunch and dinner daily), and **Patagonia Deli** (Antonio Varas 486, tel. 065/482898, lunch and dinner Mon.–Sat.), which, unfortunately, has failed to implement any tobacco-free area.

Reasonably priced **Don Lomo Donde Raúl** (Talca 84, tel. 065/254597, lunch and dinner daily) serves standard Chilean fare; figure about US$6–10 for lunch, more for dinner. **DiPiazza** (Pedro Montt 181, tel. 065/254174, lunch and dinner daily) makes good thin-crust pizza at moderate prices—individual-sized pizzas start around US$7, and inexpensive pasta plates are also on the menu.

The rejuvenated **Club Alemán** (German Club, Antonio Varas 264, tel. 065/252551, lunch and dinner daily) is a step up in both price and quality. **El Tablón del Ancla** (Antonio Varas 350, lunch and dinner daily) is a cheerful bar/restaurant that's worth a look.

Any of numerous *palafito marisquerías* (simple fish and seafood restaurants on stilts or pilings) clustered at the port of Angelmó are worth trying for fish, shellfish, and *curanto* (seafood stew), but the best option is **El Cuento del Mar** (Av. Angelmó 2476, tel. 061/271500, lunch and dinner daily), with fine fish and shellfish entrées starting around US$9–10. The management, in particular, is congenial and accommodating.

In a charming old residence that's been adapted into several intimate dining rooms, the Peruvian **Cantolao** (Baquedano 285, tel. 065/262630, www.cantolao.cl, lunch Tues.–Sun., dinner Tues.–Sat.) adds a welcome note of diversity to the local dining scene, starting with a varied choice of ceviche appetizers (US$9–11) and standards such as *ají de gallina* (chicken in a walnut sauce, US$10) and *lomo saltado* (stir-fried beef and vegetables, US$11). It also takes some chances, though, with items like scallop-stuffed ravioli (US$11).

**Heladería La Reina** (Urmeneta 508, tel. 065/253979) continues to produce Puerto Montt's finest ice cream.

## Information

Mid-December–mid-March, Puerto Montt's **Oficina Municipal de Turismo** (Varas and O'Higgins, tel. 065/261823, www.puertomonttchile.cl), just south of the Plaza de Armas, is open 8:30 A.M.–9 P.M. daily; the rest of the year, hours are 8:30 A.M.–1 P.M. and 3–5:30 P.M. weekdays only.

Within the hilltop Intendencia Regional, **Sernatur** (tel. 065/254580) is open 8:30 A.M.–5:30 P.M. Monday–Thursday, 8:30 A.M.–4:30 P.M. Friday.

Puerto Montt has **consulates** of Argentina (Pedro Montt 160, 6th floor, tel. 065/253996, 8 A.M.–1 P.M. Mon.–Fri.) and Germany (Antonio Varas 525, Oficina 306, tel. 065/252828).

Conaf's **Patrimonio Silvestre** unit (Urmeneta 977, 5th floor, tel. 065/486115) can provide national parks information.

## Services

Exchange houses include **Afex** (Diego Portales 516, tel. 065/256604) and the bus terminal's **La Moneda de Oro** (Diego Portales s/n, tel. 065/255108). **BancoEstado** (Urmeneta 444) has one of many downtown ATMs.

**Correos de Chile** (Rancagua 126) is the post office. For long-distance services and Internet access, try the **Centro de Llamados** (Urmeneta 459). **Lavandería Fast Clean** (San Martin 167, Local 6, tel. 065/258643) lives up to its name in laundry service.

The aging **Hospital Regional** (Seminario s/n, tel. 065/261134) is northeast of the hilltop Intendencia Regional, reached via O'Higgins and the zigzag Avenida Décima Región. A new, state-of-the-art facility is under construction at the northern outskirts of town, along the Panamericana.

## Getting There

Other than Santiago, Puerto Montt is the main gateway for air, land, and sea connections to Chilean Patagonia and across the Andes to Argentina. Only in summer can overland travelers begin the entire Carretera Austral by heading southeast from here, as Naviera Austral's Hornopirén–Caleta Gonzalo ferry link operates in January and February only; otherwise, it's necessary to take the ferry from Puerto Montt to Chaitén, or the occasional sailing from Castro or Quellón.

**LAN** (O'Higgins 167, Local 1-B, tel. 065/253315) flies several times daily to Santiago, usually nonstop but sometimes via Valdivia, Temuco, or Concepción, or a combination of those. It also flies at least twice daily to Balmaceda/Coyhaique and three or four times daily to Punta Arenas, occasionally stopping in Balmaceda/Coyhaique. Once a week, usually Sunday, it flies from Santiago to Puerto Montt and on to San Carlos de Bariloche, Argentina.

**Sky Airline** (Benavente 405, Local 4, tel. 065/437555) flies frequently to Santiago, far less frequently to Balmaceda/Coyhaique, and to Punta Arenas and Puerto Natales.

No carrier has lasted long on the air-taxi route to Chaitén, a major starting point for overland trips on the Carretera Austral, but **Aerocord** (tel. 065/262300, www.aerocord.cl) and **Cielomaraustral** (Quillota 254, Local 1, tel. 065/264010, cielomaraustral@surnet.cl) have resumed flights to nearby Santa Bárbara (US$85). These leave from Aeródromo La Paloma, on the hill immediately behind the downtown area.

Undergoing a major renovation that will

include a four-star hotel, Puerto Montt's **Terminal de Buses** (Av. Portales and Lota, tel. 065/283000) is about one kilometer southwest of the Plaza de Armas. Services are frequent to rural, regional, and most long-distance destinations, as well as to Bariloche, Argentina. Buses to the Chilean Patagonia destinations of Coyhaique and Punta Arenas, which pass through Argentina, are less frequent but reliable. **Cruz del Sur** (Av. Salvador Allende and Av. Presidente Ibáñez, tel. 065/483127) and its affiliated companies have opened a new terminal on higher ground near the Panamericana but continue to use the downtown terminal as well.

Several companies go to Puerto Varas (US$1.50, 30 minutes), including **Expresos JM, Expreso Puerto Varas,** and **Thaebus** (tel. 065/420120, less frequently). Thaebus also passes through Varas en route to Frutillar and Puerto Octay.

**Buses Fierro** (tel. 065/289024) goes to Lenca (US$2.50), the southerly access point to Parque Nacional Alerce Andino, five times daily except on weekends, when it goes only twice. **Buses JB** (tel. 065/290850) goes to Correntoso (US$2), the northern access point to Alerce Andino, five times daily between 7:40 A.M. and 8:30 P.M. except Sunday, when it goes at 9:10 A.M. and 12:30 and 8:30 P.M.

Monday–Saturday at 8 A.M. and at 1:30, 3, and 5 P.M., **Buses Jordán** (tel. 065/254938) goes to Hornopirén, also known as Río Negro (US$8, 3.5 hours), the summer ferry port to Caleta Gonzalo, the gateway to Parque Natural Pumalín and most of the Carretera Austral. **Kémelbus** (tel. 065/256450, www.kemelbus.cl) runs similar routes but, still, many more visitors use the ferry from Puerto Montt or from Castro or Quellón, on insular Chiloé, to reach Chaitén.

Numerous carriers serve the capital city of Santiago (US$40–75, 12–13 hours) and intermediates including Temuco (US$14, 5.5 hours. **Turismo Futaleufú** goes to Futaleufú (US$53, 11 hours) via Argentina Thursday at 7 A.M. **Trans Austral** (tel. 065/270984) goes to Coyhaique (US$45, 21 hours) Sunday and

© WAYNE BERNHARDSON

**Puerto Montt's new bus terminal will soon include a waterfront hotel.**

Thursday via Argentina. Chiloé destinations include Ancud (US$7, two hours) and Castro (US$10, three hours).

Several companies operate between Puerto Montt and Punta Arenas (US$85, 28 hours) via Argentina, including **Buses Pacheco** (tel. 065/252926), **Pullman Bus** (tel. 065/316561), **Queilen Bus** (tel. 065/253468), and **Turibús** (tel. 065/253245), all of which normally begin in Castro (Chiloé) and pick up passengers here and in Osorno. These are through-buses, not permitted to drop passengers in Argentina. Queilen also goes to Coyhaique (US$60, 22 hours) Monday, Wednesday, and Friday at noon.

Four companies cross the Andes to San Carlos de Bariloche, Argentina (US$23–27, six hours), via Osorno and the Cardenal Samoré pass: **Andesmar** (tel. 065/252926), **Buses Norte Internacional** (tel. 065/254731), **Cruz del Sur** (tel. 065/254731), **Tas Choapa** (tel. 065/254828), and **Vía Bariloche** (tel. 065/253841).

**Andina del Sud** (Antonio Varas 437, tel. 065/257797) sells tickets for the bus-boat relay to Bariloche (US$230) via Puerto Varas, Ensenada, Petrohué, and Peulla. These leave Puerto Montt in the morning, arriving early evening in Bariloche; summer departures are daily, but the rest of the year they're weekdays only and require an overnight stay in Peulla.

From Puerto Montt there are passenger and passenger/vehicle ferries or bus-ferry combinations to Chiloé and Chaitén in Region X, Puerto Chacabuco (the port of Coyhaique) in Region XI (Aisén), and Puerto Natales in Region XII (Magallanes). Since these routes follow the sheltered inland sea, seasickness is usually a minor problem except on the open-ocean crossing of the Golfo de Penas (literally, Gulf of Sorrows), en route to Puerto Natales. In the new passenger terminal, the two main companies are **Naviera Austral** (Av. Angelmó 1673, tel. 065/270430, www.navieraustral.cl) and **Navimag** (Av. Angelmó 1735, tel. 065/432 360, www.navimagferries.com); vehicles, however, still board at the **Terminal de Transbordadores** (Av. Angelmó 2187), about 500 meters west.

Naviera Austral runs routes between Puerto Montt and Chaitén (8–12 hours) on the cramped, aging rustbucket *Pincoya* and the newer, sleeker *Don Baldo* five times weekly. Fares are US$45 per person for reclining seats. Vehicle rates are US$185 for passenger vehicles and small trucks; bicycles cost US$20 and motorcycles US$41.

Substitution of the *Evangelistas* for the smaller *Puerto Edén* has reduced some of the passenger pressure on Navimag's Puerto Montt–Puerto Natales route, but reservations are still advisable in the summer peak; if in Santiago, visit the Navimag office there. Still, it's worth trying for a last-minute berth or cabin. Fares depend on the season and the quality of the accommodations but range US$300–2,470 per person with full board. Bicycles cost an additional US$50, motorcycles US$127, passenger cars US$417, and light trucks US$492; other vehicles pay a linear meter rate.

From September–May, **Cruceros Marítimos Skorpios** (Av. Angelmó 1660, tel. 065/252996, www.skorpios.cl) operates **luxury cruises** to Laguna San Rafael that begin in Puerto Montt; rates on the 140-passenger *Skorpios II* start at US$850 per person and range up to US$2,150 per person. **Cruceros Navimag,** a branch of the ferry company, began similar services in the summer 2011, but buses its passengers to board at Castro, on the Isla Grande de Chiloé.

## Getting Around

From the bus terminal, **Buses ETM** (tel. 065/256253) connects to inbound and outbound flights at **Aeropuerto El Tepual** (tel. 065/252019), which is 16 kilometers west via the Panamericana and a paved lateral. The fare is US$2.50.

For car rentals, try **Econorent** (Antonio Varas 126, tel. 065/481261), **Hertz** (Benavente 690, tel. 065/485993), or **Europcar** (Antonio Varas 162, tel. 065/286277). Note that taking a vehicle into Argentina requires notarial permission.

## PARQUE NACIONAL ALERCE ANDINO

Occupying most of the peninsula only a short distance east of Puerto Montt and south of Lago Chapo, adjoining the Carretera Austral, Alerce Andino takes its name from the Andean false larch, which survives in and around the 39,255-hectare unit. Hiking its rugged woodland trails and camping on the shores of several alpine lakes are its main attractions; because of its proximity to Puerto Montt, it makes an ideal day trip but is also suitable for an overnight.

### Geography and Climate

Park altitudes range from sea level just east of La Arena, on the Estuario de Reloncaví, to 1,558 meters above on Cerro Cuadrado, in the easternmost sector. While altitudes are not extreme, the precipitous terrain and dense forest make off-trail travel difficult. At upper elevations, there are more than 50 lakes and tarns of glacial origins.

The park consists of three distinct sectors. From the village of Chamiza, 10 kilometers east of Puerto Montt via the Carretera Austral, a gravel road leads 19 kilometers east to the northerly Sector Correntoso and, 9 kilometers farther south, to Sector Sargazo. The Carretera Austral passes near the westerly entrance to Sector Chaicas, about 32 kilometers southeast of Puerto Montt.

With its maritime west coast climate, Alerce Andino gets up to 4,500 millimeters of rainfall per year at lower elevations and substantial snowfall above 700–800 meters. Temperatures are mild, averaging about 7°C in winter and 15°C in summer.

### Flora and Fauna

Officially designated a national monument, the long-lived *alerce* spurred the park's creation in 1982. Ranging about 400–700 meters above sea level, it mixes with other species such as *coigüe, tineo, mañío,* and *canelo.* Evergreen rainforest of *coigüe, tepa,* and *ulmo* reaches from sea level up to 900 meters or more, while nearly prostrate *lenga* covers the highest areas.

In such dense forest, wildlife is rarely seen, but there are pumas, pudus, gray fox, and skunks (pudus have been seen in Sector Correntoso's Pangal campground). Birdlife includes the Andean condor, the kingfisher, and waterfowl such as the *pato real* (Chiloé wigeon).

The most conspicuous wildlife, abundant in early summer, is the large but slow-moving biting fly known as the *tábano.* Insect repellent, long trousers, light-colored clothing, and long sleeves are all good precautions, but they're no guarantee of invulnerability.

### Sights and Recreation

Because of deadfalls and landslides, the footpath that once connected the Sargazo and Chaicas sectors is no longer viable, but shorter hikes through dense forests to lakeside campgrounds are still feasible at both.

From Sector Sargazo, **Sendero Laguna Frías** climbs 9.5 kilometers up the Río Sargazo Valley to **Laguna Frías** (tent camping allowed, but it's a feasible day hike with an early start). There are several shorter spur trails, including a 45-minute climb to placid **Laguna Sargazo** itself, where there's a picnic site with rustic tables (no camping allowed).

At Sector Chaicas, the **Sendero Laguna Chaiquenes** up the Río Chaicas Valley leads to **Laguna Chaiquenes** (5.5 kilometers), where the **Sendero Laguna Triángulo** continues another four kilometers to its namesake lake.

For the most up-to-date information on park trails, contact Conaf's Patrimonio Silvestre office in Puerto Montt or rangers at the park entrances.

### Accommodations and Food

At Sector Correntoso, Conaf's **Camping Correntoso** (US$5 for up to six persons) has six wooded sites with reasonable privacy but only two toilets and (cold) showers for all of them. At the Sector Sargazo entrance, **Refugio Laguna Sargazo** (US$10 pp with kitchen privileges and hot showers) makes a good base for day hikers. There is backcountry camping near Laguna Fría, about a 3.5-hour walk from Sargazo.

At the head of the Río Chaica valley, the

## THE REDWOOD OF THE SOUTH

Like California's redwoods, the coniferous *alerce* is long-lived (up to 4,000 years), tall (up to 70 meters), and an attractive, easily worked, and water- and insect-resistant timber. Colonial Spanish shipwrights built vessels from it, and some of Chile's historical monuments – most notably Chiloé's churches – consist of *alerce* timber. Much of the Sur Chico's vernacular architecture, from Puerto Varas's Germanic houses to Chiloé's *palafitos*, also use its lumber.

In Chile, the natural habitat of the *alerce* ranges from coastal Valdivia south to archipelagic and continental Chiloé; it has a narrower distribution across the border in Argentina. Although it grows mostly between 400 and 700 meters above sea level, it also occurs in poorly drained *ñadi* marshlands. The branches of younger specimens touch the ground, but the reddish-barked trunks of mature trees are barren.

Known to the Mapuche as the *lawen*, the species is a national monument thanks to the efforts of the conservation organization Codeff, which somehow persuaded the Pinochet dictatorship to protect the remaining *alerce* forests in 1976, a time when any activism was risky. Darwin gave the tree its botanical name, *Fitzroya cupressoides*, after the famous commanding officer of his equally famous vessel. Still, *The Voyage of the Beagle* offers only a general description.

walk-in **Camping Chaica** (US$2 pp) is the only option in the southern sector.

By the southern approach, on the highway to Hornopirén, Austrian-run **Hostal Mozart** (Carretera Austral Km 25, cell 09/8378-7566, hostalmozart@gmail.com, US$18 pp, US$44–52 d) is a comfortable guesthouse with spacious rooms that range from a five-bed dorm with a shared bath to a sea-view double with its own small deck. The Austrian owners will shuttle guests to Sector Chaicas (US$20 pp round-trip).

Just outside the park boundaries, the secluded **Alerce Mountain Lodge** (Carretera Austral Km 36, tel. 065/286969, www.mountainlodge.cl) is a luxury lodge that specializes in multi-day packages, including activities such as hiking and horseback riding. Prices start around US$1,100 single, US$1,976 double in season, for three-day, two-night packages. Off-season rates (May–October) are about 15–20 percent lower.

En route to Sector Chaicas, a popular choice with guests at Hostal Mozart, **Los Rosales de Pichi Quillaipe** (Carretera Austral Km 20, tel. 09/9920-3692) is a view restaurant that serves Pantagruelian portions of quality regional specialties, such as smoked pork or baked salmon, in the US$12 range. Light eaters might consider sharing a main dish.

### Other Practicalities

Conaf has ranger posts at Sector Correntoso, Sector Sargazo, and Sector Chaicas; park admission costs US$2 except at Correntoso, where there's no charge.

From Puerto Montt, **Buses JB** (tel. 065/290850) goes to the village of **Correntoso** (US$2, one hour), the park's northern access point, five times daily except Sunday, when it goes only thrice (early in the morning and late in the evening). There is no public transport to Sector Sargazo, which means a nine-kilometer walk for those without their own vehicles.

Southbound on the Carretera Austral, **Buses Jordán** will drop passengers at **Lenca** (US$1.50), where a seven-kilometer gravel road ascends the Río Chaica Valley to the park. As at Sargazo, there is no public transport along this route.

## HORNOPIRÉN (RÍO NEGRO) AND VICINITY

At La Arena, 45 kilometers southeast of Puerto Montt, the mouth of the Estuario de Reloncaví interrupts the graveled Carretera Austral, but

## CROSSING THE LAKES

In Walter Salles's 2004 film *The Motorcycle Diaries*, a youthful Ernesto (Che) Guevara and his friend Alberto Granados push their dying motorcycle through a freak summer snowstorm around Lago Frías en route to Chile. The two Argentines were following the **Cruce de Lagos,** a route that's become one of the South America's classics since it opened in the early 20th century.

Connecting the Chilean and Argentine lake districts, the Cruce de Lagos is a boat-bus-boat shuttle between Puerto Montt, Chile, and Bariloche, Argentina. While many people do it in a day, there are accommodations at each end of Lago Todos los Santos that offer opportunities for exploratory hikes.

The more active can go white-water rafting on the Río Petrohué, canyon up steep ravines, or even scale snowcapped Volcán Osorno, a 2,652-meter peak that's a technical challenge. There are fewer places to stay on the Argentine side, except between Bariloche and Puerto Pañuelo. A good network of footpaths makes it possible to hike part of the route. Quite a few cyclists pedal the roads between the water segments of the trip.

The Cruce de Lagos (www.crucedelagos.com) is open all year but best from October to April. While through trips cost around US$230 per person, budget-conscious travelers can do it for less by paying for each leg separately, on the spot – if space is available. For day-trippers and overnighters, Turismo Peulla (San Juan 430, Puerto Varas, tel. 065/437127, www.turismopeulla.cl) offers organized excursions, including hiking (two hours, US$30), horseback riding (1-3 hours, US$40-44), and fly-fishing (three hours, US$70).

Here is a sample itinerary for those who wish to tour both sides of the Andean lakes district by rental car. It's easier to arrange a border-crossing vehicle on the Chilean side. It is important to clarify the insurance situation, as Chilean liability coverage is not normally valid in Argentina. Alternatively, it's simpler to rent a car separately on either side, especially if the bus-boat-bus crossing to Bariloche is on the docket.

© WAYNE BERNHARDSON

**Bariloche-bound passengers board the bus outside Hotel Peulla in Parque Nacional Vicente Pérez Rosales.**

**Day 1**

Arrive in the morning at Santiago's Aeropuerto Internacional Arturo Merino Benítez, make a quick connection to **Puerto Montt,** and overnight in nearby **Puerto Varas;** alternatively, you could spend an afternoon sightseeing in **Santiago,** with a seafood lunch at the Mercado Central, and take a comfortable sleeper bus to Puerto Varas or Puerto Montt.

**Day 2**

For orientation, take a leisurely drive around **Lago Llanquihue** via **Frutillar, Puerto Octay, Ensenada,** and Puerto Varas. With an early start, it's possible to continue south from Ensenada to **Cochamó** and **Puelo,** along the Estuario de Reloncaví, and come back to Puerto Montt or Puerto Varas via the Caleta Puelche ferry shuttle.

**Days 3-4**

From Puerto Varas, depart in the morning for **Bariloche,** Argentina, on the bus-boat-bus

CHILEAN LAKES DISTRICT

crossing via **Lago Todos los Santos.** Find accommodations in or near Bariloche.

The next day, take a morning tour of Bariloche, followed by an excursion on the **Circuito Chico** loop in **Parque Nacional Nahuel Huapi,** including a stiff trail hike to **Cerro López.**

**Days 5-6**
Via rental car, preferably, plan a morning departure for **Villa La Angostura,** on Lago Nahuel Huapi's north shore, leaving most of the day for hiking, mountain biking, or kayaking in the vicinity. The next morning, take a long but not taxing day hike to the myrtle forest of **Parque Nacional Los Arrayanes** and back; those with less stamina can take a comfortable boat either or both ways.

**Day 7**
Drive to **San Martín de los Andes** via the leisurely **Siete Lagos** (Seven Lakes) route. Take an afternoon boat excursion on **Lago Lácar** or a tour of city.

**Days 8-9**
Leave in the morning for the north shore of Lago Huechulafquen in **Parque Nacional Lanín,** via **Junín de los Andes.** Use in-park accommodations or camp so you can go hiking, horseback riding, or fishing.

The following morning, take a full-day hike through *pewen* forest on the south shore of **Lago Huechulafquen** and **Lago Paimún.**

**Day 10**
Return to Bariloche via Junín de los Andes and RN 40, pausing at **Estancia Fortín Chacabuco** for a horseback ride and an *asado* (barbecue).

**Days 11-12**
Drive south on RN 40 to the turnoff for Parque Nacional Nahuel Huapi's **Ventisquero Negro** (Black Glacier), south of Bariloche. After the scenic detour, arrive in the afternoon at **El Bolsón.**

The following morning, if it's market day visit the lively Feria Artesanal and then enjoy a short afternoon hike at **Parque Nacional Lago Puelo;** if it's not market day, hike to the summit of **Cerro Piltriquitrón** for a panoramic view of the Andes along the Chilean border, to the west.

**Day 13**
Make an early return to Bariloche for your bus connection to Puerto Montt or Puerto Varas.

**Day 14**
Depart in the morning for Santiago. Spend the day sightseeing, then catch an evening flight home.

## IF YOU HAVE MORE TIME . . .

**Day 14**
Plan a morning departure for **Ancud,** Chiloé, with an afternoon visit to the mixed Magellanic and Humboldt penguin colony at **Monumento Natural Islotes de Puñihuil.**

**Days 15-16**
Leave in the morning for **Castro** and **Cucao** in Parque Nacional Chiloé, where there are short hikes near park headquarters. There are simple B&B and cabaña accommodations near the park entrance.

The next morning, take a full-day hike along the Pacific shoreline of **Parque Nacional Chiloé,** returning to Puerto Montt or Puerto Varas for accommodations.

**Days 17-18**
One possible excursion is from Castro to the port of **Quellón** for a day's blue whale-watching in the Golfo de Corcovado, then returning to Puerto Montt or Puerto Varas for accommodations. Alternatively, you could overnight at **Parque Tantauco,** on Chiloé's remote southwestern shore, which is reached by motor launch only.

**Day 19**
Catch an early flight to Santiago, leaving the afternoon free for sightseeing and lunch at one of Barrio Bellavista's fine restaurants, followed by an evening departure from Santiago's Aeropuerto Internacional Arturo Merino Benítez.

frequent ferries cross the water to Puelche, where the road continues to Hornopirén (also known as Río Negro), 48 kilometers farther south. Hornopirén (population about 1,500) is the access point for its little-visited namesake national park, only a few kilometers east; it is also the northern port for the summer vehicle/passenger ferry to Caleta Gonzalo and Parque Natural Pumalín.

### Parque Nacional Hornopirén

Only a short distance east of town, Parque Nacional Hornopirén is an almost totally undeveloped 48,232-hectare park surrounded by several volcanoes, including 1,210-meter Apagado, 1,572-meter Hornopirén, and 2,187-meter Yates. Access is difficult, though, because of bad roads.

### Accommodations and Food

Rates at the aging but charming **Hotel Hornopirén** (Ignacio Carrera Pinto 388, tel. 065/217256, www.hotelhornopiren.cl, US$24 pp with shared bath) include breakfast; lunch and dinner are optional. In addition, there's a cluster of inexpensive *hospedajes* (family-run lodgings) opposite the ferry ramp, as well as the more developed **Hostería Catalina** (Ingenieros Militares s/n, tel. 065/217359, www.hosteriacatalina.cl, US$15 pp with shared bath, US$45 s, US$58 d with private bath).

At the ferry ramp, several simple *cocinerías* (eateries) prepare fresh fish for those awaiting the *Mailén*.

### Other Practicalities

From Puerto Montt, **Buses Jordán** (tel. 065/254938) and **Kémelbus** (tel. 065/256450, www.kemelbus.cl) each go to Hornopirén (US$8, 3.5 hours) three or four times daily except Sunday, when they go only twice. In summer, the scheduled 2:30 P.M. departures from Hornopirén wait for the ferry from Caleta Gonzalo.

Both buses and private vehicles must cross from La Arena to Puelche over the Estuario de Reloncaví, where **Naviera Puelche** (tel. 065/270000, www.navieraparedes.cl) shuttles the ferries *Trauco* and *Gobernador Figueroa* 6:15 A.M.–12:30 A.M. The half-hour voyage costs US$20 for cars and light trucks, US$14 for motorcycles, US$5 for bicycles; passengers pay US$1 per person.

In January and February only, Naviera's Austral's ferry *Mailén* (cell 09/9939-7895) sails from Hornopirén to **Caleta Gonzalo** (five hours) at 9 A.M. Sunday, Monday, and Tuesday; the rest of the year, it has only one service monthly. Passengers pay US$21 per person, cyclists an extra US$13, and motorcyclists US$25. Automobiles and light trucks pay US$140, while larger vehicles pay per linear meter.

## Insular Chiloé



The heartland of Chilean folklore, greener than Washington and Oregon, rain-soaked Chiloé is an archipelago whose wild western woodlands are darker than the Black Forest and traversed by trails leading to secluded ocean beaches with rolling dunes. Its cultural landscape is a mosaic of field and forest, and its seas yield some of Chile's most diverse seafood.

Chiloé also includes the associated mainland area that is inaccessible overland. The main island is the Isla Grande de Chiloé; some 180 kilometers long and 50 kilometers wide, one of about 40 islands in the group, it is not only Chile's largest island but South America's second largest—only Tierra del Fuego is larger. The sheltered inlets on its more densely populated east coast are ideal for sea kayaking, linking peasant villages with a unique vernacular architecture of elaborately shingled houses—a handful of them stilted *palafitos*—and churches.

Though it can rain in any season, summer is the best time to visit, as days are long enough at least to hope for a break in the drizzle. On the Pacific side, penguins—the ranges of the Humboldt and Magellanic species overlap here—also breed in summer.

## HISTORY

Pre-Columbian Chiloé was the province of the Huilliche, the southernmost branch of the Mapuche, who netted and trapped fish, gathered shellfish such as sea urchins, and cultivated maize and especially potatoes in its cool, damp climate. Their insularity bred a self-reliance that persists to the present, as residents have ingeniously adapted native materials into technologically simple but useful artifacts.

Spain founded the city of Castro in 1567, but Jesuit missionaries soon established a circuit around what they called the "last outpost of Christianity." Before their 1767 expulsion from the Americas, the Jesuits encouraged the construction of wooden churches and chapels that were predecessors of the 50-plus scattered around the archipelago, which led to its designation as a UNESCO World Heritage Site.

Refugees fleeing the mainland Mapuche insurrection of the early 17th century found a haven here, creating the first permanent European presence. Their geographical isolation took political form in a conservatism that made them the Spanish empire's last holdouts in Chile, which failed to conquer the fortress of Ancud until 1826.

Economically, isolation meant poverty, though not starvation. Darwin remarked, a few years after Spain's expulsion, that "there is no demand for labour, and consequently the lower orders cannot scrape together money sufficient to purchase even the smallest luxuries," and that barter was pervasive. Emigration for employment became a way of life—buses still leave the Isla Grande for southern Patagonia every day—but developments of the past two decades have improved the economy and reduced isolation. Ferries constantly shuttle across the Canal Chacao to the mainland, and salmon farming, despite serious environmental drawbacks, has brought a measure of prosperity. In summer, the tourist trade also makes a substantial contribution.

## ANCUD

On a sheltered harbor with good ocean access, the late colonial outpost of San Carlos de Ancud defended Spain's Pacific coastline from foreign powers and privateers so well that it held out for nearly a decade after Chile's 1818 declaration of independence. Only the Peruvian port of Callao stayed in Spanish hands longer.

The former fortress was once a major port of entry, but the 1912 arrival of the railroad to Puerto Montt undercut its economic base, and it now relies on fishing for its livelihood. It is now Chiloé's largest town, and its headlands provide exceptional coastal views.

### Orientation

On the Isla Grande's northern coast, facing the Canal Chacao, which divides the archipelago from the mainland, San Carlos de Ancud (population about 30,000) is 90 kilometers southwest of Puerto Montt, 27 kilometers west of the Pargua–Chacao ferry crossing. Some 87 kilometers north of Castro via the Panamericana, which skirts the city's eastern approach, it occupies a hilly peninsular site whose irregular terrain has generated an equally irregular but compact city plan around the trapezoidal Plaza de Armas.

### Sights

At the southwest corner of the Plaza de Armas, the **Museo Azul de las Islas de Chiloé,** alternatively known as the **Museo Aurelio Bórquez Canobra,** is the regional museum (Libertad 370, tel. 065/622413, 9:30 A.M.–8 P.M. daily, closing at 7:30 P.M. Sat., Jan.–Feb.; 10 A.M.–5:30 P.M. Tues.–Fri., 10 A.M.–2 P.M. weekends and holidays the rest of the year, US$1.25 for adults, US$0.25 for children). Colloquially known as the Museo Chilote, it reopened in February 2011 after a major renovation that's improved the exhibits on the archipelago's natural environment and wildlife (with a major nod to Darwin), regional archaeology, European settlement (including Dutch exploration), ecclesiastical art and architecture, stunning photographs of the 1960 earthquake and tsunami

© WAYNE BERNHARDSON

Ancud's renovated Museo Azul de las Islas de Chiloé includes a full blue whale skeleton.

(which literally shook the island into the present), the Castro–Ancud railway (destroyed by the quake), and a vivid relief map of the archipelago. The patios feature items such as petrified logs and a full blue whale skeleton.

New in 2010, the **Fundación Amigos Iglesias de Chiloé** (Errázuriz 227, tel. 065/621046, www.iglesiasdechiloe.cl, 9 A.M.–7 P.M. daily in summer, 9 A.M.–6 P.M. weekdays only the rest of the year, free) has converted the former Convento Inmaculada Concepción into a museum that provides an outstanding overview of Chiloé's UNESCO heritage of wooden churches. It has not only meticulously crafted models of many of them, with descriptions in good English, but also a sample of doors, windows, and other architectural features salvaged from the original structures.

Guarding the harbor from a promontory just west of the intersection of Cochrane and San Antonio, the colonial **Fuerte San Antonio** (1770) was Spain's last Chilean stronghold during the independence struggles—revolutionary forces finally lowered the Spanish flag and raised their own in 1826. Its cannon emplacements are still intact. It's now fenced and open 9 A.M.–8 P.M. daily; there is no admission charge.

## Entertainment and Events

Performing-arts events take place at the **Teatro Municipal de Ancud** (Blanco Encalada 660), on the east side of the Plaza de Armas, and the **Casa de la Cultura** (Libertad 663, tel. 065/628164), alongside the museum.

Late January's **Semana Ancuditana** (Ancud Week) celebrates the city's founding, the island's folkloric music and dance, and traditional food. Throughout December and January, though, there are similar events in nearby communities.

For drinks, try the **Retro Pub** (Maipú 615) or the nearby **Lumiere Bar** (Ramírez 278).

## Shopping

Chiloé's crafts offerings include ceramics, wood carvings, and woolens. Outlets include the **Museo Chilote** (Libertad 370) and the **Mercado Municipal** (Dieciocho between Libertad and Blanco Encalada). **Austral Adventures** (Av. Costanera 904, tel. 065/625977) carries a small selection of quality crafts, including liqueurs made from *calafate* and *arrayán* berries.

## Accommodations

Ancud has plenty of accommodations, ranging from camping to mostly midrange choices, with a handful of not-quite-upmarket alternatives.

Surveying the shoreline from its location above Playa Gruesa, about 600 meters north of downtown, **Camping Arena Gruesa** (Costanera Norte 290, tel. 065/623428, www.arenagruesa.cl, US$8 pp) has 60 lighted sites with improved privacy, hot showers, firewood, and other conveniences; on the same site, it's also added the cheerful new **Hostal Arena Gruesa** (US$36 s, US$56 d with private bath). In this residential neighborhood, the major drawbacks are barking dogs and crowing roosters.

Under new management who've invested it with *buena onda* (good vibes), the best budget choice is immaculate **Hostal Terramar** (Bellavista 457, tel. 065/620493, www.terramarhostel.com, US$14 pp in dorms, US$24–30 s, US$36–40 d), engagingly decorated with painted flowers on its doors, walls, and even furniture. The rooms aren't large, but they're well furnished, and those with private baths are only slightly more expensive; the common areas are spacious and inviting. It lacks parking.

Run by a Chilean-Colombian couple, **Hostal Chiloé Mágico** (Baquedano 156, tel. 065/628476, parrillahostalchiloemagico@gmail.com, US$20 pp) affects a rustic style, what with its rough-hewn timbers and irregular stairsteps, but it's deceptively modern, if less than luxurious, inside. The beds are comfortable and firm, there are plenty of power outlets, and wireless Internet reaches the rooms easily from the office. On weekends, though, when its downstairs restaurant hosts private events that go late, it can get noisy.

All rooms at **Hotel Madryn** (Bellavista 491, tel. 065/622128, www.hotelmadryn.cl, US$40 s, US$50 d) come with private baths, cable TV, and breakfast, and some have sea views. Some rooms are a little irregular in shape but still functional.

**Hostal Vista al Mar** (Av. Salvador Allende 918, tel./fax 065/622617, www.vistaalmar.cl, US$20 pp in dorms, US$36–48 s, US$48–56 d) has moderately priced accommodations with shared baths but has added others with private baths and even some cabañas.

Arguably Ancud's best value, the nearly pristine, Swiss-run **Hostal Mundo Nuevo** (Av. Costanera Salvador Allende 748, tel. 065/628383, www.newworld.cl, US$17–19 pp in dorms, US$50–72 d) provides spacious rooms, firm new beds, panoramic sunsets through the glassed porch, a fine breakfast, an ample kitchen for the budget-conscious, and secure parking. Given its popularity, reservations are advisable.

For the best views, at least from the common areas, there's **Hotel Ancud** (San Antonio 30, tel. 065/622340, Santiago tel. 02/2349610, www.panamericanahoteles.cl, US$90 s or d); since its acquisition by the Panamericana group, the facilities and service have improved. Still, the common areas outshine the rooms, which are on the small side.

**Hotel Don Lucas** (Av. Costanera 906, tel. 065/620950, www.hoteldonlucas.cl, US$58 s, US$92 d) lacks the imposing location of Hotel Ancud, but its upper rooms still enjoy good ocean views, and they're considerably larger than the older hotel's. Some local operators prefer it for their overseas clients, but it does front on a busy avenue.

**Hotel Galeón Azul** (Libertad 751, tel. 065/622567, www.hotelgaleonazul.cl, US$80 s, US$96 d) is cheerful and central but wins no points for truth in labeling—the "Blue Galeon" sports a bright yellow paint job.

## Food

Most restaurant menus are similar in content—fish and shellfish—and in price, mostly in the US$9–12 range for most items. Salads are easily large enough for two.

At **Kurantón** (Prat 94, tel. 065/622216, lunch and dinner daily) the specialty is, obviously, their signature seafood stew, *curanto* (US$12), but the menu also stresses fish, mostly hake and salmon, with seafood sauces for around US$11. It has an eclectic decor of folkloric figures from Chiloé (with a soundtrack to match), plus bullfight posters, maritime memorabilia, and photos, but the kitchen can be slow.

More elaborate seafood venues include the nearby **La Pincoya** (Prat 61, tel. 065/622613, lunch and dinner daily), **Polo Sur** (Av. Salvador Allende 630, tel. 065/622200, lunch and dinner daily), and especially **Mascarón de Proa** (Baquedano 560, tel. 065/621979, lunch and dinner daily), which is the best view restaurant.

New in 2011, the rustically elegant **El Patagon de Chiloe** (Pudeto 15, tel. 065/620499) has a great waterfront location and perhaps more potential than any other restaurant in town. Dishes such as grilled hake (US$9) with a choice of side dishes (try the *merkén*-spiced potatoes) are fine, but it lacks personality (the odd Led Zeppelin track doesn't fit, even for those who like Led Zep).

The **Retro Pub** (Maipú 615, tel. 065/626410, lunch and dinner daily) breaks the local mold by daring to serve pizza and even some Mexican dishes. For a relatively elegant splurge, **Casa Mar** (Costanera Salvador Allende and Errázuriz, tel. 065/624481, lunch and dinner daily) has a more elaborate menu that includes more sophisticated versions of traditional fish and seafood and also extends to sushi.



## Information

**Sernatur** (Libertad 665, tel. 065/622800, infochiloe@sernatur.cl) is the island's best-equipped office in terms of maps, brochures, and up-to-date accommodations data. In summer, it's open 8:30 A.M.–8 P.M. weekdays, 9 A.M.–1 P.M. and 2:30–7 P.M. weekends. The rest of the year, hours are 8:30 A.M.–5:30 P.M. weekdays only.

On the Plaza de Armas, the helpful **Oficina Municipal de Turismo** (Pudeto and Blanco Encalada, tel. 065/487624, oficinaturismo@muniancud.cl) is open 8:30 A.M.–9 P.M. weekdays in summer, 8:30 A.M.–6 P.M. weekdays the rest of the year. At the Mercado Municipal, its satellite office (Dieciocho s/n, tel. 065/628163, turismomuniancud@gmail.com) is open 9 A.M.–7:30 P.M. daily in summer, 8:30 A.M.–6 P.M. daily the rest of the year.

## Services

Ancud has no exchange houses, but **BancoEstado** (Ramírez 222) has one of several ATMs.

For postal services, **Correos de Chile** is at Pudeto and Blanco Encalada. **Zona PC** (Pudeto 276, Local 2) has Internet access and phones.

**Clean Center** (Pudeto 45, tel. 065/623838) does the washing.

**Hospital de Ancud** (Almirante Latorre 301, tel. 065/622355) can handle medical matters.

## Getting There and Around

Ancud's long-distance **Terminal de Buses** (Aníbal Pinto and Marcos Vera), about 1.2 kilometers east of downtown, is relatively new but increasingly rundown. **Cruz del Sur** (Los Carrera 850, tel. 065/622249, www.busescruzdelsur.cl) has opened its own glistening new terminal, which is more convenient to downtown.

There are many northbound buses to Puerto Montt and on to Santiago and intermediates, southbound buses to Castro and Quellón, and services to Punta Arenas via Argentina with **Queilen Bus** (tel. 065/621140) and **Turibús** (tel. 065/622289).

Typical destinations, times, and fares include Castro (US$4, one hour), Chonchi (US$5, 1.5 hours), Puerto Montt (US$8, two hours), Temuco (US$18–26, seven hours), Santiago (US$42–62, 15 hours), and Punta Arenas (US$50–70, 32 hours).

For buses to destinations other than those on or along the Panamericana, the **Terminal de Buses Rurales** is at Pedro Montt and Colo Colo.

**Transmarchilay** (www.tmc.cl) and **Cruz del Sur** ferries sail between Pargua and Chacao, charging US$19 for automobiles and light trucks, US$11 for motorcycles, US$3 for bicycles; foot passengers go for US$1.25.

## VICINITY OF ANCUD

Ancud's U.S.-Peruvian **Austral Adventures** (Av. Costanera 904, tel./fax 065/625977, www.austral-adventures.com) conducts multi-day hikes along the island's wild northwest coast and custom sea kayak trips. Its specialty, though, is extended explorations of the archipelago's inner waters and points south on the 15-meter *Cahuella,* whose exterior resembles a traditional Chilote fishing boat but whose interior has contemporary comforts.

In a kiosk at the Mercado Municipal, **Aki Turismo** (Dieciocho s/n, tel. 065/545253, www.akiturismochiloe.cl) arranges local excursions, such as trips to the Puñihuil penguin colony and to the island's churches and chapels.

### Monumento Natural Islotes de Puñihuil

About 27 kilometers southwest of Ancud, the offshore islets of Puñihuil are home to summer breeding colonies of both Magellanic and Humboldt penguins, whose ranges overlap here. Ancud's **Austral Adventures** (Av. Costanera 904, tel. 065/625977, 9 A.M.–7 P.M. daily) handles reservations for the comfortable boats that Chilote fishers use to shuttle penguin-watchers from the sandy beach into the surrounding waters. Two hours advance notice is necessary; at Puñihuil, those with reservations have priority.

**Bahía Puñihuil,** one of several restaurants along the beach, serves simple but artful fish and seafood dishes at modest prices (around US$8 with a side dish).

### Chepu

About 40 kilometers southwest of Ancud via Ruta 5 and a gravel road, set among Chiloé's rugged western mountains, the village of Chepu has a nascent kayak scene on wetlands created by the massive 1960 tsunami that struck the area. Today its "sunken forest" is a prime **birding** destination. Here a relocated Santiago couple has created an eco-campground (US$8), with wind turbines, solar-powered hot water, and toilets overlooking the river. There are also simple but stylish four-bed dormitories (US$10 pp), using the campground's shared toilets, and newer ones with private baths (US$60 s or d). Cooking facilities are limited, but the owners can help arrange meals, including lamb barbecues, at nearby locations.

In addition to kayaking, there are excursions to a nearby penguin colony, reached by boat and a hike. Children under 18 are not permitted because of safety concerns about the river. For more information, contact English-speaking Fernando Claude at **Chepu Adventures** (P.O. Box 402, Ancud, tel. 09/9379-2481, www.chepuadventures.com).

Only a couple kilometers west, the more rustic **Los Senderos de Chepu** (tel. 09/9260-2423, www.actiweb.es/senderoschepu, US$30 pp with full board) gets high marks from local operators and guests alike for charm and graciousness, as well as excursions including guided horseback rides (US$20 for four hours). There's also the unique *maderocarril* (a short-line railcar that runs on wooden "rails" and ends at a forest grove where there's a good hour's hike).

Every Monday, Wednesday, and Friday, there are two buses daily from Ancud to Chepu, which pass directly by the entrance to Chepu Adventures but turn around before reaching Los Senderos de Chepu. The first leaves at 6:30 A.M. from the Esso service station at the corner of Prat and Goycolea; the second departs at 4 P.M. from the Terminal de Buses Rurales (Pedro Montt and Colo Colo). For US$10 per person, Fernando Claude will also pick up passengers at kilometer 25 on the Panamericana for those who have booked cabañas or kayak trips. A taxi from Ancud costs about US$24–30 but can be shared by several people.

## CASTRO

The Isla Grande's first urban settlement, Castro dates from 1567, when Martín Ruiz de Gamboa made it the base for evangelizing the southern Huilliche and Chonos. Despite the activities of Franciscan, Mercedarian, and Jesuit missionaries, it remained a poor and isolated backwater, subject to earthquakes, tsunamis, fires, and sacking by privateers.

© WAYNE BERNHARDSON

At high tide, the water reaches more than halfway up Castro's *palafitos*.

In 1834, barely two decades after Chilean independence was declared, Charles Darwin found Castro to be "a most forlorn and deserted place." Even in the early 20th century, it had barely a thousand inhabitants, and its isolation had fostered a distinctive townscape still characterized by its surviving *palafitos,* the stilted waterfront houses with their elaborately carved shingles. By 1912, a narrow-gauge railroad linked it with Ancud and the rest of the country, as farm products increased port activity.

The 1960 earthquake devastated the city, but salmon farming sparked a recovery that has continued to this day. Improved ferry services have brought regular tourist traffic of Chileans and foreigners, especially Argentines.

## Orientation

Castro (population about 37,000), 88 kilometers south of Ancud via the Panamericana, is a central location for Isla Grande excursions. Its compact central grid occupies a broad plain above the Estero de Castro, a sheltered ocean inlet, while Avenida Pedro Montt curves around the shoreline at sea level.

## Sights

Castro's sights give it greater tourist appeal than any other city on the island, but it's also a fine base for excursions.

On the north side of the refurbished Plaza de Armas, the landmark **Iglesia San Francisco** represents both change and continuity in Chiloé's architectural tradition. After fire destroyed its Franciscan-built predecessor in 1902, ecclesiastical authorities broke with tradition in hiring an Italian architect, Eduardo Provasoli, who incorporated both neo-Gothic and classical elements into the twin-tower structure. At the same time, employing local master builders and artisans ensured that Chilote elements would survive in the ironclad wooden building, which was begun in 1906 but not completed until 1912.

Now a national monument, the church has changed its colors without surrendering its flamboyance—instead of salmon and violet, its galvanized-iron exterior is now banana yellow with violet towers and dashes of reddish trim—but its repainting is long, long overdue. The burnished-wood interior is more somber, embellished with traditional Catholic statuary—some of it grisly renderings of the crucifixion.

Half a block south of the Plaza de Armas, bursting at the seams of its cramped facilities, the **Museo Regional de Castro** (Esmeralda 255, tel. 065/635967, 9:30 A.M.–7 P.M. Mon.–Fri., 9:30 A.M.–6:30 P.M. Sat., 10:30 A.M.–1 P.M. Sun. in summer; 9:30 A.M.–1 P.M. Mon.–Sat., 3–6:30 P.M. weekdays only the rest of the year, free but donations welcome) displays Huilliche artifacts and ethnographic materials, "appropriate technology" from the surrounding countryside, accounts of the island's urban development, and excellent photographic exhibits. As of 2011, though, it still looks as if its move to new waterfront quarters for Chile's 2010 bicentennial may have to wait until the tricentennial.

Now sitting in the newly developed **Plazuela El Tren,** a waterfront park on Avenida Pedro Montt, the **Locomotora Ancud-Castro** hauled passengers and freight on the narrow-gauge railroad between 1912 and 1960, when an earthquake and tsunami ended the island's train service. The route either followed or paralleled the present-day Panamericana.

Occupying airy, well-lighted quarters that once were warehouses, the **Museo de Arte Moderno de Chiloé** (MAM, Galvarino Riveros s/n, tel. 065/635454, www.mamchiloe.cl, free) stresses up-and-coming Chilean (mostly Chilote) painters, sculptors, and multimedia specialists. On the grounds of the Parque Municipal, the MAM is open 10 A.M.–6 P.M. daily in January and February, when invited artists show their latest work. In November, December, and March, hours are 11 A.M.–2 P.M. daily, but it's closed the rest of the year except by appointment.

Until the 1960 earthquake and tsunami, shingled, stilted *palafitos* lined nearly all the Isla Grande's eastern shore estuaries, but only a handful survive today, most notably in Castro and its vicinity. Traditionally, Chilote fishermen would tie their vessels to the pilings out their back doors, but the houses themselves front on city streets.

Castro has the largest remaining assortment of this unique vernacular architecture, along the Costanera Avenida Pedro Montt at the northern approach to town, only two blocks from the Plaza de Armas at the Costanera's south end, and on both sides of the Río Gamboa bridge, southwest of the city center via the Panamericana.

At the south end of the Costanera, the waterfront **Feria Artesanal** integrates tourist appeal—typical woolens, souvenir basketry, and *palafito* seafood restaurants—with practical items such as food (including edible algae) and fuel (blocks of peat). While Dalcahue's Sunday crafts market gets more hype, this daily market rates nearly as highly.

## Entertainment and Events

The **Centro Cultural de Castro** (Serrano 320, tel. 065/635531) is Castro's main performing-arts venue, but it also offers special art exhibitions plus myriad classes and other activities.

Mid-February's **Festival Costumbrista** is a weekend event with island crafts, folkloric music and dance, traditional foods such as *curanto* (seafood stew) and *yoco* (a pork dish), and liquors such as *chicha* (cider, usually made from apples).

## Shopping

In addition to the Feria Artesanal, the **Almacén de la Biodiversidad** (Lillo 1) carries a selection of quality handicrafts, such as woolens and even scale models of Chilote churches, by island artisans.

Castro has two excellent bookstores, **El Tren Libros** (Thompson 299, tel. 065/633936) and **Anay Libros** (Serrano 437, tel. 065/630158).

## Accommodations

Of several budget accommodations, the best central value is **Hospedaje Mirador** (Barros Arana 127, tel. 065/633795, www.hostalelmiradorcastro.cl, US$20 pp, US$50 d with breakfast), an immaculate place on a pedestrian staircase overlooking the port; the more expensive rooms have private baths.

Castro's most distinctive new accommodations can be found at the **Palafito Hostel** (Ernesto Riquelme 1210, tel. 065/531008, www.palafitohostel.com, US$24 pp, US$40 s, US$60 d), near the Gamboa Bridge. The owners have completely rebuilt and expanded an existing *palafito* and turned it into a luminous eight-room designer hostel that's more of a B&B—all rooms, even the dorms, have private baths, and the building incorporates elements of the island's maritime heritage, such as curved walls. Even travelers normally wary of a hostel should consider staying here.

One of Castro's best-kept secrets is **Hostal Casa Kolping** (Chacabuco 217, tel. 065/633273, www.kolping.cl, US$36 s, US$50 d), an immaculate and architecturally notable place in a quiet location south of the plaza, but enough people know about it that reservations are advisable. All the rooms have central heating, unusual in a building of this vintage, but the singles are small. Off-season rates, about 25 percent lower, are a steal.

Embellished with native wood and carpeted floors, **Hostal Casita Española** (Los Carrera 359, tel. 065/635186, www.hosteriadecastro.cl/ce, US$46 s, US$62 d) is operated under the same management as the pricier Hostería de Castro.

Dating from 1910, a hotel only since 1986, the quirky **Hotel Unicornio Azul** (Pedro Montt 228, tel. 065/632359, www.hotelunicornioazul.cl, US$80 s, US$95 d) was once a budget hotel, but steady improvements have driven prices upward. Rooms vary considerably in size, shape, and view, so don't take anything without seeing it first.

Seemingly taking its cues from the nearby Palafito Hostel, the **Palafito 1326 Hotel Boutique** (Ernesto Riquelme 1326, tel. 065/530053, www.palafito1326.cl, US$77–99 s, US$88–110 d) has done an even more spectacular transformation and expansion of a stilted house, with a dozen smartly furnished rooms decorated with native woods. Rates vary according to whether the room has street-side or sea views, but everyone can make use of the decks and spectacular rooftop terrace, which face the water.

Despite its offbeat chalet design (on an island that rarely gets snow), the **Hostería de Castro Hotel & Spa** (Chacabuco 202, tel. 065/632301, www.hosteriadecastro.cl, US$90 s, US$108 d) traditionally vies for the honor of being Castro's best hotel in its price range. Amenities include sea views, a restaurant and bar, an indoor pool, and wireless Internet. It has remodeled two rooms into more elaborate (and expensive) suites.

## Food

Facing the plaza, **La Brújula del Cuerpo** (O'Higgins 308, tel. 065/633229) now calls itself a grill, but the café menu of breakfasts, sandwiches, coffee, and desserts hasn't really changed much. It remains popular, though.

Most of the best are seafood venues, such as **Sacho** (Thompson 213, tel. 065/632079, lunch and dinner daily), **Dónde Eladio** (Lillo 97, tel. 065/635285, lunch and dinner daily), and **El Bucanero** (Lillo s/n, tel. 065/637260, lunch and dinner daily).

**Octavio** (Av. Pedro Montt 261, tel. 065/632855, lunch and dinner daily) offers waterfront dining with style and fine service at moderate prices with a diverse menu. Entrées range from US$7 (chicken) to US$19 (king crab), but most fishes dishes fall into the US$9–10 range. It has occasional live music, but, on the minus side, the pisco sours are a little small, and switching off the TV would enhance the experience.

The ambitious **Hicamar** (Gamboa 413, tel. 065/532655, lunch and dinner daily) has a large menu of meat, game, and fish dishes that mostly fall into the US$12–16 range. The portions are not excessive, but neither are they tiny—rather, they strike a happy medium. The service is exemplary.

Castro's best new restaurant, though, is **El Embrujo** (Thompson 244-B, tel. 065/533032, www.elembrujo.cl, dinner Mon.–Sat.), which has a wide choice of fish dishes with shellfish sauces ranging from scallops to shrimp to king crab, for around US$15; side orders include stir-fried native potatoes (Chiloé is a center of genetic diversity for spuds). The homemade blueberry and raspberry ice cream is excellent, the pisco sours are fine, the wine list outstanding for a provincial city (with several varietals by the glass), and service is conscientious.

### Information

Directly on the Plaza de Armas, the municipal **Oficina de Información Turística** (tel. 065/547706) is open 9:30 A.M.–8 P.M. weekdays, 10:30 A.M.–8 P.M. Saturday, 11 A.M.–8 P.M. Sunday in summer. The rest of the year, hours are 10 A.M.–7 P.M. weekdays only.

**Conaf** (Gamboa 424, tel. 065/532501, 8:30 A.M.–5 P.M. weekdays only) can provide information on Parque Nacional Chiloé.

### Services

**Cambio Julio Barrientos** (Chacabuco 286) changes foreign money. **BancoEstado** (San Martín 397) has an ATM.

**Correos de Chile** (O'Higgins 388) handles the mail. The **Centro de Llamados** (Blanco 398) is one of several long-distance telephone providers.

The **Clean Center** (Balmaceda 220, tel. 065/633132) does laundry for about US$2 per kilo.

For medical assistance, contact the **Hospital de Castro** (Freire 852, tel. 065/632445).

### Getting There and Around

Most local and long-distance bus companies use the deceptively named **Terminal de Buses Rurales** (San Martín 667). **Cruz del Sur** (San Martín 486, tel. 065/632389) has its own terminal, also used by **Turibús** (tel. 065/632389) and **Transchiloé** (tel. 065/635152). Some companies have ticket agents at both sites.

Cruz del Sur goes south to Chonchi and north to Ancud and Puerto Montt, offering continuing service to Santiago and intermediates. Transchiloé has similar routes. Several carriers go to Punta Arenas, including **Queilen Bus** (tel. 065/632173), **Buses Pacheco** (tel. 065/631188), and Turibús.

At the Terminal de Buses Rurales, **Buses Arroyo** (tel. 065/635604) goes three times daily to Cucao (US$3), the gateway to Parque Nacional Chiloé; **Buses Ojeda** (065/573488) and **Interlagos** (tel. 09/9772-1222) have additional services on the same route. **Dalcahue Expreso** (tel. 065/635164) goes at least half hourly to Dalcahue on weekdays but less frequently on weekends. **Buses Lemuy** and **Buses Gallardo** (tel. 065/630529) serve Chonchi (US$1.50). *Taxi colectivos* to Chonchi leave from the corner of Chacabuco and Esmeralda.

Sample destinations, fares, and times include Ancud (US$4, one hour), Puerto Montt (US$12, three hours), Temuco (US$22–30, eight hours), Santiago (US$46–66, 17 hours), and Punta Arenas (US$55–75, 34 hours).

In summer only, Sunday at 9 A.M., **Naviera Austral** (Esmeralda 198, tel. 065/635254) sails the slow ferry *Pincoya* to Chaitén (eight hours) from the modernized port on the Costanera. Fares are US$32 per person, US$15 per bicycle, US$35 per motorcycle, and US$165 for an automobile or light truck.

LAN and perhaps Sky Airline are due to begin flights to Castro in 2012, but details are not yet available.

## VICINITY OF CASTRO

Several companies conduct day trips and longer tours, including destinations such as Dalcahue, Chonchi, Parque Nacional Chiloé, and offshore islands. Among them are **Turismo Quelcún** (San Martín 581, tel. 065/632396), **Turismo Queilen Bus** (San Martín 667, tel. 065/632173), at the Terminal de Buses Rurales, and **Pehuén Turismo** (Latorre 238, tel. 065/635254, www.turismopehuen.cl).

### Dalcahue

Artisans from around Chiloé customarily present their best at Dalcahue's Sunday market, still its biggest attraction, but this modest fishing village (population about 6,500), about 20 kilometers northeast of Castro, is gaining importance as a base for sea kayaking among the islands off the archipelago's sheltered eastern shore.

Nothing remains of Dalcahue's original *palafitos,* obliterated by the 1960 tsunami, but a handsome new construction, comprising a gaggle of seafood eateries, puts a modern twist on the typical Chilote style. Alongside it, the vendors and their clients at the sharp new **Mercado Artesanal** no longer have to dodge the rain squalls that pass through here. The 19th-century **Iglesia Parroquial** is one of the architectural monuments that helped the island's wooden churches gain UNESCO World Heritage Site status.

Mid-February's **Semana Dalcahuina** is the town's major festival.

Dalcahue makes a better day trip than an overnight, as its modest accommodations are inferior to their counterparts in Ancud and Castro. The exception is the stylishly Chilote **Hotel La Isla** (Av. Mocopulli 113, tel. 065/641246, hotellaisla@hotmail.com, US$51 s, US$68 d), which has some modern comforts. Mostly interchangeable, the new *palafito* restaurants have fried and grilled fish and empanadas.

Frequent **Dalcahue Expreso** buses to and from Castro stop at both the main bus terminal (Freire and O'Higgins) and the waterfront Feria Artesanal. There are also *taxi colectivos* to and from Castro.

## Chonchi

Nicknamed the Ciudad de los Tres Pisos (City of Three Levels) for its sheer hillsides and steep streets, San Carlos de Chonchi (population 4,629) was one of Chiloé's first Jesuit missions, thanks to its strategically central location. Not founded officially until 1767, it managed to keep its own spontaneous street plan and avoid the imposition of the regulation Spanish colonial grid, which would have played havoc with its hilly topography. With one of the island's best concentrations of traditional architecture, it is 22 kilometers south of Castro.

Even if the 1960 tsunami split Chonchi's *palafitos* into toothpicks, the accompanying earthquake spared its historic **Iglesia San Carlos de Chonchi** (1900) and many houses along **Calle Centenario,** an area designated a *zona típica* national monument; the church's exterior has undergone restoration—though its tower fell in 2008 and had to be replaced, improvements to the interior are palpable. The **Museo de las Tradiciones Chonchinas** (Centenario 116, tel. 065/672802, 9:30 A.M.–1 P.M. and 3–7 P.M. Tues.–Sun., US$1) replicates a typical Chilote kitchen and displays impressive photographs of the 1960 tsunami.

New in 2008, the **Mercado Municipal** (Irarrázaval s/n) has helped renovate Chonchi's waterfront, where regular cleanups are keeping the beach presentable. Like its counterpart in Dalcahue, the market blends the traditional and the contemporary, and contains a clutch of modest seafood restaurants with ocean views, but taggers have defaced parts of it.

Late January's **Semana Verano Chonchi** is the city's summer festival, featuring folkloric music, dance, and art, along with rural skills such as rodeo.

Chonchi is renowned for its *licor de oro,* a milk-based liqueur resembling Drambuie.

Having undergone substantial restoration, the classic **Hotel Huildín** (Centenario 102, tel. 065/671388, www.hotelhuildin.cl, US$20–23 pp with breakfast and shared bath) once again deserves consideration.

Set on spacious grounds with fruit trees and a gazebo, with English-speaking ownership, the seaside **Hospedaje La Esmeralda** (Irarrázabal s/n, tel. 065/671328, www.esmeraldabythesea.cl, US$14–20 pp with shared bath, US$20–30 pp for more spacious rooms with private baths and in-room heating) is a backpackers' favorite that's added more private rooms. Breakfast costs extra; other meals—salmon dinners and on-the-beach *curantos* (seafood stews)—are also available, along with rental bikes, a rowboat, fishing gear, and boat tours.

Don't miss the *pastel de jaiva* (crab soufflé, US$9) at the waterfront **El Trébol** (Irarrázaval 187, tel. 065/671203, lunch and dinner daily); the lack of frills keeps prices down, but the service is still excellent. The *mostaza de ajo* (garlic mustard) enhances the homemade bread. One block inland, **La Quila** (Andrade 183, tel. 065/671389, lunch and dinner daily) is

©WAYNE BERNHARDSON

Iglesia San Carlos de Chonchi

comparable. **Los Tres Pisos** (O'Higgins 359, tel. 065/671433, lunch and dinner daily) serves sandwiches, empanadas, and kuchen.

The municipal **Oficina de Información Turística** (Sargento Candelaria and Centenario, www.municipalidadchonchi.cl) is open 9:30 A.M.–8:30 P.M. daily in summer only, with a branch at the Mercado Municipal.

**BancoEstado** (Centenario 28) has an ATM. **Correos de Chile** (Sargento Candelaria 134) is the post office.

In shared offices, **Cruz del Sur** and **Transchiloé** (Pedro Montt 233, tel. 065/671218) have frequent services between Castro and Chonchi; *taxi colectivos* to Castro (US$1.50) are also frequent. Buses from Castro bound for Cucao (Parque Nacional Chiloé) stop at Chonchi's Terminal Municipal (Alonso de Ercilla s/n).

## PARQUE NACIONAL CHILOÉ

South of Ancud and west of the Panamericana, Chiloé's Pacific coast is an almost roadless area of abrupt headlands, broad sandy beaches, and sprawling dunes at the foot of forested mountains dissected by transverse rivers. Much of this landscape, in fact, differs little from Darwin's description in *The Voyage of the Beagle* as he rode west toward Cucao, now the gateway to Parque Nacional Chiloé:

> *At Chonchi we struck across the island, following intricate winding paths, sometimes passing through magnificent forests, and sometimes through pretty cleared spots, abounding with corn and potato crops. This undulating woody country, partially cultivated, reminded me of the wilder parts of England, and therefore had to my eye a most fascinating aspect. At Vilinco [Huillinco], which is situated on the borders of the lake of Cucao, only a few fields were cleared.*

Since its creation in 1982, Parque Nacional Chiloé has protected a representative sample of the Isla Grande's natural habitat and wildlife, while providing recreational access to growing numbers of outdoors enthusiasts, both

© WAYNE BERNHARDSON

At Cucao, Parque Nacional Chiloé has a handsome new visitors center.

Chileans and foreigners. For many years, the Conaf administration failed to integrate the area's indigenous Huilliche residents into its activities—matters had changed little from the 19th century, when Darwin observed "they are very much secluded from the rest of Chiloé, and have scarcely any sort of commerce"—but substantial areas of former parkland are now under Huilliche control.

## Geography and Climate

On the thinly settled, densely forested Pacific coast, Parque Nacional Chiloé comprises 42,567 hectares in five discrete sectors: **Sector Anay,** west of Chonchi near the village of Cucao; **Sector Chepu,** southwest of Ancud; **Sector Cole Cole,** north of Chanquín; the 50-hectare **Sector Islote Metalqui,** a rugged offshore island; and the Conaf administration area west of Cucao.

Altitudes range from sea level to 850 meters in the Cordillera de Piuchén. Annual rainfall varies from about 2,000 millimeters on the coast to 3,000 millimeters at the highest elevations. Temperatures are mild, averaging about 10°C over the course of the year, with few extremes of either heat or cold.

## Flora and Fauna

At some lower elevations, mixed evergreen forest of the endemic *coigüe* or *roble de Chiloé* covers the valleys and slopes, along with the coniferous *mañío* and climbing vines; in others, enormous ferns cover the soil beneath the *ulmo, arrayán,* and the twisted *tepu.* Near its northern limit, the world's most southerly conifer, the *ciprés de los Guaitecas,* grows in swampy soils alongside the *tepu;* the *alerce* reaches the southern limit of its geographical range at altitudes above 600 meters.

In such dense forest, it's rare to see mammals, though the pudu and the Chiloé fox (*Dusicyon fulvipes,* first identified by Darwin) survive here. Both sea otters and sea lions inhabit coastal areas, while the 110 bird species include Magellanic and Humboldt penguins, oystercatchers, and cormorants on the coast. The dense forest is home to the elusive *chucao.*

## Sights and Recreation

**Chanquín** is the base for visiting Sector Anay, the park's most accessible area, which has several hiking trails of varying length. The damp climate makes wool socks and water-resistant boots advisable for hikers.

Near Conaf's Centro de Información Ambiental at Chanquín, just across the river from the village of Cucao, the 750-meter **Sendero Interpretivo El Tepual** makes as many twists and turns as the *tepu* trunks over which it passes in boggy, slippery terrain. A short distance west, the **Sendero Playa de Cucao** winds through vestigial forest and traverses a broad dunefield to arrive at a long, white sandy beach, 1.4 kilometers to the west; at about the midway point, a short lateral climbs to a scenic overlook. Violent surf, treacherous currents, and frigid Pacific waters make it unsuitable for swimming, so the scenery is the main attraction.

North of Cucao, the road continues eight kilometers past **Lago Huelde** to the Río Chanquil; from there, it's necessary to walk to the **Río Cole Cole,** which has a 10-site campground administered by the community of Huentemó. Eight kilometers beyond Cole Cole, Conaf has a *refugio* on the north bank of the **Río Anay,** but until completion of a pedestrian suspension bridge it will not be open.

For nonhikers, inexpensive rental horses are available at Chanquín, but they're not suitable for forest trails such as El Tepual, and because they're untrained for amateur riders, there have been accidents.

## Accommodations and Food

In and around Chanquín, several Huilliche-run campgrounds charge around US$2–3 per person. Conaf's **Camping Chanquín** (US$6 pp) and nearby cabañas (US$100 for up to six persons) have reopened under concessionaire Bernabé Leal (tel. 09/9507-2559). Staying at Conaf *refugios* along trails costs US$4 per person, but camping is free of charge.

Noncampers can try any of several Cucao *hospedajes,* such as **Hospedaje El Paraíso** (cell 09/9296-5465, US$13 pp with breakfast), which also serves meals.

At Chanquín, just across the bridge, the German-run **Parador Darwin** (tel. 09/9799-9923, paradordarwin@hotmail.com, US$30 s, US$50 d) has four attractive rooms but only one shared bath; its restaurant prepares excellent fish and seafood, as well as homemade bread and spreads made from local ingredients such as seaweed. A bit farther west, the exterior is a bit weathered at **Hostal El Fogón de Cucao** (tel. 09/9946-5685, elfogondecucao@hotmail.com, US$25 pp, US$70 d), but the interior is immaculate and attractive. It has one tiny single and two more comfortable doubles with shared bath downstairs, plus four more elaborate rooms with private baths upstairs. The reception is at its namesake restaurant, just across the road, where it also operates a campground.

**Cucao** and **Chanquín** both have minimarkets, and it's possible to buy fresh fish, potatoes, and the like from local fisherfolk and farmers, but supplies are more diverse and cheaper in **Castro** and **Chonchi.**

## Information

About 500 meters beyond the concrete bridge over the Río Cucao, rangers collect a US$2 per person admission at Chanquín, where Conaf's glistening new **Centro de Información Ambiental** is open 9 A.M.–7 P.M. daily; they also provide an informative map (Spanish only). Within, it contains exhibits on the park's flora and fauna, the aboriginal Huilliche, mining history, and regional legends and traditions. The surrounding grounds contain samples of Chilote technology, including a cider press and wooden sleighs used to drag heavy loads over boggy ground.

## Getting There and Around

**Cucao,** the park's easiest access point, is 52 kilometers southwest of **Castro** and 32 kilometers west of **Chonchi** via the Panamericana and a paved road with a few potholes; public transportation now continues to **Chanquín.** From Castro to Cucao and Chanquín, there are 2–5 or even more buses daily, depending on the season, with **Buses Arroyo** (tel. 065/635604),

**Ojeda** (tel. 065/573488), and **Interlagos** (tel. 09/9772-1222). Normally these stop at Chonchi en route.

## QUELLÓN

Nondescript Quellón is a 20th-century port that really only came into its own after an alcohol and acetone distillery, using native woods from dense nearby forests, installed itself here in 1905. After the 1960 tsunami, most inhabitants moved to higher ground away from the port, which is home to a small fishing fleet and regular ferries to continental Chiloé and Aisén. It is technically the Chilean terminus of the Panamericana, though an alternative route goes farther south in Argentine Patagonia.

Quellón hopes for a tourist influx because of the presence of a large **blue whale feeding colony** in the waters to the southwest, but commercial operators have only recently begun to make inroads here; at the kelp-gathering hamlet of **Chaiguao,** 11 kilometers east of town, it's sometimes possible to observe blue whales and humpbacks from the shore. To the southwest, current Chilean president Sebastián Piñera has created Parque Tantauco, a conservation project similar to Parque Pumalín that's begun to draw attention. For the moment, though, it's still the ferries that bring the tourists.

### Orientation

On the southeastern coast of the Isla Grande, Quellón (population about 12,000) is 92 kilometers south of Castro via the Panamericana, which becomes Calle Ladrilleros as it enters town. The townsite rises steeply above the harbor. Most points of interest and services are on or near the Costanera Pedro Montt, which runs along the shoreline.

### Accommodations and Food

**Residencial Esteban** (Aguirre Cerda 353, tel. 065/681438, US$16 pp with shared bath, US$30 s, US$40 d with private bath, with breakfast and cable TV) is on a quiet block; the newer rooms at the back, with private baths, are far more spacious and comfortable. It also has a better-than-average downstairs restaurant, **Rincón del Sur.**

**Hostal Chiloé Verde** (Ladrilleros 186, tel. 065/680083, cafeislasandwich@gmail.com, US$24 pp with breakfast) has everything going for it but its location along Quellón's busiest street, though the three rooms face in the other direction. While they all share one bath at present, additional baths are in the planning stages; oddly, it provides no toilet paper. The downstairs **Café Isla Sandwich** serves the obvious as well as kuchen and coffee.

On the waterfront, **Hotel El Chico Leo** (Pedro Montt 325, tel. 065/681567, irma1.0@hotmail.com, US$14 pp, US$44 d) has a choice of rooms with shared or private baths, and a restaurant with good seafood and service. **Hotel Tierra del Fuego** (Pedro Montt 445, tel. 065/682079, manoba71@hotmail.com, US$36 s, US$54 d with private bath) has a restaurant with a unique boat-shaped bar.

Atop a wooded slope at the west end of town, Quellón's top hotel choice is cordial **Hotel Patagonia Insular** (Ladrilleros 1737, tel. 065/681610, www.hotelpatagoniainsular.cl, US$90 s, US$98 d), whose clientele often consists of Japanese fishing entrepreneurs. New in 2007, it has 30 spacious rooms with built-in work areas and cable TV; some have French balconies, with views to snow-covered Andean peaks across the water, and the suites have Jacuzzis and walk-in closets. In a town not known for its accommodations, the Patagonia Insular is a pleasant surprise; its mostly seafood restaurant is no more expensive than several lesser choices—try the seafood risotto (US$10)—but it lacks atmosphere.

In addition to hotel dining rooms, seafood restaurants dot the waterfront, with a handful of venues elsewhere. **Hostería Romeo Alfa** (Capitán Luis Alcázar 554, tel. 065/680177, lunch and dinner daily) has an exceptional *chupe de jaiva* (crab casserole, US$9)—good enough to overlook the glacially slow, if well-intentioned, service. They also do pretty good grilled fish (salmon, hake, conger eel, corvina)

## WHALE-WATCHING FROM CHILOÉ

For decades now, Argentina's Península Valdés, where southern right whales spend the winter months mating and giving birth, has been South America's prime whale-watching site. Chile's Isla Carlos Tercero, in the western Strait of Magellan, is a feeding ground for southern humpbacks, but more recently, biologists have identified the Golfo de Corcovado south and east of Chiloé as a major feeding ground for both blue whales (the largest of the whales) and humpbacks.

While whale-watching from shore is possible (if uncertain) at the hamlet of Chaiguao, near Quellón, the surest place to see the whales is at Melinka, in the Archipiélago de las Guaitecas, about two hours south of Quellón via high-speed launch. At Quellón, English-speaking veterinarian Jorge Oyarce has founded the company **Darwin Adventure** (tel. 09/95304355, www.darwinadventure.cl) to offer day trips to Melinka and longer charter photo-safaris around the Golfo de Corcovado; he is also interested in birds and dolphins.

From Quellón, it's also possible to fly to Melinka with Puerto Montt's **Aerocord** (tel. 065/262300, www.aerocord.cl) or **Pewen Servicios Aéreos** (tel. 065/224000, www.pewenchile.com) for about US$40. At Melinka, there are accommodations as well as boats that will take passengers more cheaply than from Quellón, as it's closer to the feeding grounds.

for around US$8 (including a side dish, such as *merkén*-spiced mashed potatoes).

**El Madero** (Ramón Freire 430, tel. 065/681330, 12:30–11 P.M. Mon.–Sat.) has better atmosphere than the Patagonia Insular, and a similarly interesting menu, but the kitchen can be slow and the service erratic. On a good day, it gets raves from diners, but it overcooks the barbecued lamb (US$11); the most reliable items are the sandwiches (around US$6) and the homemade ice cream, especially Swiss chocolate and pistachio.

**Rincon del Sur** (Ladrilleros 125, tel. 065/680685, lunch and dinner daily) prepares an exquisite *chupe de locos* (abalone casserole, US$10) and serves its *sopaipillas* (fry bread) with a surprisingly spicy *pebre* spread. Other choices include ceviche (US$8), crab crepes (US$10), a diversity of fish (US$10 plus extra for sauces), and a *parrillada* for two (US$28).

### Information

Two blocks north of the waterfront, staffed by interns whose knowledge varies considerably, Quellón's **Caseta de Información Turística** (Gómez García and Santos Vargas, www.comunaquellon.co.cl) is an information kiosk open 10 A.M.–6:30 P.M. daily October–April.

### Services

Services are fewer than in Ancud or Castro. **BCI** (22 de Mayo 343) has an ATM. **Correos de Chile** (22 de Mayo and Ladrilleros) handles the mail. **BancoEstado** (22 de Mayo 399) has an ATM. There are numerous call centers and Internet locales along Ladrilleros.

For medical help, try the **Hospital de Quellón** (Dr. Ahués 305, tel. 065/681443).

### Getting There and Around

**Cruz del Sur** and **Transchiloé** (both at Aguirre Cerda 52, tel. 065/681284) have frequent service to Chonchi, Castro, Ancud, and Puerto Montt. There are also *taxi colectivos* to Castro.

**Naviera Austral** (Pedro Montt 457, tel. 065/682207, www.navieraustral.cl) sails to Chaitén on the *Don Baldo* Friday at midnight. Fares range from US$23 per person for fixed seats to US$40 per person for bunks. Vehicle rates are US$160 for passenger vehicles and small trucks, and US$44 per linear meter for other vehicles; bicycles cost US$15 and motorcycles US$35. The *Don Baldo* also sails to Puerto Chacabuco (Aisén) via Melinka, Raúl Marín Balmaceda, Puerto Cisnes, and other remote destinations Tuesday at 6 P.M. Fares to Puerto Chacabuco are US$75 per person in seats, US$85–90 per person in berths. Shipping a vehicle costs US$270.

## PARQUE TANTAUCO

Doug Tompkins may have started something. Since the U.S. environmental philanthropist succeeded in having Parque Pumalín declared a formal nature sanctuary under Chilean law, Sebastián Piñera—elected Chile's president in 2010—has created his own private nature reserve in the virtually roadless southwestern sector of the Isla Grande de Chiloé.

Since acquiring the property and declaring it a park in 2006, Piñera—who consulted with Tompkins about the project—has built an attractive guesthouse, an elegant campground with modern bathrooms and a spacious *quincho* for cooking, several hiking trails, and a series of *refugios* (shelters) along those trails for hikers who brave the park's nearly incessant rain and soggy forests. At the same time, he's created a plant nursery to reforest areas damaged by fire and logging, most notably near the park's overland entrance at Chaiguata, near the city of Quellón.

The park's centerpiece is its headquarters at **Caleta Inío,** a settlement created some 30 years ago to exploit the area's extensive kelp beds. Accessible only by foot or motor launch from Quellón (2.5–6 hours away, depending on the vessel), Inío has a permanent population of about 50. Many of them are now park employees; others benefit from the park's presence by offering lodging, meals, and handicrafts for sale. Given Inío's isolation, they also benefit because Tantauco's daily launch takes them to and from Quellón for free, on a space-available basis (paying passengers have priority).

Though Tantauco's really in its early days, one trek appears likely to become an instant classic: the five-day, 52-kilometer **Sendero Transversal** from Chaiguata (reachable by bus from Quellón) to Caleta Inío, where hikers catch the launch back to Quellón. En route, they stay at four simple *refugios,* with bunks, that eliminate the need to carry a tent. They also have cooking facilities and latrines (not flush toilets).

© WAYNE BERNHARDSON

Parque Tantauco headquarters at Caleta Inío

At first glance, the daily distances suggested—ranging from 7.5 to 15 kilometers per day—sound pretty modest for experienced hikers at low altitudes (the trail's highest point is only about 250 meters above sea level). That's misleading, though, because a good part of the route crosses soggy (sometimes muddy) terrain and involves climbing up, over, and down fallen tree trunks. Many but not nearly all of those trunks have steps cut into them; even then, they are often slippery and require caution to avoid falls and sprains. In some areas, though, boardwalks and staircases make things easier.

For visitors who arrive at Inío, there are shorter hikes, such as the **Sendero Punta Rocosa,** which climbs to a solar-powered lighthouse erected by the park and then loops through a rocky peninsula that has several small, secluded beaches. Tantauco, in fact, may have some of South America's most secluded beaches, even if the South Pacific is a bit too chilly for swimming except on the warmest summer days.

Another worthwhile excursion is the **Sendero Quilantar,** a two-day, 22-kilometer loop from Caleta Inío that includes a night at Refugio Quilantar. All trails are clearly marked with bright metallic triangles every 100 meters; at regular intervals, they also have numbers that indicate progress along the route. Still, given the area's copious rainfall and winter storms that often knock down trees, maintenance is a major issue.

Combined with **whale-watching** in the Golfo de Corcovado, Parque Tantauco could make Quellón and vicinity a huge ecotourism destination. At the same time, it lacks some of the attention to detail that Tompkins brings to Pumalín and his other projects—Tantauco's guesthouse, for instance, lacks double-paned windows, there are no books (though there are bookshelves), and there are no towels (bring your own). Electricity comes from a diesel generator (there are no suitable sites for a hydropower turbine, but wind power is a real possibility).

It's hard to imagine that Piñera can't afford a wind turbine for Tantauco—his fortune, made largely through LAN Airlines and the pioneering implementation of credit card payment systems in Chile, must be immeasurably larger than Tompkins's. On the other hand, for the Chilean president, Tantauco is just one of many projects; Tompkins's entire life is conservation.

For more information, contact the Quellón offices of Parque Tantauco (Av. La Paz 068, tel. 065/680066, www.parquetantauco.cl). Before visiting the park, it's imperative to make arrangements for transportation and accommodations, including the park *refugios,* which hold a maximum of eight persons. There is a central office in Santiago at the Fundación Futuro (Apoquindo 3000, 19th floor, Las Condes, tel. 02/4227322, www.fundacionfuturo.cl).

# AISÉN AND CONTINENTAL CHILOÉ

With the smallest population of any Chilean region, Aisén is a natural wonderland of islands, mountains, fjords, lakes, rivers, and forests that's drawing ever more visitors since the Carretera Austral's completion from Caleta Gonzalo in the north to Villa O'Higgins in the south. Its only sizable city is the regional capital of Coyhaique, which has a state-of-the-art airport and is a good base for exploring the area. Some visitors, though, begin at the ferry port of Chaitén—which was devastated by volcanic ash and flooding in May 2008—and move south by road. Others arrive at Coyhaique's Puerto Chacabuco, via ferry or catamaran from Puerto Montt.

In addition to the Carretera Austral and several national parks, Aisén's big draw is Parque Nacional Laguna San Rafael, where the ice meets the ocean, but it's accessible only by sea or by air taxi. The climate resembles that of coastal British Columbia, with the seasons reversed (December, January, and February are summer). Consequently, weather can be wet, windy, and cool at any time, especially at higher elevations, so hikers should carry good trekking and rain gear and hope for the best. Summer highs can climb above 25°C around Coyhaique, but cooler temperatures are the rule. Midsummer days are long, with sunsets around 10 P.M.

Thanks to tourism, Aisén is increasingly prosperous, but agriculture, forestry, and mining are also important. The salmon-farming industry has brought both prosperity and controversy, as its environmental cost is greater than some residents believe it's worth.

© WAYNE BERNHARDSON

## HIGHLIGHTS

**Parque Nacional Laguna San Rafael:** Southwest of Coyhaique, the ice still reaches the sea at Laguna San Rafael – though it's receding alarmingly fast (page 287).

**Parque Nacional Queulat:** The hanging glacier at this park once reached what is now the northern Carretera Austral; while it's receded dramatically over the past two centuries, it still provides a clue as to what Yosemite Valley might have looked like before its own glaciers melted (page 291).

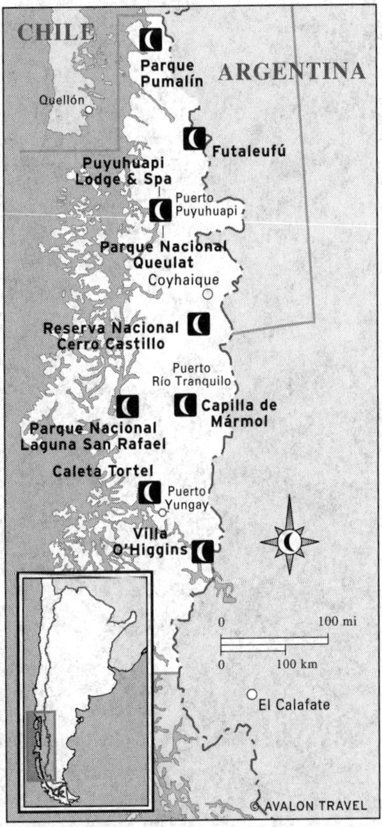


**Puyuhuapi Lodge & Spa:** It's not really an island, but this surprisingly affordable hot-springs resort might as well be, due to its splendid isolation opposite the northern Carretera Austral (page 294).

**Futaleufú:** Almost every rafter and kayaker places the Río Futaleufú among the world's top 10 white-water rivers, and many put it atop the list (page 296).

**Parque Pumalín:** It's been politically controversial, but South America's largest private conservation project is winning acceptance for its commitment to preserving huge extents of midlatitude rainforest and making them accessible to the public (page 301).

**Reserva Nacional Cerro Castillo:** Growing in popularity, the trekking beneath the spires of this readily accessible reserve on Chile's southern Carretera Austral makes it second only to Torres del Paine, probably, in its popularity with multi-day hikers. It's a distant second, though, so there's no Paine gridlock (page 305).

**Capilla de Mármol:** Accessible by water only, the sinuous walls of these blue/white grottos line the western shores of Lago General Carrera (page 309).

**Caleta Tortel:** A road reaches its outskirts now, but the only way to get around this quaint seaside fishing village is still on foot, via the boardwalks and staircases that connect its waterfront and scattered houses and businesses (page 317).

**Villa O'Higgins:** In scenic mountain surroundings, this orderly outpost of bureaucracy is almost the end of the road – the Carretera Austral stops just south of here – but it's also the starting point for the new Cruce de Lagos to Argentina's trekking capital of El Chaltén (page 318).

LOOK FOR TO FIND RECOMMENDED SIGHTS, ACTIVITIES, DINING, AND LODGING.

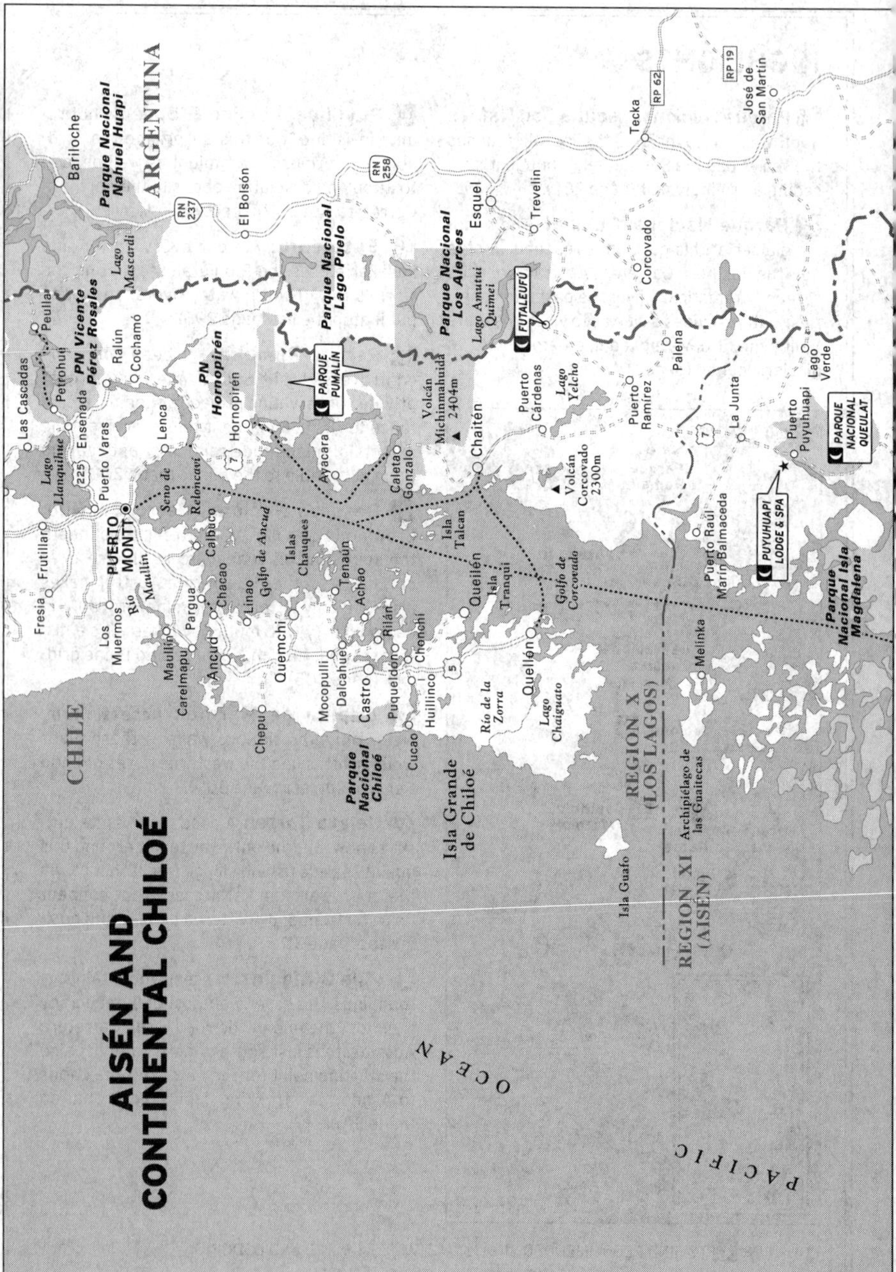
AISÉN AND CONTINENTAL CHILOÉ
CHILE
ARGENTINA
PACIFIC OCEAN
REGION X (LOS LAGOS)
REGION XI (AISÉN)
Bariloche
Parque Nacional Nahuel Huapi
Lago Mascardi
RN 237
El Bolsón
RN 258
Esquel
Trevelin
Tecka
RP 62
RP 19
José de San Martín
Corcovado
Parque Nacional Lago Puelo
Parque Nacional Los Alerces
Lago Amutui Quimei
FUTALEUFÚ
Palena
Lago Verde
Peulla
PN Vicente Pérez Rosales
Ralún
Cochamó
Petrohué
Las Cascadas
Ensenada
Lago Llanquihue
225
Puerto Varas
Frutillar
Fresia
Los Muermos
PUERTO MONTT
Río Maullín
Maullín
Carelmapu
Pargua
Chacao
Calbuco
Seno de Reloncaví
Lenca
PN Hornopirén
Hornopirén
7
PARQUE PUMALÍN
Ayacara
Caleta Gonzalo
Volcán Michinmahuida 2404m
Chaitén
Puerto Cárdenas
Lago Yelcho
Puerto Ramírez
La Junta
Volcán Corcovado 2300m
Puerto Puyuhuapi
PARQUE NACIONAL QUEULAT
PUYUHUAPI LODGE & SPA
Puerto Raúl Marín Balmaceda
Parque Nacional Isla Magdalena
Melinka
Archipiélago de las Guaitecas
Isla Guafo
Golfo de Corcovado
Isla Tranqui
Queilén
Isla Talcan
Islas Chauques
Golfo de Ancud
Tenaún
Achao
Linao
Quemchi
Ancud
Chepu
Mocopulli
Dalcahue
Castro
Rilán
Chonchi
Puqueldón
Huillinco
Cucao
5
Parque Nacional Chiloé
Río de la Zorra
Quellón
Lago Chaiguato
Isla Grande de Chiloé

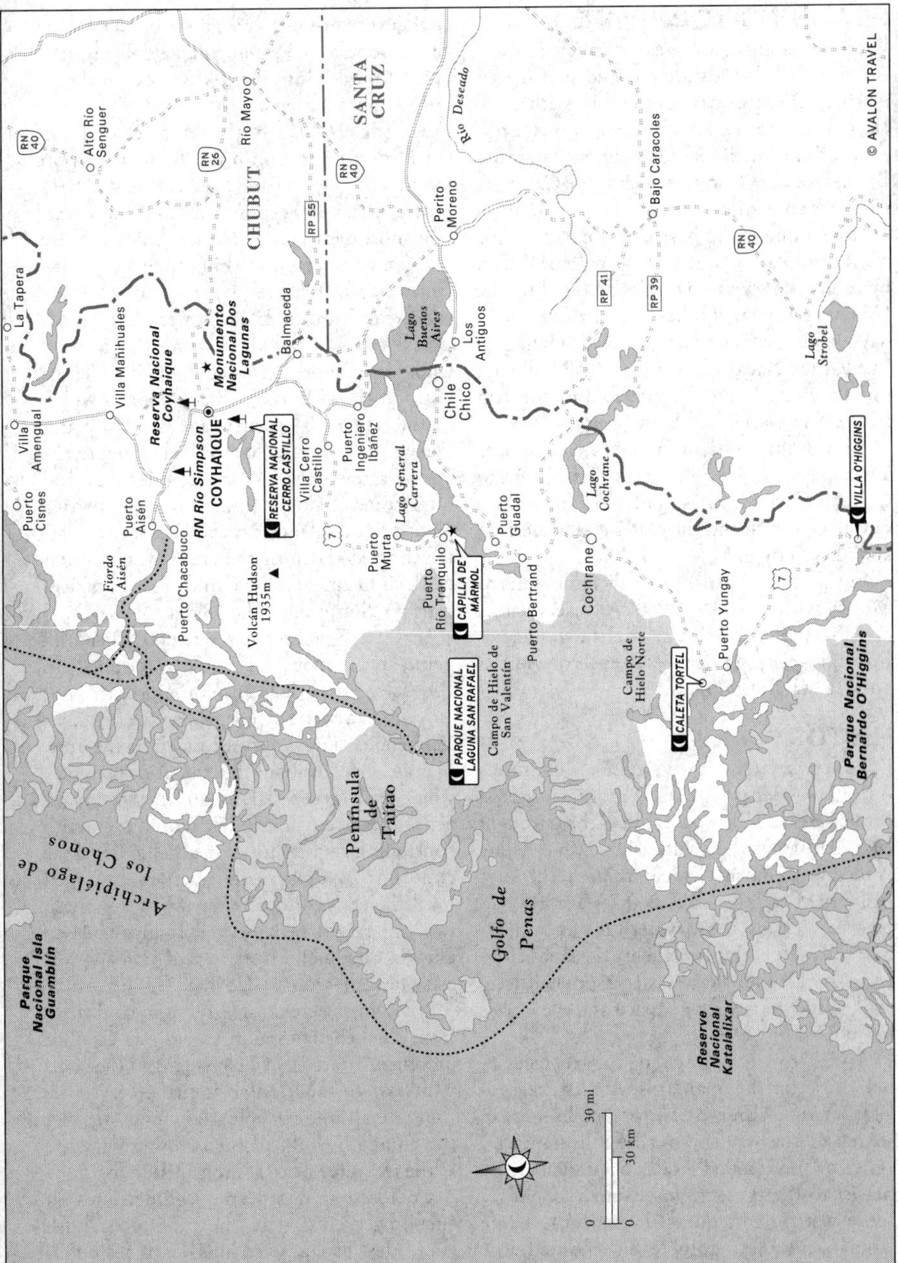


© AVALON TRAVEL

## PLANNING YOUR TIME

Because distances are great, public transport is limited, and roads are few and slow, Aisén justifies a rental car, preferably with high clearance. Vehicles are also few, so rental reservations are advisable for visitors flying into Balmaceda/Coyhaique, which is the Carretera Austral's approximate midpoint.

Coyhaique is the best base for excursions north and south, and to Laguna San Rafael by catamaran or air taxi. Northbound on the Carretera Austral, it takes at least a week or 10 days to see roadside or near-roadside highlights like Parque Nacional Queulat, the Puyuhuapi hot springs, Parque Pumalín, and the Río Futaleufú's world-class white water.

Southbound on the highway, it requires at least a week to enjoy Cerro Castillo, Lago General Carrera, the singular fishing village of Caleta Tortel, and the road's end wilderness at Villa O'Higgins.

For visitors heading south from Puerto Montt with rental cars, ferry reservations are advisable, especially for the January–February-only service between Hornopirén and Caleta Gonzalo.

## HISTORY

Europeans first viewed Aisén's channels in 1553, when Pedro de Valdivia ordered Francisco de Ulloa to explore the Strait of Magellan from the Pacific side. When Ulloa landed on Península Taitao, though, the forerunners of today's Kawéskar (Alacaluf) had been navigating those waterways for millennia; on the nearby continent, the Tehuelche (Aónikenk) and their predecessors had long stalked the steppes for guanaco and the forests for huemul.

Aisén's thinly populated, rugged recesses held little for the Spaniards. At first, tales of "Trapananda" drew a few fortune hunters in search of the wealthy but literally fantastic "City of the Caesars" (tales of hidden riches persist to the present, and a small Conaf reserve near Coyhaique still bears the name Trapananda). As gold fever subsided, the Spaniards settled temperate areas where they could extract tribute and labor from the indigenous population, a more dependable source of wealth until introduced diseases greatly reduced their numbers.

In the 1670s, both Bartolomé Díaz Gallardo and Antonio de Vea came upon Laguna San Rafael and the Campo de Hielo Norte, the northern continental ice sheet. The most dedicated explorers, though, were Jesuit missionaries, working their way south from insular Chiloé by land and sea until their expulsion from the Americas in 1767. The list of non-Spaniards reads like a who's who: John Byron, grandfather of poet George Gordon (Lord Byron), suffered a shipwreck in the late 18th century, and Fitz Roy and Darwin saw Laguna San Rafael on board the *Beagle* a few decades later. Under Admiral Sir Thomas Baker, commanding the British navy's South American Squadron, the latter charted much of the area's waters, their work supplemented by Chilean naval officer Enrique Simpson in the 1870s.

In 1798, Spain made the region's first land grant, an enormous tract between the northern Río Yelcho and the southern Río Bravo, but Argentine overland explorers were the first non-indigenous travelers to see much of the area. Despite concern about the Argentine presence, which led to territorial disagreements only recently resolved, Chile had trouble enough controlling areas south of the Biobío, let alone remote Aisén. Consequently, settlement lagged until the early 20th century, when it granted the Valparaíso-based Sociedad Industrial Aisén a huge concession for sheep ranching and forestry near present-day Coyhaique.

News of the concession set off a land rush, from the heartland and Argentina's Chubut province, by settlers who challenged the company's state-sanctioned dominance. While these smallholders held their own against the company, both of them, along with the Chilean state, bear responsibility for massive deforestation under a misguided law that encouraged cutting and burning to establish land titles. Today, when hillsides of deciduous *ñirres* turn red in autumn, it's a pale reminder of what the entire region must have looked like seven decades ago, before both deliberate and unintentional wildfires denuded countless slopes, leaving pale trunks scattered among pasture grasses, from Mañihuales in the north to Puerto Ibáñez in the south. Silt carried by the Río Simpson, from erosion triggered by deforestation and grazing, clogged the harbor of Puerto Aisén, the region's main port, necessitating its shift to Puerto Chacabuco.

Since the 1970s, the major development has been construction of the Carretera Austral, parts of which are now being paved, to Villa O'Higgins. Improved relations with Argentina have brought better cross-border contacts, and pressure has increased to open up the area to controversial hydroelectric projects on the Futaleufú, Baker, and Pascua Rivers, all of them prime recreational resources. While Aisén seems likely to grow, it seems unlikely to attract the large-scale immigration advocated by some regional politicians.

# Coyhaique

Originally known as Baquedano, today's regional capital was once so obscure that letters addressed here could end up in an eponymous Atacama Desert rail junction. After a decade of confusion following its 1929 founding, its name became Coyhaique, but it did not become the provincial capital until it succeeded Puerto Aisén in 1973.

Founded as a service center for the Sociedad Industrial Aisén, its growth spurred by the colonists who flooded the region in its wake, Coyhaique is a mostly modern city whose infrastructure hasn't quite matched its growth—in heavy rain, streets drain poorly and the flow of water is so broad that city workers place temporary pedestrian bridges across the gutters. Improvements, though, include a redesigned Plaza de Armas and conversion of congested Calle Horn into Paseo Horn, a pedestrian mall that's become a popular gathering place.

Still the region's only substantial city, Coyhaique has a complete array of services, including fine restaurants, pubs, and travel agencies. The virtual midpoint of the Carretera Austral, it also offers an alternative route into Argentina.

## ORIENTATION

Beneath the basaltic barricade of Cerro Macay, Coyhaique (population about 52,000) sits at the confluence of the Río Simpson and the Río Coyhaique, 455 kilometers south of Caleta Gonzalo and 566 kilometers north of Villa O'Higgins. It is 634 kilometers from Puerto Montt via the Carretera Austral.

Westbound, a paved highway leads to Puerto Aisén and Puerto Chacabuco, while another leads southeast to Balmaceda and the Argentine border at Paso Huemules. On the Argentine side, the mostly paved road continues to the Atlantic port of Comodoro Rivadavia, 600 kilometers east on the so-called

© WAYNE BERNHARDSON

**New wind turbines outside Coyhaique suggest alternative energy futures for Aisén.**

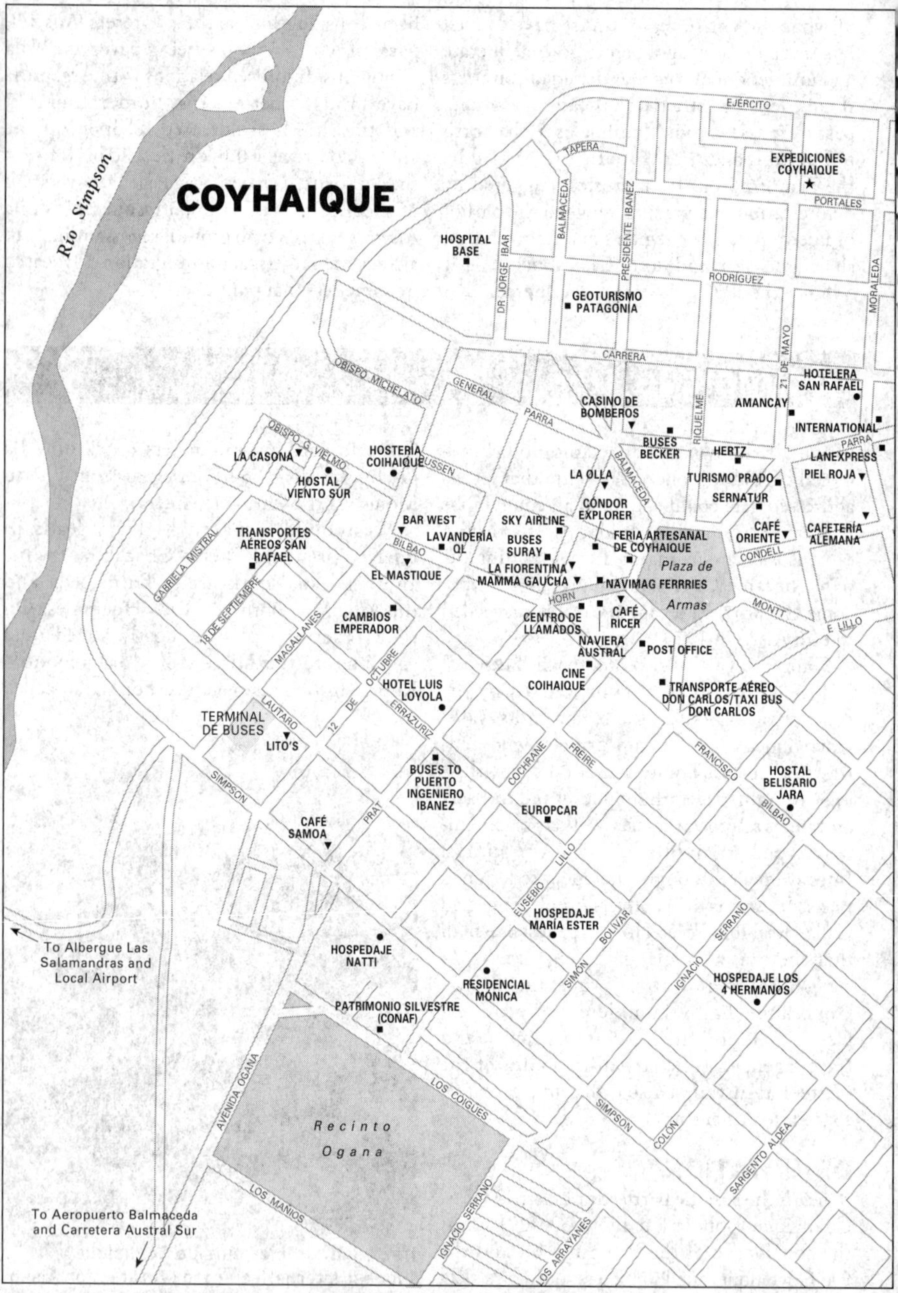
COYHAIQUE
Río Simpson
EJÉRCITO
TAPERA
EXPEDICIONES COYHAIQUE
PORTALES
BALMACEDA
PRESIDENTE IBANEZ
HOSPITAL BASE
DR JORGE IBAR
RODRIGUEZ
MORALEDA
GEOTURISMO PATAGONIA
21 DE MAYO
CARRERA
HOTELERA SAN RAFAEL
OBISPO MICHELATO
GENERAL PARRA
CASINO DE BOMBEROS
RIQUELME
AMANCAY
INTERNATIONAL
OBISPO G. VIELMO
BUSES BECKER
HERTZ
PARRA
LANEXPRESS
LA CASONA
HOSTERÍA COIHAIQUE
LUSSEN
HOSTAL VIENTO SUR
LA OLLA
BALMACEDA
TURISMO PRADO
PIEL ROJA
SERNATUR
CÓNDOR EXPLORER
BAR WEST
SKY AIRLINE
CAFÉ ORIENTE
CAFETERÍA ALEMANA
TRANSPORTES AÉREOS SAN RAFAEL
LAVANDERÍA QL
BUSES SURAY
FERIA ARTESANAL DE COYHAIQUE
BILBAO
CONDELL
GABRIELA MISTRAL
EL MASTIQUE
LA FIORENTINA
MAMMA GAUCHA
Plaza de Armas
NAVIMAG FERRRIES
18 DE SEPTIEMBRE
HORN
MONTT
CAMBIOS EMPERADOR
CAFÉ RICER
E LILLO
CENTRO DE LLAMADOS
MAGALLANES
NAVIERA AUSTRAL
POST OFFICE
12 DE OCTUBRE
CINE COIHAIQUE
HOTEL LUIS LOYOLA
TRANSPORTE AÉREO DON CARLOS/TAXI BUS DON CARLOS
TERMINAL DE BUSES
LAUTARO
ERRÁZURIZ
LITO'S
FREIRE
COCHRANE
FRANCISCO BILBAO
HOSTAL BELISARIO JARA
BUSES TO PUERTO INGENIERO IBANEZ
SIMPSON
EUROPCAR
CAFÉ SAMOA
PRAT
LILLO
EUSEBIO
SERRANO
HOSPEDAJE MARÍA ESTER
BOLÍVAR
To Albergue Las Salamandras and Local Airport
HOSPEDAJE NATTI
RESIDENCIAL MÓNICA
SIMÓN
IGNACIO
HOSPEDAJE LOS 4 HERMANOS
PATRIMONIO SILVESTRE (CONAF)
LOS COIGUES
AVENIDA OGANA
Recinto Ogana
SIMPSON
COLÓN
SARGENTO ALDEA
LOS MANIOS
IGNACIO SERRANO
LOS ARRAYANES
To Aeropuerto Balmaceda and Carretera Austral Sur

Corredor Bioceánico (Bi-Oceanic Corridor) with Puerto Chacabuco.

Based on a pair of concentric pentagons, the inner one surrounding the Plaza de Armas, Coyhaique's street plan is not for the geometrically challenged. Beyond this, it's more regular and less disorienting but still presents problems for those unaccustomed to irregular angles at intersections.

Avenida Baquedano, on the northeast edge of town, connects the paved Puerto Chacabuco road with the gravel road leading east to the border at Coyhaique Alto. Avenida Ogana is the main route to the southbound Carretera Austral and Balmaceda.

## SIGHTS

Nearly all first-time visitors to the disorienting **Plaza de Armas,** where 10 streets radiate like spokes from a hub, get lost returning to their accommodations. Bewildered walkers can blame policeman Luis Marchant González, who in 1929 chose the Carabineros' five-sided badge as a city-planning template. Relandscaped a few years ago, the plaza still boasts many mature trees, but the sight lines are better and new fountains add a touch of distinction.

Closed as of early 2011 to make room for a major expansion of its facilities in the Casa de la Cultura, the **Museo Regional de la Patagonia** (Eusebio Lillo 23) documents regional history through a well-presented series of historical photographs and early settlers' household implements.

Nearby, on the Baquedano median strip, the **Monumento al Ovejero** commemorates Aisén's pioneer sheep farmers. The series of statues consists of a mounted shepherd, his flock, and his dogs. There are fine views of the Río Coyhaique valley from the newly landscaped **Plaza Mirador Río Coyhaique,** at the east end of Condell.

## ENTERTAINMENT AND SHOPPING

Coyhaique has a growing number of bars, but their aspirations exceed their appeal. **Piel Roja** (Moraleda 495, tel. 067/236635), for instance, has pizza and pub grub, psychedelic decor that probably infringes Fillmore copyrights, and a 7–9 P.M. happy hour, but something's lacking.

Despite its pioneer-style house, swinging doors, pistols on the wall, and cold beer on tap, **Bar West** (Bilbao 110, tel. 065/210007) serves mediocre pisco sours and plays too much insipid pop music.

**Peña Quilantal** (Baquedano 791, tel. 065/234394) sometimes showcases live folkloric music but is just as likely to offer run-of-the-mill pop. The **Cine Coihaique** (Cochrane 321) shows occasional recent films, but also hosts live music, usually folkloric.

At the **Feria Artesanal de Coyhaique,** on the west side of the Plaza de Armas, local horse gear is the main attraction, supplemented by wood carvings and woolens. **Amancay** (21 de Mayo 340, tel. 067/216099) has custom chocolates.

## ACCOMMODATIONS

Coyhaique's accommodations scene is unusual, with plenty of budget and midrange choices and few upmarket options. With some exceptions, budget accommodations are only so-so.

### US$25-50

Reached by a staircase so narrow your elbows can touch both walls, some rooms at **Hospedaje Los 4 Hermanos** (Colón 495, tel. 067/232647, US$14–16 pp without breakfast) can be claustrophobic, but it's often full and singles are at a premium—phoning ahead is a good idea. Cheerful **Residencial Mónica** (Eusebio Lillo 664, tel. 067/234302, US$14–20 pp with breakfast) has shared and private bath options, but in some rooms too many beds nearly cover all of the floor space.

The backpackers' best is Spanish-run **Albergue Las Salamandras** (Sector los Pinos s/n, tel. 067/211865, www.salamandras.cl, US$15 pp, US$30 s, US$48 d with kitchen access), on piney grounds about two kilometers southwest of town on the old airport road. Most rooms in this attractive building, with large communal spaces, are dorms, but there are a few doubles. Camping (US$10 pp) is also possible.

For the price, it's hard to find anything better than pristine, friendly **Hospedaje María Ester** (Lautaro 544, tel. 067/233023, www.hospedajemariaester.cl, US$16 pp with shared bath, US$30 pp with private bath). The comparable **Hospedaje Natti** (Almirante Simpson 417, tel. 067/231047, US$20 pp with breakfast) is a good alternative; camping is possible (US$8 pp).

Perhaps Coyhaique's best value, **Hostal Gladys** (General Parra 65, tel. 067/245288, patagoniagladys@hotmail.com, US$26–34 s, US$40–60 d with cable TV and wireless Internet) has built a stylish eight-room addition, with high ceilings, that contrasts with the simple but pleasant family-run B&B it always was. Quiet, well-located, spotless, and tobacco-free, it has a couple of drawbacks: Only the street-side rooms have windows (though all have skylights), and a couple of the older rooms are cramped with too many beds. Breakfast (US$6 extra) varies in quality; prices in the new sector may well rise.

### US$50-100

Under new ownership, on a quiet block, **Hostal Viento Sur** (Obispo Vielmo 71, tel. 067/232707, US$44 s, US$60 d) is luminous and spacious, but the open floor plan still lets noises carry into the upstairs sleeping quarters. **Hotelera San Rafael** (Moraleda 343, tel. 067/233733, www.hotelerasanrafael.cl, US$65 s, US$78 d without IVA) has tasteful, spacious, and sunny hotel rooms as well as cabaña-style accommodations.

In a residential neighborhood, **Hostal Español** (Sargento Aldea 343, tel./fax 067/242580, www.hostalcoyhaique.cl, US$60 s, US$83 d with continental breakfast) is a polished product with upstairs view rooms. Despite its unimpressive street-side exterior—hard to see unless you're really looking for it—**Hotelera San Sebastián** (Av. Baquedano 496, tel. 067/233021, US$67 s, US$84 d) has large comfortable rooms with views over the Río Coyhaique.

In some rooms at **Hotel Los Ñires** (Av.

Baquedano 315, tel./fax 067/232261, www.hotellosnires.cl, US$74 s, US$88 d), large beds occupy almost all the floor space, but the baths are spacious and it has a quality restaurant.

New in 2010, overlooking the river, **Raíces Bed & Breakfast** (Baquedano 444, tel. 067/210490, www.raicesbedandbreakfast.com, US$90 s or d) enjoys modern conveniences but a rustic style, with blond pine details.

**Hotel Luis Loyola** (Prat 455, tel./fax 067/234200, www.hoteloyola.cl, US$73 s, US$91 d) is modern, central, and comfortable.

### Over US$100

On sprawling west-side grounds, motel-style **Hostería Coyhaique** (Magallanes 131, tel. 067/231137, www.hotelcoyhaique.cl, US$88 s, US$112 d) has recovered from a fire, but there is no indication yet of a projected remodel that could include a casino.

On a site overlooking the Río Coyhaique, genial **Hotel El Reloj** (Baquedano 828, tel./fax 067/231108, www.elrelojhotel.cl, US$102 s, US$143 d with breakfast and without IVA) is one of Coyhaique's best values, with an exceptional restaurant as well.

Overseas tour operators often choose **Hostal Belisario Jara** (Bilbao 662, tel./fax 067/234150, www.belisariojara.cl, US$118 s, US$156 d), which has more architectural distinction and personality than most hotels here.

## FOOD

**Cafetería Alemana** (Condell 119, tel. 065/231731, lunch and dinner Mon.–Sat.) makes outstanding sandwiches, *onces* (afternoon tea), and desserts; down the block is its sister, **Café Oriente** (Condell 201, tel. 065/231622, lunch and dinner Mon.–Sat.). For inexpensive light meals, try **Café Samoa** (Prat 653, tel. 065/232864, lunch and dinner Mon.–Sat.).

For home cooking with class, try the lunches (US$6) at **El Mastique** (Bilbao 141, tel. 067/235594, lunch and dinner Mon.–Sat.); its dinner menu is more limited. Despite an almost foreboding exterior, **Lito's** (Lautaro 147, tel. 067/254528, lunch and dinner Mon.–Sat.) has a spacious dining area with an attractive bar and above-average versions of Chilean beef (US$8–12), fish, and seafood.

With a Chilean menu enhanced by top-quality ingredients, the **Casino de Bomberos** (General Parra 365, tel. 065/231437, lunch and dinner daily) is an institution, but it's one of the country's more expensive fire-station restaurants. **La Fiorentina** (Prat 230, tel. 065/238899, lunch and dinner daily) has good pizza, *pastel de choclo,* and crisp service at moderate prices (US$8 and up).

For light cooking to international standards, Hotel El Reloj's **El Ovejero** (Baquedano 828, tel./fax 065/231108, lunch and dinner daily) comes highly recommended for entrées such as *congrio al ajillo* (conger eel with garlic, US$15) and Patagonian desserts, including rhubarb mousse; grab a window table for views over the river.

New in late 2010, **Mamma Gaucha** (Paseo Horn 47, tel. 067/210721) has been an overwhelming success for remarkable thin-crusted pizzas, light on cheese, with a far greater variety of toppings than available even in Santiago's best pizzerias—think shredded chicken with sautéed red onions and cilantro (US$10). The kitchen may be a little slow, but the service is cheerful and the ambience is totally tobacco-free.

A favorite with locals and visitors alike, **Café Ricer** (Paseo Horn 48, tel. 067/232920, www.ap.cl/restaurante.htm, 8:30 A.M.–2 or 3 A.M. daily) serves Patagonian specialties such as barbecued lamb (about US$13); humongous sandwiches and snacks are cheaper. Most people dine in the downstairs café; the upstairs restaurant has more style, its walls lined with historic photographs, but it's home to the city's surviving smokers.

Another good option, best for seafood, is **La Casona** (Obispo Vielmo 77, tel. 067/238894, lunch daily, dinner Mon.–Sat.), for lamb, *pastel de jaiva* (crab soufflé), and other regional entrées in the US$9–15 range. The service equals or surpasses the food.

## INFORMATION

**Sernatur** (Bulnes 35, tel. 067/240290, infoaisen@sernatur.cl, 8:30 A.M.–9 P.M. weekdays,

10 A.M.–6 P.M. Sat., and 9 A.M.–4 P.M. Sun. in summer; 8:30 A.M.–7 P.M. weekdays only the rest of the year) has English-speaking staff.

Directly on the Plaza de Armas, Coyhaique's private **Cámara de Turismo** operates a summer-only office (9:30 A.M.–9 P.M. weekdays, 10 A.M.–1 P.M. and 3:30–7 P.M. weekends and holidays).

Conaf's **Patrimonio Silvestre** (Los Coihues s/n, tel. 067/212125, aysen@conaf.cl) provides information on national parks and reserves.

## SERVICES

Coyhaique has the region's most complete services. Changing money, in particular, is easier than elsewhere on the Carretera Austral.

**Turismo Prado** (21 de Mayo 417) and **Cambios Emperador** (Freire 171) both exchange cash and travelers checks. **BancoEstado** (Moraleda 502) and several other banks have ATMs.

For postal services, **Correos de Chile** (Cochrane 202) is near the Plaza de Armas.

## THE DICTATOR'S HIGHWAY?

The highway where Santiaguinos come to test their SUVs, rather than on the avenues of Las Condes and Vitacura, the **Carretera Austral** is so crucial to Aisén that Coyhaique's museum used to devote its largest exhibit to it. Many residents still give General Pinochet the credit – one conspicuous photo showed a grandfatherly Pinochet, in civilian dress, beaming at a local schoolboy. A frequent comment is that the military regime was "the last one to pay attention to the region," and one Pinochet partisan claimed that "the politicians would never have built this highway. There are no votes here."

But Pinochet may get more credit than he deserves. The original highway studies date from 1968, during President Eduardo Frei Montalva's Christian Democrat government, and the project advanced during Salvador Allende's Socialist administration until Pinochet's 1973 coup. Work accelerated during the dictatorship, but civilian contractors actually did more than the military.

The Carretera's final irony is that the man who finished it, President Ricardo Lagos (2000–2006), is the man who boldly stared down Pinochet in 1988, through a TV camera: "You promise the country another eight years of torture, disappearances, and human rights violations." Lagos's bravery probably turned the tide in a plebiscite that ended Pinochet's reign. Maps once labeled "Carretera Longitudinal Austral Presidente Pinochet" now say "Carretera Longitudinal Austral."

Despite its sympathy for the far-right UDI (Unión Demócratica Independiente), the entire town of Villa O'Higgins showed up in April 2000, when the newly elected Lagos, Pinochet's nemesis, formally dedicated the Río Bravo–Villa O'Higgins segment, the final piece in the puzzle.

The notoriously timid huemul, the emblematic, endangered Andean deer that graces Chile's coat-of-arms (along with the Andean condor and the motto "by reason or force") is surprisingly common and even docile along this last segment. In a sense, it's a tangible symbol of change and the openness that the highway represents – not force alone, but reason as well. The highway that began as a military exercise now belongs to everyone.

Some pioneer settlements along the Carretera Austral are acquiring an air of permanence, but this is still wild country, with just enough creature comforts for those on bigger budgets. Prices are highest and public transport most frequent in January and February, when most Chileans take their vacations. The spring months of October and November and the autumn months of March and April can be good times to travel, though public transport is less frequent.

While the Carretera Austral may be one of the continent's loveliest roads – there's no bad scenery – it's also one of the most hazardous. Blind curves in dense forests and sheer mountains, narrow segments with steeply sloping shoulders, and frequent loose gravel all require drivers to pay the closest attention to avoid head-on collisions, rollovers, and other accidents.

**CTC Centro de Llamados** (Paseo Horn 40) has phones and fax service; **Trapananda Cyber** (General Parra 86) provides Internet access.

Intensive **Spanish classes** with room and full board cost US$375 per week or US$950 per month at **Baquedano International Language School** (Baquedano 20, tel. 067/232520, www.balasch.cl); rates include four hours of instruction Monday–Saturday.

For laundry, try **Lavandería QL** (Bilbao 160, tel. 067/232266) or **Lavandería All Clean** (General Parra 55, Local 2, tel. 067/219635), alongside Residencial Gladys.

For medical attention, contact the **Hospital Base** (J. M. Carrera s/n, tel. 067/231286).

## GETTING THERE

Coyhaique is the region's transportation hub, with flights north and south as well as bus service along the Carretera Austral to Region X (Los Lagos) and Region XII (Magallanes) via Argentina, and to Argentina itself. Chilean buses to destinations in other regions are prohibited from dropping passengers in Argentina.

### Air

Commercial jets land at modern **Aeropuerto Balmaceda,** 50 kilometers southeast of Coyhaique. Small planes still use convenient **Aeródromo Teniente Vidal,** only five kilometers southwest of town.

**LAN** (Moraleda 402, tel. 065/231188) flies several times daily to Puerto Montt and Santiago, Saturday only to Punta Arenas. **Sky Airline** (Prat 203, tel. 067/240825) flies daily to Puerto Montt and the Chilean capital, and south to Punta Arenas.

**Transportes Aéreos San Rafael** (18 de Septiembre 469, tel. 067/573083, sanrafael@123.cl) flies to the remote island settlement of Melinka (US$47) Tuesday and Thursday.

### Bus

More carriers now use the **Terminal de Buses** (Lautaro and Magallanes), but several still prefer their own offices elsewhere. Services north and south along the Carretera Austral are most frequent in summer and may be considerably reduced in winter.

To Puerto Aisén (US$3) and Puerto Chacabuco (US$4, one hour), there are frequent departures with **Buses Suray** (Prat 265, tel. 067/238387).

At the main terminal, **Buses São Paulo** (tel. 067/255726) goes north to Mañihuales (US$3, one hour) and Puerto Cisnes (US$12, six hours) daily at 12:30 P.M. via the paved Viviana junction, and to off-highway destinations such as Villa Ortega and La Tapera.

Because of the eruption and its aftermath, northbound services to Chaitén are in flux. **Buses Becker** (General Parra 329, tel. 067/232167) normally goes there four times weekly, but as of early 2011 it was going Tuesday and Saturday at 8 A.M. to Futaleufú (US$40, 10.5 hours) via Puerto Puyuhuapi (US$16), La Junta (US$20, seven hours), and Villa Santa Lucía (US$30, 8.5 hours). At the terminal, **Buses Altamirano** (tel. 067/314143) goes weekdays to La Junta (US$20) at 4 P.M.

At the main terminal, **Terra Austral** (tel. 067/254335) goes to Puerto Cisnes daily at 6 A.M.

To Puerto Ingeniero Ibáñez (US$8, two hours), on Lago General Carrera's north shore, **Buses Carolina** (tel. 067/255726) connects with the Chile Chico ferry; a combined ticket costs US$12. Ibáñez-bound minibuses usually pick up passengers at their homes or hotels; carriers include **Darío Figueroa Castro** (tel. 09/8977-9737) and **Miguel Acuña** (Manuel Rodríguez 143, tel. 067/251579). Some of these also stop at the corner of Prat and Errázuriz.

Other southbound minibuses go as far as Villa Cerro Castillo (US$7, 1.5 hours), where the pavement ends on the Carretera Austral: **Minibuses Amin Alí** (tel. 09/9313-1402) and **Minibuses Tomás Urreta** (cell 09/9950-0276) leave from Prat and Lautaro, near the restaurant Moneda de Oro, but with a day's notice they'll come to your hotel.

From the main terminal, **Acuario 13** (tel. 067/255726) goes beyond Cerro Castillo to Cochrane (US$26, nine hours) and intermediates at 9:30 A.M. Wednesday and Sunday; **Buses São Paulo,** at the same office, goes

## THE PHANTOM CAPITAL

For better or worse, wrote the 19th-century Argentine-American naturalist William Henry Hudson in his classic *Idle Days in Patagonia*, Argentine Patagonia's destiny was to remain a desert: "During the last twenty years the country has been crossed in various directions, from Atlantic to the Andes, and from the Río Negro to the Straits of Magellan, and has been found all barren." Hudson disparaged the delusions of early explorers who fantasized a "City of the Caesars," an austral El Dorado, adding that "The mysterious illusive city, peopled by whites, which was long believed to exist in the unknown interior, in a valley called Trapananda, is to moderns a myth, a mirage of the mind, as little to the traveler's imagination as the glittering capital of great Manoa, which Alonzo Pizarro and his false friend Orellana failed to discover."

What, then, would Hudson say of the three Chilean cities that, in 2001, were aiming to "capitalize" on the Patagonian mystique by claiming to be the political and cultural center of a region that transcends borders and exists at least partly in the imagination? In Chile, at least, "Patagonia" has no juridical reality, but that didn't stop Puerto Montt, Punta Arenas, and Coyhaique from conducting public press campaigns to champion their claims to a title that, each one thought, would help promote its tourist industry.

The furor started in early 2001, when the Punta Arenas city council sent a note to Chile's Interior Ministry protesting Puerto Montt mayor Rabindranath Quinteros's claim that Puerto Montt was "capital of Patagonia." Punta Arenas mayor Juan Morano argued that "By tradition and history the title is ours, and nobody's adventurous phrases will change that, no matter how much authority they may have." The council even considered a complaint to the Servicio Nacional de Consumidores (National Consumer Protection Service, Sernac), on the grounds that Puerto Montt authorities were lying to tourists.

Morano said that "it's the community itself that determines who is the capital, because people have internalized it – the agreements of politicians and leaders cannot change historic reality, and in the end the people will decide which is the real capital." Meanwhile,

Tuesday, Thursday, and Saturday. **Don Carlos** (Subteniente Cruz 63, tel. 067/232981) goes Wednesday and Friday, while **Águilas Patagónicas** (Lautaro 104, tel. 067/211288), across from the terminal, also goes to Cochrane Sunday at 2 P.M.

Other southbound fares include Puerto Río Tranquilo (US$16, 5.5 hours), Puerto Guadal (US$20, seven hours), and Puerto Bertrand (US$22, eight hours).

From the main terminal, **Queilen Bus** (tel. 067/240760) goes to Puerto Montt (US$60, 22 hours) via Argentina at 4 P.M. Monday, Wednesday, and Friday.

In the same main terminal office (tel. 067/232067), **Transaustral** serves Comodoro Rivadavia (US$40, nine hours), Argentina, via Río Mayo and Sarmiento, with northbound connections to Esquel and Bariloche. Departures take place Monday and Friday at 9 A.M.

### Sea

Coyhaique is not a seaport, but the local office of **Navimag Ferries** (Paseo Horn 47-D, tel. 067/223306) sells ferry berths from Puerto Chacabuco to Puerto Montt, and to Parque Nacional Laguna San Rafael.

**Naviera Austral** (Paseo Horn 40, Oficina 101, tel. 067/210727, www.navieraustral.cl) operates ferries to Chaitén, Puerto Montt, and throughout the Chiloé archipelago.

**Geoturismo Patagonia** (Balmaceda 334, tel. 067/573461, www.geoturismopatagonia.cl) is the agent for Catamaranes del Sur, which has high-speed service to Parque Nacional Laguna San Rafael from Puerto Chacabuco.

## GETTING AROUND

### To the Airport

Taxis to **Aeropuerto Teniente Vidal** are cheap enough (about US$5), but air-taxi

Coyhaique mayor David Sandoval and his city council added their two centavos' worth, declaring their city the capital of this questionable imaginary region.

Coyhaique's argument was that the efforts of its pioneers, the linguistic heritage of the Tehuelche, Chonos, and Kawéskar people, and cartography as far back as Magellan justified their cause. According to Sandoval, "Puerto Montt's pretensions owe more to publicity motivations than to historical and geographical factors." Coyhaique's regional secretary said that the governor had been "clear in soliciting from the Subsecretaria de Desarollo Regional (Subsecretary of Regional Development) a definition of what constitutes Patagonia; in this sense we consider any argument over the title sterile."

Sandoval stressed that "what we are trying to do is to brake the arrogance of Puerto Montt in trying to establish criteria completely unrelated to history and geography. What we want to do is sit down and talk, because tomorrow Argentina could easily pick a city according to the same criteria as capital of Patagonia, or it could be Punta Arenas, and that's not the idea either." At the same time, Punta Arenas's private Cámara de Turismo (Tourism Bureau) called on locals to defend their city's claims, because "we should not lose nor let others take away this title, because it could affect our tourist image."

Former Chilean president Ricardo Lagos, though, took the most sensible approach. Diplomatically avoiding any direct criticism of the three contenders, he commented that "it's better to project yourselves as a city than to arrogantly claim the idea of capital of Patagonia." Hudson, even if he never expected to see cities in the region, would probably agree.

Even more recently, though, the northern lakes district region of La Araucanía has quietly entered the fray in promoting itself as part of Patagonia. In reality, given its history as Chile's Mapuche frontier, the presence of the signature monkey puzzle tree that gives the region its name, and the fact that Argentines consider their bordering province of Neuquén an integral of Patagonia, this is not an unreasonable assertion – and it's certainly a savvy marketing move.

companies usually provide their own transfers. To **Aeropuerto Balmaceda** about 45 minutes away, door-to-door minivan services (US$8 pp) include **Transfer Velásquez** (tel. 067/250413) and **Transfer Valencia** (tel. 067/233030).

### Car Rental

Even shoestring travelers indulge themselves on car rentals in Aisén, since public transport is less frequent than elsewhere and some sights are off the main north–south route. Because the fleet is limited and demand can be high, summer reservations are advisable—even essential.

Among Coyhaique's rental agencies are **Traeger** (Av. Baquedano 457, tel. 067/231648, traeger@patagoniachile.cl), **Europcar** (Errázuriz 454, tel. 067/255171), **Hertz** (General Parra 280, tel. 067/245780), and **International** (General Parra 97, tel. 067/214770).

## VICINITY OF COYHAIQUE

Coyhaique is an ideal base for activities like hiking, fly-fishing, rafting, and even winter skiing. **Fishing** probably tops the list, as the season runs November–May in the numerous lakes and rivers.

Among reliable operators are fly-fishing specialist **Aisén Bridges Travel** (tel./fax 067/233302, www.aisen.cl), which is easiest to contact by phone (English is spoken); **Cóndor Explorer** (Condell 87, tel. 067/573634, www.condorexplorer.com); U.S.-run, Puerto Bertrand–based **Patagonia Adventure Expeditions** (Casilla 8, Cochrane, cell 09/8182-0608, www.adventurepatagonia.com), which offers extended fishing and backcountry trips; and U.S.–Chilean **Salvaje Corazón** (Casilla 311, tel. 067/211488, www.salvajecorazon.com)—English, Hebrew, Portuguese, and some French are also spoken.

## Reserva Nacional Coyhaique

Few cities anywhere have so much wild country so near as this mountainous 2,676-hectare reserve, with its top-of-the-world views of Coyhaique, Cerro Macay, and Cerro Castillo to the south, the Río Simpson Valley to the west, and the Patagonian plains sprawling eastward. Local residents enjoy weekend picnics and barbecues here, only five kilometers north of town, but there's always space away from the crowds, and weekdays it's almost empty.

Altitudes range from 400 meters to 1,361 meters on Cerro Cinchao's summit. More than a meter of rain and snow falls throughout the year, but summers are mild and fairly dry, with an average temperature of 12°C.

While the reserve is wild and almost undeveloped, it's not exactly pristine. Forests of *coigüe (Nothofagus betuloides)* and *lenga (Nothofagus pumilio)* blanket the hillsides, but plantations of exotic pines and larches have supplanted some of the native forest devastated in the 1940s. So close to the city, birds are the most conspicuous wildlife.

The main sights are literally that—the seemingly infinite panoramas in every direction. Several trails offer different perspectives on those panoramas: the 800-meter **Sendero Laguna Verde,** the four-kilometer **Sendero Laguna Venus,** and the **Sendero Las Piedras,** which leads to Cerro Cinchao's summit.

Most visitors stay in town, but Conaf (tel. 067/212125 in Coyhaique) has a rustic six-site campground at **Laguna Verde** and a 10-siter at **Casa Bruja.** Each charges US$9 for up to six persons; two of the Laguna Verde sites have roofed shelters. All have picnic tables, freshwater, and fire pits; Casa Bruja has toilets and hot showers. Bring as much food as necessary. At the entrance, Conaf collects an admission fee of US$4 for adults, US$1 for children.

Three kilometers north of town via the paved highway to Puerto Chacabuco, a dirt lateral climbs steeply east to the reserve. The road is passable for most vehicles in summer but difficult or impossible with rain. It's close enough to the city, though, that anyone in decent physical condition should be able to hike from the highway to the park entrance in about half an hour.

## Reserva Nacional Río Simpson

Northwest of Coyhaique, midway to Puerto Chacabuco, paved Ruta 240 passes through the Río Simpson Valley, flanked by the steep walls and canyons that form this accessible 41,634-hectare forest reserve.

Altitudes are about 100 meters along the river but rise to 1,878 meters in the cordillera. Because it's mostly lower than Reserva Nacional Coyhaique, the weather is milder (15–17°C in summer), but it's also wetter, as westerly storms drop up to 2,500 millimeters of precipitation en route inland.

As at Coyhaique, Río Simpson's forests are mostly native southern beeches (*Nothofagus* species), but the rainfall fosters verdant undergrowth of ferns, fuchsias, and the like. Huemul are found in the more remote areas, as are puma and pudu. Bird species, which include the Andean condor, diminish in autumn and winter, returning in spring.

At kilometer 37, look for the **Cascada La Virgen,** a waterfall that plunges vertically through intense greenery on the highway's north side. Two kilometers east of park headquarters, Conaf's eight-site **Camping San Sebastián** (Ruta 240 Km 30, US$9 per tent) has bathrooms with hot showers.

Conaf's **Centro de Información Ambiental** (Ruta 240 Km 32) boasts a small natural-history museum (8:30 A.M.–5:30 P.M. daily, admission US$2) and botanical garden. From Coyhaique, Don Carlos or Suray buses will drop passengers at the campground, museum, or anywhere along the route.

## Puerto Chacabuco and Vicinity

The forests that thrived here before the 1940s wildfires were more than just embellishments on the landscape; their foliage softened the impact of heavy storms and impeded soil erosion. One effect of the fire-fed devastation was to increase the Río Simpson's sediment load and silt up Puerto Aisén's harbor, forcing authorities to build new port facilities at Puerto Chacabuco, 14 kilometers west.

Now the region's main maritime gateway, Chacabuco is also the departure point for excursions to Parque Nacional Laguna San Rafael and a stopover on some voyages between Puerto Montt and Laguna San Rafael.

### Parque Aiken del Sur

Just 10 kilometers east of Puerto Chacabuco, Aiken del Sur (www.parqueaikendelsur.cl) is a private 250-hectare nature preserve and botanical garden, with several hiking trails at Lago Riesco's south end. Owned by the same company as Catamaranes del Sur and Hotel Loberías del Sur, it's most often visited as part of a hotel stay, including a midday lamb barbecue.

### Accommodations and Food

With 60 rooms in three separate modules, **Hotel Loberías del Sur** (J. M. Carrera 50, tel. 067/351115, www.catamaranesdelsur.cl, US$150 s, US$180 d with buffet breakfast) may be the region's best pure hotel (as opposed to lodges and resorts, though it also does packages). Everything runs like clockwork, including a fine restaurant, catamaran excursions to Laguna San Rafael, and its own 250-hectare forest reserve nearby. The rooms are spacious, with bay windows and king-sized beds; amenities include a gym and sauna, but the wireless Internet signal has a few black holes—check before taking the room.

### Getting There and Around

Buses shuttle frequently between Puerto Chacabuco and Coyhaique, 82 kilometers east via Ruta 240.

Both long-distance ferries and excursions to Parque Nacional Laguna San Rafael leave from the **Terminal de Transbordadores,** part of the port complex. **Naviera Austral** (Coyhaique tel. 067/210727) operates passenger/vehicle ferries from Puerto Chacabuco to Quellón (Chiloé) on Thursday only. Passengers pay US$75. Shipping a vehicle costs US$274; motorcyclists pay US$46 more, bicyclists US$18 more.

## PARQUE NACIONAL LAGUNA SAN RAFAEL

Flowing ice meets frigid sea at Parque Nacional Laguna San Rafael, where frozen pinnacles tumble from the crackling face of Ventisquero San Rafael, a 60-meter-high glacier that descends from the Campo de Hielo Norte, to become bobbing icebergs. Misleadingly named, Laguna San Rafael is really an ocean inlet, though its salinity is low as the icebergs slowly thaw and the receding glacier—a palpable victim of global warming that may no longer touch the water within a few years—discharges freshwater into it.

One of Chile's largest national parks (1,742,000 hectares of rugged terrain), Laguna San Rafael is a UNESCO World Biosphere Reserve for its extraordinary scenery and environments. While remote from any settlement, it's a popular summer excursion for Chileans and foreigners, accessible all year.

### History

For a place so thinly populated and rarely visited, Laguna San Rafael has an intriguing history. Its first European visitor was Spaniard Bartolomé Díaz Gallardo, who crossed the low-lying Istmo de Ofqui (Isthmus of Ofqui) from the Golfo de Penas. Jesuit missionaries visited in 1766 and 1767, bestowing its present name, but the Spanish king soon expelled them from the continent.

British naval officer John Byron, grandfather of the famous poet Lord Byron, was once marooned here in winter. During the voyage of the *Beagle,* Darwin made extensive observations here, while Chilean naval officer Enrique Simpson delivered the first official report in 1871. In 1940, the government started a canal across the isthmus to simplify communications with the far south but soon gave up the project. In 1959 it declared the area a national park, but as late as the 1980s it entertained proposals to build a road for cargo transshipments.

### Geography and Climate

Laguna San Rafael is 225 kilometers southwest of Puerto Chacabuco via a series of

Parque Nacional Laguna San Rafael

narrow channels, but only 190 kilometers from Coyhaique as the air taxi flies. To the east rises the rugged Patagonian mainland; to the west lie the myriad islands of the Archipiélago de Chonos and the Península de Taitao.

Altitudes range from sea level to 4,058-meter Monte San Valentín, the southern Andes's highest peak. Sea-level temperatures are fairly mild, about 8°C, with upwards of 2,500 millimeters of rainfall per year; at higher elevations, precipitation doubles, temperatures are colder, and the snowfall feeds 19 major glaciers that form the 300,000-hectare Campo de Hielo Norte. Pacific storms can darken the skies for weeks on end, but views are stunning when the overcast lifts.

## Flora and Fauna

In areas not covered by ice, up to about 700 meters, mixed Valdivian forest grows so dense that, in Darwin's words, "our faces, hands and shin-bones all bore witness to the maltreatment we received, in attempting to penetrate their forbidding recesses." The main trees are two species of the southern beech *coigüe,* the coniferous *mañío macho (Podocarpus nubigena), tepu,* and other species, with a dense understory of shrubs, ferns, mosses, and vines. Above 700 meters, there is almost equally dense forest of the southern beeches *lenga* and *ñire,* with occasional specimens of the coniferous Guaiteca cypress.

Most of the easily visible wildlife congregates around the shoreline, beginning with eye-catching seabirds, such as the flightless steamer duck and Magellanic penguin, the soaring black-browed and sooty albatrosses, and various gulls. Marine mammals include the southern elephant seal, southern sea lion, and southern sea otter.

Forest-dwelling animals are harder to see, but pudu and huemul graze the uplands, while foxes and pumas prowl for their prey.

## Sights and Recreation

Calving off the face of **Ventisquero San Rafael,** indigo icebergs bob and drift in the waters of **Laguna San Rafael,** an oval body of water measuring 6–9 kilometers in width and connected to the southern canals by the narrow Río Témpanos. The world's lowest-latitude tidewater glacier, Ventisquero San Rafael may not be so much longer; in continuous retreat since 1960, it could be a casualty of global warming.

Few visitors set foot in the park, as most arrive by ferry or catamaran, transferring to inflatables to meander among the bergs and approach the glacier's face. Those who manage to land can hike through seven kilometers of evergreen forest on the **Sendero al Ventisquero** to a glacial overlook.

## Accommodations and Food

At park headquarters, Conaf's three-site **Camping Laguna Caiquenes** (US$7 per site for up to six campers) allows no campfires. Its **Casa de Huéspedes Laguna Caiquenes** (US$140), with kitchen facilities, accommodates up to six persons, park admission included. For reservations, contact Conaf's Coyhaique Patrimonio Silvestre office (Los Coihues s/n, tel. 067/212125).

No supplies except fresh water are available—bring everything from Coyhaique or Puerto Chacabuco. Ferries and catamarans feed their passengers; the catamarans usually have an open bar and chill the whiskey with ice chipped off passing bergs.

## Information

Conaf's administration and ranger station is on Laguna San Rafael's northeastern shore. Anyone who literally sets foot in the park pays a US$6 admission fee, but boat people do not, as offshore waters fall under naval rather than Conaf jurisdiction; according to Conaf statistics, which exclude maritime passengers, the park hosted only 158 visitors in 2009.

## Getting There

Unfortunately, there's no cheap and easy way of reaching the park. Air travel usually means only an overflight, while sea travel can be relatively fast (in a catamaran) or slow (on a cruise ship) but still expensive. Catamarans spend only a couple hours at the glacier, while cruise ships spend longer but are even more expensive. From the town of Puerto Río Tranquilo, on the north arm of Lago General Carrera, a new gravel road has reached Bahía Exploradores, only about 65 kilometers north of the glacier, but its completion has not eliminated the need for boat travel, only shortened it.

Air taxis rarely land at the 775-meter gravel airstrip, but Coyhaique-based charter companies can carry up to five passengers on overflights for around US$1,900. The current options are **Transporte Aéreo Don Carlos** (Subteniente Cruz 63, tel./fax 067/231981) and **Transportes Aéreos San Rafael** (18 de Septiembre 469, tel./fax 067/573080).

**Navimag Cruceros** now operates small cruise ships from Castro (Chiloé) and Puerto Chacabuco, overnighting at the glacier. From Castro, summer fares for the five-day, four-night voyage on the *Mare Australis* start around US$780 per person; from Puerto Chacabuco, the comparable round-trip fares for three days and two nights start at US$600 per person. For more detail, contact Navimag offices in Santiago, Puerto Montt, Coyhaique, or Puerto Chacabuco, or see its website (www.navimagcruceros.cl).

September–May, **Cruceros Marítimos Skorpios** (Augusto Leguía 118, Las Condes, Santiago, tel. 02/2311030, www.skorpios.cl) offers four-day, three-night cruises from Puerto Montt on the 130-passenger *Skorpios II.* Rates range from US$850 per person in low season to US$2,100 per person in high season (mid-December–mid-March), depending on the cabin; some voyages include a side trip to hot springs in the Quitralco fjord.

Rates on **Catamaranes del Sur**'s *Chaitén* (US$400 pp) include full meals and an open bar; Coyhaique's **Geoturismo Patagonia** (Balmaceda 334, tel. 067/573461, www.geoturismopatagonia.cl) can make reservations, but they're not very knowledgeable about details.

As of early 2011, a new operator, affiliated with Coyhaique's Cóndor Explorer and Puerto Río Tranquilo's El Puesto, is taking hikers by sea to the park for day trips, and for one- and two-night packages with tent camping. It's not cheap—about US$180 for the day trip and US$300 for the overnight, not counting transportation to the end of the Río Exploradores valley road—but the price compares favorably to the catamaran and cruise ship excursions.

# The Northern Carretera Austral

From Coyhaique, the paved Carretera Austral is briefly contiguous with Ruta 240 to Puerto Aisén and Puerto Chacabuco, but after nine kilometers it becomes a gravel road veering northeast to Villa Ortega. Ruta 240 continues west and, passing through the **Túnel Farellón** above the Río Simpson, it reaches the Viviana junction after 39 kilometers. Here, a smooth paved highway turns northeast up the Río Mañihuales Valley and intersects the Carretera Austral about 13 kilometers southeast of Villa Mañihuales.

Heavy rains can and do close the highway north to Chaitén, sometimes for several days.

## VILLA MAÑIHUALES

Villa Mañihuales, a pioneer village 76 kilometers north of Coyhaique via the roundabout Viviana junction, is the headquarters for **Reserva Nacional Mañihuales,** a 3,596-hectare forest reserve that takes its name from the native *mañío* (podocarpus) forest.

Facilities at Conaf's five-site **Camping Las Lavanderas** (US$7.50 for up to six persons) include picnic tables and toilets, but cold showers only. **Residencial Mañiguales** (Ibar 280, tel. 067/431403, US$24 pp with breakfast) has rooms with shared baths (which are numerous); there are a few simple eateries.

All buses from Coyhaique pass through town en route to northbound Carretera Austral destinations.

## VILLA AMENGUAL

About 58 kilometers north of Villa Mañihuales, overlooking the Río Cisnes Canyon beneath 2,095-meter Cerro Alto Nevado, Villa Amengual dates from 1983; it owes its existence to the Carretera Austral. A few kilometers south, an eastbound gravel road climbs the valley to the settlement of La Tapera and a rarely used border crossing to Argentina.

Distinguished by its shingled chapel, built in the Chilote immigrant style, Amengual is an important stop for cyclists, as one of few places with food and accommodations between Mañihuales and Puerto Puyuhuapi, another 60 kilometers north over rugged terrain.

### Practicalities

There are several modest *hospedajes* (family-run lodgings) in the US$10–12 per person range, including **Residencial El Encanto** (Castro 33-A), **Residencial El Paso** (Arias 12), and **Café y Residencial El Indio** (Arias s/n), all of which also serve meals.

Amengual's spiffy **Oficina de Información Turística** (Arias and Castro, 2–8 P.M. Mon.–Sat. summer only) doubles as a crafts shop.

All northbound buses from Coyhaique pass through Amengual, but some turn west toward Puerto Cisnes from a junction just a few kilometers north of town.

## PUERTO CISNES

At the mouth of its namesake river, Puerto Cisnes (population about 2,600) owes its origins to a 1920s lumber mill but still serves as a key port for scattered fishing hamlets in and around Canal Puyuhuapi; rarely visited Parque Nacional Isla Magdalena is just across the water to the west.

Construction of a link to the Carretera Austral has partially reoriented the town inland, and in recent years the economy has diversified with salmon farming and tourism (primarily fly-fishing).

One of Aisén's architectural oddities, facing the Plaza de Armas, is Cisnes' **Biblioteca Pública Genaro Godoy** (Sotomayor s/n), a wooden structure with hexagonal neoclassical columns and a pediment with bas reliefs based on Greek mythology.

Visitors can hire a launch to the 157,616-hectare **Parque Nacional Isla Magdalena,** occupying most of its namesake island and several smaller islands, but day trips cost around US$85 (for up to eight or ten people). Operators include Jorge Coronado at Tour Bella Vista (Séptimo de Línea 112, tel. 067/346408, www.

tourbellavista.cl), Javier Catalán (tel. 09/6848-9601, 09/99179487), and Juan Cárcamo (tel. 09/9833-6649).

### Accommodations and Food

Puerto Cisnes has several passable accommodations, starting with the reasonably priced **Hospedaje Bella Vista** (Séptimo de Línea 112, tel. 067/346408, US$14 pp with shared bath). **Hostería El Gaucho** (Holmberg 140, tel. 067/346514, US$20 pp) is slightly dearer.

Well-kept **El Guairao** (Piloto Pardo 58, tel. 067/346473, US$50 s, US$60 d) has motel-style rooms with satellite TV; it also has the best restaurant, but there are other options along the waterfront.

### Information

Occupying municipal offices, **Sernatur** (Sotomayor and José María Caro, tel. 09/7663-7208, pepabecker@gmail.com) has a seasonal representative, but this is subject to change. Hours are generally 10 A.M.–1:30 P.M. and 3–7 P.M. daily, again subject to change.

### Getting There

Several companies go to Coyhaique (US$12, six hours), including **Transportes Terra Austral** (Piloto Pardo 368, tel. 067/346757) and **Patagonia Norte** (Arturo Prat s/n, cell 09/8226-3651), but schedules are in flux.

**Buses Entre Verdes** (Gabriela Mistral s/n, cell 09/8426-0959) goes to La Junta (US$12, 3.5 hours) at 4 P.M. Monday, Wednesday, and Friday; otherwise, for northbound connections, wait at the highway junction or backtrack toward Coyhaique.

## PARQUE NACIONAL QUEULAT

From the Cisnes junction, the Carretera Austral zigzags over the 500-meter Portezuelo Queulat as it enters 154,093-hectare Parque Nacional Queulat, which rises from the ocean fjords of Canal Puyuhuapi through nearly impenetrable evergreen forests that, except on a few well-kept trails, deter all but the most intrepid hikers. Beneath snowcapped summits, meltwater cascades off hanging indigo glaciers into frigidly limpid rivers that have cut deep canyons en route to the sea.

Queulat's accessibility has made it a popular destination for those exploring the Carretera Austral, but most see only a sample of its attractions. Many visitors come to enjoy the fishing in particular, but Queulat could be a poster child for climate change—as late as 1837, its hanging glacier came within 100 meters of the sea, but that distance is now 7.8 kilometers. Much of this change dates from a 1960 flood.

### Geography and Climate

Roughly midway between Chaitén and Coyhaique, Queulat ranges from sea level on Canal Puyuhuapi to the 2,225-meter summit of Cerro Alto Nevado. Up to 4,000 millimeters of precipitation, evenly distributed throughout the year, feeds its upper snowfields and glaciers, rushing rivers, and peaceful finger lakes; the more westerly areas are wettest. The mean annual temperature is around 8°C.

### Flora and Fauna

At lower elevations, Queulat's humid climate fosters dense evergreen forests of the southern beech *coigüe* and *tepa,* which reaches heights of 30 meters or more, with a dense understory of bamboo-like *quila,* fuchsia, and ferns. On some slopes, the coniferous Guaiteca cypress shades massive specimens of the broad-leaved shrub *nalca,* while at higher altitudes the *coigüe* mixes with the related *lenga.*

Even along the highway, look for the timid pudu, no bigger than a border collie, as it emerges from the forest. Foxes, pumas, and Patagonian skunks are also present. The seldom-seen *chucao* is a solitary songbird that, legend says, brings good luck if it sings on your right, but bad luck if it sings on your left. The elegant black-necked swan paddles the fjords and even some lakes.

### Sights and Recreation

Many points of interest are on or near the Carretera Austral; the best operations base is **Sector Ventisquero,** where Conaf's Centro de Información, 22 kilometers south of Puerto Puyuhuapi via the highway and a short eastbound lateral, marks the start of several dead-end trails. Even the most sedentary can walk the 200-meter **Sendero El Mirador** to a vista point that looks up the valley to the **Ventisquero Colgante,** a hanging glacier that suggests what California's Yosemite Valley must have looked like before the ice melted. Even when the sun shines brightly, the trail winds through rainforest so dark that you nearly need a flashlight at midday.

Crossing its eponymous river on a suspension bridge, the 600-meter **Sendero Río Guillermo** trail arrives at **Laguna Témpanos** (Iceberg Lake); despite the name, it's iceberg-free. On the turbulent river's north bank, the 3.5-kilometer **Sendero Ventisquero Colgante** climbs unrelentingly to even more breathtaking views of the hanging glacier. As the afternoon sun warms the atmosphere, ice chunks tumble onto the rocks below.

West of the bridge crossing, on the south bank, the 350-meter **Sendero Interpretativo El Aluvión** loops through part of the valley where the 1960 flood carried huge boulders and flattened tall trees. It's signed in Spanish and pretty good English.

Just beyond Guardería Pudú, the park's southern entrance, the 1.7-kilometer **Sendero Río de las Cascadas** trail winds through dripping rainforest before arriving at a granite amphitheater where ribbons of glacial meltwater mark the river's source. Farther on, where the highway begins to switchback into the Río Queulat Valley, a short staircase trail approaches the **Salto Río Padre García,** a waterfall named for the Chiloé-based Jesuit who, in 1766–1767, may have been the first European to see the area.

Queulat's numerous rivers and lakes, particularly the northern **Lago Risopatrón** and **Lago Rosselot,** are prime fly-fishing destinations.

## Accommodations and Food

Accommodations are decentralized, to say the least, but there are options from La Junta in the north to the Río Ventisquero and vicinity in the south. Other nearby accommodations can be found in Puerto Puyuhuapi and La Junta.

Near the main trailheads, Conaf's **Camping Ventisquero** (US$10 for up to six persons) has 10 relatively barren sites with sheltered cooking areas and immaculate toilets, but if the shower water were any colder the pipes would freeze. Cheap firewood is also available.

On Lago Risopatrón's western shore, 12 kilometers north of Puerto Puyuhuapi, Conaf's five-site **Camping Angostura** (US$10 for up to six persons) has similar facilities in a humid temperate rainforest with soggy soils.

Thirty kilometers south of Puerto Puyuhuapi, fly-fishing is the focus at **Fiordo Queulat Ecolodge** (tel. 067/233302 in Coyhaique, www.aisen.cl, US$185 s or d with half board), but it has branched out to include other activities such as hiking and sea-kayaking, leaving directly from its own property. Formerly just a cluster of cabañas, it has added a handsome new clubhouse with a fireplace and comfortable common areas, and it has 24-hour electricity from a water-driven turbine. Lunches and dinners cost US$25 each per person.

About half an hour north of Puerto Puyuhuapi on Lago Risopatrón, ☾ **Cabañas El Pangue** (Km 240, tel. 067/325128, www.elpangue.cl, US$110 s, US$129 d) offers spacious cabins with natural wood, large double beds, and sunken tubs in a woodsy setting; off-season rates are about 40 percent lower. Larger units, sleeping up to seven, cost less on a per-person basis; breakfasts and other meals, including lamb barbecues, are also available. The management also rents canoes, rowboats, motorboats, and horses. A sauna and hot tub are available. El Pangue has begun to offer multi-day, all-inclusive packages as well.

## Other Practicalities

At Conaf's informative **Centro de Información Ambiental** at Sector Ventisquero, rangers provide guidance on hiking and other activities. Visitors can also consult with rangers at Guardería Pudú (the park's southern entrance) and Guardería El Pangue (northern entrance).

Conaf collects a US$6 admission charge (US$2 for children) at Sector Ventisquero only.

Buses from Coyhaique to Puerto Puyuhuapi

and Chaitén pass directly through the park, though they drop passengers at least half an hour's walk west of Sector Ventisquero.

## PUERTO PUYUHUAPI

Thanks to its history as a pioneer port established by Sudeten German immigrants in the 1930s, Puerto Puyuhuapi has a greater air of permanence than any other Carretera Austral settlement between Coyhaique, 225 kilometers to the south, and Chaitén, 195 kilometers to the north. Many of its streets, residents, and businesses still bear names like Hopperdietzel, Grosse, Ludwig, Rossbach, and Übel.

At the north end of Seno Ventisquero, a sheltered extension of the larger Canal Puyuhuapi, Puerto Puyuhuapi (population about 600) is also a gateway to Parque Nacional Queulat and the hot-springs resort of Termas de Puyuhuapi.

### Alfombras de Puyuhuapi

Since its 1940 founding by textile engineer Walter Hopperdietzel, Alfombras de Puyuhuapi (Aysén s/n, cell 09/9359-9515, www.puyuhuapi.com) has produced handmade woolen carpets, tinted with Swiss dyes, for both local and export markets. Some sell for upwards of $1,000, but there are smaller, more affordable pieces as well. Most of the 20 employees are female weavers from Chiloé. The benchmark price is about US$150 per square meter.

The factory is open for tours 8:30 A.M.–1:30 P.M. and 3–6:30 P.M. Monday–Friday; admission is free. The sales office keeps identical hours but is also open 9:30 A.M.–noon Saturday.

### Termas Ventisquero de Puyuhuapi

Six kilometers south of town, nestled between the road and the shoreline, Ventisquero de Puyuhuapi (tel. 067/325228, www.termasventisqueropuyuhuapi.cl, 9 A.M.–11 P.M. daily) is an upstart hot-springs center with outdoor pools suitable for a hot soak and, for the more daring, a plunge into the sea. Given its accessibility, Ventisquero is drawing visitors who otherwise might spend the day at upscale Puyuhuapi Lodge & Spa (reached only by boat).

Ventisquero de Puyuhuapi charges US$23 per person for use of the baths. Upstairs, it has a handsome café that prepares espresso, quality teas, sandwiches, and kuchen, and has recently added lunch and dinner to its offerings.

### Accommodations and Food

After being closed for many years, the classic **La Casona** (Av. Otto Übel 1, tel. 067/325221, US$30 s, US$44 d) is once again open to the public. Set among delightful gardens, the seven-room **Hostería Alemana** (Av. Übel 450, tel. 067/325118, www.hosteriaalemana.cl, US$30 s, US$50 d) is good enough but is otherwise utilitarian.

Now open all year, with exceptional ownership, tobacco-free **Casa Ludwig** (Av. Übel 202, tel./fax 067/325220, www.casaludwig.cl, US$27–45 s, US$40–71 d) is a 10-room bed-and-breakfast in a cavernous four-story landmark house. Attic rooms with shared baths are cheaper than the downstairs rooms (some of which have sea views) but are still comfy and cozy, and the breakfast is excellent. English and German are spoken; the sitting room has a German-language library with a few English titles. There is wireless Internet as well.

If you wish to venture from hotel dining rooms, salmon dinners and kuchen are served with inconsistent quality at **Café Rossbach** (Aysén s/n, tel. 067/325203, lunch and dinner daily), alongside the carpet factory. **Aonikenk** (Hamburgo 16, lunch and dinner daily) is a little more daring than some small-town restaurants, even offering vegetarian dishes, but fish and pasta are the specialties. It makes a genuine effort at pleasing decor. Next door to Casa Ludwig, the excellent **Lluvia Marina** (Av. Übel 720, lunch and dinner daily) is only open in summer.

### Information and Services

The privately run **Oficina de Información Turística** (Otto Übel s/n, tel. 067/325244, www.puertopuyuhuapi.cl, 9:30 A.M.–1:30 P.M. and 3–8 P.M. Wed.–Mon. Oct.–Apr.) has flyers for self-guided tours, written in good English, to the town and its surroundings. It also offers free wireless Internet.

### Getting There and Around

Services change rapidly here, but as of early 2011 **Buses Becker** (Übel s/n, tel. 067/325195) and **Buses Altamirano** (O'Higgins 39, tel. 067/325130) were passing through here from Coyhaique (US$16) en route to Villa Santa Lucía and Futaleufú.

Starting from Puerto Cisnes, **Buses Entre Verdes** (O'Higgins 39, tel. 067/325130) stops here Monday, Wednesday, and Friday en route to and from La Junta.

## PUYUHUAPI LODGE & SPA

South of Puerto Puyuhuapi, sumptuous in style but more affordable than it looks, Puyuhuapi Lodge & Spa (Bahía Dorita s/n, tel. 067/325129) is a secluded spa that's not literally an island, but since there's no road and the only access is by launch across the Seno Ventisquero (Glacier Sound), it might as well be. Both hotel guests and day visitors can enjoy naturally heated outdoor pools and hiking trails that veer through the forest understory of dense *quila* (solid bamboo) thickets, *chilco* (firecracker fuchsia), rhubarb-like *nalcas* with leaves the size of umbrellas, and colossal tree ferns.

Hotel guests only, though, have access to spa facilities, including a gym, heated indoor pool, and massage room (perched in a tower, it enjoys 360-degree views of its scenic surroundings). When the weather lifts, the panorama is Queulat's Andean front range, where snow lingers even at summer's end.

Spacious waterfront rooms, stocked with genteel touches like terrycloth robes and individual umbrellas, look onto the dock where the catamaran *Patagonia Express* starts its weekly run to Parque Nacional Laguna San Rafael, on the final day of package holidays that range from four days and three nights to six days and five nights. Activities like hiking, fly-fishing, and excursions along the Carretera Austral are additional.

While the hotel works mainly with packages, overnight accommodations are possible on a space-available basis, normally Thursday and Friday only. In peak season (Christmas–mid-March), rates start at US$220 single or double with buffet breakfast; the rest of the year, they're about 20 percent lower. Spa access costs US$18 per person more. Fixed-price lunches and dinners cost US$37, while deluxe buffet dinners cost US$50.

While it sounds exclusive, Puyuhuapi also lets the riffraff in for day use of the outdoor pools and baths (US$17 per adult, US$8 pp per child) and of the spa (US$44 per adult, US$22 per child). The cafeteria at the outdoor pools, open only in daytime, has a cheaper but more limited menu than the restaurant.

Launches from its mainland information center on the Carretera Austral, 14 kilometers south of Puerto Puyuhuapi, are free for package guests; otherwise they cost US$10 per adult, US$5 per child round-trip. Scheduled departures from the hotel are at 9:30 A.M. and 12:30, 3, 5, and 6:30 P.M., returning half an hour later, but there are occasional unscheduled crossings as well.

Termas de Puyuhuapi's main office is **Patagonia Connection** (Fidel Oteíza 1951, Oficina 1006, Providencia, Santiago, tel. 02/2256489, www.patagonia-connection.com).

## LA JUNTA AND VICINITY

At the crossroads town of La Junta, new penetration roads proceed west along the Río Palena toward the port of Raúl Marín Balmaceda and east up the Río Figueroa valley toward the Argentine border. Local businesses, thus, are placing themselves as a "place of encounter" for exploring the Cuenca de Palena, the Río Palena drainage.

On a broad plain at the confluence of the two rivers, just south of the regional border between Aisén and Los Lagos, La Junta (population about 1,200) is the main access point to **Reserva Nacional Lago Rosselot,** a 12,725-hectare forest reserve whose longitudinal finger lake is known for its fishing.

La Junta gained a measure of notoriety when,

in 2001, local authorities erected an unauthorized monument to General Pinochet—still popular with some residents for building the north–south highway. Others, though, find this embarrassing; with a project to widen the highway through town, they may have an excuse to remove it without ruffling feathers—or raising hackles.

## Sights

Only 200 meters south of Hotel Espacio y Tiempo, Conaf's **Sendero Mirador La Roca** leads to two scenic overlooks within Reserva Nacional Lago Rosselot. Climbing steeply from the highway for about 25 minutes, the trail's first viewpoint looks west toward the dormant snow-covered cone of 2,400-meter Cerro Melimoyu. At the second, about 15 minutes on, there are even better views of the Río Rosselot and the Córdon Barros Arana to the northeast.

From the north end of town, there is Monday and Friday minibus service on a scenic new road that leads 65 kilometers northeast, including a short ferry connection, to the small island port of **Raúl Marín Balmaceda.** The modest **Hospedaje Melimoyu** (tel. 09/6222-4944, US$40 with full board) is a good budget alternative here, while **Fundo Los Leones Lodge** (cell 09/7898-2956, www.fundolosleones.com, US$100–156 s, US$100–180 d) is a seaside ecolodge that offers excursions that include sea kayaking, visits to a nearby sea lion colony, and fly-fishing among its options. Formerly the property of environmental philanthropists Doug and Kris McDivitt Tompkins, its four cabañas still bear the founders' rustically elegant style, and the food is remarkable—light but flavorful quiches and pies, diverse salads, and even homemade truffles.

## Accommodations and Food

La Junta has many simple accommodations, the best of which is probably **Residencial Valdera** (Antonio Varas s/n, tel. 067/314105, luslagos@hotmail.com, US$20–30 d), where rates include breakfast; the higher price corresponds to rooms with private baths. The elite choice, though, is the nine-room **Hotel Espacio y Tiempo** (Carretera Austral s/n, tel. 067/314141, www.espacioytiempo.cl, US$75 s, US$108 d with breakfast and private bath), where a cordon of conifers encloses the lawns and gardens of a small but appealing roadside inn that also offers fishing and other excursions. The rooms themselves are spacious and even sophisticated, and the outstanding restaurant, open to the public, serves a diverse menu of meats and fish that even includes the odd Peruvian dish, such as *picante de pollo* (US$12), a shredded chicken casserole with a little bite to it. There is also wireless Internet.

Immediately north of Espacio y Tiempo, **Alto Melimoyu B&B** (Carretera Austral s/n, tel. 067/314320, nicolas.troncoso@inasa.cl, US$52–66 s, US$75–95 d) is a shiny new construction with luminous common areas and nine rooms—four smaller rooms with shared bath and five significantly larger ones with private baths and TV.

For breakfasts, lunches, and desserts, **Mi Casita de Té** (Carretera Austral and Patricio Lynch, tel. 067/314206) makes an ideal break. It also offers wireless Internet and has outdoor seating—a mixed blessing when trucks pass by on the dusty highway.

## Information

On the Plaza de Armas, La Junta's **Oficina de Información Turística** (www.cuencadelpalena-queulat.cl, 10 A.M.–1 P.M. Mon.–Sat., 3–7:30 P.M. Mon.–Fri., and 3–5 P.M. Sat.) is planning to move to new quarters elsewhere on the plaza.

## Getting There and Around

Like other Carretera Austral villages, La Junta is a regular stop for buses en route between Coyhaique and continental Chiloé. **Entre Verdes** (Antonio Varas s/n, tel. 067/314725) goes to Puerto Cisnes (US$12, 3.5 hours) at 7 A.M. Monday, Wednesday, and Friday. Monday, Tuesday, Friday, and Saturday at 6 A.M., **Transportes Altamirano** (Moraleda 13, tel. 067/314143) goes to Chaitén (US$20), with connections to Futaleufú in Villa Santa

Lucía. Weekdays, it goes Coyhaique at 5:30 A.M. (US$21). **Terra Austral** (Manuel Montt s/n, tel. 067/314400, tel. 09/8241-5526) also goes Futaleufú and Coyhaique.

## LAGO YELCHO

About 30 kilometers north of La Junta, where the highway bridges the Río Palena, lies the boundary between Region XI (Aisén) and Region X (Los Lagos). Los Lagos's first major attraction is elongated Lago Yelcho, stretching from Puerto Cárdenas in the north to Puerto Ramírez in the southeast, which formed the lacustrine part of the highway between Chaitén and Futaleufú until the overland route eliminated the need for ferries. Kayakers, though, can still paddle from Puerto Ramírez to Puerto Cárdenas and even to the Pacific.

At **Villa Santa Lucía,** 70 kilometers north of La Junta and 78 kilometers south of Chaitén, the main highway continues north but the eastbound lateral Ruta 235 drops steeply to the lakeshore and **Puerto Ramírez,** continuing southeast toward Palena and a minor border crossing. The alternative Ruta 231 proceeds northeast toward the white-water-rafting and kayaking capital of Futaleufú and a far more efficient crossing.

Midway between Villa Santa Lucía and Puerto Cárdenas, on the west side of the Carretera Austral, the north side of the **Puente Ventisquero** (Glacier Bridge) is the trailhead for a two-hour hike through soggy evergreen forest to the **Ventisquero Cavi,** a hanging glacier. **Camping Ventisquero** (www.ventisqueroyelcho.cl) is a no-frills facility with a token per-person charge. It also operates a summer café, with sandwiches and fresh fruit kuchen.

Across the highway from the Ventisquero Cavi, the lakeside **Hotel Yelcho en la Patagonia** (tel. 065/731337, www.yelcho.cl, US$120 s, US$132 d) is a fashionable fishing lodge whose comfortable upstairs rooms offer lake views through groves of *arrayanes;* the ground-level bar/restaurant has high-beamed ceilings and decent-enough food for a place that specializes in fly-fishing holidays. On the same grounds, it also has 15 campsites (US$60 for up to four persons) with electricity, roofed shelters, and hot showers.

## FUTALEUFÚ

With its reputation for world-class white-water rafting—some say it's *the* best—Futaleufú draws outdoor recreationists like a magnet. But what works for this tidy village, its forested mountains, and its namesake river—spectacular natural beauty, cleanliness, and isolation—also works against it. The 1,200 or so who live here may be on borrowed time, possibly powerless to fend off Endesa, the powerful Spanish electric utility company that wants to build three massive dams where at least three international rafting and kayaking enterprises have elaborate summer camps and several Chilean operators spend at least part of the season.

More recent threats have been a gold mine in the upper reaches of the Río Espolón drainage, and the 2008 eruption of Volcán Chaitén, which left substantial amounts of ash in and around the town. The eruption, though, also stopped construction on a new road from Chaitén that would have left the valley open to hydroelectric development.

As of 2011, the "Fu" remains one of the world's cleanest and most challenging rivers. Both foreign and Chilean operators hope to kindle local and national enthusiasm for preserving the river and its surroundings, and the March 2000 Whitewater Challenge World Championships brought rafters and kayakers from 14 different countries. Fly-fishing has also had a substantial impact on the economy, but the unfortunate introduction of the so-called "toilet paper alga" is threatening the clear waters in some of the Fu's tributaries.

### Orientation

Only eight kilometers west of the Argentine border, at the confluence of the Río Espolón and the Río Futaleufú, the village is 155 kilometers southeast of Chaitén via the Carretera Austral, Ruta 235 from Villa Santa Lucia, and Ruta 231 from Puerto Ramírez.

Futaleufú's plan is a rectangular grid whose focus, if not its precise center, is the manicured

Plaza de Armas. On the plaza's south side, Bernardo O'Higgins leads east toward the Argentine border, while Arturo Prat, on the west side, leads south toward westbound Ruta 231.

## Recreation

White water is the major attraction, but hiking, climbing, mountain biking, and horseback riding are also grabbing attention. Several U.S. **rafting/kayaking** operators maintain summer camps in the vicinity October–April.

The Class III Espolón is a good starter river, though the 2008 eruption of Volcán Chaitén has affected it more than any other river here. Even parts of the Fu are suitable for those with limited experience, but rapids like the Class V Terminator can challenge even top professionals.

According to former U.S. Olympic kayaker Chris Spelius, who runs a camp here, "Big water can be forgiving to a certain extent, but this river's so big that it can take a normal human being with a life jacket and hold him under water longer than he can hold his breath." Even on commercially rafted Class IV stretches there are "Death Spots" that need a professional guide to be avoided. According to Lawrence Alvarez, another U.S. operator, about 10 percent of Fu rafters become "swimmers" at some point.

For a half-day Class IV descent on the Fu, figure about US$100 per person, though some Chilean companies might do it for as little as US$70; this involves descent of the river "between the bridges," a nonstop succession of Class III–IV rapids; novices get out before tackling the Class V Casa de Piedra rapid.

For **hikers,** one of the best trails follows the Fu's south bank, starting on an undulating oxcart road opposite the Expediciones Chile camp about 10 kilometers west of town; ask for directions at **Expediciones Chile** (Gabriela Mistral 296, tel. 065/721386). The trail continues past peasant homesteads above rapids like the Terminator before continuing through southern beech forest so dense that in midafternoon on a sunny day, it's as dark as dusk. The trail eventually emerges onto a terrace with new trophy houses; a nearby bridge recrosses the river to Ruta 231.

© WAYNE BERNHARDSON

White-water rafters take on the mighty Río Futaleufú.

## THE *HUASO* AND THE RODEO

Less celebrated than the Argentine gaucho, the Chilean *huaso* resembles his trans-Andean counterpart in many ways but differs dramatically in others. Both, of course, are horsemen, but the gaucho arose from a background of fierce independence on the Pampas, while the subservient *huaso* originated on the landed estates that dominated economic and social life in colonial and republican Chile.

Though the *huaso* was a hired hand or even a peon attached to the property, on Sundays he and his colleagues could blow off steam by racing their horses, betting, and drinking. As the spontaneous rodeo grew too raucous, though, it drew the disapproval of landowners, who responded by organizing competitions that, over time, became more genteel versions of their *huaso* origins.

Though Chilean rodeo remains popular, it is now, according to historian Richard Slatta, a nostalgic exercise that's "a middle- and upper-class pastime, not a profession," as it has become in North America. Riders wear colorful ponchos, flat-brimmed hats, oversized spurs, and elaborately carved wooden stirrups.

Chilean rodeo's signature event is the *atajada,* in which a pair of *jinetes* (riders) guide and pin a calf or steer to the padded wall of the *medialuna,* the semicircular rodeo ring. Since it's harder to control the steer by the body than the head – the chest is best – the horsemen get more points for this. They lose points if the steer strikes any unpadded part of the wall or escapes between the horses.

There are no cash prizes, though the event ends by acknowledging the champions and other riders with wine and empanadas. Compared to Canada, the United States, and even Mexico, Chilean rodeo is truly *machista* – women prepare and serve food, dress in costume, and dance the traditional *cueca* with the men, but they do not ride.

An hour south of Santiago, Rancagua is the capital of Chilean rodeo, drawing thousands of spectators to March's national festival. In small settlements along the Carretera Austral, though, rodeo probably comes closest to its historic roots.

For river rafting and other activities, drop-in visitors can try local operators and offices including **Cara del Indio** (Ruta 231 Km 35, tel. 02/1964239, www.caradelindio.cl), which has a camp and cabañas on the Fu 35 kilometers west of town; **Cóndor Fu** (Sector Nordeste No. 1, cell 09/8579-5242, www.condorfu.com), which has drawn praise from overseas operators; **Futaleufú Explore** (O'Higgins 772, tel. 065/721527, www.futaleufuexplore.com); and the U.S. operator **Expediciones Chile** (Gabriela Mistral 296, tel. 065/721386, www.exchile.com).

For **horseback riding,** contact **Rancho las Ruedas** (Piloto Carmona 337, tel. 065/721294. www.rancholasruedas.cl), in the woods at the north end of Arturo Prat.

### Accommodations

Futaleufú has more and better accommodations than any other place its size on or along the Carretera Austral; most are utilitarian, but several have both character and style.

Just south of town on Ruta 231, prior to crossing the bridge over the river, **Aldea Puerto Espolón** (puertoespolon@gmail.com, cell 09/9447-7448, US$8 pp) has shady campsites with grass, clean toilets, and hot showers. It also rents two-person tepees (US$20 d) on the ground and domes (US$24 d) on elevated platforms.

Affordable accommodations with breakfast and shared baths include **Residencial Carahue** (O'Higgins 332, tel. 065/721221, carlosespinozapinto@yahoo.es, US$12 pp), which also has one room with private bath (US$40 d), and **Hotel Continental** (Balmaceda 595, tel. 065/721222, US$16 pp). Wireless-Internet-equipped **Hospedaje Adolfo** (O'Higgins 302, tel. 065/721256, pettyrios@hotmail.com, US$16 pp with shared bath) is a step above the others, though some rooms have low ceilings, and it sometimes fills with laborers on short-term jobs here.

**Hospedaje Cañete** (Gabriela Mistral 347, tel. 065/721214, elocovi@hotmail.com, US$17 pp) gets high marks from local operators for their overseas clients who want to stay within a limited budget. Rates include private bath and wireless Internet. **Posada Ely** (Balmaceda 409, tel. 065/721205, posada.ely.futaleufu@gmail.com, US$24 pp with breakfast) has rooms with private baths.

**Hostería Río Grande** (O'Higgins 397, tel. 065/721320, www.pachile.com, US$70 s, US$110 d) has pleasant common areas, a bar/restaurant, and a dozen simple, tastefully decorated rooms with twin beds. At this rate, though, it's overpriced compared with some cheaper options.

Rooms at rustically styled, family-run **Hotel El Barranco** (O'Higgins 172, tel. 065/721314, www.elbarrancochile.cl, US$151 s, US$182 d with breakfast, with half board and full board options) look into lush woods at the west end of town. In terms of comforts, this is clearly the top choice in town.

## Food

Like the accommodations, the food is a bit better than in most other towns of Futaleufú's size, though Chilean standards like beef, chicken, and sandwiches are the rule. In addition to Hostería Río Grande's dining room, choices include **El Encuentro** (O'Higgins 653, tel. 065/721247, lunch and dinner daily), **Escorpio** (Gabriela Mistral 265, tel. 065/721228, lunch and dinner daily), and the rather bland **Futaleufú** (Sargento Aldea 265, tel. 065/9247-5678, lunch and dinner daily).

**Sur Andes** (Aguirre Cerda 308, tel. 065/721405, lunch and dinner daily) has varied espresso drinks, huge tasty sandwiches, rich desserts including kuchen, and homemade chocolates. It also has good wireless Internet.

Though overbuilt for a burg of Futa's size, the ambitious **Martín Pescador** (Balmaceda 603, tel. 065/721279, lunch and dinner daily) offers a cozy living-room-style atmosphere for an aperitif, good salmon, and a small English-language library (not a book exchange).

## Information and Services

Futaleufú's **Oficina de Turismo Municipal** (O'Higgins 536, tel. 065/721241, www.futaleufu.cl, 9 A.M.–9 P.M. daily Dec.–Mar.) is on the south side of the Plaza de Armas.

For visitors arriving from or bound for Argentina, the border is open 8 A.M.–8 P.M. daily.

**BancoEstado** (O'Higgins 603), the only place to change money, now has an ATM (MasterCard only). **Correos de Chile** (Balmaceda 501) is the post office. **Telefónica del Sur** (Balmaceda 419) has long-distance telephone service, while Ciber Loren@ (O'Higgins 564) has Internet service.

**Señora Vicky** (Sargento Aldea 273, tel. 065/721276) does the washing.

## Getting There and Around

Since the eruption of Volcán Chaitén, services to and from Futaleufú via Argentina are more abundant, but subject to abrupt changes. There is no bus terminal, and companies will either pick you up or tell you where to wait, especially as services often begin in La Junta.

Several companies now operate between Futaleufú and Puerto Montt (US$53, 11 hours) via Argentina: **Buses Transaustral** (Balmaceda 501, tel. 065/721360), which has larger, more comfortable buses; **Feryval** (Pedro Agurre Cerda 415, tel. 065/721312); and **Lago Espolón** (O'Higgins 505, tel. 065/721215, www.lagoespolon.cl).

**Transportes Altamirano** (Balmaceda 597, tel. 065/721453) goes daily except Thursday to Chaitén, and makes connections for La Junta (US$20) in Villa Santa Lucía Monday, Tuesday, Friday, and Saturday. **Buses Becker** (Balmaceda 501, tel. 065/721360, busesbecker@hotmail.com) connects directly with Coyhaique US$40, 10.5 hours) and intermediates Sunday at 9 A.M.

Feryval and **Turismo Futaleufú** (Pedro Aguirre Cerda 436, tel. 065/721458) go to the Argentine border in the morning and afternoon on Monday and Friday, with connections to Esquel and beyond. Otherwise, the only option is a taxi.

## CHAITÉN

Between the snowy volcanic cones of Michinmahuida and Corcovado, the modest port of Chaitén was long the main gateway to continental Chiloé. Receiving regular ferries and occasional catamarans from Puerto Montt and insular Chiloé, it's the starting point for many trips down the Carretera Austral and the year-round access point for Parque Natural Pumalín, U.S. entrepreneur Douglas Tompkins's controversial conservation initiative.

In May 2008, though, a nearby volcanic eruption and subsequent flooding forced the evacuation of the port of Chaitén and the downwind village of Futaleufú, Chile's white-water kayaking and rafting capital, where several inches of ash fell. As of early 2011, though, the eruption had subsided, and the new Chilean government had agreed to restore electricity and water, with telephones to follow (cell service never ceased). Though some parts of town are beyond salvation, and the population is only about 500 (before the eruption, it exceeded 4,000), ferries are again arriving, and accommodations, food, and fuel are all available. Still, before traveling along the northernmost Carretera Austral, readers should inquire locally and look for updates at the author's blog (www.southernconetravel.com).

### Orientation

Chaitén is 46 kilometers north of Puerto Cárdenas by a Carretera Austral segment that is paved almost to just beyond Termas de Amarillo, and 56 kilometers south of Caleta Gonzalo, a summer-only ferry port that's also the headquarters of Parque Pumalín.

### Accommodations and Food

Even before the government's decision to restore utilities, accommodations and food service had resumed—in fact, they had resumed for nearly two years despite the presumed intention to move the settlement to Santa Bárbara.

For budget accommodations, try the waterfront **Hostería Llanos** (Corcovado 378, cell 09/9084-1978, US$14–17 pp with shared bath or private bath and breakfast), but its water supply has been spotty. **Hospedaje Rita** (Arturo Prat 229, cell 09/9778-2351, US$14–20) is comparable, but it sometimes fills with short-term workers as Chaitén rebuilds.

Attractive **Hotel Schilling** (Corcovado 230, cell 09/6826-0680, hotel_schilling@telsur.cl, US$48 s, US$60 d with private bath) is more than a step up. Thanks to its own well and generator, **Cabañas Pudú** (Corcovado 668, tel. 09/8227-9602, puduchaiten@hotmail.com, US$70 d) has managed to avoid problems with the water and electricity supplies; it also serves lunch or dinner for as little as US$5. **Cabañas Brisas del Mar** (Corcovado 278, tel. 09/9515-8808, cababrisas@telsur.cl, US80 d) is immaculate and spacious.

Other than hotel restaurants, Chaitén has few eateries. **El Quijote** (O'Higgins 42, lunch and dinner daily) serves huge sandwiches, such as the steak-and-cheese Barros Luco. **El Refugio** (Todesco 2, lunch and dinner daily) has been the best dining choice, but the resurrected Flamengo (Corcovado 218) also deserves a look.

### Information and Services

At the bus terminal, run by Nicholas La Penna, **Chaitur** (O'Higgins 67, tel. 09/7468-5608, www.chaitur.com) is a good year-round information source, with Spanish-, English-, and French-speaking staff. In addition to leading trips to Pumalín, including hikes to the volcano's cinder cone, Nicholas also sells maps, has a small book exchange, and provides up-to-date bus schedules.

### Getting There and Around

Chaitén has air links with Puerto Montt, sea links with Puerto Montt and Chiloé, and roads south to Futaleufú and Coyhaique and north to Caleta Gonzalo. All of them, though, are subject to change and, in the case of bus service, to demand.

Chaitén's airfield is at Santa Bárbara, about 10 kilometers north of town. The local representative of **Aerocord** is Jacqueline Pineda (cell 9884-2643, jpineda@aerocord.cl).

Chaitén's ferry dock is a short distance northwest of town via the Costanera. In summer, **Naviera Austral** (Corcovado 266, cell 097976-0342, www.navieraustral.cl) sails twice weekly to Castro, with the slow vehicle ferry *Pincoya,* but it also sails twice weekly to Quellón with the faster and more comfortable *Don Baldo;* for most of the year, there is direct service to Puerto Montt. Passenger fares to Quellón are US$40 per adult, US$32 per child under age six, and US$2.50 for infants. Vehicle rates are US$160 for passenger vehicles and small trucks, and US$44 per linear meter for other vehicles; bicycles cost US$15 and motorcycles US$35.

In January and February only, Naviera Austral normally sails the ferry *Mailén* from Caleta Gonzalo, 56 kilometers north of Chaitén, to the town of Hornopirén, a service that resumed in early 2011 after two years' closure because of the eruption of Volcán Chaitén.

Nearly all buses stop at the main **Terminal de Buses** (O'Higgins 67, tel. 067/731429), but services are also in flux here. The main destinations are Futaleufú, Coyhaique, and intermediates, but occasional services go north to Caleta Gonzalo (Parque Pumalín). Schedules change frequently; for monthly updates, check the Chaitur website (www.chaitur.com).

When full service resumes, buses to Coyhaique (US$40, 12 hours) are once or twice daily in summer, three or four times weekly the rest of the year, with **Buses Becker** and **Buses Daniela.** Departure time is usually around 9–10 A.M. **Buses Altamirano** goes daily except Thursday to Futaleufú (US$15, 3.5 hours) and Monday, Tuesday, Friday, and Saturday to La Junta (US$15, 3.5 hours), with connections to Coyhaique.

Since the northbound road reopened, **Chaitur** (O'Higgins 67, cell 09/7468-5608, www.chaitur.com) has resumed service to Caleta Gonzalo (US$16, two hours), linking up with the Hornopirén ferry. Rates can rise or fall, though, depending on the number of passengers.

## VICINITY OF CHAITÉN

Tourist services in Chaitén are limited, but visitors with their own transportation can still see the sights.

### Casa Avión

About 20 kilometers southeast of Chaitén, on the south side of the Carretera Austral, stands one of the region's most offbeat landmarks. In 1974, well before the highway's completion, the Chilean Air Force crashed a DC-3 in the vicinity; unable to fly it out, they salvaged the engine and left the fuselage. Using two oxcarts, farmer Carlos Anabalón hauled it to his roadside property, divided it into three rooms, and lived in the Casa Avión (Airplane House) until the year 2000, when he traded it to a Chaitén policeman for a four-wheel-drive Jeep. At present, though, the interior has been gutted and there are no apparent plans to remodel it.

### Termas El Amarillo

At a highway junction about 25 kilometers southeast of Chaitén, a gravel road turns north for five kilometers to the forested, no-frills hot springs of Termas El Amarillo. Admission to the outdoor pools costs US$5 per person; it also has walk-in campsites (US$7 per tent).

## PARQUE PUMALÍN

In 1991, U.S. businessman Douglas Tompkins and his wife, Kris McDivitt Tompkins, cashed out their equity from the Esprit and Patagonia clothing empires to purchase blocks of temperate rainforest to create the region's largest destination—literally so—in Parque Pumalín, a 317,000-hectare private nature reserve straddling the highway north of Chaitén. Since then, says the *New York Times,* only General Pinochet's name has appeared more in the Chilean press than Tompkins, who's even received death threats from ultranationalists who accuse him of trying to split the country in half. Tompkins has many Chilean supporters, though, and most criticisms are far less extreme.

Tompkins has allayed much of that criticism by building trails, cabins, campgrounds,

## THE PUMALÍN SAGA

In the 15-plus years since he purchased 17,000 hectares of temperate rainforest on continental Chiloé's Fiordo Reñihué, Californian **Douglas Tompkins** has become the gringo Chile knows best – or at least the one many Chileans think they know best. During that time, as Tompkins acquired a total of about 360,000 hectares in southernmost Region X (Los Lagos), his name appeared constantly in the Chilean press.

One of Chile's largest landholders, Tompkins is a polarizing figure, but not in the usual sense. Objections to large landholdings usually come from the political left, which fought to redistribute *latifundios* to peasants until the 1973 coup. The right, by contrast, upheld the private property status quo, and their position seemingly triumphed after 1973.

Tompkins, founder of the Esprit clothing empire, turned conventional politics on its head. Taking advantage of openness toward foreign investment, he used the proceeds from selling Esprit to consolidate undeveloped properties not for profit, but for preservation. As other entrepreneurs were clear-cutting native forest and replanting with fast-growing exotics to turn a quick profit, Tompkins formed a Chilean trust to turn his lands into a private *santuario de la naturaleza* (nature sanctuary).

Tompkins expected that his Proyecto Pumalín, in a thinly populated and once-inaccessible area south of Hornopirén and north of Chaitén, would make him a hero. In fact it did – among the small if growing Chilean environmental movement for whom forest preservation was a hot-button issue, and who distrusted the growing power of multinationals. For them, the millionaire capitalist who believed in philanthropy and biodiversity was a real, if improbable, hero.

On the other hand, Tompkins's actions aroused the distrust and hostility of conservative sectors with whom, economically at least, he would seem to have much in common. He ran afoul of business, military, and religious interests, all with different but overlapping objections for opposing the project.

Tompkins has many local and national supporters, though. Both Christian Democrat deputy Gabriel Ascensio, of Chiloé, and Partido por la Democracia (PPD) deputy Leopoldo Sánchez, of Chaitén, favored the park and its tourist potential. PPD deputy Guido Girardi, an outspoken conservationist, said that opposition to Pumalín was a combination of "extreme nationalism" and lobbying by forestry companies. The Lagos administration was supportive, though, and on August 19, 2005, it granted final approval to convert Pumalín into a natural sanctuary administered by a seven-member, all-Chilean board of directors.

Even some of Tompkins's supporters agree his actions have not been so transparent as they might have been – his earliest purchases, in particular, seemed almost surreptitious. As the project has developed, though, public access has improved through hiking trails, campgrounds, cabañas, a very good restaurant, and a visitors center, not to mention small-scale sustainable agriculture experiments and other features to benefit the small local population.

So successful has Pumalín been that, in 2005, center-right businessman Sebastián Piñera – now Chile's president – followed Tompkins's model in creating **Parque Tantauco** (www.parquetantauco.cl) through his own Fundación Futuro. At the southern tip of the Isla Grande de Chiloé, Tantauco has limited access, but this should improve in the coming years.

At the same time, through **Conservación Patagónica** (www.conservacionpatagonica.org), Tompkins and his wife, Kris McDivitt Tompkins, also purchased the Aisén region's **Estancia Valle Chacabuco,** which is in the process of being turned into a national park that would create a protected area almost from Lago General Carrera to Lago Cochrane. The proposed Parque Nacional Patagonia would also incorporate Reserva Nacional Jeinimeni and Reserva Nacional Tamango, with its key huemul habitat.

For more details on Pumalín in Chile, contact **Parque Pumalín** (Klenner 299, Puerto Varas, tel. 065/250079 or 065/251911, www.parquepumalin.cl); in the U.S., contact the Foundation for Deep Ecology (Building 1062, Fort Cronkhite, Sausalito, CA 94965, tel. 415/229-9339, www.deepecology.org).

and a restaurant and visitors center that have lured visitors from Chaitén to the summer ferry port of Caleta Gonzalo, on the Reñihué fjord, and other points along the highway and the park's extensive shoreline. In late 2004, at a ceremony in Santiago, Pumalín finally received formal legal recognition from President Ricardo Lagos's government. A few years ago, a plan to reroute the Carretera Austral and run a 2,300-kilometer power line from a proposed hydroelectric project in southern Aisén to Puerto Montt and farther north threatened Pumalín's ecological integrity, but, ironically, the 2008 eruption of Volcán Chaitén has complicated those plans.

## Geography and Climate

Pumalín stretches from 42° south latitude, where it's contiguous with Parque Nacional Hornopirén, to nearly 43° south, east of Chaitén in the south. Most visitors, though, see the areas along both sides of the Carretera Austral between Chaitén and Caleta Gonzalo.

Elevations range from sea level to snow-capped 2,404-meter Volcán Michinmahuida, in the southernmost sector, but even these statistics are misleading—the topography rises so steeply in some areas that trails require ladders rather than switchbacks.

Pumalín wouldn't look like it does without rain—lots of rain. While there are no reliable statistics, probably more than 4,000 millimeters of rain falls every year. At higher elevations, of course, it accumulates as snow.

## Flora and Fauna

Pumalín takes its name from the puma or mountain lion, but the main reason for its creation was to protect the temperate southern rainforest, whose single most significant species is the *alerce* (false larch). There are also several species of southern beech, not to mention numerous other rainforest species common to southern Chile.

In addition to the puma, the pudu inhabits the sopping woodlands, while foxes prowl along the shoreline and other open areas. Southern sea lions inhabit headlands and rookeries, stealing salmon from the fish farms that float just beyond the park boundaries—and placing themselves at risk from the powerful companies that bring in much of the region's income.

Hikers here and in other parts of the southern rainforests should watch for tiny *sanguijuelas* (leeches), which can work their way into boots and trousers (some leeches are used for medical purposes in Chile).

## Sights and Recreation

Because of the eruption of Volcán Chaitén, within the park boundaries, Pumalín was closed for the summer season in 2009, but it reopened in December of 2010.

From a trailhead near Café Caleta Gonzalo, the **Sendero Cascadas** climbs and winds through thick rainforest to a high falls; figure about 1.5 hours each way. At the Centro de Información, it's possible to arrange a tour of the apiaries at **Fundo Pillán,** across the Fiordo de Reñihué, and to obtain fishing licenses.

From a trailhead about 12 kilometers south of Caleta Gonzalo, west of the highway, the **Sendero Laguna Tronador** crosses a *pasarela* (hanging bridge) before ascending a string of slippery stepladders to the **Mirador Michinmahuida,** a platform where, on clear days, there are astounding views of the volcano's wintry summit. The trail continues through nearly pristine forest, dropping gradually to the amphitheater lake where Tompkins's staff have built a stylish two-site campground with picnic tables, a deck, and an outhouse. It's about 1.5 hours to or from the trailhead.

A short distance farther south, on the highway's east side, the mostly boardwalk **Sendero los Alerces** crosses the Río Blanco to a large *alerce* grove. Just a little farther south on the west side, the **Sendero Cascadas Escondidas** is longer and more strenuous than the signposted three hours might suggest. It's mostly boardwalk—through the swampy, soggy forest—and catwalk along precipitous rock walls, with some steep stepladders as well. The hardest part, though, is boulder-hopping the river on slippery granite or, better and perhaps safer, wading across. On the other side, the trail climbs steeply another 15–20 minutes, then drops into a narrow canyon where, on a dangerous-looking stepladder anchored by a rope, the bravest hikers can continue around the rock to get the best view of the "hidden" falls.

Seventeen kilometers south of Caleta Gonzalo, at its namesake campground, **Sendero Lago Negro** leads 800 meters through dense forest to reed-lined Lago Negro. Just north of the park entrance on the Chaitén–Caleta Gonzalo road, the **Sendero Interpretativo** is a 1.8-kilometer walk in the woods starting from the Volcán ranger station, which provides an explanatory map.

From Chaitén, it's possible to reach the southern **Sendero Ventisquero Amarillo,** via a northbound road at the highway's junction of the turnoff to Termas El Amarillo. Since the eruption damaged part of the trail, though, it's being rerouted, and information here is subject to change.

## Organized Tours

**Al Sur Expediciones** (Aconcagua 8, Puerto Varas, tel./fax 065/232300, www.alsurexpeditions.com) arranges activity-oriented excursions—hiking, sea kayaking, and sailing—throughout the park.

Chiloé-based **Austral Adventures** (Av. Costanera 904, Ancud, tel./fax 065/625977, www.austral-adventures.com) offers customized cruises on the 15-meter motor vessel *Cahuella*.

## Accommodations and Food

At Caleta Gonzalo, the walk-in **Camping Río Gonzalo** (US$3 pp) has forested sites with fire pits (firewood is for sale), clean toilets, and cold showers. There's a separate large shelter for cooking. Those without tents can rent one of three *fogones* (US$10), roofed shelters with fire pits normally reserved for picnickers during the daytime; *fogón* No. 3 has wide benches that can sleep three tentless campers comfortably, presuming they have their own sleeping pads.

Fourteen kilometers south of Caleta Gonzalo, **Auto-Camping Cascadas Escondidas** has four drive-in sites (US$10) with clean toilets, cold showers, and roofed decks for pitching tents and eating without having to sit on soggy ground.

Seventeen kilometers south of Caleta Gonzalo, **Camping Lago Negro** (US$10 per roofed site) resembles Cascadas Escondidas, with four roofed sites and an open tent-camping area. Accessible by an 800-meter footpath, the nearby **Camping Punta del Lago** has two lakeside sites. Three kilometers farther south, **Camping Lago Blanco** (US$10) resembles Camping Lago Negro, with half a dozen roofed sites. Slightly beyond, near the park entrance, **Camping El Volcán** (US$10 per roofed site) has a small store at the ranger station.

Tompkins's seven cozy but stylish **Cabañas Caleta Gonzalo** (Puerto Varas tel. 065/250079, reservas@parquepumalin.cl, US$110 s, US$150 d) accommodate 3–6 people each. All have private baths and hot water, but no kitchen facilities, so it's bring your own food and cook at the campground, or eat at the nearby café.

Dignified by a stone fireplace with a copper vent, the airy tobacco-free **Café Caleta Gonzalo** (near the ferry ramp, 7:30 A.M.–10 P.M. daily) serves quality organic fruit, vegetables, dairy products, meat, and seafood. The breakfast (US$12) really shines with homemade bread, local honey, butter, and cheese; there's also a sandwich menu, omelets, and juices. Four-course lunches or dinners, with fresh bread, cost around US$25.

## Information

At Caleta Gonzalo, Pumalín's **Centro de Visitantes** distributes brochures, provides information, and displays informational panels with large black-and-white photographs of the park; it also sells books, maps, film, park products like organic honey and jam, and local crafts. If it's not open, café personnel can unlock it on request.

Pumalín maintains additional **information offices** in Puerto Varas (Klenner 299, tel. 065/250079, info@parquepumalin.cl) and in the United States (The Conservation Land Trust, Building 1062, Fort Cronkhite, Sausalito, CA 94965, tel. 415/229-9339, www.theconservationlandtrust.org).

Pumalín also has a detailed website (www.parquepumalin.cl, in Spanish and English).

### Getting There

In January and February only, **Naviera Austral's** *Mailén* sails Sunday, Monday, and Tuesday to Hornopirén (six hours) at 3:30 P.M.; vehicle reservations are advisable. Passengers pay US$21 per person, while cyclists pay an extra US$13 and motorcyclists US$25. Automobiles and light trucks pay US$140, while larger vehicles pay per linear meter. This service is subject to major changes.

Since the northbound road reopened, **Chaitur** (O'Higgins 67, Chaitén, cell 09/7468-5608, www.chaitur.com) has resumed service to Caleta Gonzalo (US$16, two hours), linking up with the Hornopirén ferry. Rates can rise or fall, though, depending on the number of passengers.

# The Southern Carretera Austral

Even more thinly settled than north of Coyhaique, southern Aisén is wild country, with few and scattered services; barely 10,000 people live in nearly 46,000 square kilometers. The only towns with more than a thousand inhabitants are Chile Chico, near the Argentine border on Lago General Carrera, and Cochrane, directly on the Carretera Austral.

The highway is now paved to Villa Cerro Castillo, 98 kilometers south of Coyhaique, as is the Puerto Ibáñez lateral. In late 1999, it finally reached its terminus at Villa O'Higgins, though the last 100-kilometer stretch still requires a ferry shuttle from Puerto Yungay to Río Bravo.

## RESERVA NACIONAL CERRO CASTILLO

Straddling the Carretera Austral beyond the Balmaceda turnoff, marking the divide between the Río Simpson and Río Ibáñez drainages, Cerro Castillo is a 179,550-hectare unit whose map boundaries look like jigsaw puzzle pieces. Its signature landmark is Cerro Castillo itself, whose soaring basaltic battlements, above the tree line, truly resemble a medieval castle.

Elevations range from about 500 meters to Cerro Castillo's 2,320-meter summit, embellished by three south-facing glaciers. Like most of the region, it gets substantial rainfall and snow at higher altitudes, but some east-facing areas enjoy a rain-shadow effect.

Nearly pure stands of the southern beech *lenga* dominate the forest landscape up to about 1,200 meters, along with the related *coigüe, ñire,* and many shrubs. Steppe-like grasslands typify the rain shadow areas.

Mammals include the puma, huemul, two fox species, and skunks. Birds are common, including the Andean condor, various owls, the *tordo* (austral blackbird), and the *cachaña* (austral parakeet).

### Sights and Recreation

About eight kilometers south of Laguna Chiguay, a handsome new sign marks the faint westbound road that's the starting point for **Sendero Las Horquetas,** a four-day backpacking trail that climbs the Estero la Lima Valley to pass beneath the spires of Cerro Castillo before descending to the roadside village of Villa Cerro Castillo. This is easier from the north than from the south, where the approach is steeper and more rugged.

### Practicalities

At the reserve's northeastern edge, Conaf's woodsy five-site **Camping Laguna Chiguay** (Km 67, US$7 per site) is just west of the highway. At the southern approach, there are simple accommodations at Villa Cerro Castillo, just outside the reserve boundary.

Conaf maintains a ranger station on

## THE CARRETERA AUSTRAL

For the most part, this is a Chilean road trip itinerary through some of the continent's wildest scenery, but there's an optional detour into Argentine territory. Because public transportation is so limited along the southern highway, a rental car is almost essential, unless time is no object. A high-clearance vehicle is a good idea, but four-wheel drive is not necessary.

### Days 1-2

Arrive in the morning at Santiago's Aeropuerto Internacional Arturo Merino Benítez, connecting onward to **Balmaceda.** Transfer to a **Coyhaique** hotel.

If you're not too tired, take a brief excursion to the nearby **Reserva Nacional Coyhaique.** The next morning, plan a full-day excursion to **Parque Nacional Laguna San Rafael,** by high-speed catamaran from Puerto Chacabuco.

### Day 3

Depart in the morning, northbound to **Puerto Puyuhuapi,** breaking for a hike to the hanging glacier at **Parque Nacional Queulat.** If space is available, overnight at the **Puyuhuapi Lodge & Spa** hot-springs hotel; if not, stay in Puerto Puyuhuapi at simpler but more than acceptable B&B accommodations.

### Days 4-5

In the morning visit the **Alfombras de Puyuhuapi** carpet factory, then depart northbound to volcano-struck **Chaitén** and **Caleta Gonzalo** (Parque Natural Pumalín), with a possible hiking detour to the hanging glacier west of Lago Yelcho. Find accommodations in Chaitén or, preferably, camp or stay in cabañas in Caleta Gonzalo.

The next morning, choose one of several full-day hiking excursions within **Parque Natural Pumalín.**

### Days 6-7

Plan a morning departure to the village of **Futaleufú.** Take short afternoon excursions from town, after making preparations for rafting or other activities.

The next morning, spend an exhilarating full day rafting or kayaking on the Class IV-V **Río Futaleufú,** one of the world's top white-water experiences.

### Days 8-9

Leave early for the historic Welsh mill town of **Trevelin,** Argentina, and **Parque Nacional Los Alerces,** where options include camping, cabañas, and a hotel within the park. The next morning, plan a full-day lake excursion to the park's signature *alerce* woodlands.

### Day 10

In the morning head for **Cholila,** site of Butch Cassidy's Patagonian home, and **Leleque,** site of Benetton's impressive museum, looping back to **Esquel** or Trevelin for accommodations. At Trevelin, eat a late afternoon Welsh tea in lieu of dinner.

### Day 11

Make a return loop to Chile via the village of Palena, with accommodations at La Junta's **Hostal Espacio y Tiempo** or **Cabañas El Pangue,** at Parque Nacional Queulat's north end, or Puerto Puyuhuapi.

### Day 12

Return overland to Coyhaique, taking a late-afternoon excursion to **Reserva Nacional Coyhaique** or planning easy rafting or kayaking on the **Río Simpson.**

### Day 13

Leave in the morning for **Reserva Nacional Cerro Castillo,** taking a day hike to the reserve and/or visiting pre-Columbian rock art near Villa Cerro Castillo; find simple accommodations in Cerro Castillo or **Puerto Ingeniero Ibáñez.**

### Day 14

Ferry across **Lago General Carrera** from Puerto Ingeniero Ibáñez to **Chile Chico.** One possible excursion is to **Lago Jeinimeni.**

### Day 15

Depart in the morning for **Puerto Guadal, Puerto Bertrand,** and **Cochrane** via Lago General Carrera's thrilling south shore road.

Guadal and Bertrand both have excellent accommodations, but Cochrane has more complete services.

**Day 16**

Leave early for **Caleta Tortel,** a uniquely scenic fishing village with boardwalks in lieu of streets and simple, or not-so-simple, bed-and-breakfast accommodations. Alternatively, drive to **Estancia Valle Chacabuco,** a new private conservation initiative by the creators of Parque Pumalín, staying at the new lodge or campgrounds.

**Days 17-18**

Depart in the morning for **Villa O'Higgins,** via the Fiordo Mitchell ferry (delays are possible if demand is heavy); for those who have visited Valle Chacabuco, a short side trip to Caleta Tortel is still feasible. The next morning, plan a full-day hiking excursion on the **Sendero de Chile** or a boat excursion to the **Glaciar O'Higgins.**

**Day 19**

Leave early for Cochrane and **Puerto Río Tranquilo,** which has bed-and-breakfast accommodations. Wind permitting, take a half-day boat ride to lakeside limestone caverns at **Capilla de Mármol.**

**Day 20**

If the wind has let up, there's time to retry the Capilla de Mármol. Either way, you'll have a leisurely return to Coyhaique via Cerro Castillo, with plenty of time for photography.

**Day 21**

Catch an early northbound flight from Balmaceda, leaving the afternoon free for sightseeing and a seafood lunch at the Mercado Central in **Santiago,** followed by an evening departure from Aeropuerto Internacional Arturo Merino Benítez.

© WAYNE BERNHARDSON

**South of Coyhaique, Reserva Nacional Cerro Castillo is the Aisén region's prime hiking destination.**

the highway opposite the Laguna Chiguay campground.

All public transportation between Coyhaique, to the north, and Puerto Ibáñez and Villa Cerro Castillo to the south, passes through the reserve's northern sector.

## PUERTO INGENIERO IBÁÑEZ

Prior to the Carretera Austral's completion, Puerto Ibáñez was a major lake port, connecting Coyhaique with Chile Chico and other settlements on Lago General Carrera's south shore. Its current livelihood derives from agriculture, both livestock and tree fruit like apples and pears.

Since completion of the highway bypass, it's lost economic clout, but the ferry from here to Chile Chico, for an easy border crossing to Argentina, is quicker and cheaper than the roundabout (but scenic) roads. It's about 110 kilometers south of Coyhaique via the Carretera Austral and a paved lateral that bears south about 10 kilometers east of Villa Cerro Castillo. There's also a rugged road but scenic border crossing along the lake's north shore (in Argentina, it's called Lago Buenos Aires).

### Accommodations

Lodging is available at simple **Residencial Vientos del Sur** (Dickson 283, tel. 09/8972-6519, US$20 pp with shared bath). The comparable **Residencial Emmanuel** (Ronchi 210, tel. 09/8358-6514, US$20 pp) also has more spacious cabaña accommodations (US$70 d).

### Getting There and Around

Several companies operate minibuses to Coyhaique (US$8, two hours): **Transportes Yamil Alí** (tel. 067/250346), **Darío Figueroa Castro** (cell 09/8977-9737), and **Minibus Eben Ezer** (tel. 067/423203).

**Mar del Sur** (Baquedano 146, Coyhaique, tel. 067/231255) sails the ferry *Pilchero* to Chile Chico (2.5 hours) daily except for Wednesday (no service) and Thursday (twice); schedules are subject to change. Fares are US$8 per adult. Bicycles pay an additional US$3.50, motorcycles US$7. Passenger vehicles and light trucks pay US$34; larger vehicles pay US$13 per linear meter.

## VILLA CERRO CASTILLO

Founded in 1966, the frontier outpost of Villa Cerro Castillo is finally acquiring an air of permanency, though its exposed site makes it one of the Carretera Austral's bleaker settlements. Just south of here, 89 kilometers from Coyhaique, the pavement ends and the gravel begins. Hikers who begin the trek through Reserva Nacional Cerro Castillo at Las Horquetas will exit the reserve here.

### Alero de las Manos

Five kilometers south of town, via a lateral off the highway, the positive and negative hands of the pre-Columbian rock art at Alero de las Manos resemble those of the famous Argentine site at Cueva de las Manos. Beneath a volcanic overhang, these paintings differ in that they are fewer, younger (only about 3,000 years old), and include no animals. In some cases, rocks have split from the overhang and fallen to the ground, probably concealing even more images.

Alero de las Manos (admission US$2 pp including a guided tour) is open 10 A.M.–6 P.M. daily. There's a small visitors center with clean toilets.

### Practicalities

Though improving, accommodations other than inexpensive campgrounds are limited and fill up fast.

**Hospedaje La Querencia** (O'Higgins 460, US$12 pp) has firm beds, good food, and improved bathroom facilities (all of them shared). **Hospedaje Villarrica** (O'Higgins 592, tel. 067/419200, US$30 pp) has upgraded its rooms, runs a cheerful restaurant, and has added cabañas (US$75 d).

Open long hours November–March only, the **Oficina de Información Turística** (O'Higgins s/n, www.rioibanez.cl) provides a town map and list of services.

Several **minibus** services have early morning departures for Coyhaique (US$7, 1.5

hours); all regularly scheduled services between Coyhaique, to the north, and Puerto Río Tranquilo and Cochrane, to the south, pass by the entrance to town.

## BAHÍA MURTA AND VICINITY

West of Villa Cerro Castillo, the Carretera Austral climbs above the Río Ibáñez valley before veering south to **Lago General Carrera** and the lakeside hamlet of **Bahía Murta,** one of the best areas to see fall colors. Murta's also the gateway to **Puerto Sánchez,** 23 kilometers south, for boat trips to the **Cavernas de Mármol,** a series of small islands opposite Puerto Río Tranquilo's Capilla de Mármol.

From early November to late March, Murta's **Oficina de Información Turística** (5 de Abril s/n, www.rioibanez.cl) supposedly keeps long hours.

### Accommodations and Food

There are several simple in-town accommodations, including **Hospedaje Mariela** (Av. 18 de Septiembre 476, US$10 pp) and **Residencial Patagonia** (Pasaje España 64, US$12 pp); the latter has a convenient branch at the highway junction (US$15 pp), with good beds, a small museum, and squeaky floors. All use the same community telephone (tel. 067/419600) and charge around US$5 more for breakfast.

## PUERTO RÍO TRANQUILO AND VICINITY

Until the Carretera Austral's completion, Puerto Río Tranquilo (population about 550) was a port with a weekly supply boat from Puerto Ibáñez; today it's a small but steadily growing settlement at Lago General Carrera's west end, 25 kilometers south of Puerto Murta. At the north end of town, a new road toward Bahía Exploradores, an inlet of the larger Estero Capquelán, is nearly finished, and there are now summer boat-and-hike connections to Laguna San Rafael.

### Capilla de Mármol

The area's best excursion is a launch trip to Capilla de Mármol, a string of swirling marble grottos on the shoreline. The 1.5-hour trip costs around US$50 for up to five persons, but it's difficult if winds are high. It's best in late summer or fall, when water levels permit launches to approach more closely and explore more thoroughly. In season, there are now roadside stands that assemble groups to visit the site.

### Valle Exploradores

Westbound from Río Tranquilo, a smooth but narrow penetration road will eventually reach the Pacific, but at present it goes only about 60 kilometers, past Lago Bayo and the Glaciar Exploradores, an impressive but receding continental glacier that's scoured the mountainside, leaving lateral and terminal moraines; small icebergs still calve off its face and float down its namesake river.

While the road will eventually reach Parque Nacional Laguna San Rafael, most of the land is private property. **El Puesto** (Km 52, Tranquilo tel. 02/1964555) charges US$6 for climbing the trail to its Mirador Exploradores, a 20-minute woodland walk that yields spectacular views from a hilltop deck. More ambitious hikers can arrange for a full-day ice hike at Tranquilo or here, if guides are available.

### Accommodations and Food

Río Tranquilo has above-average accommodations for a town its size; unless otherwise indicated, all use the same community telephone (tel. 067/419500) for messages.

Two blocks west of the highway, local favorite **Residencial Darka** (Los Arrayanes 330, US$16 pp) has smallish rooms with twin beds and shared baths.

With 10 rooms divided by a corridor, friendly, family-run **Hostal Los Pinos** (Godoy 51, tel. 067/411576, US$50 s or d) has spotless accommodations with breakfast and either shared or private baths. Low-season prices are about 10–15 percent cheaper. Its restaurant is also above average, serving fixed-price lunches or dinners for US$10–12 in a tobacco-free dining room.

Right on the highway, rebuilt after a major fire, **Hostería Costanera** (Carretera Austral

9, trapananda1@gmail.com, US$30 pp) is a major improvement over its predecessor, with an additional floor, larger rooms, and private baths. **Hostal El Puesto** (Pedro Lagos 258, tel. 02/1964555, www.elpuesto.cl, US$80 s, US$110 d) is closer in style to high-priced fishing lodges than to traditional roadside accommodations (actually, it's a couple blocks west of the highway).

In the Valle Exploradores, German-owned **Albergue Campo Alacaluf** (Km 44, campoalacaluf@yahoo.de, US$36–48 pp) has four rooms with either shared or private baths in a rustically handsome house with 24-hour electricity from its own water-driven turbine. Rates include breakfast, and other simple home-cooked meals cost about US$12.

### Information and Getting There

From mid-November to mid-April, there's an **Oficina de Información Turística** (9 A.M.–2 P.M. and 3–6:30 P.M. Mon.–Sat, 10 A.M.–2 P.M. Sun.) directly on the highway, across from the gas station.

Scheduled buses between Coyhaique and Cochrane drop and pick up passengers here. Many backpackers try hitching here, which means heavy competition for a handful of rides.

## HACIENDA TRES LAGOS

Cruce El Maitén, about 50 kilometers south of Puerto Río Tranquilo at Lago General Carrera's westward outlet, is only a crossroads with the eastbound highway to Puerto Guadal and Chile Chico. Almost at the junction, though, Hacienda Tres Lagos (Km 274, tel./fax 067/411323, from US$266 s, US$298 d) is one of the highway's best accommodations.

Oriented toward packages of three days or more, its spacious, well-lighted cabañas are appealing enough, but its newer suites, separated from the main building, are even more so. Amenities include a good restaurant, a sauna, a game room and bar, wireless Internet, and even a cinema, while activities include horseback riding, fishing, and excursions to sights on and off the highway. In Santiago, contact Hacienda Tres Lagos (Zurich 255, Oficina 24, Las Condes, tel./fax 02/3334122, www.haciendatreslagos.com).

## PUERTO GUADAL

Another former lake port, at Lago General Carrera's west end, Puerto Guadal is more picturesque than most area towns. It lies 13 kilometers east of El Maitén; from here, a rugged and narrow road leads northeast to Chile Chico and the Argentine border at Los Antiguos.

The cheapest accommodations are **Hostería Huemules** (Las Magnolias 382, tel. 067/411202, US$10 pp with shared bath), which also has a restaurant. **Cabañas Antué** (Los Pinos 456, tel. 067/431215, US$70 for up to five persons) has hot showers, full kitchens, and wood stoves; check in at Supermercado Plaza (Las Camelias 147).

On Guadal's eastern outskirts, the wooded grounds at elegantly simple **☾ Terra Luna** (Km 1.5, Camino a Chile Chico, tel. 067/431263, www.terra-luna.cl) enjoy lake panoramas. While the French-run resort specializes in weeklong activities-oriented packages, it also rents inexpensive "ministudio" accommodations; rooms in the main lodge go for US$100 off-season, US$160 in summer. Breakfast is included, but other meals are extra; the kitchen can do a lot with a little, even on short notice. English and French are spoken; the Santiago contact is Azimut 360 (General Salvo 159, Providencia, tel. 02/2363880, www.azimut360.com).

Other than the Terra Luna, **Café de la Frontera** (Los Lirios 399, tel. 067/431234, lunch and dinner daily) is the best place for standard Chilean food.

To Chile Chico (US$12, three hours), try **Turismo Seguel** (Los Notros 560, tel. 067/431214) Monday at 4 P.M.; **Transportes ECA** (Las Magnolias 306, tel. 067/431224) Tuesday, Wednesday, and Friday at 7 A.M.; **Transportes Jarita** (O'Higgins 426, tel. 067/431271) Wednesday and Friday at 7 A.M.; and **Buses Ale** (tel. 067/522242), which passes through here en route from Cochrane. Seguel also goes to Coyhaique (US$20) and intermediates Tuesday at 8:30 A.M.

## CHILE CHICO AND VICINITY

Settled from Argentina in the early 20th century, on Lago General Carrera's south shore, Chile Chico developed in isolation from the rest of Chile, and connections are still better with Argentina. One of the region's easiest border crossings, it also enjoys access to remote protected areas like Reserva Nacional Lago Jeinimeni and is the starting (or finishing) point for the wild rugged highway to or from Puerto Guadal.

Despite brief mining booms, Chile Chico's enduring economic base has been the production of temperate fruits, thanks to its mild lakeshore microclimate. This has not exactly brought prosperity, though—even after the 1952 completion of the first motor road from Coyhaique to Puerto Ibáñez, it remained remote from any sizable market. Ashfall from Volcán Hudson's 1991 eruption depressed fruit production, which has only recently recovered.

Improvements are under way, with many more paved streets, a refurbished Plaza de Armas, and a newly paved road to the border town of Los Antiguos. From Los Antiguos, travelers can make connections to the town of Perito Moreno and the Atlantic-coast city of Caleta Olivia, the northern Argentine Patagonian cities of Esquel and Bariloche, and southern Argentine Patagonian destinations such as El Chaltén and El Calafate.

Motorists can fill the tank far more cheaply in Los Antiguos.

### Orientation

Only five kilometers west of the border, Chile Chico (population about 4,500) is 122 kilometers northeast of Cruce El Maitén via the narrow, precipitous road along Lago General Carrera's south shore. Avenida O'Higgins, one block south of the lakeshore, is the main thoroughfare; the central grid extends about 10 blocks from east to west, and four blocks from north to south. The Plaza de Armas is in the northwest corner of town.

### Museo de la Casa de la Cultura

Improved, but still lacking interpretive panels, Chile Chico's museum (O'Higgins and Lautaro, tel. 067/411268, free) displays regional

© WAYNE BERNHARDSON

Young kayakers get their start at Chile Chico, on Lago General Carrera.

## THE LEGACY OF VOLCÁN HUDSON

In the vicinity of Lago General Carrera, which continues east across the Argentine border as Lago Buenos Aires, travelers will see the results of the August 1991 eruption of the remote, 1,935-meter Volcán Hudson, northwest of Villa Cerro Castillo. Chile's second-largest 20th-century eruption deposited more than one cubic kilometer of ash in Chile, about two cubic kilometers in Argentine Patagonia, and another two cubic kilometers over the South Atlantic Ocean; in some areas, the accumulated ashfall reached a depth of more than 1.5 meters. Northwesterly winds carried the ash plume southeast to the Falkland Islands and South Georgia, in the South Atlantic, and eventually as far as Australia. Fierce winds, in excess of 100 kilometers per hour, also remobilized already-fallen ash to cover pasture and watercourses, resulting in the deaths of tens of thousands of cattle and sheep. Today, though, plantlife is steadily recolonizing parts of Aisén's Hudson ashfall – perhaps a hopeful precedent for the aftermath of the Chaitén eruption of 2008.

© WAYNE BERNHARDSON

**Ash from the 1991 eruption of Volcán Hudson filled the Río Murta valley and killed many trees, creating the "Bosque Inundado" (Drowned Forest).**

painting and sculpture along with paleontological materials, historical artifacts from early colonists, and, connected to the second story by a walkway leading straight to its deck, the restored *Los Andes,* which once ferried passengers and cargo around the lake. Hours are supposedly 10 A.M.–7 P.M. Monday–Saturday, December–March only, but the actual schedule can be erratic.

Part of the museum's collections are now on display in the tourist office, two blocks west, where the hours are more reliable.

### Reserva Nacional Lago Jeinimeni

South of Chile Chico, a four-wheel-drive-only road parallels the border to Reserva Nacional Lago Jeinimeni, an infrequently visited protected area of 161,000 hectares. There is little infrastructure except a campground (US$7 per tent); Conaf rangers collect US$2 admission for adults, US$1 for children.

### Accommodations

The quantity of accommodations is increasing and their quality is improving. Half a block south of the plaza, **Hospedaje Don Luis** (Balmaceda 175, tel. 067/411384, US$12–25 pp with breakfast) is one of the best values. Traditional budget choice **Hospedaje Brisas del Lago** (Manuel Rodríguez 443, tel. 067/411204, US$22 pp) has added cabañas (US$70 s or d).

In a distinctive deco-style brick structure, run by an obliging family, **Hotel Plaza** (Balmaceda 102, tel. 067/411215, US$20 pp) has cheerful rooms but no frills (shared bath only, no breakfast). Some interior walls are a bit thin, but the major downside is that one exterior wall adjoins a thunderous Saturday disco (the hotel proprietors are candid about potential noise). On other nights, it's fine.

**Hotel Ventura** (Carrera 290, tel. 067/411311, US$18–28 pp with shared or private bath) is good and central. **Hotel Austral** (O'Higgins 501, tel. 067/411815, US$36 s, US$50 d with private bath) is also worth consideration.

On the eastern outskirts, the Belgian-Chilean **Hostería de la Patagonia** (Camino Internacional s/n, tel./fax 067/411337, www.hosteriadelapatagonia.cl, US$40 s, US$68 d) is an ivy-covered inn with large, rustically decorated but cozy rooms with private baths and breakfast (excellent homemade bread); there's one tiny single with shared bath for US$20 and some slightly larger ones for US$25. Camping and additional meals are available.

New in late 2010, within walking distance of the border complex, **Posada del Río** (Camino Internacional Km 5, tel. 09/9647-0968, www.chile-chico.cl, US$68 s, US$84 d) is a purpose-built lodge with only eight spacious rooms and inviting common areas. The owners also have cabañas in town.

## Food

There's nothing exceptional, though the dining room at **Hostería de la Patagonia** (Camino Internacional s/n, tel./fax 067/411337, www.hosteriadelapatagonia.cl) is pretty good. On the east side of the plaza, **Café Loly y Elizabeth** (González 25, tel. 067/411288) serves reliable breakfasts, sandwiches, lunches, and *onces* (afternoon tea).

## Information and Services

The privately run **Oficina de Información Turística** (O'Higgins s/n, tel. 067/411638, www.chilechico.cl) is open 8 A.M.–10 P.M. daily except weekends, when it opens at 10 A.M. For national parks information, contact **Conaf** (Blest Gana 121, tel. 067/411325).

**Expediciones Patagonia** (O'Higgins 416, tel. 067/411140, www.expeditionspatagonia.com) leads excursions to Jeinimeni and other nearby attractions, rents cars, and posts additional information on the town and vicinity on its website.

**Banco del Estado** (González 112, 10 A.M.–1 P.M. weekdays only) is slow to change both U.S. cash and travelers checks, but it now has an ATM (MasterCard only).

**Correos de Chile** (O'Higgins 223) is the post office. **Entel** (O'Higgins 426) provides long-distance telephone and Internet connections. **Conect@t** (O'Higgins 408, Local 3) has Internet service.

Opposite the Copec gas station near the ferry dock, **Lavandería Ayken** (Rodríguez s/n, cell 09/9575-8134) does the laundry.

**Hospital Chile Chico** (Lautaro 275, tel. 067/411334) provides medical services.

## Getting There and Around

Except for minibus shuttles to Los Antiguos, transportation out of town can be difficult. Bus and boat capacity are limited, so reserve as early as possible—backpackers crossing from Argentina have been stranded here for several days until space has become available.

Minibuses to Los Antiguos (US$5, 30 minutes) leave from in front of Entel long-distance offices (O'Higgins 426); carriers include **Transporte Jaime Acuña** (Augusto Grosse 150, tel. 067/411904) and **Buses Karla** (tel. 09/9470-4442). There are four or five Monday–Saturday, but only one or two on Sunday.

**Transportes Seguel** (O'Higgins 394, tel. 067/411443) goes to Puerto Guadal (US$12, three hours) Monday and Thursday at 7 A.M. **Transportes Ale** (Rosa Amelia 880, tel. 067/411739) goes Wednesday and Saturday at 1 P.M. to Puerto Guadal and Cochrane (US$26, six hours).

From new dockside quarters, **Mar del Sur** (Manuel Rodríguez s/n, tel. 067/411864) sells tickets for the vehicle-passenger ferry *Pilchero,* which sails north to Puerto Ibáñez daily (2.5 hours); schedules are subject to change. Fares are US$8 per adult. Bicycles pay an additional US$3.50, motorcycles US$7. Passenger vehicles and light trucks pay US$34; larger vehicles pay US$13 per linear meter.

# PUERTO BERTRAND AND VICINITY

Separated from Lago General Carrera by a short and narrow channel, Lago Bertrand is the source of the Río Baker, Chile's largest river in terms of its flow. Beautifully sited on the lake's southeastern shore, the village of Puerto Bertrand is a convenient base for exploring the area, though there are several handsome lodges in the vicinity. It is 11 kilometers south of Cruce El Maitén.

### Sights and Recreation

For water sports—rafting, kayaking, and fly-fishing—the **Río Baker** itself is the big draw. Because it has few rocks and play spots, the Class II and III rapids draw fewer rafters and kayakers than the rugged Futaleufú, but its fast current, huge flow, large waves, and occasional deep holes make it lively enough for beginners. Fly-fishing lodges line the highway south of town, beneath the glistening backdrop of the northern Patagonian ice field.

September–April, Bertrand-based, U.S.-run **Patagonia Adventure Expeditions** (Casilla 8, Cochrane, tel./fax 067/411330, www.adventurepatagonia.com) arranges adventure excursions in the vicinity; there is also a specialist fly-fishing guide. It no longer does half-day trips down the Baker but has added more ambitious expeditions, such as the 212-kilometer, eight-day descent to the ocean. Its specialty, though, is the Aysén Glacier Trail, a 10-day trek with porter-guides that goes through nearly uncharted territory on the eastern edge of Parque Nacional Laguna San Rafael and ends with a float down the Río Baker to Caleta Tortel.

Meanwhile, **Baker Patagonia Adventure** (Costanera s/n, tel. 067/419900) has taken over the half-day rafting trips on the Río Baker (US$60 pp).

### Practicalities

There are primarily budget accommodations in Bertrand itself and package-oriented fishing lodges in the vicinity; if space is available, lodges will take drop-in guests.

The upstairs front room at **Hostería Bertrand** (Costanera s/n, tel./fax 067/419900, US$20 pp shared bath, US$50 d private bath) has central heating of a sort—the chimney pipe from the first-floor woodstove rises directly through the room. Rates include an adequate breakfast, and its restaurant is decent enough for other meals.

On a steep S-curve street up from the lakefront, **Cabañas Campo del Hielo Norte** (Ventisquero Nef s/n, US$20 pp) occupies a house with one spacious double with private bath and two somewhat cramped twin rooms that share a bath; the management is the friendliest and perhaps most attentive in town.

Also in town, Argentine-run **Lodge Río Baker** (tel./fax 067/411499, US$80 s or d) enjoys a stunning riverside location with great fly-fishing possibilities, but its absentee Argentine owner (tel. 261/4202196) doesn't seem to have the same commitment to it he once did.

On the highway just south of town, the friendly and rustically appealing **Green Baker Lodge** (Lote C, Lago Bertrand, tel. 02/1960409, www.greenbakerlodge.com, US$65 s or d with IVA discount) has both cabañas and hotel rooms along the lake, offers wireless Internet, and has a decent restaurant with three-course dinner for US$18.

Also south of town, the six-room **Patagonia Baker Lodge** (tel. 067/411903, US$130 s, US$160 d with breakfast, slightly more for a larger suite) is a sterile riverside facility that stresses fly-fishing. In Santiago, contact Patagonia Baker Lodge (Av. del Parque 5455, D84, Ciudad Empresarial, Huechuraba, tel. 02/7280018, www.pbl.cl).

Three kilometers south of town, the **Cabañas Rápidos del Río Baker** (tel. 067/411150, www.rapidosdelriobaker.cl, US$80 d) has two-bedroom cabins with kitchen facilities, but it's less attractive than the cheaper Green Baker Lodge.

**Buses** between Coyhaique and Cochrane, and between Chile Chico and Cochrane, stop at Hostería Bertrand for about 15 minutes.

## CRUCE PASO ROBALLOS AND VICINITY

At the confluence of the Río Baker and Río Nef, 15 kilometers south of Puerto Bertrand, the **Cascada Nef Baker** is a thunderous waterfall, but since the highway was rerouted it's no longer visible from the road. There is free trail access to the river, though, from a clearly signed parking area on the west side of the highway—only about a 10-minute walk from the falls. Visitors must carry out their trash, must not start fires, and are not allowed to camp.

The highway continues south to Cochrane and Villa O'Higgins, while an eastbound lateral ascends the Río Chacabuco Valley to 647-meter Paso Roballos, the region's most southerly border crossing for motor vehicles (others farther south are for nonmotorized transport only). Across the border, at the bleak crossroads of Bajo Caracoles (where gasoline sometimes runs out), Argentina's once dusty Ruta Nacional 40 is steadily being paved south to El Calafate and Chile's Parque Nacional Torres del Paine.

Between the highway junction and the border, **Estancia Valle Chacabuco** is a former sheep ranch acquired by conservationist Kris McDivitt Tompkins and the foundation Conservación Patagonia, who outbid Chilean interests concerned—or obsessed—with the Patagonian property acquisitions of McDivitt's husband Doug Tompkins, creator of Parque Pumalín. The plan is to donate the land as a national park, and they have opened a shining new lodge, campgrounds, and a restaurant on the property.

Should the plan proceed, Aisén will have a large, nearly unbroken swath of national park and reserve land stretching from Reserva Nacional Jeinimeni, just south of Chile Chico, through the Chacabuco Valley to Reserva Nacional Cochrane. Over the next several years, substantial parts of Valle Chacabuco will open to the public.

## COCHRANE

Once literally the end of the road, the tidy town of Cochrane may still have more horses than automobiles, but, says one immigrant, "If you park your horse in front of the bar now, you'll get a ticket for shitting on the sidewalk." Tidy enough for a frontier settlement, thanks to a neatly landscaped Plaza de Armas and broad paved streets, its main appeal lies in the surrounding countryside of **Reserva Nacional Lago Cochrane,** north and northeast of town. If and when Valle Chacabuco achieves protected status, Cochrane could see a major outdoor recreation boom.

Cochrane is still an obligatory stop for southbound wanderers, partly because it offers the last accommodations and food for nearly 300 kilometers and partly because it's home to **Casa Melero,** Patagonia's greatest general store. It's *the* place to buy camping gear, canoes, chainsaws, chocolate, fine wines, firearms, fishing gear, and almost anything else you can't find between here and Antarctica.

### Orientation

Cochrane (population about 2,800) is 345 kilometers south of Coyhaique and 225 kilometers north of Villa O'Higgins. Its core is a rectangular grid that's only about three blocks from north to south but about nine blocks from west to east, where the Río Cochrane marks its limit.

Recent changes have meant inconsistencies in street numbers, but the town is small enough that orientation remains fairly simple.

### Reserva Nacional Lago Cochrane

Informally known as Reserva Nacional Tamango, Reserva Nacional Lago Cochrane is most notable as home to the endangered huemul, the south Andean deer that appears on Chile's coat of arms. On the north shore of its namesake lake, the 6,925-hectare reserve is six kilometers northwest of Cochrane. Admission at the Guardería Húngaro entrance costs US$5 per adult, US$1.50 per child.

Huemul-watching excursions to the east end of the lake, by launch, cost US$50–80 for up to eight people. While there is no regular public transportation to the reserve, it's close enough that hitching is possible, and even a taxi's not that expensive.

On the Río Cochrane's north bank, Conaf's **Camping Las Correntadas** (US$16) has four sites with picnic tables, wash basins, and fire pits. A four-person cabaña (US$50) has a bathroom and hot shower, but needs some maintenance work.

Accessible only by a 45-minute boat ride (US$30) or an eight-kilometer hike, Conaf's lakeside **Camping Playa Paleta** has four campsites and three cabañas with baths but without showers. Prices are identical to Camping Las Correntadas.

## Accommodations

The simple **Residencial Cochrane** (Dr. Steffens 451, tel. 067/522377, US$12 pp without breakfast) also offers camping space (US$4 pp).

A steep rickety staircase leads to six simple rooms with shared baths at **Residencial El Arriero** (San Valentín 750, tel. 067/522137, US$16 pp with an above-average breakfast). The beds are comfortable, the shared baths are tidy and the showers excellent, and some rooms even have balconies, but the doors and floors are creaky. Ask at the downstairs supermarket to see the rooms.

Rooms vary at **Residencial Sur Austral** (Arturo Prat 334, tel. 067/522150, US$20–30 pp), but a recent remodel has improved many of them—even if the walls are a little thin—and the management is obliging. Another budget favorite is family-run **Hostal Latitud 47° Sur** (Lago Brown 564, tel. 067/522280, latitud47sur_patagonia@hotmail.com, US$20 pp).

Popular with cycling groups, comfortably furnished **Residencial Rubio** (Teniente Merino 871, tel. 067/522173, US$18–30 pp) has spacious, spotless rooms with twin beds, private baths, and breakfast (some cheaper rooms have shared baths).

On barren grounds long awaiting landscaping, Spanish-run ☾ **Hotel Ultimo Paraíso** (Lago Brown 455, tel./fax 067/522361, hotelultimoparaisochile@hotmail.es, US$84 s, US$100 d) is otherwise exceptional, with eight well-heated, spacious, and attractive rooms with private baths. The guests-only restaurant serves lunch and dinner.

## Food

**El Fogón** (San Valentín 651, lunch and dinner daily) is no longer the best, but it's still not bad. The name implies a *parrilla,* but the menu is more diverse than that, with fish (including conger eel, hake, and salmon) and fowl, in the US$8–12 range. The specialty, though, is still beef.

Thanks to outstanding homemade meals, family-run ☾ **Ñirrantal** (O'Higgins 650-C, tel. 067/522604, lunch and dinner daily) prepares diverse entrées ranging from sandwiches and salmon to beef and everything in between; entrées cost as little as US$8 including a side dish. While the service can be erratic, it's so well intentioned and the food is so good that's only a minor drawback.

Ñirrantal has competition, though, from **Ada's** (Teniente Merino 374, tel. 09/8399-5889, 11 A.M.–midnight daily), a cheerful place whose offerings range from sandwiches to individual pizzas (US$6, a little heavy on the cheese), seafood, and roast lamb (US$11), in attractive surroundings. It's also tobacco-free.

## Information and Services

December–March only, the municipal **Oficina de Información Turística** (www.cochranepatagonia.cl, 9 A.M.–1:30 P.M. and 2:30–6 P.M. Mon.–Fri., 9 A.M.–1:30 P.M. Sat.) works from a kiosk at the southeast corner of the Plaza de Armas; the staff can range from very helpful to indifferent. For information on nearby parks and reserves, visit **Conaf** (Río Nef 417, tel. 067/522164).

On the east side of the Plaza de Armas, **Banco del Estado** (Esmeralda 460) now has an ATM (MasterCard only). At the southwest corner of the plaza, **Correos de Chile** (Dr. Steffens and Golondrinas) handles postal needs. **Mazal** (O'Higgins 650) provides fast Internet access, including wireless Internet, and also has coffee, fresh kuchen, and other sweets.

In addition to its accommodations, **Hostal Latitude 47° Sur** (Dr. Steffen 576, tel. 067/522280) arranges fly-fishing and other excursions. **La Lavandería** (Los Helechos 336) washes and irons for about US$8.

**Hospital Cochrane** (O'Higgins 755, tel. 067/522131) provides medical assistance.

## Getting There

Several companies connect Cochrane with Coyhaique (US$26, nine hours) and intermediates, including **Buses Don Carlos** (Prat 281, tel. 067/522150), **Buses São Paulo** (Río Baker 349, tel. 067/255726), **Buses Acuario 13** (Río Baker 349, tel. 067/522143), **Aguilas Patagónicas** (Dr. Steffen and Golodrinas, tel. 067/212020), and **Buses Sabra** (Teniente Merino 372).

**Buses Ale** (Las Golondrinas 399, tel. 067/522448) goes to Puerto Guadal and Chile Chico (US$26, six hours) Thursday and Sunday at 10 A.M. **Buses Aldea** (Río Baker 349, tel. 09/8180-9162) goes to Caleta Tortel (US$12, three hours) at 9:30 A.M. Tuesday, Thursday, Friday, and Sunday.

Acuario 13 provides service to Villa O'Higgins (US$24, seven hours) Thursday and Sunday at 9 A.M. This is a subsidized route on which locals have priority.

# CALETA TORTEL

Where the Río Baker greets the sea, Caleta Tortel is a distinctive fishing village with no streets in the traditional sense—boardwalks and staircases link its houses and businesses. For nearly half a century the only access to this isolated hamlet (founded 1955) was slow or expensive—or both—by air, river, or sea. Since the road link opened from the Carretera Austral, though, it's accessible overland.

Over the last few years, Tortel has seen a minor building boom of handsome roofed riverside plazas, as well as a massive Municipalidad, which have enhanced its traditional charm. In addition to the town itself, there is hiking to destinations such as **Cerro La Bandera** or, more ambitiously, to **Cascada Pisagua,** which requires hiring a launch to the trailhead.

Caleta Tortel (population about 625) is roughly 130 kilometers southeast of Cochrane via the Carretera Austral and a westbound lateral along the Río Baker's south bank. Motor vehicles arrive at a parking lot at the Rincón Alto sector, from which it's necessary to wheel or haul your baggage down the steep staircases (and back up when you leave).

## Accommodations and Food

Traditionally the town's best, **Hostal Costanera** (tel. 067/211876, US$20 pp with

© WAYNE BERNHARDSON

At Caleta Tortel, the streets are boardwalks and the plazas have roofs to keep off the rain.

shared bath) has one exceptional room with high ceilings and sea views, but all the others are more than acceptable. In its range, though, it's got competition from several other places and across-the-boardwalk **Hospedaje Estilo** (US$20 s, US$36 d), which also serves meals, and **Hospedaje Don Adán** (Rincón Alto, hospedaje_donadan@chile.com, US$19 pp).

In a class of its own, though, is the six-room **Entre Hielos Lodge** (Sector Base, tel. 02/1960271, US$95 s, US$120 d) an engaging place remodeled by a Santiago architect who now lives here with her local husband. He, in fact, designed and built the furniture and decoration, which has a contemporary sensibility without turning its back on local tradition. The rooms are midsize, all with private baths; a chef prepares meals for lodge guests only, and the wine list would be a good one even in a large city.

For the freshest fish, head to **El Mirador** (Sector Base s/n, lunch and dinner daily), whose picture windows provide broad panoramas of the harbor and mountains. This is river salmon, not farmed, and while the preparation may be unsophisticated, the quality is high; there are often catch-of-the-day specials, such as *merluza* (hake). A three-course meal costs US$10–12. **Sabores Locales** (Sector Base s/n, lunch and dinner daily) is less elaborate but makes savory fresh seafood soups (US$6) and larger plates as well.

### Information and Services

At the parking lot, the Municipalidad maintains a small but helpful tourist office that has has maps and offers suggestions for hikes and excursions; from mid-October to mid-April, it keeps long hours, but it is closed the rest of the year. They can also help arrange six-hour boat trips to nearby glaciers (around US$500 for up to eight people).

### Getting There

From the parking lot above town, **Buses Aldea** goes to Cochrane (US$12, three hours) at 3 P.M. Tuesday, Thursday, Friday, and Sunday. In high season, **Hielo Sur** offers Thursday and Sunday service to Villa O'Higgins (US$30, four hours).

## PUERTO YUNGAY

Until 1999, Puerto Yungay, on Fiordo Mitchell, was the highway's end point, but now it's the port for a free car and passenger ferry to a ramp at Río Bravo and Villa O'Higgins, the highway's most southerly outpost. When the road opened late that year, according to Sergeant Eduardo Martínez of the Cuerpo Militar de Trabajo (CMT, Chile's Army Corps of Engineers), it was the site of the highway's biggest traffic jam: "There were so many cars backed up that we were working from 7 A.M. until midnight. Some days we couldn't handle all of them, so they had to camp and wait until the next day."

The CMT may someday carve a road along the sheer rock wall of the fjord's north side, but it will never be as fast as the half-hour ferry to Río Bravo, where the road resumes. There, some visionary (or hallucinatory) politicians envision a further southern link to Parque Nacional Torres del Paine, a project that could take decades and still require eight or nine ferry crossings (a segment of this road has been under construction, but the process is slow).

In November 2005, the car ferry *Padre Antonio Ronchi* replaced the tiny old CMT ferry on this run; space is available free on a first-come, first-served basis. Summer departures are at 10 A.M., noon, and 6 P.M. daily; return times from Río Bravo are at 11 A.M., 1 P.M., and 7 P.M. The rest of the year, services may be reduced; for more information, contact Cochrane's Departamento de Vialidad (Av. O'Higgins and Esmeralda, tel. 067/521242).

There are no other services at Puerto Yungay except for a small café that, in season, prepares hot tea or coffee and has a small selection of groceries and snacks. At the Río Bravo, there's a new passenger shelter with clean toilets; late-arriving cyclists have camped inside.

## VILLA O'HIGGINS

Over the last several years, tiny Villa O'Higgins has become something of a backpackers' mecca as the start or finish of the still rugged overland crossing to and from the Argentine trekking capital of El Chaltén—while waiting for

© WAYNE BERNHARDSON

Villa O'Higgins is the southernmost settlement on the Carretera Austral.

the boat that begins the track south or the bus north to Caleta Tortel or Cochrane, there's not much choice but to stay here. Still, O'Higgins has plenty to do in its own right, including hiking and fishing amid extraordinary scenery, and its services are rapidly improving.

From its founding in 1954 until completion of the Carretera Austral in 1999, O'Higgins (population about 550) was accessible only by air taxi from Coyhaique or by water from Argentina. It depended on Argentine supplies, and highway construction materials entered via Argentine roads and ferries on Lago O'Higgins (Lago San Martín to Argentines). Now, though, the Puerto Yungay ferry drops passengers and vehicles at Río Bravo, a boat ramp 100 kilometers to the northwest, for the Carretera Austral's last leg.

When the new road finally opened, said ex-policeman Arturo Gómez, curious tourists overran the town. "We were at full capacity, and most of the people here have scarce resources and couldn't arrange things so soon." People camped, slept in spare rooms, and rented a handful of cabañas. "We didn't evolve step-by-step," said then-mayor Alfredo Runín. "We went from horseback to jet."

Today, Villa O'Higgins is booming with new construction, and the town has big plans. Thanks to work on the Sendero de Chile trail, and the motor launch that helps link the town with remote parts of the lake and El Chaltén, the backcountry is increasingly hiker-friendly. A new road has also been built to Río Mayer, on the Argentine border to the northeast, for a border crossing that may soon open.

One measure of O'Higgins's growth is that its Petrobras gas station is the first one south of Cochrane on the Carretera Austral (with the priciest fuel in the country, approaching US$2 per liter). Still, the services here are about 15 years behind El Chaltén's (not necessarily a bad thing).

## Sights and Recreation

On the south side of the Plaza de Armas, the **Museo Antonio Ronchi** was the town's first church and still preserves the spartan bedroom

## THE NEW CRUCE DE LAGOS

The traditional lake-land-lake crossing from Chile to Argentina goes from Puerto Montt to Bariloche, but if Aisén and Santa Cruz authorities have their druthers, the next big thing will be the route from Villa O'Higgins to El Chaltén.

Increasing numbers of hardy travelers are making the journey from **Villa O'Higgins** to the nearby lake port of **Bahía Bahamóndez** for the twice-weekly, 50-kilometer, 3.5-hour journey (US$80) on the 60-passenger motor launch *Quetru* to the Chilean border post of Candelario Mancilla. From **Candelario Mancilla,** the *Quetru* makes an optional excursion to **Glaciar O'Higgins** and **Glaciar Chico** (US$40 more) before returning to Mancilla (to pick up arrivals from Argentina) and return to Bahamóndez.

At Candelario Mancilla, where there are simple accommodations (US$12 pp), camping (US$4 per tent), and meals, Chilean Carabineros handle immigration and customs procedures. By foot, bicycle, horseback, or vehicle, it's another 15 kilometers to the international border and 7.5 kilometers more to the Argentine Gendarmería, who handle customs and immigration there. In some cases, hikers may need to ford the appropriately named Río Obstáculo (Obstacle River); beyond the borderline, the existing road becomes a footpath unsuitable for cyclists, who will have to push or even carry their bikes. At Candelario Mancilla, it's possible to hire a guide (US$25) and horses (US$30 pp plus US$40 for each pack animal); these leave the day after arrival on the boat. Make arrangements as far in advance as possible, as both horses and personnel are few, and the guide can take no more than three or four persons.

From the Gendarmería post, at the north end of **Laguna del Desierto,** there are passenger launches (US$25, 30-45 minutes, plus US$5 per bicycle) to the south end of the lake at 1:30 and 4:45 P.M. Alternatively, hikers can walk the 15 kilometers in about five hours. At the south end, where the launches leave for the border at 10:45 A.M. and 2 P.M., there is also **Camping Estancia Lago del Desierto** (US$7.50 pp), offering wooded sites with fire pits and toilets with hot showers.

From Laguna del Desierto, there are buses to **El Chaltén** (US$25, one hour) at 2:30 and 8:30 P.M. Buses from El Chaltén to Laguna del Desierto leave at 8:30 A.M. and 3 P.M.; schedules are subject to change.

There are environmental issues here – deforestation and erosion, for example – and romantics may deplore the loss of frontier feeling as buses replace bicycles. Whatever the ultimate result, though, crossing the borders here is a huge improvement over the days when Chilean and Argentine forces exchanged gunfire – including an incident that killed a Carabinero in 1965 – over what was one of the last outstanding border disputes between the two countries.

of the apparently ascetic priest for whom it was named. Also containing artifacts of early colonists, it keeps no regular hours, but the tourist office on the plaza will open it on request.

At the east end of Río Pascua street, a footpath leads to a scenic overlook that's part of **Parque Cerro Santiago,** Chile's first municipal nature reserve. Hoping to attract adventurous hikers and climbers, local authorities have patched together a trail by signing existing forest paths to a backwoods shelter near the **Ventisquero Mosco** (Mosco Glacier), a 12-hour round-trip.

Villa O'Higgins lies in the broad valley of the **Río Mayer,** a prime trout stream. Just outside town, a southbound secondary road crosses the river on the **Puente Colgante August Grosse,** a 123-meter suspension bridge; from the bridge's south side, an exposed zigzag trail leads west above **Lago Ciervo,** a scenic route that eventually drops onto the shore of **Lago Negro,** where camping is possible. With an early start, this can also be a long day hike, but the trail is tiring because it conserves altitude poorly and is difficult to follow in some spots.

© WAYNE BERNHARDSON

Glaciar O'Higgins is a full-day excursion from VIlla O'Higgins.

To the west, the steeply rising peaks of the **Campo de Hielo Sur,** the southern Patagonian icecap, may be the next big thing for hikers for whom Torres del Paine is too tame. Beyond the bridge, the road continues south to **Bahía Bahamóndez,** where a launch carries tourists up Lago O'Higgins to the **Glaciar O'Higgins** in a full-day excursion.

It is possible, however, to cross the Argentine border by taking the boat to the south end of **Lago O'Higgins** and making a long and sometimes difficult hike through rugged country to **Laguna del Desierto.** From this point there's a road to the Argentine village of **El Chaltén,** in Parque Nacional Los Glaciares.

## Accommodations and Food

Until not so long ago, Villa O'Higgins had only one permanent lodge, the simple but well-kept **Hospedaje Patagonia** (Río Pascua 191, tel. 067/431818, US$20 pp), opposite the Plaza de Armas, with comfortable beds and a decent breakfast. In summer, it serves lunch and dinner as well. **Hospedaje Carretera Austral** (Río Colorado 40, tel. 067/431819, US$14 with breakfast) is a similar family-run hostelry with good meals, but the walls seem a little thin if it's really crowded.

Spanish-run **Hostería El Mosco** (Carretera Austral Km 1240, tel. 067/431819, www.patagoniaelmosco.com, US$20 pp in dorms, US$36–60 s, US$56–80 d) is a hybrid B&B (six upstairs doubles, three of them with private baths), hostel (four six-bed dorms at street level), and a fairly barren campground (US$10 pp). Both levels have ample common areas, including kitchens; campers may also use the downstairs areas. Arguably, it's a travelers' social center, and also provides a sauna and a hot tub (for an extra charge).

Directly across from El Mosco, far more ambitious than anything else in town, the **Robinson Crusoe Deep Patagonia Lodge** (Carretera Austral s/n, www.hielosur.com, US$200 s or d) is a new 12-room lodge with a big central clubhouse area and bar with high ceilings, plus two separate wings of comfortable doubles or triples with double-paned windows.

© WAYNE BERNHARDSON

Cyclists crowd the boat from Villa O'Higgins to Candelario Mancilla.

O'Higgins now has two pretty good restaurants. In an attractive building at the north end of town, **Entre Patagones** (Carretera Austral 1, tel. 067/431810, www.entrepatagones.cl, lunch and dinner daily) makes great soups and a genuine effort to make its dishes visually appealing, but the main menu is limited to one or two dishes (about US$12), usually beef-based, per night. Though a bit less aesthetically pleasing, **San Gabriel** (Lago O'Higgins s/n, no phone, lunch and dinner daily) has a more diverse menu (including lamb in the evening) and excellent service. The lamb, though, is a bit overcooked.

## Information and Services

There's a small but helpful information kiosk, keeping irregular hours, on the Plaza de Armas. The de facto tourism office, though, is Hans Silva's **Hielo Sur** (Carretera Austral 267, tel. 067/431821, www.hielosur.com), which maintains an informative website in both Spanish and English. Silva also operates the twice- or thrice-weekly excursion to Glaciar O'Higgins (US$120 pp), one leg of which also transports passengers to Candelario Mancilla (US$80 pp) for the crossing to Argentina.

Half a block south of the plaza, the **Biblioteca Pública** (Public Library) has free Internet access in half-hour blocks, by reservation only (the wait is rarely long), but the town has added free wireless Internet that works reasonably well. Across the street, there's a long-distance telephone office.

## Getting There and Around

From the airstrip directly opposite the main drag, there are flights to and from Coyhaique, but a new carrier is due to take them over, and as of press time no further details were available.

Buses to Cochrane (US$24, 6.5 hours) remain infrequent and subject to change, with preference for local residents. Presently the only carrier is **Buses Aldea** (cell 09/8180-9162) at 9 A.M. Thursday and Sunday, but **Hielo Sur** (tel. 067/431821) has begun service to Caleta Tortel (US$30, four hours), where there are onward connections to Cochrane.

# SOUTHERN ARGENTINE PATAGONIA

Argentina's second- and third-largest provinces, stretching from the Atlantic to the Andes, Santa Cruz and Chubut might be considered Argentina's "Deep South," whose vast open spaces and scattered population lend themselves to Patagonia's "wild and remote" stereotype. That said, there are substantial cities and towns with hotels and other services, many good roads (plus others not so good), and decent public transportation.

Southern Argentine Patagonia's most dramatic sight (and sound) is the Perito Moreno Glacier at Parque Nacional Los Glaciares—along with Buenos Aires and Iguazú, it's one of the top reasons people travel to Argentina. Many spend entire days gazing upon and listening to this relentless river of ice. More-active visitors take the bus to the hamlet of El Chaltén, where trailheads offer access to wild backcountry and, for climbers, some of the continent's most challenging technical peaks. Even day hikers, though, will appreciate its striking Andean scenery.

Even then, the barren coastline draws many visitors to Península Valdés and other sites where packs of penguins waddle ashore in the southern spring, elephant seals give birth in summer, and the great right whales breed and birth in sheltered shallows in winter and spring. The coast and steppe also feature picturesque towns, such as the Welsh settlement of Gaiman and the historic ports of Puerto Deseado and Puerto San Julián. On the Santa Cruz steppe, there are several petrified forests and the landmark rock art of Cueva de las Manos, a UNESCO World Heritage Site.

© PATRICK POENDL/123RF

# HIGHLIGHTS

**Área Natural Protegida Península Valdés:** It's hard to choose among coastal Patagonia's countless wildlife reserves, but Península Valdés has everything: guanacos, rheas, penguins, elephant seals, sea lions, orcas, and the great right whales. It doesn't have everything at the same time, though, so every season's a different experience (page 336).

**Área Natural Protegida Punta Tombo:** Every austral spring, 200,000 pairs of Magellanic penguins waddle ashore to mate in this remote spot, where there are also plenty of other seabirds and shorebirds (page 350).

LOOK FOR ☾ TO FIND RECOMMENDED SIGHTS, ACTIVITIES, DINING, AND LODGING.

**Bahía Bustamante:** An unique kelp-gathering community hosts visitors in comfortable accommodations to visit the nearby sights of the **Parque Interjurisdiccional Marino Costero Patagonia Austral** (page 352).

**Puerto Deseado:** On a picturesque setting by an estuary, the town is the base for exploring the several penguin, cormorant, and sea lion colonies along the *ría* (estuary) and on the islands of a new coastal park (page 357).

**Parque Nacional Monte León:** Where the tides strike the headlands, the South Atlantic has molded the most varied shapes in this coastal park – and there's plenty of wildlife, including penguins and guanacos (page 364).

**Estancia Monte Dinero:** On the coastal steppe southeast of Río Gallegos, Monte Dinero is a model working ranch that also provides homey accommodations and access to the giant penguin colony and other sights at Cabo Vírgenes (page 370).

**Eolo Lodge:** Southwest of El Calafate, this country lodge re-creates the style of the original Patagonia *estancias*, with vast panoramas and modern luxuries (page 383).

**Parque Nacional Los Glaciares:** The constantly calving 60-meter face of groaning Glaciar Moreno, west of El Calafate, is one of the continent's most awesome sights (and sounds). Sector Fitz Roy, near the hamlet of El Chaltén, offers some of the Andes's most exhilarating scenery, hiking, and climbing (page 383).

**Parque Nacional Perito Moreno:** West of RN 40, Argentina's loneliest highway, what may be Patagonia's wildest park offers endless vistas and varied terrain – ranging from sub-Antarctic forest to high Andean pastures (page 402).

**Cueva de las Manos:** This UNESCO World Heritage Site's rock art includes hundreds of human hands and other more abstract designs nearly 10,000 years old (page 404).

Note that southern Argentine Patagonia, for the purposes of this guide, includes sections of RN 40 from Río Turbio, along the Chilean border, and north to the town of Perito Moreno; northern Argentine Patagonia includes northern RN 40, from the Río Negro provincial border to the southern Chubut town of Río Mayo.

## PLANNING YOUR TIME

Southern Argentine Patagonia's highlights are limitless, but distances are great and flying is almost imperative for short-term visitors—overland transportation is too time-consuming to visit widely separated sights like Península Valdés's wildlife and the Perito Moreno Glacier (Glaciar Perito Moreno).

Perito Moreno Glacier visitors should make additional time—perhaps at least a week—to hike Parque Nacional Los Glaciares's Sector Fitz Roy and even Chile's Parque Nacional Torres del Paine (dedicated climbers may wait the entire summer for the weather to clear at these latitudes). Many choose an extension to Tierra del Fuego as well.

For those with time, money, and a vehicle, the ideal way to see the region is to drive south on RN 3—all the way to the Perito Moreno Glacier or even Tierra del Fuego—and return via RN 40 to Bariloche or beyond. Besides a sturdy vehicle, this requires at least a month, preferably two, and ideally three.

Coastal Patagonia's best base is Puerto Madryn, which has the best services, and access to secondary attractions like the Welsh settlements of Trelew and Gaiman. For the national parks along the Andes, El Calafate and El Chaltén, along with full-service *estancias,* are the top options.

January and February are the most popular months, but also the most expensive. The shoulder months of November–December and March–April have less crowding, lower prices, and equally good (sometimes better) weather. By April the days are getting shorter, but winter whale-watching has become big business at Puerto Pirámides.

Overland transportation schedules change seasonally and annually, and they can be disrupted by weather.

© JAVARMAN JAVARMAN/123RF

Parque Nacional Los Glaciares

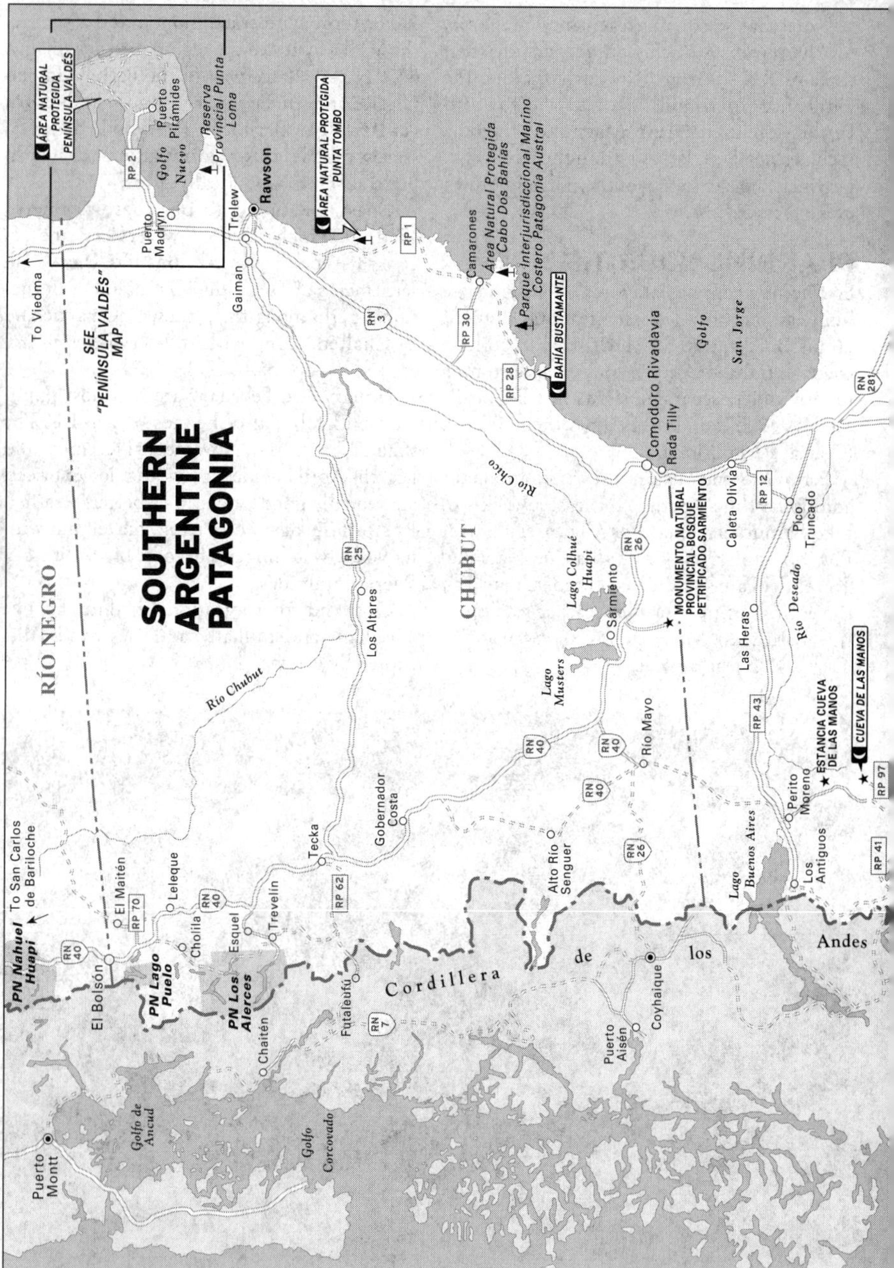

SOUTHERN ARGENTINE PATAGONIA
RÍO NEGRO
CHUBUT
SEE "PENÍNSULA VALDÉS" MAP
To Viedma
To San Carlos de Bariloche
ÁREA NATURAL PROTEGIDA PENÍNSULA VALDÉS
ÁREA NATURAL PROTEGIDA PUNTA TOMBO
BAHÍA BUSTAMANTE
MONUMENTO NATURAL PROVINCIAL BOSQUE PETRIFICADO SARMIENTO
ESTANCIA CUEVA DE LAS MANOS
CUEVA DE LAS MANOS
Puerto Pirámides
Golfo Nuevo
Reserva Provincial Punta Loma
Puerto Madryn
Trelew
Rawson
Gaiman
Camarones
Área Natural Protegida Cabo Dos Bahías
Parque Interjurisdiccional Marino Costero Patagonia Austral
Comodoro Rivadavia
Rada Tilly
Caleta Olivia
Pico Truncado
Golfo San Jorge
Río Chico
Río Chubut
Río Deseado
Lago Colhué Huapi
Lago Musters
Sarmiento
Los Altares
Las Heras
Río Mayo
Gobernador Costa
Tecka
Alto Río Senguer
Perito Moreno
Los Antiguos
Lago Buenos Aires
Trevelín
Esquel
Leleque
El Maitén
Cholila
El Bolsón
PN Nahuel Huapi
PN Lago Puelo
PN Los Alerces
Futaleufú
Chaitén
Cordillera de los Andes
Coyhaique
Puerto Aisén
Puerto Montt
Golfo de Ancud
Golfo Corcovado
RP 2
RP 1
RN 3
RP 30
RP 28
RN 281
RP 12
RN 26
RN 25
RP 43
RN 40
RP 97
RP 41
RP 62
RP 70
RN 7

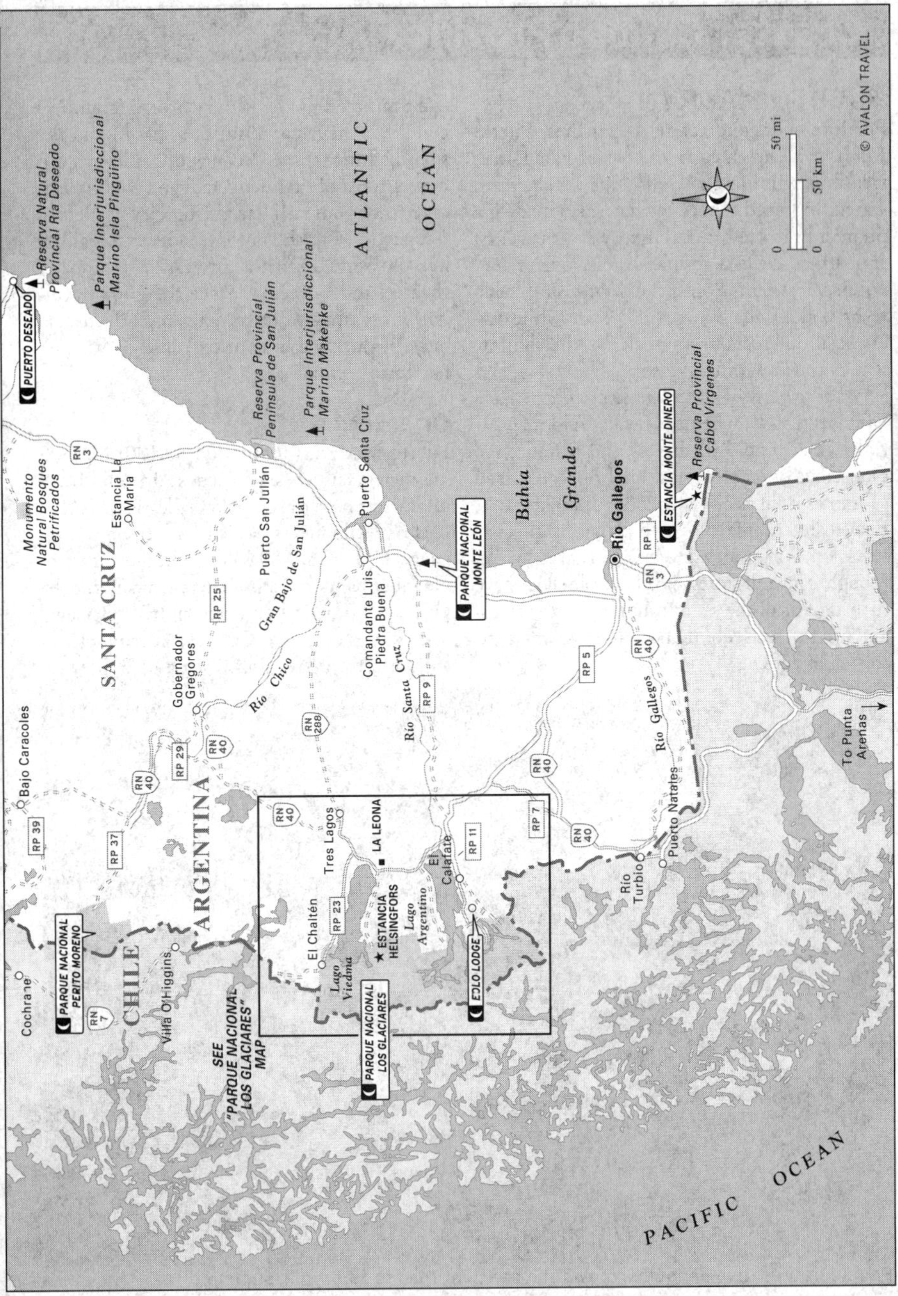


S. ARGENTINE PATAGONIA

# Coastal Chubut Province

## PUERTO MADRYN

For foreigners and many Argentines, Puerto Madryn is the gateway to coastal Patagonia's wealth of wildlife; the Golfo Nuevo's sheltered waters and sandy shoreline have also made it a premier beach resort. In January and February, sunbathers, cyclists, in-line skaters, joggers, and windsurfers irrupt onto the *balnearios* (beach resorts) along the Boulevard Brown, while divers seek out reefs and wrecks as the shallow waters warm with the season.

Madryn's tourist season weakens after Semana Santa until July, when Península Valdés's great right whales help fill hotels and restaurants. Conscious of its ecological birthright, Madryn promotes itself as an ecofriendly destination; its Ecocentro complex, focused on maritime conservation, is a positive development. Meanwhile, though, souvenir stores and chocolate shops have turned parts of the waterfront into tourist traps, and bright green suburban lawns have worsened the water deficit.

Stimulated by the Muelle Storni (commercial pier), the Aluar aluminum plant, and the fishing fleet, three decades of rapid growth have almost obliterated Madryn's Welsh heritage (though it still has a sister city in Nefyn, Gwynedd). On the positive side, cultural life has blossomed with a university campus, a theater, and a cinema. Since the 2002 devaluation, many visitors have been Chileans, especially during that country's mid-September patriotic holidays.

### Orientation

Puerto Madryn (population 80,100) is 1,308 kilometers southwest of Buenos Aires and 1,219 kilometers northeast of Río Gallegos via RN 3. It is 670 kilometers east of Esquel via several paved highways; 680 kilometers southeast of Neuquén; and 960 kilometers from Bariloche via Esquel. It is 65 kilometers north of Trelew.

Most services are within a few blocks of the waterfront Avenida Roca and Boulevard

© WAYNE BERNHARDSON

People, rather than penguins, crowd the beach at Puerto Madryn in summer.

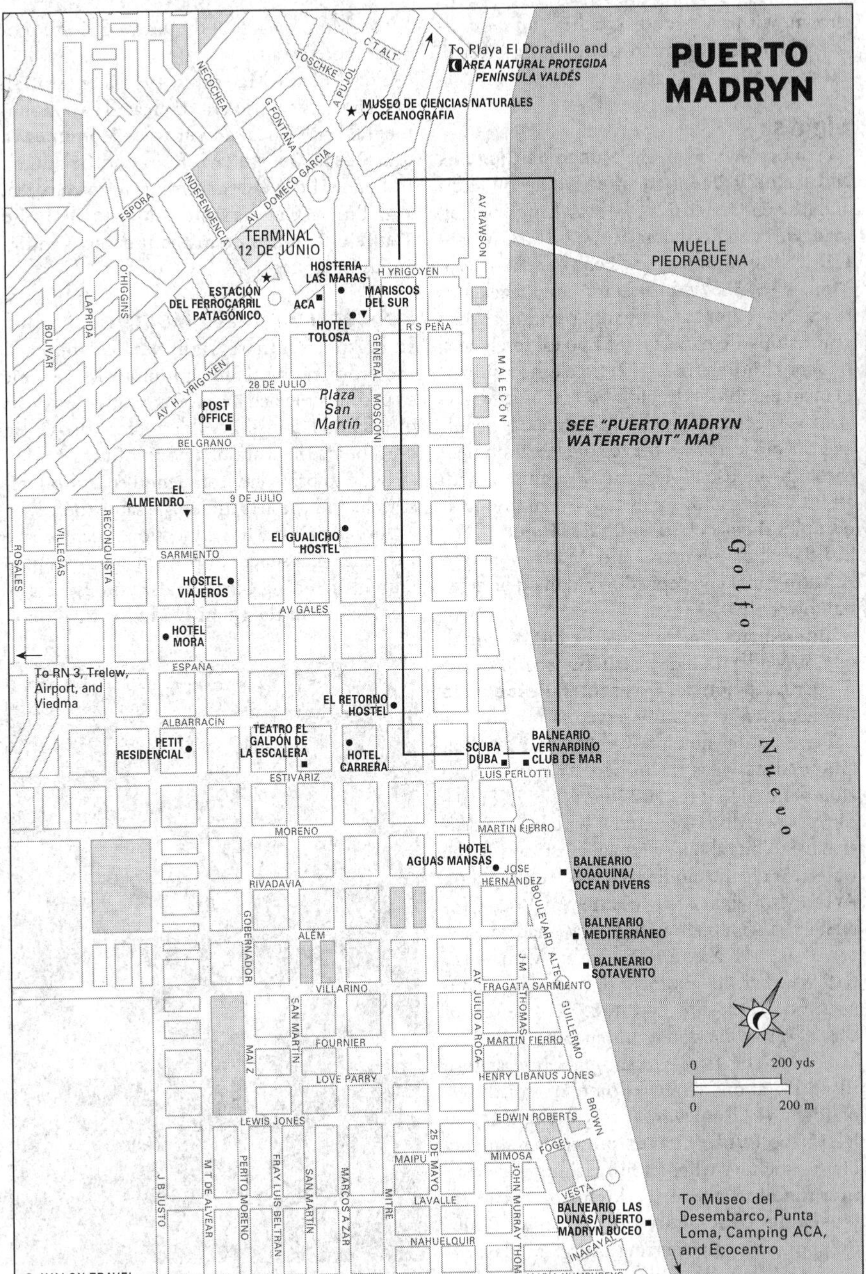
PUERTO MADRYN
To Playa El Doradillo and
AREA NATURAL PROTEGIDA PENÍNSULA VALDÉS
MUSEO DE CIENCIAS NATURALES Y OCEANOGRAFIA
TERMINAL 12 DE JUNIO
ESTACIÓN DEL FERROCARRIL PATAGÓNICO
HOSTERIA LAS MARAS
ACA
MARISCOS DEL SUR
HOTEL TOLOSA
MUELLE PIEDRABUENA
POST OFFICE
Plaza San Martín
SEE "PUERTO MADRYN WATERFRONT" MAP
EL ALMENDRO
EL GUALICHO HOSTEL
HOSTEL VIAJEROS
HOTEL MORA
To RN 3, Trelew, Airport, and Viedma
EL RETORNO HOSTEL
PETIT RESIDENCIAL
TEATRO EL GALPÓN DE LA ESCALERA
HOTEL CARRERA
SCUBA DUBA
BALNEARIO VERNARDINO CLUB DE MAR
HOTEL AGUAS MANSAS
BALNEARIO YOAQUINA/ OCEAN DIVERS
BALNEARIO MEDITERRÁNEO
BALNEARIO SOTAVENTO
BALNEARIO LAS DUNAS/ PUERTO MADRYN BUCEO
To Museo del Desembarco, Punta Loma, Camping ACA, and Ecocentro
Golfo Nuevo
0 200 yds
0 200 m
C T ALT
TOSCHKE
A PUJOL
NECOCHEA
G FONTANA
AV DOMECQ GARCIA
INDEPENDENCIA
ESPORA
AV RAWSON
H YRIGOYEN
R S PEÑA
O'HIGGINS
LAPRIDA
BOLIVAR
AV H YRIGOYEN
28 DE JULIO
GENERAL MOSCONI
MALECÓN
BELGRANO
9 DE JULIO
VILLEGAS
RECONQUISTA
ROSALES
SARMIENTO
AV GALES
ESPAÑA
ALBARRACIN
ESTIVARIZ
LUIS PERLOTTI
MORENO
MARTIN FIERRO
JOSE HERNÁNDEZ
RIVADAVIA
BOULEVARD ALTE GUILLERMO BROWN
GOBERNADOR MAIZ
ALEM
J M THOMAS
VILLARINO
FRAGATA SARMIENTO
AV JULIO A ROCA
SAN MARTÍN
FOURNIER
MARTIN FIERRO
LOVE PARRY
HENRY LIBANUS JONES
LEWIS JONES
EDWIN ROBERTS
25 DE MAYO
MAIPU
MIMOSA
FOGEL
J B JUSTO
M T DE ALVEAR
PERITO MORENO
FRAY LUIS BELTRAN
SAN MARTÍN
MARCOS A ZAR
MITRE
JOHN MURRAY THOMAS
VESTA
LAVALLE
NAHUELQUIR
INACAYAL
DORREGO
MARIA HUMPHREYS
© AVALON TRAVEL

Brown, with their sandy beaches and *balnearios,* which are the main points of interest in the city itself.

## Sights

North of downtown, the **Museo de Ciencias Naturales y Oceanografía** (Domecq García and Menéndez, tel. 02965/451139, museopujolmadryn@yahoo.com.ar, 9 A.M.–8 P.M. Mon.–Fri., 4–8 P.M. Sat. Dec.–Feb.; 9 A.M.–7 P.M. Mon.–Fri., 3–7 P.M. Sat. and long weekends Mar.–Nov.; also Sat. and Sun. mornings when cruise ships are in port, US$1.50 for foreigners, free for children under 12) holds the semipermanent exhibition El Hombre y el Mar, which stresses the interaction of the Tehuelche people and the pioneers with the regional environment through the use of its natural resources, with an interesting account of traditional myths. It occupies the neoclassical **Chalet Pujol** (1917), built by businessman and Madryn mayor Agustín Pujol and topped by a domed hexagonal tower.

Immediately in front of the bus terminal, one of Madryn's oldest structures (1889), the former **Estación del Ferrocarril Patagónico** (train station) previously served as a bus terminal and houses now the **Centro de Estudios Históricos** (Av. Hipólito Yrigoyen and Independencia, tel. 02965/471777, 8:30–11:30 A.M. Mon.–Fri., free), which has occasional exhibits about the town's history. On the waterfront is the modest **Museo Municipal de Arte** (Municipal Art Museum, Av. Roca 444, tel. 02965/453204, museodearte@madryn.gov.ar, 10 A.M.–1 P.M. and 6–9 P.M. Mon.–Fri., 6–9 P.M. Sat. in summer; 10 A.M.–1 P.M. and 5–8 P.M. Mon.–Fri., 5–8 P.M. Sat. the rest of the year, free but donations encouraged).

Where the first Welshmen came ashore in 1865, about three kilometers southeast of town via Boulevard Brown, the **Parque Histórico Punta Cuevas** preserves remnants of the shelters whose foundations they dug into the bluff above the high-tide mark. Its **Museo del Desembarco** (Blvd. Brown 3600, no phone, www.puntacuevas.org.ar, 10 A.M.–noon and 5–9 P.M. daily in summer, 3–7 P.M. Wed.–Mon. the rest of the year, US$1.25) provides more details.

For Puerto Madryn's 1965 centennial, Porteño artist Luis Perlotti created two monumental sculptures: downtown's **Monumento a la Gesta Galesa** (Av. Roca and Belgrano), to honor the Welsh contribution to the area, and Punta Cuevas's **Monumento al Indio Tehuelche,** a tribute to the province's indigenous inhabitants.

## Ecocentro Puerto Madryn

In season, southern right whales approach the promontory of this luminous Magellanic structure, crowned by a tower that yields views of distant Península Valdés across the Golfo Nuevo. It's the work of a nonprofit institution striving to bring environmental education, research, and the arts under the same roof.

As a maritime-life educational center, the Ecocentro has superb displays of South Atlantic fauna, including birds, seals, and especially whales; one of the finest is a living tidal pool.

© WAYNE BERNHARDSON

Ecocentro Puerto Madryn

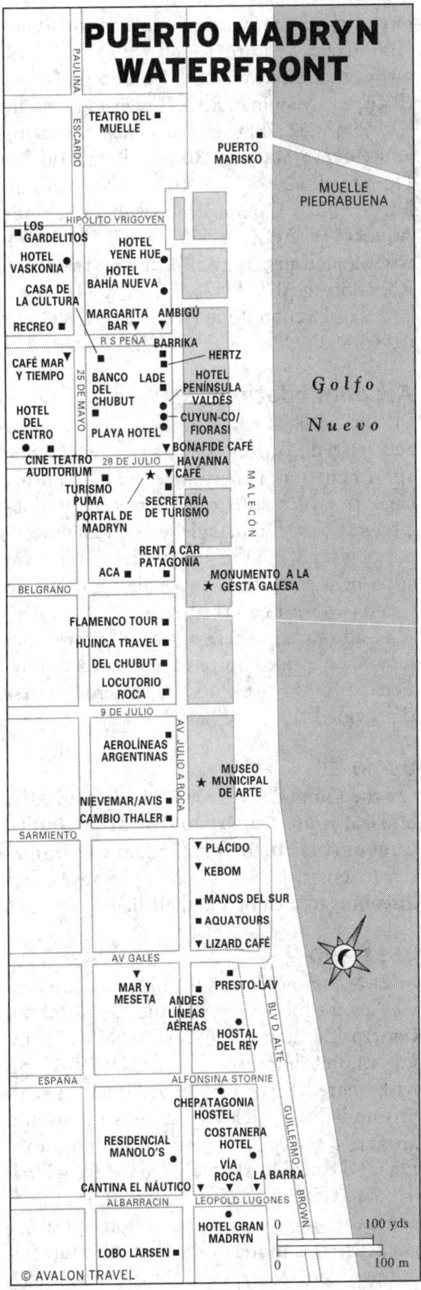


Even the surrounding gardens serve a didactic purpose—in lieu of residential Madryn's water-hungry lawns, the directors have chosen to preserve the native coastal desert flora.

Reached by a spiral staircase, the three-level tower holds a library, an exhibition room for local artists and authors, and a reading room. Painting, photography, and sculpture are all on display; the ground-floor atrium accommodates the largest works. Other features include a 150-seat theater for concerts and lectures, a crafts and souvenir shop, and a café with a great view.

Reached by Boulevard Almirante Brown, about five minutes from downtown by taxi, 15 minutes by bicycle, and 40 minutes on foot, the Ecocentro (Julio Verne 3784, tel. 02965/457470, www.ecocentro.org.ar, US$10 foreign adults, US$6 foreign children ages 6–12) is open 5–9 P.M. daily January–February, plus 10 A.M.–1 P.M. when cruise ships are in port. Hours are 3–7 P.M. Wednesday–Monday in March and July–September, 3–7 P.M. Wednesday–Sunday April–June, and 3–8 P.M. Wednesday–Monday October–December.



## Entertainment and Events

Madryn has an active cultural calendar, starting with the **Teatro del Muelle** (Rawson 60, tel. 02965/450307), which offers theater programs, usually on weekends. The **Casa de la Cultura** (Roque Sáenz Peña 86, tel. 02965/472060) hosts a variety of events.

The **Cine Teatro Auditorium** (28 de Julio 129, tel. 02965/455653) shows current movies and also offers live theater. The **Teatro El Galpón de la Escalera** (Estivariz and San Martín, tel. 02965/15-578922) is a newer theater company with a good reputation.

For occasional live music, try the **Margarita Bar** (Roque Sáenz Peña 15), which has pub grub (with outstanding midday specials from US$9) and costlier drinks. **Los Gardelitos** (Av. Hipólito Yrigoyen 144) is another popular bar, with live music on weekends and occasional tango during the week.

July 28's **Fundación de la Ciudad** celebrates the initial Welsh landing at Punta Cuevas. Festivities continue for several days.

## Shopping

The waterfront avenues are full of souvenir shops, but the best option remains **Manos del Sur** (Av. Roca 516, tel. 02965/472539).

**Recreo** (Roque Sáenz Peña 101; Av. Roca and 28 de Julio, at Portal de Madryn Shopping Mall, tel. 02965/472971) carries a fine selection of books on Patagonia, some in English. **Barrika** (Av. Roca 109, tel. 02965/450454) has the best wine selection.

**Del Chubut** (Av. Roca 369, tel. 02965/451311) sells takeaway *alfajores* (cookies sandwiched around sweet fillings like *dulce de leche*) and delicious *torta galesa* (the traditional Welsh pioneer's black cake).

## Sports and Recreation

Water sports are the attraction on the crescent of sandy beaches stretching from Muelle Storni in the north almost to Punta Cuevas in the south. In these sheltered waters, hazards like rip currents are nonexistent, but at low tide the water retreats hundreds of meters on the gently sloping beach.

At the beaches along Boulevard Almirante Brown, several *balnearios* (beach resorts) rent water-sports equipment and have snack bars and restaurants, including (from north to south and centrally located) **Balneario Vernardino Club de Mar** (Blvd. Brown 860, tel. 02965/474289, www.vernardinoclubdemar.com.ar), **Balneario Yoaquina** (Blvd. Brown 1050, tel. 02965/456058), **Balneario Mediterráneo** (Blvd. Brown 1070, tel. 02965/458145), **Balneario Sotavento** (Blvd. Brown 1300, tel. 02965/470070), and **Balneario Las Dunas** (Blvd. Brown and Inacayal, tel. 02965/457403).

*Balnearios* also rent items like in-line skates and mountain bikes. Some operators who arrange diving excursions and other activities have space here; others are scattered around town.

Divers favor Madryn because of its clear waters, natural and artificial reefs, and shipwrecks; most operators do initial dives for novices, PADI certification courses, and underwater photography. Operators working out of the *balnearios* include **Ocean Divers** (Balneario Yoaquina, tel. 02965/472569, www.oceandivers.com.ar), **Patagonia Buceo** (Balneario Maminas, Blvd. Brown and Castelli, tel. 02965/452278, www.patagoniabuceo.com), and **Puerto Madryn Buceo** (Balneario Las Dunas, tel. 02965/15-564422, www.madrynbuceo.com). Operators elsewhere include **Aquatours** (Av. Roca 550, tel. 02965/451954, www.aquatours.com.ar), **Lobo Larsen** (Av. Roca 885, tel. 02965/470277, www.lobolarsen.com), and **Scuba Duba** (Blvd. Brown 893, tel. 02965/452699, www.scubaduba.com.ar).

## Accommodations

In addition to current hotel prices, the Secretaría de Turismo keeps a register of rental apartments on a daily, weekly, or monthly basis. In peak season, most hotels charge double rates even for a single guest. Hotel occupancy is high, but the summer trend is toward apartment complexes, as people come here to spend two weeks on the beach.

In addition to these options, Madryn has reasonably priced hostels for shoestring travelers. In most cases, wireless Internet access is provided.

### US$10-25

On the Punta Cuevas road, the wooded ACA 800-campsite **Complejo Turístico Punta Cuevas** (tel. 02965/452952, www.acamadryn.com.ar, US$15 for two persons) offers discounts to members and affiliates.

### US$25-50

Most accommodations in this range are hostels, except for basic places such as **Hotel del Centro** (28 de Julio 149, tel. 02965/473742, www.hotel-delcentro.com.ar, US$9–15 pp with shared bath, US$23 s, US$30 d with private bath), which has spotless rooms and attractive shady patios, but serves no breakfast, and **Hotel Vaskonia** (25 de Mayo 43, tel. 02965/472581, US$25 s, US$30 d).

Freshly modernized, set among pleasing gardens, the motel-style **Hostel Viajeros** (Gobernador Maíz 545, tel. 02965/456457, www.hostelviajeros.com, US$13 pp dorm, US$28 s, US$43 d, US$48–54 d at the *hostería*) is an amiable place with dorms, legitimate single rooms, and doubles with private baths. Newer private rooms at its *hostería* in the same location offer equivalent comfort to a good modern hotel.

Though a little farther from the beach, homey **El Retorno Hostel** (Mitre 798, tel. 02965/456044, www.elretornohostel.com.ar, from US$13 pp dorm, US$55 d) has several private rooms in a beautifully appointed place.

Only half a block from the beach, Israeli favorite **Chepatagonia Hostel** (Alfonsina Storni 16, tel. 02965/455783, www.chepatagoniahostel.com.ar, US$14 pp dorm, US$40–45 d with shared bath) is an independent hostel with mostly dorm accommodations, but it's spotless and pleasant. It offers free use of bikes.

Madryn's HI affiliate is the exceptional **El Gualicho Hostel** (Marcos A. Zar 480, tel. 02965/454163, www.elgualichohostel.com.ar, US$17 pp dorm, US$65 d with private bath). Comfortably furnished and attractively decorated, it also has a shady patio that encourages socializing.

Though it's less central than others, all rooms at **Hotel Mora** (Juan B. Justo 654, tel. 02965/471424, www.morahotel.com.ar, US$43 d with breakfast) have private baths, and it's a good choice. Set back from the busy avenue, centrally located **Residencial Manolo's** (Av. Roca 763, tel. 02965/472390, manolos@speedy.com.ar, US$50 s or d) has firm beds but slightly cramped rooms.

### US$50-100

The spartan **Petit Residencial** (Marcelo T. de Alvear 845, tel. 02965/451460, hotel_petit@hotmail.com, US$35 s, US$53 d) is a friendly place with small motel-style rooms and ample parking.

Though its smallish rooms don't get many style points, the homey, well-kept **Hotel Carrera** (Marcos A. Zar 844, tel. 02965/450759, www.hotelcarrera.com.ar, US$63 s, US$67 d) offers personalized service in a quiet neighborhood, with a very decent breakfast to boot. At the comparable, well-located **Hotel Gran Madryn** (Lugones 40, tel. 02965/472205, www.hotelgranmadryn.com, US$78–98 s or d), the pricier rooms are newer and more comfortable, and some have sea views.

Overpriced for its category, tranquil **Hotel Aguas Mansas** (José Hernández 51, tel. 02965/473103, www.aguasmansas.com, US$85 s or d) is still a pleasant contemporary place with a swimming pool on a residential block very close to the beach. It offers cash discounts.

### OVER US$100

Madryn's top-end hotels continue to follow the unfortunate policy of charging foreigners more, often substantially more, than they do Argentines.

**Playa Hotel** (Av. Roca 187, tel. 02965/451446, www.playahotel.com.ar, US$105 s or d) draws its character from its age, which doesn't make it necessarily attractive. Though overpriced in high season and lacking views, **Hostería Las Maras** (Marcos A. Zar 64, tel. 02965/453215, www.hosterialasmaras.com.ar, US$90–110 s, US$110–120 d) is still an attractive choice, in a convenient location with easy access to the beach and the bus terminal, very comfortable superior rooms, and an attentive staff.

Re-creating the style of Madryn's early Welsh houses, but with contemporary comforts, **Hotel Bahía Nueva** (Av. Roca 67, tel./fax 02965/451677, www.bahianueva.com.ar, US$97 s, US$124 d) also has spacious gardens and ample parking in a central beachfront location. Rooms are comfy, but not large, and there is an extra charge for any of the four rooms with sea views.

Though well-established, central, and redecorated in 2010, **Hotel Tolosa** (Roque Sáenz Peña 253, tel. 02965/471850, www.hoteltolosa.com.ar, US$135–155 s or d) isn't quite so good as some cheaper places. It's worth paying extra for the larger superior rooms with sea views.

**Hotel Península Valdés** (Av. Roca 155, tel. 02965/471292, www.hotelpeninsula.com.ar,

US$168–236 s or d) has fine standard rooms, but spectacular ocean views make the larger panoramic and even the top superior rooms at the eighth floor worth consideration.

Facing the beach, **Hotel Yenehue** (Av. Roca 33, tel. 02965/471496, www.hotelesaustralis.com.ar, US$187–208 s, US$208–232 d) is a spa hotel with high-rise ocean views from the rooms that front on the avenue. In addition to saunas, massages, and other treatments (which are open to nonguests), amenities include a restaurant, a swimming pool, and good accessibility for travelers with disabilities.

At the south end of town, emulating a massive shearing shed in its exterior style, **Hotel Territorio** (Blvd. Brown 3251, tel. 02965/470050, www.hotelterritorio.com.ar, from US$256 s or d) is a top-end 36-room hotel offering high comfort, functionality, spectacular ocean views from all rooms, a spa, and a restaurant open only to guests. It's owned by Ecocentro's founder, and a small patch of protected dunes separates the hotel from the coastal road.



## Food

Puerto Madryn's dining scene is mostly uninspired, with diminished creativity and innovation, but there are exceptions.

Good choices for breakfast, snacks, light lunches, and coffee include **Café Mar y Tiempo** (Roque Sáenz Peña and 25 de Mayo) and the **Lizard Café** (Av. Roca and Gales, tel. 02965/458333), also a decent pizzeria. The **Bonafide Café** (Av. Roca and 28 de Julio) and the **Havanna Café,** across the street, are probably the best *confiterías.*

In an eclectic ambience that includes nine TVs in silent mode plus music, **Ambigú** (Av. Roca and Roque Sáenz Peña, tel. 02965/472541, lunch and dinner daily) is excellent value for its pastas and tasty sauces (for about US$10) and top quality pizzas (from US$8). It is also a popular choice that fills up fast in the evening.

Part of its namesake *balneario,* **Vernardino** (Blvd. Brown 860, tel. 02965/474289, lunch and dinner daily) has stuffed pastas (around US$8–17), fish from US$12 and house wine by the glass, but it's a little *too* family-friendly for a quiet dinner. Down the block, the comparable **Yoaquina** (Blvd. Brown 1050, tel. 02965/456058, lunch and dinner daily) has a varied menu, including fish of the day (US$11) and raspberries with cream for dessert.

**Cantina El Náutico** (Av. Roca 790, tel. 02965/471404, lunch and dinner daily) and slightly cheaper **Puerto Marisko** (Av. Rawson 77, tel. 02965/450752, lunch and dinner daily) are traditional seafood choices. The former is especially popular; the latter has its seaside location to recommend it, but service is erratic and the kitchen slow. They serve fish dishes from US$7, scallops at US$11, and a *tabla* of varied seafood costs US$12.

Made in the metal-clad Magellanic style, **Mariscos del Sur** (Mitre and Roque Sáenz Peña, tel. 02965/470991, lunch and dinner daily) is a very popular and family-friendly place that serves fish from US$8, scallops in a white wine sauce (US$8), and a seafood *parrillada* (US$15).

**Mar y Meseta** (Av. Gales 32, tel. 02965/458740, www.marymeseta.com.ar, lunch and dinner daily) boasts intriguing dishes like gnocchi with lamb (US$13) and crab cannelloni in a shrimp sauce (US$18), but not everything is available every night. Consider also the *abadejo* (pollock) in a honey sauce (US$14).

Named for the almond tree that shades its entrance, **El Almendro** (Marcelo T. de Alvear and 9 de Julio, tel. 02965/470525, dinner only) is one of few Madryn restaurants that provide quiet dining in sophisticated surroundings at reasonable prices, with items such as *sorrentinos* stuffed with Patagonian lamb along with fines herbes sauce (US$10), plus simple well-executed dishes such as *lomo tres pimientas* (three-pepper steak, US$14). With good desserts, a decent wine list, and attentive service, this is probably the city's top choice.

The kitchen can be creative at **Plácido** (Av. Roca 506, tel. 02965/455991, www.placido.com.ar, lunch and dinner daily), but the appetizers, desserts, and drinks are unconscionably expensive by Argentine standards—a modest malbec by the glass, for instance, costs almost as much as an entire bottle of pretty good wine in some other places. Entrées are reasonably priced instead and are in the US$12–17 range.

Madryn has fine ice cream at **Kebom** (Av. Roca 540, tel. 02965/474094).

## Information

The exemplary and tireless **Secretaría de Turismo** (Av. Roca 223, tel. 02965/453504 or 02965/456067, www.madryn.gov.ar/turismo) provides information in Spanish and English and helps find accommodations when beds are scarce. Hours are 7 A.M.–11 P.M. weekdays, 8 A.M.–11 P.M. weekends mid-December–mid-March; in other seasons, hours are 7 A.M.–9 P.M. weekdays, 8 A.M.–9 P.M. weekends and holidays. There is also an information point at the bus terminal (Dr. Ávila s/n, tel. 02965/475971, 7 A.M.–9 P.M. weekdays, 8 A.M.–9 P.M. weekends).

For motorists, **ACA** (tel. 02965/453546) is at Avenida Hipólito Yrigoyen and Marcos A. Zar.

## Services

**Banco del Chubut** (25 de Mayo 154) has one of many ATMs. The only currency exchange house is **Cambio Thaler** (Av. Roca 493).

**Correo Argentino** is at Belgrano and Gobernador Maíz; the postal code is 9120.

**Locutorio Roca** (Av. Roca and 9 de Julio) has phone, fax, and Internet services. Madryn now has free public wireless Internet along the beachfront.

**Presto-Lav** (Av. Brown 605, tel. 02965/451526) can do the washing.

The **Hospital Subzonal** (tel. 02965/451999) is at Roberto Gómez 383.

## Getting There

Commercial flights traditionally land at Trelew, 65 kilometers south, but Puerto Madryn's **Aeropuerto El Tehuelche** (tel. 02965/456774) gets some commercial flights. **Andes Líneas Aéreas** (Av. Roca 624, tel. 02965/452355, www.andesonline.com) flies to and from Buenos Aires's Aeroparque Jorge Newbery. **LADE** (Av. Roca 119, tel. 02965/451256) has southbound flights to Ushuaia via Comodoro Rivadavia and Río Gallegos, and to Bariloche and Viedma, but schedules may change.

**Aerolíneas Argentinas** (Av. Roca 427, tel. 02965/451998) flies out of Trelew twice to thrice daily to Buenos Aires's Aeroparque Jorge Newbery and daily to El Calafate and Ushuaia from August to January.

Madryn's bus terminal, **Terminal 12 de Junio** (Dr. Ávila s/n, tel. 02965/451789, www.terminalmadryn.com), stands directly behind the former railroad station. It has frequent service to Trelew with **Línea 28 de Julio** (tel. 02965/472056) and **Mar y Valle** (tel. 02965/450600) plus extensive regional and long-distance connections. **Mar y Valle** also goes off season to Puerto Pirámides at 9:45 A.M. daily, and at 6:30 A.M. and 4 P.M. Monday, Wednesday, and Friday; in summer it goes at 8:55 A.M. and 5 and 6:55 P.M. daily, and at 6:30 A.M. Monday, Wednesday, and Friday.

Sample destinations, times, and fares include Trelew (US$2.50–3, one hour), Puerto Pirámides (US$4.50, 1.5 hours), Comodoro Rivadavia (US$23–26, six hours), Esquel (US$43, nine hours), Neuquén (US$49–60, 9–11 hours), Bariloche (US$46–63, 13–14 hours), Río Gallegos (US$72–108, 16–18 hours), and Buenos Aires (US$72–108, 18–21 hours).

## Getting Around

For flights from Madryn's Aeropuerto El Tehuelche, **Transporte Aitué** (tel. 02965/15-272444, transporteaitue@hotmail.com) provides shuttle service for US$4 per person. A taxi or *remise* costs US$6.50.

For flights to and from Trelew, **Transportes Eben-Ezer** (tel. 02965/472474 or 02965/15-660463) charges US$9 per person for door-to-door shuttle service, but a taxi or *remise* costs around US$50.

Most hostels rent bikes, but also try **Balneario Vernardino Club de Mar** (Blvd. Brown 860, tel. 02965/455633).

Because the area's attractions are spread out and the roads are decent, renting a car is a good option. Agencies include **Avis** (Av. Roca 493, tel. 02965/475422), **Fiorasi** (Av. Roca 165, tel. 02965/456300), and **Rent A Car Patagonia** (Av. Roca 293, Local 8, tel. 02965/471797).

## VICINITY OF PUERTO MADRYN

Madryn's tour agencies go farther afield as well, to Trelew, Gaiman, Punta Tombo, and, of course, Península Valdés. Operators include **Cuyun-Co** (Av. Roca 165, tel. 02965/451845, www.cuyunco.com), **Huinca Travel** (Belgrano 198, Oficinas 1 and 2, tel. 02965/450720, www.huincatravel.com), **Nievemar** (Av. Roca 493, tel. 02965/455544, www.nievemartours.com.ar), and **Turismo Puma** (28 de Julio 46, tel. 02965/451063, www.turismopuma.com). Full-day excursions to Península Valdés cost US$45, not including meals or park admission fees; while springtime excursions usually include a stop at Punta Delgada, later in summer they visit Punta Norte instead. Whale-watching starts at US$45 per person.



### Área Natural Protegida Punta Loma

Close enough to Madryn for a mountain-bike excursion, Punta Loma lacks the sheer wildlife numbers and diversity of Península Valdés, but its ample sea lion colonies, along with cormorants, giant petrels, gulls, terns, and snowy sheathbills, are reason enough to visit. Only 15 kilometers southeast of Madryn via an undulating gravel road, it gets far fewer visitors than Valdés.

Near the sea lion colony, there's a visitors center and an overlook that permits good views of the animals. Hours are 8 A.M.–8 P.M. daily; admission costs US$7 for foreigners, US$2 for Argentine residents, and US$0.75 for Chubut residents. There's no scheduled transportation, but Madryn operators will arrange excursions, or a small group can go for about US$32 by *remise.*

### Área Protegida Municipal El Doradillo

From Playa El Doradillo's headlands, 15 kilometers northeast of Madryn via RP 42, deep water lets whales approach the shore—the next best choice to an in-the-water view at Península Valdés. Like Punta Loma, this is close enough for a bike ride or a shared taxi.

## ÁREA NATURAL PROTEGIDA PENÍNSULA VALDÉS

Coastal Patagonia's top destination, the World Heritage Site of Península Valdés is the place where the great southern right whale arrives to breed and birth in the winter months. Protected since 1937, the *ballena franca* occupies a nearly unique position as a "natural monument"—a designation normally reserved for territorial ecosystems—within the Argentine national park system.

Península Valdés itself, a provincial reserve rather than a national park, has more to offer than just whales. Some marine mammal species—ranging from sea lions to southern elephant seals and orcas—cover the beaches or gather in the Golfo San José, Golfo Nuevo, or the open South Atlantic all year. There are also concentrations of burrowing Magellanic penguins and flocks of other seabirds, plus herds of grazing guanacos and groups of sprinting rheas in the interior grasslands.

The main activity center is the hamlet of **Puerto Pirámides,** which, like Puerto Madryn, enjoys a longer tourist season because of the whale- and orca-watching periods. Once the export point for salt from the Salina Grande depression, it has grown haphazardly, and water continues to be a problem in this desert environment. After an election in 2010, the street names have changed: 25 de Septiembre (National Whale Day) replaces Primera Bajada, and 14 de Julio (the town's anniversary) replaces Segunda Bajada. Other new street names include those of Antonio Soto and Facón Grande, leaders of the Santa Cruz anarchist rebellion of 1921, and of the writer Osvaldo Bayer, whose book *Los Vengadores de la Patagonia Trágica* helped to reveal the facts.

Sometimes called Puerto Pirámide, the village has since reasserted its plurality. According to local accounts, when the Argentine navy

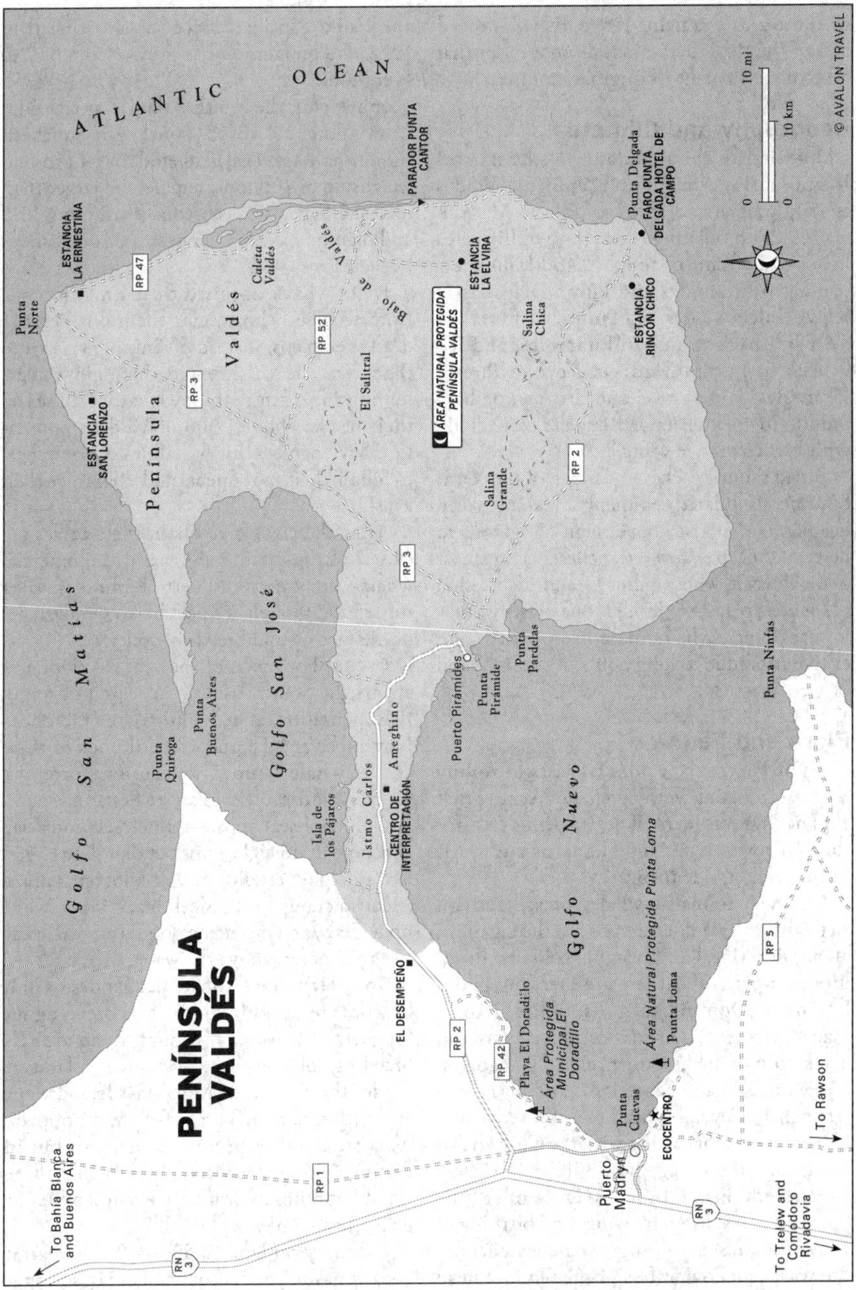
PENÍNSULA VALDÉS
ATLANTIC OCEAN
Golfo San Matías
Golfo San José
Golfo Nuevo
Península Valdés
Punta Norte
ESTANCIA LA ERNESTINA
ESTANCIA SAN LORENZO
RP 47
RP 3
RP 52
RP 2
RP 42
RP 1
RP 5
RN 3
Caleta Valdés
Bajo de Valdés
El Salitral
PARADOR PUNTA CANTOR
ESTANCIA LA ELVIRA
ÁREA NATURAL PROTEGIDA PENÍNSULA VALDÉS
Salina Chica
Salina Grande
ESTANCIA RINCÓN CHICO
Punta Delgada
FARO PUNTA DELGADA HOTEL DE CAMPO
0 10 mi
0 10 km
© AVALON TRAVEL
Punta Quiroga
Punta Buenos Aires
Isla de los Pájaros
Istmo Carlos Ameghino
CENTRO DE INTERPRETACIÓN
Puerto Pirámides
Punta Pirámide
Punta Pardelas
Punta Ninfas
EL DESEMPEÑO
Playa El Doradillo
Área Protegida Municipal El Doradillo
Área Natural Protegida Punta Loma
Punta Loma
Punta Cuevas
ECOCENTRO
Puerto Madryn
To Bahía Blanca and Buenos Aires
To Trelew and Comodoro Rivadavia
To Rawson

used the area as a firing range, they destroyed two of the three pyramidal promontories that gave the settlement its original moniker.

## Geography and Climate

Connected to the mainland by the narrow Istmo Carlos Ameghino, Península Valdés is 45 kilometers northeast of Puerto Madryn via RP 2, but visiting the major wildlife sites involves a circuit of roughly 400 kilometers to Puerto Pirámides and Punta Delgada via RP 2, Caleta Valdés and Punta Norte via RP 47, RP 3 back to Puerto Pirámides, and RP 2 back to Puerto Madryn. Beyond Puerto Pirámides, loose gravel and dirt can be hazardous to inexperienced drivers, especially with low-clearance vehicles.

Broad sandy beaches line much of the coast, but unconsolidated sediments make the steep headlands that rise above them dangerous to descend. Sheep *estancias* (ranches) occupy most of the interior, whose Salina Grande depression (42 meters below sea level) is one of the world's lowest points. The climate is dry, with high evaporation due to long hours of sunlight and perpetual winds.

## Flora and Fauna

Most of Península Valdés consists of rolling *monte* (scrubland) with patches of pasture that expand in wet years. The stocking rate for sheep is low, permitting guanacos and rheas to thrive alongside them.

Marine mammals—whales, orcas, southern elephant seals, and sea lions—are the big draw, along with Magellanic penguin colonies. In addition to penguins, there are breeding populations of Dominican gulls, white herons, black-crowned night herons, olivaceous and black cormorants, steamer ducks, Patagonian crested ducks, and Magellanic and black oystercatchers. Several species of gulls, terns, and plovers are visitors, along with the Chilean flamingo and the snowy sheathbill.

**Whales:** From June to December, the breeding, breaching, blowing, and birthing of *Eubalaena australis* brings whale-watchers to the warm shallow waters of the Golfo Nuevo and Golfo San José. Since the first census in 1971, the population has grown from 580 to over 3,000.

Inhabiting the South Atlantic at latitudes from about 20° to 55° south, the southern right whale reaches 17 meters in length and weighs up to 100 tons; females are larger than males. They are baleen whales, filtering krill and plankton as seawater passes through sieves in their jaws.

Right whales acquired their English name from whalers who sought them out because dead specimens, instead of sinking, floated to the surface; hence, they were the "right whales" for hunting. Identifiable by keratin calluses on their heads, about 1,300 of Valdés's population have names; this has allowed researchers to follow their movements and even trace their kinship.

After the cows give birth, their calves get closest to the catamarans that do commercial whale-watching from Puerto Pirámides. Over the season, though, it's possible to see all stages of the mating and breeding cycle.

**Orcas:** For much of the year, *Orcinus orca* swims the South Atlantic in search of squid, fish, penguins, and dolphins, but October–November and February–April pods of these "killer whales" prowl the Punta Norte and Caleta Valdés shorelines for sea lions and southern elephant seal pups—a nine-meter orca can consume up to eight pups per day. The largest of the dolphin family, the 950-kilogram animal is conspicuous for its sleek black body, white underbelly, and menacing dorsal fin, which can rise two meters above the water.

**Southern elephant seals:** Valdés's sandy beaches are the only continental breeding site for *Mirounga leonina,* though there are also breeding colonies on sub-Antarctic islands in Chile, the Falkland (Malvinas) Islands, and at South Georgia. Largest of the pinnipeds, it's a true seal with no external ear, but its distinguishing characteristic is the male's inflatable proboscis, which truly resembles an elephant's trunk.

Ungainly on land, 2,500–4,000-kilogram "beachmaster" males come ashore in spring to

© ELNAVEGANTE/123RF

Puerto Pirámides is the prime whale-watching site on Península Valdés.



dominate harems that number up to 100 females (who weigh only about 500 kilograms each). Reaching seven meters in length, the beachmasters defend their harems in fights with younger bachelors that leave all parties bloody, scarred, and even disfigured.

Females spend most of their pregnancy at sea, giving birth on returning to land in spring. Pups spend only a few weeks nursing, gaining weight quickly, before the mother abandons them (some die crushed beneath battling males). At sea, the elephant can plunge up to 600 vertical meters in search of squid before surfacing for air half an hour later.

**Sea lions:** Present all year on the beaches and reefs beneath the península's headlands, *Otaria flavescens* is common from southern Brazil and Uruguay all the way around the tip of South America and north to Perú. With its thick mane, the 300-kilogram 2.3-meter male resembles an African lion, but Spanish speakers call it *lobo marino* (sea wolf). The female, about 1.8 meters long, weighs only about 100 kilograms.

Unlike the larger southern elephant seal, the sea lion has external ears. Also unlike the southern elephant seal, it propels itself on land with both front and rear flippers, and the male is quick enough to drag away elephant pups. More often, though, it feeds on krill and the odd penguin.

For Spanish speakers, by the way, this is the *lobo marino de un pelo;* the *lobo marino de dos pelos,* or southern fur seal *(Arctocephalos australis),* whose pelt was more valuable to commercial sealers, is found farther south.

**Penguins:** *Spheniscus magellanicus,* the braying and burrowing jackass, is normally the only penguin species here. From September to March or April, it breeds and raises its young at isolated Caleta Valdés and Punta Norte, but summer swimmers have had close encounters at Puerto Pirámides.

## Sights and Recreation

Many visitors book excursions in Madryn, but day trips are too brief for more than a glimpse of the best—especially if the operators spend too much time at lunch. Staying at Puerto Pirámides and contracting tours there is ideal for whale-watching, as you have the flexibility to pick the best time to go out.

Six Pirámides operators, some with offices in Madryn as well, offer whale-watching in semirigid rafts (which get closer to the animals) or larger catamarans: **Tito Bottazzi** (25 de Septiembre s/n, tel. 02965/495050, www.titobottazzi.com), **Hydrosport** (25 de Septiembre s/n, tel. 02965/495065, www.hydrosport.com.ar), **Whales Argentina** (25 de Septiembre s/n, tel. 02965/495015, www.whalesargentina.com.ar), **Punta Ballena** (14 de Julio s/n, tel. 02965/495112, www.puntaballena.com.ar), **Peke Sosa** (14 de Julio s/n, tel. 02965/495010, www.pekesosa.com.ar), and **Southern Spirit** (Av. de las Ballenas and 25 de Septiembre, tel.02965/495094, www.southernspirit.com.ar). Prices start around US$45 but can cost more, depending on the vessel and the tour's duration.



In Golfo San José, 800 meters north of the isthmus, penguins, gulls, cormorants, and herons all nest on **Isla de los Pájaros,** an offshore bird sanctuary; it's off-limits to humans, but a stationary shoreline telescope magnifies the breeding birds. Near the telescope is a replica chapel of Fuerte San José, the area's first Spanish settlement (1779, but destroyed by Tehuelches in 1810).

**Puerto Pirámides** has the major concentration of services, including the most affordable accommodations and food. June–December, whales are the main attraction, but beachgoers take over in January and February. Carless visitors can hike or bike to the sea lion colony at Punta Pirámide, four kilometers west, for vast panoramas and sunsets over the Golfo Nuevo.

Beneath the headlands at the peninsula's southeastern tip, **Punta Delgada** is home to southern elephant seal and sea lion colonies, reached by trail from the lighthouse at the former naval station (now a hotel-restaurant). Hotel concessionaires provide English-speaking guides to lead tour groups and individuals, but they collect a small charge for those who do not eat at the restaurant. They have also turned the lighthouse into a museum and offer horseback tours of the area.

On the peninsula's eastern shore, about midway between Punta Delgada and Punta Norte, **Caleta Valdés** is a sheltered bay that's fast becoming a lagoon as its ocean outlet fills with sediment. Meanwhile, though, Magellanic penguins swim north to a breeding colony and southern elephant seals haul up onto shore in the mating season. Even guanacos may be seen along the beach.

Where RP 47 and RP 3 meet at the peninsula's northern tip, **Punta Norte** features a mixed colony of southern elephant seals and sea lions, but October–April this is also the best place to see orcas, which lunge onto the beach to grab unwary pups. Punta Norte also has a museum that places marine mammals in both natural and cultural context, thanks to exhibits on the indigenous Tehuelche and a historical account of the sealing industry.

Near Punta Norte, reached by a northwesterly road off RP 3, **Estancia San Lorenzo** (www.pinguinospuntanorte.com.ar) conducts tours of its own Magellanic penguin colony but does not offer accommodations.

## Accommodations and Food

**Puerto Pirámides** has sprouted many more places to stay, eat, and recreate than ever before, but demand is high. Most accommodations, including the *estancias,* have added wireless Internet service. In summer and in the whale-watching season, reservations are advisable. Rates rise notably in the second half of the year, and some hotels keep those well into the summer months, while others apply lower rates once the whale-watching season is over. There are *estancia* accommodations scattered around Punta Delgada, Caleta Valdés, and Punta Norte, but no camping is permitted beyond Puerto Pirámides.

Immediately behind the dunes, the shoreline **Camping Municipal** (tel. 02965/15-699161, US$7 pp) charges separately for the timed showers (US$2.50). The bathrooms are clean, and a store carries basic supplies, but few sites have shade.

On the access to town, simple hostel accommodations are found at **Bahía Ballenas** (tel. 02965/15-567104, www.bahiaballenas.com.ar, US$15 pp), which hosts up to 24 people in two large dorms on a gender basis.

**Motel ACA** (tel. 02965/495004, www.motelacapiramides.com, US$50 s, US$63 d for members; US$73 s, US$89 d for nonmembers) was once Pirámides's top choice together with its restaurant, and has recently been spruced up. At the member price, which members of foreign affiliates can take advantage of, it's an excellent value.

At **Hostería La Estancia del Sol** (Av. de las Ballenas s/n, tel. 02965/495007, www.interpatagonia.com/estanciadelsolpiramides, US$73 d), plain but reasonably spacious rooms, immaculately clean, are the rule. Its restaurant serves seafood for US$15, plus the usual Argentine standards.

New in 2008, set back from the main drag, the **Hostería Ecológica del Nómade** (Av. de las Ballenas s/n, tel. 02965/495044, www.ecohosteria.com.ar, US$160–190 s or d, open mid-Aug.–mid-Apr.) is an eight-room accommodation designed to minimize its carbon footprint and water consumption in this desert area; it does so without sacrificing style.

Its handsome brick superstructure mimicking Chubut's Welsh heritage, the inviting **Hostería The Paradise** (Av. de las Ballenas s/n, tel./fax 02965/495030, www.hosteriatheparadise.com.ar, US$180–218 s or d) is a substantial improvement on the usual utilitarian choices. Its restaurant offers fixed-price lunches or dinners that cost slightly more for foreigners than for Argentines, and the menu also has meals such as scallops in a white wine sauce (US$15) and rice with seafood (US$20 for two people).

Top-end **Las Restingas Hotel de Mar** (tel. 02965/495101, www.lasrestingas.com, US$240–300 s or d) is a seafront hotel with only 12 functional rooms, a few of which have balconies at the upper floor, others with decks and individual access to the beach, and some without ocean views at lower rates. It has a restaurant, gym, and spa. Post-whale-watching rates are much lower.

In a casual ambience blending traditional artifacts and artwork with pop music, **La Estación** (Av. de la Ballenas s/n, tel. 02965/495047) serves excellent fresh fish and salads (US$8–13), but the kitchen is slow and the service amateurish.

On the bluffs overlooking Punta Delgada, alongside the lighthouse at RP 2's east end, **Faro Punta Delgada Hotel de Campo** (tel. 02965/458444 or 02965/15-406304, www.puntadelgada.com, closed May–June) is an upgraded property on lease from the navy. It offers a lovely location and good access to wildlife, including penguins and southern elephant seals. With 27 comfortable rooms, its high-season rates (Sept.–Feb.) are US$235 single or US$275 double with breakfast, US$280 single or US$365 double with half board, and US$325 single or US$455 double with full board; low-season rates (Mar.–Apr. and July–Aug.) are 20–30 percent lower. Tour buses often stop at its restaurant, which is open to nonguests.

Near Punta Delgada, run by a young Madryn couple, the best tourist-oriented *estancia* is **Estancia Rincón Chico** (Blvd. Brown 1783, tel. 02965/15-304581, Puerto Madryn tel. 02965/471733, www.rinconchico.com.ar, US$465 s, US$660 d). Four kilometers southwest of RP 2, its purpose-built hotel has eight well-furnished doubles. From September to November they host elephant-seal researchers, as the seals frequent their long coastal frontage. Rates are all-inclusive, with all meals and activities but not drinks; they normally close from April to mid-September.

In a sheltered depression west of Caleta Valdés, along RP 47, **Estancia La Elvira** (Av. Hipólito Yrigoyen 257, Local 2, tel. 02965/15-666283, Puerto Madryn tel. 02965/474248, www.laelvira.com.ar, open Sept.–Mar. and Semana Santa, US$230 s, US$340 d half board, US$260 s, US$395 d full board) lacks Rincón Chico's mature landscaping, but the rooms and common areas are attractive enough. Rates include all organized activities. Near the elephant seal colony, they also operate the roadside **Parador Punta Cantor,** which gets lunchtime tour buses.

Toward Punta Norte, just west of RP 47, the amiable six-room **Estancia La Ernestina** (tel. 02965/15-661079, www.laernestina.com, open Sep.–Nov. and Mar.–Apr., US$450 s, US$550 d with full board) offers easy access to Estancia San Lorenzo's large penguin colony. Three of the rooms have only two baths among them. Rates include drinks and excursions.

### Information

At El Desempeño, at the west end of the Istmo de Ameghino, a provincial toll booth collects an admission fee of US$18 for foreign adults, US$9 for foreign children aged 6–12, and US$5 for Argentines (it's free for all children under 6). About 22 kilometers east, the **Centro de Interpretación** (7:30 A.M.–9 P.M. daily) exhibits a complete right whale skeleton and also historical materials ranging from Tehuelche times to Spanish colonization and Argentine settlement for salt mining and sheep ranching. An observation tower offers panoramas across the northerly Golfo San José to the southerly Golfo Nuevo, and east across the peninsula's interior.



The **Dirección de Turismo** (25 de Septiembre s/n, tel. 02965/495048, www.puertopiramides.gov.ar), the municipal tourist office, serves visitors 8 A.M.–8 P.M. daily in summer, 9 A.M.–6 P.M. daily the rest of the year.

### Getting There and Around

In summer, from Puerto Madryn, **Mar y Valle** (tel. 02965/450600) has daily buses to Puerto Pirámides (US$4.50, 1.5 hours) at 8:55 A.M. and 5 and 6:55 P.M.; return buses leave at 11 A.M. and 7 and 8:45 P.M. All year-round there is also a 6:30 A.M. bus from Madryn Monday, Wednesday, and Friday, returning at 8:10 A.M. Off-season there is also a daily bus from Madryn at 9:45 A.M., and at 4 P.M. Monday, Wednesday, and Friday, with returning buses at 6 P.M. daily and at 11:45 A.M. Monday, Wednesday, and Friday.

On a space-available basis, tour buses may allow passengers to disembark at Pirámides and return another day, but make advance arrangements.

Distances from Pirámides to other peninsula destinations are too great for nonmotorized transport, so it's worth considering a **rental car** in Puerto Madryn. Many consider day trips from Madryn too rushed.

## TRELEW

Less obviously tourist-oriented than Puerto Madryn, the Río Chubut city of Trelew retains more visible remnants of its Welsh birthright than its ocean-side sister city. It also offers access to the lower Chubut Welsh communities of Gaiman and Dolavon, the dolphin-watching beach resort of Playa Unión, and the massive penguin colonies at Punta Tombo. Its own attraction, though, is the state-of-the-art paleontological museum that documents Argentina's dramatic dinosaur discoveries of recent decades.

Dating from 1886, when the railroad united Puerto Madryn with the lower Chubut's farm towns, Trelew takes its name from Welsh colonist and railroad promoter Lewis Jones (in Welsh, *tre* means town, while *lew* was an abbreviation of Lewis). It has since absorbed several waves of immigration—Italians and Spaniards, as well as Argentines from elsewhere in the country—and boom-and-bust cycles thanks to the wool industry, customs preferences, and industrial promotion.

Despite the changes, Trelew has retained its Welsh identity in events like the Eisteddfod del Chubut (a poetry and music festival) and other cultural activities.

On the Río Chubut's north bank, Trelew (population 99,200) is 65 kilometers south of Puerto Madryn and 375 kilometers northeast of Comodoro Rivadavia via RN 3. It is 608 kilometers west of Esquel via several paved highways.

### Sights

On the pleasingly landscaped **Plaza Independencia,** the Victorian-style **Kiosco del Centenario** (1910) marked the centennial of Argentine independence. To the southwest, once isolated by walls and gates, the former **Distrito Militar** (army headquarters),

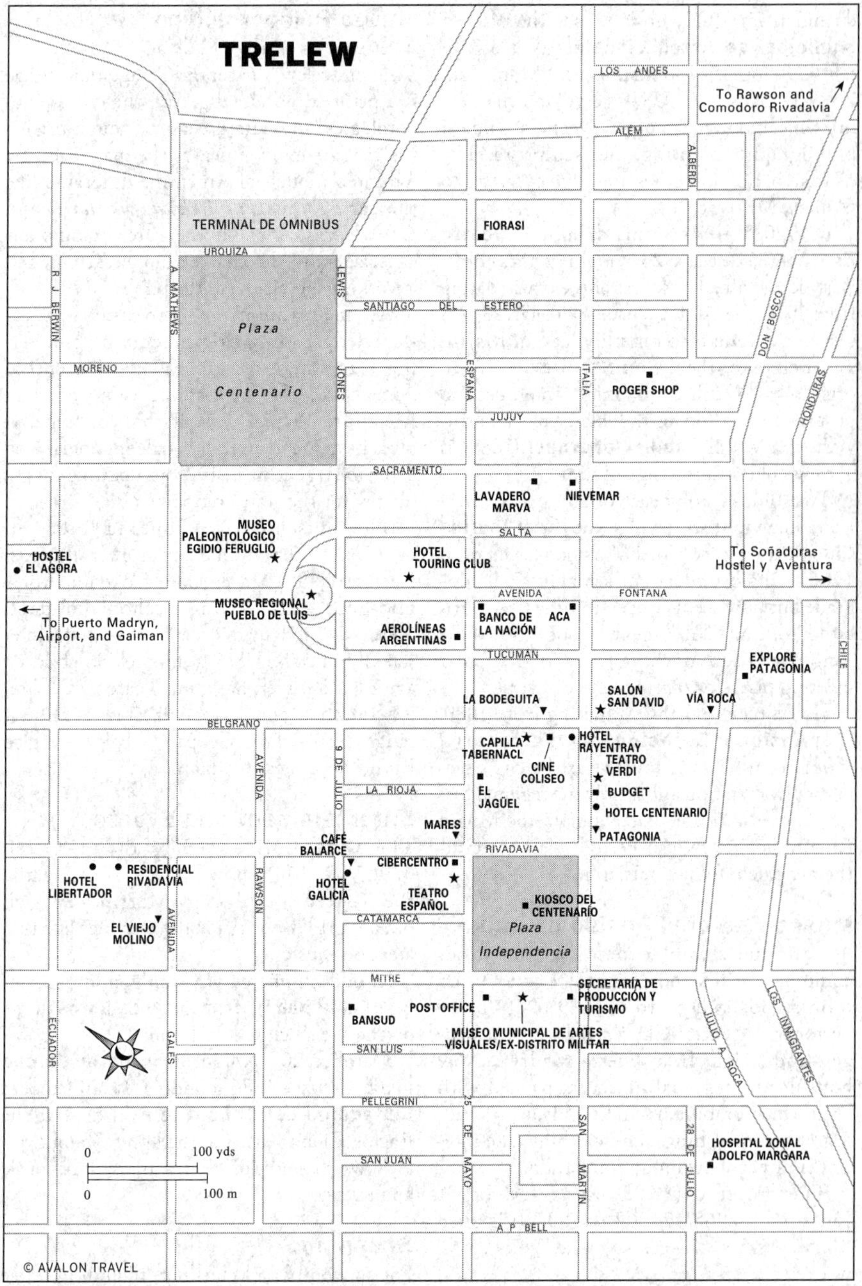
TRELEW
LOS ANDES
To Rawson and Comodoro Rivadavia
ALEM
ALBERDI
TERMINAL DE ÓMNIBUS
FIORASI
URQUIZA
R J BERWIN
A. MATHEWS
LEVIS
SANTIAGO DEL ESTERO
Plaza Centenario
DON BOSCO
MORENO
JONES
ESPAÑA
ITALIA
ROGER SHOP
HONDURAS
JUJUY
SACRAMENTO
LAVADERO MARVA
NIEVEMAR
MUSEO PALEONTOLÓGICO EGIDIO FERUGLIO
SALTA
HOSTEL EL AGORA
HOTEL TOURING CLUB
To Soñadoras Hostel y Aventura
MUSEO REGIONAL PUEBLO DE LUIS
AVENIDA FONTANA
To Puerto Madryn, Airport, and Gaiman
BANCO DE LA NACIÓN
ACA
AEROLÍNEAS ARGENTINAS
TUCUMÁN
EXPLORE PATAGONIA
CHILE
SALÓN SAN DAVID
LA BODEGUITA
VÍA ROCA
BELGRANO
CAPILLA TABERNACL
CINE COLISEO
HOTEL RAYENTRAY
TEATRO VERDI
AVENIDA
9 DE JULIO
EL JAGÜEL
LA RIOJA
BUDGET
HOTEL CENTENARIO
MARES
PATAGONIA
CAFÉ BALARCE
RIVADAVIA
CIBERCENTRO
HOTEL LIBERTADOR
RESIDENCIAL RIVADAVIA
RAWSON
HOTEL GALICIA
TEATRO ESPAÑOL
KIOSCO DEL CENTENARIO
CATAMARCA
EL VIEJO MOLINO
AVENIDA
Plaza Independencia
MITHE
SECRETARÍA DE PRODUCCIÓN Y TURISMO
BANSUD
POST OFFICE
LOS INMIGRANTES
JULIO A ROCA
MUSEO MUNICIPAL DE ARTES VISUALES/EX-DISTRITO MILITAR
ECUADOR
GALES
SAN LUIS
PELLEGRINI
25 DE MAYO
SAN MARTÍN
28 DE JULIO
0
100 yds
0
100 m
HOSPITAL ZONAL ADOLFO MARGARA
SAN JUAN
A P BELL
© AVALON TRAVEL

dating from 1900, now houses the **Museo Municipal de Artes Visuales** (Mitre 350, tel. 02965/433774, 8 A.M.–8 P.M. Mon.–Fri., 2–8 P.M. Sat.–Sun., US$0.50 voluntarily), exhibiting historical photos as well as modern photography, painting, and sculpture. The tourist office occupies its adjacent **Anexo** (Annex, Mitre 387).

In 1920, Trelew's Spaniards built the **Teatro Español** (25 de Mayo 237), on the plaza's northwest side. Half a block east of the plaza, dating from 1914, the **Teatro Verdi** (San Martín 128) served the Italian community; at San Martín and Belgrano, the **Salón San David** (1913), originally a Welsh community center, used to host the Eisteddfod festival. Half a block northwest, the Welsh **Capilla Tabernacl** (1889) is Trelew's oldest surviving building.



Two blocks northeast of the plaza, early Patagonian tourists stayed at the **Hotel Touring Club** (formerly the Hotel Martino, dating from 1906), which underwent a major 1920s upgrade but now seems frozen in time (the moribund Touring Club Argentino once rivaled the Automóvil Club Argentino). It is still a popular meeting place for *trelewenses,* however.

Half a block northwest, dating from 1889, the **Antigua Estación del Ferrocarril** (Fontana and Lewis Jones) was the city's second railway station and is now the regional history museum; immediately north, the Museo Paleontológico Egidio Feruglio is a state-of-the-art paleontology museum.

## Museo Regional Pueblo de Luis

An antique steam locomotive and other equipment still stand outside Trelew's former train station, where, from 1889 to 1961, the Ferrocarril Central Chubut delivered passengers and freight from Puerto Madryn. Now housing the regional museum, packed with Welsh memorabilia, including historical photographs, furnishings, and clothing, the interior is rather short on interpretation.

The museum (Av. Fontana and Lewis Jones, tel. 02965/424062, US$0.50) is open 8 A.M.–7:45 P.M. weekdays and 2–7:45 P.M. weekends.

## Museo Paleontológico Egidio Feruglio (MEF)

West of Trelew, the central Patagonian steppe is a prime dinosaur dig, and the city's paleontological museum is reason enough to visit the city. Its main appeal is the magnificently mounted models of Argentine dinosaurs like the carnivorous *Pianitzkysaurus floresi* and *Carnotaurus sastrei,* but there are also dinosaur eggs, a genuine touchable dinosaur femur, and a working lab visible to the public.

At the same time, the museum acknowledges the achievements of pioneering Patagonian researchers like Florentino Ameghino, George Gaylord Simpson, and Alejandro Pianitzky in its hall of fame. It owes its name to an Italian paleontologist who came to Argentina in 1925 as a petroleum geologist for the state company YPF.

The museum (Av. Fontana 140, tel. 02965/432100, www.mef.org.ar, 10 A.M.–6 P.M. weekdays, 9 A.M.–8 P.M. weekends Apr.–mid-Sept. except winter school holidays; 9 A.M.–8 P.M. daily mid-Sept.–Mar. and winter school holidays, US$9 adults, US$6 children age 12 and under) has a small café (with wireless Internet) and a souvenir shop. It also arranges excursions to Geoparque Paleontológico Bryn Gwyn, near Gaiman.

## Entertainment and Events

The **Cine Coliseo** (Belgrano 371, tel. 02965/425300) shows recent films, while the **Teatro Verdi** (San Martín 128, tel. 02965/431398) occasionally provides live theater and music.

In odd-numbered years only, mid-September's **Certamen Internacional de Coros** draws on the Welsh choral tradition.

October 20's **Aniversario de la Ciudad** marks Trelew's 1886 founding. Late October's **Eisteddfod del Chubut** festival held at the Racing Club focuses on the lower Chubut valley's Welsh traditions, particularly folk music and poetry.

## Shopping

For souvenirs and clothing, including horse

© WAYNE BERNHARDSON

*Pianitzkysaurus* at Trelew's Museo Paleontológico Egidio Feruglio



gear, leather, and woolens, visit **El Jagüel** (25 de Mayo 140, tel. 02965/422949).

**Roger Shop** (Moreno 463, tel. 02965/430690) is the place to purchase traditional black cake and *teisenbach* (a Welsh cake), good as snacks.

## Accommodations

For backpackers, Trelew has two well-run hostels, both spotless, with wireless Internet and breakfast included. About 12 blocks southeast of downtown, **Soñadores Hostel y Aventura** (Pasaje Lamadrid 1312, tel. 02965/436505, www.soñadoreshostel.com.ar, US$13 pp, US$63 d) has dorms and private rooms with their own bathrooms, and four blocks from bus terminal, the smaller **Hostel El Ágora** (Edwin Roberts 33, tel. 02965/426899, www.hostelagora.com.ar, US$15 pp, US$35 d) has a small backyard, dorms, and a double, all sharing bathrooms.

The serviceable staff of **Residencial Rivadavia** (Rivadavia 55, tel. 02965/434472, www.cpatagonia.com/rivadavia, US$33 s, US$42 d, breakfast US$3.50 extra) helps overcome, at least in part, the basic comfort of the smallish rooms. But in the poor local hotel scene, this still offers one of the best value accommodations.

For a touch of old Patagonia—perhaps because it's well past its prime—try the landmark **Hotel Touring Club** (Av. Fontana 240, tel. 02965/433998, www.touringpatagonia.com.ar, US$38 s, US$63 d). Though its rooms have been impersonally modernized, the building still keeps signs of more glamorous times.

**Hotel Centenario** (San Martín 150, tel. 02965/420542, www.hotelcentenario.com.ar, US$65 s, US$73 d) is a large hotel with covered parking, and a room renovation was in progress in 2011.

Four-star in designation, the 80-room **Hotel Libertador** (Rivadavia 31, tel./fax 02965/420220, www.hotellibertadortw.com, from US$75 s, US$93 d) has lost its dull style thanks to continuous renovation, offering now mostly comfortable standard rooms and suites in contemporary ambience.

The central 110-room **Hotel Rayentray** (Belgrano and San Martín, tel. 02965/434702, www.cadenarayentray.com.ar, US$113 s, US$125 d) has amenities including a restaurant, a gym, a sauna, and a swimming pool.

Overpriced **Hotel Galicia** (9 de Julio 214, tel. 02965/433802, www.hotelgalicia.com.ar, US$100 s, US$135 d) has an impressive staircase, if slightly less impressive rooms. Rates for foreigners are almost double those for Argentines.

## Food

Even those who don't stay at the hotel should take breakfast or coffee at the **Confitería Touring Club** (Av. Fontana 240, tel. 02965/433998) to partake of its timeless ambience. **Café Balcarce** (Rivadavia and 9 de Julio, tel. 02965/424021, 8 A.M.–12:30 A.M. Mon.–Thurs., 8 A.M.–2 A.M. Fri., 8:30 A.M.–2 A.M. Sat.) is not only good for its sweets and desserts, but also for short orders, serving set menus (from US$9) and a daily special, including fish (from US$8).



**Sugar** (25 de Mayo 247, tel. 02965/435978, 7:30 A.M.–12:30 A.M. daily) is a sandwich and short-order option, but also serves elaborate dishes, such as risotto with seafood (US$12) and lamb in a fines herbes sauce (US$14).

In an uninspiring restaurant scene, **Patagonia** (San Martín 188, tel. 02965/437280, 11 A.M.–3 P.M. and 7 P.M.–1 A.M. daily), with its all-you-can-eat offer of *parrilla* for US$11, ends up as an excellent value in town.

**La Bodeguita** (Belgrano 374, tel. 02965/437777, lunch and dinner daily) serves good pasta (particularly cannelloni) and pizza, with decent service. Most entrées are US$10–14.

In an elegantly recycled flour mill dating from 1896, **El Viejo Molino** (Av. Gales 250, tel. 02965/428019, lunch and dinner daily) is Trelew's most ambitious restaurant; its best dishes are variations on the traditional *parrilla,* lamb (US$12) being one of its specialties.

For ice cream, try **Mares** (25 de Mayo 195) or **Vía Roca** (Belgrano and Roca).

## Information

At Plaza Independencia's southwest corner, the well-organized municipal **Secretaría de Producción y Turismo** (Mitre 387, tel. 02965/420139, www.trelewpatagonia.gov.ar, 8 A.M.–8 P.M. weekdays and 9 A.M.–9 P.M. weekends) usually has an English speaker on hand. There are also offices at the bus terminal (8:30 A.M.–8:30 P.M. weekdays and 9 A.M.–9 P.M. weekends) and the airport (for arriving flights only).

For motorists, **ACA** (tel. 02965/435197) is at Avenida Fontana and San Martín.

## Services

Many visitors stay in Puerto Madryn, but Trelew agencies also do excursions to destinations like Rawson and Playa Unión, the lower Chubut valley's Welsh villages, Punta Tombo, and even Península Valdés.

Several banks have ATMs, including **Banco de la Nación** (Av. Fontana and 25 de Mayo), which also exchanges money and travelers checks.

**Correo Argentino** is at Calle 25 de Mayo and Mitre; the postal code is 9100. **Cybercentro** (25 de Mayo 219), at Plaza Independencia's northwest side, has telephone and Internet services. The area around Plaza Independencia is a wireless Internet zone.

**Nievemar** (Italia 98, tel. 02965/434114, www.nievemartours.com.ar) arranges excursions to the Welsh settlements and Punta Tombo. **Explore Patagonia** (Julio A. Roca 94, tel. 02965/437860, www.explore-patagonia.com.ar) also offers tours.

**Lavadero Marva** (Sarmiento 363, tel. 02965/434233) washes clothes.

For medical needs, contact the **Hospital Zonal Adolfo Margara** (28 de Julio 160, tel. 02965/427543).

## Getting There

**Aerolíneas Argentinas** (25 de Mayo 33, tel. 0810/2228-6527) flies twice or thrice daily to Buenos Aires's Aeroparque Jorge Newbery and daily to El Calafate and Ushuaia from August to January.

With offices in the bus terminal, **LADE** (Urquiza 150, tel. 02965/435740) flies sporadically to Aeroparque Jorge Newbery as well as to some Patagonian destinations.

The **Terminal de Ómnibus** (Urquiza 150, tel. 02965/420121) is six blocks northeast of Plaza Independencia. A small boarding tax is charged to all long-distance tickets.

**Mar y Valle** (tel. 02965/432429) has regular service to Puerto Pirámides, leaving Trelew at 8:30 A.M., with additional summer service. **El Ñandú** (tel. 02965/427499) goes to the coastal town of Camarones at 8 A.M. Monday, Wednesday, and Friday.

Typical destinations, times, and fares include Camarones (US$10, four hours), Puerto Pirámides (US$7, three hours), Comodoro Rivadavia (US$21–26, five hours), Esquel (US$28–40, 8–8.5 hours), Neuquén (US$54–65, 10–12 hours), Río Gallegos (US$69–103, 15–18 hours), Bariloche (US$43–60, 12–13 hours), and Buenos Aires (US$75–112, 19–21 hours).

### Getting Around

**Aeropuerto Internacional Marcos A. Zar** (RN 3 s/n, tel. 02965/433443) is five kilometers north of town on the east side of the Puerto Madryn highway. Cabs or *remises* cost about US$7.

**Mar y Valle** (tel. 02965/432429) alternates with **Línea 28 de Julio** (tel. 02965/432429), running frequent buses to Puerto Madryn (US$2.50–3, one hour). Línea 28 de Julio also goes every half hour to Gaiman (US$1) and less frequently to Dolavon (US$2), though weekend services are fewer.

Both Línea 28 de Julio and **Empresa Rawson** (tel. 02965/481915) go frequently to Rawson (US$1), while **Transportes Bahía** (tel. 02965/482317) goes hourly to Puerto Rawson and Playa Unión (US$1.50), via Rawson.

Car-rental agencies include **Budget** (San Martín 146, tel. 02965/434634) and **Fiorasi** (Urquiza 310, tel. 02965/435344).

## RAWSON AND PLAYA UNIÓN

Rawson (population 30,800) is Chubut's low-profile capital, and in truth there's little to see in this nondescript bureaucratic outpost. Its suburb of Playa Unión, though, is an ecotourism destination for the *toninas overas,* the glossy black-and-white Commerson's dolphins, which are not uncommon in other coastal destinations but here dart around and under launches that motor through the waters fronting its long sandy beach.

Though dolphin watching is not assured with every excursion, sea lions and various birds may also be seen. At rather picturesque Puerto Rawson (at Playa Unión's south end), contact **Estación Marítima** (Av. Marcelino González s/n, tel. 02965/15-591514, www.estacionmaritima.com.ar); the watching season runs from July to April and excursions cost US$38 per person. While waiting, or afterward, try a seafood lunch (for about US$11) at the dockside **Cantina Marcelino** (tel. 02965/496960).

The small seaside resort of Playa Unión has very good accommodations two blocks off the beach at **Hotel Punta León** (Juan de la Piedra y José Hernández, tel. 02965/498042, www.puntaleon.com.ar, US$62 s, US$73 d), with wireless Internet, buffet breakfast, comfortable rooms, and some bathrooms with bathtubs.

Playa Unión has its own **Dirección General de Turismo** (Av. Rawson and Juan Manuel de Rosas, tel. 02965/496887, www.rawson.gov.ar/turismo, 8 A.M.–9:30 P.M. daily in summer, 8 A.M.–8 P.M. weekdays and 10 A.M.–8 P.M. weekends the rest of the year).

Playa Unión to Trelew **Transportes Bahía** buses run hourly, with a central stop at Juan Manuel de Rosas between Avellaneda and Rivadavia.

## GAIMAN AND VICINITY

More than any other lower Chubut settlement, Gaiman has sustained and capitalized on its Welsh heritage. Though it's known for tourist teahouses, sturdy stone buildings, and community events like the youth Eisteddfod festival, several B&Bs have recently made it a destination rather than just an excursion.

Gaiman (population 8,100), 17 kilometers east of Trelew via RN 25, dates from 1874, when Welsh farmers first harnessed the river to irrigate their fields and orchards. The Tehuelche gave it the name Gaiman (Stony Point).

## Sights

The best starting point is the **Amgueddfa Hanesyddol** (Sarmiento and 28 de Julio, tel. 02965/491007, 3–8 P.M. Tues.–Sun. in summer, closing at 6 P.M. the rest of the year, US$0.75), the regional historical museum in the former train station. Staffed by Welsh- and English-speaking volunteers, it holds documents, photographs, and possessions of early immigrants.

Two blocks northwest, Dolavon-bound trains no longer chug through the **Twnnel yr Hen Reilfford,** a 300-meter brick tunnel that's now open to pedestrians only. A block west of the tunnel exit, dating from 1906, the **Coleg Camwy** (Michael D. Jones and Bouchard) may have been Patagonia's first secondary school. Other original Welsh colony buildings can be seen nearby, such as the **Yr Hen Bost,** the old post office (Michael D. Jones 222), and, dating from 1874, the town's first house, which opens as a small museum (J. C. Evans between Av. Eugenio Tello and 28 de Julio). At the east end of 28 de Julio, historic headstones, many of them in Welsh, dot the **Mynwent** (cemetery).

At the west end of town is **Parque El Desafío** (Av. Almirante Brown s/n), a unique site where late artist Joaquín Alonso turned everyone else's trash, including thousands of bottles and aluminum cans, automobiles, TVs, refrigerators, and washing machines, into lighthearted objets d'art. It closed in 2011 after Alonso's death, but it's worth asking if it has reopened.

## Geoparque Paleontológico Bryn Gwyn

Exposed by meanderings of the Río Chubut after an earlier subtropical sea evaporated, Bryn Gwyn's sedimentary badlands are an open book of Tertiary fossils. The oldest beds are too recent for dinosaur bones, but there is evidence of marine mammals, such as seals, dolphins, and whales, along with penguins, giant anteaters, and ungulates from times when this was savanna.

Visitors to the park, eight kilometers south of Gaiman via RP 7, can hike the well-organized trail, which climbs gradually and then steeply up the cliffs from the southside *confitería.* There are at least a dozen excavations, with some fossils in the open and others preserved in glass cases.

Affiliated with Trelew's Museo Paleontológico Egidio Feruglio, Bryn Gwyn charges US$2.50 admission for adults, US$1.25 for children; groups larger than 20 can arrange guided visits. Hours are 10 A.M.–6 P.M. Tuesday–Sunday in summer and over winter holidays, 11 A.M.–5 P.M. Tuesday–Sunday the rest of the year. There's no scheduled transportation, but *remises* from Gaiman are not unreasonable.

## Shopping

For crafts, visit the **Paseo Artesanal Crefft Werin** (Av. Eugenio Tello and Michael D. Jones, tel. 02965/491134), opposite Plaza Roca.

## Accommodations

The quality of accommodations is fine, as top teahouses now offer B&B. Options are still limited, though, so reservations are advisable.

Gaiman's only purpose-built hotel, the rehabbed **Hotel Unelem** (Av. Eugenio Tello and 9 de Julio, tel. 02965/491663, www.hotelunelem.com.ar, US$40 d) is a good shoestring choice with large rooms with baths, in a somewhat timeless ambience.

In a century-old house, friendly **Hostería Yr Hen Ffordd** (Michael D. Jones 342, tel. 02965/491394, www.yrhenffordd.com.ar, US$38 s, US$45 d) has simple and functional rooms.

**Hostería Plas y Coed** (Michael D. Jones 123, tel. 02965/491133, www.plasycoed.com.ar, US$63 d) is a B&B annex of Gaiman's landmark teahouse, with wireless Internet and only three comfortable rooms.

**Hostería Ty Gwyn** (9 de Julio 111, tel. 02965/491009, www.tygwyn.com.ar, US$43 s, US$63 d) is a quality teahouse with several stylishly furnished rooms—the beds are handsome, and antique sewing machines serve as desks. Rooms have balconies facing the river that might be welcoming for summer mosquitoes. Breakfast is a delicious reprise of the previous afternoon's tea.

### Food

Gaiman may be picturesque, but it's pointless to come here without indulging yourself on cakes, jams, scones, pies, and a bottomless teapot. Since tea starts around 2:30–3 P.M., either skip lunch or go later and then skip dinner; for about US$15 per person, it's a de facto all-you-can-eat. When tour buses are parked outside, slow service is almost certain.

Gaiman's oldest teahouse is **Plas y Coed** (Michael D. Jones 123, tel. 02965/491133, www.plasycoed.com.ar), which wins points for exceptional sweets and personalized service. Ivy-covered **Ty Nain** (Av. Yrigoyen 283, tel. 02965/491126) is the most stylish, but **Ty Gwyn** (9 de Julio 111, tel. 02965/491009, www.tygwyn.com.ar) is also appealing. The newest teahouse, **Ty Cymraeg** (A. Mathews 74, tel. 02965/491010, www.gaimantea.com) blends a traditional style but lacks the historical patina of, say, Plas y Coed; still, its scones, grape jam, and lemon pie are outstanding.

Quite a long way across the river, reached by a roundabout route over the bridge at the south end of J. C. Evans, **Ty Te Caerdydd** (tel. 02965/491510) is an enormous teahouse set among its own irrigated fields, which produce fresh fruits and berries for its own products, and elaborate flower gardens. Lady Diana, as Princess of Wales, was once a celebrity guest.

Overnighters can't gorge themselves on Welsh teas every day. For short orders and sandwiches, **Plas y Coed** (Av. Yrigoyen 320, tel. 02965/491133, www.plasycoed.com.ar, 2–9 P.M. Jan.–Feb., 2–7 P.M. daily Mar.–Apr. and July–Dec., closed May–June) has a small place open when everywhere else is closed in the early afternoon. Other restaurants, where entrées are US$8–15, include the *parrilla* **Cornel Wini** (Av. Eugenio Tello 199, tel. 02965/491397, 11:30 A.M.–2:30 P.M. Wed.–Mon., from 8 P.M. Thurs.–Mon.) and **Clave Celta** (Michael D. Jones 440, tel. 02965/491615, 12:30–4 P.M. Sat.–Sun., 8:30 P.M.–midnight Tues.–Sat.).

### Other Practicalities

Next to the east end of the railway tunnel is the municipal **Oficina de Informes** (Belgrano s/n, tel. 02965/491571, www.gaiman.gov.ar, 9 A.M.–8 P.M. Mon.–Sat., noon–8 P.M. Sun. in summer, 9 A.M.–6 P.M. Mon.–Sat. the rest of the year.

**Correo Argentino** is at J. C. Evans and Av. Yrigoyen, just north of the bridge over the river; the postal code is 9105. There's a ***locutorio*** on Avenida Tello between 25 de Mayo and 9 de Julio.

**Línea 28 de Julio** buses (Trelew tel. 02965/432429) eastbound to Trelew and westbound to Dolavon stop on Plaza Roca. Note that a few bus services a day run the more attractive Trelew–Gaiman–Dolavon *valle* route in both directions across farms and passing by some old Welsh chapels.

## DOLAVON

Unlike Gaiman, sleepy Dolavon (population 2,481) has never become a tourist town, but the brick buildings along its silent streets evince a greater architectural harmony than its larger neighbor—even though, founded in 1919, it's much newer. Its major landmark, the **Molino Harinero** (1930), is a former grain mill with a restaurant annex; **La Molienda** (Maipú 61, tel. 02965/492290) serves pastas and lamb, with local wines (US$9–18). *Norias* (waterwheels) decoratively set along the downtown canal represent what was a common practice for the irrigation of the nearby fields and orchards.

From the Trelew terminal, **Línea 28 de Julio** (Trelew tel. 02965/432429) runs buses almost every hour daily to Dolavon via Gaiman. Try to take those going along the *valle* route for a more picturesque journey.

## LOS ALTARES

From Trelew, passing Gaiman and Dolavon, paved westbound RN 25 stays atop the steppe for about 150 kilometers before dropping into the Río Chubut valley at Valle de los Mártires, where the landscape resembles Utah's Bryce Canyon, with striking sandstone hoodoos resisting the ravages of erosion. The road continues through the Valle de las Ruinas, slightly less impressively, and from the floodplain hamlet

## THE WILDLIFE ROUTES OF COASTAL CHUBUT

For Patagonia travelers, arrow-straight RN 3 is the quickest ticket south, but visitors with their own wheels – whether two or four – should explore coastal Chubut's dusty back roads. It's common enough to rent a car for Península Valdés, where a bicycle is awkward because camping is prohibited, but the loop from Rawson south to Punta Tombo and Camarones, returning via RN 3, is an intriguing alternative for automobiles, motorbikes, and bicycles.

Along southbound RP 1, the big attraction is Punta Tombo's penguins, but most visitors see them on a tour. Rather than returning to Puerto Madryn or Trelew, the self-propelled can get an *estanciero*'s view of the thinly settled area by following the dusty, narrow, but smooth gravel road south past desolate Cabo Raso, with its steep gravel beach, and on to picturesque Camarones.

From Camarones, the provincial wildlife reserve at Cabo Dos Bahías makes an ideal excursion before returning to RN 3 via a paved lateral and heading back north – perhaps for tea in Gaiman – or continuing south toward Bahía Bustamante, the kelp-gathering community that's part of the new Parque Interjurisdiccional Marino Costero Patagonia Austral along the Atlantic shoreline, and Comodoro Rivadavia. With an early start, the Punta Tombo-Camarones-Gaiman circuit could be a day trip, but an overnight in Camarones is a better option.



of Los Altares through the Valle Paso de los Indios, where it rejoins the steppe.

At Los Altares, a wide spot on the road with only about 120 inhabitants, there's a municipal campground with decent facilities. The only other lodging is the **ACA Motel** (RN 25 Km 321, tel. 02965/499003, US$30 s, US$45 d), a tidy but worn facility, where everything works, and there's hot water, but it's on such a shoestring budget that, when a light bulb fails, they have to go out and buy one. The rooms are spartan and dark.

While the accommodations are no prize, **Parrilla El Vasco** across the highway offers better-than-expected food at reasonable prices.

### ÁREA NATURAL PROTEGIDA PUNTA TOMBO

On barren South Atlantic shores, 126 kilometers south of Trelew, about 200,000 pairs of Magellanic penguins waddle ashore every austral spring to nest on only 210 hectares at Punta Tombo. Despite its isolation, more than 100,000 visitors a year—and up to 2,500 in a single day—find their way down RN 3 and a shortcut to a dusty southeasterly lateral and the continent's largest single penguin colony. Besides penguins, there are giant petrels, kelp and dolphin gulls, king and rock cormorants, and shorebirds including oystercatchers and flightless steamer ducks—not to mention offshore whales.

Despite their numbers, penguin populations here and at Península Valdés may be in trouble. A late 2006 article in *Science* concluded that continued overfishing of the Patagonian anchovy, which constitutes half the penguins' diet (and also sustains elephant seals, dolphins, and other South Atlantic species) could cause a population collapse.

Tours from Trelew (around US$40 pp) arrive around 11 A.M., but the birds are so dispersed that it rarely seems crowded. Authorities have marked off the nesting grounds, and human visitors must stay on marked trails and boardwalks. Still, since penguins do not respect fences, it's possible to get up-close-and-personal photos while respecting the birds' space (their beaks can inflict a nasty gash).

Tombo's infrastructure remains limited, though a large visitors center is due to open in late 2011.

At the entrance, provincial authorities collect US$9 per person for foreigners, US$3 for

Argentine residents, and a small fee per vehicle. No camping is permitted. Season runs from September to April; the park is closed for visits out of that period.

While it's also possible for a group to hire a taxi for a day trip to the reserve, renting a car in Trelew or Puerto Madryn would make it possible to follow the scenic desert coastline south past the ghost town of Cabo Raso to the picturesque fishing port of Camarones and Cabo Dos Bahías, a reserve with both penguins and sea lions. From Camarones it's possible to return to Trelew or Puerto Madryn via paved RN 3.

## CAMARONES AND VICINITY

Toward the south end of its namesake bay, Camarones is a sleepy fishing port with just two paved streets but so many wide gravel roads that it seems to be waiting for something to happen. Its citizens may wait a while, but Camarones is just picturesque enough, close enough to the wildlife reserve at Cabo Dos Bahías, and an interesting enough jaunt from Punta Tombo via the Cabo Raso route that it's an ideal off-the-beaten-road loop for anyone with a vehicle. Its museum also deserves a look.

Alternatively, there's public transportation via RN 3 either southbound from Trelew or northbound from Comodoro Rivadavia, and then eastbound on RP 30, a distance of about 260 kilometers from both cities. The town holds a **Fiesta Nacional del Salmón** (National Salmon Festival) in early February.

### Museo de la Familia Perón

Camarones's Perón family museum occupies a shiny new replica of Juan Domingo Perón's boyhood home—the caudillo's father, Tomás Perón, was justice of the peace and ran a sheep *estancia* on the town's western outskirts in the early years of the 20th century (Juan Domingo was born in 1895). It differs from other Perón museums not in that it's professionally organized—so is Buenos Aires's Museo Eva Perón—but in that it admits that Perón was a controversial and contradictory figure whose loyalists even engaged each other in firefights in the 1970s (right- and left-wing factions were each convinced the general was on their side).

While the museum leans toward the interpretations of Argentina's current left-of-center Peronists, it avoids the polemics so common in Argentine politics. Not only that, but the English translations that accompany the exhibits are well above average.

The Museo de la Familia Perón (Estrada 467, tel. 0297/4963014, museoperon.camarones@gmail.com, free) is open 9 A.M.–7 P.M. daily in summer, 9 A.M.–7 P.M. weekdays and 2–7 P.M. weekends the rest of the year.

### Área Natural Protegida Cabo Dos Bahías

Only 30 kilometers southeast of Camarones, the 12,000-strong Magellanic penguin colony Dos Bahías is smaller than Punta Tombo's, but Dos Bahías's open terrain makes it easier to appreciate the colony's extent. In addition to penguins, it boasts a southern sea lion colony on offshore **Isla Moreno,** though they're hard to see without binoculars. Besides many of the same seabirds that frequent Punta Tombo, terrestrial wildlife includes armadillos, foxes, guanacos, and rheas.

Unlike at Punta Tombo, it's possible to camp at beaches en route to Dos Bahías, though there are no other services. There is no scheduled transportation either, though it's possible to hire *remises* in Camarones. At the reserve's entrance, provincial authorities collect a US$5 admission fee from adult foreigners, US$1.50 for Argentines.

### Accommodations and Food

Open all year, the waterfront **Camping Camarones** (Espora s/n, tel. 02965/15-322906, campingcamarones@gmail.com, US$4 pp plus US$4 per vehicle) has sheltered sites with electricity, clean bathrooms with hot showers, and a cantina serving fish and seafood (US$9–13).

The **Indalo Inn** (Sarmiento and Roca, tel. 0297/4963004, www.indaloinn.com.ar, US$60 s, US$68 d) has comfortable rooms and also good cabañas, and a reliable restaurant for fish and seafood (entrées for about US$20).

### Information and Services

Near the shoreline at the foot of Calle Roca, Camarones's **Centro de Informes** (Espora s/n, tel. 0297/4963013, www.camarones.gov.ar) is open 8 A.M.–9 P.M. weekdays, 9 A.M.–9 P.M. weekends.

**Correo Argentino** is at Roca and Estrada. **Banco Chubut** (San Martín 570) has an ATM.



### Getting There

From the terminal at 9 de Julio and Rivadavia, **El Ñandú** (tel. 02965/427499 in Trelew) has buses to Trelew (US$10, four hours) at 4 P.M. Monday, Wednesday, and Friday, while **ETAP** (tel. 0297/4482750 in Comodoro Rivadavia) has buses to Comodoro Rivadavia (US$9, 3.5 hours) at 6 A.M. Tuesday and Friday.

## BAHÍA BUSTAMANTE

Declared in 2008 along the Chubut shoreline south of Camarones and Área Natural Protegida Cabo Dos Bahías, **Parque Interjurisdiccional Marino Costero Patagonia Austral** comprises only a strip of Argentina's South Atlantic coastline, exactly one nautical mile out to sea and 1.5 kilometers (nearly one statute mile) inland. The easiest access point for the park is the unique Bahía Bustamante, 30 kilometers east of the main highway turnoff by a good gravel road, and a sort of company town based not on mining but on seaweed! Dating from about 1953, it once had 400 residents—most of them employees—but now has only about 40 or so. Many of them gather seaweed along the shoreline; it is then dried in the sun and trucked to Gaiman, where a factory processes it into food additives.

All Bahía Bustamante's streets are named for species of seaweed, and its restaurant at **La Proveeduría** serves intriguing meals that often use seaweed as a condiment. Only a handful of the houses are occupied, but some of those—the former administrators' houses—have been transformed into stylishly retrofitted guesthouses by the sea, now called Casas del Mar,

rheas on the steppe behind Bahía Bustamante

available at premium prices on an all-inclusive basis. At the simpler Casas de la Estepa, cheaper accommodations with kitchen are offered, but meals and excursions on a space-available basis are extra.

From Bahía Bustamante, it's possible to take multiple excursions, including one to offshore islands that are part of the park and home to thousands of Magellanic penguins, cormorants, dolphin gulls, and steamer ducks as well as large colonies of southern sea lions and South American fur seals. This is possible only at high tide, though, as the five-meter tidal range makes it impossible for the flat-bottom launch to navigate at low tide.

At low tide, there are other options: Beyond the limits of the park, Bustamante possesses a remarkable badlands that features a sprawling petrified forest equivalent to Santa Cruz province's Monumento Natural Bosques Petrificados and Chubut's own Monumento Natural Bosque Petrificado de Sarmiento.

Accommodations at Bahía Bustamante (access at RN 3 Km 1674, tel. 0297/4801000,

Buenos Aires tel. 011/5032-8677, www.bahiabustamante.com, open Aug.–Apr.) are at the all-inclusive **Casas del Mar** (US$360 s, US$430 d with full board, lower rates for three or four people) and at the less elaborate **Casas de la Estepa** (US$120 for the house for up to three people).

## COMODORO RIVADAVIA

Comodoro Rivadavia's motto is "a city with energy," and Chubut's southernmost city is really Houston by the Sea. For nearly a century, ever since water-seeking drillers hit a crude gusher instead, it has been the locus of Argentina's petroleum industry. Thanks to the former state oil company Yacimientos Petrolíferos Fiscales (YPF), it has an outstanding petroleum museum.

On the surrounding hills, the landscape remains a jumble of drilling rigs, pipelines, storage tanks, and seismic survey markers. Ironically, though, Cerro Chenque's high-tech windmills herald alternative energy.

A frequent stopover for southbound motorists, hilly Comodoro (population 173,300) is 375 kilometers southwest of Trelew and 780 kilometers north of Río Gallegos via RN 3; it's 581 kilometers southeast of Esquel via several paved highways. Most services are on or near east–west San Martín, within a few blocks of the ocean.

### Sights

For a panorama of Golfo San Jorge's curving coastline, take the road up to **Cerro Chenque,** immediately north of downtown. Nearly barren, and prone to landslides that have covered RN 3, it's now one of the sites of **Parque Eólico Antonio Morán,** South America's largest windmill farm.

On the Avenida Rivadavia median strip, a stiff climb from downtown, the orderly but uninspiring **Museo Regional Patagónico Antonio Garcés** (Rivadavia and Chacabuco, tel. 0297/4477101, museogarces@yahoo.com.ar, 9 A.M.–4:30 P.M. weekdays, 1–5 P.M. Sat. and holidays, free) chronicles Comodoro's development through fossils, aboriginal artifacts, and photographs.

In Comodoro's old railway station, the **Museo Ferroportuario** (Rivadavia and 9 de Julio, ferroportuariocomriv@gmail.com, 9 A.M.–5 P.M. weekdays, 1–5 P.M. Sat., free) chronicles the train that hauled wool and produce from the city of Sarmiento, 149 kilometers west; intended to reach Lago Buenos Aires, it never went beyond Sarmiento, though it also carried crude from nearby oilfields to the port.

About three kilometers north of downtown, the Universidad Nacional de la Patagonia's **Museo Nacional del Petróleo** (San Lorenzo 250, tel. 0297/4559558, museodelpetroleo@gmail.com, 9 A.M.–5 P.M. Tues.–Fri., 3–6 P.M. Sat., US$5 foreigners, slightly less for Argentines) is a YPF legacy. On the grounds of Comodoro's initial gusher, it presents a professional account of Argentina's oil industry, from the natural and cultural environment to petroleum technology and its social and historical consequences. From San Martín between 25 de Mayo and Carlos Pellegrini, take the No. 4 Saavedra or No. 5 Universidad bus, and also other northbound buses.

Nearby, on sprawling shoreline grounds, dating from 1923, the **Museo Chalet Huergo** (tel. 0297/4550225, chalethuergo@gmail.com, 10 A.M.–5 P.M. weekdays, 1–5 P.M. Sat., free) was the residence of YPF administrators and during the oil boom years hosted guests like the shah of Iran. Today, though, it's the centerpiece of a public park and home to special events and exhibitions.

### Entertainment

A classic of its era, the **Cine Teatro Español** (San Martín 664, tel. 0297/4477700, www.cinecr.com.ar) offers recent movies and theater productions. There's also the **Cine Coliseo** (San Martín 570, tel. 0297/4445500), inside a mall.

### Accommodations

Because Comodoro is the largest city in almost 1,000 kilometers of highway, hotels can fill up fast, and reservations are advisable.

**Hotel del Mar** (Ameghino 750, tel. 0297/4472025, hoteldelmar@hotmail.com,

US$43 s, US$62 d) is one of several plain but acceptable accommodations, with wireless Internet and cheaper rooms without bath, along with **Hostería Rua Marina** (Belgrano 738, tel. 0297/4468777, US$42 s, US$65 d).

Rehabbed **Hotel Azul** (Sarmiento 724, tel. 0297/4474628, www.hotelazul.com.ar, US$69 s, US$75 d) always had pretty good rooms, which have wireless Internet now, and the common areas are more presentable. Slightly cheaper **Residencial Comodoro** (España 919, tel. 0297/4462582, tilsamendieta55@hotmail.com, US$60 s, US$72 d) is comparable.

With improved services in a modern location, **Nuevo Hotel Español** (9 de Julio 940, tel. 0297/4460116, www.nuevohotelespanol.com.ar, US$53 s, US$78 d) also has a small restaurant.

The traditional **Comodoro Hotel** (9 de Julio 770, tel. 0297/4472300, www.comodoro-hotel.com.ar, US$76–113 s, US$87–126 d) continues to lag behind some newer options.

Really two hotels in one, the **Austral Express** (Moreno 725, tel. 0297/4472200, www.australhotel.com.ar, US$97–113 s, US$108–125 d) and the newer **Austral Plaza** (from US$180 s, US$192 d) share a reception area, telephones, bar, *confitería,* and restaurant. The Express's rooms are comfy enough, if a little small, but they're less extravagant than the Plaza's. Guests at both enjoy the same buffet breakfast.

**Lucania Palazzo Hotel** (Moreno 676, tel. 0297/4499300, www.lucania-palazzo.com, from US$167 s, US$186 d) is a four-star high-rise with all the amenities and skyrocketing rates.

## Food

A popular local bakery has its own pleasant café, **Barile Express** (San Martín 514), which serves good breakfasts.

**Pizzería Giulietta** (Belgrano 851, tel. 0297/4461201, lunch and dinner daily) serves pizzas from US$14 and fine pasta as well (around US$10); in the same vein, there's **Cayo Coco** (Rivadavia 102, tel. 0297/4473033, lunch and dinner daily).

Comodoro has several quality *parrillas,* including **Bom Bife** (España 789, tel. 0297/4468412, lunch and dinner daily) and **La Rastra** (Rivadavia 348, tel. 0297/4443623, lunch and dinner daily), where entrées cost around US$15.

Waterfront **Puerto Cangrejo** (Av. Costanera 1051, tel. 0297/4444590, lunch and dinner daily) serves ample portions of fish and seafood in the US$15–20 range.

The Hotel Austral Plaza's **Tunet** (Moreno 725, tel. 0297/4472200, lunch and dinner daily) is Comodoro's top restaurant, with an elaborate fish and seafood menu that also includes tapas (entrées cost around US$23; tapas are US$8–10).

**Chocolate's** (San Martín 231, tel. 0297/4464488) serves Comodoro's best ice cream.

## Information

The municipal **Secretaría de Turismo** (Av. Rivadavia and Carlos Pellegrini, tel. 0297/4440664, www.comodoroturismo.gob.ar) is open 8 A.M.–8 P.M. weekdays and 9 A.M.–8 P.M. weekends November–March, and 8 A.M.–7 P.M. weekdays, 9 A.M.–7 P.M. weekends April–October.

For motorists, **ACA** (tel. 0297/4464036) is at Dorrego and Alvear.

## Services

**Banco de la Nación** (San Martín 102) has one of several ATMs along the street. **Cambio Thaler** (Mitre 943) is the only currency exchange house.

**Correo Argentino** is at Avenida San Martín and Moreno; the postal code is 9000. There are a few *locutorios* with phone and Internet services, mainly on Avenida Rivadavia or on San Martín, and one at Moreno 830.

The **Chilean consulate** (tel. 0297/4462414) is at Almirante Brown 456, Oficina 3.

For medical assistance, try the **Hospital Regional** (Hipólito Yrigoyen 950, tel. 0297/4442287).

## Getting There

**Aerolíneas Argentinas** (Rivadavia 156, tel. 0297/4440050) flies 3–5 times daily to Buenos Aires's Aeroparque Jorge Newbery, and twice weekly to Neuquén. **LAN** (tel. 0297/4548171 at the airport) also flies to Buenos Aires. **Sol** (tel. 0810/4444765) has northbound services to Rosario via Neuquén, Mendoza, and Córdoba, and southbound to Ushuaia via Río Gallegos.

Comodoro is a hub for **LADE** (Rivadavia 360, tel. 0297/4470585), which flies northbound to Bariloche, Aeroparque Jorge Newbery, and intermediate towns, westbound to Perito Moreno, and southbound to El Calafate, Río Gallegos, and Ushuaia.

Comodoro's **Terminal de Ómnibus Teniente General Ángel Solari** (Pellegrini 730) has regional, long-distance, and limited international service to Coyhaique, Chile.

At 8 A.M. Wednesday and Saturday, **Transaustral** (tel. 0297/4474841) departs for Coyhaique (US$33, 10 hours); these buses usually run full and schedules can vary, so reservations are essential.

Other sample destinations, times, and fares include Caleta Olivia (US$9, 1.5 hours), Puerto San Julián (US$23–30, six hours), Trelew (US$21–26, five hours), Puerto Deseado (US$29, 4.5 hours), Puerto Madryn (US$23–26, six hours), Los Antiguos (US$37, 6.5 hours), Sarmiento (US$7, 2.5 hours), Camarones (US$9, 3.5 hours), Esquel (US$32–37, eight hours), Río Gallegos (US$42–55, 10–11 hours), Bariloche (US$50–63, 13–15 hours), and Buenos Aires (US$89–133, 24–27 hours).

### Getting Around

Behind the bus terminal, the Palazzo Standard bus goes to **Aeropuerto General Mosconi** (RN 3, tel. 0297/4548093), which is nine kilometers north of town.

Car-rental agencies include **Avis** (Moreno 725, at Austral Plaza Hotel, tel. 0297/4464828, comodoro@avis.com.ar) and **Dubrovnik** (Moreno 941, tel. 0297/4441844, www.rentacardubrovnik.com).

## VICINITY OF COMODORO RIVADAVIA

### Rada Tilly

About 12 kilometers south of Comodoro via RN 3, Rada Tilly is Comodoro's main beach resort and the access point for a sea lion colony at **Punta del Marqués,** where the animals are visible from an overlook. The **Museo Regional** (Combate de Martín García 143, tel. 0297/4451598, 9 A.M.–1 P.M. and 2–6 P.M. Tues.–Fri., 3–6 P.M. Sat., Sun., and holidays in summer; 9 A.M.–noon and 2–6 P.M. Tues.–Fri., 2–6 P.M. Sat., Sun., and holidays the rest of the year, US$0.25) has exhibits on natural history, ethnography, and rock art.

For further information, Rada Tilly's **Dirección de Turismo** (Av. Brown and Seguí, tel. 0297/4452423, www.radatilly.com.ar) is open 8 A.M.–8 P.M. daily in summer, shorter hours the rest of the year. There are frequent buses from Comodoro's downtown terminal.

### Sarmiento

In what was once Tehuelche territory, 149 kilometers west of Comodoro Rivadavia, Sarmiento (population about 11,000) is an oil town and farming service center. It sits between two large lakes, Lago Musters and Lago Colhué Huapi, part of whose waters flow eastward via a pipeline to relieve the thirst of arid Comodoro Rivadavia.

Uninteresting in its own right, Sarmiento is the gateway to impressive petrified forests a short distance south, while westbound RP 20 to Río Mayo runs through colorful badlands.

In Sarmiento the best accommodations fill up fast. In town, the best is **Hotel Ismar** (Patagonia 248, tel. 0297/4893293, US$25 s, US$38 d with shared bath, US$33 s, US$50 d with private bath), though the management's a little brusque and would do well to oil the hinges.

Ten kilometers west of town via RP 20, just over the Río Senguer bridge, **Hostería Labrador** (tel. 0297/4893329, www.hosterialabrador.com.ar, US$60 s, US$85 d) is a working farm that also offers accommodations and breakfast that include its own fresh fruit, chocolates, and other regional products; lunch and dinner may also be served. The owners speak English and Dutch as well as Spanish.

There's no elaborate food, but **Heidy's** (Perito Moreno 600, tel. 0297/4898308) serves large portions of pretty good ravioli at low prices and an excellent flan for dessert.

© WAYNE BERNHARDSON

Fossil logs lie scattered across the badlands at Monumento Natural Provincial Bosque Petrificado Sarmiento.

Sarmiento's hard-working **Dirección Municipal de Turismo** (Av. Regimiento de Infantería 25 and Pietrobelli, tel. 0297/4898220, www.coloniasarmiento.gov.ar) keeps long hours daily.

**ETAP** (tel. 0297/4482750) has several buses to and from Comodoro, and others to Río Mayo and Esquel as well.

## Monumento Natural Provincial Bosque Petrificado Sarmiento

Thirty kilometers south of Sarmiento, fossil stumps, trunks, and chips of wood and bark litter the polychrome shale-and-sandstone landscape of this petrified forest. Here, 75 million years ago, a two-tier tropical to subtropical forest covered what is now a brilliantly colored desert. Probably uprooted by hurricanes, then buried by ash blown westward as volcanism and tectonic uplift built the Andes, the fallen trees petrified as ensuing climatic change turned the densely vegetated fluvial landscape into a desert. The petrified trees, often exceeding a meter in diameter, may have reached 100 meters in height.

From the park visitors center (tel. 0297/4898282), there's a stunningly scenic 1.5-kilometer nature trail that passes through the modern moonscape that was once the forest. It's best when the slanting afternoon sun brings out the hues of Cerro Colorado, to the southeast, but worthwhile at any time. Souvenir taking is absolutely prohibited.

At the park entrance, reached by a gravel road from Sarmiento, rangers collect a US$5 per person admission charge for foreigners. This is a common day tour from Comodoro, but it's also possible to hire a *remise* from Sarmiento for about US$40. Hours are 9 A.M.–7 P.M. daily October–March, 10 A.M.–6 P.M. daily April–September.

# Coastal Santa Cruz Province

## CALETA OLIVIA

South of Comodoro Rivadavia, there's heavy truck traffic and plenty of reckless drivers on winding RN 3 (a four-lane freeway is under construction) before arriving at the unattractive oil port of Caleta Olivia. Rapidly growing without much planning, suffering frequent water shortages, Caleta (population about 60,000), 79 kilometers from Comodoro, is a crossroads for westbound traffic to Lago Buenos Aires and the Chilean border at Chile Chico. It's 346 kilometers north of Puerto San Julián but only 216 kilometers northwest of Puerto Deseado, an underrated wildlife destination.

The only conspicuous sight, dominating a rotary that marks the town center, is the **Monumento al Obrero Petrolero** (1969), popularly known as "El Gorosito." Facing north, Pablo Daniel Sánchez's 10-meter sculpture of a muscular shirtless worker turning an oil valve symbolizes thinly peopled Patagonia's contribution to (or exploitation by) the populous heartland. It's also an oblique reference to authoritarian president Juan Domingo Perón, whose most devoted followers were working-class *descamisados* ("shirtless ones").

### Accommodations and Food

With a helpful staff that do their best, **Hostería Don David** (Hipólito Yrigoyen 2385, tel. 0297/4857661, posadadondavid@hotmail.com, US$46 s, US$55 d) is, however, a rather basic place that has a small restaurant, self-service breakfast, and larger doubles for a small extra amount.

Expanded **Hotel Robert** (Av. San Martín 2151, tel. 0297/4856500, www.hotelrobert.com.ar, US$52–67 s, US$60–73 d, small cash discount, breakfast US$5) has comfortable rooms; its restaurant, **La Rosa** comes recommended, serving fish (US$8–16).

**El Puerto** (Av. Independencia 1060, tel. 0297/4851313, lunch and dinner daily) is best for fish and seafood, serving salmon (from US$17), shrimp (US$20), and a daily special (US$13–15).

**Heladería Centro** (Av. Independencia 1175, tel. 0297/4853721) has fine ice cream.

### Information and Services

The municipal **Oficina Central de Informes Turísticos** (Av. San Martín and Güemes, tel. 0297/4850988, www.caletaolivia.gov.ar) is open 7 A.M.–9 P.M. daily in summer, shorter hours the rest of the year.

**Banco de la Nación** (Av. Eva Perón 135) has one of several ATMs.

**Correo Argentino** is at Hipólito Yrigoyen 2194. **Telefonía Caleta** (Av. San Martín 5) has long-distance services and Internet, while **Cyber Centro** (Av. Independencia and Fagnano) has Internet connections as well.

### Getting There

From the **Terminal de Ómnibus** (Av. Tierra del Fuego 850), 16 blocks west of the Gorosito sculpture, there are northbound and southbound services along RN 3, plus westbound connections to Los Antiguos and Chile Chico via paved RP 12 and RP 43.

Typical destinations, times, and fares include Comodoro Rivadavia (US$9, 1.5 hours), Puerto Deseado (US$21, three hours), Río Gallegos (10 hours, US$32–48), Los Antiguos (US$33, five hours), and Buenos Aires (US$93–137, 25–28 hours).

## PUERTO DESEADO AND VICINITY

Bypassed by RN 3—but not by nature or history—Puerto Deseado is one of Patagonia's underrated pleasures. Visited by Magellan, settled by Spanish whalers, explored by Charles Darwin in 1833, and resettled half a century later, it clings to its pioneer ambience in what Francisco P. Moreno called "the most picturesque place on the eastern Patagonian coast." The star, though, is the Ría Deseado, where strong tides rush up the estuary to create a wildlife-rich environment that supports a growing ecotourism sector. Also wildlife-rich offshore islands and the shores south of Deseado are now part of the Parque Marino Isla Pingüino. At the same time, Deseado has become a home port for the South Atlantic shrimp fishery, and some businesses keep signs in Spanish, English, and Russian.

On the Ría Deseado's north shore, Puerto Deseado (population about 15,000) is 216 kilometers southeast of Caleta Olivia and 295 kilometers from Comodoro Rivadavia via RN 3 and paved RN 281 (but 126 kilometers from the RN 3 junction).

## Sights

For a small town, Deseado has plenty to see. The big draw is the **Reserva Natural Ría Deseado,** but various historical monuments all have good stories behind them.

By the late 19th century, Deseado seemed destined to become a rail port, as authorities planned a northwesterly freight-and-passenger line to Bariloche. It never advanced beyond Las Heras, 283 kilometers northwest, and closed in 1977, leaving the stately **Estación del Ferrocarril Patagónico** (Eufrasia Arias s/n, tel. 0297/4870601, 4–7 P.M. Mon.–Sat., also Sun. in summer, free but donations encouraged) as a surprisingly good museum staffed by former railroad workers.

© JAVARMAN JAVARMAN/123RF

Darwin's viewpoint, Puerto Deseado

Several monuments date from this era, most notably the railroad's **Vagón Histórico** (1898), a historical railcar in a small plaza at San Martín and Almirante Brown. Immediately across the street, **Banco de la Nación** has preserved its classic lava-block style, but the supermarket that occupies the former **Compañía Argentina del Sud** (1919) has concealed its vintage details with hideous painted signs on all sides (pointlessly, as it has no competition in town). One block west stands the **Sociedad Española** (1915).

Along the waterfront, the **Museo Regional Mario Brozoski** (Colón and Belgrano, tel. 0297/4871358, 10 A.M.–5 P.M. weekdays and 2–5 P.M. weekends in summer, shorter hours the rest of the year, free) holds artifacts from the English corvette *Swift,* sunk nearby in 1770 and rediscovered in 1982. Four kilometers northeast, **Balneario Las Piletas** is a volcanic beach area where retreating tides leave pools warm enough for swimming, at least in summer.

At the north end of Almirante Zar, after passing beneath a railroad bridge, the road leads five kilometers into the isolated **Cañadón Quitapenas** and excellent camping sites (no services). Thirteen kilometers west of town, a southbound lateral leads to the **Gruta de Lourdes,** a secluded pilgrimage site where the faithful have left devotional plaques. Rare rainstorms produce ephemeral waterfalls here.

## Reserva Natural Provincial Ría Deseado

One of coastal Patagonia's primo wildlife sites, the Ría Deseado submerges a long narrow valley that once carried more fresh water. As the fresh water flow diminished, seawater penetrated farther and farther inland, creating new islands and other fauna-rich habitats.

Several operators organize wildlife-watching excursions in and around the *ría* (estuary) to locations such as the Magellanic penguin colonies at **Isla Chaffers** and **Isla de los Pájaros,** and cliff-side colonies of rock cormorants and gray or red-legged cormorants at **Barranca de**

## DEATH RODE THE RAILS

The handsome wooden railcar now at the corner of San Martín and Almirante Brown in Puerto Deseado is more than an object of train-spotter nostalgia. During the Santa Cruz anarchist rebellion of 1921 (a struggle dramatized in Osvaldo Bayer's novel-based film *La Patagonia Rebelde*), it was the mobile command center for Colonel Héctor Benigno Varela, who led government forces against striking farm workers throughout the territory. At Jaramillo station, near the present-day junction of RN 281 and RN 3, Varela personally executed gaucho insurgent José Font (known as "Facón Grande" or "Big Knife") under false pretenses (appropriately enough, Varela died from a bomb and bullets by German anarchist Kurt Gustav Wilckens in Buenos Aires in 1923).

As a symbol of military brutality – in total, some 1,500 people died at the hands of Varela's forces – the car is an enduring monument. Nearly six decades later, in December 1980, in a defiant demonstration against Argentina's fiercest dictatorship ever, Deseado residents encircled the historic railcar with 40 private automobiles to prevent its removal by truck. Not only did the demonstrators challenge armed authority – in a town with a tank regiment – but they bravely signed their names and ID card numbers in a petition to Santa Cruz's military governor. Astonishingly, the de facto government backed down.



**los Cormoranes,** where deep water permits close approach to the nests. On any excursion, swiftly swimming *toninas overas* (Commerson's dolphins) breach and dive around and under the outboard launches; in mating season, they leap out of the water. Some operators also follow Darwin's route up the *ría* where, wrote the great naturalist, "I do not think I ever saw a spot which appeared more secluded from the rest of the world, than this rocky crevice in the wild plain."

In handsome quarters that include a sea-view *confitería,* **Darwin Expediciones** (España 2551, tel. 0297/15-6247554, www.darwin-expeditions.com) has extensive experience here and also does sea kayaking. Half-day trips along the Ría Deseado cost US$42 per person with a six-passenger minimum; full-day trips, following Darwin's estuary route, cost US$110 per person with a six-passenger minimum.

**Puerto Penacho** (tel. 0297/15-4058472, www.puertopenacho.com.ar) does similar maritime itineraries, and **Turismo Aventura Los Vikingos** (Estrada 1275, tel. 0297/4870020, www.losvikingos.com.ar) adds other overland excursions to the usual nautical journeys.

For horseback rides, try **El Noble Argento** (tel. 0297/15-4216475, www.elnobleargento.blogspot.com), which organizes one- and two-hour excursions along nearby *cañadones* from US$45 per person. Their grounds are three kilometers northeast of town and there's a roadside sign on the highway.

### Parque Interjurisdiccional Marino Isla Pingüino

While in the process of being declared in 2011, this park protects the wildlife-rich seashores south from Ría Deseado to Bahía Laura and several small offshore islands, including **Isla Pingüino.** Exploited until the 19th century for its populous sea lion colonies, this 1.25-square kilometer island about 20 kilometers southeast of Deseado has breeding sea lions, occasional elephant seals, two species of the skuas and their hybrids, and the world's northernmost colony of the tireless rockhopper penguin, which braves crashing waves up steep stone faces to reach its nesting sites.

Full-day boat excursions to Isla Pingüino are run by Deseado operators **Darwin Expediciones** (España 2551, tel. 0297/15-6247554, www.darwin-expeditions.com), **Puerto Penacho** (tel. 0297/15-4058472, www.puertopenacho.com.ar), and **Turismo Aventura Los Vikingos**

© JAVARMAN JAVARMAN/123RF

a rockhopper penguin near Puerto Deseado



(Estrada 1275, tel. 0297/4870020, www.losvikingos.com.ar) for about US$100 per person with a six-passenger minimum.

## Accommodations and Food

Reservations are advisable in summer for the limited accommodations.

At the western approach to town, the sheltered **Camping Cañadón Giménez** (tel. 0297/15-4663815, US$2.50 pp) also charges US$5 per tent.

Some of the singles are tiny at labyrinthine **Residencial Los Olmos** (Gregores 849, tel. 0297/4870077, www.losolmosresidencial.com.ar, US$37 s, US$48 d with discounts for cash), but the management is friendly, and amenities include (balky) wireless Internet and private parking.

At **Hotel los Acantilados** (España 1611, tel. 0297/4872167, www.rend3r.com.ar/hotelosacantilados, US$43–63 s, US$50–75 d), downstairs rooms come with small but serviceable baths; upstairs rooms have sea views and better furniture, but the baths are equally small. Its bar is one of the best places to watch the sunset.

**Hotel Isla Chaffers** (San Martín and Moreno, hotelislachaffers@hotmail.com, tel. 0297/4872246, US$43 s, US$53 d) has decent enough rooms at a central location.

Its slogan says *pizzas con historia* (pizzas with history), and **La Cueva** (Eufrasia Arias s/n, tel. 0297/4870601, dinner Sat.–Sun.), located at the former train station, tries to keep an old-time atmosphere. **El Refugio de la Ría** (San Martín 1456, lunch and dinner daily) serves seafood and is a *parrilla* as well. **Puerto Cristal** (España 1698, tel. 0297/4870387, lunch Thurs.–Tues. and dinner daily) has decent seafood, excellent pastas, and a good service; its entrées range US$9–15. **Lo de Armando** (San Martín 1494, tel. 0297/4871399), though, is the only place in town that makes an effort at creativity in both its menu and decor. The shrimp *sorrentinos* (US$13) are excellent, but stay away from the house wine.

## Information and Services

The **Dirección Municipal de Turismo** (Av. San Martín 1525, tel. 0297/4870220, www.puertodeseado.tur.ar) is open 9 A.M.–9 P.M. daily in summer, 9 A.M.–7 P.M. daily the rest of the year.

**Banco de la Nación** (San Martín and Brown) has an ATM.

**Correo Argentino** (San Martín 1075) is the post office; the postal code is 9050. **Nuevo Centro** (Almirante Brown 571) has telephones and Internet connections.

For medical services, try the **Hospital Distrital** (España 991, tel. 0297/4870200).

## Getting There and Around

From the **Terminal de Ómnibus** (Sargento Cabral 1302), about 10 blocks northeast of downtown, there are buses to Caleta Olivia (US$21, three hours) and Comodoro Rivadavia (US$29, 4.5 hours) with **La Unión** (tel. 0297/4870188, three buses daily) and **Sportman** (tel. 0297/4870013, two daily).

# MONUMENTO NATURAL BOSQUES PETRIFICADOS

One of RN 3's most desolate stretches is the 350 kilometers between Caleta Olivia and

Puerto San Julián, but just north of the halfway point there's an incomparable detour to this 60,000-hectare badlands. In Jurassic times, before the Andes rose in the west, this was a humid region of coniferous *Proaraucaria* woodlands. After volcanic eruptions flattened the forests and buried them in ash 130 million years ago, water and wind gradually uncovered the now-petrified trunks.

Measuring up to three meters in diameter and 35 meters in length, *Proaraucaria* was a forerunner of the Andean araucaria. Until 1954, when the area became a natural monument (meriting Argentina's highest possible level of protection), the best and biggest specimens were regularly looted.

Solitary Bosques Petrificados, 50 kilometers west of RN 3 via graveled RP 49, gets only a few thousand visitors per year, mostly in summer. In addition to its petrified forests, it has desert steppe vegetation and wildlife including guanacos and rheas. It has no water, and there is no public transportation, but Puerto Deseado operators will organize excursions to the site.

For camping, try **Estancia La Paloma** (tel. 0297/15-4305255, nikourri@yahoo.com.ar), roughly midway between RN 3 and the forest. Otherwise, about 90 kilometers north of the access to the park, basic accommodations and food are offered at the villages of Fitz Roy and Jaramillo (www.jaramillo.tur.ar), including **Cabañas Dormis Fitz Roy** (tel. 0297/15-4277433, dptofitzroy@yahoo.com.ar) and Jaramillo's **Camping Comunal** (tel. 0297/4443503), on the road to Puerto Deseado. About 40 kilometers south of the access to the park, on RN 3, a basic hotel and restaurant (tel. 02962/454294, estaciontrescerros@hotmail.com) is an annex of Tres Cerros's gas station.

For more information, contact Caleta Olivia's **APN** office (Hipólito Irigoyen 2031, tel. 0297/4851000, bosquespetrificados@apn.gov.ar).

## PUERTO SAN JULIÁN AND VICINITY

Coastal Patagonia's single most important historical site, windswept San Julián was where Magellan's crew wintered in 1520 during the first circumnavigation of the globe. Both Magellan and Sir Francis Drake (half a century later) faced mutinies that they repressed ruthlessly, while Antonio de Viedma founded a short-lived Spanish colony at nearby Floridablanca—southern Patagonia's first European settlement—in 1780. Darwin, who found the countryside "more sterile" than Deseado, uncovered a llama-like fossil with an elephantine trunk here.

In the 1890s, British settlers from the Falkland Islands and Scotland finally established a permanent presence through the powerful San Julián Sheep Farming Company. Even in the late 1930s, according to John Locke Blake, "English was spoken freely round town," and the company's extensive holdings—175,000 hectares of pastureland—dominated life into the 1960s. Today, it's a secondary ecotourism destination for its dolphins and penguins, and a common stopover between Caleta Olivia and Río Gallegos. In 2011 a long stretch of the coast and its ocean waters south from Cabo Curioso (25 kilometers north of San Julián) is to be protected as part of the **Parque Interjurisdiccional Marino Makenke.**

San Julián (population about 8,500) is 351 kilometers south of Caleta Olivia and 360 kilometers north of Río Gallegos via RN 3. It is a well-kept town, and Avenida San Martín, the main thoroughfare, is an extension of the eastward lateral that connects the town with the highway.

### Sights

In the bay just north of town, **Isla Cormorán** has a Magellanic penguin colony; there's a king cormorant colony nearby at the sardonically named **Isla Justicia,** where Magellan stopped a mutiny by decapitating one rebel, quartering another, and leaving two others to starve. Headquartered in an adapted shed, **Pinocho Excursiones** (Av. Costanera and Mitre, tel. 02962/454600, www.pinochoexcursiones.com.ar) takes visitors on harbor tours (US$38 pp), with English-speaking guides, that include dolphin- and penguin-watching; when winds are too strong, the rigid inflatables may not sail.

At the foot of Avenida San Martín, San Julián's most conspicuous waterfront attraction is a Disneyish scale model of Magellan's ship that holds the **Museo Temático Nao Victoria.** It's tempting to describe this as "Pirates of the South Atlantic," but it makes an effort to cover local history. Admission costs US$1 for kids, US$2 for Argentine adults, and US$3 for foreigners; it's open 8 A.M.–10 P.M. or dark, whichever is earlier.

Temporarily closed in 2011, the **Museo de los Pioneros Rosa Novak de Hoffman** (Vieytes and Rivadavia) is a small archaeological and historical museum.

Immediately across from the museum, the memorial **Plazoleta Albino Argüelles** commemorates one of the army's victims in the 1921 anarchist rebellion. From here, the coastal Avenida Hernando de Magallanes leads north past the marked grave of *Beagle* crewman Robert Sholl, who died on the voyage prior to Darwin's. The road continues to the **Frigorífico Swift,** a mutton freezer that operated from 1912 to 1967; its crumbling shell and pier appeal to postindustrial photographers.

About 50 kilometers south from Puerto San Julián on RN 3, there's a viewpoint onto the vast natural depression of the **Gran Bajo de San Julián,** whose lowest point at Laguna del Carbón is 105 meters below sea level, marking the continent's deepest site.

## Accommodations

The waterfront **Autocamping Municipal** (Av. Hernando de Magallanes 650, tel. 02962/454506, US$1.25 pp plus US$2.50 per vehicle) has well-sheltered sites with picnic tables and fire pits, clean bathrooms, hot showers, laundry facilities, and even a playground.

**Hostería La Casona** (9 de Julio s/n, tel. 02962/452434, US$28 s, US$55 d) is a B&B in a recycled waterfront house—the most distinctively Patagonian lodgings in town. It has comfortable beds, spacious and attractive common areas with wireless Internet, and a kitchen for a basic self-serve breakfast.

Under the same ownership as La Casona, the 12-room **Hostería Miramar** (Av. San Martín 210, tel. 02962/454626, www.hosteria-miramar.com, US$45 s, US$60 d) looks better on the surface than La Casona, but the rooms are just OK.

**Hotel Sada** (Av. San Martín 1112, tel. 02962/452013, www.hotelsada.com.ar, US$50 s, US$60 d) has 18 rooms with private baths, but it's their **Posada de Drake** (Mitre and Rivadavia, tel. 02962/452523, www.posadadedrake.com.ar, US$50 s, US$60 d), new in 2007, that deserves attention for immaculate quarters; it also has wireless Internet.

Government-owned but privately run, the **Hotel Municipal Costanera** (25 de Mayo and Urquiza, tel. 02962/452300, www.costanerahotel.com, US$45 s, US$70 d) has 21 comfortable and spotless rooms, a restaurant, and wireless Internet.

**Hotel Bahía** (Av. San Martín 1075, tel. 02962/453144, www.hotelbahiasanjulian.com.ar, US$63 s, US$70–80 d) is an attractive hotel that fills up fast. Its only drawback is its location on the main avenue.

## Food

Popular **La Rural** (Ameghino 811, tel. 02962/454066, lunch and dinner daily) has a menu of Argentine standards, such as its *bife de chorizo* at US$12, plus very good fish (from US$6) and seafood all at reasonable prices. Its fine pastas include *sorrentinos* at US$8.

Right on the waterfront, **Naos** (9 de Julio and Mitre, tel. 02962/452714, lunch and dinner daily) is another quality restaurant that may get crowded in the evening, serving lamb, fish, and seafood (entrées US$10–15). **Popeye** (Moreno 1070, tel. 02962/452045, lunch and dinner daily) has the best pizza from US$10.

**M&M** (Av. San Martín 387, tel. 02962/454419) has superb ice cream.

## Information and Services

On the main avenue median, the municipal **Centro de Informes "Boulevard"** (Av. San Martín between Mariano Moreno and Rivadavia, tel. 02962/454396, www.sanjulian.gov.ar) is open 8 A.M.–10 P.M. weekdays in summer, much shorter hours the rest of the year.

At the bus terminal, the **Centro de Informes "La Terminal"** (Av. San Martín 1570, tel. 02962/452301) is open 7 A.M.–midnight daily in summer, with much shorter hours the rest of the year.

**Banco de la Nación** (Mitre 101) has an ATM.

**Correo Argentino** is at Avenida San Martín 155; the postal code is 9310. For phone and Internet services there is **Telefónica** (Moreno and Mitre).

For medical services, try the **Hospital Distrital Miguel Lombardich** (9 de Julio s/n, tel. 02962/452020).

### Getting There

On a highway the length of RN 3, somebody has to draw the short straw, and most San Julián buses arrive and leave between midnight and 4 A.M. There are several services to Buenos Aires and intermediate towns, and also south to Río Gallegos. The bus terminal (Av. San Martín 1570) is 15 blocks northwest of several services on the shore.

**Cerro San Lorenzo** (tel. 02962/452403) and **Cañadón León** (Gobernadores Gregores tel. 02962/491172) go daily to Gobernador Gregores (US$25, four hours).

## ESTANCIA LA MARÍA

Though it's 150 kilometers northwest of San Julián via graveled RP 25 and RP 77, Estancia La María attracts visitors to pre-Columbian rock-art sites that resemble the far more famous Cueva de las Manos, in western Santa Cruz. With nearly 90 caves in a dozen valleys and canyons, it's home to an active archaeological research project operated by the Universidad Nacional de la Plata (www.arqueologialamaria.com.ar).

Open November–early March, the *estancia* itself offers accommodations (US$20 pp with shared bath, US$70 d with private bath), a cabaña for five people (US$80), camping (US$7 plus US$3 pp), and meals (US$22 pp for lunch or dinner, US$4 pp for breakfast). They also offer a full board package with private accommodations and one excursion included for US$180 per person. For details, contact Josefina Ortolá or Lorena Behm (Saavedra 1168, San Julián, tel. 02962/452328 or 02966/15-527467).

## COMANDANTE LUIS PIEDRA BUENA

When Charles Darwin and the *Beagle* crew ascended the Río Santa Cruz in 1834, swift currents beyond Isla Pavón obliged them to walk the shore and drag their boats on lines, limiting their progress to about 10 miles per day. Twenty-five years later, naval explorer Luis Piedra Buena first raised the Argentine flag where his namesake town now stands; naval officer Valentín Feilberg first ascended the river in 1873 to its source at Lago Argentino, followed four years later by Perito Moreno, who sailed the lake and went beyond, reaching Lago Viedma and Lago San Martín.

Piedra Buena (population about 6,000) has little to see, but its services make it worth a lunch break or even an overnight stay before seeing Parque Nacional Monte León. On the Río Santa Cruz's north bank, it's 127 kilometers south of Puerto San Julián and 237 kilometers north of Río Gallegos via RN 3. About 45 kilometers south, westbound RP 9 provides a bumpy motorist's or cyclist's shortcut along the Río Santa Cruz valley to El Calafate.

While the town is nondescript, **Isla Pavón,** reached by a turnoff from the bridge over the Río Santa Cruz about three kilometers south of the highway junction, is a wooded beauty spot that's popular for fishing; a small museum honors Piedra Buena's efforts.

### Accommodations and Food

On the island, the campsite at **Complejo Turístico Isla Pavón** (tel. 02966/15-389953, islapavon@hotmail.com, US$7 per tent plus US$1 pp) has electricity, clean toilets, and hot showers (US$0.65).

Despite its unappealing and unimaginative name, the spacious rooms at **Hotel Sur Atlantic Oil** (RN 3 Km 2404, tel. 02962/497008, suratlantic@infovia.com.ar, US$43 d, breakfast extra from US$3), part of the YPF gas station complex, fill up early (and it does not take reservations). Popular with southbound travelers, it also has a remarkable restaurant (entrées US$9–13) with particularly choice pastas (take lunch in the restaurant proper, rather than the adjacent *confitería*).

Across the highway, newer **Hotel Río Santa Cruz** (tel. 02962/497245, h_riosantacruz@yahoo.com.ar, US$50 s or d) is a good backup choice.

On the access road, **Doña Ana** (Av. Belgrano and Benigno Fernández, tel. 02966/15-458719, lunch and dinner daily) serves local trout, as well as traditional Patagonian lamb, for US$10–15.



### Getting There and Around

Northbound and southbound services along RN 3 use the **Terminal de Ómnibus** (Av. Ibáñez 157), but it's also possible to flag down buses on the highway. At the same terminal, check at the **Centro de Información Turística** (tel. 02966/15-573065) to see if there are regular transfer services for Parque Nacional Monte León; in 2011 they were operated by **Terramar** (tel. 02966/15-475311, pamefeu@hotmail.com, US$25 return) Wednesday, Friday, and Sunday mornings, departing at 9 A.M. from Puerto Santa Cruz, stopping at Piedra Buena's terminal at 9:45 A.M. (only if seats were previously booked), and returning from the park at 4 P.M., after a five-hour stay.

## PARQUE NACIONAL MONTE LEÓN

Donated to the APN by the Fundación Vida Silvestre and the Patagonia Land Trust via environmental philanthropists Doug Tompkins and Kris McDivitt Tompkins, 62,000-hectare Monte León's 30-kilometer shoreline and headlands are an ecological wonderland of copious wildlife and uncommon landscapes. Little known and less visited, this former *estancia* is Argentina's second coastal national park, after Parque Nacional Tierra del Fuego.

### Flora and Fauna

Monte León's coastline is home to some 150,000 Magellanic penguins, as well as

© WAYNE BERNHARDSON

A *pichi* (armadillo) hides in the brush of Santa Cruz province's arid steppe.

gray and king cormorants, snowy sheathbills, Patagonian crested and steamer ducks, Dominican gulls, and sea lions, while its interior grazes guanacos and rheas and shelters armadillos and *liebres* (Patagonian hares). The vegetation is primarily grasses and prostrate shrubs of the Patagonian steppe. There are also pumas as well as red and gray foxes.

### Sights and Recreation

Wildlife-watching is the principal activity, but the landscape is special: Where the tides meet the headlands, the sea has eroded deep caverns. Seen from the steppe above, **La Olla** (The Kettle) took its name from its almost perfectly circular opening, but heavy rains and seas caused it to collapse in October 2006.

Unlike much of the South Atlantic, the coastline here abounds with offshore rocks and stacks. Guano collectors worked one of these, **Isla Monte León,** by stringing a still-existing cable tram from the headland. At low tide, exploring La Olla's remnants and Isla Monte León's base is possible, but be aware of the tides to avoid being stranded in a dangerous situation—the route is slippery, and the tide comes in fast. Try to descend about an hour before low tide—the park rangers there will advise on times.

### Accommodations and Food

Camping is possible at Monte León proper in **Camping Kimiri** (tel. 02966/15-625411, www.kimiri.com, US$15 per site), next to an attractive *confitería* and shop. More comfortable accommodations and personalized attention are found at **Hostería Monte León** (RN 3 Km 2399, Buenos Aires tel. 011/4621-4780, www.monteleon-patagonia.com, US$270 s, US$390 d with half board, open Nov.–Apr.), the former *estancia*'s *casco* (manor). While donating the *estancia* to the park service through their Patagonia Land Trust, Tompkins and McDivitt have retained about 330 hectares and left the *hostería*'s management to former owner Silvia Braun and her Swiss-Argentine husband, Juan Kuriger. The *casco* itself is a spacious, high-ceilinged beauty with four guest rooms and a small museum; much of the produce comes from Silvia Braun's organic garden.

### Other Practicalities

Six kilometers northeast of the park's entrance at the former *estancia*'s *casco* is the **Oficina de Informes del Centro Operativo Monte León,** where free registration is necessary prior to the visit and information is provided, especially on the tides and the state of the washout-prone road. Access to the park from RN 3 Km 2405 (31 kilometers south of Piedra Buena) is via graveled RP 63, which reaches the coast after about 20 kilometers. The park closes from April to November; after rains in season the access road might be closed due to bad conditions. APN's office is in Puerto Santa Cruz (San Martín 112, tel. 02962/498184, www.pnmonteleon.com.ar).

A transfer service from Puerto Santa Cruz via Piedra Buena to Monte León in high season may be operating; in 2011 it was run by **Terramar** (tel. 02966/15-475311) Wednesday, Friday, and Sunday mornings. Tours are organized from Puerto Santa Cruz by **Kimiri Aike Tours** (tel. 02966/15-625763, martaboillos@hotmail.com).

## RÍO GALLEGOS

Travelers often dismiss windy Río Gallegos as merely a port and service center for Anglo-Argentine wool *estancias* and, more recently, the petroleum industry. Dating from 1885, near continental Argentina's southern tip, it has a handful of museums, historical landmarks, and other distinctive Magellanic buildings as well as a handsomely redeveloped waterfront; it's also the gateway to one of the continent's largest penguin colonies and several historic *estancias* open to visitors. It's no longer the main gateway to El Calafate since construction of the new international airport there, but travelers bound for Punta Arenas (Chile) and Tierra del Fuego may have to spend the night here.

Río Gallegos (population about 100,000) is 780 kilometers south of Comodoro Rivadavia and 360 kilometers south of Puerto San Julián via RN 3, and 67 kilometers north of the

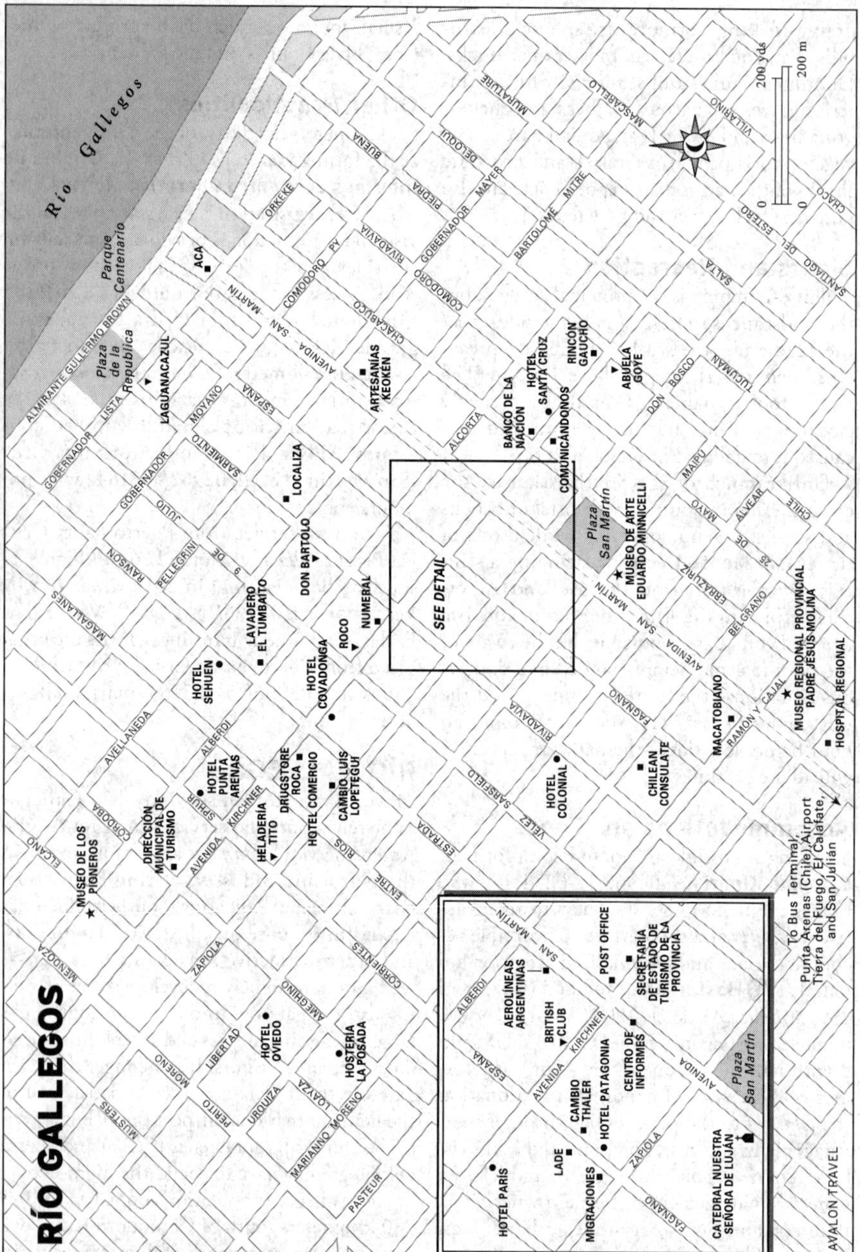
RÍO GALLEGOS
Río Gallegos
Parque Centenario
Plaza de la República
ACA
LAGUANACAZUL
ARTESANÍAS KEOKEN
HOTEL SANTA CRUZ
RINCÓN GAUCHO
BANCO DE LA NACIÓN
COMUNICÁNDONOS
ABUELA GOYE
LOCALIZA
DON BARTOLO
LAVADERO EL TUMBAITO
NUMERAL
ROCO
SEE DETAIL
Plaza San Martín
MUSEO DE ARTE EDUARDO MINNICELLI
HOTEL SEHUEN
HOTEL COVADONGA
HOTEL PUNTA ARENAS
DRUGSTORE ROCA
HOTEL COMERCIO
CAMBIO LUIS LOPETEGUI
DIRECCIÓN MUNICIPAL DE TURISMO
HELADERÍA TITO
MUSEO DE LOS PIONEROS
HOTEL COLONIAL
CHILEAN CONSULATE
MACATOBIANO
MUSEO REGIONAL PROVINCIAL PADRE JESÚS MOLINA
HOSPITAL REGIONAL
HOTEL OVIEDO
HOSTERÍA LA POSADA
To Bus Terminal, Punta Arenas (Chile), Airport Tierra del Fuego, El Calafate, and San Julián
AEROLÍNEAS ARGENTINAS
BRITISH CLUB
POST OFFICE
SECRETARÍA DE ESTADO DE TURISMO DE LA PROVINCIA
CENTRO DE INFORMES
CAMBIO THALER
HOTEL PATAGONIA
LADE
HOTEL PARÍS
MIGRACIONES
CATEDRAL NUESTRA SEÑORA DE LUJÁN
ALMIRANTE GUILLERMO BROWN
LISTA
GOBERNADOR
MOYANO
SARMIENTO
JULIO
9 DE
PELLEGRINI
RAWSON
MAGALLANES
AVELLANEDA
ALBERDI
SPHUR
KIRCHNER
AVENIDA
CÓRDOBA
ELCANO
MENDOZA
ZAPIOLA
LIBERTAD
MORENO
MUSTERS
PERITO
URQUIZA
LOAYZA
MARIANNO MORENO
PASTEUR
AMEGHINO
CORRIENTES
ENTRE RÍOS
ESTRADA
SARSFIELD
VÉLEZ
RIVADAVIA
FAGNANO
ESPAÑA
AVENIDA SAN MARTÍN
ORKEKE
COMODORO PY
CHACABUCO
BUENA
PIEDRA
GOBERNADOR MAYER
DELOQUI
MURATURE
BARTOLOMÉ MITRE
ALCORTA
MASCARELLO
VILLARINO
SANTIAGO DEL ESTERO
CHACO
SALTA
TUCUMÁN
DON BOSCO
MAIPÚ
25 DE MAYO
ALVEAR
CHILE
ERRAZURIZ
BELGRANO
RAMÓN Y CAJAL
0 200 yds
0 200 m
© AVALON TRAVEL

Chilean border post of Monte Aymond. From Monte Aymond it's another 196 kilometers to Punta Arenas or, alternatively, 571 kilometers to Ushuaia, Tierra del Fuego (including a ferry crossing at Primera Angostura). It's 305 kilometers southeast of El Calafate via RN 3, RP 5, RN 40, and RP 11, all paved.

The city's main thoroughfare, Avenida Roca, was renamed in 2010 as Avenida Presidente Doctor Néstor C. Kirchner, only a few days after the Gallegos-born former president's death, in a political decision that has not pleased every citizen.

## Sights

Opposite Plaza San Martín, the **Catedral Nuestra Señora de Luján** (1899) was the work of Salesian priest Juan Bernabé, who was also responsible for the cathedrals of Punta Arenas and Ushuaia. Like other pioneer buildings, it reflects the wood-framed metal-clad Magellanic style.

On the plaza's southwest side, the **Museo de Arte Eduardo Minnicelli** (Maipú 13, tel. 02966/436323, www.museominnicelli.com.ar, 8 A.M.–7 P.M. Tues.–Fri., 3–7 P.M. Sat.–Sun. and holidays, closed Dec. 20–Feb. 10, free) showcases provincial artists such as its namesake sculptor.

Three blocks southwest, the comprehensive **Museo Regional Provincial Padre Jesús Molina** (Ramón y Cajal 51, tel. 02966/423290, museopadremolina@yahoo.com.ar, 10 A.M.–5 P.M. weekdays, 1–5 P.M. weekends in summer, and 9 A.M.–7 P.M. weekdays, 11 A.M.–7 P.M. weekends the rest of the year, free) holds material on geology, paleontology, natural history, ethnology, and local history, including a good photographic collection.

In a pioneer house that belonged to Arthur and Victor Fenton, the city's first physicians, the **Museo de los Pioneros** (Elcano and Alberdi, tel. 02966/437763, pioneros@riogallegos.gov.ar, 10 A.M.–7:30 P.M. daily in summer, in winter closing as early as 6 P.M., free) documents southern Patagonia's early settlers. A guide may explain the details in English.

The late president's family tomb is becoming something of a pilgrimage site at the **Cementerio Municipal** (Av. Beccar and Tucumán), southwest of downtown.

## Shopping

**Rincón Gaucho** (Av. Kirchner 619, tel. 02966/420669) specializes in horse gear and the like. **Artesanías Keokén** (Av. San Martín 336, tel. 02966/420335) specializes in woolens but also sells leather goods and food items (preserves and candies).

## Accommodations

Traditionally expensive, scarce, and of mediocre quality, accommodations have substantially improved in comfort and amenities such as wireless Internet, now present in all listed hotels. Demand is high, so reservations are advisable.

Friendly **Hotel Punta Arenas** (Federico Sphur 55, tel. 02966/431924, US$25–55 s, US$35–63 d) has newer comfortable rooms but also keeps the old and cheaper ones with or without bath, which are a little rough around the edges. Breakfast takes place in its adjacent Something Café, which has a small but tasty snack menu.

With gracious and conscientious ownership, **Hotel Colonial** (Urquiza and Rivadavia, tel. 02966/422329, ines_frey@hotmail.com, US$25 s, US$38–45 d) is the best shoestring choice in a partly renovated 1930s building with spotless rooms, of which some doubles are cheaper with shared bath. Though no breakfast is served, the kitchen may be used.

A reliable classic, **Hotel Covadonga** (Av. Kirchner 1244, tel. 02966/420190, hotelcovadongargl@hotmail.com, US$49–57 s or d) has preserved much of its original attractive 1930s style, especially in its common areas, while rooms are simple with both shared and private baths, as well as parking.

Well-kept **Hotel Oviedo** (Libertad 746, tel. 02966/420118, US$38 s, US$53 d, breakfast US$4 extra) is a very good value choice, where the original mid-20th-century style has been preserved in its spacious rooms; all bathrooms have bathtubs.

Reservations are almost essential for friendly, well-kept **Hotel Sehuen** (Rawson 160, tel. 02966/425683, www.hotelsehuen.com, US$48 s, US$60–65 d), where singles are too small perhaps; some doubles have baths with bathtubs.

Ill-planned remodeling has cost **Hotel París** (Av. Kirchner 1040, tel. 02966/420111, elhotelparis@yahoo.com.ar, US$53 s, US$62 d with cash discounts) most of its original charm, but under new ownership renovation works have led finally to a respectable result. At the back, there are modern motel-style rooms with high ceilings and firm single beds.

Nondescript **Hotel Santa Cruz** (Av. Kirchner 701, tel. 02966/420601, www.hotelsantacruzrgl.com.ar, US$75–93 s, US$98–119 d) has newer and good superior rooms, though slightly overpriced in general.

Rehabbed **Hotel Comercio** (Av. Kirchner 1302, tel. 02966/420209, reservas@hotelcomercio.net, US$80 s, US$111 d) is a good value central choice with comfortable rooms and a self-serve breakfast. There's a 10 percent discount for cash.

It took 20 years to finish, but the 85-room **Hotel Patagonia** (Fagnano 54, tel. 02966/444969, www.hotel-patagonia.com, US$125–213 s, US$140–225 d), under the same ownership as El Calafate's Hotel Los Alamos, has established itself as the city's best, with a gym, a spa, a business center, and a restaurant with a short and reasonably priced menu. The higher rates correspond to four larger suites.

## Food

Top-quality chocolate shop and ice cream parlor, the southernmost branch of Bariloche's **Abuela Goye** (Av. Kirchner and Chile, tel. 02966/433500) is an attractive café and also a small restaurant for pizzas, omelets, creative sandwiches, and more elaborate food served as meals of the day (US$12).

For a diverse menu of specialties like salmon ravioli with pesto (US$10) or the local *róbalo* fish (snook) in a champagne sauce (US$13), in enormous portions, popular **RoCo** (Av. Kirchner 1157, tel. 02966/420203, lunch and dinner daily) is worth consideration.

Highly regarded as a pizzeria and *parrilla,* **Don Bartolo** (Sarmiento 124, tel. 02966/427297, lunch and dinner daily) serves pizzas from US$10, lamb at US$15, and a *parrillada* for two people at US$49.

Anyone who's ever been, or aspired to be, an Anglo-Argentine wool baron will want to dine at the atmospheric **British Club Restaurant** (Av. Kirchner 935, tel. 02966/432668, www.britishclub.com.ar, lunch and dinner daily), which offers live jazz some nights. The menu is short but highly creative, including seafood, beef, fish, and lamb, even using a wok, and managing to combine the Andean quinoa cereal with a Yorkshire pudding in one single dish. Entrées start at US$10. A set menu for US$13 is served at lunchtime.

A blue Magellanic house on a waterfront park provides a lovely atmosphere for chef Mirko's superb cooking at **Laguanacazul** (Gobernador Lista y Sarmiento, tel. 02966/444114, laguanacazul@hotmail.com, lunch and dinner daily). Its creative menu includes fine regional produce, including several lamb-based meals, and adding in certain times of the year unusual dishes such as *choique* (rhea) steak and *milanesa de lomo de guanaco* (breaded guanaco steak). Entrées are US$13–20. Reservations are advisable for dinner.

For ice cream, **Abuela Goye** (Av. Kirchner and Chile) is the best, while the traditional favorite for locals is **Heladería Tito** (Zapiola and Corrientes, tel. 02966/422008).

## Information

The well-organized **Secretaría de Estado de Turismo de la Provincia** (Av. Kirchner 863, tel. 02966/437412, www.santacruzpatagonia.gob.ar, 9 A.M.–4 P.M. Mon.–Fri., opening one hour later in Jan.) has maps and details on accommodations, excursions, and transportation.

The **Dirección Municipal de Turismo** (Av. Kirchner 1587, tel. 02966/436920, www.turismo.riogallegos.gov.ar) is open 8 A.M.–5 P.M. weekdays only; it also maintains two other

**Centro de Informes:** one occupies an old railcar known as *El Carretón* (Av. San Martín and Av. Kirchner, tel. 02966/422365, ext. 1138, 8 A.M.–8 P.M. weekdays, 8 A.M.–2 P.M. and 4–8 P.M. weekends Oct.–Apr. only), and another one is at the bus terminal (RN 3 and Charlotte Fairchild, tel. 02966/442159, 7 A.M.–8 P.M. weekdays, 7 A.M.–noon and 4–8 P.M. weekends and holidays).

For motorists, **ACA** (Orkeke 10, tel. 02966/420477) is at the north end of Avenida San Martín.

## Services

**Cambio Luis Lopetegui** (Zapiola 469, tel. 02966/421202) and **Cambio Thaler** (Monseñor Fagnano 20, tel. 02966/436052) exchange U.S. dollars, Chilean pesos, and travelers checks. **Banco de la Nación** (Av. Kirchner 799) has one of many ATMs.

**Correo Argentino** (Av. Kirchner 893) occupies a historic building; the postal code is 9400. **Comunicándonos** (Av. Kirchner 780) has phone and Internet services.

For visa matters, **Migraciones** (Monseñor Fagnano 95, tel. 02966/420205) is open 8 A.M.–4 P.M. weekdays only. The **Chilean consulate** (Mariano Moreno 148, tel. 02966/422364) is open 8 A.M.–1 P.M. weekdays.

**Lavadero El Tumbaito** (Alberdi 397, tel. 02966/422452) handles the laundry.

For medical attention, try the **Hospital Regional** (José Ingenieros 98, tel. 02966/420025).

## Getting There

Air services are fewer since El Calafate's airport opened. Overland, there are westbound bus connections to El Calafate and Parque Nacional Los Glaciares as well as the coal town of Río Turbio, and to Chile's Puerto Natales and Parque Nacional Torres del Paine; southbound links are to Punta Arenas, Chile, and to Argentine Tierra del Fuego.

**Aerolíneas Argentinas** (Av. San Martín 545, tel. 0810/2228-6527) flies daily to Buenos Aires's Aeroparque Jorge Newbery and twice weekly to Ushuaia. **LADE** (Fagnano 53, tel. 02966/422316) flies northbound to Comodoro Rivadavia; westbound to El Calafate; and southbound to Ushuaia.

**LAN** (tel. 02966/457189) flies to Aeroparque Jorge Newbery four times a week; for details, contact travel agencies. **Sol** (tel. 0810/4444765) flies southbound to Río Grande and Ushuaia, and northbound to Comodoro Rivadavia, Neuquén, Mendoza, Córdoba, and Rosario.

About two kilometers southwest of downtown, Río Gallegos's **Terminal de Ómnibus Manuel Álvarez** (RN 3 and Charlotte Fairchild, tel. 02966/442159) fronts on RN 3 near Avenida Eva Perón. There are provincial, long-distance, and international services to Chile.

Daily in high season, there's direct service to Río Grande (US$58, eight hours) and Ushuaia (US$73, 11 hours), in Argentine Tierra del Fuego, with **Tecni-Austral** (tel. 02966/442447) and **Marga** (tel. 02966/442671).

**Taqsa** (tel. 02966/442194) goes daily to Gobernador Gregores (US$33, seven hours), the quasi-gateway to Parque Nacional Perito Moreno (*not* the location of the famous Perito Moreno Glacier).

**TPS** (02966/442687) goes Tuesday, Thursday, and Sunday to El Chaltén (US$33, seven hours).

Other typical destinations, times, and fares include San Julián (US$21–27, 4–6 hours), Río Turbio (US$19, five hours), El Calafate (US$20, 4.5 hours), Comodoro Rivadavia (US$42–55, 10–11 hours), Trelew (US$69–103, 15–18 hours), Puerto Madryn (US$72–108, 16–18 hours), and Buenos Aires (US$124–172, 36–38 hours).

Several carriers go to Punta Arenas, Chile (US$23, four hours), including **El Pingüino** (tel. 02966/442169), **Buses Ghisoni** (tel. 02966/457047), and **Pacheco/Magallanes Tour** (tel. 02966/442765). El Pingüino goes Tuesday and Saturday to Puerto Natales (US$23, five hours), the gateway to Torres del Paine, but it's also possible to bus to Río Turbio, where there are frequent shuttles to Natales.

### Getting Around

Taxis and *remises* (about US$8) are the only public transport to **Aeropuerto Internacional Piloto Civil Norberto Fernández** (tel. 02966/442340), about five kilometers west of town on RN 3.

From downtown Avenida Kirchner, city buses A and B (US$0.65) go directly to the Terminal de Ómnibus, on the southwestern outskirts of town, while cabs charge about US$6.

Car-rental agencies include **Localiza** (Sarmiento 245, tel. 02966/436717) and **Riestra** (Av. San Martín 1508, tel. 02966/421321, www.riestrarentacar.com), near the traffic circle junction with RN 3.

## VICINITY OF RÍO GALLEGOS

Given its proximity to historic *estancias* and wildlife sites, most notably the Cabo Vírgenes penguin colony, Río Gallegos is earning a newfound respect even though it's not a major destination itself. Gallegos travel agencies such as **Macatobiano** (Av. San Martín 1093, tel. 02966/422466, www.macatobiano.com) arrange excursions to outlying attractions such as Cabo Vírgenes (US$63 pp with a three-passenger minimum plus US$4 reserve admission fee for foreigners).

Returning from Cabo Vírgenes, Chile-bound travelers with their own vehicles can take the RP 51 shortcut to the Monte Aymond border post but should ask directions before doing so, as it's not always obvious or clearly signed.

### Estancia Monte Dinero

From a junction about 15 kilometers south of Río Gallegos, RP 1 swerves southeast through rolling pasturelands where gas-and-oil derricks remind you that Santa Cruz is an energy storehouse. The gravel road is smooth to the picture-postcard settlement of **Estancia Cóndor** (neighboring farmers consider the Benetton empire, which now owns Cóndor, to be indifferent to its neighbors, who traditionally help each other out).

Beyond Cóndor, the road deteriorates toward Estancia Monte Dinero, a pioneer sheep farm open to overnighters and day-trippers. Some 120 kilometers from Río Gallegos, 26,000-hectare Monte Dinero benefits from proximity to the Cabo Vírgenes penguin colony, but it's also interesting as a ranch that, unlike most others in the area, has subdivided its fragile pastures into smaller paddocks to manage its 17,000 sheep more intensively. Also unlike other *estancias*, it trains its contract shearers to use manual rather than electric shears, pays them a premium to do so, and shears ewes before lambing to ensure a higher lambing rate.

Founded by the Fentons, another pioneer Patagonian family, **Hostería Monte Dinero** has four downstairs bedrooms with private baths and two upstairs (with a shared bath), plus wireless Internet and satellite TV; with renovation works in 2011, more accommodations will be added. The *casco*'s former sun porch has been expanded into an attractive and spacious, but not extravagant, bar and dining room. A small museum holds family keepsakes, and there's also a billiard table (*not* a pool table).

Estancia Monte Dinero (tel./fax 02966/428922, www.montedinero.com.ar, US$130 pp with half board, US$150 pp with full board, excluding drinks) is open year-round. Rates include farm activities such as dog trials, sheep shearing, and hiking.

For nonguests, there's a *día de campo* (day-use fee, US$90 pp) that includes farm activities and lunch but not drinks.

### Reserva Provincial Cabo Vírgenes

Beyond Monte Dinero, the road improves as it approaches Cabo Vírgenes, second only to Punta Tombo among Argentina's Magellanic penguin colonies. With more than 120,000 breeding pairs, the rapidly growing colony has increased by at least a third in a decade-plus.

The abundance of brush here means the birds are less visible than at Dos Bahías, and there's no direct beach access. A 1,500-meter nature trail, though, permits close approach to the birds, and there's an interpretive brochure in good English. There's an admission fee of US$4 for foreigners, less for Argentine and Santa Cruz residents.

At the reserve's northeast corner, the rehabbed hilltop **Faro Cabo Vírgenes,** the historic Argentine lighthouse, includes a small museum. Outside, facing the ocean, there remain foxholes dug to repel British commandos who might have landed here during the 1982 Falklands war (Britain conducted operations in Argentine Patagonia and Tierra del Fuego, escaping into Chile with collusion from the Pinochet dictatorship, which feared an Argentine attack if the Brits lost).

At the so-called **Cementerio Histórico,** the only truly legitimate tomb may be that of Conrado Assinbom, a hermit who lived in the shack beneath the lighthouse. One older cross is almost illegible, and it's not certain anyone's buried there.

At the reserve's southern edge, visitors can cross the border—technically illegally—to see **Faro Punta Dungeness** (1897), the lighthouse at the east end of Chile's narrow latitudinal strip along the Strait of Magellan. When duties permit, Chilean navy personnel show visitors around the facility.

Estancia Monte Dinero has the nearest accommodations, and its sparkling *confitería,* **Al Fin y al Cabo,** has become the place to stop for lunch and sweets—try the rhubarb cake. The quality is excellent and the building has magnificent shoreline views southeast to Punta Dungeness.



# Interior Santa Cruz Province

## EL CALAFATE

Spreading along the south shore of Lago Argentino, a giant glacial trough fed by meltwater from the Campo de Hielo Sur, fast-growing El Calafate is the poster child for Argentina's tourism boom. The gateway to Parque Nacional Los Glaciares and its spectacular Glaciar Perito Moreno, it now has a major point of interest in the Glaciarium, a new museum of and about the rivers of ice. While the growth of services, including hotels and restaurants, has slowed, it remains southwestern Santa Cruz's most important destination and transport hub.

Calafate owes its growth to (1) a new international airport that has nearly eliminated the overland route from Río Gallegos for long-distance passengers; (2) the competitive Argentine peso; (3) the fact that the late Argentine president Néstor Kirchner, a Santa Cruz native, built a home here and invited high-profile international figures, such as Brazilian president Luis Inácio Lula da Silva and former Chilean president Ricardo Lagos, to admire the Glaciar Perito Moreno with him.

The boom has had drawbacks, though. As the population has more than doubled in a decade, real-estate prices have skyrocketed. Unfortunately, a prime downtown location that once housed the old power plant—admittedly a noisy eyesore—has become the site of a new casino, no less an eyesore even if less noisy.

### Orientation

El Calafate (population about 18,000) is 320 kilometers northwest of Río Gallegos and 32 kilometers west of northbound RP 40, which leads to the wilder El Chaltén sector of Parque Nacional Los Glaciares and an adventurous overland route to Chile. While only about 50–60 kilometers from Torres del Paine as the crow flies, the town is 215 kilometers from the Cerro Castillo border crossing and about 305 kilometers from Puerto Natales via Argentine highways RN 40, RP 5, and RP 11, plus a small additional distance on the Chilean side.

A former stage stop, El Calafate has an elongated city plan that has spread barely a few blocks north and south of its main east–west thoroughfare, the pompously named Avenida del Libertador General José de San Martín (for Argentina's independence hero). Most services

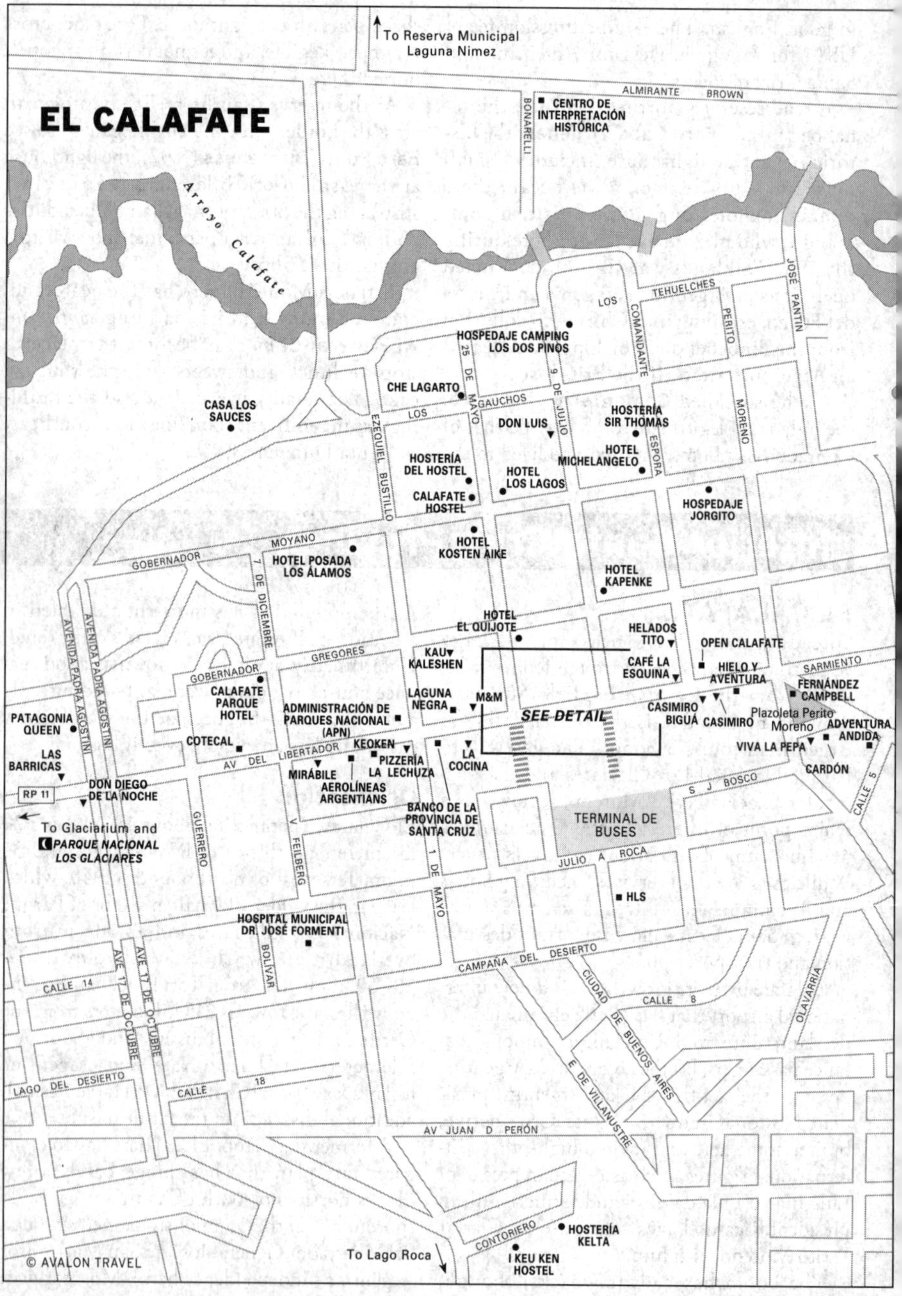


© AVALON TRAVEL

S. ARGENTINE PATAGONIA

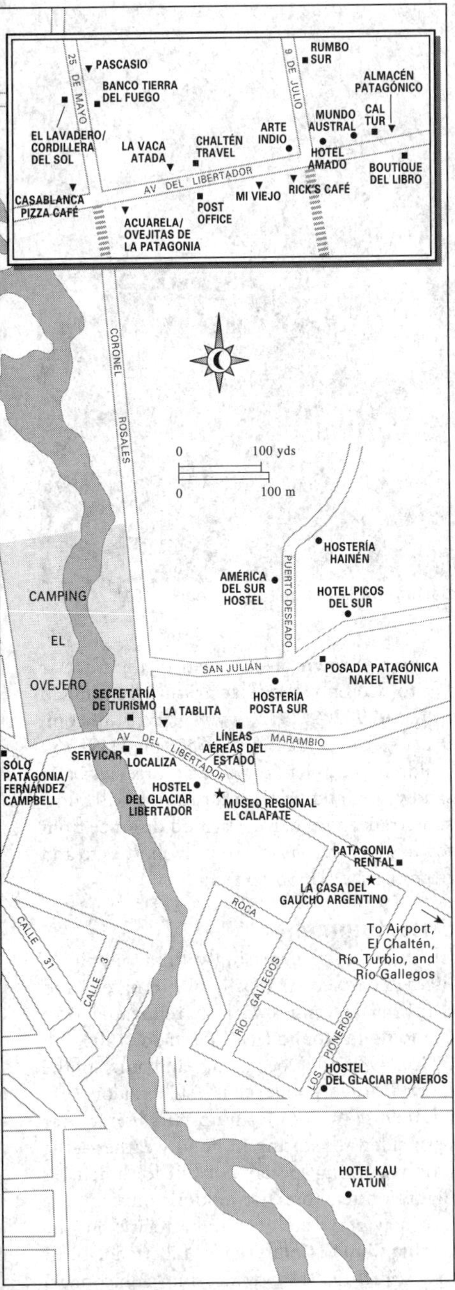


and points of interest are close to "Avenida Libertador" or "San Martín," as the street is variously called, but explosive hotel growth has taken place to the east, on and near the former airfield.

## Sights

After years of near abandonment, the **Museo Regional El Calafate** (Av. Libertador 575, tel. 02902/491924, 10 A.M.–5 P.M. weekdays, free) has reopened, but it's hard to say that the sparse and poorly presented exhibits on paleontology, natural history, geology, and ethnology were worth the wait. The pioneer families' photographic histories show promise, but it still lacks an explanation of the 1920s labor unrest that led to several shooting deaths on the *estancias.*

More promising is the **Centro de Interpretación Histórica** (Almirante Brown and Bonarelli, tel. 02902/492799, www.museocalafate.com.ar, 10 A.M.–8 P.M. daily Sept.–Semana Santa, 10 A.M.–6 P.M. daily the rest of the year, US$6, US$5 for seniors over 65, US$4 for children ages 6–12), whose sophisticated timeline puts southern Patagonia's natural, cultural, and historical events in context; it has many photographs, good English translations, and a quality library. Admission includes *remise* transportation from downtown.

At the north edge of town, a onetime sewage pond is now **Reserva Municipal Laguna Nimez,** a freshwater body now frequented by more than 100 bird species. Guides from the Universidad de la Patagonia now take visitors for interpretive walks (US$5 pp) through the wetlands and along the lakeshore.

One sight that locals know but few foreigners recognize is the **Casa Kirchner** (Los Gauchos and Namuncurá), the home of the late president Néstor Kirchner and his wife, current president Cristina Fernández de Kirchner.

### GLACIARIUM

New in 2011, the Glaciarum is a first-of-its-kind "Museo de Hielo Patagónico," placing the Patagonian ice sheets in natural and historical perspective, in state-of-the-art hilltop facilities.

© WAYNE BERNHARDSON

On the western outskirts of El Calafate, the Glaciarium museum opened in early 2011.

Within its walls (shaped to mimic the angular blocks of ice on a glacier's tongue), there are sophisticated exhibits on the formation of the southern Patagonian fields, their original coverage and present extent, and details on individual glaciers on both the Argentine and Chilean sides of the border. There are also detailed accounts of discovery and research, with special emphasis on explorer and conservationist Francisco P. Moreno—in fact, there's even a robot of an elderly Moreno at his desk, writing his memoirs with an out-loud narration of his thoughts.

Built with private funds, the museum's real purpose, though, is to promote public consciousness of climate change and environmental deterioration. The consulting glaciologist is Pedro Skvarca, an early mountaineer in the region who found his life's calling in the preservation of the massive rivers of ice and the summits that surround them. In addition to the regular exhibits, there is an art space and a 120-seat theater that offers a 3-D tour of the glaciers themselves—worthwhile for those who lack time to visit all of them.

West of town on the road to the Glaciar Perito Moreno, the Glaciarium (RP 11 Km 6, tel. 02902/497912, www.glaciarium.com, 9 A.M.–9 P.M. Tues.–Sun., US$18 pp, US$12.50 children 6–12) has a *confitería* for snacks and sandwiches and, in the near future, will add a subterranean ice bar. It's a good distance from town, so it offers its own hourly shuttles to and from the site (US$6 pp round-trip).

## Entertainment

El Calafate is surprisingly light on nightlife, which consists mostly of dining out and drinking at venues such as renovated **Don Diego de la Noche** (Av. Libertador 1603, tel. 02902/493270). Open all day and much of the night, **Borges y Álvarez** (Av. Libertador 1015, tel. 02902/491464) is an upstairs literary bar with sidewalk seating in good weather—the food is nothing special, but OK for lunch. At night, it often hosts live folkloric music.

It may be an architectural atrocity, but the **Casino Club El Calafate** (Av. Libertador 1061, tel. 02902/495911, www.casino-club.com.ar)

does have live entertainment—mostly cabaret acts, but sometimes more rewarding programs that include folkloric performers.

## Shopping

Downtown Avenida del Libertador is lined with souvenir shops such as **Open Calafate** (Av. Libertador 996, tel. 02902/491254), which also sells books and maps.

**Boutique del Libro** (Av. Libertador 1033, tel. 02902/491363) carries a broad selection of books (many in English) on Antarctica, Argentina, and Patagonia, including Moon handbooks and novels.

For premium homemade chocolates, try **Ovejitas de la Patagonia** (Av. Libertador 1197, tel. 02902/491736), **Laguna Negra** (Av. Libertador 1250, tel. 02902/492423), or any of several similar locales.

**Cardón** (Emilio Amado 835, tel. 02902/492074) is a casual clothing counterpart to Esprit or Patagonia. **Arte Indio** (Av. Libertador 1108, tel. 02902/492131, www.puebloindio.com.ar) carries high-end crafts from around the country, including ceramics, silverwork, and tapestries. **La Casa del Gaucho Argentino** (Av. del Libertador 351, tel. 02902/491281) stocks gaucho apparel and riding gear.

## Accommodations

El Calafate has diverse high-standard accommodations ranging from camping to five-star extravagance. Its custom-built hostels, with stylish architecture, engaging common areas with stunning views, and even restaurants and bars, far surpass the dingy no-frills reputation that the word sometimes implies. In addition to dorms, several have excellent private rooms that shame some hotels.

Occupancy rates are at all-time highs, and places that once stayed open only in summer now stay open all year, but the increased capacity has helped stabilize prices. Unless otherwise indicated, those listed are for high season, usually October–April, but dates vary, and if business is slow, rates can be negotiable. Every place in categories over US$50 includes breakfast; less expensive places may or may not provide it. Wireless Internet has become almost universal. Argentine hotels, unlike those in Chile, do not discount IVA to foreign visitors.

### CAMPING

Flanking the Arroyo Calafate, the municipal **Camping El Ovejero** (José Pantín s/n, tel. 02902/493422, www.campingelovejero.com.ar, US$5 pp) has reopened under a private concessionaire. Fenced and forested, it has good common toilets and hot showers, and each site has its own fire pit; areas east of the creek are for walk-in campers only. It's also added hostel quarters (US$10 pp).

On the grounds of its namesake *hospedaje,* **Camping Jorgito** (Moyano 943, tel. 02902/491323, US$5 pp) is decent enough. **Camping Los Dos Pinos** (9 de Julio 218, tel. 02902/491271, www.losdospinos.com, US$6 pp plus US$2 per car) has improved and expanded.

### US$10-25

Custom-built **Che Lagarto** (25 de Mayo 311, tel. 02902/496670, www.chelagarto.com, US$11 pp dorm, US$42–48 d) is a hostel with large and luminous common areas, but some of the dorms are cramped with up to a dozen beds. Even some of the dorms have balconies, though, which add a touch of style to its amenities.

Expanded **Hospedaje los dos Pinos** (9 de Julio 358, tel./fax 02902/491271, www.losdospinos.com, US$10–12 pp dorm, US$55 d) provides plain but spacious and immaculate rooms—ranging from hostel dorms to private doubles and cabañas (its tours, though, have drawn some criticism). Breakfast costs extra.

The **I Keu Ken Hostel** (Pontoriero 171, tel. 02902/495175, www.patagoniaikeuken.com.ar, US$18 pp, US$63 d) is a purpose-built hostel in the Magellanic style, with truly inviting common areas. All rooms are quadruple dorms with lockers and shared baths; rates include breakfast. It's a windy location uphill from downtown, but there are free transfers from the bus terminal.

Near the old airfield, a short walk from América del Sur, the **Marco Polo Inn** (Calle 405 No. 82, tel. 02902/493899, www.marcopoloinncalafate.com, US$12–16 pp dorm, US$45–50 s, US$50–55 d, with breakfast) is part of a chain with others in Puerto Iguazú and Bariloche. Amenities include a kitchen, a bar, and a restaurant, and there are half a dozen private rooms in addition to the dorms.

### US$25-50

Several hostels in this category also have private accommodations that are excellent values in this price range, which otherwise has few options.

East of the arroyo, open October–mid-April, the HI affiliate **Hostel del Glaciar Pioneros** (Los Pioneros 251, tel./fax 02902/491243, www.glaciar.com, US$13 pp dorm, US$40 s, US$50 d) has extensive common spaces, including a large lounge with wireless Internet, kitchen space, and laundry facilities. The higher rates are for larger and comfortable but no-frills hotel-style rooms with breakfast; it also offers its own Glaciar Perito Moreno excursions.

Under the same management, the newer and more stylish **Hostel del Glaciar Libertador** (Av. Libertador 587, tel./fax 02902/491792, www.glaciar.com, US$15 pp dorm, US$71 s, US$77 d) has 22 rooms with private baths; some are four-bed dorms, while others are twins or doubles. Both hostels offer roughly 15 percent discounts for HI members, and 30 percent low-season discounts in October and April (except for Semana Santa).

Friendly **Hospedaje Jorgito** (Moyano 943, tel. 02902/491323, hospedajejorgito@cotecal.com.ar, US$15–20 pp) has decent multibed rooms with shared or private baths, best for small groups of friends.

**Hostería Sir Thomas** (Espora 257, tel. 02902/492220, www.sirthomas.com.ar, US$40 s, US$45 d) is reliable; breakfast costs US$2.50 more.

"Think big" seems to be the motto at **Calafate Hostel** (Gobernador Moyano 1296, tel. 02902/492450, www.calafatehostels.com,

© WAYNE BERNHARDSON

Hostel del Glaciar Pioneros is one of several stylish budget accommodations in El Calafate.

US$16 pp dorm), which has dorms with shared baths and balconies in a stylish building with vast common areas; it also has better rooms with private baths (US$43 s, US$58 d, with breakfast).

On the hilltop immediately east of the municipal campground, custom-built **América del Sur Hostel** (Puerto Deseado s/n, tel. 02902/493525, www.americahostel.com.ar, US$19 pp dorm, US$80 s or d) has friendly management, spectacular common spaces with panoramic views, and well-designed rooms in which the toilet and shower are separate and the vanity is outside of both. Rates include breakfast and free transfers from the bus terminal; off-season rates are about 20 percent less.

### US$50-100

Directly across from the América del Sur hostel, **Hostería Hainén** (Puerto Deseado 118, tel. 02902/493874, www.hosteriahainen.com, US$63 s or d) is a handsome wooden structure with wainscoted midsize rooms in soothing colors. Owner-operated, it lacks elaborate amenities but compensates with peace and quiet (except for the nearly incessant winds at this exposed location).

Sometimes serving as an overflow option from the nearby Calafate Hostel, tidy **Hotel Los Lagos** (25 de Mayo 220, tel. 02902/491170, www.loslagoshotel.com.ar, US$63 s, US$70 d with breakfast) has come up in the world—as have its rates. The rooms, though, are on the small side.

Alongside the Calafate Hostel, under the same management but with a separate reception area, the **Hostería del Hostel** (25 de Mayo and Gobernador Moyano, www.calafatehostels.com, US$55 s, US$73 d) is a smart modern building with immaculate midsize rooms, all of which have Internet-connected computers. When business is slow, rates may fall by a third or so.

Surpassed by newer options, **Hotel Michelangelo** (Gobernador Moyano 1020, tel. 02902/491045, www.michelangelohotel.com.ar, US$87 s, US$100 d) has smallish rooms with limited natural light, but its restaurant draws raves for lunch or dinner. Some rooms are small, but the management and service are professional, and it's now tobacco-free.

### US$100-200

The hillside **Hostería Kelta** (Portoriero 109, tel. 02902/491966, www.kelta.com.ar, US$83 s, US$101 d) is a handsome hotel with views across the lake; the larger lake-view rooms are no more expensive than the smaller interior rooms, and on request, the staff will shift guests to better rooms as they open up.

Near the old airfield, the rooms at owner-operated **Hostería Posta Sur** (Puerto San Julián 490, tel./fax 02902/492406, www.hosteriapostasur.com.ar, US$100 s, US$105 d) are small for the price and some lack even closets, but it's well-regarded. Off-season rates fall by half.

Nearby **Hotel Picos del Sur** (Puerto San Julián 271, tel. 02902/493650, www.hotelpicosdelsur.com.ar, US$97 s, US$108 d) has overcome some service problems—it's truly congenial now—to become a good choice. Rates include an airport pickup and drop-off.

At first glance, the interior of **Posada Patagonia Rebelde** (José R. Haro 442, tel. 02902/494495, www.patagoniarebelde.com, US$88 s, US$110 d) seems more a well-stocked antiques shop than a boutique hotel in a distinctive Patagonian style. Ironically, much of the recycled material that built the building came from the Buenos Aires barrio of La Boca, and its own rustic sophistication contrasts dramatically with the sophisticated design hotels elsewhere in town. Though it's not for everyone, everyone who's read *In Patagonia* is likely to love it.

The renovated **Hotel Kapenke** (9 de Julio 112, tel. 02902/491093, www.kapenke.com.ar, US$109 s, US$119 d) has added a handsome new wing to an already attractive hotel, with rates stabilizing or even dropping a bit.

When El Calafate was smaller, **Hotel Kau Yatún** (tel. 02902/491259, www.kauyatun.com, US$108 s, US$124 d, US$157–199 d, with breakfast) was part of Estancia 25 de Mayo; the older part was the *casco,* whose suites have whirlpool tubs, fireplaces, and other amenities, but it's not kept pace with with trends here. Note that its business address, Avenida Libertador 1190, is not the same as the property itself; the hotel is east of the arroyo and up the hill from the Albergue del Glaciar.

New in 2005, atop a hill near the eastern approach to town, the upper-midsize rooms at **Hotel Alto Calafate** (RP 11 s/n, tel. 02902/494110, www.hotelaltocalafate.com.ar, US$145–245 s or d plus taxes) command views of the entire Lago Argentino basin and the Andes to the southwest, or of the "Balcón de Calafate" that rises immediately behind it. The service is exemplary, and its bar-restaurant precludes the need to dine or drink in town (though a free shuttle is available every 15 minutes). There are no neighbors to make any noise around this Kirchner-owned property, but the wind can wail at the exposed location.



Located close to everything but just beyond the crowded center, **Patagonia Queen** (Av. Padre Agostini 49, tel. 02902/496701, www.patagoniaqueen.com.ar, US$150 s, US$165 d) is a 20-room boutique hotel done in stunning natural wood with earnest Korean-Argentine ownership. The rooms are only midsize, but all the baths have whirlpool tubs, and it's tobacco-free throughout.

Its exterior handsomely rehabbed in wood and glass, the pastel rooms at well-located **Hotel El Quijote** (Gregores 1191, tel. 02902/491017, www.quijotehotel.com.ar, US$150 s, US$175 d) make it one of El Calafate's most stylish hotels. A recent remodel enlarged the rooms and made them more comfortable, but it has also meant thinner walls that conduct noise more easily.

The 60-room **Hotel Kosten Aike** (Gobernador Moyano 1243, tel. 02902/492424, www.kostenaike.com.ar, US$184 s or d) is an impressive four-star facility with every modern convenience, including a well-regarded restaurant, a gym and a spa, and facilities for disabled guests. Though it's not a view hotel, the large and comfy quarters, with Tehuelche-derived decor, have drawn uniformly positive comments—as has its personnel.

**Hotel Mirador del Lago** (Av. Libertador 2047, tel. 02902/493176, www.miradordel-lago.com.ar, US$130–185 s, US$140–195 d) is more than two decades old, but a rehab and expansion have left it looking like new. From its knoll on the east side of the road, it has fine lake views, but rooms in the newer wing are larger and significantly better than the older ones. It has a well-regarded restaurant, and the staff often anticipates (rather than reacts to) its guests' needs.

### OVER US$200

New in 2007, on the western outskirts of town, the **Imago Hotel & Spa** (Calle 669 No. 40, tel. 02902/496501, www.imagohotelspa.com, US$200–600 s or d) is another outpost of the Kirchner empire, and a symbol of their presence in Santa Cruz province. It embodies a modern Patagonian style, with a quarried stone facade and glistening wood details, with midsize to large rooms equipped with the latest technology; some have balconies with lake views. Its spa is one of the most complete in town, in a class with Hotel Posada Los Álamos and Design Suites Calafate.

On the western outskirts of town, **Xelena Deluxe Suites** (René Favaloro 3548, tel. 02902/496201, www.xelena.com.ar, US$210–487 s or d) is a seven-story, 70-room hotel that looks far smaller than it is because three ample floors, including guest rooms and a spa (with an indoor-outdoor pool), lie below the street-level reception area. Even standard rooms have exceptional lake views, while the suites enjoy a more panoramic aspect; all the baths have Jacuzzis.

On a blustery bluff north of the old airfield, the architecturally audacious **Design Suites Calafate** (Calle 598 No. 190, tel. 02902/494525, www.designsuites.com, US$215–285 s or d plus taxes) enjoys spectacular panoramas—at least from the higher-priced suites that face the lake. Slightly smaller standard rooms face an unappealing part of the steppe. Given its relative isolation, though, it's surprising that its hourly downtown shuttle doesn't begin until 6 P.M.

© WAYNE BERNHARDSON

El Calafate's Design Suites offers panoramic views of Lago Argentino.



Though well-regarded by its guests, rates for the midsize-plus rooms at **Calafate Parque Hotel** (7 de Diciembre and Gobernador Gregores, tel. 02902/492970, www.calafateparquehotel.com.ar, US$165–248 s or d plus taxes) seem a little high. Facilities include a third-floor gym and spa as well as a fairly elaborate restaurant. With discounted rates through its website, though, it can be an excellent value.

In a sense, every room is a presidential suite at **Casa Los Sauces** (Los Gauchos 1352, tel. 2902/495854, www.casalossauces.com, US$250–500 s or d plus taxes), as it's the property of President Cristina Fernández. Its 36 rooms, in several buildings over three willow-studded hectares, adjoin the presidential weekend house, and the rates seem more suitable for kings. Some operators, though, have complained about the oppressive security when the president and her family are here.

**Hotel Posada Los Álamos** (Gobernador Moyano 1355, tel. 02902/491144, www.posadalosalamos.com, US$233–508 s or d plus taxes) may be Calafate's most complete hotel, with a pool, a spa, and a convention center. Breakfast takes place in the restaurant across the street, where it also operates the compact nine-hole (three holes with three different tees each) Campo de Golf Pinar. The rooms, though, are a little undersized for its category.

## Food

El Calafate has the province's best restaurants, and in southernmost Argentine Patagonia, only Ushuaia can match it for quality. Prices have risen considerably, although the quality remains high.

Unfortunately, unlike Ushuaia, it has not yet banished tobacco from the food scene; some individual restaurants have done so, and others have tobacco-free areas, though some of those are merely symbolic.

The best breakfast spot is **Cafetería Don Luis** (9 de Julio 265, tel. 02902/491550), with the best coffee, the most succulent croissants, and many other treats to try throughout the day.

Several decent *confiterías* offer short orders,

sandwiches, coffee, and the like. Among them are **Café La Esquina** (Av. Libertador 1000, tel. 02902/492334) and the tobacco-heavy wireless-Internet-equipped **Casablanca Pizza Café** (Av. Libertador 1202, tel. 02902/491402).

**Pizzería La Lechuza** (Av. Libertador and 1° de Mayo, tel. 02902/491610, lunch and dinner daily, US$8–10) deserves special mention for its *super cebolla y jamón crudo* (onion and prosciutto) and its empanadas. The pasta-oriented **La Cocina** (Av. Libertador 1245, tel. 02902/491758, lunch and dinner daily) has expanded its menu to include high-end meats in the US$15-plus range.

**Mirábile** (Av. del Libertador 1329, tel. 02902/492230, closed Mon.) has plenty of tough competition in the pastas category, but has moderate prices (most entrées under US$10, but a complex sauce can add another US$5 per dish) and excellent service. King crab *sorrentinos* (US$15) are the prestige item on the menu.

**Viva la Pepa** (Emilio Amado 833, Local 1, tel. 02902/491880, lunch and dinner daily) offers outstanding sweet and savory crepes (US$10–12.50) that are an ideal antidote for anyone who's overdosed on beef, lamb, or other Patagonian staples. The small wine list stresses Patagonian vintages.

**Kau Kaleshen** (Gobernador Gregores 1256, tel. 02902/491118) is a reinvented teahouse and vegetarian restaurant with moderately priced entrées such as pumpkin-stuffed *sorrentinos* (US$12) and pizzas, in a cozy environment.

Despite its name, **La Vaca Atada** (Av. Libertador 1176, tel. 02902/491227, lunch and dinner daily) is Calafate's best choice for fish, such as trout in a shrimp sauce (US$12), though it also serves beef, pastas, and soups. On the down side, the bread is basic, it gets a little noisy with families, and the small wine list relies on major bodegas, though there are some by-the-glass selections. The service is decent but slightly absent-minded.

Remodeled **Rick's Café** (Av. Libertador 1105, tel. 02902/492148, lunch and dinner daily) and **La Tablita** (Coronel Rosales 28, tel. 02902/491065, lunch and dinner daily) are both well-regarded *parrillas.* The former has a grilled beef buffet for US$16, but the latter has made a transition toward more creative cuisine.

Despite a utilitarian decor, **Mi Viejo** (Av. Libertador 1111, tel. 02902/491691, lunch and dinner daily, US$10–20) serves fine lamb with roasted potatoes (US$20) and exceptional pepper steak along with especially tasty creamed potatoes (also US$20). The service is efficient, but the only style points come from the staked lamb in the window fire pit.

**Casimiro** (Av. Libertador 963, tel. 02902/492590, www.casimirobigua.com, lunch and dinner daily) would be a good choice almost anywhere in the world; the plate of smoked Patagonian appetizers is exquisite. There's a US$19 lunch that includes a main dish, dessert, and a glass of wine, but entrées such as almond-crusted lamb (US$19) and black hake (US$28) make this a special outing at dinnertime. It's also a by-the-glass wine bar, with an imposing list reaching several hundred dollars per bottle (though there are other more affordable, and still palatable, choices).

A few doors west, under the same ownership, **Casimiro Biguá** (Av. del Libertador 993, tel. 02902/493993, www.casimirobigua.com, lunch and dinner daily) has an overlapping menu, but it's best to stick with its *parrilla* specialties of grilled beef and lamb. Entrées start around US$15, and, as at its siblings, its rapidly rising prices make it a lesser value than it once was.

In the same vein as Casimiro, **Pascasio** (25 de Mayo 52, tel. 2902/492055, lunch and dinner daily) is a gourmet restaurant with starters such as lamb carpaccio (US$8), pastas with a regional touch, meats in the US$15–19 range, and occasional game dishes such as Patagonian hare.

A spinoff from its near namesakes, **Casimiro Biguá Trattoria** (Av. Libertador 1359, tel. 02962/492993, lunch and dinner daily) specializes in Patagonian-inspired pastas such as lamb ravioli (US$20). The flavors are rich, the portions generous, and the wine list diverse, but the service can border on indifferent or inattentive.

Often accommodating tour groups, **Las Barricas** (Av. Libertador 1610, tel. 02902/493414, www.barricasdeenopio.com.ar, lunch and dinner daily) prepares meat, fish, and game dishes, plus smoked meats. Desserts are only so-so, but there's a big list of premium wines in the US$20–50 range; decent by-the-glass house wines are moderately priced.

Two blocks west of Barricas, **Pura Vida** (Av. Libertador 1876, tel. 02902/493356, lunch and dinner Thurs.–Tues.) gets few foreigners for quality versions of traditional Argentine and Patagonian dishes such as gnocchi (US$10) with a saffron sauce, *carbonada* (a motley stew large enough for two hungry diners, US$16), and *cazuela de cordero* (a lamb casserole, US$17). Self-consciously casual—no two chairs or menu cards are alike—it has mezzanine seating with views over Laguna Nimes and, in the distance, Lago Argentino; the main floor, though, is cozier. The menu rarely changes, and the wine list is modest (with nothing by the glass).

El Calafate went nearly a decade without a quality ice creamery, but now it has two outstanding ones. **Acuarela** (Av. Libertador 1197, tel. 02902/491315) can aspire toward Buenos Aires's best, but **Tito** (Espora 33, tel. 02902/494602) is also fine.

## Information

At the eastern approach to town, the **Secretaría de Turismo de la Municipalidad de El Calafate** (Coronel Rosales s/n, tel. 02902/491090, www.elcalafate.gov.ar, 8 A.M.–8 P.M. daily) maintains a database of hotels and other services, as well as maps and brochures. A separate office at the Terminal de Ómnibus (Av. Roca 1004, tel. 02902/491476, www.elcalafate.gov.ar, 8 A.M.–8 P.M. daily) also has a message board; both have English-speaking personnel.

The **Administración de Parques Nacionales** (APN, Av. Libertador 1302, tel. 02902/491755 or 02902/491545, losglaciares@apn.gov.ar) is open 8 A.M.–8 P.M. weekdays, 9:30 A.M.–8 P.M. weekends.

There is a useful private website, www.losglaciares.com, with considerable information on El Calafate and surroundings.

## Services

**Cambio Thaler** (Av. del Libertador 963, tel. 02902/493245) is the only currency exchange house. Both **Banco de Santa Cruz** (Av. Libertador 1285) and **Banco Tierra del Fuego** (25 de Mayo 40) have ATMs.

**Correo Argentino** (Av. Libertador 1133) is the post office.

The **Cooperativa Telefónica de Calafate** (Cotecal, Av. Libertador 1486, tel. 02902/491900) has the best and cheapest Internet service; there are no collect phone calls, though. **Open Calafate** (Av. Libertador 996, tel. 02902/491254) provides some competition in both telephone and Internet service, but its connections are slower.

**El Lavadero** (25 de Mayo 43, tel. 02902/492182) charges around US$6 per laundry load.

The **Hospital Municipal Dr. José Formenti** (Av. Roca 1487, tel. 02902/491001 or 02902/491173) handles medical matters.

## Getting There

El Calafate is the transport hub for western Santa Cruz thanks to its new airport, road connections to Río Gallegos, and improving links north and south along RN 40.

### AIR

**Aerolíneas Argentinas** (Av. del Libertador 1361, tel. 02902/492815) normally flies north to Trelew and Buenos Aires's Aeroparque Jorge Newbery, and south to Ushuaia, but it sometimes has service to or from Bariloche as well.

**LAN Argentina** (airport tel. 02902/495548, www.lan.com) has an increasing number of flights; travel agencies can arrange seats, but it's better to try online.

**LADE** (Jean Mermoz 160, tel. 02902/491262, ladecalafate@cotecal.com.ar) flies northbound to Comodoro Rivadavia and Buenos Aires, and southbound to Río Gallegos, Río Grande, and Ushuaia.

### BUS

El Calafate's **Terminal de Ómnibus** overlooks the town from its perch at Avenida Roca 1004; for pedestrians, the easiest approach is a staircase from the corner of Avenida Libertador and 9 de Julio. There has been little progress on plans to move it to the former airfield terminal just west of the bridge over the arroyo so that buses would no longer enter town. For long-distance connections to most of the rest of the country, it's necessary to backtrack to Río Gallegos, but there are services to Puerto Natales and Torres del Paine, Chile.

**Taqsa** (tel. 02902/491843, www.taqsa.com.ar) and **Sportman** (tel. 02902/492680) shuttle between El Calafate and the Santa Cruz provincial capital of Río Gallegos (four hours, US$18–20), where there are northbound connections to Buenos Aires and intermediate towns, and southbound connections to Punta Arenas (Chile). These buses will also drop passengers at the Río Gallegos airport.

Three carriers connect El Calafate with El Chaltén (4.5 hours, US$18–20) in the Fitz Roy sector of Parque Nacional Los Glaciares: **Cal Tur** (tel. 02902/491842), **Chaltén Travel** (tel. 02902/491833), and Taqsa. Most services leave 7:30–8 A.M., though there are sometimes afternoon buses 5–6 P.M. Winter services are fewer but normally go at least daily among the three companies.

**RP Transportes** (tel. 02902/494680) now goes to Tres Lagos and Gobernador Gregores (US$30, six hours) Thursday and Sunday at 5 P.M., and is due to begin service to Puerto Madryn.

From September to April, Taqsa now has a daily afternoon service to Perito Moreno (the town, not the glacier) and Los Antiguos (15 hours, US$85), along desolate RN 40, for connections to Chile Chico. While this is more expensive than comparable distances elsewhere, it's also more direct, quicker, and even cheaper than the roundabout routes via coastal RN 3, especially if you factor in accommodations. Taqsa also goes to Bariloche, but uses the longer coastal route before turning inland toward Esquel.

December–April or so, Chaltén Travel also provides alternate-day bus service from El Calafate to Perito Moreno and Los Antiguos (15 hours, US$72); Bariloche-bound passengers have to spend the night in Perito Moreno. Passengers from El Chaltén can board the northbound bus from El Calafate at the junction of RN 40 and RP 23 without having to return to El Calafate. Buses depart Calafate on odd-numbered days and return from Los Antiguos on even-numbered days. **Cal Tur** operates the same route, as far as Perito Moreno and Los Antiguos.

In summer, **Turismo Zaahj/Bus Sur** (tel. 02902/491631, www.turismozaahj.co.cl) and **Cootra** (tel. 02902/491444) alternate daily services to Puerto Natales, Chile (4.5 hours, US$20); occasionally there are direct services to Parque Nacional Torres del Paine. In winter, these services may operate only weekly.

## Getting Around

**Ves Patagonia** (tel. 02902/494355, www.vespatagonia.com.ar) provides door-to-door shuttles to **Aeropuerto Internacional El Calafate** (tel. 02902/491220, clientesfte@londonsupply.net, US$8 pp), 23 kilometers east of town and just north of RP 11. A *remise* costs about US$23 for up to four passengers.

Car-rental agencies include **Hertz** (Av. Libertador 1822, tel. 02902/492525), **Localiza** (Av. Libertador 687, tel. 02902/491398, localizacalafate@hotmail.com), **Nunatak** (Gobernador Gregores 1075, tel. 02902/491987, nunatakrentacar@cotecal.com.ar), **Patagonia Rental** (Av. Libertador 290, tel. 02902/493707, calafate@alamoargentina.com.ar), and **Servicar** (Av. del Libertador 695, tel. 02902/492301, servicar@cotecal.com.ar).

Half a block south of the bus terminal, **HLS** (Buenos Aires 173, tel. 02902/493806) rents bicycles.

# VICINITY OF EL CALAFATE

Tours and transport to the Glaciar Perito Moreno and other nearby attractions are possible with a variety of competent operators. In alphabetical order, they include **Aventura**

**Andina** (Av. del Libertador 761, Local 4, tel. 02902/491726, aventura@cotecal.com.ar), **Cal Tur** (Av. Libertador 1080, tel. 02902/492217, www.caltur.com.ar), **Cordillera del Sol** (25 de Mayo 43, tel. 02902/492822, www.cordilleradelsol.com), **Eurotur** (Av. del Libertador 1025, tel. 02902/492190, www.eurotur.com.ar), **Mundo Austral** (Av. Libertador 1080, tel. 02902/492365, mundoaustral@cotecal.com.ar), and **Rumbo Sur** (9 de Julio 81, Local 2, tel. 02902/492155, www.rumbosur.com.ar).

### El Galpón del Glaciar

Formerly the *casco* (big house) of Estancia Alice, west of El Calafate en route to the Glaciar Perito Moreno, El Galpón del Glaciar (RP 11 Km 22) is open for day tours that may include activities such as birding and horseback riding, as well as exhibitions of sheep herding and shearing, afternoon tea, and a barbecued-lamb dinner. Rates are around US$60 pp plus transportation to and from the farm (US$6 pp); drinks and horseback rides are extra.

El Galpón also offers accommodations (US$130 s or d; US$385–430 s or d for a two-night program, with limited activities included). For details, contact Agroturismo El Galpón (Av. Libertador 761, El Calafate, tel. 02902/491793, www.elgalpondelglaciar.com.ar).

### Eolo Lodge

On the 4,000-hectare Estancia Alice, Eolo is an exclusive mountainside lodge with 17 spacious suites and equally spacious common areas, all with "big sky" views that include either Lago Argentino to the east, the Valle de Anita immediately south, the Brazo Rico to the west, or a combination of them. On a clear day, there are even glimpses across the border to Torres del Paine.

Eolo owes its style to the *cascos* of the great Patagonian wool *estancias,* with corrugated metal siding, antique furnishings, and English tea settings. Contemporary technology such as double-paned windows, though, allows far greater natural light and better views than the poorly insulated buildings of the late 19th and early 20th centuries. The baths are also modern.

Like those houses, though, the suites at Eolo lack modern conveniences such as television and Internet (though there's a satellite TV and DVD lounge, as well as wireless Internet in common areas). There's a sheltered interior patio studded with Technicolor lupines in summer, a small indoor pool, and a restaurant (also open to nonguests, by reservation only).

Open mid-September through April, Eolo (RP 11 Km 23, tel. 2902/492042, www.eolo.com.ar, from US$995 s, US$1,440 d, for a two-night program with full board) also has a Gran Buenos Aires contact (Laprida 3278, Oficina 39, San Isidro, tel. 011/4700-0705). Eolo helps arrange excursions to the Perito Moreno Glacier and other nearby sights but does not organize them itself.

### Hostería Alta Vista

Once a separate *estancia,* since absorbed by adjacent Estancia Anita, Hostería Alta Vista (RP 15 Km 35, tel./fax 02902/499902, www.hosteriaaltavista.com.ar, US$650 s, US$862 d) is an outpost of the Braun-Menéndez dynasty that dominated the Patagonian wool industry of Chile and Argentina. As such, its seven-room *casco* is the place to be spoiled; surrounded by luxuriant gardens in a sheltered location at the foot of 1,294-meter Cerro Freile, it has a guests-only bar-restaurant, a separate *quincho* for lamb *asados,* and flawless service from its English-speaking staff.

Alta Vista also offers excursions that include horseback riding in the nearby hills, which offer a small lagoon full of wild fowl with condors soaring above, and distant views of the Glaciar Perito Moreno. Two-night packages that include excursions to the glacier and other more remote sights are slightly more expensive.

Accommodations are all-inclusive except for incidentals such as telephone charges and laundry. Alta Vista also offers activities-oriented packages at rather higher prices.

## PARQUE NACIONAL LOS GLACIARES AND VICINITY

On the eastern Andean slopes, Parque Nacional Los Glaciares comprises over 750,000 hectares, where slowly flowing ice gives birth to clear frigid rivers and vast lakes, interspersed with Magellanic forests, along the Chilean border west and north of El Calafate. A UNESCO World Heritage Site, it's famous for the Glaciar Perito Moreno (Perito Moreno Glacier), which draws thousands of sedentary visitors for day trips but also pulls in scientists absorbed in glaciology and climate studies. The northern sector—a 3.5-hour bus trip from El Calafate—attracts those seeking to spend several days in vigorous exercise, for either trekking or the far more demanding and dangerous technical climbing.

## Geography and Climate

As the Pleistocene ended and the Campo de Hielo Sur receded, it left behind the two huge glacial troughs that are now Lago Argentino and, to the north, the roughly parallel Lago Viedma. While these lakes lie only about 250 meters above sea level, the Andean summits along the border rise to 3,375 meters on Cerro Fitz Roy and nearly as high on pinnacles such as 3,102-meter Cerro Torre, which match Chile's Torres del Paine for sheer majesty.

Most of these bodies of water lie beyond park boundaries, but the eastern Andean slopes still contain their remnants, some of the world's most impressive, and accessible, glaciers. Thirteen major glaciers flow toward the Argentine side, including the benchmark Glaciar Perito Moreno; ice covers 30 percent of the park's surface.

Despite its accumulated snow and ice, the Argentine side is drier than the Chilean, receiving only about 400 millimeters of precipitation on the eastern steppe, rising to about 900 millimeters at its forested western elevations. The warmest month is February, with an average maximum temperature of 22°C and a minimum of 9°C; the coolest is August, when the maximum averages only 5°C and the minimum is -1°C. As elsewhere in Patagonia, it gets ferocious winds, strongest in spring and summer.

## Flora and Fauna

Where rainfall is insufficient to support anything other than *coirón* bunch grasses and thorny shrubs such as the *calafate (Berberis buxifolia)* that gave the nearby town its name, the guanaco grazes the Patagonian steppe. Foxes and Patagonian skunks are also conspicuous, the flightless rhea or *ñandú* scampers across the open country, the *bandurria* (buff-necked ibis, with its conspicuous curved beak) stalks invertebrates, and flocks of upland geese browse the swampy lakeshores. The Andean condor soars above the plains and even the highest peaks, occasionally landing to feast on carrion.

In the forests, the predominant tree species are the southern beeches *lenga* and the *coigüe,* also known here as *guindo.* The puma still prowls the forest, while the huemul and perhaps the pudu survive near Lago Viedma. Squawking flocks of austral parakeets flit among the trees, while the Patagonian woodpecker pounds on their trunks. Perching calmly, awaiting nightfall, the austral pygmy owl is a common late-afternoon sight.

Along the lakeshores and riverbanks, aquatic birds such as coots and ducks are abundant. The most picturesque is the Patagonian torrent duck, which dives for prey in the rushing creeks.

## Sights and Recreation

In general, the park's southerly sector, west of El Calafate, gets day visitors for passive sightseeing. The northerly sector—a 3.5-hour bus trip from El Calafate—attracts hikers and mountaineers. Gregory Crouch's *Enduring Patagonia* (New York: Random House, 2001) details one mountaineer's experiences on Cerro Fitz Roy and Cerro Torre.

Backpackers should note that no campfires are permitted within the park—carrying a camp stove is obligatory for cooking.

### GLACIAR PERITO MORENO

Where a low Andean pass lets Pacific weather systems cross the cordillera, countless storms have deposited immeasurable meters of snow that, over millennia, have compressed into the Perito Moreno Glacier, the groaning, rasping river of ice that's one of the continent's greatest sights and sounds. Fifteen times during the

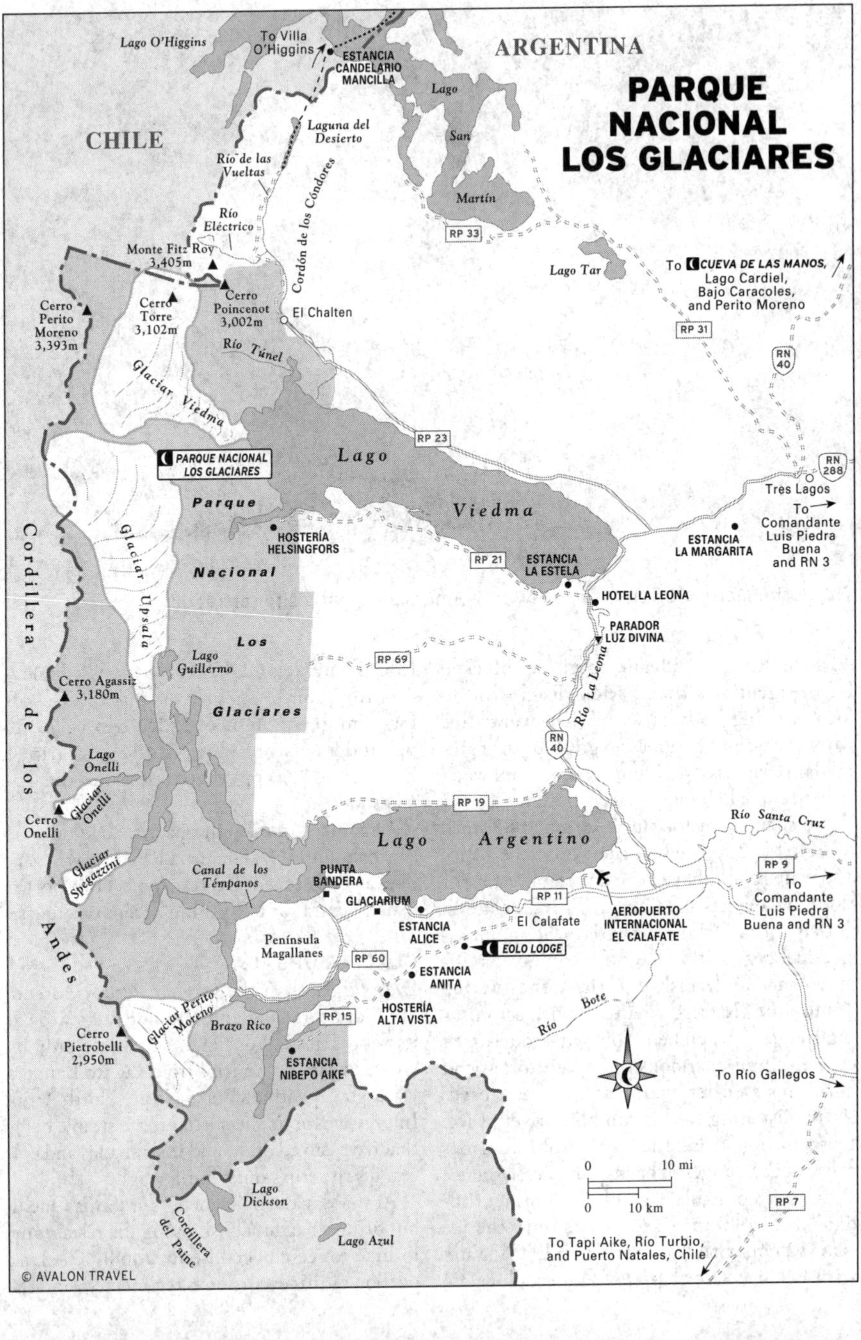


S. ARGENTINE PATAGONIA

© ELNAVEGANTE/123RF

The Perito Moreno Glacier is one of South America's great visitor attractions.

20th century, the advancing glacier blocked Lago Argentino's **Brazo Rico** (Rico Arm) to form a rising body of water that eventually, when the weight became too great for the natural dam, triggered an eruption of ice and water toward the lake's main glacial trough.

No such event took place from 1988 until March 14, 2004, when the avalanche of ice and water could have been a metaphor for the flood of tourists that invaded El Calafate in anticipation. On any given day, though, massive icebergs still calve off the glacier's 60-meter face and crash into the **Canal de los Témpanos** (Iceberg Channel) with astonishing frequency. Perched on newly modernized catwalks and overlooks, many visitors spend entire days either gazing at or, eyes closed, simply listening to this rumbling river of ice. Descending to lake level is prohibited because of the danger of backwash and flying ice chunks; it's possible, though, to contract full-day "minitrekking" excursions onto the ice (US$125 pp with transport from El Calafate) with **Hielo y Aventura** (Av. Libertador 935, El Calafate, tel. 02902/491053, www.hieloyaventura.com). Hielo y Aventura also offers a more strenuous Big Ice trip (US$150 pp) and a passive Safari Náutico boat trip (1 hour, US$12.50 pp) that approaches the glacier's face.

Organized tours to the glacier, 80 kilometers southwest of El Calafate via RP 11, leave every day, as does scheduled transport; transport is usually extra for everything except bus tours.

### GLACIAR UPSALA

Even larger than the Glaciar Perito Moreno, 50 kilometers long and 10 kilometers wide at its foot, Upsala Glacier is accessible only by crowded catamaran trips from Puerto Bandera via Lago Argentino's Brazo Norte (North Arm). Impressive for its sheer extent, the sizable bergs that have calved off it, and their shapes and colors, it's the trip's outstanding sight.

At midday the boat anchors at Bahía Onelli, but bring a bag lunch (skipping the restaurant) to hike to ice-clogged **Lago Onelli.** The land portion of this excursion is regimented, and the

## HOSTERÍA HELSINGFORS

In an incomparably dramatic setting at the base of glacier-covered mountains, on Lago Viedma's secluded south shore, Helsingfors was one of southwestern Santa Cruz's earliest *estancias* (ranches), and also one of the first to open its gates to tourists. Though its services, elevated prices, and isolation imply exclusivity, it's surprisingly unpretentious – the comfortable *casco* (big house) has an inviting reception area, a cozy sitting room with beamed ceilings, a large brick fireplace, a bar, and a dining room with an Italian-born chef.

One of Helsingfors's recreational highlights is a 2.5-hour hike through meadows and *lenga* forest to Laguna Azul, a cirque lake beneath a hanging glacier. Despite the name, it's more turquoise than blue. There is also a rigid inflatable Zodiac for excursions to Glaciar Viedma, wind and weather permitting.

Legally, Helsingfors may not even be an *estancia,* as the founders apparently never registered their title and the land on which it sits probably belongs to Parque Nacional Los Glaciares. Laguna Azul and other surrounding areas certainly are part of the national park, and Helsingfors's owners are concerned that Calafate operators could bring an influx of day hikers that could impact a nearly pristine part of the park and, of course, reduce its appeal to affluent overnighters.

Most visitors spend two or three nights at Helsingfors, which is 179 kilometers from El Calafate via eastbound RP 11, northbound RN 40, and westbound RP 21. It has nine double rooms, some of them detached from the *casco.* Open mid-October–mid-April, **Hostería Helsingfors** (San Martín 516, Río Gallegos, tel. 02966/420719; Av. Córdoba 827, 11° A, C1054AAH Buenos Aires, tel. 011/4315-1222, www.helsingfors.com.ar, US$260–340 s, US$480–550 d) includes full board, transportation to and from El Calafate, and all excursions. Children under age eight pay half. The higher rates correspond to peak season (Dec. 21–Mar. 23).

Tuesday, Thursday, and Sunday, Helsingfors provides its own transfers to and from El Calafate for its overnight guests.



guide-suggested pace—30 minutes from dock to lakeshore—is suitable for those on crutches. Smoking is prohibited on the forest trail.

Visitors should realize that this is a mass-tourism excursion that may frustrate hikers accustomed to freedom of the hills. If you take it, choose the biggest available ship, which offers the most deck space to see the Spegazzini and Upsala Glaciers. On board, the freshest air is within the cabin of the *ALM,* whose seats are cramped but where smoking is prohibited; on deck, desperate smokers congregate even in freezing rain. Reasonably priced cakes, sandwiches, coffee, tea, and hot chocolate are available on board.

Puerto Bandera is 45 kilometers west of Calafate via RP 11 and RP 8. For information and reservations, contact concessionaire **Fernández Campbell** (Av. Libertador 867, El Calafate, tel. 02902/491155 or 02902/491428, www.fernandezcampbell.com.ar). The full-day trip costs about US$90 per person; this now includes transfers to Puerto Bandera but not the US$25 park fee for non-Argentines.

On its small cruiser *Leal,* **Cruceros Marpatag** (9 de Julio 57, Local 10, El Calafate, tel. 02902/492118, www.crucerosmarpatag.com) offers a full-day excursion, with a six-course gourmet lunch (wine included), to the Spegazzini and Upsala glacier fields (US$245 pp, including transfers and park admission). In the near future, the triple-decked, 22-cabin catamaran *Santa Cruz* is due to begin three-day, two-night cruises to Upsala and Spegazzini, with a final day's lunch facing the Perito Moreno Glacier.

### LAGO ROCA

Also known as La Jerónima, the park's little-visited southwesterly sector along Lago Roca's Brazo Sur (South Arm) offers camping and cross-country hiking—there are no formal trails, only routes such as the one from the campground to the summit of **Cerro Cristal,** 55 kilometers from El Calafate. The landscape's most striking feature is the high shoreline—dry from the days when the lake backs up behind the advancing Glaciar Perito Moreno. Unlike other sectors, Lago Roca charges no admission fee.

### SECTOR FITZ ROY

In the park's most northerly sector, the Fitz Roy range has sheer spires to match Torres del Paine, but even if you're not a top technical climber, trails from the village of El Chaltén to the base of summits such as **Cerro Fitz Roy** and **Cerro Torre** make for exhilarating hikes. It's even possible to traverse the southern Patagonian ice fields, but visitors seeking a sedate outdoor experience will find a handful of former sheep *estancias,* onetime Patagonian wool producers that have reinvented themselves as tourist accommodations.

From a signposted trailhead at El Chaltén's north end, just south of the former Camping Madsen, the **Sendero Laguna Torre** is an 11-kilometer track gaining about 200 meters in elevation as it winds through southern beech forests to the climbers' base camp for Cerro Torre; figure 3–3.5 hours. At the lake, in clear weather, there are extraordinary views of Cerro Torre's 3,102-meter summit, crowned by the so-called ice-and-snow "mushroom" that technical climbers must surmount. While Italian Cesare Maestri claimed that he and Austrian Toni Egger reached the summit in 1959 (Egger died in an avalanche, taking the expedition's camera with him), Italian Casimiro Ferrari made the first undisputed ascent in 1974.

From the Madsen pack station, the more demanding **Sendero Río Blanco** trail rises steeply at the outset before leveling out through boggy beech forest and continuing to the Fitz Roy base camp, climbing about 350 meters in 10 kilometers. About midway to Río Blanco, a signed lateral leads south to **Laguna Capri,** which has backcountry campsites.

From Río Blanco, a vertiginous zigzag trail ascends 400 meters in just 2.5 kilometers to

© JAVERMAN JAVARMAN/123RF

the Fitz Roy range

S. ARGENTINE PATAGONIA

**Laguna de los Tres,** a glacial tarn whose name commemorates three members of the French expedition—René Ferlet, Lionel Terray, and Guido Magnone—who summited Fitz Roy in 1952. Truly a top-of-the-world experience, Laguna de los Tres offers some of Patagonia's finest Andean panoramas.

From the Río Blanco campground (reserved for climbers), a northbound trail follows the river's west bank north to **Laguna Piedras Blancas,** whose namesake glacier continually calves small icebergs. The trail continues north to the Río Eléctrico, beyond the park boundaries, where a westbound trail climbs the river to Piedra del Fraile and a possible circuit of the Campo de Hielo Sur, only for experienced snow-and-ice trekkers. At the Río Eléctrico, it's also possible to rejoin the road from El Chaltén to Lago del Desierto.

From the park visitors center, a short ascent (about 45 minutes) leads to the **Mirador de los Cóndores,** for good views of El Chaltén and the confluence of the Río de las Vueltas and the Río Fitz Roy.

From the same trailhead, the hike to **Loma del Pliegue Tumbado** is a 500-meter elevation gain that yields some of the area's best views—weather permitting, the panorama takes in Fitz Roy, Cerro Torre, Cerro Solo, Glaciar Torre, and Lago Torre, but the wind at the overlook can be overpowering. Four hours is about right for an average hiker, but the truly fit can do it three; the descent takes about 2.5 hours.

### GLACIAR VIEDMA

From Lago Viedma's north shore, south of El Chaltén, the park's best lake excursion is the *Viedma Discovery*'s full-day catamaran voyage to Viedma Glacier, which includes an ice-climbing component.

Sailing from Bahía Túnel, the vessel rounds the ironically named **Cabo de Hornos** (Cape Horn) to enter an iceberg-cluttered area before anchoring in a rocky cove. After disembarking, visitors hike to an overlook (the glacier is Argentina's largest, though its lakeside face is small) with additional views of 2,677-meter Cerro Huemul. Those who want to can strap on crampons and continue onto the glacier for about 2.5 hours (even some sedentary city dwellers do so).

The bilingual guides know glaciology and provide more personalized service than the Fernández Campbell excursion from Puerto Bandera. While the price here does not include lunch, they do provide an aperitif on the glacial rocks.

Departure time from El Chaltén is 8:30 A.M., while the boat sails from Bahía Túnel at 9 A.M.; the cost is US$110 per person including transportation from El Chaltén. For details, contact **Patagonia Aventura** (Güemes s/n, tel. 02962/493110, El Chaltén, www.patagonia-aventura.com).

### LAGO DEL DESIERTO AND VICINITY

Beyond the park borders, 37 kilometers north of El Chaltén, Lago del Desierto is a scenic end-of-the-road destination with hiking trails, boat excursions, and even a challenging border crossing to the Chilean settlement of Villa O'Higgins.

From the lake's south end, a short trail winds west through dense southern beech forest to a vista point and the hanging glacier at **Laguna Huemul;** the Estancia Lago del Desierto campground collects a US$4.50 admission charge. A longer route follows the eastern shore to the border, a 20-kilometer trek over gentle terrain. Every year several hundred cyclists and hikers cross the Argentine-Chilean border in a zone that was once so contentious that a Chilean Carabinero even lost his life in a firefight with Argentine border guards in 1965. Despite objections by a handful of Chilean nationalists, the matter is resolved, the border is peaceable, and determined hikers or even mountain bikers can readily reach Villa O'Higgins.

About midway to to Lago del Desierto, **Estancia Los Huemules** (Km 17, Buenos Aires tel. 011/4765-8085, www.loshuemules.com) is a hybrid real estate development and nature reserve—open to the public, more than 95 percent of its 5,786 hectares is devoted to forest and high country preservation. Four of five planned trails, up to four or five hours one-way, are open to the public; within a year or two, there will be rustic shelters for overnighters. The professionally arranged visitor center is accessible at no charge; trail usage, though, costs US$10 per person per day. Hours are 9 A.M.–6 P.M. daily.

From El Chaltén, **Transporte Las Lengas** (Viedma 95, tel. 02962/493023, laslengaselchalten@yahoo.com.ar) minibuses go to El Pilar (US$10 pp), Río Eléctrico (US$13), and Lago del Desierto (US$25 one-way or round-trip) at 8:30 A.M. and 3 P.M. daily, returning at 2:30 and 8:30 P.M. Hitching is feasible, but vehicles are few and often full. At the lake itself, the 40-passenger *Huemul* carries passengers to the north end and back (US$25 pp).



## Accommodations and Food

Since most Glaciar Perito Moreno visitors stay at El Calafate, the park's southern sector has only limited accommodations, but they're increasingly abundant in and around El Chaltén in the Fitz Roy sector.

Hikers should note that campfires are prohibited—camp stoves are obligatory for cooking. Rangers assert that park water is potable throughout.

### GLACIAR PERITO MORENO

The only accommodations near the glacier, multi-day packages with full board and excursions are the rule at the lavish **Hostería Los Notros** (tel. 02902/499510, daily rates start at US$457 s, US$550 d). It rivals Torres del Paine's Hotel Salto Chico in the "room with a view" competition; all 32 rooms face the ice. For details, contact Hostería Los Notros (Arenales 1457, 7th floor, Buenos Aires, tel. 011/4814-3934, www.losnotros.com).

Also at the glacier, **Nativos de la Patagonia** operates both a snack bar (sandwiches for US$6–8, plus coffee and desserts) and a separate restaurant with set meals (around US$20); there's also an à la carte menu. These facilities are undergoing expansion that will include a sheltered picnic area for those who bring their own food.

### LAGO ROCA

La Jerónima's **Camping Lago Roca** (tel. 02902/499500, lagoroca@yahoo.com.ar, US$8 pp) also has four-bed dorm-style cabañas (US$37 d, US$58 quadruple) with exterior baths. Hot showers are available, and its *confitería* serves decent meals.

At the terminus of RP 15, 56 kilometers southwest of El Calafate, the *casco* at Croatian-founded **Estancia Nibepo Aike** (El Calafate tel./fax 02966/492797, www.nibepoaike.com.ar, US$135 pp half board, US$180 pp with full board and activities) preserves its original rustic style but is now an 11-room guesthouse with contemporary conveniences. Open October–April, it also has a newer **Quincho Don Juan** where day-trippers can lunch or dine; overnight guests can choose to dine there or in the main house's dining room. "Day in the country" excursions (US$58 pp) include grilled lamb and dessert for either lunch or dinner (plus US$17 pp for transportation).

### LAGO DEL DESIERTO

At the south end of the lake, **Camping Estancia Lago del Desierto** (US$7.50 pp) offers wooded sites with fire pits and toilets with hot showers.

## Information

At the Río Mitre entrance, the main Glaciar Perito Moreno approach, the Administración de Parques Nacionales (APN) collects a US$25 admission fee (payable in pesos only) from nonresidents of Argentina. At present, the Lago Roca and El Chaltén sectors continue to be fee-free.

At the southern approach to El Chaltén, the **APN** (tel. 02962/493004, 9 A.M.–5 P.M. daily, occasionally until 8 P.M.) has turned a former *hostería* into a visitors center. In addition to natural history exhibits, it provides a decent trail map (scale 1:75,000) and also issues climbing permits (free).

Hikers may want to consult Tim Burford's *Chile and Argentina: The Bradt Trekking Guide* (Chalfont St. Peter, United Kingdom: Bradt Travel Guides, 2001) or Carolyn

McCarthy's *Trekking in the Patagonian Andes* (Melbourne: Lonely Planet, 2009). The former has thorough text but needs an update; the latter has better maps. There is also Miguel A. Alonso's locally available, bilingual *Trekking en Chaltén y Lago del Desierto* (Buenos Aires: Los Glaciares, 2003), which covers numerous hikes in the vicinity. Alonso has also written *Lago Argentino & Glaciar Perito Moreno Handbook* (Buenos Aires: Zagier & Urruty, 2004), a more general guide that's available in English, Italian, German, and French.

For an informed guide who leads backcountry trips in the El Chaltén sector, contact retired ranger **Adrián Falcone** (tel. 02962/493064, aefalcone@gmail.com), who speaks English and even a smattering of Japanese.

### Getting There and Around

The Glaciar Perito Moreno is about 80 kilometers west of El Calafate by RP 11, which is now completely paved; the trip takes slightly over an hour. Both **Cal Tur** (tel. 02902/491842) and **Taqsa** (tel. 02902/491843, www.taqsa.com.ar) at El Calafate's bus terminal have scheduled services at 9 A.M. daily (US$25 round-trip), returning in the afternoon.

In addition to regularly scheduled services, guided bus tours are frequent, but both are less frequent in winter. Competent operators include **Aventura Andina** (Av. del Libertador 761, Local 4, tel. 02902/491726, andina@cotecal.com.ar), **Cal Tur** (Av. Libertador 1080, tel. 02902/492217, www.caltur.com.ar), **Cordillera del Sol** (25 de Mayo 43, tel. 02902/492822, www.cordilleradelsol.com), **Eurotur** (Av. del Libertador 1025, tel. 02902/492190, www.eurotur.com.ar), **Mundo Austral** (Av. Libertador 1114, tel. 02902/492365, mundoaustral@cotecal.com.ar), and **Rumbo Sur** (9 de Julio 81, Local 2, tel. 02902/492155, www.rumbosur.com.ar).

El Calafate's **Albergue del Glaciar** runs its own guided minivan excursions (US$50 pp), leaving about 8:30 A.M. and returning about 5 P.M. These include more hiking and a navigation for a waterside view of the lake.

## EL CHALTÉN

Billing itself as "Capital Nacional del Trekking," Argentina's national trekking capital, El Chaltén has become popular for easy access to Fitz Roy range trailheads in Parque Nacional Los Glaciares. Many trails are suitable for overnight backpacking, but access is so easy that day hikers can cover nearly as much ground.

Exposed to fierce westerly winds and to potential floods from the Río de las Vueltas, El Chaltén has somehow managed to achieve a sense of permanence in what, just a few years back, seemed a bleak outpost of government offices aimed to uphold Argentina's presence in a disputed border zone (the last of many Chilean-Argentine territorial quarrels, over Lago del Desierto to the north, was finalized a few years ago). With the highway from the RN 40 junction recently paved, it's growing so rapidly that some fear it will become the next El Calafate, where real estate development (and speculation) are rampant.

With the highway completely paved, travel time from El Calafate has fallen to about three hours. Meanwhile, the town is enjoying improvements as the streets are paved to keep down the dust, and a new bus terminal is one of many new and improved services.

El Chaltén (population about 100) is 220 kilometers northwest of El Calafate via eastbound RP 11 to the Río Bote junction, northbound RN 40, and westbound RP 23 along Lago Viedma's north shore. It's worth mentioning that, while street addresses are increasingly common, locals pay little attention to them.

### Entertainment and Events

Immediately behind Albergue Rancho Grande, **La Tanguería** (Lionel Terray 330) brings the urban sensibility of Buenos Aires to fast-growing Chaltén, in tango shows and lessons.

El Chaltén celebrates several events, including October 12's **Aniversario de El Chaltén,** marking its formal founding in 1985; November 10's **Día de la Tradición,** celebrating the gaucho heritage; and early February's weeklong **Fiesta Nacional del Trekking.**

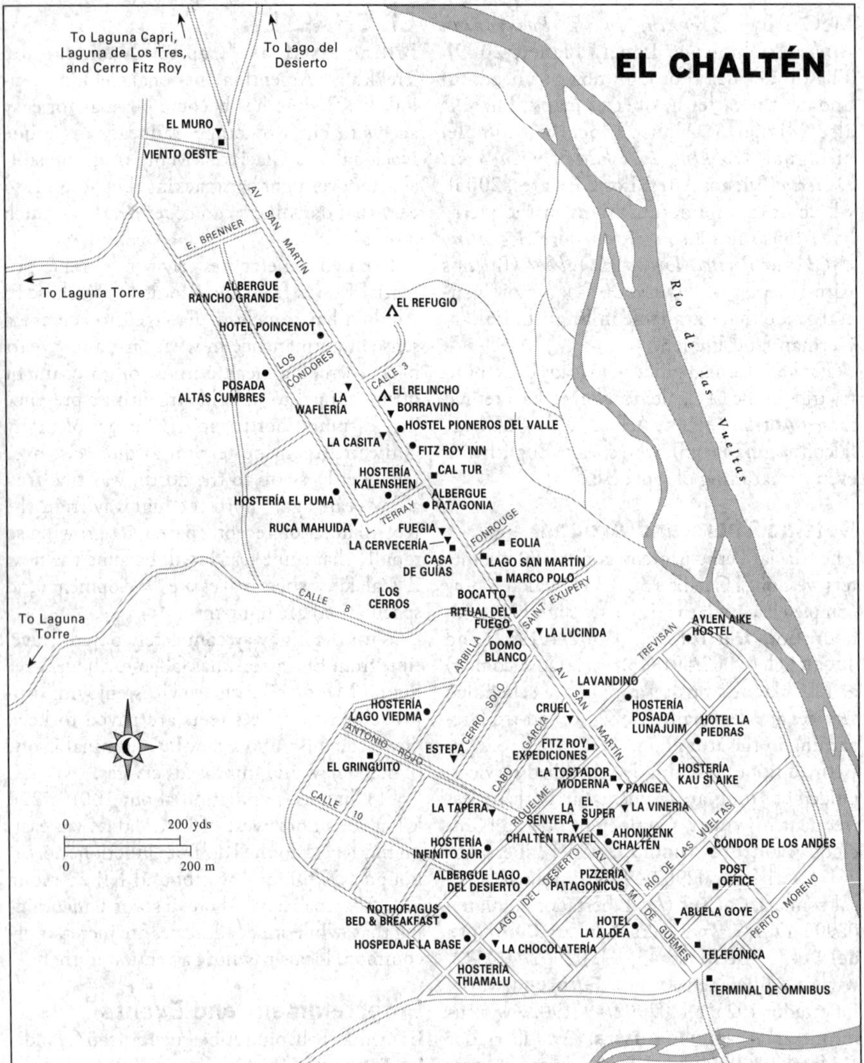


S. ARGENTINE PATAGONIA

## Shopping

**Marco Polo** (San Martín 249, tel. 02962/493122) sells books, maps, and CDs, with English-language titles including guidebooks and novels.

## Recreation

There are extensive hiking and climbing opportunities in nearby Parque Nacional Los Glaciares.

From here, it's possible to arrange a one-day trek and ice climb on Glaciar Torre (US$95 pp) with **Fitz Roy Expediciones** (Av. San Martín 56, tel. 02962/493178, www.fitzroyexpediciones.com.ar), which also offers lengthier guided hikes—nine-day expeditions, really—on the Campo de Hielo Sur, the Southern Continental Ice Field. **Oscar Pandolfi Expediciones** (Calle 2 No. 23, tel. 02962/493043, www.caminoabierto.com) and **Alta Montaña** (Lionel Terray 55, tel. 02962/493018, altamont@infovia.com.ar) are also guides.

**NYCA Adventure** (Cabo García 122, tel. 02962/493185, www.nyca.com.ar) offers half-day excursions that include activities such as climbing, hiking, mountain biking, rafting, and rappelling. **Lago San Martín** (Av. San Martín 275, tel. 02962/493045) arranges excursions to and from Lago San Martín, across the mountains to the northeast, with *estancia* accommodations. The **Casa de Guías** (Av. San Martín 310, tel. 02962/493118, www.casadeguias.com.ar) is another possibility.

At the north end of town, **Viento Oeste** (San Martín 898, tel. 02962/493200, vientooeste@infovia.com.ar) rents and sells climbing, camping, and wet-weather gear, as does **La Brecha** (Costanera Sur 246, tel. 02962/493151). **Eolia** (Pasaje Fonrouge 45, tel. 02962/493066, www.patagoniamagica.com) also rents gear and provides guide service.

## Accommodations

El Chaltén has a reasonable selection of accommodations, some of them very good, but high summer demand makes reservations advisable. Most places close in winter, but there's usually something available. Wireless Internet is almost universal, but often slow because of heavy demand on the town's limited bandwidth.

### US$10-25

Commercial campgrounds, which offer hot showers and shelter for cooking, include **Camping El Refugio** (San Martín s/n, tel. 02962/493221, US$7.50 pp) and **Camping El Relincho** (San Martín 505, tel. 02962/493007, elrelincho@cotecal.com.ar, US$7.50 pp). There are other campgrounds along the road to Lago del Desierto.

At the south end of town, **Ahonikenk Chaltén** (Güemes 23, tel. 02962/493070, ahonikenkchalten23@yahoo.com.ar, US$10 pp dorm, US$40 d) is the cheapest of hostel accommodations, though the dorms-only **Albergue Lago del Desierto** (Lago del Desierto 137, tel. 02962/493245, hosteldellago_elchalten@yahoo.com.ar, US$10 pp dorm) is about the same.

### US$25-50

Like El Calafate, El Chaltén has little that's exclusive to this range, but several hostels also offer private rooms that are excellent values for around the same price or a little more.

Having more than doubled its capacity by adding a second floor, the HI affiliate **Albergue Rancho Grande** (San Martín 724, tel./fax 02962/493005, www.ranchograndehostel.com, US$15 pp dorm, US$63 s or d) has drawn some flak for failing to insulate the between-floors gap for sound. It does offer B&B packages with transportation from El Calafate; for reservations, contact Chaltén Travel (Av. Libertador 1174, El Calafate, tel. 02902/492212, www.chaltentravel.com).

Open all year except June, the HI affiliate **Albergue Patagonia** (San Martín 392, tel. 02962/493019, www.elchalten.com/patagonia, US$15 pp dorm, US$45 s or d, US$60–70 s or d) provides utilitarian dorms—four beds per room—but also has shared-bath doubles and a separate wing of more spacious and comfortable doubles and twins with private baths; the latter include continental breakfast. On the

S. ARGENTINE PATAGONIA

hostel side, it also provides cooking facilities, laundry service, a small book exchange, and bike rentals, and organizes excursions. Its main drawback is that the hostel toilet and shower facilities, while good enough, are arguably too few. English and Dutch are spoken.

Owned and operated by Cal Tur, **Hostel Pioneros del Valle** (San Martín 451, tel. 02962/493298, US$15 pp) is a dorms-only facility whose spacious common areas partially compensate for cramped sleeping quarters. **Aylen Aike Hostel** (Trevisan 125, tel. 02962/493317, aylen-aike@hotmail.com, US$18 pp) is a dorms-only hostel that's made good first impressions.

**Cóndor de los Andes** (Av. Río de las Vueltas and Halvorsen, tel. 02962/493101, www.condordelosandes.com, US$17–20 pp dorm, US$70 d) has four- and six-bed dorms, each with its own bath, kitchen facilities, and spacious common areas with exceptional views. It has also added private rooms.



### US$50-100

Family-run **Hospedaje La Base** (Lago del Desierto 97, tel./fax 02962/493031, labase@elchaltenpatagonia.com.ar, US$52 s or d) has two firm beds per room, which are two-bedroom cabañas that share a kitchen but have private baths. Like many other places, it closes June–November.

Cozy, friendly ☾ **Nothofagus Bed & Breakfast** (Calle 10 No. 40, tel. 02962/493087, www.nothofagusbb.com.ar, US$42–63 s, US$45–65 d, with breakfast) has seven rooms in a handsome house with convivial common areas; rates vary according to whether the room has a shared or private bath.

Expanded **Posada Altas Cumbres** (Lionel Terray 342, tel. 02962/493060, www.altascumbreschalten.com.ar, US$63 s, US$70 d) has a dozen spacious rooms and friendly management, but many of the rooms are underfurnished, and those closest to the reception area have thin walls (though it doesn't draw a noisy crowd).

Friendly **Hostería Thiamalu** (Lago del Desierto 99, tel. 02962/493736, www.thiamalu.com.ar, US$65 s, US$75 d, with breakfast) isn't up to the level of the Nothofagus, though all its rooms do have private baths.

Open October–March, **Hostería Lago Viedma** (Arbilla 71, tel. 02962/493089, hosterialagoviedma@hotmail.com, US$45–50 s, US$70–75 d with breakfast) has small but well-designed rooms with private baths. **Hotel Cumbres Nevadas** (Cerro Solo 95, tel. 02962/493160, www.elchalten.com/cumbresnevadas, US$75 s or d) is an excellent value at this price.

New in late 2008, ☾ **Hostería Infinito Sur** (Riquelme 208, tel. 02962/493325, www.infinitosurelchalten.com, US$83 s, US$90 d) is a boutique-style hotel with just nine rooms in a building of quarried stone and rough-hewn wood. Only the bar/breakfast room, though, enjoys views of Fitz Roy. Rates fall by about 20–25 percent outside January–February.

Combining a traditional Patagonian style with contemporary comforts in its standard rooms, **Hostería Kau Si Aike** (Lago del Desierto 365, tel. 02962/493279, www.elchalten.com/kausiaike, US$90 s or d) also has split-level apartments suitable for 4–5 guests (US$150–175).

In a new building with clean modern lines, **Hotel Poincenot** (San Martín 688, tel. 02962/493252, www.hotelpoincenot.com, US$93 s or d) has cozy midsize rooms, some with wheelchair access. Its bar has a sandwich menu and a good wine selection, but no elaborate meals.

Rates at the venerable (by Chaltén standards) **Fitz Roy Inn** (San Martín 545, tel. 02962/493062, www.hosteriafitzroyinn.com.ar, US$96 s or d) drop considerably outside the November–March high season; it also has multi-day packages with half or full board, but the full-board option would preclude eating at other good places.

### US$100-200

At the southern edge of town, the 25-room **Hotel La Aldea** (Av. Güemes 95, tel. 02962/493040, www.hotellaaldea.com.ar, US$92 s, US$103 d with breakfast) is more a motel-style complex, with the rooms separate from a two-story reception area that includes a restaurant and bar.

**Hostería Kalenshen** (Lionel Terray 30, tel. 02962/493108, www.kalenshen.com, US$100 s, US$110 d, with breakfast) has 17 rooms with handmade furniture and another six cabañas (US$225, for up to four people). Unusually for this town, it has a heated swimming pool.

Rates have risen at expanded, upgraded **Hotel Las Piedras** (Lago del Desierto 423, tel./fax 02962/493015, www.elchalten.com/lacasadepiedra, US$112–290 s, US$120–330 d), which provides large and comfy but tackily decorated rooms with private baths. It has well-tended grounds and is quiet, since the nearby power plant has a noise-reducing structure.

With improved landscaping, **Hostería Posada Lunajuim** (Trevisan 45, tel. 02962/493047, www.posadalunajuim.com.ar, US$121 s, US$148 d) continues to make a good impression with appealing common areas (including a bar/restaurant) and rooms with private baths, central heating, and breakfast.

North of town, in an out-of-the-way location bordering the Lago del Desierto road, **Hostería El Pilar** (RP 23 s/n, tel./fax 02962/493002, Buenos Aires tel. 011/5031-0755, www.hosteriaelpilar.com.ar, US$137 s, US$152 d with breakfast) has the classic style of a Patagonian *casco,* but it's really a recent construction (1996). Reservations are essential for this cozy and increasingly popular place, open October–April, but it's possible to dine in the restaurant without being a guest, although reservations are advisable. Shuttle transportation from El Chaltén is free for guests.

The 12-room **Hostería El Puma** (Lionel Terray 212, tel. 02962/493095, www.hosteriaelpuma.com.ar, US$143 s, US$176 d) and its Terray restaurant make another impressive addition to Chaltén's accommodations scene. Prices with half board are an additional US$30 per person.

### OVER US$200

Atop a hillock with panoramic views of the Río de la Vueltas, under the same ownership as Hostería Los Notros at Glaciar Perito Moreno, **Los Cerros** (San Martín 260, tel. 02962/493182, Buenos Aires tel. 011/4814-3934, www.loscerrosdelchalten.com, US$278–408 s, US$329–494 d) works mainly with multi-day packages but takes other guests on a space-available basis. Spacious and luminous, with baths all featuring whirlpool tubs, the rooms have massive picture windows; the common areas, many of them decorated with historic maps, have soaring cathedral ceilings that flood them with natural light.

## Food

Hikers and climbers stock up on supplies at **El Super** (Lago del Desierto 248), **El Gringuito** (Cerro Solo 108), or **La Tostadora Moderna** (Av. San Martín 36). For its size, though, El Chaltén offers a fine and improving restaurant selection.

**La Chocolatería Josh Aike** (Lago del Desierto 105, tel. 02962/493109, roughly 10 A.M.–7 P.M. daily) is more than it sounds—the desserts are good enough, but the breakfasts and pizzas are also excellent, and the Bailey's-spiked hot chocolate is comforting on a cold night. **La Senyera del Torre** (Lago del Desierto 240, tel. 02962/493063, breakfast, lunch, and dinner daily) prepares Argentine comfort food such as the *locro* (a hearty stew) and excellent desserts.

In bright new quarters, **Domo Blanco** (San Martín 164) serves exceptional ice cream, with local ingredients such as raspberries and strawberries.

**Bocatto** (Av. San Martín 229, Local 3, tel. 02962/493214, 11 A.M.–11 P.M. daily) makes the best takeaway empanadas, in several varieties, all a little larger than the Argentine standard. **Cruel** (San Martín 84, tel. 02962/493167, lunch and dinner daily) is best for a quick sandwich.

Chaltén's first wine bar, **La Vinería** (Lago del Desierto 265, tel. 02962/493301, 2–10 P.M. daily) also serves empanadas, sandwiches, and platters of cheeses, cold cuts, and smoked Patagonian meats—not to mention great cycling advice (in English, from a couple who cycled from Ushuaia to Alaska and lived several years in Anchorage). New in 2011, **La Lucinda** (San Martín 175, tel. 02962/493202, 7 A.M.–1 A.M. daily) is an art-themed café that displays photographs and works by local talent.

**La Tapera** (Antonio Rojo 76, tel. 02962/493138, lunch and dinner daily) is an exceptionally friendly restaurant/tapas bar with a small but excellent menu of fixed-price dinners (US$15) that include soup and a choice of four entrées—one of the best values in town.

Informal but pleasant and subdued, with only a few small tables and one long one flanked by equally long benches, **La Waflería** (San Martín 640, tel. 02962/493093, lunch and dinner daily) prepares savory waffles such as roast lamb (US$10), but most of the rest are suitable for desserts.

Focused on pizza and pastas (US$9–15), **Borravino** (San Martín 520, tel. 02962/493353, lunch and dinner daily) also prepares meats like lamb in a beer sauce with rosemary-tinged potatoes (US$17). There's plenty of room between tables, and it's not noisy, but the service and kitchen can be slow even when the crowd is small.

**La Cervecería** (San Martín 320, tel. 02962/493109, lunch and dinner daily) is a pizza pub with its own microbrew beer; it also prepares an outstanding *locro* (US$7), a meal-in-itself northwestern Argentine stew that's ideal for a cool Chaltén evening.

Open in summer only, **Ruca Mahuida** (Lionel Terray 55, tel. 02962/493018, lunch and dinner daily) is one of Chaltén's most imaginative eateries—try the lamb ravioli in mint sauce (US$15)—with improved service. It's open for lunch but most people come at dinnertime after their hikes. There are fine appetizers (US$6–8), but most entrées cost nearly US$20 and up. With only four (big) tables, it's something of a communal experience, but an expansion is underway.

Lamb is the specialty at **La Casita** (San Martín 430, tel. 02962/493042, lunch and dinner daily), which otherwise serves a standard Argentine menu—beef, pizza, pasta, and the like. Its major downside is the cramped and tobacco-heavy atmosphere. In midsummer it can be hard to get a table at popular **Pizzería Patagonicus** (Güemes 57, tel. 02962/493025, lunch and dinner daily), one of few Argentine eateries to have lamb on the pizza menu; the decor, with natural wood and mountaineering photos, embodies Chaltén's evolving style. **Pangaea** (Lago del Desierto 330, tel. 02962/493084, lunch and dinner daily) has decent pizza and a really excellent wine list.

Reservations are advisable for **Fuegia** (San Martín 342, tel. 02962/493019, lunch and dinner daily), Albergue Patagonia's bistro-style restaurant, though it's expanded to accommodate demand for dishes like rack of lamb and Patagonian trout (US$15). Likewise, plan ahead for the unpretentious **Estepa** (Cerro Solo 86, tel. 02962/493069, lunch and dinner daily), a snug, tobacco-free, six-booth place with views of Fitz Roy. Offering home-style cooking at a high level, its enduring specialty is the *cordero estepa* (US$16) lamb with *calafate* sauce, but there are also pizzas and empanadas, with most other entrées in the US$8–15 range. In daytime hours, it has an adjacent sandwich shop.

At the north end of town, the tiny but luminous **El Muro** (San Martín 948, tel. 02962/493248, lunch and dinner daily) is a bistro-style restaurant that gets crowded, but the kitchen pays minute attention to diners' tastes. The service can be distracted when it gets busy—especially with only two waitresses—but dishes such as grilled lamb or lamb and mushroom lasagna (both about US$14) are well worth minor inconveniences. Special mention goes to the light-crusted empanadas, including lamb and beef.

**Ritual del Fuego** (San Martín 219, tel. 02962/493173, www.ritualdelfuego.com.ar, lunch and dinner daily) is a small if noisy bistro with diverse menu of well-presented and flavorful dishes such as lamb curry and sirloin in a rhubarb sauce with scalloped sweet potatoes (US$14). Other choices include arugula gnocchi in a sauce of tomato, eggplant, basil, and mozzarella (US$10) and the standard *bife de chorizo* (US$13). The service is attentive.

### Information and Services

In the new bus terminal, El Chaltén's **Dirección de Turismo, Medio Ambiente y Pesca** (Perito Moreno 28, tel. 02962/493370, www.elchalten.com, 8 A.M.–11 P.M. daily in summer, 9 A.M.–5 P.M. weekdays the rest of the year) has maps and other information, and will help phone for accommodations.

**Correo Argentino** (Andreas Madsen 22) is the post office. **Telefónica** (Güemes 109) has long-distance phone and Internet service, but wireless Internet is now routine in many accommodations and restaurants.

There are no formal exchange houses, but **Banco de Santa Cruz** operates an ATM in the bus terminal; still, as it often runs out of bills, it's better to bring as much cash as is feasible. Some businesses will accept U.S. dollars, euros, Brazilian reais, and Chilean pesos in exchange for services, but few handle credit cards.

**Lavandino** (San Martín and Trevisan) handles the washing, though many accommodations also do so at reasonable prices.

**Mountain Repair** (Av. Güemes 142) keeps long summer hours to patch clothes, replace zippers, and repair boots and sleeping bags.

### Getting There

All buses now leave from the new **Terminal de Ómnibus** (Perito Moreno 28, tel. 02962/493370), at the southern edge of town. Several companies connect El Chaltén with El Calafate (3.5 hours, US$15–20): **Cal Tur** (tel. 02962/493150), **Chaltén Travel** (tel. 02962/493392), and **Taqsa** (Antonio Rojo 88, tel. 02962/493370). There are several buses daily in summer, but this can fall to about one daily in winter.

With Chaltén Travel and Cal Tur, it's possible to travel north on RN 40 (La Cuarenta), to the towns of Perito Moreno and Los Antiguos in Chubut province (13 hours, US$64); the former continues to Esquel (US$95), El Bolsón (US$111), and Bariloche (US$114). Chaltén Travel leaves Chaltén on alternate days in summer; passengers from El Calafate can board the bus at the RN 40 junction, but continuing beyond Perito Moreno requires an overnight at Perito's Hotel Belgrano. The rest of the year, there may be only one bus weekly. Taqsa also serves Perito Moreno, but goes to Bariloche (US$112–125) only via the roundabout coastal Ruta 3.

**Transporte Las Lengas** (tel. 02962/493370, laslengaselchalten@yahoo.com.ar) provides direct service to Aeropuerto Internacional El Calafate (3.5 hours, US$21) at 6:30 and 10:30 A.M. daily, returning at 1:30 and 7 P.M.

Also in summer, at 6:30 A.M. Monday, Wednesday, and Friday, **Transpatagonia Servicios** (tel. 02962/493370) provides door-to-door service to Río Gallegos (five hours, US$33), which makes it feasible to connect with buses to Argentine Tierra del Fuego and to Punta Arenas, Chile.

### Getting Around

When the national park shuttles don't meet your needs, consider a meterless taxi service, such as **Remises Chaltén Móvil** (tel. 02962/493061), an economical option if shared by several riders.

## RN 40 SOUTH

Southeast of El Calafate, RN 40 and RP 5 are contiguous for 132 kilometers as far as La Esperanza, where there's a gas station and a restaurant, and RN 40 doglegs back toward Tapi Aike, a wide spot in the road where there's another gas station and a convenience store, but Estancia Tapi Aike no longer offers accommodations. In fact, the Argentine government appears to have fudged on its pledge to pave all of RN 40 by selectively renumbering the roads here—at El Cerrito, a southbound gravel shortcut that used to be north–south RN 40 is now RP 7, which was formerly the east–west route from La Esperanza.

From Tapi Aike, the road continues southwest toward the border crossing at **Cancha Carrera,** the easiest access to Torres del Paine, with occasional direct summer bus connections. Many travelers, though, enter Chile at Río Turbio, an otherwise bleak coal town with a mining museum, a historical narrow-gauge railway, and a modern ski resort.

## Estancia Rupai Pacha

From Tapi Aike, RN 40 leads southwest past the **Hotel Fuentes del Coyle,** a bare-bones roadhouse (now closed) that's a local landmark; about 22 kilometers southwest via a detour from the new route, the Sturtzenbaum family's **Estancia Rupai Pacha** (Piedra Buena 129, Río Gallegos, tel. 02902/494057, www.rupai-pacha.com, US$100 s, US$120 d with breakfast) provides organic produce for El Calafate and raises sheep on 26,000 hectares of rolling steppe. With views of Torres del Paine to the southwest, it also offers congenial farm-stay accommodations, plus hiking, riding, and especially bird-watching on its marshy lowlands. Founded in 1973, it's not a historic *estancia,* but the gardens are a treasure, with delectable raspberries and other fresh fruits in season, and there's also a handicrafts shop.

About 180 kilometers south of El Calafate and 70 kilometers north of Río Turbio, Rupai Pacha is about 10 kilometers west of the new RN 40 from a signed junction. Rates include breakfast, while additional meals are available (US$32 pp); there is also a sheltered campground (US$16 d). English and German are spoken.

## Río Turbio

In one of Argentina's remotest corners, the gritty coal town of Río Turbio had been declining as its underground seams neared exhaustion, but it got an ironic shot in the arm with the 2002 peso meltdown—as locals could no longer afford to shop in Chile, supermarkets and other businesses here opened and even expanded during the country's worst economic crisis ever. Even Chileans began to cross the border for cheaper Argentine goods.

Even the mines recovered as national fuel shortages made the local mineral a competitive energy source, but this had a downside as well. In mid-2004 an underground fire killed 14 miners, plunging the community into mourning and raising questions about cost-cutting measures by the private concessionaire. The federal government, though, has taken over the mine and begun to build a new coal-fired 240-megawatt power plant that would seem to suggest confidence in dirty energy.

Though it's no beauty spot, Río Turbio holds some interest for its mining museum and aging locomotives and railcars—the narrow-gauge railway still carries coal to Punta Loyola, near Río Gallegos—and for its modest winter-sports center.

Río Turbio (population about 9,500) is 270 kilometers west of Río Gallegos via RN 40, and 30 kilometers north of Puerto Natales, Chile. It's 242 kilometers south of El Calafate via RN 40 and RP 11.

Near the Villa Dorotea border post, about four kilometers south of town, the **Centro de Deportes de Invierno Valdelén** (tel. 02902/421900, angeli@oyikil.com.ar) is a modest but lighted ski area, with elevations ranging 180–690 meters; there are about 12 hectares of downhill slopes and 160 suitable for cross-country. Hours are 10 A.M.–10 P.M. daily when snow is sufficient, usually June–August.

For those who speak Spanish, miners themselves conduct 45-minute tours of the **Museo Minero** (Mina 3, 8 A.M.–5 P.M. weekdays, free, but donations welcome), on Ruta 40 about three kilometers east of town. Part of the school used to train miners, it gives a good introduction to underground mining, its evolving technologies, and its dangers.

Whatever its shortcomings as a hometown, Río Turbio has decent accommodations, starting with **Hospedaje Yenu** (2 de Abril 170, Barrio Islas Malvinas, tel. 02902/421694, US$25 s, US$45 d). Another good option is **Hotel Nazo** (Gobernador Moyano 464, tel. 02902/421334, nazo@oyikil.com.ar, US$50 s, US$58 d); its **Fond du Cave** (Gobernador Moyano 474, tel. 02902/421800) is the best full-service restaurant.

Río Turbio's helpful **Centro de Información Turística** (Plazoleta Agustín del Castillo s/n, tel. 02902/421950, rioturbio@santacruzpatagonia.gov.ar) is presumably open 8 A.M.–9 P.M. weekdays and 9 A.M.–9 P.M. weekends; in practice it keeps irregular hours.

**Banco de Santa Cruz** (Gobernador Lista s/n) has an ATM. For postal services, **Correo**

© WAYNE BERNHARDSON

Miners themselves lead tours of Río Turbio's coal museum.

**Argentino** is at Avenida de los Mineros and Roque Sáenz Peña.

**LADE** (Av. de los Mineros 375, tel. 02902/421224) flies sporadically to Río Gallegos and Río Grande (Tierra del Fuego).

Río Turbio has no central bus terminal, but all the companies are fairly close to each other. **Cootra** (Teniente del Castillo 01, tel. 02902/421448) operates 5–7 buses daily to Puerto Natales (1 hour, US$6) except on weekends, when there are only two or three. **Bus Sur** (Av. de los Mineros 262) goes once or twice daily.

**Taqsa** (Teniente del Castillo 130, tel. 02902/421422) goes to Río Gallegos (4.5 hours, US$15) at 2:30 and 11:30 A.M. and 4 P.M. daily.

## RN 40 NORTH

About 30 kilometers east of El Calafate, northbound RN 40 covers some 600-plus kilometers of once rugged gravel road in the Andes's arid eastern foothills, before arriving at the cow town of Perito Moreno near Lago Buenos Aires, the oasis of Los Antiguos, and the Chilean border town of Chile Chico. Now roughly half paved, this desolate highway has seen more and more overland travelers, but mixed reviews indicate it's not for everyone: The unrelenting westerlies bowl over cyclists and bikers alike, sharp rocks still blow tires and shatter windshields, and vehicles can break down in the middle of nowhere.

Still, this segment of La Cuarenta—running from Río Gallegos almost to the Bolivian border, RN 40 is Argentina's longest interior highway—has a mystique all its own. Some love it, some loathe it, and others are ambivalent, but no one forgets it.

### La Leona and Vicinity

Since 1916, the landmark **Hotel de Campo La Leona** (Buenos Aires tel. 011/5032-3415, www.hoteldecampolaleona.com.ar, US$60 s, US$75 d, with breakfast) has been a rural roadhouse where today's travelers brake for chocolate and lemon pie, banana bread, and tea and coffee. Though the exterior looks much

## THE CHANGING CUARENTA

From the Bolivian border near La Quiaca to its terminus near Río Gallegos, RN 40 has been Argentina's great unfinished interior highway. Some segments of "La Cuarenta" (*cuarenta* means "40") in the central Cuyo provinces have long been smoothly paved, while others in the Andean northwest remain rough and rugged. None of those, though, has enjoyed the notoriety of the segment between the El Calafate junction and the town of Perito Moreno, on the cusp between the Patagonian steppe and the icy southern Andes.

It's no longer Argentina's loneliest road – some of the cul-de-sac tracks that spin off it seem simply *abandoned* – but for Argentines and foreigners alike it's been the standard for adventurous driving and cycling thanks to its secluded Andean lakes, isolated *estancias*, plentiful wildlife, and rare sights like the pre-Columbian rock art of Cueva de las Manos. Even the advent of ever more frequent public transportation has not diminished its mystique.

When the author first drove the roughly 600 kilometers of "La Cuarenta" in early 1991, its "gravel" was sometimes the size of a fist, services were almost nil, and he saw only three other vehicles in four days. Since then, traffic has not exactly burgeoned, but the summer season sees a growing procession of motorists, motorcyclists, and bicyclists. Some, at least, appreciate Charles Darwin's insight that the appeal of the bleak Patagonian plains was "the free scope given to the imagination."

It's clearly not for everyone, though, and a trip up or down La Cuarenta still requires planning. With accommodations and supplies few and far between, bicyclists and motorcyclists *must* carry tents and cold-weather gear, even in midsummer, and plenty of food. A GPS and/or maps, like ACA's newest regional sheets, are essential. Some motorists might feel more comfortable with two spare tires.

Also carry extra fuel – between El Calafate and Perito Moreno, the only reliable supplies



as it did a century ago, a Buenos Aires investor has totally transformed the interior, with a small souvenir shop in addition to a more spacious and cheerful dining room (with equally cheerful personnel). The four remodeled rooms have private baths. Camping costs US$12 per person, breakfast not included.

Little more than a wide turnout alongside the road, at junction of RN 40 and westbound RP 21, it's a useful stop for cyclists, either northbound or southbound, who don't care to set up the tent and want amenities like wireless Internet.

Under the same ownership, west of the highway, the more luxurious **Estancia La Estela** (www.estancialaestela.com.ar, US$125 s, US$150 d) offers custom-built accommodations with views of Lago Viedma and the Fitz Roy range, plus activities that include rafting, riding, and even archery. An entire house, sleeping six, is available for US$350.

Nearby, the **Bosque Petrificado La Leona** is a badlands reserve of petrified forests and dinosaur fossils on nearby Estancia Santa Teresita, visited by guided tour only. For details on this full-day excursion (US$75 including a picnic lunch), contact any El Calafate travel agency.

### Tres Lagos and Vicinity

Beyond La Margarita, RN 40 climbs over the volcanic Meseta Escorial before dropping into the enigmatically named hamlet of Tres Lagos (Three Lakes; however, the only nearby water is the humble Río Shehuen). Northbound motorists *must* fill up at the YPF station, which has the only gasoline until Gobernador Gregores, about 210 kilometers northeast, and Bajo Caracoles, 338 kilometers north.

Tres Lagos has few other services, though its municipal **Camping Don Jorge Cepernic** (US$11 per tent) has undergone a major upgrade, with new baths and a *confitería*. Sandwiches and lesser snacks are available at the YPF station.

are at El Chaltén (a 90-kilometer detour), Tres Lagos, Gobernador Gregores (which sometimes runs out), and Bajo Caracoles (which also sometimes runs out, but now benefits from a tanker truck parked there in summer). Some tourist *estancias* will sell gasoline to their clients or in an emergency, but don't count on it.

Road hazards are numerous. Bicyclists and motorcyclists must contend with powerful Patagonian winds that can knock them down in an instant, and in some areas deep gravel still adds to the danger. Even high-clearance vehicles are vulnerable to flipping on loose gravel, especially when braking suddenly, and 50-knot-plus gusts make things worse. Though four-wheel drive is not essential, some drivers prefer it to avoid fishtailing on gravel.

Chipped, cracked, and even shattered windshields are par for the course on the unpaved areas and other graveled roads. Normally, rental-car insurance policies do *not* cover such damage, and replacements are expensive in Argentina (though fairly cheap in Punta Arenas, Chile). Approaching vehicles usually brake to minimize the possibility of damage, but some drivers find they need to play chicken to slow down an onrushing pickup truck or SUV.

The big news is that, as of early 2011, about half of this segment of RN 40 is paved and, with work proceeding rapidly, the rest of it seems likely to be completed by late 2012. Because of rerouting, it now passes through rather than around Gobernador Gregores (anyone nostalgic for the old route can still take on the graveled shortcut of RP 29, formerly part of La Cuarenta).

If driving or cycling doesn't appeal to you, but you still want to see the "loneliest highway," summer bus and minivan services now connect El Calafate and El Chaltén, at the south end, with Perito Moreno and Los Antiguos at the north end of Santa Cruz province, and with Bariloche.



## Lago Cardiel and Vicinity

North of Tres Lagos, RN 40 winds north over the Meseta Cascajosa before coming within sight of Lago Cardiel, a deep interior drainage lake that's a bellwether for ongoing climate-change studies. It also enjoys a certain popularity for fishing, but it's so remote that there's little competition.

On the west side of the highway, 22 kilometers south of the RP 29 junction to Gobernador Gregores, **Estancia La Siberia** (Río Gallegos tel. 02966/426972, lasiberia2436@yahoo.com.ar) is the casual doppelgänger of the stereotypical tourist *estancia*. With little livestock, set among an aging orchard of apricot, cherry, pear, and plum trees, it's open October–mid-April and rents rooms (US$25 pp in hostel-style accommodations with breakfast, US$38 s, US$63 d with private baths and hot showers); inexpensive camping (US$10 pp with shower access) makes it popular with cyclists. Lunches and dinners (US$18) are also available.

## Estancia La Angostura and Vicinity

About 60 kilometers northwest of La Siberia on RN 29, which used to be RN 40 and is still a more direct route north than via Gobernador Gregores, an eastbound dirt road drops into the Río Chico marshlands, dotted with birds that include upland geese, coots, and lapwings. Sheltered by densely planted trees, La Angostura has six comfortable guest rooms (US$100 s or d with breakfast) and also a decent campground (US$10 pp) on a farm that leans toward the rustic end of the *estancia* continuum. The food is heavy on Argentine standards like *milanesa* (breaded cutlet). Estancia La Angostura (RP 29 Km 91.5, tel. 02902/491501, www.estancialaangostura.com.ar) is open mid-October through March. With RN 40 rerouted to Gobernador Gregores, this will be an off-the-paved-track shortcut to experience the old highway.

North of La Angostura, the 200 or so

kilometer stretch of northbound RN 40 to Bajo Caracoles is almost service-free, especially since the owner's death forced closure of the landmark Hotel Las Horquetas, an out-of-the-wind dive near the junction with westbound RP 37. Some campers like the free sites beneath the bridge over the Río Chico near the junction of RN 40 and RP 29, but the best spots go early.

## Gobernador Gregores

Though it's 60–70 kilometers east of the former RN 40 shortcut, Gobernador Gregores (population about 4,900) can be an essential detour for bikers or motorists running short of gasoline. It's also the easiest place to obtain other supplies and to hire a car and driver to Parque Nacional Perito Moreno, some 200-plus kilometers northwest. RN 40's presumed paving and rerouting to Gregores figures to reinvigorate the town as a tourist service center, especially as a base for improved park access.



The **Camping Municipal Nuestra Señora del Valle** (Roca and Chile, tel. 02962/491228, free) has hot showers. The best accommodations are at **Hotel Cañadón León** (Roca 397, tel. 02962/491082, US$43 s, US$60 d), which also has the best restaurant. The next best dining is at **Pizzería Chicho** (Belgrano 319, tel. 02962/491391).

The **Dirección Municipal de Turismo** (Av. San Martín 514, tel. 02962/491259, gregores@epatagonia.gov.ar) can help with general information; it also keeps a kiosk at the western approach to town. The **APN** (San Martín 882, tel./fax 02962/491477, peritomoreno@apn.gov.ar) deals with Parque Nacional Perito Moreno.

**Cerro San Lorenzo** (San Martín and Alberdi) has buses to San Julián (US$25) at 6 P.M. Monday–Saturday. **Cañadón León** (Roca 673, tel. 02962/491172) serves this route daily.

**Taqsa** (Paradelo 956, tel. 02962/491102) goes to Río Gallegos (5.5 hours, US$33) daily at 7 A.M. and 5 P.M. **RP Transportes** (Av. San Martín 1022, tel. 02966/15-313454) goes to El Calafate (US$30, six hours) Monday and Friday at 2 P.M.

## Estancia Río Capitán

Some 56 kilometers northwest of the junction of RN 40 and RP 29, graveled RP 35 leads southwest to a border crossing that, when a new bridge is finished, will provide direct access to the Chilean settlement of Villa O'Higgins, at the southern end of the Carretera Austral. Meanwhile, Estancia Río Capitán (RP 35 Km 55, tel. 02286/420938, www.estanciariocapitan.com.ar, US$80 s, US$110 d with half board) provides the only accommodations along the route. Its half dozen rooms are primarily for fly-fishing fans.

## Parque Nacional Perito Moreno

The Sierra Colorada's intensely colored sedimentary summits are the backdrop for the lake-laden, wind-whipped, and wildlife-rich high country of Parque Nacional Perito Francisco P. Moreno, named for the founder of Argentina's park system. Possibly Patagonia's wildest park, where Paleo-Indians covered cave walls with images of guanacos and human hands, it's a major reason travelers have braved the past rigors of La Cuarenta.

Comprising 115,000 hectares of Patagonian steppe, sub-Antarctic forest, glacial lakes and fjords, and high Andean pastures, the park is 220 kilometers northwest of Gobernador Gregores via RP 25, RN 40, and RP 37. It's 310 kilometers southwest of the town of Perito Moreno via RN 40 and RP 37.

At 900 meters above sea level, its base altitude is higher than Los Glaciares, and its climate is colder, wetter, and more unpredictable. Its highest summit is 2,254-meter Cerro Mié, but snowcapped 3,700-meter Cerro San Lorenzo, north of the park boundary, is even higher.

In the drier eastern steppes, the dominant vegetation consists of bunch grasses known collectively as *coirón;* to the west there's a transitional wind-flagged forest of *lenga* and *ñire,* the ubiquitous southern beeches. In more sheltered areas, there are dense and nearly pure *lenga* stands along the shores of Lago Azara and Lago Nansen.

Troops of guanacos patrol the steppes and even some of the high country where there's summer pasture; the huemul (Andean deer) grazes the uplands in summer but winters at lower altitudes. The puma is the alpha predator, but there are smaller killers in red and gray foxes. The *pilquín* or *chinchillón anaranjado* is a species of viscacha unique to Santa Cruz province and southernmost Chile.

The largest birds are the Andean condor and the flightless rhea, but other impressive species include the *águila mora* (black-chested buzzard eagle), the large owl *ñacurutú,* Patagonian woodpeckers, and the *carancho* (crested caracara). The many lakes and streams support abundant wildfowl, including flamingos, black-necked swans, grebes, wild geese, and steamer ducks. Unlike other Patagonian lakes, those within the park have remained free of introduced fish species.

### SIGHTS AND RECREATION

While **Lago Burmeister** is worth a visit, the cave paintings have been closed to public access. There are large troops of guanacos on **Península Belgrano,** reached by an isthmus immediately west of Estancia Belgrano (which is not a tourist *estancia*).

One of the best day hikes is 1,434-meter **Cerro León,** a 2.5-hour climb immediately north of Estancia La Oriental, which offers the area's best easily accessible panoramas (hikers must be prepared for the changeable weather). The volcanic overhang known as the **Cerro de los Cóndores** is the flight school for condor chicks.

### ACCOMMODATIONS AND FOOD

There are free but barren campsites with pit toilets at the APN's Centro de Informes, at the park entrance; the more appealing Lago Burmeister campground consists of Tehuelche-style lean-tos in dense *lenga* forest. The water is potable, but no supplies are available; campers must bring everything.

Open November–April, on Lago Belgrano's north shore, **Estancia La Oriental** (Rivadavia 936, San Julián, Buenos Aires tel./fax 011/4152-6901, laorientalpatagonia@yahoo.com.ar, US$90 s, US$115 d) has both conventional accommodations (seven rooms sleeping up to 22 guests) and protected campsites (US$22 per tent for up to three people, with hot showers) near the lodge. The US$10 breakfasts of homemade scones, bread, jam, ham, and cheese deserve a detour, but the dinners (US$28 pp) are nothing special.

Just outside the park boundary, **Estancia Menelik** occupies a windy, oddly exposed site—most *estancieros* chose protected valley-bottom locations—but the popular explanation is that its original German homesteader wanted to advertise his presence and spot the approach of any strangers. Despite the barren landscape, the welcome is warm at both the comfortably furnished farmhouse, which has ample bedrooms (US$125 pp with full board) plus a large sitting room (with library) and dining areas, and at its simpler **Refugio Río Belgrano** (a rehabbed bunkhouse with kitchen access, US$25 pp). Though well off the beaten path, it does get tour groups, so reservations are advisable; for details, contact Cielos Patagónicos (Buenos Aires tel. 011/4836-3502, www.cielospatagonicos.com). Given Menelik's isolation, the quality of the food (breakfast US$8, lunch or dinner US$20) is good. It's open November–April.

### OTHER PRACTICALITIES

Rangers at the Centro de Informes, at the park entrance, provide maps and brochures and offer guided hikes and visits; they can also be reached through the APN (Av. San Martín 882, tel./fax 02962/491477, peritomoreno@apn.gov.ar) in Gobernador Gregores. You can also write for information at their postal address: Casilla de Correo 103 (9311), Gobernador Gregores.

Rental cars offer the greatest flexibility, though it's possible to hire a car and driver in Gobernador Gregores or the town of Perito Moreno. Hitching from the highway junction is feasible but uncertain.

## Bajo Caracoles

Midway between Las Horquetas and the town of Perito Moreno, barren Bajo Caracoles is an oasis for automobiles and motorcycles, with the only gas station in nearly 500 kilometers (though the newly designated RN 40 via Gobernador Gregores offers an alternative). Southbound travelers should fill the tank here; others should buy enough to reach Perito Moreno, 128 kilometers north. With a tanker trailer parked here in summer, occasional shortages are less frequent than they used to be.

Bajo Caracoles is also the southern gateway to the rock-art site of Cueva de las Manos, 41 kilometers northeast via RP 97, but there are alternative access points farther north. RP 39 leads east to the hamlet of Hipólito Yrigoyen and **Lago Posadas,** near the Chilean border, while RP 41, a short distance north of Bajo Caracoles, goes directly to the border crossing at **Paso Roballos.**



Better than expected in this remote outpost, with recently modernized bathrooms, the legendary **Hotel Bajo Caracoles** (tel. 02963/490100, US$53 s or d) fills up early despite its cantankerous operator. It also has groceries and surprisingly good meals.

The hotel has shoestring competition in the nearby **Hostel Ruta 40** (US$10 pp dorm, US$37 s or d), and there's also cheap camping across the highway.

### Lago Posadas and Vicinity

Bajo Caracoles is not known for its beauty, but it's hard to improve on aquamarine Lago Posadas, 90 kilometers west, and nearby Lago Pueyrredón, nudging the Chilean border. While the main route from Bajo Caracoles to the border passes Lago Ghío, along RP 41 to the north, southerly RP 39 via Lago Posadas is a more scenic alternative. The westbound road continues to Paso Roballos, a spectacular border area with access to Valle Chacabuco, the audacious new conservation project that should soon create Chile's Parque Nacional Patagonia.

### Cueva de las Manos and Vicinity

Beyond Baja Caracoles, rugged RN 40 traverses the northern steppe until the point where, over millions of years, the Río Pinturas has cut a deep, scenic canyon. In the process, erosion has left countless *aleros,* stony overhangs often mistakenly called *cuevas* (caves). One of these is the Cueva de las Manos, a UNESCO World Heritage Site where stencils of hundreds of human hands, guanacos, and abstract forms cover the walls in orange, red, and yellow tones.

Dating from around 7370 B.C., the oldest paintings represent hunter-gatherers from immediate postglacial times, but the more abstract designs, which are fewer, are more recent. Oddly enough, nearly all the hands from which the site takes its name are left hands.

Along with Parque Nacional Perito Moreno, this is one of La Cuarenta's finest detours, with two main access points. From Bajo Caracoles in the south, gravel RP 41 goes directly to the visitors center, where the province now collects an admission fee of US$12.50 (US$4 for Argentines) that includes a guided tour; the center itself contains informational panels in imperfect but passable English. Metal screens now block close access to the paintings, to discourage vandalism and prevent repeated touching that could damage the paintings, but they do not obstruct the view.

Another access point is **Estancia Cueva de las Manos,** another 23 kilometers north and four kilometers east in the Pinturas drainage; from there, another 18-kilometer access road leads to a parking area and a trailhead, where it's a two-kilometer hike that includes a sandy, slippery descent, with many loose rocks. By this route, mountain bikers can avoid backtracking to RN 40 by walking their bikes down the slope and then over the river (there's a suspension footbridge, but the stream is usually shallow in any event) and out the other direction.

**Estancia Cueva de las Manos** (Buenos Aires tel. 011/5237-4043, www.cuevadelasmanos.net) has nine attractive, modern rooms with private baths (US$100 s, US$115 d, with breakfast) as well as hostel accommodations (US$30 pp, with breakfast) in two vast dorms, each with 18 beds, three toilets, and three showers. Restaurant lunches and dinners, including dishes such as pumpkin-stuffed

© WAYNE BERNHARDSON

The pre-Columbian paintings at Cueva de las Manos have made it a UNESCO World Heritage Site.



*sorrentinos* and excellent desserts, cost about US$28; the wine list has some good but moderately priced vintages.

It's open November–March and sometimes for Semana Santa. It also offers additional excursions besides Cueva de las Manos proper. It has no phone or Internet access here, but they check their mail in town every couple of days.

## Perito Moreno

Where RN 40 meets the smoothly paved international highway from Comodoro Rivadavia to Chile Chico, nondescript Perito Moreno marks the return to civilization for northbound travelers and the start of the adventure for the Calafate-bound. Often confused with its namesake national park, as well as the eponymous glacier in Parque Nacional Los Glaciares, it has pretty good services, but many visitors prefer the lakeside town of Los Antiguos to the west.

Perito Moreno (population about 8,000) is 398 kilometers southwest of Comodoro Rivadavia via Caleta Olivia, and 58 kilometers east of Los Antiguos via paved RP 43. It is 124 kilometers south of Río Mayo, Chubut province, via one of RN 40's rougher stretches, which continues toward Esquel and the Andean Lake District. There is only infrequent public transportation between Perito Moreno and Río Mayo.

Early February's **Festival Folklórico Cueva de las Manos** is a musical event that capitalizes on the proximity of the world heritage site. A new **Museo Regional de la Cueva de las Manos** is under construction; part of it is already operative in the **Café Iturrioz,** a handsome brick structure at San Martín and Rivadavia.

### ACCOMMODATIONS AND FOOD

Opposite Laguna de los Cisnes, the city park at Perito's south end, the sheltered **Camping Municipal** (Roca and Moreno, tel. 02963/432130, US$2.50 pp plus US$2.50 per vehicle or tent) is small but has flawless bathrooms with hot showers for a small extra charge.

Otherwise, the pickings are slim. Used by Chaltén Travel buses for the overnight break between El Calafate and Bariloche, **Hotel Belgrano** (Av. San Martín 1001, tel. 02963/432019, US$17 in dorms, US$45 s, US$60 d) also has a restaurant, but the best option is the homey three-room B&B **Posada del Caminante** (Rivadavia 937, tel. 02963/432204, posadadelcaminante@yahoo.com.ar, US$50 s, US$70 d); phone or email first, as it's often booked far ahead.

**Hotel y Restaurante El Viejo Bar** (Av. San Martín 990, tel. 02963/432538, US$50 s, US$58 d) has leapt ahead of most local competitors in its accommodations and bar/restaurant facilities. **Café Iturrioz** (San Martín and Rivadavia) has snacks, sandwiches, drinks, and wireless Internet in a museum atmosphere.

### INFORMATION AND SERVICES

In new quarters, the **Dirección de Turismo** (Av. San Martín and Gendarmería Nacional, tel. 02963/432732, peritomoreno@santacruzpatagonia.gob.ar) is open 7 A.M.–11 P.M. daily in summer; the rest of the year, it keeps the same hours on weekdays but is open only 10 A.M.–7 P.M. on weekends.

**Banco de la Nación** (Av. San Martín 1385) has an ATM.

**Correo Argentino** is at Avenida Juan D. Perón 1331; the postal code is 9040. The **Call Center** (Rivadavia 1055) has long-distance phones, while **CTC** (San Martín and Estrada) has Internet access.

**Zoyen Turismo** (Av. Perón 1008, tel. 02963/432207, cell 0297/15-6238811, www.zoyenturismo.com.ar) offers local excursions including Cueva de las Manos (US$45 plus the admission fee) via Estancia Cueva de las Manos and a short end-of-the-road hike. Bilingual **Harry Nauta** (tel. 02963/432303, jarinauta@yahoo.com.ar, jarinauta@santacruz.com.ar) now freelances on excursions that include Cueva de las Manos and Cañadón del Arroyo Feo.

For medical services, try the **Hospital Distrital** (Colón 1237, tel. 02963/432045).

### GETTING THERE

**LADE** (Av. San Martín 1065, tel. 02963/432055) has occasional flights into and out of Perito Moreno but is hard to rely on.

The sharp new **Terminal de Ómnibus** is at the north end of town, where RN 40 (Av. San Martín) meets RP 43. **La Unión** (tel. 02963/432638) and **Sportman** (tel. 02963/432177) have westbound service to Los Antiguos (1 hour, US$9) and eastbound service to Comodoro Rivadavia (five hours, US$32). Sportman and **Taqsa** (tel. 02963/432675) both have daily service to Río Gallegos (14 hours, US$68). Taqsa now goes to El Chaltén and El Calafate (US$100) as well.

**Chaltén Travel** buses (El Calafate tel. 02902/492480) from Los Antiguos to El Calafate will pick up passengers at the terminal here; the service runs on alternate days December–April or so. Passengers from El Chaltén can board the northbound bus from El Calafate at the junction of RN 40 and RP 23 without having to return to El Calafate. Buses depart Calafate on odd-numbered days and return from Los Antiguos on even-numbered days. For southbound travel to El Chaltén, Chaltén Travel links up with its own buses between El Calafate and El Chaltén. It now takes passengers onward to Bariloche, but they have to spend the night at Hotel Belgrano. **Cal Tur** now has similar services to and from El Calafate and El Chaltén, and onward to Los Antiguos, but does not go to Bariloche.

## Los Antiguos

Rows of upright poplars announce the approach to Los Antiguos, a garden spot where vivid flowerbeds fill the median strip of Avenida 11 de Julio, flats of soft fruits like raspberries, cherries, and strawberries go for a song, and baskets of apples, apricots, pears, peaches, plums, and prunes adorn the storefronts.

Its microclimate has made Los Antiguos a getaway since Tehuelche times. Its Spanish name ("the ancient ones") is derived from an indigenous term meaning "place of the elders." After August 1991, when the eruption of Chile's nearby Volcán Hudson buried the area in ash, both the fruit harvest and the tourist trade suffered, but it has recovered nicely. Fishing and hiking are the main attractions.

On Lago Buenos Aires's south shore, Los Antiguos (population about 2,500) is 58 kilometers west of Perito Moreno via RP 43. Entering town, the highway becomes Avenida 11 de Julio, which continues to the Chilean border; the Argentine border post is at the western end, while the Chilean Carabineros are across the Río Jeinimeni, about five kilometers farther.

Early January's three-day **Fiesta de la Cereza** (Cherry Festival) can put a strain on accommodations. February 5's **Día de los Antiguos** marks the town's anniversary, while **Día del Lago Buenos Aires** takes place October 29.

For fresh fruit as well as preserves, try any of several farms, such as **Chacra El Porvenir** (walking distance from Avenida 11 de Julio).

## ACCOMMODATIONS AND FOOD

Protected by poplars and cypresses, the lakeshore **Camping Municipal** (Av. 11 de Julio s/n, tel. 02963/491265, US$1.25 pp plus US$5 per tent plus US$4 per car) provides picnic tables and fire pits at every site. Hot showers are available 5:30–10 P.M. only, and cost US$1.25.

Chaltén Travel has opened **Albergue Padilla** (San Martín 44, tel. 02963/491140, mia_padilla@hotmail.com, US$15 pp dorm, US$50 d), with a dozen beds for shoestring travelers and some private rooms. **Hotel Antiguos Cerezos** (Av. 11 de Julio 850, tel. 02963/491132, hotel_losantiguoscerezos@hotmail.com, US$45 s, US$60 d) is a utilitarian hotel with a decent restaurant. On the eastern outskirts of town, **Hostería Antigua Patagonia** (RP 43 s/n, tel. 02963/491038, www.antiguapatagonia.net, US$83 s, US$99 d) is a three-story lakeshore hotel with a restaurant. **Chacra Refugio de Rocas** (Chacra 127, Parcela 10, tel. 0297/15-4010787, www.refugioderocas.com, US$83 s, US$120 d) is a new spa hotel on a traditional berry farm parcel.

Dutch-run **Viva El Viento** (Av. 11 de Julio 477, tel. 02963/491109, www.vivaelviento.com) is a new restaurant and wine bar, with live music and wireless Internet, that does a superb leg of lamb with rosemary and garlic potatoes (US$20), with ample portions. The service, though, can be appallingly distracted.

## INFORMATION AND SERVICES

The **Secretaría de Turismo** (Av. 11 de Julio 432, tel. 02963/491261, www.losantiguos.gov.ar) is open 8 A.M.–midnight daily December–April, 8 A.M.–8 P.M. daily the rest of the year.

**Banco de Santa Cruz** (Av. 11 de Julio 531) has an ATM.

**Correo Argentino** is at Gobernador Gregores 19; the postal code is 9041. **Locutorio Los Antiguos** (Alameda 436) has long-distance telephone services. Wireless Internet is abundant but slow.

## GETTING THERE

From the new **Terminal de Buses** (Av. Tehuelches 157), **La Unión** (tel. 02963/491078) and **Sportman** (tel. 02963/491175) both provide bus service to Perito Moreno (US$9, one hour), Caleta Olivia (five hours, US$32), and Comodoro Rivadavia (six hours, US$40). Sportman also has daily service to Río Gallegos (US$77).

Chilean minibuses from Chile Chico shuttle back and forth across the border here (US$5, 30 minutes); carriers include **Transporte Jaime Acuña** (Augusto Grosse 150, Chile Chico, tel. 067/411904) and **Buses Karla** (Chile Chico tel. 09/9470-4442). There are four or five Monday–Saturday, but only one or two on Sunday.

For up-to-date information on Chaltén Travel buses to El Chaltén (13 hours, US$57) and El Calafate (14 hours, US$72) via southbound RN 40, contact **Albergue Padilla** (San Martín 44, tel. 02963/491140). At the terminal, **Cal Tur** (tel. 0297/15-6234882) has similar services.

# MAGALLANES

Thanks to the Torres del Paine, the magnificent granite needles that rise above the Patagonian plains, Chile's most southerly region has acquired international fame. Pacific storms drench the nearly uninhabited western cordillera, feeding alpine and continental glaciers and rushing rivers, but relentless winds buffet the rolling eastern grasslands of the Andean rain shadow. Along the Strait of Magellan, the city of Punta Arenas is the center for excursions to various attractions, including easily accessible penguin colonies and Tierra del Fuego's remote fjords. The region has no direct road connections to the rest of Chile—travelers arrive by air, sea, and through Argentine Patagonia.

Administratively, Region XII (Magallanes) includes all Chilean territory beyond 49° south latitude—technically to the South Pole, as Chile claims a slice of Antarctica between 53° and 90° west longitude. It also takes in the Chilean sector of the Tierra del Fuego archipelago.

Improved communications have meant that many visitors to southern Argentina also visit Chile to see Puerto Natales, Torres del Paine, and other attractions. January and February are the peak months, but the season is broadening. Prices drop in winter, though many places also close.

## PLANNING YOUR TIME

Punta Arenas can be a sightseeing base, but only for a day or two; for those who haven't seen Magellanic penguins elsewhere, it's worth scheduling or waiting for the boat to Isla Magdalena. It's also home port for the

© PATRICK POENDL/123RF

## HIGHLIGHTS

**Casa Braun-Menéndez (Museo Regional de Magallanes):** Magallanes's regional museum now occupies what was once the mansion of Patagonia's wool aristocracy (page 415).

**Monumento Natural Los Pingüinos:** In the summer season, penguins occupy every square centimeter of Isla Magdalena, also home to a historic lighthouse (page 426).

**Parque Nacional Pali Aike:** Hugging the Argentine border, the volcanic caves of northern Magallanes's steppe feature some of the continent's prime early human sites (page 431).

**The Fjords of Fuegia:** It may be expensive to cruise the ice-clogged inlets of the archipelago of Tierra del Fuego, from Punta Arenas to Ushuaia, Cape Horn, and back, but it's still cheaper than chartering your own yacht. Even backpackers sometimes splurge for a leg of this unforgettable itinerary (page 433).

**Torres del Paine:** The granite needles that rise above the Patagonian steppe are a beacon drawing travelers from around the world to Chile's premier national park, Parque Nacional Torres del Paine (page 453).

**Cuernos del Paine:** This jagged interface between igneous and metamorphic rock, also in Parque Nacional Torres del Paine, is some of the world's most breathtaking alpine scenery (page 454).

**Puerto Williams:** On Isla Navarino, across the Beagle Channel from Ushuaia, tiny Williams retains much of the "uttermost part of the earth" ambience that the Argentine city once offered. It also provides access to the rugged hiking trails of the Dientes de Navarino, a series of summits that rise like inverted vampire's fangs (page 463).

LOOK FOR [icon] TO FIND RECOMMENDED SIGHTS, ACTIVITIES, DINING, AND LODGING.



spectacular cruise to Tierra del Fuego's remotest fjords and Cape Horn via Ushuaia (Argentina), a three- or four-day excursion in either direction. Based on an island in the western Strait of Magellan, summer whale-watching is drawing a small but growing crowd on three-day excursions.

Exploring the thinly populated Chilean sector of Tierra del Fuego requires a vehicle or an airplane—connections to Puerto Williams, though it's not far from Ushuaia as the crow flies, are haphazard except by air from Punta Arenas. Once you're there, hiking the Dientes de Navarino circuit takes at least a week.

Puerto Natales, the urban gateway to Torres del Paine, is mainly a place to prepare for trekking, but its seaside setting, youthful exuberance, and nearby hiking excursions can extend

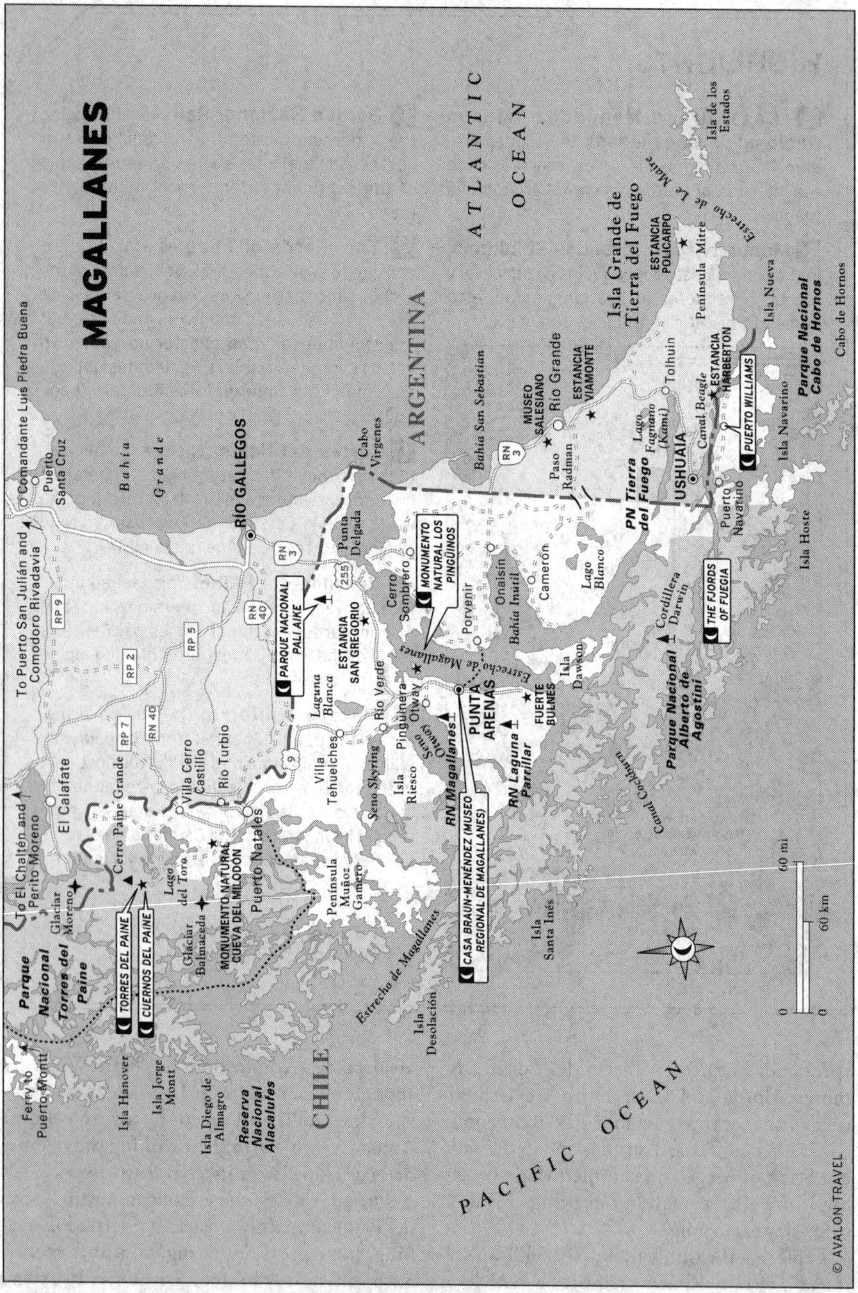


© AVALON TRAVEL

the stay. The park deserves no less than a week, for day-hikers and overnight trekkers alike, but even an abbreviated day trip—some people do it, despite the time and difficulty of getting here—is worth the trouble.

Another attraction is the *Skorpios III* cruise through the fjords on the west side of the Campos de Hielo Sur, across the ice from Torres del Paine. In summer, this five-day, four-night excursion visits many otherwise inaccessible areas.

## HISTORY

Some of the continent's oldest archaeological evidence for human habitation comes from volcanic rock shelters in and near Parque Nacional Pali Aike, along the Argentine border. Pleistocene hunter-gatherers once stalked now-extinct species such as giant ground sloths and native American horses, but they later switched to a broader subsistence that included marine and coastal resources. These peoples were the predecessors of the few surviving Tehuelche and Kawéskar (Alacaluf) peoples and the nearly extinct Selk'nam (Ona) and Yámana (Yahgan), who gathered shellfish and hunted guanaco and rhea with bows and arrows and *boleadoras.*

The European presence dates from 1520, when Portuguese navigator Fernando Magalhaes, under the Spanish flag, sailed through the strait that bears his name (Magallanes in Spanish, Magellan in English). Ranging 3–25 kilometers in width, the strait became a major maritime thoroughfare en route to the Pacific.

Spain's colonization attempts failed miserably, as did early Chilean and Argentine efforts, but the city of Punta Arenas took hold after 1848—thanks partly to the fortuitous discovery of gold in California just a year later. Gold fever soon subsided, but the introduction of sheep brought a wool and mutton boom that benefited from the 1870s Franco-Prussian War and helped create sprawling *estancias* (ranches) that dominated regional political, social, and economic life for nearly a century.

While the livestock industry hangs on, commercial fisheries, the state-run oil industry, and the tourist trade have superseded it in the economy. Even these industries have proved vulnerable to fluctuations, declining reserves, and international developments beyond their control, but Chile's energy shortages have spurred new exploration and investment. The Zona Franca free-trade zone, which once drew immigrants from central Chile, is not the engine of growth it once was, but Magallanes still has Chile's lowest unemployment rate at about 4.5 percent.

At the same time, isolated Magallanes is probably Chile's most politically volatile region, as a week-long strike against President José Piñera's decree increasing natural gas prices showed in early 2011. By blocking roads, highways, and ferry docks, as well as border crossings into Argentina, the strikers virtually shut down the regional economy—including the tourism sector—and forced Piñera to back off.



# Punta Arenas

Patagonia's largest city, Punta Arenas is also the regional capital and the traditional port of entry, whether by air, land, or sea. Stretching north–south along the Strait of Magellan, the city boasts an architectural heritage that ranges from the Magellanic vernacular of corrugated metal-clad houses with steeply pitched roofs to elaborate Francophile mansions commissioned by 19th-century wool barons. Home to several museums, it's a base for excursions to historical sites and nearby penguin colonies.

The diverse economy depends on fishing, shipping, petroleum, duty-free retail, and tourism. Historically, it's one of the gateways to Antarctica for both research and tourism, but the Argentine port of Ushuaia has absorbed much of that traffic. Ironically, in a region that grazes millions of sheep, it's hard to find woolens here because of the influx of artificial fabrics through the duty-free Zona Franca.

## HISTORY

After the collapse of Chile's initial Patagonian settlement at Fuerte Bulnes, Governor José Santos Mardones relocated north to a site on the western shore of the Strait of Magellan, long known to British seamen as "Sandy Point." Soon expanded to include a penal colony, the town adopted that name in Spanish translation.

The timing was propitious, as California's 1849 Gold Rush spurred a surge of shipping that helped keep the new city afloat—even if supplying sealskins, coal, firewood, and lumber did not exactly portend prosperity. A mutiny that resulted in Governor Benjamín Muñoz Gamero's death did not improve matters, and traffic soon fell off.

What did bring prosperity was Governor Diego Dublé Almeyda's introduction of breeding sheep from the Falkland Islands. Their proliferation on the Patagonian plains, along with a vigorous immigration policy that brought entrepreneurs such as the Portuguese José Nogueira, the Spaniard José Menéndez, and the Irishman Thomas Fenton—not to mention the polyglot laborers who made their fortunes possible—helped transform the city from a dreary presidio to the booming port of a pastoral empire. Its mansions matched many in Buenos Aires, though the maldistribution of wealth and political power remained an intractable issue well into the 20th century.

As the wool economy declined after World War II, petroleum discoveries on Tierra del Fuego and commercial fishing sustained the economy. Creation of Zona Franca duty-free areas gave commercial advantages to Punta Arenas in the 1970s, and tourism has flourished since Pinochet's dictatorship ended in 1989.

## ORIENTATION

Punta Arenas (population about 125,000) is 210 kilometers southwest of Río Gallegos via

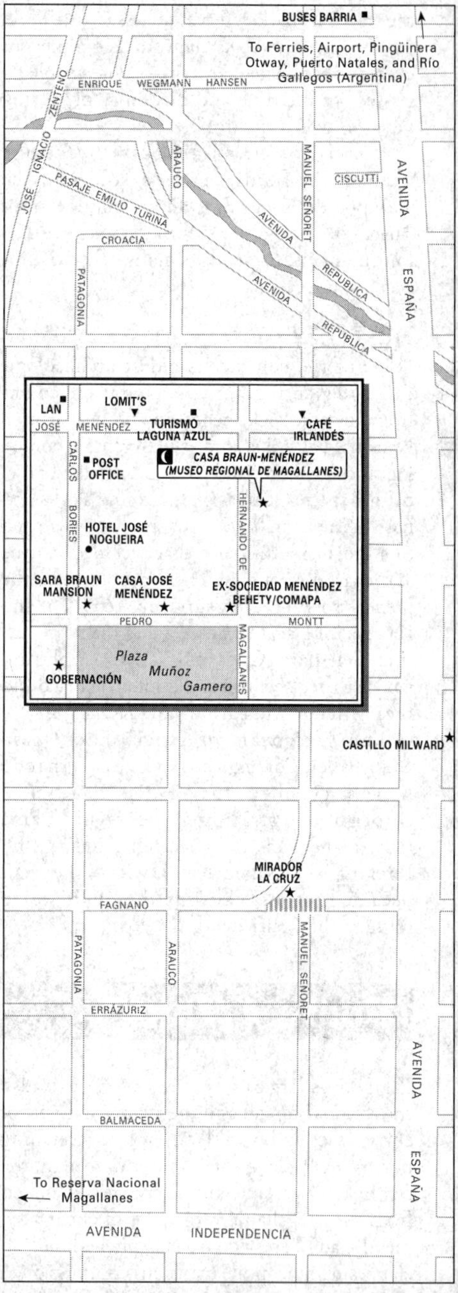

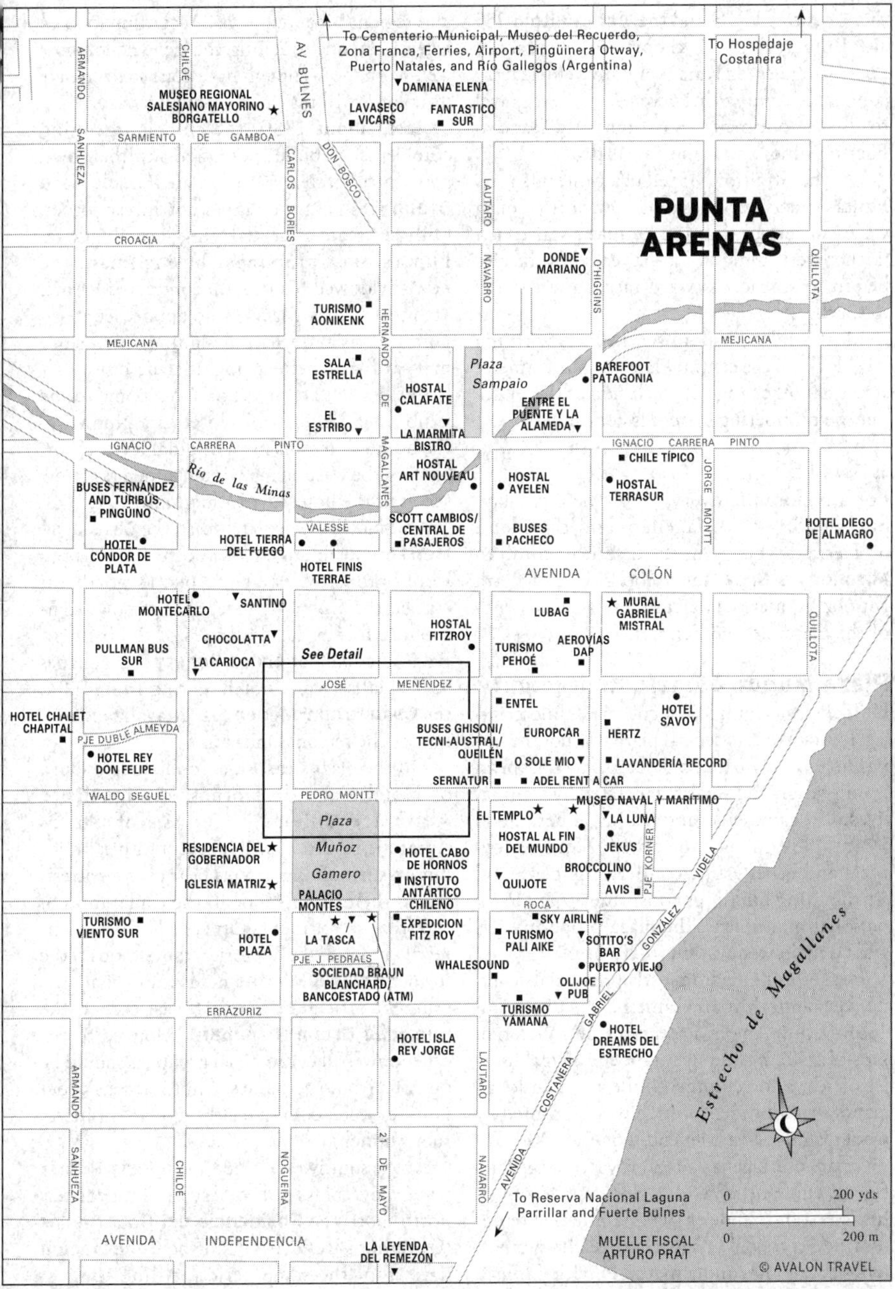
PUNTA ARENAS
To Cementerio Municipal, Museo del Recuerdo, Zona Franca, Ferries, Airport, Pingüinera Otway, Puerto Natales, and Río Gallegos (Argentina)
To Hospedaje Costanera
MUSEO REGIONAL SALESIANO MAYORINO BORGATELLO
DAMIANA ELENA
LAVASECO VICARS
FANTASTICO SUR
DONDE MARIANO
TURISMO AONIKENK
SALA ESTRELLA
HOSTAL CALAFATE
Plaza Sampaio
BAREFOOT PATAGONIA
ENTRE EL PUENTE Y LA ALAMEDA
EL ESTRIBO
LA MARMITA BISTRO
HOSTAL ART NOUVEAU
HOSTAL AYELEN
CHILE TÍPICO
HOSTAL TERRASUR
Río de las Minas
BUSES FERNÁNDEZ AND TURIBÚS, PINGÜINO
HOTEL CÓNDOR DE PLATA
HOTEL TIERRA DEL FUEGO
HOTEL FINIS TERRAE
SCOTT CAMBIOS/ CENTRAL DE PASAJEROS
BUSES PACHECO
HOTEL DIEGO DE ALMAGRO
HOTEL MONTECARLO
SANTINO
CHOCOLATTA
PULLMAN BUS SUR
LA CARIOCA
See Detail
HOSTAL FITZROY
LUBAG
MURAL GABRIELA MISTRAL
TURISMO PEHOÉ
AEROVÍAS DAP
HOTEL CHALET CHAPITAL
HOTEL REY DON FELIPE
ENTEL
HOTEL SAVOY
BUSES GHISONI/ TECNI-AUSTRAL/ QUEILÉN
EUROPCAR
HERTZ
O SOLE MIO
LAVANDERÍA RECORD
SERNATUR
ADEL RENT A CAR
MUSEO NAVAL Y MARÍTIMO
EL TEMPLO
LA LUNA
Plaza Muñoz Gamero
RESIDENCIA DEL GOBERNADOR
IGLESIA MATRIZ
HOTEL CABO DE HORNOS
HOSTAL AL FIN DEL MUNDO
JEKUS
BROCCOLINO
INSTITUTO ANTÁRTICO CHILENO
QUIJOTE
AVIS
PALACIO MONTES
TURISMO VIENTO SUR
HOTEL PLAZA
LA TASCA
EXPEDICION FITZ ROY
SKY AIRLINE
TURISMO PALI AIKE
SOTITO'S BAR
WHALESOUND
PUERTO VIEJO
SOCIEDAD BRAUN BLANCHARD/ BANCOESTADO (ATM)
OLIJOE PUB
TURISMO YAMANA
HOTEL DREAMS DEL ESTRECHO
HOTEL ISLA REY JORGE
Estrecho de Magallanes
To Reserva Nacional Laguna Parrillar and Fuerte Bulnes
LA LEYENDA DEL REMEZÓN
MUELLE FISCAL ARTURO PRAT
ARMANDO SANHUEZA
CHILOÉ
AV BULNES
CARLOS BORIES
DON BOSCO
HERNANDO DE MAGALLANES
LAUTARO
NAVARRO
O'HIGGINS
JORGE MONTT
QUILLOTA
SARMIENTO DE GAMBOA
CROACIA
MEJICANA
IGNACIO CARRERA PINTO
VALESSE
AVENIDA COLÓN
JOSÉ MENÉNDEZ
PJE DUBLE ALMEYDA
WALDO SEGUEL
PEDRO MONTT
PJE KORNER
ROCA
PJE J PEDRALS
ERRÁZURIZ
NOGUEIRA
21 DE MAYO
AVENIDA INDEPENDENCIA
AVENIDA COSTANERA
GABRIEL GONZÁLEZ VIDELA
0 200 yds
0 200 m
© AVALON TRAVEL

the Argentine RN 3 and the Chilean Ruta 255 and Ruta 9; it is 241 kilometers southeast of Puerto Natales via Ruta 9. A daily vehicle ferry connects Punta with Porvenir, while a gravel road, the continent's most southerly, leads to Fuerte Bulnes and Cabo San Isidro.

On the Strait of Magellan's western shore, Punta Arenas occupies a narrow north–south wave-cut terrace, but the ground rises steeply farther west. Only in recent years has the city begun to spread eastward rather than north to south.

Most landmarks and services are within a few blocks of the central Plaza Muñoz Gamero; street names change on each side of the plaza, but the numbering system is continuous.

## SIGHTS

For a panoramic overview of the city's layout, the Strait of Magellan, and the island of Tierra del Fuego in the distance, climb to **Mirador La Cruz,** four blocks west of Plaza Muñoz Gamero via a staircase at the corner of the Fagnano and Señoret.



### Plaza Muñoz Gamero and Vicinity

Unlike plazas founded in colonial Chilean cities, Punta Arenas's central plaza was not the initial focus of civic life, but thanks to European immigration and wealth generated by mining, livestock, commerce, and fishing, it became so by the 1880s. Landscaped with Monterey cypress and other exotic conifers, the plaza and surrounding buildings constitute a *zona típica* national monument; the plaza proper underwent a major renovation in 2004.

It takes its name from early provincial governor Benjamín Muñoz Gamero, who died in an 1851 mutiny. Among its features are a Victorian kiosk (1910), now housing the municipal tourist office, and sculptor Guillermo Córdova's elaborate monument, which was sponsored by wool magnate José Menéndez on the 400th anniversary of Magellan's 1520 voyage. Magellan's figure, embellished with a globe and a copy of his log, stands above a Selk'nam native representing Tierra del Fuego, a Tehuelche symbolizing Patagonia, and a mermaid with Chilean and regional coats-of-arms. According to local legend, anyone touching the Tehuelche's now well-worn toe—enough have done so to change its color—will return to Punta Arenas.

After about 1880, the city's burgeoning elite began to build monuments to their own good fortune, such as the ornate **Palacio Sara Braun** (1895) at the plaza's northwest corner. Only six years after marrying José Nogueira, Punta's most prominent businessman, the newly widowed Sara Braun contracted French architect Numa Mayer, who applied contemporary Parisian style in designing a two-story mansard that helped upgrade the city's earlier utilitarian architecture. Now home to the Club de la Unión and Hotel José Nogueira, the building retains most original features, including the west-facing winter garden that now serves as the hotel's bar/restaurant.

Mid-block, immediately east, the **Casa José Menéndez** belonged to another of Punta's wool barons, while at the plaza's northeast corner, the Comapa travel agency now occupies the former headquarters of the influential **Sociedad Menéndez Behety** (Magallanes 990). Half a block north, dating from 1904, the **Casa Braun-Menéndez** (Magallanes 949) houses the regional museum.

On the plaza's east side, immediately south of Hotel Cabo de Hornos, the **Instituto Antártico Chileno** is the site of Chile's Antarctic research entity; several other buildings in surrounding streets bear plaques attesting to their significance in the exploration of the frozen continent. On the south side, directly opposite the Victorian tourist kiosk, the former **Palacio Montes** holds municipal government offices; at the southeast corner, the **Sociedad Braun Blanchard** belonged to another powerful commercial group (as should be obvious from the names, Punta Arenas's first families were, commercially at least, an incestuous bunch).

At the southwest corner, the **Iglesia Matriz** (1901) now enjoys cathedral status. Immediately north, both the **Residencia del Gobernador** (Governor's Residence) and the **Gobernación** date from the same period, filling the rest of the block with offices of the Intendencia Regional, the regional government.

### Casa Braun-Menéndez (Museo Regional de Magallanes)

Like European royalty, Punta's first families formed alliances sealed by matrimony, and the Casa Braun-Menéndez (1904) is a classic example: the product of a marriage between Mauricio Braun (Sara's brother) and Josefina Menéndez Behety (daughter of José Menéndez and María Behety, a major wool-growing family in Argentina—though international borders meant little to wool barons).

Still furnished with the family's belongings, preserving Mauricio Braun's office and other rooms virtually intact, the house boasts marble fireplaces and other elaborate architectural features. The basement servants' quarters expose the early-20th-century's upstairs-downstairs divisions.

Today, the Casa Braun-Menéndez (Magallanes 949, tel. 061/244216, www.museodemagallanes.cl, 10:30 A.M.–5 P.M. Mon.–Sat., 10:30 A.M.–2 P.M. Sun., US$2 adults, US$1 children) serves as the regional museum, replete with pioneer settlers' artifacts and historical photographs. There are imperfect but readable English descriptions of the exhibits. On some days, a pianist plays beneath the atrium's stained-glass skylight.

### Museo Regional Salesiano Mayorino Borgatello

From the 19th century, the Salesian order played a key role in evangelizing southern Patagonia and Tierra del Fuego, on both sides of the border. Punta Arenas was their base, and, while their rosy view of Christianity's impact on the region's native people may be debatable, figures such as the Italian mountaineer priest Alberto de Agostini (1883–1960) made key contributions to both physical geography and ethnographic research.

Agostini left a sizable collection of photographs in the museum, which also has a library and a regionally oriented art gallery. Permanent exhibits deal with regional flora and fauna, a

© WAYNE BERNHARDSON

The Braun-Menéndez mansion in Punta Arenas is now the regional history museum.

## I HEARD IT THROUGH THE GRAPEVINE

When the Patagonian wool barons built their mansions and *cascos* in the 19th century, one amenity they all required was a glassed-in greenhouse or conservatory. In a region where high winds, hail, and snowstorms were not unusual at any season, they could enjoy balmy indoor sunshine on long summer days and grow vegetables like eggplants and tomatoes that could never survive the climate outdoors.

Both Argentina and Chile are famous for their grapes (thanks largely to their wine industries), but the two countries can also boast the world's southernmost grape arbors. The most readily seen is the one at the conservatory restaurant at Punta Arenas's **Hotel José Nogueira,** the former Sara Braun mansion, at 53° 9' south. So far, though, even visiting experts have been unable to identify its origins.

According to Sara Braun's descendant, Julia Braun, vines at the *casco* of Estancia Sara, on the Argentine side of Tierra del Fuego, push the grape line to 53° 25' south. The original *casco* at Estancia María Behety (53° 48' south), west of the city of Río Grande, may have had vines, but the house burned to the ground several years back.

One of the most luxuriant austral grapevines, though, flourishes in **Government House** in Stanley, in the Falkland Islands. Introduced by Governor Cosmo Haskard in the 1960s, at 51° 45' south, it's not as far south as Punta Arenas or Estancia Sara, but its Black Hamburg table grapes may provide the most abundant harvest of any of them.

In the Islands, grapes have been such a luxury that Government House dinner guests eat them dipped in chocolate during the March-April harvest. According to Stanley market gardener Tim Miller, he purchases the surplus and labels them "'by Royal Appointment,' as the governor is the queen's representative at the end of the day!"



handful of early colonial artifacts, regional ethnography, the missionization of Isla Dawson and other nearby areas, cartography, and the petroleum industry. For Darwinians, there's a scale model of the *Beagle* and, for Chilean patriots, one of the *Ancud,* which sailed from Chiloé to claim the region in 1843.

The Museo Regional Salesiano (Av. Bulnes 336, tel. 061/221001, www.museomaggiorinoborgatello.cl, US$4 adults, US$0.40 children) is open 10 A.M.–12:30 P.M. and 3–5:30 P.M. Tuesday–Sunday.

### Museo Naval y Marítimo

Pleasantly surprising, Punta Arenas's naval and maritime museum provides perspectives on topics like ethnography—in the context of the Strait of Magellan's seagoing peoples—even while stressing its military mission. It features interactive exhibits, such as a credible warship's bridge, a selection of model ships, and information on the naval history of the southern oceans.

The most riveting material, though, concerns Chilean pilot Luis Pardo Villalón's 1916 rescue of British explorer Ernest Shackleton's crew at Elephant Island, on the Antarctic peninsula. On the cutter *Yelcho,* with neither heat, electricity, nor radio in foggy and stormy winter weather, Pardo soon returned the entire crew to Punta Arenas; he later served as Chilean consul in Liverpool.

The Museo Naval y Marítimo (Pedro Montt 981, tel. 061/205479, www.museonaval.cl, US$2 adults, US$0.60 children) is open 9:30 A.M.–12:30 P.M. and 2–6 P.M. daily Tuesday–Saturday.

### Museo del Recuerdo

Run by the Instituto de la Patagonia, part of the Universidad de Magallanes, the Museo del Recuerdo is a mostly open-air facility of pioneer agricultural implements and industrial machinery, reconstructions of a traditional house and shearing shed, and a restored shepherd's trailer house (hauled across the Patagonian plains on wooden wheels). In addition to a modest botanical garden, the institute has a library/bookshop with impressive cartographic exhibits.

The Museo del Recuerdo (Av. Bulnes 01890, tel. 061/207056, 8:30 A.M.–11 A.M. and 2–6 P.M. Mon.–Sat., US$2 adults, free for children) can be reached from downtown Punta Arenas by *taxi colectivos* (duty-free to the Zona Franca), which stop directly opposite the entrance.

## Other Sights

Four blocks south of Plaza Muñoz Gamero, at the foot of Avenida Independencia, naval vessels, freighters, cruise ships, Antarctic icebreakers, and yachts from many countries dock at the **Muelle Fiscal Arturo Prat,** the city's major port facility until recently. It's still a departure point for cruises to the fjords of Tierra del Fuego and to Antarctica, but, unfortunately, international security hysteria has closed it to spontaneous public access.

The late, gifted travel writer Bruce Chatwin found the inspiration for his legendary vignettes of *In Patagonia* through tales of his eccentric distant relative Charley Milward, who built and resided at the **Castillo Milward** (Milward's Castle, Av. España 959). Described by Chatwin as "a Victorian parsonage translated to the Strait of Magellan," with "high-pitched gables and gothic windows," the building features a square street-side tower and an octagonal one at the rear.

At the corner of Avenida Colón and O'Higgins, gracing the walls of the former **Liceo de Niñas Sara Braun** (Sara Braun Girls' School), and honoring Chile's Nobel Prize poetess, the weathering seven-meter **Mural Gabriela Mistral** has undergone a recent restoration.

Ten blocks north of Plaza Muñoz Gamero, the **Cementerio Municipal Sara Braun** (Av. Bulnes 029) is home to the extravagant crypts of José Menéndez, José Nogueira, and Sara Braun; the multinational immigrants who worked for them—English, Scots, Welsh, Croat, German, and Scandinavian—repose in more modest circumstances. A separate

© WAYNE BERNHARDSON

Punta Arenas's Cementerio Municipal is full of elaborate crypts and topiaries.

monument honors the vanished Selk'nam (Ona) people who once flourished in the Strait, while another memorializes German fatalities of the Battle of the Falklands (1914).

## ENTERTAINMENT

Except on Sunday, when the city seems deader than the cemetery, there's usually something to do.

Punta Arenas has one surviving cinema, the **Sala Estrella** (Mejicana 777, tel. 061/241262).

**El Templo** (Pedro Montt 951, tel. 061/223667) is primarily a dance club. The stylish **Olijoe Pub** (Errázuriz 970) has the feel of an upscale English pub, with paneled walls, ceiling, and bar, and reasonably priced drinks; the music, though, can get a little loud for conversation. The Sara Braun mansion's basement **Taberna Club de la Unión** (Plaza Muñoz Gamero 716, tel. 061/617133) is popular on weekends.

**Santino** (Av. Colón 657, tel. 061/710882, www.santino.cl) is a spacious and informal pub where everyone (except nonsmokers) feels welcome; there's also food, but it's not the star.

At the north end of town, **Makanudo** (El Ovejero 474, cell 09/6492031) has 7–10 P.M. happy hours Monday–Thursday, and live music Friday and Saturday nights from around 1:30 A.M.

The **Club Hípico** (municipal racetrack) fronts on Avenida Bulnes between Coronel Mardones and Manantiales, north of downtown. Professional soccer matches take place at the **Estadio Fiscal** (stadium), a few blocks north at Avenida Bulnes and José González.

## SHOPPING

Though it's faltered in recent years, Punta's major shopping destination is the duty-free **Zona Franca,** four kilometers north of downtown but easily reached by *taxi colectivo* from Calle Magallanes. Consumer electronics were once the big attraction—Santiaguinos even flew here for the bargains—but price differentials are smaller now.

For crafts such as metal (copper and bronze), semiprecious stones (lapis lazuli), and woollens, visit **Chile Típico** (Ignacio Carrera Pinto 1015, tel. 061/225827). For books (including some local guidebooks and travel literature in English), maps, and keepsakes, try **Southern Patagonia Souvenirs & Books,** which has outlets at the airport (tel. 061/211591) and at Hotel Dreams (O'Higgins 1235).

## ACCOMMODATIONS

Sernatur maintains a complete list of accommodations with up-to-date prices. What in many other parts of Chile would be called *residenciales* are *hostales* (B&Bs) here. Some relatively expensive places have cheaper rooms with shared baths that can be excellent values.

### US$10-25

With the Chilean peso's recent appreciation, finding truly shoestring accommodations has become more difficult. However, friendly **Barefoot Backpackers** (O'Higgins 646, cell 09/6848-8110, www.barefoot.cl, US$10 pp) occupies an old but well-kept house, with 4–8 beds per room, kitchen access, decent bathrooms, and abundant computers plus wireless Internet.

### US$25-50

East of the racetrack at the foot of Quillota, the shoreline **Hospedaje Costanera** (Rómulo Correa 1221, tel. 061/240175, hospedajecostanera@hotmail.com, US$13–15 pp in dorms, US$20–50 s, US$36–50 d) has drawn favorable commentary. The cheaper doubles have shared baths.

**Hostal Fitz Roy** (Lautaro Navarro 850, tel./fax 061/240430, www.hostalfitzroy.com, US$16 pp, US$30–40 s, US$40–50 d) is an old-fashioned B&B offering some modern comforts—notably cable TV and phones in each room—along with peace and quiet, thoughtful English-speaking ownership, and an excellent breakfast that includes fresh homemade bread and eggs. Returned to their original configuration, the rooms are spacious, but buildings of this vintage still have creaky floors and staircases. The higher rates correspond to rooms with private baths; there are separate cabañas with private baths (US$60 d). Parking is ample.

In a large old house that's been subdivided, rooms at **Hostal al Fin del Mundo** (O'Higgins 1026, tel. 061/710185, www.alfindelmundo.cl, US$20 pp with shared bath, US$32 s, US$50 d with private bath) vary in size and quality, but it has its good points (including proximity to some of the city's best restaurants).

## US$50-100

Rehabbed **Hotel Montecarlo** (Av. Colón 605, tel. 061/222120, www.montecarlohotel.cl, US$20 pp, US$44 s, US$56 d) is once again worth consideration; the more expensive rooms have private baths.

In upgraded new quarters, with delightfully attentive management, **Hostal Calafate** (Magallanes 671, tel. 061/241281, www.calafate.cl, US$44–54 s, US$54–67 d) has become a nine-room guesthouse in a lovingly restored, vintage Magellanic house with contemporary amenities except for the double-paned windows—which, surprisingly, it had from the first. All rooms are luminous, and have gleaming new private baths, though the third-floor rooms share a separate bath on the floor below. As with any building of this age, though, the floors still creak. There is parking.

**Hostal Ayelen** (Lautaro Navarro 763, tel. 061/242413, www.ayelenresidencial.com, US$50 s, US$70 d) is a friendly family-run hostelry with small but efficient singles and larger doubles and triples. Rates include satellite TV, wireless Internet, and parking, but at midday the yippy poodles in the garden can be a nuisance (they're indoors, and quiet, at other hours).

Across from Hostal Ayelen, **Hostal Art Nouveau** (Lautaro Navarro 762, tel. 061/228112, www.hostalartnouveau.cl, US$50 s, US$72 d) is less pretentious than it sounds—a restored period house with attractive common spaces and a breakfast. Some of the rooms, though, lack exterior windows, and others are on the small side.

Low-key **Hostal Terrasur** (O'Higgins 723, tel. 061/225618, www.hostalterrasur.cl, US$56 s, US$76 d) is one of the more appealing B&B-style places in its range. Rates include cable TV, telephone, and continental breakfast.

The deco-style **Hotel Cóndor de Plata** (Av. Colón 556, tel. 061/247987, www.condordeplata.cl, US$75 s, US$85 d) has always been a good choice, but the strong peso has made its prices less competitive.

New in late 2007, the 11-room **Hotel Chalet Chapital** (Sanhueza 974, tel. 061/730100, www.hotelchaletchapital.cl, US$85 s, US$95 d) occupies a handsomely restored historic building, with contemporary furnishings, wireless Internet, and whirlpool tubs in every room.

## US$100-200

Across from the Hotel Chalet Chapital, **Hotel Rey Don Felipe** (Armando Sanhueza 965, tel. 061/295000, www.hotelreydonfelipe.com, US$100 s, US$120 d) is a good new hotel. **Hotel Isla Rey Jorge** (21 de Mayo 1243, tel. 061/222681, www.islareyjorge.com, US$119 s, US$146 d) has been a favorite with foreign tour groups, but it's showing signs of deferred maintenance. Half a block south of Plaza Muñoz Gamero, **Hotel Plaza** (Nogueira 1116, tel. 061/241300, www.hotelplaza.cl, US$98–127 s or d) is a classic of its era, but it would benefit from a restoration.

The contemporary **Hotel Tierra del Fuego** (Av. Colón 716, tel./fax 061/226200, www.puntaarenas.com, US$125 s, US$140 d) is a business-oriented facility that's managed to hold prices steady. Overlooking the rejuvenated waterfront, the modern **Hotel Diego de Almagro** (Av. Colón 1290, tel. 061/208800, www.dahoteles.com, US$153 s, US$164 d) is a welcome addition to Punta's accommodations roster; the spacious corner rooms have especially panoramic views, and the service is noteworthy. **Hotel Finis Terrae** (Av. Colón 766, tel. 061/228200, www.hotelfinisterrae.com, US$154 s, US$185 d) is another fine newer hotel.

The most historic accommodations, though, can be found at the **Hotel José Nogueira**

(Bories 959, tel. 061/711000, www.hotelnogueira.com, US$170 s, US$190 d), which occupies part of the Sara Braun mansion. Its greenhouse bar/restaurant, with its snaking grape arbor, merits a visit even if you can't afford to book a room (some of which are small).

## Over US$200

New in 2010, **Hotel Dreams del Estrecho** (O'Higgins 1235, tel. 061/204500, www.mundodreams.com, US$173 s, US$207 d) is a glass palace casino hotel with 88 rooms including 16 suites. From the outside, it contrasts shockingly with the old waterfront, but it's agreeable within except for the adjoining casino, which makes a kitschy use of the neoclassic columns of the former gymnasium. In addition to the slots and tables, it has a restaurant, wine bar, convention center, rooftop bar, and heated pool, plus subterranean parking.

Built by the Sociedad Ganadera Tierra del Fuego, the 1960s high-rise **Hotel Cabo de Hornos** (Plaza Muñoz Gamero 1025, tel. 061/715000, www.hoteles-australis.com, US$190 s, US$210 d) has undergone not just a face-lift but a full-scale makeover under new ownership—the same as the Cruceros Australis cruise line. The public spaces are spectacular and the rooms attractive, but they have their shortcomings—the ethernet cables, for instance, are short and remote from the any potential workspace.



## FOOD

Punta Arenas's fast-improving gastronomic scene ranges from fast food to haute cuisine. With the appreciating Chilean peso, prices are increasing rapidly.

**Quijote** (Lautaro Navarro 1087, tel. 061/241225) serves inexpensive lunches. The best fast-food alternative, though, is **Lomit's** (José Menéndez 722, tel. 061/243399), a dependable sandwich-and-beer chain that's almost always packed. Sandwiches cost around US$5–7. **La Carioca** (José Menéndez 600, tel. 061/224809), by contrast, is a one-of-a-kind sandwich outlet that also serves passable pizza, pasta, and draft beer.

Friendly **Chocolatta** (Bories 852, tel. 061/221129) has the best coffee drinks and hot chocolate, along with desserts and muffins, and good wireless Internet. It also has a branch in the new Hotel Dreams alongside the casino, but that locale permits smoking.

**Dónde Mariano** (O'Higgins 504, tel. 061/245291, lunch and dinner daily) delivers on its modest pretensions, serving simply prepared fish entrées for around US$10 and a king crab casserole for US$15.

On the former site of the landmark restaurant La Luna (and under the same management), **O Sole Mio** (O'Higgins 974, tel. 061/242026, lunch and dinner daily) serves pastas with creative touches—spinach gnocchi, for instance—and excellent seafood sauces. Prices are moderate, around US$7 for the lunch special and US$14 for a three-course dinner that that might include lasagna or a seafood stew. It's kept most of La Luna's informal atmosphere and decor, including classic (and newer) movie posters.

In a new location half a block south, **La Luna** (O'Higgins 1017, tel. 061/228555, lunch and dinner daily) still buzzes with activity—pins stuck on wall maps indicate the origins of the clientele—but the transition seems to have cost it some of its informality. The *chupe de centolla* (king crab casserole, US$15) is still the signature dish.

Alongside La Luna, **Jekus** (O'Higgins 1021, tel. 061/245851, jekus.patagonia@gmail.com, lunch and dinner daily) has a sunken bar and dining room of natural woods, with a separate upstairs for smokers. The food is demonstrably Patagonian in dishes such as the king crab cannelloni (US$11) and roast lamb (US$13).

Stick with the meat at **El Estribo** (Ignacio Carrera Pinto 762, tel. 061/244714, lunch and dinner daily); its fish is only so-so, but the beef and lamb dishes (US$9–11 and up) are consistently strong, and Patagonian game dishes have earned a spot on the menu. The English menu translation is occasionally hilarious, but the service is attentive.

**La Marmita Bistro** (Plaza Sampaio 678, tel. 061/222056, lunch and dinner daily) has risen to near the top of Punta's restaurant scene for creative seafood (no Italian would recognize the scallop appetizer as "lasagna," but it's outstanding), unusual vegetarian plates (US$10–14), a lamb casserole (US$14), and even game dishes such as guanaco (US$15). With a casual historical atmosphere, it also serves varied desserts.

It's not faultless, but Punta's first Peruvian restaurant, tobacco-free **Entre el Puente y la Alameda** (O'Higgins 694, tel. 061/222818, lunch and dinner Mon.–Sat.) was worth the wait for traditional dishes such as *ají de gallina* (chicken in a walnut sauce, US$13) and pisco sours well balanced between sweet and tart, as well as the ceviche starter (US$11). On the down side, it can run short of fish, and the wines—none of them by the glass—come only from the largest Chilean producers.

In expanded quarters, the nautically themed **Puerto Viejo** (O'Higgins 1166, tel. 061/225103) continues doing bang-up business with an almost exclusively seafood menu. Open for lunch and dinner, with knowledgeable waiters and terrific service, it serves specialties such as *centolla* (king crab) and *merluza* (hake).

Under the same management as Puerto Viejo, a couple kilometers north of the plaza, **Los Ganaderos** (Av. Bulnes 0977, tel. 061/214597, www.parrillalosganaderos.cl, lunch and dinner daily) is a classy *parrilla* specializing in succulent Patagonian lamb grilled on a vertical spit (US$15). There is also a more diverse *parrillada* for two (US$28), and pasta dishes, with simple sauces, are in the US$10 range. Try the regional Patagonian desserts, such as *mousse de calafate* and *mousse de ruibarbo* (rhubarb).

Four blocks south of the plaza, the creative **La Leyenda del Remezón** (21 de Mayo 1469, tel. 061/241029, lunch and dinner daily) serves game dishes (beaver and guanaco are farmed in the region) in the US$20–24 range—not cheap, obviously, but unique. For US$13, the *pastel de choclo* made with king crab (instead of the traditional chicken) is worth a taste.

In the old Centro Español, the upstairs **La Tasca** (Plaza Muñoz Gamero 771, tel. 061/242807, lunch and dinner daily) is a cheerful midrange to upmarket Spanish restaurant with creative variants on traditional dishes, such as *merluza* (hake) stuffed with king crab and avocado (US$13). The pisco sours are excellent, and the wine list is good, but it's unfortunately a free-fire zone for smokers.

**Broccolino** (O'Higgins 1049, tel. 061/710479, lunch and dinner daily) serves a fine rack of lamb (US$24), plus fish dishes such as such as conger eel with *centolla* and scallops in a white wine sauce (US$15). Traditionally, the expanded **Sotito's Bar** (O'Higgins 1138, tel. 061/245365, lunch and dinner daily) has set the seafood standard here, and it still deserves consideration.

In a magnificent period house whose several small dining rooms give it a real intimacy, **Damiana Elena** (Magallanes 341, tel. 061/222818) is widely considered the city's best; in its new location, it now has a tobacco-free section that it lacked before. Appetizers include *ostiones al pil pil* (a garlicky scallop dish, US$13), while main dishes are items such scallops with palm heart cannelloni (US$15) and lamb chops with polenta (US$17). It also has gracious ownership, though the wine list focuses on big producers such as Errázuriz and Concha y Toro.

## INFORMATION

One block east of the plaza, **Sernatur** (Lautaro Navarro 999, tel. 061/225385, infomagallanes@sernatur.cl, 8:30 A.M.–7 P.M. weekdays all year, with identical hours on summer weekends) is one of Chile's better regional offices, with English-speaking personnel and up-to-date accommodations and transportation information.

In summer, Plaza Muñoz Gamero's municipal **Kiosko de Informaciones** (tel. 061/200610, informacionturistica@puntaarenas.cl) is open 8 A.M.–5:30 P.M. weekdays except Monday, when it closes an hour earlier, and 9 A.M.–6 P.M. Saturday.

**Conaf** (Av. Bulnes 0309, 4th floor, tel. 061/238581) provides information on national parks.

## SERVICES

Punta Arenas is one of the easier Chilean cities in which to change both cash and travelers checks, especially at travel agencies along Lautaro Navarro. Most close by midday Saturday, but **Scott Cambios** (Av. Colón and Magallanes, tel. 061/245811) will cash travelers checks then.

Several banks around Plaza Muñoz Gamero have ATMs, such as **BancoEstado** (Plaza Muñoz Gamero 799), which occupies the historical Sociedad Braun Blanchard.

Just north of Plaza Muñoz Gamero, **Correos de Chile** (Bories 911) is the post office. **Entel** (Lautaro Navarro 931) has a long-distance call center.

The **Argentine consulate** (21 de Mayo 1878, tel. 061/261912) is open 10 A.M.–3:30 P.M. weekdays only.

For clean clothes, try **Lavandería Record** (O'Higgins 969, tel. 061/243607) or **Lavaseco Vicars** (Sarmiento de Gamboa 726, tel. 061/241516).

Punta Arenas's **Hospital Regional** (Arauco and Angamos, tel. 061/244040) is north of downtown.

## GETTING THERE

Punta Arenas has good air links with mainland Chile, frequent flights to Chilean Tierra del Fuego, infrequent flights to Argentine Tierra del Fuego, and regular weekly service to the Falkland Islands. There are roundabout overland routes to mainland Chile via Argentina, regular bus service to Argentine Tierra del Fuego via a ferry link, direct ferry service to Chilean Tierra del Fuego, and expensive (but exceptionally scenic) cruise-ship service to Ushuaia, in Argentine Tierra del Fuego.

### Air

**LAN** (Bories 884, tel. 061/241232) flies several times daily to Santiago, normally via Puerto Montt, but some flights stop at Balmaceda, near Coyhaique. It also flies three times weekly to Ushuaia, Argentina, and Saturday to the Falkland Islands; one Falklands flight per month stops in the Argentine city of Río Gallegos.

**Sky Airline** (Roca 935, tel. 061/710645) now flies north to Balmaceda/Coyhaique, Puerto Montt, and Santiago, with connections to northern Chilean cities.

**Aerovías DAP** (O'Higgins 878, tel. 061/616100, www.aeroviasdap.cl) flies seven-seat Cessnas to and from Porvenir (US$40), in Chilean Tierra del Fuego, at least once a day except Sunday, more often in summer. Daily except Tuesday and Sunday, it flies 20-seater Twin Otters to and from Puerto Williams on Isla Navarino (US$112). In addition, it has extensive charter services and occasionally goes to Antarctica.

## AIR ANTARCTICA

For many visitors, one of the great disincentives to Antarctic travel is the fact that, even though southern South America offers the closest approach to the frozen continent, it usually involves a stomach-churning two-day crossing of the stormy Drake Passage – in each direction. If Chilean entrepreneurs have their way, though, well-heeled travelers will soon skip the seasickness.

In the summer of 2004, Punta Arenas-based **Antarctica XXI** organized the first commercial air-sea excursion to the South Shetland Islands, eliminating the Drake Passage segment. Arriving at the Base Aérea Presidente Eduardo Frei Montalva, the Chilean air force's main Antarctic base on Isla Rey Jorge, passengers almost immediately board the Danish-built, 62-passenger *Ocean Nova* for a five-day cruise in the relatively sheltered waters between the South Shetlands and the Antarctic Peninsula.

The convenience comes at a price, though; the cheapest rate for the all-inclusive tour is US$8,990 per person, triple occupancy. For more details, contact Antarctica XXI (Lautaro Navarro 987, 2nd floor, Punta Arenas, tel. 061/614100, www.antarcticaxxi.com).

## Bus

Punta Arenas has no central terminal, though some companies share facilities and the **Central de Pasajeros** (Av. Colón and Magallanes, tel. 061/245811) sells tickets for all of them. Most terminals are within a few blocks of each other, north of Plaza Muñoz Gamero. Services vary seasonally but are most numerous in January and February.

Carriers serving Puerto Natales (US$8–12, three hours) include **Pullman Bus Sur** (José Menéndez 552, tel. 061/614224, www.bus-sur.cl), with four buses daily; **Buses Fernández** (Armando Sanhueza 745, tel. 061/242313, www.busesfernandez.com), eight daily; and **Buses Pacheco** (Av. Colón 900, tel. 061/225527, www.busespacheco.com), five daily.

In addition to its Puerto Natales services, Bus Sur goes to the Chilean cities of Osorno (US$50–70, 32 hours), Puerto Montt, and Castro Monday at 9 A.M., via Argentina. **Queilen Bus** (Lautaro Navarro 975, tel. 061/222714) does the same route on Friday, while **Turibús** (Armando Sanhueza 745, tel. 061/227970) goes to Osorno (US$50) Tuesday, Thursday, and Saturday at 9:30 A.M.

Several carriers go to Río Gallegos (US$16, four hours): Bus Sur, **Buses El Pingüino** (Armando Sanhueza 745, tel. 061/223898), **Buses Ghisoni** (Lautaro Navarro 975, tel. 061/613420, busesghisoni@123.cl), and Buses Pacheco.

**Tecni-Austral** (Lautaro Navarro 975, tel. 061/222078) goes to Río Grande (US$50, eight hours) and Ushuaia (US$60, 11 hours), in Argentine Tierra del Fuego, Tuesday, Thursday, and Saturday at 8:30 A.M. **Buses Pacheco** goes Monday, Wednesday, and Friday at 9 A.M. to Río Grande, with connections to Ushuaia, but also has direct services Tuesday, Thursday, and Saturday at 10 A.M. Bus Sur has also added services to Ushuaia.

## Sea

**Transbordadora Austral Broom** (Av. Bulnes 05075, tel. 061/218100, www.tabsa.cl) sails from Punta Arenas to Porvenir (2.5 hours) at 9 A.M. daily except Sunday, when sailing time is 9:30 A.M. Adult passengers pay US$10 per person except for the drivers, whose fare is included in the US$60 charge per vehicle (motorcyclists pay US$20 but bicyclists board for

© WAYNE BERNHARDSON

Both cruise ships and merchant vessels use the port of Punta Arenas.

free). The rate for children is half the adult fare. The new *Crux Australis* ferry has greater vehicle capacity than the one it replaced, but reservations are still advisable; it leaves from Terminal Tres Puentes, at the north end of town but easily reached by *taxi colectivo* No. 15 from the Casa Braun-Menéndez, on Magallanes half a block north of Plaza Muñoz Gamero.

Broom also operates the ferry *Bahía Azul* to Puerto Williams (32 hours) every Wednesday at 6 P.M., returning Friday at 10 P.M. The fare is US$210 for a bunk, US$175 for a reclining seat; children up to age 10 pay half.

It's neither cheap nor a conventional way of getting to Argentina, but the luxury cruisers *Via Australis* and *Stella Australis* shuttle to Ushuaia as part of a weeklong circuit through the fjords of Chilean Tierra del Fuego, and passengers can disembark in Ushuaia (or board there, for that matter). Normally both ships require reservations well in advance: contact **Cruceros Australis** (www.australis.com).

### GETTING AROUND

**Aeropuerto Presidente Carlos Ibáñez del Campo** is 20 kilometers north of town on Ruta 9, the Puerto Natales highway. **Transfer Austral** (Lautaro Navarro 975, tel. 061/617202, www.transferaustral.com) arranges door-to-door transfers (US$6 pp in a shared van).

Buses returning from Puerto Natales will normally drop passengers at the airport to meet outgoing flights on request, but make arrangements before boarding. Natales-bound buses will also pick up arriving passengers, but again make arrangements in advance.

Punta Arenas has numerous car-rental options, including **Adel Rent a Car** (Pedro Montt 962, tel. 061/224819, www.adel.cl), **Europcar** (O'Higgins 964, tel./fax 061/202720, anselmo.cares@europcar.cl), **Avis** (Roca 1044, tel./fax 061/241182, rentacar@viaterra.cl), **Hertz** (O'Higgins 931, tel. 061/613087), and **Lubag** (Av. Colón 975, tel./fax 061/710484, luis_barra@entelchile.net).



## Vicinity of Punta Arenas

Punta Arenas's myriad travel agencies operate excursions to nearby destinations such as Reserva Nacional Magallanes, Fuerte Bulnes, the Seno Otway penguin colony, Río Verde, Estancia San Gregorio, and even Parque Nacional Torres del Paine. The most popular half-day excursions, such as Fuerte Bulnes and Otway, cost around US$25 per person, while full-day trips such as Pali Aike cost around US$60 per person, with a three-person minimum.

Among the established operators are **Aventour** (Patagonia 779-A, tel. 061/241197, www.aventourpatagonia.com), **Turismo Aónikenk** (Magallanes 570, tel. 061/228616, www.aonikenk.com), **Turismo Laguna Azul** (José Menéndez 786, tel. 061/225200, www.lagunaazul.cl), **Turismo Pali Aike** (Lautaro Navarro 1125, tel. 061/615750, www.turismopaliaike.com), **Turismo Viento Sur** (Fagnano 585, tel. 061/222590, www.vientosur.com), and **Turismo Yámana** (Errázuriz 932, tel. 061/240056, www.yamana.cl).

### RESERVA NACIONAL MAGALLANES

Only eight kilometers west of downtown, 13,500-hectare Reserva Nacional Magallanes is a combination of Patagonian steppe and southern beech forest that, in good winters, amasses enough snow for skiing. Despite its proximity to Punta Arenas, official statistics say it gets barely 11,500 visitors per year, and fewer than 1,800 of those are foreigners.

Westbound Avenida Independencia, a good gravel road that may require chains in winter, climbs gradually to a fork whose southern branch leads to **Sector Andino,** where the local Club Andino's **Centro de Esquí Cerro Mirador** includes a *refugio* that serves meals, as well as a ski school and a single well-maintained chairlift. In summer, try the **Sendero**

## *PINGÜINOS* AND *PINGÜINERAS*

Chilean Patagonia's largest city, Punta Arenas, is close to two breeding colonies of the burrowing Magellanic penguin, *Spheniscus magellanicus.* The Otway Sound colony (Pingüinera Seno Otway) is about a 45-minute drive from the city, and is interesting enough. The larger colony on Isla Magdalena (Monumento Natural Los Pingüinos), an island in the Strait of Magellan, is two hours away by ferry or slightly less by bus and rigid inflatable.

Also known to English speakers as the jackass penguin because its call resembles that of a braying burro, the Magellanic is present from October to April. It's most numerous in January and February, when the chicks hatch in the sandy burrows that the birds have dug beneath the coastal turf. After the chicks have hatched, the parents alternate fishing trips in search of food that they later regurgitate to their young (combined with the scent of bird droppings, this makes any visit to a penguin colony an olfactory as well as a visual and auditory experience).

While the birds appear tame, they are wild animals and their sharp beaks can draw blood – maintain a respectful distance for photography. Though both the Otway and Magdalena colonies have fenced walking routes to restrain tourists, the birds themselves frequently cross these routes.

Besides the countless seabirds and dolphins en route, the Magdalena trip has the added bonus of a historical lighthouse that's now a visitors center on an island that's one enormous warren of penguin burrows. While neither trip is strenuous, any walk in Patagonia's roaring winds can be a workout.



**Mirador,** a two-hour loop hike that winds through the forest and crosses the ski area; there's also a mountain-bike circuit.

The northwesterly **Sector Las Minas,** which includes a gated picnic area, charges US$2 per person for adult admission, but nothing for kids. A longer footpath links up with the trail to the El Mirador summit, which offers panoramas east toward Punta Arenas, the strait, and Tierra del Fuego, and west toward Seno Otway.

Though some travel agencies offer tours to the reserve, it would also be a good mountain-bike excursion from town.

## PINGÜINERA SENO OTWAY

Burrowing Magellanic penguins abound along Argentine Patagonia's Atlantic shoreline, but they are fewer in Chile. Barely an hour from Punta Arenas, though, the Otway colony of *Spheniscus magellanicus* is the closest to any major city on the continent. Administered by the nonprofit Fundación Otway, it grew in a decade from no more than 400 penguins to about 10,000 (5,000 breeding pairs) at present. From October, when the first birds arrive, to April, when the last stragglers head to sea, it draws up to 40,000 visitors. The peak season is December–February.

While the site is fenced to keep human visitors out of critical habitat, the birds are relatively tame and easy to photograph; on the downside, this fence did not prevent stray dogs from killing more than a hundred birds in 2001. The landowning Kusanovic family has taken over management from the Fundación Otway.

During the season, any number of Punta Arenas operators shuttle visitors to and from Otway for about US$25 per person, not including the US$10 per person admission charge. Half-day tours take place either in morning (which photographers may prefer) or afternoon. For visitors with private vehicles, there's also a US$2 toll.

Otway is only about 65 kilometers northwest of Punta Arenas via Ruta 9 and a gravel road that leads west from a signed junction at Parque Chabunco, about 19 kilometers north of the city.

While Otway is a worthwhile excursion, visitors with flexible schedules and a little more money should consider the larger Isla Magdalena colony in Monumento Natural Los Pingüinos, in the Strait of Magellan. For more details, contact **Turis Otway** (Mejicana 122, tel. 061/614650, www.turisotway.cl) or virtually any other local travel agency.

## MONUMENTO NATURAL LOS PINGÜINOS

From early October, nearly 70,000 breeding pairs of Magellanic penguins paddle ashore and waddle to burrows that cover nearly all of 97-hectare **Isla Magdalena,** 20 nautical miles northeast of Punta Arenas, before returning to sea in April. Also the site of a landmark lighthouse, Isla Magdalena is the focal point of Monumento Natural Los Pingüinos, one of Conaf's smallest but most interesting reserves.

While the mainland Otway colony gets upwards of 40,000 visitors per year, Isla Magdalena gets only about half that number—80 percent of them foreigners—because of relative inaccessibility. In summer, though, the ferry *Melinka* visits the island daily from Punta Arenas. Though more expensive than Otway tours, these excursions also offer the chance to see penguins and dolphins in the water, as well as black-browed albatrosses, cormorants, kelp gulls, skuas, South American terns, and other seabirds in the surrounding skies.



From a floating dock on the east side of the island, a short trail leads along the beach and up the hill to Scottish engineer George Slight's **Faro Magdalena** (1901), a lighthouse whose iron tower rises 13.5 meters above the island's highest point; still functioning, the light has a range of 10 nautical miles. A narrow spiral staircase ascends the tower.

In the building's first five decades, a resident caretaker maintained the acetylene light, but after its automation in 1955 the building was abandoned and vandalized. In 1981, though, the Chilean navy entrusted the building to Conaf; declared a national monument, it has since become a visitors center (unfortunately, the tower is now closed to visitors). It boasts remarkably good accounts of the island's history, including discovery, early navigation, cartography, and the lighthouse's construction, and natural history in both Spanish and English (though the English text is less complete). U.S. archaeologist Junius Bird, best known for his 1930s work at the mainland site of Pali Aike, also undertook excavations here.

For ferry excursions to Isla Magdalena, contact **Turismo Comapa** (Magallanes 990, tel. 061/200200, tcomapa@entelchile.net). In December, January, and February, the ferry *Melinka* normally makes a daily passengers-only trip to Isla Magdalena (US$50 pp, US$25 for minors) from Terminal Tres Puentes; sometimes the larger, more comfortable *Crux Australis* substitutes for it. Sailing time is 4 P.M. (bring food—the *Melinka*'s snack bar is pretty dire, the *Crux Australis*'s only a bit better). Visitors spend about 1.5 hours on the island, returning to Punta Arenas around 9:30 P.M.

Passengers on the luxury Cruceros Australis voyages through Tierra del Fuego's fjords stop here on the return leg of the trip, but there's also an intermediate alternative that's more frequent than either of the above. **Solo Expediciones** (José Nogueira 1255, tel. 061/710219, www.soloexpediciones.com) offers half-day excursions (US$75 pp) that shuttle passengers from the mainland in covered Zodiacs and include an approach to nearby Isla Marta, where the overflow from penguin-saturated Magdalena has migrated.

## FUERTE BULNES

In 1584, Spanish explorer Pedro Sarmiento de Gamboa organized an expedition of 15 ships and 4,000 men to control the Strait of Magellan, but after a series of disasters only three ships with 300 colonists arrived to found **Ciudad del Rey don Felipe** at Punta Santa Ana, south of present-day Punta Arenas. Even worse for the Spaniards, the inhospitable climate and unsuitable soils made agriculture impossible; when British privateer Thomas Cavendish landed three years later, in 1587, he found only a handful of survivors and gave it the name Port Famine, which has survived as the Spanish **Puerto del Hambre.**

For many years, the consensus was that

© WAYNE BERNHARDSON

Magellanic penguins crowd the beach at Isla Magdalena, in the Strait of Magellan.



starvation alone determined the fate of Puerto Hambre, but regional historian Mateo Martinic has suggested that disease, mutual acts of violence, Tehuelche attacks, and a simple sense of anguish or abandonment contributed to its demise. Unfortunately, the Chilean military controls much of the area, making archaeological excavations that might resolve the question difficult.

The area remained unsettled until 1843, when President Manuel Bulnes ordered the cutter *Ancud* south from Chiloé with tools, construction materials, food, and livestock to take possession for the expansionist Chilean state. The result was Fuerte Bulnes, a military outpost that survived only a little longer than the original Spanish settlement before being relocated to Punta Arenas in 1848.

Modern Fuerte Bulnes, on the site of the first Chilean settlement, is a national monument more for its site than for its reconstructions of 19th-century buildings and the defensive walls—with sharpened stakes—that surround them. Among the structures were residences, stables, a blockhouse, a chapel, a jail, and warehouse.

Archaeologists located nearby remnants of Ciudad del Rey don Felipe in 1955, and later excavations turned up human remains, bullets, tombs, and ruins of Puerto Hambre's church. A more recent plaque (1965) celebrates the 125th anniversary of the Pacific Steam Navigation Company's ships *Chile* and *Perú* and their routes around the Horn.

Puerto Hambre and Fuerte Bulnes are 58 kilometers south of Punta Arenas via Ruta 9, which is paved about halfway; the rest is bumpy but passable. There is no regular public transportation, but most Punta Arenas tour operators offer half-day excursions. Admission is free of charge.

## RESERVA NACIONAL LAGUNA PARRILLAR

About 45 kilometers southwest of Punta Arenas via paved Ruta 9 and a gravel westbound lateral, Laguna Parrillar attracts barely 7,000 visitors per year to its 18,000 hectares of forest and

## THE WHALES OF MAGALLANES

For decades, the great whales have drawn travelers to Mexico's Baja California lagoons, the shallows of Argentina's Península Valdés, and other breeding and feeding sites. From late December to April, Chile's Parque Marino Francisco Coloane, in the Strait of Magellan southwest of Punta Arenas, joins the whale-watching sweepstakes.

Established in July 2003, named in honor of a Chilean author who chronicled the southern seas, the 67,000-hectare park is the result of five years' research that pinpointed the waters near Isla Carlos III as feeding grounds for the southern humpback *(Megaptera novaeangliae)* from mid-December to late April. In addition to the humpbacks, which migrate south from Colombia, the park's seas and shorelines are home to breeding populations of Magellanic penguins, cormorants, many other southern seabirds, fur seals, and sea lions. Orcas are also present.

The Punta Arenas company Whalesound operates the motor yacht *Esturión*, which sails south through the strait; as it spies Isla Dawson to the east, black-browed albatrosses, giant petrels, and Magellanic penguins circle the ship above and in the water. It then passes the Cabo Froward lighthouse where, by tradition, Pacific and Atlantic waters mix beneath the **Cruz de los Mares,** an illuminated hilltop cross that marks the terminus of an overland trek from the road's end at Cabo San Pedro. Construction materials for the cross arrived by boat and, after being beached here, were helicoptered to the summit.

Turning west into the strait, the ship reaches Carlos III by late afternoon and, after unloading luggage at the camp, usually takes a spin around nearby rocks to see breeding colonies of fur seals and sea lions, as well as Magellanic oystercatchers, kelp geese, and small birds. The main attraction, though, is the humpbacks that dive and breach in the open strait.

Carlos III itself is a sheltered island of bonsai beeches that's also home to the world's southernmost conifer, the *ciprés de las Guaitecas* (Guaiteca cypress, *Pilgerodendron uviferum*). At low tide, a fur seal colony is only 20 minutes away on foot.

After trolling for whales the next morning, the boat circumnavigates wooded **Isla Rupert,** with a breeding colony of 22,000 Magellanic penguins. Unfortunately, the burrowing Magellanics have undermined the southern beech forest and, with their excrement and urine, are putting the woodland under serious stress.

From Isla Rupert, the *Esturión* sails west to **Isla Santa Inés** and its **Canal Ballena,** where the water shifts from deep blue to a blue-gray that it owes to sediments from a glacier that, though it reaches the sea, is receding quickly.



wetland. While it's open to day use only, it has picnic areas and hiking trails to recommend it and makes a worthwhile excursion from the city. Admission costs US$2.

## PARQUE MARINO FRANCISCO COLOANE

Established in July 2003, named for a Chilean author who chronicled the southern seas, this 67,000-hectare maritime park is the result of five years of biological investigations that pinpointed the area around Isla Carlos III, in the southwestern Strait of Magellan, as summer feeding grounds for the southern humpback whale. In addition to the humpbacks, which migrate the length of the South American coast from Colombia, the park's seas and shores are home to breeding Magellanic penguins, cormorants, many other southern seabirds, fur seals, and sea lions. Orcas are also present.

From mid-December to late April, **Whalesound** (Lautaro Navarro 1175, 2nd floor, Punta Arenas, tel. 061/710511, ext. 201, cell 09/9349-3862, www.whalesound.com) offers three-day expeditions (US$960 pp, minimum two persons) to the park, where guests sleep in geodesic dome tents, with comfortable

In an area as scenic as Tierra del Fuego's fjords, there is little wildlife except for nesting rock cormorants and, surprisingly, a clutch of condors despite the scarcity of carrion.

Leaving Santa Inés, where Whalesound offers sea kayaking and intends to build a trail for overnight treks, the ship returns to Carlos III by early evening. The next morning, it returns to the continent via **Fiordo Jerónimo**, part of southernmost **Isla Riesco**'s wild scenery, in Conaf's **Reserva Nacional Alacalufes.** At Seno Otway, passengers meet a vehicle for the return to Punta Arenas.

### PRACTICALITIES

**Whalesound** (Lautaro Navarro 1163, 2nd floor, Punta Arenas, tel. 061/710511, cell 09/9349-3862, www.whalesound.com) offers three-day expeditions (US$960 pp, minimum two persons) to Isla Carlos III, where guests sleep in geodesic dome tents, with comfortable Japanese beds and solar-powered electricity. The cost includes daily excursions with specialized bilingual guides and gourmet meals from a French-trained Chilean chef. There is also a four-day program (US$1,600 pp) that includes sea kayaking.

The *Esturión II* sails from Fuerte Bulnes, an hour south of Punta Arenas by road; if seas are too rough, they may go overland via Isla Riesco and then a shorter hop to Carlos III on rigid inflatables. For those with more money than time, there are half-day helicopter trips.

Purchased in Buenos Aires after service on the calmer Río de la Plata, the *Esturión* is an 11-meter launch that does just eight knots. It carries up to ten passengers and can sleep seven in close quarters; in addition, it has a galley, sofa, and an open-air observation deck (which served it better on the balmy Río de la Plata than the stormy Strait of Magellan).

Carlos III's sturdy dome tents are spacious but unheated; sleeping bags with fitted mummy sheets cover their single-sized platform beds. Boardwalks connect them to separate baths (hot showers with a view!) and the combination kitchen/dining room/bar, but it can be a wet, cold walk if you need the toilet in the middle of the night.

Food is excellent both on board and on land, with exceptional ceviche, fresh fish, beef, fruit, and Chilean wines. The boat's crew is friendly, the guides are knowledgeable, and the service is attentive.

New in 2008, **Expedición Fitz Roy** (Roca 825, Oficina 3, tel. 061/613933, www.expedicionfitzroy.com, from US$875 pp for two-day, two-night packages, with three-day, two-night packages for US$1,100 pp) offers similar services, but passengers sleep aboard the reconditioned M/V *Forrest,* which once hauled wool around the Falkland Islands.



Japanese beds and solar-powered electricity, on Isla Carlos III. The cost includes daily excursions with specialized bilingual guides and gourmet meals from a French-trained Chilean chef. Sea kayaks are also available.

## RÍO VERDE

Some 43 kilometers north of Punta Arenas on Ruta 9, a gravel road loops northwest along Seno Otway to Seno Skyring and Estancia Río Verde, which has seemingly made the transition from a shipshape sheep farm to a model municipality of exquisitely maintained public buildings in the Magellanic style. Note particularly the manicured gardens surrounding the **Escuela Básica,** the local boarding school.

In one wing of the boarding school, the **Museo Comunal Río Verde** has exhibits on local history, natural history (taxidermy), ethnology, and local and regional literature, but it's open only erratically. The admission charge is nominal.

Unfortunately, only the foundations of the recently created Municipalidad remain, after it burned to the ground a couple years back and museum exhibits were lost; municipal offices have since moved to the former Hostería Río Verde, 90 kilometers from Punta Arenas and six kilometers south of the *estancia*.

Across from the former *hostería,* a small ferry shuttles vehicles and passengers to **Isla Riesco** (warning: it's free to the island but costs US$40 to get your vehicle back to the mainland; the ferry operates 8:30 A.M.–noon and 2–7 P.M. daily). Nearby, Paola Vizzani González's *Escultura Monumental,* a beached whale built of concrete and driftwood, honors the region's early colonists. Also nearby, the **Hito El Vapor** marks the final resting place of the steamer *Los Amigos,* which carried coal to outlying farms until it ran aground in a storm.

The loop road rejoins Ruta 9 at Villa Tehuelches, a wide spot in the road about 90 kilometers from Punta Arenas. This makes a good alternative route north or south for both motorists and mountain bikers (the terrain is comparable, but the loop is more scenic even though it's about 13 kilometers longer).

While the *hostería* at the ferry crossing no longer provides accommodations, the Chilean-Uruguayan **Estancia Río Verde** (Km 98 Norte, tel. 061/311123 or 061/311131, www.estanciarioverde.cl, US$110 s, US$154 d) offers stylish accommodations (one suite has a sunny tower with sea and Pampas views), day tours that can include horseback riding and fishing, and *asados,* lunches, and tea in its restaurant. Open November to March, it's a bargain by *estancia* standards and has gracious English-speaking ownership.



## ESTANCIA RÍO PENITENTE

Founded by Falkland Islands immigrants in 1891, Río Penitente has turned one of the best-preserved historic houses on any Patagonian sheep ranch into a guesthouse that feels like a step back in time but still has essential comforts, such as private baths. Most guest rooms in this two-story Victorian have period furniture, in immaculate condition, and fireplaces for heat. Activities include horseback riding and fly-fishing in its namesake river, but it's an ideal place for just relaxing. The restaurant serves lamb-on-a-stake barbecues to tour groups on weekends.

**Hostería Estancia Río Penitente** (Ruta 9 Km 137, tel. 061/331694, www.hosteriariopenitente.com, US$126 s, US$146 d with breakfast) is open October to Semana Santa (Holy Week).

## RÍO RUBENS

About midway between Villa Tehuelches and Puerto Natales, Río Rubens is a prime trout stream that flows northeast into Argentina. At kilometer 183 on Ruta 9, the nearby **Hotel Posada Río Rubens** (cell 09/9254-7943, www.hotelriorubens.cl, US$30 s, US$50 d with shared bath, breakfast included) has largely resisted the temptation to upgrade itself from a modest rural inn with a decent restaurant at modest prices, though it has added cabañas and camping.

## ESTANCIA SAN GREGORIO

From a highway junction about 45 kilometers north of Punta Arenas, paved Ruta 225 leads east/northeast to the Argentine border at Monte Aymond, passing the former Estancia San Gregorio, once one of Chilean Patagonia's largest landholdings. Part of the Menéndez wool empire, San Gregorio dates from the 1890s, though it reached its peak between 1910 and 1930. Besides wool, it produced frozen mutton, hides, and tallow.

Now run as a cooperative, 120 kilometers from Punta Arenas, San Gregorio is a *zona típica* national historical monument. It exemplified the Anglo-Scottish model of the Patagonian sheep *estancia,* in which each unit was a self-sufficient hierarchy with a nearly omnipotent administrator at the top. Geographically, it consisted of discrete residential and production sectors: The former included the administrator's house, employee residences, shearers' dormitories, chapel, and the like, while the latter comprised the shearing shed, warehouses, a smithery, company store, and similarly functional buildings. It had its own pier and railroad to move the wool clip directly to freighters.

Most of San Gregorio's constructions date from the 1890s, but a descendant of the Menéndez dynasty still occupies French architect Antoine Beaulier's **Casa Patronal**

© WAYNE BERNHARDSON

The rusting hulk of the British clipper *Ambassador* rests on the shoreline at San Gregorio.

(1925). The farm featured an extensive system of windbreaks ranging upwards of five meters in height, later planted with Monterey cypress for beautification.

While technically not open to the public, many of San Gregorio's buildings line both sides of the highway to Monte Aymond. Beached on shore are the corroded hulks of the British clipper *Ambassador* (a national monument) and the company steamer *Amadeo,* which gave up the ghost in the 1940s.

## PUNTA DELGADA

About 30 kilometers east of San Gregorio, paved Ruta 257 leads southeast to Punta Delgada, the port for the ferry crossing to Tierra del Fuego via the Primera Angostura narrows. Depending sometimes on tidal conditions, the ferries *Patagonia* and *Pionero* shuttle across the channel every 1.5 hours 8:30 A.M.–1:30 A.M. Fares are US$3 per person for passengers, US$1.50 for kids ages 10–14, US$28 for automobiles, and US$9 for motorcycles. Most buses to Argentine Tierra del Fuego use this route because the longer ferry to Porvenir goes only once daily and is subject to delay or cancellation for rough seas.

## PARQUE NACIONAL PALI AIKE

Hugging the Argentine border north of Kimiri Aike and west of the Monte Aymond border crossing, little-visited Pali Aike is an area of volcanic steppe and rugged lava beds that once supported megafauna such as the ground sloth milodon and the native American horse, both of which disappeared soon after humans first inhabited the area some 11,000 years ago.

While Paleo-Indian hunters may have contributed to their extinction, environmental changes after the last major glaciation may also have played a role. In the 1930s, self-taught archaeologist Junius Bird, of New York's American Museum of Natural History, conducted the earliest systematic excavations of Paleo-Indian sites such as Cueva Pali Aike, within the park boundaries, and Cueva Fell, a short distance west. These archaeologically rich volcanic shelters (not caves in the strictest sense of the word) are the prime reason Chilean authorities have nominated the area as a UNESCO World Heritage Site.

Findings at Pali Aike include human remains that have yielded insights on Paleo-Indian funerary customs, while materials from Cueva

MAGALLANES

Fell have helped reveal the transition from relatively simple hunting to more complex forms of subsistence. These include sophisticated hunting tools such as the bow and arrow and *boleadoras,* and a greater reliance on coastal and marine resources. There are also indicators of ceremonial artifacts.

## Geography and Climate

Part of arid eastern Magallanes, 5,030-hectare Pali Aike consists of rolling steppe grasslands whose porous volcanic soils and slag absorb water quickly. Almost constant high winds and cool temperatures make it a better summer or autumn excursion.

## Flora and Fauna

While the milodon and native horse may have disappeared, the park's grasslands swarm with herds of wild guanaco and flocks of rheas, upland geese, ibis, and other birds. Pumas and foxes are the major predators.

## Sights and Recreation

Accessible by road, **Cueva Pali Aike** is a volcanic tube seven meters wide and five meters high at its mouth; it is 17 meters deep but tapers as it advances. In the 1930s, Bird discovered both human and megafauna remains, at least 8,600 years old and probably much older, in the cave.

Tours from Punta Arenas visit Cueva Pali Aike and usually hike the 1.7-kilometer trail through the **Escorial del Diablo** (the appropriately named Devil's Slag Heap, which is hell on hiking boots). The trail ends at the volcanic **Crater Morada del Diablo.**

From Cueva Pali Aike, a nine-kilometer footpath leads to **Laguna Ana,** where waterfowl are abundant, and the main road, five kilometers from the park entrance. Mountain bikes should be ideal for this sort of rolling terrain, but it could be even tougher on tires than it is on boots.

## Practicalities

As of 2009, a campground was supposedly in the works, but there are no tourist services as yet, so bring supplies.

At the main entrance, Conaf has a ranger station but collects no admission fee. A great destination for solitude seekers, Pali Aike

© WAYNE BERNHARDSON

guanacos, Parque Nacional Pali Aike

officially gets only about 1,500 visitors per year, about a third of them foreigners.

Parque Nacional Pali Aike is 196 kilometers northeast of Punta Arenas via Ruta 9, Ruta 255, and a graveled secondary road from the hamlet of Cooperativa Villa O'Higgins, 11 kilometers beyond Kimiri Aike. Just south of the Chilean border post at Monte Aymond, a hard-to-follow dirt road also leads to the park.

There is no public transportation, but Punta Arenas travel agencies can arrange visits. Hiring a car, though, is probably the best option, especially if shared among several people.

## THE FJORDS OF FUEGIA

Short of Antarctica itself, some of the Southern Hemisphere's most awesome scenery occurs in the Beagle Channel and southern Tierra del Fuego. And as usual, Charles Darwin left one of the most vivid descriptions of the channel named for the vessel on which he sailed:

> *The scenery here becomes even grander than before. The lofty mountains on the north side compose the granitic axis, or backbone of the country, and boldly rise to a height of between three and four thousand feet, with one peak above six thousand feet. They are covered by a wide mantle of perpetual snow, and numerous cascades pour their waters, through the woods, into the narrow channel below. In many parts, magnificent glaciers extend from the mountain side to the water's edge. It is scarcely possible to imagine anything more beautiful than the beryl-like blue of these glaciers, and especially as contrasted with the dead white of the upper expanse of the snow. The fragments which had fallen from the glacier into the water, were floating away, and the channel with the icebergs presented, for the space of a mile, a miniature likeness of the Polar Sea.*

Even today, few visitors see Tierra del Fuego's splendid fjords, little changed—except for the receding glaciers—since Darwin described them in 1833. Many of those do so onboard weeklong excursions from Punta Arenas to the Argentine port of Ushuaia and back on the Chilean vessel *Via Australis* or the larger and more luxurious *Stella Australis* (every cabin on the *Stella* has a huge picture window, and it has additional lounges with audiovisual gear, and even a top-deck gym with running tracks and stationary bicycles).

Unlike the Navimag ferry from Puerto Montt to Puerto Natales, these are cruises in the traditional sense—the passengers are waited on hand and foot, and they're not cheap. Yet for the foreseeable future, this remains the only way to see the area short of sailing your own yacht or chartering someone else's, and for that reason it's worth consideration even for those with limited finances.

One common alternative is to do either leg of the voyage separately—either five days and four nights from Punta Arenas to Ushuaia, or four days and three nights from Ushuaia to Punta Arenas. The boats sometimes undertake variants, and there's usually some duplication; both legs, for instance, usually visit Cape Horn and the western Beagle Channel's **Glaciar Pía,** and sometimes the boats are there simultaneously. Routes can also vary depending on weather conditions in this notoriously capricious climate.

After an evening departure from Punta Arenas's Muelle Prat, the vessel usually crosses the Strait of Magellan to enter the **Seno del Almirantazgo** (Admiralty Sound), a westward maritime extension of the freshwater Lago Fagnano trough. Passengers usually go ashore at **Bahía Ainsworth,** near the **Glaciar Marinelli,** where there's a short hiking trail through what was once forest until feral beavers dammed the area into a series of ponds; the most interesting site for most visitors is a small elephant seal colony. Farther west, at **Isla Tucker,** there's a small Magellanic penguin colony (observed from an inflatable Zodiac), and it's also possible to see the rare striated caracara, *Phalcoboenus australis.*

After a night's sailing that includes Canal Cockburn, where open ocean swells can rock the boat at least briefly, the vessel turns into the

© WAYNE BERNHARDSON

*Stella Australis* passengers in front of Glaciar Pía



calmer **Canal Ocasión** and eventually enters the Beagle Channel's north arm, sailing past the so-called **Avenida de los Glaciares,** a series of glaciers named for various European countries. After entering **Fiordo Pía** (Pía Fjord), where dozens of waterfalls cascade down sheer metamorphic slopes, passengers normally disembark at **Glaciar Pía,** where a short hike leads to an overlook as sharp seracs collapse off the glacier's face and into the sea.

Darwin, again, described the dangers of travel in a land that sea kayakers are just beginning to explore:

> *The boats being hauled on shore at our dinner hour, we were admiring from the distance of half a mile a perpendicular cliff of ice, and were wishing that some more fragments would fall. At last, down came a mass with a roaring noise, and immediately we saw the smooth outline of a wave traveling toward us. The men ran down as quickly as they could to the boats; for the chance of their being dashed to pieces was evident. One of the seamen just caught hold of the bows, as the curling breaker reached it: he was knocked over and over, but not hurt; and the boats, though thrice lifted on high and let fall again, received no damage.... I had previously noted that some large fragments of rock on the beach had been lately displaced; but until seeing this wave, I did not understand the cause.*

After traveling through the night, the ship anchors at **Cabo de Hornos** (Cape Horn), and, wind permitting (less than 45 knots), passengers disembark in a rocky cove to hike to the stylized iron albatross silhouette that symbolizes sailors who lost their lives "rounding the Horn." At the lighthouse, tended by a Chilean naval officer with his family, there is now a small gift shop.

Again, if weather permits, the captain can choose to round the Horn before proceeding north to **Bahía Wulaia,** on Isla Navarino's western shore. Here passengers visit the site of an early mission where, in a notorious incident, the Yámana massacred all but one of the Anglicans and their crew. There is then the option of a short but steep hike with panoramic views of the bay, or an easier shoreline walk to see birdlife, including Magellanic oystercatchers.

Before continuing to Argentina, the vessel stops at **Puerto Navarino,** at the western end of **Isla Navarino,** for immigration formalities (the crew carries the documents ashore and back by Zodiac). Proceeding to **Ushuaia,** passengers spend the night aboard; those returning to Punta Arenas have the day free in Ushuaia before returning to the ship, while new passengers check their bags downtown before boarding in late afternoon.

After reentering Chile at Puerto Navarino, the ship sails south to Cape Horn again for an early morning disembarkation and stops again at Wulaia as well. Returning to the Beagle Channel, it veers westward through the Beagle Channel's north arm, again passing the Avenida de los Glaciares. It re-enters Canal Cockburn, rounding Península Brecknock to the **Fiordo Chico** (Little Fjord), where passengers board Zodiacs for an easy shoreline walk to the receding **Glaciar Águila.** On the final morning, the boat sails north to **Isla Magdalena** before returning to Punta Arenas.

## Practicalities

Well-organized without being regimented, the cruise is informal in terms of dress and behavior. At the start, passengers sign up for meal tables; places are fixed for the duration, though some small groups join their tables. In general, passengers are grouped according to language, though they often place together people who speak English as a second language. The staff themselves can handle Spanish, English, German, French, and some other languages.

After introduction of the captain and crew, and an obligatory safety drill, there's a welcome drink and a brief folklore show (in Punta Arenas) or tango demonstration (in Ushuaia). Smoking is prohibited everywhere except the exterior decks; bar consumption is included in the package.

The cabins themselves are reasonably spacious, with either a double or twin beds, built-in reading lights, closet with hangers and shelves (with a small lock box for valuables), and private bath with excellent hot shower. Some also have a fold-down bunk for children or a third person. The food is abundant and often excellent, though breakfasts can be a little monotonous; the wine is superb, and the service exceptional. Vegetarian menus are available on request.

For those who tire of the landscape or when the weather is bad, onboard activities include karaoke, slide lectures on history and flora and fauna, engine-room tours, knot-tying demonstrations, and documentary films on topics such British explorer Ernest Shackleton and local wildlife. The farewell dinner is a fairly gala affair, followed by champagne on the topmost deck.

Punta Arenas is the home port for fjord-bound cruises; check-in takes place at Turismo Comapa (Magallanes 990, tel. 061/200200) 1–5 P.M., while boarding takes place 5–6 P.M. at the entrance to Muelle Prat. Some passengers begin or end the trip in Argentine Tierra del Fuego, where check-in takes place at Comapa's Ushuaia office (San Martín 245, tel. 02901/430727, 9 A.M.–4 P.M.); boarding takes place 5–6 P.M. at the Muelle Comercial, at the foot of 25 de Mayo.

Often this popular cruise runs full September–April, but the combination of the debut of the *Stella Australis* and the 2010 global economic slowdown brought at least a temporary overcapacity; this made it possible, for instance, to book late and even to upgrade to a private cabin without paying a single supplement. In December and January, days are so long that it's possible to enjoy the landscape until after 11 P.M., and there's sufficient light to read by at 4 A.M.

Make reservations through **Cruceros Australis** (Av. Bosque Norte 0440, 11th floor, Las Condes, Santiago, tel. 02/4423110, fax 02/2035173, www.australis.com), which also has offices in Buenos Aires (Pacheco de Melo 1833, 6th floor, Recoleta, tel. 011/4139-8400) and in Miami (4014 Chase Ave., Suite 202, Miami Beach, FL 33140, tel. 305/695-9618 or 877/678-3772). Per-person rates for four days and three nights start at US$840–1,150 in low season and go up to US$1,328–1,980 in high season. For five days and four nights, the comparable rates are US$1,120–2,010 in low season to US$1,770–3,110 in high season.

# Puerto Natales

In the past few decades, Puerto Natales has changed from a sleepy wool and fishing port on what seemed the aptly named Seno Última Esperanza (Last Hope Sound) to a bustling tourist town whose season has lengthened well beyond the traditional summer months. Its proximity to the famous Torres del Paine, coupled with its status as the southern terminus for the scenic ferry route from Puerto Montt, has placed it on the international travel map, utterly transforming the local economy.

While Natales has no knockout attractions in its own right, the town enjoys a magnificent seaside setting, with the snowcapped Cordillera Sarmiento and Campo de Hielo Sur, the southern Patagonian ice cap, visible over the water to the west. The waterfront is more presentable than in the past, and there are numerous excursions in the vicinity that make it more than just a stopover en route to Paine.

In addition, it's a more attractive town than it used to be, with a rejuvenated Plaza de Armas that includes a sunken amphitheater, and the main commercial street, Eberhard, features wider and handsomely tiled sidewalks. New park benches along Eberhard and other central streets increase Natales's pedestrian appeal, along with new and upgraded hotels and an improving gastronomic scene.



For visitors to Paine and other regional sights, Natales has abundant services, including tour operators and rental equipment, plus convenient connections to the Argentine town of El Calafate and Parque Nacional Los Glaciares. The strength of the Chilean peso has reduced its competitiveness with nearby Argentine attractions such as the Glaciar Perito Moreno, however, and the lack of a suitable airport limits its accessibility compared to El Calafate.

## HISTORY

Última Esperanza acquired its name because expeditions led by 16th-century explorers Juan Ladrilleros and Pedro Sarmiento de Gamboa failed to find a westbound route to the Pacific here. Puerto Natales proper dates from the early 20th century, a few years after German explorer Hermann Eberhard founded the area's first sheep *estancia* at Puerto Prat. Within a few years, the Sociedad Explotadora de Tierra del Fuego had built a slaughterhouse at nearby Bories to process and pack mutton for the export market. While the livestock economy declined in the second half of the 20th century, the tourist boom has reactivated and diversified the economy.

## ORIENTATION

On the eastern shores of Seno Última Esperanza, Puerto Natales (population about 19,700) is 250 kilometers northwest of Punta Arenas via paved Ruta 9. It is 150 kilometers south of Parque Nacional Torres del Paine, also by Ruta 9, which is paved as far as the town of Cerro Castillo.

Entering town from the north, Ruta 9 becomes the roughly north–south Costanera Pedro Montt; most services and points of interest are within easy walking distance to the east. The principal commercial streets are east–west Manuel Bulnes and north–south Avenida Baquedano. A new northwesterly route has cut the distance to the park border and made a loop through the park feasible.

## SIGHTS

The Sociedad Explotadora de Tierra del Fuego, owner of large pasture tracts in both Chile and Argentina, financed construction of Natales's gingerbread-style **Municipalidad,** dating from 1929 (many might have said the powerful Sociedad Explotadora was the region's de facto government). Immediately east, dating from the same era, the **Iglesia Parroquial María Auxiliadora** shares its Magellanic style.

In the same exterior fashion but with a roomier interior that displays its holdings to advantage, the **Museo Histórico Municipal** (Bulnes 285, tel. 061/411263, muninata@ctcinternet.cl, 8 A.M.–7 P.M. weekdays, 10 A.M.–1 P.M. and

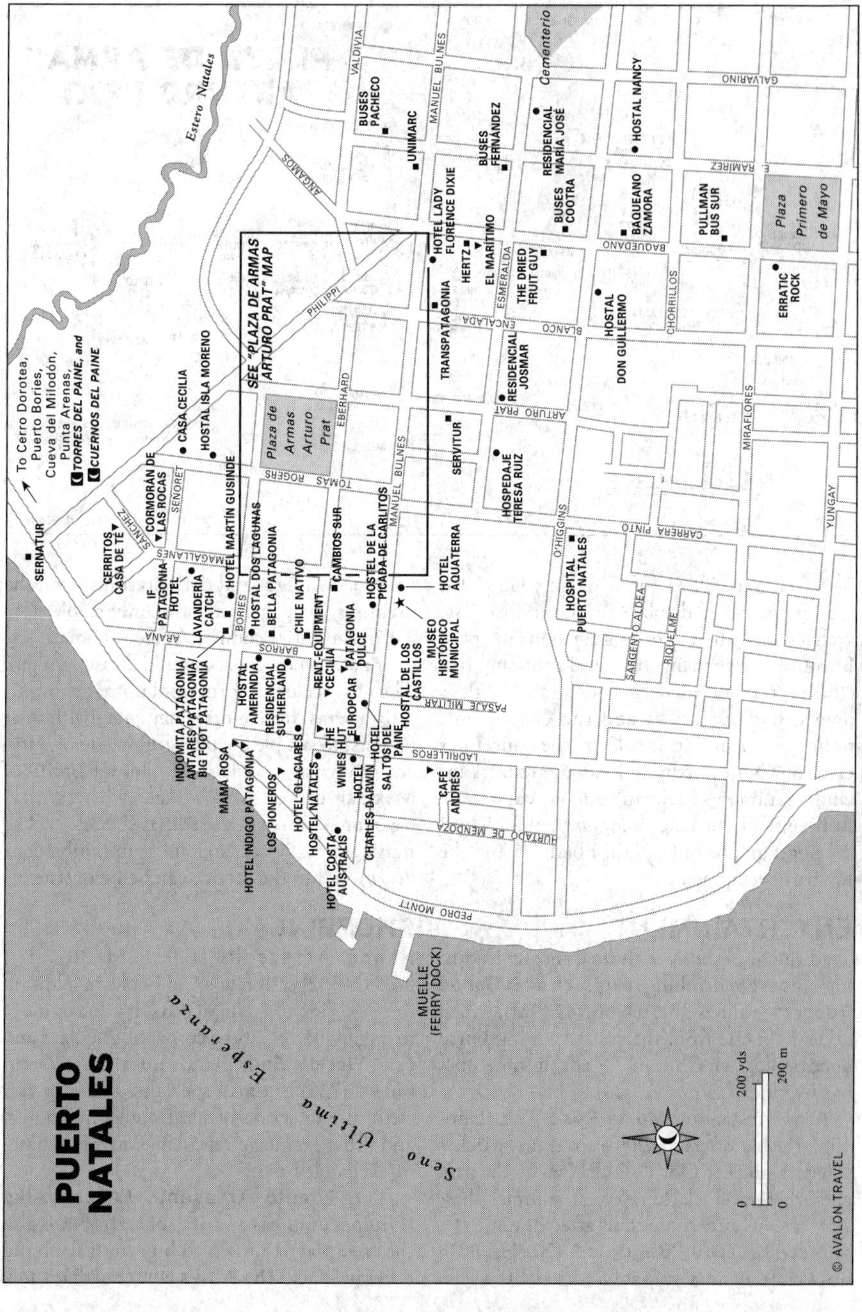
PUERTO NATALES
Seno Última Esperanza
Estero Natales
To Cerro Dorotea, Puerto Bories, Cueva del Milodón, Punta Arenas, TORRES DEL PAINE, and CUERNOS DEL PAINE
SERNATUR
CERRITOS CASA DE TÉ
CORMORÁN DE LAS ROCAS
CASA CECILIA
HOSTAL ISLA MORENO
IF PATAGONIA HOTEL
LAVANDERÍA CATCH
HOTEL MARTÍN GUSINDE
HOSTAL DOS LAGUNAS
BELLA PATAGONIA
CHILE NATIVO
CAMBIOS SUR
RENT-EQUIPMENT
CECILIA
PATAGONIA DULCE
HOSTEL DE LA PICADA DE CARLITOS
HOTEL AQUATERRA
MUSEO HISTÓRICO MUNICIPAL
HOSTAL DE LOS CASTILLOS
HOTEL SALTOS DEL PAINE
HOTEL CHARLES DARWIN
EUROPCAR
THE WINES HUT
HOSTAL AMERINDIA
RESIDENCIAL SUTHERLAND
INDOMITA PATAGONIA/ ANTARES PATAGONIA/ BIG FOOT PATAGONIA
MAMÁ ROSA
HOTEL INDIGO PATAGONIA
LOS PIONEROS
HOTEL GLACIARES
HOSTEL NATALES
HOTEL COSTA AUSTRALIS
CAFÉ ANDRÉS
MUELLE (FERRY DOCK)
SEE "PLAZA DE ARMAS ARTURO PRAT" MAP
Plaza de Armas Arturo Prat
SERVITUR
HOSPEDAJE TERESA RUIZ
RESIDENCIAL JOSMAR
TRANSPATAGONIA
HOTEL LADY FLORENCE DIXIE
HERTZ
EL MARÍTIMO
THE DRIED FRUIT GUY
BUSES FERNÁNDEZ
UNIMARC
BUSES PACHECO
RESIDENCIAL MARÍA JOSÉ
BUSES COOTRA
BAQUEANO ZAMORA
HOSTAL NANCY
PULLMAN BUS SUR
Plaza Primero de Mayo
ERRATIC ROCK
HOSTAL DON GUILLERMO
HOSPITAL PUERTO NATALES
Cementerio
ARANA
MAGALLANES
SEÑORET
SÁNCHEZ
BORIES
BARROS
EBERHARD
TOMÁS ROGERS
MANUEL BULNES
PHILIPPI
ANGAMOS
VALDIVIA
ESMERALDA
ENCALADA
BLANCO
ARTURO PRAT
O'HIGGINS
CARRERA PINTO
PASAJE MILITAR
LADRILLEROS
HURTADO DE MENDOZA
PEDRO MONTT
CHORRILLOS
MIRAFLORES
YUNGAY
SARGENTO ALDEA
RIQUELME
GALVARINO
E. RAMÍREZ
BAQUEDANO
0 200 yds
0 200 m
© AVALON TRAVEL

3–7 P.M. Sat., US$1 for Chileans, US$2 for foreigners) offers displays on natural history, archaeology, the region's indigenous peoples, European settlement, the rural economy (including the Sociedad Explotadora), Natales's own urban evolution, and the Carabineros police, who played a role in the museum's creation. Noteworthy individual artifacts include a Yámana (Yahgan) dugout canoe and Aónikenk (Tehuelche) *boleadoras,* plus historical photographs of Captain Eberhard and the town's development.

## ENTERTAINMENT

Traditional nightlife is limited mostly to dining out and to drinking spots such as **El Bar de Ruperto** (Bulnes 371, tel. 061/413921), which takes its name from the pisco-swilling burro once popular on Chilean TV ads. It sometimes has live music.

At the restaurant **Mamá Rosa** (Ladrilleros 105), the bar offers snacks, pisco sours, wireless Internet, and occasional slide shows on the park and other travel-related topics. In summer, these start late because sunset falls after 10 P.M.

New in 2010, **Baguales** (Bories 430, 061/411920) is a stylishly casual brewpub, with its own light and dark draft made on the premises, that's perhaps the only smoke-free bar in the entire country (there is a small outdoor patio where tobacco junkies can light up). The absence of airborne contaminants, ironically, means that children may enter (with their parents) to sample the pub-grub menu of burgers, sandwiches, and salads, plus a handful of Mexican dishes such as tacos with carnitas (two for US$8) and quesadillas (US$7–9). The music normally isn't so loud as to inhibit conversation, but the service can be inconsistent.

## SHOPPING

**Ñandú Artesanía** (Eberhard 301, tel. 061/414382) sells maps and books in addition to a selection of quality crafts; it's due to move to larger quarters at the corner of Eberhard and Prat. **World's End** (Blanco Encalada 226, tel. 061/414725) is a map specialist that also carries a big selection of used books in English and other languages, available on a purchase-or-exchange basis.

The **Pueblo Artesanal Ehterh Aike** (Philippi 660) has a variety of crafts but is also the best place in town to buy fresh fruit and other produce. **The Wines Hut** (Eberhard 145, tel. 061/415436) carries varietals and blends from various regions, but all of them belong to the Concha y Toro empire.

## ACCOMMODATIONS

Natales has developed one of Chile's densest offerings of accommodations. This is especially true in the budget category, where competition keeps prices low, and in exceptional new upscale options—but there are plenty of mediocre and ordinary places in all ranges. Off-season rates can drop dramatically at upscale places, but many close at least briefly. Nearly every place now offers wireless Internet.

### US$10-25

Natales's Israeli favorite, **Residencial María José** (Esmeralda 869, tel. 061/412218, juan_lasa@hotmail.com, US$10 pp) has simple doubles, triples, and quadruples with shared bath.

**Hospedaje Teresa Ruiz** (Esmeralda 463, tel. 061/410472, freepatagonia@hotmail.com, US$12 pp) gets high marks for congeniality, cleanliness, and outstanding breakfasts with homemade rhubarb preserves.

**Residencial Josmar 2** (Esmeralda 517, tel. 061/411685, www.josmar.cl, US$10 pp with shared bath, US$36 d with private bath) has also built a spacious campground (US$7–9 pp) with clearly delineated sites, privacy from the street, shelter from the wind, electricity, hot showers, and a place to barbecue. Campers can use the hotel's common spaces.

### US$25-50

Among the most traditional of budget accommodations, friendly **Residencial Sutherland** (Barros Arana 155, tel. 061/410359, US$14 pp, US$36 s or d) now has rooms with private baths.

Friendly **Residencial Patagonia Aventura** (Tomás Rogers 179, tel. 061/411028, www.apatagonia.com, US$16 pp, US$40 d) provides a bit more privacy than others in its range, with knowledgeable operators who also rent equipment. Unlike many hostels, it has no kitchen access.

The expat-operated hostel **Erratic Rock** (Baquedano 719, tel. 061/410355, www.erraticrock.com, US$18–24 pp) occupies a creaky house with character. It also serves a better-than-average breakfast, has a large book exchange, and rents quality gear for Paine-bound travelers. It also has a unique special: Anyone who can do 150 pushups nonstop gets one free night.

Relocated in improved quarters, popular **Hostal Nancy** (Ramírez 540, tel. 061/410022, www.nataleslodge.cl, US$28–40 d with breakfast) has rooms with either shared or private bath.

At friendly **Hostal Dickson** (Bulnes 307, tel. 061/411871, www.hostaldickson.com, US$20–28 s, US$36–40 d), look at the rooms closely—some have windows so small that they feel like jail cells. On the other hand, there's central heating, the beds are good, the shared baths are numerous, there are now rooms with private baths, and rates include breakfast in a nicely remodeled nook.

Open all year, in an older house with substantial character and attentive ownership, the five-room ☾ **Hostal Dos Lagunas** (Barros Arana 104, tel. 061/415733, www.hostaldoslagunas.com, US$20 pp, US$36 s, US$50 d with shared bath) is steadily upgrading. Rates include an ample and varied breakfast; owner Alejandro Cárdenas, who speaks English and German, conducts off-season trips to Paine.

In an off-the-beaten-sidewalk location, looking more expensive than it is, the immaculate ☾ **Hostal Don Guillermo** (O'Higgins 657, tel./fax 061/414506, www.hostaldonguillermo.com, US$16–40 s, US$28–50 d) is underpriced compared to nearby competitors. Though the singles are small, some rooms now have private baths, and the breakfast is excellent; rates can vary according to whether the room has cable TV.

### US$50-100

Nearly new, **Hostal South Wind** (Eberhard 568, tel. 061/412766, www.southwindhostel.cl, US$48 s, US$60 d) offers spacious and comfortable rooms, with contemporary furnishings and private baths; the rooms mostly lack windows but get ample illumination from skylights. The upside to the windowless rooms is that they get almost no street noise.

Despite its name, the eight-room **Hostel de la Picada de Carlitos** (Bulnes 280, tel. 061/414885, picadadecarlitos@gmail.com, US$30 pp) is more of a B&B. All the rooms have fine furniture, small flat-screen TVs, and private baths; there are legitimate singles for solo travelers, but those go early.

**Hostal Isla Morena** (Tomás Rogers 68, tel. 061/414773, www.islamorena.cl, US$40 s, US$64 d) enjoys fine natural light in modern rooms with private baths; a couple lack exterior windows but have skylights. It also has a restaurant with a limited nightly menu.

A recent expansion for an improved breakfast nook has virtually eliminated its signature rose garden, but **Hostal de los Castillos** (Bulnes 241, tel. 061/413641, US$50 s, US$70 d with breakfast) remains both friendly and immaculate. All room now have private baths, central heating, and cable TV, as well as wireless Internet.



Now a Natales institution, **Casa Cecilia** (Tomás Rogers 60, tel. 061/613560, www.casaceciliahostal.com, US$28–60 s, US$48–70 d) deserves credit for improving accommodations standards here—it's such a legend that, on occasion, nonguests even ask for tours of the Swiss-Chilean B&B. The rooms are simple, and some are small, but all enjoy central heating and some have private baths and cable TV. The cheerful atrium is a popular gathering place, and rates include a diverse breakfast with fresh homemade bread.

Expanded **Hostal Amerindia** (Barros Arana 135, tel. 061/411945, www.hostelamerindia.com, US$32–40 s, US$60–76 d, 6 percent surcharge for credit cards) is an artfully decorated 13-room B&B, in two buildings separated by a garden that may become an expanded reception area. It serves a diverse buffet breakfast. Seven of the rooms have private baths, but the other six share three baths. Free tea and cookies are available all day.

A few years ago, **Hostel Natales** (Ladrilleros 209, tel. 061/410081, www.hostelnatales.cl, US$29 pp, US$72 s, US$94 d) transformed the dreary Hotel Palace into warm, luminous accommodations with private baths; some rooms have two or four bunk beds—expensive by hostel standards—while others have doubles for couples. The lobby and atrium (which includes a fountain) are spacious and inviting, with comfortable chairs and sofas, but the rooms are sparsely furnished and sounds carry from the lobby (which is also an Internet café) to the nearest ones. An ample breakfast costs US$5 extra.

## US$100–200

The striking **Hotel Lady Florence Dixie** (Manuel Bulnes 659, tel. 061/411158, www.chileanpatagonia.com/florence, US$80–95 s, US$112–130 d) has expanded and upgraded what was already a good hotel. The comparable **Hotel Glaciares** (Eberhard 104, tel./fax 061/411452, www.hotelglaciares.com, US$107 s, US$119 d) has kept its prices more stable.

Just a few years ago **Hotel Aquaterra** (Bulnes 299, tel. 061/412239, www.aquaterrapatagonia.com, US$125 s, US$140 d), a purpose-built 13-room hotel that combines style (native woods) and substance (comfortable furnishings), was almost unique. Though the competition has more than caught up, it's still worth consideration, though its previously excellent restaurant has slipped more than a notch.

Recently acquired by the neighboring casino, the expanding **Hotel Martín Gusinde** (Bories 278, tel. 061/412770, www.martingusinde.com, US$130 s, US$140 d) lacks the subdued character it once had. Arguably, the improvements have been insufficient to keep up with hotel trends here.

If only for honoring history's greatest scientist, **Hotel Charles Darwin** (Bulnes 90, tel. 061/412478, www.hotelcharlesdarwin.com, US$127 s, US$153 d with discounts for Internet bookings) deserves some attention; painted in pastels, the 23 rooms range from smallish to midsize, but they're flooded with natural light. Management is accommodating and the location is excellent, but it sometimes

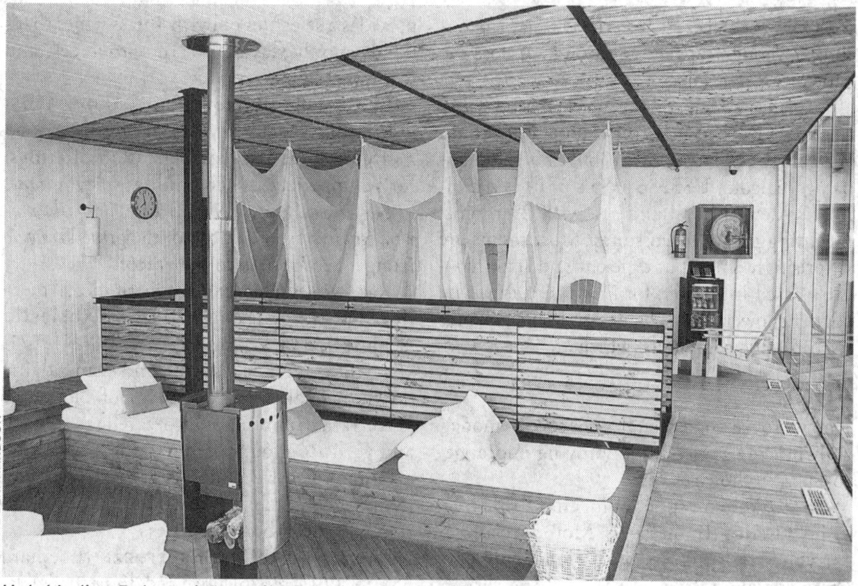

© WAYNE BERNHARDSON

Hotel Indigo Patagonia's rooftop spa is popular with guests.



fills up with groups. The handsome **Hotel Saltos del Paine** (Bulnes 156, tel. 061/413607, www.saltosdelpaine.cl, US$150 s or d) is more spacious than the Darwin.

Clearly drawing its inspiration from Hotel Indigo Patagonia (despite assertions to the contrary), the luminous 15-room **IF Patagonia Hotel** (Magallanes 73, tel. 061/410312, www.hotelifpatagonia.com, US$150 s, US$170 d) includes two suites and seven rooms with panoramic sea views; the rest face the city or Cerro Dorotea. The standard rooms are on the small side; the fourth-floor terrace offers both sorts of views.

Replacing an identically named predecessor on a deep narrow lot, **Hotel Natalino** (Eberhard 371, tel. 061/414345, www.hotelnatalino.com, US$160 s, US$190 d) offers 23 mostly small but maximally efficient rooms, reached by a gently rising staircase (with its own gentle waterfall) along one side of the building. Behind the modernistic facade, where blue-lighted slabs of glass mimic the face of a glacier, the third floor has a spa and small pool, and a deck for fine weather. One room is suitable for disabled access.

Natales's most distinctive accommodations are at the subtly landscaped **Hotel Altiplánico del Sur** (Ruta 9 Norte, Huerto 258, tel. 061/412525, www.altiplanico.cl, US$180 s, US$220 d), which has built all its rooms into the hillside along the Paine highway about two kilometers north of town. Only the windows and roof rise above ground level, while blocks of peat insulate the concrete structure and help integrate it into its site. The common areas, the rooms, and the furnishings all display an elegant simplicity.

## Over US$200

After suffering a serious fire that cost it the entire 2009 summer season, the waterfront classic **Hotel Costa Australis** (Costanera Pedro Montt 262, tel. 061/412000, www.hoteles-australis.com, US$220–470 s, US$248–490 d) has reopened; standard rates depend on whether the room has a city or sea view, and the highest rates correspond to suites. It's hard-pressed to keep up with newer choices such as the Altiplánico and Indigo, though the new addition may close the gap at least partially.

New in late 2006, on the site of what was once a modest B&B, **Hotel Indigo Patagonia** (Ladrilleros 105, tel. 061/413609, www.indigo-patagonia.com, US$286–385 s or d) is a minimalist-design hotel and spa with 29 rooms, including half a dozen suites. Most rooms are surprisingly small but efficient and striking—the glassed-in shower, for instance, has a huge copper showerhead. The design theme extends to the public computers, which are iMacs.

## FOOD

Known for seafood, Natales has several moderately priced eateries and improving midrange-to-upscale choices.

To stock up on supplies for that Paine trek, visit **Unimarc** (Bulnes 742). More specialized, for your trail mix, is **The Dried Fruit Guy** (Baquedano 443).

On the east side of the Plaza de Armas, the British-run vegetarian **El Living** (Arturo Prat 156, tel. 061/411140, 11 A.M.–11 P.M. daily, closed May–mid-Oct., US$6–7 for sandwiches) also serves breakfast, economical sandwiches, and desserts. The owner arrived here by way of Torres del Paine's extravagant Hotel Salto Chico, but his food is more upmarket than his prices.

**El Marítimo** (Baquedano 379-A, tel. 061/413166, lunch and dinner daily) and **Los Pioneros** (Pedro Montt 166, tel. 061/410783, www.lospioneroschile.cl, lunch and dinner daily) set the standard in quality fish and seafood at moderate prices; the former makes an outstanding *chupe de centolla* (king crab casserole, US$13), while the latter's grilled hake with a garlic sauce (US$8) is a flavorful bargain. Both have good service, but lack ambience and flair. Another option is **Café Andrés** (Ladrilleros 381, tel. 061/412380, lunch and dinner daily), for cooked-to-order seafood.

The best *parrilla* is **El Asador Patagónico** (Prat 158, tel. 061/413553, lunch and dinner daily), facing the Plaza de Armas, which prepares meat to order (including lamb on a stake), provides a selection of by-the-glass wines that's uncommonly flexible for the provinces, and features assiduous service.

**La Burbuja** (Bulnes 300, tel. 061/414204, lunch and dinner daily) specializes in seafood and meats but also has vegetarian offerings; for an appetizer, try the mildly spicy *ostiones al pil pil* (scallops, US$12), and the *paila marina* (seafood stew, US$9) or the grilled *congrio* (conger eel, US$10) for an entrée.

Rarely does Chilean pizza merit special mention, but the thin-crusted pies at **Mesita Grande** (Arturo Prat 196, tel. 061/411571, www.mesitagrande.cl, lunch and dinner daily) do. Individual pizzas (US$5–11), of four ample slices, range from simple mozzarella to spinach and garlic to ground lamb and just about everything in between; diners sit at either of two long but solid tables that encourage conversation with neighboring parties.

Underrated **Última Esperanza** (Eberhard 354, tel. 061/413626, lunch and dinner daily) deserves more attention than it gets for exceptional seafood at modest prices with outstanding service. Sample dishes include scallop and squid appetizers (US$8), conger eel (US$10), and grilled Patagonian lamb and potatoes (US$12).

Hotel Indigo's adjacent restaurant **Mamá Rosa** (Ladrilleros 105, tel. 061/413609, ext. 218, lunch and dinner daily) offers bayview dining on sophisticated versions of regional ingredients, such as king crab ravioli in a red pepper sauce (US$14) or pork chops in a citrus marinade with polenta (US$18). The flavors are delicate and the side orders thoughtfully assembled.

Reopened and relocated after an unfortunate absence, **Angélica's** (Bulnes 501, tel. 061/410007, lunch and dinner daily) has great fish and seafood, such as king crab cannelloni (US$15), but the service is an anomaly—often great when it's crowded, but distracted when it's barely a third full. The decor is underwhelming, but this would be a quality kitchen just about anywhere.

Reserve a window table at the new **Cormorán de las Rocas** (Sánchez 72, tel. 061/615131, www.cormorandelasrocas.

com)—the panoramas of Última Esperanza, plus the line of peaks and glaciers, including Monte Balmaceda and Paine Grande, are awe-inspiring at the city's top view restaurant. At the same time, it offers quality food at moderate prices—a substantial avocado and shrimp salad (US$8), *entraña* (grilled skirt steak, US$9), and hake in a white wine sauce (US$14), for instance. The service is impeccable, and the pisco sour a near perfect balance of the tart and sweet. It has separate wine bar that, unfortunately, permits smoking.

The surprising **Afrigonia** (Eberhard 343, tel. 061/412232, lunch and dinner daily) attempts to fuse Patagonian standards with East African touches in dishes such as shrimp and scallop curry (US$15). It's certainly Natales's most sophisticated restaurant and, by consensus, probably its best.

**Patagonia Dulce** (Barros Arana 233, tel. 061/415285, www.patagoniadulce.cl) serves several variations on coffee, tea, and hot chocolate (US$3–6 each), plus exquisite pastries and desserts (around US$4 each, mostly chocolate but also with fresh fruit), along with rich homemade chocolates by weight. Unfortunately it doesn't open until 11 A.M. For fine days, there are a couple of outdoor tables.

Across from Cormorán de las Rocas, **Cerritos** (Sánchez 11, tel. 061/412989) is a teahouse with a view—almost identical to, but a bit lower than, that of its neighbor. The pastries here—a rhubarb and *calafate* kuchen, for instance—are more sugary than those at Patagonia Dulce.

At **Helados Bruna** (Bulnes 585), *calafate* and rhubarb are the regional ice cream specialties. Patagonia Dulce also has ice cream.

## INFORMATION

In a freestanding waterfront chalet, the local delegation of **Sernatur** (Pedro Montt 19, tel./fax 061/412125) is open 8 A.M.–7:30 P.M. weekdays all year; December–March, it's also open 10 A.M.–1 P.M. and 2:30–6 P.M. weekends. It has helpful personnel, occasionally English-speaking, and fairly thorough information on accommodations, restaurants, and transportation.

Since its recent sale, the monthly tabloid *Black Sheep*, which provided regularly updated information on Natales, Torres del Paine, and services throughout the region, has declined in quality and shrunk in size. Still useful, for free at least, it's widely available around town.

## SERVICES

Puerto Natales has several exchange houses, including **Cambio Mily** (Blanco Encalada 266) and **Cambios Sur** (Eberhard 285). On Plaza Arturo Prat, **BancoEstado** (Bories 492) has an ATM.

**Correos de Chile** (Eberhard 429), at the southwest corner of Plaza Arturo Prat, is the post office.

Long-distance operators include **Telefónica CTC** (Blanco Encalada and Bulnes). Internet connections are improving and cheapening, with new outlets appearing all the time and wireless Internet ubiquitous.

**Lavandería Catch** (Bories 218) can do the washing. **Rent-Equipment Cecilia** (Eberhard 224, tel. 061/412589, agenciacecilia@yahoo.es) is one of many places that rent tents, sleeping bags, and other outdoor gear.

**Hospital Puerto Natales** (Ignacio Carrera Pinto 537, tel. 061/411582) handles medical emergencies.



## GETTING THERE

### Air

LAN no longer keeps a separate office here, but **Turismo Comapa** (Eberhard 555, tel. 061/414300, www.comapa.com) handles reservations and tickets. Punta Arenas–bound buses will drop passengers at that city's Aeropuerto Presidente Carlos Ibáñez del Campo.

Up to three times weekly in summer only, **Sky Airline** (Bulnes 682, Local 4, tel. 061/410646, www.skyairline.cl) offers service from Santiago, stopping in Punta Arenas before continuing here and then back to Santiago.

### Bus

As of early 2011, Puerto Natales had completed a new Terminal Rodoviario on Santiago Bueras (the eastward extension of Yungay). Individual companies, though, have rebelled at the terms of use and continue to prefer their scattered, but mostly central, bus terminals. There's frequent service to and from Punta Arenas and Torres del Paine, and regular but less frequent service to the Argentine destinations of Río Turbio, Río Gallegos, and El Calafate.

Carriers serving Punta Arenas (US$8, three hours) include **Bus Sur** (Baquedano 668, tel. 061/614224, www.bus-sur.cl), **Buses Fernández** (Ramírez 399, tel. 061/411111, www.busesfernandez.com), and **Buses Pacheco** (Ramírez 224, tel. 061/415123, www.busespacheco.com). Round-trip tickets offer small discounts but less flexibility. Pacheco goes to Ushuaia (Argentina) Sunday–Friday at 7:30 A.M. (US$70, 14 hours), which involves changing buses just outside Punta Arenas; Bus Sur offers similar services Tuesday–Sunday; on some days, this also requires a change of bus in Río Grande.

Services to Torres del Paine (US$16, 2.5 hours) vary seasonally, and there is frequent turnover among agencies; again, there are small discounts for round-trip fares. Carriers include Bus Sur, **Buses J.B.** (Prat 258, tel. 061/410242), **Buses Gómez** (Arturo Prat 234, tel. 061/411971, www.busesgomez.com), **Buses María José** (Esmeralda 869, tel. 061/412218), and **Trans Vía Paine** (Bulnes 518, tel. 061/413672).

For the Argentine border town of Río Turbio (US$8, one hour), where there are connections to El Calafate and Río Gallegos, try **Buses Cootra** (Baquedano 454, tel. 061/412785), which has services at 8:30 A.M. and 6:15 P.M. daily.

To El Calafate itself (US$22, five hours), the carriers are Buses Cootra and **Turismo Zaahj** (Prat 236, tel. 061/412260, www.turismozaahj.co.cl). Services are frequent in high season, but in winter they may be weekly only.

### Ferry

**Turismo Comapa/Navimag** (Eberhard 555, tel. 061/414300, www.navimag.cl) operates the weekly car/passenger ferry MV *Evangelistas* to the mainland Chilean city of Puerto Montt. In early season, it's fairly easy to get a northbound berth, but later in the season reservations are advisable.

Northbound departures are normally Tuesday at 6 A.M., but weather and tides can change schedules. Passengers usually spend the night on board before these early-morning departures, but Navimag also has a *sala de espera* (waiting room) immediately across from the new pier.

## GETTING AROUND

The selection of rental cars is growing, though it's bigger in Punta Arenas. Agencies include **Europcar** (Bulnes 100, tel. 061/4144475), **Hertz** (Blanco Encalada 353, tel. 061/414519), **Punta Alta** (Blanco Encalada 244, tel. 061/410115, www.puntaalta.cl), and **Transpatagonia** (Blanco Encalada 330, tel. 061/413593, www.transpatagonia.cl). **World's End** (Blanco Encalada 226, tel. 061/414725) rents bicycles and motorcycles.



# Vicinity of Puerto Natales

A growing number of operators arrange excursions to nearby sites of interest and, of course, to Parque Nacional Torres del Paine and even Argentina's Parque Nacional Los Glaciares. Day tours of Paine, more feasible since completion of a new road permits loops rather than time-consuming backtracking to return to Natales, cost around US$40 per person (plus the park entrance fee, of course). The most reliable are **Tour Express** (Manuel Bulnes 769, tel. 061/410734, www.tourexpress.cl), **Turismo Comapa** (Eberhard 555, tel. 061/414300, www.comapa.com), and **Kipaventour Patagonie** (Bulnes 90-B, tel. 061/413615, www.kipaventourpatagonie.com).

Several operators supply services, including accommodations and meals at park *refugios*, and activities within the park. These include **Fantástico Sur** (Esmeralda 661, tel. 061/614184, www.fslodges.com), with its own accommodations; **Turismo Stipe** (Baquedano 571, tel./fax 061/411125, turismostipe@

entelchile.net); **Chile Nativo** (Eberhard 230, tel. 061/411385, www.chilenativo.travel) for riding, trekking, and birding; **Fortaleza Patagonia** (Tomás Rogers 235, tel. 061/613395, www.fortalezapatagonia.cl); and **Servitur** (Prat 353, tel./fax 061/411858, www.servitur.cl). **Baqueano Zamora** (Baquedano 534, tel. 061/613530, www.baqueanozamora.com) specializes in horseback trips in the park and is also the concessionaire for Hostería El Pionero.

Three companies have united to form the **Centro de Turismo Aventura de Patagonia** (Bories 206), all with different contacts: **Antares Patagonia** (tel. 061/414611, www.antarespatagonia.com) for trekking; **Indómita Patagonia** (tel. 061/414525, www.indomitapatagonia.com) for kayaking and sea kayaking; and **Big Foot Patagonia** (tel. 061/414525, www.bigfootpatagonia.com) for expeditions.

Several other companies work together on sea kayaking in particular, including Fortaleza Patagonia; **Sendero Aventura** (Tomás Rogers 179, tel. 061/415636, www.senderoaventura.com), in the same building as Residencial Patagonia Aventura; and **La Maddera** (Arturo Prat 297, tel. 061/412138, www.aventurakallpamayu.com), though the latter is more a gear rental place.

## FRIGORÍFICO BORIES

Four kilometers north of Puerto Natales, the Sociedad Explotadora de Tierra del Fuego built this state-of-the-art (for its time) meat freezer to process livestock, primarily sheep, for shipment to Europe. Built of brick between 1912 and 1914, in the Magellanic style, it's the only plant of its kind in a reasonable state of preservation. After its 1971 expropriation by the Allende government, the plant was partially dismantled and finally shut down a few years back.

Among the remaining structures are the rendering plant, which converted animal fat into tallow; the tannery, which prepared hides for shipment; and the main offices, smithery, locomotive repair shop (Bories had its own short line), freight jetty, power plant, and boilers.

Closed at last pass, the entire complex is undergoing a major redevelopment project that will include a 57-room luxury hotel, **The Singular Patagonia** (www.thesingular.com), due to open in November 2011. Meanwhile, the best accommodations are at **Bories House** (tel. 09/9732-9998, www.borieshouse.com, US$130–170 s or d), a stylish expansion of an existing Patagonian house that offers large, comfortable, well-furnished rooms and is only a short cab ride from Puerto Natales; it is due to add a restaurant and spa to its offerings. The Anglo-Chilean owners also offer horseback excursions from their *estancia* at Puerto Consuelo, about 15 minutes north.

Otherwise, accommodations and food are also available at the moribund **Hotel Cisne Cuello Negro** (tel. 061/411498, US$80 s, US$112 d); make reservations through **Turismo Pehoé** (José Menéndez 918, Punta Arenas, tel. 061/244506, www.pehoe.com). Rates include private bath and breakfast.

## PUERTO PRAT AND VICINITY

About 15 kilometers northwest of Puerto Natales via a gravel road, sheltered Puerto Prat is the nearest thing to a beach getaway for Natalinos—on rare hot days, its shallow waters warm up enough to let the truly intrepid dip their toes into the sea. It's also the paddling point for half-day sea kayak trips to **Fiordo Eberhard** (about US$105 pp); for details, contact any of several kayaking companies in Puerto Natales. A new luxury hotel is due to begin construction here.

A short distance north, settled by Captain Hermann Eberhard, **Estancia Puerto Consuelo** was the area's first sheep farm. It's open to the public for horseback excursions; a beginner's two-hour ride through scenic rolling seaside terrain costs US$44, a half-day excursion to the Cueva del Milodón and back costs US$84, and a full-day ride to Villa Luisa is US$120 with lunch and drinks. A full-day combination of kayaking and riding, with lunch included, costs US$172. For details, contact **Estancia Travel** (tel. 061/412221, www.estancia travel.com), which has native and Chilean English-speaking personnel, at Puerto Bories.

## DIFUNTA CORREA SHRINE

About six kilometers east of Puerto Natales, on the south side of Ruta 9, the spreading mountain of water-filled plastic bottles at this spontaneous roadside shrine suggests one of two things: Either many Argentines are traveling here, or Chileans are becoming devoted to Argentina's favorite folk saint, a woman who presumably died in the desert, with a live baby suckling at her breast, in the 19th century. Or it may be a changing combination of the two, ever since the Argentine economic crisis of early 2002 reversed the traditional flow of Argentine tourists into Chile.

## CERRO DOROTEA

About seven kilometers east of town on Ruta 9, nudging the Argentine border, the hike to the Sierra Dorotea ridge makes an ideal half-day excursion, offering some of the area's finest panoramas. Well-marked with red blazes and signs, the route to Cerro Dorotea's 549-meter summit is, after the initial approach, unrelentingly uphill but never exhaustingly steep. This is not pristine nature, though—much of the lower slopes consists of cutover *lenga* forest, some of which has regenerated itself into an even-aged woodland. The ridge itself is barren, with a telephone relay antenna on the top.

Trailhead access is over private property, where farmer Juan de Dios Saavedra Ortiz collects US$8 per person. The fee, though, includes a simple but welcome Chilean *onces* (afternoon tea with homemade bread, butter, ham, and cheese) on your return from the hike. Cabalgatas Cerro Dorotea (www.cabalgatascerrodorotea.cl) offers the option of riding to the ridge for US$50 or, on a different route, mountain biking.

## MONUMENTO NATURAL CUEVA DEL MILODÓN

Northwest of present-day Puerto Natales, on the shores of a small inlet known as Fiordo Eberhard, the giant Pleistocene ground sloth known as the mylodon *(Mylodon darwini)* took shelter in this wave-cut grotto some 30 meters high and 80 meters wide at its mouth, and 200 meters deep. While the mylodon has been extinct for nearly as long as humans have inhabited the area—some 11,000 years—the discovery of its remains caused a sensation, as their state of preservation induced some European scientists to speculate the animal might still be alive.

German pioneer Hermann Eberhard gets credit for discovering the cave in 1895, but Erland Nordenskjöld (1900) was the first scientist to study it, taking sample bones and skin back to Sweden. Its manure has been carbon-dated at roughly 10,400 years before the present, meaning the large herbivore coexisted with humans, but it was most definitely *not* a domesticate. In all probability, hunting pressure contributed to its demise (and that of other Pleistocene megafauna). Oddly enough, no complete skeleton has been found.

The mylodon has gained a spot in the Western imagination, among both scientists and the lay public. U.S. archaeologist Junius Bird described the animal in his journals, published as *Travel and Archaeology in South Chile* (University of Iowa Press, 1988), edited by John Hyslop of the American Museum of Natural History. Family tales inspired Bruce Chatwin to write his masterpiece *In Patagonia,* which relates far-fetched legends that Paleo-Indians penned the mylodon in the cave and that some animals survived into the 19th century.

Conaf's **Museo de Sitio** (8:30 A.M.–8:30 P.M. daily) has excellent information on the 192-hectare park, which attracted 71,739 visitors in 2009, about 40 percent of them foreigners. A tacky life-sized statue of the mylodon stands in the cave itself.

Summer admission costs US$6 for adult foreigners, US$3 for Chilean residents, with nominal rates for children. Many Natales-based tours take in the sight, but there is no regular public transport except for Paine-bound buses that pass on Ruta 9, five kilometers east. Mountain-bike rental could be a good option.

## GLACIAR BALMACEDA (PARQUE NACIONAL BERNARDO O'HIGGINS)

Chile's largest national park, covering 3,525,901 hectares of islands and icecaps from near Tortel in Region XI (Aisén) to Última Esperanza in Region XII (Magallanes), largely lacks easy access points, but the Balmaceda Glacier at the Río Serrano's outlet is one of them. From Puerto Natales, the closest approach is a four-hour sail northwest—where Juan Ladrilleros and Pedro de Sarmiento de Gamboa ended their futile quests for a sheltered route to the Pacific—past Puerto Bories, several wool *estancias* reachable only by sea, and nesting colonies of seabirds and breeding colonies of southern sea lions, among U-shaped valleys with glaciers and waterfalls. Andean condors have been sighted in the area.

At the end, passengers disembark for an hour or so at **Puerto Toro,** where a half-hour walk through southern beech forest leads to the fast-receding Glaciar Balmaceda. Visitors remain for about an hour before returning to Natales, unless they take advantage of the option to travel upriver to Torres del Paine, which may be visible in the distance.

Another option for visiting remote parts of the park, in comfort, is the five-day, four-night *Skorpios* cruise on the so-called Ruta Kawéskar.

### Accommodations and Food

The park lacks formal accommodations. Across the sound from Puerto Toro, though, in virtually the most peaceful location imaginable—but for the wind—is the nearly new **Hostería Monte Balmaceda** (c/o Turismo 21 de Mayo, Eberhard 560, Puerto Natales, tel. 061/411978, www.turismo21demayo.cl, US$150 s, US$180 d with breakfast); lunch and dinner cost another US$25 each.

As it's mostly accessible by sea, a stay here is usually part of a package including a visit to the park and/or Torres del Paine. There is, however, a footpath suitable for a two-day trek to or from Torres del Paine.

### Getting There

Natales operators sail up the sound to the Balmaceda Glacier, usually daily in summer, less frequently the rest of the year. Bad weather and high winds may cause cancellations at any time of year.

The traditional operator is **Turismo 21 de Mayo** (Eberhard 560, tel. 061/411978, www.turismo21demayo.cl), which sails its eponymous cutter or the yacht *Alberto de Agostini* from a new pier at Puerto Bories. Fares are US$130 per person; on the return the boat stops for an *asado* at Estancia Los Perales.

Recently, though, **Agunsa Patagonia** (Blanco Encalada 244, tel. 061/415940, www.agunsapatagonia.cl) has provided competition with newer catamarans that cover the route faster, in greater comfort (US$145 pp), with decent food on board.

Instead of returning to Puerto Natales, it's possible to continue upriver to Torres del Paine with either Turismo 21 de Mayo or Agunsa Patagonia. In open Zodiac rafts, supplying all passengers with warm rain gear, the route traverses scenic areas not normally seen by Paine visitors, makes a lunch stop, and requires a brief portage around the Serrano rapids before arriving at the Río Serrano campground. The total cost ranges from US$130–145 with lunch; the excursion can also be done in the opposite direction, or as a round-trip from either Puerto Natales or the park.

## FIORDO DE LA MONTAÑA

Almost directly west of Puerto Natales, the Fiordo de la Montaña is a deep, narrow waterway on the Península Roca between the nearly vertical slopes of the Cordillera Sarmiento on the Pacific side, and the lower Cordillera Riesco that borders Golfo Almirante Montt. Though disconnected from the Campo de Hielo Sur, it includes a series of five impressive glaciers, four of which reach the sea. Only recently begun as a day trip, it's in many ways a superior alternative to the Balmaceda Glacier excursion up Última Esperanza. Unlike Balmaceda, though, the Fiordo de la Montaña does not permit upriver access to Torres del Paine.

## THE CHANNELS OF THE KAWÉSKAR

From the Golfo de Penas to Tierra del Fuego, southwestern Patagonia is one of the planet's most thinly peopled, least visited areas. Its pre-Columbian inhabitants were "Canoe Indians," a term applied to the Yámana and Kawéskar people, who used precarious vessels to hunt seals and gather shellfish. Never numerous, they prospered on local resources until catastrophic contact with Europeans – first violence and then disease – nearly obliterated them.

Today, ironically enough, it's possible to explore the dramatically scenic channels and icy fjords of the Kawéskar – also known as the Alacaluf – on a comfortable cruiser. Long known for its voyages from Puerto Montt to Laguna San Rafael, the Skorpios line has incorporated the glacial fjords between Puerto Natales and Puerto Edén into a **Ruta Kawéskar** itinerary that pays symbolic homage, at least, to the last sad survivors.

The *Skorpios III* normally sails late Saturday from the company's new jetty, four kilometers north of Puerto Natales. At the beginning, it follows Navimag's northbound ferry route as far as Isla Chatham, where it turns east to enter **Parque Nacional Bernardo O'Higgins** and anchor briefly at the remote fishing camp of **Caleta Villarrica.** It then enters **Fiordo Amalia,** where **Glaciar Amalia**'s floating tongue protrudes from the southern continental ice field, almost directly opposite Torres del Paine. Here passengers transfer onto double-hull, flat-bottomed boats that are really mini-icebreakers, slicing through pack ice to approach the glacier's face (flat roofs keep off the rain and snow – except when wind makes the rain horizontal).

From Amalia, the ship sails north to **Fiordo Calvo,** a site of magnificent hanging glaciers, a sea lion colony, and a rock cormorant colony. Unfortunately, when the icebreakers'



From Puerto Natales, the comfortable 150-passenger catamaran *Orca* navigates the Golfo Almirante Montt, the narrow Canal Kirke, and Paso Vicuña before entering the fjord, where it makes stops at the Zamudio, Bernal, Hermann, Alsina and Paredes glaciers. All except the partially visible Hermann, hidden by a winding valley, still reach the sea; the Bernal, though, barely touches salt water and in a few years may no longer do so. On the other hand, it has several impressive moraines and emerald lagoons. The Alsina also barely reaches the sea, but, with a greater mass, it may outlast the Bernal.

Though Skorpios cruises have been visiting it for several years now, only in late 2010 did this begin as a day trip on the *Orca,* which includes a 20-seat VIP deck. There is abundant birdlife along the route, including gulls, cormorants, terns, and skuas, as well as sea lions and dolphins. The guides are capable, pointing out cultural as well as natural features, though their English is less than perfect. The food is palatable but nothing memorable; as on most trips of this sort, the service includes whiskey on the glacial rocks.

The standard cost for the 10-hour excursion, which sails Fridays only at 7:30 A.M., is US$175 per person including lunch and snacks. The VIP seating on the second deck costs US$230 per person. There are, however, occasional specials as low as US$130—about one-third the price of the catamaran to Laguna San Rafael (admittedly, a more impressive individual glacier than any of those on this route). For more details, contact **Punta Alta** (Blanco Encalada 244, tel. 061/410115, www.puntaalta.cl).

## PUERTO EDÉN AND VICINITY

Thanks to nearly incessant rains, Puerto Edén is as verdant as Adam and Eve's biblical garden, but red-tide conditions have placed the shellfish livelihood of the remaining 15 or so Kawéskar people at risk. Their only other income sources are government handouts and some crude crafts—tiny carved

noisy diesels approach too closely, the lions and their pups scramble over the rocks and into the sea.

Retracing its route and then sailing south, the ship eventually enters the **Fiordo de la Montaña,** a sheer-sided canyon between the Cordillera Sarmiento and Cordillera Riesco, just west of Puerto Natales. Also reachable by day trips from Natales, it includes the cruise's only other shore-based excursion – a hike to the relatively small **Glaciar Bernal.** The last night on board, which includes a dinner-dance, is spent en route to and at anchor in Natales, where guests spend the night aboard ship.

Accommodating only 110 passengers in 48 cabins, *Skorpios III* is small for a cruise ship. Decorated with handsome wood veneer, with view windows rather than portholes, the cabins also have excellent bathrooms and showers. The food and wine are excellent, and the service personalized.

The Kochifas family, Greek-Chilean shipbuilders based in Puerto Montt, have pioneered an appealing itinerary. What the Ruta Kawéskar trip lacks is information: The guides' main task seems to be pointing out photo opportunities – already obvious enough in this extraordinary landscape. The *Skorpios III* would benefit from a library of books on the region, and presentations on history, environment, and ecology – instead, it's simply "eat well, sip your pisco sours, and snap your shutter."

The *Skorpios III* operates early September-late April, sailing Tuesdays and Fridays on four-day, three-night voyages; high-season is mid-December-late February. Rates range US$1,200-2,000 per person, depending on the season and level of accommodations. For more detail, contact **Cruceros Skorpios** (Augusto Leguía Norte 118, Las Condes, Santiago, tel. 02/4771900, www.skorpios.cl).



canoes and shells, for instance. Alcoholism is sadly common.

Vicinity is a relative term with respect to Puerto Edén (population about 300), the last outpost of the Kawéskar, which is about 400 kilometers northwest of Puerto Natales. It is on the weekly Navimag ferry route to and from Puerto Montt and also gets *Skorpios III* cruise-ship passengers and private yachts, which can explore the ice fields of the Campo de Hielo Sur, in Parque Nacional Bernardo O'Higgins, from the west.

Cruise passengers typically spend a couple hours on shore, where the subsidized Proyecto Yekchal has built a boardwalk over soggy terrain to an overlook where, on clear days, the view is magnificent. There's also a replica of a traditional Kawéskar dwelling, but nobody lives in these anymore.

Accommodations and meals are available at **Hospedaje Yekchal** (tel. 02/1969650, yekchal@entelchile.net, US$36 pp with full board), on the boardwalk north of the boat dock. Ships of any size cannot get close to shore and need to shuttle passengers on smaller boats.

## CERRO CASTILLO AND VICINITY

North of Natales, one of Chile's most thinly populated municipalities, the *comuna* of Torres del Paine had only 739 inhabitants according to the 2002 census; more than half reside in the hamlet of Cerro Castillo, 60 kilometers north of Puerto Natales on Ruta 9, alongside the Río Don Guillermo border crossing. Called Cancha Carrera on the Argentine side, this is the most direct route from Parque Nacional Torres del Paine to El Calafate (Argentina) and Parque Nacional Los Glaciares. Previously seasonal, it's now open all year.

Formerly an *estancia* of the powerful Sociedad Explotadora de Tierra del Fuego, Cerro Castillo has an assortment of services, including a dismal museum at the municipal **Departamento de Turismo** (Av. Bernardo

O'Higgins s/n, tel. 061/691932) and the only gas station north of Puerto Natales (if continuing to Argentina, fill up there; gasoline is significantly cheaper on the Argentine side, diesel less so).

En route to and at Cerro Castillo, there are several accommodations options. The most southerly, on the site of an older namesake that burned to the ground, **Hotel Tres Pasos** (Km 38 Norte, tel. 02/1969630 or 02/1969631, www.hotel3pasos.cl, US$120 s, US$148 d) is a contemporary roadside inn that's above average for the area. Lunch or dinner costs US$17 at its restaurant.

At Cerro Castillo itself, there are basic accommodations at **Residencial Loreto Belén** (tel. 061/413285, US$56 d) and more elaborate lodgings at **Hostería El Pionero** (Baquedano 534, Puerto Natales, tel. 061/613531, www.baqueanozamora.com, US$42 pp, US$115 s, US$123 d); their cheaper rates correspond to an annex *refugio*. Open September–April only, El Pionero also serves meals to nonguests and rents horses.

On what is still a working sheep ranch on Estancia Cerro Guido, about midway between Cerro Castillo and Torres del Paine, **Lodge Cerro Guido** (tel. 02/1964807, Punta Arenas tel. 061/227716, www.lodgecerroguido.cl, US$260–320 s or d) has rehabbed and modernized its historical *casco* and another structure into attractive guesthouses with 10 total rooms. About 12 kilometers north of the road that leads to the park's Laguna Amarga entrance, Cerro Guido gets less traffic than Paine's accommodations, but its facilities equal or better most of them; there's also a restaurant/bar whose wines come from the ownership's own Matetic family vineyards near Valparaíso. Rates include breakfast, while lunch or dinner costs about US$30 extra. Activities include horseback riding (multi-day excursions are possible), hiking, and observing farm activities such as summer shearing.



# Parque Nacional Torres del Paine (Chile)

Some years ago, when a major Pacific Coast shipping company bought a two-page spread in Alaska Airlines' in-flight magazine, the landscape chosen to represent Alaska's grandeur was...Torres del Paine! While an uninformed photo editor was the likely culprit—fittingly enough for a Southern Hemisphere destination, the image was reversed—the soaring granite spires of Chile's premiere national park have truly become an international emblem of alpine majesty.

But there's more—unlike many South American parks, Torres del Paine has an integrated network of hiking trails suitable for day trips and backpack treks, endangered species such as the wild guanaco in a UNESCO-recognized World Biosphere Reserve, and accommodations options from rustic campgrounds to cozy trail huts and five-star luxury hotels. It's so popular that some visitors prefer the shoulder seasons of spring (November–December) or fall (March–April)—the park receives more than 140,000 visitors annually, almost two-thirds of them foreigners. While Torres del Paine has become a major international destination, it's still wild country.

Almost everybody visits the park to behold extraordinary natural features such as the **Torres del Paine,** the sheer granite towers that defy erosion even as the weaker sedimentary strata around them have weathered, and the jagged **Cuernos del Paine,** with their striking interface between igneous and metamorphic rocks. Most hike its trails uneventfully, but for all its popularity, this can still be treacherous terrain. Hikers have disappeared, the rivers run fast and cold, the weather is unpredictable, and there is one documented case of a tourist killed by a puma.

## ORIENTATION

Parque Nacional Torres del Paine is 112 kilometers northwest of Puerto Natales via Ruta 9 through Cerro Castillo; 38 kilometers beyond Castillo, a westbound lateral traces the southern shore of Lago Sarmiento de Gamboa to the park's isolated Laguna Verde sector. Three kilometers beyond the Laguna Verde junction, another westbound lateral leaves Ruta 9 to follow Lago Sarmiento's north shore to Portería Sarmiento, the main gate; it continues southwest for 37 kilometers to the Administración, the park headquarters at the west end of Lago del Toro.

Twelve kilometers east of Portería Sarmiento, another lateral branches northwest and, three kilometers farther on, splits again; the former leads to Guardería Laguna Azul, in the little-visited northern sector, while the latter enters the park at Guardería Laguna Amarga, the most common starting point for the popular Paine Circuit, and follows the south shore of Lago Nordenskjöld and Lago Pehoé en route to the Administración visitors center. Most public transportation takes this route.

Recently completed, a new bridge over the Río Serrano now permits access to park headquarters via Cueva del Milodón and Lago del Toro's western shore, but this has not affected regular public transportation.

## THE TORRES DEL FUEGO

In February 2005, in an incident that will have consequences for decades or more, a careless Czech camper overturned his camp stove, starting a fire that burned for nearly a month in Parque Nacional Torres del Paine. The conflagration scorched 15,470 hectares of native vegetation, including forest, scrubland, and steppe, in the park's popular northeastern sector.

Most of the burned area consisted of steppe grasses and shrubs that are recovering nicely, but the 2,400 hectares of slow-growing southern beech forest are more problematic. West of the Río Paine and the Lago Paine road, Conaf is placing priority on restoring 800 hectares of *lenga* and *ñirre*. In spring of 2006, at a cost of about US$1,700 per hectare, the government forestry agency collected seeds and built several greenhouses to nurture seedlings for transplanting to the burned area. As of early 2011, according to Conaf's Juan Ivanovich, 100,000 seedlings have been planted in the fire area, now fenced off to prevent humans trampling them and guanacos from feeding off them.

Some parts of the park may be off-limits to hikers for several years, though it's possible trails may be rerouted. While the fire came perilously close to the Hostería Las Torres and the Cascada EcoCamp (since relocated), it damaged no major structures.

## GEOGRAPHY AND CLIMATE

Parque Nacional Torres del Paine comprises 181,414 hectares of Patagonian steppe, lowland and alpine glacial lakes, glacier-fed torrents and waterfalls, forested uplands, and nearly vertical granite needles. Altitudes range from only 50 meters above sea level along the lower Río Serrano to 3,050 meters atop Paine Grande, the central massif's tallest peak.

Paine has a cool temperate climate characterized by high winds, especially in spring and summer. The average summer temperature is about 11°C, with highs reaching around 23°C, while the average winter minimum is around freezing. Average figures are misleading, though, as the weather is changeable. The park lies in the rain shadow of the Campo de Hielo Sur, where westerly storms drop most of their load as snow, so it receives only about 600 millimeters of rainfall per year. Still, snow and hail can fall even in midsummer. Spring is the windiest season; in autumn, March and April, winds tend to moderate, but days are shorter.

It should go without saying that at higher elevations temperatures are cooler and snow is likelier to fall. In some areas it's possible to hut-hop between *refugios*, eliminating the need for a tent and sleeping bag—but not for warm clothing and impermeable rain gear.

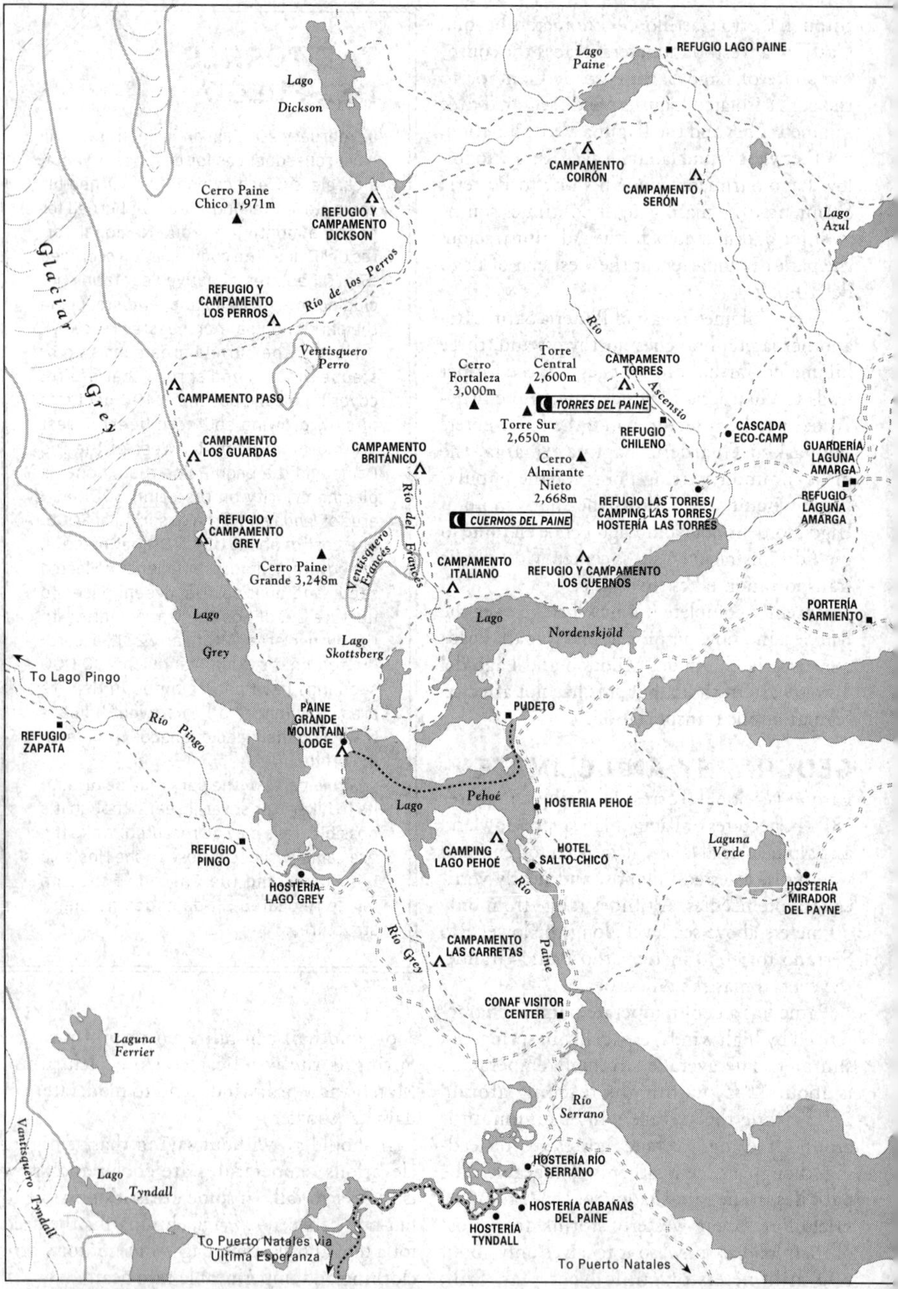

Lago Dickson
Lago Paine
REFUGIO LAGO PAINE
CAMPAMENTO COIRÓN
CAMPAMENTO SERÓN
Lago Azul
Cerro Paine Chico 1,971m
REFUGIO Y CAMPAMENTO DICKSON
Glaciar Grey
Río de los Perros
REFUGIO Y CAMPAMENTO LOS PERROS
Ventisquero Perro
CAMPAMENTO PASO
Cerro Fortaleza 3,000m
Torre Central 2,600m
Torre Sur 2,650m
CAMPAMENTO TORRES
Río Ascensio
TORRES DEL PAINE
REFUGIO CHILENO
CASCADA ECO-CAMP
GUARDERÍA LAGUNA AMARGA
REFUGIO LAGUNA AMARGA
CAMPAMENTO LOS GUARDAS
CAMPAMENTO BRITÁNICO
Cerro Almirante Nieto 2,668m
REFUGIO LAS TORRES/ CAMPING LAS TORRES/ HOSTERÍA LAS TORRES
CUERNOS DEL PAINE
REFUGIO Y CAMPAMENTO GREY
Río del Francés
Ventisquero Francés
Cerro Paine Grande 3,248m
CAMPAMENTO ITALIANO
REFUGIO Y CAMPAMENTO LOS CUERNOS
Lago Grey
Lago Skottsberg
Lago Nordenskjöld
PORTERÍA SARMIENTO
To Lago Pingo
REFUGIO ZAPATA
Río Pingo
PAINE GRANDE MOUNTAIN LODGE
PUDETO
Lago Pehoé
HOSTERIA PEHOÉ
REFUGIO PINGO
CAMPING LAGO PEHOÉ
HOTEL SALTO CHICO
Laguna Verde
HOSTERÍA MIRADOR DEL PAYNE
HOSTERÍA LAGO GREY
Río Paine
Río Grey
CAMPAMENTO LAS CARRETAS
CONAF VISITOR CENTER
Laguna Ferrier
Río Serrano
Ventisquero Tyndall
Lago Tyndall
HOSTERÍA RÍO SERRANO
HOSTERÍA CABAÑAS DEL PAINE
HOSTERÍA TYNDALL
To Puerto Natales via Ultima Esperanza
To Puerto Natales

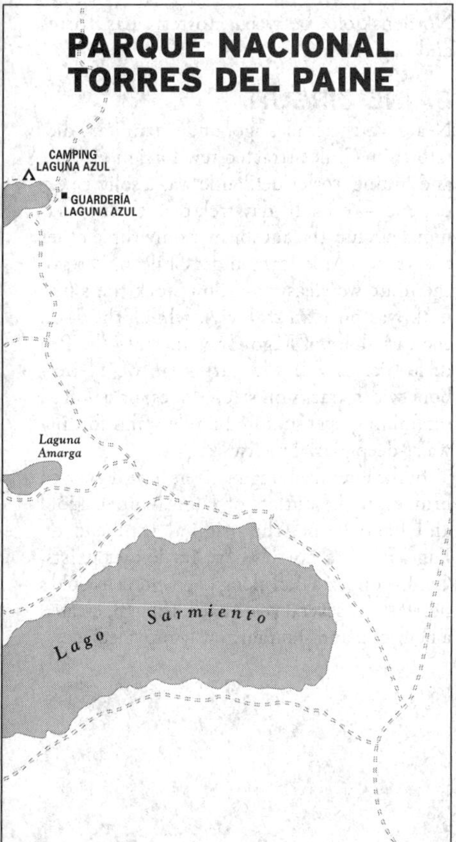


## FLORA AND FAUNA

Less diverse than in areas farther north, Paine's vegetation still varies with altitude and distance from the Andes. Bunch grasses of the genera *Festuca* and *Stipa,* known collectively as *coirón,* cover the arid southeastern steppes, often interspersed with thorny shrubs such as the *calafate (Berberis buxifolia),* which produces edible fruit, and *neneo.* There are also miniature ground-hugging *Calceolaria* orchids, such as the *zapatito* and *capachito.*

Approaching the Andes, deciduous forests of southern beech *(Nothofagus)* species such as *lenga* blanket the hillsides, along with the related evergreen *coigüe de Magallanes* and the deciduous *ñirre.* At the highest elevations, little vegetation of any kind grows among alpine fell fields.

Among Paine's mammals, the most conspicuous is the llama-relative guanaco, whose numbers—and tameness—have increased dramatically. Many of its young, known as *chulengos,* fall prey to the puma. A more common predator, or at least a more visible one, is the gray fox, which feeds off the introduced European hare and, beyond park boundaries, off sheep. The endangered huemul (Andean deer) is a rare sight.

The monarch of South American birds, of course, is the Andean condor, not a rare sight here. Filtering the lake shallows for plankton, the Chilean flamingo summers here after breeding in the northern altiplano. The *caiquén* (upland goose) grazes the moist grasslands around the lakes, while the black-necked swan paddles peacefully on the surface. The fleet flightless rhea or *ñandú* scampers over the steppes.

## TORRES DEL PAINE

Some of the Andes's youngest peaks, the Torres del Paine are among the most emblematic in the entire range. Some 10 million years ago, a magma intrusion failed to reach the earth's surface, cooling underground into resistant granite; in the interim, water, ice, and snow have eroded softer terrain to liberate the spires as one of the world's most dramatic landscapes.

So strong a draw are the Torres that some visitors pressed for time settle for day tours that allow only a few hours in the park. Others walk to the base of the Torres from Hostería Las Torres, a relatively easy day hike where it's hard to avoid the crowds. A longer and more tiring alternative, up the steep canyon of the Río Bader, provides a different perspective and the Andean solitude that many hikers seek.

## CUERNOS DEL PAINE

Many park visitors misidentify the Cuernos del Paine (Horns of Paine) as the Torres. Located almost immediately south of the Torres proper, the saw-toothed Cuernos retain a cap of darker but softer metamorphic rock atop a broader granitic batholith that, like the Torres, never reached the surface before cooling. It's the contrast between the two that gives the Cuernos their striking aspect.

As with the Torres, day-trippers can admire the Cuernos from the highway through the park. The best views, though, come from the "W" trail along the north shore of Lago Nordenskjöld, between Hostería Las Torres and Lago Pehoé.

## PAINE CIRCUIT

Nearly three decades ago, under a military dictatorship, Chile attracted few foreign visitors, and hiking Torres del Paine was a solitary experience—on a 10-day trek over the now-famous circuit, the author met only three other hikers, two Americans and a Chilean. Parts of the route were easy-to-follow stock trails (the park was once an *estancia*), while others, on the east shore of Lago Grey and into the Río de los Perros Valley in particular, were barely boot-width tracks on steep slopes, or involved scrambling over granite boulders and fording waist-deep glacial meltwater.

In the interim, as raging rivers have destroyed bridges at the outlets of Lago Nordenskjöld and Lago Paine, the original trailhead on Lago Pehoé's north shore no longer exists. Completion of a trail along Lago Nordenskjöld's north shore several years back, though, created a new loop and simultaneously provided access

© PAWEL PASKA/123RF

Cuernos del Paine

to the Torres's south side, offering easier access up the Río Ascencio and Valle del Francés on the shorter "W" route to Lago Pehoé. Where the former circuit crossed the Río Paine and continued along its north bank to the Laguna Azul campground, the new circuit now follows the river's west bank south to Laguna Amarga (a Laguna Azul exit or entrance is still feasible, though, by crossing the Río Paine by a cable raft at the river's Lago Dickson outlet, with help from the staff at Refugio Dickson).

In the interim, trail maintenance and development have improved, rudimentary and not-so-rudimentary bridges have replaced fallen logs and traversed stream fords, and comfortable *refugios* and organized campgrounds have supplanted the lean-tos and *puestos* (outside houses) that once sheltered shepherds. Though it's theoretically possible to complete most of the circuit without a tent or even a sleeping bag, showering and eating at the *refugios,* hikers must remember that this is still rugged country with unpredictable weather.

Most hikers now tackle the circuit counterclockwise from Guardería Laguna Amarga, where buses from Puerto Natales stop for passengers to pay the park admission fee. An alternative is to continue to Pudeto and take a passenger launch to Refugio Pehoé, or else to the park's Administración (involving a longer and less interesting approach); both of these mean doing the trek clockwise.

At least a week is desirable for the circuit; before beginning, registration with park rangers is obligatory. Camping is permitted only at designated sites, a few of which are free. Purchase supplies in Puerto Natales, as only limited goods are available with the park, at premium prices.

### Accommodations and Food

For counterclockwise hikers beginning at Laguna Amarga, there is no *refugio* until Lago Dickson (roughly 11 hours), though there is a fee campground at **Campamento Serón** (4–5 hours).

All the *refugios* are presently under concession to Puerto Natales's **Vértice Patagonia** (Esmeralda 671, tel. 061/412742, Puerto Natales, www.verticepatagonia.cl), including **Refugio Lago Grey** and **Refugio Lago Dickson,** where there are also campgrounds and backpackers still crash at the old *puesto,* plus the **Campamento Río de los Perros.**

Both *refugios* resemble each other, with 32 bunks charging US$30 per person, with kitchen privileges and hot showers, but without sheets or sleeping bags, which are technically available for rental but sometimes scarce. Breakfast costs US$10, lunch US$13, dinner US$18; a bunk with full board costs US$68 per person. Campers pay US$7 each (*refugio* guests, though, have shower priority). Rental tents, sleeping bags, mats, and camp stoves are also available.

Replacing the cramped and overcrowded Refugio Lago Pehoé, the **Paine Grande Mountain Lodge** (tel. 02/1960051) is the newest option along the Paine Circuit. Rates are US$44–61 per person without breakfast (US$10 extra); lunch (US$13) and dinner (US$17) are available separately, but full-board packages (US$78–95 pp) mean a small savings. Camping costs US$9 per person (US$51 with full board), with rental tents, pads, and sleeping bags available. There's also phone and even (expensive) Internet access.

## THE "W" VARIANT

From Guardería Laguna Amarga, a narrow undulating road crosses the Río Paine on a narrow suspension bridge to the grounds of **Estancia Cerro Paine,** at the foot of 2,640-meter Monte Almirante Nieto. The *estancia* operates a hotel, *refugios,* and campgrounds, and the staff also shuttles hikers back and forth from Laguna Amarga for US$5 per person.

From Estancia Cerro Paine, a northbound trail parallels the route from Guardería Laguna Amarga, eventually meeting it just south of Campamento Serón. The *estancia* is more notable, though, as the starting point for the "W" route to Lago Pehoé, a scenic and popular option for hikers lacking time for the full circuit. On the western edge of the grounds, the trail crosses the Río Ascencio on a footbridge to a junction where a northbound lateral climbs the river canyon to Campamento Torres, where a short but steep trail ascends to a nameless glacial tarn at the foot of the Torres proper. Weather permitting, this is an easy day hike from the *estancia,* though many people prefer to camp or spend the night at the *refugio.*

From the junction, the main trail follows Lago Nordenskjöld's north shore, past another *refugio* and campground, to the free Campamento Italiano at the base of the **Río del Francés** valley. While the main trail continues west toward Lago Pehoé, another northbound lateral climbs steeply up the valley, between the striking metamorphic Cuernos del Paine to the east and the 3,050-meter granite summit of Paine Grande to the west, to the free Campamento Británico.

Hikers in search of peace and quiet can make a strenuous detour up the **Valle Bader,** a steep rugged river valley that's home to a climber's camp at the base of the Cuernos. The route is mostly unmarked, but experienced cross-country walkers can handle it.



### Accommodations and Food

Technically outside park boundaries, most of the "W" route belongs to **Fantástico Sur** (Sarmiento 846, Punta Arenas, tel./fax 061/360360, www.fslodges.com), which runs the 96-bunk **Refugio Las Torres Norte** and the new, nearby **Refugio Las Torres Central** on the *estancia*'s main grounds; the 36-bunk **Refugio Chileno** in the upper Río Ascencio Valley; and the 28-bunk **Refugio Los Cuernos,** all of which also have campgrounds. Fantástico Sur's *refugios* are more spacious, diverse, and attractive in design than the Conaf *refugios,* and the food is better as well.

Bunks at Fantástico Sur *refugios* cost US$37–46 per person (US$80–89 pp with full board), except for the slightly more expensive Las Torres Central (US$41–50 pp, US$84–93 pp with full board). Camping costs US$9 per person with hot showers. Refugio Los Cuernos also has two-person cabañas (US$131 d with breakfast and hot tub, US$174 s, US$217 d with full board).

Separately, breakfast costs US$10, lunch US$14, or dinner US$19; a full meal package costs US$43. Rental tents, sleeping bags, mats, and stoves are also available.

## OTHER TRAILS

After heavy runoff destroyed the once-sturdy bridge at Lago Paine's outlet in the early 1980s, the Río Paine's north shore became, and has remained, isolated from the rest of the park. A good road, though, still leads from Guardería Laguna Amarga to Laguna Azul's east end, which has a campground and cabañas, as well as the **Sendero Lago Paine,** a four-hour walk to the lake and a simple *refugio.* A trekkers' alternative is the **Sendero Desembocadura,** which leads north from Guardería Laguna Amarga through open country to Laguna Azul's west end and continues to Lago Paine, but this takes about eight hours. From the north shore of Lago Paine, the **Sendero Lago Dickson** (5.5 hours) leads to the Dickson Glacier.

Several easy day hikes are possible near Guardería Lago Pehoé, directly on the road from Laguna Amarga to the Administración visitors center. The short **Sendero Salto Grande** trail leads to the thunderous waterfall, at Lago Sarmiento's outlet, that was the circuit's starting point until unprecedented runoff swept away the iron bridge to Península Pehoé in 1986. From Salto Grande, the **Sendero Mirador Nordenskjöld** is a slightly longer but still easy walk to a lakeshore vista point, directly opposite the stunning Cuernos del Paine.

From Guardería Lago Grey, 18 kilometers northwest of the Administración by road, a short footpath leads to a sandy beach on Lago Grey's south shore, where steady westerlies often beach icebergs from Glaciar Grey. The longer and less visited **Sendero Lago Pingo** ascends the Río Pingo Valley to its namesake lake (5.5–6 hours); a basic *refugio* and two free campgrounds are along the route.

## FURTHER RECREATION

Though popular, hiking is not Paine's only recreational option.

Despite similar terrain, Paine attracts fewer

climbers than Argentina's neighboring Parque Nacional Los Glaciares, perhaps because fees for climbing permits have been high here. At present, permits are free of charge; before being granted permission, though, climbers must present Conaf with climbing résumés, emergency contacts, and authorization from their consulate.

When climbing in sensitive border areas (meaning most of Andean Chile), climbers must also have permission from the Dirección de Fronteras y Límites (Difrol, www.difrol.cl) in Santiago. It's possible to do this through a Chilean consulate overseas or at Difrol's Santiago offices or, preferably, online; if you arrive in Puerto Natales without permission, it's possible to request it through the **Gobernación Provincial** (tel. 061/411423, fax 061/411992), the regional government offices on the south side of Plaza Arturo Prat. The turnaround time is 48 hours.

While climbing and mountaineering activities may be undertaken independently, local concessionaires can provide training and lead groups or individuals with less experience on snow and ice. **Rutas Patagonia** (tel. 02/1960761, www.rutaspatagonia.com) has a Refugio Grey base camp, where it leads half-day traverses of Glaciar Grey's west side (US$130 pp). Except for warm, weatherproof clothing, the company provides all equipment.

Kayaking specialist **Indómita** (Bories 206, tel./fax 061/414525, www.indomitapatagonia.com) arranges guided three-day, two-night descents of the Río Serrano (US$600–742 pp, depending on group size).

Río Serrano–based **Baqueano Zamora** (Baquedano 534, Puerto Natales, tel. 061/613531, www.baqueanozamora.com) offers horseback riding within the park; just outside the park boundaries, though, Hostería Las Torres has its own stables. Other operators are now allowed to enter the park with their horses, on trips that take as long as two weeks from Puerto Natales.

## ACCOMMODATIONS AND FOOD

Park accommodations range from free trailside campgrounds to first-rate luxury hotels with just about everything in between; in summer, reservations are almost obligatory at hotels and advisable at campgrounds and *refugios.*

### Camping

At Estancia Cerro Paine, **Camping Las Torres** (US$9 pp, US$50 pp with full board) draws hikers heading up the Río Ascencio Valley to the Paine overlook and/or west on the "W" route to Lago Pehoé, or finishing up the circuit here. Formerly insufficient shower and toilet facilities have improved.

On a bluff above Refugio Las Torres, the **Cascada EcoCamp** (www.ecocamp.travel) is a geodesic dome-tent facility designed for minimum-impact accommodations; on raised platforms, each tent is five meters wide, with wooden floors and two single beds, with towels and bedding including down comforters. Two larger domes contain a common living area, dining rooms, and kitchen; the separate bathrooms have hot showers and composting toilets (from some domes, it's a long walk for middle-of-the-night toilet visits).

Electricity comes from solar collectors, windmills, and a small hydroelectric turbine. Cascada's organized tour clients have priority, but its half-dozen luxury "Dome Suites" (with woodstoves, king-size beds, private baths and showers, and exterior decks with views of the Torres) are available to private parties on a space-available basis. Contact them through the website or, alternatively, through their Puerto Natales office (Barros Arana 166, tel. 061/414442).

On the small peninsula on its namesake lake's eastern shore, just west of the road to the Administración, sites at concessionaire-run **Camping Lago Pehoé** (tel. 02/1960377, www.campingpehoe.com, US$9 pp) hold up to six people; fees include firewood and hot showers. About six kilometers south of park headquarters, **Vista Paine Camping** (www.campingchile.com, US$7.50 pp) has undertaken considerable improvements, including cooking shelters at each site.

In Paine's remote northeastern sector, which some visitors prefer, is **Camping Laguna Azul** (tel. 061/613531 in Puerto Natales, www.baqueanozamora.cl, US$7.50 pp).

### *Hosterías* and Hotels

Reachable by road along Lago Sarmiento's south shore or by foot or horseback from the Río Paine, well-regarded **Hostería Mirador del Payne** (tel. 061/410498, www.miradordelpayne.com, US$190 s, US$234 d) lies in the isolated southeastern Laguna Verde sector. Its decor, particularly the garish bedspreads, could use an update.

Where Lago Grey becomes the Río Grey, the 30-room **Hostería Lago Grey** (US$261 s, US$308 d with breakfast) hosts visitors to the park's lesser-visited western sector; it also has a restaurant open to the public. For reservations, contact the hotel through **Turismo Lago Grey** (tel. 061/712100, www.lagogrey.cl).

The park's oldest hotel, on a five-hectare island linked to the mainland by a footbridge, the 25-room **Hostería Pehoé** (US$195–213 s, US$213–269 d) has improved since the operator began to reinvest in what had been a run-down facility, with substandard service, in an undeniably spectacular setting. For reservations, contact **Turismo Pehoé** (José Menéndez 918, Punta Arenas, tel. 061/241373, www.pehoe.com).

At Estancia Cerro Paine, seven kilometers west of Guardería Laguna Amarga, the sprawling but well-run **Hostería Las Torres** (Sarmiento 846, Punta Arenas, tel. 061/360360, www.lastorres.com, US$245–267 s, US$270–305 d) is a gem for its setting beneath Monte Almirante Nieto, its professionalism, the recent addition of a spa offering saunas and massages, and even wireless Internet access (expensive because of a costly satellite link). While it's an elite option that's leaning toward all-inclusive packages, it's conscientiously ecofriendly in terms of waste disposal, and management is constantly seeking feedback from guests. It now offers all-inclusive packages as well as just lodging. Off-season hotel rates are about half. Open to both guests and nonguests, the tobacco-free restaurant prepares quality food in cruise-ship quantities.

Open for packages only, **Hotel Salto Chico** is a mega-luxury resort that, somehow, manages to blend inconspicuously into the landscape while providing some of the grandest views on the globe. Rates start at US$3,760 single, US$5,560 double for four nights in the least expensive room, ranging up to US$11,400 single, US$15,200 double for eight nights in the costliest suite, including transfer to and from Punta Arenas and unlimited excursions. Low-season rates are about 20 percent cheaper. For details and/or reservations, contact **Explora Hotels** (Américo Vespucio Sur 80, 5th floor, Las Condes, Santiago, tel. 02/2066060, www.explora.com).

Just beyond park boundaries, reached by launch over the Río Serrano, the stylish **Hotel Lago Tyndall** (tel. 061/614682, www.hoteltyndall.cl, US$162–176 s, US$176–208 d) enjoys peace, quiet, and magnificent views. Nearby is the less stylish **Hotel Cabañas del Paine** (tel. 061/210179 in Punta Arenas, www.cabanasdelpaine.cl, US$240 s, US$250 d).

## INFORMATION

Conaf's principal facility is its **Centro de Informaciones Ecológicas** (tel. 061/691931, ptpaine@conaf.cl, 8 A.M.–8 P.M. or later daily in summer), at the Administración building on the shores of Lago del Toro near the Río Paine outlet, with good natural-history exhibits.

Ranger stations at Guardería Laguna Amarga, Portería Lago Sarmiento, Guardería Laguna Azul, Guardería Lago Verde, and Guardería Lago Grey can also provide information.

The private Hostería Las Torres has an excellent audiovisual salon with sophisticated environmental exhibits.

### Entry Fee

For foreigners, Torres del Paine is Chile's most expensive national park—the entry fee is US$30 per person except May–September, when it's US$15. Rangers at Portería Lago Sarmiento, Guardería Laguna Amarga (where most inbound buses now stop), Guardería Lago Verde, or Guardería Laguna Azul collect the fee, issue receipts, and provide a 1:100,000 park map that's useful for trekking.

### Books and Maps

In English, the best available trekking guide is Rudolf Abraham's *Torres del Paine* (Milnthrope, Cumbria, United Kingdom, 2010; www.cicerone.co.uk), which has fine full-color maps and photographs to accompany a thorough text. Climbers should look for Alan Kearney's *Mountaineering in Patagonia* (Seattle: The Mountaineers, 1998), which includes both historical and practical information on climbing in Torres del Paine and Argentina's Parque Nacional Los Glaciares. Gladys Garay N. and Oscar Guineo N. have collaborated in *The Fauna of Torres del Paine* (1993), a locally produced guide to the park's animal life.

## GETTING THERE

Most people find the bus the cheapest and quickest way to and from the park, but the more expensive trip up Seno Última Esperanza and the Río Serrano by cutter and Zodiac is a viable, more interesting alternative.

The new road from Puerto Natales has opened, so tour companies usually enter the park at Laguna Amarga and loop back on the new road, but regular bus services continue to use the old highway.

### Bus

Bus companies enter the park at Guardería Laguna Amarga, where many hikers begin the Paine Circuit, before continuing to the Administración at Río Serrano and then returning by the same route. Round-trips from Natales are slightly cheaper, but companies do not accept each others' tickets.

In summer only, there may be direct bus service to and from El Calafate, Argentina (US$50, five hours), the closest town to that country's Parque Nacional Los Glaciares. Inquire in Puerto Natales at Calafate Travel (Baquedano 459, tel. 061/414456).

### River

Transportation up and down the Río Serrano, between the park and Puerto Natales, has become a popular if more expensive alternative to the bus. Visitors who only want to see this sector of the river, without continuing to Puerto Natales, can do so as a day trip to Puerto Toro and back.

The traditional operator is **Turismo 21 de Mayo** (Eberhard 560, Puerto Natales, tel. 061/411978, www.turismo21demayo.cl), which sails its eponymous cutter or the yacht *Alberto de Agostini* from a new pier at Puerto Bories. Fares are US$130 per person; on the return the boat stops for an *asado* at Estancia Los Perales.

Recently, though, **Agunsa Patagonia** (Blanco Encalada 244, Puerto Natales, tel. 061/415940, www.agunsapatagonia.cl) has provided competition with newer catamarans that cover the route faster, in greater comfort (US$145 pp), with decent food on board.

## GETTING AROUND

Buses to and from Puerto Natales will also carry passengers along the main park road, but as their schedules are similar, there are extended daily periods with no public transportation. Hitching is common, but competition is heavy and most vehicles are full with families. There is a regular shuttle between Guardería Laguna Amarga and Estancia Cerro Paine (Hostería Las Torres, US$5 pp) that meets arriving and departing buses.

October–April, reliable transportation is available from Pudeto to Refugio Pehoé (US$22 one-way, 30 minutes; US$38 round-trip) with the catamaran ***Hielos Patagónicos*** (Los Arrieros 1517, Puerto Natales, tel. 061/411380). The first two weeks of October and in April, there is one departure daily, at 12:30 P.M., from Pudeto, returning at 1 P.M. From mid-October to mid-November and the last fortnight of March, there's an additional service at 6 P.M., returning at 6:30 P.M. From mid-November to mid-March, there are departures at 9:30 A.M., noon, and 6 P.M., returning at 10 A.M., 12:30 P.M., and 6:30 P.M. Schedules may be postponed or canceled due to bad weather, and there are no services on Christmas and New Year's Day.

Also in season, the catamaran *Grey II* goes daily from Hotel Lago Grey to Glaciar Grey (US$40 one-way, US$80 round-trip) at 9 A.M. and 3 P.M. daily; on the return, it cruises the glacier's face, so the reverse direction costs US$64 one-way.

# Chilean Tierra del Fuego

Across the Strait of Magellan from Punta Arenas, thinly populated Chilean Tierra del Fuego has only one major settlement, the town of Porvenir, on its northerly steppes. To the south, its rugged alpine terrain is a westward extension of the Argentine cordillera, with scenic fjords that few other landscapes can match. Across the Beagle Channel, Isla Navarino's Puerto Williams, the world's southernmost permanent settlement, is part of an archipelagic maze that stretches south to the celebrated Cape Horn.

## PORVENIR

Chilean Tierra del Fuego's main town, Porvenir sits on a sheltered harbor on the Strait of Magellan's eastern shore. It dates from the 1880s, when the area experienced a brief gold rush, but stabilized with the establishment of wool *estancias* around the turn of the 20th century. After the wool boom fizzled in the 1920s, it settled into an economic torpor that has left it a collection of corroding metal-clad Magellanic buildings. Construction of a salmon-processing plant has jump-started the local economy, and it's more presentable now.



Porvenir's inner harbor is ideal for spotting kelp geese, gulls, cormorants, steamer ducks, and other seabirds, but the lack of public transportation to the Argentine border has marginalized the tourist sector—all buses from the mainland to Argentine Tierra del Fuego take the longer Primera Angostura route, with a shorter and more frequent ferry crossing.

Only 30 nautical miles east of Punta Arenas, Porvenir (population about 5,500) occupies a protected site at the east end of Bahía Porvenir, an inlet of the Strait of Magellan. Its port at Bahía Chilota, though, is five kilometers west of the town proper. Because the Sunday ferry to Punta Arenas sails late (at 5 P.M.), it allows curious visitors to spend the day here rather than return immediately.

From Porvenir, Ruta 215 (a smooth gravel road) leads south and then east along the Bahía Inútil shoreline to the Argentine border at San Sebastián, 150 kilometers away; an alternative route leads directly east through the Cordón Baquedano before rejoining Ruta 215 about 55 kilometers to the east. If it's too late to catch the ferry back to Punta Arenas, another gravel road follows the coast to Puerto Espora, 141 kilometers northeast.

### Sights

Directly on the water, **Parque Yugoslavo** memorializes the earliest gold-seeking immigrants, mostly Croats; it's also one of Porvenir's best birding spots. The tourist office provides a small map/brochure, in English, of the city's architectural heritage; many of its houses and other buildings were also Croatian-built.

Most public buildings surround the neatly landscaped **Plaza de Armas,** two blocks north of Parque Yugoslavo. Among them is the **Museo de Tierra del Fuego Fernando Rusque Cordero** (Zavattaro 402, tel. 061/581800, www.museoporvenir.cl, 9 A.M.–5 P.M. Mon.–Thurs., 9 A.M.–4 P.M. Fri., 11 A.M.–2 P.M. and 3–5 P.M. weekends and holidays, US$1), a regional museum dealing with the island's natural history, indigenous heritage, the early gold rush, the later but longer-lasting wool rush, and even cinematography—German-born filmmaker José Bohr went to Hollywood in 1929 and enjoyed a long if inconsistent career. It has added a skillfully produced replica of an early rural store and a good photographic display on local architecture.

Due to move to newly constructed quarters next door, the museum takes its name from a Carabineros officer who helped found it—and was no doubt responsible for the permanent exhibit on police uniforms.

### Accommodations and Food

There's no sign outside expanding **Hospedaje Shinká** (Santos Mardones 333, tel. 061/580491, US$24 s, US$36 d), but this still homey place offers better facilities and amenities—immaculate midsize rooms with comfortable beds, private baths, and cable TV—for less money than any other place in town. The breakfast is forgettable, but that's a minor fault for a place this good.

All rooms at **Hotel Rosas** (Philippi 269, tel. 061/580088, hotelrosas@chile.com, US$36 s, US$48 d with breakfast) have cable TV and private baths; its restaurant is one of the better values in a town with limited choices.

All rooms have private baths at upgraded and expanded **Hotel España** (Croacia 698, tel. 061/580160, www.hotelespana.cl, US$30 s, US$50 d), whose utilitarian addition masks large new rooms; in the older section, some slightly smaller rooms are still adequate. It also has a restaurant.

Under new management, in a restored Magellanic house with greater character than any other lodging in town, **Hostería Yendegaia** (Croacia 702, tel. 061/581919, www.hosteriayendegaia.com, US$36 s, US$52 d) has spacious rooms in their original configuration, with high ceilings and contemporary comforts including flat-screen TVs.

Other than hotel restaurants, the main dining options include the basic **Puerto Montt** (Croacia 1169, tel. 061/580207, lunch daily, dinner Mon.–Sat.) and the **Club Social Catef** (Zavattaro 94, tel. 061/581399, lunch daily, dinner Mon.–Sat.). On the waterfront, the slightly more formal **Club Social Croata** (Señoret 542, tel. 061/580053, lunch daily, dinner Mon.–Sat.) has a tobacco-free dining room and good fish in ample portions—try the conger eel in a king crab and scallop sauce for US$14.

## Information and Services

In the same offices as the museum, Porvenir's helpful **Oficina Municipal de Turismo** (Padre Mario Zavattaro 434, tel. 061/581800, www.muniporvenir.cl) keeps the same hours as the museum (9 A.M.–5 P.M. Mon.–Thurs., 9 A.M.–4 P.M. Fri., 10 A.M.–1:30 P.M. and 3–5 P.M. weekends and holidays).

**BancoEstado** (Philippi 263) has an ATM.

**Correos de Chile** (Philippi 176) is at the southwest corner of the Plaza de Armas. Almost alongside the bank, the **Centro de Llamados** (Philippi 277) has long-distance telephones. There is free municipal wireless Internet on and around the plaza.

For medical services, try the **Hospital Porvenir** (Carlos Wood s/n, between Señoret and Guerrero, tel. 061/580034).

## Getting There and Around

Porvenir has regular but infrequent connections to the mainland but none to the San Sebastián border crossing into Argentina; those with their own vehicles (including cyclists) will still find this a shorter route from Punta Arenas to Ushuaia.

**Aerovías DAP** (Manuel Señoret s/n and Muñoz Gamero, tel. 061/580089) operates air taxi service to Punta Arenas (15 minutes, US$40) at least daily, often more frequently.

At 3:45 P.M. Tuesday and Friday there's a municipal bus from the DAP offices on Señoret to Camerón and Timaukel (two hours, US$3.50) in the southwestern corner of the island; another goes to **Cerro Sombrero** (1.5 hours, US$5.50) at 5 P.M. Monday, Wednesday, and Friday from Zavattaro 432.

In the same office as DAP, **Transbordadora Broom** (Manuel Señoret s/n, tel. 061/580089) sails the comfortable car-passenger ferry *Crux Australis* to Punta Arenas (2.5 hours) Tuesday–Sunday, seas permitting. The ferry leaves from Bahía Chilota, about five kilometers west of town. Adult passengers pay US$10 per person except for the drivers, whose own fare is included in the US$65 per-vehicle charge (motorcycles pay US$18). Children cost US$5 each.

From Bahía Chilota, shared taxis to town cost US$2 per person; from town, a regular taxi costs US$6 (for up to four passengers).

# VICINITY OF PORVENIR

"Vicinity" is a relative term on Tierra del Fuego, as some fascinating locales are difficult or expensive—or both—to reach. To reach the remote south-side fjords, the main option is the luxury cruises on the Cruceros Australis line.

## Monumento Natural Laguna de los Cisnes

International birding groups often detour to this 25-hectare saline lake reserve, which sometimes dries out, just north of Porvenir. While it takes its name from the elegant black-necked swan, it's home to many other species.

## Cordón Baquedano

After Chilean naval officer Ramón Serrano Montaner found gold in the rolling hills east of Porvenir in 1879, panners from Chile and Croatia flocked to the Río del Oro valley, between the Cordón Baquedano and the Sierra Boquerón. Living in sod huts that shielded them from the wind and cold, hoping to eke out a kilogram per year, more than 200 worked the placers until they gave out. By the turn of the century, California miners introduced dredges and steam shovels, but decreasing yields ended the rush by 1908–1909. A century later, a few hardy panners hang on.

From Porvenir, the eastbound road through the Cordón Baquedano passes several gold-rush sites, some marked with interpretive panels; the literal high point is the **Mirador de la Isla,** an overlook 500 meters above sea level. In many places guanacos, which seem to outnumber sheep, gracefully vault meter-high fences that stop the sheep cold.



## Onaisín

About 100 kilometers east of Porvenir, a major north–south road crosses Ruta 215 at Onaisín, a former Sociedad Explotadora *estancia* whose **Cementerio Inglés** is a national historical monument. Northbound, the road goes to the petroleum company town of Cerro Sombrero, while southbound it goes to Camerón and Lago Blanco.

## Lago Blanco

Some 50 kilometers southwest of Onaisín, the road passes through **Camerón,** an erstwhile picture-postcard *estancia* that is now a municipality. The road then angles southeast to Lago Blanco, an area known for its fishing, and continues toward Yendegaia, though it'll be a while before it's finished; in summer there's a bumpy border crossing to Río Grande, Argentina, via a dirt road with many livestock gates and a ford of the Río Rasmussen. The Argentine border post is called Radman.

## Estancia Yendegaia

Visited primarily by Chilean cruise ships and private yachts, Yendegaia conserves 44,000 hectares of Fuegian forest in the Cordillera Darwin between the Argentine border and Parque Nacional Alberto de Agostini. While the owners hope to establish a private national park and create an unbroken preservation corridor along the Beagle Channel (Yendegaia borders Argentina's Parque Nacional Tierra del Fuego), there's government pressure to pave the airstrip at Caleta María, at the property's north end, and a road south from Lago Blanco has reached the Chilean side of Lago Fagnano; to continue beyond, as construction continues, it's necessary to ask permission from the Ministerio de Obras Públicas (Public Works) in Punta Arenas. The owners, for their part, would rather see the border opened to foot traffic from Argentina, but they have consulted with public-works officials to minimize the road's environmental impact.

In the meantime, the *estancia* is open to visitors, although access is difficult without chartering a plane or boat, or taking an expensive cruise through the Fuegian fjords; even Cruceros Australis stops only occasionally. Naval boats between Punta Arenas and Puerto Williams may drop passengers here but are so infrequent that getting back could be problematic.

# CERRO SOMBRERO

About 70 kilometers north of Onaisín and 43 kilometers south of the Puerto Espora ferry landing, Cerro Sombrero is a company town where employees of the Empresa Nacional de Petróleo (ENAP, National Petroleum Company) reside in orderly surroundings with remarkable amenities for a town with only about 150 houses. Dating from the early 1960s, it boasts an astronomical observatory, a bank,

© WAYNE BERNHARDSON
Estancia Yendegaia in the Cordillera Darwin

a botanical garden, a cinema, a hospital, recreational facilities that include a heated swimming pool, and restaurants. Buses between Río Grande and Punta Arenas take a meal break at **Restaurant El Conti** just outside town.

Overnighters will find accommodations at vastly improved **Hostería Tunkelén** (Arturo Prat 101, tel. 061/296696, US$78 s, US$95 d), which also has a good (but expensive) restaurant.

## PUERTO WILLIAMS

On Isla Navarino's north shore, across the Beagle Channel from Argentine Tierra del Fuego, Puerto Williams is the so-called "Capital of Antarctica" and gateway to the rugged Dientes de Navarino backcountry circuit, a five-day slog through soggy mountainous terrain. Local residents look forward to a permanent ferry link to nearby Argentina, but there is political opposition across the channel because myopic Ushuaia impresarios fear losing business to tiny Williams—however unlikely that possibility.

Founded in the 1950s, formerly known as Puerto Luisa, the town (population about 2,000) has paved sidewalks but gravel streets. Most residents are Chilean naval personnel living in relatively stylish prefabs, but there are also some 60 remaining Yámana descendants, only a few of whom speak the language—now a hybrid including many Spanish and English words—among themselves.

### Sights

Overlooking the harbor is the **Proa del Escampavía Yelcho,** the prow of the cutter that, under Luis Pardo Villalón, rescued British explorer Ernest Shackleton's crew from Elephant Island on the Antarctic Peninsula in 1916. A national monument, the bow survived collisions with icebergs to reach its destination; returning to Punta Arenas, the entire ship makes a cameo appearance in original newsreel footage in British director George Butler's *Endurance,* an extraordinary documentary of Shackleton's adventure.

Very professional for a small-town museum, Williams's **Museo Martin Gusinde** (Aragay 1, tel. 061/621043, www.museoantropologicomartingusinde.cl, 9 A.M.–1 P.M. and 2:30–7:18 P.M. Mon.–Thurs., 2:30–6:30 P.M. Sat.–Sun., free) has exhibits on geology, plants, and taxidermy, a marker for the former post office, and a sign for the coal mine at Caleta Banner, on nearby Isla Picton, which provisioned the *Yelcho* on its rescue mission. Nearby is the **Parque Botánico Omora,** an organized selection of native plants.

Built in Germany for operations on the Rhine, the **MV *Micalvi*** shipped supplies between remote *estancias* and other settlements before sinking in Puerto Williams's inner harbor in 1962; the upper deck and bridge remain as the yacht club's bar-restaurant.

### Accommodations, Food, and Entertainment

At **Residencial Pusaki** (Piloto Pardo 242, tel. 061/621116, pattypusaki@yahoo.es, US$23 s, US$50 d), rates vary according to shared or private bath. **Refugio Coirón** (Ricardo Maragaño

168, tel. 061/621227, www.simexpeditions.com, US$20–30 pp) has good accommodations with kitchen privileges and either shared or private baths, but it has had to close on occasion because of labor shortages.

The top choice is the utterly transformed 24-room **Hotel Lakutaia** (tel. 061/621733, www.lakutaia.cl, US$220 s, US$250 d), which is more a destination than just a hotel, with multi-day activities programs; it also has a fine restaurant. Off-season (May–mid-Oct.) rates are about 25 percent lower.

South America's southernmost bar-restaurant, the **Club de Yates Micalvi,** occupies the main deck and bridge of the historic vessel that lies grounded in the inner harbor.

The **Pingüino Pub** is at the Centro Comercial.

### Services

Nearly all services are concentrated around the Centro Comercial, a cluster of storefronts just uphill from the Muelle Guardián Brito, the main passenger pier. These include the post office, several telephone offices, Banco de Chile, the Cema-Chile crafts shop, and Manualidades, which rents mountain bikes.



### Getting There

**Aerovías DAP** (tel. 061/621051), at the Centro Comercial, flies 20-seat Twin Otters to Punta Arenas (US$112) Monday and Wednesday–Saturday April–October. Flights leave Monday–Saturday the rest of the year. DAP flights are often heavily booked, so make reservations well in advance.

Regular connections between Puerto Williams and Ushuaia, on Argentine Tierra del Fuego, continue to be problematic, but there are occasional crossings from Puerto Navarino, 54 kilometers west; contact the **Gobernación Marítima** (tel. 061/621090), the **Club de Yates** (tel. 061/621041, ext. 4250), or **Sim Expeditions** (tel. 061/621150). There are occasional charter flights as well.

In summer, the **ferry** *Bahía Azul* sails to Punta Arenas (34 hours) at 10 P.M. Saturday. Fares are US$210 for a bunk, US$175 for a reclining seat.

## VICINITY OF PUERTO WILLIAMS

The Williams-based German-Venezuelan **Sea & Ice & Mountains Adventures Unlimited** (Austral 74, tel. 061/621227, tel./fax 061/621150, www.simexpeditions.com) organizes trekking, climbing, and riding expeditions on Isla Navarino and the Cordillera Darwin, week-long yacht excursions around the Beagle Channel and to Cape Horn, and even excursions to Antarctica. Advance booking is imperative.

### The Coastal Road

From Puerto Williams, a coastal road runs 54 kilometers west to the village of Puerto Navarino, now a legal port of entry, and 28 kilometers east to Caleta Eugenia; only two kilometers east of Williams, **Villa Ukika** is the last Yámana refuge. From Caleta Eugenia, the road is advancing southeast to **Puerto Toro,** where some 60 boats employ about four workers each in search of *centolla* (king crab).

### Dientes de Navarino

Immediately south of Puerto Williams, Cordón de los Dientes de Navarino is a range of jagged peaks rising more than 1,000 meters above sea level that offers the world's southernmost trekking opportunities. There are, however, few trails through this rugged countryside—anyone undertaking the four- to five-day "circuit" should be experienced in route finding and carry a GPS.

# ARGENTINE TIERRA DEL FUEGO

If Patagonia is exciting, the archipelago of Tierra del Fuego (Land of Fire)—the "uttermost part of the earth"—is electrifying. In the days of sail, the reputation of its sub-Antarctic weather and ferocious westerlies obsessed seamen whether or not they had ever experienced the thrill—or terror—of "rounding the Horn." After Richard Henry Dana survived the southern seas en route to California in November 1834, he vividly recounted conditions that could change from calm to chaos in an instant:

> *"Here comes Cape Horn!" said the chief mate; and we had hardly time to haul down and clew up, before it was upon us. In a few moments, a heavier sea was raised than I had ever seen before, and...the little brig... plunged into it, and all the forward part of her was under water; the sea pouring in through the bow ports and hawse-hole, and over the knight-heads, threatening to wash everything overboard.... At the same time sleet and hail were driving with all fury against us.*

In Dana's time, that was the price of admission to one of the earth's most spectacular combinations of sea, sky, land, and ice. In a landscape whose granite pinnacles jut nearly 2,000 meters out of the ocean, only a handful of hunter-gatherers foraging in the fjords and forests could know the area with any intimacy. Today, fortunately, there are ways to reach Tierra del Fuego that involve less hardship—not to mention motion sickness—than Dana and his shipmates suffered.

© RITA MELVILLE/123RF

## HIGHLIGHTS

**Museo Marítimo de Ushuaia:** Much more than its name suggests, Ushuaia's best museum needs more than one visit to absorb its maritime heritage and appreciate the way in which one of the world's most remote prisons affected the city's development (page 471).

**Beagle Channel Boat Excursions:** Following the wake, not just the footsteps, of Fitz Roy and Darwin should be part of every visit to the uttermost part of the earth. Choose a small vessel, though, that lets you go ashore on its islands (page 480).

**Estancia Harberton:** East of Ushuaia, this historic *estancia* is, arguably, the nucleus of the "uttermost part of the earth" (page 481).

**Glaciar Martial:** Whether entirely by foot or partly by chairlift, the climb to Ushuaia's nearby glacier, part of **Parque Nacional Tierra del Fuego,** rewards visitors with panoramic views of the city and the storied Beagle Channel (page 483).

**Misión Salesiana:** North of Río Grande, the priests at this national historical monument did their best to salvage the remains of Fuegia's indigenous cultures from the European onslaught, but they themselves inadvertently contributed to the holocaust (page 487).

LOOK FOR [icon] TO FIND RECOMMENDED SIGHTS, ACTIVITIES, DINING, AND LODGING.



In his memoirs, pioneer settler Lucas Bridges labeled Tierra del Fuego the "uttermost part of the earth" for its splendid isolation at the continent's southern tip. It's still a place where fur seals, sea lions, and penguins cavort in the choppy seas of the strait named for the celebrated navigator Ferdinand Magellan, where Darwin sailed on the *Beagle* and the first 49ers found their route to California. From the seashore, behind its capital of Ushuaia, glacial horns rise like sacred steeples. The beaches and southern beech forests of Parque Nacional Tierra del Fuego, west of the city, are the terminus of the world's southernmost highway.

Tierra del Fuego is not just one island, but an archipelago, though the Isla Grande de Tierra del Fuego is South America's largest island. Chile shares the territory with Argentina; while parts of the Argentine side are urbanized, the Chilean side has just a few small towns and isolated *estancias.* Roads are few but improving, and some are now paved, especially on the Argentine side; the unpaved roads can be hell on windshields, which are most cheaply replaced in the Chilean mainland city of Punta Arenas.

Two ferry routes connect the Chilean mainland to Tierra del Fuego: a shuttle from

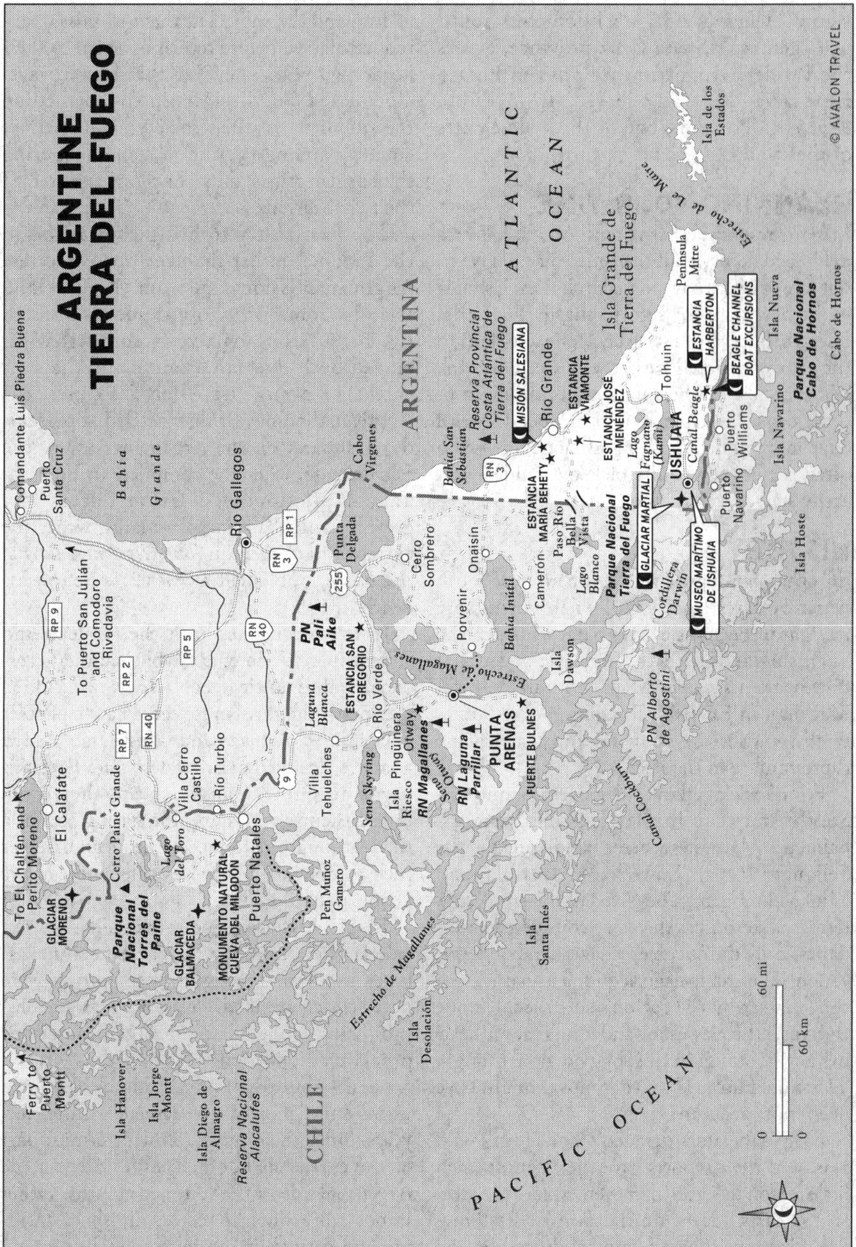
ARGENTINE TIERRA DEL FUEGO
© AVALON TRAVEL
ATLANTIC OCEAN
PACIFIC OCEAN
ARGENTINA
CHILE
Comandante Luis Piedra Buena
Puerto Santa Cruz
Bahía Grande
To Puerto San Julián and Comodoro Rivadavia
RP 9
RP 2
RP 5
RP 7
RN 40
RN 3
RP 1
255
9
Río Gallegos
Cabo Vírgenes
Punta Delgada
To El Chaltén and Perito Moreno
El Calafate
GLACIAR MORENO
Cerro Paine Grande
Parque Nacional Torres del Paine
Lago del Toro
Villa Cerro Castillo
Río Turbio
GLACIAR BALMACEDA
MONUMENTO NATURAL CUEVA DEL MILODÓN
Puerto Natales
Pen Muñoz Gamero
Villa Tehuelches
Laguna Blanca
PN Pali Aike
ESTANCIA SAN GREGORIO
Río Verde
Seno Skyring
Isla Riesco
Pingüinera Otway
RN Magallanes
Seno Otway
RN Laguna Parrillar
PUNTA ARENAS
FUERTE BULNES
Estrecho de Magallanes
Porvenir
Onaisin
Cerro Sombrero
Bahía Inútil
Isla Dawson
Camerón
Lago Blanco
Paso Río Bella Vista
ESTANCIA MARÍA BEHETY
Bahía San Sebastián
Reserva Provincial Costa Atlántica de Tierra del Fuego
MISIÓN SALESIANA
Río Grande
ESTANCIA VIAMONTE
ESTANCIA JOSÉ MENENDEZ
Lago Fagnano (Kami)
Tolhuin
Parque Nacional Tierra del Fuego
GLACIAR MARTIAL
USHUAIA
MUSEO MARÍTIMO DE USHUAIA
Canal Beagle
ESTANCIA HARBERTON
BEAGLE CHANNEL BOAT EXCURSIONS
Isla Grande de Tierra del Fuego
Península Mitre
Estrecho de Le Maire
Isla de los Estados
Puerto Williams
Puerto Navarino
Isla Navarino
Isla Nueva
Isla Hoste
Parque Nacional Cabo de Hornos
Cabo de Hornos
Cordillera Darwin
PN Alberto de Agostini
Canal Cockburn
Isla Santa Inés
Isla Desolación
Ferry to Puerto Montt
Isla Hanover
Isla Jorge Montt
Isla Diego de Almagro
Reserva Nacional Alacalufes
0
60 mi
60 km

Punta Delgada, only 45 kilometers south of Argentina's Santa Cruz province, across the Primera Angostura narrows to Puerto Espora, and a daily service from Punta Arenas to Porvenir, one of the widest parts of the strait.

## PLANNING YOUR TIME

Like the rest of southern South America, Tierra del Fuego deserves all the time you can give it, but most visitors have to make choices. Ushuaia is the best base for sightseeing in Tierra del Fuego proper, given its access for excursions to the nearby national park, the Beagle Channel, and Estancia Harberton, with a minimum of three days. Hikers may wish to spend several days more and fly-fishing aficionados—who often prefer the vicinity of Río Grande—can easily stay a week or two.

## HISTORY

European familiarity with southernmost South America dates from 1520, when Portuguese navigator Fernando Magalhaes, under the Spanish flag, sailed through the strait that now bears his name (Magallanes in Spanish, Magellan in English). Ranging 3–25 kilometers in width, the strait became a maritime thoroughfare to the Pacific.

Prior to Magellan's "discovery," southern South America's insular extremes were inhabited by hunter-gatherer bands such as the Selk'nam (Ona), Kawéskar (Alacaluf), and Yámana (Yahgan). They lived off maritime and terrestrial resources that they considered abundant—only European eyes saw a land of deprivation. The archipelago acquired its name from the fires set by the region's so-called "Canoe Indians," the Kawéskar and Yámana, for heating and cooking; in this soggy region, though, Tierra del Humo (Land of Smoke) might have been more accurate.

Early navigators dreaded Cape Horn's wild seas, and their reports gave their countrymen little reason to settle in or even explore the area. In the early 1830s, on the *Beagle*'s first voyage, Captain Robert Fitzroy abducted several Yámana, including the famous Jemmy Button, to England; he subjected them to missionary indoctrination before returning them to their home two years later. On that later voyage, a perplexed Charles Darwin commented on the simplicity of their society: "The perfect equality among the individuals composing the Fuegian tribes, must for a long time retard their civilization."

The first to try to bring civilization to the Yámana, rather than the opposite, were Anglican missionaries from the Falkland Islands, some of whose descendants still live here. After abortive attempts that included both Fuegian assaults and the starvation of evangelist Allen Gardiner, the Anglican Thomas Bridges settled at present-day Ushuaia, on the Argentine side of the Isla Grande, where he compiled an English-Yámana dictionary. His son Lucas, who grew up with Yámana playmates, wrote the extraordinary memoir *The Uttermost Part of the Earth*, published a few years before his death in 1950.

In the meantime, both the Chilean and Argentine governments established their presence, and gigantic sheep *estancias* occupied the sprawling grasslands where native peoples once hunted guanaco and other game. As the guanaco declined and the desperate Fuegians began to hunt domestic sheep, they often found themselves facing the wrong end of a rifle—though introduced European diseases such as typhoid and measles killed more native people than did bullets.

In 1979, the two countries nearly went to war over three small Beagle Channel islands in an archipelago whose borders were never clearly defined. Positions were uncompromising—one adamant Argentine poster proclaimed "We will never surrender what is ours!"—but papal mediation averted open warfare and brought a settlement within a few years. Since then, travel to the uttermost part of the earth has boomed, especially on the Argentine side in the summer months. Other important economic sectors are sheep farming and petroleum, on both the Chilean and Argentine sides.

# Ushuaia

Beneath the Martial range's serrated spires, on the Beagle Channel's north shore, the city of Ushuaia is both an end (the virtual terminus of the world's southernmost highway) and a beginning (the gateway to Antarctica). The surrounding countryside attracts activities-oriented visitors for hiking, mountain biking, fishing, and skiing. In the summer season, the city gets hundreds of thousands of visitors, many of them merely day-trippers from the hundreds of cruise ships that anchor here.

After more than two decades of economic growth and physical sprawl, the provincial capital is both declining and improving. On the one hand, the duty-free manufacturing, fishing, and tourist boom that transformed a onetime penal colony and naval base into a bustling city has weakened. On the other, it has spruced up the waterfront and restored historic buildings, some of them becoming hotels or B&Bs. The streets are cleaner (though San Martín is tourist-trap ugly) and there are more parks, plazas, and green spaces. Still, Ushuaia has particulate pollution problems because high winds kick up dust in its unpaved newer neighborhoods.

## HISTORY

Ushuaia dates from 1870, when the Anglican South American Missionary Society decided to place the archipelago's first permanent European settlement here. Pioneer missionary Thomas Bridges and his descendants have left an enduring legacy in Bridges's Yámana (Yahgan) dictionary, his son Lucas's memoir, and the family *estancia* at nearby Harberton (the Yámana whom Thomas Bridges hoped to save, though, succumbed to introduced diseases and conflict with other settlers).

Not long after Ushuaia's settlement, Argentina, alarmed by the British presence, moved to establish its own authority at Ushuaia

© WAYNE BERNHARDSON

city of Ushuaia, with the Martial range in the background

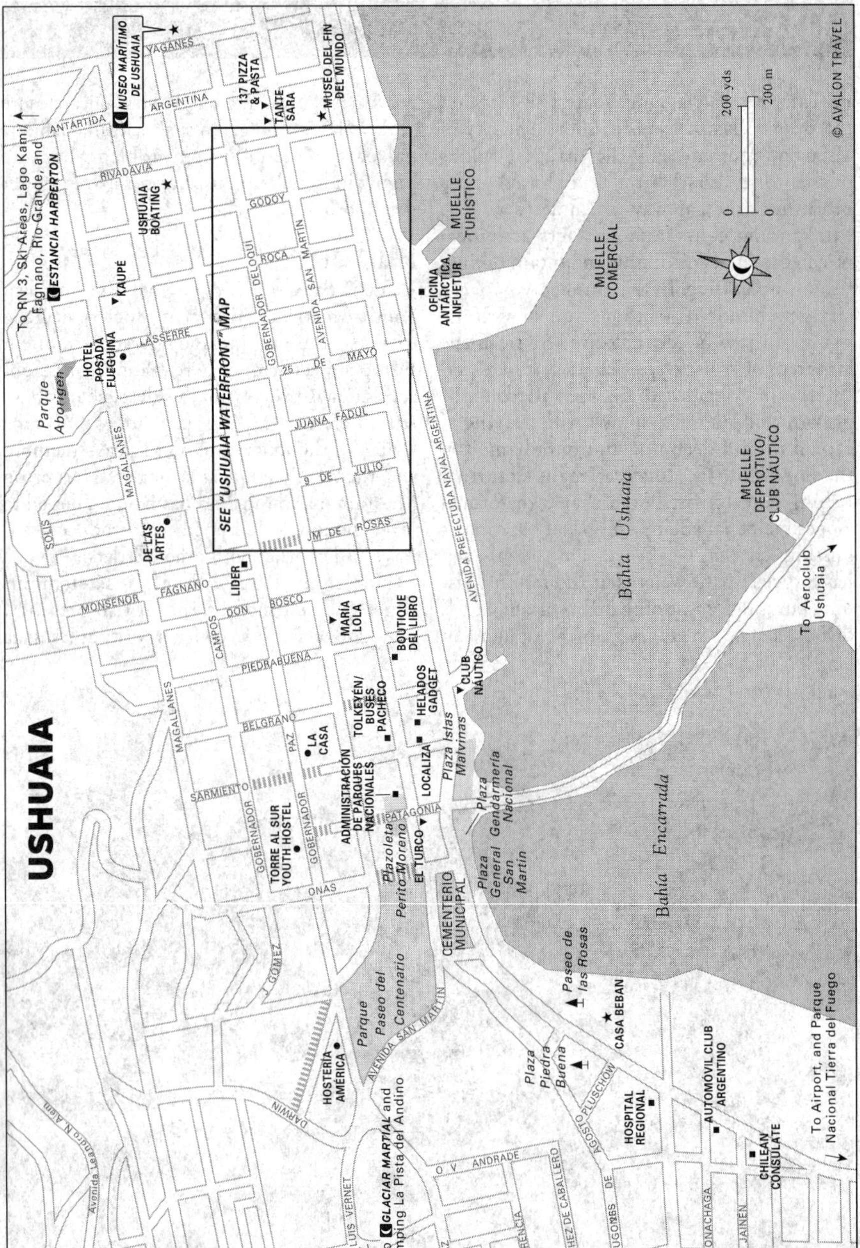
USHUAIA
To RN 3, Ski Areas, Lago Kami/Fagnano, Río Grande, and ESTANCIA HARBERTON
MUSEO MARÍTIMO DE USHUAIA
YAGANES
ARGENTINA
ANTÁRTIDA
RIVADAVIA
137 PIZZA & PASTA
TANTE SARA
MUSEO DEL FIN DEL MUNDO
USHUAIA BOATING
GODOY
ROCA
GOBERNADOR DELOQUI
AVENIDA SAN MARTÍN
KAUPÉ
HOTEL POSADA FUEGUINA
LASSERRE
Parque Aborigen
SEE "USHUAIA WATERFRONT" MAP
25 DE MAYO
JUANA FADUL
9 DE JULIO
JM DE ROSAS
MAGALLANES
SOLÍS
DE LAS ARTES
MONSEÑOR
FAGNANO
LÍDER
DON BOSCO
CAMPOS
MARÍA LOLA
BOUTIQUE DEL LIBRO
PIEDRABUENA
HELADOS GADGET
TOLKEYEN/BUSES PACHECO
CLUB NÁUTICO
BELGRANO
LA CASA
PAZ
SARMIENTO
ADMINISTRACIÓN DE PARQUES NACIONALES
LOCALIZA
TORRE AL SUR YOUTH HOSTEL
GOBERNADOR
PATAGONIA
Plazoleta Perito Moreno
EL TURCO
Plaza Islas Malvinas
Plaza Gendarmería Nacional
Plaza General San Martín
ONAS
CEMENTERIO MUNICIPAL
OFICINA ANTÁRTICA INFUETUR
MUELLE TURÍSTICO
MUELLE COMERCIAL
AVENIDA PREFECTURA NAVAL ARGENTINA
MUELLE DEPROTIVO/CLUB NÁUTICO
Bahía Ushuaia
To Aeroclub Ushuaia
Bahía Encarrada
200 yds
200 m
0
© AVALON TRAVEL
J. GÓMEZ
Parque Paseo del Centenario
AVENIDA SAN MARTÍN
HOSTERÍA AMÉRICA
Paseo de las Rosas
CASA BEBAN
Plaza Piedra Buena
PLUSCHOW
HOSPITAL REGIONAL
AUTOMÓVIL CLUB ARGENTINO
CHILEAN CONSULATE
To Airport, and Parque Nacional Tierra del Fuego
DARWIN
Avenida Leandro N. Alem
To GLACIAR MARTIAL and Camping La Pista del Andino
LUIS VERNET
O V ANDRADE
SÁNCHEZ DE CABALLERO
AGOSTO
LUGONES
DE
FLORENCIA
PAZ
ONACHAGA
JAINEN

and did so with a penal settlement for its most infamous criminals and political undesirables. It remained a penal settlement until almost 1950, when Juan Domingo Perón's government created a major naval base to support Argentina's Antarctic claims. Since the 1976–1983 dictatorship ended it has become a tourist destination, visited by cruise ships as well as overland travelers and air passengers who come to see the world's southernmost city.

## ORIENTATION

Stretching east–west along the Beagle Channel's north shore, Ushuaia (population about 56,500) is 3,220 kilometers south of Buenos Aires and 212 kilometers southwest of Río Grande, the island's only other city.

Bedecked with flowerbeds, the main thoroughfare is Avenida Maipú, part of RN 3, expanded into a divided boulevard; it continues west to Bahía Lapataia in Parque Nacional Tierra del Fuego. The parallel San Martín, one block north, is the main commercial street; the focus of Ushuaia's nightlife, it gets gridlocked on summer nights as surely as any avenue in Buenos Aires. From the shoreline, the perpendicular northbound streets rise steeply—some so steeply that they become staircases.

## SIGHTS

Even if it has leveled off, Ushuaia's economic boom provided the wherewithal to preserve and even restore some of the city's historic buildings. Two of them are now museums: Dating from 1912, the waterfront former branch of the **Banco de la Nación** (Av. Maipú 173) houses the historical Museo del Fin del Mundo, while the former **Presidio de Ushuaia** (Yaganes and Gobernador Paz), dating also from the early 20th century, is now the misleadingly named Museo Marítimo (while not insignificant, its maritime exhibits are less interesting than those on the city's genesis as a penal colony).

Three blocks west of the Museo del Fin del Mundo, dating from 1893, the classically Magellanic **Antigua Casa de Gobierno** (Av. Maipú 465) once housed the provincial government and is now part of the museum. Five blocks farther west, the **Antigua Capilla de la Merced** (Av. Maipú and Rosas) is a chapel originally dating from 1898 and restored in 1999. A branch of the municipal tourist office occupies the **Biblioteca Sarmiento** (1926) at San Martín 674, the city's first public library (built by prisoners). At the west end of downtown, the waterfront **Casa Beban** (Av. Maipú y Plüschow) is a reassembled pioneer residence dating from 1913; it now houses an exhibition center.

### Museo del Fin del Mundo

Its block-style exterior handsomely restored, Ushuaia's evolving historical museum contains exhibits on the Yámana, Selk'nam, and other Fuegian natives as well as on early European voyages. There remain permanent exhibits on the presidio, an early general store, Banco de la Nación's original branch (which occupied the building for more than 60 years), and natural history, including run-of-the-mill taxidermy. Its celebrity artifact is a rare copy of Thomas Bridges's Yámana–English dictionary.

An open-air sector re-creates a Yámana encampment and dwellings alongside machinery used in early agriculture and forestry projects. The Museo del Fin del Mundo (Av. Maipú 173, tel. 02901/421863, www.tierradelfuego.org.ar/museo, 10 A.M.–7 P.M. weekdays and noon–7 P.M. weekends and holidays Oct.–Apr., noon–7 P.M. Mon.–Sat. the rest of the year, US$8) also contains a bookstore/souvenir shop and a specialized library on southernmost Argentina, the surrounding oceans, and Antarctica. The exceptional website places much of this material online. Guided tours are offered at 10:30 A.M. and 2 P.M. October–April.

Admission includes access to the former Casa de Gobierno (Government House, Av. Maipú 465), with guided tours noon and 3:30 P.M.

### Museo Marítimo de Ushuaia

Misleadingly named, Ushuaia's maritime museum (Yaganes and Gobernador Paz, tel. 02901/437481, www.museomaritimo.com, US$15, US$9 for foreign students, US$33

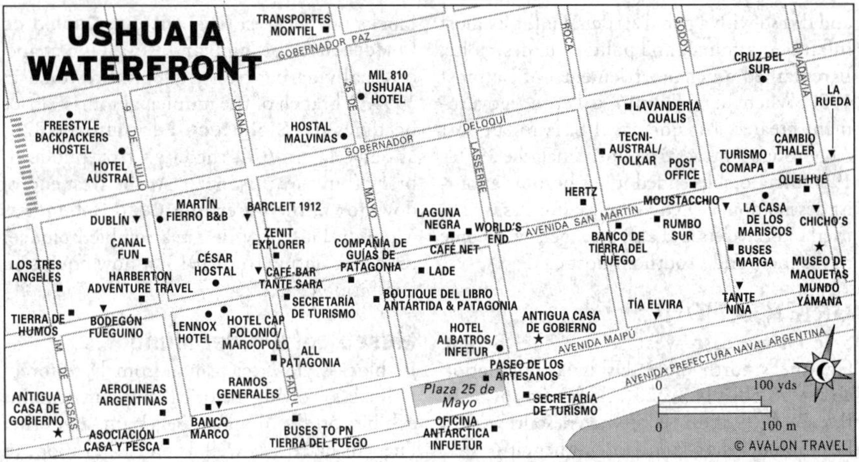


for a family ticket; Argentines and locals get a discount) most effectively tells the story of Ushuaia's inauspicious origins as a penal settlement for both civilian and military prisoners. Alarmed over the South American Missionary Society's incursions among the Beagle Channel's indigenous peoples, in 1884 Argentina reinforced its territorial claims by building a military prison on Isla de los Estados (Staten Island), across the Strait of Lemaire at the southeastern tip of the Isla Grande.

Barely a decade later, in 1896, it established Ushuaia's civilian Cárcel de Reincidentes for repeat offenders; after finally deciding that Isla de los Estados was a hardship post even for prisoners, the military moved its own facility to Ushuaia in 1902. Then, in 1911, the two institutions fused in this building, which held some of the country's most famous political prisoners, celebrated rogues, and notorious psychopaths of the first half of the 20th century, until it closed in 1947.

Divided into five two-story pavilions, with 380 cells intended to house one prisoner each, it held up to 600 prisoners at a time. Its most famous inmates were political detainees, such as Russian anarchist bomber Simón Radowitzsky, who killed Buenos Aires police chief Ramón Falcón in 1909; Radical politicians Ricardo Rojas, Honorio Pueyrredón, and Mario Guido (the deceptively named Radicals are an ineffectual middle-class party); and Peronist politician Héctor Cámpora, who was briefly president in the 1970s.

Many, if not most, prisoners, though, were long-termers or lifers, such as the diminutive strangler Cayetano Santos Godino, a serial killer dubbed "El Petiso Orejudo" for his short height and his oversized ears (the nickname also describes a large-eared bat native to the archipelago). Julio Ordano has written a play, performed in Buenos Aires, about Santos Godino.

Life-sized figures of the most infamous inmates, modified department-store dummies clad in prison stripes, occupy many cells. One intriguing exhibit is a wide-ranging comparison with other prisons that have become museums, such as San Francisco's Alcatraz and South Africa's Robben Island.

The museum does justify its name with a collection of scale models of ships that have played a role in local history, such as Magellan's galleon *Trinidad,* the legendary *Beagle,* the South American Missionary Society's three successive sailboats, each known as the *Allen Gardiner,* and Antarctic explorer and conqueror Roald Amundsen's *Fram.* In addition, there are materials on Argentina's Antarctic presence since the early 20th century, when the corvette *Uruguay* rescued Otto Nordenskjöld's Norwegian expedition, whose crew included the Argentine José María Sobral. On the grounds stands a full-size replica of the Faro San Juan de Salvamento, the Isla de los Estados (Staten Island) lighthouse that figures in Jules Verne's story "The Lighthouse at the End of the World."

In addition, the museum contains a philatelic room, natural history and marine art exhibits, and admirable accounts of the region's indigenous peoples. It has only two drawbacks: There's too much to see in a single day, and the English translations could use some polishing—to say the least.

The Museo Marítimo is open 9 A.M.–8 P.M. daily November–April, and 10 A.M.–8 P.M. daily May–October.

On request, staff will validate your admission ticket for another day; since there's so much here, splitting up sightseeing sessions is a good idea. It has an excellent book and souvenir shop as well as a *confitería* for snacks and coffee.

### Museo de Maquetas Mundo Yámana

While both the Museo del Fin del Mundo and Museo Marítimo do a creditable job on Tierra del Fuego's indigenous heritage, this small private museum (Rivadavia 56, tel. 02901/422874, 9 A.M.–8 P.M. daily, US$6) consists of skillfully assembled dioramas of pre-European life along the Beagle Channel, at a scale of 1:15. It also includes cartographic representations of the Yámana and their neighbors, interpretations of the European impact, and panels of historical photographs. The staff speak fluent English.

## ENTERTAINMENT AND EVENTS

Ushuaia has sprouted a plethora of pubs, some but not all with Irish aspirations or pretensions, such as **Dublin** (9 de Julio 168, tel. 02901/430744), with a standard menu of *minutas* (short orders).

April's **Festival Internacional de Ushuaia** (www.festivaldeushuaia.com) is a varied program of classic music concerts by Argentine and international artists, held at Las Hayas Resort Hotel in April for two weeks. A free concert at a local stadium is always included in the program.

© WAYNE BERNHARDSON

Ushuaia's Boutique del Libro Antártida & Patagonia is a thriving travel bookstore.

## SHOPPING

**Boutique del Libro Antártida & Patagonia** (25 de Mayo 62, tel. 02901/432117, www.antartidaypatagonia.com.ar) carries a wide choice of Argentine and imported books in Spanish, English, and other languages on the "uttermost part of the earth" and its surroundings, including Moon Handbooks at moderate markups; there are also novels for that long voyage across the Drake Passage to Antarctica. In spacious quarters, its other **Boutique del Libro** (San Martín 1120, tel. 02901/424750) offers an excellent selection of Spanish-language books and a smaller choice of English-language titles.

Along with many similar venues along Ushuaia's main shopping street, **World's End**

## BOUND FOR THE ICE

Ushuaia has become the main jumping-off point for Antarctic excursions, using ships such as Russian icebreakers. (Despite being chartered under U.S. officers, the Russian ships sometimes still show the hammer and sickle of the Soviet Union on their bows.) For travelers with flexible schedules, it has been possible to make last-minute arrangements at huge discounts – no ship wants to sail with empty berths – but heavy demand has made it difficult to pay anything less than US$4,500-5,000 for 10 days, including several days' transit across the stormy Drake Passage (seasickness medication advised).

On the waterfront Muelle Comercial, Ushuaia's **Oficina Antártica Infuetur** (tel. 02901/430015, antartida@tierradelfuego.org.ar) has the latest information on Antarctic cruises. At present, even last-minute arrangements go through Ushuaia travel agencies for the October-March season.

© WAYNE BERNHARDSON

Canada's Polar Star and Russia's Akademik Iofee both serve Antarctic tourists.



(San Martín 505, tel. 02901/422971, also at San Martín 702, tel. 02901/422665, and other branches) has many kitschy souvenirs but also maps and books. Nearby **Laguna Negra** (San Martín 513, tel. 02901/431144) specializes in locally produced chocolates.

**Tierra de Humos** (San Martín 861, tel. 02901/433050, www.tierradehumos.com) stocks locally produced leather, fleeces, handicrafts, and silverwork. For purchases directly from the artisans, there's the **Paseo de los Artesanos** (Av. Maipú and Lasserre), at the entrance to the Muelle Comercial port.

**Quelhué** (San Martín 214, tel. 02901/435882, www.quelhue.com.ar) carries a fine selection of Argentine wines and imported duty-free liquors.

## ACCOMMODATIONS

Ushuaia has abundant accommodations, but it has long been one of the country's most expensive destinations. Demand is also high, especially in the summer months of January and February, when prices rise and reservations are advisable. One heartening development is the proliferation of good but moderately priced backpacker hostels and the arrival of several bed-and-breakfasts—known by the semi-

English acronym ByB—some of them excellent alternatives. Wireless Internet services are widely available.

## US$10-25

A stiff climb to the northwest of downtown, **La Pista del Andino** (Av. Leandro N. Alem 2873, tel. 02901/435890, www.lapistadelandino.com.ar, US$6 pp) has slightly sloping campsites at its ski area and a *refugio* with a *confitería,* a kitchen for the campers' use, and a dining room.

## US$25-50

Perched at downtown's western edge, with spectacular Beagle Channel views, **Torre al Sur Youth Hostel** (Gobernador Paz 1437, tel. 02901/430745, www.torrealsur.com.ar, US$15 pp dorm) has been one of Argentina's finest backpacker facilities, but overcrowding and noise have meant mixed reviews recently. Rooms have 2–6 beds as well as lockers; there's free luggage storage.

The central **Cruz del Sur** (Deloqui 242, tel. 02901/434099, www.xdelsur.com.ar, US$15 pp dorm) is a hostel with cheerfully colored four- and six-bed dorms, plus a garden for barbecues, parking, and free luggage storage.

Half a block from the Líder bus terminal, **Freestyle Backpackers Hostel** (Gobernador Paz 866, tel. 02901/432874, www.ushuaiafreestyle.com, US$18–20 pp dorm, US$53 d) is a gleaming purpose-built hostel with youthful energy, a spacious lounge and kitchen facilities, and secondary amenities including laundry service and parking.

The HI affiliate **Albergue Los Cormoranes** (Kamshen 788, tel. 02902/423459, www.loscormoranes.com, US$20 pp dorm, US$83 d with private bath) has attractive common areas, including a wind-sheltered garden, and better sleeping facilities than Torre al Sur. Most easily reached by climbing Don Bosco to its end and then taking a left, it's about eight steep blocks north of the waterfront (arrival transfers are free).

**De las Artes** (9 de Julio 462, tel. 02901/431862, www.bbdelasartes.com.ar, US$38 s, US$50 d), a small bed-and-breakfast with shared baths, has tidy cheerful rooms, hostel facilities such as kitchen use, and a large breakfast table for socializing.

## US$50-100

Owner, designer, and host Silvia Casalaga makes you feel at home at her six-room **La Casa** (Gobernador Paz 1380, tel. 02901/423202, www.silviacasalaga.com.ar, US$45 s, US$57 d), which is far enough from noisy San Martín, but still central, and with plain, spotless rooms with baths to share.

Only a short walk from downtown, in an oasis neighborhood of sheltered gardens, **Galeazzi-Basily B&B** (Gobernador Valdez 323, tel. 02901/423213, www.avesdelsur.com.ar, US$46 s, US$67 d) is a comfortable family house where its few private rooms share bathrooms. It also has exterior cabañas, which are excellent value (from US$75 for two people in low season). The hosts speak English fluently and are a great source of information on the rest of the island, especially Estancia Harberton.

**Hostal Malvinas** (Deloqui 615, tel. 02901/422626, www.hostalmalvinas.net, US$80 s, US$90 d) provides simple but quiet and immaculate rooms with large baths and no frills.

**Hotel Austral** (9 de Julio 250, tel. 02901/422223, www.hotel-austral.com.ar, US$95 s or d) is a 10-room hotel with soaring, light-filled common areas that offer panoramic views of the Beagle Channel (at least until new constructions block them some years from now). Painted in pastels, the rooms themselves are spacious and comfortable.

Rehabbed **César Hostal** (San Martín 753, tel. 02901/421460, www.hotelcesarhostal.com.ar, US$63 s, US$97 d) has become one of the better values in a congested central area, and it has a restaurant.

On the hillside, the contemporary **Martín Fierro B&B** (9 de Julio 175, tel. 02901/430525, www.martinfierrobyb.com.ar, US$75 s, US$100 d) has two bunks in each of four small but well-designed rooms with shared baths. Host Javier Jury has created tasteful common areas that are simultaneously spacious and cozy, and the breakfast is varied and filling; the tiny shower stalls, though, make bathing with a friend impossible without being *really* intimate. Two downstairs "apart-hotel" rooms (US$100 s, US$138 d), with separate kitchens, sleep up to three people each.

## US$100-200

Responsive **Hostería América** (Gobernador Paz 1665, tel. 02901/423358, www.hosteriaamerica.com.ar, US$88–100 s, US$100–113 d) is a decent choice in a fine location above the Parque Paseo del Centenario. Higher rates correspond to channel views.

Hillside **Hotel Ushuaia** (Lasserre 933, tel. 02901/430671, www.ushuaiahotel.com.ar, US$98 s, US$127 d) is a good value in its price range and has a restaurant.

In dense woods about 1.5 kilometers northeast of downtown, **Patagonia Villa Lodge** (Bahía Buen Suceso 563, tel. 02901/435937, www.patagoniavilla.com, US$180–260 d) has just four rooms in luminous semidetached cabins and a new lodge with magnificently rustic architecture and comforts including whirlpool tubs in two of its suites. There is one double (US$110 s, US$140 d) that lacks significant natural light but suffers only by comparison with the others; elsewhere, it would count among the best in town. Owner Luciana Lupotti, a former Florida exchange student, speaks fluent English.

From its cul-de-sac perch, **Hotel Posada Fueguina** (Lasserre 438, tel. 02901/423467, www.posadafueguina.com.ar, US$110–123 s, US$148–180 d) offers awesome views, especially from its deluxe rooms, which also have Jacuzzis. It has cabañas as well to handle any overflow.

Only its busy location and the differential rates (around 25 percent higher for foreigners) detract from the bright and cheerful **Hotel Cap Polonio** (San Martín 746, tel. 02901/422131, www.hotelcappolonio.com.ar, US$155 s or d, with breakfast). All rooms are carpeted and baths have tubs as well as showers. There's a good restaurant *confitería,* and a playroom for children open Wednesday–Monday from 5 P.M.

Though it's not really a view hotel, the 30-room **Mil 810 Ushuaia Hotel** (25 de Mayo 245, tel. 02901/437710, www.hotel1810.com, US$163 s or d) is a central design hotel that occupies a prominent hillside site just a couple of blocks from the waterfront, close enough to walk everywhere but just beyond the congested center.

The spacious, rejuvenated **Hotel Albatros** (Av. Maipú 505, tel. 02901/437300, www.albatroshotel.com.ar, US$180 s or d) is the pick of the waterfront accommodations, with a spa and a restaurant.

About four kilometers west of downtown, in a still-developing neighborhood that's mostly residential, family-run **Hostería Tierra de Leyendas** (Tierra de Vientos 2448, tel. 02901/446565, www.tierradeleyendas.com.ar, US$189–229 s or d) is a five-room boutique hotel with expansive views of the Beagle Channel. Owner Sebastián García Cosoleto, who cooked for eight years at the Buenos Aires Marriott Plaza Hotel, is also chef of its French-influenced restaurant (open for dinner and for guests only).

## Over US$200

Renovated in 2010, the interior is more impressive than the surprisingly plain exterior at the luxury **Hotel del Glaciar** (Luis Martial 2355, tel. 02901/430640, www.hoteldelglaciar.com, US$209–219 s or d), at kilometer 3.5 on the road to the Martial Glacier. Each room has either a mountain view or an ocean view (which is slightly more expensive), but it's questionable whether staffing is sufficient for a hotel of its category—and price.

At kilometer 3 on the glacier road, the **Las Hayas Resort Hotel** (Luis Martial 1650, tel. 02901/430710, www.lashayashotel.com, from US$290 s or d) enjoys nearly all conceivable luxuries, including an elaborate buffet breakfast, a gym, a sauna, a hot tub, and a heated indoor pool; it picks up guests at the airport and offers a regular shuttle to and from downtown. Behind its surprisingly utilitarian exterior, some of its 93 rooms and suites suffer from hideous decor—the wallpaper is to cringe at—but all are comfortable, and its staff is highly professional.

## FOOD

Although the 2001–2002 peso collapse briefly reined in prices, they've since rebounded, and there are some truly expensive dining choices; the financially challenged should look for *tenedor libre* specials or be cautious with extras like dessert and coffee.

Hotel Cap Polonio's **Marcopolo** (San Martín 746, tel. 02901/436612) is a café-restaurant that serves excellent coffee, chocolate, and croissants for breakfast—try the *submarino* for a cold morning's pickup.

**El Turco** (San Martín 1440, tel. 02901/424711, lunch and dinner Mon.–Sat.), though lacking variety, is a good shoestring choice where entrées are US$7–12 and pizzas start at US$10. Well-established **Barcleit 1912** (Juana Fadul 148, tel. 02901/433015, lunch and dinner daily) has fallen a step behind some of the other pizzerias with pizzas from US$10, but also offers moderately priced short orders and a convenient fixed-price menu (US$10).

In luminous quarters, **Tante Sara Resto Bar** (San Martín 175, tel. 02901/433710, lunch and dinner daily) made its name in sweets and snacks, which are still abundant, but it also produces a limited menu of well-crafted lunch and dinner dishes, such as a rib-eye with a Malbec sauce (US$15) and others in the US$11–18 range. For breakfast, coffee, sandwiches, and desserts, try its **Café-Bar Tante Sara** (San Martín 701, tel. 02901/423912).

**137 Pizza & Pasta** (San Martín 137, tel. 02901/435005, lunch and dinner daily) still sets the pace in diverse pastas with a broad selection of imaginative sauces, as well as pizza. Most entrées, such as ravioli with king crab, fall into the US$7–12 range, with sauces for US$5–10 extra.

Facing the waterfront, **Ramos Generales** (Av. Maipú 749, tel. 02901/424317, www.ramosgeneralesushuaia.com, 9 A.M.–midnight daily) is a bar and restaurant that re-creates a pioneer general store with humor and museum-quality artifacts. It may romanticize the era, but its snacks (including sandwiches) and sweets reinforce the style to make it a must for any Ushuaia visitor. The menu is not elaborate, but the quality is outstanding. Its entrées range US$12–20.

In an artfully restored historical house, **Bodegón Fueguino** (San Martín 859, tel. 02901/431972, lunch and dinner daily) specializes in Fuegian lamb prepared in a variety of styles (US$20), but it also has pasta, pizza, tangy beef empanadas, and good desserts.

**La Rueda** (San Martín 193, tel. 02901/436540, lunch and dinner daily) charges US$22 per person for its own buffet *parrilla* and cold dishes, drinks extra. The well-established **Moustacchio** (San Martín 298, tel. 02901/423308, lunch and dinner daily) stresses seafood (its king crab costs US$25) but also serves beef and other meats, including lamb (US$19).

Ushuaia has a wider choice of seafood restaurants than almost any other Argentine provincial city. **La Casa de los Mariscos** (San Martín 232, tel. 02901/421928, lunch and dinner daily) specializes in *centolla* (king crab, US$23) but has many other fish and shellfish options (US$13–16).

With a 30-year history and portside views, **Tante Nina** (Gobernador Godoy 15, tel. 02901/432444, www.tanteninarestaurant.com.ar, lunch and dinner daily) focuses on Fuegian fish and seafood, including 10 varieties of king crab (from US$23); the food is fine and the service is efficient, but the ambience feels institutional. **Chicho's** (Rivadavia 72, tel. 02901/423469, lunch and dinner daily) also handles large crowds efficiently, serving dishes such as king crab (US$23), hake (US$23), and Fuegian trout stuffed with crab, prawns, and champignons (US$15).

Other possibilities include **Tía Elvira** (Av. Maipú 349, tel. 02901/424725), where king crab is served for US$25; and **Kaupé** (Roca 470, tel. 02901/422704, www.kaupe.com.ar, lunch and dinner daily), which serves an exclusively (and exclusive) à la carte menu (entrées US$20–25). Kaupé has specialties such as king crab crêpes in saffron sauce (US$25), exquisite lemon ice cream, and wine by the glass.

Equally top-of-the-line—both literally and geographically—is the dining room with a panoramic view at **Chez Manu** (Luis Martial 2135, tel. 02901/432253, lunch and dinner daily), immediately below Hotel del Glaciar. Using local ingredients such as king crab and lamb, the French-run restaurant is *the* place for a truly elaborate meal, with entrées starting at US$15. This is one Ushuaia restaurant with food to match its views, although portions are on the small side.

On a promontory, in a recycled building that once transmitted Argentina's first-ever color TV program—the 1978 World Cup—**María Lola** (Deloqui 1048, tel. 02901/421185, www.marialolaresto.com.ar, lunch and dinner Mon.–Sat.) may be Ushuaia's best restaurant, period. For items ranging from relatively simple but delicate pastas to more elaborate dishes, such as stir-fried Patagonian lamb with vegetables, prices range US$15–20. The bar serves a diversity of mixed drinks at moderate prices.

In bright new quarters, **Helados Gadget** (San Martín 1256, tel. 02901/434864) has all the conventional Argentine ice cream flavors—good enough in their own right—but also incorporates regional specialties such as *calafate*.

## INFORMATION

Ushuaia's well-organized municipal **Secretaría de Turismo** (Av. Maipú s/n, tel. 02901/437666, www.turismoushuaia.com, 9 A.M.–6 P.M. daily) occupies spacious quarters opposite the tourist pier and also has a downtown branch (San Martín 674, tel. 02901/424550, 9 A.M.–10 P.M. weekdays, 9 A.M.–8 P.M. weekends and holidays). English-speaking staff are normally present. There's also an airport subsidiary (tel. 02901/423970) that's open for arriving flights only.

Motorists can consult the **Automóvil Club Argentino** (ACA, Malvinas Argentinas and Onachaga, tel. 02901/421121, 24 hours).

The **Administración de Parques Nacionales** (APN, San Martín 1395, tel. 02901/421315, tierradelfuego@apn.gov.ar) is open 9 A.M.–4 P.M. Monday–Friday.

At the waterfront Muelle Comercial, the **Oficina Antárctica Infuetur** (tel. 02901/430015, antartida@tierradelfuego.org.ar, 9 A.M.–6 P.M. weekdays Oct.–Mar., also for scheduled cruise arrivals or departures on weekends) has the latest information on Antarctic sailings and tours.

## SERVICES

Several banks have ATMs, including **Banco Macro** (Av. Maipú 761) and **Banco de Tierra del Fuego** (San Martín 396); the latter accepts travelers checks at a 2 percent commission. **Cambio Thaler** (San Martín 209, tel. 02901/421911) also takes about the same commission but keeps longer hours in summer (10 A.M.–8 P.M. Mon.–Sat.).

**Correo Argentino** (San Martín 309) is the post office.

**Café Net** (San Martín 565, tel. 02901/430037) provides telephone, fax, and Internet access, including wireless Internet.

The **Chilean consulate** (Jainén 50, tel. 02901/430909) is open 9 A.M.–1 P.M. weekdays only.

The **Dirección Nacional de Migraciones** (Fuegia Basket 187, tel. 02901/422334) is open 9 A.M.–5 P.M. weekdays only.

**Los Tres Angeles** (Juan Manuel de Rosas 139, tel. 02901/435262) offers quick and reliable laundry service but can be overwhelmed in high season; try instead **Lavanderías Qualis** (Deloqui 368, tel. 02901/421996).

The **Hospital Regional** (12 de Octubre and Fitz Roy, tel. 02901/441000, tel. 107 for emergencies) handles medical issues.

## GETTING THERE

Ushuaia has air links to Buenos Aires and intermediate points, and improving overland transportation from mainland Argentina and from Chile. Maritime transportation is either tenuous or expensive.

### Air

**Aerolíneas Argentinas** (Av. Maipú 823, tel. 02901/421218) normally flies two or three times daily to Buenos Aires's Aeroparque Jorge Newbery, adding more services in high season and sometimes via Trelew or El Calafate and Bariloche; it also flies twice weekly to Río Gallegos. Occasional Buenos Aires–bound flights land at the international airport Ezeiza instead of Aeroparque.

**Sol** (tel. 0810/4444765, www.sol.com.ar) flies to Río Gallegos, Comodoro Rivadavia, Neuquén, Mendoza, Córdoba and Rosario.

**LAN** flies daily to Aeroparque Jorge Newbery, and in high season it flies to El Calafate. LAN tickets can be purchased at any local travel agency, including **All Patagonia** (Juana Fadul 60, tel. 02901/433622, www.allpatagonia.com), **Canal Fun** (9 de Julio 118, Local 1, tel. 02901/437395, www.canalfun.com), **Rumbo Sur** (San Martín 350, tel. 02901/421139, www.rumbosur.com.ar), **Tolkar** (Roca 157, Local 1, tel. 02901/431408, www.tolkarturismo.com.ar), and **Tolkeyén** (San Martín 1267, tel. 02901/437073, www.tolkeyenpatagonia.com).

**LADE** (San Martín 542, Local 5, tel. 02901/421123) flies irregularly to Río Gallegos, El Calafate, Comodoro Rivadavia, Bariloche, and Buenos Aires.

For Puerto Williams, across the Beagle Channel in Chile, it may be possible to arrange a private charter through the **Aeroclub Ushuaia** (tel. 02901/421717 or 02901/421892, www.aeroclubushuaia.org.ar).

### Bus

At the foot of Juana Fadul, a parking area now serves as a bus station, even though companies have their offices elsewhere. **Líder** (Gobernador Paz 921, tel. 02901/436421, www.lidertdf.com.ar) and **Montiel** (Gobernador Paz 605, tel. 02901/421366) have several daily services to Tolhuin (US$15, 1.5 hours) and Río Grande (US$23, 3.5 hours).

Represented by Tolkar (Roca 157, tel. 02901/431408), **Tecni-Austral** goes daily at 5 A.M. to Río Grande (US$15) and Río Gallegos (US$73, 12 hours).

**Marga** (Gobernador Godoy 41, tel. 02901/435453) also goes at 5 A.M. daily in high season (a few weekly services off-season) to Tolhuin (US$15), Río Grande (US$20), and Río Gallegos (US$73), continuing to El Calafate (US$90, 18 hours).

Several carriers go to Punta Arenas early in the morning (US$48–63, 12 hours), including Tecni-Austral, Pacheco, Bus Sur, and Barría, whose tickets can be purchased at travel agencies **Tolkar** (Roca 157, tel. 02901/431408), **Tolkeyén** (San Martín 1267, tel. 02901/437073), **Comapa** (San Martín 245, tel. 02901/430727), and at Marga's office (Gobernador Godoy 41, tel. 02901/435453). Some services may require changing buses at Río Grande. A few of these companies offer connections to Puerto Natales (US$65–75).

### Sea

The Chilean cruisers MV *Stella Australis* and MV *Via Australis* offer luxury sightseeing cruises to Puerto Williams, Cape Horn, and through the fjords of Chilean Tierra del Fuego to Punta Arenas; while not intended as simple transportation, they can serve that purpose for those who can afford them. It's possible to either disembark in Punta Arenas (four days) or return to Ushuaia (in a week). These cruises are usually booked far in advance, but on occasion—normally just before Christmas—it may be possible to make on-the-spot arrangements.

For Puerto Williams, across the Beagle Channel, **Fernández Campbell** (www.fernandezcampbell.com) does one crossing Friday, Saturday, and Sunday in summer (US$125 pp each way plus US$6 boarding tax, 1.5 hours); tickets can be purchased at **Zenit Explorer** (Juana Fadul 126, tel. 02901/433232, www.zenitexplorer.com.ar). **Ushuaia Boating** (Gobernador Paz 233, tel. 02901/436193 or 02901/15-609030, www.ushuaiaboating.com.ar) shuttles passengers daily in summer across the channel to Puerto Navarino and then overland to Puerto Williams (US$125 pp each way plus US$6 boarding tax, two hours).

## GETTING AROUND

### To the Airport

A causeway links the city with **Aeropuerto Internacional Malvinas Argentinas,** which has the country's highest airport taxes: US$7 for flights elsewhere in Argentina, and US$20 for international flights. Taxis and *remises* cost about US$7 with **Remiscar** (San Martín 895, tel. 02901/422222, www.remiscar.com.ar).

### Bus

From the staging point at Avenida Maipú and Juana Fadul, in summer **Transporte Lautaro** (tel. 02901/444393) and **Transporte Ushuaia** (tel. 02901/15-608600) alternatively run hourly services between 9 A.M. and 4 P.M. to Parque Nacional Tierra del Fuego (US$14 pp round-trip); it's normally possible to camp in the park and return the following day. **Transporte Lautaro** also runs one summer service at 10 A.M. to the chairlift at the Glaciar Martial (US$7 pp), returning at 4 P.M. It may add services in ski season.

### Car Rental

Car rentals start around US$50 per day and range up to US$210 per day for four-wheel-drive vehicles. Some agencies offer unlimited mileage within Tierra del Fuego province, but others limit mileage to as few as 100 kilometers per day, so verify it before signing any contract.

Rental agencies include **Budget** (Gobernador Godoy 49, tel. 02901/437373, ushuaia@budgetargentina.com.ar), **Hertz** (San Martín 409, tel. 02901/437529, hertzushcentro@speedy.com.ar), and **Localiza** (Sarmiento 81, tel. 02901/437780, localizaush@speedy.com.ar).

# Vicinity of Ushuaia

Ushuaia has more than a dozen travel agencies offering excursions in and around Ushuaia, ranging from double-decker-bus city tours (US$10, one hour) to Parque Nacional Tierra del Fuego (US$38, four hours) and historic Estancia Harberton (US$68, eight hours). They also organize activities such as hiking, climbing, horseback riding, fishing, and mountain biking.

Local operators include **All Patagonia** (Juana Fadul 60, tel. 02901/433622, www.allpatagonia.com), which is the AmEx representative; **Canal Fun** (9 de Julio 118, Local 1, tel. 02901/437395, www.canalfun.com); **Rumbo Sur** (San Martín 350, tel. 02901/421139, www.rumbosur.com.ar); **Tolkar** (Roca 157, tel. 02901/431408, www.tolkarturismo.com.ar); and **Tolkeyén** (San Martín 1267, tel. 02901/437073, www.tolkeyenpatagonia.com).

The **Compañía de Guías de Patagonia** (San Martín 628, tel. 02901/437753, www.companiadeguias.com.ar) specializes in trekking.



## BEAGLE CHANNEL BOAT EXCURSIONS

From the Muelle Turístico, at the foot of Lasserre, there are boat trips to Beagle Channel wildlife sites such as **Isla de los Lobos,** home to the southern sea lion *(Otaria flavescens)* and the rarer South American fur seal *(Arctocephalus australis),* and **Isla de los Pájaros,** a cormorant nesting site. These excursions cost around US$40 per person for a 2.5-hour trip on oversized catamarans such as the *Ushuaia Explorer, Mariana I,* and *Ana B.* With summer extensions to the penguin colony at Estancia Harberton and a visit to the *estancia* itself, the cost is about US$68.

Rumbo Sur, Catamaranes Canoero, and Tolkeyén sell tickets for these excursions from offices at the foot of the Muelle Turístico, where Héctor Monsalve's **Tres Marías** (tel. 02901/436416, www.tresmariasweb.com) operates four-hour trips (US$45–58 pp) on smaller vessels (four passengers minimum,

10–12 maximum) that can approach Isla de los Lobos more closely than the large catamarans. They also land on Isla H, a small island with a diverse birdlife. A short walk on Islas Bridges is added to the conventional itinerary in a few excursions operated by Rumbo Sur, as well as on **Catamaranes Canoero** (tel. 02901/433893, www.catamaranescanoero.com.ar) and **Patagonia Adventure Explorer** (tel. 02901/15-465842, www.yatespatagonia.com.ar) on their four-hour excursions (US$45 pp) on boats of up to 26 passengers.

A US$2 boarding tax is added to all excursion fees; verify also if Harberton or national park admission charges are included.

## FERROCARRIL AUSTRAL FUEGUINO (TREN DEL FIN DEL MUNDO)

During Ushuaia's early days, prison labor built a short-line, narrow-gauge steam-driven railroad west into what is now Parque Nacional Tierra del Fuego to haul the timber that built the city. Only a few years ago, commercial interests rehabilitated part of the rail bed to create an antiseptic tourist version of the earlier line that pretty much ignores its unsavory history to focus on the Cañadón del Toro's admittedly appealing forest scenery.

The train leaves from the **Estación del Fin del Mundo** (tel. 02901/431600, www.trendelfindelmundo.com.ar), eight kilometers west of Ushuaia. There are two to three departures daily September–April; the rest of the year there's only one, or perhaps two if demand is sufficient. The two-hour-plus excursion costs US$33 per person in tourist class (free for children under 5), US$50 per person in first class, and US$75 per person with food service. Fares do not include the US$17 park entry fee. From its office at the Muelle Turístico, a return ticket for one adult in tourist class, including transfers and park admission fee, costs US$62.

## SKI AREAS

Most visitors see Ushuaia in summer, but it's also becoming a winter sports center given its proximity to the mountains. Downhill skiing, snowboarding, cross-country skiing, and even dogsledding are possibilities.

The major ski event is mid-August's **Marcha Blanca.** Luring upwards of 400 skiers, it's a 21-kilometer cross-country race along the Valle de Tierra Mayor.

There are two downhill ski areas. The aging **Centro de Montaña Glaciar Martial** (Luis Martial 3995, tel. 02901/15-503767, escuela@tierradelfuego.org.ar), seven kilometers northwest of town at the end of the road, has a single 1,130-meter run on a 23-degree slope, with a double-seat chairlift capable of carrying 224 skiers per hour. Daily passes for skiers cost US$15 for foreigners, Ar$50 (about US$12.50) for Argentines. Daily passes for pedestrians cost US$13 for foreigners, Ar$35 (about US$9) for Argentines.

East of Ushuaia, **Cerro Castor** (RN 3 Km 26, tel. 02901/499301, www.cerrocastor.com) has up-to-the-minute facilities, including four lifts and 25 different runs. In high season (July), lift tickets cost US$50 per day, with discounts for multi-day packages; in low and shoulder seasons, there are additional discounts.

Other areas east of town, along RN 3, are for cross-country skiers. These include **Tierra Mayor** (Km 21, tel. 02901/437454, www.tierramayor.com), **Villa Las Cotorras** (Km 25, tel. 02901/499300), **Haruwen** (Km 36, tel. 02901/421306, www.haruwen.com.ar), and other several options. All of them rent equipment and offer transfers from Ushuaia. Access is free.

## ESTANCIA HARBERTON

Historic Harberton dates from 1886, when missionary Thomas Bridges resigned from Ushuaia's Anglican mission to settle at his new *estancia* at Downeast, later renamed for the Devonshire hometown of his wife, Mary Ann Varder. Thomas Bridges, of course, was the author of the famous English-Yámana dictionary, and their son Lucas continued their literary tradition with *The Uttermost Part of the Earth,* an extraordinary memoir of a boyhood and life among the indigenous Yámana and Ona (Selk'nam).

© WAYNE BERNHARDSON

Estancia Harberton is one of Patagonia's most historic ranches.

Harberton continues to be a family enterprise—its present manager and part-owner, Tommy Goodall, is Thomas Bridges's great-grandson. While the wool industry that spawned it has declined in recent years, the *estancia,* which still has about 1,000 cattle, has opened its doors to organized English- and Spanish-language tours of its grounds and outbuildings; these include the family cemetery, flower gardens, woolshed, woodshop, boathouse, and a native botanical garden whose Yámana-style lean-tos are more realistic than their Disneyfied counterparts along the Ferrocarril Austral Fueguino tourist train. Photographs in the woolshed illustrate the process of cutting firewood with axes and transporting it by raft and oxcart, and the tasks of gathering and shearing sheep.

In addition, American biologist Rae Natalie Prosser (Tommy Goodall's wife) has created the **Museo Acatushún de Aves y Mamíferos Marinos Australes** (www.acatushun.com, 10 A.M.–7 P.M. daily mid-Oct.–mid-Apr., US$5), a bone museum stressing the region's marine mammals but also seabirds and a few shorebirds. It's also possible to visit Magellanic penguin rookeries at **Isla Martillo** (Yécapasela) with Piratour for US$50 per person; a small colony of gentoo penguins has established itself on the island, making this a more intriguing trip for those who've seen Magellanic penguins elsewhere.

Estancia Harberton (www.estanciaharberton.com; for further enquiries contact Alejandro Galeazzi, Ushuaia tel. 02901/423213) is 85 kilometers east of Ushuaia via paved RN 3 and gravel RC-j (now RP 33). The *estancia* is open for guided tours (US$10 pp) 10 A.M.–7 P.M. daily mid-October–mid-April except Christmas, New Year's Day, and Easter. Because of Harberton's isolation, there is no telephone, and email communications can be slow.

With written permission, free **camping** is permitted at unimproved sites; the *estancia* offers accommodation at the shepherds' house (two triple rooms with private baths, US$130 pp). Dinner or lunch costs an additional US$30 per person.

Harberton's teahouse, **Mánacatush,** serves a three-course lunch without drinks for US$30. A separate afternoon tea is offered for nonguests.

In summer, several companies provide round-trip transportation from Ushuaia, but renting a car is more convenient. From Ushuaia's Muelle Turístico, **Piratour** (tel. 02901/435557, www.piratour.com.ar) offers a US$82 package with overland transportation and a visit to the penguin colony, but without enough time for the one-hour farm tour. It also operates out of **Harberton Adventure Travel** (San Martín 847, tel. 02901/424834).

Catamaran tours from Ushuaia include the farm-tour fee, and time spent on land can vary depending on the operator.

# Parque Nacional Tierra del Fuego

For pilgrims to the uttermost part of the earth, mecca is Parque Nacional Tierra del Fuego's **Bahía Lapataia,** where RN 3 ends on the Beagle Channel's north shore. It's a worthy goal, but most visitors see only the area on and around the highway, because most of the park's mountainous interior, with its alpine lakes, limpid rivers, blue-tinged glaciers, and jagged summits, is closed to public access.

## GEOGRAPHY AND CLIMATE

About 12 kilometers west of Ushuaia, Parque Nacional Tierra del Fuego hugs the Chilean border as its 63,000 hectares stretch from the Beagle Channel north across Lago Fagnano (Kami). Elevations range from sea level to 1,450 meters on the summit of Monte Vinciguerra.

The park has a maritime climate, with frequent high winds. Rainfall is moderate, about 750 millimeters per year, but humidity is high, as cool temperatures inhibit evapotranspiration—the summer average is only about 10°C. The record maximum temperature is 31°C, while the minimum is a fairly mild -12°C. At sea level, snow rarely sticks, but higher elevations have permanent snowfields and glaciers.

## FLORA AND FAUNA

As in southernmost Chile, thick southern beech forests cover the Argentine sector of Tierra del Fuego. Along the coast, the deciduous *lenga (Nothofagus pumilio)* and the Magellanic evergreen *coigüe* or *guindo (Nothofagus betuloides)* are the main tree species; at higher elevations, the stunted, deciduous *ñire (Nothofagus antarctica)* forms nearly pure stands. In some low-lying areas, where cool annual temperatures inhibit complete decomposition, dead plant material compresses into *sphagnum* peat bogs with a cover of ferns and other moisture-loving plants; the insectivorous *Drosera uniflora* swallows unsuspecting bugs.

Argentina's first coastal national park, Parque Nacional Tierra del Fuego has a seashore protected by thick kelp beds that help incubate fish fry. Especially around Bahía Ensenada and Bahía Lapataia, the shoreline and inshore waters swarm with cormorants, grebes, gulls, kelp geese, oystercatchers, flightless and flying steamer ducks, snowy sheathbills, and terns. The black-browed albatross skims the Beagle's waters, while the Andean condor sometimes soars overhead. Marine mammals, mostly sea lions but also fur seals and elephant seals, cavort in the ocean. The rare southern river otter *(Lontra provocax)* exists here.

Inland areas are fauna-poor, though foxes and guanacos are present in small numbers. The most conspicuous mammals are the European rabbit and the Canadian beaver, both of which were introduced for their pelts but have proved to be pests.

## GLACIAR MARTIAL

Technically within park boundaries but also within walking distance of Ushuaia, the Glaciar Martial is the area's best single hike, offering expansive views of the Beagle Channel and

© WAYNE BERNHARDSON

hikers at Glaciar Martial, Parque Nacional Tierra del Fuego

even the jagged peaks of Chile's Isla Navarino. Reached by the zigzag Camino al Glaciar (also known as Luis Martial), which climbs northwest out of town, the trailhead begins at the Aerosilla del Glaciar, the ski area's chairlift, which operates 10 A.M.–4:15 P.M. daily. The 1.2-kilometer chairlift (US$17 pp) reduces the two-hour climb to the foot of the glacier to a mere 10 minutes. **Transporte Lautaro** runs one summer service at 10 A.M. to the chairlift (US$7 pp), returning at 4 P.M., leaving from the corner of Avenida Maipú and Juana Fadul. Although it is easy to follow, the trail—especially the middle segment—is steep, and the descent requires particular caution because of loose rocks and soil. There is no admission charge to this sector.

## OTHER SIGHTS AND ACTIVITIES

Where freshwater Lago Roca drains into the sea at Bahía Lapataia, the park's main sector has several short nature trails and a few longer ones; most of the backcountry is off-limits to casual hikers. Slightly less than one kilometer long, the **Senda Laguna Negra** uses a boardwalk to negotiate boggy terrain studded with ferns, wildflowers, and other water-tolerant species. The 400-meter **Senda de los Castores** (Beaver Trail) winds among southern beeches gnawed to death to form dams and ponds where the beavers themselves occasionally peek out of their lodges.

The five-kilometer **Senda Hito XXIV** follows Lago Roca's northeastern shore to a small obelisk that marks the Chilean border. If Argentine and Chilean authorities can someday get it together, this would be an ideal entry point to Estancia Yendegaia's wild backcountry, but at present it's illegal to continue beyond the marker. From a junction about one kilometer up the Hito XXIV trail, **Senda Cerro Guanaco** climbs four kilometers northeast up the Arroyo Guanaco to its namesake peak's 970-meter summit.

From Bahía Ensenada, near the park's southeastern edge, there are summer boat shuttles (10 A.M.–5 P.M.) to **Isla Redonda** (US$28 pp) and to Bahía Lapataia (US$33 pp).

## PRACTICALITIES

### Accommodations and Food

Camping is the only option in the park itself, where there are free sites with little or no infrastructure at **Camping Bahía Ensenada, Camping Río Pipo, Camping Las Bandurrias,** and **Camping Laguna Verde.** While these are improving, they're less tidy than the commercial **Campamento Organizado Lago Roca** (tel. 02901/15-412649, www.confiterialagoroca.com.ar, US$6 pp for foreigners plus US$5 per tent), which has hot showers, a grocery, a *refugio* accommodating up to 20 people (US$13 pp), and the restaurant *confitería* **La Cabaña del Bosque.**

### Information

At the park entrance on RN 3, the APN collects a US$17 per person entry fee; Argentine residents get a 75 percent discount. Farther west, 700 meters from the shores of Lago Roca, there is the **Centro de Visitantes Alakush** (RN

3 Km 3057, tel. 02901/15-519727, www.centroalakush.com.ar), with some exhibits on the park's natural history and ethnography. It also has a restaurant, a bookstore, and a gift shop.

Several books have useful information on the park, including William Leitch's *South America's National Parks* (Seattle: The Mountaineers, 1990), which is now out of print. Two good hiking guides are the fifth edition of Tim Burford's *Chile & Argentina: The Bradt Trekking Guide* (Chalfont St. Peter, United Kingdom: Bradt Travel Guides, 2001) and the fourth edition of *Trekking in the Patagonian Andes* (Melbourne: Lonely Planet, 2009).

Birders may want to acquire Claudio Venegas Canelo's *Aves de Patagonia y Tierra del Fuego Chileno-Argentina* (Punta Arenas: Ediciones de la Universidad de Magallanes, 1986), Ricardo Clark's *Aves de Tierra del Fuego y Cabo de Hornos* (Buenos Aires: Literature of Latin America, 1986), or Enrique Couve and Claudio Vidal Ojeda's bilingual *Birds of the Beagle Channel and Cape Horn* (Punta Arenas: Fantástico Sur Birding & Nature, 2000).

### Getting There and Around

In Ushuaia, from the staging point at Avenida Maipú and Juana Fadul, in summer **Transporte Lautaro** (tel. 02901/444393) and **Transporte Ushuaia** (tel. 02901/15-608600) alternatively run hourly buses between 9 A.M. and 4 P.M. to Parque Nacional Tierra del Fuego (US$14 pp round-trip); it's normally possible to camp in the park and return the following day. **Transporte Lautaro** also runs one summer service at 10 A.M. to the chairlift at the Glaciar Martial (US$7 pp), returning at 4 P.M. It may add services in ski season.

Car rentals start around US$50 per day and range up to US$210 per day for four-wheel-drive vehicles. Some agencies offer unlimited mileage within Tierra del Fuego province, but others limit mileage to as few as 100 kilometers per day, so verify it before signing any contract.

Rental agencies in Ushuaia include **Budget** (Gobernador Godoy 49, tel. 02901/437373, ushuaia@budgetargentina.com.ar), **Hertz** (San Martín 409, tel. 02901/437529, hertzushcentro@speedy.com.ar), and **Localiza** (Sarmiento 81, tel. 02901/437780, localizaush@speedy.com.ar).

## Río Grande and Vicinity

Most visitors who stay in and around Río Grande, on the Isla Grande's blustery Atlantic shoreline, do so for the fishing. For the rest, this once-desolate city is more a place to change buses, but thanks to smoothly paved streets, the huge dust clouds that once blew through this wool and oil burg have subsided. There are limits to beautification, though—all the trees planted in Plaza Almirante Brown are stiffly wind-flagged.

Bus schedules used to dictate that travelers spend the night here, but recent improvements mean quicker overland connections to Ushuaia. Still, services have improved, and there's enough to do that an afternoon spent here need not be a wasted one.

On the north bank of its namesake river, Río Grande (population about 65,000) is 89 kilometers southeast of the Chilean border post at San Sebastián via paved RN 3 and gravel RC-i and 212 kilometers northeast of Ushuaia via RN 3, which is now completely paved, though work is in progress in 2011 along some deteriorating segments.

### SIGHTS AND ENTERTAINMENT

Occupying the former storehouses of the Asociación Rural de Tierra del Fuego, the **Museo Municipal Virginia Choquintel** (Alberdi 555, tel. 02964/430647, 9 A.M.–5 P.M. Mon.–Fri., 3–7 P.M. Sat., free) does a lot with a little, with good materials on natural history, sophisticated exhibits on ethnology and indigenous subsistence, and historic displays on maps and mapmaking, island communications, and astronomy.

Río Grande has few architectural landmarks—or few buildings of any antiquity, for that matter—but the **Obras Sanitarias** waterworks tower (Lasserre 386), at the plaza's northeast corner, dates from the Juan Perón era (circa 1954).

**El Cine 1 & 2** (Av. Perito Moreno and 9 de Julio, tel. 02962/433260) shows current films in modern facilities, but it sometimes cranks up the volume to excruciating levels—bring or improvise ear plugs, just in case.

## ACCOMMODATIONS

Accommodations are few and uninspiring. Nearly every midrange-to-upscale place offers discounts for cash payment.

The simple but spotless family-run **Hospedaje Noal** (Obligado 557, tel. 02964/427516, US$18 pp, US$38 d with private bath) has spacious rooms with shared baths but plenty of closet space and good beds, and some rooms have private baths. No breakfast is served. **B&B El Puesto** (Juan Bautista Thorne 345, tel. 02964/420923, bybelpuesto@yahoo.com.ar, US$35 s, US$45 d), the only one of its kind, is the best budget choice.

Possibly Río Grande's best value for money, rehabbed **Hotel Villa** (Av. San Martín 281, tel. 02964/424998, hotelvilla@live.com, US$73 s or d) has cheerful contemporary rooms and assiduous service.

With its rooms and public areas upgraded, **Hotel Federico Ibarra** (Rosales 357, tel. 02964/430071, www.federicoibarrahotel.com.ar, US$83 s, US$99 d) is worth consideration for its substantial discount for cash payment, though rooms are rather small.

Río Grande's most professional operation, **Posada de los Sauces** (Elcano 839, tel. 02964/432895, posadadelossauces@speedy.com.ar, US$88–105 s, US$100–165 d) is easily top of the line. One of the suite bathrooms could hold a hot-tub party, and the restaurant is the city's most elegant.

Despite the dubious exterior style, suites at the **Status Hotel Casino** (Av. San Martín 268, tel. 02964/435700, www.statushotelcasino.com, from US$100 s or d) are very comfortable, plainly decorated, and have all the amenities of a hotel of its range, with attractive promotional rates.

On the airport road, the top-end **Grande Hotel** (Echelaine 251, tel. 02964/436500, www.grandehotel.com.ar, from US$138 s or d) has 64 contemporary rooms and suites, all with whirlpool tubs, a restaurant, and an indoor pool.

## FOOD

**Mamá Flora** (Av. Belgrano 1101, tel. 02964/424087, breakfast and lunch daily) is a good breakfast choice that also has coffee and exquisite chocolates. Also good is **Bonafide Café** (Piedra Buena 520, tel. 02964/425910, 9 A.M.–9 P.M. Mon.–Sat.).

**Tante Sara** (Av. Belgrano 402, tel. 02964/424366, 8 A.M.–midnight daily), like its homonymous counterpart in Ushuaia, is a fine café-restaurant with a varied menu where most entrées are in the US$10–15 range.

**La Nueva Colonial** (Av. Belgrano 489, tel. 02964/425353, lunch and dinner daily) serves abundant pastas, such as lasagna for US$10, plus sauces ranging US$4–6.

**Leymi** (25 de Mayo 1335, tel. 02964/421683, lunch and dinner Mon.–Sat.) serves fixed-price lunches for US$10 including drinks, and has a broad *parrilla* and pasta menu, plus good homemade desserts. A full dinner costs around US$18.

Several hotels have their own restaurants, most notably the **Posada de los Sauces** (Elcano 839, tel. 02964/432895, lunch daily, dinner Mon.–Sat.), which deserves special mention for superb service and the cooked-to-order *lomo a la pimienta* (pepper steak, US$17). There's also a 10 percent cash discount.

**Canela** (Moyano and Libertad, tel. 02964/425570) is a fine ice creamery.

## INFORMATION

On Plaza Almirante Brown, Río Grande's **Dirección de Turismo** (Rosales 350, tel. 02964/431324, www.riogrande.gov.ar, 9 A.M.–5 P.M. Mon.–Fri.) is exceptionally helpful.

The provincial **Instituto Fueguino de Turismo** (Infuetur, Av. Belgrano 319, tel. 02964/422887) is open 9 A.M.–4 P.M. weekdays only.

## SERVICES

**Cambio Thaler** (Espora 631, tel. 02964/421154) is the only currency exchange house. Banks with ATMs include **Banco de Tierra del Fuego** (Av. San Martín 193) and **HSBC** (Av. San Martín 194).

**Correo Argentino** (Rivadavia 968) is two blocks west of San Martín; the postal code is 9420. **Centro Integral de Comunicaciones** (Av. Belgrano 568) has long-distance telephone and Internet services.

**Welcome** (Moyano 343) handles the washing.

For medical services, contact the **Hospital Regional** (Ameghino 755, tel. 02964/422086).

## GETTING THERE

**Aerolíneas Argentinas** (Av. San Martín 607, tel. 0810/2228-6527) flies nonstop to Buenos Aires several days a week. **LADE** (Lasserre 447, tel. 02964/422968) flies to Ushuaia, Río Gallegos, and El Calafate, and to other northbound destinations including Buenos Aires, but with several stops.

**Sol** (tel. 0810/4444765, www.sol.com.ar) flies to Río Gallegos, Comodoro Rivadavia, Neuquén, Mendoza, Córdoba, and Rosario.

The **Terminal Fueguina** (Obligado and Finocchio) is Río Grande's bus terminal, but companies also keep some more central offices. **Líder** (Av. Perito Moreno 635, tel. 02964/420003, www.lidertdf.com.ar) and **Transportes Montiel** (25 de Mayo 712, tel. 02964/420997) have multiple departures to Tolhuin (US$15, 1.5 hours) and Ushuaia (US$23, 3.5 hours). At the terminal, **Buses Pacheco** (tel. 02964/425611, www.busespacheco.com) goes to Punta Arenas, Chile (US$38, nine hours), at 10 A.M. Tuesday, Thursday, and Saturday and has connections to Puerto Natales, Chile.

**Tecni-Austral** (Moyano 516, tel. 02964/430610) goes to Punta Arenas at 8:30 A.M. Monday, Wednesday, and Friday, to Río Gallegos (US$58, nine hours) at 8:30 A.M. daily, and to Ushuaia (US$15, three hours) at 4 P.M. daily.

**Buses Marga** (tel. 02964/434316) goes daily to Río Gallegos (US$58, nine hours) and to Ushuaia (US$20, three hours).

## GETTING AROUND

City bus Línea A goes directly to **Aeropuerto Internacional Río Grande** (tel. 02964/420699), a short distance west of downtown on RP 5, for US$0.70. A cab charges around US$4.

Car rentals include **Hertz** (Av. San Martín 236, tel. 02964/426754).

## VICINITY OF RÍO GRANDE

As the surrounding area lacks a well-developed transport infrastructure, hiring a vehicle is worth consideration.

### Reserva Provincial Costa Atlántica de Tierra del Fuego

From Cabo Nombre, at Bahía San Sebastián's north end, to the mouth of the Río Ewan, southeast of Río Grande, the Isla Grande's entire shoreline is a bird sanctuary because of the abundant plovers and sandpipers in summer, including the *Charadrius falklandicus* (two-banded plover), the *Numenius phaeopus* (whimbrel), the *Limosa haemastica* (Hudsonian godwit), the *Calidris canutus* (red knot), and the *Calidris fuscicollis* (white-rumped sandpiper), some of which cover one of the world's longest migration routes yearly between the Arctic and South America. In winter, other birds can be spotted, such as the *Chionis alba* (snowy sheathbill), which migrates from Antarctica.

### Misión Salesiana

One exception to Río Grande's lack of historic sites is the Salesian mission (RN 3 Km 2800, tel. 02964/430667, www.misionrg.com.ar), founded by the order to catechize the Selk'nam; after the indigenous people died out from unintentionally introduced diseases and intentional slaughter, the fathers turned their attention to educating rural youth in

North of Río Grande, the Salesian chapel was the focus of efforts to catechize the Selk'nam in the early 20th century.

their boarding school. The well-preserved **Capilla** (chapel), a national historic monument, and similar Magellanic buildings make up part of the mission's **Museo de Historia, Antropología y de Ciencias Naturales** (3–6 P.M. Tues.–Sun. in summer, 9:30 A.M.–noon and 3–6 P.M. Tues.–Sun. the rest of the year, US$1.25 adults, US$0.50 children), whose facilities display their natural history and ethnography exhibits far better than in the not-too-distant past.

From Río Grande, the Línea D bus goes hourly to the Misión Salesiana, about 11 kilometers north of Río Grande, 7:30 A.M.–8:30 P.M.



## Historic *Estancias*

Several of the region's largest and most important *estancias* are in the vicinity of Río Grande. Founded by the Menéndez dynasty's Sociedad Explotadora de Tierra del Fuego, **Estancia María Behety** (tel. 02964/430345, www.maribety.com.ar), 17 kilometers west via gravel RC-c (now RP 5), is home to the world's largest shearing shed. It's open to guided visits (US$30 pp) and it keeps two exclusive fishing lodges.

Also Sociedad Explotadora property, **Estancia José Menéndez,** 16 kilometers southwest of town via RN 3 and RC-b (now RP 8), is one of the island's most historic ranches with its exclusive **Villa María** fishing lodge (Buenos Aires tel. 011/4801-1008, U.S. toll-free tel. 877/637-8420, www.vmarialodge.com) on the shores of the Río Grande. RP 8 continues west to an obscure border post (open Nov.–Apr. only) at **Radman,** known also as **Río Bella Vista,** where few visitors of any kind (best in 4WD vehicles) cross the line to Lago Blanco on the Chilean side.

For potential overnighters, though, the Sea View Guest House at the Simon and Carolina Goodall family's **Estancia Viamonte** (tel. 02964/430861, www.estanciaviamonte.com, US$160 pp with half board, US$195 pp with full board, including wine and soft drinks, open Nov.–Mar.) is the only place on the island that can offer the opportunity to sleep in Lucas Bridges's bedroom. Directly on RN 3, about 42 kilometers southeast of Río Grande, it fronts on a bird-rich beach; the house itself can sleep up to six people with two shared baths, plus living and dining rooms. There are extensive gardens and chances for fishing, riding, and farm activities.

### Lago Fagnano (Kami)

Named for the priest who spearheaded Salesian evangelism among the Selk'nam, this elongated lake fills a structural depression that stretches across the Chilean border to the west. Also known by its Selk'nam name, Kami, its shoreline is nearly 200 kilometers long, and its surface covers nearly 600 square kilometers.

The lake's most westerly part, along the Chilean border, lies within Parque Nacional Tierra del Fuego but is virtually inaccessible except by boat. As might be expected, the lake is popular with fishing enthusiasts.

At the east end, about midway between Río Grande and Ushuaia, pilgrims pause at the town of **Tolhuin** to sample the goods at **Panadería La Unión** (www.panaderialaunion.com), a legendary bakery that has the usual fine bread but also loads of *facturas* (pastries), *alfajores* (cookies sandwiched around sweet fillings like *dulce de leche*), and sandwiches; what it lacks, astonishingly for Argentina, is any coffee other than machine-dispensed instant.

For accommodations and a full meal, five kilometers west of Tolhuin on the shores of Lago Fagnano try rehabbed **Hostería Kaikén** (RN 3 Km 2958, tel. 02964/15-615102, www.hosteriakaiken.com, US$98–113 s or d), which has comfortable doubles with lake views, of which the most expensive ones have a whirlpool tub. Its restaurant serves regional specialties such as lamb and trout for about US$14 each.

## FISHING IN FUEGIA

Fishing for Atlantic salmon, brown trout, and rainbow trout is a popular pastime throughout Argentine Tierra del Fuego, but fees differ according to the period of time, the lake or river in question, and residence status.

The season runs November-April. Daily rates range US$25-113 for nonresidents; there's a weekly license for US$75-250, and seasonal rates are US$105-355. Neighboring countries and Argentine residents pay a fraction of these rates.

In Ushuaia, licenses are available at the **Asociación Caza y Pesca** (Av. Maipú 822, tel. 02901/423168, cazpescush@infovia.com.ar). In Río Grande, contact the **Asociación Riograndense de Pesca con Mosca** (Montilla 1040, tel. 02964/421268, arpmosca@ciudad.com.ar).

# THE FALKLAND ISLANDS (ISLAS MALVINAS)

In 1982, the isolated Falkland Islands made world headlines when Britain and Argentina fought a 10-week South Atlantic war that ended in a decisive British victory and, serendipitously, ended a brutal military dictatorship. The territorial dispute over the Islands, which Argentina claims as the Malvinas, has not gone away, but the Islands' tourism profile has risen as a destination for cruise ships and a select group of independent travelers interested primarily in sub-Antarctic wildlife.

What the Falklands can offer, as a Patagonian outlier 500 kilometers east of the South American continent, is enormous colonies of seabirds (the five penguin species include easy access to the uncommon king and gentoo), black-browed albatrosses and several species of cormorants in particular, and marine mammals including elephant seals, sea lions, and fur seals. Most of these are rarely seen on the continent, and many of them would require a trip to either remote South Georgia or Antarctica.

Despite their small permanent population, only about 2,500, the Islands have good tourist infrastructure in the capital city of Stanley and in main island and offshore lodges, close to wildlife sites, that are the local counterpart to Argentine and Chilean *estancias*. The big drawback is that most, though not all, of these sites are only accessible by relatively expensive air taxis that require good timing.

## PLANNING YOUR TIME

Because of infrequent international commercial flights—weekly at best—unless your time is almost unlimited, organizing your itinerary before

© WAYNE BERNHARDSON

# HIGHLIGHTS

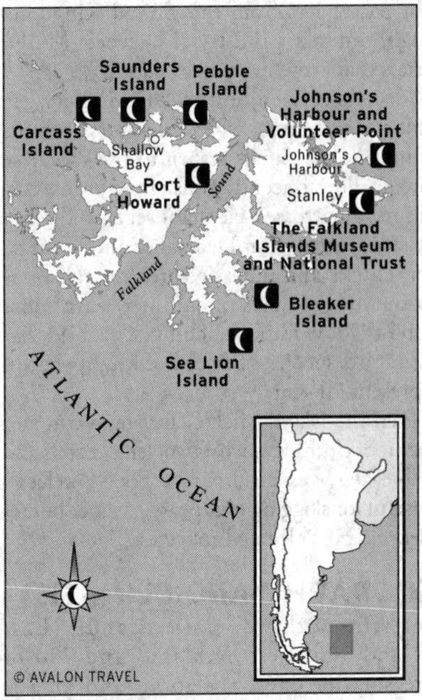


LOOK FOR ☾ TO FIND RECOMMENDED SIGHTS, ACTIVITIES, DINING, AND LODGING.

**The Falkland Islands Museum and National Trust:** In only an hour or so, visitors can get a grasp of the Islands' local, maritime, military, and natural history, with a touch of Antarctica to boot, before exploring the rest of Stanley (page 500).

**Johnson's Harbour and Volunteer Point:** Johnson's Harbour on East Falkland is a key stop for its large and growing king penguin colony, which spends the entire year at the lagoon at scenic Volunteer Point. There's even more to see in the summer (page 508).

**Bleaker Island:** For visitors on a budget, Bleaker has excellent accommodations and much of the same wildlife as Sea Lion, but its penguins, cormorants, and petrels are more dispersed (page 510).

**Sea Lion Island:** Sea Lion may be one of the Falklands' most expensive destinations, but there's more wildlife in a smaller area than any other easily accessible part of the Islands (page 510).

**Port Howard:** On West Falkland, guests at Port Howard Lodge can enjoy the comforts of the former manager's house in what is now the last survivor of the large sheep farms that once monopolized the Islands' wool industry. Since construction of the West Falklands road, it's a great base for visiting other settlements and wildlife sites on the island (page 512).

**Pebble Island:** In addition to penguin and petrel colonies, Pebble has endless crescent beaches and lagoons full of wildfowl, all within easy reach of one of the Islands' best-run lodges, Pebble Island Lodge (page 514).

**Saunders Island:** Both the hiking and the wildlife – especially the black-browed albatrosses – are extraordinary on mountainous Saunders, whose historic resources include ruins of Britain's original 18th-century outpost (page 515).

**Carcass Island:** The Falklands may be a more commercial destination than they were 20 years ago, but Rob and Lorraine McGill's wildlife-rich West Falkland ranch still feels like a throwback to the days when it would never have occurred to any islander to charge for bed and breakfast (page 517).

arrival is essential. Without your own plane or yacht, visits shorter than a week are nearly impossible, and two weeks would be desirable. Charter flight passengers from the United Kingdom, though, can take Ministry of Defence (MOD) charters that arrive every five or six days.

Most visitors enjoy the Islands between October and March, when migratory seabirds and marine mammals return to the shoreline to breed. The concentrations of penguins, cormorants, albatrosses, elephant seals, and other species are greatest in December and January, when chicks and pups are present; these are also the longest days of summer, with more flexibility for wildlife-watching. That said, signature bird species such as the king penguin are present all year.

Given the Islands' fickle climate, warm and waterproof clothing, such as woolen sweaters and windbreakers, is essential. Rubber boots ("wellies") are useful for slogging over peaty ground, but it's sometimes possible to borrow them.

## GEOGRAPHY AND CLIMATE

Consisting of two main islands (East Falkland and West Falkland) and 700 or more smaller ones, the total land area is about 4,700 square miles (12,173 square kilometers). Roughly the size of Connecticut, they measure about 155 miles (250 kilometers) from east to west; the Falkland Sound separates the two main islands.

Except for East Falkland's softly undulating southern peninsula of Lafonia, the topography ranges from hilly to mountainous, though the highest point, East Falkland's Mount Usborne, reaches only 2,312 feet (705 meters). The most striking landforms are the periglacial "stone runs," quartzite boulder fields that descend like rivers from the ridges and summits of the two main islands. The heavily indented coastline, with its sandy and gravelly beaches, bays, estuaries, inlets, and scenic headlands, provides habitat for the abundant wildlife.

Over the past decade, the road network on both East and West Falkland has improved dramatically, making some destinations more accessible, but air taxis still link the relatively populous East with the West and smaller offshore islands, only a handful of which are inhabited. A twice-weekly ferry from East to West Falkland now connects the two.

While it might be fair to describe the climate as "sub-Antarctic" because low annual average temperatures (around 6°C) inhibit plant growth and decomposition as well, the latitude is comparable to that of London, and the surrounding South Atlantic alleviates the winter cold. Summer temperatures rarely rise to 75°F (25°C) and average around 59°F (15°C), while winter temperatures rarely remain below freezing for days on end. Humidity is high but rainfall is moderate, reaching about 24 inches (600 millimeters) at Stanley, but West Falkland is drier. The climate's most trying feature is the almost incessant westerlies—the average annual wind speed is nearly 14 knots.

## FLORA AND FAUNA

The Islands' relatively simple flora comprises mostly extensive grasslands and prostrate shrubs; there are no native trees. Fringing parts of the coastline is the high, dense tussock grass *(Parodiochloa flabellata),* a prime wildlife habitat so dense and verdant that passing European mariners mistook it for forest. Because it was vulnerable to fire and overgrazing, its range has diminished and its abundance has declined. Most native pasture is "white grass" *(Cortaderia pilosa),* which covers much of the interior but is less nutritious for livestock.

It's the fauna, though, that draws visitors. Five penguin species breed here, of which only the Magellanic is normally seen on the South American continent; the gentoo, the majestic king, and the crested rockhopper are easily sighted, while the occasional macaroni nests among rockhoppers, which it resembles. Other species, such as the chinstrap, make the odd appearance but do not breed here.

Large numbers of king cormorants nest among the rockhoppers, while predatory skuas raid the colonies to steal eggs. The most interesting bird of prey, though, is the striated caracara or Johnny rook, so fearless that it will approach humans on foot and steal small, shiny objects.

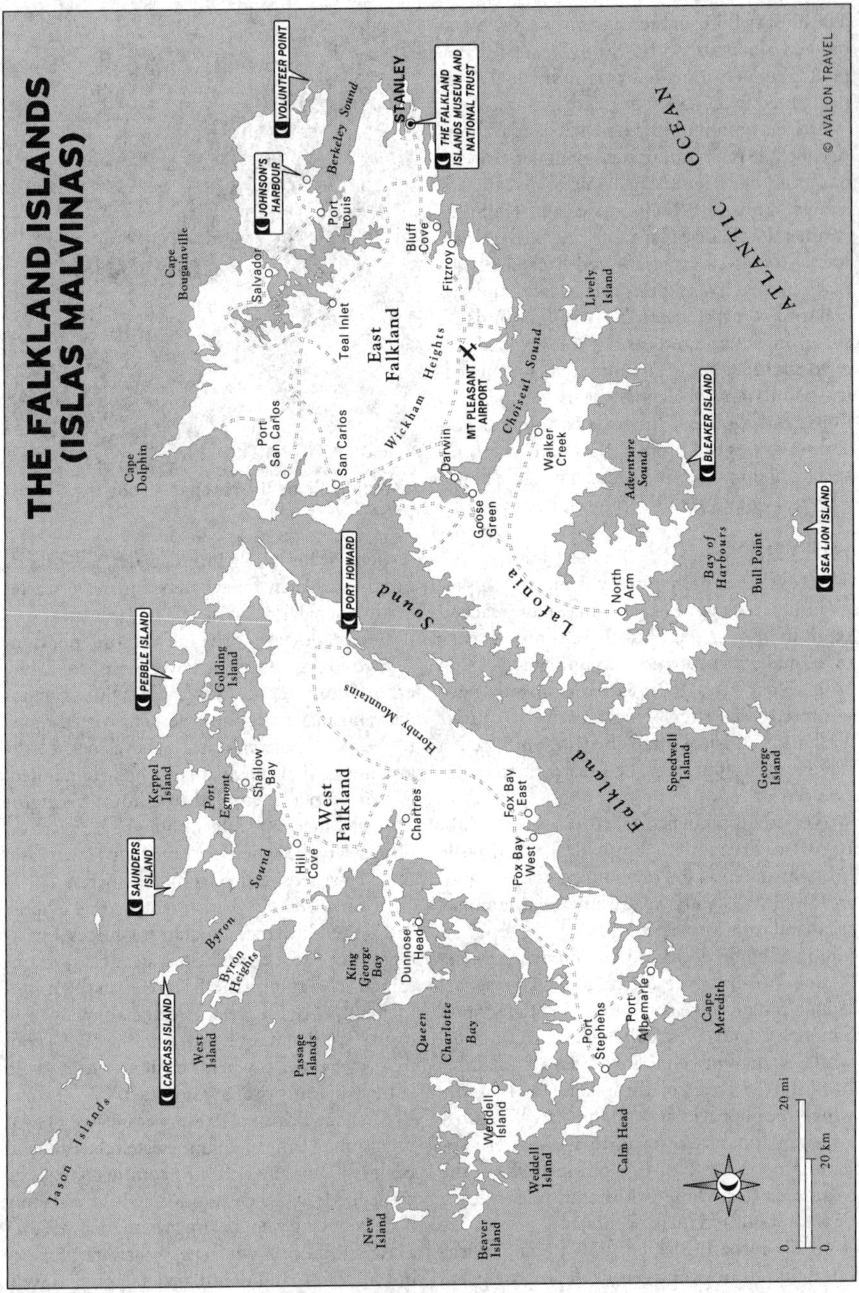
THE FALKLAND ISLANDS (ISLAS MALVINAS)
© AVALON TRAVEL
VOLUNTEER POINT
JOHNSON'S HARBOUR
STANLEY
THE FALKLAND ISLANDS MUSEUM AND NATIONAL TRUST
Berkeley Sound
Port Louis
Bluff Cove
Fitzroy
Salvador
Cape Bougainville
Teal Inlet
East Falkland
Wickham Heights
MT PLEASANT AIRPORT
Choiseul Sound
Lively Island
ATLANTIC OCEAN
Port San Carlos
San Carlos
Darwin
Goose Green
Walker Creek
Adventure Sound
BLEAKER ISLAND
SEA LION ISLAND
Cape Dolphin
PORT HOWARD
Falkland Sound
Lafonia
North Arm
Bay of Harbours
Bull Point
PEBBLE ISLAND
Golding Island
Hornby Mountains
Keppel Island
Port Egmont
Shallow Bay
West Falkland
Chartres
Fox Bay East
Fox Bay West
Speedwell Island
George Island
SAUNDERS ISLAND
Hill Cove
Byron Sound
Byron Heights
King George Bay
Dunnose Head
CARCASS ISLAND
West Island
Passage Islands
Queen Charlotte Bay
Port Stephens
Port Albemarle
Cape Meredith
Jason Islands
Weddell Island
Calm Head
New Island
Beaver Island
0
20 mi
0
20 km

The most striking of breeding birds is the black-browed albatross, so flawlessly beautiful that photographs can make living individuals look like perfectly preserved museum specimens.

Other common birds on the Islands' shoreline include rock cormorants, giant petrels, various gulls, black and Magellanic oystercatchers, snowy sheathbills, kelp geese, and flightless steamer ducks. The grasslands and wetlands are home to crested caracaras, red-backed hawks, black-necked swans, peregrine falcons, and several species of sheldgeese. Nearly all the birds are surprisingly tame and easily photographed.

In addition, marine mammals include breeding populations of elephant seals, southern sea lions, and southern fur seals (whose inaccessible colonies are more difficult to visit), six species of dolphins, and orcas. The large South Atlantic whales are uncommon, however.

© WAYNE BERNHARDSON

A Magellanic oystercatcher strolls the beach on Saunders Island.

## HISTORY

The Falklands' early history is murky. In pre-Columbian times, Fuegians may have reached them in bark canoes, but there is no evidence of permanent occupation; an unidentified ship from Magellan's 1520 expedition may have wintered here after being blown off course. Various Spanish, Dutch, British, and French navigators frequented the area over the next two centuries.

Nobody established a settlement, though, until the Frenchman Louis de Bougainville brought colonists to Port Louis, East Falkland, in 1764 (the Islands' Spanish name, Malvinas, is an adaptation of St. Malo, the English Channel home port for many French vessels).

In 1766, unaware of the French presence, Britain built its own garrison at Port Egmont on Saunders Island, West Falkland. In 1767, meanwhile, Spain replaced France at Port Louis after invoking the Treaty of Tordesillas (1494), under which the pope had divided the New World between Spain and Portugal. In 1770, after happening upon the Port Egmont settlement, the Spaniards ejected the British but, under threat of war, permitted them to return.

In 1774, the British left Port Egmont without relinquishing their claims. A desolate penal settlement for nearly four decades, the Islands became a haven for whalers and sealers after Spain's departure in 1811.

A decade later, the newly independent United Provinces of the River Plate sent a governor whose tenure was short, while Buenos Aires businessman Louis Vernet asserted rights to the seal fishery and the feral livestock, cattle, and horses that the Spaniards had abandoned. When Vernet attempted to enforce his rights against American sealers, though, a U.S. naval officer wrecked the Port Louis settlement and forced Vernet's return to Buenos Aires.

In early 1833, a British naval vessel evicted the United Provinces' remaining forces, but its Argentine successor state has steadfastly maintained its claim to the Islands, usually diplomatically—but it never became an overt issue until Juan Perón took power in the 1940s and, more aggressively, when a military dictatorship launched a surprise invasion in 1982.

After the British takeover, Montevideo-based Englishman Samuel Lafone created the Falkland Islands Company (FIC) to commercialize the cattle herds and then transformed the economy by introducing wool-bearing sheep. For well over a century, the FIC owned nearly half the property in the Islands and dominated shipping as well, though other immigrants created similar large sheep farms with a resident labor force.

About half the population, which grew slowly and has never exceeded about 2,500, lived on the farms; the other half resided in the port capital of Stanley, established in 1844. Starting in the 1970s, though, political uncertainty and the wool industry's decline led farm owners to sell off their properties; nearly all of them are now family farms, but the population has shifted dramatically toward the capital for reasons that have only partly to do with the wool industry.

### The South Atlantic Conflict

The Falklands' peculiar political status, as an isolated British possession in the decolonization era that followed World War II, led to negotiations that might have resulted in their absorption by Argentina—despite Islanders' determination to remain British (perhaps a dozen Argentines, nearly all of them married to Islanders or other British citizens, resided on the Falklands). Granting Argentina's military airline LADE the first regular routes from the continent to the Islands, a 1971 communications agreement also gave Buenos Aires a de facto say in immigration and other matters.

The 1976–1983 military dictatorship, which increased Islanders' misgivings about Argentine instability, was collapsing beneath the weight of its own brutality, corruption, and ineptitude when it made a last-gasp grab for domestic popularity by invading the Falklands on April 2, 1982. The Argentine generals and admirals, though, underestimated British prime minister Margaret Thatcher's resolve; even worse, they misjudged her military's ability to organize the force that retook the Islands within 10 weeks (Argentine forces, for their part, had not fought a real shooting war since 19th-century conflicts with Paraguay and the Mapuche).

### The Post-War Period

In the conflict's aftermath, Britain's declaration of a fisheries protection zone and licensing regime made the Islands in general, and Stanley in particular, one of the world's most prosperous places on a per-capita basis. While the Islanders themselves did not crew the ships that came from Europe and Asia, the revenue from squid licenses and joint ventures enabled local government to invest in schools, medical care, and roads, and individuals to improve their living standards. Tourism revenues also increased dramatically, as 'round-the-Horn and Antarctica-bound cruise ships called to visit the Islands' capital and enjoy the spectacular coastal wildlife.

Meanwhile, relations with the continent remained distant through the 1980s but improved in the 1990s as Argentine president Carlos Menem's administration attempted to persuade skeptical Islanders of its goodwill. The biggest step forward was a communications agreement that allowed the Chilean airline LAN to fly weekly from Santiago and Punta Arenas to the Islands' Mount Pleasant International Airport. That remains the only commercial international air link, and subsequent Argentine governments have taken a harder line—in 2003, President Néstor Kirchner's administration revoked LAN's permission for Mount Pleasant–bound charter flights that simplified cruise-ship passenger exchange. In 2010, Kirchner's wife, current president Cristina Fernández, even ordered that ships en route to the Falklands could not pass through Argentina's 200-mile maritime economic zone without permission—a flagrant violation of international law that no vessel has yet seen fit to challenge.

Stanley benefited most from the newfound prosperity and the population shift, as family-owned farms did not need—and could not afford—the large labor force employed by traditional sheep ranches. More recently, there has been offshore exploration for oil—probably the main reason for Argentina's maritime embargo—though there is no certainty that oil is present in commercial quantities.

## RECREATION

For most visitors, **wildlife-watching** is the main activity. Because of the Islands' isolation and small human population, many species show no fear of people, but the Falklands Islands Countryside Code, adapted from rules for comparable sites in Antarctica, recommends that visitors get no closer than six meters to birds and marine mammals. Be especially cautious with the southern sea lion, which can be aggressive and surprisingly quick on land.

**Fishing** for sea trout no longer requires a license, but there are daily bag limits; for more information, such as open seasons, contact Stanley's Environmental Planning Department (St. Mary's Walk, tel. 27390).

Opportunities for **hiking** are almost limitless, but government and some landowners discourage camping because of fire danger and livestock disturbances. Since nearly all land is privately held, hikers must seek permission from the landowner; the Tourist Board (tel. 22215, info@falklandislands.com) in Stanley can provide a list of contacts.

**Diving** among the Islands' numerous shipwrecks, kelp forests, and reefs is possible with Stanley operator Dave Eynon's **Falklands Underwater** (Boathouse Gallery, Ross Rd.,

## EIGHT DAYS IN THE FALKLANDS

For visitors to southernmost Patagonia, the Falkland Islands make an intriguing detour, but an inflexible one. There is only one weekly flight, on Saturday, from the Chilean city of Punta Arenas to the Islands' Mount Pleasant International Airport. Likewise, travel within the Islands requires, for the most part, using air taxis whose itineraries depend on demand rather than fixed schedules. For a visit this short, and with limited accommodations, advance arrangements are almost essential; depending on availability, other sites could be substituted for those mentioned.

**Day 1**

Arrive at Mount Pleasant International Airport and make an immediate FIGAS flight connection to Pebble Island, West Falkland. Overnight at Pebble Island Lodge, with a visit to 1982 combat sites and nearby seabird and marine mammal colonies. Alternatively, take a flight to Saunders Island, with self-catering accommodations; visit 18th-century ruins of the earliest British settlement and the bird-rich shoreline.

**Day 2**

Enjoy a full-day exploration of Pebble Island wildlife sites, with gentoo and rockhopper penguins, the occasional king penguin, and sea lions. Alternatively, on Saunders, take a long but rewarding hike to diverse penguin and black-browed albatross colonies at "The Neck," or to similar wildlife at "The Rookery."

**Days 3-4**

Catch the FIGAS flight to Carcass Island, West Falkland, with elephant seal colonies and many birds, including an abundance of the rare striated caracara, a remarkably tame predator. Stay at the Carcass Island ranch.

**Day 5**

Take a FIGAS flight to Sea Lion Island, East Falkland, home to three penguin species, large elephant seal and sea lion colonies, giant petrels, uncommon small birds, and the Falklands' largest remaining stands of native tussock grass, more than two meters high. Stay at Sea Lion Lodge.

Alternatively, visit Bleaker Island, which has most of the same wildlife as Sea Lion, with considerably less expensive but still comfortable accommodations.

**Day 6**

Do morning sightseeing on Sea Lion or Bleaker, with an afternoon FIGAS flight to Stanley. Find hotel or B&B accommodations in town.

**Day 7**

Take a full-day overland excursion to Volunteer Point to visit the king penguin colony, also with gentoos and Magellanics, returning to Stanley in the afternoon. Do a Friday-night pub crawl, if desired.

**Day 8**

Your morning is free for sightseeing in Stanley, with an early-afternoon departure for Punta Arenas.

Stanley, tel. 21145, www.falklands-underwater.com), which rents equipment and organizes tours, and has recently added a 14-meter catamaran to its fleet.

**Golfers** seeking a real challenge can take on the 12-green, 18-tee course at Stanley, as the Islands' nearly constant winds complicate play even more. Arranged through local agencies, greens fees are £5.

## HEALTH AND SAFETY

Probably one of the world's safest destinations—serious crime is virtually nonexistent—the Falklands pose no major health problems and have good medical infrastructure in case of illness or injury. It is worth mentioning, though, the unfortunate legacy of landmines laid by the Argentine military; though dangerous, minefields are fenced and clearly marked, and no civilian has been injured since hostilities ceased in 1982. Entering minefields or tampering with signs can expose you to fines of £1,500 and a year in jail. To report landmines or other questionable objects, contact the Joint Service Explosive Ordnance Disposal (tel. 22229).

While the weather can be changeable, the Falklands' intense sunshine and brisk winds make visitors vulnerable to sunburn even with very brief exposure. A good sunscreen is imperative.

## GETTING THERE

Chile's **LAN** (www.lan.com) offers the only regular commercial flight to the Falklands' **Mount Pleasant International Airport (MPN),** 35 miles (60 kilometers) southwest of Stanley, every Saturday from Santiago and Punta Arenas; it turns around immediately. One Saturday per month in each direction, it picks up passengers in Río Gallegos, Argentina; the following Saturday, it drops them off.

LAN fares from Santiago start at US$833 round-trip; from Punta Arenas, it's US$664 round-trip. Through fares from Europe or North America can be cheaper for those already planning to visit South America; from the United Kingdom, the economy fare is £863 round-trip, with one stopover permitted. From Río Gallegos, though, the fare is only US$207.

LAN also has good connections from North America, Mexico, Australia, and New Zealand. LAN's U.S. gateways are Miami (US$1,930 to Mount Pleasant), New York (US$2,010), Los Angeles (US$1,930), and San Francisco (US$1,985). From Toronto, the fare is US$2,290; from Sydney, it's US$2,800; and from Auckland, US$2,700.

Britain's **Ministry of Defence (MOD)** charters six or seven flights per month from RAF Brize Norton, near Burford, Oxfordshire, via the tiny South Atlantic island of Ascension. The flight takes 18 hours, including an hour's stopover for refueling on Ascension; fares start around £2,222 round-trip with a 28-day advance purchase, considerably more expensive than the Santiago–Punta Arenas route, but Chile-bound travelers can purchase one-way tickets. The MOD baggage limit is normally 60 pounds (27 kilograms); enforcement is irregular, but overweight charges run £13.40 per pound.

For reservations on MOD flights, contact the Travel Coordinator at **Falkland House** (14 Broadway, Westminster, London SW1H 0BH, tel. 020/7222-2542, fax 020/7222-2375, travel@falklands.gov.fk); in the Islands, contact the **Falkland Islands Company West Store** (Ross Rd., tel. 27633, fic.travel@horizon.co.fk). In the Falklands, for both LAN and MOD flights, contact **International Tours and Travel Ltd** (1 Dean St., tel. 22041, fax 22042, www.falklandislands.travel.com).

Passengers flying from Mount Pleasant pay an international departure tax of £22 or its equivalent in U.S. dollars or euros. This can also be prepaid at Customs & Immigration in Stanley.

## GETTING AROUND

Except between Stanley and Mount Pleasant International Airport, there is no regular public transportation on roads, though **taxis** and **rental cars** (with or without guides) are available on both East and West Falkland. Rental cars are not allowed off-road; in any event, driving is not advisable for drivers without local experience, who frequently get "bogged" in the soggy terrain and have to call or trek for help. Visitors may use their own state or national driver's licenses in the Falklands for up to 12 months.

To West Falkland and offshore islands, the only regular public transportation is the **Falkland Islands Government Air Service (FIGAS)** (tel. 27219), an air-taxi service that flies 10-seater Norman-Britten Islander aircraft to grass airstrips throughout the Islands. At the approximate rate of £1.40 per minute, the fare from Stanley to Saunders Island, north of West Falkland, is about £170 round-trip. For safety reasons, pilots enforce the baggage limitation of 30 pounds (14 kilograms) per passenger.

In 2008, the freight-and-passenger ferry M/V *Concordia Bay* (Globe Offices, Philomel St., Stanley, tel. 22301, www.workboat.co.fk) began to operate between the East Falkland port of New Haven and the West Falkland settlement of Port Howard every Friday, Sunday, and alternate Wednesdays. Return passenger fares are £30 per adult, £10 per child under age 16, and £5 per child under five. The vehicle rate of £50 return includes the driver's fare; motorbikes cost £10 return.

# Stanley and Vicinity

Its setting often compared with the moorlands of Scotland's outer isles, fast-growing Stanley claims to be the "world's smallest capital." It's modernizing rapidly as commercial fishing, tourism, and (tentatively) oil supplant wool in the Islands' economy. The sweet scent of smoldering peat no longer permeates the evening atmosphere, as heating oil now warms the houses and fuels the cookstoves of most aging stone cottages and newer kit constructions alike, and streets once lined with utilitarian Land Rovers now sport shiny new SUVs.

While few Islanders work directly in the fishery, their joint ventures with overseas fishing companies and local government's infrastructural investments have, since the 1982 South Atlantic conflict, transformed a forlorn-looking village into a much more presentable place. Many local residents have remodeled and repainted their houses, or built new ones; many continue their tradition of self-sufficiency by tending tidy kitchen gardens even though more commercial produce is now available.

## HISTORY

After the Colonial Office shifted the Islands' capital from Port Louis to sheltered Port Jackson (soon renamed Stanley Harbour) in 1844, Stanley became the new seat of government, but its permanent population was a ragtag assortment of roving mariners, holdover gauchos, and military pensioners. Except in emergencies, 'round-the-Horn shipping avoided the Islands, because Stanley gained a reputation for cargo-shipping losses—"condemned at Stanley" became a cliché among insurers.

In the early days, feral cattle rather than sheep roamed the Islands' pastures, and low-value hides attracted little commercial interest. After midcentury, though, when the newly founded Falkland Islands Company (FIC) shifted from cattle to sheep and other recently created farms followed suit, Stanley grew rapidly as the transshipment point for wool between camp—which is the local term for the countryside—and the United Kingdom.

In addition to being the Islands' largest landholder, the FIC dominated commerce as the Islands' only significant merchant house and Stanley's biggest employer, and it remained so for more than a century. Its impact on the townscape was palpable—many if not most Stanley houses belonged to the company, whose workers lived in them only so long as they remained employees.

With declining wool prices after World War II,

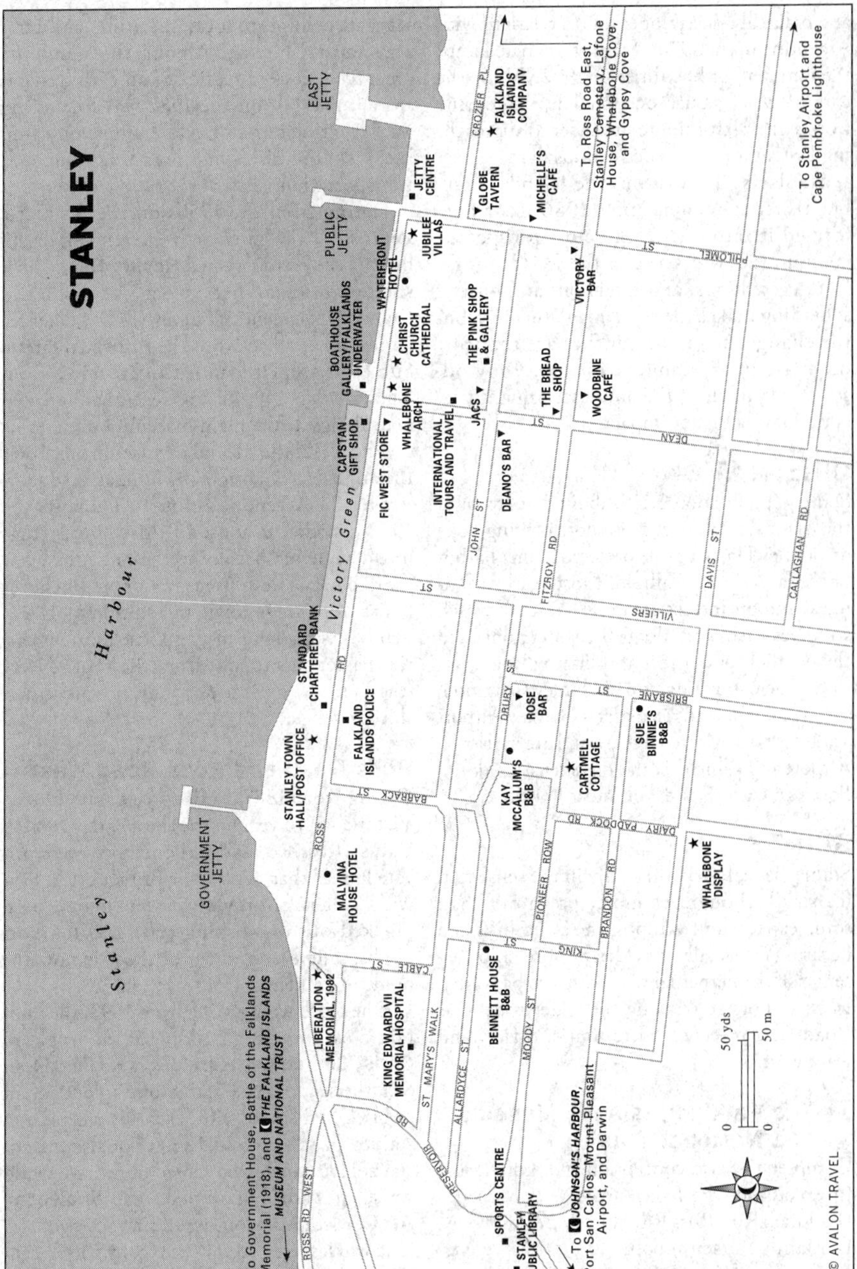
STANLEY
Stanley Harbour
EAST JETTY
PUBLIC JETTY
GOVERNMENT JETTY
Victory Green
JETTY CENTRE
FALKLAND ISLANDS COMPANY
GLOBE TAVERN
MICHELLE'S CAFÉ
JUBILEE VILLAS
WATERFRONT HOTEL
BOATHOUSE GALLERY/FALKLANDS UNDERWATER
CHRIST CHURCH CATHEDRAL
WHALEBONE ARCH
THE PINK SHOP & GALLERY
VICTORY BAR
THE BREAD SHOP
WOODBINE CAFÉ
JACS
INTERNATIONAL TOURS AND TRAVEL
CAPSTAN GIFT SHOP
FIC WEST STORE
DEANO'S BAR
STANDARD CHARTERED BANK
STANLEY TOWN HALL/POST OFFICE
FALKLAND ISLANDS POLICE
ROSE BAR
KAY McCALLUM'S B&B
CARTMELL COTTAGE
SUE BINNIE'S B&B
MALVINA HOUSE HOTEL
WHALEBONE DISPLAY
LIBERATION MEMORIAL, 1982
KING EDWARD VII MEMORIAL HOSPITAL
BENNETT HOUSE B&B
SPORTS CENTRE
STANLEY PUBLIC LIBRARY
CROZIER PL
PHILOMEL ST
DEAN ST
JOHN ST
FITZROY RD
DAVIS ST
CALLAGHAN RD
VILLIERS ST
DRURY ST
BRISBANE ST
ROSS RD
BARRACK ST
DAIRY PADDOCK RD
PIONEER ROW
BRANDON RD
KING ST
CABLE ST
ST MARY'S WALK
ALLARDYCE ST
MOODY ST
RESERVOIR RD
ROSS RD WEST
To Ross Road East, Stanley Cemetery, Lafone House, Whalebone Cove, and Gypsy Cove
To Stanley Airport and Cape Pembroke Lighthouse
To Government House, Battle of the Falklands Memorial (1918), and THE FALKLAND ISLANDS MUSEUM AND NATIONAL TRUST
To JOHNSON'S HARBOUR, Port San Carlos, Mount Pleasant Airport, and Darwin
0 50 yds
0 50 m
© AVALON TRAVEL

and political uncertainties due to relations with Argentina in the 1970s, Stanley stagnated until the outbreak of hostilities in 1982. While the capital was heavily occupied by Argentine troops, their last-minute surrender to approaching British forces avoided serious damage.

Stanley still transships the Islands' wool, but fisheries income since 1986 has transformed it into one of the most prosperous communities of its size in the world. It's far from pretentious, and the boom-and-bust of squidding makes the economy vulnerable, but the changes since the conflict are the most dramatic in the capital's history. Only oil, still not confirmed in commercial quantities, could have a bigger impact.

## ORIENTATION

Stanley (population 2,115, about 85 percent of the Islands' total) occupies a north-facing slope on Stanley Harbour, the protected inner harbor of the larger Port William. Most points of interest and businesses are on Ross Road, which stretches east–west along the waterfront, and the parallel John Street and Fitzroy Road.

On the windy ridgetop of Stanley Common, south of town, roads lead east to Stanley Airport and west to Mount Pleasant International Airport and camp destinations such as Darwin, Port San Carlos, and Volunteer Point.

## SIGHTS

Stanley is pedestrian-friendly in the sense that it's small, though it's more spread out than some expect, and walking the steep hills can be tiring (especially for elderly cruise-ship passengers); the perpetual wind can also be trying. Most visitors start along the waterfront Ross Road, at the Jetty Centre tourist office, and walk west.

### The Falkland Islands Museum and National Trust

Comprehensive in conception and professional in execution, the Falkland Islands Museum (Holdfast Rd., Ross Rd. W., tel. 27428, www.falklands-museum.com, 9:30 A.M.–4 P.M. Mon.–Fri., 2–4 P.M. Sat.–Sun., £3) dedicates separate exhibits to local, maritime, military, and natural history. Among the standouts are a well-stocked replica of an early general store, materials on the 1982 war (including an Argentine bunker), and exhibits on camp life, including changing communications and transportation.

Dating from the 1950s on the Antarctic Peninsula, the museum's current prize exhibit is the reconstructed **Reclus Hut,** which sheltered researchers from the Falkland Islands Dependencies Survey (FIDS), later renamed and still active as the British Antarctic Survey (BAS). Dismantled and removed from Antarctica in 1996, it was recently re-erected here alongside the main museum building.

The Falkland Islands Museum occupies Britannia House, originally built as headquarters for the Argentine airline LADE; after the 1982 conflict, it housed British forces commanders before becoming the museum a few years back. The museum is open whenever cruise ships are in town, in addition to its regular hours; at that time, a shuttle minibus carries passengers to and from the tourist jetty (the shuttle is open to anybody, not just cruise ship passengers).

### Ross Road and Ross Road West

Dating from 1887, built to celebrate Queen Victoria's 50th year on the throne, the **Jubilee Villas** (Ross Rd. and Philomel St.) were private homes that, with their British brick, bay-window, terraced-row style, seem to have been plucked out of working-class London boroughs. The easternmost of them is now the home of Falklands Conservation.

One block west, dating from 1892, the capital's most imposing building is the Anglican **Christ Church Cathedral** (Ross Rd. and Dean St.), the seat of the Church of England. Built of brick and stone, with a soaring steeple and stained-glass windows, its interior also memorializes local men who served in the two world wars. The cathedral overlooks the **Whalebone Arch,** a sculpture joining the jawbones of two blue whales, erected for the colony's 1933 centennial in the center of an open green.

© WAYNE BERNHARDSON

On the Stanley waterfront, the Liberation Memorial honors the soldiers that died in the 1982 conflict with Argentina.

Stretching west along the waterfront from Dean Street, **Victory Green** commemorates the Allied triumph in World War I; several cannons from the Port Louis settlement, functional 19th-century Hotchkiss guns (fired on ceremonial occasions), and the mizzenmast of HMS *Great Britain* punctuate the neatly trimmed lawns.

One block west, the rehabbed **Stanley Town Hall** is home to the post office, public meetings, and events such as May dances. A block farther, the **Liberation Memorial** (1982) honors the British soldiers and sailors who died in the 1982 conflict with Argentina; every June 14, Stanley residents gather for a memorial service here.

Appointed by London, the colony's highest officials have resided in **Government House** (Ross Rd. W.) since the mid-19th century. Bright yellow in summer, spiny gorse hedges and broad lawns separate the house from the street, but not so long ago it was customary for all island visitors to sign the guest register. With all the economic activity and personnel movement since the 1982 war, the governor has more to do than just socialize, and it's now open by invitation only.

On the shoreline side of Government House, the **Monument to the Battle of the Falklands** (1918) is an obelisk commemorating the 1914 confrontation in which British naval forces surprised and sank several German vessels. Farther west, one of few still-identifiable Stanley Harbour shipwrecks, the Liverpool-built barque *Jhelum,* tilts offshore after being scuttled here in 1870; on the green itself, a new **Solar Systems Sculpture** walk begins with a replica of the sun, made of recycled materials. Nearby is the excellent Falkland Islands Museum (Holdfast Rd.).

## Central Stanley

Many of Stanley's surviving stone houses from the 19th century line John Street, one block south of Ross Road. Erected for the Chelsea pensioners, mid-19th century kit houses line **Pioneer Row,** directly uphill from Stanley Town Hall; one of these, **Cartmell Cottage** (7 Pioneer Row), is now open, by appointment only, as part of the Falkland Islands Museum.

Admission costs £1 separately but is included in the museum's £3 admission charge.

Two blocks farther uphill, local conservationist Mike Butcher displays part of his salvaged **whalebone collection,** including the skull, jaws, and teeth of a gigantic sperm whale, in his yard at Dairy Paddock Road and Davis Street. The exhibit also includes a harpoon gun that, according to Butcher, killed 20,000 whales between 1936 and 1965.

### Ross Road East and Vicinity

East of Philomel Street, the **Falkland Islands Company** headquarters occupies most of block-long Crozier Place, beyond which Ross Road resumes as Ross Road East and passes **Stanley Cemetery,** whose weathering tombstones tell a great deal about the origins of the Islands' immigrant population. The **Memorial Wood** is a tribute to the British military who died in the 1982 war.

At the east end of Stanley Harbour, **Whalebone Cove** is the final resting place for several rusting hulks, most notably the handsome three-masted freighter *Lady Elizabeth,* left here after striking a reef in 1913. To the north, still a feasible walk from town, **Gypsy Cove** is home to about 320 breeding pairs of Magellanic penguins, as well as cormorants, night herons, oystercatchers, and small birds; stick to the signed nature trail, as landmines left by the Argentines in 1982 are still a potential hazard on the beach and in some other areas.

Farther east, about seven miles from town, **Cape Pembroke Lighthouse** (1854) is a bit distant for most hikers, but it's a common destination for tours out of Stanley. During the 1982 conflict, lighthouse keeper Reginald Silvey used a hidden radio to keep British forces informed of Argentine movements. Visitors can enter the lighthouse with the loan of a key (£5, nonrefundable) from the museum.

© WAYNE BERNHARDSON

Cape Pembroke Lighthouse is part of the Falklands Museum, which keeps the key to it.

## ENTERTAINMENT

For some Stanley residents, nightly entertainment involves watching videos at home, but there's always a pub crawl starting at the relatively low-key **Victory Bar** (1-A Philomel St., tel. 21199, www.victorybar.com), commonly known as "the Vic." One block north, the **Globe Tavern** (Crozier Place and Philomel St., tel. 22703) is the capital's traditional and, in some ways, more colorful watering hole. To the west, **Deano's Bar** (40 John St., tel. 21296) and the **Rose Bar** (1 Brisbane Rd., tel. 21067) are additional options.

Live music with local bands, and occasional visitors, takes place in the pubs and on occasion in Stanley Town Hall. Occasionally, after the pubs close, Stanley's Fighting Pig Band (www.fightingpigband.com) hosts a show and dance at its tobacco-free home sty The Trough, a remodeled assemblage of eight military Portakabins on Stanley Airport Road. Admission costs £3, and since it has no liquor license, it's BYOB only.

## EVENTS

New Year's Day is an occasion for the annual **Sea Cadets Raft Race,** for which competitors build their own vessels. Under the sponsorship

## FALKLANDS PHILATELY

Until the 1982 South Atlantic conflict, the Falkland Islands had a low international profile except among one serious constituency – they made their mark in philately. Since the Islands' first postage stamps appeared in 1878, collectors have treasured Falklands issues, and for more than a century, they were one of the colony's main revenue earners. Economically, they're no longer so important, but neither are they insignificant.

Unlike many newly independent countries in post-colonial Africa and Asia, the Falklands never flooded the market, and thus they've kept their credibility among collectors. Falklands stamps are also works of art, thanks to local talents like illustrators Ian Strange and Tony Chater, and painter James Peck.

In Stanley Town Hall, adjacent to the post office, the **Philatelic Bureau** (Ross Rd., tel. 27159, www.falklandstamps.com, 9 A.M.-noon and 1:15-4 P.M. Mon.-Fri.) sells Falklands stamps and first-day covers for up to a year after their initial appearance. It keeps longer hours when cruise ships are in port.

of the Falkland Islands Horticultural Society, March's **Horticultural Show** is a competitive event which, at the end of the day, finishes with an auction of produce and baked goods from Stanley and the camp.

August's Town Hall **Crafts Fair** showcases the efforts of leatherworkers (whose bridles, stirrups, and other gear resemble those of early gauchos), weavers, artists, and photographers.

On Boxing Day, the day after Christmas, **Stanley Sports** features horse racing (betting is legal), footraces, and gymkhana competitions. **Camp Sports** takes place in late February or early March, after the end of shearing, at venues such as Goose Green (East Falkland) and Port Howard or Fox Bay (West Falkland).

## SHOPPING

Locally produced items include knitted woollens and leatherwork, and children's toys with penguin motifs, but many souvenirs are imported from the United Kingdom.

Stanley has a growing number of outlets, starting with books and maps at the **Jetty Centre** (Ross Rd. and Philomel St.). Directly opposite Whalebone Arch, the **Boathouse Gallery** (Ross Rd., tel. 21145, fax 22674) has a photo gallery, with landscape, wildlife, and underwater prints, and also sells local crafts and standard souvenirs. Immediately west, the FIC's **Capstan Gift Shop** (Ross Rd., tel. 27654) also carries local souvenirs and photographic equipment.

In new quarters, **The Pink Shop & Gallery** (John St., tel. 21399) has prints and crafts by local artists, as well as books and maps.

**Studio 52** (Ross Rd., tel. 51552, www.studio52.co.fk), on Victory Green alongside Town Hall, is a photo print gallery and souvenir shop.

## SPORTS AND RECREATION

Immediately south of Government House, Stanley's **Sports Centre** (Reservoir Rd., tel. 27291) includes a public swimming pool, but hours vary—phone ahead or ask the tourist office.

For **fishing,** the nearest site is the Murrell River at the west end of Ross Road, but the improved road network has made other East Falkland sites almost equally accessible.

**South Atlantic Marine Services** (Ross Rd. and Dean St., tel. 21145, www.falklands-underwater.com) rents diving equipment and does dive tours. In and around Stanley, shipwrecks, kelp forests, and reefs (with their sea lions and elephant seals) are great attractions for divers.

## ACCOMMODATIONS

Reservations are almost essential, since accommodations are limited even though quality is good. For emergencies, the tourist board keeps a list of local people who will take in roomless visitors.

Where Davis Street East intersects the Airport Road, the hostel-style **Wickham Heights Lodge** (VPC Rd., tel. 22834, £30 pp with full board) is the shoestring visitor's choice, but it's often full.

Conspicuous for its colorful flowerbeds and even more colorful garden gnomes, **Kay McCallum's B&B** (14 Drury St., tel. 21071, kay@horizon.co.fk, £25 pp for B&B) is homey and comfy, with excellent lunches and dinners at modest prices; she's particularly good at curries. She also allows camping for £5 per tent, plus £4 for shower and meal.

The comparable **Susana Binnie's B&B** (3 Brandon Rd, tel. 21051, £25 pp) is a comfortable traditional house with soft-spoken, Spanish-speaking ownership. **Bennett House B&B** (14 Allardyce St., tel. 21191, celiastewart@horizon.co.fk, £30–35 pp) is a comfortable house whose charming hostess, Celia Stewart, has a double and a triple room with shared bath, plus a double with private bath. She provides a filling English-style breakfast. Camping is possible for £15 per person.

At the east end of town, **Shorty's Motel** (West Hillside, tel. 22861, £38s £54 d) is an immaculate prefab often used by visiting military from Mount Pleasant. It's part of a small complex that includes a pretty good cafeteria-style restaurant with a diverse menu.

In a quiet location beyond the cemetery, **Lafone House** (Ross Rd. E., tel. 22891, arlette@horizon.co.fk, £55 s, £90 d with shared bath, £65 s £110 d with private bath, both with breakfast) is an immaculate and spacious five-room B&B, with coffee and tea available all day. Proprietor Arlette Betts is also one of Stanley's most hospitable innkeepers.

The upgraded, centrally located **Waterfront Hotel** (36 Ross Rd., tel. 22331, thewaterfronthotel@cwimail.fk, £75 pp) offers B&B accommodations in a rambling house with harbor views.

Generally considered Stanley's best, the expanding **Malvina House Hotel** (3 Ross Rd., tel. 21355, fax 21357, www.malvinahousehotel.com, £104 s, £136 d with breakfast) is a contemporary lodging on attractive grounds, with a conservatory restaurant, a cozy bar, and wireless Internet throughout. It's also the only Stanley hotel with hot tub and sauna.

## FOOD

It's worth mentioning that, while the food has improved dramatically over the last decade-plus, Stanley restaurants still have their ups and downs.

For the largest selection of groceries, there's the FIC's **West Store** (Ross Rd. and Dean St., tel. 27660), which has also opened a café and a delicatessen. Open early, **The Bread Shop** (Dean St., tel. 21273) has outstanding fresh bread, pies, pizzas, sausage rolls, sandwiches, and Chilean-style empanadas. **Jacs** (John St., tel. 21143) offers pastries, cupcakes, and coffee.

There are several good takeaway choices, starting with the **Woodbine Café** (29 Fitzroy Rd., tel. 22696, 10 A.M.–2 P.M. Tues.–Sat., 6:30–8:30 P.M. Mon., Wed., Fri.) for fish and chips, and **Michelle's Café** (2 Philomel St., tel. 21123), which also serves breakfast and lunch.

Tobacco-free **Shorty's Diner** (Snake Hill and Davis St. E., tel. 22855, www.shortys-diner.com, 9 A.M.–8:30 P.M. daily, 9 A.M.–8 P.M. weekends and holidays) has panini and other sandwiches, short orders such as sweet-and-sour chicken (£6), and desserts. It is licensed to serve alcohol with meals. **Deano's Bar** (40 John St., tel. 21296, 10 A.M.–11 P.M. Mon.–Thurs., 10 A.M.–11:30 P.M. Fri.–Sat., noon–10:30 P.M. Sun.) serves pub grub including fish and chips, burgers, and curries and fishcakes.

With a new chef from the United Kingdom, the conservatory restaurant at **Malvina House Hotel** (3 Ross Rd., tel. 21355) has taken over the top spot among Stanley restaurants, with full meals in the £16 range but also excellent lunch specials for only about £5–6 per entrée. Appetizers include upland goose pâté; entrées start with succulent roast lamb in a country where the default option used to be aging mutton. It's popular enough that reservations are advisable for both lunch and dinner.

## INFORMATION

At the foot of Philomel Street, the **Jetty Visitor Centre** (Ross Rd., tel. 22281, www.visitorfalklands.com, 10 A.M.–5 P.M. weekdays, 9 A.M.–5 P.M. Sat., 9 A.M.–4 P.M. Sun.) keeps longer hours when cruise ships are in port.

The Falkland Islands Tourism Board publishes the annual *Visitor Guide*, a glossy full-color booklet with brief descriptions of sights and services both in Stanley and throughout the Islands. It's free of charge at the Jetty Centre.

**Falklands Conservation** (41 Ross Rd., tel. 22247, www.falklandsconservation.com) is the leading conservation organization, offering advice and information on visiting wildlife sites throughout the Islands; it also has a small shop in its Jubilee Villas headquarters.

In the Falkland Islands Community School, the **Stanley Public Library** (Reservoir Rd., tel. 27290) holds a large collection of books and papers relating to the Falklands (including the author's 781-page doctoral dissertation!) and Antarctica. Hours are 9 A.M.–noon Monday–Friday, plus 1:30–5:45 P.M. Monday, Tuesday, and Thursday, 2:30–5:30 P.M. Wednesday, 3–6 P.M. Friday, and 1:45–5 P.M. Saturday.

## SERVICES

**Standard Chartered Bank** (Ross Rd. between Barrack and Villiers Streets, 8:30 A.M.–3 P.M. Mon.–Fri.) changes U.S. dollars and euros to British and local pounds. There's no ATM, but they'll issue cash advances against MasterCard and Visa. The Falkland Islands Company's **West Store** (Ross Rd. and Dean St.) will also change money (unofficially).

The **post office** (Ross Rd. at Barrack St., tel. 27180, 8 A.M.–noon and 1:15–4:30 P.M. Mon.–Fri.) occupies part of Town Hall. It keeps longer hours, as well as weekend hours, when cruise ships are in port.

**Public phones,** in the Jetty Visitor Centre, the FIC West Store, and some other locations, require prepaid Cable and Wireless phone cards. Internet service at the Jetty Centre, with new broadband connections, is expensive at £6 per hour.

### MAKING THE CONTINENTAL CONNECTION

Because Buenos Aires has prohibited Chilean charters from using Argentine airspace en route to the Falklands, LAN's scheduled Saturday flights to and from Punta Arenas are increasingly full of cruise-ship passengers. This means that independent travelers need to make travel plans carefully or they might have to remain longer than expected in the Falkland Islands.

Returning from the Islands, if disembarking in Río Gallegos, Argentina, insist that immigration officials stamp your passport; some travelers exiting Argentina at more northerly border posts have had problems with immigration officials who have accused them of entering the country illegally or overstaying their visas. Some, on the other hand, have backdated entry stamps to the date the individual arrived in the Falklands – which Argentina considers its territory.

There is one advantage in flying from Río Gallegos to the Falklands – since Argentina considers this a "domestic" route, the fare is about one-third the cost of that from Punta Arenas.

For efficiently arranging a visit to the Islands, especially for short-term guests, try **International Tours and Travel** (Dean St., tel. 22041, www.falklandislands.travel), which is also the LAN airline rep here. **Falkland Islands Holidays** (Airport Rd., tel. 22622, www.falklandislandsholidays.com) is also reliable.

East of Philomel Hill, the **Customs & Immigration Department** (H Jones Rd. 3, tel. 27340) also sells nautical charts of the Islands. For emergencies, contact the **Falkland Islands Police** (Ross Rd. between Barrack St. and Villiers St., tel. 28100).

**King Edward VII Memorial Hospital** (St. Mary's Walk, tel. 28000) has 90 staff members

## AIRBORNE WITH EDDIE

For anyone who enjoys small planes, Falkland Islands Government Air Service (FIGAS) flights are a treat. With an excellent safety record, the government air service covers every remote settlement, though weight restrictions limit access to some airstrips, particularly on small islands like West Point and New Island. Still, there's no better overview of the Islands, and, because flight schedules are demand-driven, tourists sometimes get a lengthy aerial tour before reaching their final destination.

Though the odds are against it, one of FIGAS's outstanding experiences is sharing the cockpit headphones with head pilot Eddie Anderson, who can identify every farmstead and islet he flies over. An outspoken conservationist, he's been buying up prime conservation sites such as the outer Passage Islands and Elephant Keys, the key breeding site for the notoriously timid giant petrel.

© WAYNE BERNHARDSON

**A FIGAS Islander prepares to board.**

and 28 beds; in true emergencies, British military specialists are also available. Care is on a fee-for-service basis, though, and visitors must have insurance, including medical evacuation coverage, to enter the Islands.

The hospital **pharmacy** (tel. 27329) can fill prescriptions, also on a fee-for-service basis.

## GETTING THERE

For several years after the 1982 war, the only way to reach the Islands was an expensive Royal Air Force flight from England via Ascension Island. That route still exists, with an irregular schedule, but for the last several years LAN (www.lan.com) has offered Saturday flights to and from Punta Arenas (US$664 roundtrip); one flight per month picks up and drops off passengers in the Argentine city of Río Gallegos (where the fare is only US$207).

## GETTING AROUND

**FIGAS** (tel. 27219, tel. 27303 at check-in desk) flies 10-seat Norman-Britten Islanders to grass airstrips around the Islands on demand, but clients may need to be flexible; it now takes credit cards. **Stanley Airport** is about four kilometers east of town.

Typical FIGAS destinations and one-way fares include Bleaker Island (£54), Port Howard (£66), Sea Lion Island (£48), Pebble Island (£66.80), Saunders Island (£84.40), and Carcass Island (£100.40).

For international flights, **Falkland Islands Tours & Travel** (tel. 21775, fitt@horizon.co.fk) offers door-to-door bus service (£15 pp) to Mount Pleasant International Airport. The Falkland Islands Company (tel. 27633) does it for one pound less.

**Bonner's Taxi** (tel. 51126) and **Town Taxi** (tel. 52900) provide service around town; the average fare is about £3, but Stanley airport transfers cost £6.

For rental cars, try **FIC Automotive** (Crozier Place and Hebe St., tel. 27680), **Stanley Services** (tel. 22622), or **Raymond Poole** (tel. 51037). Rates start around £38 per day.

# East Falkland

East Falkland still has the Islands' best road network, though little beyond town is paved. The best is the Stanley–Mount Pleasant Highway, which links the capital with the airport, continuing to Darwin and Goose Green, but even this is mostly gravel and requires caution. From Pony's Pass, about eight miles west of town on this route, the North Camp Road leads to Estancia, where it forks north to Port Louis and Johnson's Harbour, and west to Teal Inlet, Douglas Station, and Port San Carlos. Rental cars may not be taken off-road.

Several Stanley-based operators offer tours in and around Stanley, and overland on East Falkland by road and off-road. In alphabetical order, they include Patrick Watts's **Adventure Falklands** (P.O. Box 223, Stanley, tel. 21383, pwatts@horizon.co.fk), which covers Stanley, wildlife sites at Volunteer Point and Cape Bougainville, and 1982 battlefields (Patrick manned the FIBS radio coverage during the 1982 Argentine invasion); Charlene Rowland's **Charley's Tours** (19 Jeremy Moore Ave., tel. 51588, rowland@cwimail.fk) for off-road trips to wildlife sites; Tony Smith's **Discovery Falklands** (38 Ross Rd., tel. 21027, www.discoveryfalklands.com), which does natural history, historical, and battlefield excursions throughout East Falkland; Graham France's **Falklands Forays** (7 Snake Hill, tel. 21624, france@cwimail.fk), which focuses on Stanley and vicinity, including golf and Gypsy Cove; **Harbour Excursions** (tel. 22260, cheryl@beauchenefishing.co.fk) for boat trips around Stanley Harbour, Port William, and Berkeley Sound; and John Birmingham's **Top Town Tours** (tel. 21443, jay.bee@horizon.co.fk), which also rents bicycles.

## KIDNEY COVE

For visitors stuck in Stanley, whether by weather, unavailability of flights, or shortage of camp accommodations, nearby Kidney Cove is more than just a consolation prize—bird-watchers can count on seeing gentoo, Magellanic, and rockhopper penguins here. On a good day, they can also bag kings and macaronis for their life list, though there's no guarantee given the relatively small numbers of those species here.

Murrell Farm owners Adrian and Lisa Lowe live close enough to Stanley that they can pick up passengers in town and Rover them to a large gentoo colony with the occasional king that also has plenty of Magellanics nearby. Alternatively, they can head overland to the scenic southern shore of Berkeley Sound, where rockhoppers scale the steep headlands to an exposed site where, in the spring hatching season, skuas swoop down to steal newborn chicks. Either trip costs £35 per person, but for £60 per person the Lowes will combine the two for an excursion that can be done comfortably in about five hours. That said, they place no time limit at any site—the visitors themselves determine when to move on; for more than four people, there are discounts.

In addition, there are fishing trips on the Murrell for £75 per person, gear included, and full-day minibus tours to Goose Green, San Carlos, and back via Teal Inlet (£45 pp, with a minimum of three persons). For more information, contact Adrian or Lisa Lowe at **Kidney Cove Safari Tours** (Murrell Farm, tel./fax 31001, www.kidneycove.com). When cruise ships are in port, though, individual tours are on hold.

## PORT LOUIS

Open to the public only occasionally, Port Louis still holds ruins of Louis de Bougainville's French settlement of 1764, of Louis Vernet's early-19th-century colony, and the tomb of Vernet's deputy Matthew Brisbane, who took charge after the British displaced Buenos Aires in 1833 (Brisbane died at the hands of renegade gauchos, and other colonists had to flee to an offshore island for their lives). Dating from 1843, the handsome ivy-covered farmhouse is the Islands' oldest habitable building; a museum may be in the works.

Several hours north of the settlement, **Seal Bay** is one of East Falkland's finest wildlife sites, with southern sea lions and many penguins, including Magellanics, rockhoppers, and the occasional macaroni. While access is restricted, some Stanley operators may get permission.

For information on Port Louis, contact farm owner Peter Gilding (tel. 51060).

## JOHNSON'S HARBOUR AND VOLUNTEER POINT

Northeast of Port Louis settlement by a good road, Johnson's Harbour is an essential stop on the Islands' tourist circuit for its thousands-strong colony of king penguins, which are present all year, at its easterly Volunteer Point sector. In addition, there are gentoos, Magellanics, cormorants, and many other birds.

The colorful king, the Islands' largest penguin, has an unusual breeding cycle that can range from 10 months (in the Falklands, at the northern limit of its range) to 14 months (at sub-Antarctic South Georgia). Moreover, that cycle is much less season-specific than that of its migratory counterparts or even the gentoo, which is also present throughout the year. At the site itself, do not enter the stone circle intended to mark an undisturbed king penguin area.

Recently sold to Jan Cheek of Stanley, Johnson's Harbour is a 36,000-acre (14,570-hectare) sheep farm that charges £15 per person per day to visit the colony. From the settlement, the soggy four-wheel-drive track is open for tour operators only and can be difficult even for locally experienced drivers. The season generally runs November–March; fee camping is possible at the warden's cottage.

### THE CAMP

Traditionally, in the Falklands, everything outside Stanley is camp, and camp has been a synonym for hospitality. The term itself derives from the Spanish *campo* (countryside), and it's a common usage among Anglo-Argentines and Anglo-Chileans as well.

In the heyday of sheep farming, Falklands settlements were small company towns on or near sheltered harbors. Since the land reform and subdivision of the 1980s, though, this pattern has changed; many campers have moved to Stanley, the settlements have fewer residents, and many farmers now live in isolated homesteads, at what were once "outside houses." Still, on East and West Falkland, an improved road network has partly compensated for the decline of traditional settlements and their social amenities.

While many camp residents are still involved in sheep farming, an increasing number work wholly or partially in tourism and cottage industries. Some of the best wildlife sites – Sea Lion, Bleaker, Pebble, Saunders, and Carcass Islands, for instance – now boast comfortable lodges and/or self-catering accommodations.

Not so long ago, the idea of charging someone who came to spend a weekend in camp was almost unthinkable – though it was customary to present the host with rum or another small gift. Now, for better or worse, the custom of a free bed has nearly disappeared. Pebble Island Hotel's Allan White claims, "I preferred the old way," but the pressure for economic diversification has nearly – though not entirely – eliminated that option. Even so, the hospitality remains.

## SALVADOR AND CAPE BOUGAINVILLE

Northwest of Stanley via Estancia, Teal Inlet, and Douglas Station, Salvador is the gateway to Cape Bougainville, home to large rockhopper colonies and the occasional macaroni, plus other seabirds and a plethora of sea lions. In the hands of the same family since its Gibraltarian founder, Andrés Pitaluga, arrived from South America in the 1830s, it also has elephant seal and sea lion colonies on Centre Island in the estuary of Port Salvador (Salvador Water), near the settlement.

© WAYNE BERNHARDSON

**Rockhoppers emerge from the ocean at Cape Bougainville.**

From Stanley, Cape Bougainville is a full-day excursion; there are no accommodations, but it has a Portakabin shelter, with sofas and chairs, in case of rough weather.

## PORT SAN CARLOS AND CAPE DOLPHIN

At the end of the North Camp Road, the settlement of Port San Carlos is the gateway to Cape Dolphin, a wildlife-rich area that's a long day's excursion from Stanley. Its long white-sand beach and headlands are home to gentoo penguins, king and rock cormorants, and sea lions, while black-necked swans, grebes, and teal paddle its ponds.

A protected wildlife reserve, Cape Dolphin is irregularly open to the public—it's best to go with a tour from town or at one of the farms. At **Racepoint Farm** (tel. 41012, jhjones@horizon.co.fk, £25 pp, two-person minimum) John and Michelle Jones offer self-catering accommodations, plus coastal tours for up to three persons for £100, as well as horseback rides for £20 per hour.

Ben Berntsen also provides self-catering at nearby **Elephant Beach House** (tel. 41020, benebf@horizon.co.fk, £20 pp for adults, £10 pp for kids age 5–10); meals, usually a roast with vegetables (£20), are also available. Camping costs £10 per person, while coastal tours are available for £100 per vehicle, with guide.

From Stanley, Port San Carlos (commonly known as "KC" for the initials of founder Keith Cameron) is about two hours by road, but the overland track to the cape is slower.

## DARWIN AND GOOSE GREEN

Where a slender isthmus links East Falkland's mountainous north with its undulating southern peninsula of Lafonia, about 60 miles west of Stanley, Darwin once had a population of nearly 200 that has fallen to a just a few, as most of the farm buildings and houses shifted to nearby Goose Green in the 1920s. The peninsula, whose highest point is only 90 meters above sea level, takes its name from Montevideo merchant Samuel Fisher Lafone, founder of what became the Falklands Islands Company; Lafone's gauchos hunted feral cattle to be slaughtered, their hides processed, at his *saladero*.

Darwin is a historic site, starting with the circular **corral** that dates from *saladero* days before sheep replaced cattle, and it became the center of the FIC's camp operations for more than a century; the weathering headstones at **Darwin Cemetery** tell part of the story. In 1982, the South Atlantic war's deadliest combat took place at Goose Green; military landmarks include a **monument** to British Colonel H. Jones, who died leading an assault on Argentine positions, and the **Argentine military cemetery.**

At Goose Green itself, part of the FIC jetty, the decaying remains of the barque ***Vicar of Bray*** (1841) belong to the only surviving ship to have served San Francisco during the California Gold Rush. After spending several decades coasting the Islands, it was blown ashore here in 1912 and incorporated into the jetty.

South of Goose Green, dating from 1927, the **Bodie Creek Bridge** is the world's southernmost suspension span. In the middle of the FIC camp, it simplified communications with the outlying Walker Creek and North Arm settlements.

The tastefully modernized **Darwin Lodge** (tel. 31313, darwin_house@cwimail.fk, £61 pp with full board, £80 pp with full board) is under new management. Two of the nonsmoking facility's five comfortable guest rooms have private baths, while the others share baths. Common areas include a sunny north-facing conservatory, large sitting and dining rooms, a substantial library, and a small bar.

## BLEAKER ISLAND

For wildlife-oriented visitors on a budget, Bleaker Island is an exceptional alternative to more distant and/or costly destinations like Sea Lion and Carcass Islands, which require longer flights and have more expensive accommodations and food. Bleaker can't quite match the diversity of those islands, but it has a scenic rocky shoreline with Magellanic, rockhopper, and gentoo penguins, as well as the occasional king, plus king cormorants and night herons, and a breeding colony of giant petrels.

Because Bleaker has no cats, it also has thriving populations of small birds, and owners Mike and Phyl Rendell are removing rats from offshore islands to further encourage the diminutive species like tussock birds. While there are no breeding sea lions or elephant seals, Bleaker gets occasional visitors.

Bleaker's **Cobb's Cottage** (tel. 32491 or 21084, mrendell@horizon.co.fk, £30 pp) is a comfortable and attractive self-catering kit house with three bedrooms, sleeping a maximum of five persons; if it's full, the Rendells can accommodate extra people in the main house. A new lodge called Cassard House (£45 pp self-catering) opened in 2011. Named after a French ship that was wrecked at the south end of the island in 1906, the lodge consists of four rooms with private baths. Full board is available at Cobb's Cottage or Cassard House for £25 per person, pre-prepared meal packs for £20 per person; there's a small store for supplementary needs.

At its closest, Bleaker is barely half a mile from East Falkland; FIC managers used to ride 20 miles southeast from North Arm and row across to Bleaker, but today's visitors prefer FIGAS air taxis. Most wildlife is within easy walking distance of the settlement, but there's a Land Rover available for rent (on Bleaker's "hard camp," unlike much of East Falkland, getting bogged is not a serious hazard).

## SEA LION ISLAND

For wildlife-lovers who can afford it, compact Sea Lion offers more in a smaller area than any other destination in the Islands. Five miles long and barely a mile wide, with landscapes ranging from broad sandy beaches to rocky tussock-topped cliffs, it can boast 47 breeding bird species (including three penguins and five predators), plus large breeding colonies of elephant seals and sea lions.

Sea Lion's single most impressive feature may be the sprawling mixed colonies of rockhopper

© WAYNE BERNHARDSON

a massive king cormorant colony on Bleaker Island

penguins and king cormorants—for both their visual impact and their odor—but the most exciting one may be the dense plantations of native tussock grass that sometimes conceal the bull sea lions that gave the island its name. An unexpected encounter with these large, fierce beasts can be disconcerting.

In the summer breeding season, some 2,000 elephant seals nearly blanket the sandy beaches within a few minutes' walking distance of the island's comfortable lodge. Frequenting the nearby tussock, the striated caracara or Johnny rook *(Phalcoboenus australis)* is one of the world's rarest predatory birds, but it's remarkably tolerant of the human presence.

Owned by the Falkland Islands Development Corporation (FIDC), Sea Lion has very few sheep since its 1990s purchase from Terry and Doreen Clifton, who had restored the native tussock for both wildlife habitat and controlled grazing. In 1986, FIDC chose Sea Lion for the Islands' first dedicated wildlife lodge, where those who are staying only a day can see a bit of everything, while those spending several days can orient themselves and then choose where they wish to concentrate their efforts.

Under a 150-year lease, a British company now operates **Sea Lion Lodge** (tel. 32004, fax 32003, www.sealionisland.com, £90–145 pp with full board). Purpose-built from a kit, with a Chilean cook and mostly Chilean staff, the 19-bed lodge is probably the most economically successful of the Islands' wildlife destinations. Rates vary seasonally, with the highest November through March.

# West Falkland

Beyond the Falkland Sound, which runs northeast–southwest, the west was the site of Britain's first settlement, at Port Egmont on Saunders Island. Nobody settled West Falkland proper, though, until J. L. Waldron founded a sheep station at Port Howard in the late 1860s, and settlements like Fox Bay, Hill Cove, and Port Stephens followed in short order. Some of these farms remained in the same hands for over a century, while others became FIC property. Several offshore islands, some of them exceptional wildlife destinations, were home to small independent farmers; one of them, Keppel Island, witnessed a curious experiment in missionizing native people from Tierra del Fuego.

While the population of West Falkland has been declining since the agrarian reform of the 1980s, there's hope that the improved road network and the establishment of Fox Bay Village, on the south coast, as a wool transshipment point, will revitalize the island. The only other surviving large settlement, still run as a traditional sheep station, Port Howard has fewer than 20 permanent residents. One local humorist has suggested that it would be easy to repopulate the west by enforcing prohibition in Stanley and declaring open licensing hours here.

## PORT HOWARD AND VICINITY

Every house has a view at Port Howard, West Falkland's only surviving large farm and the starting point for an improving road system. Most of the island's wildlife sites are a bit distant, but a visit here offers insights into how the large sheep stations worked. Since its sale to former employees in 1987, though, hard times in the wool industry have caused unemployment, population has fallen from 40 into the twenties, and the school closed because there was only a single school-age child (served by a traveling teacher and radio instruction).

One of Howard's outstanding features is the former **manager's house,** now a visitors' lodge. In its present state, this is a gem, but in the past it could also be a burden. According to one experienced observer, a large house was not necessarily a luxury, especially as labor became more scarce and expensive:

> *Managers' houses have tended to be large not for the convenience of the managers – rather the opposite. They have been used as free hotels by official visitors – OK when servants were obtainable but a burden on wives in particular since in general they were not.*

Still, as it grazes 42,000 sheep on about 200,000 acres, Port Howard offers possibilities for hiking near Mount Maria, fishing in the Warrah River, golf on a nine-hole par-three course, and highway and off-road tours. Occupied by a thousand Argentines in 1982, it saw no serious combat, but there's a small **war museum** here, and the British military's occasional live-fire exercises are a reminder of the continuing territorial dispute.

**Port Howard Lodge** (tel./fax 42187, porthowardlodge@cwimail.fk, £90 pp with full board, discounts for children depending on age) provides a glimpse into the apparent comforts that came with privilege—spacious, well-furnished bedrooms with private baths, a large sitting room that now serves as a bar, a dining room that's now the restaurant, and a sunny conservatory that yields luscious grapes in summer. The operators have preserved historic features like the antique crank telephone exchange (since replaced by a digital network); a handsome assortment of gaucho-style horse gear adorns the walls.

In addition, Howard Lodge offers farm tours (£5 pp) and eight-hour four-wheel-drive and wildlife tours (£40 pp, with a two-person minimum).

## HILL COVE AND VICINITY

Almost directly west of Port Howard, now reached by a good road, Hill Cove acquired

## THE FALKLANDS BOOKSHELF

For a good general account of history and natural history, look for Ian J. Strange's *The Falkland Islands* (London: David & Charles, 1983); however, it barely anticipates the dramatic economic and political changes since the 1982 South Atlantic war. Robert Fox's *Antarctica and the South Atlantic: Discovery, Development and Dispute* (London: BBC Books, 1985) places the territorial controversy in historical context. For military and political details on the war, try Max Hastings's and Simon Jenkins's *Battle for the Falklands* (London: Pan, 1983).

For detail on natural history, try Strange's *Field Guide to the Wildlife of the Falkland Islands and South Georgia* (London: Harper Collins, 1992), illustrated with the author's exceptional color and black-and-white drawings and black-and-white photographs. Also well illustrated, Robin Woods's *Guide to Birds of the Falkland Islands* (Oswestry, Shropshire, United Kingdom: Anthony Nelson, 1988) focuses exclusively on birds, while Strange covers marine mammals, introduced land mammals, and flora as well.

For a Darwinian perspective, based on archival research at Cambridge, there's Patrick Armstrong's *Darwin's Desolate Islands: A Naturalist in the Falklands, 1833 and 1834* (Chippenham, United Kingdom: Picton, 1992). Based on private papers, Michael Mainwaring's *From the Falklands to Patagonia* (London: Allison & Busby, 1983) chronicles one 19th-century shepherd's family's departure from the Islands to pioneer an *estancia* on "The Coast" of Argentine Patagonia.

In cooperation with the Falkland Islands Trust, the small British publisher Bluntisham Books (www.bluntishambooks.co.uk) has a series of well-illustrated booklets that include T. H. Davies's and J. H. McAdam's *Wild Flowers of the Falkland Islands* (1989), John Smith's historical *Those Were the Days* (1989) on Stanley's past, and Julian Fisher's *Walks and Climbs in the Falkland Islands* (1992).

The annual *Falklands Islands Journal* covers a variety of historical and natural-history topics, including local memoirs. It's available in Stanley or in the United Kingdom from Jim McAdam (Department of Applied Plant Science, Queens University, Newforge Ln., Belfast BT9 5PX, Northern Ireland, jim.mcadam@afbini.gov.uk).

Beautifully illustrated with color photographs, and with contributions from local writers, Debbie Summers's excellent *Visitor's Guide to the Falkland Islands* (London: Falklands Conservation, 2001) makes an ideal souvenir; it's available in the Islands for £9.

a certain fame for being the only place in the Islands where a forest plantation, primarily conifers such as pines and Sitka spruce, has been successful. Some specimens reach 50 feet in a land where most ornamentals are stunted and wind-flagged, but recently they've suffered parasitic attacks that have killed many of them.

Since its subdivision and sale, the settlement is a lesser focus than the outside houses, some of which offer accommodations. On the site of the initial settlement, northeast of Hill Cove proper, Paul and Davina Peck's **Shallow Bay Guest House** (tel. 41007, psb@horizon.co.fk, £20 pp self-catering, £30 pp with full board) occupies one of the Islands' oldest stone houses.

Rates at Peter and Shelley Nightingale's **West Lagoons Farm** (tel. 41194, shelley@cwimail.fk, £33 pp) include full board.

## PORT STEPHENS AND VICINITY

Now accessible by road, from Port Howard via Fox Bay Village, the far western settlement of Port Stephens lies on the edge of one of the Islands' most scenic and wildlife-rich areas. Unfortunately, it lacks formal tourist facilities, but for visitors with time and flexibility it's worth exploring the options—perhaps by renting a vehicle at Port Howard, about three hours away.

Just southwest of the settlement, the wildlife sites include **Wood Cove** and **Stephens**

**Peak,** home to enormous mixed colonies of cormorants and rockhopper penguins, and Magellanic and gentoo penguins. **Calm Head,** about two hours from the settlement, provides some of the Islands' most spectacular coastal panoramas. Peter and Anne Robertson, who own this area, do not permit vehicles to enter it; visitors *must* hike from the settlement.

Formerly part of Port Stephens, **Port Albemarle** was the site of an industrial sealing station, a Colonial Development Corporation fiasco that—fortunately—failed to commercialize sea lion oil after World War II. Most of its ruins have been dismantled, but the factory was a suitable metaphor for the misjudgments and neglect that so long characterized London's attitude toward the Islands.

Beyond the former sealing station, a large gentoo colony faces the stunning **Arch Islands,** where the South Atlantic seas have eroded a passageway in the largest of the group.

Prospective visitors need permission from landowners Peter and Anne Robertson (tel. 42307, par@horizon.co.fk) at the settlement, and Gonzalo Hobman and Helen Wallace (tel. 42250) at Albemarle Station. When it's not needed for shearers, the Robertsons rent the **Cadet's Quarters** on a self-catering basis (£25 pp, half that for kids under 16).

## PEBBLE ISLAND

Just off West Falkland's north coast, Pebble Island takes its name from the colorful agates, sometimes polished and turned into jewelry, that litter its westernmost beaches. Visitors come to the 24-mile-long offshore island for its diverse wildlife and landscape: East of the settlement isthmus, a pond-filled plain teems with wildfowl while sea lions breed along the shore; to the west, several penguin species have colonized the coastal greens and headlands, along with giant petrels. There are more than 40 resident bird species.

Immediately north of the settlement, horseshoe-shaped **Elephant Bay** has no elephant seals, but its white crescent beach is the starting point for a two-hour walk to **Little Wreck Point;** at the end, there's a shoreline graveyard of beaked whale skulls, ribs, and vertebrae. Magellanic penguins breed here and swim in the large pond.

On the night of May 14–15, 1982, Pebble was the site of a British commando raid that destroyed 11 Argentine spotter planes—an action that made their naval counter-invasion of East Falkland feasible. On the slope of **First Mount,** just west of the settlement, there's a monument to HMS *Coventry,* which sank with at least 10 British helicopters onboard after being hit by a missile, about 10 miles to the north. A nearby gravesite marks the resting place of two Argentine pilots whose Learjet came down a short distance from here, but the remains went undetected until 1992.

Some distance west, on a coastal green, there's a substantial gentoo colony with the occasional king, and a midsize rockhopper colony with the odd macaroni. Giant petrels also nest on a nearby slope, but visitors should not approach too closely as these easily disturbed birds may abandon their nests.

The former manager's house, **Pebble Island Lodge** (tel./fax 41093, www.pebblelodge.com, £99 pp with full board for adults, half-price for children 5–15) has six spacious doubles and one odd compact single entered through its own bathroom; all baths are private but have showers rather than tubs. The enormous sitting room, with excellent natural light, has a self-service bar on the honor system. There is 24-hour electricity from a wind turbine and storage batteries, and 24-hour hot water.

The food is well above average by camp standards, with very fine homemade bread and good desserts. There's a respectable choice of wines, mostly Chilean.

Islanders Allan White and Jacqui Jennings, who run Pebble Lodge, offer eight-hour Land Rover tours (£60 pp) that cover western Pebble thoroughly; Allan, who has substantial cruise ship experience in both the South Atlantic and South Pacific, is particularly knowledgeable on natural history but also on the 1982 conflict ("When I was in England in school, I watched the TV news every night to see what was happening . . . ," he says). As of late 2010, the lodge was up for sale.

For hikers, the lodge has Land Rover drop-off service whose cost depends on the distance from the settlement.

## KEPPEL ISLAND

Immediately west of Pebble and north of Hill Cove, rarely visited Keppel has wildlife including penguins and black-browed albatrosses, no permanent inhabitants, and the most extraordinary history of any offshore island. In the early 1850s, the South American Missionary Society (SAMS) occupied Keppel as part of an ambitious project to make Fuegians abandon their livelihood as mobile hunter-gatherers and become sedentary horticulturalists—evangelizing them, of course, in the process.

Among the inhabitants at Cranmer, as the SAMS settlement was known, was Jemmy Button, history's most famous Fuegian. Having traveled to England with Captain Fitzroy on the *Beagle,* learned English, and even met the Queen, Button returned to Tierra del Fuego and resumed his aboriginal ways, though he spent five months on Keppel shortly after it opened. In 1859, in an incident that's still subject to much speculation, he was implicated in the murder of SAMS missionaries at Tierra del Fuego but acquitted in a Stanley trial.

At remote Keppel, the SAMS operated with little government oversight and even less transparency, leading to suspicions of forced labor and abuse. Many Fuegians died at Cranmer, their graves unmarked, but in all probability crowded living fomented diseases like tuberculosis. In their homeland, living in the open air, the Fuegians survived almost without clothing.

Despite these setbacks, Keppel remained a missionary station until 1898, and while the number of Fuegians decreased, its produce brought substantial income on the Stanley market. Sold in 1911 to Dean Brothers, owners of nearby Pebble, it operated as a sheep farm until 1992.

Cruise ships sometimes stop at Keppel, where a high relief SAMS emblem embellishes the arch of the mission's woolshed. Several other mission structures are fairly intact, and there remain foundations of several Yámana houses. More recent buildings are in good condition.

While it's hard to reach Keppel other than on cruise ships, because FIGAS planes cannot land unless there is someone there in case of emergency, some locals have spoken of offering boat tours from nearby Pebble or Saunders, so it's worth asking around. In conjunction with the Falkland Islands Museum and National Trust, the Liverpool Museum has published an excellent, well-illustrated, and laminated *Keppel Island Site Guide,* available in Stanley.

## SAUNDERS ISLAND

Better than any other island in the archipelago, Saunders blends the attractions of natural history and history—its wildlife is abundant and accessible, but it's also a case study in the Falklands/Malvinas controversy.

The Falklands' second-largest offshore island, at 31,000 acres, Saunders is a roughly U-shaped landmass nearly cut into unequal segments by the east–west Brett Harbour. The settlement, though, occupies a site near Port Egmont, on the relatively sheltered east coast, almost facing Keppel.

### History

British marines first established themselves here in 1765, but after France withdrew from Port Louis, Spain discovered and expelled the Port Egmont settlement two years later—nearly sparking a shooting war in Europe. Under pressure, the Spaniards restored the Saunders settlement, but, in 1774, Britain suspended its presence for, it said, budgetary reasons. After the British departure, Spanish forces leveled the settlement.

Just north of the current settlement, Port Egmont's surviving ruins include extensive foundations and even some walls, jetties, and garden terraces that, by one account, yielded plentiful produce—mostly root crops such as potatoes and carrots, but also green vegetables such as broccoli, celery, lettuce, and spinach.

Ironically enough, long after Britain regained the Islands from Buenos Aires, Saunders became Argentine property. Scottish sheep farmer John Hamilton, who came to the Islands as an FIC shepherd in the late 19th century, re-emigrated to Santa Cruz territory, where he became a major *estanciero;* never losing interest in the Falklands, he purchased several island properties including Saunders. When Hamilton died, though, his Argentine children inherited the property, and until its sale to resident employees in 1987, its ownership was a sore point among Islanders.

## Sights

For wildlife-oriented visitors, the big attraction is **The Neck,** a sandy isthmus about four hours' walk from the settlement on the north side of Brett Harbour. On its north side, facing the open ocean, a large gentoo colony and a smaller contingent of 30 or so kings breed; for some years, a solitary chinstrap penguin made its home among the gentoos, but it's apparently headed back to the Antarctic.

The Neck's real highlight is the enormous breeding colonies of rockhopper penguins, cormorants, and especially black-browed albatrosses, who need the steep cliffs and stiff northwesterly winds beneath **Mount Richards** to launch themselves into flight. On land, these stunningly beautiful birds are ungainly but, nearly fearless of humans, they will reward photographers by waddling into close-up range.

For tireless hikers, this scenic northeastern coastline is an ideal way to return to the settlement, but its steepness, slipperiness, and high winds make it potentially hazardous. Beneath **Rookery Mountain,** more albatrosses, rockhoppers, and king cormorants breed near a new house and an old Portakabin that both offer accommodations; it is more easily accessible from the settlement proper.

Immediately west of The Neck, Magellanic penguins burrow in the coastal greens en route to **Elephant Point** (another four hours on foot), which has a substantial elephant-seal colony, as well as kelp gulls, skuas, and other birds.

February–May, there are whales offshore.

© WAYNE BERNHARDSON

trumpeting chinstrap penguin, a rare Antarctic visitor to Saunders Island

## Accommodations and Food

In the settlement proper, farm owners/managers David and Suzan Pole-Evans (tel. 41298, fax 41296, davidpe@horizon.co.fk) rent the self-catering, six-bed **Stone Cottage,** dating from 1875 but with a modernized interior, and the separate 10-bed **R&R House,** sometimes used by military guests from Mount Pleasant. Rates are £30 per person.

Wildlife enthusiasts, though, usually prefer the converted **Portakabin** (£50 pp) at The Neck, which has electricity and hot water and can sleep up to eight. It also has a gas cookstove and a full bathroom with a tub and flush toilet.

Beneath Rookery Mountain, about 50 minutes' ride north from the settlement near rockhopper and albatross colonies, **Freddie's Karavan** (£10 pp) has two bunks, hot and cold water, a peat stove, 24-hour electricity, and a small gas cookstove. Nearly alongside, the sparkling new **Rookery Inn** (£50 pp) is a comfortable modern house with two ample bedrooms, plus a combination living/dining room and kitchen.

The Pole-Evanses also permit camping (£10 pp) anywhere except near the Portakabin at The Neck proper (though it's possible not too far away, where there's piped spring water and a latrine). The farm has a small store and may sell fresh milk and eggs, but visitors should bring most supplies from Stanley. Payment is possible in British sterling or in U.S. dollars.

Children under age 10 pay half price for accommodations, with children under 5 free.

For those staying in the settlement, full board is available (£60 pp, minimum of six).

### Getting Around

Farm schedules permitting, the Pole-Evanses can provide Land Rover transfers to The Neck (£50 pp round-trip), or to The Rookery for visitors who stay at the settlement (£30 pp). Children under age 16 go free of charge.

## CARCASS ISLAND

For many Islanders and visitors alike, remote and tiny Carcass is their favorite island in the Falklands. At the northwestern edge of the archipelago, it's full of wildlife, but at the same time, it's equally notable for a home-style hospitality that belies its dependence on the tourist trade.

On the island's south shore, Carcass settlement is a sheltered beauty spot whose honeysuckle aroma and 10-foot dracaenas lend it an almost tropical aura. Curious caracaras perch in the Monterey cypress windbreaks outside the lodge's dining-room windows, the younger ones playing like kittens with string that droops from the limbs.

Unlike the larger islands, Carcass has always been a family farm, though it's changed hands several times in nearly a century and a half. The present owners, Rob and Lorraine McGill, run only about 800 sheep and make much of their living from brief cruise-ship visits and overnight guests. On meeting the FIGAS flight, Rob McGill even offers chocolates and juice on the Rover ride into the settlement.

On the shoreline in front of the settlement, the birdlife is abundant and diverse, with kelp geese, steamer ducks, Magellanic

© WAYNE BERNHARDSON

elephant seal pups, Northwest Point, Carcass Island

oystercatchers, Patagonian crested ducks, Cobb's wren, and tussock birds (small birds flourish in the absence of cats, rats, and mice). South of the settlement, there's a large tussock grass plantation with gentoo and Magellanic penguins.

At Northwest Point, several miles from the settlement but not far from the airstrip, there's a colony of perhaps 200 elephant seals. The highest point, 723-foot Mount Bing, yields views of the remote, uninhabited Jason Islands to the northwest.

Carcass, which takes its name from the 18th-century naval vessel HMS *Carcass,* has rooms with private baths in the main house (£100 pp with full board). Thanks to a wind turbine and backup generator, it now enjoys 24-hour electricity. For reservations and/or information, contact Rob or Lorraine McGill (tel. 41106, lorraine@horizon.co.fk).

## WEST POINT ISLAND

Southwest of Carcass, separated from West Falkland by a narrow strait called The Woolly Gut, West Point Island has been in the same family since 1879. Like Carcass, it gets plenty of cruise-ship visitors to see its black-browed albatrosses, Johnny rooks, Magellanic penguins, and rockhoppers, and owner Roddy Napier replanted native tussock grass on much of the shoreline. Unfortunately, because of its short and thrilling airstrip—probably too thrilling for timid fliers—FIGAS can no longer land passengers here, but Michael Clarke (tel. 41105) will shuttle passengers to and from nearby Carcas by boat; he also runs excursions to remote Steeple Jason Island (£575 for up to six persons).

## WEDDELL ISLAND

On the southwestern edge of the archipelago, sprawling Weddell is the Falklands' third-largest island, with a representative sample of wildlife and an intriguing history. Like Saunders Island, Weddell belonged to Scottish *estanciero* John Hamilton, and he and his managers undertook audacious agricultural experiments here.

### THE STAATS ISLAND GUANACOS

West of Weddell, uninhabited Staats Island is notable for supporting a population of roughly 300 guanacos, first introduced by John Hamilton in the 1930s. In such a restricted habitat, as its 500 hectares of natural vegetation declined under grazing pressure, biologists would expect large die-offs to keep the population in equilibrium. Into the 1950s, though, hunting kept the population in check – on sporadic visits, islanders culled upwards of a hundred in a week.

The culling records are, in fact, scratched into the walls of **Waldron's Shanty,** where the hunters sought shelter from wind and rain. The remarkably stable numbers since then have piqued biologists' interest in the species' population dynamics in what is, for all practical purposes, an ideal natural laboratory. The current owners have still been culling occasionally to maintain the numbers, and plan to fence off the island's north end for tussock restoration.

Some of these projects, such as replanting native tussock grass, cultivating experimental forests, and diversifying the livestock with dozens of Highland cattle and more than a hundred Shetland ponies, were commendable even if they met limited success. Others, such as introducing Patagonian foxes, were foolish; expected to provide pelts, the proliferating foxes not only caused high lamb mortality but also preyed on bird eggs.

Like Saunders, Weddell became Argentine property, but after the war it was sold to its resident managers; it has since changed hands again to a British owner. Visitors can go to Loop Head, the best wildlife site, for its gentoo and Magellanic penguins, giant petrels, great skuas, night herons, and striated caracaras. Open to visitors once again, the island offers self-catering accommodations at **Mountain View Cottage** (tel. 42398).

## NEW ISLAND

In more than one sense, New Island has always been the Falklands' "Wild West." Its rugged, precipitous headlands bursting with wildlife, including rockhopper penguins, black-browed albatrosses, and southern fur seals, it was also a lawless refuge for British and North American sealers and whalers in the late 18th and early 19th centuries. In one celebrated case, during the War of 1812, New England whaler Charles Barnard spent 18 months marooned here after being abandoned by British marines he had rescued from a shipwreck.

Remains of **Barnard's House** (now a visitors center) still stand here, as do rusting ruins of an early-20th-century **Norwegian Whaling Factory** that folded for lack of whales. In all, New Island has 41 breeding bird species, including crested and striated caracaras, and the rare thin-billed prion.

Most New Island visitors come from cruise ships, as the airstrip no longer permits FIGAS to land here (though improvement work is underway). The owners manage the property as nature reserves, and only about 50 sheep remain, primarily for food. No smoking is permitted anywhere on the island.

Ian J. Strange established the **New Island South Conservation Trust** (tel. 42317, www.newislandtrust.com) to protect wildlife colonies and historical constructions on the island.

For an account of Barnard's New Island stranding, look for his memoir *Marooned* (Middletown, Connecticut: Wesleyan University Press, 1979), edited and with an illuminating introduction by Bertha S. Dodge.

# BACKGROUND

## The Land

Patagonia's diverse geography rises from sea level through desert steppe to Andean forests and fell-fields to continental glaciers. On the Chilean side, west of the Andes, Patagonia is a well-watered and often lushly forested region, while the sparsely vegetated eastern Argentine side lies mostly in the rain shadow of the cordillera.

### GEOGRAPHY

Because there's no agreement as to Patagonia's boundaries, it's hard to calculate its size, but it's larger than most of the world's countries. From its northernmost point at the source of Argentina's Río Colorado, around 36° south latitude, it's about 2,200 kilometers as the crow flies to Cape Horn, at nearly 56° south. At the widest point, roughly 40° south, it measures nearly 1,000 kilometers from the Atlantic to the Pacific, but it narrows to barely 400 kilometers toward the tip of the continent.

Argentine Patagonia, traditionally comprising the provinces of Neuquén, Río Negro, Chubut, Santa Cruz, and Tierra del Fuego, has an area of 786,983 square kilometers, larger than Texas and about the same size as Turkey. This calculation excludes similar areas of Buenos Aires province north of the Río Negro and south of the Río Colorado, Argentine Patagonia's traditional boundary.

© WAYNE BERNHARDSON

Some contemporary analyses include La Pampa province and even parts of Mendoza.

Chilean Patagonia's limits are even more imprecise. South of the traditional Mapuche frontier on the Río Biobío, La Araucanía, Los Lagos, and the new Los Ríos region, plus the more southerly regions of Aisén and Magallanes, add up to 339,914 square kilometers, only a little smaller than present-day Germany. Counting only the "truly" Patagonian regions of Aisén and Magallanes, though, it would be just 241,058 square kilometers—still as large as the United Kingdom.

Together, the Argentine and Chilean sectors of Patagonia would total 1,126,897 square kilometers, about the size of France, Germany, and the United Kingdom combined, or of California and Texas combined.

### Mountains

Patagonia's most imposing physiographic feature is the longitudinal Andean range that extends the length of the continent to southernmost Patagonia, where it gradually disappears beneath the Pacific Ocean. The southern Patagonian Andes are lower than the uplands of Peru, Bolivia, and northernmost Chile and Argentina, but still have many glaciated peaks because of their higher latitude.

One of the world's most seismically active countries, Chile lies at the juncture of the Nazca and South American tectonic plates. Positioned along the so-called Pacific "ring of fire," it also has numerous active volcanoes—some *very* active—and many active earthquake faults. The 1960 earthquake centered near the southern city of Valdivia brought a tsunami that devastated coastal areas from Concepción to Chiloé and left many thousands homeless, and the more northerly 2010 quake had similar consequences. Seismic safety has improved, but earthquakes are not going to disappear.

### Steppes

In Patagonia's high latitudes, in the Andean rain shadow, bunch grasses and shrubs punctuate the arid, mostly level meseta (small mesa) that stretches to the Atlantic. In a few areas, eastward-flowing rivers have cut deep, scenic canyons through the bedrock.

### Rivers

On both sides of the Andes, rushing transverse rivers create recreational rafting runs and water to irrigate the vineyards of Neuquén. Some Argentine rivers reverse direction to flow through gaps into the Pacific on the Chilean side, while others, like the Río Negro and the Río Santa Cruz, traverse the Patagonian steppe to reach the Atlantic.

Chile's largest and most important rivers are the Futaleufú, still providing recreational thrills, and the remote Baker, which carries the largest flow of any Chilean river. Both, as well as other rivers, are threatened with major hydroelectric projects.

### Lakes

Both Argentina and Chile are famous for their Andean lakes districts, where the melting ice of Pleistocene glaciers has left a legacy of indigo-filled troughs. Chile's remote Aisén region and Argentina's Chubut and Santa Cruz provinces have countless large lakes barely touched by anglers. There are also large interior drainage lakes such as Chubut's Lago Musters and Lago Colhué Huapi, and Santa Cruz's Lago Cardiel.

## CLIMATE

In the Southern Hemisphere, Patagonia's seasons are reversed from the Northern Hemisphere: The summer solstice falls on December 21, the autumn equinox on March 21, the winter solstice on June 21, and the spring equinox on September 21. For most Argentines and Chileans, the summer months are January and February, when schools are out of session and families take their holidays.

In far southern latitudes, blustery maritime conditions are the rule and seasonal variations can be dramatic, but it's difficult to generalize about climate. Moreover, altitude plays a major role in all areas.

Because its receding glaciers are particularly sensitive to warming, Patagonia is a living laboratory for climate-change studies. While it's the coolest part of both countries, its inclemency is often overstated—despite its geographical position at the southern tip of the continent, it is not Antarctica. Eastern portions of Argentina's Patagonian provinces are even arid steppe, with low rainfall but frequent high winds, especially in summer. Climatically, Tierra del Fuego is an extension of mainland Patagonia.

# Flora and Fauna

Much of Patagonia's flora and fauna will be novel to foreign visitors, especially those from the Northern Hemisphere.

## CONSERVATION ORGANIZATIONS

Argentina, Chile, and the Falkland Islands all have their own conservation-oriented entities, both governmental and nongovernmental.

### Argentina

For information on protected areas and national parks, contact the **Administración de Parques Nacionales** (Av. Santa Fe 690, Retiro, Buenos Aires, tel. 011/4314-9325, www.parquesnacionales.gov.ar).

Argentina's main wildlife advocacy organization is the **Fundación Vida Silvestre Argentina** (Defensa 251, Monserrat, Buenos Aires, tel. 011/4331-3631, www.vidasilvestre.org.ar). Annual membership rates start around US$37; it publishes the bimonthly magazine *Revista Vida Silvestre,* which is excellent reading for those proficient in Spanish.

For bird-watchers, it's the **Asociación Ornitológica del Plata** (Matheu 1246/1248, Buenos Aires, tel. 011/4943-7216, www.avesargentinas.org.ar); hours are 3–9 P.M. weekdays.

The international conservation organization **Greenpeace** also has a Buenos Aires branch (Zabala 3873, Chacarita, tel. 011/4551-8811, www.greenpeace.org.ar).

For general information on mountaineering, contact the **Centro Andino Buenos Aires** (Rivadavia 1255, Oficina 2, tel. 011/4381-1566, www.caba.org.ar). There are also local and provincial mountaineering clubs.

### Chile

Chile's primary government environmental organization, in charge of national parks and other protected areas, is the **Corporación Nacional Forestal** (Conaf, Av. Bulnes 291, Santiago, tel. 02/3900282, 02/3900125, www.conaf.cl), which provides information and also sells maps, books, and pamphlets at its Santiago offices. It also has offices in every regional capital and some other cities, and visitors centers and/or ranger stations at nearly all its units.

Since the 1989 return to democracy, nonprofit environmental advocacy organizations have proliferated—so much so that their abundance may have diluted their influence. Many focus on forest preservation, arguably the country's most hot-button issue, but the country's wild and scenic southern rivers are getting ever more attention.

**Renace** (Seminario 774, tel. 02/2234483, Ñuñoa, Santiago, www.renace.cl) is a loose alliance of environmental organizations. The highly professional **Fundación Terram** (General Bustamante 24, 5-I, Providencia, Santiago, tel. 02/2694499, www.terram.cl) emphasizes sustainable development.

Chile's oldest environmental organization is the **Comité de la Defensa de Flora y Fauna** (Committee for the Defense of Flora and Fauna, or Codeff, Ernesto Reyes 035, Providencia, Santiago, tel. 02/7772534, www.codeff.cl). Since 1968, it has focused on practical projects to preserve and restore native plants and animals, often in cooperation with government agencies such as Conaf.

### Falkland Islands

**Falklands Conservation** (Jubilee Villas, 41 Ross Road, P.O. Box 26, Stanley FIQQ 1ZZ, tel. 22247, www.falklandsconservation.com) is the main conservation organization. It also has a U.K. office (14 East Hatley, Bedfordshire SG 19 3JA, tel. 1767/650639).

## VEGETATION ZONES

Floral associations are strongly, but not perfectly, correlated with latitude and altitude.

### Broadleaf and Coniferous Forest

In the Patagonian lakes region, various species of broadleaf southern beech (*Nothofagus* species), both evergreen and deciduous, are the most abundant trees. Notable conifers include the *paraguas* (umbrella) or monkey puzzle tree *(Araucaria araucana),* so called because its crown resembles an umbrella and its limbs resemble the form of a monkey's curled tail. The long-lived *alerce* or *lawen (Fitzroya cupressoides)* is an endangered species because of its high timber value, though most stands are now protected; it is more common on the well-watered Chilean side.

© WAYNE BERNHARDSON

araucaria trees, Parque Nacional Lanín

Except for specialists, Argentines and Chileans refer indiscriminately to conifers as *pinos* (pines), even though the Southern Hemisphere's only true pines (of the genus *Pinus*) occur as garden ornamentals or plantation timber.

### Temperate Rainforest

In southwestern Chilean Patagonia, heavy rainfall supports dense and verdant coastal and upland forests of mostly *Nothofagus,* though there are many other broadleaf trees and even the occasional conifer, such as the *ciprés del los Guaitecas* (Guaytecas cypress). In some areas, though, this forest has suffered severe depredations at the hands of corporations and colonists.

### Patagonian Steppe

In the Andean rain shadow, on the eastern Patagonia plains, Chilean Magallanes, and even parts of Tierra del Fuego, decreased rainfall supports extensive grasslands where the wind blows almost ceaselessly. In some areas, thorn scrub such as the fruit-bearing barberry *calafate (Berberis buxifolia)* is abundant. From the late 19th century, sheep grazing for wool had a tremendous detrimental impact on these natural pastures, but some are recovering as some *estancias* (ranches) have folded.

### Magellanic Forest

From southern Patagonia to the tip of Tierra del Fuego, Argentine and Chilean woodlands consist primarily of dense *Nothofagus* forests that, because of winds and climatic extremes, are nearly prostrate except where high mountains shelter them.

## FAUNA

As with the flora, Patagonian wildlife is largely correlated with latitude and altitude.

### Marine, Coastal, and Aquatic Fauna

The temperate to sub-Antarctic southern Atlantic and Pacific, with their lengthy coastlines and many estuaries, are a storehouse of biological wealth. That wealth, though, is more abundant in sheer numbers than in species diversity.

Upwelling nutrients and the north-flowing Peru (Humboldt) Current make Chile's coastline one of the world's richest fishing grounds (giving Chile's cuisine its character). In the far south, peoples like the Yámana and Kawéskar lived largely on maritime resources.

The main pelagic **fish** in the southern oceans include *congrio* (conger eel) *cojinova, corvina,* and the overexploited *merluza* (hake) and *merluza negra* (Chilean sea bass or Patagonian toothfish). Shellfish and crustaceans, all of them edible, include the commonplace mussel, *centolla* (king crab), the *ostión* (scallop), and *calamares* (squid, both *Loligo gahi* and *Ilex argentinus*), the target of a burgeoning fishery between the Argentine mainland and the Falklands. Particularly notable in Chile are the *loco* (abalone), *erizo* (sea urchin), and *picoroco* (giant barnacle).

**Marine mammals** include the *lobo marino* (southern sea lion), which inhabits the coastline from the Río de la Plata all the way south to Tierra del Fuego and well north into the Pacific. From Argentina's Chubut province south, the southern elephant seal and southern fur seal are both on Appendix II of the Endangered Species List (CITES), classified as threatened or regionally endangered.

The most famous of Argentine whales is the southern right whale, which breeds in growing numbers in the waters around Península Valdés. Other cetaceans found in southern waters include the blue whale, humpback whale, fin whale, sei whale, minke whale, pygmy right whale, and beaked whales. The orca or killer whale is also present, along with smaller marine mammals such as Commerson's dolphin.

## Terrestrial Fauna

Patagonia's land animals, especially large mammals, are often nocturnal or otherwise inconspicuous, but they are a diverse lot.

The largest, most widely distributed carnivore is the secretive puma or mountain lion. The smaller Andean cat *(Felis jacobita)* is an endangered species.

© WAYNE BERNHARDSON

elephant seal, Northwest Point, Carcass Island, in the Falklands

The southern river otter is an endangered species, while the Argentine gray fox qualifies as threatened.

Wild grazing mammals include the widely distributed guanaco *(Lama guanicoe),* a relative of the domestic llama and alpaca, which is most abundant on the Patagonian steppe but also inhabits parts of the high Andes. Domestic livestock like cattle, horses, burros, and goats are, of course, very common.

The South Andean huemul, a cervid that appears on Chile's coat-of-arms, is the subject of a joint conservation effort between the two countries. In the mid-19th century, there were some 22,000 in both countries, but at present only about 1,000 survive in each country south of Chile's Río Biobío because of habitat destruction, contagious livestock diseases, and unregulated hunting.

The pudu is a miniature deer found in densely wooded areas on both sides of the Patagonian Andes; like the huemul, it's difficult to spot.

Chile lacks poisonous snakes, but some species of the venomous, aggressive pit vipers known collectively as *yarará* range into the northernmost parts of Argentine Patagonia, even south of Península Valdés. They are less common in the southern part of their range than in the subtropical north, however.

## Freshwater Fish

In the Andean lakes district, introduced species include brook trout, European brown trout, rainbow trout, and landlocked Atlantic salmon. Native species (catch-and-release only) include *perca bocona* (big-mouthed perch), *perca boca chica* (small-mouthed perch), *puyén,* Patagonian *pejerrey,* and *peladilla.*

## Birds

Southern Patagonia's steppes, seacoasts, oceans, and forests can be a wonderland for birders; for visitors and especially dedicated birders from the Northern Hemisphere, the great majority are new additions to their life lists.

The Argentine Pampas' signature species may be the southern lapwing or *tero,* whose local name derives from its call, but it and

© WAYNE BERNHARDSON

gentoo penguins at Wood Cove, Port Stephens, in the Falklands

other similar species have a wide distribution. With its curved beak, the buff-necked ibis or *bandurria* is a striking presence.

The Andean condor soars along the length of the cordillera, while migratory birds like flamingos, along with coots, ducks, and geese, frequent shallow steppe lakes like Lago Musters and even much smaller bodies of water.

In northern Patagonia's dense forests, some birds are heard as often as seen, especially the reticent songbird *chucao*. Others, like the flocks of squawking Patagonian parakeets that flit through the woods, are more conspicuous.

Some 240 bird species inhabit the south Atlantic coastline and Tierra del Fuego, including the wandering albatross, with its four-meter wingspan; the black-necked swan; Coscoroba swan; flightless steamer duck; kelp gull; and several penguin species, most commonly the Magellanic or jackass penguin. Its close relative, the Humboldt penguin, is an endangered species that ranges far north on the Chilean side. Several other penguin species inhabit the Falklands.

Its numbers reduced on the Pampas, where it roamed before cattle, horses, and humans turned native grasslands into ranches and granaries, the ostrich-like *choike* or *ñandú* (greater rhea) still strides across some less densely settled parts of Argentine and Chilean Patagonia. The smaller *ñandú petiso* (lesser rhea) is fairly common in the provinces of Neuquén, Río Negro, Chubut, and Santa Cruz.

### Invertebrates

For purely practical purposes, visitors should pay attention to pests and dangers like mosquitoes, flies, and ticks, which can be disease vectors, even though maladies like malaria and dengue are almost unheard of (the mosquito vector for dengue has been spreading southward from the tropics, but the disease itself has not yet been detected). In well-watered rural areas, mosquitoes can be a real plague, so a good repellent is imperative.

The reduviid, or assassin bug, which bears trypanosomiasis (Chagas' disease) is present in Argentina, though it is hardly cause for hysteria.

# The Cultural Landscape

While Patagonia's natural landscapes, flora, and fauna are fascinating and enchanting, the region also has a cultural landscape, one transformed by human agency over the millennia. Few areas are truly pristine, but their landscapes are no less interesting for all that.

Most of pre-Columbian Patagonia was a thinly populated place of hunter-gatherers who left few conspicuous landmarks—notwithstanding globally significant aboriginal rock-art sites such as Santa Cruz province's Cueva de las Manos. Some of the continent's most important early archaeological sites are just over the border from Santa Cruz, in Chile's Magallanes region, and at Monte Verde near Puerto Montt.

In immediate pre-Columbian times, bands of nomadic hunter-gatherers peopled much of Patagonia. Living in smallish bands with no permanent settlements, they relied on wild game like the guanaco (related to the domestic llama) and the flightless *ñandú* (rhea), as well as fish, for subsistence. What remains of their material culture is primarily lithic (arrowheads, spear points, and the rounded stone balls known as *boleadoras*).

## AGRICULTURE AND THE LANDSCAPE

From the Pampas south, the European invasion utterly transformed Argentina's landscape into, first, an open range cattle zone, and, then, large fenced sheep and cattle ranches known as *estancias* that dominated the rural economy for a century-plus. In Patagonia, this took the form of the sheep *estancia,* an extensive unit producing wool for export to Europe and North America.

© WAYNE BERNHARDSON

sorting sheep at Estancia Monte Dinero, Argentina

Beyond the Biobío, in the Andean lakes district, southern Chile's pre-Columbian peoples were shifting cultivators and, as such, their impact on the landscape was not always obvious. Because they cut the forest and used fire to clear the fields before planting, their impact was significant, but long fallow periods allowed the woodlands to recover. Much of what seems virgin forest today may in fact be secondary growth.

Because Araucanians on both sides of the Andes resisted the advance of the Spaniards and, then, the Argentines and Chileans, Patagonia's agricultural colonization was spotty until the late 19th century (this, though, did not prevent the Araucanians from adopting European livestock and planting orchards of European fruits such as apples). By the early 1880s, though, Argentine general Julio Roca's ruthless military campaign against them and Chile's advance south of the Biobío ended indigenous autonomy.

On the Chilean side of the border, European settlers transformed the landscape by deforesting large areas for dairy farms and croplands; in the Aisén region, government incentives encouraged settlers to slash and burn the forest even when they lacked manpower to produce crops that, in any event, had no market.

On the drier Argentine side, irrigation was necessary to develop the Patagonian fruit basket in localities such as the Río Negro and Río Chubut valleys. A few remote localities achieved a certain success, such as Argentina's Los Antiguos and, just across the border, Chile Chico, but their remoteness made it difficult to get their products to market.

The greatest factors in transforming the natural landscape of the Falklands have been the introduction of domestic animals, first cattle and then sheep, and the impact of fire. Both have nearly eliminated the lush and nutritious native tussock grass, which fringed virtually the entire coastline before the Islands were settled. Other plant species, better adapted to grazing and trampling, have flourished over the landscape.

## SETTLEMENT LANDSCAPES

When the Spaniards took control of present-day Argentina and Chile, they tried to institute a policy of *congregación* or *reducción*. This meant concentrating native populations in villages or towns to achieve political control, impose tribute or taxes, and stimulate religious evangelization. This model had limited success in the northernmost parts of Chile's lakes district, and small, dispersed populations made it utterly impractical elsewhere in Patagonia.

Cities, of course, differ greatly from the countryside. By royal decree, Spanish-American cities were organized according to a rectangular grid surrounding a central plaza where all the major public institutions—*cabildo* (town council), cathedral, and market—were located. The logical outgrowth of *reducción* policies, Buenos Aires, Santiago, and other cities were no exception to the rule; the transformation from colonial city to modern metropolis obliterated some landmarks, but the essential grid pattern became an almost universal model for the former Spanish empire.

In the Mapuche countryside south of the Biobío, traditional *rucas* (plank houses with thatched roofs erected with community labor rather than by individual families) have nearly disappeared; they are more common on the Chilean side, where the indigenous population is larger and more cohesive. On the Chiloé archipelago, some neighborhoods of precarious *palafitos* (fishers' houses on stilts or pilings) have withstood earthquakes and tsunamis.

In colonial cities and towns, houses fronted directly on the street or sidewalk, with an interior patio or garden for family use; any setback from the street was almost unheard of. This general pattern has persisted, though building materials have mostly changed from adobe to concrete, and high-rise apartment blocks have replaced single-family houses in many urban neighborhoods. Covered by metal cladding and topped by corrugated zinc roofs, southernmost Patagonia's wood-framed, 19th-century Magellanic houses affect a Victorian style.

In recent decades, wealthier Argentines and Chileans have built houses with large gardens, on the North American suburban model, in a frenzy of conspicuous consumption—but still surrounded by high fences and state-of-the-art security. Some lie within so-called "gated communities," known in Argentina as *"countries,"* but these are uncommon in Patagonia.

On the Falkland Islands, in the camp (anything outside the "city" of Stanley is the camp), settlement landscapes resemble those of Patagonia's sprawling *estancias*—in fact, these were the prototype for the mainland as landless shepherds emigrated to take up farming in Chile and Argentina. In the Falklands' case, they were located close to the shore, to simplify the transfer of wool to Stanley.

Stanley, the Islands' only real "urban" settlement, reminds many visitors of towns and villages in Scotland or Ireland. The capital's older stone houses fit that mold, but the Magellanic style of brightly painted, metal-clad houses is as common here as it is on the southern Patagonia mainland and Tierra del Fuego.

# Environmental Issues

Like other countries, Argentina and Chile suffer from environmental degradation, though not all indicators are negative.

## AIR, WATER, AND NOISE POLLUTION

Aging diesel buses may be the primary culprit in deteriorating urban air quality, but private vehicles (some of which still run on leaded gasoline in Argentina) and taxis contribute more than their share (many taxis and private vehicles, though, run on natural gas). Superannuated factories, with subsidized smokestacks, are another source.

In Patagonia, a different sort of atmospheric problem is critical. Deterioration of the Antarctic ozone layer has exposed both humans and livestock to dangerous ultraviolet radiation in summer; though ozone depletion from aerosols is a global problem over which Argentines and Chileans have relatively little control, they suffer the consequences of the growing ozone hole.

Just as motor vehicles cause urban air pollution, so they produce most of its noise pollution, due partly to inadequate mufflers. Buses and motorcycles are the worst offenders, but Jet Skis and other "personal watercraft" on otherwise limpid, placid lakes are a source of growing concern.

Drinking water is normally potable, but a historical legacy of polluted waterways derives from, first, the proliferation of European livestock, followed by the processing of hides and livestock, and then by industry. Mining is also a factor; near the city of Esquel, Chubut, there has been concern and vociferous opposition to a Canadian project that would use cyanide, which might find its way into streams and aquifers, to extract gold from local ores.

Salmon farming, a booming and increasingly concentrated industry, causes problems with runoff, from Chile's Andean lakes region south into Aisén. Moreover, salmon often escape to colonize streams and seas at the expense of native fish, and some farmers have been accused of killing sea lions that prey on the caged fish.

## SOLID WASTE

Like other urban and rural areas, Patagonian cities can produce prodigious amounts of garbage; though the landfills are isolated, gusting winds can carry their contents for dozens of kilometers or more.

Despite the disposal problems, city streets are relatively clean even if, in the rush toward "development," there's an unfortunate reliance on disposable beverage containers and other undesirable packaging. The town of El Calafate, though, has been one of the first Patagonian municipalities to ban plastic bags.

## ENERGY

Argentina is nearly self-sufficient in fossil fuels and has substantial hydroelectric resources in the subtropical north and along the Andean foothills, but recently it's had to import petroleum from Venezuela because low prices have discouraged local producers from exploration and extraction. Argentine governments have promoted nuclear power since the 1950s; not known for its transparency, the **Comisión Nacional de Energía Atómica** (CNEA, National Atomic Energy Commission) is located in San Carlos de Bariloche.

Even hydroelectricity is no panacea, as it threatens key natural sites in both Argentina and Chile. The most threatened areas are the basins of Chile's Río Futaleufú, one of the world's top white-water rivers, and the isolated Río Baker.

## DEFORESTATION AND SOIL CONSERVATION

Native forest conservation is a hot-button issue for many Chilean activists, who have led determined and successful opposition to schemes like the Cascada Chile wood chip project in Region X (Los Lagos), which was canceled in early 2001. Clandestine logging of protected *alerce* trees in the Andean lakes district has caused occasional scandals.

According to the industry-oriented Corporación de Madera (Corma), 90 percent of the timber that arrives in Chilean factories comes from forest plantations and only 10 percent from native forests. This figure is misleading, though, in that plantations of eucalyptus and Monterey pine have replaced heavily logged native woodlands. Moreover, of the 10 million cubic meters of wood used annually for heating and cooking in Chilean households, 70 percent comes from native forests. Hydroelectric projects planned for Aisén, near the town of Cochrane, would require a 2,300-kilometer power line that would deforest a lengthy strip of land along the Carretera Austral.

Centuries of livestock activities, both grazing and trampling, have already caused serious erosion even in areas where there were never native forests, such as the Pampas and the Patagonian steppes. Even today, some forested national parks—most notably Argentina's Lanín and Los Glaciares—have failed to eliminate grazing within their boundaries. There has been pressure to create presumably sustainable forest-exploitation projects in Tierra del Fuego's Magellanic woodlands, and building roads into these areas has caused substantial damage.

### FISHING

What happens beneath the seas may be less observable than deforestation or air pollution, but there is serious concern that both small and large fisheries are overfished on both sides of the Andes. Pelagic species such as the Patagonian toothfish (often known as Chilean sea bass) are vulnerable to industrial overfishing, and inshore shellfish such as *locos* (abalone) are traditionally at risk of exploitation.

This has repercussions in the region's natural assets—overfishing for squid, for instance, *may* have contributed to Magellanic penguin deaths in the Falklands, but this controversial issue is a reasonable hypothesis rather than proven fact. Such issues, unfortunately, often get tied up in political disputes, such as Argentina's territorial claims to the Falklands or Chilean fishers' assertions that predation by sea lions is reducing their catches.

The Falklands' big environmental issue for most of its history had been the deterioration of overgrazed pastures, due to high stocking rates and insufficient fencing. In the 1980s, though, the "Squid Rush" of Asian and European fishing fleets forced the British government to declare a conservation zone and licensing regime in offshore waters that had previously been a free-for-all. Commercial fishing has revolutionized the economy and given the Islands some of the world's highest per-capita income and living standards. At the same time, some have worried that the fishery could collapse if, under pressure to maintain those standards, authorities grant too many licenses.

Meanwhile, petroleum exploration in the Falkland Islands' stormy offshore waters could also put fish and other wildlife at risk.

## History

Patagonia has an epic and complex multinational history that started long before it lodged in the European imagination.

### PREHISTORY

Human occupation of the Americas is relatively recent. The earliest immigrants reached North America from East Asia more than 12,500 years ago, when sea levels fell during the last major continental glaciation and united the two continents via a land bridge across the Bering Strait. Some researchers believe this migration, interrupted by various interglacials during which rising sea levels submerged the crossing, began tens of thousands of years earlier. In any event, by the time the bridge last closed about 10,000 years ago, the entire Western Hemisphere was populated, at least thinly, with hunter-gatherer bands occupying environments that ranged from barren, torrid deserts to sopping rainforests to frigid uplands and everything in between.

One of the continent's oldest confirmed archaeological sites is at Monte Verde, Chile, near present-day Puerto Montt. Radiocarbon dating here has given a figure of 14,000 years at a site that, according to University of Kentucky archaeologist Tom Dillehay, has some of the continent's earliest evidence of architecture, as well as use of wild potatoes and other native tubers. The most geographically proximate early human sites—later than Monte Verde—are 900 kilometers or more to the north.

At least 11,000 years ago, probably several thousand years earlier, the first inhabitants arrived as aboriginal hunter-gatherers who subsisted on guanaco, rhea, and other wild game and may even have contributed to extinction of megafauna like the ground sloth (*Mylodon* species) and the native American horse *(Onohippidium saldiasi)*.

In cave sites ranging from present-day Neuquén to Tierra del Fuego, they left clues as to the peopling of Patagonia. Their successors left vivid visual evidence of their way of life in rocky overhangs like Cueva de las Manos, in Santa Cruz province. These were essentially self-sufficient bands; only much later, around A.D. 1000, does ceramic evidence suggest contact between northernmost Patagonia and the central Andean civilizations.

As important as hunting was to the first Americans, gathering wild foods probably contributed more to the diet. As the population gradually reached saturation point under hunter-gatherer technology, they began to rely on incipient agriculture, one of whose hearths was the Peruvian highlands, but sedentary farming did not arrive in what is now Patagonia until much later.

In any event, from around 6000 B.C., beans, squash, and potatoes became the staples of an agricultural complex that, as population grew, supported a settled village life and, eventually, great Andean civilizations. Maize was a later addition, acquired from Mexico.

When the Spaniards finally arrived, according to one scholar, they found "the richest assemblage of food plants in the Western Hemisphere." Domestic animals were few, though—only the dog (sometimes raised for food), the guinea pig (definitely raised for food), and the llama and alpaca (both raised for food and fiber, with the llama also serving as a pack animal).

Slower to develop than the Andean region, at least partly due to late demographic saturation, most Patagonian peoples remained nomadic or semi-sedentary until shortly before the Spanish invasion. Some sustained a hunter-gatherer way of life even into the 20th century.

## PRE-COLUMBIAN CULTURES

In Pre-Columbian times, then, the area that is now Chile and Argentina comprised a diversity of native peoples who ranged from small isolated bands of hunter-gatherers to semi-urbanized outliers of Inka Cuzco (in present-day Peru). The Inkas' southernmost penetration took them beyond present-day Santiago, but they never managed to conquer the Araucanians—the semi-sedentary Mapuche and the closely related Pehuenche and Puelche withstood both the Inka expansion and, for more than three centuries, the invading Spaniards and their successors. More numerous on the Chilean side of the Andes, they survived because of distance from Cuzco, their mobility as shifting cultivators, and their decentralized political structure—not easily conquered or co-opted by the bureaucratic Inka.

In Patagonia, groups like the Chonos, Tehuelche (Aónikenk), Kawéskar (Alacaluf), Yámana (Yahgan), and Selk'nam (Ona) subsisted by hunting, fishing, and gathering, but introduced European diseases and outright extermination devastated their already small numbers, and sheep displaced the guanaco and rhea on which their livelihood depended.

Toward the end of the 15th century, then, just prior to the Spanish invasion of the New World, southernmost South America was a mosaic of remote peoples who either resisted domination from "civilized" outsiders or had little or no contact with them.

## EARLY HISTORY

Early Patagonian history is complex because of multiple currents of European exploration and settlement. Ferdinand Magellan's legendary expedition of 1519 spent the winter of 1520 in San Julián, Santa Cruz province, before rounding the Horn; Magellan died before returning to Spain on the first circumnavigation of the globe, but his Italian chronicler Antonio Pigafetta aroused European imaginations with exaggerated tales of Patagonian "giants." This first meeting between Europeans and Patagonians was cordial, but many succeeding encounters were not.

Pigafetta's fanciful description of the Tehuelche was not the only one of its kind, and it took more than two and a half centuries for this sort of exaggeration to fade away. As late as the 1770s, John Byron, grandfather of the celebrated poet Lord Byron, fabricated tales of Patagonians whose "middle stature seemed to be about eight feet; their extreme nine feet and upwards."

The word Patagonia itself is a matter of confusion. One explanation is that it derived from the Tehuelches' supposedly oversized feet, but the Spanish word *pata* more correctly means "paw." More probably, it came from the Spanish romance *Primaleón,* in which a giant named Patagón inhabits an island of fur-wearing hunter-gatherers.

Though little explored, the Patagonian interior was also a source of tall tales like the kingdom of Trapalanda or Trapananda, a southern El Dorado (ironically enough, no European saw real geographical marvels such as the Glaciar Perito Moreno until the 19th century). If Patagonia was a source of tall tales, though, it also saw scientifically serious expeditions like those of the Englishman John Narborough, the Frenchman Louis de Bougainville, the Spaniard Alejandro Malaspina, and, of course, Charles Darwin on the *Beagle.* It was Darwin who credibly debunked the lingering legends of "Patagonian giants":

> *We had an interview at Cape Gregory with the famous so-called gigantic Patagonians, who gave us cordial reception. Their height appears greater than it really is, from their large guanaco mantles, their long flowing hair, and general figure; on an average their height is about six feet, with some men taller and only a few shorter; and the women are also tall; altogether they are certainly the tallest race which we anywhere saw.*

### From the North

Christopher Columbus's so-called "discovery" of the New World was, of course, one of the signal events of human history. While he may have bungled his way into fame—according to geographer Carl Sauer, "The geography in the mind of Columbus was a mixture of fact, fancy, and credulity"—the incompetently audacious Genoan sailor excited the interest and imagination of Spaniards and others who, within barely half a century, brought virtually all of present-day Latin America under at least nominal control.

Europeans had roamed the Caribbean for more than three decades after Columbus's initial voyage, but the impulse to conquest in South America came from Mexico and especially Panama, which Francisco Pizarro and his brothers used as a base to take Peru. From Peru, in 1535, Pizarro's partner/rival Diego de Almagro made the first attempt to take Chile by traveling south through what is now northwestern Argentina. Crossing the 4,748-meter Paso de San Francisco from the east, Almagro's poorly organized expedition ended in grisly failure—most of his personnel, retainers, and even livestock died—but this marked the start of the Spanish presence in Argentina and Chile.

Four years later, after defeating an uprising by Almagro, Pizarro designated Pedro de Valdivia to undertake Chile's conquest, and by 1541 Valdivia had founded Santiago. In short order, he founded several other cities on or south of the Biobío, including Concepción, Villarrica, and his namesake city Valdivia.

Valdivia met his match, his own former Araucanian slave Lautaro, at the Battle of Tucapel. Before his death—according to some accounts, Valdivia pleaded for his life by offering his captors unimaginable wealth, before dying from a blow to the head—he had laid the groundwork for the country that was to become Chile.

Spanish institutions were most easily imposed in areas that had been under Inka influence, as a long history of hierarchical government made it possible for the Spaniards to place themselves atop the pyramid. In much of Spanish America, peoples accustomed to paying tribute to the Inka's delegate now paid it to the *encomendero,* the Spanish crown's representative, but Patagonia developed differently.

## COLONIAL PATAGONIA

Not permanently settled until 1580, Buenos Aires was not Patagonia, but what happened there affected Patagonia dramatically. On the surrounding Pampas, the Querandí and other indigenous groups had subsisted on guanacos, rheas, and other game, in addition to edible fruits and plants they gathered, but these resources were inadequate, and culturally inconceivable, for the Spaniards.

The failed Pedro de Mendoza expedition of 1535, though, had left behind horses that proliferated on the lush but thinly populated Pampas pastures, and the multiplication of escaped cattle from Juan de Garay's 1580 expedition rapidly transformed the Buenos Aires backcountry and northernmost Patagonia into a fenceless feral cattle ranch. The abundance of horses and cattle, nearly free for the taking, fostered Argentina's famous gaucho culture.

After 1776, when Buenos Aires became capital of the newly created Virreinato del Río de la Plata (Viceroyalty of the River Plate), the Spaniards began to establish a presence in Atlantic Patagonia, founding the cities of Carmen de Patagones and Viedma.

South of the Chilean heartland, the Araucanians quickly adopted the Spanish-introduced horse—bringing mounts across the Andes from Argentina—and staved off the Spaniards and then the Chileans for more than three centuries. In fact, the territory south of the Biobío was widely known as a separate country called "Arauco." In distant Patagonia and Tierra del Fuego, the situation was even more tenuous, as tentative Spanish colonization efforts failed disastrously because of poor planning and environmental conditions for which they were unprepared.

### The Demise of Colonial Spain

When Napoleon invaded Spain, in the early 19th century, the glue that held its colonial possessions together began to dissolve, leading to independence in several steps. Patagonia was marginal to this struggle, in which an evolving sense of metropolitan identity contributed to political change.

In the early generations, people identified themselves as Spaniards, but over time criollos (American-born Spaniards) began to differentiate themselves from *peninsulares* (European-born colonists). It bears mention that while the mestizos and even the remaining indigenous population may have identified more closely with Argentina or Chile than Spain, it was the criollo intelligentsia to whom independence had the greatest appeal.

The South American independence movements commenced on the periphery, led by figures such as Argentina's José de San Martín, Venezuela's Simón Bolívar, and Chile's Bernardo O'Higgins, but their heroism rested on a broad base of support. In Buenos Aires, this base developed as opportunistic and unauthorized British forces, taking advantage of Spain's perceived weakness, occupied the city in 1806 and 1807, but a grassroots uprising ejected the invaders and gave the Porteños confidence.

Returning from Spain, San Martín led criollo forces against royalist armies deployed from Peru, in what is now northwestern Argentina and over the Andes into Chile. As both countries soon declared independence, the polities that would rule Patagonia began to take shape; San Martín honorably refused to head the new Chilean government, leaving it to his colleague O'Higgins.

## THE SETTLEMENT OF PATAGONIA

Political independence meant less in Patagonia than it did in the rest of Argentina and Chile, though the isolationist dictator Juan Manuel de Rosas of Buenos Aires dominated a loose confederation of provinces from 1829 until his overthrow in 1852. In the 1830s, he drove the Araucanians westward out of Buenos Aires province toward the Andean lakes district, but the real challenge was the Patagonian frontier to the south and west.

In immediate pre-Columbian times, the semi-sedentary Mapuche and their other Araucanian allies crossed the northern Patagonian Andes freely, occupying Tehuelche territory and mixing with them, and they continued to do so after the Spanish invasion. Acquisition of the Old World horse, which the Mapuche soon mastered, allowed them to keep their autonomy even as the Spaniards and then the Argentines advanced southward. After Darwin met Rosas, he sorrowfully foretold the aborigines' demise:

> *Every one here is fully convinced that this is the justest war, because it is against*

*barbarians. Who would believe that in this age in a Christian civilised country that such atrocities were committed?...Great as it is, in another half century I think there will not be a wild Indian in the Pampas north of Río Negro.*

The Argentines and their European immigrant allies advanced on several fronts, by differing means. In the 1860s foreign minister Guillermo Rawson struck a deal granting Welsh dissidents farms in coastal Chubut, from where they moved westward up the river to the Andes. General Julio Argentino Roca, though, wanted to complete the job begun by Rosas, while the Araucanians, for their part, continued to raid the frontier for cattle and horses.

In 1879, the politically ambitious Roca initiated his euphemistically titled Conquista del Desierto (Conquest of the Desert), a merciless military campaign that rode across La Pampa, Neuquén, and Río Negro to displace the Mapuche and other Araucanians in favor of settlers' cattle and sheep; at the same time, it was a preemptive strike against Chilean territorial ambitions. On the strength of his success, Roca became president in 1880; the subsequent arrival of the railway from the coast accelerated the process and opened the fertile Río Negro valley to agricultural development.

Around the same time, the government began to encourage Scottish settlers, many of them from the Falkland Islands, into the southern territories of Chubut, Santa Cruz, and Tierra del Fuego, to conquer Patagonia with sheep. With the definitive settlement of southern Patagonia, Argentina reached its maximum territorial expansion, though precise boundaries with Chile remained to be settled.

Meanwhile, at the same time Chile warred with Bolivia and Peru for control of nitrate-rich northern deserts, it also turned its attention to the troublesome Araucanian frontier and, soon thereafter, consolidated its position in Patagonia. In 1881, treaties with the Mapuche paved the way for European, largely German, immigration beyond the Biobío. The war with Bolivia and Peru probably cost Chile much of what is now far southern Argentina, but the growth of Punta Arenas, thanks to the California Gold Rush and the subsequent wool boom, contributed to the country's newfound prosperity.

Argentine Patagonia remained peripheral to, though hardly exempt from, the turmoil of 20th-century Argentine phenomena like Peronism and the countless coups that eventually culminated in the 1976–1983 "Dirty War," in which a bloodthirsty military dictatorship tortured and killed thousands of mostly leftist opponents and presumed opponents. It led the country into a foolish war with Great Britain over the Falklands (known to Argentines as the Malvinas).

Only a few years earlier, in 1978, the Argentine and Chilean dictatorships had nearly gone to war over three small islands in the Beagle Channel, south of Ushuaia. Papal mediation resolved that conflict without bloodshed, but General Augusto Pinochet's regime clearly looked the other way when British forces used Chilean territory to conduct mainland commando operations against Argentina in the Falklands war.

Southernmost Patagonia also played a role in the campaign against "subversives" that followed Pinochet's 1973 coup against constitutional president Salvador Allende. Once a Salesian missionary outpost, remote Isla Dawson, southwest of Punta Arenas, served the regime as an inescapable prison camp.

## PATAGONIA TODAY

Today, thanks to fishing, industrial preferences, and tourism, Argentine Patagonia (including Tierra del Fuego) is the country's fastest-growing region, with the most positive demographic indicators. Between 1980 and 2010, Tierra del Fuego's population more than quadrupled, while Neuquén's and Santa Cruz's more than doubled. Chubut grew by 79 percent.

Patagonia now has some of Argentina's highest employment rates outside of Buenos Aires, and some of the highest mean monthly incomes, lowest poverty rates, and lowest mortality rates. It has the highest percentage rate of potable water and sewer service, and the highest literacy rates.

Ironically, the Argentine economic implosion of 2001–2002 revived the wool industry, as the new exchange rate made the Argentine clip more competitive internationally; at the former one-to-one rate with the U.S. dollar, production costs were impossibly high. At the same time, Australia's drought-depleted flocks and wool stocks raised demand elsewhere, and oil price increases made wool more competitive with synthetic petroleum-based fibers: Prices that were US$3 per kilogram rose to US$9 per kilogram and, in peso terms, earnings quadrupled. More recently, they have fallen to US$2–5 per kilogram, depending on the fiber diameter, quality, and yield, but the price of lamb and mutton doubled in 2009–2010, so that even fine wool growers are paying more attention to improving lambing rates.

Likewise, in 2002, mutton exports from Santa Cruz doubled, thanks partly to worries about mad cow disease in Europe. At present, a state-of-the-art abattoir owned by provincial growers has helped improve exports to Spain and the European Union, and also to Middle Eastern countries, which, with their Muslim populations and Halal dietary laws, lead global demand.

Before World War II, Santa Cruz province had 1,500 *estancias* with 7.5 million sheep, a figure that fell in the 1990s from four million on 1,200 to two million on 600. After a series of bad winters and a natural disaster in the ash-laden 1992 eruption of Chile's Volcán Hudson, some farms were abandoned. Some economically desperate *estancieros* may have even set fires to collect on insurance, and perhaps set outbuildings afire to avoid their designation as historic structures that they would have been obliged to maintain (with no economic assistance).

More recently, though, a promotional sheep law and low interest loans with easy terms have helped repopulate the pastures, which now graze some 2.4 million sheep. Chubut, the top wool-growing province, has 3.8 million sheep, while Río Negro has 1.45 million and the Argentine side of Tierra del Fuego 380,000. Neuquén's sheep population is minimal, having been displaced by Hereford cattle.

Some beneficiaries of the boom have been foreign companies who bought the best properties at bargain prices. In Santa Cruz, sheep still outnumber humans by ten to one, and Patagonia's largest wool producer, the Italian conglomerate Benetton, owns flagship ranches like Estancia El Cóndor near Río Gallegos. Now running some 250,000 sheep on about 900,000 hectares, Benetton has introduced sustainable production techniques on its pastures, has planted windbreaks against erosion, and has purchased a 30 percent interest in an Italian-owned wool-processing plant in Trelew so that it can export its produce in final form.

Devaluation also made tourism competitive. For much of the 1990s, Argentines took their vacations in Chile or other "inexpensive" countries like the United States, but the exchange rate trend has since reversed, so that Chileans and other foreigners are flocking to Argentine Patagonia. Summers since 2003 have been a bonanza for Patagonian tourism; increased demand has brought steadily rising prices, but they're still reasonable by international standards.

Chilean Patagonia's population has also grown, but less dramatically than Argentina's. Since the 1982 census, thinly settled Aisén's population has grown by 58 percent, but Magallanes by only 21 percent. Much closer and more accessible to Santiago than comparable Argentine provinces, the regions of La Araucanía and Los Lagos grew by 38 and 53 percent respectively.

As the Chilean peso has strengthened against the dollar and held its own with the euro, the reversal of the exchange rate has made Chile expensive for Argentine tourists, most of whom have had to take their vacations in their own country instead of Pucón or Puerto Varas. Unlike in Argentina, the Chilean wool sector has not benefited from devaluation and falling production costs for export.

Chile's relatively high costs have not yet deterred overseas visitors, though—there's only one Torres del Paine, so Patagonian tourism continues to grow.

# Government and Politics

In both Chile and Argentina, Patagonian politics differ from those of the rest of the country in some important ways. Argentine federalism has encouraged a certain provincial autonomy, while Chilean unitarianism has engendered skepticism and even resentment in both Aisén and Magallanes. In the latter case, it's not unusual to see unofficial flags and bumper stickers of the "República Independiente de Magallanes" (Independent Republic of Magallanes).

These are not just theoretical issues. During the Argentine financial collapse of 2001–2002, for instance, Santa Cruz's then-governor (later president), Néstor Kirchner, was able to shift US$660 million in provincial oil revenues to overseas banks, thus avoiding the pesification and devaluation of the province's financial assets (it's worth adding that Santa Cruz residents objected to President Kirchner's meddling in provincial issues). Chilean citizens of Magallanes, meanwhile, argue that the decisions that affect their daily lives take place in Santiago, not Punta Arenas.

Traditionally, one of Patagonia's hot-button issues has been "territorial integrity," as the two countries have argued over accurate borders for nearly a century. In the 20th century, border guards even died in shootouts, and full-scale war nearly broke out over three small Beagle Channel islands in 1978. All these disagreements have now been settled, but a handful of extreme nationalists on both sides still grit their teeth and grimace. Some Chileans fret and the more extreme seethe over U.S. environmental philanthropist Douglas Tompkins's initiatives to create private nature reserves and national parks in continental Chiloé (Los Lagos region) and Aisén, in their belief that these compromise the country's territoriality.

The highest-profile territorial issues, though, are Argentina's claims to the Islas del Atlántico Sur (including the British-ruled Falkland/Malvinas Islands and South Georgia) and Antártida Argentina (an Antarctic wedge below 60° south latitude between 25° and 74° west longitude). Many Argentine politicians and citizens of the southern Patagonian provinces, especially Santa Cruz and Tierra del Fuego, are vociferous on the Malvinas controversy—especially since petroleum exploration has begun there.

While Argentina is persistent and vocal in its claims to the Falklands and South Georgia, it acknowledges that Antarctic claims are on hold by international treaty. Chile reserves an Antarctic area between 53° and 90° west longitude, but the oldest Antarctic claim belongs to Great Britain: British Antarctic Territory lies between 20° and 80° west latitude. Fortunately, these overlapping claims have not precluded international cooperation on the frozen continent.

## ORGANIZATION

### Argentina

Argentina's federal system superficially resembles that of the United States, with executive, legislative, and judicial branches at the national level and parallel institutions for each of the 23 provinces and the Ciudad Autónoma de Buenos Aires (Autonomous City of Buenos Aires).

At the national level, the Congreso Nacional (legislative branch) consists of a 257-member Cámara de Diputados (Chamber of Deputies) and a 72-member Senado (Senate, with three members for each province and the city of Buenos Aires). In reality, as head of the executive branch, the president wields great discretionary powers, often governs by decree, and frequently intervenes in provincial affairs.

Provincial governments establish their own budgets, but the federal government funds them through revenue-sharing—a formula that has led to irresponsibly large deficits in some provinces that the feds are obliged to cover. This varies from province to province—oil-rich Santa Cruz, for instance, is solvent, but Neuquén's extensive social services have put a strain on local revenues.

### Chile

Chile's national government consists of separate

and legally independent executive, legislative, and judicial branches, but its 14 regions, plus the Metropolitan Region of Santiago, lack the autonomy of Argentina's provinces—their governors, for instance, are appointed from the president's office in Santiago. At the same time, municipalities do have considerable autonomy in local matters.

At the national level, the bicameral Congreso Nacional (National Congress) consists of a 38-member Senado (Senate) and a 120-member Cámara de Diputados (Chamber of Deputies), both based in Valparaíso. Constitutional reform has eliminated eight so-called "institutional" senators, a dictatorial legacy that included ex-presidents and former armed forces heads. Based in Santiago, the 21-member Corte Suprema is the highest judicial authority.

### Falkland Islands

As a British Overseas Territory, the Falkland Islands are a political anomaly. The governor is an appointee of the Foreign and Commonwealth Office (FCO) in London; the United Kingdom controls foreign and civil service affairs, but the local Legislative Council (Legco) is an elected eight-member body with considerable autonomy. Legco members serve four-year terms, and selected members advise the governor as part of his Executive Council (Exco), along with the chief executive (normally an expatriate Briton recruited and appointed by local government) and financial secretary.

Local political issues are mostly practical matters, including education and public works. On an international level the biggest concern is Argentina, which most Islanders instinctively have distrusted even before the 1982 invasion. Related practical issues include air links with Chile, on which Islanders rely for both their own convenience and for the tourism and fisheries industries. Connections with Punta Arenas, their preferred airport, are subject to permission to fly over Argentine territory; the South Atlantic fishery, which is the Falklands' main revenue source, relies on migratory stocks that move from Argentine offshore waters into local seas, and vice versa.

Islanders are virtually unanimous that they wish to remain British, but some are disposed toward friendlier commercial and political relations than others. Those opposed argue that there needs to be greater reciprocity on the Argentine side.

## BUREAUCRACY

The government institutions most travelers are likely to come into contact with are immigration, customs, and police. Most visitors have little contact with the Argentine or Chilean military, who were notorious for political repression in the 1970s and 1980s but now keep a low profile.

### Argentina

Argentine immigration and customs generally treat foreigners fairly, but the police are notoriously corrupt. The capital's Policía Federal are generally superior to provincial forces, some of whom are infamous for shaking down motorists for bribes for minor equipment violations, but this is less common in the Patagonian provinces.

### Chile

Unlike most other Latin American countries, Chile has a reputation for honesty in public administration—regularly, the country receives the region's highest rating from the anti-corruption organization Transparency International.

Chile's immigration, customs, and police are trustworthy as institutions; the Carabineros (national police) might be best categorized as "firm but fair." There have been instances, though, of renegade cops who rob, steal, and intimidate, especially in lower-class neighborhoods.

### Falkland Islands

The Falklands bureaucracy is exemplary in terms of honesty, but unyielding in enforcing rules "by the book." Immigration officials, for instance, invariably question arriving visitors as to their local accommodations, admit them for exactly the time their resources permit, and make it clear that nonresidents may not work. Like the Chilean Carabineros, local police are firm but fair (and do not carry firearms).

# Economy

## ARGENTINA

To most foreign observers, Argentina's economy is an enigma. Rich in natural resources, with a well-educated populace and modern infrastructure, for most of seven decades it has lurched from crisis to crisis, with the notable exception of the stable, prosperous 1990s. In late 2001, it stunned the world and even many Argentines by defaulting on part of its US$141 billion foreign debt, triggering a political and economic meltdown comparable to the Great Depression of the 1930s.

Much of the problem was attributable to high-level corruption and a rigid exchange policy that was particularly tough on Patagonia, where production costs for wool remained high in international terms. The subsequent devaluation, though, made Patagonian wool an attractive international commodity, and competitive prices spurred a tourism boom throughout the country, but especially in Patagonia.

International tourism, which accounts for about 8 percent of Argentine exports, and domestic travel are significant economic factors. As Argentina's main gateway, the city of Buenos Aires benefits more than any other locality from the tourist trade, but Patagonia is the ultimate destination for many of the more than two million who pass through the capital.

## CHILE

While not Latin America's largest economy, Chile is one of the region's most stable and dynamic. For nearly two decades, its economic performance has been one of almost uninterrupted growth, though the dramatic 7.6 percent average for the decade that ended in 1998 has fallen into the 5 percent range. With a fishing and retail boom, the southern Patagonian Region XII (Magallanes) has enjoyed growth in the 5–6 percent range and a relatively low unemployment rate of only 5.5 percent in the third quarter of 2010.

Perhaps the economy's most obvious weakness is its continuing dependence on mining in general and copper in particular. It's also vulnerable to energy shortages, which have fostered pressure to develop Aisén's remote rivers for hydroelectricity, with high transmission costs and even greater environmental risk. A general economic contraction in Aisén, though, has put on additional pressure to complete such projects.

After mining, the single most important export contributor is forestry, constituting roughly 13 percent of exports. It's a controversial sector for environmental reasons, as overharvesting of native forests and their subsequent replacement by plantations of exotics like Monterey pine and eucalyptus have created biological deserts. It's also controversial for social and political reasons, as forestry companies have occupied ancestral lands of the Mapuche, who are increasingly vocal in seeking their return.

One interesting agricultural development is a plan to establish organic agricultural standards for all of Region XI (Aisén), which would ease the export of products like beef to the European community. This could also apply to fruit growing in the small but productive "banana belt" around Lago General Carrera, and even to fish farming.

Thanks to the productive north-flowing Humboldt or Peru Current, which parallels the coast, Chile has become one of the world's leading fisheries countries. A more recent development is salmon farming in the cool ocean inlets and glacial lakes from the Andean Lakes district south through Aisén and into Magallanes, but this flourishing industry has had high environmental costs.

Tourism is a key economic sector from Chile's lakes district to the tip of Cape Horn. Once nearly limited to January and February, the season is lengthening, and overseas visitors, in particular, have flocked to Aisén and Magallanes. Chile's lakes district lost much of its traditional market, at least temporarily, with the Argentine economic collapse of 2001–2002, and Chilean vacationers aggravated the situation by passing their own holidays at giveaway prices in Argentina.

According to most surveys, poverty is declining throughout most of the country, but southern Patagonian rates in Aisén (Region XI) actually increased by 5.6 percent since 2008. Aisén and Magallanes (Region XI), though, had relatively low rates of 12 and 9.3 percent compared with the region of La Araucanía (Region IX), where the rate was 27.1 percent. The Araucanía's level, the country's highest, correlates with the impoverished Mapuche population.

## FALKLAND ISLANDS

For more than a century, wool dominated the Falklands' economic life through sprawling sheep farms that closely resembled or were even the forerunners of the Patagonian sheep *estancia.* Since 1986 it's a distant second or even third to fishing and tourism. There are about 460,000 sheep on 88 farms, with an average of around 5,200 sheep on about 25,000 acres. Most of the population lives in Stanley, though, where the main employers are government, the Falkland Islands Company (FIC), and small businesses.

In 1986, establishment of an exclusive fishing zone around the Islands led to a licensing regime whose revenues transformed the economy into one that, given the small population, now enjoys one of the world's highest per-capita GDPs (around US$32,000 per person, having fallen because of the weak British pound) and standards of living.

In the 2008–2009 fiscal year, fisheries revenue amounted to £11.2 million (about US$18.5 million). Though it's the economy's most vigorous sector, it's also vulnerable to boom and bust as squid, the most valuable species, has a short life cycle. In 2004, with apparently falling stocks, local government had to reduce the number of licenses and make budget cuts.

Some observers worry that a collapse in squid and other fish stocks could cause revenue shortfalls that would make it impossible to support the Falklands' infrastructure of ports, roads, schools, and a new hospital—not to mention the 600 or so civil servants who administer and maintain them. There's hope that offshore petroleum might pick up the slack, but results so far have been mixed—petroleum is present, but it's not clear that the quantity recoverable and the cost of extraction would justify the effort.

For an isolated archipelago, the tourism sector is well developed. In the 2009–2010 season, 48,359 cruise-ship passengers disembarked in the wildlife-rich Islands at £18 per head in landing fees. The total revenue of some £870,462 (about US$1,319,000) made this local government's second-largest revenue earner after fishing. Private sector farmers with wildlife sites also earn landing fees (around £10 per head), a valuable supplement to wool and mutton income, and service providers such as wildlife lodges, bus and taxi services, a market garden, and a butcher have also benefited.

# The People

## ARGENTINA

According to the October 2010 census, Argentina has 40,091,539 inhabitants, but detailed results are not yet available. The Patagonian provinces, though, are thinly populated—among them, Neuquén, Río Negro, Chubut, Santa Cruz, and Tierra del Fuego total slightly more than 5 percent of the country's population in more than 28 percent of its territory.

Argentina is a country of immigrants, both recent and not-so-recent, and Patagonia's population reflects that history. Spaniards, of course, first colonized what is now Argentina, but a 19th-century tsunami of Italians, Basques, English, Irish, Welsh, and other nationalities have spread throughout the country. In Patagonia, Anglo-Argentines and Yugoslavs have a high profile, along with

## *EL VOSEO*

Along with Uruguayans, Paraguayans, and some Central Americans, Argentines commonly use the distinctive second-person familiar form of address known as *el voseo* (use of the pronoun *vos*). Spaniards and most other Latin Americans, by contrast, employ the *tuteo* (use of the pronoun *tú*) in most circumstances.

Use of the *voseo*, a mostly archaic form dating from the 16th and 17th centuries, involves different verb endings for all regular and most irregular verbs. This means adding a final-syllable accent for stress – instead of *tú hablas*, for instance, Argentines will say *vos hablás*. Likewise, with an irregular verb such as *decir* (to say), Argentines will also say *vos decís* rather than *tu dices*.

In the imperative form, there are also differences – instead of *ven* (come), Argentines say *vení*. Negative imperatives, though, are the same in both *tuteo* and *voseo;* e.g., *no vengas* (don't come). Some very common verbs, such as *ir* (to go) and *estar* (to be) are similarly irregular in both *voseo* and *tuteo*, but others are not. In the *voseo*, for instance, *tu eres . . .* becomes *vos sos . . . .*

Despite differing verb forms, Argentines still use the possessive article *tu* and the reflexive or conjunctive object pronoun *te (¿te vas?)*. Alert travelers will quickly recognize the differences but should hesitate before using the form, considered substandard in some contexts. Visitors may wish to refrain from using *voseo* unless absolutely certain it's appropriate. The *tuteo* is never incorrect, though it may sound quaint in some contexts.

working-class Chilotes from the Chilean archipelago of Chiloé.

Argentina has the smallest indigenous population of any South American country except Uruguay, though certain provinces and regions have significant concentrations. There are no definitive statistics, but perhaps 40,000–90,000 Mapuches reside in La Pampa, Neuquén, and Río Negro provinces, with far smaller numbers of Tehuelches and others in the southern provinces of Chubut, Santa Cruz, and Tierra del Fuego.

## CHILE

According to a 2010 estimate (the next census will take place in 2012), Chile's population is 17,094,270, but, as in Argentina, the distribution is skewed. More than 40 percent of Chileans live in the Santiago Metropolitan Region, and nearly a third in the capital city itself. Fewer than 2.2 million, only about 14 percent, live in the regions of La Araucanía, Los Ríos, and Los Lagos, and the Patagonian regions of Aisén and Magallanes, which together compose about 45 percent of Chilean territory.

In the truly Patagonian jurisdictions of Aisén and Magallanes, the statistics are even more extreme; only about 260,000 people, barely 1.5 percent of the population, live on nearly a third of the country's surface. In Aisén alone, only about 104,000 residents, barely half a percent of all Chileans, inhabit about 15 percent of the country's territory.

Chile's population is largely mestizo, of mixed Spanish and indigenous heritage, but roughly a million Mapuche inhabit the area south of the Biobío—not to mention Santiago boroughs such as Cerro Navia, La Pintana, El Bosque, Pudahuel, and Peñalolén (80 percent of Chile's indigenous population lives in urban areas, only 20 percent in the countryside).

The Mapuche, whose vernacular language of Mapudungun is vigorously used, constitute about 90 percent of Chile's total indigenous population; there are remnants of the Kawéskar (Alacaluf) and Yámana (Yahgan) in the southern fjords and rainforests of Aisén and Magallanes.

The surnames of Chile's nonindigenous populations suggest a potpourri of nationalities, from Spanish to Basque, Italian, German, Anglo, and many others, but they do not form such obvious ethnic communities as, say, Italian-Americans in New York or Irish-Americans in Boston. Chilean Patagonia's population resembles that of Argentine Patagonia, with a particularly strong representation of Croats.

## FALKLAND ISLANDS

On a much smaller scale, the Falklands' population distribution is even more extreme than that of either Argentine or Chilean Patagonia. According the the 2006 census, the permanent population is 2,478 (excluding 477 civilian support workers at the Mount Pleasant military base). Mount Pleasant is home to about 1,200 people, including British troops, both officers and "squaddies" on four-month tours of duty.

Of the Falklands' permanent residents, 2,115 (about 85 percent) live in the capital of Stanley. The rest are dispersed among the 12,173 square kilometers of the two main islands, East Falkland and West Falkland, and the smaller offshore islands. Some 1,339 (about 54 percent) were Falklands-born, with as many as seven generations of history in the Islands. Most of the rest came from the United Kingdom, but there is a Chilean contingent of 161, as well as nearly 60 other nationalities. Of the Mount Pleasant support workers, about 400 came from the South Atlantic island of St. Helena.

Most of the original 19th-century immigrants were English and Scottish laborers and shepherds, some of whom migrated to "The Coast" of Patagonia, as they referred to it. At the same time, Britain has long remained "home," and prosperous landowners traditionally sailed there to escape the austral winter and even sent their children there for secondary and university education.

Today, Falklands schools are on a United Kingdom schedule, so that students who finish their A levels here may now continue their university education in the United Kingdom without a break. Thanks to fishing revenues, local government funds university education—"even their beer money," according to one local commentator—even for indifferent students. This, ironically, is the other extreme from the time when university education was the privilege of landowners' children.

## LANGUAGE

Spanish is Argentina's official language, but English is widely spoken in the tourist and business sectors of the economy. Foreign language use is also vigorous among ethnic communities such as Italian-Argentines, Anglo-Argentines, and German-Argentines. The Anglo-Argentine and business communities even support a daily tabloid, *The Buenos Aires Herald,* while the German-Argentine community has the weekly *Argentinisches Tageblatt.* Welsh is making a comeback in Chubut province.

Spanish, likewise, is Chile's dominant language, but perhaps 400,000 speak the Mapuche vernacular of Mapudungun, with half of those active users. As in Argentina, English is a fairly common second language in the tourism sector and the business community, and the government's policy is to broaden the use of the language.

In the Falklands, English is the official language and the language of preference. Many locals handle basic Spanish or better, but some are reluctant to speak it because of their antipathy toward Argentina. At the same time, others are taking Spanish lessons to improve their business communications with the South American continent—preferably with Chile.

# Arts and Entertainment

Both Argentina and Chile have made contributions to the arts and literature well beyond the size of their relatively small populations (there are about 17 million Chileans and 40 million Argentines). Patagonia, though, is still a frontier in Southern Cone arts and entertainment.

## LITERATURE

Much of Argentine literature is urban and urbane, but not all of it. In the 19th century, even as the free-roaming gaucho was becoming a wage laborer on the *estancias,* Argentine literature enshrined his most positive qualities in José Hernández's epic poem *Martín Fierro* (1872 and 1879), available in many editions and in English translation. This so-called *gauchesco* (gauchesque) tradition has never completely disappeared.

Born of U.S. immigrant parents in Buenos Aires province, William Henry Hudson (1841–1922) left Argentina for London at the age of 33, but his memoir *Long Ago and Far Away* (1922) is a staple of Argentine public education. An accomplished amateur naturalist, he also wrote *Idle Days in Patagonia* (1893), about his birding explorations. Argentines know him as Guillermo Enrique Hudson.

Chile is famous for its poets; the progenitor of them all was the conquistador Alonso de Ercilla (1533–1594), who paid his indigenous adversaries tribute in the 16th-century epic *La Araucana,* about the southern frontier that is now the lakes district. The first Chilean-born poet of note was Pedro de Oña (1570–1643), whose *Arauco Domado* (Arauco Tamed) extols the Spaniards' martial achievements, particularly those of García Hurtado de Mendoza, whom Ercilla had disparaged.

## VISUAL ARTS

Buenos Aires is a city of monuments. Unfortunately, many if not most are pretentious busts of ostensible statesmen and colossal equestrian statues of military men like Patagonian invader Julio Argentino Roca, who also makes a horseback appearance in Bariloche's landmark Centro Cívico.

Chilean public art can be comparably pompous, but there are agreeable surprises like Castro's Museo de Arte Moderno (Modern Art Museum), on the Isla Grande de Chiloé.

## ARCHITECTURE

Argentine architect Alejandro Bustillo, who designed many luxurious Buenos Aires buildings, also created a magnificent northern Patagonian style with Bariloche's landmark Centro Cívico. His many imitators, though, have failed to achieve the same harmony of nature and culture, and many European-styled structures in the region are derivative.

Indigenous architecture survives in thatched Mapuche *rucas,* which are more common on the Chilean side of the Andean lakes district. In Chilean towns like Puerto Varas, 19th-century German immigration has left a legacy of shingled houses that seem straight out of Bavaria. The archipelago of Chiloé has become a UNESCO World Heritage Site for its churches and chapels—the diversity of shingle designs is truly extraordinary—but its remaining *palafitos* (houses on stilts or pilings) are a treasure of vernacular architecture.

Southernmost Patagonia, especially the Chilean city of Punta Arenas, is notable for the mansions erected during the wool boom of the late 19th and early 20th centuries but also for more modest wooden-framed, metal-clad Magellanic houses. Some of the best are in the town of Porvenir, on the Chilean side of the Isla Grande de Tierra del Fuego, but many remain along Argentine Patagonia's Atlantic coastline and on its side of Tierra del Fuego.

## MUSIC

It's hard to identify a distinctive Patagonian music, but even high culture has reached the provinces. Punta Arenas tenor Tito Beltrán (born 1965), a Swedish resident for a decade

© KAMILA KOWALSKA/123RF

Castro's Iglesia San Francisco, an example of the architectural tradition of Chiloé, Chile

and a half, is widely considered one of the world's best opera singers in his range and has sung alongside Luciano Pavarotti.

## CINEMA

Like the American West, thinly populated Patagonia has a hold on the imagination, but that hasn't quite translated into a comparable cinematic notoriety. Nevertheless, cinephiles can explore the region on video, DVD, and occasionally the big screen.

Chileans have played a greater role in global cinema than most people realize, though it's best not to exaggerate. It has its origins, surprisingly enough, in the tiny Tierra del Fuego town of Porvenir, where German-born José Bohr made an early movie before eventually finding an erratic career in Hollywood.

With state support in the late 1960s and early 1970s, talented but noncommercial Chilean filmmakers, such as Miguel Littín (born 1942), did some truly audacious work; he's best known for *Alsino and the Condor* (1983), filmed in exile in Nicaragua, which earned an Academy Award nomination for Best Foreign Film. His most recent effort, though, is *Tierra del Fuego* (2000), characterized by the director as an "existentialist western." Filmed on both sides of the Argentine-Chilean border, Chilean director Alex Bowen's *Mi Mejor Amigo* (My Best Enemy, 2005) is a tragicomedy about the 1978 near-war between the two countries.

The classic Patagonian film, though, is Argentine director Héctor Olivera's *La Patagonia Rebelde* (1974), based on Osvaldo Bayer's fictional treatment of the anarchist uprising in Santa Cruz province in the early 1900s. Tristan Bauer's *Iluminados por el Fuego* (Blessed by Fire, 2005) tells the tale of the 1982 Falklands war between Argentina and Britain from the viewpoint of Argentina's maltreated conscripts; the closing scenes were actually shot in the Islands.

Fans of the offbeat can look for director Emilio Vieyra's *Sangre de Virgenes* (Blood of the Virgins, 1967), presumably the finest vampire flick ever filmed in Bariloche and available on DVD through the British distributor

MondoMacabro (www.mondomacabro.co.uk). In Brazilian director Walter Salles's *The Motorcycle Diaries* (2004), a young Ernesto "Che" Guevara tours the region.

Starting with a bungled Buenos Aires bank robbery, Marcelo Piñeyro's *Wild Horses* (1995) becomes a road romance that ends with a chase in the Patagonian province of Chubut.

## CRAFTS

The artisanal heritage of Argentina and Chile, especially in Patagonia, is less evident than, say, the indigenous textile traditions of the Peruvian or Guatemalan highlands. Still, both the city and the countryside have characteristic crafts.

Indigenous weaving traditions are apparent in Mapuche blankets, ponchos, sweaters, and similar garments on both sides of the Andean lakes district. Mapuche silversmiths are heir to an equally impressive tradition.

Befitting their origins on the Río de la Plata (literally, River of Silver), Argentine silversmiths create truly intricate jewelry, as well as adornments such as the large-bladed *facón* (knife) and *espuelas* (spurs) that accompany traditional gaucho clothing.

Expert leatherworkers, in turn, produce gaucho-style clothing and horse gear such as *rastras* (belts), reins, and saddles. Both these traditions come together in the production of paraphernalia for *mate,* the herbal "Paraguayan tea," whose consumption is a cultural bellwether. Traditionally, *mate* (the herb) is sipped with a silver *bombilla* (straw) from a *mate* (gourd, the same word in a different context), which may be mounted in a leather holder.

Throughout the Chilean heartland and well into the south, *huaso* horse gear has its own unique features—look for the elaborately carved wooden stirrups in particular. Carvers in the Chiloé archipelago produce model *dalcas* (dugouts), *palafitos* (houses on pilings), and dolls.

## ENTERTAINMENT

Even in the Patagonian provinces, Argentines are night people—discos and dance clubs, for instance, may not even *open* until 1 A.M. or so and stay open until dawn. Chileans are less so, but by North American or Northern European standards, they often keep remarkably late hours.

### Bars, Clubs, and Discos

Patagonian cities like Bariloche have the largest numbers of places to dance and drink; rock and techno, but sometimes Latin styles like salsa, are the music of choice. Cavernous dance clubs *(boliches)* can have state-of-the-art sound systems and recorded techno, but some smaller, more interesting venues have live folk, rock, and even jazz.

In Argentina, the distinction between cafés and bars is not always obvious—in fact, it's often more a continuum than a dichotomy. Some of the more stylish (or pretentious) bars often go by the English "pub" but call themselves Irish.

### Cinemas

In some provincial cities, the central cinemas have closed but multiplexes have also opened in suburban areas. Cultural centers and universities in regional capitals often reprise classics or show less commercial movies.

Most imported films appear in the original language, with Spanish subtitles. The major exceptions are animated and children's films, which are invariably dubbed into Spanish.

## HOLIDAYS, FESTIVALS, AND EVENTS

Government offices and most businesses close on national holidays, most of which are religious observations. The summer months of January and February, when most leave on vacation, are generally a quiet time; things pick up after school starts in early March.

Traditionally, many Chileans take "sandwich holidays" between official holidays and the weekend, but the government is attempting to eliminate the practice by moving some holidays to the nearest Monday.

January 1 is **Año Nuevo** (New Year's Day), an official holiday in both countries and the Falkland Islands.

**Semana Santa** (Holy Week) is widely observed in both Argentina and Chile, though only the days from **Viernes Santo** (Good Friday) through **Pascua** (Easter) are official holidays. Many use the long weekend for a mini-vacation.

May 1 is **Día del Trabajador** (International Labor Day), an official holiday in both countries.

October 12 is **Día de la Raza** (equivalent to Columbus Day), an official holiday in both countries.

November 2's **Día de los Muertos** (All Saints' Day or Day of the Dead) is the occasion for Argentines and Chileans to visit the graves of their loved ones, though it's not the colorful event it is in, say, Mexico or Guatemala.

December 25 is **Navidad** (Christmas Day), an official holiday in both countries and the Falkland Islands.

## Argentina

On May 25, Argentines observe the **Revolución de Mayo** (May Revolution of 1810), when the Porteños of Buenos Aires made their first move toward independence by declaring the viceroy illegitimate. This is not, however, the major independence celebration, which takes place July 9.

June 10 is **Día de las Malvinas** (Malvinas Day), an official holiday commemorating Argentina's claim to the British-governed Falkland Islands. June 20, also an official holiday, is **Día de la Bandera** (Flag Day).

July 9, **Día de la Independencia,** celebrates Argentina's formal declaration of independence at the northwestern city of Tucumán, in 1816. Later in the month, when school lets out, many Argentines take ***vacaciones de invierno*** (winter holidays), when flights and even buses out of the capital fill up fast.

August 17 is **Día de San Martín,** the official observance of the death (not the birth) of Argentina's independence hero.

## Chile

On May 21, **Glorias Navales** commemorates the Battle of Iquique, a naval skirmish in the War of the Pacific with Peru.

**Corpus Christi** (May 30) is a religious holiday, as are the **Día de San Pedro y San Pablo** (Saint Peter and Saint Paul's Day) on June 29 and **Asunción de la Virgen** (Assumption) on August 15.

September 18's **Día de la Independencia Nacional** (Independence Day) is immediately followed by September 19's **Día del Ejército** (Armed Forces Day); together, they constitute the **Fiestas Patrias.**

December 8 marks the **Inmaculada Concepción** (Immaculate Conception), a religious holiday.

## Falkland Islands

The Falklands celebrate many of the same holidays as Argentina and Chile, but several others are either derived from the British tradition or unique to the Islands. January 10, for instance, is **Margaret Thatcher Day,** as the Islanders acknowledge the birthday of the British prime minister who responded to the 1982 invasion by ordering a naval task force to expel the Argentines.

June 14 is **Liberation Day,** commemorating the date on which the British forced the Argentine surrender. The first Monday of October is the **Spring Holiday.**

December 8 acknowledges the **Battle of the Falklands,** a World War I confrontation with Germany that took place within sight of Stanley. The day after Christmas is **Boxing Day,** a movable holiday that can change if Christmas falls on a Saturday or Sunday.

# ESSENTIALS

## Getting There

Most overseas visitors arrive in Patagonia by air, via Buenos Aires or Santiago, but some will arrive overland and others by ship.

### BY AIR

Buenos Aires and Santiago have regular air links with North America, Europe, and Australia/New Zealand, plus less-frequent routes from southern Africa across the Atlantic (some via Brazil). Both, though, are relatively expensive destinations during peak periods such as the Christmas/New Year's and Holy Week holidays; an Advance Purchase Excursion (Apex) fare can reduce the bite but may have minimum- and maximum-stay requirements, allow no stopovers, and impose financial penalties for changes. Economy-class (Y) tickets, valid for 12 months, are more expensive but allow maximum flexibility. Travelers staying longer than a year have to cough up the difference for any interim price increases.

Discount ticket agents ("consolidators" in North America and "bucket shops" in Britain) may offer the best deals through so-called "bulk fares," but often have other drawbacks—they may not, for instance, allow mileage credit for frequent-flyer programs. Courier flights, on which passengers surrender some or all of their baggage allowance to a company sending equipment or documents to overseas affiliates

© GALINA BARSKAYA/123RF

## INTERNATIONAL AIRLINES IN BUENOS AIRES

Unless otherwise indicated, the addresses below are in the Microcentro and vicinity.

- **Aerolíneas Argentinas:** Perú 2, Monserrat, tel. 011/4320-2000, www.aerolineas.com.ar
- **Aeroméxico:** Paraguay 555, tel. 011/5648-2205, www.aeromexico.com
- **AeroSur:** Av. Santa Fe 849, 1st floor, tel. 011/4516-0999, www.aerosur.com
- **Air Canada:** Av. Córdoba 656, tel. 011/4327-3640, www.aircanada.com
- **Air Europa:** Av. Santa Fe 850, tel. 011/5219-4545, www.aireuropa.com
- **Air France:** San Martín 344, 23rd floor, tel. 011/4317-4700, www.airfrance.com
- **Alitalia:** Suipacha 1111, 28th floor, Retiro, tel. 011/4310-9999, www.alitalia.com
- **American Airlines:** Av. Santa Fe 881, Retiro, tel. 011/4318-1111, www.aa.com
- **Avianca:** Carlos Pellegrini 1163, 4th floor, Retiro, tel. 011/4394-5990, www.avianca.com
- **British Airways:** Av. del Libertador 498, 13th floor, tel. 0800/2220075, www.britishairways.com
- **Continental Airlines:** Carlos Pellegrini 527, tel. 0800/3330425, www.continental.com
- **Copa:** Emma de la Barra 353, 7th floor, Puerto Madero, tel. 011/4132-3535, www.copaair.com
- **Cubana de Aviación:** Sarmiento 552, 11th floor, tel. 011/4326-5291, www.cubana.cu
- **Delta:** Av. Santa Fe 899, Retiro, tel. 011/4898-8170, www.delta.com
- **Gol:** tel. 0810/2663131, www.voegol.com
- **Iberia:** Carlos Pellegrini 1163, 1st floor, Retiro, tel. 011/4131-1000, www.iberia.com
- **KLM:** San Martín 344, tel. 011/4317-4700, www.klm.com
- **LAN:** Cerrito 866, Retiro, tel. 0800/9999526, www.lan.com
- **Lufthansa:** Marcelo T. de Alvear 590, 6th floor, Retiro, tel. 011/4319-0600, www.lufthansa.com
- **Pluna:** Libertad 1133, 4th floor, Retiro, tel. 011/4132-4444, www.flypluna.com
- **Qantas:** Av. Madero 900, 27th floor, Puerto Madero, tel. 011/4114-5800, www.qantas.com.au
- **South African Airways:** Av. Santa Fe 846, Retiro, tel. 011/4319-0099, www.flysaa.com
- **Swiss International:** Av. Santa Fe 846, Retiro, tel. 011/4319-0000, www.swiss.com
- **Taca Airlines:** Carlos Pellegrini 1075, Retiro, tel. 0810/3338222, www.taca.com
- **Transportes Aéreos de Mercosur (TAM):** Cerrito 1030, Retiro, tel. 011/4819-4800, www.tam.com.br
- **United Airlines:** Av. Eduardo Madero 900, 9th floor, Retiro, tel. 0810/7778648, www.united.com

or customers, may be even cheaper. Available for short periods only, though, they often leave on short notice and are less common to Latin America than to other parts of the world.

Other options include Round the World (RTW) and Circle Pacific routes that permit numerous stopovers on longer multi-continental trips, but assembling an itinerary requires effort and patience. The fourth edition of Edward Hasbrouck's *The Practical Nomad* (Berkeley, California: Avalon Travel, 2007; the fifth edition is due out in late 2011) is a key resource for researching airfares and other aspects of international travel.

Many airlines reduced their services to Argentina after the economic collapse of

2001–2002, as debt default and a steep devaluation meant fewer Argentines could splurge on overseas travel. With the tourism boom, though, services have rebounded and even increased.

Buenos Aires's international airport is **Aeropuerto Internacional Ministro Pistarini** (BUE), operated by the private concessionaire Aeropuertos Argentinos 2000 (tel. 011/5480-6111, www.aa2000.com.ar). Popularly known as "Ezeiza" for the Buenos Aires province suburb where it's located, the airport is 35 kilometers southwest of downtown Buenos Aires.

Recovering from damage in the February 2010 earthquake, Santiago's international airport is the state-of-the-art **Aeropuerto Internacional Arturo Merino Benítez** (SCL,

## INTERNATIONAL AIRLINES IN SANTIAGO

This list includes airlines that fly to and from Santiago, though several other foreign airlines also have local representatives. Unless otherwise noted, the offices are in Santiago Centro.

- **Aerolíneas Argentinas:** Roger de Flor 2921, Las Condes, tel. 02/2109300, www.aerolineas.com.ar
- **Aeroméxico:** Isidora Goyenechea 2939, Oficina 602, Las Condes, tel. 02/3901000, www.aeromexico.com
- **Air Canada:** Andrés Bello 2687, 16th floor, Las Condes, tel. 02/6901108, www.aircanada.com
- **Air France:** Americo Vespucio Sur 100, Oficina 202, Las Condes, tel. 02/2909330, www.airfrance.com
- **Alitalia:** Av. Providencia 1998, Oficina 208, Providencia, tel. 02/3351010, www.alitalia.com
- **American Airlines:** Huérfanos 1199, tel. 02/6790000, www.aa.com
- **Avianca:** Isidora Goyenechea 3365, Oficina 1201, Las Condes, tel. 02/2706600, www.avianca.com
- **British Airways:** Don Carlos 2929, Oficina 1105, Las Condes, tel. 02/3308610, www.britishairways.com
- **Copa:** Fidel Oteíza 1921, Oficina 703, Providencia, tel. 02/2002100, www.copaair.com
- **Delta:** Isidora Goyenechea 2939, Oficina 601, Las Condes, tel. 02/2801600, www.delta.com
- **Iberia:** Bandera 206, 8th floor, tel. 02/8701010, www.iberia.com
- **LAN:** Huérfanos 926, tel. 02/5263000, www.lan.com
- **Lufthansa:** Av. El Bosque Norte 500, 16th floor, Las Condes, tel. 02/6301655, www.lufthansa.com
- **Malaysia Airlines:** Zurich 221, Oficina 13, Las Condes, tel. 02/3341758, www.malaysiaairlines.com
- **Pluna:** Barros Errázuriz 1954, Oficina 1302, Providencia, tel. 02/5952879, www.flypluna.com
- **Qantas:** Isidora Goyenechea 2934, Oficina 301, Las Condes, tel. 02/2329562, www.qantas.com.au
- **South African Airways:** Av. 11 de Septiembre 1881, Oficina 713, Providencia, tel. 02/3769040, www.flysaa.com
- **Swiss International:** Barros Errázuriz 1954, Oficina 810, Providencia, tel. 02/9402907, www.swiss.com
- **Taca Airlines:** Barros Borgoño 105, 2nd floor, Providencia, tel. 02/3528200, www.taca.com
- **Transportes Aéreos Mercosur (TAM):** Av. Vitacura 2943, Edificio Milenium, Las Condes, tel. 02/6767900, www.tam.com.br
- **United Airlines:** Av. Andrés Bello 2867, 16th floor, Las Condes, tel. 02/3370000, www.united.com

tel. 02/6901753, www.aeropuertosantiago.cl). One of the most modern and well monitored in the world, it's in the western suburb of Pudahuel, 26 kilometers west of downtown.

### From North America

The main gateways to Buenos Aires are Miami, Atlanta, Washington, D.C. (Dulles), New York (JFK), Dallas, Houston, Los Angeles, and San Francisco. Canadian passengers may also use Toronto.

Aerolíneas Argentinas is the traditional carrier, but other options include AeroSur, American Airlines, Avianca, Continental, Copa, Delta, Gol, LAN and LAN Argentina, Transportes Aéreos Mercosur (TAM), TACA, United Airlines, and US Airways. Aerolíneas Argentinas, American, Continental, LAN, United, and US Airways have the only nonstop or direct services; others require changing planes elsewhere in Central or South America.

Air Canada flies from Toronto to Buenos Aires via Santiago, three or four times per week. By taking this route, non-Canadians can avoid the hassle of getting a U.S. visa just for transit purposes.

### From Mexico, Central America, and the Caribbean

Services from Mexico to either Santiago or Buenos Aires almost always require changing planes in Central America or elsewhere in South America; the main exception is LAN, which flies nonstop from Mexico City to Santiago, with connections to Buenos Aires.

Other carriers from Mexico City include Aeroméxico; Copa, which requires changing planes in Panama; and Taca Airlines, via Lima, Perú. Cubana has two or three flights weekly from Havana, while Avianca has connections to the Caribbean, Central America, and Mexico via Bogotá.

### From Europe

From Europe, there are direct services to Buenos Aires with Aerolíneas Argentinas (from Rome and Madrid); Air France (from Paris); Alitalia (from Milan and Rome); British Airways (from London); Iberia (from Barcelona and Madrid); KLM (from Amsterdam); Lufthansa (from Frankfurt via São Paulo); and Swiss International (from Geneva and Zurich). TAM has connections from Paris via São Paulo.

Many Buenos Aires services continue to Santiago, but there are also direct services to the Chilean capital with LAN and Iberia. There are also connections via Brazil with Gol. From Madrid, Uruguay's Pluna takes a Rio de Janeiro–Montevideo–Santiago route.

### From Asia, Africa, and the Pacific

The most direct service from the Pacific has been Aerolíneas Argentinas' twice-weekly service from Sydney via Auckland, but LAN now also has direct flights from Australia and New Zealand. From Australia, Qantas links up with LAN flights via Tahiti, Easter Island, and Santiago, or with LAN via Los Angeles. Air New Zealand also links up with LAN. From Japan, it's easiest to make connections via Los Angeles.

From Johannesburg, South African Airways flies five times or so weekly to São Paulo, where TAM and Gol offer connections to Buenos Aires.

### Within South America

Buenos Aires and Santiago have connections to neighboring republics of Uruguay, Brazil, Paraguay, Peru, and Bolivia, and elsewhere on the continent as well. There are no flights to the Guyanas, however.

For passengers on a Patagonian trip, the most important connections might be between Buenos Aires and Santiago, which are frequent on many South American and trans-Atlantic carriers.

LAN has the only flights to the Falkland Islands, every Saturday from Santiago and Punta Arenas; they return the same day. Once a month, these flights also stop in Río Gallegos, Argentina.

## OVERLAND

Overland travel from the north can be challenging, but once you reach Argentina or Chile, it's easy enough.

### From North America, Mexico, and Central America

Overland travel from North America is problematic because Panama's Darien Gap to Colombia is time-consuming, impassable for motor vehicles, and difficult and potentially dangerous even for those on foot. The route passes through areas controlled by drug smugglers, guerrillas, and/or brutal Colombian paramilitaries.

Those visiting Patagonia and other parts of the continent for an extended period should consider shipping a vehicle. To locate a shipper, check the Yellow Pages of your local phone directory under Automobile Transporters, who are normally freight consolidators rather than the company that owns the ship, which will charge higher container rates. Since many more people ship vehicles to Europe than to South America, finding the right shipper may take patience; one reliable U.S. consolidator is **McClary, Swift & Co.** (360 Swift Ave., South San Francisco, CA 94080, tel. 650/872-2121, www.mcclaryswift.com), which has affiliates at many U.S. ports.

Argentine bureaucracy has improved in recent years, and clearing customs is simpler than it used to be. Vehicles arrive at the Puerto Nuevo's **Estación Marítima Buenos Aires** (Av. Quartino s/n, Retiro, tel. 011/4310-1428 or 011/4310-1431); here it is necessary to present your passport, vehicle title, and the original *conocimiento de embarque* (bill of lading), and to fill out a customs application. You will then obtain an appointment with a customs inspector to retrieve the vehicle, which will cost about US$450 port charges and another US$400 for the shipper; if the vehicle has been in port longer than five days, there will be additional charges. The vehicle can remain in Argentina legally for eight months, with an eight-month extension possible; any visit to a neighboring country restarts the clock. In event of any difficulty, consult a private *despachante de aduana* (customs broker), such as **José Angel Vidal Labra** (tel. 011/4345-7887, vidla@sinectis.com.ar).

Chile's ports are less bureaucratic and even safer for the vehicle than those of Argentina. The likely ports of entry are San Antonio, southwest of Santiago, and Valparaíso, northwest of the capital. It pays to be there within a couple of days of the vehicle's arrival, or storage charges can mount. Leave the gas tank as empty as possible (for safety's sake) and leave no valuables, including tools, in the vehicle.

To arrange a shipment from San Antonio or Valparaíso, contact the Santiago consolidator **Ultramar** (Av. Bosque Norte 500, 18th floor, Vitacura, tel. 02/6301000, www.ultramar.cl). For a trustworthy customs broker to handle the paperwork, contact **Juan Alarcón Rojas** (Fidel Oteíza 1921, 12th floor, Providencia, Santiago, tel. 02/3285100, fax 02/3285140, www.alarcon.cl).

Bicycles, of course, can be partially dismantled, packaged, and easily shipped aboard airplanes, usually for a small additional charge.

## Crossing Patagonian Borders

Argentina and Chile have numerous border crossings, in Patagonia and elsewhere. In both countries' lakes districts, trans-Andean bus service is fairly common, but many southerly crossings lack public transportation.

Crossing the border is normally routine and, given the similarities between the two countries' visa regimes, poses few unexpected obstacles for any nationality. That said, Chilean customs and immigration posts tend to be quicker and more efficient than their Argentine counterparts, whose personnel are often poorly trained, with outdated technology (and technological skills). Argentina's customs regulations, at the same time, can be far more arbitrary than Chile's; while this mostly affects Argentine citizens, it slows everyone down. At some remote crossings, Chilean Carabineros (national police) and the Argentine Gendarmería (Border Patrol) handle all formalities.

In many border areas, especially where the towns are close together (as in Chile Chico and Los Antiguos, and Puerto Natales and Río Turbio), Chilean and Argentine currencies are accepted on both sides of the line. However, they are usually *not* acceptable for official transactions, such as postal services.

## OVERLAND CROSSINGS

In northern Patagonia, Argentina-bound buses cross from Temuco to Neuquén over the 1,884-meter Paso de Pino Hachado via Curacautín and Lonquimay; the alternative 1,298-meter Paso de Icalma is slightly to the south. Other options include a regular bus service from Temuco to San Martín de los Andes via the Paso de Mamuil Malal (Paso Tromen to Argentines); a bus-boat combination from Panguipulli to San Martín de los Andes via the 659-meter Paso Huahum and Lago Pirehueico; a paved highway from Osorno to Bariloche via the Paso de Cardenal Samoré that's the second-busiest crossing between the two countries; and the classic bus-boat shuttle from Puerto Montt and Puerto Varas to Bariloche.

There are many southern Patagonian crossings, but roads are often bad and only a few have public transportation. Those with scheduled services include the mostly gravel road from Futaleufú, Chile, to Esquel (local buses only); Coyhaique to Comodoro Rivadavia on a mostly paved road via Río Mayo on long-distance coaches; Chile Chico to Los Antiguos (shuttles with onward connections in either direction); Puerto Natales to El Calafate via Río Turbio on a steadily improving route, much of it now paved; Punta Arenas to Río Gallegos via an almost entirely paved highway; and Punta Arenas to Río Grande and Ushuaia, a route that includes a ferry crossing on the Chilean side.

In addition, many border crossings are suitable for private motor vehicles and mountain bikes, and a few by foot.

## BY WATER

The main international crossings are the popular and scenic but increasingly expensive bus-boat-bus route between the Argentine resort town of San Carlos de Bariloche and the Chilean city of Puerto Montt, and the relatively short cruise (three-plus days) that carries passengers between Punta Arenas (Chile) and Ushuaia (Tierra del Fuego). There is also a rugged boat-bus route between Villa O'Higgins (Chile) and El Chaltén (Argentina) that also requires travelers to cover part of the route on foot, bicycle, or horseback.

# Getting Around

## BY AIR

### Argentina

In addition to international air service, Argentina has a large network of domestic airports and a handful of airlines centered on Buenos Aires; indeed, to fly between Argentine cities, changing planes in Buenos Aires is often unavoidable. Most domestic flights use Aeroparque Jorge Newbery, the city airport, but a few use the international airport at Ezeiza.

Aerolíneas Argentinas has domestic as well as international flights, while its affiliate Austral (the two are almost indistinguishable) serves many Patagonian destinations from Buenos Aires south to Ushuaia, Tierra del Fuego.

Other domestic airlines come and go, with the exception of Líneas Aéreas del Estado (LADE, www.lade.com.ar), the air force's heavily subsidized commercial branch. Miraculously surviving budget crises and privatizations, it flies to southern Buenos Aires province and out-of-the-way Patagonian destinations on a wing and an overdrawn bank account.

Other private airlines have consistently failed, but expanding LAN Argentina, an affiliate of Chile's LAN, seems likelier to survive.

Airfares fell with the 2002 devaluation and

have remained reasonable, though foreigners are ineligible for discount fares available to Argentine citizens and residents. This means, in effect, that foreigners are paying full Y-class fares, but it also means greater flexibility in purchasing one-way *cabotaje* tickets, "open-jaws" itineraries that land at one city and depart from another, and to mix and match airlines.

Available only in conjunction with international travel to Buenos Aires, Aerolíneas Argentinas' "Visit Argentina" pass offers a series of discount fares to foreigners and nonresident Argentines, which requires some planning to gain maximum advantage from them. Fares are notably lower if the international travel takes place on Aerolíneas Argentinas.

### Chile

In addition to Santiago's international airport, there are domestic airports with commercial flights at Temuco, Pucón, Osorno, Puerto Montt, Chaitén, Balmaceda (Coyhaique), and Punta Arenas; some of these have short international hops to Argentina. Coyhaique has a separate aerodrome for flights to Laguna San Rafael.

LAN dominates the domestic market, but its planes are fairly spacious for a country whose longest domestic flight is only about three hours. There are big discounts at inconvenient hours, such as the middle-of-the-night flight from Punta Arenas to Santiago.

No competitor has had sustained success challenging LAN's supremacy, but Sky Airline now holds about 20 percent of the domestic market and serves the airports at Temuco, Puerto Montt, Balmaceda, and Punta Arenas.

Chilean domestic airfares are generally reasonable, but purchasing tickets a few days ahead of time can result in substantial discounts. For overseas visitors LAN also has a "Visit Chile" pass that can mean substantial savings, but it's not promoting this as much as it has in the past.

For student discounts on both international and domestic flights, try the **Student Flight Center** (Hernando de Aguirre 201, Oficina 401, Providencia, Santiago, tel. 02/4112000, www.sertur.cl).

## BY BUS

In both Argentina and Chile, buses along the principal highways, and those connecting other main cities and resorts, are frequent and almost invariably spacious and comfortable—sometimes even luxurious. A handful on back-roads routes are only marginally better than Central American "chicken buses," and they may be infrequent, but distances are relatively short.

So-called Pullman buses have reclining seats, and for short to medium runs, say up to six or seven hours, they're more than adequate. Seats are guaranteed. For the longest distances, many travelers prefer the more spacious *servicio diferencial* or the *coche cama* service, which provide greater legroom in seats that recline almost horizontally. Fares are reasonable by international standards—the 20-hour trip from Buenos Aires to Bariloche, in northern Patagonia, is only about US$100.

Most cities have a central *terminal de buses* (bus terminal), but a few have multiple terminals for long-distance, regional, and rural services, or for individual companies. Some companies also have separate ticket offices in more central locations than the terminals themselves.

Services are so frequent that reservations are rarely necessary except for a few infrequently traveled routes and some international services, or during holiday periods like Semana Santa (Holy Week), September's Chilean patriotic holidays, Christmas/New Year's periods, and occasionally during the January/February summer and July/August winter vacation seasons. Fares can rise and fall with demand, depending on the season.

## BY RAIL

Once the primary mode of interurban transportation, Argentine domestic rail service is now limited to a handful of long-distance domestic services. In Argentine Patagonia, the only long-distance service connects the Río Negro provincial capital of Viedma with the resort city of Bariloche.

In addition to regular passenger trains, there are also tourist excursions, including the

© ELNAVEGANTE/123RF

the narrow-gauge train known as La Trochita

narrow-gauge La Trochita in Río Negro and Chubut provinces; the latter was immortalized in Paul Theroux's overrated bestseller *The Old Patagonian Express.*

Chile no longer offers rail service from Santiago to Temuco and Puerto Montt, but, for possible changes, check the website of the governmental Empresa de Ferrocarriles del Estado (www.efe.cl).

## BY CAR AND MOTORCYCLE

Driving conditions in Argentina and Chile have similarities, but there are also dramatic differences. In the Falkland Islands, where roads are few and many of the most interesting destinations are inaccessible except by air or bad tracks best left to locals, driving is inadvisable for short-term visitors.

Note that members of the American Automobile Association (AAA), Britain's Automobile Association (AA), and other foreign automobile clubs are often eligible for limited roadside assistance through the **Automóvil Club Argentino** (ACA, Av. del Libertador 1850, Buenos Aires, tel. 011/4808-4000, www.aca.org.ar) and through the Automóvil Club Chileno (Acchi, Av. Andrés Bello Norte 1863, Providencia, Santiago, tel. 02/4311000, www.automovilclub.cl). Both have representatives in larger cities, and many smaller towns, throughout each country.

### Argentina

Driving in Argentina, especially Buenos Aires, is not for the timid. In the words of *Buenos Aires Herald* columnist Martín Gambarotta, this is a country "where pedestrians and not cars have to stop at a zebra crossing." According to the NGO Luchemos for la Vida (www.luchemos.org.ar), the traffic death rate of 1,066 per million vehicles is South America's highest, more than five times that of the United States.

Argentine highways are divided into *rutas nacionales* (abbreviated here as RN), for which the federal government is responsible, and *rutas provincials* (RP), which each province maintains. Generally, but not necessarily, federal highways are better maintained; one exception is prosperous Santa Cruz province, which has large oil royalty revenues.

Speed limits on most highways are generally around 100 kilometers per hour but 120 km/hr on four-lane divided roads (of which Patagonia has none). Officially, helmets are obligatory for motorcyclists, but enforcement is lax, especially in northwestern cities. The most thickheaded riders appear to believe their skulls are strong enough, but emergency-room statistics have proved them wrong.

## Chile

The longitudinal Panamericana or Ruta 5, which stretches from the Peruvian border to Puerto Montt and the Isla Grande de Chiloé, is Chile's main transport artery; on the mainland south of Santiago, it's a smoothly paved, four-lane divided highway, though it's recovering from damage to both surfaces and bridges damaged in the February 2010 earthquake. Even so, and despite the presence of call boxes, rest areas, and *peajes* (toll booths), there are occasionally loose animals, pedestrians crossing at unsuitable places, and even vendors hawking items ranging from sweets and ice cream to fresh produce and cheese to dressed kid goat, ready for barbecue.

Many more roads are paved or smoothly graded, though Ruta 7, the legendary Carretera Austral (Southern Highway), is often narrow, mostly gravel, and occasionally precarious (the author has wrecked two four-wheel-drive vehicles on it, with extenuating circumstances). Heavy truck traffic can make all these routes dangerous, but most Chileans are courteous and cautious drivers despite occasional road-rage incidents in Santiago. Watch carefully for Argentine license plates, as many trans-Andean visitors drive more aggressively.

Speed limits on most highways are generally around 100 km/hr but are 120 km/hr on most segments of the Panamericana that are four-lane divided roads. Carabineros (the national police) with radar guns are common sights along all highways.

## Vehicle Documents, Driver's Licenses, and Equipment

Most South American countries, including Argentina and Chile, have dispensed with the cumbersome *Carnet de Passage en Douanes,* which required depositing a large bond in order to import a motor vehicle. Officials at the port of arrival or border post usually issue a 90-day permit on presentation of the vehicle title, registration, bill of lading (if the vehicle is being shipped), and your passport. For shipped vehicles, port charges can rise rapidly if the vehicle has been stored more than a few days.

Before traveling, many visitors obtain an International or Interamerican Driving Permit, available through the American Automobile Association (AAA) or your home country's counterpart and normally valid for one calendar year from date of issue. Police in both countries, though, now acknowledge state and national driver's licenses.

The police pay closer attention to vehicle documents—*tarjeta verde* (green card) registration for Argentine vehicles, customs permission for foreign ones, and liability insurance (though many Argentines drive without it). Vehicles without registration may be impounded on the spot. Argentine vehicles should have proof of a *verificación técnica* (safety inspection); Chile's equivalent is the *revision técnica.*

At roadside checkpoints, Argentine police are rigid about obligatory equipment such as headrests for the driver and each passenger, *valizas* (triangular emergency reflectors), and *matafuegos* (1-kg fire extinguishers). In any instance of document irregularity or minor equipment violation, provincial police may threaten fines while really soliciting *coimas* (bribes), though this is less common in the Patagonian provinces. A firm but calm suggestion that you intend to call your consulate may help overcome any difficulty.

Chilean checkpoints are far less common than they were under the Pinochet dictatorship, but always stop when the Carabineros signal you to do so; this is usually a routine document check. Unlike many Argentine police, nearly all Carabineros will refuse bribes; offering one can get you in serious trouble. If you've committed an *infracción* (traffic violation), the best thing to do is reason with the officer, and you may get off unless your offense is truly flagrant or particularly dangerous. Note also that the slang term *paco* for a policeman is widely considered an insult—never use it to a cop's face.

Be sure to obtain Chilean liability insurance, which is available in major cities. *Seguro mínimo,* a cheap no-fault policy with limited personal injury coverage, is obligatory but inadequate for any serious accident.

In remote areas where gas stations are few, carry additional fuel.

## Road Hazards

Argentine traffic can be fast and ruthless, many roads are narrow with little or no shoulder, and others are poorly surfaced or potholed. Heavy truck traffic can make all routes dangerous, and not just because of excess speed—impatient Argentine drivers often try to pass in dangerous situations, and head-on crashes are disturbingly common, even between passenger buses.

Porteño drivers in the city and stray cattle in the provinces might seem to be enough to deal with, but the economic crisis since 2001–2002 has led to a major increase of *piquetes* (roadblocks) of demonstrators protesting unemployment and other issues. *Piqueteros* (picketers), while they tend to focus on stopping commercial traffic, manage to slow everything else down as well; never try to run a roadblock, which can raise the picketers' wrath. Rather, try to show solidarity and, in all likelihood, you'll pass without incident. Patagonia's main focus of picketing activity has been the western Neuquén oil town of Plaza Huincul.

Unleaded fuel is available everywhere, though some older vehicles still use leaded. In remote areas where gas stations are few, carry additional fuel.

In both the city and the countryside, watch for *lomas de burro* (speed bumps), also colloquially known as *pacos acostados* (sleeping policemen) in Chile. Night driving is inadvisable in some rural areas, as domestic livestock and inebriated campesinos may roam freely.

## Expenses

Prior to devaluation, Argentina had some of the most inexpensive gasoline in the Americas except for Uruguay, but prices have begun to rise in both peso and dollar terms. Average prices are about US$0.87 per liter for regular, US$0.97 for super, and US$1.17 for Fangio. *Gasoil* (diesel) is typically cheaper than most gasolines, about US$0.88 per liter, but the differential is shrinking. Because gasoline prices are unregulated, they may rise quickly.

Note, however, that so-called "Patagonian prices" south of Sierra Grande on RN 3 and El Bolsón on RN 40 are more than one-third cheaper for gasoline; there is no price differential for diesel.

Partly because Chile imports more than 90 percent of its oil, operating a gasoline-powered vehicle is more expensive than in the United States (though it's still cheaper than in Europe). The cost of 93-octane *bencina* (gasoline) has risen to around US$1.50 per liter (roughly US$5.70 per U.S. gallon) in Santiago; prices generally increase with distance from the capital, reaching US$2 per liter (US$7.60 per gallon) or upward in remote Aisén. These prices are subject to fluctuations in the exchange rate and international crude oil prices.

Unleaded fuel is available everywhere, but some older vehicles still use leaded. There's no price difference between lower octane leaded *(con plomo)* and unleaded *(sin plomo)* fuels; higher octane unleaded is only slightly more expensive. Diesel fuel, though, is about 20 to 30 percent cheaper than gasoline.

In both countries, repairs are cheap in terms of labor, but parts can be expensive, as many of them must be imported; generally, parts are cheaper in Chile. Fortunately, skilled Argentine and Chilean mechanics can rehabilitate virtually any salvageable part.

## Car Rental

Both Buenos Aires and Santiago have such good public transportation that it's hardly worth risking aggressive drivers (especially in the Argentine capital), traffic congestion, and lack of parking. In Patagonia's wide-open spaces, though, a car makes it easier to explore otherwise inaccessible places, especially when time is limited. To rent a car, you must present a valid driver's license, a valid credit card, and be at least 25 years old.

Rental prices are generally lower and terms are better in Chile, where unlimited mileage deals are more common. With major local agencies, rates start around US$45 per day or US$282 per week for economy vehicles and around US$65 per day or US$408 per week or up for twin-cab pickup trucks. Even more expensive are four-wheel-drive vehicles, commonly referred to as *doble tracción* or *cuatro por cuatro* (the latter usually written "4X4"). On the other hand, if they're shared among a group, they can be fairly reasonable. International agencies such as Avis and Hertz are more expensive but have larger vehicle fleets and can usually guarantee a rental for overseas clients.

Local agencies may have somewhat lower rates, but insurance is normally additional and may not completely cover you against losses—there is almost always a deductible of several hundred dollars or more in case of serious damage, total destruction, or theft of the vehicle.

It's possible to rent camper vehicles and motor homes in Buenos Aires and Argentine Patagonia through **Gaibu Motorhome Time** (Av. Maipú 2517, Olivos, Vicente López, Buenos Aires province, tel./fax 011/5368-1544, www.gaibu.com).

In Chile, camping vehicles ranging from pickup trucks with shells to fully equipped motor homes are available through **Holiday Rent** (Los Leones 2300, Providencia, tel. 02/2582000, fax 02/2324975, www.holiday-rent.cl) or **Trekker Chile** (Viña Andrea s/n, Sector Alto Lircay, Talca, tel. 071/1972757, www.trekkerchile.com).

Note that taking a Chilean vehicle into Argentina, or vice versa, involves additional paperwork and a surcharge, as well as supplementary insurance. Returning a vehicle to an office other than the one you rented from, which is impossible with the cheapest local companies, usually means a hefty drop-off charge.

## Buying a Vehicle

If you're visiting Chile and Argentina for several months, buying a vehicle is worth consideration. The process is simpler in Chile, especially as Argentine regulations prohibit nonresidents from taking Argentine-registered vehicles out of the country—even if they have been legally purchased there—without notarial permission.

Santiago has the largest selection; be circumspect about purchasing a vehicle in Region XII (Magallanes), where *zona franca* (duty-free) regulations limit purchases of many vehicles to permanent residents. Only a vehicle that is legally *liberado* may be sold in and taken outside the region.

To purchase a Chilean car, you need a RUT (Rol Único Tributario) tax ID number, which takes only a few minutes at any Servicio de Impuestos Internos (SII, Internal Revenue Service) office; you need not be a legal resident of Chile. The SII issues a provisional RUT, valid for any purpose, and sends the permanent card to a Chilean address that you designate.

Before purchasing the vehicle, request a *Certificado de Inscripción y Anotaciones Vigentes* from any office of the Registro Civil (Civil Registry); this inexpensive document will alert you to title problems if any, as well as pending legal issues (such as accident settlements). To be licensed, the vehicle also needs an up-to-date *revisión técnica* (safety and emissions test).

Registering the sale, at any Registro Civil office, involves a *compraventa* (bill of sale, about US$10) and an official *Transferencia de Dominio de Vehículos Motorizados* (title transfer, about US$42), plus a transfer tax set at 1.5 percent of the sale price. The Registro then issues a provisional title and mails the permanent title, usually within a month, to the address on your RUT.

Legally, the *compraventa* and other documents entitle you to take the vehicle out of the country, but since purchase of a Chilean vehicle by foreigners is still uncommon, it may be worth making a special request to accelerate the issuance of the permanent title, which requires a brief letter to the head of the Registro. Personnel at the office can help with this.

## BY BICYCLE

For the physically fit, or those intending to become physically fit, with enough time, cycling can be an ideal way to see Patagonia. Because so many roads are unpaved, a *todo terreno* (mountain bike) trumps a touring bike. Cyclists should know basic mechanics, though the increasing availability of mountain bikes means that parts and mechanics are easier to find than they once were. In an emergency, it's easy to put a bicycle on board a bus.

Some cyclists dislike the main Argentine highways because their narrowness, coupled with fast drivers and the lack of shoulders, can make them unsafe, but there are many alternative routes with less traffic. Frequent high winds can make cycling difficult on Argentine Patagonian roads, such as coastal RN 3 and the interior RN 40.

Likewise, some cyclists dislike Chile's busy Panamericana, much of which is also relatively uninteresting, but its completion as a four-lane divided highway with broad paved shoulders should make it safer, at least. There are many interesting alternatives, though—the scenic Carretera Austral, especially, is a mountain biker's delight.

## BY FERRY AND CATAMARAN

From Puerto Montt south through the Aisén and Magallanes regions, lacustrine and maritime transportation fills the gaps in Chile's highway network. This is true even in parts of the Andean lakes district, where passenger ferries on finger lakes like Lago Todos los Santos form part of trans-Andean routes to Argentina. In addition to ferries, high-speed catamarans cover some of these routes and also serve some isolated tourist destinations.

From Puerto Montt, there are ferries and catamarans to Chaitén and Puerto Chacabuco, and to the ice fields of Parque Nacional Laguna San Rafael, a route also traveled by the cruise ship *Skorpios* and the luxury passenger catamaran *Patagonia Connection*.

Navimag's *Magallanes* connects Puerto Montt with Puerto Natales, a three-day journey through the scenic fjords of Aisén and northern Magallanes.

Transmarchilay runs a shuttle ferry across the mouth of the Reloncaví estuary, from

© WAYNE BERNHARDSON

Ferry passengers enjoy the sunshine on the Seno de Reloncaví (Reloncaví Sound).

La Arena to Puelche, about 45 kilometers southeast of Puerto Montt. The village of Hornopirén, 60 kilometers farther southeast, is the port for Transmarchilay's summer-only ferry to Caleta Gonzalo, the gateway to Parque Pumalín, Chaitén, and the Carretera Austral.

Ferries also connect the mainland port of Pargua, southwest of Puerto Montt, with Chacao, on the Isla Grande de Chiloé. There are also ferries from Quellón, at the south end of the Isla Grande, to Chaitén and occasionally to Puerto Chacabuco.

From the Aisén village of Puerto Ingeniero Ibáñez, on Lago General Carrera's north shore, the car ferry *Pilchero* sails to the south shore border town of Chile Chico; while Chile Chico is also accessible by a road around the lake, the ferry is faster and cheaper.

In Magallanes, there's a daily ferry from Punta Arenas across the Strait of Magellan to Porvenir, on the Chilean side of the Isla Grande de Tierra del Fuego; a more frequent shuttle ferry crosses the strait from Primera Angostura, northwest of Punta Arenas.

## LOCAL TRANSPORTATION

Though cars clog the streets of Buenos Aires and Santiago, most Argentines and Chileans still rely on public transportation to get around, even in small towns.

### Underground

Buenos Aires and Santiago have the Southern Cone's only subway systems. Buenos Aires's **Subte** (www.metrovias.com.ar) dates from 1913, but carries city residents efficiently and is expanding to underserved neighborhoods; Santiago's exemplary **Metro** (www.metrosantiago.cl) looks as good as the day it opened in 1975.

### *Colectivos* and *Micros* (Buses)

Even small cities and towns are well served by local buses, which often run 24/7. Fares mostly range US$0.35–0.75 but vary according to distance. Argentines use the term *colectivo,* while Chileans normally say *micro* or, for smaller buses, *liebres* (literally, hares). Santiago's new integrated bus system, **Transantiago** (www.transantiagoinforma.cl), got off to a rocky start in 2007 but has since stabilized.

One of the great conveniences in Chilean public transport is the *taxi colectivo,* which operates like a city bus on a fixed route. Only slightly more expensive than a city bus, it's usually faster and often more comfortable. *Taxi colectivos* are identifiable by the illuminated plastic signs on top of their roofs, which show major destinations along the route.

In Buenos Aires and some other localities, some buses have fare boxes that make change, but these are due to be phased out in favor of rechargeable cards. In other localities they may require *fichas* (tokens) or cards; in a few, drivers still handle the task.

### Taxis and *Remises*

Buenos Aires, Santiago, and other cities have abundant fleets of taxis, mostly painted black with yellow roofs. Since a spate of robberies that began some years ago, nearly all Buenos Aires cabs are now *radio taxis*—some people prefer the security of phoning for a cab—but many Argentines still flag them down in the street. If in doubt, lock the back doors so that no one can enter by surprise.

All regular cabs have digital meters. In Buenos Aires, it costs about US$1.20 to *bajar la bandera* ("drop the flag"; i.e., switch on the meter) and another US$0.12 per 200 meters; provincial cities tend to be a little cheaper. Verify that the meter is set at zero.

Drivers do not expect tips; sometimes, to avoid making change, they will even round the fare *down.* Carry small bills rather than rely on the driver's making change, especially if he has just come on shift; to deter a potentially dishonest driver when paying with a large note, ask whether he has the proper change for that amount.

*Remises* are Argentine radio taxis that charge an agreed-upon rate based on distance; the dispatcher will let you know the fare when you call, based on the pickup and drop-off points.

Hotels, restaurants, and other businesses will gladly ring radio taxis and *remises* for customers and clients, especially when the hour is late.

### Bicycle

Cycling may not be the safest way of navigating chaotic city traffic, but the number of cyclists is growing rapidly. If riding around Buenos Aires, Santiago, or other cities, side streets may be safer than fast-moving avenues, but they are also narrower, with less room for maneuvering. Weekend traffic is not so wild as on weekdays, and downtown areas may be virtually deserted on Sunday. There are few dedicated bike paths, most of which go through city parklands.

### Walking

Most Argentine cities are compact enough that walking suffices for sightseeing and other activities, but the first rule of pedestrian safety is that that you are invisible—for an overwhelming majority of Argentine drivers, crosswalks appear to be merely decorative. While making turns, drivers weave among pedestrians rather than slowing or stopping to let them pass. Jaywalking is endemic, perhaps because it's not much more hazardous than crossing at the corner with the light.

Compared with most Argentines, Chilean motorists respect crosswalks and are courteous to pedestrians. A substantial minority, though, seem to drive distractedly at times, so it pays to be attentive.

Despite the hazards, pedestrians can often move faster than automobiles in congested areas.

# Visas and Officialdom

## ARGENTINA

Citizens of neighboring countries—Bolivians, Brazilians, Uruguayans, and Paraguayans—need only national ID cards, but most other nationalities need passports. U.S. and Canadian citizens, along with those of the European Union and Scandinavian countries, Switzerland, Israel, Australia, and New Zealand, and other Latin American countries need passports but not advance visas. Citizens of nearly every African and Asian country, except for South Africa and Japan, need advance visas.

Regulations change, though, and it may be helpful to check the visa page of Argentina's **Ministerio de Relaciones Exteriores** (Foreign Relations Ministry, www.mrecic.gov.ar), which also includes contacts of the most important Argentine embassies and consulates overseas. The most recent change is the application of a "reciprocity fee" for citizens of countries that collect visa fees from Argentine applicants—in this case, those of the United States (US$140, valid for 10 years), Australia (US$100, single entry), and Canada (US$70, single entry). At present, this is collected only on arrival at Buenos Aires's international airport at Ezeiza, but that could change.

Argentina routinely grants foreign visitors 90-day entry permits in the form of a tourist card. Theoretically, this card must be surrendered on departure; in practice, it's the passport stamp that counts. For 100 pesos, or about US$33, entry is renewable another 90 days at the **Dirección Nacional de Migraciones** (Av. Argentina 1355, Retiro, Buenos Aires, tel. 011/4317-0237, 8 A.M.–1 P.M. Mon.–Fri.).

In the provinces, renewal can be done at any office of the Policía Federal (Federal Police), but in smaller towns the police may not be accustomed to doing so.

Formally, arriving visitors must have a return or onward ticket, but enforcement is inconsistent—if you have a Latin American, North American, or Western European passport, for instance, it's unlikely you will be asked to show the return ticket (in the Western Hemisphere, only Cubans need advance visas to enter Argentina). The author has entered Argentina dozens of times over many years, at Buenos Aires's international airport and some of the most remote border posts, without ever having been asked for either.

Foreign airlines, though, may not permit a passenger without a round-trip ticket to

## ARGENTINE CONSULATES IN OTHER COUNTRIES

Embassies and consulates are often, though not always, at the same address. Consulates, rather than embassies, are primarily responsible for dealing with individuals traveling for either business or pleasure, however. Intending visitors should visit consulates for visas or other inquiries; this list includes overseas consulates and others in countries that border Argentina and Chile.

**Australia:**

- 7 National Circuit, 2nd floor, Barton ACT, tel. 02/6273-9111, www.argentina.org.au
- 44 Market St., 20th floor, Sydney NSW, tel. 02/9262-2933

**Bolivia:**

- Aspiazu 497, La Paz, tel. 2/241-7737, www.bolivia.embajada-argentina.gov.ar

**Brazil:**

- Praia de Botafogo 228, Sobreloja, Rio de Janeiro, tel. 21/2553-1646
- Av. Paulista 1106, Entreloja, São Paulo, tel. 11/3897-9522, www.brasil.embajada-argentina.gov.ar

**Canada:**

- 81 Metcalfe, 7th floor, Ottawa, ON K1P 6K7, tel. 613/236-2351, www.canada.embajada-argentina.gov.ar
- 5001 Yonge St., Suite 201, Toronto, ON M2N 6P6, tel. 416/955-9075
- 2000 Peel St., Suite 600, Montréal, QC H3A 2W5, tel. 514/842-6582

**Chile:**

- Vicuña Mackenna 41, Santiago, tel. 2/582-2606, www.embargentina.cl
- Pedro Montt 160, 6th floor, Puerto Montt, tel. 65/253996
- 21 de Mayo 1878, Punta Arenas, tel. 61/261912

**New Zealand:**

- 142 Lambton Quay, Level 14, Wellington, tel. 4/472-8330, www.arg.org.nz

**Paraguay:**

- Palma 319, 1st floor, Asunción, tel. 21/442151, www.embajada-argentina.org.py
- Artigas 960, Encarnación, tel. 71/201066

**United Kingdom:**

- 27 Three Kings Yard, London W1Y 1FL, tel. 20/7318-1340, www.argentine-embassy-uk.org

**United States:**

- 1811 Q St. NW, Washington, DC 20009, tel. 202/238-6460, www.embassyofargentina.us
- 5550 Wilshire Blvd., Suite 210, Los Angeles, CA 90036, tel. 323/954-9155, www.consuladoargentino-losangeles.org
- 1101 Brickell Ave., Suite 600, North Tower, Miami, FL 33131, tel. 305/373-1889, www.consuladoargentinoenmiami.org
- 245 Peachtree Center Ave., Suite 2101, Atlanta, GA 30303, tel. 404/880-0805, www.consuladoargentinoatlanta.org
- 205 N. Michigan Ave., Suite 4209, Chicago, IL 60601, tel. 312/909-0308, www.chicago.argentinaconsul.ar
- 12 W. 56th St., New York, NY 10019, tel. 212/603-0400, www.congenargentinany.com
- 2200 West Loop South, Suite 1025, Houston TX 77027, tel. 713/871-8935, www.consuladoarhouston.com

**Uruguay:**

- Wilson Ferreira Aldunate 1281, Montevideo, tel. 2/902-8623, www.consuladoargentinomontevideo.com
- Av. General Flores 209, Colonia, tel. 52/22086
- Edificio Espigón Gorlero, Av. Gorlero and Calle 19 (Comodoro Gorlero), Sala H, Punta del Este, tel. 42/446162 (mid-Dec.-mid-Mar. only)

board an Argentina-bound flight. Likewise, if the arriving passenger presents an Eastern European, Asian, or African passport, he or she may well be asked for proof of return transport. Immigration officials have a great deal of discretion in these matters.

Always carry identification, since either the federal or provincial police can request it at any moment, though they rarely do so without reason. Passports are also necessary for routine transactions like checking into hotels, cashing travelers checks, or even credit card transactions.

Dependent children under age 14 traveling without both parents presumably need notarized parental consent, but the author's minor daughter visited Argentina many times with only one parent and was never asked for such a document.

Argentine-born individuals, even if their parents were not Argentines or if they have been naturalized elsewhere, sometimes attract unwanted attention. Generally, they may enter the country for no more than 60 days on a non-Argentine document. Argentine passports renewed outside the country expire on reentry, often requiring a time-consuming renewal at the Policía Federal.

### Lost or Stolen Passports

Visitors who suffer a lost or stolen passport must obtain a replacement at their own embassy or consulate. After obtaining a replacement passport, visit the Dirección Nacional de Migraciones to replace the tourist card.

### Customs

Traditionally notorious for flagrant corruption, Argentina's improved customs system normally presents no obstacle to tourists. Short-term visitors may import personal effects including

## FOREIGN CONSULATES IN BUENOS AIRES

As a major world capital, Buenos Aires has a full complement of embassies and consulates that provide services to foreign visitors. A country's embassy and consulate often share an address, but when the addresses are separate this list provides the address of the consulate, as they are primarily responsible for dealing with individuals traveling for either business or pleasure. It includes major overseas consulates as well as those from countries that border Argentina.

**Australia:** Villanueva 1400, Palermo, tel. 011/4779-3500, www.argentina.embassy.gov.au

**Bolivia:** Bartolomé Mitre 2815, 1st floor, Balvanera, tel. 011/4381-0539, www.consuladoboliviano.com.ar

**Brazil:** Carlos Pellegrini 1363, 5th floor, Retiro, tel. 011/4515-6500, www.brasil.org.ar

**Canada:** Tagle 2828, Palermo, tel. 011/4808-1000, www.dfait-maeci.gc.ca/argentina

**Chile:** Roque Sáenz Peña 547, 2nd floor, tel. 011/4331-6228, www.consuladodechile.org.ar

**New Zealand:** Carlos Pellegrini 1427, 5th floor, Retiro, tel. 011/4328-0747, www.nzembassy.com

**Paraguay:** Viamonte 1851, Balvanera, tel. 011/4812-0075, www.consuladoparaguay.com.ar

**Peru:** Av. Rivadavia 1501, Microcentro, tel. 011/4382-3916, www.consuladoperubaires.org

**United Kingdom:** Dr. Luis Agote 2412, Recoleta, tel. 011/4808-2200, www.ukinargentina.fco.gov.uk

**United States:** Colombia 4300, Palermo, tel. 011/5777-4533, http://buenosaires.usembassy.gov

**Uruguay:** Av. Las Heras 1915, 5th floor, Recoleta, tel. 011/4807-3032, www.embajadadeluruguay.com.ar

clothing, jewelry, medicine, sporting gear, camping gear and accessories, photographic and video equipment, personal computers and the like, as well as 400 cigarettes, two liters of wine or alcoholic beverages (adults over 18 only), and up to US$300 in new merchandise.

Customs inspections are usually routine, but at Buenos Aires's international airports, river ports, and at some land borders, incoming checked baggage may pass through X-rays; do not put undeveloped photographic film in checked baggage. Fresh food will be confiscated at any port of entry.

At some remote border posts, the Gendarmería Nacional (Border Patrol) handles all formalities, from immigration to customs to agricultural inspections. Visitors arriving from drug-producing countries such as Colombia, Peru, and Bolivia may get special attention, as may those from Paraguay, with its thriving contraband economy.

### Police and Military

Argentina is so notorious for police corruption that Porteños and other Argentines scornfully call both federal and provincial police *la cana*—an insult that should never be used to their face.

The Policía Federal (Federal Police) are more professional than provincial forces, which are often despised for harassing motorists for minor equipment violations and, even worse, for their *gatillo fácil* (hair-trigger) response to minor criminal offenses. Officers often solicit *coimas* (bribes) at routine traffic stops. To avoid paying a bribe, either state your intention to contact your consulate, or else use broken Spanish even if you understand the language well. Either one may frustrate a corrupt official sufficiently to give up the effort.

Since the 1976–1983 dictatorship ended, the Argentine military has lost prestige and appears to have acknowledged its inability to run the country, despite occasional coup clamor by fringe figures. Still, security is heavy around military bases and photography is taboo—though the Sentry Will Shoot signs have mostly disappeared.

## CHILE

Argentines, Brazilians, Uruguayans, and Paraguayans need only national identity cards, but every other nationality needs a passport. U.S. and Canadian citizens, along with those of the European Union, Switzerland, Norway, Israel, Mexico, Australia, and New Zealand, need passports but not advance visas.

Nationalities that *must* obtain advance visas include Indians, Jamaicans, Koreans, Poles, Russians, and Thais. For contacts of overseas Chilean embassies and consulates, see the website of the Ministerio de Relaciones Exteriores (Foreign Ministry, www.minrel.gov.cl).

Chile routinely grants 90-day entry permits to foreign visitors, in the form of a tourist card that must be surrendered on departure from the country. Formally, visitors must have a return or onward ticket, but the author has entered Chile dozens of times over many years, both at the international airport and some of the most remote border posts, without ever having been asked for a return or onward ticket.

An unpleasant surprise, though, is the hefty *arrival* tax that the Foreign Ministry has imposed on certain nationalities: US$23 for Mexicans, US$95 for Australians, US$131 for U.S. citizens, and US$132 for Canadians. These are one-time fees, valid for the life of the user's passport and collected only at airports.

The rationale behind these fees, officially described as a *gasto administrativo de reciprocidad* (administrative reciprocity charge), is that the governments of those countries require Chilean citizens to pay the same amounts simply to apply for a visa (with no guarantee of being issued one). That's a reasonable argument, but the misunderstandings provoked when unsuspecting arrivals are diverted to a special line to pay those additional fees often generate ill will.

Ninety-day extensions can take several days and cost roughly US$100, plus two color photos, at the **Departamento de Extranjería** (Moneda 1342, Santiago Centro, tel. 02/6725320) or in regional capitals. Visitors close to the Argentine, Peruvian, or Bolivian border may find it quicker and cheaper to dash across the line and return. For lost tourist cards, request a replacement from the **Policía Internacional** (General Borgoño 1052, Independencia, Santiago, tel. 02/7371292), or from offices in regional capitals.

Always carry identification, since the Carabineros (national police) can request it at any moment, though they rarely do so without reason. Passports are also necessary for routine transactions like checking into hotels and cashing travelers checks.

## Lost or Stolen Passports

Visitors who suffer a lost or stolen passport must obtain a replacement at their own embassy or

## CHILEAN EMBASSIES AND CONSULATES ABROAD

Chile has embassies and consulates throughout much of the world; those listed should be most useful to potential visitors. For a complete list, check the website of the foreign-relations ministry (Ministerio de Relaciones Exteriores, www.minrel.cl).

**Argentina:**

- San Martín 439, 9th floor, Buenos Aires, tel. 011/4327-2435

**Australia:**

- 10 Culgoa Circuit, O'Malley, ACT 2606, tel. 02/6286-2430
- 80 Collins St., Level 43, Melbourne, Victoria 3000, tel. 03/9654-4982
- 44 Market St., Level 18, Sydney, NSW 2000, tel. 02/9299-2533

**Bolivia:**

- Calle 14 No. 8042, Calacoto, La Paz, tel. 2/2797331

**Brazil:**

- Praia do Flamengo 344, 7th floor, Flamengo, Rio de Janeiro, tel. 21/2552-5349
- Av. Paulista 1009, 10th floor, São Paulo, tel. 11/3284-2148

**Canada:**

- 50 O'Connor St., Suite 1413, Ottawa, ON K1P 6L2, tel. 613/235-4402
- 2 Bloor St. W., Suite 1801, Toronto, ON M4W 3E2, tel. 416/924-0106
- 1010 Sherbrooke St. W., Suite 710, Montréal, QC H3A 2R7, tel. 514/499-0405
- 1250-1185 W. Georgia St., Vancouver, BC V6E 4E6, tel. 604/681-9162

**New Zealand:**

- 7th floor, Willis Corroon House, 1-3 Welleston St., Wellington, tel. 4/471-6270

**Paraguay:**

- Capitán Emilio Neudelmann 351, Asunción, tel. 21/613855 or 21/662756

**United Kingdom:**

- 12 Devonshire St., London W1N 2DS, tel. 20/7580-1023

**United States:**

- 1736 Massachusetts Ave. NW, Washington, DC 20036, tel. 202/785-3159
- 6100 Wilshire Blvd., Suite 2140, Los Angeles, CA 90048, tel. 323/933-3697
- 870 Market St., Suite 1062, San Francisco, CA 94105, tel. 415/982-7662
- 800 Brickell Ave., Suite 1230, Miami, FL 33131, tel. 305/373-8623
- 875 N. Michigan Ave., Suite 3352, Chicago, IL 60611, tel. 312/654-8780
- 79 Milk St., Suite 600, Boston, MA 02109, tel. 617/426-1678
- 866 United Nations Plaza, Suite 601, New York, NY 10017, tel. 212/355-0612
- Public Ledger Building, Suite 1030, 6th St. & Chestnut St., Philadelphia, PA 19142, tel. 215/829-9520
- Edificio American Airlines, Suite 800, 1509 López Landrón, Santurce, San Juan, PR 00911, tel. 809/725-6365
- 1360 Post Oak Blvd., Suite 2330, Houston, TX 77056, tel. 713/621-5853

**Uruguay:**

- Andes 1365, 1st floor, Montevideo, tel. 2/902-6316

consulate. After obtaining a replacement, it's necessary to visit the Policía Internacional to replace the tourist card.

## Customs

Visitors may import personal effects including clothing, jewelry, medicine, sporting gear, camping equipment and accessories, photographic and video equipment, personal computers and the like, and wheelchairs for disabled individuals, as well as 500 grams of tobacco, three liters of wine or alcoholic beverages (adults over 18 only), and small quantities of perfume.

Customs inspections are usually routine, but at Santiago's international airport and some land borders, incoming checked baggage passes through X-rays; do not put photographic film in your checked baggage overland from Mendoza, Argentina, to Santiago, for instance. At the international airport, there are drug-sniffing beagles.

Travelers bound from Region XII (Magallanes) will undergo internal customs checks because the region has *zona franca* (duty-free) status. At many borders, the Servicio Agrícola Ganadero (SAG, Agriculture and Livestock Service) conducts agricultural inspections—fresh food will be confiscated—and sometimes levies a small charge for doing so.

At some remote border posts, the Carabineros handle all formalities, from immigration to customs to agricultural inspections.

## Police and Military

Chile's Carabineros are probably the continent's most professional police, with a reputation for integrity and a low tolerance for bribery and similar corruption (Argentine motorists, accustomed to bribing police following traffic violations in their own country, have had their vehicles confiscated for trying to do so in Chile). Known popularly but scornfully as *pacos* by some Chileans (do not use this form of address to a Carabinero!), the Carabineros are normally polite and helpful in public, but can be stern with lawbreakers—or individuals they suspect of being lawbreakers.

## FOREIGN EMBASSIES AND CONSULATES IN SANTIAGO

All major European and South American states, plus many others, have diplomatic representation in Santiago. The bordering countries of Argentina, Bolivia, and Peru have consulates in several other cities.

**Argentina:** Vicuña Mackenna 41, tel. 02/5822609, www.consuladoargentino.tie.cl

**Australia:** Isidora Goyenechea 3621, 13th floor, Las Condes, tel. 02/5503500, www.chile.embassy.gov.au

**Bolivia:** Av. Santa María 2796, Providencia, tel. 02/2328180, www.consuladodebolivia.cl

**Brazil:** MacIver 225, 15th floor, tel. 02/8205800, www.consuladodebrasil.cl

**Canada:** Nueva Tajamar 481, 12th floor, Las Condes tel. 02/6523800, www.canadainternational.gc.ca/chile-chili

**New Zealand:** El Golf 99, Oficina 703, Las Condes, tel. 02/2909802, www.nzembassy.com

**Paraguay:** Huérfanos 886, Oficina 514, tel. 2/6394640

**Peru:** Bucarest 162, Providencia, tel. 02/2318020, www.conpersantiago.cl

**United Kingdom:** Av. El Bosque Norte 0125, 3rd floor, Las Condes, tel. 02/3704100, www.ukinchile.fco.gov.uk

**United States:** Av. Costanera Andrés Bello 2800, Las Condes, tel. 02/2322600, chile.usembassy.gov

**Uruguay:** Pedro de Valdivia 711, Providencia, tel. 02/2047988

During the Pinochet dictatorship, the military were feared, but since the return to constitutional government and, especially, since Pinochet's detention and arrest in London, they keep a low public profile.

## FALKLAND ISLANDS

All visitors, including Britons, must have passports to visit the Falklands. Visitors from Britain, the European Union, most Commonwealth countries, Chile, and the Mercosur countries do not need visas, but others should contact a British consulate. Tourists must have return tickets and sufficient funds to cover their stay, and they may need to arrange accommodations in advance. Visa or MasterCard is proof of sufficient funds. Visitors must also have adequate medical coverage, including emergency evacuation insurance.

### Lost or Stolen Passports

Visitors who suffer a lost passport here—theft is unlikely—may have problems, as there are no foreign consulates. United Kingdom and European Union citizens should be able to arrange a temporary passport through Customs and Immigration, but other nationalities could need to obtain a formal Declaration of Identity through their nearest embassy and obtain permission from any other country through which they might pass, with consular assistance required at the transit airport. Consequently there could be delays in departing the Islands.

### Customs

Local customs regulations permit the importation of almost anything except illegal drugs, though there are taxes on alcoholic beverages (which are readily available locally). For details, contact Customs and Immigration (3 H Jones Rd, Stanley, tel. 27340, admin@customs.gov.fk).

### Police and Military

Falklands police resemble their British counterparts; they do not carry firearms and rarely have to deal with anything more serious than a traffic violation or a bar brawl.

The British military presence is substantial, but most live at Mount Pleasant Airport and visitors rarely come in contact with them. Some soldiers do take advantage of R&R to visit wildlife sites, where they may meet tourists.

# Outdoor Recreation

Patagonia provides exciting options for hiking, climbing, and mountain biking in the Andes; bird-watching on its Atlantic and Pacific shorelines, the interior drainage lakes, the southern steppes, and southern rainforest fjords; and viewing marine mammals ranging from seals, sea lions, and dolphins to orcas and the great right and blue whales.

On both sides of the Andes, the runoff permits white-water rafting and kayaking from the Andean lakes district in the north to Chubut province and Aisén in the south, and sea kayaking in the southern fjords and glacier-fed lakes.

## NATIONAL PARKS AND OTHER PROTECTED AREAS

Both Argentina and Chile have impressive rosters of national parks, reserves, and monuments, and some significant provincial reserves as well. In fact, Argentina and Chile were pioneers in setting aside land for conservation purposes, even if they haven't always backed up legislation with sufficient funding and have sometimes surrendered to commercial pressures.

Given a land tenure situation in which nearly all its territory is privately owned, the Falkland Islands have no formal national parks, but the northwesterly Jason Islands and some other areas are Crown Reserves. Many farms protect their wildlife zealously, and some have designated parts of their properties, particularly offshore islands, as nature reserves.

## Argentina

Argentina's main conservation agency is the Administración de Parques Nacionales (APN, Av. Santa Fe 690, Retiro, Buenos Aires, tel. 011/4311-0303, www.parquesnacionales.gov.ar, 10 A.M.–5 P.M. weekdays). While its selection of brochures on national parks and other protected areas continues to improve, the staff members themselves are best informed on the highest-profile destinations, such as Parque Nacional Los Glaciares. The APN also maintains branch offices in cities such as San Martín de los Andes, San Carlos de Bariloche, El Calafate, and Ushuaia, while rangers staff information offices at many of its parks and reserves.

Argentina has three categories of protected areas: *parques nacionales* (national parks), *reservas nacionales* (national reserves), and *monumentos naturales* (natural monuments), though the practical distinctions among them are not always clear. According to law, the national parks are "areas to be preserved in their natural state, which are representative of biogeographical region and have natural beauty or scientific interest." Often contiguous with national parks, national reserves may be buffers that permit "conservation of ecological systems...or the creation of independent conservation zones."

Natural monuments are "places, things, and live animal or plant species, of aesthetic, historic, or scientific interest, to which is granted absolute protection." They usually have one outstanding feature, such as the petrified forest of Santa Cruz province, but may also consist of a rare or endangered species such as the southern right whale or the huemul (Andean deer).

## Chile

Chile's main conservation agency is the Corporación Nacional Forestal (Conaf, National Forestry Corporation), which manages the Sistema Nacional de Áreas Silvestres Protegidas (Snaspe, National Protected Areas System). Within Snaspe, Chile has three principal categories of protected areas: *parques nacionales* (national parks), *reservas nacionales* (national reserves), and *monumentos naturales* (natural monuments). In addition, Chilean law allows for *reservas naturales privadas* or *santuarios de la naturaleza,* private nature reserves of which there are only a few as yet.

Conaf defines each of its *parques nacionales* as "a generally extensive area where there exist either unique or biologically representative environments, not significantly affected by human intervention and capable of self-sustainability, whose flora and fauna or geological formations are of special educational, scientific, or recreational interest." Management objectives are to preserve samples of these environments, their cultural and scenic characteristics, the continuity of natural processes, and to promote activities associated with education, research, and recreation.

*Monumentos naturales* are generally smaller areas "characterized by the presence of native flora and fauna, or the existence of geologically relevant sites of scenic, cultural, or scientific interest." Management objectives are similar to those of national parks.

*Reservas nacionales* are areas "whose natural resources require special attention because of their susceptibility to degradation or importance to the welfare of nearby communities." The primary management objectives are soil and watershed conservation, the preservation of endangered wild flora and fauna, and the application of appropriate technologies to those ends.

## Falkland Islands

The Falklands have no national parks per se, but there are 27 "national nature reserves" totaling about 400 square kilometers. Several farms are de facto wildlife reserves, and a handful have been formally designated so, most notably the **New Island South Wildlife Reserve.** The remote 790-hectare **Steeple Jason Island** belongs to the Wildlife Conservation Society of New York, while the neighboring **Grand Jason Island** is government property, a Crown Reserve.

## HIKING

Both Argentina and Chile have plenty of ideal hiking terrain, and the number of parks and reserves with integrated and well-maintained trail systems is increasing, but there are still shortcomings. Each country has an Instituto Geográfico Militar whose topographic maps, at a scale of 1:50,000, are available for parts of the country, but many trails lack clearly signposted junctions—multiple tracks are the rule. If necessary, try to contract a local guide.

Prime hiking and backpacking areas include the lakes districts on both sides of the Andes, where the season tends to be longer than in the far south; throughout the region, the Argentine side tends to be drier than the Chilean side, which receives the brunt of Pacific storms. Of the more northerly parks, the best for hiking are Nahuel Huapi and Lanín on the Argentine side, and Huerquehue, Villarrica, and Puyehue on the Chilean side.

South of the temperate lakes districts, Patagonia can be inclement at any time of year. In Argentina, the northern El Chaltén sector of Parque Nacional Los Glaciares has the best trail network, but things are improving at hard-to-reach Parque Nacional Perito Moreno, which is much less crowded.

Farther south on the Chilean side, the best hiking destinations are Parque Pumalín, whose unique trails include ladders through vertiginously steep forest terrain; Reserva Nacional Cerro Castillo, the best multi-day hiking choice in the Aisén region; and of course Parque Nacional Torres del Paine, whose season is consistently lengthening. Popular Paine is the most crowded hikers' destination in all of Patagonia, but motivated walkers can still find solitude on its lesser-known trails.

In the Falkland Islands, where wildlife-watching is the main tourist activity and the coastal sites are distant from each other, most people travel by air taxi and four-wheel-drive vehicle. That said, there's plenty of open country and hiking opportunities for those willing to confront the incessant westerlies.

## CLIMBING

In both Argentine and Chilean Patagonia, the long Andean cordillera offers a climber's

© WAYNE BERNHARDSON

The "trekking capital" of El Chaltén occupies a scenic site on Río de las Vueltas.

buffet, or for truly committed pilgrims it can be a mecca. For serious technical climbers, the biggest draws are the vertical spires of the Fitz Roy range in Parque Nacional Los Glaciares's El Chaltén sector, or even Parque Nacional Nahuel Huapi's ice-covered 3,478-meter Monte Tronador. Other options include the rest of Parque Nacional Nahuel Huapi near Bariloche and 3,776-meter Volcán Lanín near Junín de los Andes. A warning: Even experienced mountaineers in prime condition have died on these peaks.

Across the Andes, Chile's volcanoes are a particular attraction—from the northernmost lakes district to remotest southern Aisén region, Chile is part of the Pacific "ring of fire"—but there is snow, ice, and rock climbing on all kinds of surfaces. Summer is the season for most climbers.

The most frequently climbed Chilean volcano, near the resort town of Pucón, is 2,847-meter Volcán Villarrica, which is also one of the most active; it's a day excursion that's sometimes canceled when Conaf determines that the crater is a little too lively. A local guide is obligatory. Volcán Osorno, near the town of Puerto Varas, is also commercially climbed but is more technical.

For general information on mountaineering in Argentina, try the **Centro Andino Buenos Aires** (Av. Rivadavia 1255, Oficinas 2/3, tel. 011/4381-1566, www.caba.org.ar). There are also local and provincial mountaineering clubs.

Capable independent climbers can tackle many Chilean summits on their own, but peaks near international borders require clearance from the Foreign Ministry's **Dirección de Fronteras y Límites** (Difrol, Teatinos 180, 7th floor, Santiago, tel. 02/8275900, fax 02/3810179, www.difrol.cl). For this permission, which may be done prior to arrival, each participant must present complete name, passport number, nationality, birth date, residence address, profession, arrival and departure dates in Chile, and a detailed itinerary. Issuing permission usually takes 2–3 days; climbers must present this permission to the nearest Carabineros police station before actually undertaking the climb.

For general information on climbing in Chile, including suggestions on dealing with the bureaucracy, contact the **Federación de Andinismo** (Almirante Simpson 77, tel. 02/2220888, www.feach.cl). See also the bilingual online **Chile Climbing Page** (www.chilemountains.info).

While the Falkland Islands are not a climber's destination per se, the rocky summits of both main islands, though they barely reach 700 meters, can provide challenging recreation.

## CYCLING AND MOUNTAIN BIKING

Both long-distance riders and recreational mountain bikers will find Patagonia's spectacular landscapes appealing and rugged terrain challenging. Because many roads have dirt or gravel surfaces, and because paved roads are often so narrow that riding on the shoulder is imperative, a mountain bike is the best option. Riders without their own bikes will find rentals readily available in tourist towns like Bariloche and Pucón, but their condition varies widely—check brakes, tires, and everything else before renting.

If touring, carry rain gear, a tent, and supplementary camping gear, and acquire a knowledge of bicycle repairs—some of the finest riding areas have almost no services. Possible routes are countless, but the most popular area is the scenic lakes district on both sides of the Andes.

Increasing numbers of cyclists, some of them through riders from Alaska to Tierra del Fuego, are braving the changeable weather on Chile's Carretera Austral, a discontinuous 1,100-kilometer penetration road from Puerto Montt that's now complete to the southern outpost of Villa O'Higgins, and even onwards to El Chaltén, on the Argentine side. Mostly gravel except for a few paved segments around the regional capital of Coyhaique, it still requires several ferry crossings as it passes through some of the continent's most spectacular wild terrain. East of the Andes, between Esquel and

El Calafate, Argentina's dusty but charismatic RN 40 parallels the Carretera Austral, but riders need tremendous stamina and sense of balance, as the powerful winds can either slow progress to a crawl or blow a rider over.

Feasible as early as October, the southernmost Patagonian routes are probably best December–April. As work progresses on the Sendero de Chile, intended to link the Andean uplands for pedestrians, bicycles, and horseback riders only, this will become an even more adventurous alternative.

## HORSEBACK RIDING

Gaucho Argentina was born on horseback, and recreational riding is common even in and around Buenos Aires. It's most interesting in the provinces, though, especially in the rugged terrain of the Andean lakes around Junín de los Andes and Bariloche. Trips range from morning or afternoon trail rides to hard-riding excursions of several days, and nearly all *estancias* offer riding as an optional activity.

Likewise, Chile's strong *huaso* tradition makes riding a popular pastime in many lakes district and southern Patagonian destinations. The most challenging options are around Pucón and the Cochamó area near Puerto Varas, and in Parque Nacional Torres del Paine.

## SKIING

Since the seasons are reversed in southern South America, Patagonia's Andean slopes reach their peak in August. While Argentina's international and regional ski resorts may not have the reputation of Chile's best, the mountains near Bariloche have long drawn skiers from around the continent and the world. There are also options at San Martín de los Andes, Villa La Angostura, Esquel, and even Ushuaia.

Chile's famous international ski resorts are close to the capital city of Santiago, but Parque Nacional Villarrica (near the town of Pucón) and Antillanca in Parque Nacional Puyehue (near the city of Osorno) are respectable choices.

## BIRDING

Patagonia's diverse natural environments—ranging from Atlantic and Pacific shorelines to boundless steppes with surprising wetlands and from Andean woodlands to the sub-Antarctic—mean an opportunity to add lots of new species to your life list. The finest birding areas are the Atlantic and Pacific coasts, the arid eastern steppes, and both sides of the temperate Andean woodlands in the lakes district.

For birding suggestions in Argentina, contact the **Asociación Ornitológica del Plata** (Matheu 1246, Buenos Aires, tel. 011/4943-7216, www.avesargentinas.org.ar). **Hostería Las Torres,** in Chile's Parque Nacional Torres del Paine, is also a birding specialist with English-speaking personnel. Many tour operators offer birding excursions.

## WATER SPORTS

Argentines and Chileans have traditionally flocked to their countries' beaches, riversides, and southern lakes, but have only recently begun to enjoy active water sports like surfing, sea kayaking, windsurfing, diving, and white-water rafting and kayaking.

### White-Water Rafting and Kayaking

Descending steeply from the Andes, Chile's transverse Patagonian rivers are world-class—more than a few rafters and kayakers consider the powerful Futaleufú, in a remote area near the southern Argentine border, the world's *best* white water. The Trancura near Pucón, the Fuy near Panguipulli, the Petrohué near Puerto Varas, and the Baker south of Coyhaique all blend wild water with exquisite scenery, but none of them quite matches the Futaleufú's adrenaline level.

On the rain-shadow side of the Andes, Argentine rivers mostly lack the tremendous spring snowmelt that turns Chilean rivers into raging white water, but there are commercially viable rivers from the Aluminé in northern Neuquén to Esquel in northern Chubut, and the number is growing. The country's top river is the Class IV Río Manso, south of Bariloche.

Nearly all Patagonian rivers may be run from the first October runoff to the early days of April.

### Diving

Diving may not be an obvious activity in Patagonia, much of whose waters are cold and lack reefs, but in summer the Argentine city of Puerto Madryn, in Chubut province, has a cluster of diving outfitters and operators for the warm and shallow waters of the Golfo Nuevo.

### Surfing and Windsurfing

The good news is that, with a long coastline and small surfer population, Patagonia means little competition for waves; the bad news is that Argentina's Atlantic surf is generally tamer than Chile's Pacific, which is wilder but much colder (wet suits are essential here).

Shallow waters and wide tidal ranges may be further deterrents in Argentine Patagonia, but places like desolate Cabo Raso (where competition is zero) are suitable. The waters of the Golfo Nuevo, at Puerto Madryn, are too sheltered for big waves, but the blustery Patagonian winds make it a windsurfer's paradise.

Most Chilean surfers frequent areas well north of the Andean lakes district, but there are possibilities near the coastal city of Valdivia. Windsurfing is best on some of the lakes, rather than on the ocean.

### Sea Kayaking

The Chilean village of Dalcahue, on the Isla Grande de Chiloé, is a center for commercial sea kayaking, though there are many other suitable locations, among them Puerto Natales and Tierra del Fuego's spectacular Cordillera Darwin. The channels of Pacific Chile offer exceptional opportunities, such as the river to ocean route from the mouth of the Río Futaleufú to Chaitén via Lago Yelcho and the Río Yelcho.

While Argentine Patagonia's exposed coastline lacks the sheltered channels and inlets of Pacific Chile, Nahuel Huapi and other large glacial lakes are a more-than-adequate substitute for sea kayakers.

### Fishing

Both Argentine and Chilean Patagonia draw fly-fishing enthusiasts eager to test their skills on lakes, rivers, and fjords from both sides of the Andean lakes district to Tierra del Fuego's southernmost tip.

Along the eastern Andean slopes, the rivers of Neuquén and Río Negro provinces have Argentina's greatest concentration of fly-fishing choices. Along Chile's Carretera Austral, in the Aisén region, there are numerous specialized fishing lodges and other resorts that include fly-fishing among their offerings.

## Accommodations

Argentine and Chilean Patagonia both have accommodations in all categories, from campgrounds to youth-hostel dormitories to extravagant luxury suites and everything in between, but peak summer season demand can stress the resources of some localities. National and municipal tourist officials offer accommodations lists and brochures, but these often exclude budget options and may even omit some midrange and high-end places.

Argentine prices may be negotiable; do not assume the *tarifa mostrador* (rack rate) is etched in stone. Visitors should not take hotel ratings too literally as they often represent an ideal rather than a reality, and some one- or two-star places are significantly better than others that formally rank higher.

Prices in Buenos Aires and Santiago often fall during the summer months of January and February, as business travel slows to a crawl; for Patagonian destinations, though, prices usually rise. Other peak seasons, when prices may rise, are Semana Santa (Holy Week), July's winter school vacations, which coincide with

Argentine patriotic holidays, and mid-September's Chilean patriotic holidays.

Note that Argentine hotels levy 21 percent in *impuesto al valor agregado* or IVA (value-added tax). Unless otherwise indicated, rates in this guide include IVA, but if there's any question at the front desk, ask for clarification to avoid unpleasant surprises when paying the bill.

Midrange to upscale Chilean hotels levy 19 percent IVA but can legally discount that to tourists with the appropriate documentation—passport and tourist card—who pay in dollars or by international credit card. Foreign residents of Chile are *not* eligible for this discount. At the same time, the discount can be smaller than expected if the hotel's exchange rate is unfavorable.

## CAMPING

Organized camping is common throughout Patagonia; campgrounds are generally spacious affairs, with shade, clean toilets, and bathrooms with hot showers, and even groceries and restaurants. They are often surprisingly central and are usually cheap, rarely more than a few dollars per person, but some Chilean campgrounds charge for a minimum of four or five persons.

In the peak summer season and on weekends, the best sites can be crowded and noisy, as families on a budget take advantage of bargain prices. It's usually possible to find a quiet—but less desirable—site on the periphery. Remember that Argentines stay up late—very late—for their barbecues.

In the wilder, more remote areas like Santa Cruz and Aisén, it's possible to camp just about anywhere for free, though there are restrictions in the most popular destinations like Parque Nacional Los Glaciares and Parque Nacional Torres del Paine.

## HOSTELS

For youth and budget travel, Argentina and Chile have growing hostel networks, plus many independent hostels, where bunks start around US$8–10 per person. In Argentina, since the 2002 devaluation, these are no longer the only budget options, but they do offer an opportunity to get together with like-minded travelers. In addition to the customary dorm accommodations, many hostels offer more expensive private rooms for individuals and couples.

Note that Argentine hostels usually avoid the term *albergue;* in Argentine Spanish, an *albergue transitorio* means a by-the-hour hotel. Many have adapted the English word hostel, or Hispanicized it into *hostal,* a term more common in Chile, where it's a step above a *hospedaje.*

For up-to-the-minute information on official Argentine hostels, contact **Hostelling International Argentina** (Florida 835, 3rd floor, Oficina 319-B, tel. 011/4511-8723, www.hostels.org.ar). For their Chilean counterparts, contact **Hostelling International Santiago** (Cienfuegos 151, Santiago Centro, tel. 02/6718532, fax 02/6728880, www.hostelling.cl) or the **Asociación Chilena de Albergues Turísticos Juveniles** (Hernando de Aguirre 201, Oficina 602, Providencia, Santiago, tel. 02/2333220, fax 02/2322555, hostelling@hostelling.cl).

Numerous independent hostels have opened in both countries, sometimes in loosely affiliated groups such as Chile's **Backpacker's Best** (www.backpackersbest.cl) and **Backpackers Chile** (www.backpackerschile.com). These often have private rooms in addition to dorm-style accommodations.

## OTHER BUDGET ACCOMMODATIONS

Budget accommodations in Argentina and Chile can cost as little as US$8–10 per person; they go by a variety of names that may camouflage their quality—ranging from dingy fleabags with mattresses that sag like hammocks to simple but cheerful and tidy places with firm new beds.

A *hospedaje* is generally a family-run lodging with a few spare rooms; *pensiones* and *casas de huéspedes* (guesthouses) are comparable, nearly interchangeable terms. All may have long-term residents as well as overnight guests. *Residenciales* (singular *residencial*) are generally

## A DAY (OR MORE) IN THE COUNTRY

Over the past decade-plus, facing economic reality, many of Argentina's great rural estates have opened themselves to the tourist trade. From the subtropical north to the sub-Antarctic south, diversification has become the word for *estancia* (ranch) owners, some of which earn more income from hosting visitors than they do growing grain or raising livestock. For many visitors, staying at an *estancia* is their entire vacation.

According to the Buenos Aires-based Red Argentina de Turismo Rural (Ratur), more than 1,000 *estancias* are open to the public, and hundreds of thousands of people spend some time in the countryside every month. For nearly all of these farms, tourism makes up a significant portion of their income, and for some of them, most notably in Patagonia, it exceeds 90 percent.

Throughout the country, some *estancias* are reasonably priced places with limited services, but others are magnificent properties with castle-like *cascos* (big houses), elaborate service that includes gourmet meals, and recreational activities such as horseback riding, tennis, and swimming. Some *estancias* aim at day-trippers – weekending in the countryside of Buenos Aires province has become an increasingly popular option for escaping the capital – but most of them prefer overnight guests.

Many *estancias* get detailed individual coverage in this guide, but various others are open to the public. Several groups of them have formed networks to promote themselves as tourist destinations.

Affiliated with the Sociedad Rural Argentina, the traditionally powerful landowners' organization, the **Red Argentina de Turismo Rural** (Ratur, Florida 460, 4th floor, Buenos Aires, tel. 011/4328-0499, www.raturestancias.com.ar) represents a number of *estancias* in northern and southern Buenos Aires province, and a few more in Mesopotamia, the Cuyo region, and Patagonia.

**Estancias Argentinas** (Diagonal Roque Sáenz Peña 616, Oficina 910, Buenos Aires, tel. 011/4343-2366, www.estanciasargentinas.com) has expanded in recent years, with a broader geographical representation than it once had, but not all of its members are *estancias* – some are even urban hotels.

The best-organized provincial group is **Estancias de Santa Cruz** (Suipacha 1120, Retiro, Buenos Aires, tel./fax 011/4325-3098 or 011/4325-3102, www.estanciasdesantacruz.com). Most of its affiliates are in the southwestern corner of its home province, but there are also a few members on the Argentine side of Tierra del Fuego.

© WAYNE BERNHARDSON

Estancia Anita's Hostería Alta Vista in Argentina's Santa Cruz province

buildings constructed with short-stay accommodations in mind, but they may also have semi-permanent inhabitants. All such places may even go by the term *hotel,* though that term usually means a more formal category.

All these categories may have some exceptionally good values. Most will have shared bath and toilet *(baño general* or *baño compartido),* but some offer a choice between shared and private bath *(baño privado);* bathtubs are unusual. In some cases, they will have ceiling fans and even cable TV, but there is often an extra charge for cable and almost always a surcharge for air-conditioning.

Travelers intending to stay at budget accommodations should bring their own towels, though some provide towels. Many but by no means all include breakfast in their rates; ask to be certain.

### Showers

Many Argentine and Chilean showers use natural gas in a *calefón,* which heats the water as it passes through the gas-run water heater. Opening the tap normally triggers the *calefón,* presuming the *piloto* (pilot) is lit, but some budget-conscious accommodations light the pilot only when someone wants to take a shower. Before getting in and turning on the tap, be sure the pilot is lit.

## MIDRANGE ACCOMMODATIONS

Midrange hotels generally offer larger, more comfortable, and better-furnished rooms than even the best budget places. This category almost always includes a private bath. Ceiling fans, cable TV, and even air-conditioning are common, but there may not be on-site parking. Some have restaurants. Rates can range anywhere from US$50 up to US$100 d; some are better values than their high-end counterparts.

## HIGH-END ACCOMMODATIONS

Luxury hotels with top-flight service are most common in the capital cities of Buenos Aires and Santiago and major resort areas, but they are increasingly abundant throughout Patagonia. In capital cities, these will usually offer amenities like restaurants, swimming pools, gym facilities, business centers, Internet connections, and conference rooms; outside capital cities, these are mostly resort hotels and may lack the business facilities. Invariably they will offer secure parking.

Some of the best options are hot-springs hotels and country-inn resorts on *estancias,* which offer traditional hospitality and ambience with style unmatchable at other high-end places. Prices range upwards of US$100, often substantially upwards.

# Food and Drink

Food and drink range from the economical and ordinary to the truly elegant and everything in between. In Argentina, for most of the 1990s, eating well at restaurants was financially challenging except for cheap cafeteria lunches and *tenedor libre* (all-you-can-eat—literally, "free fork") buffets, but the peso collapse of 2002 has made it possible to eat diverse and imaginative food for a fraction of its former price—at least for visitors with dollars or euros in their bank accounts.

Stereotypically, the Argentine diet consists of beef and more beef. This common perception is not entirely mistaken, but the diet has always had a Spanish touch and, for more than a century, a marked Italian influence with pizza and pasta. Over the past decade, though, the restaurant scene has become far more cosmopolitan, adventurous, and nuanced, with Brazilian, Japanese, Thai, Vietnamese, and many other once-exotic cuisines—not to mention high-quality variations on regional dishes.

Chile's long, rich coastline and productive farmland provide seafood, meat, fresh fruit, and vegetables in abundance. While the

## DINING VOCABULARY AND ETIQUETTE

In both Argentina and Chile, dining vocabulary is mostly straightforward. The usual term for menu is *la carta; el menú* is almost equally common but can also mean a fixed-price lunch or dinner. The bill is *la cuenta. Cubiertos* are silverware, while a *plato* is a plate and *vaso* a glass. A *plato principal* is a main dish or entrée.

Note that one might ask for a *vaso de agua* (glass of water), but never for a *vaso de vino* (literally but incorrectly, a glass of wine); rather, ask for a *copa de vino*. When speaking English, native Spanish speakers often make a comparable error in requesting "a cup of wine."

Many but not all Argentine restaurants assess a small *cubierto* (cover charge) for dishes, silverware, and bread. This is not a *propina* (tip); generally, a 10 percent tip is the norm, but Argentines themselves often ignore this norm, especially in times of economic crisis. Women in a group will often tip little or nothing, but a good rule of thumb is that anyone able to afford a restaurant meal can afford a tip.

It's worth emphasizing that the occupation of waiter is traditionally male and professional, rather than a short-term expedient for university students or aspiring actors, but this is changing in the new, stylish restaurants, where servers are just as likely to be young and female. Note, though, that *mozo,* a common and innocuous term for an Argentine waiter, implies an insulting servility in Chile. When in doubt, use *mesero* or *jóven,* even if the individual in question is not particularly young; for a female, use *señorita* unless the individual is at least of late middle age.

everyday Chilean diet may have some shortcomings, in most areas visitors will have no difficulty finding appealing food and drink.

On both sides of the border, it's becoming more common to find "Patagonian" cuisine that stresses fresh regional products, including wild game, lamb, seafood, greens, and soft fruits like raspberries.

## WHERE TO EAT

In Argentina, places to eat range from hole-in-the-wall *comedores* (eateries) or fast-food *bares* (unavoidably but misleadingly translated as "bars") with no formal menu, in bus and train stations, to *cafés, confiterías* (teahouses), and elegant *restaurantes* in Buenos Aires and other major tourist centers.

Likewise, in Chile, *restaurante* can cover a seemingly infinite range of possibilities. About the only hard and fast rule is to avoid places in which single men—or groups of men—sit and drink beer.

Restaurant terminology—the words used to describe various eateries—overlaps in Argentina and Chile, but there are some differences.

### Argentina

*Restaurante* (occasionally *restorán* or, more fashionably, *restó*) usually means a place with sit-down service, but within this definition there can be great differences. Most often, the term refers to a locale with a printed menu and table service, but even this can range from any place with a basic beef and pasta menu to truly elegant settings with celebrity chefs, complex cuisine, elaborate wine lists, and professional service.

The usual international fast-food villains have franchises in Buenos Aires, but the best cheap food normally comes from *rotiserías* (delicatessens), which serve excellent takeaway fare and may have basic seating. Likewise, supermarkets such as Coto and Disco have budget *cafeterías* that are excellent budget options.

*Bares* and *comedores* are no-frills eateries, with indifferent service, offering *minutas* (short orders); the term *comedor* can also mean a hotel breakfast nook or dining room. A *café,* by contrast, is a place whose patrons may dawdle over coffee and croissants, but its real purpose is to promote social interaction in personal affairs, business deals, and other transactions—even though it also serves snacks, *minutas,* and alcoholic beverages.

*Confiterías,* by contrast, serve breakfast, light meals like sandwiches, snacks like cakes and other desserts, and coffee-based drinks. Generally more formal than *cafés*—some of them prestigious—they are suitable for afternoon tea; some have full-scale restaurant menus, often in a separate section.

### Chile

*Cocinería* can be a synonym for *comedor,* but there are several other terms not used in Argentina. *Fuente de soda* (literally, "soda fountain") signifies a place with a modest menu that lacks a liquor license. *Cafeterías* provide plain meals, usually without table service, but the misleadingly named *salón de té* (literally, "teahouse") can be more like a European-style café, sometimes with sidewalk seating. *Hosterías* are generally country-style restaurants serving large numbers of customers on weekend or holiday outings. *Hostería* can also mean a type of accommodations, though such places often have restaurants as well.

One distinctively Chilean term is the *picada,* a small family-run eatery that begins informally, often with just a couple tables in a spare room facing the street, but can develop into something more elaborate. (In both Chile and Argentina, by the way, *picada* can mean a snack, and in Argentina, it can also refer to a trail or footpath.)

*Marisquerías* are simple but often very good fish and seafood eateries in locations where they can buy the morning's catch straight off the boat.

## WHAT TO EAT

According to historian John C. Super, whatever the negative consequences of the Spanish invasion, it actually improved a late pre-Columbian diet that was, by some accounts, nutritionally deficient (often protein-poor). In Super's opinion,

> *The combination of European and American foods created diversified, nutritionally rich diets. Crop yields were higher than those in Europe, and longer or staggered growing seasons made fresh food available during much of the year. The potential for one of the best diets in the history of the world was evident soon after discovery of the New World. For Europeans, the introduction of livestock and wheat was an essential step in creating that diet.*

When Europeans first set foot in South America, in the densely populated Andean region, the staples were beans, squash, and a variety of potatoes and other tubers, but the diet was low in animal protein—only the llama, alpaca, guinea pig, and wild game were readily available, and not in all areas. Spanish introductions such as wheat and barley, which yielded only a four-to-one harvest ratio in Europe, were usually double or triple that in the Americas.

The Spanish introductions blended with the indigenous base to create many edibles found on Argentine and Chilean tables today. The abundance of seafood, combined with European animal protein and high-productivity European fruits like apples, apricots, grapes, pears, and many others, resulted in a diverse food production and consumption system, which, however, is changing today.

### Cereals

*Trigo* (wheat), a Spanish introduction, is most common in *pan* (bread) but also appears in the form of pasta. *Arroz* (rice) is a common *agregado* or *guarnición* (side dish).

*Maíz* (maize or corn) is a main ingredient in many dishes, including the Italian-derived polenta. Maize leaves often serve as a wrapping for traditional dishes like *humitas,* equivalent to Mexican tamales in northwestern Argentina and throughout Chile.

### Legumes, Vegetables, and Tubers

Salads are almost always safe, and all but the most sensitive stomachs probably need not be concerned with bugs from greens washed in tap water. In Argentine restaurants, green salads are usually large enough for two diners.

*Porotos* (beans of all sorts except green beans) are traditional in families of Spanish descent. Other common legumes include *chauchas* (green beans), *arvejas* (peas), *lentejas* (lentils), and *habas* (fava beans).

In many varieties, *zapallo* (squash) is part of the traditional diet, as is the *tomate* (tomato). Old World vegetables include *acelga* (chard), *berenjena* (eggplant), *coliflor* (cauliflower), *lechuga* (lettuce), and *repollo* (cabbage). *Chiles* (peppers) are relatively uncommon; neither Argentine nor Chilean cuisine is really *picante* (spicy), except for dishes from Argentina's Andean northwest, and even those rarely challenge palates accustomed to Mexican or Thai cuisine.

Native to the central Andes, *papas* (potatoes) grow in well-drained soils at higher elevations in northwestern Argentina and as far south as the Chilean archipelago of Chiloé; *papas fritas* (french fries) are almost universal, but spuds also appear as *purée* (mashed potatoes) and in Italian-derived dishes such as Argentine *ñoquis* (gnocchi). Other common tubers include *zanahorias* (carrots) and *rábanos* (radishes).

## Vegetarianism

While vegetarian restaurants are few outside of Buenos Aires and Santiago, the ingredients for vegetarian meals are easy to obtain, and many eateries prepare dishes such as pasta and salads that are easily adapted to vegetarian preferences. Before ordering any pasta dish, verify whether it comes with a meat sauce—*carne* means "beef" in the Southern Cone. Waiters or waitresses may consider chicken, pork, and similar items another category—sometimes called *carne blanca* (literally, "white meat"). Faced with an unwilling kitchen, you can always plead *alergia* (allergy).

## Fruits

As its seasons are reversed from the Northern Hemisphere, the temperate Southern Cone produces many of the same fruits, often available as fresh juices. Items like *manzana* (apple), *pera* (pear), *naranja* (orange), *ciruela* (plum), *sandía* (watermelon), *membrillo* (quince), *durazno* (peach), *frambuesa* (raspberry), and *frutilla* (strawberry) will be familiar to almost everyone. When requesting *jugo de naranja* (orange juice) in Argentina, be sure it comes *exprimido* (fresh-squeezed) rather than out of a can or box. In Chile, fresh-squeezed juice is a *vitamina*.

Also widely available, mostly through import, are tropical and subtropical fruits like banana and *ananá* (pineapple). Mango, *maracuyá* (passion fruit), cherimoya, and similar tropical fruits are less common but not unknown.

The *palta* (avocado), a Central American domesticate known as *aguacate* in its area of origin, often appears in Argentine and Chilean salads.

## Meats and Poultry

Prior to the Spaniards, South America's only domesticated animals were the *cuy* (guinea pig, rare in what is now Argentina and Chile), the llama and alpaca, and the dog, sometimes used for food. The Spaniards enriched the American diet with their domestic animals, including cattle, sheep, pigs, and poultry (chickens and ducks).

Red meat consumption, the hallmark of the Argentine diet, may be decreasing among the more affluent but it remains the entrée of choice among lower classes. Thanks to the Italian immigrant influence, pasta is available almost everywhere. Traditionally, Chileans consume less red meat than Argentines, but it remains the entrée of choice for many.

*Carne,* often modified as *carne de vacuno,* or *bife* (beef), is the most common menu item in both countries. Specifically Argentine terms include *bife de chorizo* (sirloin or rump steak), *bife de lomo* (tenderloin), *asado de tira* (rib roast), and *matambre* (rolled flank steak). *Milanesa* is a breaded cutlet or chicken-fried steak that, at cheaper eateries, can be greasy.

The widest selection is usually available in the *parrillada* or *asado,* a mixed grill that includes prime cuts but also *achuras,* a broad term that encompasses offal such as *chinchulines* (small intestines, known as *chunchules* in Chile), *mollejas* (sweetbreads), *criadillas* (testicles), *morcilla* (blood sausage), and *riñones* (kidneys). *Asado* can also mean a simple roast.

## CATTLE CULTURE ON THE PAMPAS

From his hotel room on the Avenida de Mayo, U.S. poet Robert Lowell once wrote, he could hear "the bulky, beefy breathing of the herds." Ever since feral livestock changed the face of the Pampas in the 16th century, displacing the native guanaco and rhea, cattle have been a symbol of wealth and the foundation of the Argentine diet. Riding across the Pampas, Charles Darwin found the reliance on beef remarkable:

> *I had now been several days without tasting any thing besides meat: I did not at all dislike this new regimen; but I felt as if it would only have agreed with me with hard exercise. I have heard that patients in England, when desired to confine themselves exclusively to an animal diet, even with the hope of life before their eyes, have scarce been able to endure it. Yet the Gaucho in the Pampas, for months together, touches nothing but beef.... It is, perhaps, from their meat regimen that the Gauchos, like other carnivorous animals, can abstain long from food. I was told that at Tandeel, some troops voluntarily pursued a party of Indians for three days, without eating or drinking.*

Recent research has suggested that this diet has not been quite so universal as once imagined – urban archaeologist Daniel Schávelzon has unearthed evidence that, for instance, fish consumption was much greater in colonial Buenos Aires than once thought – but there is no doubt that the *parrilla* is a culinary institution. Beef may not be healthy in the quantities that some Argentines enjoy, and many of them will even admit it. But few can bypass traditional restaurants, where flamboyantly clad urban gauchos stir the glowing coals beneath grilled meat on a vertical spit, without craving that savory beef.

For most Argentines, *bien cocido* (well done) is the standard for steak, but *jugoso* (rare) and *a punto* (medium) are not uncommon. In Patagonia, though, the standard is just as often well-grilled lamb.

*Chimichurri* is a garlic-based marinade that often accompanies the Argentine *parrillada.*

Sausages such as the slightly spicy Argentine *chorizo* may also form part of the *asado;* in a hot-dog bun, it becomes *choripán. Panchos* are basic hot dogs, while *fiambres* are processed meats.

*Cordero* (lamb), often roasted on a spit over an open fire, is common in Patagonia. *Cerdo* (pork) appears in many forms, ranging from simple *jamón* (ham) to *chuletas* (chops) to *lomito* (loin) and *matambre de cerdo* (pork flank steak). *Chivo* (goat) or *chivito* (the diminutive) is a western Argentine specialty that sometimes appears on menus in the capital and occasionally in Patagonia; note that the Uruguayan *chivito* means something else—a steak sandwich or plate slathered with eggs, fries, and other high-calorie extras.

Argentine stews and casseroles include *carbonada* (beef, rice, potatoes, sweet potatoes, corn, squash, and fruit like apples and peaches) and *puchero* (beef, chicken, bacon, sausage, *morcilla,* cabbage, corn, garbanzos, peppers, tomatoes, onions, squash, and sweet potatoes). Broth-cooked rice serves as a garnish.

*Ave* (poultry) most often means *pollo* (chicken), which sometimes appears on menus as *gallina* (literally, hen) in a casserole or stew; eggs are *huevos. Pavo* (turkey) is becoming more common.

In Chile, the most common poultry dish is *cazuela de ave,* a stewed piece of chicken in a thin broth with potato, corn on the cob, and other vegetables.

### Fish and Seafood

Argentine fish and seafood may not have the international reputation of its beef, but the long coastline, territorial seas, and freshwater rivers and lakes provide abundant options. Buenos Aires and other coastal cities have fine seafood restaurants, but these are less common in the interior. Chilean cuisine makes better use of its abundant ocean resources.

Seafood, among the most abundant animal-protein sources in pre-Columbian times, includes both *pescado* (fish) and *mariscos* (shellfish and crustaceans). The most common fish are *congrio* (conger eel, covering a variety of species), sometimes called *abadejo; lenguado* (sole or flounder), *merluza* (hake), and freshwater *trucha* (trout); *salmón* (salmon) normally comes from Patagonian fish farms.

The cheapest restaurants often ruin perfectly good fish by preparing it *frito* (deep fried), but on request almost all will prepare it *a la plancha* (grilled, usually with a dab of butter) or *al vapor* (steamed). Higher-priced restaurants will add simple or sometimes elaborate sauces, often including shellfish.

Among the shellfish, visitors will recognize the relatively commonplace *almejas* (clams), *calamares* (squid), *camarones* (shrimp), *cangrejo* or *jaiva* (crab), *centolla* (king crab), *mejillones* (mussels), *ostiones* or *callos* (scallops, but beware—*callos* can also mean tripe), *ostras* (oysters), and *pulpo* (octopus). Spanish restaurants normally serve the greatest variety of fish and shellfish.

Chilean cuisine also makes use of *cholgas* and *choritos* (different varieties of mussels) and *machas* (razor clams), as well as more unusual items like the *choro zapato* ("shoe mussel," so called because of its enormous size); *erizos* (sea urchins, definitely an acquired taste, frequently exported to Japan); the oddly named *locos* (giant abalone, literally "crazies"); *picoroco* (giant barnacle); and *piure* (resembling a dirty sponge, according to food writer Robb Walsh). Many shellfish have closed seasons, when they may not be taken.

Seafood often appears on the menu in the form of ceviche, raw fish or shellfish marinated in lime juice and spiced with cilantro. Other seafood specialties worth looking for are *chupes* (casseroles) of *congrio, jaiva,* and *locos,* and *curanto,* a kitchen-sink stew that can include fish, shellfish, beef, chicken, lamb, pork, potato, and vegetables.

## "Fast Food" Snacks

Despite the invasion of international franchises, Argentina retains some of the continent's best snack food. Best of the best is the empanada, a flaky turnover most often filled with ground beef, hard-boiled egg, and olive, but it may also come with ham and cheese, chicken, onion, and (rarely) with tuna or fish. The spicier ground beef *salteña* comes from northwestern Argentina but may be available elsewhere; the tangy *empanada árabe* (lamb with a touch of lemon juice) is more difficult to find. Empanadas *al horno* (oven-baked) are lighter than *fritas* (fried, sometimes in heavy oil).

Argentine pizza is also exceptional, though less diverse in toppings than in North America. For slices, try the cheeseless *fugazza* with Vidalia-sweet onions or its cousin *fugazzeta,* enhanced with ham and mozzarella. Argentines embellish their slices with *fainá,* a baked chickpea dough that fits neatly atop.

Chileans also eat pizza, but it generally lacks zest. Chilean empanadas are larger, with a heavier crust; the standard is the *empanada de pino* of ground beef, hard-boiled egg, and olive, but ham and cheese is an option. Only at Easter does seafood appear in Chilean empanadas.

## Desserts

At home, the standard Argentine *postre* is fresh fruit, ranging from grapes (many single-family homes have their own arbors) to apples, pears, and oranges. In restaurants, this becomes *ensalada de frutas* (fruit salad) or, more elaborately, *macedonia. Postre vigilante,* consisting of cheese and *membrillo* (quince) or *batata* (sweet potato) preserves, is another fruit-based dessert; it also goes by the name *queso y dulce.*

Often topped with whipped cream, *arroz con leche* (rice pudding) and flan (egg custard) are also good choices, as is the Spanish custard *natillas.* An acquired taste is *dulce de leche,* which one international travel magazine referred to as "its own major food group." Argentines spread prodigious quantities of this sickly sweet caramelized milk, which Chileans call *manjar,* onto just about anything and even eat it directly out of the jar.

Though it stems from the Italian tradition, Argentine ice cream lacks the high international profile of gelato—when a pair of Porteños opened an ice creamery in the author's hometown of Oakland, California, they chose the compromise name of Tango Gelato, stressing its Italian roots without suppressing its Buenos Aires stopover. Argentina has countless quality ice creameries, and a diversity of flavors, ranging from the standard vanilla and chocolate (with multiple variations on those, including white chocolate and bittersweet chocolate) to lemon mousse, *sambayón* (resembling eggnog), *dulce de leche,* and countless others.

Chilean ice cream is also popular, but the quality is usually only so-so except in the capital, where *elaboración artesanal* (small-scale production) is more common, and in Patagonia, where regional flavors like *ruibarbo* (rhubarb) appear on the menu. Chile's German immigrants have left a legacy of kuchen (pastries such as apple strudel and raspberry tarts) in the south.

### International and Ethnic Food

Buenos Aires and Santiago (an underappreciated gastronomic center) have the greatest variety of international food, though some tourist-oriented areas also have good selections. Italian and Spanish are the most common foreign cuisines, but French and Chinese venues are also numerous. Peruvian food has become popular in Santiago and Buenos Aires, but it's rare elsewhere.

Brazilian, Mexican, and Middle Eastern restaurants are less common; some popular world-food cuisines, such as Japanese, Thai, and Vietnamese, have made inroads. Given the raw material that Chile's oceans offer, sushi can be a real treat here.

## MEALS AND MEALTIMES

Despite some regional differences, Argentine food is relatively uniform throughout the country, except in Buenos Aires, where diverse ethnic and international cuisine is abundant; in Patagonia, game dishes are not unusual (most of this, such as venison, is either farmed or culled on *estancias* where populations have risen too high).

By North American and European standards, both Argentines and Chileans are late eaters except for *desayuno* (breakfast); Chileans, though, are notorious late risers. *Almuerzo* (lunch, sometimes called *colación* in Chile) usually starts around 1 P.M., *cena* (dinner) around 9 P.M. or later—sometimes much later in Argentina. Argentines bide their time between lunch and dinner with a late-afternoon *té* (tea) that consists of a sandwich or some sort of pastry or dessert; the Chilean counterpart is *onces.*

Since Argentines often eat *after* the theater or a movie, around 11 P.M. or even later on weekends, anyone entering a restaurant before 9 P.M. may well dine alone.

### Breakfast and Brunch

Most Argentines eat a light breakfast of coffee or tea and *pan tostado* (toast, occasionally with ham and/or cheese) or *medialunas* (croissants) or *facturas* (pastries, also eaten for afternoon tea); *medialunas* may be either *de manteca* (buttery and sweet) or *salada* (saltier, baked with oil). *Mermelada* (jam) usually accompanies plain *tostados.*

As a side dish, eggs may be either *fritos* (fried) or *revueltos* (scrambled), or sometimes *duros* (hard-boiled). In some fashionable restaurant zones, a more elaborate Sunday brunch has become an option.

Chilean breakfasts are similar, but usually without the croissants or pastries; North American breakfast foods like corn flakes have also made inroads. *Avena* (oatmeal) is common in wintertime.

### Lunch

Lunch is often the day's main meal, usually including an *entrada* (appetizer), followed by a *plato principal* (entrée, often *plato de fondo* in Chile), accompanied by a *guarnición* (side dish, *agregado* in Chile) and a *bebida* (soft drink) or *agua mineral* (mineral water) and followed by *postre* (dessert).

Upscale restaurants often offer fixed-priced lunches that make it possible to eat stylishly without busting the budget. It's also possible to find local fast-food items like *hamburguesas* (hamburgers), sandwiches, pizza, and pasta, without resorting to international franchises.

### *Té* and *Onces*

Filling the time between lunch and the late-dinner hour, the Argentine *té* and the Chilean *onces* can range from a late-afternoon sandwich to a full afternoon tea, with cakes and cookies, and is often a social occasion. Presumably intended to tide people over until their relatively late dinnertime, it often becomes larger and more elaborate than the name would imply.

### Dinner

Dinner resembles lunch, but in formal restaurants it may be substantially more elaborate (and more expensive), and it can be a major social occasion. Argentines and Chileans dine late—9 P.M. is early, and anything before that will likely earn incredulous "What are you doing here?" stares from waiters. The exception to this rule is at tourist-oriented areas like Buenos Aires's Puerto Madero complex, where restaurateurs have become accustomed to North Americans and Europeans who, lodged at nearby luxury hotels, can't wait any later than 7 P.M.

## BUYING GROCERIES

In Argentina, North American–style supermarkets carry a wide selection of processed foods but often a lesser variety (and quality) of fresh greens than is available in produce markets. Many of them have cheap cafeterias with surprisingly good food.

In areas where supermarkets are fewer, almost all neighborhoods have corner shops with basic groceries and fresh produce, usually within just a few minutes' walk. Butchers are numerous, fishmongers less so.

Virtually every Chilean city, town, village, and hamlet has a central market where it's possible to buy fresh produce. Even in locales without central markets, small shops almost always carry groceries.

## BEVERAGES

### Coffee, Tea, and Chocolate

Caffeine junkies feel comfortable in Argentina, where espresso is the norm even in small provincial towns. *Café chico* is a dark viscous brew in a miniature cup, supplemented with enough sugar packets to make it overflow onto the saucer. A *cortado* comes diluted with milk—for a larger portion request a *cortado doble*—and follows lunch or dinner. *Café con leche,* equivalent to a latte, is a breakfast drink; ordering it after lunch or dinner is a serious faux pas.

Most Chilean coffee, by contrast, is a disappointment—powdered Nescafé remains the norm, though espresso is becoming more common. *Café negro* is Nescafé mixed with hot water; *café con leche* (coffee with milk) is usually Nescafé dissolved in warm milk.

*Té negro* (black tea) usually comes in bags and is insipid by most standards. Visitors wanting British-style tea with milk should ask for tea first and milk later; otherwise, they may get a tea bag immersed in lukewarm milk. Herbal teas range from the nearly universal *manzanilla* (chamomile) and *rosa mosqueta* (rose hips) to *mate de coca* (coca leaf). *Yerba mate* (Paraguayan tea) is one of Argentina's most deeply embedded customs.

In addition to the usual, Chilean herbal teas also include specialties such as *llantén* (plantain), *cedrón* (lemon verbena), *paico* (saltwort), *boldo,* and many others. In Patagonia, some Chileans follow the Argentine custom of *mate.*

Chocolate lovers will enjoy the Argentine *submarino,* a bar of semisweet chocolate that dissolves smoothly in steamed milk from the espresso machine. Powdered chocolate is also available, but less flavorful.

It's possible to get a good cup of *chocolate* (hot chocolate) in Santiago and much of Chile's Lakes district, where Swiss-German influence is most significant. Elsewhere, it will be powdered chocolate mixed with hot water.

## Water, Juices, and Soft Drinks

Tap water is potable nearly everywhere; ask for *agua de la canilla* in Argentina or *agua de la llave* in Chile. For ice, request it *con hielo.*

Visitors with truly sensitive stomachs might consider bottled water, which is widely available. Ask for *agua pura* or *agua mineral;* some brands are spring water, while others are purified. For carbonated water, add *con gas* or, in Argentina, ask for the even cheaper *soda,* which comes in large siphon bottles.

*Gaseosas* (in the plural) are sweetened bottled soft drinks (including most of the major transnational brands but also local versions such as the Argentine tonic water Paso de los Toros).

Fresh-squeezed *jugos* (fruit juices) are good though limited in their diversity. *Naranja* (orange) is the standard; to ensure freshness, ask for *jugo exprimido* or, in Chile, a *vitamina.*

Chilean *licuados* are fruit-based drinks mixed with water or blended with *leche* (milk). Unless your sweet tooth is insatiable, ask to have them prepared without sugar *(sin azúcar, por favor);* this can be a problem even with fresh-squeezed juices other than orange.

## Alcoholic Beverages

Argentina is less famous for its wines than Chile, perhaps because domestic consumption traditionally overshadows exports, but it's the world's fifth-largest wine producer and its international profile is rising fast. Most production takes place in the western and northwestern provinces of Mendoza, San Juan, and Salta, but the northern Patagonian provinces of Neuquén and Río Negro have earned a niche market.

Chile, of course, is one of the world's major wine producers, and exports have boomed since worldwide boycotts ended along with the Pinochet dictatorship. Its signature varietal is Carmenere, destroyed by phylloxera in France but rediscovered here (where it was long mistaken for merlot) in the 1990s.

*Tinto* is red wine, while *blanco* is white. The best restaurants have a wide selection, usually in full bottles though sometimes it's possible to get a *media botella* (half bottle) or, increasingly, wine by the glass. Argentines often mix their table wines—even reds—with soda water or ice.

For more information on Southern Cone wines, look for Christopher Fielden's *The Wines of Argentina, Chile, and Latin America* (New York: Faber and Faber, 2001), though it doesn't account for some recent developments. Harm de Blij's *Wine Regions of the Southern Hemisphere* (Rowman and Littlefield, 1985) is a more intellectually sophisticated overview, though it too is out of date in some respects.

While the wines are more than worthwhile, both Argentines and Chileans are leaning more toward beer, which tastes best as *chopp,* direct from the tap, rather than from bottles or cans.

Hard liquor is less popular in Argentina, but whiskey, gin, and the like are readily available. *Ginebra bols* (differing from gin) and *caña* (cane alcohol) are local specialties.

Chile is, along with Peru, a major producer of the potent grape brandy known as pisco, the base of the legendary pisco sour. Another popular aperitif is the *vaina,* a concoction of port, cognac, cocoa, and egg white that some Chileans consider a "woman's drink."

In both Argentina and Chile, as well as the Falklands, the legal drinking age is 18.

# Conduct and Customs

Argentines and Chileans have many things in common, but some traits differ dramatically. In both countries, politeness goes a long way with officials, shopkeepers, and others with whom you may have contact. It's always good form to offer the appropriate polite salutation: *buenos días* (good morning), *buenas tardes* (good afternoon), or *buenas noches* (good evening or good night), depending on the time of day.

In terms of general conduct, both women and men should dress conservatively and inconspicuously when visiting churches, chapels, and sacred sites. This, again, is an issue of respect for local customs, even if locals themselves don't always observe it.

Argentines and especially Porteños (like New Yorkers) are known as extroverts, with a stereotyped reputation for brusqueness; some even gripe about their compatriots that "nobody respects anybody here any more." Chileans, by contrast, have a reputation as the "Victorians of South America" for their reluctance to display their emotions publicly. This is a stereotype as well—many Chileans are gregarious—but on balance Argentines are probably more outgoing.

## PHOTOGRAPHIC ETIQUETTE

Unlike some countries with large indigenous populations, Argentines are not exactly camera-shy, though an in-your-face approach is not necessarily appropriate. Especially when inclusion of people is incidental to, say, a landscape, it's not a problem. However, if a person is the photograph's primary subject, try to establish a rapport before asking permission to photograph, if you can manage Spanish or have another language in common. Photographers should be particularly respectful of Patagonia's indigenous peoples.

### PHOTOGRAPHIC ETIQUETTE – AND A WARNING

Most Argentines, especially Porteños, are not exactly camera-shy, but do be cautious about photographing political protests – the police are notorious for cataloguing dissidents, so protestors may be suspicious of unknowns with cameras. Likewise, avoid photography near military installations, although "the sentry will shoot" signs are a thing of the past.

Generally, if a person's presence in a photograph is incidental, as in a townscape, it's unnecessary to ask permission, but avoid the in-your-face approach. If in doubt, ask; if rejected, don't insist. If you're purchasing something from a market vendor, he or she will almost certainly agree to be photographed.

There is one absolute no-no – without explicit permission, do not even think about photographing Israeli or Jewish community sites anywhere in Argentina. Since car-bomb attacks on Retiro's Israeli Embassy in 1992 and Once's Jewish cultural center in 1994, federal police are stationed outside all these sites. They will politely or, if necessary, not-so-politely discourage would-be clickers.

Likewise, Chileans in general are accustomed to cameras, but photographing the Mapuche of the Andean lakes district or other indigenous people without first establishing a rapport would be a serious error of judgment.

# Tips for Travelers

## EMPLOYMENT OPPORTUNITIES

The unemployment situation may be better in Patagonia than elsewhere in Argentina or Chile, but well-paid work can be hard to come by even for legal residents, let alone visitors on tourist or student visas. Nevertheless, foreigners have found work in the tourist industry, or casual labor in bars or restaurants. Such jobs, though, may be seasonal (in the case of tourism) or poorly paid (in the case of restaurants, except in a handful of places where tips are high).

Ideally, obtaining a work permit from an Argentine consulate is better than attempting to obtain one in country, as employment may not begin until the permit is actually granted. Nevertheless, it still requires submitting documents and takes time.

Legal residence in Chile, which permits eligibility for a greater number of better-paying jobs, usually requires local or foreign sponsorship, a substantial investment, marriage to a Chilean spouse or other permanent resident, or a reliable retirement income. In theory, temporary working visas can lead to residence, but some workers have continued on them for several years, as the Interior Ministry bureaucracy turns slowly.

## BUSINESS TRAVEL

Argentina's economy has rebounded since the 2001–2002 collapse, while Chile's has remained the continent's most stable and one of the most productive.

There are few legal restrictions on foreign businesses operating in Argentina, but the recent business climate, thanks largely to debt default and banking restrictions, has encouraged investment by those accustomed to dealing with risk. Political corruption continues to be a disincentive.

The best investment bets include travel and tourism services, a key Patagonian sector. Devaluation had made residential real estate a bargain but, in recent years, prices have rebounded. In any event, before signing any business deal, consult a local lawyer recommended by your embassy, consulate, or a truly trusted friend.

Chile's institutional stability and low corruption levels have made it an investor's favorite. That, however, does not eliminate the need to understand the cultural and legal context of investing in the country.

## ORGANIZED TOURS

Because of Patagonia's complex travel logistics, organized tours can be a useful option for visitors with limited time, and many reputable U.S., Argentine, and Chilean operators offer and even coordinate tours on both sides of the border. Within each category, the companies appear in alphabetical order.

### North America-Based Operators

The **American Geographical Society** (P.O. Box 938, 47 Main St., Suite 1, Walpole, NH 03608-0938, tel. 888/805-0884, www.amergeog.org) regularly offers upmarket tours to Patagonia and Antarctica, with highly qualified geographers in charge.

Primarily but not exclusively for cyclists, **Backroads** (801 Cedar St., Berkeley, CA 94710, tel. 510/527-1555 or 800/462-2848, www.backroads.com) offers a five-day Argentina's Lake District Biking tour that takes in Bariloche, Villa La Angostura, and the Siete Lagos area, for US$4,798–5,398 per person. Their eight-day Patagonia Walking trip stays at luxury lodgings in and around Argentina's Parque Nacional Los Glaciares; rates range US$4,498–5,298 per person, with accommodations at places like Eolo Lodge, Los Cerros, and Estancia Cristina.

**Bio Bio Expeditions** (P.O. Box 2028, Truckee, CA 96160, tel. 800/246-7238, www.bbxrafting.com) offers weeklong kayaking and multi-sport programs in the US$3,200–3,500 range, not including transportation, at its cozy base camp on Chile's Río Futaleufú.

From its own deluxe camp on the Río Futaleufú, **Earth River Expeditions** (180 Towpath Rd., Accord, NY 12404, tel. 845/626-2665 or 800/643-2784, www.earthriver.com) offers 10-day rafting and multi-sport trips on and around the river for US$3,100 from Puerto Montt. It also offers fly-in backcountry kayaking trips in remotest Aisén at a slightly higher cost, or can combine the two for US$5,600.

For travelers at least 55 years of age, **Exploritas** (formerly Elderhostel, 11 Avenue de Lafayette, Boston, MA 02111, tel. 800/454-5768, www.exploritas.org) offers a variety of southern South America trips, including a 15-day Patagonia and the Andean Lake Region tour (from US$4,194) that takes in Chile and Argentina, including the Punta Tombo and Península Valdés wildlife reserves, and a 15-day Hiking at the End of Earth trip (from US$5,696) that visits southern Argentine Patagonia and Tierra del Fuego.

A pioneer on the Río Futaleufú, former U.S. Olympian Chris Spelius's **Expediciones Chile** (P.O. Box 752, Sun Valley, ID 83353, tel. 888/488-9082, www.exchile.com) has its own sprawling and secluded but cozy Campo Tres Monjas on the river's south bank. While the company specializes in kayaking the Fu, it also offers rafting and multi-sport holidays that include birding, hiking, and horseback riding. Weeklong stays (from US$1,795) at Tres Monjas include plenty of time and instruction on the river, and transportation from Bariloche or Esquel, Argentina; there are also shorter options, but a week is ideal here.

**Mountain Travel Sobek** (1266 66th St., Emeryville, CA 94608, tel. 888/687-6235, fax 510/594-6001, www.mtsobek.com) does a variety of Patagonian trips, including an 11-day Trekking the Paine Circuit Tour (from US$3,995 pp). The 15-day Patagonia Explorer Tour (US$7,295 pp) includes four nights cruising through the Fuegian fjords of Tierra del Fuego on the *Terra Australis* and a variety of day hikes in southernmost Argentina and Chile.

**Nature Expeditions International** (7860 Peters Rd., Suite F-103, Plantation, FL 33324, tel. 954/693-8852 or 800/869-0639, fax 954/693-8854, www.naturexp.com) operates upscale "soft adventure" and culture-oriented tours to Argentina and Chile, among other destinations. Its 15-day Chile: Land of Extremes Tour (land cost from US$5,660) takes in Puerto Varas, Chiloé, Laguna San Rafael, and Torres del Paine, while the 15-day Argentina: Journey to Patagonia includes Buenos Aires, Península Valdés, Punta Tombo, Trelew, and Bariloche, with a brief detour to Iguazú falls. The bi-national Patagonia Wilderness Adventure (from US$4,625 pp) visits Torres del Paine, El Calafate, and Buenos Aires.

**Orvis** (1711 Blue Hills Dr., Roanoke, VA 24012-8613, tel. 800/547-4322, www.orvis.com) arranges fishing holidays in the vicinity of Argentine lakes district destinations of Junín de los Andes and Bariloche, as well as Chubut province, and northern Chilean Patagonia's Río Baker.

Owned by native Patagonians (from Neuquén and Río Gallegos), California-based **Patagonia Travel Adventures** (P.O. Box 22, Ben Lomond, CA 95005, tel. 831/336-0167, www.patagoniaadventures.com) focuses on small group tours to Península Valdés and Punta Tombo, Parque Nacional Los Glaciares, the little-visited Patagonian steppe along RN 40, and even Chile's Parque Nacional Torres del Paine.

**Powderquest Tours** (7108 Pinetree Rd., Richmond, VA 23229, tel. 970/455-4790, www.powderquest.com) runs five or six 9- to 13-day Southern Cone ski tours annually. Argentine Patagonia resorts include Chapelco, Cerro Bayo, Catedral Alta Patagonia, and Ushuaia, while Chilean Patagonia sites include Las Araucarias (east of Temuco) and Pucón.

**REI Adventures** (P.O. Box 1938, Sumner, WA 98390, tel. 800/622-2236, www.rei.com) offers a diversity of Patagonian trips, including a 10-day Northern Patagonia Multisport tour (US$3,999 pp) of Argentina and Chile; destinations include Bariloche, Villa La Angostura, San Martín de los Andes, and Pucón. The 13-day Fitz Roy and Paine Hiking tour (US$4,599 pp) focuses on Argentina's Chaltén area and Chile's Torres del Paine.

Affiliated with the Smithsonian Institution, **Smithsonian Journeys** (P.O. Box 23182, Washington, DC 20077-0843, tel. 202/357-4700 or 877/338-8687, www.smithsonianjourneys.org) offers a 14-day Patagonia excursion (US$3,549 pp) that visits Bariloche, Puerto Varas, Punta Arenas, Puerto Natales, Torres del Paine, El Calafate and the Glaciar Perito Moreno, and Ushuaia.

**Wilderness Travel** (1102 9th St., Berkeley, CA 94710, tel. 510/558-2488 or 800/368-2794, fax 510/558-2849, www.wildernesstravel.com) offers trips including a 16-day, hiking-oriented In Patagonia Excursion (US$6,395 pp) that focuses mostly on Argentina but also visits Torres del Paine.

**Wildland Adventures** (3516 NE 155th St., Seattle, WA 98155, tel. 800/345-4453, fax 206/363-6615, www.wildland.com) operates small group tours (2–8 persons) through locally based guides. In Argentina, the 10-day Best of Patagonia Tour (US$4,550 pp) takes in the Perito Moreno Glacier and other sights via Buenos Aires. The 14-day In the Wake of Magellan Trip (from US$7,395) includes both Torres del Paine and a segment of the scenic luxury cruise between Punta Arenas and Ushuaia, as well as Argentina's Glaciar Perito Moreno.

## United Kingdom-Based Operators

**Explore Worldwide** (Nelson House, 55 Victoria Rd., Farnborough, Hants GU14 7PA, tel. 0845/0131537, www.exploreworldwide.com) organizes 13- to 18-day tours primarily to the northern Andean lakes district and the more southerly Torres del Paine and Argentina's El Calafate area. Rates are in the £2,583 range, flights included.

**Journey Latin America** (12/13 Heathfield Terrace, Chiswick, London W4 4JE tel. 020/8747-8315, www.journeylatinamerica.co.uk) specializes in small group tours throughout Latin America, including Argentina, Chile, and the Falkland Islands.

**Muir's Tours** (97a Swansea Rd., Reading RG1 8HA, tel. 0119/950-2281, www.nkf-mt.org.uk) is a fair-trade adventure and cultural-travel operator that offers Torres del Paine hiking packages of 5, 7, and 10 days. Rates run about US$1,880 per person, with accommodations at the Cascada EcoCamp when not actually on the trail. Horseback trips, with different itineraries, are also possible.

## Australia-Based Operators

**Peregrine Adventures** (380 Lonsdale St., Melbourne, Victoria 3000, tel. 03/9662-2700, fax 03/9662-2422, www.peregrineadventures.com) organizes tours to southernmost Patagonia, covering both sides of the border.

One of Australia's biggest operators, **World Expeditions** (71 York St., Level 5, Sydney, NSW 2000, tel. 02/8270-8400, www.worldexpeditions.com.au) has a variety of Patagonian tours. It also has branches in Melbourne (393 Little Bourke St., Melbourne, Victoria 3000, tel. 03/8631-3300, travel@worldexpeditions.com.au) and several other Australian cities, as well as Auckland, New Zealand (Level 2, 35 High Street, Auckland CBD, tel. 09/3684161, enquiries@worldexpeditions.co.nz).

## Argentina-Based Operators

The operators below invariably have English-speaking personnel and have services in many parts of the country. Many locally focused operators, though, have very good services as well. Argentina's country code is 54.

The Buenos Aires–based **Asatej Group** (Florida 835, Oficina 320, tel. 011/4114-7600, www.asatej.com) is Argentina's youth- and budget-oriented operator, which has refocused on incoming tourism since the early 2002 peso collapse.

Based in El Chaltén, activity-oriented **FitzRoy Expediciones** (San Martín 56, tel. 02293/436424 or 02962/493178, www.fitzroyexpediciones.com.ar) focuses on that geographical area, organizing expeditions onto the southern Patagonian ice sheets and other less-demanding day trips.

Bariloche-based **Magellanica** (Calle 4, Meli 12040, San Carlos de Bariloche, tel. 02944/520669, www.magellanica.com.ar) is an adventure travel company whose custom-made journeys for solo travelers, small groups, or families make the most of the best hiking, sea kayaking, backcountry skiing, and mountaineering sites and itineraries in Patagonia and the lakes district of Chile and Argentina. Trained at the National Outdoor Leadership School (NOLS) in Wyoming, owner Diego Allolio and his staff adhere to the "Leave No Trace" principle.

Also Bariloche-based, **Meridies** (tel./fax 02944/512073, www.meridies.com.ar) is primarily an adventure-oriented climbing company that does strenuous trips like Volcán Lanín, but it also does a weeklong driving and hiking trip along the southern portion of RN 40 (La Cuarenta).

Buenos Aires–based **Sendero Sur** (Perú 359, Oficina 608, Monserrat, tel./fax 011/4343-1571, www.senderosur.com.ar) does a series of activity-oriented trips that include cycling in the Argentine and Chilean lakes districts, visits to Patagonian *estancias,* and hiking and ice trekking in and around Parque Nacional Los Glaciares and Ushuaia.

## Chile-Based Operators

Several Chile-based operators focus on Chilean Patagonia and Tierra del Fuego, and some also work the Argentine side of the border. Chile's country code is 56.

**AlSur Expediciones** (Aconcagua and Imperial, Puerto Varas, tel./fax 065/232300, www.alsurexpeditions.com) operates tours and activities in the lakes district and specializes in Parque Pumalín, Douglas Tompkins's large private nature reserve.

Based in summer only at the town of Dalcahue on the Isla Grande de Chiloé, **Altué Sea Kayaking** (tel. 09/9419-6809, www.seakayakchile.com) has extensive itineraries around the eastern shore of the archipelago. For reservations, its Santiago contact is Altué Active Travel (General Salvo 159, Providencia, Santiago, tel. 02/2351519, www.altue.com).

**Antares Patagonia Adventure** (Barros Arana 111, Puerto Natales, tel. 061/414611, www.antarespatagonia.com) operates activities-oriented trips to Patagonia, mostly but not exclusively in Parque Nacional Torres del Paine, where it has concessions for activities like ice hiking, kayaking, and mountaineering. It offers a diverse set of packages ranging from 4 days/3 nights to 13 days/12 nights for US$1,050–3,510 per person, depending on the number of passengers and choice of accommodations. Its U.S. representative is Americas Travel (348 Hayes St., San Francisco, CA 94102-4421, tel. 415/703-9955 or 800/267-6129, mdiaz@antarespatagonia.com). Kayaking programs last 1–3 days.

U.S./Peruvian–run **Austral Adventures** (Av. Costanera 904, Ancud, Chiloé, tel./fax 065/625977, www.austral-adventures.com) offers custom boat tours from Ancud south to Parque Pumalín, as well as land-based programs on the Isla Grande de Chiloé. Full-day tours with bilingual guides in the vicinity of Ancud start around US$70, while four-day expeditions to Parque Pumalín with gourmet meals cost around US$966.

French-owned **Azimut 360** (General Salvo 159, Providencia, Santiago, tel. 02/2351519, www.azimut360.com) offers Patagonian excursions ranging from traditional lakes district trips to northern Patagonian ice fields and technical climbs of summits such as Aisén's 4,058-meter Monte San Valentín.

**Campo Aventura** (San Bernardo 318, Puerto Varas, tel./fax 065/232910, www.campoaventura.cl) offers four-day, three-night horseback explorations of the spectacularly scenic Cochamó backcountry southeast of Puerto Varas, for US$450 per person, but shorter and longer options are possible.

Santiago-based **Cascada Expediciones** (Don Carlos 3219, Las Condes, tel. 02/2329878, North America tel. 800/901-6987, U.K. tel. 0800/051-7095, www.cascada.travel) offers activity-oriented excursions to destinations such as Pucón, Futaleufú, and Torres del Paine (where its domed Eco-camp is the most distinctive accommodations option).

Aisén-based **Catamaranes del Sur** (Pedro de Valdivia Norte 0210, Providencia, Santiago, tel. 02/2311902, www.catamaranesdelsur.cl) goes to Laguna San Rafael from its hotel at

Puerto Chacabuco, and has longer programs with additional activities in the region.

October–April, **Cruceros Australis** (Av. Bosque Norte 0440, 11th floor, Las Condes, Santiago, tel. 02/4423115, www.australis.com) offers three-, four-, and seven-day cruises from Punta Arenas through southern Tierra del Fuego's fjords to Ushuaia and Cape Horn on the luxury vessel *Via Australis* and the somewhat larger *Stella Australis.* Rates change from low-season (October and April) to mid-season (November–mid-December and all of March) and high-season (mid-December–February). Per-person rates for four days and three nights start at US$840–1,150 in low season and go up to US$1,328–1,980 in high season. For five days and four nights, the comparable rates are US$1,120–2,010 in low season to US$1,770–3,110 in high season. Cruceros Australis also has U.S. offices (4014 Chase Ave., Suite 215, Miami Beach, FL 33140, tel. 305/695-9618 or 877/678-3772).

September–May, **Cruceros Marítimos Skorpios** (Augusto Leguía 118, Las Condes, Santiago, tel. 02/4771900, www.skorpios.cl) operates a fleet of small cruise ships (around 100 passengers) from Puerto Montt and Puerto Chacabuco to Laguna San Rafael, and from Puerto Natales to the fjords of Campo de Hielo Sur, the southern continental ice field west of Torres del Paine.

**Explora Hotels** (Américo Vespucio Sur 80, 5th floor, Las Condes, Santiago, tel. 02/2066060, U.S. tel. 866/750-6699, www.explora.com) offers expensive, all-inclusive packages, ranging from three days to a week, at its magnificently sited hotel in Parque Nacional Torres del Paine, with overland *travesías* (extensions) to El Chaltén on the Argentine side.

**Navimag Ferries** (Av. El Bosque Norte 0440, Las Condes, 11th floor, tel. 02/4423114, www.navimag.com) sails between the Patagonian town of Puerto Natales and the mainland city of Puerto Montt. While these are not cruises in the traditional sense, they are more than just transportation as they pass through Pacific Chile's spectacular fjordlands.

**Pachamama by Bus** (Agustinas 2113, Santiago, tel. 02/6888018, www.pachamamabybus.com) is a weekly hop-on, hop-off backpackers' bus between Santiago and Puerto Montt (to the south). While it's more expensive than regular buses, it has English-speaking guides, stops at roadside attractions, permits clients to stop over and board a subsequent bus at no additional charge, and has no time limit. Scheduled trips leave even with one passenger; the maximum is 13.

U.S.-run, Puerto Bertrand–based **Patagonia Adventure Expeditions** (Casilla 8, Cochrane, tel./fax 067/411330, www.adventurepatagonia.com) is a trekking, fishing, and white-water rafting operator. Its signature trip is the nine-day Aisén Glacier Trail, an exclusive 10-day hiking trip (US$2,700 pp) through the wild backcountry of Parque Nacional Laguna San Rafael and adjacent private lands.

**Patagonia Connection** (Fidel Oteíza 1951, Oficina 1006, Providencia, Santiago, tel. 02/2256489, www.patagonia-connection.com) offers four-day/three-night to six-day/five-night packages based at its Termas de Puyuhuapi hot-springs resort in Aisén; these include a full-day catamaran excursion to Parque Nacional Laguna San Rafael. Prices are lower in the fall and spring shoulder seasons than in the January–February summer peak.

Puerto Williams–based, German-run **Sea & Ice & Mountains Adventures Unlimited** (tel./fax 061/621150 or 061/621227, www.simexpeditions.com) operates summer yacht tours through Tierra del Fuego and Cape Horn.

Based in Puerto Montt, British-run **Darwin's Trails Chile** (Av. Angelmó 2456, 2nd floor, tel./fax 065/262099, www.darwinstrails.com) is an experienced resource for the southernmost Sur Chico, setting up adventure travel excursions with the most reliable local operators.

## TRAVELERS WITH DISABILITIES

For people with disabilities, Patagonia can be problematic, as the infrastructure is mostly unsuitable in a region whose main attractions are outdoors. Even in cities, narrow and uneven sidewalks, not to mention the fast-moving traffic, are unkind to people with disabilities, especially those who need wheelchairs. Public transportation rarely accommodates passengers with disabilities, though Avis Argentina offers rental vehicles with hand controls.

Few older buildings are specifically equipped for handicapped people, but many of these are single-story and can often accommodate people with disabilities. In newer high-rise hotels, accessibility is obligatory.

## TRAVELING WITH CHILDREN

Argentina and Chile are child-friendly countries. In fact, since many Argentines and Chileans enjoy large extended families, they may feel little in common with people in their late twenties and older who do *not* have children, and traveling with kids can open doors.

Many parks and plazas have playground equipment, and it's easy to mix with families there. What foreign parents may find unusual is that even toddlers may be out on the swings and slides with their families at 11 P.M. or later, even in small isolated communities. Likewise, kids are off across the street, around the neighborhood, and even on the buses at ages when North American helicopter parents are driving their kids three blocks to school and waiting anxiously until the doors close safely behind them.

On public transportation, strangers may spontaneously but gently touch small children and even set them on their laps. While foreigners may find this disconcerting, it's not necessarily inappropriate in cultural context.

## WOMEN TRAVELERS

Like other Latin American societies, Argentina and Chile have strong *machista* (chauvinist) elements. Argentine and Chilean women are traditionally mothers, homemakers, and children's caregivers, while men are providers and decision-makers, but there are increasing numbers of professionals and other working women.

Many Argentine and Chilean men view foreign women as sexually available, but this is not necessarily discriminatory—they view women of their own nationality the same way. In Argentina, harassment often takes the form of *piropos,* sexist comments that are often innocuous and can even be poetic, but are just as likely to be vulgar. It's best to ignore verbal comments, which are obvious by tone of voice even if you don't understand them; if they're persistent, seek refuge in a café or *confitería.*

Despite problems, Argentine and Chilean women have acquired political prominence. The most prominent and notorious, of course, was Evita Perón, but her rise to the top was an unconventional one. The highest-profile women in current politics are Argentina's President Cristina Kirchner—wife of the late president Néstor Kirchner but a formidable politician in her own right—and former Chilean president Michelle Bachelet.

## GAY AND LESBIAN TRAVELERS

Despite its conspicuous Catholicism, Argentina is a fairly tolerant country for both gay males and lesbians, and public displays of affection—men kissing on the cheek, women holding hands—are common even among heterosexuals. In 2003, in fact, the city of Buenos Aires passed an ordinance permitting same-sex civil unions, and in 2010 the country enacted same-sex marriage.

This does not mean that homosexuals can always behave as they wish in public—the police have beaten and jailed individuals who have offended their sense of propriety. If in doubt, be circumspect.

Certain Buenos Aires districts, most notably Recoleta, Barrio Norte, and Palermo, have a number of openly gay entertainment venues and even accommodations, but these are less conspicuous in provincial cities.

Conservative Chile may be less publicly tolerant of homosexuality, but Santiago has a lively (though not exclusively) gay scene in Barrio Bellavista. Certainly times are better than in the 1930s, when authoritarian president General Carlos Ibáñez del Campo's regiment rounded up homosexuals and threw them into the ocean with concrete footwear.

# Health and Safety

Midlatitude Buenos Aires and Santiago offer no major health risks beyond those associated with any large city; public health standards are good and tap water is potable almost everywhere.

A good general source on foreign health matters is Dr. Richard Dawood's *Travelers' Health* (New York: Random House, 1994), a small encyclopedia on the topic. The 13th edition of Stuart R. Rose's and Jay Keystone's *International Travel Health Guide* (Northampton, Massachusetts: Travel Medicine Inc., 2006) is regionally focused. Try also the fifth edition of Dirk G. Schroeder's *Staying Healthy in Asia, Africa, and Latin America* (Berkeley, California: Avalon Travel, 2000).

For information on health issues throughout the Southern Cone, one source is the U.S. Centers for Disease Control (CDC, www.cdc.gov), though some of its suggestions for Patagonian countries sound alarmist, with inappropriate boilerplate text (to mention two examples—there are no monkeys in Chile except in zoos, and no one is likely to swim outdoors in the Falklands).

## BEFORE YOU GO

Theoretically, Argentina and Chile demand no proof of vaccinations, but if you are coming from a tropical country where yellow fever is endemic, authorities could ask for a vaccination certificate.

Traveling to Patagonia or elsewhere without adequate medical insurance is risky. Before leaving your home country, purchase a policy that includes evacuation in case of serious emergency. Foreign health insurance may not be accepted in either country, so you may be required to pay out of pocket for later reimbursement. Often, however, private medical providers accept international credit cards in return for services.

Numerous carriers provide medical and evacuation coverage; an extensive list, including Internet links, is available at the U.S. State Department's website (www.travel.state.gov).

## GENERAL HEALTH MAINTENANCE

Common sense precautions can reduce the possibility of illness. Washing hands frequently with soap and water, and drinking only bottled, boiled, or carbonated water reduces the risk of contagion for short-term visitors (though Argentine and Chilean tap water is potable almost everywhere).

Where purified water is impossible to obtain, such as backcountry streams where there may be livestock or problems with human waste, pass drinking water through a one-micron filter and further purify it with iodine drops or tablets (but avoid prolonged consumption of iodine-purified water).

## FOOD- AND WATER-BORNE DISEASES

Few visitors to Patagonia run into problems of this sort, but contaminated food and drink are not unheard of. In many cases, it's simply exposure to different sorts of bugs to which the body soon becomes accustomed, but if symptoms persist the problem may be more serious.

### Traveler's Diarrhea

Colloquially known as *turista,* the classic traveler's diarrhea usually lasts just a few days and almost always less than a week. Besides "the runs," symptoms include nausea, vomiting, bloating, and general weakness. The usual cause is the *Escherichia coli* bacterium from contaminated food or water; in rare cases *E. coli* infections can be fatal.

Fluids, including fruit juices, and small amounts of bland foods such as freshly cooked rice or soda crackers, may relieve symptoms and help regain strength. Dehydration can be serious, especially for children, who may need an oral rehydration solution of carbohydrates and salt.

Over-the-counter remedies like Pepto-Bismol, Lomotil, and Immodium may relieve symptoms but can also cause problems. Prescription drugs such as doxycyline and trimethoprim/sulfamethoxazole can also shorten the cycle. These may not, however, be suitable for children, and everyone should avoid them if at all possible.

Worsening symptoms, including bloody stools, may mean dysentery, a serious ailment that requires a physician's attention.

### Dysentery

Bacterial dysentery, resembling a more intense form of traveler's diarrhea, responds well to antibiotics, but the more serious amoebic dysentery can lead to intestinal perforation, peritonitis, and liver abscesses. Like diarrhea, its symptoms include soft and even bloody stools, but some people may be asymptomatic even as they pass on *Entamoeba hystolica* through unsanitary toilet and food-preparation practices. Metronidazole, known by the brand names Flagyl or Protostat, is an effective treatment, but a physician's diagnosis is advisable.

### Cholera

Resulting from poor hygiene, inadequate sewage disposal, and contaminated food, modern cholera is less devastating than its historical antecedents, which produced rapid dehydration, watery diarrhea, and imminent death without almost equally rapid rehydration. While today's strains are highly infectious, most carriers do not even suffer symptoms. Existing vaccinations are ineffective, so health authorities now recommend against them.

Treatment can only relieve symptoms. On average, about 5 percent of victims die, but those who recover are immune. Not a common problem in either Argentina or Chile, it's rare in Patagonia.

### Hepatitis A

Usually passed by fecal-oral contact under conditions of poor hygiene and overcrowding, hepatitis A is a virus. Of limited efficacy, the traditional gamma globulin prophylaxis wears off in just a few months. New hepatitis A vaccines, though, are more effective and last longer.

### Typhoid

Typhoid is a serious disease common under unsanitary conditions, but the recommended vaccination is an effective prophylaxis.

## INSECT-BORNE DISEASES

Patagonia is malaria-free, but the disease may exist in northern subtropical Argentina; a few other insect-borne diseases may be present if not exactly prevalent.

### Dengue Fever

Like malaria, dengue is a mosquito-borne disease of the lowland tropics, but it's less common than malaria and rarely fatal. Eradicated in Argentina in 1963, the mosquito vector *Aedes egypti* is once again present as far south as Buenos Aires. There were several confirmed cases in lowland subtropical areas of Salta province in 1998, and a single case identified in a Buenos Aires suburb in 2007. The best prophylaxis is to avoid mosquito bites by covering exposed parts of the body with insect repellent or appropriate clothing.

### Chagas' Disease

Also known as South American trypanosomiasis, Chagas' disease is most common in Brazil but affects about 18 million people between Mexico and Argentina; 50,000 victims die every year. Not a tropical disease per se, it has a discontinuous distribution—Panama and Costa Rica, for instance, are Chagas-free.

Since Chagas spreads by the bite of the night-feeding conenose or assassin bug, which lives in adobe structures, avoid such structures (these still exist in the countryside); if it's impossible to do so, sleep away from the walls. DEET-based insect repellents offer some protection. Chickens, dogs, and opossums may carry the disease.

Chagas' disease's initial form is a swollen bite often accompanied by fever, which soon subsides. In the long run, though, it may cause heart damage leading to intestinal constipation, difficulty in swallowing, and sudden death; there is no cure.

## HANTAVIRUS

Hantavirus is an uncommon but deadly disease contracted by breathing, touching, or ingesting feces or urine of the long-tailed rat. Primarily a rural phenomenon and most prevalent in Patagonia, the virus thrives in enclosed areas; when exposed to sunlight or fresh air, it normally loses potency. Avoid places frequented by rodents, particularly abandoned buildings—but there have been cases in which hikers and farm workers have apparently contracted the disease in open spaces.

## RABIES

Rabies, a virus transmitted through bites or scratches by domestic animals (like dogs and cats) and wild mammals (like bats), is a concern; many domestic animals go unvaccinated in rural Patagonia. Human prophylactic vaccination is possible.

Untreated rabies can cause an agonizingly painful death. In case of an animal bite or scratch, clean the affected area immediately with soap and running water, and then with antiseptic substances like iodine or 40 percent-plus alcohol. If possible, try to capture the animal for diagnosis, but not at the risk of further bites; where rabies is endemic, painful post-exposure vaccination may be unavoidable.

## SNAKEBITE

Poisonous snakes are rare in Patagonia (Chile has none), but the aggressive pit viper *yarará*, responsible for most of Argentina's snakebite incidents, ranges into northern Chubut province. The venom paralyzes the nervous system, but strikes are uncommon. Death is not instantaneous and antivenins are available, but it's best to be alert and avoid confrontation. If bitten, get to medical facilities as quickly as possible, but avoid excessive movement that helps the venom circulate.

## ALTITUDE SICKNESS

At the highest elevations, above about 3,000 meters, *apunamiento* or *soroche* can be an annoyance and even a danger, particularly for older people with respiratory problems. Most of the Patagonian uplands are lower than the central and northern Andes, but even among young, robust individuals, a quick rise from sea level to the sierra, in the space of a couple hours, can cause intense headaches, vertigo, drowsiness or insomnia, shortness of breath, and other symptoms. Combined with hypothermia, it can be life-threatening.

For most people, rest and relaxation help relieve symptoms as the body adapts to reduced oxygen at higher altitudes; aspirin or a similar painkiller will combat headache. Should symptoms persist or worsen, moving to a lower elevation usually has the desired effect. Do not overeat, avoid alcohol consumption, and drink extra fluids.

The second edition of Stephen Bezruchka's *Altitude Illness, Prevention & Treatment* (Seattle: The Mountaineers, 2005) addresses the topic in detail; the sixth edition of James A. Wilkerson's edited collection *Medicine for Mountaineering & Other Wilderness Activities* (Seattle: The Mountaineers, 2010) discusses other potential problems as well.

## HYPOTHERMIA

Hypothermia is a dangerously quick loss of body heat, most common in cold and damp weather at high altitudes or high latitudes, with large day-to-night temperature variations. Symptoms include shivering, disorientation, loss of motor functions, skin numbness, and physical exhaustion. The best remedy is warmth, shelter, and food; unlike cottons, woolen clothing retains warmth even when wet. Avoid falling asleep; in truly hazardous conditions, you may not regain consciousness. Carry high-energy snacks and drinking water.

## SUNBURN

In southernmost Patagonia and Tierra del Fuego, ozone-destroying aerosols have increased the entry of ultraviolet radiation, contributing to skin problems (including melanomas) for people and even for livestock like cattle and sheep. For all outdoor activities, use a heavy sunblock; on city streets, walk in the shade whenever possible.

## SEXUALLY TRANSMITTED DISEASES

While life-threatening AIDS is the most hazardous of sexually transmitted diseases (STDs) and gets the most press, other STDs are more prevalent and serious if left untreated. All are spread by unprotected sexual conduct; the use of latex condoms by males reduces the possibility of contracting STDs but does not necessarily eliminate it.

Most STDs, including gonorrhea, chlamydia, and syphilis, are treatable with antibiotics, but some strains have developed immunity to penicillin and alternative treatments. If taking antibiotics, complete the prescribed course, since an interrupted or incomplete treatment may not kill the infection and could even help it develop immunity.

The most common STD is **gonorrhea,** characterized by a burning sensation during urination and penile or vaginal discharge; it may cause infertility. **Chlamydia** has milder symptoms but similar complications. **Syphilis,** the only major disease that spread from the Americas to Europe after the Spanish invasion, begins with ulcer and rash symptoms that soon disappear; long-term complications, though, can include cardiovascular problems and even derangement.

**Herpes,** a virus that causes small but irritating genital ulcers, has no effective treatment. It's likely to recur, easily spread when active, and can contribute to cervical cancer. **Hepatitis B,** though not exclusively an STD, can spread through the mixing of bodily fluids such as saliva, semen, and menstrual and vaginal secretions. It can also spread through unsanitary medical procedures, inadequately sterilized or shared syringes, during body piercing and tattooing, and similar circumstances. Like hepatitis A, it can lead to liver damage but is more serious; vaccination is advisable for high-risk individuals but is expensive.

As in most countries, **HIV/AIDS** is an issue of increasing concern. It is not exclusively an STD (IV drug users can get it by sharing needles), but unprotected sexual activity is a common means of transmission; the use of latex condoms reduces the possibility of infection.

## SMOKING

Approximately 40 percent of Argentines smoke, including nearly half the male population; tobacco directly causes 40,000 deaths per annum. According to a survey several years back, 3 of every 10 Argentine *cardiologists* smoke, and few of those make any recommendation to their own patients on the subject. Future fatalities start early—3 of 10 students between the ages of 13 and 15 are smokers.

Still, there is widespread recognition that the habit is unhealthy, and effective smoking restrictions are making rapid progress—in Buenos Aires, for instance, all restaurants and bars are, in principle, tobacco-free, though they may allow smoking in patio or sidewalk seating.

Enforcement hasn't been perfect, but it's been surprisingly good. Beyond the capital, provincial laws are a hodgepodge, even if the trend is to restrict smoking. If faced with inappropriate second-hand smoke, it's easiest to appeal to courtesy with a white lie such as *"soy asmático"* ("I'm asthmatic").

Smoking is more widespread in Chile than in the United States, but less so than in Europe. A complex law has prohibited smoking on public transportation and in other public areas; restaurants that permit smoking may not serve anyone under 18, and are not required to have a tobacco-free area even though many do. Chilean smokers generally respect limitations on their habit.

## LOCAL DOCTORS

Top-quality medical services, with the latest technology, are readily available in Buenos Aires and Santiago, and even in some provincial cities. Foreign embassies sometimes maintain lists of English-speaking doctors, who often have overseas training and are numerous in the capitals and other large cities.

### PHARMACIES

Pharmacies serve an important public health role in Argentina and Chile, but they also carry certain risks. Pharmacists may provide drugs on the basis of symptoms that they may not completely comprehend, especially if there's a language barrier; while the societal impact may be positive, individual recommendations may be erroneous.

Many medications available by prescription only in North America or Europe may be sold over the counter in Argentine or Chilean pharmacies. Travelers should be circumspect about self-medication even when such drugs are available; check expiration dates, as out-of-date drugs sometimes remain on the shelf.

In large cities and even some smaller towns, pharmacies remain open all night for emergency prescription service on a rotating basis. The *farmacia de turno* and its address will usually be posted in the window of other pharmacies or advertised in the newspaper.

### CRIME

Many Argentines and Chileans believe assaults, rapes, homicide, and property crimes are increasing, but both countries are safe by international standards, and Patagonia particularly so. Because citizens keep late hours, there are plenty of people on the street at most times—rarely will you find yourself walking alone down a dark alleyway.

Still, certain precautions almost go without saying—most crimes are crimes of opportunity. Never leave luggage unattended, store valuables in the hotel safe, watch your belongings closely at sidewalk cafés, and carry a photocopy of your passport with the date of entry into the country. Avoid carrying amounts of cash (money belts or leg pouches are good alternatives for hiding currency), do leave valuable jewelry at home, and do keep conspicuous items such as photo and video cameras out of sight. Do not presume that any area is totally secure.

If accosted by anyone with a firearm or other potentially lethal weapon, do not resist. While guns are uncommon—knives are the weapon of choice—and violent crime against tourists is unusual (and almost unheard of in Patagonia), a misjudgment can have lethal consequences.

One phenomenon that has disturbed Argentines in recent years is the so-called *secuestro exprés* (express kidnapping), in which criminals hold an individual for a small ransom or, alternatively, force someone to withdraw money from an ATM. Far more common in Buenos Aires province than in the capital or elsewhere in the country, these crimes have *not* targeted tourists—rather, they appear to concentrate on individuals whose movements are familiar to the lawbreaker.

More common is the crime of distraction, in which an individual bumps into the victim and spills a substance like ice cream or mustard; while the perpetrator apologizes profusely, an accomplice surreptitiously lifts items of value. Pickpocketing is also common on public transportation; carry wallets and other items of value in a front trouser pocket or, even better, an interior jacket pocket.

## Information and Services

### MONEY

While traveling in Patagonia, consider a variety of money alternatives. International credit cards are widely accepted, and foreign ATM cards work almost everywhere. Because ATMs are open 24 hours, many visitors prefer this alternative, but in remotest Patagonia there are sometimes no banks. It makes sense to have a cash reserve in U.S. dollars (rather than euros; though the European currency is gaining credibility, it's not an everyday item, especially outside Buenos Aires and Santiago). Travelers checks may be the safest way to carry money, since they're usually refundable in case of loss or theft, but changing them outside Buenos Aires or Santiago can be a nuisance, especially in Argentina.

If carrying an emergency cash reserve, use an inconspicuous leg pouch or money belt—not the bulky sort that fits around the waist, which thieves or robbers easily recognize, but a zippered leather belt that looks like any other.

## Currency

Argentina's unit of currency is the peso (Ar$). Banknotes exist in denominations of Ar$2, Ar$5, Ar$10, Ar$20, Ar$50, and Ar$100. Coins exist in denominations of 1, 5, 10, 25, and 50 centavos, but 1-centavo coins have nearly disappeared and businesses generally round off prices to the nearest 5 or 10 centavos. There are also Ar$1 and Ar$2 coins.

Counterfeiting of both U.S. and local currency appears to be increasing in Argentina. Merchants will often refuse a U.S. banknote with the smallest tear or writing on it; ironically, they will accept any peso note that is not flagrantly *trucho* (bogus). On Argentine banknotes, look for the conspicuous watermark with the initials of the historical figure depicted—J.S.M. for José de San Martín on the 5-peso note, for instance.

Chile's unit of currency is also the peso (Ch$), with coins in denominations of Ch$5, Ch$10, Ch$50, Ch$100, and Ch$500. Banknotes come in values of Ch$1,000, Ch$2,000, Ch$5,000, Ch$10,000, and Ch$20,000.

Equivalent to British sterling, the Falkland Islands pound (£) is the official currency, but U.S. dollars and euros are widely accepted, as are travelers checks. MasterCard and Visa are also widely accepted, at least in Stanley, but other credit cards are not. Stanley's Standard Chartered Bank has no ATM, but British visitors with a guarantee card can cash personal checks up to £50.

## Exchange Rates

Following Argentina's early 2002 debt default, caretaker president Eduardo Duhalde's government devalued the peso from 1 to 1.4 per dollar, but, when that proved unsustainable, he floated the currency. By mid-year, the peso had fallen to 3.5 to the dollar before stabilizing and then gradually depreciating—by early 2011, it was trading at around 4 per dollar. The euro's strength against the dollar has made the country cheaper for European travelers, but even it has faltered recently.

With Chile's more stable economy, the currency has fluctuated far less and even gained against foreign currencies; as of early 2011, it was trading at just under Ch$500 per dollar. Rates tend to be highest in Santiago and lower in the regions, but this is less meaningful than it used to be as credit card payments become increasingly common.

For the latest exchange rates, consult the business section of your daily newspaper or an online currency converter such as www.oanda.com.

In the Falkland Islands, the local pound is equivalent to the British sterling, which circulates alongside it. Falklands currency, though, is useless outside the Islands.

## ATMs

Foreign ATM cards work almost everywhere, but in Argentina economic instability and occasional regulations that limit cash withdrawals for Argentines have made Argentine ATMs iffy at times; carry a cash reserve in U.S. dollars. Argentine ATMs impose fees (about US$4) on each withdrawal, so it pays to make fewer withdrawals of larger amounts. The maximum is Ar$1,000, but sometimes the ATM charge means you must withdraw a slightly smaller amount.

Conditions are similar in Chile, but some small villages do not even have banks, let alone ATMs, so be sure to change enough money to get you to the next major town. Likewise, in the countryside, carry smaller bills—for a small shopkeeper with limited resources, changing a Ch$5,000 note may be impossible. Nearly all ATMs charge a fee here too; at present, only Banco del Estado and Banco Security (which has only a handful of branches) do not.

In the Falkland Islands, U.S. dollars, euros, and pounds are widely accepted, and Stanley's Standard Chartered Bank will change travelers checks and give advances on Visa. There are no ATMs, however.

## Travelers Checks and Refunds

Despite their safeguards, travelers checks have drawbacks in Patagonia, particularly the Argentine side. In addition to the time-consuming bureaucracy of changing them at banks and exchange houses, they may carry a substantial commission penalty—up to 3 percent or even more in some cases. Businesses other than exchange houses may not accept them, and in really out-of-the-way places almost nobody will. Travelers checks, unfortunately, should be a last-resort means of carrying and changing money here; cash (despite the risks) and ATM cards are better options.

## Bank Transfers

Many Argentine exchange houses, post offices, and other businesses are affiliated with Western Union, making it relatively straightforward to send money from overseas. For a list of Western Union affiliates in Argentina and Chile, see its website (www.westernunion.com). The American Express Money Gram is another alternative; American Express has headquarters in Buenos Aires and Santiago, and affiliates throughout both countries.

In an emergency, it's possible to forward money to U.S. citizens via the U.S. Embassy in Buenos Aires or Santiago by establishing a Department of State trust account through its Overseas Citizens Services (Washington, D.C. 20520, tel. 202/647-5225); there is a US$30 service charge for setting up the account. It's possible to arrange this as a wire or overnight-mail transfer through Western Union (tel. 800/325-6000 in the U.S.); for details, see the State Department's website (www.travel.state.gov).

## Credit and Debit Cards

Credit cards have been common currency for many years in both Argentina and Chile. During the 2002 peso crisis, when Argentines could not withdraw their savings from frozen bank accounts, their use became even more widespread. Visa and MasterCard are most widely accepted, but there are inconsistencies—some businesses prefer American Express, sometimes to the exclusion of others, or even Diner's Club. Debit cards with Visa or MasterCard affiliation are also widely accepted.

There can be drawbacks to credit cards, though. During the 1990s boom, Argentine merchants generally refrained from the *recargo,* a surcharge on credit-card purchases because of slow bank payments; many have reinstituted the *recargo,* up to 10 percent, to cut potential losses due to slow bank reimbursement. Note that hotels in particular may offer equivalent cash discounts.

Fluctuating exchange rates may also affect the charge that eventually appears on your overseas account. If the rate has changed in the interim between your payment in Patagonia and its posting to the home account, it may be either greater or smaller in terms of dollars (or other foreign currency), depending on the peso's performance.

In general, *propinas* (gratuities) can *not* be added to charged Argentine restaurant meals, but Chile is more flexible. Still, keep some cash, either dollars or pesos, for tips.

## Costs

For most of the 1990s, **Argentina** was South America's most expensive country, so much so that even North Americans and Europeans cringed at the cost. Wealthy Argentines, meanwhile, partied in Miami, Madrid, Rome, and other "inexpensive" destinations.

This anomaly was a function of then economy minister Domingo Cavallo's "convertibility" exchange-rate policy, which reduced previous hyperinflation to near zero. It also, however, froze prices at a relatively high but unsustainable level that eventually made Argentine exports noncompetitive and contributed to the late-2001 default.

After the 2002 peso float, Argentina became a bargain for visitors from hard currency countries. Though the peso has solidified since then—some even argue that it's undervalued—travel remains relatively inexpensive by global standards. Much depends on the traveler's expectations; there are suitable services for everyone from bare-bones budget backpackers to pampered international business travelers. Budget travelers will still find hostel or hotel rooms for US$10 per person or so, and some excellent values for only a little more money. Prices have rebounded at hotels and resorts of international stature, such as the Hyatt and Sheraton chains and their local equivalents, which had to lower rates during the crisis.

Likewise, meals range from a few dollars or less at the simplest *comedores,* but restaurants with sophisticated international cuisine can charge a lot more; even the latter, though, often serve moderately priced lunchtime specials.

As of press time, true shoestringers could still get along on US$25 per day or conceivably less for accommodations and food. For US$50 or so per day it's possible to live comfortably and eat a bit better, but a budget over US$100 per day is far from extravagant. It's worth adding that economic volatility—hyperinflation was a recurrent phenomenon in the late 20th century—makes it impossible to guarantee that prices will not rise.

By global standards, travel in **Chile** is moderately priced, but much depends on the traveler's expectations and where in the country he or she goes. Truly disciplined travelers in rural areas might get away with as little as US$25 or less per day by staying in the cheapest accommodations, buying groceries, and cooking for themselves, or eating market food. Public transportation is moderately priced, especially given the long distances on some routes, but the fact that Chile imports nearly all its oil makes the sector vulnerable to fluctuations.

The **Falkland Islands,** by contrast, are substantially more expensive than either Argentine or Chilean Patagonia, because accommodations are few, wages are high, and local transportation relies on costly air-taxis. For most visitors, US$100 per day for meals and accommodations alone will be a modest budget.

Prices are comparable to those in the United Kingdom for hotels and wildlife lodges (the latter, with full board, cost upwards of £100 pp per day in some cases). On the other hand, self-catering cottages in camp go for as little as £20–30 per person, and B&B accommodations in Stanley for only a little more. Camping is an option in a few areas, but nearly all land is private, and many farmers worry about fire.

Food costs except for fresh meat (mainly mutton) are also high, as many items must be imported by air or sea, and Stanley's market garden is a capital-intensive hydroponic facility. Stanley's best couple of restaurants would be good anywhere and have prices to prove it, but there are also moderately priced snacks like burgers and pub grub like fish and chips.

Internal transportation is expensive because of high capital investments for a relatively small market. Government air-taxi service links the two main islands and many smaller ones, but visitors pay higher rates than residents.

## Taxes

**Argentina** imposes a 21 percent *impuesto al valor agregado* (IVA, value added tax) on goods and services, though this is normally included in the advertised price; if in doubt, ask for clarification *("¿Incluye los impuestos?").* Tax evasion is a national sport, though, and hotel owners often ignore the tax for cash payments.

Tourists may request IVA refunds for purchases of Argentine products valued more than about US$25 from shops that display a "Global Refund" decal on their windows. Always verify, though, that the decal is not out of date.

When making any such purchase, request an invoice and other appropriate forms. Then, on leaving the country, present these forms to Argentine customs; customs will then authorize payment to be cashed at Banco de la Nación branches at the international airport.

At smaller border crossings, though, do not expect officials to be prepared to deal with tax refunds. Some crossings do not even have separate customs officials but rather are staffed by the Gendarmería (Border Patrol), a branch of the armed forces.

**Chile** levies a 19 percent IVA on goods and services. Most midrange to upscale hotels, however, legally discount IVA for foreign visitors, who receive a *factura de exportación* (export receipt) with their hotel bill.

### Tipping

In formal restaurants with table service, a 10 percent gratuity is customary, but in family-run eateries the practice is rare. Taxi drivers are customarily not tipped, but rounding off the fare to the next highest convenient number is appropriate. Where there is no meter, this is not an issue.

### Bargaining

Bargaining is less common in Argentina and Chile than it is in some other Latin American countries, but in flea or crafts markets the vendor may start at a higher price than he or she expects to receive—avoid insultingly low offers, or such a high offer that the vendor will think you a fool. Depending on your language and bargaining skills, you should reach a compromise that satisfies everybody.

### Student and Senior Discounts

Student discounts are relatively few, and prices are so low for most services that it's rarely worth arguing the point. Students, though, may be eligible for discount international airfares; visit a student-oriented travel agency to see if such a deal is available.

Travelers above age 62 may be eligible for *tercera edad* discounts for museums, transportation, and some other services.

## COMMUNICATIONS AND MEDIA

### Postal Services

Though it's been renationalized, Correo Argentino is still more reliable than in the past. Domestic services remain generally cheap, international services more expensive. Major international couriers provide fast, reliable services at premium prices.

General delivery at Argentine and Chilean post offices is *lista de correos,* literally a list arranged in alphabetical order. There is a small charge for each item addressed to you.

Note that, in Spanish-language street addresses, the number follows rather than precedes the name; instead of "1343 Washington Avenue," for example, a comparable Spanish-language address would read "Avenida Providencia 2134." Spanish speakers normally omit the word *calle* (street) from addresses; where an English speaker might write "499 Jones Street," for instance, a Spanish speaker would simply use "Tucumán 272." It's not unusual for street addresses to lack a number, as indicated by *s/n* (*sin número,* without a number), especially in small provincial towns.

Falklands postal services are dependable but infrequent, as they rely on weekly flights from Chile and less-frequent RAF charters from the United Kingdom. Large parcels go by sea, four or five times per annum. Air taxis deliver mail to outer settlements and islands, sometimes without landing.

### Telephone and Fax

**Argentina's** country code is 54; the *característica* (area code) for the Capital Federal and Gran Buenos Aires is 011, but there are a bewildering number of area codes for individual cities, smaller cities and towns, and rural areas. All telephone numbers in the Capital Federal and Gran Buenos Aires have eight digits, while those other in provincial cities and rural areas vary. When calling out of the area code, it's necessary to dial zero first.

Cellular phone numbers in Buenos Aires all have eight digits, prefixed by 15. In addition, certain toll-free and other specialty numbers have six or seven digits with a three-digit prefix. In the provinces, the cell phone number follows the area code.

Public telephones are abundant; some operate with coins only, but most also accept rechargeable account cards. The basic local phone rate is Ar$0.25 (about US$0.08) for five minutes or so; domestic long distance is more expensive. Phone cards are convenient for in-country calls but less useful for more expensive overseas calls.

For long-distance and overseas calls, and faxes, it's simplest to use *locutorios* (call centers), which are abundant in both Buenos Aires and the provinces. Prices now tend to be much cheaper than placing *cobro revertido* (collect) or *tarjeta de crédito* (credit card) calls to the U.S.

or any other country. Calls are more expensive during peak hours, 8 A.M.–8 P.M. Monday–Friday and 8 A.M.–1 P.M. Saturday.

Opening a cell-phone account without a permanent Argentine address is something of a nuisance, but "caller pays" card phones are a good alternative if you're going to be in-country for a while. Rental phones are available from Nolitel (tel. 011/4311-3500, www.nolitelgroup.com) in Buenos Aires.

**Chile's** country code is 56; there are a number of area codes for individual cities and, in some cases, entire regions. All telephone numbers in Santiago and a few other cities have seven digits; those in the other regions generally have six, but in some rural areas they have seven digits beginning with 1.

Cellular phones all have eight digits, prefixed by 07, 08, or 09. In addition, certain toll-free and other specialty numbers have six digits with a three-digit prefix.

Public telephones are abundant; some operate with coins only, but most also accept rechargeable account cards. The basic local phone rate is Ch$100 (about US$0.20) for five minutes or so; domestic long distance is inexpensive. For long-distance and overseas calls and faxes, it's simplest to use *centros de llamados* (call centers), which are abundant in both Santiago and the regions.

The **Falkland Islands** country code is 500, valid for numbers in Stanley and in camp. Cable and Wireless PLC operates both local and long-distance telephone services; all local numbers have five digits. All telecommunications are fairly expensive, though local technology is state-of-the-art; calls may be made from private phones or Stanley's Cable and Wireless office.

Local calls cost £0.06 per minute, calls to the United Kingdom are £0.99 per minute (except weekends, holidays, and evenings, when it's £0.80 per minute), and calls to other countries are £1.10 per minute (except weekends, holidays, and evenings, when it's £0.99 per minute). Operator-assisted calls are more expensive and have a three-minute minimum, so it's best to buy a phone card. There's also a surcharge for collect calls (local only).

Mobile phone packages are also available for visitors. For details, contact Cable & Wireless (Ross Road West, www.cwfi.co.fk).

## Internet Access

In the last few years, public Internet access has become abundant and so cheap that, if price trends continue, providers will soon be paying customers to use their services. Rarely does access cost more than US$1 per hour, and it's often even cheaper. Many Argentine *locutorios* offer access, but there are many Internet cafés in both Argentina and Chile. High-speed and wireless Internet coverage are increasing rapidly in both countries.

In the Falklands, broadband Internet service is relatively expensive at £0.10 per minute; some Stanley hotels have wireless Internet. As with phone calls, it's more convenient to purchase a card.

## Media

Buenos Aires papers are also—some to a greater degree than others—national papers sold throughout **Argentina.** The middle-of-the-road tabloid *Clarín* is the Spanish-speaking world's largest-circulation daily, while the *Buenos Aires Herald* is an English-language daily whose niche market correlates highly with hotel occupancy. It stresses commerce and finance but also produces intelligent analyses of political and economic developments; its thicker Sunday edition relies on material from the *Washington Post, Bloomberg News,* and other international sources, and includes a locally published version of *Newsweek.*

What was once a state broadcast monopoly is now far more diverse, thanks to privatization and the advent of cable, but conglomerates like the Clarín and El Cronista groups control much of the content.

**Chile** may have emerged from dictatorship, but the press remains in the hands of large consortia like the pro-Pinochet El Mercurio group, which publishes its namesake daily and many other papers. Pinochet's arrest and subsequent legal troubles, however, opened up a whole new space for irreverently satirical papers such as *The Clinic,* whose bimonthly circulation of some 40,000 is a remarkable success story (the paper named itself for the London clinic at which the late dictator was detained). For an English-language summary of the Chilean daily press, plus occasional original reporting, look at the Internet-only *Santiago Times* (www.santiagotimes.cl).

In contrast with the print media, radio and TV journalism are more pluralistic, at least in terms of ownership, as private media with foreign capital have competed with local sources since the early 1990s. That said, the state-run Television Nacional (TVN) and the Universidad Católica's Canal 13 (Channel 13) are still the most important broadcast outlets.

The only print medium in the **Falkland Islands** is the weekly *Penguin News,* which often raises the hackles of local politicians. The Falkland Islands Radio Service (96.5 FM or AM 550) provides local radio programming, but Islanders also get radio and TV from the BBC and the British Forces Broadcasting System (BFBS). The nightly radio announcements, at 6:30 P.M., include the following day's Falkland Islands Government Air Service flight schedules.

## MAPS AND TOURIST INFORMATION

Argentina, Chile, and the Falkland Islands all have good sources for maps and tourist information, but others are available overseas.

### Maps

**International Travel Maps and Books** (ITMB, 12300 Bridgeport Rd., Richmond, BC V6V 1J5, tel. 604/273-1400, www.itmb.com) publishes a series of maps that cover all or parts of Patagonia at a variety of scales, including Argentina (1:2,200,000), Chile (1:1,130,000), Patagonia (1:2,000,000) and Tierra del Fuego (1:750,000), and the Falkland Islands (1:300,000).

For **Argentina,** the **Automóvil Club Argentino** (ACA, Argentine Automobile Club, Av. del Libertador 1850, Palermo, Buenos Aires, tel. 011/4808-4000, www.aca.org.ar) publishes Argentina's most comprehensive series of highway maps, covering every province and including major city plans. Members of overseas affiliate automobile clubs, like the AAA in the United States, can buy these at discount prices. For official topographic maps, the source is Argentina's **Instituto Geográfico Militar** (Av. Cabildo 381, Palermo, Buenos Aires, tel. 011/4576-5576, www.igm.gov.ar). Recent creations by Bariloche-based Pixmap (cell 02944/15-642152, www.macarenaperez.com) are pretty much the best available recreational maps now, and also cover parts of Chile.

In **Chile,** the oil retailer Copec has recently taken over the annually updated three-volume *Turistel* guidebook series (Spanish only), which contains the most current road maps at the back of its *Norte* (North), *Centro* (Center), and *Sur* volumes, along with numerous useful city maps, which, unfortunately, lack scales.

Chile's own **Instituto Geográfico Militar** (IGM, Dieciocho 369, Santiago Centro, tel. 02/410963, www.igm.cl) publishes detailed topographic maps covering the entire country at a scale of 1:50,000; some of these, however, are "proprietary" as they adjoin what the military consider to be sensitive border areas. They are also expensive at about US$15 and up. The Instituto also sells a variety of city maps, road atlases, and books useful to the everyday visitor, and the staff members are professional and efficient.

For the **Falkland Islands,** the locally available *Falkland Islands Explorer,* published in the United Kingdom, depicts the Islands' roads and topography at a scale of 1:365,000, plus a basic city map of Stanley and text on history and natural history.

In Stanley, the **Secretariat** (Ross Rd., tel. 27242) offers Directorate of Overseas Surveys (DOS) topographic maps of the entire Falkland Islands at a scale of 1:50,000, but there's also a two-sheet (1:250,000) series that's adequate for most purposes. Customs & Immigration (3 H Jones Rd., tel. 27340) has maritime charts.

### Tourist Offices

Argentina's **Ministerio de Turismo** (www.turismo.gov.ar), recently promoted to ministry status, has its main office in Buenos Aires, but every province also maintains a tourist-information representative in the capital.

Each Argentine province also operates an information office in its own capital, and often in specific destinations as well. Almost every other locality has its own tourist office—even in very small towns; these normally keep long summer hours but may be limited the rest of the year.

**Sernatur** (www.sernatur.cl), Chile's national tourism service, maintains public information offices in Santiago and all regional capitals, and in Puerto Natales. Most are normally open weekdays only, but in summer and in some localities they are open weekends.

Many cities and towns have their own municipal tourist offices, especially in Andean lakes district resorts like Villarrica, Pucón, and Puerto Varas, which keep long summer hours but are limited the rest of the year. Many smaller towns have summer-only (January and February) offices.

The **Falkland Islands Tourist Board** (www.visitorfalklands.com) is a public-private partnership with offices in Stanley and representatives in the United Kingdom. For details on and suggestions for travel to, from, and in the Islands, consult the thorough, well-organized website.

In the United Kingdom, **Falkland House** (14 Broadway, Westminster, London SW1H 0BH (tel. 20/7222-2542, reception@falklands.gov.fk) is the Islands' official representative and de facto tourist office.

Based at Stanley's Jetty Centre, **Falklands Conservation** (P.O. Box 26, Stanley, Falkland Islands, tel. 22247, fax 22288, www.falklandsconservation.com) provides information on wildlife and conservation issues. It also has a U.K. representative (14 East Hatley, Sandy, Bedfordshire SG19 3JA, tel. 1767-650639).

## PROVINCIAL TOURIST OFFICES IN BUENOS AIRES

Every Patagonian province in Argentina maintains a tourism representative in Buenos Aires.

**Chubut:** Sarmiento 1172, San Nicolás, tel. 011/4831-3493, www.chubutur.gov.ar

**Neuquén:** Maipú 48, Microcentro, tel. 011/4343-2324, www.neuquentur.gov.ar

**Río Negro:** Tucumán 1916, Balvanera, tel. 011/4371-5599, www.rionegrotur.gob.ar

**Santa Cruz:** Suipacha 927, Retiro, tel. 011/4313-4880 or 011/4311-7906, www.epatagonia.gov.ar

**Tierra del Fuego (Instituto Fueguino de Turismo):** Esmeralda 783, Retiro, tel. 011/4328-7040, www.tierradelfuego.org.ar

## FILM AND PHOTOGRAPHY

For those who still use color print film, it is still available, but color slide film much less so. As film tends to be cheaper in North America and Europe, it's best to bring as much as possible. If purchasing film in Argentina, check the expiration date, especially in out-of-the-way places. In the capital and larger tourist centers, competent print-film processing is readily available and moderately priced, but it's better to hold slide film until returning to your home country if possible (but store it under cool, dark, and dry conditions).

Environmental conditions can affect the quality of your shots and the type of film you should use. Bright sun can wash out photographs; in these circumstances, it's best to use a relatively slow film, around ASA 64 or 100, and a polarizing filter to reduce glare. A polarizing filter also improves contrast, dramatizing the sky and clouds, but can result in a dark foreground.

## WEIGHTS AND MEASURES

### Time

Argentina is three hours behind GMT for most of the year and does not observe daylight saving time in the summer. When the U.S. eastern time zone is on daylight saving time, during the

Northern Hemisphere summer, and Argentina is on standard time, Buenos Aires is one hour ahead of New York; the rest of the year, there is two hours' difference.

Across the Andes, Chile is four hours behind GMT and one hour behind Argentina except in summer, when Chile goes on daylight saving time and it's two hours behind.

Like Chile, the Falkland Islands are four hours behind GMT. In summer, Stanley goes on daylight saving time, but parts of camp remain on standard time—according, apparently, to the whims of individual farmers.

## Electricity

Throughout Argentina and Chile, nearly all outlets are 220 volts, 50 cycles, so converters are necessary for some North American appliances that do not have dual voltage power supplies. Traditional plugs have two rounded prongs, but more recent Argentine plugs have three flat blades that form, roughly, an isosceles triangle; cheap adapters are widely available.

Adequately powered converters are hard to find, so it's better to bring one from overseas.

Falkland Islands outlets also run on 220 volts, 50 cycles, but plugs are identical to those in the United Kingdom.

## Measurements

The metric system is official, but this doesn't completely eliminate the variety of vernacular measures that Argentines and Chileans use in everyday life. Rural folk often use the Spanish *legua* (league) of about five kilometers as a measure of distance, and the *quintal* of 46 kilos is also widely used, especially in wholesale markets and agricultural statistics.

Likewise, the metric system is now official in the Falklands, but locals still use vernacular English measures such as miles in everyday situations.

# RESOURCES

## Glossary

***aduana*** customs
***aduana paralela*** "parallel customs"; corrupt Argentine customs officials
***agregado*** side dish
***agua de la canilla*** in Argentina, tap water; in Chile, this is *agua de la llave*
***albergue juvenil*** youth hostel; the word "hostel," however, is now widely used in both Argentina and Chile
***albergue transitorio*** a by-the-hour-hotel, frequently used by young and not-so-young couples in search of privacy
***andén*** platform at train station or bus terminal
***anexo*** telephone extension
***argentinidad*** nebulous notion of Argentine nationalism, often associated with the gaucho
***asado*** generally, a barbecue; in context, can also mean short ribs or roast prime rib
***autopista*** freeway
***avenida*** avenue
***balneario*** bathing or beach resort
***baño compartido*** shared bath (in a hotel or other accommodations)
***baño general*** shared or general bath (in a hotel or other accommodations)
***baño privado*** private bath
**barrio** borough or neighborhood
***boleadoras*** rounded stones, tied together with leather thong, used for hunting by Pampas and Patagonian peoples; also known as *bolas*
***bronca*** a singularly Porteño combination of aggravation and frustration; there is no precise English equivalent, the closest being "wrath" or, in Britain, "aggro"
***cabildo*** colonial governing council
***cabotaje*** full-fare domestic airline ticket
**cacique** indigenous chief or headman
***cajero automático*** automatic teller machine (ATM)
***calle*** street
***camarote*** sleeper berth on a train
***camioneta*** pickup truck
**campo** countryside
***característica*** in Argentina, telephone area code
***carbonada*** stewed beef
***carne*** in Argentina, beef; other kinds of meat are *carne blanca* (literally, "white meat")
***carretera*** highway
***cartelera*** in Argentina, discount ticket agency
***casa chorizo*** house on a deep, narrow lot in Buenos Aires
***casa de cambio*** official money-exchange facility, often just *cambio*
***casco*** "big house" of an *estancia*
***casilla*** post office box
**caudillo** in early independence times, a provincial Argentine warlord, though the term is often used for any populist leader, such as Juan Domingo Perón
***cazuela de ave*** chicken soup with potato, corn on the cob, and other vegetables
***cerro*** hill
**Chilote** inhabitant or native of the Chiloé archipelago
***chivito*** roast kid goat; alternatively, in Uruguay, a steak sandwich
***chopp*** draft beer
***cobro revertido*** collect or reverse-charge telephone call

***coche cama*** spacious, fully reclining long-distance bus seat
***cocinería*** small restaurant, often in a market complex
***coima*** bribe
***colectivo*** in Argentina, a city bus
***comedor*** simple eatery or dining room
***comuna*** political subdivision in Chile, ranging in size from the borough of a city to sprawling rural areas
***confitería*** in Argentina, a restaurant/café with a menu of *minutas* (short orders)
***corralito*** unpopular banking restrictions imposed by Argentine government during the debt default and devaluation of 2001-2002
***costanera*** any road along a seashore, lakeshore, or riverside
**criollo** in colonial times, an American-born Spaniard; in the present, normally a descriptive term meaning "traditionally" Argentine or Chilean
***curanto*** meat and/or shellfish stew, cooked in the earth or a large pot
***desaparecido*** "disappeared one," victim of the military dictatorships of the 1970s and 1980s
***día de campo*** "day in the countryside" on a tourist *estancia*
***dique*** deep-water basin dredged in the harbor of Buenos Aires
***doble tracción*** four-wheel drive, also known as *cuatro por cuatro* (the latter written as "4X4")
***edificio*** building
***encomienda*** in colonial times, a grant of indigenous labor within a given geographical area; the *encomendero* (holder of the *encomienda*) incurred the reciprocal obligation to provide instruction in the Spanish language and Catholic religion, though such obligations were rarely honored
***estancia*** cattle or sheep ranch controlling large extents of land, often with an absentee owner, dominant manager, and resident employees
***estanciero*** owner of an *estancia*
***estero*** estuary
***facón*** gaucho knife
***farmacia de turno*** pharmacy remaining open all night for emergencies, on a rotating basis
***feria*** artisans' market, outdoor crafts or antiques fair; alternatively, an outdoor bookstall
***filete*** traditional colored sign painting of Buenos Aires
***gasoil*** in Argentina, diesel fuel
***gauchesco*** adjective describing romantic art or literature about, as opposed to by, gauchos
***golfo*** gulf
***golpe de estado*** coup d'etat
**Gran Aldea** Great Village; Buenos Aires prior to influx of 20th-century immigrants
***guarnición*** side dish
***heladería*** ice creamery
***hipódromo*** horserace track
***hospedaje*** family-run lodging
***hostería*** B&B or a small hotel; can also mean rural restaurant
***humita*** corn dish resembling Mexican tamale
***indígena*** indigenous person
***indigenista*** adjective describing romantically pro-indigenous literature, music, and art
***infracción*** traffic violation
***isla*** island
***islote*** islet
***istmo*** isthmus
***lago*** lake
***laguna*** lagoon
**latifundio** large landholding, usually an *estancia*
***local*** numbered office or locale, at a given street address
***locutorio*** in Argentina, a telephone call center
***lunfardo*** Porteño street slang that developed in working-class immigrant barrios but is now more widely used in Argentine Spanish, though not in formal situations
***machista*** male chauvinist
**Magellanic architecture** traditional architecture of southernmost Patagonia, wooden houses with metal cladding
***marisquería*** a simple seafood restaurant
***matambre de cerdo*** pork flank steak
***mate*** the dried leaf of *Ilex paraguayensis*, a holly relative prepared in a gourd and sipped through a straw by Argentines, Uruguayans, and others in the Southern Cone countries
***mate de coca*** tea made from the coca leaf

***media pensión*** half board, at a hotel or guesthouse
***menú*** menu; also, a fixed-price meal
**meseta** Patagonian steppe
**mestizo** individual of mixed indigenous and Spanish ancestry
***milonga*** informal neighborhood dance club, which often includes tango as a participant rather than spectator activity
***minuta*** in Argentina, a short-order meal like pasta
**mirador** overlook or viewpoint
***mozo*** in Argentina, a term of address for a restaurant waiter; in Chile, though, this would be extremely rude
***museo*** museum
***oligarquía terrateniente*** traditional landowning "aristocracy" of the Pampas
***onces*** Chilean afternoon tea
***palacete*** mansion
***palafito*** house on stilts or pilings, in the Chiloé archipelago
**Pampa** broad, flat expanse in and around Buenos Aires province
**pampero** southwesterly cold front on the Argentine Pampas
***parada*** bus stop
***parque nacional*** national park
***parrilla*** grill restaurant
***parrillada*** mixed grill
***pasarela*** catwalk in wet or marshy area
***paseaperros*** professional dog walker in Buenos Aires
***pastel de choclo*** Chilean corn casserole with beef, chicken, onions, and/or hard-boiled egg slices
***payador*** spontaneous gaucho singer
***peaje*** tollbooth
***peatonal*** pedestrian mall
***peña*** a community meeting place, with cheap food and drink
***pensión*** family-run accommodation
***pensión completa*** full board, at a hotel or guesthouse
***picada*** in Chile, a simple restaurant, usually in a private home; in both Chile and Argentina, a snack; alternative meaning in Argentina, a footpath
***picante*** spicy hot; the Argentine and Chilean tolerance for spicy food is low, however, and most visitors may find foods labeled as spicy relatively bland
***pingüinera*** penguin colony
***piquete*** protestors' roadblock
***piropo*** sexist remark, ranging from humorous and innocuous to truly vulgar; also, on *filete*, an aphorism
***playa*** beach
**Portakabin** military container-style housing, brought to the Falklands after the 1982 war; now mostly used for storage
**Porteño** native or resident of Buenos Aires
***propina*** tip, as at a restaurant
***puchero*** stewed meat and vegetables
***puente*** bridge
***puerto*** port
**Pullman** first-class bus, with reclining seats and luggage storage underneath
***pulpería*** general store, often the only retail outlet in a rural area
***rastra*** studded gaucho belt
***recargo*** surcharge on credit-card purchases, common in Argentina
***reducción*** colonial settlement where missionaries concentrated the indigenous population for catechization
***remise*** meterless radio taxi charging a fixed rate within a given zone
***reserva nacional*** in Chile, a national reserve, a category of Conaf-protected land
***residencial*** permanent budget accommodations, often also called hotel
***restó*** fashionable, even pretentious, term for a restaurant, especially in Buenos Aires
***río*** river
***rotisería*** delicatessen
***ruca*** Mapuche plank house with thatched roof
***ruta*** route or highway
***ruta nacional*** federal highway
***ruta provincial*** provincial highway
***saladero*** meat-salting plant of late-colonial and early republican times
***sendero*** footpath or trail
***sorrentino*** stuffed pasta resembling ravioli, but larger and round instead of square
***tango canción*** "tango song," with music and lyrics expressing nostalgia

***tanguero*** tango dancer

***tarifa mostrador*** hotel "rack rate," from which there are often discounts

***tenedor libre*** literally "free fork"; an all-you-can-eat restaurant

***terma*** hot springs (normally appears in plural *termas*)

***toldo*** tent of animal skins, inhabited by mobile Pampas natives in pre-Columbian times

***trucho*** bogus, in Argentine slang

***turco*** Argentine of Middle Eastern descent

***ventanilla*** ticket window at bus terminal or train station

***viveza criolla*** in Argentina, "artful deception," ranging from small-scale cheating to audacious chutzpah

***voseo*** use of the second person singular pronoun *vos* and its distinct verb forms in Argentina, Uruguay, Paraguay, and some other countries; most others, though, use the *tuteo* (the pronoun *tú* and its forms)

## ABBREVIATIONS AND ACRONYMS

**ACA** Automóvil Club Argentino

**APN** Administración de Parques Nacionales (National Parks Administration, Argentina)

**Av.** *avenida*, or avenue

**Codeff** Consejo de Defensa de la Flora y Fauna (Council for the Defense of Flora and Fauna, Chile)

**Conaf** Corporación Nacional Forestal (National Forestry Corporation, Chile)

**Conama** Comisión Nacional del Medio Ambiente (National Environmental Commission, Chile)

**IVA** *impuesto al valor agregado* (value-added tax)

**RN** Ruta Nacional (National Highway, Argentina)

**RP** Ruta Provincial (Provincial Highway, Argentina)

**s/n** *sin número*, a street address without a number

# Spanish Phrasebook

Spanish is Argentina's official language, but the stereotypical Porteño intonation – equivalent to a Bronx accent in New York – is unique, for better or worse. Argentine Spanish in general is distinctive, often Italian-inflected, most notable for pronouncing both the "ll" diphthong and "y" as "zh." "Llegar" (to arrive), for example, is pronounced "zhe-gar," while "yo" (I) sounds like "zho."

Another distinguishing feature is the familiar pronoun "vos" instead of "tú." Verb forms of the *voseo* differ from those of the *tuteo*, although Argentines will always understand speakers who use "tú."

Spanish is also Chile's official language, but the local variant, which often drops terminal consonants and glides over some internal ones, may confuse those who learned Spanish elsewhere. At tourist offices, airlines, travel agencies, and upscale hotels in both countries, English is often spoken. In the provinces and regions, it's less common, though its use is spreading, especially in the travel-and-tourism sector.

## PRONUNCIATION GUIDE

Spanish may be more phonetic than English, but there are still occasional variations in pronunciation, especially in Argentina.

### Consonants

**c** as "c" in "cat," before "a," "o," or "u"; like "s" before "e" or "i"

**d** as "d" in "dog," except between vowels, then like "th" in "that"

**g** before "e" or "i," like the "ch" in Scottish "loch"; elsewhere like "g" in "get"

**h** always silent

**j** like the English "h" in "hotel," but stronger

**ll** in Argentina, like the "z" in "azure"; in Chile, like the English "y"

**ñ** like the "ni" in "onion"

**r** always pronounced as strong "r"

**rr** trilled "r"

**v** similar to the "b" in "boy" (not as English "v")

**y** in Argentina, like "ll," it sounds like the "z" in

azure (when standing alone, it's pronounced like the "e" in "me"); in Chile, equivalent to its English counterpart
**z** like "s" in "same"
**b, f, k, l, m, n, p, q, s, t, w, x** as in English

## Vowels

**a** as in "father," but shorter
**e** as in "hen"
**i** as in "machine"
**o** as in "phone"
**u** usually as in "rule"; when it follows a "q" the "u" is silent; when it follows an "h" or "g," it's pronounced like "w," except when it comes between "g" and "e" or "i," when it's also silent (unless it has an umlaut, when it is pronounced as English "w," as in "Gûemes")

## Stress

Native English speakers frequently make pronunciation errors by ignoring stress – all Spanish vowels – a, e, i, o and u – may carry accents that determine which syllable of a word gets emphasis. Often, stress seems unnatural to nonnative speakers – the surname Chávez, for instance, is stressed on the first syllable – but failure to observe this rule may mean that native speakers may not understand you.

# NUMBERS

**0** *cero*
**1** *uno* (masculine)
**1** *una* (feminine)
**2** *dos*
**3** *tres*
**4** *cuatro*
**5** *cinco*
**6** *seis*
**7** *siete*
**8** *ocho*
**9** *nueve*
**10** *diez*
**11** *once*
**12** *doce*
**13** *trece*
**14** *catorce*
**15** *quince*
**16** *diez y seis*
**17** *diez y siete*
**18** *diez y ocho*
**19** *diez y nueve*
**20** *veinte*
**21** *veinte y uno*
**30** *treinta*
**40** *cuarenta*
**50** *cincuenta*
**60** *sesenta*
**70** *setenta*
**80** *ochenta*
**90** *noventa*
**100** *cien*
**101** *ciento y uno*
**200** *doscientos*
**1,000** *mil*
**10,000** *diez mil*
**1,000,000** *un millón*

# DAYS OF THE WEEK

**Sunday** *domingo*
**Monday** *lunes*
**Tuesday** *martes*
**Wednesday** *miércoles*
**Thursday** *jueves*
**Friday** *viernes*
**Saturday** *sábado*

# TIME

While Argentine and Chileans normally use the 12-hour clock (A.M. and P.M.), they sometimes use the 24-hour clock, usually associated with plane or bus schedules. Under the 24-hour clock, for example, *las diez de la noche* (10 P.M.) would be *las 22 horas* (2200 hours).

**What time is it?** *¿Qué hora es?*
**It's one o'clock** *Es la una.*
**It's two o'clock** *Son las dos.*
**It's at two o'clock** *A las dos.*
**It's ten to three** *Son tres menos diez.*
**It's ten past three** *Son tres y diez.*
**It's three fifteen** *Son las tres y cuarto.*
**It's two forty five** *Son tres menos cuarto.*
**It's two thirty** *Son las dos y media.*
**It's 6 A.M.** *Son las seis de la mañana.*
**It's 6 P.M.** *Son las seis de la tarde.*
**It's 10 P.M.** *Son las diez de la noche.*
**Today** *hoy*

**Tomorrow** *mañana*
**Morning** *la mañana*
**Tomorrow morning** *mañana por la mañana*
**Yesterday** *ayer*
**Week** *la semana*
**Month** *mes*
**Year** *año*
**Last night** *anoche*
**The next day** *el día siguiente*

## USEFUL WORDS AND PHRASES

Argentines, Chileans, and other Spanish-speaking people consider formalities important. Whenever approaching anyone for information or some other reason, do not forget the appropriate salutation – good morning, good evening, etc. Standing alone, the greeting *hola* (hello) can sound brusque.

Most of the words and phrases below are fairly standard, common to all Spanish-speaking countries. Many, however, have more idiomatic equivalents; refer to the glossary for these.

**Hello.** *Hola.*
**Good morning.** *Buenos días.*
**Good afternoon.** *Buenas tardes.*
**Good evening.** *Buenas noches.*
**How are you?** *¿Cómo está?*
**Fine.** *Muy bien.*
**And you?** *¿Y usted?*
**So-so.** *Más o menos.*
**Thank you.** *Gracias.*
**Thank you very much.** *Muchas gracias.*
**You're very kind.** *Muy amable.*
**You're welcome** *De nada* (literally, "It's nothing").
**Yes** *sí*
**No** *no*
**I don't know.** *No sé.*
**Please** *por favor*
**It's fine; okay** *Está bien.*
**Good; okay** *Bueno.*
**Please** *por favor*
**Pleased to meet you.** *Mucho gusto.*
**Excuse me (physical)** *Perdóneme.*
**Excuse me (speech)** *Discúlpeme.*
**I'm sorry.** *Lo siento.*
**Good-bye** *adiós*
**See you later** *hasta luego* (literally, "until later")
**More** *más*
**Less** *menos*
**Better** *mejor*
**Much, a lot** *mucho*
**A little** *un poco*
**Large** *grande*
**Small** *pequeño, chico*
**Quick, fast** *rápido*
**Slowly** *despacio*
**Bad** *malo*
**Difficult** *difícil*
**Easy** *fácil*
**He/She/It is gone; as in "She left," "He's gone."** *Ya se fue.*
**I don't speak Spanish well.** *No hablo bien el español.*
**I don't understand.** *No entiendo.*
**How do you say . . . in Spanish?** *¿Cómo se dice . . . en español?*
**Do you understand English?** *¿Entiende el inglés?*
**Is English spoken here? (Does anyone here speak English?)** *¿Se habla inglés aquí?*

## TERMS OF ADDRESS

When in doubt, use the formal *usted* (you) as a form of address. If you wish to dispense with formality and feel that the desire is mutual, you can say *Me podés tutear* (you can call me "*tú*") even though Argentines use the slightly different verb forms that correlate with the familiar pronoun "*vos.*" In Chile, of course, the equivalent would be *Me puedes tutear.*

**I** *yo*
**You (formal)** *usted*
**You (familiar)** *vos* (Argentina)
**You (familiar)** *tu* (Chile)
**He/him** *él*
**She/her** *ella*
**We/us** *nosotros*
**You (plural)** *ustedes*
**They/them (all males or mixed gender)** *ellos*
**They/them (all females)** *ellas*
**Mr., sir** *señor*
**Mrs., madam** *señora*

**Miss, young lady** *señorita*
**Wife** *esposa*
**Husband** *marido or esposo*
**Friend** *amigo* (male), *amiga* (female)
**Sweetheart** *novio* (male), *novia* (female)
**Son, daughter** *hijo, hija*
**Brother, sister** *hermano, hermana*
**Father, mother** *padre, madre*
**Grandfather, grandmother** *abuelo, abuela*

## GETTING AROUND

**Where is . . . ?** *¿Dónde está . . . ?*
**How far is it to . . . ?** *¿A cuanto está . . . ?*
**from . . . to . . .** *de . . . a . . .*
**Highway** *la carretera*
**Road** *el camino*
**Street** *la calle*
**Block** *la cuadra*
**Kilometer** *kilómetro*
**North** *norte*
**South** *sur*
**West** *oeste; poniente*
**East** *este; oriente*
**Straight ahead** *al derecho; adelante*
**To the right** *a la derecha*
**To the left** *a la izquierda*

## ACCOMMODATIONS

**Is there a room?** *¿Hay habitación?*
**May I (we) see it?** *¿Puedo (podemos) verla?*
**What is the rate?** *¿Cuál es el precio?*
**Is that your best rate?** *¿Es su mejor precio?*
**Is there something cheaper?** *¿Hay algo más económico?*
**Single room** *un single*
**Double room** *un doble*
**Room for a couple** *matrimonial*
**Key** *llave*
**With private bath** *con baño privado*
**With shared bath** *con baño general; con baño compartido*
**Hot water** *agua caliente*
**Cold water** *agua fría*
**Shower** *ducha*
**Electric shower** *ducha eléctrica*
**Towel** *toalla*
**Soap** *jabón*
**Toilet paper** *papel higiénico*
**Air-conditioning** *aire acondicionado*
**Fan** *ventilador*
**Blanket** *frazada; manta*
**Sheets** *sábanas*

## PUBLIC TRANSPORT

**Bus stop** *la parada*
**Bus terminal** *terminal de buses*
**Airport** *el aeropuerto*
**Launch** *lancha*
**Dock** *muelle*
**I want a ticket to . . .** *Quiero un pasaje a . . .*
**I want to get off at . . .** *Quiero bajar en . . .*
**Here, please.** *Aquí, por favor.*
**Where is this bus going?** *¿Adónde va este autobús?*
**Round-trip** *ida y vuelta*
**What do I owe?** *¿Cuánto le debo?*

## FOOD

**Menu** *la carta, el menú*
**Glass** *taza*
**Fork** *tenedor*
**Knife** *cuchillo*
**Spoon** *cuchara*
**Napkin** *servilleta*
**Soft drink** *agua fresca*
**Coffee** *café*
**Cream** *crema*
**Tea** *té*
**Sugar** *azúcar*
**Drinking water** *agua pura, agua potable*
**Bottled carbonated water** *agua mineral con gas*
**Bottled uncarbonated water** *agua sin gas*
**Beer** *cerveza*
**Wine** *vino*
**Milk** *leche*
**Juice** *jugo*
**Eggs** *huevos*
**Bread** *pan*
**Watermelon** *sandía*
**Banana** *banana*
**Apple** *manzana*
**Orange** *naranja*
**Peach** *durazno*
**Pineapple** *ananá*
**Meat (without)** *carne (sin)*

**Beef** *carne de res*
**Chicken** *pollo; gallina*
**Fish** *pescado*
**Shellfish** *mariscos*
**Shrimp** *camarones*
**Fried** *frito*
**Roasted** *asado*
**Barbecued** *a la parrilla*
**Breakfast** *desayuno*
**Lunch** *almuerzo*
**Dinner, or a late-night snack** *cena*
**The check, or bill** *la cuenta*

### MAKING PURCHASES

**I need . . .** *Necesito . . .*
**I want . . .** *Deseo . . .* or *Quiero . . .*
**I would like . . . (more polite)** *Quisiera . . .*
**How much does it cost?** *¿Cuánto cuesta?*
**What's the exchange rate?** *¿Cuál es el tipo de cambio?*
**May I see . . . ?** *¿Puedo ver . . . ?*
**This one** *ésta/ésto*
**Expensive** *caro*
**Cheap** *barato*
**Cheaper** *más barato*
**Too much** *demasiado*

### HEALTH

**Help me please.** *Ayúdeme, por favor.*
**I am ill.** *Estoy enfermo.*
**It hurts.** *Me duele.*
**Pain** *dolor*
**Fever** *fiebre*
**Stomachache** *dolor de estómago*
**Headache** *dolor de cabeza*
**Vomiting** *vomitar*
**Diarrhea** *diarrhea*
**Drugstore** *farmacia*
**Medicine** *medicina*
**Pill, tablet** *pastilla*
**Birth control pills** *pastillas anticonceptivas*
**Condom** *condón, preservativo*

## Suggested Reading

### ARCHAEOLOGY, ETHNOGRAPHY, AND ETHNOHISTORY

McEwan, Colin, Luis A. Borrero, and Alfredo Prieto, eds. *Patagonia: Natural History, Prehistory and Ethnography at the Uttermost End of the Earth.* Princeton, New Jersey: Princeton University Press, 1997. First published under the auspices of the British Museum, this collection of academic but accessible essays ranges from Patagonia's natural environment to early human occupation, first encounters between Europeans and indigenes, the origins of the Patagonian "giants," and even travel literature.

### GUIDEBOOKS AND TRAVELOGUES

Burford, Tim. *Chile & Argentina: The Bradt Trekking Guide.* Chalfont St Peter, United Kingdom: Bradt Publications, 2001. Needs an update, but still a useful source for planning many hiking trips in the two countries.

Chatwin, Bruce. *In Patagonia.* New York, Summit Books, 1977. One of the continent's classic travelogues, even if—perhaps because—Chatwin blurs the line between experience and fiction.

Crouch, Gregory. *Enduring Patagonia.* New York: Random House, 2001. Details one mountaineer's experiences on Cerro Fitz Roy and Cerro Torre in Parque Nacional Los Glaciares.

Darwin, Charles. *Voyage of the Beagle* (many editions). Perhaps the greatest travel book ever written, Darwin's narrative of his 19th-century journey bursts with insights on the people, places, and even politics he saw while collecting the plants and animals that led to his revolutionary theories.

Foster, Dereck, and Richard Tripp. *Food and Drink in Argentina.* El Paso, Texas: Aromas y Sabores, 2006. A fine short introduction to Argentine food, with an extensive Spanish-English glossary, by the longtime restaurant critic of the *Buenos Aires Herald* and a U.S. collaborator.

Green, Toby. *Saddled with Darwin.* London: Phoenix, 1999. Audacious if uneven account by a young, talented writer of his attempt to retrace the hoofprints—not the footsteps—of Darwin's travels through Uruguay, Argentina, and Chile. Self-effacing but still serious, the author manages to compare Darwin's experience with his own, reflect on contemporary distortions of the great scientist's theories, and stay almost completely off the gringo trail.

Guevara, Ernesto. *The Motorcycle Diaries: A Journey around South America.* New York and London: Verso, 1995. Translated by Ann Wright, this is an account of an Argentine drifter's progress from Buenos Aires across the Patagonian Andes and up the Chilean coast by motorcycle and, when the bike broke down, by any means necessary. The author is better known by his nickname, "Che," a common Argentine interjection.

Keenan, Brian, and John McCarty. *Between Extremes.* London: Black Swan, 2000. During four years as hostages in Lebanon, Keenan and McCarty fantasized about riding through Patagonia on horseback. Years after their release, they did it.

Leitch, William. *South America's National Parks.* Seattle: The Mountaineers, 1990. Dated in detail, but still a good summary of several national parks in Chile and Argentina.

Lista, Ramón. *A Journey to the Southern Andes.* Olivos, Argentina: El Calafate Editores, 2000. Originally published in 1892, this journal by the governor of Santa Cruz territory recounts an arduous steamer navigation up the Río Santa Cruz, duplicating the route of Fitzroy, to Lago Argentino and Lago Viedma. Some of the naval officer's natural-history observations are badly mistaken.

McCarthy, Carolyn. *Trekking in the Patagonian Andes.* Melbourne: Lonely Planet, 2009. Long overdue update, with good maps.

Meadows, Anne. *Digging Up Butch and Sundance.* 3rd edition. Lincoln, Nebraska: University of Nebraska Press, 2003. The classic biography of the world's most famous outlaws since Robin Hood.

Moreno, Francisco Pascasio. *Perito Moreno's Travel Journal: A Personal Reminiscence.* Buenos Aires: Elefante Blanco, 2002. Absorbing translation of the great Patagonian explorer's northern Patagonian letters and journals, including his thrilling escape down the Río Limay from his indigenous captors.

Muir, John. *John Muir's Last Journey.* Washington, D.C.: Island Press, Shearwater Books, 2001. Edited by Michael P. Branch, this annotated collection of Muir's correspondence and notes on his eight-month odyssey through South America and Africa includes his search for native araucaria forests in Chile's northern Andean lakes district.

Murphy, Dallas. *Rounding the Horn.* New York: Basic Books, 2004. A hybrid of historical and contemporary navigation in the world's wildest waters, Murphy's travelogue conveys the travails of advancing against the winds of the "Furious Fifties." But it also communicates the mystique of South America's southernmost tip.

Reding, Nick. *The Last Cowboys at the End of the World.* New York: Crown Publishing, 2001. Anthropological in its approach, this account of isolated gauchos in Chilean Patagonia's upper Río Cisnes rings true for the author's refusal to romanticize people with whom he clearly sympathizes and empathizes.

Roosevelt, Theodore. *A Book Lover's Holiday in the Open.* New York: Scribner's, 1916. After retiring from politics, the still vigorous U.S. president undertook numerous overseas adventures; among other stories, this collection retells his crossing of the Andes from Chile into the lake district of northern Argentine Patagonia, and his meeting with legends like Perito Moreno.

Symmes, Patrick. *Chasing Che: A Motorcycle Journey in Search of the Guevara Legend.* New York: Vintage, 2000. Symmes follows the treadmarks of Che's legendary early 1950s trip from Buenos Aires through Argentina and Chile.

Wangford, Hank. *Lost Cowboys.* London: Victor Gollencz, 1995. A British country musician and experienced travel writer—whose band's name and book title are identical—follows the gauchos and other Latin American horsemen.

Willis, Bailey. *A Yanqui in Patagonia.* Palo Alto, California: Stanford University Press, 1947. Out of print but well worth seeking, this U.S. geologist's memoir is a vivid account of the early 20th century's northern Patagonian frontier. It's also fascinating for his assessment of the region's potential, and for his account of intrigues within the Argentine governments of the day.

## HISTORY

Crow, John A. *The Epic of Latin America,* 3rd ed. Berkeley: University of California Press, 1980. A comprehensive history of the region, told more through narrative than analysis, in an immensely readable manner. Several chapters deal with Argentina.

Nouzeilles, Gabriela, and Gabriela Montaldo, eds. *The Argentina Reader: History, Culture, Politics.* Durham, North Carolina: Duke University Press, 2002. It's too big and heavy to carry along on the road, but this diverse collection of essays and extracts is an excellent introduction to the country through the eyes of Argentines, and visitors to Argentina, since colonial times.

Parry, J. H. *The Discovery of South America.* London: Paul Elek, 1979. Well-illustrated account of early voyages and overland explorations on the continent.

Rock, David. *Argentina 1516–1987: From Spanish Colonization to the Falklands War and Alfonsín.* London: I. B. Taurus, 1987. Comprehensive narrative and analysis of Argentine history prior to Carlos Menem's presidency.

Slatta, Richard. *Cowboys of the Americas.* New Haven and London: Yale University Press, 1990. Spectacularly illustrated comparative analysis of New World horsemen, including both Argentine gauchos and Chilean *huasos.*

## GOVERNMENT AND POLITICS

Caviedes, César. *The Southern Cone: Realities of the Authoritarian State.* Totowa, New Jersey: Rowman & Allanheld, 1984. Comparative study of the military dictatorships of Chile, Argentina, Uruguay, and Brazil of the 1970s and 1980s.

## LITERATURE AND LITERARY CRITICISM

Aira, César. *The Hare.* London and New York: Serpent's Tail, 1998. Touching the dangerous territory of magical realism, Aira's novel of a wandering English naturalist on the Pampas is a complex tale that ties up neatly at the end.

Hudson, William Henry. *Far Away and Long Ago.* London: Eland Publishing, 1982. Originally published in 1922, this is Hudson's memoir of his childhood in Argentina, including trips to the edge of Patagonia.

Hudson, William Henry. *Idle Days in Patagonia.* Berkeley: Creative Arts Book Company, 1979. Originally published in 1893, this title covers Hudson's travels and natural history observations in northern Argentine Patagonia.

Martínez, Tomás Eloy. *The Perón Novel.* New York: Pantheon Books, 1988. Based on the author's own lengthy interviews with the exiled caudillo, for which fiction seemed the appropriate outlet. According to Jorge Castañeda, "Whether Perón ever actually uttered these words is in the last analysis irrelevant: He could have, he would have, and he probably did."

Wilson, Jason. *Traveler's Literary Companion: South & Central America, Including Mexico.* Lincolnwood, Illinois: Passport Books, 1995. An edited collection of excerpts from literature, including fiction, poetry, and essays, that illuminates aspects of the countries from the Río Grande to the tip of Tierra del Fuego, including Argentina, Buenos Aires, and Chile.

## ENVIRONMENT AND NATURAL HISTORY

Clark, Ricardo. *Aves de Tierra del Fuego y Cabo de Hornos.* Buenos Aires: Literature of Latin America, 1986. Spanish-language field guide to birds in "the uttermost part of the earth."

Couve, Enrique, and Claudio Vidal Ojeda. *Birds of the Beagle Channel and Cape Horn.* Punta Arenas: Fantástico Sur Birding & Nature, 2000. Bilingual field guide to coastal Tierra del Fuego.

Hudson, William Henry. *The Bird Biographies of W.H. Hudson.* Santa Barbara, California: Capra Press, 1988. A partial reprint of the romantic naturalist's detailed description of the birds he knew growing up in Buenos Aires province, with illustrations.

Venegas Canelo, Claudio. *Aves de Patagonia y Tierra del Fuego Chileno-Argentina.* Punta Arenas: Ediciones de la Universidad de Magallanes, 1986. Well-illustrated field guide to the region's birds.

# Internet Resources

## ARGENTINE WEBSITES

### Administración de Parques Nacionales
**www.parquesnacionales.gov.ar**

Primary government agency in charge of national parks and other conservation areas.

### Aerolíneas Argentinas
**www.aerolineas.com.ar**

Home page for Argentina's recovering flagship airline.

### Aeropuertos Argentinos 2000
**www.aa2000.com.ar**

Private concessionaire operating most of Argentina's international and domestic airports, including Buenos Aires's Ezeiza and Aeroparque. In English and Spanish.

### Argentina Travel Net
**www.argentinatravelnet.com**

Portal for Argentine travel sites, though not all of the links are closely related to travel. In Spanish and English.

### Asociación Argentina de Albergues de la Juventud (AAAJ)
**www.aaaj.org.ar**

Argentine hostelling organization, with limited facilities throughout the country.

### Asociación Ornitológica del Plata
**www.avesargentinas.org.ar**

Buenos Aires–based birding and conservation organization.

**Automóvil Club Argentino (ACA)**
**www.aca.org.ar**
Argentine automobile association, useful for both information and up-to-date road maps. Offers discounts for members of affiliated clubs, such as AAA in the United States and the AA in Britain.

***Buenos Aires Herald***
**www.buenosairesherald.com**
Abbreviated online version of the capital's venerable English-language daily, worthwhile for its editorials alone.

***Clarín***
**www.clarin.com**
Outstanding online version of the capital's tabloid daily, the Spanish-speaking world's largest-circulation newspaper.

**Festival de Tango**
**www.festivaldetango.com.ar**
The capital's increasingly popular series of autumn (March–April) tango events, following Brazilian Carnaval.

**Fundación Vida Silvestre Argentina**
**www.vidasilvestre.org.ar**
Nongovernmental wildlife and habitat advocates.

**Greenpeace**
**www.greenpeace.org.ar**
Argentine affiliate of the international conservation organization.

**Hostelling International Argentina**
**www.hostels.org.ar**
Argentine Hostelling International affiliate, with information on travel and activities throughout the country.

**Instituto Geográfico Militar**
**www.igm.gov.ar**
Military Geographical Institute, preparing and selling maps of Argentina.

**Instituto Nacional de Estadísticas y Censos**
**www.indec.mecon.ar**
Homepage for the federal government's statistical agency.

**Interpatagonia**
**www.interpatagonia.com**
Probably the most complete site for content and services on both the Argentine and Chilean sides of the Southern Cone's southernmost region.

**Líneas Aéreas del Estado (LADE)**
**www.lade.com.ar**
Commercial passenger arm of the Argentine air force, which serves primarily Patagonian destinations.

**Metrovías**
**www.metrovias.com.ar**
Details on Buenos Aires's subway system.

**Ministerio de Relaciones Exteriores**
**www.mrecic.gov.ar/consulares/pagcon.html**
Argentine foreign ministry, with information on visas and consulates, in English and Spanish.

**Páginas Amarillas**
**www.paginasamarillas.com.ar**
Yellow pages for the entire country.

**Secretaría Nacional de Turismo**
**www.turismo.gov.ar**
National tourism authority, with information in Spanish and English.

## CHILEAN WEBSITES

**Automóvil Club Chileno**
**www.acchi.cl**
Motorist organization that also provides services to members of overseas affiliates.

**Chile Information Project**
**www.chip.cl**
English-language site with daily Chilean news summaries and a useful travel section.

**Comité de la Defensa de Flora y Fauna**
**www.codeff.cl**
Well-established group oriented toward wildlife and habitat conservation.

**Corporación de Promoción Turística**
**www.visitchile.org**
Public-private Chilean site in English and Spanish.

**Corporación Nacional de Desarrollo Indígena**
**www.conadi.cl**
Official government page for indigenous affairs, in Spanish only.

**Corporación Nacional Forestal**
**www.conaf.cl**
Official page of quasi-governmental agency in charge of Chile's national parks and other protected areas; in Spanish only.

***El Mercurio***
**www.emol.com**
Santiago's traditional daily newspaper, with conservative editorial line; in Spanish.

**Federación de Andinismo**
**www.feach.cl**
Site devoted to climbing, including bureaucratic obstacles in sensitive border areas.

**Fundación Terram**
**www.terram.cl**
Nonprofit promoting sustainable development in Chile.

**FutaFriends**
**www.futafriends.org**
Nonprofit organization dedicated to preserving the Río Futaleufú.

**Hostelling International Santiago**
**www.hostelling.cl**
Chilean affiliate of Hostelling International, with information on hostels and activities throughout the country.

**Instituto Geográfico Militar**
**www.igm.cl**
Chilean government agency in charge of mapping, map sales, and general geographic information.

***La Tercera***
**www.latercera.cl**
Best of the Chilean tabloid dailies, serious but with a rigidly conservative editorial policy.

**Parque Natural Pumalín**
**www.parquepumalin.cl**
Exceptional site, in Spanish and English, for what may be the most audacious (and controversial) private conservation effort in the world.

**Publiguías**
**www.amarillas.cl**
Chilean yellow pages.

**Renace**
**www.renace.cl**
Alliance of Chilean environmental organizations.

**Sernatur**
**www.sernatur.cl**
Chilean government tourism bureau; in Spanish and English.

**Viña Cousiño Macul**
**www.cousinomacul.cl**
Classic winery within Santiago's city limits, open for tours and tasting.

## FOREIGN AND GENERAL INTEREST WEBSITES

**Centers for Disease Control**
**www.cdc.gov**
U.S. government page with travel health advisories.

**CIA Factbook**
**www.odci.gov/cia/publications/factbook**
The world's most notorious spooks perform at least one admirable public service in their annual encyclopedia of the world's countries, which appears complete online.

**Currency Converter**
**www.oanda.com**
Present and historic exchange-rate information.

**Department of Health**
**www.doh.gov.uk**
British government agency with country-by-country health advice.

**Department of State**
**www.travel.state.gov**
Travel information and advisories from the U.S. government; while it has a great deal of useful material, its warnings are often exaggerated.

**Latin American Network Information Center (LANIC)**
**http://lanic.utexas.edu**
Organized by the University of Texas, this site has a huge collection of quality links to Argentina, Chile, and other Latin American countries.

**Mercopress News Agency**
**www.falkland-malvinas.com**
Montevideo-based Internet news agency covering politics and business in the Mercosur common-market countries of Argentina, Brazil, Uruguay, and Paraguay, as well as Chile and the Falkland/Malvinas Islands. In English and Spanish.

## USENET DISCUSSION GROUPS

**Soc.culture.argentina**
No-holds-barred discussion group that touches on many other issues besides travel.

**Soc.culture.chile**
Similar to its Argentine counterpart.

**Rec.travel.latin-america**
Regional discussion group dealing with all Latin American countries, with a steady number of postings on Argentina and Chile. Since it's unmoderated, critical reading is imperative.

# Index

## N



## OP

## QR

## T

## UV



## WXYZ

# List of Maps

Acknowledgments

Like my previous efforts on Argentina, Chile, and Buenos Aires, this guide owes its existence in its present form to numerous individuals in North America, Argentina, Chile, and elsewhere. Once again, praise to Bill Newlin, whose prerogative helped make this title a priority, and his Berkeley staff at Avalon Travel.

In the course of 30 years' experience in South America, two-thirds of that as a guidebook writer, I owe enormous debts to friends, acquaintances, and officials throughout the region. My apologies to anyone I may have overlooked or perhaps omitted through an errant keystroke. Their names appear by region in no particular order, though some are grouped by workplace.

In Buenos Aires and vicinity, thanks to Joaquín Allolio; Eduardo Birabén; Dan Perlman; and my nephews José, Juan, and Manuel Massolo. A special mention to Nicolás Kugler, who did an excellent job of updating most of the coverage of Argentine Patagonia.

In Santiago, acknowledgments to Pablo Fernández of Hostelling International; Cristina Cáceres of ADS Mundo; Marco Vergara of Cruceros Australis and Adrien Champagnat of Navimag; Yerko Ivelic and Javier López of Cascada Expediciones; Maureen Wahl of AyR Hoteles; and Eduardo Núñez of Conaf.

In northern Argentine Patagonia, thanks to Diana Seijo of Neuquén; Diego Allolio of Bariloche; and Charly Moreno of Trevelin. In southern Argentine Patagonia, I would add Matías Soriano of Bahía Bustamante; Silvia Braun and Juan Kuriger of Hostería Monte León; Ricardo Pérez of Puerto Deseado; María Elisa Rodríguez, Sebastián Bruna, and Dany Feldman of El Calafate; and Ricardo Brondo and Rubén Vasquez of El Chaltén. In Argentine Tierra del Fuego, regards to Javier Jury and Luciana Lupotti.

In the Chilean lakes district, special mention to Hans Schoendorfer of the Andenrose, Curacautín; Armin Dübendorfer of Puerto Octay; Beat Zbinden of Villarrica; Andreas La Rosé and Carolina Morgado of Puerto Varas; Britt Lewis of Ancud; and administrator Alan Bannister of Parque Tantauco.

In Chilean Patagonia, including Aisén and vicinity, thanks to Nicholas La Penna of Chaitén; Chris and Rosi Spelius of Futaleufú; Gabriela Neira Morales of Sernatur, Coyhaique; Jonathan Leidich of Puerto Bertrand; Francisco Sánchez of Sernatur, Punta Arenas; Alejandro Cárdenas Lobos of Puerto Natales; Werner Ruf and Cecilia Chaura of Casa Cecilia, Puerto Natales; Hernán Jofré of Antares Patagonia, Puerto Natales; Arturo Báez Hernández of Kipaventour Patagonie, Puerto Natales; and Milenko Buljan of Agunsa Chile, Punta Arenas.

In Stanley, Falkland Islands, thanks to tourism manager Paul Trowell and marketing officer Louise Taylor, Sally Ellis and Jennie Forrest of International Tours & Travel, María Strange, Tony Smith, Sally Poncet, and Ian Bury. Ray and Nancy Poole deserve special mention for putting me up—and putting up with me—as their house guest. I'd also like to acknowledge Jane Cameron, the dedicated and irreplaceable government archivist, and express my sadness at her accidental death in Argentine Patagonia. In camp, where I couldn't spend as much time as I might have liked, thanks to Rob McGill of Carcass Island, Mike Rendell of Bleaker Island, and Peter and Ann Robertson of Port Stephens.

Stateside, thanks to Ursula Velarde and Victoria Mellado of LAN Airlines, Miami, for help in arranging transportation.

And finally, thanks to my wife, María Laura Massolo, and daughter, Clío Bernhardson-Massolo, for their patience, and to my Alaskan malamute Malbec, who reminds me when I need to get out of my office for a walk.

www.falklandislands.com

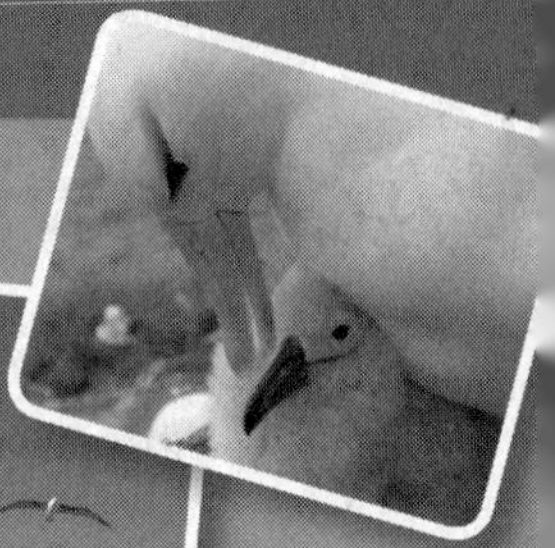

# The Falkland Islands

## A photographic paradise at the bottom of the world!

| Unrivalled access to incredible wildlife | 5 breeding species of penguin
| Enviable photo opportunities | History & battlefield tours | Friendly local hospitality
| Epic landscapes | 80% of the world's black-browed albatross population

**Contact Us:**
**T:** + 500 22215 **F:** + 500 27020
**E:** info@falklandislands.com

Falkland Islands
TOURIST BOARD